W9-DAZ-923

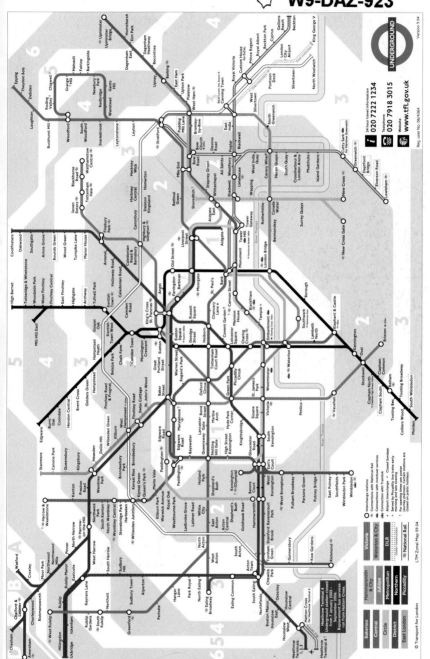

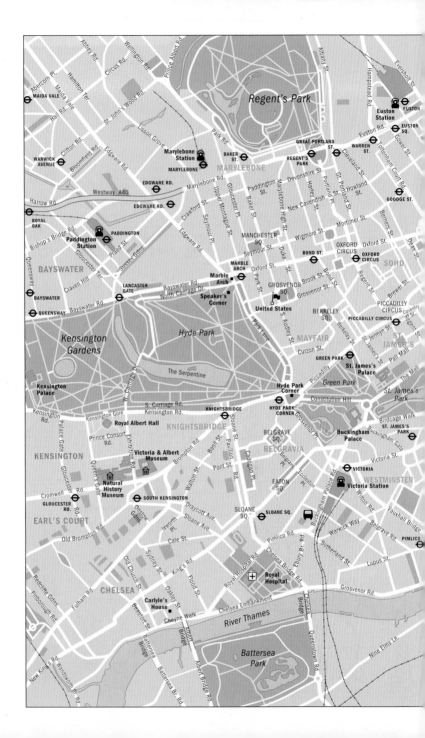

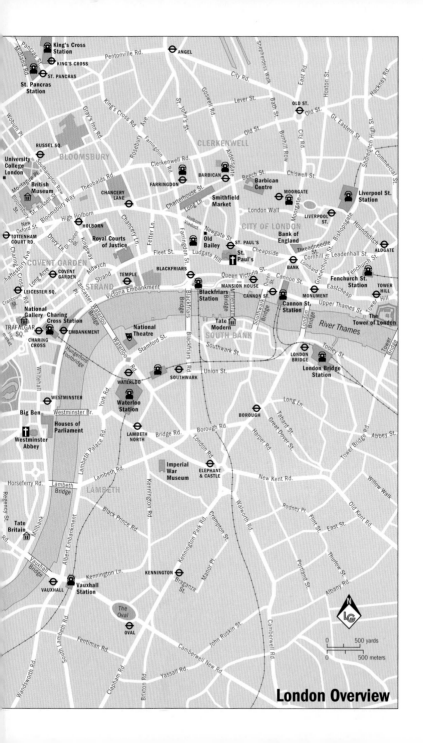

London Overview

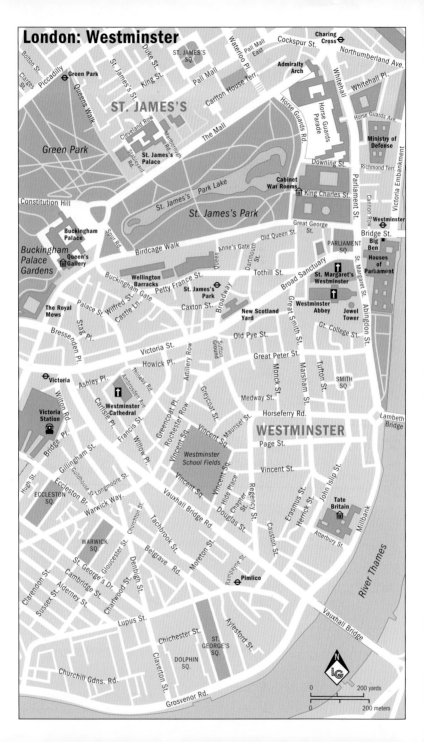

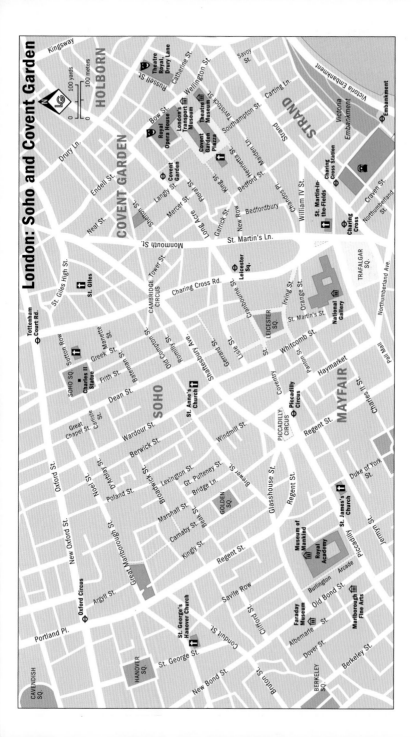

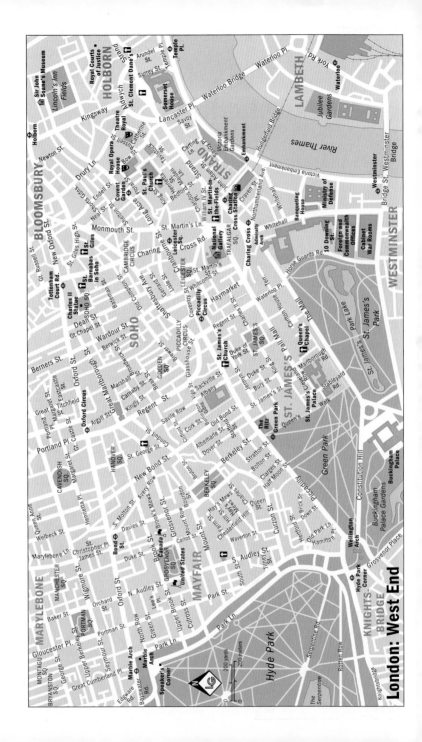
London: West End

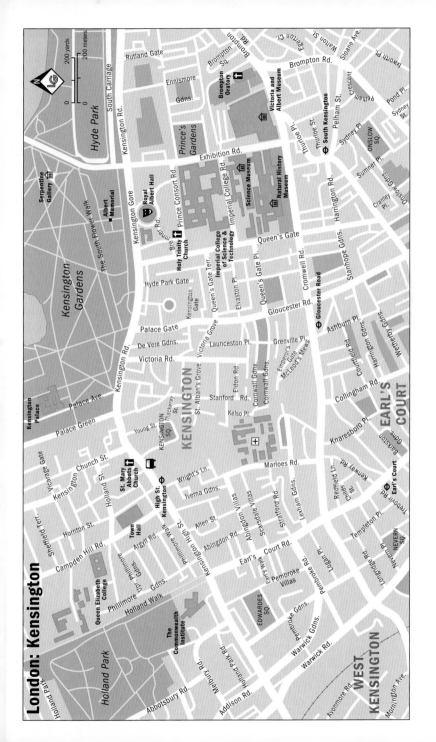

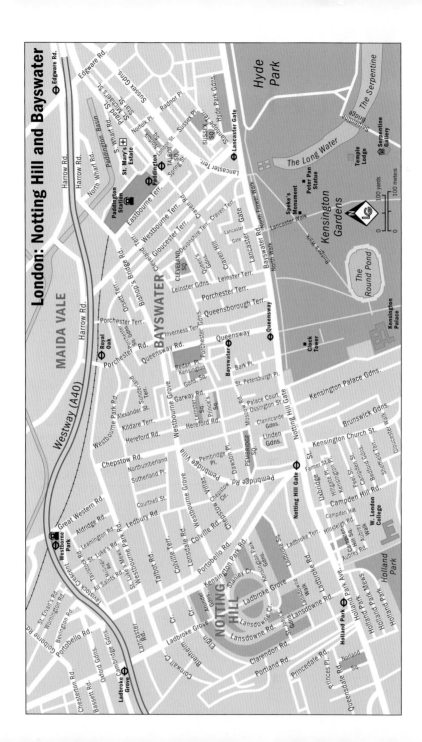

London: Notting Hill and Bayswater

LET'S GO PUBLICATIONS

TRAVEL GUIDES

Australia 8th edition
Austria & Switzerland 12th edition
Brazil 1st edition
Britain 2006
California 10th edition
Central America 9th edition
Chile 2nd edition
China 5th edition
Costa Rica 2nd edition
Eastern Europe 12th edition
Ecuador 1st edition
Egypt 2nd edition
Europe 2006
France 2006
Germany 12th edition
Greece 8th edition
Hawaii 3rd edition
India & Nepal 8th edition
Ireland 12th edition
Israel 4th edition
Italy 2006
Japan 1st edition
Mexico 21st edition
Middle East 4th edition
New Zealand 7th edition
Peru 1st edition
Puerto Rico 2nd edition
South Africa 5th edition
Southeast Asia 9th edition
Spain & Portugal 2006
Thailand 2nd edition
Turkey 5th edition
USA 23rd edition
Vietnam 1st edition
Western Europe 2006

ROADTRIP GUIDE

Roadtripping USA

ADVENTURE GUIDES

Alaska 1st edition
Pacific Northwest 1st edition
Southwest USA 3rd edition

CITY GUIDES

Amsterdam 4th edition
Barcelona 3rd edition
Boston 4th edition
London 15th edition
New York City 15th edition
Paris 13th edition
Rome 12th edition
San Francisco 4th edition
Washington, D.C. 13th edition

POCKET CITY GUIDES

Amsterdam
Berlin
Boston
Chicago
London
New York City
Paris
San Francisco
Venice
Washington, D.C.

LET'S GO

■ PAGES PACKED WITH ESSENTIAL INFORMATION

"Value-packed, unbeatable, accurate, and comprehensive."

—The Los Angeles Times

"The guides are aimed not only at young budget travelers but at the independent traveler; a sort of streetwise cookbook for traveling alone."

—The New York Times

"Unbeatable; good sight-seeing advice; up-to-date info on restaurants, hotels, and inns; a commitment to money-saving travel; and a wry style that brightens nearly every page."

—The Washington Post

■ THE BEST TRAVEL BARGAINS IN YOUR BUDGET

"All the dirt, dirt cheap."

—People

"Let's Go follows the creed that you don't have to toss your life's savings to the wind to travel—unless you want to."

—The Salt Lake Tribune

■ REAL ADVICE FOR REAL EXPERIENCES

"The writers seem to have experienced every rooster-packed bus and lunar-surfaced mattress about which they write."

—The New York Times

"[Let's Go's] devoted updaters really walk the walk (and thumb the ride, and trek the trail). Learn how to fish, haggle, find work—anywhere."

—Food & Wine

"A world-wise traveling companion—always ready with friendly advice and helpful hints, all sprinkled with a bit of wit."

—The Philadelphia Inquirer

■ A GUIDE WITH A SPIRIT AND A SOCIAL CONSCIENCE

"Lighthearted and sophisticated, informative and fun to read. [Let's Go] helps the novice traveler navigate like a knowledgeable old hand."

—Atlanta Journal-Constitution

"The serious mission at the book's core reveals itself in exhortations to respect the culture and the environment—and, if possible, to visit as a volunteer, a student, or a teacher rather than a tourist."

—San Francisco Chronicle

LET'S GO
BRITAIN
2006

ANNIE M. LOWREY EDITOR
EOGHAN O'DONNELL ASSOCIATE EDITOR

RESEARCHER-WRITERS
MADELEINE BÄVERSTAM
MARY KATE BURKE
TERRENCE COSTELLO
LINDSAY CROUSE
JOHN ARTHUR EPLEY

KATHERINE J. THOMPSON MAP EDITOR
ADRIENNE TAYLOR GERKEN MANAGING EDITOR

ST. MARTIN'S PRESS ✕ NEW YORK

HELPING LET'S GO. If you want to share your discoveries, suggestions, or corrections, please drop us a line. We read every piece of correspondence, whether a postcard, a 10-page email, or a coconut. **Address mail to:**

> **Let's Go: Britain**
> **67 Mount Auburn St.**
> **Cambridge, MA 02138**
> **USA**

Visit Let's Go at **http://www.letsgo.com,** or send email to:

> **feedback@letsgo.com**
> **Subject: "Let's Go: Britain"**

In addition to the invaluable travel advice our readers share with us, many are kind enough to offer their services as researchers or editors. Unfortunately, our charter enables us to employ only currently enrolled Harvard students.

Maps by David Lindroth copyright © 2006 by St. Martin's Press.

Distributed outside the USA and Canada by Macmillan.

ISBN: 0-312-34888-6
EAN: 978-0-312-34888-5
First edition
10 9 8 7 6 5 4 3 2 1

CONTENTS

RESEARCHER-WRITERS

Madeleine Bäverstam *Northern England, Edinburgh, Southern and Central Scotland*

An old-school Bostonian with Scandinavian fortitude and the umlaut to show, Madeleine jumped from big-city Edinburgh to bird sanctuary with good humor and her trusty violin on her back. This history and literature enthusiast and musician produced immaculate coverage and entertaining features and came away with a love of the *ceidleh* and—surprisingly—an intact violin.

Mary Kate Burke *Midlands, Heart of England, Southwest, and Northern England*

Mary Kate tackled a chameleon-like route—from multimillion person cities to nobody-can-hear-you-scream countryside, exclusive nightspots to equally exclusive tea-cozy villages, the coast to the dales and back again. Faced with an impenetrable transport system and a birthday spent on a tor, this New Yorker buckled down and came through in characteristic style.

Terrence Costello *Glasgow, Central Scotland, Highlands and Islands*

It's always the quiet ones. This Boston native took his wee car and drove it to the ends of the earth on a whirlwind tour of tors, Stone-Age monuments, and the swankiest cafe-bars by the North Sea. When stranded in a storm, with no money, on a remote island, he called to inform his editors that he had just discovered a croft house and eaten a snack. That says it all. We'd trust our children to him anyday.

Lindsay Crouse *South and Heart of England, Midlands, East Anglia, Yorkshire*

X-treme RW and *Let's Go* vet, Lindsay impressed us with immaculate copy and unfailing professionalism despite transportation nightmares, public holidays, strict deadlines, and a few choice dates with public school boys. When not busy running between listings (no—actually running, like, with her own legs), Lindsay hit up moors and small towns on a jam-packed itinerary.

John Arthur Epley *Wales, Isle of Man*

Arthur *is* his middle name—we should have known that John would rule Britain (well, at least Wales) on a mythic scale. TeamBri's very own Tom Sawyer, John Southern-charmed the metaphorical pants off of every motorcyclist, old age pensioner, winemaker, tipsy bachelorette, fortune teller, and sheep he met on the rural road. This Arkansas native produced stellar copy and hilarious features.

CONTRIBUTING WRITERS

Emma Beavers *Dublin*

Much like a trench-coated detective, Emma employed six senses to cut through Dublin's underbelly, scoping out the club scene, national museums, and everything in between.

Chris Schonberger *Northern Ireland*

A three year Let's Go veteran, this marathoner researched in Northern Ireland. Despite (or thanks to?) his taste for Guinness, Chris delivered impeccable and entertaining reports on his route.

Amber Johnson *London*

Hailing from Orange County, CA, Amber graduated from Stanford University in 2001 and is now a student at the Harvard School of Public Health.

Yaran Noti *London*

A veteran of *Let's Go: Italy*, Yaran integrated himself into true London culture. A die-hard researcher, Yaran is known for his funny notes. While in London, Yaran became addicted to British *Big Brother*.

Rachel Nolan *Editor, Let's Go: Ireland 2006*

Kevin Feeney *Associate Editor, Let's Go: Ireland 2006*

David Blazar *Editor, Let's Go: London 2005*

Simon Schama is an author and a professor at Columbia University. He writes for *The New Yorker* and was recently the writer and host of the BBC's *History of Britain*.

Lily Brown graduated from Harvard University in 2004 with a degree in Women, Gender, and Sexuality Studies.

HOW TO USE THIS BOOK

COVERAGE LAYOUT. *Let's Go: Britain* launches out of **London** and follows with a whirling tour through **England.** From the idyllic **South,** venture to the criminally picturesque **Southwest,** through the storybook **Heart of England,** to the fens of **East Anglia** and the countryside of the **Midlands.** Cross the cities and lakes of the **Northwest** (with a quick hop to the **Isle of Man**) and the moors of the **Northeast.** Your travels restart in **Wales,** sweeping from Cardiff, through **South Wales,** into mountainous **North Wales.** In Scotland, wheel from Edinburgh to **Southern Scotland** to Glasgow, then trek north to the castles of **Central Scotland.** Continue to the rugged **Highlands and Islands.** Next, it's across the sea to the Emerald Isle. Begin in Belfast and then tour the Giant's Causeway. Bid farewell to the UK for a daytrip through **Dublin.**

TRANSPORTATION INFO. Information is generally listed under a transport's arrival location; look to where you're going to for how to get there. Parentheticals usually provide the trip duration, the frequency, and the price, in that order. For general information on travel, consult the **Essentials** (p. 11) section.

COVERING THE BASICS. The first chapter, **Discover Britain** (p. 1), contains highlights of the Britain and **Suggested Itineraries** for short and long trips. The **Essentials** (p. 11) section contains practical information on planning a budget, making reservations, and staying safe. The section also contains useful tips for traveling in Britain. Take some time to peruse the **Life and Times** sections, which introduce each country (England, p. 64; Wales, p. 433; Scotland, p. 515; Northern Ireland, p. 669) and sum up its history, culture, and customs. The **Appendix** (p. 702) has climate information, a list of bank holidays, measurement conversions, and a glossary. For information on studying, volunteering, or working in Britain, **Beyond Tourism** (p. 53) is all you need.

SCHOLARLY ARTICLES. Two contributors with unique regional insight wrote articles for *Let's Go: Britain.* Columbia University professor and renowned British historian **Simon Schama** discusses his favorite ruins (p. 10) and Harvard graduate **Lily Brown** reflects on her experience studying at Oxford (p. 59).

FEATURES. Britain's expensive. There's no getting around that. But *Let's Go's* features and tipboxes are meant to guide you to the very best deals, the very best sights, and the very best places to splurge. Other features give you insight into local lore, small-scale city tours, or stories from the *Let's Go* researchers.

PRICE DIVERSITY. Our researchers list establishments in order of value, from best to worst. Our absolute favorites are denoted by the *Let's Go* thumb-pick (🌅). Since the lowest price does not always mean the best value, we have incorporated a system of price ranges for food and accommodations; see p. xiii.

PHONE CODES AND TELEPHONE NUMBERS. Area codes for each city or region appear opposite the its name and are denoted by the ☎ icon. Phone numbers in text are also preceded by the ☎ icon. For more on dialling, see p. 38.

A NOTE TO OUR READERS. The information for this book was gathered by *Let's Go* researchers from May through August of 2005. Each listing is based on one researcher's opinion, formed during his or her visit at a particular time. Those traveling at other times may have different experiences since prices, dates, hours, and conditions are always subject to change. You are urged to check the facts presented in this book beforehand to avoid inconvenience and surprises.

ACKNOWLEDGMENTS

LET'S GO

TEAM BRITAIN THANKS: Our researchers—we're proud and still jealous. Adrienne, we just heart you. Katherine, Seth, and Stuart. Our proofers, tech support, and the extra hands that helped us with the book. The Eagle-Scoutish (always prepared) MEs. The other eds. And Ireland.

ANNIE THANKS: Eoghan and Adrienne; the researchers; Seth, Stuart, Katherine—to all of you I owe infinite gratitude. Kevin, Rachie, Dusty, and Maya; the gentlemen of and visitors to 1679; an office at large; Charlotte, Jack, Caitlin, Mum, Dad, Gram, and Stella. All best.

EOGHAN THANKS: Annie, Adrienne, and Katherine; the MEs; Ireland; London; my parents; the Dickson St. Bookshop; the tenman; Ms. Fine; Arkansas; Berwick-upon-Tweed.

KATHERINE THANKS: Annie and Eoghan, for providing Pimms, picking up slack, and playing nice with my other island bookteam; Adrienne for being generally fantastic and loving the nachos; my great RWs, for color-coding, pointing out dinosaur-shaped lochs, and always improving; Seth and Stuart for making me take this job, and David, Jess, and Kelly for making it easy; Ella, Laura, and Jeremy for sharing a summer of construction work and mice; my family, who taught me English; and Cocksburnpath, Uckfield, and Loch Lochy, for just being themselves.

Publishing Director
Seth Robinson
Editor-in-Chief
Stuart J. Robinson
Production Manager
Alexandra Hoffer
Cartography Manager
Katherine J. Thompson
Editorial Managers
Rachel M. Burke, Ashley Eva Isaacson, Laura E. Martin
Financial Manager
Adrienne Taylor Gerken
Publicity Manager
Alexandra C. Stanek
Personnel Manager
Ella M. Steim
Production Associate
Ansel S. Witthaus
IT Director
Jeffrey Hoffman Yip
Director of E-Commerce
Michael Reckhow
Office Coordinator
Matthew Gibson

Director of Advertising Sales
Jillian N. London
Senior Advertising Associates
Jessica C.L. Chiu, Katya M. Golovchenko, Mohammed J. Herzallah
Advertising Graphic Designer
Emily E. Maston

Editor
Annie M. Lowrey
Associate Editor
Eoghan O'Donnell
Managing Editor
Adrienne Taylor Gerken
Map Editor
Katherine J. Thompson
Typesetter
Teresa Elsey

President
Caleb J. Merkl
General Manager
Robert B. Rombauer
Assistant General Manager
Anne E. Chisholm

 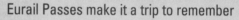

PRICE RANGES>>BRITAIN

Our researchers list establishments in order of value from best to worst; our favorites are denoted by the Let's Go thumbs-up (🗹). Since the best value is not always the cheapest price, however, we have also incorporated a system of price ranges, based on a rough expectation of what you'll spend. For **accommodations,** we base our range on the cheapest price for which a single traveler can stay for one night. For **restaurants** and other dining establishments, we estimate the average amount a traveler will spend (thus, an excellent sandwich shop may be a 1 or a 3). The table tells you what you'll *typically* find in Britain at the corresponding price range; keep in mind that no system allows for every individual establishment's quirks, and that generally you'll get more for your money in small towns than in large cities, particularly London.

ACCOMMODATIONS	RANGE	WHAT YOU'RE *LIKELY* TO FIND
1	under £12	Dorm-style. Expect bunk beds, a communal bath, and drunk backpackers. You may have to rent or bring sheets and towels.
2	£12-20	Upper-end hostels, small hotels, and lower-end B&Bs. You may have an ensuite bath or communal facilities. Some amenities, such as a television, may be included.
3	£21-30	Equivalency to a basic chain hotel room; decent but basic amenities (telephone and TV) and a private bath. Breakfast may be included.
4	£31-59	Similar to 3. However, expect A/C, TV, private bath, fridge, curtains, and pervasive cleanliness. Some offer tourist services, Internet, and breakfast.
5	£60 and up	Large hotels, chain hotels, nice B&Bs, even castles. If it's a 5 and doesn't have the perks you want, you've paid too much.

FOOD	RANGE	WHAT YOU'RE *LIKELY* TO FIND
1	under £6	Mostly street-corner stands, food trollies, sandwiches, shawarma, take-away, and tea shops. Rarely a sit-down meal.
2	£6-10	Often take-away ethnic foods (curry!) and basic sit-down options outside of London. In London, see 1.
3	£11-15	Entrees more expensive, but a sit-down meal. Good pub grub, chain restaurants, and local joints.
4	£16-23	Fancier food, higher prices, and better service. Likely, you're paying for decor and ambience. An excellent meal.
5	£24 and up	The best—or at least the best-looking—bangers and mash you've ever had.

ABOUT LET'S GO

NOT YOUR PARENTS' TRAVEL GUIDE

At Let's Go, we see every trip as the chance of a lifetime. If your dream is to grab a machete and forge through the jungles of Brazil, we can take you there. If you'd rather bask in the Riviera sun at a beachside cafe, we'll set you a table. We write for readers who know that there's more to travel than sharing double deckers with tourists and who believe that travel can change both themselves and the world—whether they plan to spend six days in London or six months in Latin America. We'll show you just how far your money can go, and prove that the greatest limitation on your adventures is not your wallet, but your imagination.

BEYOND THE TOURIST EXPERIENCE

To help you gain a deeper connection with the places you travel, our fearless researchers scour the globe to give you the heads-up on both world-renowned and off-the-beaten-track attractions, sights, and destinations. They engage with the local culture, only to emerge with the freshest insights on everything from local festivals to regional cuisine. We've also opened our pages to respected writers and scholars to hear their takes on the countries and regions we cover, and asked travelers who have worked, studied, or volunteered abroad to contribute first-person accounts of their experiences. In addition, we increased our coverage of responsible travel and expanded each guide's Beyond Tourism chapter to share more ideas about how to give back while on the road.

FORTY-SIX YEARS OF WISDOM

Let's Go got its start in 1960, when a group of creative and well-traveled students compiled their experience and advice into a 20-page mimeographed pamphlet, which they gave to travelers on charter flights to Europe. Four and a half decades later, we've expanded to cover six continents and all kinds of travel—while retaining our founders' adventurous attitude toward the world. Laced with witty prose and total candor, our guides are still researched and written entirely by students on shoestring budgets, experienced travelers who know that train strikes, stolen luggage, food poisoning, and marriage proposals are all part of a day's work.

THE LET'S GO COMMUNITY

More than just a travel guide company, Let's Go is a community. Our small staff comes together because of our shared passion for travel and our desire to help other travelers see the world the way it was meant to be seen. We love it when our readers become part of the Let's Go community as well—when you travel, drop us a postcard (67 Mt. Auburn St., Cambridge, MA 02138, USA), send us an e-mail (feedback@letsgo.com), or post on our forum (http://www.letsgo.com/connect/forum) to tell us about your adventures and discoveries.

For more information, visit us online: www.letsgo.com.

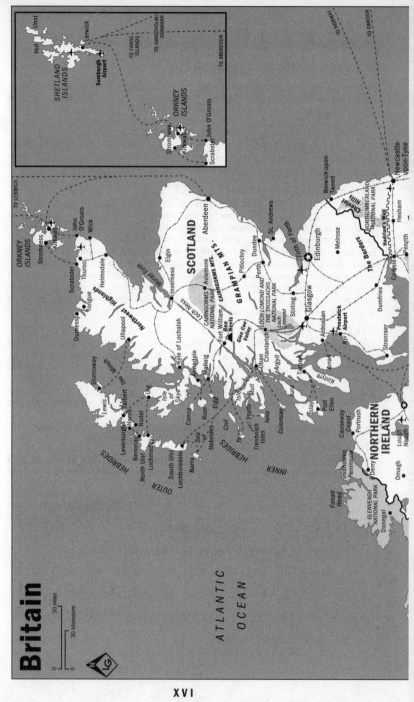

Britain

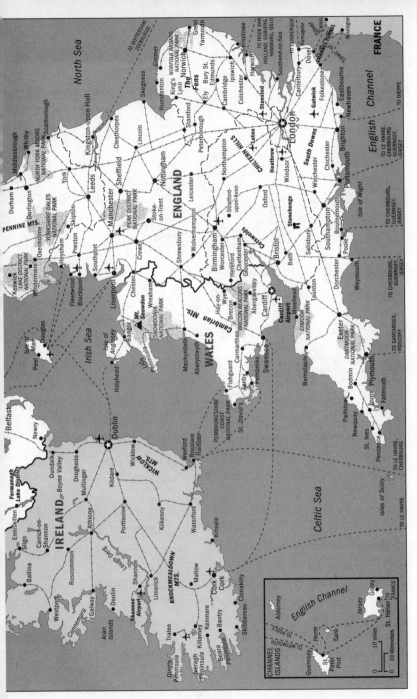

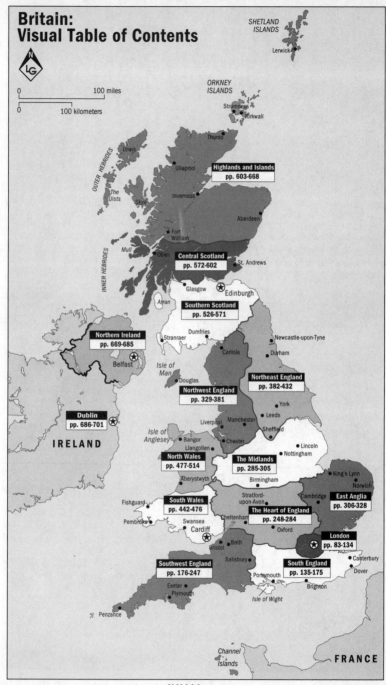

Britain: Visual Table of Contents

DISCOVER
BRITAIN

Welcome to Britain. You've arrived on an island half the size of Spain with a population almost twice that of California, whose people have managed to colonize two-fifths of the globe and win just about every war they've gotten into. Though small, Britain has enough regional flavor to keep you occupied for your entire stay and then some. The rolling farms of the south and the rugged peaks of the north are only hours apart by train, and even on a two-week trip, you'll come across London clubbers, Yorkshire football hooligans, Welsh students, and Scottish crofters. Prepare to experience a multiplicity of cultures living in remarkably close quarters, a historic quirk that has left Britain dotted with fortresses, subterranean dungeons, and ruins. Inheriting a nation and a language born from rivalry (Celtic/Roman, Anglo-Saxon/Norman, to name a few), Britons embrace and even adopt from other cultures; you'll eat as many curries and Shawarmas as scones with lemon curd. So boot up in your wellies, grab your *Let's Go*, and discover.

FACTS AND FIGURES

POPULATIONS: England, 49.9 million; Wales, 2.9 million; Scotland, 5.1 million; Northern Ireland, 1.7 million.

PATRON SAINTS: George (England), David (Wales), Andrew (Scotland).

MONARCHS: Kings: 35. Queens: 7. Longest reign: 64 years (Victoria). Shortest reign: 9 days (Lady Jane Grey).

SUN STATS: Average hours of sunshine per day in England: 4.65, in Wales: 4, in the Scottish Highlands: 3. Hours of darkness, midsummer, Shetland Islands: 0.

MOST COMMON NAMES: Jack (it's a boy!), Emily (it's a girl!), Max (it's a dog!), The Red Lion (it's a pub!).

BEVERAGES: Tea (per person per year): 860 cups. Beer: 228 pints.

WHEN TO GO

Britain's popularity as a tourist destination makes it wise to plan around high season (June to August). Spring or autumn (April to May and September to October) are also appealing times to visit; the weather is still pleasant and flights are cheaper. If you intend to visit the cities and linger indoors, the low season (November to March), is cheapest. Keep in mind, however, that sights and accommodations often run reduced hours or close completely, especially in rural areas.

"Rain, Rain, Go Away" is less a hopeful plea than an exercise in futility. Regardless of when you go, **it will rain.** Have warm, waterproof clothing on hand at all times. Relatively speaking, April is the driest (and cruellest) month. The mild weather has few extremes; excluding Highland altitudes, temperatures average around 15-20°C (mid-60° F) in summer and 5-7°C (low 40° F) in winter. And note that the British Isles are farther north than you may think; Newcastle is on the same latitude as Moscow. In Scotland, the midsummer sun lasts almost all day, and in winter sets as early as 3:45pm.

THINGS TO DO

With Manchester's clubs only an hour from the Lake District fells, and Land's End only 16 hours from John O'Groats by car, Britain provides unparalleled opportunities in an amazingly compact space. For more specific regional attractions, see the **Highlights** box at the start of each chapter.

AU NATURAL

Forget the madding crowds: the diversity of Britain's natural landscapes is worthy of a continent. Discover your inner romantic (or Romantic) among the gnarled crags and crystalline waters of the peaceful **Lake District** (p. 360). The **South Downs Way** (p. 148) ambles through the gentle hills of Southern England. Limestone cliffs hang over the Irish Sea at the gorgeous **Pembrokeshire Coast National Park** (p. 466), where you can go coasteering and cliff-diving. **Loch Lomond and the Trossachs** (p. 588), now in Scotland's first national park, lie along the **West Highland Railway,** which travels north from Glasgow, past Loch Lomond and **Ben Nevis** (p. 647). Farther north, the misty peaks of the **Isle of Skye** (p. 629) and the **Northwest Highlands** (p. 647) lend themselves to postcard snapshots from just about any angle. In the windy, isolated **Orkneys** (p. 653) find wildlife, geological phenomena, and Iron-Age monuments. In Northern Ireland, the honeycomb columns of the **Giant's Causeway** (p. 684) are a geological anomaly among Antrim's rocky outcrops and pristine white beaches.

HISTORY, PRE-1066

Britain was popular long before the arrival of William the Conqueror and the Normans. Walk through a perfectly preserved Neolithic village at **Skara Brae** (p. 658) in the Orkneys. **Stonehenge** (p. 182) is the best-known marker of Bronze Age inhabitants, while nearby **Avebury** (p. 183) is a bigger, less-touristed site. On Scotland's Isle of Lewis, the **Callanish Stones** (p. 640) reveal the ancient Celtic tribes' knowledge of astronomy, while the burial tomb of Wales's **Bryn Celli Ddu** (p. 507) pokes up from the middle of a modern farm. Fabulous mosaics and a theater have been excavated at **St. Albans** (p. 248), once the capital of Roman Britannia, while **Bath** (p. 183) provided a regenerative retreat for Roman colonists. **Hadrian's Wall** (p. 429) marks an emperor's frustration with rebellious tribes to the north. Finding the light in the Dark Ages, early Christianity got its start in Canterbury, where the **Church of St. Martin** (p. 135) is Britain's oldest house of worship. But a new era of British history was soon to be inaugurated in that fateful year when William trounced the Saxons at **Hastings** (p. 147).

CHURCH AND STATE

Early Britons never held back when a fortress, castle, or cathedral could be defiantly built or defiantly razed. Edward I of England had a rough time containing the Welsh; his massive fortresses—like **Caernarfon** (p. 502), the Robocop of Welsh castles, or **Caerphilly** (p. 448)—mark the northwestern Welsh coast. Two castles, equally grand, top extinct volcanoes in Scotland, one ringed with gargoyles, in **Stirling** (p. 586), the other perched high above **Edinburgh** (p. 526). **Dover Castle** (p. 144) has protected the southern coast since England ruled half of France. Join the camera-toters if you must at **Eilean Donan Castle** (p. 647), but you can't leave Scotland without visiting **Dunnottar Castle** (p. 609); it's even more mind-exploding on a stormy day. On your way south, stop by the ruined **St. Andrews Castle** (p. 576) and scurry through Britain's only surviving countermine tunnel. In central England, get the full medieval experience at **Warwick Castle** (p. 285), complete with banquets, jousts, and wax figures. You can also play the lord or lady at hilltop **Durham Castle** (p. 415), which lets out its rooms to travelers, as does 15th-century **St. Briavel's Castle** (p. 452), now a hostel near Tintern. The sumptuous **Castle Howard** (p. 391), not strictly a castle at all, and the magnificent **Alnwick Castle** (p. 426) both afford a heady taste of how the other 0.001% still lives.

In northeast England, **York Minster** (p. 388), the country's largest Gothic house of worship, jockeys with **Durham Cathedral** (p. 415) to inspire the most awe in its visitors, while **Canterbury Cathedral** (p. 135) has attracted pilgrims since even before the time of Geoffrey Chaucer. **Salisbury Cathedral** (p. 180) sets a record of its own with England's tallest spire. In London, thousands flock to **Westminster Abbey** (p. 104) and **St. Paul's Cathedral** (p. 105), where Poets' Corner and the Whispering Gallery take their breath away. Up in Scotland, the ruined Border Abbeys—**Jedburgh** (p. 549), **Melrose,** (p. 547), **Kelso** (p. 550), and **Dryburgh** (p. 547)—draw fewer visitors, but way more introspection.

LITERARY LANDMARKS

Even if you've never been to Britain, its landscape may seem familiar from your English Lit notes. Jane Austen grew up in **Winchester** (p. 170), wrote in **Bath** (p. 183), and took the odd trip to **Lyme Regis** (p. 204). Farther north, the Brontës—Charlotte, Emily, and Anne—lived in the parsonage in **Haworth** (p. 394) and captured the wildness of the **Yorkshire Moors** (p. 404) in their novels. Thomas Hardy was a **Dorchester** (p. 202) man, whose fictional county of Wessex mirrored Southwest England perfectly. Sir Arthur Conan Doyle set Sherlock Holmes's house on 221b Baker St. in **London** (p. 83), but sent the sleuth to **Dartmoor** (p. 212) to find the Hound of the Baskervilles. Virginia Woolf drew inspiration for her novel *To the Lighthouse* from **St. Ives** (p. 239) and the **Isle of Skye** (p. 629). Long after shuffling off his mortal coil, William Shakespeare lives on in **Stratford-upon-Avon** (p. 264). William Wordsworth grew up in the **Lake District** (p. 360) and his best bud Samuel Taylor Coleridge envied him deeply for it—much of their poetry was inspired by walks near its waters and mountain ridges. J.R.R. Tolkien and C.S. Lewis chatted fantasy over pints at The Eagle and Child in **Oxford** (p. 253). Welshman Dylan Thomas was born in **Swansea** (p. 463), moved to **Laugharne** (p. 472), and today enjoys a fanatical following in both locations. Scotland's national poet is Robert Burns, and every town in Dumfries and Galloway (p. 551) pays tribute to him, while **Edinburgh** (p. 526) cherishes its favorite Scott, Sir Walter.

A SPORTS FAN'S PARADISE

Football (soccer, if you must) fanaticism is unavoidable: the Queen Mum was an Arsenal fan, and the police run a National Hooligan Hotline. At the football grounds of London, become a gunner for a day at Highbury, chant for the Spurs at White Hart Lane, or don the Chelsea blue. Then head up to **Old Trafford** (p. 347), Manchester United's hallowed turf on Sir Matt Busby Way, or move west to the stadia of bitter rivals **Everton** and **Liverpool** (p. 335). Rugby scrums are held in gaping Millennium Stadium, **Cardiff** (p. 442). Discouraged by the terrace yobs and the mud? Throwers of tree-trunks and other wearers of kilts reach their own rowdy heights annually at the festival-like Highland Games in **Braemar** (p. 609) and other Scottish towns. Cricket is more refined; watch the men

DISCOVER

✎ LET'S GO PICKS

BEST PLACE FOR A PINT: In Penzance, the **Admiral Benbow** (p. 235) adorns its walls with shipwreck relics. Students prowl **"The Turf"** (p. 253) in Oxford. Tradition mandates a pub crawl in **Edinburgh** (p. 541). Nottingham's **Ye Old Trip to Jerusalem,** carved from rock and established in 1189, is England's oldest pub and still serves a mean pint.

BEST QUIRKY MUSEUMS: A collection of antiquities and architectural marvels, **Sir John Soane's Museum** (p. 121) is worth a look. In Boscastle, the **Museum of Witchcraft** (p. 227) confirms the hocus pocus with biographies of living witches. The **Dog Collar Museum** in Leeds Castle (p. 141) displays medieval pooch attire. Near Shrewsbury, the **Land of Lost Content** (p. 296) salvages souvenirs of popular culture from trash cans.

BEST PLACE TO BE A ROCK STAR: Rock gods like Oasis cut their teeth at **The Water Rats,** in London (p. 126). Find three friends and strut the crosswalk in front of **Abbey Road Studios** (p. 118) in St. John's Wood. Or channel the Beatles in the **Cavern Club** (p. 342), Liverpool's tourist mecca. Radiohead filmed the video for "Creep" at Oxford's **The Zodiac** (p. 263).

BEST INDULGENCES: It is easy to overload on clotted cream and cucumber sandwiches as you sip **high tea** in London (p. 83). Sate chocolate cravings and Willy Wonka fantasies at **Cadbury World,** in Birmingham (p. 290). Check out **Cheddar** (p. 196), but don't forget to bring biscuits.

BEST WAY TO TEMPT FATE: Nappers on Snowdonia's **Cader Idris** (p. 497) will awake either as poets or madmen, according to legend. In Snowdonia, mountaineers celebrate reaching the summit of **Tryfan** (p. 499) by jumping between its two peaks. And watch out for spitting tourists hoping to avoid beheading at Edinburgh's **Mercat Cross** (p. 536).

BEST SUNSETS: The walled Welsh city of **Caernarfon** (p. 502) sits on the water, facing the western horizon full on. The extreme northern location of **Shetland** (p. 662) makes for breathtaking skies, while **Arthur's Seat** (p. 538) grants 360° views of the shimmering Edinburgh skyline.

BEST LIVESTOCK: Don't pet Northumberland's psychotic **Wild Cattle,** inbred for seven centuries (p. 426). The Highlands have the harrowing **Bealach-na-ba ("Cattle") Pass** (p. 648), featuring plunging cliffs, hairpin turns, and daredevil cows. They aren't really livestock, but the tailless **Manx cats** on the Isle of Man (p. 376) are still pretty rad. Famous **seaweed-eating sheep** sustain themselves on North Ronaldsay's beaches (p. 661).

BEST NIGHTLIFE: Brighton (p. 152) does native son Fatboy Slim proud. Students command most of **Newcastle** (p. 417), while funkier folks try Oldham St. in **Manchester** (p. 343), home of the famous Factory Records club nights, or Broad St. in **Birmingham** (p. 287). Oh, and **London** (p. 83) is rumored to have the odd club, here and there.

BEST OF THE MACABRE: The morbid can sample the gallows at Nottingham's **Galleries of Justice** (p. 300). Some 250,000 bodies supposedly slumber around Edinburgh's **Greyfriars Tollbooth and Highland Kirk** (p. 538), while corpses are put to more interesting use at **Moyses' Hall Museum** (p. 326) in Bury St. Edmunds. Don't lose your head at the **Tower of London** (p. 104). A walk through the somber ruins of **Kilmainham Gaol** (p. 700) will leave you chilled to the bone.

in white at London's Lords grounds. Tennis, too, demands genteel conduct, at least with the strawberries-and-cream at Wimbledon. The Royal Ascot horse races and the Henley regatta draw Britain's blue-bloods, but the revered coastal "links" golf courses of **St. Andrews** (p. 572) attract enthusiasts from all over. Surfers catch a wave along the Atlantic coast at alternative **Newquay** (p. 228), artsy **St. Ives** (p. 239), and hardcore **Lewis** (p. 638). Go canyoning or whitewater rafting at **Fort William** (p. 623), or try the more tranquil punting at **Oxford** (p. 253) or **Cambridge** (p. 307). **Snowdonia National Park** (p. 492) and the **Cairngorm Mountains** (p. 611) challenge hikers, while every park has cycling trails. Any town will offer spontaneous kickabouts: go forth and seek your game.

FEELING FESTIVE?

Britons throw many lavish and large festivals. The concurrent **Edinburgh International** and **Fringe Festivals** (p. 544) take over Scotland's capital with a head-spinning program of performances. The whole of Scotland hits the streets to welcome the New Year for **Hogmanay**, while torch-lit Viking revelry ignites the Shetlands during **Up Helly Aa** (p. 665). Back in London, things turn fiery during the **Chinese New Year.** In Manchester's Gay Village, **Mardi Gras** (p. 343) is the wildest of street parties, while the summer **Notting Hill Carnival** blasts the streets of London with Caribbean color. The three-day **Glastonbury Festival** (p. 197) is Britain's biggest homage to rock, drawing the banner names (and crowds) year after year. **T in the Park, Reading Festival, Leeds Festival, V Festival, and** the **Isle of Wight Festival** all draw massive musical acts and massive crowds; British summer music festivals sell over a million tickets annually. The **International Musical Eisteddfod** is Wales's version of the mega-fest, swelling modest Llangollen (p. 491) to nearly 30 times its normal size. For a celebration of all things Welsh, check out the **National Eisteddfod** (p. 440).

TOP TEN LIST

THE QUEST FOR THE HOLY GRAIL

1. Begin by waxing noble at Henry III's Round Table in the **Winchester Great Hall** (p. 172).

2. Reenact Arthur's final battle with his son Mordred at **Slaughter Bridge** (p. 224), using plastic swords bought from the nearby **Arthurian Centre** gift shop.

3. Go back to where it all began at **Tintagel Castle** (p. 226), Arthur's legendary birthplace, or poke around **Merlin's Cave** on the water just below.

4. Sleuth carefully at **Glastonbury Tor** (p. 199), an Isle of Avalon and Grail-hunter hotspot.

5. Hike up the **Brecon Beacons** (p. 454) looking for bits of Camelot sticking up through the grass (or reenacting the movie *King Arthur*, partially filmed here).

6. Get your legends straight in the caverns of **King Arthur's Labyrinth** in Machynlleth (p. 481).

7. Be wary of the Grail (and ghosts) at the legendary ruins of **Castell Dinas Brân** (p. 492).

8. Explore the **Eildon Hills** (p. 547), keeping an eye out for the underground caverns where Arthur and his knights sleep until Britain needs them once more.

9. Follow *Da Vinci Code* enthusiasts to **Rosslyn Chapel** (p. 545) and test your knowledge of Templar symbology on the thousands of stone carvings.

10. Paddle out to the end of your Quest with Monty Python fans at **Castle Aaargh** (p. 595). Don't let any rude French knights break your resolve!

SUGGESTED ITINERARIES

THE BEST OF THE UK (5 WEEKS)

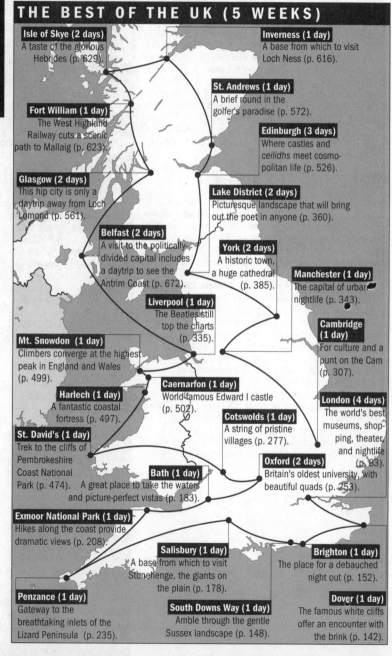

Isle of Skye (2 days)
A taste of the glorious Hebrides (p. 629).

Inverness (1 day)
A base from which to visit Loch Ness (p. 616).

St. Andrews (1 day)
A brief round in the golfer's paradise (p. 572).

Fort William (1 day)
The West Highland Railway cuts a scenic path to Mallaig (p. 623).

Edinburgh (3 days)
Where castles and *ceilidhs* meet cosmopolitan life (p. 526).

Glasgow (2 days)
This hip city is only a daytrip away from Loch Lomond (p. 561).

Lake District (2 days)
Picturesque landscape that will bring out the poet in anyone (p. 360).

Belfast (2 days)
A visit to the politically-divided capital includes a daytrip to see the Antrim Coast (p. 672).

York (2 days)
A historic town, a huge cathedral (p. 385).

Manchester (1 day)
The capital of urban nightlife (p. 343).

Liverpool (1 day)
The Beatles still top the charts (p. 335).

Cambridge (1 day)
For culture and a punt on the Cam (p. 307).

Mt. Snowdon (1 day)
Climbers converge at the highest peak in England and Wales (p. 499).

Caernarfon (1 day)
World-famous Edward I castle (p. 502).

London (4 days)
The world's best museums, shopping, theater, and nightlife (p. 83).

Harlech (1 day)
A fantastic coastal fortress (p. 497).

Cotswolds (1 day)
A string of pristine villages (p. 277).

St. David's (1 day)
Trek to the cliffs of Pembrokeshire Coast National Park (p. 474).

Oxford (2 days)
Britain's oldest university, with beautiful quads (p. 253).

Bath (1 day)
A great place to take the waters and picture-perfect vistas (p. 183).

Exmoor National Park (1 day)
Hikes along the coast provide dramatic views (p. 208).

Brighton (1 day)
The place for a debauched night out (p. 152).

Salisbury (1 day)
A base from which to visit Stonehenge, the giants on the plain (p. 178).

Penzance (1 day)
Gateway to the breathtaking inlets of the Lizard Peninsula (p. 235).

South Downs Way (1 day)
Amble through the gentle Sussex landscape (p. 148).

Dover (1 day)
The famous white cliffs offer an encounter with the brink (p. 142).

THE BEST OF ENGLAND (1 MONTH)

Lake District (2 days)
A peaceful, Wordsworthian landscape (p. 360).

Newcastle (1 day)
From a Roman fortification to the home of the famous brown ale and great nightlife (p. 417).

Liverpool (2 days)
Beatle-mania is still raging (p. 335).

Blackpool (1 day)
A terrifically gaudy weekend (p. 349).

York (2 days)
A giant cathedral in a medieval town (p. 385).

Manchester (1 day)
The post-industrial clubbing mecca (p. 343).

London (5 days)
The cosmopolitan center of everything English (p. 83).

Oxford (2 days)
A pint and a punt in the medieval university city (p. 253).

Cotswolds (2 days)
Rustic villages are separated by short hikes (p. 277).

Dover (1 day)
A panorama of the Continent from the white cliffs (p. 142).

Exmoor National Park (1 day)
Perfect for a day of rambling (p. 209).

Newquay (1 day)
An incongruous slice of surfer culture (p. 228).

Salisbury (2 days)
A base from which to explore the stone circles at Stonehenge and Avebury, with its own cathedral (p. 178).

Brighton (2 days)
The infamous "dirty weekend" on the coast (p. 152).

Penzance (2 days)
The tip of the striking Cornish coast (p. 235).

South Downs Way (1 day)
A walk in the idyllic countryside with a stop at the fairy-tale castle at Arundel (p. 148).

THE BEST OF WALES (2 WEEKS)

Caernarfon (1 day)
A Byzantine castle and Roman ruins draw visitors (p. 502).

Conwy (1 day)
Curious attractions flank a turquoise harbor (p. 483).

Llanberis (1 day)
Provides an idyllic point from which to ascend lofty Mt. Snowdon (p. 499).

Harlech (1 day)
Boasts sea, sand, and summits—not to mention Wales's most dramatic fortress (p. 497).

Snowdonia (1 day)
A spectacular landscape with stops in Machynlleth and tiny Dolgellau (p. 492).

Pembrokeshire Coast National Park (1 day)
Beckons with scenic coastal hikes (p. 466).

Wye Valley (2 days)
Bookish Hay-on-Wye sits in the midst of hills and dales (p. 449).

Chepstow (1 day)
From this picturesque town, it's just a quick jaunt to haunting Tintern Abbey (p. 450).

St. David's (1 day)
A tiny city with a majestic cathedral (p. 474).

Cardiff (2 days)
The resurgent nation's young, international capital boasts a newly developed waterfront and a flourishing arts scene (p. 442).

Tenby (1 day)
A beach resort town with flair (p. 469).

Brecon (1 day)
Trek through the rugged Brecon Beacons (p. 454).

DISCOVER

THE BEST OF HISTORY (4 WEEKS)

Orkney Islands (2 days)
Archaeological sites cover the Stone Age, Bronze Age, and Viking era (p. 653).

Stirling (1 day)
A mecca for William Wallace fans (p. 586).

Glasgow (2 days)
A city full of historical layers: from the medieval outpost to the Victorian hub to the capital of industry (p. 561).

Edinburgh (3 days)
The Royal Mile, the Scottish capital's medieval center, contains a multitude of treasures (p. 526).

Hadrian's Wall (1 day)
This wall, built at the edge of the Roman Empire, held back invaders from the north (p. 429).

Belfast (2 days)
The recent Troubles are still manifest in the graffiti on the walls (p. 672).

York (2 days)
A medieval town with a colossal cathedral (p. 385).

Cambridge (1 day)
Plenty of opportunities for punting past architectural marvels (p. 307).

Caernarfon and Conwy (2 days)
The two most impressive of Edward I's chain of castles (p. 483 and 502).

Ironbridge (1 day)
Ten museums trace the birth of the Industrial Revolution (p. 291).

London (4 days)
More sights than you could explore in a year (p. 83).

Canterbury (1 day)
The shrine of St. Thomas à Becket has drawn pilgrims from before the times of Chaucer (p. 135).

Bath (1 day)
The Roman baths have beckoned to vacationers for 1000 years (p. 183).

Oxford (2 days)
Britain's oldest University (p. 253).

Salisbury (2 days)
A base for exploring the ancient megaliths at Stonehenge and Avebury, with a spectacular cathedral of its own (p. 178).

Hastings and Battle (1 day)
The site of the 1066 battle between the Anglo-Saxons and the Normans (p. 147).

Portsmouth (1 day)
The center of Britain's naval heritage (p. 162).

THE BEST OF SCOTLAND (2 WEEKS)

Isle of Skye (2 days)
Offers enviable hiking and dramatic views of the Cuillin Mountains (p. 629).

Orkney Islands (2 days)
Ancient ruins on isolated isles (p. 653).

Inverness (1 day)
A good base for seeing Loch Ness and perhaps its infamous resident (p. 616).

Aberdeen (1 day)
For city life and a trip to clifftop Dunnottar Castle (p. 603).

Fort William (1 day)
For Scotland's highest peak, Ben Nevis (p. 623).

Stirling (1 day)
Home of Scottish heroes and a stunning castle (p. 586).

St. Andrews (1 day)
The golfer's paradise (p. 572).

Glasgow (2 days)
A city of art, culture, and nightlife and base for a daytrip to the bonnie banks of Loch Lomond (p. 561).

Edinburgh (4 days)
Fantastic during festivals in August, but sparkling year-round with unbeatable pints and the historic Royal Mile (p. 526).

THE BEST OF THE OUTDOORS (6 WEEKS)

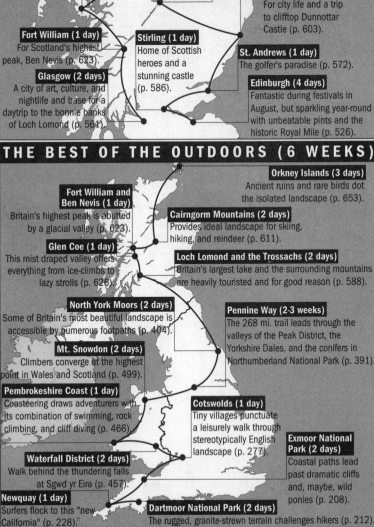

Orkney Islands (3 days)
Ancient ruins and rare birds dot the isolated landscape (p. 653).

Fort William and Ben Nevis (1 day)
Britain's highest peak is abutted by a glacial valley (p. 623).

Cairngorm Mountains (2 days)
Provides ideal landscape for skiing, hiking, and reindeer (p. 611).

Glen Coe (1 day)
This mist draped valley offers everything from ice-climbs to lazy strolls (p. 626).

Loch Lomond and the Trossachs (2 days)
Britain's largest lake and the surrounding mountains are heavily touristed and for good reason (p. 588).

North York Moors (2 days)
Some of Britain's most beautiful landscape is accessible by numerous footpaths (p. 404).

Pennine Way (2-3 weeks)
The 268 mi. trail leads through the valleys of the Peak District, the Yorkshire Dales, and the conifers in Northumberland National Park (p. 391).

Mt. Snowdon (2 days)
Climbers converge at the highest point in Wales and Scotland (p. 499).

Pembrokeshire Coast (1 day)
Coasteering draws adventurers with its combination of swimming, rock climbing, and cliff diving (p. 466).

Cotswolds (1 day)
Tiny villages punctuate a leisurely walk through stereotypically English landscape (p. 277).

Exmoor National Park (2 days)
Coastal paths lead past dramatic cliffs and, maybe, wild ponies (p. 208).

Waterfall District (2 days)
Walk behind the thundering falls at Sgwd yr Eira (p. 457).

Newquay (1 day)
Surfers flock to this "new California" (p. 228).

Dartmoor National Park (2 days)
The rugged, granite-strewn terrain challenges hikers (p. 212).

The inexpressible delight in ruin, shared by all classes and passed from generation to generation, is one of those cultural tics which make the British truly singular among the nations. This instinct to commune with melancholy, to wax wistful about the ambitions of ages past chastened and brought low by history's pratfalls, is as British as milky tea and cow parsley in the country lanes.

It's possible to enter this great British romance of ruins in many of the most celebrated piles of stones such as **Tintern Abbey,** near the River Avon where Wordsworth made intimations of mortality a national obligation. But the danger of sampling the poetry of dereliction amidst the Top Sites is, of course, the buzzing business of the present; so many tourist coaches, so much bad ice cream, so many postcards. Better by far to head to the lesser known and commune in the company of bumblebees and the occasional wandering fellow-pilgrim.

Go, for instance, to Northamptonshire to see what's left of **Lyveden New Bield,** the late 16th-century oratory of the Anglo-Catholic Thomas Tresham and a ruin almost as soon as it was constructed. An exquisite echo of French Renaissance limestone architecture, the oratory was supposed to be a place where the Elizabethan gentleman, who tried to be loyal to both his Queen and his Church, could practice his devotions safe from the prying eyes of authorities. Lyveden displays a delicate, haunting frieze of the stations of the cross on its exterior walls; and from above, the entire structure takes the form of a cross, the sign which Tresham dared not make. A great rotunda was to crown the structure, but Tresham ran out of money and time and was jailed for failing to pay the "recusancy" fines imposed for not subscribing to the official church. The entire building was left open to the elements where it stands in knee-high meadowland.

Most of the ruins in Britain are the work of sudden disaster rather than the slow crumblings of time. **Corfe Castle** (a major destination in Dorset but still worth the trip) looks the charred and blackened pile because it held out against Oliver Cromwell's besieging army to the bitter end during the Second Civil War of 1647-1648. And some of the imposing, pitted "brochs" of Iron Age **Orkney** (like Gurness) and **Shetland** look as brutal as they do, not through long centuries of decay but because, at some point they failed in their mission of holding back the oncoming wave of invaders and local rivals. Stunning, sandstone-red **Lindisfarne** occupying its heart-stopping site on the Northumbrian shore, was twice ravaged, first by Vikings who, despite their recent cultural makeover as seaborn traders, still sacked the place and slaughtered the monks. Then again predictably emptied it of its community and treasures in the Reformation. Equally sudden was the end of the spectacularly beautiful **Binham Priory** in southern Norfolk, also succumbing to the enforcers of the Protestant Reformation under Henry VIII and Edward VI who turned what had obviously been one of the most palatial and gorgeously decorated Benedictine foundations into a strangely truncated and spare parish church (where you can still hear choral concerts in the evenings). Miraculously, the Reformation's erasures of the richly painted rood screen (the screen separating the nave from the choir) have themselves become ruins, peeling away to reveal beneath some of the most astonishing church painting of saints and apostles that survived from the world of Roman Catholic England.

Some of the most powerfully evocative ruins, though, can be modern. A little way from the center of Dublin stands one of the great monuments to imperial obtuseness: Kilmainham Gaol. Now a stunning historical museum the urge to create an Irish national martyrology has been resisted for the sake of genuine historical intelligence. The exterior is just standard issue, banal, mock-castellated prison. But the interior is a cathedral of incarceration simultaneously shocking, almost operatically grand, with its multi-story iron staircase and rat-hole cells where ancient pallets and fragments of anonymous rags gather grime—morally as well as architecturally squalid. If it all gets too much, head for the tea room and munch on Irish cakes, drink in the giggly chatter of schoolchildren scripted by James Joyce and reflect that this is how ruins are supposed to get you, not a cheap rush of sentiment, much less a pang of nostalgia, but the tender inspection of ancient scars which linger obstinately to remind us of the redeeming vulnerability of the human condition.

Simon Schama is University Professor of Art History at Columbia University. He writes for The New Yorker *and was recently the writer and host of the BBC's* History of Britain. *His most recent book is* A History of Britain, Volume III: The Fate of Empire.

ESSENTIALS

PLANNING YOUR TRIP

 ENTRANCE REQUIREMENTS
Passport (p. 13). Required of all foreign nationals, though they may not be checked for citizens of the EU.
Visa (p. 14). Not required of citizens of Australia, Canada, New Zealand, the US, and many other Western countries. If you are unsure, call your local embassy or complete an inquiry at www.ukvisas.gov.uk. Students planning to study in the UK for 6 months or more must obtain a student visa.
Inoculations (p. 16). No specific inoculations, vaccinations, certificates, or the International Certificate of Vaccination is required, but check to see if an ICV is required upon re-entry into your own country.
Work Permit (p. 14). Required of all foreign nationals planning to work in the UK or Ireland.

EMBASSIES AND CONSULATES

UK CONSULAR SERVICES ABROAD

For addresses of British embassies in countries not listed here, consult the **Foreign and Commonwealth Office** (☎020 7008 1500; www.fco.gov.uk). Some cities have a local British consulate that can handle most of the same functions as an embassy.

Australia: Commonwealth Ave., Yarralumla, ACT 2600 (☎61 (0)2 6270 6666; bhc.britaus.net). Consular Section (UK passports and visas), Piccadilly House, 39 Brindabella Circuit, Brindabella Business Park, Canberra Airport, Canberra ACT 2609 (☎33 1902 941 555). **Consulates-General** in Brisbane, Melbourne, Perth, and Sydney; Consulate in Adelaide.

Canada: 80 Elgin St., Ottawa, ON K1P 5K7 (☎1-613-237-1530; www.britainincanada.org). **Consulate-General,** 777 Bay St., ste. 2800, Toronto, ON M5G 2G2 (☎1-416-593-1290). Other Consulates-General in Montreal and Vancouver; Honorary Consuls in Quebec City, St. John's, and Winnipeg.

Ireland: 29 Merrion Rd., Ballsbridge, Dublin 4 (☎353 (0)1 205 3700; www.britishembassy.ie).

New Zealand: 44 Hill St., Thorndon, Wellington 1 (☎64 (0)4 924 2888; www.britain.org.nz); mail to P.O. Box 1812, Wellington. **Consulate-General:** 151 Queen St., Auckland (☎64 (0)9 303 2973); mail to Private Bag 92014, Auckland.

US: 3100 Massachusetts Ave. NW, Washington, D.C. 20008 (☎1-900-255-6685; www.britainusa.com). **Consulate-General:** 845 Third Ave., New York, NY 10022 (☎1-212-745-0200). Other Consulates-General in Atlanta, Boston, Chicago, Houston, Los Angeles, San Francisco. Consulates in Dallas, Denver, Miami, Seattle.

IRISH CONSULAR SERVICES ABROAD

Australia: 20 Arkana St., Yarralumla, Canberra ACT 2600 (☎61 (0)2 6273 3022).

Canada: Ste. 1105, 130 Albert St., Ottawa, K1P 5G4, Ontario (☎1-613-233-6281).

New Zealand: Honorary Consul General, 6th. fl., 18 Shortland St., 1001, Auckland (☎64 (0)9 977 2252).

UK: 17 Grosvenor Pl., London SW1X 7HR (☎0870 005 6725). **Consulates:** 16 Randolph Crescent, Edinburgh EH3 7TT (☎0131 226 7711); Brunel House, 2 Fitzalan Rd., Cardiff CF24 0EB (☎029 2066 2000).

US: 2234 Massachusetts Ave. NW, Washington, D.C. 20008 (☎1-202-462-3939; www.irelandemb.org). **Consulate General:** 345 Park Ave., 17th fl., New York, NY 10154-0037 (☎1-212-319-2555). Other Consulates General in Boston, Chicago, and San Francisco.

CONSULAR SERVICES IN THE UK

Australia: Australia House, The Strand, London WC2B 4LA (☎020 7379 4334; www.australia.org.uk).

Canada: 38 Grosvenor Sq., London W1K 4AA (☎020 7258 6600; www.canada.org.uk).

Ireland: See **Irish Consular Services Abroad** (above).

New Zealand: New Zealand House, 80 Haymarket, London SW1Y 4TQ (☎020 7930 8422).

US: 24 Grosvenor Sq., London W1A 1AE (☎020 7499 9000; www.usembassy.org.uk). Consulates in Belfast, Cardiff, and Edinburgh.

TOURIST OFFICES

VISIT BRITAIN

Formerly known as the British Tourist Authority (BTA), **Visit Britain** oversees UK tourist boards and solicits tourism. The main office is located at Thames Tower, Blacks Road, London, W6 9EL (☎020 8563 3000; www.visitbritain.com).

Australia: Level 2, 15 Blue St., North Sydney NSW 2060 (☎61 (0)2 9021 4400; www.visitbritain.com/au). Open M-F 9am-4pm.

Canada: 5915 Airport Rd., ste. 120, Mississauga, Ontario L4V 1T1 (☎1-888-847-4885; www.visitbritain.com/ca). Open M-F 9am-5pm.

Ireland: 18-19 College Green, Dublin 2 (☎353 (0)1 670 8000; www.visitbritain.com/ie). Open M-F 10am-5pm.

New Zealand: Richwhite Building, 17th fl., 151 Queen St., Auckland 1 (☎64 (0)800 700 741; www.visitbritain.com/nz). Open M-F 10am-6pm.

US: 551 Fifth Ave., Ste. 701, New York, NY 10176 (☎1-800-462-2748; www.visitbritain.com/us). Open M-F 9am-5pm.

WITHIN THE UK AND IRELAND

Britain Visitor Centre, 1 Lower Regent St., Piccadilly Circus, London SW1Y 4XT (☎020 8462 2748). Open M 9:30am-6:30pm, Tu-F 9am-6:30pm, Sa-Su 10am-4pm.

Irish Tourist Board (Bord Fáilte): Baggot St. Bridge, Dublin 2 (☎353 (0)1 602 4000; www.ireland.travel.ie). Open M-F 9:30am-5:15pm.

Northern Ireland Tourist Board, 59 North St., Belfast BT1 1NB (☎028 9023 1221; www.discovernorthernireland.com). Open Oct.-May M-Sa 9am-5:30pm; June-Sept. M-Sa 9am-7pm, Su noon-5pm.

Scottish Tourism Board, 23 Ravelston Terr., Edinburgh EH4 3TP (☎0131 332 2433; www.visitscotland.com). Open M-Sa 9:30am-6pm.

Welsh Tourist Board, Brunel House, 2 Fitzalan Rd., Cardiff CF24 0UY (☎0870 830 0306; www.visitwales.com). Open daily 9am-5pm.

DOCUMENTS AND FORMALITIES

PASSPORTS

REQUIREMENTS

Citizens of all countries except the Republic of Ireland need valid passports to enter Britain and to re-enter their home countries. EU citizens should carry their passports, though they may not be checked. Britain does not allow entrance if the holder's passport expires in under six months. Returning home with an expired passport is illegal and may result in a fine.

NEW PASSPORTS

Citizens of Australia, Canada, Ireland, New Zealand, the United Kingdom, and the United States can apply for a passport at any passport office and many post offices and courts of law. New passport or renewal applications must be filed in advance of departure, although most passport offices offer rush services for a steep fee.

ONE EUROPE. Since its founding in 1958, the European Economic Community (EEC), now the **European Union (EU),** has worked to promote continental solidarity and cooperation and has become a mighty political, legal, and economic institution. On May 1, 2004, Cyprus, the Czech Republic, Estonia, Hungary, Latvia, Lithuania, Malta, Poland, Slovakia, and Slovenia were admitted to the EU, joining 15 other member states: Austria, Belgium, Denmark, Finland, France, Germany, Greece, Ireland, Italy, Luxembourg, the Netherlands, Portugal, Spain, Sweden, and the UK. A current debate rages over the induction of other countries, particularly Turkey. For foreign tourists, the EU's policy of **freedom of movement** means that border controls between the first 15 member states (minus Ireland and the UK, but plus Norway, Switzerland, and Iceland) have been abolished and visa policies harmonized. While still required to present a passport (or government-issued ID card for EU citizens) to cross an national border, a traveler admitted into one country is free to travel to other participating countries. Britain and Ireland have also formed a **common travel area,** abolishing passport controls between the UK and the Republic of Ireland. For more consequences of the EU for travelers, see **Customs in the EU** (p. 15).

PASSPORT MAINTENANCE

Photocopy all of your important travel documents, especially visas, the photo page of your passport, and traveler's checks. Leave one set of copies at home and carry one set in a part of your baggage separate from the originals. You might also consider carrying an expired passport or an official copy of your birth certificate.

If you lose your passport, immediately notify the local police and the nearest embassy or consulate of your home government. To expedite its replacement, you will need to know all information previously recorded and show ID and proof of citizenship. In some cases, a replacement may take weeks to process, and it may be valid only for a limited time. Any visas stamped in your old passport will be irretrievably lost. In an emergency, ask for immediate temporary traveling papers that will permit you to re-enter your home country.

VISAS

EU citizens, plus citizens of Iceland, Liechtenstein, Norway, and Switzerland, do not need a visa to enter Britain. Citizens of Australia, Canada, New Zealand, South Africa, and the US do not need a visa for visits shorter than six months; neither do citizens of Israel, Japan, Malaysia, Mexico, Singapore, and some Eastern European, Caribbean, and Pacific countries. Citizens of most other countries must have a visa to enter Britain; citizens of certain countries will need a visa merely to pass through Britain. If you are uncertain, contact your embassy or complete an online inquiry at www.ukvisas.gov.uk. Tourist visas cost £36 and allow you to spend up to six months in the UK. Visas can be purchased from your nearest British consulate. US citizens can take advantage of the **Center for International Business and Travel** (**CIBT; ☎** 1-800-929-2428; www.cibt.com), which secures visas for stays longer than six months for a variable service charge. If you need a **visa extension** while in the UK, contact the Home Office, Immigration and Nationality Directorate (**☎** 0870 606 7766; www.ind.homeoffice.gov.uk).

WORK AND STUDY PERMITS

Admission as a visitor does not include the right to work, which is authorized only by a work permit. Entering Britain and Ireland to **study** requires a special visa if you are planning to do so for longer than six months; see **Beyond Tourism** (p. 58).

IDENTIFICATION

When you travel, always carry at least two forms of identification on your person, including a photo ID. Never carry all of your IDs together; split them up in case of theft or loss, and keep photocopies of all of them in your luggage and at home.

STUDENT, TEACHER, AND YOUTH IDENTIFICATION

The widely accepted and eminently useful **International Student Identity Card (ISIC)** provides discounts on sights, accommodations, food, and transport; access to a toll-free 24hr. emergency helpline; and some insurance benefits for US cardholders. Some sights and establishments, such as cinemas, do not accept other forms of foreign student ID. Applicants for an ISIC must be full-time secondary or postsecondary school students. Because of the proliferation of fake ISICs, some services (particularly airlines) require additional proof of student identity.

The **International Teacher Identity Card (ITIC)** offers teachers the same insurance coverage as the ISIC and similar but limited discounts. For travelers who are 25 or under but are not students, the **International Youth Travel Card (IYTC)** also offers many of the same benefits as the ISIC, but with significantly fewer discounts.

ISIC and **ITIC** provide basic insurance benefits to US cardholders, including US$100 per day of in-hospital sickness for up to 100 days and US$10,000 of accident-related medical reimbursement (see www.isicus.com). Each of these costs $22 or equivalent. ISICs and ITICs are valid for roughly 1½ academic years; IYTC cards are valid for 1 year from the date of issue. Many travel agencies (p. 25) issue them; for a list of issuing agencies, see the **ISTC** website (www.istc.org).

The **International Student Exchange Card (ISE)** is a similar identification card available to students, faculty, and youth ages 12 to 26. The card provides discounts, medical benefits, access to a 24hr. emergency helpline, and the ability to purchase student airfares. However, it is not as widely recognized as the ISIC. The ISE costs US$25; call US **☎** 1-800-255-8000 for more info, or visit www.isecard.com.

CUSTOMS

Her Majesty's Revenue and Customs (www.hmrc.gov.uk) controls customs. Travelers from outside the EU may bring up to £145 worth of non-personal goods unintended for sale (such as gifts) into the UK, with special strictures for cigarettes, alcohol, and perfume. Upon entering Britain, you must declare items beyond the £145 allowance and pay duty. Note that goods and gifts purchased at **duty-free** shops abroad are not exempt from duty or sales tax; "duty-free" merely means that you need not pay a tax in the country of purchase. Upon returning home, likewise, you must declare all articles acquired abroad and pay a duty on the value of articles in excess of your home country's allowance. If bringing valuables from home, consider registering them with customs before traveling abroad. Be sure to keep receipts. If you're leaving for a non-EU country, you can claim back any **Value Added Tax** paid (see **Taxes**, p. 18).

The **Pet Travel Scheme (PETS)** allows dogs and cats from Western European nations, the US, and Canada to avoid a six-month quarantine. Your dog or cat must be fitted with a microchip, treated for ticks and tapeworm, vaccinated for rabies, and tested for vaccine effectiveness six months prior to arrival. For a complete description of the stringent requirements, contact the **UK Department for Environment, Food, and Rural Affairs** (www.defra.gov.uk/animalh/quarantine/index.htm) or call the **PETS helpline** (☎ 0870 241 1710).

CUSTOMS IN THE EU. As well as freedom of movement of people within the EU (see p. 13), travelers in the 15 original EU member countries can also take advantage of the freedom of movement of goods. This means that there are no customs controls at internal EU borders (i.e., you can take the blue customs channel at the airport), and travelers are free to transport whatever legal substances they like as long as it is for their own personal (non-commercial) use—up to 3200 cigarettes, 10L of spirits, 90L of wine (20L of fortified wine), and 110L of beer. Duty-free allowances were abolished in 1999 for travel between EU member states; however, travelers between the EU and the rest of the world still get a duty-free allowance when passing through customs.

MONEY

CURRENCY AND EXCHANGE

The **pound sterling** is the unit of currency in the United Kingdom. Northern Ireland and Scotland have their own bank notes (including Scottish £1 and £100 notes); the money is of equal value but may not be accepted outside Northern Ireland and Scotland. The **Republic of Ireland** switched from the Irish pound to **euro** in 2002. The currency chart below is based on August 2005 exchange rates between local currency and Australian dollars (AUS$), Canadian dollars (CDN$), European Union euros (EUR€), New Zealand dollars (NZ$), British pounds (UK£), and US dollars (US$). Check the currency converter on websites like www.xe.com or a large newspaper for the latest exchange rates. As a general rule, it's cheaper to convert money in Britain than at home. A currency exchange with obscene rates will probably be available in your arrival airport; try to exchange a small amount at home.

Try to change money at banks or bureaux de change that have no fees and at most a 5% margin between the buy and sell prices. Many British department stores, such as Marks & Spencer, also offer excellent exchange services. Convert as large a sum as possible (unless the currency is depreciating rapidly), but no more than you'll need.

ESSENTIALS

CURRENCY (£)

AUS$1 = £0.40	£1 = AUS$2.52
CDN$1 = £0.42	£1 = CDN$2.36
EUR€1 = £0.68	£1 = EUR€1.48
NZ$1 = £0.37	£1 = NZ$2.70
UK£1 = £1	£1 = UK£1
US$1 = £0.55	£1 = US$1.82

If you use traveler's checks or bills, carry some in small denominations (the equivalent of US$50 or less) for times when you are forced to exchange money at disadvantageous rates, but bring a range of denominations since charges may be levied per check cashed. Store your money in a variety of forms; ideally, at any given time you will be carrying some cash, some traveler's checks, and an ATM and/or credit card.

TRAVELER'S CHECKS

Traveler's checks are one of the safest means of carrying funds. American Express and Visa are the most-recognized brands. Many banks and agencies sell them for a small commission. Checks are accepted in heavily touristed areas and large cities, but often not in smaller towns and shops. Check issuers provide refunds if the checks are lost or stolen, and many provide additional services, such as toll-free refund hotlines abroad, emergency message services, and stolen credit card assistance. Always carry emergency cash. Visa and American Express also offer **prepaid travel cards** as a more convenient alternative to traveler's checks; call or visit their respective websites (below) for more information.

American Express: Checks available with commission at select banks, at all AmEx offices, and online (www.americanexpress.com; US residents only). American Express cardholders can purchase checks by phone (☎ 1-800-721-9768). Checks available in many currencies. Also offers the Travelers Cheque Card, a prepaid reloadable card. Cheques for Two can be signed by either of 2 people traveling together. For purchase locations or more information, contact AmEx's service centers: in Australia ☎ 1-800 688 022, in New Zealand 64 (0)423 74 409, in the UK 0800 587 6023, in the US and Canada 1-800-221-7282; elsewhere, call the US collect at 1-801-964-6665.

Travelex: Thomas Cook, MasterCard, and Visa traveler's checks available. For information about Thomas Cook MasterCard call: in the US ☎ 1-800-223-7373, in the UK 0800 622 101; elsewhere call the UK collect at 44 (0)1733 318 950. For more information, visit www.travelex.com.

Visa: Checks available (generally with commission) at banks worldwide. For the location of the nearest office, call the Visa Travelers Cheque Global Refund and Assistance Center: in the UK ☎ 0800 515 884, in the US 1-800-227-6811, elsewhere, call the UK collect at 44 (0)2079 378 091. Checks available in US dollars, GB pounds, the euro, and many other currencies. Visa also offers TravelMoney, a prepaid debit card that can be reloaded online or by phone. For more information on Visa travel services, see http://usa.visa.com/personal/using_visa/travel_with_visa.html.

CREDIT, DEBIT, AND ATM CARDS

Credit cards are widely accepted. Some small establishments—including many B&Bs—either do not take them or add a surcharge. Credit cards often offer superior exchange rates—up to 5% better than the retail rate used by banks and other currency exchange establishments. Credit cards may also offer services such as insurance or emergency help, and are sometimes required to reserve hotel rooms or rental cars. **Mastercard** and **Visa** are the most welcomed; **American Express** and **Diners Club** cards are accepted mostly in large cities.

ATM cards (a.k.a. **cash cards**) are widely used in the UK and most banks have ATMs. Depending on the system that your home bank uses, you can most likely access your personal bank account from abroad. ATMs get the same wholesale exchange rate as credit cards, but there is often a limit on the amount of money you can withdraw per day (usually around US$500). There is typically also a surcharge of US$2-5 per withdrawal. The two major international money networks are Cirrus (to locate ATMs call ☎1-800-424-7787 or visit www.mastercard.com) and Visa/ PLUS (to locate ATMs call ☎1-800-843-7587 or visit www.visa.com). The ATMs of major British and Irish banks (including Barclays, HSBC, Lloyds TSB, National Westminster, Royal Bank of Scotland, Bank of Scotland, Allied Ireland Bank, and Ulster Bank) usually accept both networks.

A debit card can be used wherever its associated credit card company (usually Mastercard or Visa) is accepted; a pound sterling account is not required. Debit cards can also be used to withdraw cash from associated banks and ATMs throughout the UK, although a steep fee (US$3-6) may be charged.

PINS AND ATMS. To use a cash or credit card to withdraw money from a cash machine (ATM) in Europe, you must have a **Personal Identification Number (PIN)**. **Credit cards** don't usually come with PINs, so if you intend to hit up ATMs in Europe with a credit card to get cash advances, call your credit card company before leaving to request one. Travelers with alphabetic, rather than numerical, PINs may also be thrown off by the lack of letters on European cash machines. The following are the corresponding numbers to use: 1=QZ; 2=ABC; 3=DEF; 4=GHI; 5=JKL; 6=MNO; 7=PRS; 8=TUV; and 9=WXY.

GETTING MONEY FROM HOME

If you run out of money while traveling, the easiest and cheapest solution is to have someone back home make a deposit to your credit card or ATM card. Failing that, consider one of the following options.

WIRING MONEY

It is possible to arrange a **bank money transfer,** in which your bank wires money to a bank in Britain. This is the cheapest way to transfer cash, but also the slowest, taking one to three days or more. Banks may release your funds in local currency, potentially at a poor exchange rate. Transfer services like **Western Union** are faster and more convenient, although they can be pricier. To find the nearest location, visit www.westernunion.com, or call US and Canada ☎1-800-325-6000, UK 0800 83 38 33, Australia 61 800 173 833, or New Zealand 64 800 27 0000. Money transfer services are also available at **American Express** and **Thomas Cook** offices.

US STATE DEPARTMENT (US CITIZENS ONLY)

In dire emergencies, the US State Department will forward money within hours to the nearest consular office, which will then disburse it according to instructions for a US$30 fee. If you wish to use this service, you must contact the Overseas Citizens Service division of the US State Department (☎1-202-647-5225, toll-free 1-888-407-4747, from overseas 1-202-501-4444).

ESSENTIALS

COSTS

The cost of your trip will vary considerably depending on where and when you go, how you travel, and where you stay. The most significant expenses will probably be your round-trip airfare (see **Getting to Britain and Ireland: By Plane,** p. 25) and a **railpass** or **bus pass** (p. 30). Before you go, spend some time calculating a reasonable daily **budget.**

STAYING ON A BUDGET

To give you a general idea, a bare-bones day in the UK (camping or sleeping in hostels/guesthouses, buying food at supermarkets) would cost about US$40 (£22/€33); a slightly more comfortable day (sleeping in hostels/guesthouses and the occasional budget hotel, eating one meal per day at a restaurant, going out at night) would cost US$91 (£50/€66); the sky's the limit. Don't forget to factor in emergency reserve funds (at least US$200) when planning how much money you'll need.

TIPS FOR SAVING MONEY

Some simpler ways to save money include finding free entertainment, splitting accommodation and food costs with trustworthy fellow travelers, and buying food in supermarkets rather than eating out. Bring a **sleepsack** (p. 19) to save on linen fees in hostels, and do your **laundry** in the sink (unless you're explicitly prohibited from doing so). Public museums in Britain are always free (excepting special exhibits). If you are eligible, consider getting an ISIC or an IYTC; many sights and museums offer reduced admission to students and youths. For getting around quickly, **bikes** are the most economical option. Renting a bike is cheaper than renting a moped or scooter. Don't forget about walking, though; you can learn a lot about a city by seeing it on foot. Drinking at bars and clubs quickly becomes expensive. It's cheaper to buy alcohol at a supermarket and imbibe before going out. That said, don't go overboard. Though staying within your budget is important, don't do so at the expense of your health or a great travel experience.

TIPPING AND BARGAINING

Tips in restaurants are often included in the bill (sometimes as a "service charge"); if gratuity is not included, you should tip your server 12.5%. Taxi drivers should receive a 10% tip, and bellhops and chambermaids usually expect £1-3. To the great relief of budget travelers from the US, tipping is not expected at pubs and bars in Britain and Ireland. Bargaining is unheard of in UK shops.

TAXES

The UK has a 17.5% **Value Added Tax (VAT),** a sales tax applied to everything but food, books, medicine, and children's clothing. The tax is **included** in the amount indicated on the price tag. The prices stated in *Let's Go* include VAT. Upon exiting Britain, non-EU citizens can reclaim VAT (minus an administrative fee) through the **Retail Export Scheme,** though the complex procedure is probably only worthwhile for large purchases. You can obtain refunds only for goods you take out of the country (i.e., not accommodations or meals). Participating shops display a "Tax Free Shopping" sign and may have a purchase minimum of £50-100 before they offer refunds. To claim a refund, fill out the form you are given in the shop and present it with the goods and receipts at customs upon departure (look for the Tax Free Refund desk at the airport). At peak times, this process can take up to an hour. You must leave the country within three months of your purchase in order to claim a refund, and you must apply before leaving the UK.

PACKING

Pack lightly. Lay out only what you absolutely need, then take half the clothes and twice the money. The Travelite FAQ (www.travelite.org) is a good resource for tips on traveling light. The online **Universal Packing List** (http://upl.codeq.info) will generate a customized list of suggested items based on your trip length, the expected climate, your planned activities, and other factors. If you plan to do a lot of hiking, also consult **The Great Outdoors, p. 38.** Some frequent travelers keep a bag packed with all the essentials: passport, money belt, hat, socks, etc. Then, when they decide to leave, they know they haven't forgotten anything.

Luggage: If you plan to cover most of your itinerary by foot, a sturdy **frame backpack** is unbeatable. (For the basics on buying a pack, see p. 46.) Toting a suitcase or trunk is fine if you plan to travel to one or two cities, but not if you plan to move frequently. A daypack (a small backpack or better, a courier bag) is also useful.

Clothing: No matter when you're traveling, it's a good idea to bring a warm jacket or wool sweater, a rain jacket to protect against ever-present British rain (Gore-Tex® is both waterproof and breathable), sturdy shoes or hiking boots, and wool socks. Flip-flops or waterproof sandals are must-haves for grubby hostel showers. You will want a classy outfit for going out at night, as well as a nicer pair of shoes.

Sleepsack: Some travelers choose to bring a sleepsack while camping, or to certain accommodations; hostels may have grungy bedding, or worse, charge extra for linens. To save yourself a few quid, make a sleepsack: fold a full-size sheet in half the long way, then sew it closed along the long side and one of the short sides.

Converters and Adapters: In Britain and Ireland, electricity is 220 volts AC, enough to fry any 120V North American appliance. 220/240V electrical appliances don't like 120V current, either. Americans and Canadians should buy an adapter (which changes the shape of the plug; US$5) and a converter (which changes the voltage; US$20-30). Don't make the mistake of using only an adapter (unless appliance instructions explicitly state otherwise, like many laptops). New Zealanders and Australians (who use 230V at home) won't need converters, but will need adapters to use anything electrical. For more on all things adaptable, check out http://kropla.com/electric.htm.

Toiletries: The basics, from toothpaste to tampons to condoms, are often available, but bring extras to save money. **Contact lenses** and solution can be expensive and difficult to find; bring enough for your entire trip. Also bring your glasses and a copy of your prescription in case you need emergency replacements.

First-Aid Kit: For a basic first-aid kit, pack bandages, pain reliever, antibiotic cream, a thermometer, a Swiss Army knife with tweezers (never in your carry-on), moleskin, decongestant, motion-sickness remedy, diarrhea or upset-stomach medication, an antihistamine for allergy emergencies, sunscreen, insect repellent, and burn ointment.

Film: Film and photo processing are expensive; bring film and develop it at home. Less serious photographers may want to bring a disposable camera or two. Despite disclaimers, airport security X-rays can fog film; consider a lead-lined pouch or ask security to hand-inspect your camera. Always pack film in your carry-on luggage as high-intensity X-rays are used on checked luggage. Although it requires a steep initial investment, a digital camera means never having to buy film again. Bring along a large memory card and extra (or rechargeable) batteries. For more info on digital cameras, visit www.short-courses.com/choosing/contents.htm.

Other Useful Items: For safety purposes, you should bring a **money belt** and small **padlock.** Basic **outdoors equipment** (plastic water bottle, compass, waterproof matches, pocketknife, sunglasses, sunscreen, hat) may also prove useful. If you want to do laundry by hand, bring detergent and string for a makeshift clothes line. Other often-forgotten items include an **umbrella;** sealable **plastic bags** (for damp clothes, soap, food, and spillables); a **travel alarm clock;** safety pins; a flashlight; earplugs; and a small **calculator.** A **cell phone** can be a lifesaver (literally) on the road (see p. 40).

Important Documents: Don't forget your passport, traveler's checks, ATM and/or credit cards, ID, and photocopies of all of these in case they get lost or stolen (p. 13). Also, if these apply: a hosteling membership card (p. 42); driver's license (p. 34); travel insurance forms; ISIC (p. 14), and rail or bus pass (p. 30).

SAFETY AND HEALTH

GENERAL ADVICE

In any type of crisis situation, the most important thing to do is **stay calm.** Your country's embassy (p. 12) is usually your best resource when things go wrong; **register** upon arrival in the UK for peace of mind and to facilitate aid.

DRUGS AND ALCOHOL

Remember that you are subject to the laws of the country in which you travel. It's your responsibility to know these laws before you go. If you carry insulin, syringes, or **prescription drugs** while you travel, it is vital to have a copy of the prescriptions and a note from your doctor. The Brits love their drink, and the vibrant pub scene is unavoidable. If you're trying to keep up with the locals, keep in mind the **Imperial pint is 20 oz.,** as opposed to the 16 oz. of a US pint. The drinking age in the UK is 18 (14 to enter, 16 for beer and wine if food is ordered).

Needless to say, **illegal drugs** are best avoided altogether. Carrying drugs across an international border can result in prison time and a "Drug Trafficker" stamp on your passport for the rest of your life. If arrested, call your country's consulate. Don't carry anyone else's luggage onto a plane.

SPECIFIC CONCERNS

DEMONSTRATIONS AND POLITICAL GATHERINGS

Sectarian violence in Northern Ireland has diminished dramatically in the past decade. but some neighborhoods and towns still experience unrest. Remain alert and cautious while traveling in Northern Ireland, especially during **Marching Season,** in the weeks leading up to July 12, and on August 12, when the **Apprentice Boys** march in Derry/Londonderry. The most common form of violence is property damage, and tourists are unlikely targets (but beware leaving a car with a Republic of Ireland license plate unattended). Use common sense and be respectful of your hosts' religious and political perspectives.

TERRORISM

The Anti-Terrorism Crime and Security Act 2001, passed in the aftermath of the September 11, 2001 attacks, strengthens the 2000 Terrorism Act, which outlaws certain terrorist groups and gives police extended powers to investigate terrorism. Britain is committed to an extensive program of prevention and prosecution. More information is available from the Foreign and Commonwealth Office (see box, below) and the Home Office (☎08700 001 585; www.homeoffice.gov.uk/terrorism). The US State Department website (www.state.gov) provides information on the current situation. To have advisories emailed to you, register with your home embassy or consulate when you arrive in Britain. If you see a suspicious unattended package or bag at an airport or other crowded public place, report it immediately at ☎999 or the **Anti-Terrorism Hotline** (☎0800 789 321).

TRAVEL ADVISORIES. The following government offices provide travel information and advisories by telephone, by fax, or via the web:

Australian Department of Foreign Affairs and Trade: ☎61 1300 555 135; www.dfat.gov.au.

Canadian Department of Foreign Affairs and International Trade (DFAIT): ☎1-800-267-8376; www.dfait-maeci.gc.ca. Call for their free booklet, *Bon Voyage...But.*

New Zealand Ministry of Foreign Affairs: ☎64 (0)44 398 000; www.mft.govt.nz/travel/index.html.

United Kingdom Foreign and Commonwealth Office: ☎020 7008 1500; www.fco.gov.uk.

US Department of State: ☎1-202-647-5225; http://travel.state.gov. Visit the website for the booklet *A Safe Trip Abroad.*

PERSONAL SAFETY

EXPLORING AND TRAVELING

EXPLORING. To avoid unwanted attention, try to blend in as much as possible. Familiarize yourself with your surroundings before setting out and carry yourself with confidence. Check maps in shops and restaurants rather than on the street. If you are traveling alone, be sure someone at home knows your itinerary and never admit that you're by yourself. When walking at night, stick to busy, well-lit streets and avoid dark alleyways. If you feel uncomfortable, leave quickly and directly.

SELF DEFENSE. There is no sure-fire way to avoid all the threatening situations you might encounter while traveling, but a good **self-defense course** will give you concrete ways to react to unwanted advances. Companies like **Impact Safety Programs** can refer you to local self-defense courses in the US (☎1-800-345-5425; www.impactboston.com/links.htm). Workshops (2-3hr.) start at US$45; full courses (20hr.) run US$350-500.

POSSESSIONS AND VALUABLES

Never leave your belongings unattended; crime occurs in even the most demure-looking hostel or hotel. Be particularly careful on **buses** and **trains;** horror stories abound about determined thieves who wait for travelers to fall asleep. Always keep your backpack in sight. When traveling with others, sleep in alternate shifts. When alone, use good judgment in selecting a train compartment: never stay in an empty one, and use a lock to secure your pack to the luggage rack. Try to sleep on top bunks with your luggage stored above you (if not in bed with you, but mind you do not sleep on or knock over your laptop).

There are a few steps you can take to minimize the financial risk associated with traveling. First, **bring as little with you as possible.** Second, buy a few combination **padlocks** to secure your belongings either in your pack or in a hostel or train station locker. Third, **carry as little cash as possible.** Keep your traveler's checks and ATM/credit cards in a **money belt**—not a fanny pack—along with your passport and ID cards. Fourth, **keep a small cash reserve separate from your primary stash.** Keep around £30 sewn into or stored in the depths of your pack, along with your traveler's check numbers and important photocopies. The best way to avoid getting **pickpocketed** is to use common sense; never flash your cash on the street, never wear your wallet in your back pocket, and do not carry open-topped bags. In large cities **con artists** often work in groups and may involve children. **Never let your passport or your bags out of your sight.** Beware of **pickpockets** on public transportation.

If you will be traveling with electronic devices, such as a laptop or a PDA, check whether your insurance covers loss, theft, or damage when you travel. If not, you might consider a low-cost policy. **Safeware** (US ☎ 1-800-800-1492; www.safeware.com) specializes in covering computers and charges US$90 for 90-day comprehensive international travel coverage up to US$4000. If you stay in any hostels on your trip, ask to store electronic valuables in a safe—most keep one in reception.

PRE-DEPARTURE HEALTH

In your **passport,** write the names of any people you wish to be contacted in case of a medical emergency and list any allergies or medical conditions. Matching a prescription to a foreign equivalent is not always easy, safe, or possible, so if you take prescription drugs, consider carrying up-to-date, legible prescriptions or a letter from your doctor stating the medication's trade name, manufacturer, chemical name, and dosage. Be sure to keep all medication with you in your carry-on luggage. For tips on packing a basic **first-aid kit** and other health essentials, see p. 19.

While no injections are specifically required for entry into the UK, travelers over two years old should make sure the following vaccines are up to date: MMR (for measles, mumps, and rubella); DTaP or Td (for diptheria, tetanus, and pertussis); OPV (for polio); HbCV (for haemophilus influenza B); and HBV (for Hepatitis B). Protection against Hepatitis A and tetanus is highly recommended. For recommendations on immunizations and prophylaxis, consult the CDC (see p. 23) in the US or the equivalent in your home country, and check with a doctor.

INSURANCE

Travel insurance covers four basic areas: medical/health problems, property loss, trip cancellation/interruption, and emergency evacuation. Though regular insurance policies may well extend to travel-related accidents, you may consider purchasing separate travel insurance if the cost of potential trip cancellation, interruption, or emergency medical evacuation is greater than you can absorb. Prices for travel insurance purchased separately generally run about US$50 per week for full coverage, while trip cancellation/interruption may be purchased separately at a rate of US$3-5 per day depending on length of stay.

Medical insurance (especially university policies) often covers costs incurred abroad; check with your provider. **US Medicare** does not cover foreign travel. **Canadian** provincial health insurance plans increasingly do not cover foreign travel; check with the Ministry of Health or Health Plan Headquarters for details. **Australians** traveling in Ireland and the UK are entitled to many of the services that they would receive at home as part of the Reciprocal Health Care Agreement. **Homeowners' insurance** (or your family's coverage) often covers theft during travel and loss of travel documents (passport, plane ticket, railpass, etc.) up to US$500.

USEFUL ORGANIZATIONS AND PUBLICATIONS

The US **Centers for Disease Control and Prevention** (**CDC;** ☎ 1-877-FYI-TRIP/394-8747; www.cdc.gov/travel) maintains an international travelers' hotline and an informative website. The CDC's comprehensive booklet *Health Information for International Travel* (The Yellow Book), an annual rundown of disease, immunization, and general health advice, is free online or US$29-40 via Elsevier Publications (☎ 1-800-545-2522; www.us.elsevierhealth.com). For quick information on health and other travel warnings call the **Overseas Citizens Services** (www.travel.state.gov; ☎ 1-888-407-4747; 1-317-472-2328 from overseas), or contact a passport agency, embassy, or consulate abroad. For information on medical evacuation services and travel insurance firms, see the US government's website (http://travel.state.gov/medical.html) or the **British Foreign and Commonwealth Office** (www.fco.gov.uk). For general health info, contact the **American Red Cross** (☎ 1-202-303-4498; www.redcross.org).

STAYING HEALTHY

Common sense is the simplest prescription for good health while you travel. Drink lots of fluids to prevent dehydration and constipation, and wear sturdy, broken-in shoes and clean socks. The British Isles are in the gulf stream; thus, temperatures are mild, around 40°F in winter and 65°F in summer. In the Scottish highlands and mountains temperatures reach greater extremes. When in areas of high altitude, be sure to dress in layers that can be peeled off as needed. Allow your body a couple of days to adjust to decreased oxygen levels before exerting yourself. Note that alcohol is more potent and UV rays are stronger at high elevations.

INSECT-BORNE DISEASES

Many diseases are transmitted by insects such as mosquitoes, fleas, ticks, and lice. Be aware of insects in wet or forested areas, especially while hiking and camping; wear long pants and long sleeves, tuck your pants into your socks, and use a mosquito net. Use insect repellents and soak or spray your gear with permethrin. **Ticks**—responsible for Lyme and other diseases—can be particularly dangerous.

FOOD- AND WATER-BORNE DISEASES

Tap water throughout Britain and Ireland is safe. When camping, purify your own water by boiling or treating it with **iodine tablets;** note that some parasites such as *giardia* have exteriors that resist iodine treatment, so boiling is more reliable.

Two recent diseases originating in British livestock have made international headlines. **Bovine spongiform encephalopathy (BSE),** better known as **mad cow disease,** is a chronic degenerative disease affecting the central nervous system of cattle. The human variety is called new variant Creutzfeldt-Jakob disease (nvCJD), and both forms involve invariably fatal brain damage. Information on nvCJD is not conclusive, but the disease is thought to be caused by consuming infected beef. The risk is extremely small (around 1 case per 10 billion meat servings); regardless, travelers might consider avoiding British beef and beef products. Milk and milk products are not believed to pose a risk.

The UK and Western Europe experienced a serious outbreak of **Foot and Mouth Disease (FMD)** in 2001. FMD is easily transmissible between cloven-hoofed animals (cows, pigs, sheep, goats, and deer), but does not pose a threat to humans, causing mild symptoms, if any. In January 2002, the UK regained **international FMD-free status.** Restrictions on rural travel have been removed.

Further information on these diseases is available through the CDC (www.cdc.gov/travel) and the British Department for Environment, Food & Rural Affairs (www.defra.gov.uk).

INFECTIOUS DISEASES

AIDS and HIV: Travelers engaging in sexual activity should always use a latex or poly, not lambskin, condom. If you believe you have been exposed to Acquired Immune Deficiency Syndrome (AIDS), immediately seek treatment from a doctor or a hospital. In the UK, call the FPA (formerly the Family Planning Association) for confidential advice (24hr. ☎0800 567 123). The Center for Disease Control (☎1-800-342-2437) and the Joint United Nations Programme on HIV/AIDS (UNAIDS), 20, ave. Appia, CH-1211 Geneva 27, Switzerland (☎41 22 791 3666; www.unaids.org) have information on prevention and treatment.

Sexually Transmitted Infections (STIs): Gonorrhea, chlamydia, HPV, syphilis, herpes, and other STIs are more common than HIV and can cause serious complications. **Hepatitis** B and C can also be transmitted sexually. Though condoms may protect you from some STIs, oral or even tactile contact can lead to transmission. If you think you may have contracted an STI, see a doctor immediately.

OTHER HEALTH CONCERNS

MEDICAL CARE ON THE ROAD

In both Britain and Ireland, medical aid is readily available and of excellent quality. For minor ailments, **chemists** (pharmacies) are plentiful. The ubiquitous **Boots** chain has a blue logo. **Late-night pharmacies** are rare even in big cities. If you need serious attention, most major hospitals have a **24hr. emergency room** (called a "casualty department" or "A&E," short for Accident and Emergency). Call the numbers listed below for assistance.

In Britain, the state-run **National Health Service (NHS)** encompasses the majority of healthcare centers (☎020 7210 4850; www.doh.gov.uk/nhs.htm). Cities may have private hospitals, but these cater to the wealthy and are not often equipped with full surgical staff or complete casualty units. Access to free care is based on residence, not British nationality or payment of taxes; those working legally or undertaking long-term study in the UK may also be eligible. **Health insurance** is a must for all other visitors. For more information, see **Insurance,** p. 22.

If you are concerned about obtaining medical assistance while traveling, you may wish to employ special support services. The *MedPass* from **GlobalCare, Inc.,** 6875 Shiloh Rd. East, Alpharetta, GA 30005, USA (☎1-800-860-1111; www.globalcare.net), provides 24hr. international medical assistance, support, and medical evacuation resources. The **International Association for Medical Assistance to Travelers (IAMAT;** US ☎716-754-4883, Canada 1-519-836-0102; www.iamat.org) has free membership, lists doctors worldwide, and offers detailed info on immunization requirements and sanitation. If your regular insurance policy does not cover travel abroad, you may wish to purchase additional coverage (p. 22).

Those with medical conditions (such as diabetes, allergies to antibiotics, epilepsy, or heart conditions) may want to obtain a **Medic Alert** membership (first year US$35, annually thereafter US$20), which includes a stainless steel ID tag and a 24hr. collect-call number, among other benefits. Contact the Medic Alert Foundation, 2323 Colorado Ave., Turlock, CA 95382, USA (☎1-888-633-4298, outside US 1-209-668-3333; www.medicalert.org).

WOMEN'S HEALTH

Women traveling are vulnerable to **urinary tract** and **bladder infections,** common and uncomfortable bacterial conditions that cause a burning sensation and painful (sometimes frequent) urination. Vaginal yeast infections are known in Britain and Ireland as **thrush** and can be treated with over-the-counter medicines like Diflucan One or Vagisil. Remember to pack **tampons, pads,** and **contraceptives** when camping, since pharmacies may be few and far between. Women who need an **abortion** or **emergency contraception** while in the UK should contact the **FPA** (formerly the Family Planning Association; ☎ 08453 101 334; www.fpa.org.uk; M-F 9am-6pm). While emergency contraception is available in the Republic of Ireland, abortions are not legal.

GETTING TO BRITAIN

BY PLANE

When it comes to airfare, a little effort can save you a bundle. If your plans are very flexible (read: you have no plans), courier fares are the cheapest. Standby seating is also a good deal, but last-minute specials, airfare wars, and charter flights often beat these fares. The key is to hunt around, be flexible, and ask about discounts. Students, seniors, and those under 26 should never pay full price for a ticket.

AIRFARES

Airfares to Britain and Ireland peak between June and September and around holidays. Midweek (M-Th morning) round-trip flights run US$40-50 cheaper than weekend flights, but they are generally more crowded and less likely to permit frequent-flier upgrades. Not fixing a return date ("open return") or arriving in and departing from different cities ("open-jaw") can be pricier than round-trip flights. Patching one-way flights together is the most expensive way to travel. Flights between London, Belfast, and Dublin and other regional hubs tend to be cheap.

If Britain is only one stop on a more extensive globe-hop, consider a round-the-world (RTW) ticket. Tickets usually include at least five stops and are valid for about a year; prices range US$1200-5000. Try **Star Alliance,** a consortium of 22 airlines including United Airlines (US ☎ 1-800-241-6522; www.staralliance.com). **Fares** for round-trip flights to London from the US or Canadian east coast cost US$400-600, US$300-500 in the low season (October-June); from the US or Canadian west coast US$800-1000/600-800 low season; from Australia AUS$3500 and up; from New Zealand NZ$3000 and up.

BUDGET AND STUDENT TRAVEL AGENCIES

While travel agents can make your life easy and help you save, they may not spend the time to find you the lowest possible fare—they get paid on commission. Travelers holding **ISICs** and **IYTCs** (see p. 14) qualify for discounts from student travel agencies. Most flights are on major airlines, but may include charter flights.

CTS Travel, 30 Rathbone Pl., London W1T 1GQ (☎ 020 7209 0630; www.ctstravel.co.uk). A British student travel agent with offices in 39 countries including the US, Empire State Building, 350 Fifth Ave., ste. 7813, New York, NY 10118 (☎ 1-877-287-6665; www.ctstravelusa.com).

ESSENTIALS

STA Travel, 5900 Wiltshire Blvd., ste. 900, Los Angeles, CA 90036, USA (24hr. reservations and info ☎1-800-781-4040; www.statravel.com). A student and youth travel organization with over 400 offices worldwide (check their website for a listing), including offices in virtually every large US city. Booking, insurance, railpasses, and more. Offices are located throughout Australia (☎61 1300 733 035), New Zealand (☎64 0508 782 872), and the UK (☎0870 1 600 599) and in many other countries.

StudentUniverse, 100 Talcott Ave. East, Watertown, MA 02472, USA (☎1-800-272-9676 within the US or 1-617-321-3100 from outside US; www.studentuniverse.com). Online-only travel service that offers dirt-cheap tickets to and from Europe.

Travel CUTS (Canadian Universities Travel Services Limited), 187 College St., Toronto, ON M5T 1P7, Canada (☎1-800-592-2887; www.travelcuts.com). Offices across Canada and the US including Los Angeles, New York, Seattle, and San Francisco.

usit, 19-21 Aston Quay, Dublin 2, Ireland (☎353 (0)1 602 1904; www.usit.ie). Ireland's leading student/budget travel agency has 13 offices throughout Northern Ireland and the Republic of Ireland.

FLIGHT PLANNING ON THE INTERNET. The Internet may be the budget traveler's dream when it comes to finding and booking bargain fares, but the array of options can be overwhelming. Many airline sites offer special last-minute deals on the Web. Try BMI (www.flybmi.com), Virgin Atlantic (www.virgin-atlantic.com), or British Airways (www.ba.com). **STA** (www.statravel.com) and **StudentUniverse** (www.studentuniverse.com) provide quotes on student tickets, while **Orbitz** (www.orbitz.com), **Expedia** (www.expedia.com), and **Travelocity** (www.travelocity.com) offer full travel services. **Priceline** (www.priceline.com) lets you specify a price, and obligates you to buy any ticket that meets or beats it; **Hotwire** (www.hotwire.com) offers bargain fares, but won't reveal the airline or flight times until you buy. Other sites that compile deals include www.bestfares.com, www.flights.com, www.lowestfare.com, www.onetravel.com, and www.travelzoo.com. Increasingly, there are online tools available to help sift through multiple offers; **SideStep** (www.sidestep.com; download required) and **Booking Buddy** (www.bookingbuddy.com) let you enter your trip information once and search multiple sites. An indispensable resource on the Internet is the **Air Traveler's Handbook** (www.faqs.org/faqs/travel/air/handbook), a comprehensive listing of links to everything you need to know before you board a plane.

COMMERCIAL AIRLINES

The commercial airlines' lowest regular offer is the **APEX** (Advance Purchase Excursion) fare, which provides confirmed reservations and allows "open-jaw" tickets. Generally, reservations must be made seven to 21 days ahead of departure, with seven- to 14-day minimum-stay and up to 90-day maximum-stay restrictions. Book high-season APEX fares early. Use **Expedia** (www.expedia.com) or **Travelocity** (www.travelocity.com) to get an idea of the lowest published fares, then try to beat those fares. Low-season fares should be appreciably cheaper than high-season (June to Sept.) fares.

Standard commercial carriers like American (☎1-800-433-7300; www.aa.com) and United (☎1-800-241-6522; www.united.com) generally offer the most convenient flights, but may be expensive without a special promotional offer. The following discount airlines offer lower fares, but often less convenient flights.

TRAVELING FROM NORTH AMERICA

Icelandair: (☎ 1-800-223-5500; www.icelandair.com.) Stopovers in Iceland for no extra cost on most transatlantic flights. US$500-800; Oct.-May US$300-$450.

Finnair: (☎ 1-800-950-5000; www.finnair.com.) Cheap round-trips from San Francisco, New York, and Toronto to Helsinki; connections throughout Europe.

Aer Lingus: (☎ 0818 365000; www.aerlingus.com.) Cheap round-trips from Boston, Chicago, Los Angeles, New York and Washington, D.C. to Birmingham, Bristol, London, Manchester, Glasgow, Dublin, and Shannon.

TRAVELING FROM AUSTRALIA AND NEW ZEALAND

Air New Zealand: (New Zealand ☎ 64 (0)800 73 70 00; www.airnz.co.nz.) Flights from Auckland to London.

Qantas Air: (Australia ☎ 61 13 13 13, New Zealand 64 (0)800 808 767; www.qantas.com.au.) Flights from Australia and New Zealand to London for around AUS$2400.

Singapore Air: (Australia ☎ 61 13 10 11, New Zealand 64 (0) 800 808 909; www.singaporeair.com.) Flies from Auckland, Sydney, Melbourne, and Perth to London, all through Singapore.

Thai Airways: (Australia ☎ 61 1300 65 19 60, New Zealand 64 09 377 38 86; www.thaiair.com.) Auckland, Sydney, and Melbourne to London, all through Bangkok.

AIR COURIER FLIGHTS

Those who travel light should consider courier flights. Couriers help transport cargo on international flights by using their checked luggage space for freight. Generally, couriers must travel with carry-ons only and deal with complex flight restrictions. Most flights are round-trip only, with short fixed-length stays (usually one week) and a limit of a one ticket per issue. Most of these flights also operate only out of major gateway cities. Generally, you must be over 21. Super-discounted fares are common for "last-minute" flights (three to 14 days ahead).

FROM NORTH AMERICA

Round-trip courier fares from the US or Canada to London cost US$200-500. Most flights leave from New York, Los Angeles, San Francisco, or Miami in the US; from Montreal, Toronto, or Vancouver in Canada. Prices quoted below are round-trip.

Air Courier Association, 1767a Denver West Blvd., Golden, CO 80401 (☎ 1-800-339-7556; www.aircourier.org). 10 departure cities in the US and Canada to London, and throughout western Europe (high-season US$130-640). 1-year membership US$49.

International Association of Air Travel Couriers (IAATC), PO Box 847, Scottsbluff, NE 69363 (☎ 1-308-632-3273; www.courier.org). From 9 North American cities to London. 1-year membership US$45.

STANDBY FLIGHTS

Traveling standby requires considerable flexibility. Companies dealing in standby flights sell vouchers rather than tickets, along with the promise to get you to your destination (or near your destination) within a certain window of time (typically 1-5 days). You call in before your specific window of time to hear your flight options and the probability that you will be able to board each flight. You can then decide which flights you want to try to make, show up at the appropriate airport at the appropriate time, present your voucher, and board if space is available. Vouchers can usually be bought for both one-way and round-trip travel. You may receive a monetary refund only if every available flight within your date range is full; if you opt not to take an available (but perhaps less convenient) flight, you can only get credit toward future travel. Carefully read agreements with any company offering standby flights as tricky fine print can leave you in the lurch. To check on a company's service record in the US, call the **Better Business Bureau** (☎ 1-703-276-0100; www.bbb.org). It is difficult to receive refunds, and clients' vouchers will not be honored when an airline fails to receive payment in time.

TICKET CONSOLIDATORS

Ticket consolidators, or **"bucket shops,"** buy unsold tickets in bulk from commercial airlines and sell them at discounted rates. The best place to look is in the Sunday travel section of any major newspaper (such as *The New York Times*), where many bucket shops place tiny ads. Call quickly, as availability is typically extremely limited. Not all bucket shops are reliable, so insist on a receipt that gives full details of restrictions, refunds, and tickets, and pay by credit card (in spite of the 2-5% fee) so you can stop payment if you never receive your tickets. For more info, see www.travel-library.com/air-travel/consolidators.html.

NOW Voyager, 315 W. 49th St. Plaza Arcade, New York, NY 10019, USA (☎ 1-212-459-1616; www.nowvoyagertravel.com) arranges discounted flights, mostly from New York to London and other major European cities. Other consolidators worth trying are **Rebel** (☎ 1-800-732-3588; www.rebeltours.com) and **Cheap Tickets** (www.cheaptickets.com). Yet more consolidators on the web include **Flights.com** (www.flights.com) and **TravelHUB** (www.travelhub.com). Keep in mind that these are just suggestions to get you started in your research; *Let's Go* does not endorse any of these agencies. As always, be cautious, and research companies before you hand over your credit card number.

BY CHANNEL TUNNEL

Traversing 27 mi. under the sea, the **Channel Tunnel (Chunnel)** is undoubtedly the fastest, most convenient, and least scenic route from France to England.

BY TRAIN. Eurostar, Eurostar House, Waterloo Station, London SE1 8SE (UK ☎ 08705 186 186; Belgium 33 (0)2 528 28 28; France 33 (0)8 92 35 35 39; www.eurostar.com) runs frequent trains between London and the continent. 10-28 trains per day run to 100 destinations including Paris (4hr., 2nd class US$80-300), Disneyland Paris, Brussels, Lille, and Calais. Book at major rail stations in the UK.

BY BUS. Eurolines and **Eurobus,** both run by National Express (UK ☎ 08705 808 080; www.nationalexpress.co.uk), provide bus-ferry combinations.

BY CAR. Eurotunnel, Customer Relations, P.O. Box 2000, Folkestone, Kent CT18 8XY (☎ 08705 35 35 35; www.eurotunnel.co.uk) shuttles cars and passengers between Kent and Nord-Pas-de-Calais. Round-trip fares for vehicle and all passengers £175-400. Same-day round-trip costs £98. Frequent specials; highly variable prices. Book online or via phone. Travelers with cars can also look into sea crossings by ferry (see below).

BY FERRY

A directory of UK ferries can be found at www.seaview.co.uk/ferries.html.

Brittany Ferries: ☎ 08703 665 333; France 33 (0)8 25 82 88 28; www.brittany-ferries.com. Plymouth to **Roscoff, France** and **Santander, Spain;** Portsmouth to **St.-Malo** and **Caen, France;** Poole to **Cherbourg;** and Cork to **Roscoff, France.**

DFDS Seaways: ☎08705 333 111; www.dfdsseaways.co.uk. Harwich to **Hamburg** and **Esbjerg, Denmark;** Newcastle to **Amsterdam, Kristiansand, Norway,** and **Gothenburg, Sweden.**

Fjord Line: ☎08701 439 669; www.fjordline.no. Newcastle to **Stavanger** and **Bergen, Norway.**

Hoverspeed: ☎08702 408 070, France 08 00 1211 1211; www.hoverspeed.co.uk. Dover to **Calais.**

Irish Ferries: ☎08705 171 717; France 33 (0)1 43 94 44 694, Ireland 353 (0)818 300 400; www.irishferries.ie.) Rosslare to **Cherbourg** and **Roscoff, France,** and Pembroke, UK; and Holyhead, UK to **Dublin.**

P&O Ferries: ☎08705 980 333; www.poferries.com. Daily ferries from Hull to **Rotterdam, Netherlands** and **Zeebrugge, Belgium;** Dover to **Calais;** Portsmouth to **LeHavre** and **Bilbao, Spain;** and several Britain to Ireland routes.

Stena Line: ☎08705 70 70 70; www.stenaline.co.uk. Harwich to **Hook of Holland;** Fishguard to **Rosslare;** Stranraer to **Belfast;** Holyhead to **Dublin** and **Dún Laoghaire;** Fleetwood to **Larne.**

GETTING AROUND BRITAIN

Fares on all modes of transportation are referred to as **single** (one-way) or roundtrip. "Period round-trips" or "open round-trips" require you to return within a specific number of days; "day round-trip" means you return on the same day. Unless stated otherwise, *Let's Go* always lists standard single fares.

BY PLANE

The recent emergence of no-frills airlines has made hopscotching around Europe (and even within the UK) by air increasingly affordable and convenient. Though these flights often feature inconvenient hours or serve less-popular regional airports, with one-way flights averaging about US$50, it's never been faster or easier to jet across the Continent. **Aer Lingus** and **British Midland Airways** fly regularly between London, Dublin, and other major cities. The cheapest Aer Lingus round-trip fares to Dublin can be as low as US$30.

If you can book in advance and/or travel at odd hours, the discount airlines listed below are a great option. A good source of offers are the travel supplements of newspapers and the airline websites. The **Air Travel Advisory Bureau** in London (☎07857 370 026; www.atab.co.uk) provides referrals to travel agencies and consolidators that offer discounted airfares out of the UK.

Aer Lingus: ☎08450 844 444; Ireland 353 (0)818 365 000; www.aerlingus.com. Services between Cork, Dublin, Galway, Kerry, Shannon, and many cities in Europe. Departures from Birmingham, Edinburgh, Glasgow, London, and Manchester in the UK.

British Midland Airways: ☎08706 070 555; www.flybmi.com. Services between Aberdeen, Belfast, Dublin, Edinburgh, Glasgow, Inverness, and London. London to Brussels, Madrid, Paris, and Frankfurt.

easyJet: ☎08706 000 000; www.easyjet.com. 210 routes between 63 European cities. Departures from Aberdeen, Belfast, Bristol, Edinburgh, East Midlands, Glasgow, Inverness, Liverpool, London, Newcastle. Frequent specials; online tickets.

EUJet: ☎08704 141 414; www.eujet.com. From Kent to Dublin, Edinburgh, Manchester, and many destinations on the continent. Online tickets.

KLM: ☎08705 074 074; www.klmuk.com. Round-trip tickets from London and other cities in the UK to Amsterdam, Brussels, Frankfurt, Düsseldorf, Milan, Paris, and Rome.

ESSENTIALS

Ryanair: ☎09062 705 656 (25p per min.); Ireland 353 1530 787 787 (33c per min.); www.ryanair.ie. From Dublin, London, and Glasgow to destinations in France, Ireland, Italy, Scandinavia, and elsewhere. As low as £1 on specials; book far in advance for greater savings.

AirBerlin: ☎08707 388 880 (8p per min.); www.airberlin.com. Departures from London, Southampton, and Manchester to over 60 European cities.

The **Star Alliance European Airpass** offers economy class fares as low as US$65 for travel within Europe to more than 200 destinations in 43 countries. The pass is available to transatlantic passengers on Star Alliance carriers, including Air Canada, Austrian Airlines, BMI British Midland, Lufthansa, Mexicana, Scandinavian Airlines, THAI, United Airlines, US Airways, and Varig, as well as on certain partner airlines. See www.staralliance.com for more information.

 TRAVELINE. An essential resource, Traveline (08706 082 608; www.traveline.org.uk) offers comprehensive and impartial information for travel planning throughout England, Scotland, and Wales—whether by train, bus, or ferry.

BY TRAIN

Britain's train network criss-crosses the length and breadth of the island. In cities with more than one train station, the city name is given first, followed by the station name (for example, "Manchester Piccadilly" and "Manchester Victoria" are Manchester's two major stations). In general, traveling by train costs more than by bus. Railpasses covering specific regions are sometimes available from local train stations and may include bus and ferry travel. Prices and schedules often change; find up-to-date information from **National Rail Inquiries** (☎08457 484 950) or online at **Railtrack** (www.railtrack.co.uk, schedules only).

TICKET TYPES. The array of available tickets on British trains is bewildering, and prices aren't always set logically—buying an unlimited day pass to the region may cost less than buying a one-way ticket. Prices rise on weekends and may be higher before 9:30am. Purchase tickets before boarding, except at unstaffed train stations, where tickets are bought on the train. There are several types of **discount tickets. APEX** (Advance Purchase Excursion) tickets must be bought at least seven days in advance (2 days for ScotRail); **SuperAdvance** tickets must be purchased before 6pm the day before you travel. **Saver** tickets are valid anytime, but may be restricted to certain trains at peak times; **SuperSaver** tickets are similar, but are only valid at off-peak times (usually Su-Th and holidays). It may seem daunting, but the general rule of thumb is simple: planning a week or more in advance can make a £30-60 difference.

BRITRAIL PASSES. If you plan to travel a great deal on trains within Britain, the **BritRail Pass** can be a good buy. Eurail passes are *not* valid in Britain, but there is often a discount on BritRail passes if you purchase the two simultaneously. BritRail passes are only available outside Britain; **you must buy them before traveling to Britain.** They allow unlimited train travel in England, Wales, and Scotland, regardless of which company is operating the trains, but they do not work in Northern Ireland or on Eurostar. Unless noted, travelers under 26 should ask for a **Youth pass** for a 25% discount on standard and first classes; **seniors** (over 60) should ask for a 15% discount on first class only. **Children** ages five to 15 can travel free with each adult pass, as long as you ask for the **Family Pass** (free). All children under 5 travel free. The **Party Discount** gets the third through ninth travelers in a party a 50% discount on their railpasses. Check with BritRail (US ☎1-866-BRITRAIL/2748-7245;

www.britrail.net) or one of the distributors for details on other passes. Prices listed do not include shipping costs (around US$15 for delivery in 2-3 days, US$30 for overnight delivery). All prices are given in US dollars.

Consecutive Pass: For consecutive days travel. 4 days standard-class $209, first-class $315; 8 days $295/455; 15 days $449/679; 22 days $575/859; 1 month $679/1019.

Flexipass: For travel within a 2-month period. Any 4 days standard-class $265, first-class $395; any 8 days $385/579; any 15 days $585/869.

England Consecutive: Travel for consecutive days, only in England. 4 days standard-class $169, first-class $249; 8 days $239/365; 15 days $365/545; 22 days $459/689; 1 month $539/815.

England Flexipass: Travel within a 2-month period, only in England. Any 4 days standard-class $209, first-class $315; any 8 days $309/465; any 15 days $469/699.

London Plus Pass: Travel between London and several popular daytrip locations, including Cambridge, Oxford, and Windsor. Travel within an 8-day period. Any 2 days standard-class $69, first-class $99; any 4 days $129/169; any 7 days within a 15 day period $169/225.

BritRail+Ireland Pass: Includes all trains in Britain, Northern Ireland, and the Republic of Ireland, plus a round-trip Stena or Irish Ferries sea crossing. No discounts apply. Travel within a 1-month period. Any 5 days standard-class $419, first-class $579; any 10 days $669/959.

BritRail Scottish Freedom Pass: Includes all Scottish trains, the Glasgow Underground, and Caledonian MacBrayne and Strathclyde ferry services. No discounts apply, except Family Pass. Standard-class travel only. Travel within a 15-day period. Any 4 days $214; any 8 days $279.

BRITRAIL DISTRIBUTORS. The distributors listed below will either sell you passes directly or tell you where to buy passes; also ask at travel agents (p. 25).

Australia: Rail Plus, Level 3, 459 Little Collins St., Melbourne, Victoria 3000 (☎61 (0)3 9642 8644; www.railplus.com.au). **Concorde International Travel,** 403 George St., Sydney, NSW 2000 (☎61 (0)2 9244 2222; www.concorde.com.au).

Canada and US: Rail Europe, 44 South Broadway, White Plains, NY 10601 (☎1-800-361-7245, 1-877-257-2887; www.raileurope.com), is the North American distributor for BritRail. Or try **Rail Pass Express** (☎1-800-RAILPASS/7245-7277; www.railpass.com/new).

Ireland: usit NOW, 19-21 Aston Quay, O'Connell Bridge, Dublin 2 (☎353 (0)1 602 1600).

New Zealand: Holiday Shoppe, Gullivers Holiday Rep: Holiday Shoppe, 5th fl., 66 Wyndham St., Auckland (☎64 (0)800 80 84 80; www.holidayshoppe.co.nz). Locations throughout New Zealand.

RAIL DISCOUNT CARDS. Unlike BritRail passes, these can be purchased in the UK. Passes are valid for one year and generally offer one-third off standard fares. They are available for young people (£20; must be 16-25 or full-time student), seniors (£20; must be over 60), families (£20), and people with disabilities (£14). Visit the **Railcards** website (www.railcard.co.uk) for details.

IN THE REPUBLIC OF IRELAND. While the **Eurailpass** is not accepted in Northern Ireland, it *is* accepted on trains in the Republic. The BritRail pass does not cover travel in Northern Ireland, but the month-long **BritRail+Ireland** works in both the North and the Republic with rail options and round-trip ferry service between Britain and Ireland (see p. 28). It's easiest to buy a Eurailpass before you arrive in Europe; contact a travel agent (p. 25). Rail Europe (p. 31) also sells point-to-point tickets.

IN NORTHERN IRELAND. Northern Ireland Railways (☎028 9066 6630; www.nirailways.co.uk) is not extensive but covers the northeastern coast. The major line connects Dublin to Belfast, then splits with one branch ending at Bangor and one at Larne. There is also service from Belfast and Lisburn west to Derry and Portrush, stopping at three towns between Antrim and the coast. BritRail passes are not valid here, but Northern Ireland Railways offers its own discounts. A valid **Translink Student Discount Card** (£7) will get you up to 33% off all trains and 15% discounts on bus fares over £1.80 within Northern Ireland. The **Freedom of Northern Ireland** ticket allows unlimited travel by train and Ulsterbus; seven consecutive days £47, three out of eight days £32, 1 day £13.

BY BUS AND COACH

The British distinguish between **buses** (short local routes) and **coaches** (long distances). *Let's Go* uses the term "buses" for both. Regional **passes** offer unlimited travel within a given area for a certain number of days; these are often called **Rovers, Ramblers,** or **Explorers.**

BUSES

In Britain, long-distance bus travel is extensive and cheap. **National Express** (☎08705 808 080; www.nationalexpress.com) is the principal operator of long-distance bus services in Britain, although **Scottish Citylink** (☎08705 505 050; www.citylink.co.uk) has extensive coverage in Scotland. Discounts are available for seniors (over 50), students, and young persons (16-25). The **Brit Xplorer passes** offer unlimited travel for a set number of days (7 days £79; 14 days £139; 28 days £219; www.nationalexpress.com). For those who plan far ahead, the best option is National Express's **Fun Fares**, available only online, which offer a limited number of seats on buses from London from, amazingly, £1; a similar option is **Megabus** (☎01738 639095; www.megabus.com), which also offers the one-quid price but has fewer buses. Tourist Information Centres carry timetables for regional buses and will help befuddled travelers decipher them.

Ulsterbus (☎028 9066 6630; www.ulsterbus.co.uk) runs extensive and reliable routes throughout Northern Ireland. Pick up a free regional timetable at any station. The **Emerald Card** offers unlimited travel on Ulsterbus; Northern Ireland Railways; Bus Éireann Expressway, Local, and city services in Cork, Galway, Limerick, and Waterford; and Intercity, DART, and Suburban Rail Iarnród Éireann services. The card works for eight days out of 15 (€218, under 16 €109) or 15 of 30 consecutive days (€375/188).

BUS TOURS

Staffed by young, energetic guides, these tours cater to backpackers and stop right at the doors of hostels. They are a good way to meet other independent travelers and get to places that public transport doesn't reach; most ensure a stay at certain hostels. "Hop-on, hop-off" tours allow you to stay as long as you like at each stop.

■ **HAGGiS,** 60 High St., Edinburgh EH1 1TB (☎0131 557 9393; www.haggisadventures.com). Specializes in 1-, 3-, 4-, 6-, and 8-day prearranged tours of Scotland with small groups and witty, super-knowledgeable guides (from £23). Sister tours **HAGGiS Britain** (same contact info) and the **Shamrocker Ireland** (☎353 (0)1 672 7651) run 3-8 days through England, Wales, and Ireland.

■ **MacBackpackers,** 105 High St., Edinburgh EH1 1SG (☎0131 558 9900; www.macbackpackers.com). Hop-on, hop-off flexitour (£65) of Scotland and 2- to 9-day tours.

Celtic Connection, 7/6 Cadiz St., Edinburgh EH6 7BJ (☎0131 225 3330; www.thecelt-icconnection.co.uk). 2- to 9-day tours of Scotland, Wales, and Ireland (£49-215).

Karibuni, (☎0118 961 8577; www.karibuni.co.uk). Runs adventure tours in England and Wales from London, with activities like biking, kayaking, surfing, horseback riding, and camping (£150-210). Longer tours available for groups of 8 or more.

BY CAR

Cars offer speed, freedom, access to the countryside, and an escape from the town-to-town mentality of trains; but they introduce the hassle of driving, parking, and the high cost of petrol (gasoline). If you can't decide between train and car travel, you may benefit from a combination of the two; BritRail pass distributors (p. 25) sell combination rail-and-drive packages.

RENTING

Renters in Britain must be over 21; those under 23 (or even 25) may have to pay hefty additional fees. Since the public transportation system in Britain is so extensive and punctual, travelers should consider using it instead. However, for longer trips, journeys into many small, obscure destinations, or into the farthest reaches of Highlands and Islands of the north and west, the convenience of a car can mean the difference between an amazing trip and a tiresome trek.

RENTAL AGENCIES. You can generally make reservations before you leave by calling ahead. Occasionally the price and availability information agencies give doesn't jive with what the local offices in your country will tell you. Try checking with both numbers to make sure you get the best price and accurate information. Local desk numbers are included in town listings. At most agencies, all you need to rent a car is a driver's license; some require additional ID. Policies and prices vary from agency to agency. Be sure to ask about insurance coverage and deductibles, and always check the fine print. The following agencies rent cars in Britain:

Auto Europe: US and Canada ☎1-888-223-5555; www.autoeurope.com.

Avis: US ☎1-800-230-4898, Canada 1-800-272-5871, UK 0870 606 0100, Australia 61 136 333, New Zealand 64 (0)800 65 51 11; www.avis.com.

Budget: US ☎1-800-527-0700, Canada 1-800-268-8900, UK 01442 276266; www.budget.com.

easyCar: ☎09063 333 333 (a whopping 60p per min.); www.easycar.co.uk.

Europe by Car: US ☎1-800-223-1516 or 1-212-581-3040; www.europebycar.com.

Europcar International: US ☎1-877-940-6900, UK 08706 075 000; www.europcar.com.

Hertz: US ☎1-800-654-3001, Canada 1-800-263-0600, UK 08705 996 699, Australia 61 9698 2555; www.hertz.com.

Kemwel: US ☎1-877-820-0668; www.kemwel.com.

LEASING. For trips longer than a few weeks, leasing can be cheaper and is often the only option for those aged 18-21. The cheapest leases are agreements to buy the car and then sell it back to the manufacturer at a prearranged price. Leases generally include insurance and are not taxed. Depending on car size, a 60-day lease starts around £725. Auto Europe, Europe by Car, and Kemwel handle leases, as does Renault Eurodrive (US ☎1-800-221-1052; www.renaultusa.com).

COSTS. Rental prices vary by company, season, and pickup point; expect to pay around £150 per week for a small car. Prices increase for 4WD and automatic cars. If possible, reserve and pay well in advance. In many cases it is less expensive to reserve a car from the US than from Europe. Rental packages can offer unlimited miles, while others offer a set number of miles per day with a surcharge per additional kilometer. National chains often allow one-way rentals, picking up in one city and dropping off in another. There is usually a minimum hire period and sometimes an extra drop-off charge.

DRIVING PERMITS AND CAR INSURANCE

INTERNATIONAL DRIVING PERMIT (IDP)

If you plan to drive in Britain, you must be over 18 and have a **valid foreign driver's license.** An **International Driving Permit (IDP)** is also advisable. Your IDP, valid for one year, must be issued in your own country before you depart. An application for an IDP usually requires one or two photos, a current local license, an additional form of identification, and a fee. To apply, contact your home country's automobile association. Be careful when purchasing an IDP online or anywhere other than your home automobile association. Many vendors sell permits of questionable legitimacy for higher prices.

Australia: Royal Automobile Club (☎ 61 13 17 03; www.rac.com.au/travel) or National Royal Motorist Association (☎ 61 13 11 12; www.nrma.com.au). AUS$50.

Canada: Canadian Automobile Association, 1145 Hunt Club Rd., ste. 200, Ottawa, Ontario K1V 0Y3 (☎ 1-613-247-0117; www.caa.ca). CDN$15.

New Zealand: New Zealand Automobile Association, 99 Albert St., Auckland (☎ 64 (0)9 377 4660; www.aa.co.nz). NZ$20.

US: American Automobile Association (AAA; ☎ 1-800-222-7448; www.aaa.com). US$10.

CAR INSURANCE

If you rent, lease, or borrow a car, you may need a **green card,** or **International Insurance Certificate,** to certify that you have liability insurance and that it applies abroad. Green cards can be obtained at rental agencies, car dealers (for those leasing cars), some travel agents, and some border crossings. Many credit cards cover standard insurance. Be aware that cars rented on an **American Express** or **Visa/MasterCard Gold or Platinum** credit cards in Britain might *not* carry the automatic insurance that they would in some other countries; check with your credit card company. Be sure to ask whether the price includes insurance against theft and collision. Insurance plans almost always come with an excess (or deductible) of around £500. The excess quote applies to collisions with other vehicles; collisions with non-vehicles, such as trees, ("single-vehicle collisions") cost more. The excess can often be reduced or waived entirely if you pay an additional charge, from £1-10 per day. If you are driving a rented vehicle on an unpaved road, you are almost never covered.

ON THE ROAD

You must be 18 to drive in Britain. Be sure you can handle **driving on the left** side of the road and driving **manual transmission** ("stick-shift" is far more common than automatic). Be particularly cautious at **roundabouts** (rotary interchanges), and remember to give way to traffic from the right. The **Association for Safe International Road Travel (ASIRT),** 11769 Gainsborough Rd., Potomac, MD 20854, USA (☎ 1-

301-983-5252; www.asirt.org), sends travelers country-specific Road Travel Reports. Road atlases for the UK are available in travel bookshops and from many Tourist Information Centres. **Petrol** (gasoline) is sold by the liter; there are about four liters to the gallon. Prices vary, but average about 85p per liter. The country is covered by a high-speed system of **motorways** ("M-roads") that connect London with major cities around the country. These are supplemented by a tight web of "A-roads" and "B-roads" that connect towns: A-roads are the main routes, while B-roads are narrower but often more scenic. **Distances** on road signs are in miles (1 mi.= 1.6km). **Speed limits** are 70mph (113km/hr.) on motorways (highways) and dual carriageways (divided highways), 60mph (97km/hr.) on single carriageways (non-divided highways), and usually 30mph (48km/hr.) in urban areas. Speed limits are marked at the beginning of town areas; upon leaving, you'll see a circular sign with a slash through it, signaling the end of the restriction. Drivers and all passengers are required to wear **seat belts**. Driving in central **London** is restricted during weekday working hours. Parking in London can be similarly nightmarish. The **Highway Code**, which details Britain's driving regulations, is accessible online (www.highwaycode.gov.uk) or can be purchased at most large bookstores or newsagents.

DRIVING PRECAUTIONS. When traveling in the summer, bring substantial amounts of water (a suggested 5 liters of **water** per person per day) for drinking and for the radiator. For long drives to unpopulated areas, register with police before beginning the trek, and again upon arrival at the destination. Check with the local automobile club for details. When traveling for long distances, make sure tires are in good repair and have enough air, and get good maps. A **compass** and a **car manual** can also be very useful. You should always carry a **spare tire** and **jack, jumper cables, extra oil, flares, a flashlight (torch),** and **heavy blankets** (in case your car breaks down at night or in the winter). If you don't know how to **change a tire,** learn before heading out, especially if you are planning on traveling in deserted areas. Blowouts on dirt roads are exceedingly common. If you do have a breakdown, **stay with your car;** if you wander off, there's less likelihood trackers will find you.

DANGERS

Learn local driving signals and wear a seatbelt. Carseats for infants are available at most rental agencies. Study route maps before you hit the road, and consider bringing spare parts. If your car breaks down, wait for the police to assist you. For long drives in desolate areas, consider investing in a cellular phone and a roadside assistance program (p. 35). Driving in rural areas often requires extra caution on single-lane roads. These roads feature occasional "passing places," which cars use to make way for passing vehicles. Cars **flash their lights** to signal that they will pull aside; the other car should take the right of way. Also be wary of roaming **livestock** along these more remote roads. Be sure to park your vehicle in a garage or well- traveled area, and use a steering wheel locking device in larger cities. **Sleeping in your car** is one of the most dangerous (and often illegal) ways to get your rest.

CAR ASSISTANCE

In the event of a breakdown, try contacting the **Automobile Association (AA; ☎ 08706 000 371;** emergency breakdown 0800 887 766; www.theaa.com) or the **Royal Automobile Club (☎ 0800 828 282;** www.rac.co.uk). Call **☎ 999** in an emergency.

BY FERRY

Caledonian MacBrayne, The Ferry Terminal, Gourock PA19 1QP (☎01475 650 100; www.calmac.co.uk). The mac-daddy of Scottish ferries, with routes in the **Hebrides** and along the west coast of Scotland.

Isle of Man Steam Packet Company serves the Isle of Man; see p. 386 for details.

P&O Ferries, 79 Pall Mall, London SW1Y 5EJ (☎020 7930 4343; www.poferries.com). Many vehicle and passenger ferries between Britain, Ireland, and the continent.

Northlink Ferries, Stromness, Orkney, KW16 3BH (☎01856 885 500, reservations 0845 600 0449; www.northlinkferries.co.uk). Sails between **Aberdeen, Lerwick, Kirkwall, Stromness,** and **Scrabster.**

HoverSpeed, King's Dock, Swansea SA1 1SF (☎08702 408 070; www.hoverspeed.co.uk). **Dover** to **Calais.**

Stena Line, 1 Suffolk Way, Sevenoaks, Kent TN13 1YL (☎08705 707 070; www.stenaline.co.uk). **Harwich** to **Hook of Holland; Fishguard** to **Rosslare; Stranraer** to **Belfast; Holyhead** to **Dublin** and **Dún Laoghaire; Fleetwood** to **Larne.**

Swansea-Cork Ferries, King's Dock, Swansea SA1 1SF (☎01792 456 116, Ireland 353 (0)21 427 1166; www.swansea-cork.ie.) **Swansea** and **Pembroke** to **Ringaskiddy.**

BY BICYCLE

Much of the British countryside is well-suited for cycling. Consult tourist offices for local touring routes and always bring along the appropriate **Ordnance Survey maps.** Keep safety in mind—even well-traveled routes often cover uneven terrain.

GETTING OR TRANSPORTING A BIKE. Many airlines will count a bike as part of your luggage, although a few charge an extra US$60-110 each way. If you plan to explore several widely separated regions, you can combine cycling with train travel; bikes often ride free on trains and ferries. A better option for some is to buy a bike in Britain and Ireland and sell it before leaving. A bike bought new overseas is subject to customs duties if brought home. **Renting** ("hiring") a bike is often preferable to bringing your own. *Let's Go* lists bike rental stores in many towns.

BICYCLE EQUIPMENT. Riding a bike with a frame pack strapped to it or your back is extremely unsafe; **panniers** are essential. You'll also need a suitable **bike helmet** (from US$30) and a U-shaped **Citadel** or **Kryptonite lock** (from US$25). British law requires a white light at the front and a red light and red reflector at the back.

INFORMATION AND ORGANIZATIONS. The **National Cycle Network** encompasses 10,000 mi. of biking and walking trails in the UK. Information and maps are available through **Sustrans** (☎0845 113 0065; www.sustrans.org.uk). The **Cyclists Touring Club,** 69 Meadrow, Godalming, Surrey GU7 3HS (☎0870 873 0060; www.ctc.org.uk), provides maps and books. Membership costs £32 (under 18s and students under 26 £12, over 65 £20) and includes a bi-monthly magazine. To purchase *England by Bike* (US$15), try the **Mountaineers Books** (US ☎1-206-223-6303; www.mountaineersbooks.org).

TOURS. Commercial tours are an alternative to cycling alone. **CBT Tours** (☎1-800-736-2453; www.cbttours.com) offers seven- to 14-day biking and hiking trips through Europe. **Bicycle Beano** (☎01982 560 471; www.bicycle-beano.co.uk) offers vegetarian tours in Wales; **Cycle Scotland** (☎0131 556 5560; www.cyclescotland.co.uk) operates "Scottish Cycle Safaris."

BY FOOT

Well-marked and well-maintained long-distance paths cover Britain, from the rolling paths of the **South Downs Way** (p. 154) to the rugged mountain trails of the **Pennine Way** (p. 396). Ordnance Survey 1:25,000 maps mark almost every house, barn, standing stone, graveyard, and pub; less-ambitious hikers will want the 1:50,000 scale maps. The **Ramblers' Association,** Camelford House, 2nd fl., 87-90 Albert Embankment, London SE1 7TW (☎020 7339 8500; www.ramblers.org.uk), publishes a *Walk Britain Yearbook* (£6, free to members) on walking and places to stay, as well as free newsletters and magazines. Their website abounds with information. (Membership £24, concessions £14.) The **National Cycle Network** (see **By Bicycle: Information and Organizations,** p. 36) includes walking trails. **Contours Walking Holidays** (www.contours.co.uk) provides both guided and self-guided walking holidays in England, Scotland, Wales, and Ireland.

BY THUMB

Let's Go never recommends hitchhiking as a safe means of transportation, and none of the information presented here is intended to do so.

Let's Go strongly urges you to consider the risks before you choose to hitchhike. Hitching means entrusting your life to a random person, risking theft, assault, sexual harassment, and unsafe driving. Nonetheless, hitching can get you where you're going, especially in rural parts of Scotland, Wales, and Ireland (England is tougher for prospective hitchers), where public transportation is sketchy. Women traveling alone should never hitch. A man and a woman are safer; two men will have a hard time, and three will go nowhere. Experienced hitchers pick a spot outside built-up areas, where drivers can stop, return to the road without causing an accident, and have time to look over potential passengers as they approach. Hitching or even standing on motorways (any road labeled "M") is illegal.

Safety precautions are always necessary, even for those not hitching alone. Safety-minded hitchers will not get into a car that they can't get out of again in a hurry (especially the back seat of a two-door car) and never let go of their backpacks. If they feel threatened, they insist on being let off, regardless of location. Acting as if they are going to open the car door or vomit usually gets a driver to stop. Hitching at night can be particularly dangerous; experienced hitchers stand in well-lit places and expect drivers to be leery.

KEEPING IN TOUCH

BY EMAIL AND INTERNET

Internet access is ubiquitous in big cities, common in towns, and sparse in rural areas. Find Internet access in the increasingly common and often cheap cybercafes; in coffee shops, particularly in chains such as Caffe Nero and Starbucks; and in public libraries. For the sneakiest of travelers, try using the computers in media shops like PC World to check your email quickly.

ESSENTIALS

Though in some places it's possible to forge a remote link with your home server, in most cases this is a much slower (and thus more expensive) option than taking advantage of free **web-based email accounts** (e.g., www.gmail.com and www.yahoo.com). **Internet cafes** and Internet terminals at public libraries or university are listed in the **Practical Information** sections of major cities. For lists of additional cybercafes in Britain, check www.cyber-star.com, www.cybercaptive.com, or www.netcafeguide.com.

Increasingly, travelers find that taking their **laptop computers** on the road with them can be a convenient option for staying connected. Laptop users can call an Internet service provider via a modem using long-distance phone cards specifically intended for such calls. They may also find Internet cafes that allow them to connect their laptops to the Internet. And most excitingly, travelers with wireless-enabled computers may be able to take advantage of an increasing number of Internet "hotspots," where they can get online for free or for a small fee. Newer computers detect these hotspots automatically; otherwise, websites like www.jiwire.com, www.wi-fispotlist.com, and www.locfinder.net can help. For information on insuring your laptop while traveling, see p. 25.

BY TELEPHONE

CALLING HOME FROM BRITAIN

Using a **calling card** is often the cheapest option for travelers. You can frequently call collect without a calling card. To obtain a calling card from your national telecommunications service before leaving home, contact the appropriate company listed below. To call home with a calling card, contact the operator for your service provider in Britain by dialing their toll-free access number. Many newsagents in the UK sell **prepaid international phonecards,** such as those offered by Swiftcall. And online sites such as www.nobelcom.com offer cards for dirt cheap. Oftentimes cards are cheap but carry a minimum charge per call. Stores such as **Call Shop** offer cheap international calls from booths and can be found in cities with large numbers of tourists or immigrants.

COMPANY	TO OBTAIN A CARD, DIAL:	TO CALL ABROAD, DIAL:
AT&T (US)	1-800-364-9292 or www.att.com	0800 89 0011 or 0500 89 0011
Canada Direct	1-800-561-8868 or www.infocan-adadirect.com	0800 559 3141 or 0800 096 0634
Ireland Direct	353 800 40 00 00	1800 218 081
MCI (US)	1-800-777-5000 or www.mci.com	0800 279 5088
Telecom New Zealand	64 (0)800 000 000 or 123	0800 890 064
Australia AAPT	61 13 88 88	0800 028 9141

To call home with a calling card, contact the operator for your service provider in Britain by dialing the appropriate toll-free access number (listed below in the second column).You can make direct international calls from **payphones,** but if you aren't using a calling card you may need to drop coins as quickly as your words. Occasionally major credit cards can also be used for direct international calls. In-room **hotel calls** invariably include an arbitrary, sky-high surcharge (as much as £6); the rare B&B that has in-room phones tends to as well. See the box for directions on how to place a direct international call. Placing a **collect call** through an international operator is even more expensive. The number for the **international operator** in Britain is ☎ 155.

PLACING INTERNATIONAL CALLS. To call Britain and Ireland from home or to call home from Britain and Ireland, dial:

1. The **international dialing prefix.** To dial *out of* Australia, dial 0011; Canada or the US, 011; the Republic of Ireland, New Zealand, or the UK, 00.
2. The **country code** of the country you want to call. To *place a call to* Australia, dial 61; Canada or the US, 1; the Republic of Ireland, 353; New Zealand, 64; the UK, 44.
3. The **city/area code.** *Let's Go* lists the city/area codes for cities and towns in Britain opposite the city or town name, next to a ☎. For international numbers, *Let's Go* writes the country code first. If the first digit of the city/area code is a zero (e.g., 020 for London), **omit the zero** when calling from abroad (e.g., dial 20 from Canada to reach London).
4. The **local number.**
5. **Examples:** To call the US embassy in London from New York, dial ☎011 44 20 7499 9000. To call the British embassy in Washington from London, dial 00 1 202 588 6500. To call the US embassy in London from London, dial 020 7499 9000.

CALLING WITHIN BRITAIN

The simplest way to call within the country is to use a coin-operated phone, but **prepaid phone cards** (available at newspaper kiosks and off licenses), which carry a certain amount of phone time depending on the card's denomination, usually save time and money in the long run. The computerized phone will tell you how much time, in units, you have left on your card. Another kind of prepaid telephone card comes with a **Personal Identification Number (PIN)** and a toll-free access number. Instead of inserting the card into the phone, you call the access number and follow the directions on the card. These cards can be used to make international as well as domestic calls. Phone rates typically tend to be highest in the morning, lower in the evening, and lowest on Sunday and late at night.

To make a call within a city or town, dial the phone code and the number. For **directory inquiries,** call ☎ 118 500 (or any of the myriad other 118 services, such as ☎118 118 or 118 888). The services normally charge a 40p connection fee and cost 15p per min. *Let's Go* lists phone codes opposite the city or town name next to the ☎ symbol; all phone numbers in that town use that phone code unless specified otherwise. To call Britain from the Republic of Ireland, or vice versa, you will have to make an international call. Northern Ireland is part of the UK phone network.

PHONE CODES

Recent changes to British phone codes have produced a system in which the first three numbers of the phone code identify the type of number being called. **Premium rate calls,** costing about 50p per minute, can be identified by the 090 phone code. **Freephone** (toll-free) numbers have a 080 code. Numbers that begin with an 084 code incur the **local call rate,** while the 087 code incurs the **national call rate** (the two aren't significantly different for short calls). Calling a **mobile phone** (cell phone) is more expensive than a regular phone call. Mobile phone numbers carry 077, 078, or 079 codes, and pager numbers begin with 076.

PUBLIC PHONES

Public payphones in Britain are mostly run by **British Telecom (BT),** recognizable by the ubiquitous piper logo, although upstart competitors such as Mercury operate in larger cities. Public phones charge a minimum of 10p for calls and don't accept

ESSENTIALS

1p, 2p, or 5p coins. The dial tone is a continuous purring sound; a repeated double-tone means the line is ringing. A series of harsh beeps will warn you to insert more money when your time is up. For the rest of the call, the digital display ticks off your credit. You may use any remaining credit on a second call by pressing the "follow on call" button (often marked "FC"). Otherwise, once you hang up, your remaining phonecard credit is rounded down to the nearest 10p. Pay phones do *not* give change, so use your smallest coins.

CELLULAR PHONES

Cell phones are ubiquitous in Britain; competitive, low prices and the variety of calling plans make them accessible even for short-term, low-budget travelers. Also, Britain has developed a text-messaging culture—for every person you see talking into a mobile, another will be typing on one.

The international standard for cell phones is **GSM**, a system that began in Europe and has spread to much of the rest of the world. Many cell phones on sale today are already **GSM-compatible**, though they may not work in the UK (see box below); check your manual or contact a retailer. You'll also need a **SIM (subscriber identity module) card,** a country-specific, thumbnail-sized chip that gives you a local phone number and plugs you into the local network. Most SIM cards are **prepaid,** meaning that they come with calling time included—you need not purchase a monthly service plan. Incoming calls are usually free and basic phones are often free with even a cheap monthly plan. When you use up the prepaid time, you can buy additional cards or vouchers at convenience stores. For more information on rates, prices, and plans, check out the companies listed below.

 GSM PHONES. Just having a GSM phone doesn't mean you're necessarily good to go when you travel abroad. The majority of GSM phones sold in the United States operate on a different **frequency** (1900) than international phones (900/1800) and will not work abroad. Tri-band phones work on all 3 frequencies (900/1800/1900) and will operate through most of the world. As well, some GSM phones are **SIM-locked** and will only accept SIM cards from a single carrier. You'll need a **SIM-unlocked** phone to use a SIM card from a local carrier when you travel.

For most visitors to Britain, a **pay-as-you-go plan** is the most attractive option. Once you arrive, pick up an eligible mobile (from £30) and recharge, or **top-up,** with a card easily purchased at an off-license, grocery store, or high street shop; on the Internet; or by phone. **Incoming calls and incoming text messages are always free.** Call rates listed here are by the minute.

Orange (☎07973 100 450; www.orange.co.uk). Phones from £30. Calls to the US from 20p; to Orange mobiles, 25p for the first 3min., then 5p thereafter; to other networks 40p; text messaging 12p.

O^2 (☎08702 257 879; www.o2.co.uk). Phones from £50. Calls to O^2 mobiles and fixed lines 25p for the first 3min., then 2-5p; to other networks 40p; text messaging 10p.

T-Mobile (☎08454 125 000; www.t-mobile.co.uk). Phones from £50; calls to US 90p flat rate; calls to any other phone from 10p if you use more than £20 of airtime per month; text messaging 10p.

TIME DIFFERENCES

Britain is on **Greenwich Mean Time (GMT).** Britain observes **daylight savings time** between the last Sunday of March and the last Sunday of October: in March, the clock moves 1hr. later; in October, the clock moves 1hr. earlier.

BY MAIL

SENDING MAIL HOME FROM BRITAIN

Airmail is the best way to send mail home from Britain. Just write "Par Avion—By Airmail" on the top left corner of your envelope, or swing by any post office and get a free Airmail label. **Aerogrammes,** printed sheets that fold into envelopes and travel via airmail, are also available at post offices. For priority shipping, ask for **Airsure;** it costs £4 on top of the actual postage, but your letter will get on the next available flight. If Airsure is not available to the country you wish to ship to, ask for **International Signed For** instead; for £3.30 your package will be signed for on delivery. **Surface mail** is the cheapest and slowest way to send mail, taking one to three months to cross the Atlantic and two to four to cross the Pacific.

Royal Mail has taken great care to standardize their rates around the world. To check how much your shipment will cost, surf to the Royal Mail Postal Calculator at www.royalmail.com. From Britain, postcards cost 21p domestically, 42p to send to Europe, 47p to the rest of the world; airmail letters (up to 20g) are 21p domestically, 42p within Europe, and 68p elsewhere. These are 2nd-class mail rates, and take two to three business days to arrive. Next day delivery is also available.

International 2nd class rates are as follows: packages up to 500g cost £5.17 and take five business days to arrive; packages up to 2kg cost £18.92 and take 5 days around the world including Australia, Canada, New Zealand, and the US.

SENDING MAIL TO BRITAIN

To ensure timely delivery, mark envelopes "Par Avion—By Airmail." In addition to the standard postage system (rates are listed below), **Federal Express** (Canada and US ☎ 1-800-463-3339, Australia 61 13 26 10, Ireland 353 1800 535 800, New Zealand 64 (0)800 733 339, UK 0800 123 800; www.fedex.com) handles express mail services to Britain; they can get a letter from New York to London in two days for US$35.

There are several ways to arrange pick-up of letters sent to you by friends and relatives while you are abroad. Mail can be sent via **Poste Restante** (General Delivery) to almost any city or town in the United Kingdom with a post office. Address *Poste Restante* letters like so:

William SHAKESPEARE
Poste Restante
2/3 Henley St.
Stratford-upon-Avon CV37 6PU
UK

The mail will go to a special desk in the central post office, unless you specify a post office by street address or postal code. It's best to use the largest post office. Bring your passport (or other photo ID) for pick-up. Have clerks check under your first name as well as your last. *Let's Go* lists post offices in the **Practical Information** section for every city and most towns.

American Express travel offices throughout the world offer a free **Client Letter Service** (mail held up to 30 days and forwarded upon request) for cardholders who contact them in advance. *Let's Go* lists AmEx office locations for most large cities in **Practical Information** sections; for a complete, free list, call ☎ 1-800-528-4800 or visit www.americanexpress.com/travel.

ACCOMMODATIONS

HOSTELS

If you want to save money, stay in a hostel. In Britain, hostels are generally clean and friendly places to spend the night, and in the larger cities students even choose to live in them for extended periods of time. They are usually laid out dorm-style, with large single-sex rooms and the inevitable bunk beds, although some offer private rooms. There are hostels with kitchens and utensils, bike or moped rentals, storage areas, transportation to airports, breakfast, and laundry facilities, but don't expect all of these in any one. Expect some to close during certain daytime "lockout" hours, enforce a curfew, or impose a maximum stay. In Britain, a hostel bed will cost about £10-13 in rural areas, £12-20 in larger cities, and £15-28 in London.

A HOSTELER'S BILL OF RIGHTS. There are certain standard features that we do not include in our hostel listings. Unless we state otherwise, you can expect that every hostel has no lockout, no curfew, a kitchen, free hot showers, some system of secure luggage storage, and no key deposit.

HOSTELLING INTERNATIONAL

Joining a national youth hostel association (listed below) grants membership privileges in **Hostelling International (HI).** Non-HI members may be allowed to stay in some hostels, but will have to pay extra to do so. HI hostels are prevalent throughout the UK and Ireland. They are run by the **Youth Hostels Association** (England and Wales), the **Scottish Youth Hostels Association, Hostelling International Northern Ireland (HINI),** and **An Óige** (an-OYJ) in the Republic of Ireland. HI's umbrella organization's web page (www.hihostels.com), which lists links and phone numbers of all national associations, can be a great place to begin researching hostels. Other comprehensive hostelling websites include www.hostels.com and www.hostelplanet.com. Most HI hostels also honor **guest memberships**—you'll get a blank card with space for six validation stamps. Each night you'll pay a nonmember supplement (about one-sixth the membership fee) and earn one guest stamp; get six stamps, and you're a member. Most student travel agencies (see p. 25) sell HI cards, as do all of the national organizations listed below. All prices listed below are for **one-year memberships** unless otherwise noted.

Youth Hostels Association (YHA), Trevelyan House, Dimple Rd., Matlock, Derbyshire DE4 3YH (☎0870 770 8868; www.yha.org.uk). £15.50, under 26 £10.

Scottish Youth Hostels Association (SYHA), 7 Glebe Crescent, Stirling FK8 2JA (☎01786 89 14 00; www.syha.org.uk). £6, under 18 £2.50.

Hostelling International Northern Ireland (HINI), 22-32 Donegall Rd., Belfast BT12 5JN (☎02890 32 47 33; www.hini.org.uk). £13, under 18 £6.

An Óige (Irish Youth Hostel Association), 61 Mountjoy St., Dublin 7 (☎353 (0)830 4555; www.irelandyha.org). €20, under 18 €10.

Australian Youth Hostels Association (AYHA), 422 Kent St., Sydney, NSW 200 (☎61 (0)2 9261 1111; www.yha.com.au). AUS$52, under 18 AUS$19.

Hostelling International-Canada (HI-C), 205 Catherine St. #400, Ottawa, ON K2P 1C3 (☎1-613-237-7884; www.hihostels.ca). CDN$35, under 18 free.

Youth Hostels Association of New Zealand (YHANZ), Level 1, Moorhouse City, 166 Moorhouse Ave., P.O. Box 436, Christchurch (☎64 (0)800 278 299; www.yha.org.nz). NZ$40, under 18 free.

Hostelling International-USA, 8401 Colesville Rd., ste. 600, Silver Spring, MD 20910 (☎1-301-495-1240; www.hiayh.org). US$28, under 18 free.

BOOKING HOSTELS ONLINE. The easiest way to ensure you've got a bed for the night is by reserving online. Surf to the **Hostelworld** booking engine through **www.letsgo.com,** and you'll have access to bargain accommodations from Argentina to Zimbabwe with no added commission.

Independent hostels tend to attract younger crowds, be located closer to city centers, and have a more relaxed attitude about lockouts or curfews than their YHA counterparts. A useful website for hostel listings throughout the UK is Backpackers UK (www.backpackers.co.uk).

BED & BREAKFASTS (B&BS)

For a cozy alternative to impersonal hotel rooms, B&Bs (private homes with rooms available to travelers) range from the horrid to the sublime. B&B owners sometimes go out of their way to be accommodating, giving personalized tours or offering home-cooked meals. Some B&Bs, however, do not provide private bathrooms (**ensuite**) and most do not provide phones. A **double** room has one large bed for two people; a **twin** has two separate beds. *Let's Go* lists B&B prices by room type unless otherwise stated. You can book B&Bs by calling directly or by asking the local **Tourist Information Centre (TIC)** to help you find accommodations; most can also book B&Bs in other towns. TICs usually charge a 10% deposit on the first night's or the entire stay's price, deductible from the amount you pay the B&B proprietor. Often a flat fee of £1-5 is added. To find B&Bs online, try www.innsite.com, www.innfinder.com, or www.bedandbreakfast.com. The British tourist boards operate a B&B **rating system,** using a scale of one to five diamonds (in England) or stars (in Scotland and Wales). Rated accommodations are part of the tourist board's booking system, but it costs money to be rated and some perfectly good B&Bs choose not to participate. Approval by the Tourist Board is legally required of all Northern Ireland accommodations. Approved accommodations in the Republic are marked with a green shamrock.

OTHER TYPES OF ACCOMMODATIONS

YMCAS

Young Men's Christian Association (YMCA) lodgings are usually cheaper than a hotel but more expensive than a hostel. Not all YMCA locations offer lodging; those that do are often located in urban downtowns. Many YMCAs accept women and families; some will not lodge those under 18 without parental permission. The **World Alliance of YMCAs,** 12 Clos Belmont, 1208 Geneva, Switzerland (☎41 22 849 5100; www.ymca.int), has listings of YMCAs worldwide.

HOTELS AND GUESTHOUSES

Basic hotel singles in Britain cost about £70 per night, doubles £95. Some hotels offer "full pension" (all meals) and "half pension" (no lunch). Smaller guest-houses are often cheaper than hotels. Not all hotels take reservations, and few accept checks in foreign currency.

UNIVERSITY DORMS

Many **colleges and universities** open their residence halls to travelers when school is not in session; some do so even during term-time. Getting a room may take a couple of phone calls and require advanced planning, but rates tend to be low, and many offer free local calls and Internet access.

HOME EXCHANGES AND HOSPITALITY CLUBS

Home exchange offers the traveler various types of homes (houses, apartments, condominiums, villas, even castles in some cases), plus the opportunity to live like a native and to cut down on accommodation fees. For more information, contact **The International Home Exchange Network,** 118 Flamingo Ave., Daytona Beach, FL 32118 (☎ 1-386-238-3633; www.homeexchange.com) or **Intervac International Home Exchange** (UK ☎ 1249 461101; www.intervac.com).

Hospitality clubs link their members with individuals or families abroad who are willing to host travelers for free or for a small fee to promote cultural exchange and general good karma. In exchange, members usually must be willing to host travelers in their own homes; a small membership fee may also be required. **Global Freeloaders** (www.globalfreeloaders.com) and **The Hospitality Club** (www.hospitalityclub.org) are good places to start. **Servas** (www.servas.org) is an established, more formal, peace-based organization, and requires a fee and an interview to join. An Internet search will find many similar organizations, some of which cater to special interests (e.g., women, gay and lesbian travelers, or members of certain professions). As always, use common sense when planning to stay with or host someone you do not know.

LONG-TERM ACCOMMODATIONS

Travelers planning to stay in Britain for extended periods of time may find it most cost-effective to rent an **apartment.** Besides the rent itself, prospective tenants usually are also required to front a security deposit (frequently one month's rent) and sometimes also the last month's rent. **UK Flatshare** (www.flatshare-flatmate.co.uk) has an extensive listing of available apartments and rooms for sublet.

THE GREAT OUTDOORS

Great Britain's mild (if rainy) weather and beautiful landscape make it a wonderful place to hike and camp. Newly instituted laws, established by the Countryside and Rights of Way Act (2000), have given hikers and walkers access to open land even if privately held. Common sense restrictions remain and camping on common land can be frowned upon; always ask the landowner before pitching a tent. Campsites are often privately owned, with basic sites costing £3 per person and posh ones costing up to £10 per person. The **Great Outdoor Recreation Pages** (www.gorp.com) provide excellent general information for travelers.

LEAVE NO TRACE. *Let's Go* encourages travelers to embrace the "Leave No Trace" ethic, minimizing their impact on natural environments and protecting them for future generations. Trekkers and wilderness enthusiasts should set up camp on durable surfaces, use cookstoves instead of campfires, bury human waste away from water supplies, bag trash and carry it out with them, and respect wildlife and natural objects. For more detailed information, contact the **Leave No Trace Center for Outdoor Ethics,** P.O. Box 997, Boulder, CO 80306, USA (☎ 1-800-332-4100 or 1-303-442-8222; www.lnt.org).

ESSENTIALS

USEFUL RESOURCES

Campers heading to Europe should consider buying an International Camping Carnet. Similar to a hostel membership, it's required at some campgrounds and provides discounts. It is available in North America from the Family Campers and RVers Association and in the UK from The Caravan Club (see below).

Automobile Association, Contact Centre, Lambert House, Stockport Rd., Cheadle SK8 2DY (☎ 0870 600 0371, international 0161 495 8945; www.theAA.com). Publishes *Caravan and Camping* guides for Europe and Britain (both £8) as well as road atlases (£7-11).

Association of National Park Authorities, 126 Bute St., Cardiff CF10 5LE (☎ 029 2049 9966; www.anpa.gov.uk). Has lists of and introductions to all British national parks, camping and hiking advice, and information on events and festivals.

The Camping and Caravanning Club, Greenfields House, Westwood Way, Coventry CV4 8JH (☎ 024 7669 4995; www.campingandcaravanningclub.co.uk). Offers online booking for campsites and travel and technical advice. Membership costs £30 per year; £5 joining fee.

The Caravan Club, East Grinstead House, East Grinstead, West Sussex, RH19 1UA, UK (☎ 44 01342 326 944; www.caravanclub.co.uk). For £32 annually, members can book sites online and receive travel equipment discounts, maps, and a monthly magazine.

The Mountaineers Books, 1001 SW Klickitat Way, ste. 201, Seattle, WA 98134, USA (☎ 1-206-223-6303; www.mountaineersbooks.org). Boasts over 600 titles on hiking, biking, mountaineering, natural history, and conservation.

Ordnance Survey, Customer Service Centre, Romsey Rd., Southampton SO16 4GU (☎ 08456 050 505, helpline 08456 050 505; www.ordsvy.gov.uk). Britain's national mapping agency (also known as the OS) publishes topographical maps, available at TICs, National Park Information Centres (NPICs), and many bookstores. Their excellent *Explorer* (£7.50) map series covers the whole of Britain in detailed 1:25,000 scale.

Sierra Club, 85 Second St., 2nd fl., San Francisco, CA 94105, USA (☎ 1-415-977-5500; www.sierraclub.org). Publishes general resource books on hiking and camping.

NATIONAL PARKS

Britain has a series of gorgeous national parks. The parks are in large part privately owned, but generally provide expansive areas for public use. There are 12 national parks in England and Wales. The Trossachs, Loch Lomond, and the Cairngorms were named Scotland's first national parks in 2002. Each park is administrated by its own National Park Authority.

WILDERNESS SAFETY

Staying **warm, dry,** and **well-hydrated** is key to a happy and safe wilderness experience. For any hike, prepare yourself for an emergency by packing a first-aid kit, a reflector, a whistle, high energy food, extra water, raingear, a hat, and mittens. For warmth, wear wool or insulating synthetic materials designed for the outdoors. Cotton is a bad choice since it dries slowly. Check **weather forecasts** often and pay attention to the skies when hiking, as weather patterns can change suddenly. Always let a friend, family member, your hostel, a park ranger, or a local hiking organization know when and where you are going hiking. See **Safety and Health,** p. 19, for information on outdoor ailments and medical concerns. If you are in trouble and can reach a phone, **call ☎ 999.** If not, six blasts on a **whistle** are standard to summon help (three are the reply); a constant long blast also indicates distress. For more information, see *How to Stay Alive in the Woods*, by Bradford Angier (Black Dog & Leventhal Books, £11).

CAMPING AND HIKING EQUIPMENT

WHAT TO BUY

Sleeping Bags: Most sleeping bags are rated by season; "summer" means 30-40°F (around 0°C) at night; "four-season" or "winter" often means below 0°F (-17°C). Bags are made of **down** (warm and light, but expensive, and miserable when wet) or of **synthetic** material (heavy, durable, and warm when wet). Prices range from US$50-250 for a summer synthetic to US$200-300 for a good down winter bag. **Sleeping bag pads** include foam pads (US$10-30), air mattresses (US$15-50), and self-inflating mats (US$30-120). Bring a **stuff sack** to store your bag and keep it dry.

Tents: The best tents are free-standing (with their own frames and suspension systems), set up quickly, and only require staking in high winds. Low-profile dome tents are the best all-around. Worthy 2-person tents start at US$100, 4-person at US$160. Make sure your tent has a rain fly and seal its seams with waterproofer. Other useful accessories include a **battery-operated lantern,** a plastic **groundcloth,** and a nylon **tarp.**

Backpacks: **Internal-frame** packs mold well to your back, keep a lower center of gravity, and flex adequately to allow you to hike difficult trails, while **external-frame packs** are more comfortable for long hikes over even terrain, as they carry weight higher and distribute it more evenly. Make sure your pack has a strong, padded hip-belt to transfer weight to your legs. There are models designed specifically for women. Any serious backpacking requires a pack of at least 4000 in^3 (65,000cc), plus 8200 in^3 for sleeping bags in internal-frame packs. Sturdy backpacks cost anywhere from US$125 to US$420, but remember that your pack (or your back) is an area where it doesn't pay to economize. Don't be afraid to strap on a few packs right in the store to find the best fit for you. Some packs include a **rain cover;** if not, pick one up (US$10-20).

Boots: Be sure to wear hiking boots with good **ankle support.** They should fit snugly and comfortably over 1-2 pairs of **wool socks** and a pair of thin **liner socks.** Break in boots over several weeks before you go to spare yourself blisters.

Other Necessities: **Synthetic layers,** like those made of polypropylene or polyester, and a pile jacket will keep you warm even when wet. A **space blanket** (US$5-15) will help you to retain body heat and doubles as a groundcloth. Plastic **water bottles** are vital; look for shatter- and leak-resistant models. Carry **water-purification tablets** for when you can't boil water. For those places (including virtually every organized campground) that forbid fires or the gathering of firewood, you'll need a **camp stove** (the classic Coleman starts at US$50) and a propane-filled **fuel bottle** to operate it. Also bring a **first-aid kit, pocketknife, insect repellent,** and **waterproof matches** or a **lighter.**

WHERE TO BUY IT

Campmor, 28 Parkway, P.O. Box 700, Upper Saddle River, NJ 07458, USA (US ☎ 1-800-525-4784, international 201-825-8300; www.campmor.com).

Eastern Mountain Sports (EMS), 1 Vose Farm Rd., Peterborough, NH 03458, USA (☎ 1-888-463-6367; www.ems.com).

Karrimor International, Ltd., Petre Rd., Clayton-le-Moors, Accrington, Lancashire BB5 5JZ, Australia (☎ 01254 893000; www.karrimor.co.uk). Many UK outlets.

L.L. Bean, Freeport, ME 04033, USA (US and Canada ☎ 1-800-441-5713; UK 0800 891 297, international 207-552-3027; www.llbean.com).

Recreational Equipment, Inc. (REI), Sumner, WA 98352, USA (US and Canada ☎ 1-800-426-4840, international 1-253-891-2500; www.rei.com).

YHA Adventure Shop, 19 High St., Staines, Middlesex, TW18 4QY, UK (☎ 01784 458 625; www.yhaadventure.com). One of Britain's largest outdoor equipment suppliers.

CAMPERS AND RVS

Renting a camper van (RV in the US) will always be more expensive than camping or hosteling, but it's cheaper than staying in hotels and renting a car (see **Rental Cars,** p. 32). Rental prices for a standard RV are around £450 per week, although prices rise considerably during the summer. The convenience of bringing along your own bedroom, bathroom, and kitchen makes it an attractive option, especially for older travelers and families with children. Try **Vivanti Motorhomes** (UK ☎ 08707 522 225, international 0126 489 830; www.vivanti.co.uk) or **Just Go** (☎ 0870 240 1918; www.justgo.uk.com).

ORGANIZED ADVENTURE TRIPS

Organized adventure tours offer another way of exploring the wild. Activities include hiking, biking, skiing, canoeing, kayaking, rafting, climbing, photo safaris, and archaeological digs. Tourism bureaus often can suggest parks, trails, and outfitters. Organizations that specialize in camping and outdoor equipment like REI and EMS (see p. 47) also are good source for info. To find an organized tour, consider contacting the **Specialty Travel Index,** P.O. Box 458, San Anselmo, CA 94979, USA (US ☎ 1-888-624-4030, international 1-415-455-1643; www.specialtytravel.com).

SPECIFIC CONCERNS

SUSTAINABLE TRAVEL

As the number of travelers on the road continues to rise, the detrimental effect they can have on natural environments becomes an increasing concern. With this in mind, *Let's Go* promotes the philosophy of **sustainable travel.** Through a sensitivity to issues of ecology and sustainability, today's travelers can be a powerful force in preserving and restoring the places they visit. **Ecotourism,** a rising trend in sustainable travel, focuses on the conservation of natural habitats and using them to build up the economy without exploitation or over-development. Travelers can make a difference by doing advance research and by supporting organizations and establishments that pay attention to their impact on their natural surroundings and strive to be environmentally friendly. Preserving Britain's open land has been a governmental priority. Even privately held land can be traversed by hikers and walkers. Short country walks in the Midlands and hiking in the Scottish highlands are particularly popular. For UK-specific trips, visit www.earthfoot.org/uk.htm.

ECOTOURISM RESOURCES. For more information on environmentally responsible tourism, contact one of the organizations below.
Conservation International, (www.conservation.org).
Green Globe 21, (☎1-612-657-9102; www.greenglobe21.com/Travellers.aspx)
International Ecotourism Society, 733 15th St. NW, Washington, D.C. 20005, USA (☎1-202-347-9203; www.ecotourism.org).
United Nations Environment Program (UNEP; ☎33 1 44 37 14 41; www.uneptie.org/pc/tourism).
Earthwatch Institute Europe, 267 Banbury Rd., Oxford OX2 7HT (☎01865 318 838; www.earthwatch.org/europe).

RESPONSIBLE TRAVEL

The impact of tourist dollars on the destinations you visit should not be underestimated. The choices you make during your trip can have potent effects on local communities—for better or for worse. Travelers who care about the destinations and environments they explore should become aware of the social and cultural implications of the choices they make when they travel. Simple decisions such as buying local products instead of globally-available products, paying a fair price for the product or service, and attempting to say a few words in the local language can have a strong, positive effect on the community.

Community-based tourism aims to channel tourist money into the local economy by emphasizing tours and cultural programs that are run by members of the host community and that often benefit disadvantaged groups. An excellent resource on community-based travel is *The Good Alternative Travel Guide* (£13), a project of **Tourism Concern** (☎020 7133 3330; www.tourismconcern.org.uk). The UK is filled with open-air historical sites such as ruinous cathedrals, Bronze-Age settlements, and other ancient monuments. It is a rare privilege that such testaments to the multicultural heritage of the British Isles survive today, and an even greater privilege to be able to walk up, in, and among them. It is up to the tourists themselves to be responsible for not taking anything or leaving anything behind, however strong the temptation to maul/be part of history may be.

TRAVELING ALONE

There are many benefits to traveling alone, including independence and greater interaction with locals. On the other hand, any solo traveler is a more vulnerable target of harassment and street theft. As a lone traveler, try not to stand out as a tourist, look confident, and be especially careful in deserted or very crowded areas. Stay away from areas that are not well-lit. If questioned, never admit that you are traveling alone. Maintain regular contact with someone at home who knows your itinerary, and always research your destination before traveling. For more tips, pick up *Traveling Solo* by Eleanor Berman (Globe Pequot Press, US$18), visit www.travelaloneandloveit.com, or subscribe to Connecting: Solo Travel Network, 689 Park Rd., Unit 6, Gibsons, BC V0N 1V7, Canada (☎1-800-557-1757; www.cstn.org; membership CDN$30-55).

WOMEN TRAVELERS

Though Britain is among the world's safest countries, women on their own inevitably face some additional safety concerns, particularly in larger cities such as London, Cardiff, Glasgow, and Belfast. The following suggestions shouldn't discourage women from traveling alone—it's easy to enjoy yourself without taking undue risks. Avoid solitary late-night treks or metro/Tube rides. Check that your hostel offers safe communal showers. Carry extra money for a phone call, bus, or taxi. If catching a bus at night, wait at a well-populated stop. Choose train or Tube compartments occupied by other women or couples. Look as if you know where you're going and approach older women or couples for directions if you're lost or uncomfortable.

Your best answer to harassment is no answer at all; feigning deafness, sitting motionless, and staring straight ahead can do a world of good. The extremely persistent can be dissuaded by a firm and loud "Go away!" Wearing a conspicuous **wedding band** may help prevent unwanted overtures. Consider carrying a whistle or rape alarm on your keychain. Mace and pepper sprays are illegal in Britain.

The national **emergency** number is ☎999. **Rape Crisis UK and Ireland** (a full list of helplines can be found at www.rapecrisis.org.uk; www.rapecrisisscotland.org.uk in Scotland) provides referrals to local rape crisis and sexual abuse counseling services throughout the UK. A self-defense course will prepare you for a potential attack and raise your level of awareness (see **Self Defense**, p. 21). For health concerns that women face when traveling, see p. 24.

GLBT TRAVELERS

Large cities, notably London, Dublin, Edinburgh, Manchester, and Brighton, are more open to GLBT culture than rural Britain, though evidence of bigotry and violence remains. The magazine *Time Out* (p. 51) has a gay and lesbian listings section, and numerous periodicals make it easy to learn about the current concerns of Britain's gay community. Visit Britain publishes the essential guide *Britain: Inside and Out* (www.gaybritain.org). The *Pink Paper* (free; ☎020 7424 7400; www.pinkpaper.com) is available from newsagents in larger cities. **Out and About** (www.planetout.com) offers a bi-weekly newsletter.

> ### ▼ FURTHER READING: BISEXUAL, GAY, AND LESBIAN.
> *Spartacus International Gay Guide 2005-2006*. Bruno Gmunder Verlag (US$33).
> *Damron Men's Travel Guide, Damron's Accommodations,* and *The Women's Traveller*. Damron Travel Guides (US$14-19). For more info, call US ☎1-800-462-6654 or international 1-415-255-0404 or visit www.damron.com.
> *The Gay Vacation Guide: The Best Trips and How to Plan Them*. Mark Chesnut. Kensington Publishing (US$15).

Gay's the Word, 66 Marchmont St., London WC1N 1AB, UK (☎020 7278 7654; www.gaystheword.co.uk). UK's largest GLBT bookshop. Mail-order service available.

International Lesbian and Gay Association (ILGA), Avenue des Villas 34, 1060 Brussels, Belgium (☎32 2 502 2471; www.ilga.org). Provides political information such as homosexuality laws of individual countries.

Ireland's Pink Pages (www.pink-pages.org). Ireland's web-based bisexual, gay, and lesbian directory. Extensive urban and regional info for both the Republic and the North.

London Lesbian and Gay Switchboard (☎020 7837 7324; www.llgs.org.uk). Confidential advice, information, and referrals. Open 24hr.

TRAVELERS WITH DISABILITIES

Traveling in Britain with a disability takes advance planning. Inform airlines and hotels of the need for special accommodations when making reservations; time may be needed to prepare special accommodations. Call ahead to restaurants, museums, and other facilities to find out if they are handicapped-accessible.

Rail may be the most convenient form of travel: many stations have ramps, and some trains have wheelchair lifts, special seating areas, and specially equipped toilets. The National Rail website (www.nationalrail.co.uk) provides general information for travelers with disabilities and assistance phone numbers; it also describes the Disabled Persons Railcard (£14), which allows one-third off most fares for one year. Most **bus** companies will provide assistance if notified ahead of time. All National Express coaches entering service after 2005 must be equipped with a wheelchair lift or ramp; call the **Additional Needs Help Line** (☎0121 423 8479) for information or consult www.nationalexpress.com. The London **Underground** is slowly improving accessibility; **Transport for London Access and Mobility** (☎020 7222 1234) can provide information on public transportation within the city.

Some major **car rental** agencies (Hertz, Avis, and National), as well as local agencies can provide and deliver hand-controlled cars. In addition, Lynx hand controls may be used with many rental cars; contact **Lynx,** Mansion House, St. Helens Road, Ormskirk, Lancashire L39 4QJ (☎01695 573 816; www.lynxcontrols.com), which can arrange an outfitted rental vehicle.

The British Tourist Boards have begun rating accommodations and attractions using the **National Accessible Scheme (NAS),** which designates three categories of accessibility. Look for the NAS symbols in Tourist Board guidebooks, or ask a sight directly for their ranking. Many **theaters** and performance venues have space for wheelchairs; some larger theatrical performances include special facilities for the hearing-impaired. Guide dogs fall under the PETS regulations (p. 15).

USEFUL ORGANIZATIONS

Access Abroad, Disability Services Research and Training, University of Minnesota, 230 Heller Hall, 271 19th Ave. S., Minneapolis, MN 55455, USA (☎1-612-626-9000; www.umabroad.umn.edu/access). A website devoted to making study abroad available to students with disabilities.

Accessible Journeys, 35 W. Sellers Ave., Ridley Park, PA 19078, USA (☎1-800-846-4537, local 610-521-0339; www.disabilitytravel.com). Designs tours for wheelchair users and slow walkers. The site has tips and forums for all travelers.

Flying Wheels, 143 W. Bridge St., P.O. Box 382, Owatonna, MN 55060, USA (☎1-507-451-5005; www.flyingwheelstravel.com). Specializes in escorted trips to Europe for people with physical disabilities; plans custom accessible trips worldwide.

The Guided Tour Inc., 7900 Old York Rd., ste. 114B, Elkins Park, PA 19027, USA (☎1-800-783-5841; www.guidedtour.com). Organizes travel programs for persons with developmental and physical challenges in the US, Ireland, Iceland, London, and Paris.

Mobility International USA (MIUSA), P.O. Box 10767, Eugene, OR 97440, USA (☎1-541-343-1284; www.miusa.org). Provides a variety of books and other publications containing information for travelers with disabilities.

Society for Accessible Travel and Hospitality (SATH), 347 Fifth Ave., ste. 610, New York, NY 10016, USA (☎1-212-447-7284; www.sath.org). An advocacy group that publishes free online travel information and the travel magazine *OPEN WORLD* (annual subscription US$13, free for members). Annual membership US$45, students and seniors US$30.

MINORITY TRAVELERS

Minorities make up about 10% of Britain's population and concentrate in London. Ireland is only beginning to experience racial diversity, while rural Scotland and Wales remain predominantly white. Minority travelers should expect reduced anonymity in the latter regions, but onlookers are usually motivated by curiosity rather than ill will and should not cause you to alter your travel plans. For information on measures to combat racism, contact the **Commission for Racial Equality (CRE)**, St. Dunstan's House, 201-211 Borough High St., London SE1 1GZ (☎020 7939 0000; www.cre.gov.uk).

DIETARY CONCERNS

Vegetarians should be able to find meals in Britain and Ireland. Virtually all restaurants have vegetarian selections and many cater specifically to vegetarians. *Let's Go* notes restaurants with good vegetarian selections. Good resources include: www.veggieheaven.com, for a comprehensive listing of restaurants; www.vrg.org/travel, for links geared toward vegetarian and vegan travel; and the **Vegetarian Society of the UK** (☎0161 925 2000; www.vegsoc.org). The travel section of the The Vegetarian Resource Group's website, at www.vrg.org/travel, has a comprehensive list of organizations and websites that are geared toward helping vegetarians and vegans traveling abroad. For more information, visit your local bookstore or health food store, and consult *The Vegetarian Traveler: Where to Stay if You're Vegetarian, Vegan, Environmentally Sensitive*, by Jed and Susan Civic (Larson Publications; US$16). Vegetarians will also find numerous resources at www.vegdining.com, www.happycow.net, and www.vegetariansabroad.com, for starters.

The prevalence of South Asian and Middle Eastern communities has made **halal** restaurants, butchers, and groceries common in large cities. Your own mosque or Muslim community organization may have lists of Muslim institutions or halal eateries. Travelers looking for halal food may find the Halal Food Authority (www.halalfoodauthority.co.uk) and www.zabihah.com to be useful resources.

Travelers who keep **kosher** should contact synagogues in larger cities for information on kosher restaurants. Your own synagogue or college Hillel may have access to lists of Jewish institutions in Britain. Orthodox communities in North London (in neighborhoods such as **Golders Green** or **Stamford Hill**), Leeds, and Manchester provide a market for kosher restaurants and grocers. A good resource is the *Jewish Travel Guide*, edited by Michael Zaidner (Vallentine Mitchell; US$19). Both halal and kosher options decrease in rural areas, but most restaurants and B&Bs will try to accommodate your dietary restrictions.

OTHER RESOURCES

Let's Go tries to cover all aspects of budget travel, but we can't put *everything* in our guides. Listed below are books and websites that can serve as jumping-off points for your own research.

USEFUL PUBLICATIONS

▨ **Time Out,** Universal House, 251 Tottenham Court Road, London, W1T 7AB, (☎020 7813 3000; www.timeout.com), is the absolute best weekly guide to what's going on in London, Edinburgh, and Dublin. The magazine is sold at every newsstand in those cities, and the website is a virtual hub for the latest on dining, entertainment, and discounts.

Rand McNally, P.O. Box 7600, Chicago, IL 60680, USA (☎ 1-847-329-8100; www.rand-mcnally.com), publishes road atlases.

WORLD WIDE WEB

Almost every aspect of budget travel is accessible via the web. In 10 minutes at the keyboard, you can book a hostel bed, get advice from other travelers, or find out how much a train from London to Scarborough costs. Because website turnover is high, use search engines (such as www.google.com) to strike out on your own.

 WWW.LETSGO.COM. Our freshly redesigned website features extensive content from our guides; community forums where travelers can connect with each other, ask questions or advice, and share stories and tips; and expanded resources to help you plan your trip. Visit us to browse by destination, find information about ordering our titles, and sign up for our e-newsletter!

THE ART OF TRAVEL

Backpacker's Ultimate Guide: www.bugeurope.com. Tips on packing, transportation, and where to go. Also tons of country-specific travel information.

BootsnAll.com: www.bootsnall.com. Numerous resources for independent travelers, from planning your trip to reporting on it when you get back.

How to See the World: www.artoftravel.com. A compendium of great travel tips, from cheap flights to self-defense to interacting with local culture.

Travel Intelligence: www.travelintelligence.net. A large collection of travel writing by distinguished writers.

Travel Library: www.travel-library.com. A fantastic set of links for general information and personal travelogues.

World Hum: www.worldhum.com. An independently produced collection of "travel dispatches from a shrinking planet."

INFORMATION ON BRITAIN

Atevo Travel: www.atevo.com/guides/destinations. Detailed introductions, travel tips, and suggested itineraries.

CIA World Factbook: www.odci.gov/cia/publications/factbook/index.html. Tons of vital statistics on British geography, government, economy, and people.

Geographia: www.geographia.com. Highlights, culture, and people of Britain.

Visit Britain: www.visitbritain.com. Exhaustive listing of British Tourist sites, from the smallest Stone Age hut to Windsor Castle.

PlanetRider: www.planetrider.com. A subjective list of links to the "best" websites covering the culture and tourist attractions of Britain.

World Travel Guide: www.travel-guides.com. Helpful practical info.

Multimap and Mapquest: www.multimap.com and www.mapquest.co.uk. Find any address, get directions, and find aerial photos.

BEYOND TOURISM

A PHILOSOPHY FOR TRAVELERS

BEYOND TOURISM HIGHLIGHTS

WORK FOR PEACE in Northern Ireland (p. 54).

REHABILITATE injured badgers and owls in Scotland (p. 55).

STUDY medieval history for a semester at the University of Cambridge (p. 58).

HARVEST gooseberries at a small farm in Staffordshire (p. 62).

The UK is rich with opportunities to diverge from the standard tourist track. Beyond the sights, there is a vibrant culture, a community enriched by a storied history. *Let's Go* believes that the connection between travelers and their destinations is an important one. We've watched the growth of the 'ignorant tourist' stereotype with dismay, knowing that many travelers care passionately about the communities and environments they explore—but also knowing that even conscientious travelers can inadvertently damage natural wonders and harm cultural environments. With this Beyond Tourism chapter, *Let's Go* hopes to promote a better understanding of the United Kingdom and enhance your experience there.

There are several options for those who seek to participate in Beyond Tourism activities. Opportunities for **volunteerism** abound, both with local and international organizations. **Studying** can also be instructive, whether through direct enrollment in a local university or in an independent research project. **Working** is a way to both immerse yourself in the local culture and finance your travels.

As a **volunteer** in the UK, you can participate in projects from archaeological digs at Norman castles to working with political groups for peace in Northern Ireland. Later in this section, we recommend organizations that can help you find the opportunities that best suit your interests, whether you're looking to pitch in for a day or a year.

Studying in the UK is another option. You can study everything from history to physics at the medieval institutions of Cambridge, Oxford, or St. Andrews. If economics is your passion, you can spend a summer or a year engaging in finance, accounting, management, and more at the London School of Economics.

Many travelers also structure their trips by the **work** that they can do along the way—either odd jobs as they go, or full-time stints in cities where they plan to stay for some time. Whether you'd like to take an internship in Parliament or teach, you can do so through a variety of organizations.

 Start your search at ▨ **www.beyondtourism.com,** *Let's Go's* searchable database of alternatives to tourism, where you can find exciting feature articles and helpful program listings divided by country, continent, and type.

VOLUNTEERING

Volunteering can be one of the most fulfilling experiences you have in life, especially if you combine it with the thrill of traveling in a new place. Though the UK is considered wealthy by world standards, there are countless aid organizations that deal with the very real issues the region faces. Civil strife continues to challenge Northern Ireland, the stunning landscapes and wildlife of northern England face threats of industrialization and ill-maintenance, and large urban communities throughout the region suffer hardships such as housing shortages.

Most people who volunteer in the UK do so on a short-term basis, at organizations that make use of drop-in or once-a-week volunteers. These can be found in virtually every city and are referenced both in this section and in our town and city write-ups themselves. The best way to find opportunities that match your interests and schedule may be to check with local or national volunteer centers that list various options. **CharitiesDirect.com** offers extensive listings and profiles on hundreds of charities in the UK, and can serve as an excellent tool in researching volunteer options. The **Council on International Educational Exchange** (☎207-553-7600; www.ciee.org) offers a searchable online database listing volunteer opportunities according to region and project type. Northern Ireland's **Volunteer Development Agency** (☎028 9023 6100; www.volunteering-ni.org) responds to inquiries concerning volunteer opportunities and holds an annual Volunteer's Week in early June. Their Freephone (☎0800 052 2212) connects callers to local volunteer bureaus.

Those looking for longer, more intensive volunteer opportunities usually choose to go through a parent organization that takes care of logistical details and often provides a group environment and support system—for a fee. There are two main types of organizations—religious and non-sectarian—although there are rarely restrictions on participation for either.

WHY PAY MONEY TO VOLUNTEER?

Many volunteers are surprised to learn that some organizations require large fees or "donations." While this may seem ridiculous at first glance, such fees often keep the organization afloat, in addition to covering airfare, room, board, and administrative expenses for the volunteers. (Other organizations must rely on private donations and government subsidies.) If you're concerned about how a program spends its fees, request an annual report or finance account. A reputable organization won't refuse to inform you of how volunteer money is spent.

Pay-to-volunteer programs might be a good idea for young travelers who are looking for more support and structure (such as pre-arranged transportation and housing), or anyone who would rather not deal with the uncertainty implicit in creating a volunteer experience from scratch.

PEACE PROCESS

The conflict in Northern Ireland has plagued Britain and Ireland for centuries. It has resulted in violence on both sides and all over the UK. Demanding international attention, the peace process has been in the works for over 30 years. Volunteering for these organizations is a good opportunity for foreigners whose primary objective is peace, not the furthering of one side over the other.

Corrymeela Community, Corrymeela Centre, 5 Drumroan Rd., Ballycastle BT54 6QU (☎028 2076 2626; www.corrymeela.org). A residential community committed to bringing Protestants and Catholics together to work for peace. Volunteer openings from 1 week to 1 year. Ages 18-30 preferred for long-term positions.

Kilcranny House, 21 Cranagh Rd., Coleraine BT51 3NN (☎028 7032 1816; www.kilcrannyhouse.org). A residential, educational, and resource center that provides a safe space for Protestants and Catholics to explore issues of non-violence, prejudice awareness, and conflict resolution. Volunteering opportunities from 6 months to 2 years. Food and accommodations provided. £26 per week.

Northern Ireland Volunteer Development Agency, 58 Howard St., 4th fl., Belfast BT1 6PG (☎028 9023 6100; www.volunteering-ni.org). Facilitates volunteer efforts in Northern Ireland. Individual fee £15.

Volunteers for Peace, 1034 Tiffany Rd., Belmont, VT 05730, USA (☎802-259-2759; www.vfp.org). Arranges 2- to 3-week placements in working camps. Most programs 18+. Registration fee US$250; some programs have additional costs.

Ulster Quaker Service Committee, 541 Lisburn Rd., Belfast BT9 7GQ (☎028 9020 1444; www.ulsterquakerservice.com). Runs programs for Protestant and Catholic children from inner-city Belfast. Accommodations and small allowance provided. 6-8 wk. summer posts and 1-2 yr. posts available. Short-term volunteers 18+, long-term volunteers 21+.

CONSERVATION AND ARCHAEOLOGY

The UK's national parks and scenic natural landscapes provide idyllic venues for community service opportunities, from trail maintenance to archaeological expeditions. The largest organization in Britain for environmental conservation is the **British Trust for Conservation Volunteers (BTCV),** Conservation Centre, 163 Balby Rd., Doncaster, South Yorkshire, DN4 0RH (☎01302 572 244; www.btcv.org). Their counterpart in Northern Ireland is **Conservation Volunteers Northern Ireland,** Beech House, 159 Ravenhill Rd., Belfast BT6 0BP (☎028 9064 5169; www.cvni.org). Many national parks have volunteer programs—the Association of National Park Authorities can contact individual park offices (see National Parks, p. 45).

Archaeological Institute of America, Boston University, 656 Beacon St., Boston, MA 02215, USA (☎617-353-9361; www.archaeological.org). The *Archaeological Fieldwork Opportunities Bulletin,* available on the website, lists fieldwork volunteer opportunities throughout the UK with a wide range of costs and durations.

Earthwatch Europe, 267 Banbury Rd., Oxford OX2 7HT (☎0186 531 8838; www.earthwatch.org/europe). Arranges 1- to 3-week programs to promote conservation of natural resources, awareness of endangered animal populations (such as the Eagles of Mull), and the study of archaeological remnants (like dinosaur footprints in Yorkshire). Fees range from US$495 to over US$3500, plus airfare.

Hessilhead Wildlife Rescue Trust, Gateside, Beith, KA15 1HT (☎01505 502 415; www.hessilhead.org.uk). Volunteers work with wild birds and mammals in Scotland.

The National Trust, Volunteering and Community Involvement Office, Rowan, Kembrey Park, Swindon, Wiltshire SN2 8YL (☎0870 609 5383; www.nationaltrust.org.uk/volunteering). Arranges numerous volunteer opportunities, including working holidays.

Orkney Seal Rescue Centre, Dyke End, South Ronaldsay, Orkney KW17 2TJ (☎01856 831 463; selkiesave@aol.com), cares for orphaned seal pups in preparation for their return to the wild. Accommodations provided. 18+.

Royal Society for the Protection of Birds (RSPB), UK Headquarters, The Lodge, Sandy, Bedfordshire SG19 2DL (☎01767 680 551; www.rspb.org.uk). Volunteer opportunities range from a day constructing nestboxes in East Anglia to several months monitoring invertebrates in the Highlands. Work for all levels of experience and for any duration.

The Wildlife Trusts, The Kiln, Waterside, Mather Rd., Newark, Nottinghamshire NG24 1WT (☎0870 036 7711; www.wildlifetrusts.org). Includes volunteer openings in conjunction with their 47 local Wildlife Trusts. Durations vary greatly.

WWF, Panda House, Weyside Park, Godalming, Surrey GU7 1XR (☎01483 426444; www.wwf.org.uk). Extensive conservation organization that lists volunteer opportunities from publicity to panda-keeping.

BEYOND TOURISM

YOUTH AND THE COMMUNITY

There are countless social service opportunities offered in the UK, including mentoring youths, working in homeless shelters, promoting mental health, and any number of more specific concerns. The following represents a sampling of options; many more can be discovered upon further research.

Christian Aid: Great Britain, 35 Lower Marsh, Waterloo, London SE1 7RL (☎020 7620 4444; www.christian-aid.org.uk). **Northern Ireland,** 30 Wellington Park, Belfast BT9 6DL (☎028 9038 1204). Individuals or groups of volunteers work in various fund-raising and administrative roles, occasionally for a small stipend.

Citizens Advice Bureau, Myddelton House, 115-123 Pentonville Rd., London, N1 9LZ (☎020 7833 2181; www.citizensadvice.org.uk). Volunteers help address issues from employment to finance to personal relationships.

Community Service Volunteers, 237 Pentonville Rd., London, N1 9NJ (☎020 7278 6601; www.csv.org.uk). Part- and full-time volunteer opportunities with the homeless, the disabled, and underprivileged youth.

Habitat for Humanity Great Britain, Southwark Habitat for Humanity, 93 Gordon Rd., London SE15 3RR (☎020 7732 0066; www.habitatforhumanity.org.uk). Volunteers build houses for low-income families. There are other offices in Liverpool, Sussex, Oxfordshire, Birmingham, and Northern Ireland.

Service Civil International (SCI), SCI USA, 5474 Walnut Level Rd., Crozet, VA 22932, USA (☎434-823-9003; www.sciint.org). Arranges placement in working camps. 18+.

SPECIAL CONCERNS

The Disability Rights Commission recently launched an Educating for Equality campaign in Britain, designed to ensure the equal rights of individuals with disabilities in the education system. Despite this progressive measure and an increasing attitude of acceptance and tolerance, those possessing physical and mental handicaps continue to face discrimination in the UK. Volunteer opportunities in this category include venues concerned with aiding the special needs of these individuals and fostering an attitude of acceptance and mutual respect.

Association of Camphill Communities, England and Wales Region, 55 Cainscross Rd., Stroud GL5 4EX (☎01453 753 142; www.camphill.org.uk). Private communities advocate Christian values and cater to both children and adults with special needs. Volunteers generally work for at least 6 months. Food, accommodation, and stipend provided. 18+.

International Volunteer Program (IVP), 678 13th St., Suite 100, Oakland, CA 94612, USA (☎510-433-0414; www.ivpsf.org). Lists 4- to 12-week volunteer programs working with the disabled, the elderly, and underprivileged youth. US$1550 and up, includes food, travel within country, and accommodations. 18+.

The Share Centre, Smith's Strand, Lisnaskea, Co. Fermanagh, Northern Ireland BT92 0EQ (☎028 677 22122; www.sharevillage.org). Volunteer openings include outdoors and arts activities leaders. Opportunities range from 1 week to 1 year. Food and accommodations provided. 16+.

Vitalise, 12 City Forum, 250 City Rd., London EC1V 8AF (☎084 5345 1972; www.vitalise.org.uk). Volunteers care for disabled people for 1-2 week working holidays. Food, accommodation, and travel within Britain provided. 16+.

Worcestershire Lifestyles, Woodside Lodge, Lark Hill Rd., Worcester WR5 2EF (☎01905 350 686; www.worcestershire-lifestyles.org.uk). Work one-on-one with disabled adults. 18+.

STUDYING

> **VISA INFORMATION**
> As of November 2003, citizens of Australia, Canada, New Zealand, and the US require a visa if they plan to study in the UK for longer than six months. Consult www.ukvisas.gov.uk to determine if you require a visa. Immigration officials will request a letter of acceptance from your UK university and proof of funding for your first year of study, as well as a valid passport from all people wishing to study in the UK. Student visas cost £36 and application forms can be obtained through the website listed above.

Study abroad programs range from basic language and culture courses to college-level classes. In order to choose a program that best fits your needs, research cost, duration, and type of accommodation as well as what kind of students participate in the program before making your decision. The **British Council,** 10 Spring Gardens, London SW1A 2BN (☎0207 930 8466; www.britishcouncil.org), is an invaluable source of information. Devoted to international student mobility, the **Council for International Education,** 9-17 St. Albans Pl., London N1 ONX (☎0207 288 4330; www.ukcosa.org.uk), is another valuable resource.

For accommodations, dorm life provides a better opportunity to mingle with fellow students, but there is less of a chance to experience the local scene. If you live with a family, there is a potential to build lifelong friendships with locals and to experience day-to-day life, but conditions can vary greatly from family to family.

UNIVERSITIES

Tens of thousands of international students study abroad in the UK every year, drawn by the prestige of some of the world's oldest and most renowned universities. Apply early, as larger institutions fill up fast.

AMERICAN PROGRAMS

If you are a US citizen, studying abroad through an American program makes your life significantly easier in terms of arranging for course credit, planning your trip, orientation once you arrive, and support during your stay. The following is a list of organizations that can help place students abroad; you can search for more at **www.studyabroad.com.**

American Institute for Foreign Study, College Division, River Plaza, 9 W. Broad St., Stamford, CT 06902 (☎800-727-2437; www.aifsabroad.com). Organizes programs for high school and college study in universities in the UK.

Arcadia University for Education Abroad, 450 S. Easton Rd., Glenside, PA 19038 (☎866-927-2234; www.arcadia.edu/cea). Operates programs at many universities throughout Britain. Costs and duration range widely.

Butler University Institute for Study Abroad, 1100 W. 42nd St., ste. 305, Indianapolis, IN 46208 (☎317-940-9336 or 800-858-0229; www.ifsa-butler.org). Organizes both term-time and summer study at British and Irish universities, including orientation and day trips. Prices vary greatly by location.

Central College Abroad, Office of International Education, 812 University, Pella, IA, 50219 (☎800-831-3629 or 641-628-5284; www.central.edu/abroad), offers internships, as well as summer ($3300), semester (US$10,500-16,900), and year-long (US$29,200) programs in Britain.

Council on International Educational Exchange (CIEE), 7 Custom House St., 3rd fl., Portland, ME 01401 (☎800-407-8839; www.ciee.org/study). Sponsors work, volunteer, academic, and internship programs in the UK.

Institute for the International Education of Students (IES), 33 N. LaSalle St., 15th fl., Chicago, IL 60602 (☎800-995-2300; www.IESabroad.org). Offers year-long (US$25,180), semester (US$13,970), and summer programs in London. Internship opportunities. Application fee US$50. Scholarships available.

Association for International Practical Training, 10400 Little Patuxent Pkwy., ste. 250, Columbia, MD 21044 (☎410-997-2200; www.aipt.org). Offers programs in the UK for college students who have completed technical study.

International Partnership for Service-Learning and Leadership, 815 2nd Ave., ste. 315, New York, NY 10017 (☎212-986-0989; www.ipsl.org). Seeks to unite service and study at the University of Surrey Roehampton in London. Courses relating to volunteer work can be combined in semester (US$10,100) or full-year (US$19,900) programs.

UK PROGRAMS

Many universities accommodate international students for summer, single-term, or full-year study. The most direct means to gather more information is to contact the university that interests you. Those listed below are only a few that open their gates to foreign students; the British Council (see p. 57) provides information on additional universities. Prices listed provide an estimate of university fees for non-EU citizens; in most cases room and board are not included. Also note that medical and other laboratory-based programs are more expensive.

Queen's University Belfast, International Office, Belfast BT7 1NN, Northern Ireland (☎02890 975 088; www.qub.ac.uk/ilo). Study in Belfast for a semester (£3305) or a full year (£6610).

University of Cambridge, Cambridge Admissions Office (CAO), Fitzwilliam House, 32 Trumpington St., Cambridge CB2 1QY (☎01223 333 308; www.cam.ac.uk). Open to overseas applicants for summer (£415-910) or year-long study (£8832-11,571).

University of Edinburgh, The International Office, University of Edinburgh, 57 George Sq., Edinburgh EH8 9JU (☎01316 504 296; www.ed.ac.uk). Offers summer programs (£950-1335) and year-long courses for international students (£9000-11,850).

University of Glasgow, Student Recruitment and Admissions Service, University of Glasgow, 1 The Square, Glasgow G12 8QQ (☎01413 304 575; www.gla.ac.uk). Offers year-long courses (£8000-10,100).

University of Leeds, Study Abroad Office, Leeds LS2 9JT (☎01333 437 591; www.leeds.ac.uk/students/study-abroad). One of largest universities in England, Leeds offers semester (£3800) and full-year (£7250) study abroad programs.

University College London, Gower St., London WC1E 6BT (☎020 7679 2000; www.ucl.ac.uk). In the center of London. Year-long programs (£10,500-13,750).

London School of Economics, The Admissions Officer, London School of Economics, P.O. Box 13401, Houghton St., London WC2A 2AE (☎020 7955 7125; www.lse.ac.uk). Year-long courses for international students (£10,500).

A LEARNING EXPERIENCE
An education on the other side of the Atlantic.

When I started to think about my year off between high school and college, the furthest possibility from my mind was participating in any program that was remotely academic. I was interested in going abroad, however, and my desire to travel soon overwhelmed my aversion to academics. In the fall of 1999, then, freshly graduated from high school and with a year of freedom ahead of me, I moved to Oxford, England to spend a semester at Oxford Tutorial College.

I participated in a program for students taking a "gap year"—European for "year off"—and while I did meet other Americans, I also met students from Russia, England, Ireland and Switzerland.

I took three classes at Oxford: English literature, creative writing, and sociology. My literature and writing groups were both small, with just seven or eight students per class, and sociology became a one-on-one tutorial after the other students in the class switched into other courses early in the semester.

One benefit of going to Oxford Tutorial was that many of the teachers were young men and women either putting themselves through graduate school or teaching at a few different schools in the area. By mid-semester, many students I knew were playing sports with their teachers on the weekends, or meeting up for a beer after class. In some cases, teachers became mentors and trusted friends as well as instructors.

Now that I can reflect on my experience in England as it relates to my four years of college in America, I see major differences between the educational systems in which I have studied. First, at Oxford, all students were encouraged to work one or two days a week at an internship organized through the school. I spent one day a week working at a school for autistic children. My experience at this school was one that prepared me well for college. I was given no formal training in working with mentally handicapped children, but I was taught instead to learn from

example and to do outside research on autism to supplement what I learned in the classroom and from interacting with the children. This experience prepared me well for the world of Harvard where students, rather than being spoon-fed, must learn to be aggressive about getting the most out of one's education.

Another difference between the systems at Oxford Tutorial College and at my American university was the very existence and protocol of the tutorial itself at Oxford. In my English literature class, each student was expected to meet with the teacher once a week to discuss readings and papers. When we wrote papers, we read them out loud to our teachers in tutorial. I will never forget the shock of finding out that I had to read a five-page paper out loud to a virtual stranger. My literature teacher, Royce, was young and very hip, and as I got to know him better, I felt more and more comfortable in our meetings—but at first I was terrified. This fear was, of course, the point. As I see it now, reading a paper aloud is a way of owning one's work in a way that I had never before experienced. This challenge dealt me by Oxford, to really experience what I had written, was a valuable one.

Reflecting on my experience now, I am struck by how great a part of my international experience took place in bars. This may sound ridiculous, but it's true. While a social life was similarly important in my four years of American college, in England, four years were compressed into four months. My roommate and I would go home after school every day to do our schoolwork, but most nights found us leaving again at ten or eleven to meet up with friends from school. Though I did take my schoolwork in England seriously, the very nature of going abroad for a semester begs one to experience all aspects of life in a new place. For this reason, my most enduring memories are of moments outside the classroom, of exploring Oxford alongside people from many different places and cultures.

Lily Brown graduated from Harvard University in 2004 with a degree in Women, Gender, and Sexuality Studies.

University of Oxford, College Admissions Office, Wellington Sq., Oxford OX1 2JD (☎0186 528 8000; www.ox.ac.uk). Large range of summer programs (£880-3780) through year-long courses (£8170-10,890).

University of St. Andrews, Admissions Application Centre, 79 North St., St. Andrews, Fife KY16 9AJ (☎01334 462 150; www.st-andrews.ac.uk/services/admissions), welcomes students for term-time study. Also houses the **Scottish Studies Summer Program,** 66 North St., St. Andrews, Fife KY16 9AH (☎01334 462 238; www.st-andrews.ac.uk/admissions/sssprog.htm). Courses in history, art history, literature, and music of the region for high-school students (£2600 all-inclusive).

University of Ulster, International Office, Shore Rd., Newtownabbey, Co. Antrim BT37 OQB, Northern Ireland (☎028 7032 4138; www.ulst.ac.uk/international), offers semester- or year-long programs for visiting international students (£2800-7725).

University of Westminster, Admissions Enquiries Office, 35 Marylebone Rd., London NW1 5LS (☎020 7911 5000; www.wmin.ac.uk). Offers a range of summer (£595) and full-year (£8125) programs of study in various fields.

WORKING

LONG-TERM WORK

If you plan to spend a substantial amount of time working in the UK, search for a job well in advance. International placement agencies are often the easiest way to find employment abroad, especially for teaching. **Internships,** usually for college students, are a good way to segue into working abroad, although they are often unpaid or poorly paid. Be wary of advertisements or companies that offer to get you a job abroad for a fee—often the same listings are available online or in newspapers. Some reputable organizations include:

Anders Elite, Capital House, 1 Houndwell Place, Southampton SO14 1 HU (☎02380 223 511; www.anderselite.com). Large job placement agency with 13 offices in Britain.

Hansard Scholar Programme, 9 Kingsway, London WC2B 6XF (☎020 7395 4000; www.hansard-society.org.uk). Combines classes at the London School of Economics with internships in British government.

IAESTE—US, 10400 Little Patuxent Pkwy., ste. 250, Columbia, MD 21044, USA (☎1-410-997-3069; www.aipt.org/iaeste.html). Arranges paid internships.

International Cooperative Education, 15 Spiros Way, Menlo Park, CA, 94025, USA (☎1-650-323-4944; www.icemenlo.com). Finds summer jobs for students in England. Costs include a $250 application fee and a $700 fee for placement.

TEACHING

The British school system is comprised of **state** (public, government-funded), **public** (independent, privately funded), and **international** (often for children of expatriates) schools, as well as **universities.** The academic year is divided into **autumn** (September to Christmas), **spring** (early January to Easter) and **summer** (Easter to late July) terms. Applications to teach at state schools must be made through the local government; independent and international schools must be applied to individually. University positions are typically only available through fellowship or exchange programs.

To obtain a permanent position, you must have **Qualified Teacher Status (QTS).** The government-run **Teacher Training Agency** (☎08456 000 991; www.canteach.gov.uk) manages teacher qualification and provides general guide-

WORK PERMIT AND VISA INFORMATION. European Economic **Area (EEA)** nationals (member countries include EU member states and Iceland, Liechtenstein, and Norway) do not need a work permit to work in the UK. If you live in a Commonwealth country (including Australia, Canada, and New Zealand) and if your parents or grandparents were born in the UK, you can apply for **UK Ancestry-Employment** and work without a permit. Commonwealth citizens ages 17-27 can work permit-free under a **working holiday visa.** Foreigners studying at an institution in the UK are able to work within restrictions permit-free. American citizens who are full-time students and are over 18 can apply for a special permit from the **British Universities North America Club (BUNAC),** which allows them to work for up to six months in the UK. Contact BUNAC at P.O. Box 430, Southbury, CT 06488, USA (☎1-203-264-0901) or 16 Bowling Green Lane, London EC1R 0QH (☎020 7251 3472; www.bunac.org.uk). Others will require a work permit to work in the UK. Applications must be made by the employer and can be obtained through the **Home Office,** Work Permits (UK), P.O. Box 3468, Sheffield (☎0114 259 4074; www.workpermits.gov.uk). Applications for work visas must be made through your local consulate. See **Facts for the Traveler: Embassies and Consulates** (p. 11).

lines for those wishing to teach in the UK. European Union-qualified teachers can work in the UK. The **British Council** (p. 57) has extensive information for people wishing to teach abroad. Placement agencies are useful in finding teaching jobs, although vacancies are also listed in major newspapers. The following organizations may be of help.

Council for International Exchange of Scholars, 3007 Tilden St. NW, ste. 5L, Washington DC 20008, USA (☎1-202-686-4000; www.cies.org). Administers the Fulbright program for faculty and professionals.

Eteach, Academy House, 403 London Rd., Camberley, Surrey GU15 3HL (☎08452 261 904; www.eteach.com). Online recruitment service for teachers.

European Council of International Schools, 21B Lavant St., Petersfield, Hampshire GU32 3EL (☎01730 268 244; www.ecis.org). Runs recruitments services for international schools in the UK and elsewhere.

International Schools Services (ISS), 15 Roszel Rd., Box 5910, Princeton, NJ 08543-5910, USA (☎1-609-452-0990; www.iss.edu). Hires teachers for more than 200 overseas schools, including some in England; candidates should have experience teaching or with international affairs, 2-year commitment expected.

The Teacher Recruitment Company, ste. G5, MLS Business Centre, 1-3 The Queensway, Redhill RH1 1NG (☎08709 220 316; www.teachers.eu.com). International recruitment agency lists positions and provides information on jobs in the UK.

SHORT-TERM WORK

Traveling for long periods of time can get expensive; therefore, many travelers try their hand at odd jobs for a few weeks at a time to help finance another month or two of touring around. Though the UK typically does not issue work permits for short-term manual or domestic labor, a popular option is to work several hours at a hostel in exchange for free or discounted room and/or board. Pub work is widely available and may not require a permit, depending on the attitude of your employer. Most often, these short-term jobs are found by word of mouth, or simply by talking to the owner of a hostel or restaurant. Due to the high turnover in the tourism industry, many places are eager for help, even if it is only temporary.

Let's Go tries to list temporary jobs like these whenever possible; look in the Practical Information sections of larger cities. **Vacation Work Publications,** 9 Park End St., Oxford, OX1 1HJ (☎01865 241 978; www.vacationwork.co.uk) publishes books on working overseas and maintains an up-to-date database of seasonal jobs in many countries including the UK. **BUNAC** (p. 61) has listings for establishments that have employed short-term workers in the past.

ENGLAND. Most English cities and larger towns have job spaces to fill, especially during the **high season,** and mainly in pubs or restaurants. **Brighton** (p. 152) is especially friendly to younger people looking for temporary work. Job hunting may be harder in the northern cities, where unemployment is higher. TICs can often be a good place to start your search (many post listings on their bulletin boards), though you will also be advised simply to check newspapers or individual establishments. **Job placement organizations** arrange temporary jobs in service or office industries. They can be found in most cities, including the Manpower office in **Manchester** (p. 343), Blue Arrow in **Cambridge** (p. 307) and throughout the southwest, and JobCentres throughout England. **Bournemouth** (p. 199), **Bristol** (p. 189), **Exeter** (p. 205), **Newquay** (p. 228) and **Torquay** (p. 217) are all good places to look for temporary work. The YHA website (www.yha.org.uk) lists openings for "general assistants"; you can also inquire personally at independent **hostels.**

WALES. Many areas of Wales are economically depressed and suffer unemployment rates higher than the British average. Picking up short-term work as a traveler may be more of a challenge here than in England. **Cardiff** (p. 442), a large, well-touristed city, is perhaps the most feasible option, especially during rugby season; smaller towns may have listings posted at TICs or outside markets. Opportunities for YHA hostel work extend to Wales as well as England (see above).

SCOTLAND. Edinburgh (p. 526) is an excellent place to look for short-term work, especially during Festival in August. The backpacker culture fosters plenty of opportunities, and most of the larger hostels post lists of job openings. **Glasgow** (p. 561) experiences a similar boom during the summer. In both cities, low-paying domestic and food service jobs are easy to procure; computer skills may net you higher-paying office work. **Inverness** has a JobCentre (p. 616) that can help you find temp placements. Archaeological digs are commonplace in both **Orkney** and **Shetland,** but the application process is competitive. The fish-processing industry in Shetland (p. 662) provides hard work but good pay and excellent scenery. The SYHA hostel network has openings listed on its website (www.syha.org.uk); independent hostels also hire short-term workers from a pool of globetrotters.

NORTHERN IRELAND. Some of the most common forms of short-term employment in Northern Ireland include **food service, domestic,** and **farm work. Belfast** is a good place to look for work and has several placement agencies.

FARMING IN THE UK

Working on a farm offers a chance to get away from the urban sprawl of London and the big cities and to wander for a time among sheep rather than tourist hordes. Run by the Home Office, the **Seasonal Agricultural Workers Scheme** is a youth-oriented program that facilitates the placement of overseas nationals, especially students ages 18-25, in seasonal positions in the agricultural industry. For more information, contact the Managed Migration division of the Home Office (☎0114 259 4074; www.workpermits.gov.uk). Below are a couple of organizations that can help set up short-term work and exchange programs in the farming industry.

Fruitfuljobs.com (☎0870 727 0050; www.fruitfuljobs.com). Sets up farm work for back-packers and students all over the UK; online application.

World Wide Opportunities on Organic Farms (WWOOF), P.O. Box 2675, Lewes BN7 1RB (☎01273 476 286; www.wwoof.org.uk). Offers a list of organic farms across the UK that welcome volunteer workers. In return for 4 to 6hr. of work, visitors receive a bed and all meals.

ADDITIONAL RESOURCES

How to Get a Job in Europe, by Sanborn and Matherly. Surrey Books, 1999 (US$23).

How to Live Your Dream of Volunteering Overseas, by Collins, DeZerega, and Heckscher. Penguin Books, 2002 (US$17).

International Directory of Voluntary Work, by Whetter and Pybus. Peterson's Guides and Vacation Work, 2000 (US$16).

International Jobs, by Kocher and Segal. Perseus Books, 1999 (US$20).

Work Abroad: The Complete Guide to Finding a Job Overseas, by Hubbs, Griffith, and Nolting. Transitions Abroad Publishing, 2000 (US$16).

Work Your Way Around the World, by Susan Griffith. Worldview Publishing Services, 2005 (US$22).

Invest Yourself: The Catalogue of Volunteer Opportunities, published by the Commission on Voluntary Service and Action (US ☎718 638 8487).

BEYOND TOURISM

ENGLAND

This blessed plot, this earth, this realm, this England...
—William Shakespeare, *Richard II*

The United Kingdom, Great Britain, England—the terms may seem interchangeable, but they refer to specific entities. England, Scotland, and Wales occupy the island of Great Britain, the larger of the British Isles. Along with Northern Ireland (Ulster), the British countries form Her Majesty's United Kingdom of Great Britain and Northern Ireland, commonly called the **UK**. England conquered Wales and Ireland by the 17th century and Scotland in 1707; the Republic of Ireland won back its independence in 1921. While Wales and Scotland retain separate cultural identities in language and customs, the two remain part of a nation administered from London. This chapter focuses on the history, literature, and culture of England; **Wales** (p. 433), **Scotland** (p. 515), and **Northern Ireland** (p. 669) are treated separately.

LIFE AND TIMES
ENGLAND OF OLD

2500-2000 BC
An ancient tribe, likely the Druids, constructs the neolithic stone circle at Stonehenge.

THE ANCIENT ISLE. Britain's residents first developed a distinct culture when the land bridge between the European continent and Britain eroded (c. 6000-5000 BC). Little is known about the island's prehistoric inhabitants, but the massive and astronomically precise stone circles left behind at **Stonehenge** (p. 182) and **Avebury** (p. 183) testify to their advanced scientific and technological prowess. The **Celts** and **Druids** emigrated from the continent in the first millennium BC, but were eradicated by the carnage-loving armies of the Roman Emperor Claudius in AD 43. The Roman conquerors held all of "Britannia" (England and Wales) by the end of the first century, despite the efforts of the mythic Celtic warrior-queen **Boudicca,** who burned London down in vengeance. Britannia marked the northernmost Roman border; the invaders established the cities of **Londinium** (London) and **Verulamium** (**St. Albans,** p. 248), as well as a resort spa at **Bath** (p. 183). Further expansion proved difficult. The Romans faced marauders from the northwest; in defense, the Emperor Hadrian constructed his eponymous wall in the 2nd century AD. By the 4th century, the Roman empire waned and the Angles and the Saxons—tribes from Denmark and northern Germany—established settlements and kingdoms in the south. The name "England" derives from "Anglaland," land of the Angles.

AD 43
Emperor Claudius successfully invades Britain and founds Londinium shortly thereafter.

AD 597
Saint Augustine converts King Æthelbert (and all Britons) to Christianity.

THE CONQUERORS. The Britons became Christian when the famed missionary **Augustine** converted King Æthelbert in AD 597 and then founded England's first Catholic church at **Canterbury** (p. 135). From the 8th to the 10th centuries, the Norse sacked Scotland and Ireland and Danish Vikings raided England's east coast. In AD 878, the legendary **Alfred the Great** defeated the Danes, curtailing their rapidly expanding influence. In 1066, the Anglo-Saxon dynasty ended and Britain was born. Allegedly **Edward the Confessor** promised the throne to a Norman named William. Better known as **The Conqueror,** William I invaded the island after Edward's death in 1066, won the pivotal **Battle of Hastings** (p. 147), slaughtered his rival Harold II (and for good measure, his two

1066
At the epic Battle of Hastings, the Norman William I, the Conqueror, defeats the Anglo-Saxon Harold II.

brothers), established the House of Norman, and promptly set about cataloguing his new English acquisitions—each peasant, cow, and bale of hay—in the epic **Domesday Book** (p. 170). A tyrant and efficient administrator, William introduced **feudalism** to Britain during the "Norman yoke," doling out vast tracts of land to his cronies and subjugating English tenants to French lords.

BLOOD AND DEMOCRACY. The Middle Ages were a bloody time of conquest and infighting. In 1154, Henry Plantagenet ascended to the throne as **Henry II**, armed with a healthy inheritance and a dowry from his wife that entitled him to most of France. During his reign he quelled internal uprisings and spread his influence across the Isles, claiming Ireland in 1171. Henry's squabbles with the insubordinate Archbishop of Canterbury, (later Saint) **Thomas à Becket**, resulted in Becket's murder at Canterbury Cathedral (p. 138). Henry's son **Richard the Lionheart** was more interested in the Crusades than domestic insurgents and spent only six months of his 10-year reign on the island. In 1215, tired of such royal pains, noblemen forced his hapless brother and successor, King John, to sign the **Magna Carta**, the precursor to the United States' Bill of Rights and a keystone of modern democracy. The first **Parliament** convened 50 years later. Defying this move toward egalitarian rule, **Edward I** absorbed Wales under the English crown in 1284 and waged war against the Scots, establishing some of Britain's greatest castles along the way (see **Caernarfon**, p. 502). While English kings expanded the nation's boundaries, the **Black Death** ravaged its population; between 1348 and 1361, one-third of all Britons died of the disease. Many more fell in the **Hundred Years' War** (or the 116 Years' War, to be precise), a costly conflict over the French throne.

In 1399, Henry Bolingbroke invaded England and usurped the throne from his cousin Richard II (on holiday in Ireland), placing the House of Lancaster in control. In 1415, Bolingbroke's son, **Henry V**, and his band of brothers defeated the French in the Battle of Agincourt, a legendary upset victory. But **Henry VI's** failure to stave off revived French resistance under Joan of Arc resulted in the loss of almost all of Britain's holdings in France. The **War of the Roses** (1455-85)—a crisis of royal succession between the houses of Lancaster and York (whose respective emblems were a red and a white rose)—culminated when Richard of York sent his nephew, the boy-king Edward V, to the Tower of London for safe-keeping. When Edward conveniently disappeared, Richard ascended.

REFORMATION, RENAISSANCE, AND REVOLUTION. The **House of Tudor** replaced the House of Lancaster in 1485, when Henry VII defeated Richard III at the Battle of Bosworth Field. England's most infamous king, **Henry VIII**, reinforced England's control over the Irish and struggled with the more intimate concern of producing a male heir. Henry's domestic troubles, ahem, led to his marriage to six women (two of whom he executed) and his establishment of the **Anglican Church** when the Pope refused his request for a divorce. Protestantism's fate was initially uncertain. Henry's only son, Edward VI, was overshadowed by his staunchly Catholic half-sister, nicknamed **Bloody Mary** for ordering the mass burnings of Protestants. Henry's daughter **Elizabeth I** inherited control after Mary's death. Elizabeth reversed the religious persecution enforced by her sister and cemented the success of the **Reformation**. Under her extraor-

1170
Followers of King Henry II assassinate the Archbishop of Canterbury, Saint Thomas à Becket.

1215
King John, brother to Richard the Lionheart, is forced to sign the Magna Carta.

1348-1361
The Black Death, a pandemic of pneumonic and Bubonic plague, kills one third of all Britons.

ENGLAND

1485
The War of the Roses, a dispute over succession within the royal house of Plantagenet, ends at the Battle of Bosworth Field.

1534
Following his excommunication from the Catholic church, Henry VIII founds the Church of England.

dinary reign, Britain became the leading Protestant power in Europe, the English defeated the **Spanish Armada** in 1588, a young man named William picked up his pen, and **Sir Francis Drake** circumnavigated the globe. Henry VII's great-granddaughter, the Catholic **Mary, Queen of Scots,** briefly threatened the stability of the throne, but her implication in a plot against the Queen's life led to her 20-year imprisonment and execution.

1603
James I (James VI of Scotland) becomes the first British monarch to rule England, Scotland, and Ireland.

The first union of England, Wales, and Scotland as Great Britain took place in 1603, when the philosopher prince James VI of Scotland ascended to the throne as **James I.** But the Catholic sympathies, extravagant spending, and insistence on divine right of kings shown by James and his less able successor, **Charles I,** aroused suspicion within the largely Puritan parliament. Thus, Charles suspended Parliament for 11 years, spurring the **English Civil War** (1642-51). The monarchy came to a violent end with the execution of Charles I and the founding of the first **British Commonwealth** in 1649.

1649
Oliver Cromwell takes control of the short-lived British Commonwealth. After the restoration of the monarchy and three years after his death from malaria, he is exhumed, drawn, quartered, and beheaded.

REPUBLICANISM AND RESTORATION. The fanatically puritanical **Oliver Cromwell** emerged as the charismatic but despotic leader of the new Commonwealth. Cromwell led a bloody conquest of Ireland, ordering the execution of all Catholic priests and every tenth Irish common soldier; he also enforced oppressive measures in Britain, outlawing swearing and the theater. To the relief of many, the Republic collapsed under the lackluster leadership of Cromwell's son Richard. According to **Thomas Hobbes** in his 1651 treatise **Leviathan,** life is "poor, nasty, brutish, and short" in the absence of an absolute sovereign; but the **Restoration** of **Charles II** to the throne in 1660 did not cure Britain's troubles. Debate raged over the exclusion of Charles's Catholic brother **James II** from the succession. Amidst the divisive politicking, England's founding political parties arose: the **Whigs,** who opposed the kings and supported reform, and the **Tories,** who supported hereditary succession.

1688
William of Orange and his wife Mary ascend to the throne, ending the wars of succession.

LAWS AND LOGIC. James II took the throne in 1685, but was deposed three years later by his son-in-law **William of Orange.** In the **Glorious Revolution of 1688,** the Dutch Protestant William and his wife Mary forced James to France and implemented a **Bill of Rights,** ensuring the Protestantism of future monarchs. Supporters of James II (called **Jacobites**) remained a threat until 1745, when James II's grandson Charles, commonly known as **Bonnie Prince Charlie,** failed in his attempt to invade and recapture the throne (p. 519). The ascension of William and Mary marked the end of a century of upheaval and a rise in liberalism and tolerance; Britain accumulated wealth and continental political clout. By the end of the **Seven Years' War** (1756-63), Britain controlled Canada, 13 unruly colonies to the west, and much of the Caribbean. **Sir Isaac Newton** theorized the laws of gravity and invented calculus on the side; Enlightenment figures **John Locke, Francis Bacon, David Hume,** and **Adam Smith** revolutionized political and philosophical thought. Religious fervor occasionally returned, with Bible-thumping **Methodists** preaching to outdoor crowds mid-century. Parliament prospered thanks to the ineffectual leadership of the Hanoverian kings, **George I, II,** and **III,** and the position of Prime Minister eclipsed the monarchy as the seat of power. Britain's uppity cross-Atlantic colonial holding declared, fought for, and won its independence between 1776 and 1783.

1687
Sir Isaac Newton publishes *Principia Mathematica.* He writes on gravity, calculus, the binomial theorem, elliptical orbits, optics, and the speed of sound.

1776
The colonies in America declare independence and win it seven years later.

ENGLAND

EMPIRE AND INDUSTRY. During the 18th and 19th centuries, Britain seized rule of more than one quarter of the world's population and more than two-fifths of its land. By 1858 Britain controlled India (the "jewel in the imperial crown") as well as Ceylon (Sri Lanka), South Africa, Hong Kong, the Falkland Islands, Australia, New Zealand, and the Western Pacific islands. The promise of overseas trade galvanized colonization: control of the Cape of Good Hope secured shipping routes to the Far East and plantations in the New World produced lucrative staples like sugar and rum. In addition to the economic imperative, Britons considered it their moral duty to "civilize" the non-Christians in their imperial domain. The **Napoleonic Wars** (1800-15) marked the renewal of the Anglo-French rivalry.

The **Industrial Revolution**—spurred by the perfection of the steam engine by **James Watt** in 1765 and by the mechanization of the textile industry—bankrolled this frenzied colonizing. Massive portions of the rural populace migrated to towns like **Manchester** (p. 343) and **Leeds** (p. 395). A wide economic gap between factory owners and laborers replaced the age-old gap between landowners and tenant farmers. The **gold standard,** which Britain adopted in 1821, stimulated international trade and ensured the pound's value.

VICTORIA AND COMPANY. The reign of **Queen Victoria** (1837-1901) marked a period of foreign and domestic stability and peace. A series of **Factory** and **Reform Acts** limited child labor, capped the average workday, and made sweeping changes in (male) voting rights. Prince Albert's 1851 **Great Exhibition** collected over 13,000 consumer goods from Britain's territories in London's **Crystal Palace,** an immense glass building. The rich and bohemian uppercrust embraced *fin de siècle* decadence: ornate art and clothing and even more ornate social rituals. Yet while commercial self-interest defined 19th-century British society, proto-socialists like **John Stuart Mill** and the members of the **Fabian Society,** including **George Bernard Shaw** and **H.G. Wells,** argued against bourgeois values. Trade unions strengthened and found a political voice in the **Labour Party,** founded in 1906. Issues with Ireland became increasingly pressing; Prime Minister **William Gladstone** failed to pass his **Home Rule Bill,** a proposal for partial Irish political autonomy. The **Suffragettes,** led by **Emmeline Pankhurst,** fought for enfranchisement for women by disrupting Parliament and staging hunger strikes. Women won the right to vote after **World War I.**

A LOST GENERATION. The **Great War** (1914-1918), as WWI was known until 1939, left two million Britons injured and one million dead. Technological advances of the 19th century begot powerful weaponry, such as the machine gun and the tank. Combined with the European militaries' outmoded strategies (predominantly, trench warfare) these advances contributed to the enormous human cost of the war. The war destroyed the Victorian dream of a peaceful, progressive society.

The 1930s brought **depression** and unemployment. A representative for the British Treasury, **John Maynard Keynes,** argued against German war reparations and for interventionism. In 1936, King Edward VIII shocked the world with the announcement of his **abdication** for the sake of twice-divorced American socialite Wallis Simpson. After Germany reoccupied the Rhineland, Prime Minister **Neville Chamberlain** pushed through a controversial and

1812-1815
The phrase *Pax Britannica* comes into usage, describing the British style of imperialism, which involves education, language, and "civilizing."

ENGLAND

1867
A special Royal Commission, reacting to a series of strikes, recognizes the legal status of trade unions (workers' unions).

1891
Anglo-Irish writer and bon vivant Oscar Wilde publishes *The Picture of Dorian Gray*, a seminal *fin de siècle* work.

1914
The French and the British engage the Germans in WWI. At the first battle, the Battle of the Marne, 500,000 soldiers die in four days.

ENGLAND

notoriously disastrous appeasement agreement with Hitler in Munich, naively promising "peace in our time." But following Hitler's invasion of Poland in 1939, Britain declared war. For the second time in 25 years Europe went up in flames. Even the Great War failed to prepare Britain for the horrors of the Holocaust and the utter devastation of **World War II.** During the prolonged **Battle of Britain** in the summer of 1940, London, Coventry, and other English cities suffered extensive damage from thunderous **"blitzkriegs,"** which left scores of Britons dead or homeless. The fall of France in 1940 precipitated the creation of a war cabinet, led by the determined and eloquent new Prime Minister **Winston Churchill.** In June 1944, Britain and the Allied Forces launched the Battle of Normandy, commonly known as the **D-Day Invasion.** The move changed the tide of the war, leading to the liberation of Paris and eventually peace in May 1945.

ENGLAND'S EVOLUTION. Following the wars, Britain suffered continued economic hardship. Rationing did not end until 1954; the government owed an enormous war debt to the United States; much of Britain's infrastructure and workforce lay in ruins. At the same time, immigration from former British colonies increased. In response, Britain adopted some socialist economic policies. In 1946, left-wing politicians established the **National Health Service,** which still provides free medical care to all Britons; Labour also nationalized many programs and utilities. In the 1960s, the Labour government relaxed laws against divorce and homosexuality and abolished capital punishment. Britain joined the **European Economic Community (EEC)** in 1971, a move that received a rocky welcome from many Britons; the relationship between Britain and the continent remains a contentious issue today. Despite its progressive policies, though, Britain could not replace the economic boon of a colonial empire. Unemployment and economic unrest culminated in a series of public service strikes during 1979's **"Winter of Discontent."**

In May 1979, conservative Tory **Margaret Thatcher** became Britain's first female Prime Minister, espousing reduced government spending, denationalization, and lower taxes. Thatcher was unpopular until the **Falkland Islands War** against Argentina in 1982 elicited a surge of patriotic feelings. Thatcher privatized nearly every industry that the Labour government had brought under public control, dismantling vast segments of the welfare state. Her policies brought dramatic prosperity to many but sharpened the divide between the haves and havenots. Aggravated by her support of the unpopular **poll tax** and resistance to the EEC, the Conservative Party conducted a vote of no confidence that led to Thatcher's 1990 resignation and the election of **John Major.** In 1995, Major forced a party election by stepping down and re-running; he won, but the Conservatives lost parliamentary seats.

Under the leadership of the charismatic and youthful Tony Blair, the Labour Party refashioned itself into the alternative for discontented middle-class voters. "New Labour" won decisively under Blair in 1997, with the biggest Labour majority to date, and garnered a second landslide victory in June 2001. (Labour also won in May 2005, although by a much reduced margin.) Blair nurtured relations with the EU and maintained inclusive, moderate economic and social positions. Britain's stance on the Kosovo crisis gained Blair the monicker of "Little Clinton."

Blair's Labour government has also tackled various constitutional reforms, beginning with domestic **devolution** in Scotland and Wales and a movement towards local governance. The Scottish Parliament (p. 520) and Welsh National Assembly (p. 437) both opened in 1999. In May 1998, London voters approved the plan for a powerful city government (currently headed by the headstrong Mayor Ken Livingstone). Progress has been more halting in attempts at **Northern Irish autonomy.** The **Good Friday Agreement** (p. 671) of 1998 began the process of a disarmament and created a Northern Ireland Assembly with limited legislative and executive powers. But the British government suspended Belfast's **Stormont Assembly** in 2000, hoping to instigate the decommissioning of arms by the IRA and the Unionists; a lack of progress led to a spate of terrorist attacks. In July 2005, Sinn Fein, the political party associated with the IRA, announced the complete disarmament of all paramilitaries, signaling the coming end of the conflict.

TODAY

RULE BRITANNIA. Britain has become one of the world's most stable constitutional monarchies without the aid of a single constitution. A combination of parliamentary legislation, common law, and convention composes the flexible system of British government. Since the 1700s the monarch has had a purely symbolic role; real political power resides with **Parliament,** consisting of the **House of Commons,** with its elected Members of Parliament (MPs), and the **House of Lords.** Power has shifted from the Lords to the Commons over time. Reforms in 1999 removed the majority of hereditary peers from the House of Lords, replacing them with Life Peers, appointed by prime ministers to serve for life. Parliament holds supreme legislative power and may change and even directly contradict its previous laws. All members of the executive branch, which includes the **Prime Minister** and the **Cabinet,** are also MPs; this fusing of legislative and executive functions, called the "efficient secret" of the British government, ensures the quick passage of the majority party's programs into bills. The Prime Minister is never elected to the post directly; rather, he or she wins a local constituency and the head of the ruling party is Prime Minister. From an elegant roost on **10 Downing Street** (or, in the case of Tony Blair and his large brood, No. 11; p. 117), the Prime Minister chooses a Cabinet, whose members head the government's departments and present a cohesive platform to the public. Political parties keep their MPs in line on most votes in Parliament and provide a pool of talent and support for the smooth functioning of the executive. Roughly, the **Labour** party, currently in power, is center-left; the **Conservatives,** or Tories, are center-right; and the smaller, feisty **Liberal Democrat** party is left. The par-

THE LOCAL STORY

A QUEEN'S BEST FRIENDS

Everybody's heard of the Queen but precious few know the entire royal family. Emma, Linnet Pharos, and Swift often go unseen and unnoticed, but they regularly shadow the Queen, keeping her company (even on her honeymoon) and scampering through her palaces.

They are the Queen's Welsh corgis, squat dogs with short legs, bobbed tails, perky ears, and endearing dispositions. With origins in South Wales, the efficient corgis have long been employed to herd cattle and sheep. According to legend, however, these dogs had more noble beginnings; ancient woodland fairies supposedly trained corgis (whose name comes from the Welsh "cor" and "ci"—dwarf and dog, respectively) to pull their magical coaches. The history of this royal breed may go back even further. In April 2004, a team of Cardiff University researchers unearthed the leg bone of a corgi-like canine on a crannog (a man-made islet) in Llangorse Lake, the hub of the 9th-century Welsh kingdom of Brycheiniog.

Recently, the Queen's family has grown. The late Princess Margaret's dachshund rendezvoused with one of the Queen's corgis, spawning the "dorgis" Brandy, Cider, and Berry. All seven pups, mutt or not, have secured a royal place in the hearts of British islanders.

ties, though, do not translate directly into American politics. Labour supported the war in Iraq, which the Conservatives opposed; the issues of gay marriage, the death penalty, and abortion have long been resolved.

CURRENT EVENTS. In the May 2005 general election, Labour won a historic victory: Tony Blair became the only post-war Prime Minister other than Thatcher to win a third term. But Labour's majority in the commons was cut to 66 seats from 167; many feel Labour won in spite of Blair, not because of him. Blair's continued support of US foreign policy and his political alliance with President George W. Bush has incited resistance, even consternation, in Britain. In February 2003, an estimated one million people gathered in London to protest military intervention in Iraq. Blair's detractors also point to the Prime Minister's stance on the **euro.** Brown and Blair's long-time position on the euro—that Britain will convert to the currency when the economy is ready—has been seen as an equivocation and a political tool. In June 2005, Blair declined to hold a referendum on the ratification of the EU constitution, again isolating Britain from the continent. The fate of the pound and Britain's participation in the EU remain heated issues, and British opinion remains, as ever, distrustful of integration with the rest of Europe.

Blair's political positions remain in contention after a spate of **terrorist attacks** in July 2005. Four suicide bombs detonated on public transport in London on the morning of July 7, killing 52; a failed second attack occurred two weeks later. The July 7 bombings marked the deadliest attack in London since WWII. In response, the British government tightened security nationwide.

A ROYAL MESS? The past decades have seen dramatic swings of public opinion on Britain's public figureheads. Opinion peaked, perversely, when the world mourned the untimely death of the "People's Princess," **Diana,** in a Paris car crash in 1997. **Queen Elizabeth II,** a matronly, practical character, won kudos when she began paying income tax in 1993 and threw a year-long Golden Jubilee for the 50th year of her reign in 2002. **Prince Charles** and his paramour **Camilla Parker-Bowles** married in April 2005 after a clandestine 30-year romance, although the Queen did not attend the service. A quick stop at a drug rehab clinic in 2002 heralded the onset of adult celebrity (and tabloid notoriety) for **Prince Harry,** the younger of Charles and Diana's sons. Harry's increasing fame still does not detract from the rapt attention devoted to second-in-line **Prince William.**

ENGLISH CULTURE

FOOD AND DRINK

English cooking, like the English climate, is a training for life's unavoidable hardships.
—Historian R.P. Lister

Historically, at least, England has been derided for its horrific cuisine. But do not fear the gravy-laden, boiled, fried, and bland traditional nosh, hungry travelers! Britain's cuisine might leave something to be desired, but food in Britain can be excellent. In the spring of 2005, a panel of more than 600 chefs, food critics and restaurateurs voted 14 British restaurants into the world's top 50; the Fat Duck in Berkshire was named the world's best. Popular television chef Jamie Oliver led a well-publicized and successful campaign to increase the British government's spending on school lunches. And travelers on a backpacker's, not bajillionaire's, budget can eat the benefits, too.

The best way to eat in Britain is to avoid British food. Thankfully, ethnic cuisine has rapidly spread from the cities to the smallest of towns, so that most any village with a pub (and you'd be hard-pressed to find one without) will have an Indian takeaway, an Asian noodle shop, or late-night Shawarma stand to feed stumbling patrons after closing. And **vegetarianism** and organic foods are popular in Britain; even the most traditional pubs and local markets, let alone the trendy cafe-bars and gastropubs, offer at least one meatless option.

All visitors to Britain should try the famed, cholesterol-filled **full English breakfast,** which generally includes fried egg, bacon, baked beans, sauteed mushrooms, grilled tomato, and black pudding (sausage made with pork blood), smothered in HP sauce and served in B&Bs, pubs, and cafes across the country. Toast smothered in jam and Marmite (the most acquired of tastes—a salty, brown spread made from yeast) is a breakfast staple. The best dishes for lunch or dinner are **roasts**—beef, lamb, and Wiltshire hams—and **Yorkshire pudding,** a type of popover drizzled with meat juices. **Bangers and mash** and **bubble and squeak,** despite their intriguing names, are just sausages and potatoes and cabbage and potatoes, respectively. Vegetables, often boiled into a flavorless mush, are typically the weakest part of the meal. Beware the British salad—often a plate of lettuce and sweetened mayonnaise called "salad cream." And beware sandwiches with hidden mayonnaise (often called "club sauce") and butter. The Britons make their **desserts** (often called "puddings" or "afters") exceedingly sweet and gloopy. Sponges, trifles, tarts, and the ill-named spotted dick (spongy currant cake) will satiate the sweetest tooth.

Pub grub is fast, filling, and a fine option for budget travelers. Try savory pies like **Cornish pasties** (PASS-tees), **shepherd's pie,** and **steak and kidney pie.** For those really on the cheap, the **ploughman's lunch** (bread, cheese, and pickles) is a staple in country pubs and can be divine. The local "chippy," or chip shop, will purvey deep-fried **fish and chips** dripping with grease, salt, and vinegar, all in a paper cone. Seek out **outdoor markets** for fresh bread and dairy—try Stilton cheese and biscuits or baps. **Boots, Benjys, Marks & Spencer,** and **Prêt à Manger** sell an impressive array of ready-made sandwiches. **Crisps,** or potato chips, come in astonishing variety, with flavors like prawn cocktail. Try Chinese, Turkish, Lebanese, and especially Indian cuisines—Britain offers some of the best **tandoori** and **curry** outside of India. Finally, for the less adventurous, American fast-food chains (McDonald's, Burger King, Pizza Hut, and Subway) are ubiquitous. But travelers should look elsewhere; they'll still be there when you get home.

British **"tea"** refers both to a drink and a social ceremony. The ritual refreshment, accompanying almost every meal, is served strong and with milk. The standard tea, colloquially known as a **cuppa,** is PG Tips or Tetley; more refined cups specify particular blends such as **Earl Grey** and **Darjeeling.** The oft-stereotyped ritual of afternoon **high tea** includes cooked meats, salad, sandwiches, and pastries. **Cream tea,** a specialty of Cornwall and Devon, includes toast, shortbread, crumpets, scones, and jam, accompanied by **clotted cream** (a cross between whipped cream and butter). The summer teatime potion **Pimm's** is a sangria-esque punch of fruit juices and gin (the recipe is a well-guarded secret). And don't forget supersweet fizzy drinks **Lilt** and **Tango** and the popular juice **Ribena.**

PUBS AND BITTER

Sir William Harcourt believed that English history was made in the pubs as much as in the Houses of Parliament. The routine inspired by the pub is considerable; to stop in at lunchtime and after work is not uncommon. Brits rapidly develop affinities for neighborhood establishments, becoming loyal to their **locals,** and pubs in turn tend to cater to their regulars and develop a particular character. Pubs are ubiquitous; even the smallest village can support a decent **pub crawl.** The drinking age is an inconsistently enforced 18, and you need only be 14 to enter a pub.

Bitter, named for its sharp, hoppy aftertaste, is the standard pub drink and should be hand-pumped or pulled from the tap at cellar temperature into government-stamped **pint** glasses (20oz.) or the more modest **half-pint.** Real **ale** retains a diehard cult of connoisseurs in the shadow of giant corporate breweries; go to www.camra.org.uk to find out more. **Brown, pale,** and **India pale ales**—less common varieties—all have a relatively heavy flavor with noticeable hop. **Stout,** the distinctive subspecies of ale, is rich, dark, and creamy; try the Irish **Guinness** (p. 700), with its silky foam head. Most draught ales and stouts are served at room temperature; if you can't stand the heat, try a **lager,** the precursor of American beer that is typically served cold. **Cider,** like **Strongbow,** is a tasty fermented apple juice served sweet or dry. Variations on the standard pint include **black velvet,** or stout and champagne;

black and tan, layers of stout and ale; and **snakebite,** lager and cider with a dash of black currant syrup or Ribena. **Alcopops,** designer drinks like **Bacardi Breezers** and hard lemonade, are particularly popular with young club-goers.

Since WWI, government-imposed **closing times** have restricted pub hours. In England and Wales, drinks are usually served 11am-11pm Monday to Saturday, and noon-3pm and 7-10:30pm Sunday; more flexible hours are in place in Scotland. A bell approximately 10 minutes before closing time signifies last call. Controversial new legislation allows pubs with special licenses to have flexible opening hours; thus, the arrival of the 24hr. pub. At any rate, pubs sometimes circumvent closing times by serving food or having an entertainment license.

CULTURE AND CUSTOMS

Great Britain, roughly the size of the state of Oregon, is home to 60 million, a dynamic and varied populace filled with local subcultures. Jane Austen, Sid Vicious, and Winston Churchill are each quintessentially "English." Stiff-upper-lipped public schoolboys and post-punk Hoxton rockers sit next to Burberry-clad football hooligans on the Tube. Thus, there is little that a traveler can do that will inadvertently cause offense. That said, the English do place weight on proper decorum, including **politeness** ("thanks" comes in many varieties, including "cheers," and you should use it), **queueing** (that is, lining up—never, ever line jump or otherwise disrupt the queue), and keeping a certain **respectful distance.** You'll find, however, that the British **sense of humor**—fantastically wry, explicit, even raunchy—is somewhat at odds with any notion of coldness and reserve.

THE ARTS

LANGUAGE AND LITERATURE

Eclipsed only by Mandarin Chinese in sheer number of speakers, the English language reflects in its history the diversity of the hundreds of millions who use it today. Once a minor Germanic dialect, English incorporated words and phrases from Danish, French, and Latin, giving even its earliest wordsmiths a vast vocabulary rivaled by few world languages. Over centuries of British colonialism, the language has borrowed endlessly from other tongues and supplied a literary and popular voice for people far removed from the British Isles. A well-chosen novel or collection of poems will illuminate any trip to Britain. Welsh (p. 438) and Scottish (p. 522) languages and literatures are treated separately.

BARDS AND BIBLES. Britain is undeniably the birthplace of much of the world's best literature. A strong oral tradition informed most of the earliest poetry in English, little of which survives. The finest piece of Anglo-Saxon (Old English) poetry is *Beowulf*, a 7th-century account of an egoistic prince, his heroic deeds, and his undoing in a battle with a dragon. The unknown author of *Sir Gawain and the Green Knight* (c. 1375) tells a romance of Arthurian chivalry in which the bedroom becomes a battlefield and a young knight seeks a mysterious destiny. **Geoffrey Chaucer** tapped into the more spirited side of Middle English; his *Canterbury Tales* (c. 1387) remain some of the sauciest, most incisive stories in the English canon and poke fun at all stations of English life. **John Wycliffe** made the Bible accessible to the masses, translating it from Latin to English in the 1380s. **William Tyndale** followed suit in 1525, translating from the original Greek and Hebrew, and his work became the model for the popular **King James** version (completed in 1611 under James I).

THE ENGLISH RENAISSANCE. English literature flourished under the reign of Elizabeth I. **Sir Philip Sidney's** sonnet sequences and **Edmund Spenser's** moral allegories (like *The Faerie Queene*) earned favor at court, while **John Donne** and **George Herbert** crafted metaphysical poetry (and some erotic verse). Playwright **Christopher Marlowe** lost his life in a pub brawl, but not before he produced popular plays of temptation and damnation, such as *Dr. Faustus* (c. 1588). **Ben Jonson,** when he wasn't languishing in jail, redefined satiric comedy in works like *Volpone* (1606). The son of a glove-maker from Stratford-upon-Avon (p. 264), **William Shakespeare** continues to loom over all of English literature. His influence and brilliance would be difficult to overstate, given his success as a playwright, poet, linguistic innovator ("scuffle," "lonely," "arouse," "skim milk"), and, in the words of literary critic Harold Bloom, the "inventor of the human."

HOW NOVEL! Britain's civil and religious turmoil in the late 16th and early 17th centuries bore a huge volume of obsessive and beautiful literature, like **John Milton's** epic *Paradise Lost* (1667) and **John Bunyan's** allegory-laden *Pilgrim's Progress* (1678). In the 18th century, **John Dryden** penned neoclassical poetry, **Alexander Pope** satires, and **Dr. Samuel Johnson** his lovably idiosyncratic dictionary. In 1719, **Daniel Defoe** inaugurated the era of the English **novel** with his swashbuckling *Robinson Crusoe*. Authors like **Samuel Richardson** (*Clarissa*, 1749) and **Fanny Burney** (*Evelina*, 1778) perfected the form, while **Henry Fielding's** wacky *Tom Jones* (1749) and **Laurence Sterne's** experimental *Tristram Shandy* (1759-67) invigorated it. **Jane Austen's** intricate narratives portrayed the modes and manners of the early 19th century. In the Victorian period, poverty and social change spawned the sentimental novels of **Charles Dickens;** *Oliver Twist* (1838) and *David Copperfield* (1849) draw on the bleakness of his childhood in Portsmouth (p. 162) and portray the harsh living conditions of working-class Londoners. Secluded in the wild Yorkshire moors (see Haworth, p. 394), the **Brontë sisters** staved off tuberculosis to conjure the tumultuous romances *Wuthering Heights* (Emily; 1847), *Jane Eyre*, and *Villette* (Charlotte; 1847 and 1853). **George Eliot** (Mary Ann Evans) wrote her intricately detailed "Study of Provincial Life," *Middlemarch* (1871). *Tess of the d'Urbervilles* (1891) and *Jude the Obscure* (1895) by **Thomas Hardy** mark a sombre end to the Victorian age.

ROMANTICISM AND RESPONSE. Partly in reaction to the rationalism of the preceding century, the **Romantic** movement garnered turbulent verse that celebrated the transcendent beauty of nature, the power of the imagination, and the profound influence of childhood experiences. Reclusive painter-poet **William Blake** published the gorgeously illustrated *Songs of Innocence and Experience* in 1794. **William Wordsworth** and **Samuel Taylor Coleridge** wrote the watershed collection *Lyrical Ballads*, which included "Lines Composed a Few Miles above Tintern Abbey" (p. 451) and "The Rime of the Ancient Mariner," in the late 1790s. Wordsworth's poetry reflects on a long, full life—he drew particular inspiration from the Lakes (p. 360) and Snowdonia (p. 492)—but many of his colleagues died tragically young. The astonishing wunderkind **John Keats,** who

THE LOCAL STORY

COUNTRY LIFE

Ah, the delightful stuffiness of the aristocracy. Despite the changes of the last century, Britain is still a land of dukes, earls, and lords. But it isn't easy being a member of the gentry these days. Due to the high cost of maintaining an estate, many in the leisure class have been forced to find creative ways of generating revenue, often opening their abodes to the paying public. It's possible to get a feel for the posh life by visiting these palaces, but paying admission and gawking at the antiques is for the common rabble.

Instead, pick up a scintillating issue of the weekly *Country Life* magazine, a notoriously snooty publication read religiously by anyone who's anyone with a string of polo ponies. After the real estate—real estates, mind you—section, every issue announces a young lady into society with a tasteful photo (often taken with a pet of noteworthy lineage) and a description of her education, where she summers and her charity of choice. Then there are articles on all the important subjects—motoring, bridge, show jumping, fox hunting—and longer inquiries into pressing issues. (Which *is* Britain's oldest family, anyway?) "Around the Salerooms" has an update on transactions made at Sotheby's and a column offers advice on common estate quandaries, like how to stop your dog from biting the help. £3; available at the poshest newsstands.

wrote the Romantic maxim "beauty is truth, truth beauty," succumbed to tuberculosis at 26. The poet **Percy Bysshe Shelley** drowned off the Tuscan coast at 29. The pansexual heartthrob **Lord Byron** defined the heroic archetype in *Don Juan* (1819-24) and died fighting in the Greek War of Independence at 36.

The poetry of the Victorian age struggled with the impact of societal changes and religious skepticism. **Alfred, Lord Tennyson** spun verse about faith and doubt for over a half-century and inspired a medievalist revival with Arthurian idylls like "The Lady of Shalott" (1842). Celebrating the grotesque, **Robert Browning** composed piercing dramatic monologues, and his wife **Elizabeth Barrett** counted the ways she loved him in *Sonnets from the Portuguese* (1850). Meanwhile, fellow female poet **Christina Rossetti** envisioned the fantastical world of "Goblin Market" (1862). **Matthew Arnold** abandoned poetry in 1867 to become the greatest cultural critic of the day. Jesuit priest **Gerard Manley Hopkins** penned tortuous verse with a unique "sprung rhythm" that make him the chief forerunner of poetic modernism.

THE MODERN AGE. "On or about December 1910," wrote **Virginia Woolf,** "human nature changed." Woolf, a key member of London's bohemian intellectual **Bloomsbury Group,** tried to capture the spirit of the time in her novels; she and Irish expatriate **James Joyce** (p. 701) were among the most ground-breaking practitioners of Modernism (c. 1910-1930). A Missouri transplant and "Pope of Russell Square," **T.S. Eliot** wrote *The Waste Land* (1922), undeniably one of the last century's most important works. Reacting to the Great War, Eliot portrays London as a barren, fragmented desert in his difficult, highly allusive work. **D.H. Lawrence** explored tensions in the British working-class family and broke sexual convention in *Sons and Lovers* (1913). Although he spoke only a few words of English when he arrived in the country at 21, **Joseph Conrad** demonstrated his mastery of the language in *Heart of Darkness* (1902). A similar disillusionment with imperialism surfaces in **E.M. Forster's** half-Modernist, half-Romantic novels, particularly *A Passage to India* (1924). Authors in the 1930s captured the tumult of the decade: **Evelyn Waugh** turned a ruthlessly satirical eye on society and **Graham Greene** explored moral ambiguity. The witty, sardonic poet **W.H. Auden,** deeply disturbed by the violence of the modern world, wrote: "We must love one another or die."

LATER TWENTIETH-CENTURY. Fascism and the horrors of WWII motivated musings on the nature of evil, while **George Orwell's** dystopic *1984* (1949) depicted a world in which memory and words were meaningless. **Anthony Burgess's** *A Clockwork Orange* (1962) imagines the violence and anarchy of a not-so-distant future. The end of empire, rising affluence, and the growing gap between classes splintered British literature. Nostalgia pervades the poems of **Philip Larkin** and **John Betjeman,** an angry working class has found its voice in **Allan Sillitoe** and **Kingsley Amis,** and postcolonial voices like Indian expatriate **Salman Rushdie** and 2002 Nobel laureate **V.S. Naipaul** have become a literary force. Driven by the success of the Man Booker Prize, given annually to novel from a Commonwealth country, Britain's hip literary circle includes working writers **A.S. Byatt, Margaret Atwood, Martin Amis, Kazuo Ishiguro, Zadie Smith,** and the masterful neo-realist **Ian McEwan.** British playwrights continue to innovate: **Harold Pinter** infused living rooms with horrifying silences, **Tom Stoppard** challenged theatrical convention in plays like *Rosencrantz and Guildenstern are Dead* (1967), and **Caryl Churchill** provides blistering commentary on "the state of Britain" in plays like *Cloud Nine* (1988).

OUTSIDE THE CLASSROOM. English literature holds its own away from the ivory tower as well. The elegant mysteries of **Dorothy L. Sayers** and **Agatha Christie** are known the world over. The espionage novels of **John le Carré** and Fleming, **Ian Fleming,** provide thrills of another sort. **P.G. Wodehouse,** creator of Jeeves, the consummate butler, hilariously satirizes the idle aristocrat. **James Herriot** (Alf Wight), beloved author of *All Creatures Great and Small* (1972), chronicled his work as a young veterinarian. **Douglas Adams** parodied sci-fi in his hilarious series *Hitchhiker's Guide to the Galaxy*, and **Helen Fielding's** hapless *Bridget Jones* speaks for singletons everywhere. British children's literature delights all ages: **Lewis Carroll's** *Alice's Adventures in Wonderland* (1865), **C.S. Lewis's** *Chronicles of Narnia* (1950-56), and **Roald Dahl's** stories, like *Charlie and the Chocolate Factory* (1964), *The Witches* (1983), *Matilda* (1988), enjoy continuing popularity. A linguist named **J.R.R. Tolkien,** Lewis's companion in letters and Oxford pub-readings (p. 258), wrote tales of elves, wizards, and rings (*The Hobbit*, 1934; *Lord of the Rings*, 1954-56). **Nick Hornby** writes cool, witty novels, like *High Fidelity* and *About a Boy*. Earning herself a fortune greater than that of the Queen, **J.K. Rowling** has enchanted the world with her saga of juvenile wizardry in the blockbuster *Harry Potter* series.

ART AND ARCHITECTURE

HOUSES OF GODS AND MEN. Early English architects often distilled continental styles, although some styles are particular to Britain. The Normans introduced **Romanesque** architecture (round arches and thick walls) in the 11th century; the British adopted the fashion in the imposing Durham Cathedral (p. 414). The **Gothic** style, originating in France (12th-15th century), ushered in intricate, elegant, and deceptively delicate buildings like the cathedrals of Wells (p. 194) and Salisbury (p. 178). By the 14th century, the English had developed the unique **perpendicular style** of window tracery, apparent at King's College Chapel in Cambridge (p. 307). Sadly, the **Suppression of Monasteries** in 1536 under Henry VIII spurred the wanton smashing of stained glass and even of entire churches, leaving picturesque **ruins** scattered along the countryside (like **Rievaulx,** p. 407; or **Glastonbury,** p. 197). After the **Renaissance,** architects utilized new engineering capabilities— attested to by **Christopher Wren's** fantastic dome on **St. Paul's Cathedral** (p. 116), built after the Great Fire of London in 1666.

LEARN A NEW LANGUAGE. A castle's **keep** is the main tower and residence hall. Some early keeps sit atop a steep mound called a **motte.** Laugh if you will, but **buttresses** are the slender external wall supports that hold up the tallest castles and the loftiest cathedrals. A **vault** is a stone ceiling; a ribbed vault is held up by spidery stone arcs or **ribs;** and the **webs** are the spaces in between ribs. Most churches are **cruciform,** or shaped like a cross. The head of the cross is the **choir,** the arms are the **transepts,** and the rest of it is the **nave,** usually flanked by **aisles.** Medieval churches usually have a three-tiered nave: the ground level is the **arcade,** the middle level (where monks used to walk and ponder scripture) is the **triforium,** and the highest level (where the light comes in) is the **clerestory.** Stained glass is awesome but usually isn't original; old or new, the **tracery** is the lacy stonework that holds it in place.

Early domestic architecture in Britain progressed from the **stone dwellings** of pre-Christian folk (see **Skara Brae,** p. 658) to the Romans' **forts and villas** (see **Hadrian's Wall,** p. 429) to the famed medieval castles. The earliest of these, the hilltop **motte-and-bailey** forts, arrived with William the Conqueror in 1066 (see **Round Tower of Windsor,** p. 252, or **Carisbrooke,** p. 169) and progressed into towering, square **Norman keeps** like the **Tower of London** (p. 104). Warmongering Edward I constructed a string of astonishing **concentric castles** along the Welsh coast (Harlech, p. 497; Caernarfon, p. 502; Beaumaris, p. 508; Caerphilly, p. 448). By the 14th century, the advent of the cannon made castles obsolete as defensive structures, yet they lived on as **palaces** for the rich (see the breathtaking **Warwick,** p. 285). During the Renaissance, the wealthy built sumptuous **Tudor homes,** like Henry VIII's Hampton Court (p. 134). In the 18th century, both the heady **baroque** style of Castle Howard (p. 391) and the severe **Palladian** symmetry of Houghton Hall (p. 320) were

ENGLAND

in vogue. **Stately homes** like Howard and Houghton (all the rage until well into the 20th century) were furnished with **Chippendale** furniture and surrounded by equally stately **gardens** (see **Blenheim Palace**, p. 264). The Victorians built in the ornate **neo-Gothic revival** (**Houses of Parliament**, p. 108) and **neo-Classical** (British Museum, p. 119) styles. Today, hotshots (and colleagues) **Richard Rogers** and **Norman Foster** vie for bragging rights as England's most influential architect, littering London with avant-garde additions like the Lloyd's Building (p. 111), City Hall, and a host of Millennium constructions (p. 106).

ON THE CANVAS. Britain's early religious art, including **illuminated manuscripts**, gave way to secular patronage and the institution of court painters; Renaissance art in England was largely dominated by foreign portraitists commissioned by the monarchy, such as **Hans Holbein the Younger** (1497-1543) and Flemish masters **Peter Paul Reubens** (1577-1640) and **Anthony Van Dyck** (1599-1641). **Nicholas Hilliard** (1547-1619) was the first English-born success of the period. Vanity, and thus portraiture, continued to flourish into the 18th century, with the satirical London scenes of **William Hogarth** (1697-1764), classically-inspired poses of **Joshua Reynolds** (1723-92), and provincial backdrops of **Thomas Gainsborough** (1727-88). Encouraged by a nation-wide interest in gardening, **landscape painting** peaked during the 19th century. Beyond the literary realm, Romanticism inspired the vibrant rustic scenes of **John Constable** and the violent sense of the sublime depicted in **J.M.W. Turner**'s stunning seascapes. The Victorian fascination for reviving old art forms sparked movements like the Italian-inspired, damsel-laden Pre-Raphaelite school, propagated by **John Everett Millais** (1829-96) and **Dante Gabriel Rossetti** (1828-82). Victorians also dabbled in new art forms like photography and took advantage of early mass media with engravings and cartoons. Modernist trends from the Continent such as Cubism and Expressionism were picked up by **Wyndham Lewis** (1882-1957) and sculptor **Henry Moore** (1898-1986). WWII broke art wide open (as it did most things), yielding experimental, edgy works by **Francis Bacon** (1909-92) and **Lucian Freud** (b. 1922), whose highly controversial portrait of the Queen was unveiled in 2002). **David Hockney** (b. 1937) and **Bridget Riley** (b. 1931) gave American pop art a dose of British wit. The monolithic, market-controlling collector **Charles Saatchi,** the success of the new Tate Modern (p. 128), the infamy of the Turner Prize, and the rise of the conceptual and sensationalist **Young British Artists (YBAs)** has invigorated Britain's contemporary art scene. The multi-media artists **Damien Hirst** (b. 1965) and **Tracey Emin** (b. 1963) have become the media-savvy *enfants terribles* of modern art. Other talented YBAs include sculptor **Bridget Riley** (b. 1931) and painter **Sarah Lucas** (b. 1962). Galleries in London (Tate Britain, p. 120; the British Museum, p. 119; the National Gallery, p. 119) are among the world's best.

FASHION. Inspired by the hip energy of London in the 1960s and movements like Op and Pop Art, England's fashion designers achieved notoriety, although not the fame of continental designers. **Mary Quant** (b. 1934) invented the miniskirt and sparked a revolution. **Vivienne Westwood** (b. 1941) is credited with originating punk fashion in the early 1970s, and her label is still known for its costume-like verve. Young British designers have made their marks at prestigious fashion houses, such as **John Galliano** (b. 1960) at Dior. In recent years, several designers have formed independent houses, as did ex-Givenchy star **Alexander McQueen** (b. 1970) and Sir Paul's daughter, ex-Chloé designer **Stella McCartney** (b. 1972).

MUSIC

CLASSICAL. In the middle ages, traveling **minstrels** sang narrative folk **ballads** and **Arthurian romances** in the courts of the rich. During the Renaissance, English ears were tuned to cathedral anthems, psalms, and madrigals, along with the odd lute performance. **Henry Purcell** (1659-95) rang in the baroque with instrumental music for Shakespeare's plays and with the opera *Dido and Aeneas*. In the 18th century, regarded as England's musical Dark Age, Britain welcomed visits of the foreign geniuses Mozart, Haydn, and **George Frideric Handel,** a German composer who wrote operas in the Italian style but spent most of his life in Britain. Thanks to Handel's influence, England experienced a wave of **operamania** in the early 1700s. Enthusiasm waned when listeners realized they couldn't understand what the performers were saying. **John Gay** satirized the opera house in *The Beggar's Opera* (1727), a low-brow comedy in which Italianate arias were set to English folk tunes. Today's audiences are familiar with the operettas of **W.S. Gilbert** (1836-1911) and **Arthur Sullivan** (1842-1900); the pair were rumored to have hated each other, but produced gems such as *The Pirates of Penzance*. A second renaissance of more serious music began under **Edward Elgar** (1857-1934), whose *Pomp and Circumstance* is often appreciated at graduation ceremonies. In contrast to his suites for military bands, **Gustav Holst** (1874-1934) adapted the Neoclassical, Romantic, and folk styles in *The Planets*. Also borrowing from folk melodies, **Ralph Vaughan Williams** (1872-1958) and **John Ireland** (1879-1962) brought musical modernism to the Isles. The world wars provided fodder for this continued musical resurgence, provoking **Benjamin Britten's** (1913-76) heartbreaking *War Requiem* and **Michael Tippett's** (1905-98) humanitarian oratorio *A Child of Our Time*. The popular **Proms** at Royal Albert Hall (p. 125) afford a rousing evening of whistle-blowing and flag-waving. Commercially lucrative music—like **Oliver Knussen's** one-act opera of Maurice Sendak's *Where the Wild Things Are* and **Andrew Lloyd Webber's** campy blend of opera, pop, and falling chandeliers—became popular in the 1980s and 90s.

IT'S ONLY ROCK 'N' ROLL (BUT I LIKE IT) A historical capsule library, sure to cause controversy...

British Invasion: The Beatles, *Revolver, Rubber Soul, Abbey Road, The White Album,* etc.; The Rolling Stones, *Exile on Main Street;* The Kinks, *Something Else by the Kinks.*

Rock, all styles: David Bowie, *The Rise and Fall of Ziggy Stardust..., Low;* Led Zeppelin, *Led Zeppelin I-IV;* Pink Floyd, *The Wall.*

Punk/post-punk/New Wave: The Clash, *London Calling;* The Sex Pistols, *Never Mind the Bollocks, Here's the Sex Pistols;* Joy Division, *Substance, Closer;* Gang of Four, *Entertainment!;* The Specials, *Specials.*

Synth-pop: Duran Duran, *Decade;* Pet Shop Boys, *Please, Actually;* Depeche Mode, *Violator;* The Police, *Synchronicity.*

Brit-pop: The Smiths, *The Queen is Dead;* The Stone Roses, *The Stone Roses;* Blur, *Parklife;* Oasis, *What's the Story (Morning Glory);* Pulp, *Different Class;* Radiohead, *The Bends, OK Computer, Kid A;* Coldplay, *Parachutes.*

Dance/UK Garage: Fatboy Slim, *You've Come a Long Way, Baby;* Chemical Brothers, *Dig Your Own Hole;* Prodigy, *Fat of the Land;* So Solid Crew, *They Don't Know;* The Streets, *Original Pirate Material, A Grand Don't Come for Free;* Dizzee Rascal, *Boy in da Corner;* M.I.A., *Arular.*

THE BRITISH ARE COMING. England's tag as "a land without music" (referring to the country's relative musical lameness, beginning in the Renaissance) can be disproved by a glance at any Billboard chart from the past 40 years. Invaded by American blues and rock 'n' roll following WWII, Britain staged an offensive unprecedented in history. The **British Invasion** groups of the 60s infiltrated the world with a daring, controversial sound. Native Liverpudlians **The Beatles** became the greatest rock band of all time. The edgier lyrics and grittier sound of the **Rolling**

ENGLAND

ENGLAND

Stones shifted teens' thoughts from "I Wanna Hold Your Hand" to "Let's Spend the Night Together." Over the next 20 years, England exported the hard-driving **Kinks,** the Urban "mod" sound of **The Who,** the psychedelia-meets-Motown **Yardbirds,** and guitar gurus Eric Clapton of **Cream** and Jimmy Page of **Led Zeppelin.**

ANARCHY IN THE UK. Despite (or perhaps because of) England's conservative national character, homosexuality became central to the flamboyant scene of the mid-70s. British rock schismed as the theatrical excesses of **glam rock** performers like **Queen, Elton John,** and **David Bowie** contrasted with the conceptual, album-oriented **art rock** emanating from **Pink Floyd** and **Yes.** Dissonant **punk rock** bands like **Stiff Little Fingers** and **The Clash** emerged from Britain's ailing industrial centers, Manchester in particular. London's **The Sex Pistols** stormed the scene with profane and wildly successful antics—their angry 1977 single "God Save the Queen" topped the charts despite being banned. Sharing punk's anti-establishment impulses, the metal of **Ozzy Osbourne** and **Iron Maiden** still attracts a cult following. Sheffield's **Def Leppard** carried the hard-rock-big-hair ethic through the 80s, while punk offshoots like **The Cure** and **goth** bands rebelled in the era of Thatcherism.

I WANT MY MTV. Buoyed by a booming economy, British bands achieved popular success on both sides of the Atlantic thanks to the advent of MTV. **Dire Straits** introduced the first computer-animated music video, while **Duran Duran,** the **Eurythmics, Boy George, Tears for Fears,** and the **Police** enjoyed top-10 hits. England also produced some of the giants of the lipstick-and-synthesizer age, including **George Michael,** the **Pet Shop Boys,** and **Bananarama.** The music scene splintered along regional and musical lines, into countless fragments of electronica, punk, and rock. Modern balladists the **Smiths** and obscure **My Bloody Valentine** developed cult followings. At the end of the decade, a crop of bands from Manchester, spearheaded by **Joy Division,** galvanized post-punk and the early **rave** movement. Any clubber worth her tube-top can tell you about England's influence on dance music, from the **Chemical Brothers** and Brighton-bred **Fatboy Slim** to the house, trip-hop, and ska sounds of **Basement Jaxx, Massive Attack,** and **Jamiroquai.** Britpop resurged in the 1990s; **Blur** and **Oasis** embodied a dramatically indulgent breed of rock 'n' roll stardom, leaving trashed hotel rooms and screaming fans in their wake. The tremendous popularity of American **grunge rock** inspired a host of posers in the UK, including then-wannabes █**Radiohead,** who have since become arguably the most influential rock band since the Beatles. The UK also produced some brilliant, awful pop, including **Robbie Williams** (survivor of the bubble-gummy **Take That**), who continues to be a stadium-filling force; sadly, the **Spice Girls** have not enjoyed the same longevity. These days, wimpy **Coldplay** is the UK's best-selling rock export. Modern post-punk and New Wave bands like **Bloc Party** and **Franz Ferdinand** enjoy indie cred and impressive fan bases. **UK Garage,** a blend of skittering beats, heavy bass, and unapologetically urban British-accented rapping, pervades every club. Super-chav Mike Skinner's **The Streets** and **Dizzee Rascal's** hardcore, nearly unintelligible flow both win fans abroad.

FILM

British film has endured an uneven history, characterized by alternation between relative independence from Hollywood and large-scale immigration of talent to America. **Charlie Chaplin** and Archibald Alec Leach (a.k.a. **Cary Grant**) were both Britain-born but made their names in US films. The **Royal Shakespeare Company** has seen heavyweight alumni like **Dame Judi Dench, Dame Maggie Smith, Sir Ian McKellen,** and **Jeremy Irons** make the transition to celluloid. Earlier Shakespeare impresario **Laurence Olivier** worked both ends of the camera in *Henry V* (the 1944 brainchild of government-sponsored WWII propaganda), and his *Hamlet* (1948) is

still the hallmark Dane. Master of suspense **Alfred Hitchcock** snared audiences with films produced on both sides of the Atlantic, terrifying shower-takers everywhere. The 60s phenomenon of "swingin' London" created new momentum for the film industry and jump-started international interest in British culture. American Richard Lester made **The Beatles'** *A Hard Day's Night* in 1963, and a year later Scot **Sean Connery** downed the first of many martinis as **James Bond** in *Dr. No*.

Elaborate costume drama and offbeat independent films characterized British film in the 80s and 90s. The sagas *Chariots of Fire* (1981) and *Gandhi* (1982) swept the Oscars in successive years. Director-producer team **Merchant-Ivory** led the way in adaptations of British novels like Forster's *A Room with a View* (1986). **Kenneth Branagh** focused his talents on adapting Shakespeare for the screen, with glossy, well-received works such as *Hamlet* (1996). **Nick Park** took claymation and British quirk to a new level with the *Wallace and Gromit* shorts and the blockbuster feature film *Chicken Run* (2000). The dashing **Guy** "Mr. Madonna" **Ritchie** tapped into Tarantino-esque conventions with his dizzying *Lock, Stock and Two Smoking Barrels* (1998), followed by the trans-Atlantic smash *Snatch* (2000), though the film's success may or may not have had something to do with American stud Brad Pitt.

Recent British films have garnered a fair number of awards. Working-class feelgoods *The Full Monty* (1997) and *Billy Elliot* (2000) received international releases. **Mike Leigh's** affecting *Secrets and Lies* (1996) and costume extravaganza *Topsy-Turvy* (1999) and the endearing comedies *Bend it Like Beckham* (2002) and *Love, Actually* (2003) have taken Academy, Cannes, and Golden Globe awards. The *Harry Potter* franchise (filmed at gorgeous Alnwick Castle (p. 426) and the Scottish Highlands) kicked off in 2001 and continues to break box office records.

MEDIA

ALL THAT'S FIT TO PRINT. In a culture with a rich print-media history, the influence of newspapers remains enormous. The UK's plethora of national newspapers yields a range of political viewpoints. *The Times*, long a model of thoughtful discretion, has turned Tory under the ownership of Rupert Murdoch. *The Daily Telegraph*, dubbed "Torygraph," is fairly conservative and old-fashioned. *The Guardian* leans left. *The Independent* respects its name. Of the infamous tabloids, *The Sun*, Murdoch-owned and better known for its Page Three topless pin-up than for its reporting, is the most influential. Among the others, *The Daily Mail*, *The Daily Express*, and *The London Evening Standard* (the only evening paper) make serious attempts at popular journalism, although the first two tend to position themselves as the conservative voice of Middle England. *The Daily Mirror*, *The News of the World*, and *The Star* are as shrill and lewd as *The Sun*. *The Financial Times*, on pleasing pink paper, distributes the news of the City of London as *The Wall Street Journal* does for Wall Street. Although associated with their sister dailies, Sunday newspapers are actually separate entities. *The Sunday Times*, *The Sunday Telegraph*, *The Independent on Sunday*, and the highly polished *Observer*, the world's oldest paper and now part of *The Guardian*, offer detailed arts, sports, and news coverage, with more "soft bits" than the dailies.

A quick glance around any High St. news agent will prove Britain has no shortage of magazines. World affairs are covered with refreshing candor and wit by *The Economist*. *The New Statesman* on the left and *The Spectator* on the right cover politics and the arts with verve. The satirical *Private Eye* is subversive, hilarious, and overtly political. Some of the best music mags in the world—the Strokes-discovering, highly biased but indispensable *New Musical Express* (called the *NME*), the more intellectual *Q*, and *Gramophone*—are UK-based. Movie and other entertainment news comes in the over-sized *Empire*. The indispensable London journal *Time Out* has an exhaustive listings guide to the city; its

website (www.timeout.com) also keeps tabs on events in Dublin and Edinburgh. Recent years have seen the explosion of "lads' mags" such as *FHM* and *Loaded*, which feature scantily-clad women and articles on beer, "shagging," and "pulling." London-born *Maxim* offers similar content for a marginally more mature crowd. Britain has excellent fashion glossies; there are British versions of *Vogue, Mademoiselle*, and *Elle*, which often come in a handy smaller size. *Tatler*, a W-cum-*Vanity Fair*, is witty, pretty, and snobby. *Hello, OK*, and a bevy of imitators feed the insatiable appetites of royal-watchers and B-list-aficionados.

ON THE AIRWAVES. The **BBC** (British Broadcasting Corporation, affectionately known as the Beeb) established its reputation for cleverly styled fairness with its radio services. The World Service provides countries around the world with a glimpse into British life. Within the UK, the BBC has **Radios 1-7,** covering news (4), sports (5), and the whole spectrum of music from pop (1) to classical and jazz (3) to catch-all (2 and 6), and recently for kids' programming (7). Each region has local commercial broadcasting services. British radio is responsible for the introduction of the **soap opera** (*The Archers* is still broadcast weekdays on Radio 4), a form now dominated by the televised *EastEnders* and *Coronation Street.*

Aside from the daytime suds, British television has brought to the world such mighty comic wonders as *Monty Python's Flying Circus, Mr. Bean, Da Ali G. Show* (innit?), and the across-the-pond hit *The Office.* The BBC has produced some stellar adapted miniseries; 1996's *Pride and Prejudice* sparked an international "Darcy-fever" for **Colin Firth** and is widely considered one of the best film versions of Austen's work. Britain currently suffers from an obsession with do-it-yourself home-improvement shows, cooking programs, and voyeur TV (remember, they invented *Big Brother* and *Pop* (aka *American Idol)*. A commercial-free repository of wit and innovation, the BBC broadcasts on two national channels. **BBC1** carries news and Britcoms, while **BBC2** telecasts cultural programs and fledgling sitcoms (like *AbFab, Blackadder, Coupling*, and the hilarious *Little Britain*). **ITV,** Britain's first and most established commercial network, carries drama, comedy, and news. **Channel 4** has morning shows, highly respected arts programming, and imported American shows. **Channel 5** features late-night sports shows and action movies. Rupert Murdoch's satellite **Sky TV** shows football, fútbol, soccer, and other incarnations of the global game on its Sky Sports channel, while its Sky One channel broadcasts mostly American shows.

SPORTS

There is a great noise in the city caused by hustling over large balls, from which many evils arise which God forbid.
    —King Edward II, banning football in 1314

FOOTBALL. It's the "beautiful game," the world's most popular sport, and a British national obsession. The top 20 English football (soccer) **clubs** (teams) occupy the **Premier League,** populated with world-class players. (The three divisions of the League and several divisions of the Conference lie below.) At the end of the season, the three clubs with the worst records in each division are relegated down, and the three top clubs promoted. The powerful Football Association (FA) regulates the British leagues and sponsors the contentious **FA Cup,** held every May in **Wembley.** (A new **National Stadium** will open in spring 2006.) The ultimate achievement for an English football club is to win the treble—the Premier League, the F.A. Cup, and the Champion's League (a competition between the top teams in several European countries). Clubs like Arsenal, Liverpool, and Everton dominate the Premier League perennially. But **Manchester United** (p. 347) is the red victory machine that every Brit loves to hate.

(And many Mancunians support Manchester City.) Fans and paparazzi alike mourned the team's loss of celebrity star **David Beckham** to Real Madrid in 2003. In the summer of 2004, Russian billionaire Roman Abramovich bought the London club **Chelsea,** purchased over £100 million worth of players, and won the Premiership.

Unfortunately, the four British international teams (England, Scotland, Wales, and Northern Ireland compete as separate countries) have not performed well in the **World Cup** or the **European Championships**—England's 1966 World Cup victory being the glorious exception. The next round of mania is slated for Germany in 2006.

Over half a million fans attend professional matches in Britain every matchday weekend from mid-August to May, and they spend the few barren weeks of summer waiting for the publication of the coming season's **fixtures** (match schedules). A match is well worth attending for a glimpse of British **football culture,** and often the lower division fans are crazier than those in the Premiership. Fans worship at post-modern cathedrals—grand, storied stadiums full of painted faces and team colors, resounding with rowdy choruses of uncannily synchronized (usually rude) songs. Intracity rivalries (London's Chelsea-Tottenham or Glasgow's "Auld Firm," p. 571) have been known to divide families. Violence and vandalism used to dog the game; matches have become safer (albeit pricier) now that clubs offer seating-only tickets, rather than standing spaces in the infamous terraces, and clubs no longer allow drinking in the stands. **Hooligans** (also called yobs or chavs) are usually on their worst behavior when the England national team plays abroad; things are tamer at home.

OTHER GAMES. According to legend, **rugby** was born one glorious day in 1823 when William Webb Ellis, an inspired (or perhaps slightly confused) Rugby School student, picked up a soccer ball and ran it into the goal. The amateur **Rugby Union** and professional **Rugby League,** both 19th-century creations, have slightly different rules and different numbers of players (15 and 13); in Britain, the former is associated with Scotland, Wales, and the Midlands, and the latter with northwest England. With little stoppage of play, no non-injury substitutions, and scanty protective gear, rugby is a melée of blood, mud, and drinking songs. An elongated ball is carried or passed backward until the team is able to touch the ball down past the goal line (a "try," worth five points) or kick it through the uprights (three points). Club season runs from September to May; the culmination of international rugby is the **Rugby World Cup,** to be hosted by France in October 2007.

Though fanatically followed in the Commonwealth, **cricket** remains a confusing spectacle to the uninitiated. The game is played by two 11-player teams on a green, marked by two **wickets,** three sticks with two bails (dowels) balancing on the top. (See www.cricket.org for explanations and diagrams of these mysterious contraptions.) In an inning, one team acts as **batsmen** and the other as **fielders.** The batting team sends up two batsmen, and a **bowler** from the fielding side throws the ball so that it bounces toward the wickets. The fielders try to get the batsmen out by **taking** the wickets (hitting the wickets so that the bails fall) or by catching the ball. The batsmen attempt to make as many runs as possible while protecting their wickets, scoring every time they switch places. The teams switch positions once 10 batsmen are out; usually both sides bat twice. Matches last one to five days. (We don't really get it either.) International games are known as **Test** matches; the **Ashes,** named for the remains of a cricket bail, are the prize in England's Test series with Australia. Cricket has its own **World Cup,** set for February and March of 2007. London's **Lords** cricket ground is regarded as the spiritual home of the game.

Tennis became the game of the upper class at the end of the 15th century, when Henry VII played in slimming black velvet. As the game developed, cooler white became the traditional color, while today almost any high-tech garb goes. For two weeks in late June and early July, tennis buffs all over the world focus their attention on **Wimbledon,** home to the only Grand Slam event played on grass.

ENGLAND

HORSES AND COURSES. The Brits have a special affinity for their horses, demonstrated in the ballyhooing of fox-killing excursions and Princess Anne's competition in **equestrian** during the 1976 Olympics. In late June, **polo** devotees flock to the **Royal Windsor Cup.** Horse-racing also pretends to noble status. An important society event, the Royal Gold Cup Meeting at **Ascot** has occurred in the second half of June every summer since 1711, though some see it as an excuse for Brits of all strata to indulge in drinking and gambling while wearing over-the-top hats. Top hats also distinguish the famed **Derby** (DAR-bee), which has been run since 1780 on Epsom Racecourse, Surrey, on the first Saturday of June.

Britain remains a force in rowing, and the annual **Henley Royal Regatta,** on the Thames in Oxfordshire, is the most famous series of rowing races in the world. The five-day regatta ends on the first Sunday in July; Saturday is the most popular day, but some of the best races are the Sunday finals. The **Boat Race** (also on the Thames, but in London), between Oxford and Cambridge, enacts the traditional rivalry between the schools. Britain is the center of Formula One racecar design, and the **British Grand Prix** is held every July at Silverstone racecourse in Northamptonshire. Meanwhile, the **T.T. Races** bring hordes of screeching motorcycles to the Isle of Man during the first two weeks of June (p. 377).

HOLIDAYS AND FESTIVALS

It's difficult to travel anywhere in the British Isles without bumping into some kind of festival. Below is a not-at-all-comprehensive list of festivals in England; the local Tourist Information Centre for any town can point you toward the nearest scene of revelry and merry-making, and *Let's Go* tries to list individual events in the appropriate towns. The chart below also includes the UK-wide **public holidays;** see the corresponding sections of Scotland (p. 525), Wales (p. 440), and Northern Ireland (p. 669) for more country-specific festivals. **Bank holidays** are listed in the Appendix.

DATE IN 2006	NAME AND LOCATION	DESCRIPTION
January 29	Chinese New Year, London	Fireworks! Lots of fireworks!
April 23	St. George's Day	Honoring England's dragon-slaying patron saint.
May	Brighton Festival	Largest mixed-arts festival in England.
May 23-25	Chelsea Flower Show	The world's premier garden event.
May 27-June 9	T.T. Races, Isle of Man	The big event in the Road Racing Capital of the World.
June	The Derby, Surrey	Horses and hats!
Late June	Glastonbury Festival	Britain's gigantic three-day homage to rock.
June 13-17	Royal Ascot, York	Hats and horses!
June 26-July 9	Wimbledon	A lot of racquets and a BIG silver dish.
June 28-July 2	Henley Royal Regatta	The world's premier boat race.
August 20-30	Manchester Pride	A wild street party in Manchester's Gay Village.
August 27-28	Notting Hill Carnival	Mad London street party.

LONDON

When a man is tired of London, he is tired of life; for there is in London all that life can afford.
    —Samuel Johnson

Beyond the blinding lights of Oxford and Piccadilly Circuses, in a world where Hugh Grant is neither the boy next door nor the Prime Minister, London is just as much a working and living city as it is a place for tourists. Comprised of 32 boroughs and two cities, London is more a conglomeration of villages than a unified whole. Locals are strongly attached to their neighborhoods; each area's heritage and traditions are alive and evolving, from the City of London's 2000-year-old association with trade to Notting Hill's West Indian Carnival. Thanks to the feisty independence and diversity of each area, the London "buzz" is continually on the move—every few years a previously disregarded neighborhood explodes into cultural prominence. In the 60s, Soho and Chelsea became achingly hip; the late 80s saw grunge rule the roost from Camden; and in the 90s the East End sprung Damien Hirst and the Britpack artists on the world. More recently, South London has come to prominence with the cultural rebirth of the South Bank and the thumping nightlife of a recharged Brixton. Plop down in the middle of Trafalgar Square one week for the annual Gay Pride Parade; come back the next week for a political protest and rally. There is no particular method to the madness of London, so throw down the map, kick up your heels, and listen to the bells in Victoria Tower singing "London Calling." If you're spending a significant amount of time in London, you'll find more extensive coverage in ▧*Let's Go: London.*

LONDON	❶	❷	❸	❹	❺
ACCOMMODATIONS	under €20	€20-34	€35-49	€50-74	€74 and up
FOOD	under €5	€5-8	€9-12	€13-16	€16 and up

LONDON HIGHLIGHTS

GO ROYAL in stately Westminster at **Westminster Abbey** (p. 104) and the **Houses of Parliament** (p. 108); take tea with the queen at **Buckingham Palace** (p. 108); gaze up at the dome of **St. Paul's Cathedral** (p. 105) and the pigeons that nest there; and watch your head at the imposing **Tower of London** (p. 104). To cover the highlights of the South Bank, follow our **"Millennium Mile" Walking Tour** (p. 106).

GAWK in the galleries of London's museums, some of the best in the world; most of the big names are free. The **British Museum** (p. 119) and the **Victoria and Albert Museum** (p. 119) recap the glory days of the British Empire, while the **National Portrait Gallery** (p. 119) chronicles the life and times of those who ran it; the **National Gallery** (p. 119) holds the first half of the national collection and the **Tate Modern** (p. 118) holds, well, everything modern. For a string of up-and-comers, head to galleries in the East End, including **Whitechapel** (p. 123) and **White Cube** (p. 123). The **Courtauld Galleries** (p. 121) at Somerset House are worth the admission fee.

SOAK in a stage-play at the **West End** (p. 126), which boasts the best of megamusicals and Andrew Lloyd Webber classics. For older drama, try **Shakespeare's Globe Theatre** (p. 127) or take a seat in the **National Theatre** (p. 127) or **Royal Court Theatre** (p. 127). Fringe theatre is alive and well at the **Almeida** (p. 127) and **Donmar Warehouse** (p. 127).

LONDON

Central London

● SIGHTS

Apsley House, 1	C4
The Barbican, 2	E3
British Library, 3	D2
British Museum, 4	D3
Buckingham Palace, 5	C4
Cabinet War Rooms, 6	D4
Chelsea Physic Garden, 7	C5
Chinatown, 8	D4
Courtaud Institute Galleries, 9	D4
Design Museum, 10	F4
The Gilbert Collection, 11	D4
Guildhall Art Gallery, 12	E3
The Houses of Parliament, 13	D4
ICA, 14	D4
Imperial War Museum, 15	E5
Kensington Palace, 16	B4
London Eye, 17	D4
Madame Tussaud's, 18	C3
Marble Arch, 19	C3
Millennium Bridge, 20	E4
Monument, 21	F4
Museum of London, 22	E3
National Gallery, 23	D4
Natural History Museum, 24	B5
National Portrait Gallery, 25	D4
Royal Academy of Arts, 26	D4
Royal Albert Hall, 27	B4
Royal Courts of Justice, 28	E3
The Royal Hospital, 29	C5

D		E		F	
The Royal Mews, 30	C4	St. Paul's Church, 41	D3	Tower Bridge, 51	F4
Royal Opera House, 31	D3	Science Museum, 42	B5	The Tower of London, 52	F4
St. Bride's Church, 32	E3	Shakespeare's Globe		Trafalgar Square, 53	D4
St. Etheldreda's, 33	E3	Theatre, 43	E4	University College London, 54	D3
St. James's Palace, 34	D4	Sir John Soane's Museum, 44	E3	Victoria and Albert Museum, 55	B5
St. John's Square, 35	E3	Smithfield Market, 45	E3	The Wallace Collection, 56	C3
St. Margaret's Westminster, 36	D4	Southwark Cathedral, 46	E4	Wellington Arch, 57	C4
St. Martin-in-the-Fields, 37	D4	Tate Britain, 47	D5	Westminster Abbey, 58	D4
St. Mary-le-Bow, 38	E3	Tate Modern, 48	E4	Westminster Cathedral, 59	D5
St. Pancras Station, 39	D2	The Temple, 49	E3	Whitehall, 60	D4
St. Paul's Cathedral, 40	E3	Theatre Royal, Dury Lane, 50	D3		

LONDON

ISLINGTON

Mornington ⊖ Crescent

Caledonia Rd.

Hampstead Rd.

Pentonville Rd.

⊖ Angel

Upper Essex Rd.

New North Rd.

Kingsland Rd.

Queensbridge Rd.

Hackney Rd.

EAST END

39 King's Cross/ St. Pancras

62

Euston Rd.

City Rd.

3

66 64

⊖ Euston
⊖ Euston Square

Woburn Pl.

Gray's Inn Rd.

Farringdon Rd.

St. John St.

Goswell Rd.

Old St.
Old Street

City Rd.

Shoreditch High St.

Bethnal Green Rd.

⊖ Warren Street

54

Russell Square

⊖ Shoreditch

BLOOMSBURY

Tottenham Court Rd.

⊖ Goodge Street

4

Holborn ⊖ Holborn

Clerkenwell Rd. 35

CLERKENWELL

Farringdon ⊖

Barbican

Beech St.

Aldersgate

2

Commercial St.

⊖ Moorgate

Liverpool Street ⊖

Commercial Rd.

Chancery ⊖ Lane

33 45

Holborn Viaduct

22

London Wall

CITY

⊖ Aldgate East Whitechapel Rd.

HOLBORN

Newgate St.

12

⊖ Aldgate

SEE "WEST END," p. 115

Covent Garden ⊖

31 50

⊖ Temple

28

32

40

Fleet St.

38

Mansion House ⊖

⊖ Bank

Cannon St. ⊖

Bishopsgate

Fenchurch St.

⊖ Tower Hill

49 Blackfriars

9 11

⊖ Leicester Square

⊖ Piccadilly Circus

8 25 23

37 ⊖ Embankment

53

14 60 ⊖ Charing Cross

Victoria Embankment

Upper Thames St.

21

Lower Thames St.

Monument ⊖

River Thames

Waterloo Bridge

20

Southwark Bridge

London Bridge

Tower Bridge

The Highway

52

51

River Thames

⊖ Temple

Blackfriars Bridge

48 43

46

10

34

6

⊖ St. James's Park

Birdcage Walk

Whitehall

17 ⊖ Waterloo

Stamford St.

Southwark

Southwark St.

London Bridge ⊖

St. Thomas St.

Tooley St.

4

St. James's ⊖ Park

36 13

58

Westminster Bridge

⊖ Westminster

SOUTH BANK

Tower Bridge Rd.

Jamaica Rd.

Lambeth North ⊖

Westminster Bridge Rd.

Borough Rd.

⊖ Borough

Victoria St.

59

WESTMINSTER

Lambeth Bridge

15

Lambeth Rd.

⊖ Elephant & Castle

New Kent Rd.

Old Kent Rd.

5

Vauxhall Bridge Rd.

Belgrave Rd.

47

⊖ Pimlico

Millbank

SEE "WESTMINSTER," p. 117

LAMBETH

Kennington ⊖

Kennington Rd.

Kennington Park Rd.

Walworth Rd.

Albany Rd.

Southampton Way

Grosvenor Rd.

Vauxhall Bridge

Vauxhall

Harleyford Rd.

Nine Elms Lane

Wandsworth Rd.

South Lambeth Rd.

Clapham Rd.

Camberwell New Rd.

Camberwell

0 — 1000 yards ⊖ Stockwell

0 — 1 kilometer

■ INTERCITY TRANSPORTATION

BY PLANE

HEATHROW

Heathrow (☎08700 000 123; www.baa.co.uk/main/airports/heathrow), 15min. from central London, is just what you'd expect from one of the world's busiest international airports. There are four terminals.

 TUB TO TERMINAL 4. London Underground service to Heathrow's Terminal 4 will be closed through September 2006. Take a replacement bus from the Tube station at Hatton Cross.

Underground: ☎7222 1234, toll-free 08453 309 880; www.thetube.com. Heathrow's 2 Tube stations form a loop on the end of the Piccadilly Line—trains stop at **Heathrow Terminal 4** and then at **Heathrow Terminals 1, 2, 3** (both Zone 6) before swinging back to central London. Stairs are an integral part of most Tube stations. (50-70min. from central London, every 4-5min. ₤4-10.)

Heathrow Express: ☎08456 001 515. A speedy, expensive connection from Heathrow to Paddington. Paddington has check-in facilities. Ticket counters at Heathrow accept foreign currency. (15min., daily every 15min. 5:10am-11:40pm. Railpasses and Travelcards invalid. ₤14, round-trip ₤26; ₤2 extra if bought on train. Discounts for day returns, students, and groups. AmEx/MC/V.)

Heathrow Connect: ☎08456 786 975; www.heathrowconnect.com. A cheaper alternative to the Express, with direct routes from Paddington, Ealing Broadway, West Ealing, Hanwell, Southall, and Hayes to Terminals 1, 2, and 3. For Terminal 4, take the first Heathrow Express train. (20min. from Paddington. Daily every 30min. 5:30am-midnight. Railcards accepted. ₤9.50 to Paddington.)

National Express: ☎08705 808 080; www.nationalexpress.com. Runs between Heathrow and Victoria Coach. (40-85min., about every 20min. Daily Heathrow-Victoria 5:35am-9:35pm, Victoria-Heathrow 7:15am-11:30pm. Railpasses and Travelcards not valid. From ₤8. AmEx/MC/V.)

Taxis: Licensed (black) cabs cost at least ₤50 and take 1-1¾hr.

GATWICK

30 mi. south of the city, Gatwick (☎0870 002 468; www.baa.co.uk/main/airports/gatwick) looks distant, but three train services make transport a breeze. The **train station** is in the **South Terminal.** Gatwick Express (☎0845 600 1515; www.gatwickexpress.com) offers service to **Victoria Station** (30-35min.; departs Gatwick every 15min. 5am-11:45pm; ₤13, round-trip ₤24). Thameslink (☎08457 484 950; www.thameslink.co.uk) also heads regularly to **King's Cross Station,** stopping at **London Bridge** and **Blackfriars** (50min., every 30 min., ₤10). Gatwick's distance from London makes **road services** slow and unpredictable. National Express's **Airbus A5** (contact info same as Heathrow) goes to **Victoria Coach Station** (1½hr., at least every hr. 4:50am-10:15pm, from ₤6.20). Never take a **taxi** from Gatwick to London; the trip will take over an hour and cost at least ₤90.

STANSTED AND LUTON

Many discount airlines (see **By Plane,** p. 25) operate from secondary airports. **Stansted Airport** (☎08700 000 303; www.baa.co.uk/main/airports/stansted) is 30 mi. north. Stansted Express (☎08457 484 950; www.stanstedexpress.co.uk)

trains run to **Liverpool St. Station** (45min.; every 15-30min.; £14.50, round-trip £24). National Express's **Airbus A6** runs to **Victoria Station** (1¼-1¾hr., about every 30min., from £8). From **Luton Airport** (☎0158 240 5100; www.londonluton.co.uk), Thameslink **trains** head to **King's Cross, Blackfriars,** and **London Bridge** (30-40min.; every 30min. M-Sa 3:20am-1am, Su less often 6am-11:15pm; £10.40); Green Line (☎08706 087 261; www.greenline.co.uk) **buses** serve **West End** and **Victoria Station** (1-1¾hr.; 3 per hr. 8am-6pm, 2 per hr. 6-11pm, every hr. 11pm-8am; £9, round-trip £12.50).

BY TRAIN

London's array of mainline stations dates from the Victorian era, when each railway company had its own city terminus; see the box below for service information. All London termini are well-served by bus and Tube; major stations sell various **Railcards,** which offer regular discounts on train travel (see **By Train,** p. 30).

LONDON TRAIN STATIONS

Charing Cross: Kent (Canterbury, Dover)

Euston: Northwest (Birmingham, Glasgow, Holyhead, Liverpool, Manchester)

King's Cross: Northeast (Cambridge, Edinburgh, Leeds, Newcastle, York)

Liverpool St.: East Anglia (Cambridge, Colchester, Ipswich, Norwich), Stansted

Paddington: West (Oxford), Southwest (Bristol, Cornwall), South Wales (Cardiff)

St. Pancras: Midlands (Nottingham), Northwest (Sheffield)

Victoria: South (Brighton, Canterbury, Dover, Hastings), Gatwick

Waterloo: South and Southwest (Portsmouth, Salisbury), Paris, Brussels

BY BUS

Most long-distance buses arrive at **Victoria Coach Station** (⊖Victoria), Buckingham Palace Rd. **National Express** is the largest intercity operator (☎08705 808 080; www.nationalexpress.com). **Eurolines** dominates international service (☎08705 143 219; www.eurolines.co.uk). **Green Line** coaches serve much of the area around London and leave from the Eccleston Bridge mall behind Victoria station. Purchase tickets from the driver. (⊖Victoria. ☎0870 608 7261; www.greenline.co.uk.)

ORIENTATION

While Greater London consists of 32 boroughs, the City of Westminster, and the City of London, *Let's Go* focuses on central London and divides this area into 13 neighborhoods, plus North, South, and East London.

BAYSWATER

Aside from a cheap place to sleep, Bayswater is nondescript. The main drags of **Westbourne Grove** and **Queensway** are frequented most by teenage mall hoppers. The longest stretch of walking is along the fringes of Kensington Gardens and Hyde Park. Use ❺Bayswater for the west; Paddington and Lancaster Gate for the east. There are two separate Paddington stations: the Hammersmith & City line runs the Paddington train station; the others run from a station underground.

⬢TIP⬢ **QUEENSWAY.** The Queensway Tube stop will be closed until summer 2006.

BLOOMSBURY

Bloomsbury is London's intellectual powerhouse, home to the British Museum, near **Russell Square,** the British Library, on **Euston Road,** and University College London, on **Gower Street.** The area resounds with the musings of the Bloomsbury Group, but its squares are some of the best places to throw books aside in the name of picnics and suntans. ❺King's Cross is the biggest interchange but not the most convenient. Goodge St. and Russell Sq. are central; Euston, Euston Sq., and Warren St. hit the north border.

CHELSEA

Chelsea would like to be considered London's artistic bohemia, a desire stemming from the 60s and 70s, when **King's Road** was the home of the miniskirt and punk rock. This makes Chelsea less stuffy than nearby Knightsbridge and Kensington, but, stifled by wealth, today's neighborhood has less stomach for radicalism. ❺Sloane Sq. to the east and South Kensington to the north will put you within distance of most attractions. The bus is critical for bad weather; most run from **Sloane Square** down King's Rd. on their way from Knightsbridge or Victoria.

THE CITY OF LONDON

The City is where London began—indeed, for most of its history, the City *was* London. Even though urban sprawl has pushed the border of London out, the City remains as tightly knit as ever, with its own mayor, separate jurisdiction, and sway over even the Queen, who must ask permission of the Lord Mayor before entering. **Upper** and **Lower Thames Streets** run along the Thames to the Tower of London; **Aldersgate Street** passes by the Barbican Centre on its way to Clerkenwell; **Ludgate Hill** extends from Fleet St. to St. Paul's Cathedral. ❺Bank and St. Paul's are within easy reach of most sights; use Tower Hill for eastern destinations.

HOLBORN AND CLERKENWELL

London's second-oldest area, Holborn was the first part of the city settled by Saxons—**Aldwych,** on the western edge, is Anglo-Saxon for "old port." **Fleet Street** remains synonymous with the British press even though the newspapers have moved on. Traveling north to Clerkenwell, **Farringdon Street** intersects **High Holborn** and **Clerkenwell Road** before becoming **King's Cross Road.** A monastic center until Henry VIII closed the priory of St. John, Clerkenwell became home to London's top artisans. During Victoria's reign, it devolved into slums, famously described by Dickens; with renewed energy, the area has recently come storming back onto the London scene. In Holborn, use ❺Holborn, Farringdon, Chancery

Ln. (closed Su), and Temple (closed Su). In Clerkenwell, everything is near ⊖Farringdon; southern and eastern parts can be reached from Barbican, western parts can be reached by Chancery Ln., and northern parts can be reached by Angel.

KENSINGTON AND EARL'S COURT

The former stomping ground of Princess Di, Kensington is divided into two distinct areas. To the west is the posh consumer mecca, **Kensington High Street,** while to the east are the museums and colleges of **South Kensington's** "Albertopolis." In the 1960s and 70s, **Earl's Court** was mainly the destination of Aussie backpackers and home to London's gay population, but today others have caught on to its combination of cheap accommodations and transportation links. One of central London's larger neighborhoods, public transportation is necessary to get around. Tube stations are helpfully named: ⊖High St. Kensington for the High St., South Kensington for the South Kensington museums, and Earl's Court for Earl's Court.

KNIGHTSBRIDGE AND BELGRAVIA

Knightsbridge and Belgravia are smug and expensive. The primary tourist draw is window-shopping on **Sloane Street** and **Brompton Road,** with shopping's biggest names, Harrods and Harvey Nichols. **Belgravia,** occupies the region east of Sloane St., with an expanse of 19th-century mansions occupied by millionaires and embassies. ⊖Knightsbridge is near the shops; most hotels in Belgravia are close to Victoria, but the north end of the neighborhood is closest to Hyde Park Corner.

MARYLEBONE AND REGENT'S PARK

Marylebone is defined by its eclectic borders. Adjacent to academic Bloomsbury in the east, beautiful **Portland Place** stands as an architectural wonder. To the west, **Edgware Road** houses London's largest Lebanese population and boasts many Middle Eastern eateries, shops, and markets. Chain-oriented **Marylebone Road** traps tourists with Madame Tussaud's wax museum but also acts as the gateway to Regent's Park. ⊖Baker St. is convenient for northern sights; Bond St. covers the south. There are two separate Edgware Rd. stations, but they're not far apart.

NOTTING HILL

Once the stopping point for those traveling between London and Uxbridge, Notting Hill has retained its appeal as an offshoot of central London; running from Oxford St., **Notting Hill Gate** actually had a gate out of (or into) the city. Its appeal has much to do with the mix of mansions, diverse ethnic culture, and an artsy/alternative vibe. **Portobello Road** may be best known for its market. ⊖Notting Hill Gate serves the south, while Ladbroke Grove deposits you close by Portobello Rd.

THE SOUTH BANK

Just across the river from the City, but lacking the business suits and the briefcases, the South Bank has long been the center of London's entertainment industry—cross the Thames on **Waterloo Road, Blackfriars Road, Borough High Street,** or **Tower Bridge Road.** Dominated by wharves and warehouses in the 19th and early-20th centuries, the South Bank was rebuilt after its destruction in WWII. Now, the "Millennium Mile" stretches from the London Eye in the west to Butlers Wharf in the east. ⊖Waterloo for inland attractions, Southwark for Bankside, and London Bridge for Borough and Butlers Wharf.

THE WEST END

The biggest, brightest, and boldest (though not always best) of London nightlife, theater, shopping, and food can be found here. See Vegas-esque **Leicester Square,** a world-renowned musical, head to **Chinatown** for dim sum, or exercise your credit cards on **Oxford Street.** The concentration of bars and clubs in **Soho** will

COUNTDOWN TO 2012

While Britain's armchair athletes are second-to-none, the country has never been known for its high concentration of world-champion sports stars. Football fans may argue to the contrary (it is true, nobody bends it like Beckham). And Britain's scrummers delighted when the nation's rugby team brought home the 2005 World Cup. And the world of curling likely objects. But, lest Britons forget, it's been over 60 years since a local won Wimbledon (tennis) and and 40 since they last won the World Cup (football) in 1966.

Come 2012, though, London will be the only city to have hosted the summer Olympics three times (previously in 1908 and 1948). So, maybe it is that Londoners are sports *fans,* rather than sports participants; this accounts for their highly publicized and glamorous Olympic bid, complete with personal pleas from Nelson Mandela and "Back the Bid" subway upholstery. With only eight years to go, London is gearing up for the games, which will be held July 27-August 12, 2012.

While some residents are concerned over the possibility of gentrification in Stratford, a historically distressed segment of East London where the Olympic Village and the center of athletic events will take place, others look

keep you busy into the morning. Stroll around the gay nightlife nexus of **Old Compton Street** or mingle with street performers (and professionals) in **Covent Garden.** If all this sounds too uncivilized, perhaps you're better suited to the posh streets of **Mayfair** and **St. James's,** which stand in sharp contrast to the West End's more touristed areas. Home to London's elite, citizens of the West End's upper class emerge to prowl the designer boutiques along **Bond Street.** Whichever lifestyle strikes your fancy, spend a little time in **Trafalgar Square** to bask in the glory of Britain's greatest days. The Tube is best for getting in and out of the West End. Use ⊖Charing Cross for Trafalgar Sq.; the stops are often only a few blocks apart. Buses are the best way to get around; stops can be found along any major thoroughfare.

WESTMINSTER
Westminster, with its postcard-friendly spires and parks, often feels like the heart of the old British Empire. It is, after all, home to the Houses of Parliament and the Queen—convenient for die-hard tourists who want to cram the biggest sights into one day. But away from the bureaucracy of **Whitehall** and the grandeur of the Abbey, Westminster is a down-to-earth district—thousands of workers make **Victoria** the busiest Tube station. South of Victoria, **Pimlico** is residential, with row after row of B&Bs. ⊖Westminster deposits you near most sights; use St. James's Park for Buckingham Palace; use Pimlico for accommodations and Tate Britain.

NORTH LONDON
What we call "North London" is actually a conglomeration of a number of distinct neighborhoods, all of which lie to the north of central London. Once the center of London's counterculture movement, **Camden Town** and **Islington** now offer more posh restaurants than punks. **Hampstead** and **Highgate** retain the feel of small sophisticated villages, removed from the bustle of downtown. **St. John's Wood** and **Maida Vale** are wealthy residential extensions of Marylebone and Bayswater. Most individual neighborhoods are walkable. Tube stops are almost all self-explanatory (i.e. Camden Town for Camden Town); also, ⊖Kentish Town for Camden; Angel for Islington; Kilburn and Swiss Cottage for St. John's Wood and Maida Vale.

SOUTH LONDON
Historically maligned for being "dodgy," areas of South London have now become hot spots for hip youngsters looking for upscale dining and all-night

parties. Once a swanky suburb, **Brixton** has been thoroughly urbanized, showcasing the charm of its Afro-Caribbean market. **Stockwell** and **Vauxhall** offer pubs galore, while **Dulwich** and **Forest Hill** have quiet streets and off-beat museums for those looking for a relaxed day outside of the urban bustle. ⊖Stockwell and Brixton. For access to some areas, overland rail service from Victoria, Waterloo, and London Bridge is necessary. From Brixton, the bus P4 will take you to all the Dulwich sites.

EAST LONDON

At Aldgate, the wealth of the City of London gives way to the historically impoverished **East End**, the heart of East London. Cheap land and nearby docks made this area a natural site for immigrants, including waves of Huguenots, Jews, and, more recently, Bangladeshis. Today the site of urban regeneration, the East End is at the center of new growth, as artists and designers colonize one of the last affordable areas in central London. There's not much reason to get off the elevated Docklands Light Railway (DLR) trains in **Docklands** until they reach **Greenwich,** home to sights documenting its maritime past. ⊖Old St. and Liverpool St. are best for the East End. Farther east, newly extended Tube lines serve Canary Wharf and Wapping. The DLR will take you to Greenwich.

▉ LOCAL TRANSPORTATION

Local gripes aside, London's public transport system is remarkably efficient. (☎7222 1234, 24hr.; www.transportforlondon.gov.uk.) The public-transport network is divided into a series of concentric zones; ticket prices depend on the zones passed. To confuse matters, there are two different zoning systems. The **Tube, rail,** and **Docklands Light Railway (DLR)** network operates on a system of six zones, with zone 1 being the most central. **Buses** reduce this to four zones. Bus zones 1, 2, and 3 are the same as for the Tube, and Tube zones 4, 5, and 6 comprise bus zone 4.

TRAVEL PASSES

You'll save money by investing in a **travel pass.** They work on the zone system and can be purchased at Tube, DLR, and rail stations, and at newsagents. Beware of **ticket touts** with second-hand passes—there's no guarantee the ticket will work, and it's illegal (penalties are stiff). Passes expire at 4:30am the morning after the expiry date. **One-Day Travelcards** are

forward to the transformation the city will see over the years leading up to the games. Plans include:

• Building a 500-acre site (including the Olympic Village) in Stratford, 7min. from central London by tube.

• Revitalizing already existing facilities in locations where events will take place: triathlon in Hyde Park, equestrian in Greenwich Park, gymnastics at the Millennium Dome, football at Wembley, and tennis—surprise, surprise—at Wimbledon.

• Improving city transportation, enough to shuttle 240,000 people to the Village each hour via Tube, train, and bus; the new Olympic Javelin will run from King's Cross St. Pancras.

• Producing a low-carbon and zero-waste Games.

• Transforming the Lea Valley into one of the largest urban parks created in Europe in the past 150 years, stretching 20 mi. from the Hertfordshire countryside to the tidal estuary of the Thames; post-Games, it will provide facilities for community use and a wildlife preserve.

• Creating 12,000 new jobs and 9000 new homes (half designated as affordable housing) in East London.

70,000 volunteers will be needed to put these plans into effect and to deliver the Games. For information on how you can volunteer, see www.volunteer2012.com.

valid for bus, Tube, DLR, and commuter rail services. There are two types of Day Travelcards: **Peak** cards (valid all day; zones 1-2 £6) and **Off-Peak** cards (M-F after 9:30am, Sa-Su all day; zones 1-2 £4.70). **Three-Day Travelcards** are also available (zones 1-2 peak and off-peak £15; zones 1-6 peak £36, off-peak £18). **Family Travelcards** and discounts for children are available. A **carnet** is a book of 10 singles, available for a Tube trip in Zone 1 (£17). **Weekend** or **Weekly Travelcards** are valid two consecutive days on weekends and public holidays or seven consecutive days, respectively. **Bus Passes** are valid only on buses.

THE UNDERGROUND

The "Tube" is best suited to longer trips; within Zone 1, adjacent stations are so close that you might as well walk, and buses are cheaper and often get you closer to your destination. The **Docklands Light Railway (DLR)** is a driverless, overland version of the Tube running in East London; the ticketing structure is the same. If you'll be traveling by Tube a lot, you'll save money with a **Travelcard.** Tickets must be bought at the start of your journey and are valid only for the day of purchase. **Keep your ticket** for the entire journey; it will be checked on the way out. Regular ticket prices depend on two factors: number of zones traveled and whether you traveled through zone 1. Individual journeys including zone 1 run: zone 1 only £2; zones 1-2: £2.30. Outside zone 1: any 1 zone £1.30; 2 zones £1.30. The Tube runs daily approximately **5:30am-midnight.** The time of the first and last train from each station is posted in the ticket hall; check if you plan to take the Tube after 11:30pm. Trains run less often early mornings, late nights, and Sundays.

BUSES

Only tourists use the Tube for short trips in central London—if it's only a couple of stops, or if it involves more than one change, a bus will likely get there faster. Excellent signposting makes the bus system easy to use; most stops display a map of local routes and nearby stops, along with a key to help you find your bus and stop. Normal buses run approximately **5:30am-midnight.** During the day, double-deckers run every 10-15min.; single-deckers arrive every 5-8min. A reduced network of **Night Buses** fills in the gap. Night Bus route numbers are prefixed with an N; they typically operate the same routes as their daytime equivalents but occasionally start and finish at different points. Buses that run 24hr. have no N in front. Bus and Night Bus fares are both £1.20. All tickets are good for traveling across the network and can be purchased at roadside machines or on the bus. **Keep your ticket** until you get off the bus, or you may face a £5 on-the-spot fine.

TAXIS

Taxis in London come in two forms: licensed taxis **(black cabs)** and **minicabs.** Fares for black cabs are regulated by the Transport for London. Taxis are obliged to take passengers anywhere in central London up to 12 mi. (20 mi. if you begin at Heathrow), even just one block; longer journeys are at their discretion—negotiate a fare in advance if you're going outside the city. A **10% tip** is expected. **Taxi One-Number** (☎08718 718 710) connects to one of the six radio taxi circuits.

Anyone with a car and a driving license can be a minicab company. As a result, competition is fierce and prices are lower than licensed cabs. **Minicabs are not always safe** for those traveling alone. Call one of the following companies ahead or take a black cab: **London Radio Cars** (☎8905 0000, or 8204 4444); **Liberty Cars** (☎7739 9080) caters to gays and lesbians, while **Lady Cabs** (☎7254 3501) provides female drivers. Always agree on a price with the driver before getting in.

ⓩ PRACTICAL INFORMATION

TOURIST AND FINANCIAL SERVICES

Tourist Information Centre: Britain Visitor Centre, 1 Regent St. (www.visitbritain.com), ⊖Oxford Circus. Open M 9:30am-6:30pm, Tu-F 9am-6:30pm, Sa-Su 10am-4pm. **London Information Centre,** 1 Leicester Pl. (☎7930 6769; www.londoninformationcentre.com) ⊖Leicester Sq. Open M-F 8am-midnight, Sa-Su 9am-6pm.

Tours: The **Big Bus Company,** 48 Buckingham Palace Rd. (☎7233 9533; www.bigbus.co.uk). ⊖Victoria, has multiple routes and buses every 5-15min. 1hr. walking tours and mini Thames cruise. Buses start at central office and at hubs throughout the city. £20. £2 discount for online purchase. AmEx/MC/V. **Original London Walks** (☎7624 3978, recorded info 7624 9255; www.walks.com) runs themed walks, from "Haunted London" to "Slice of India." Most 2hr. £6, concessions £4, children under 16 free.

Financial Services: American Express, 84 Kensington High St. (☎7795 6703 or 0800 521 313; www.americanexpress.com), ⊖High St. Kensington. Open M-Sa 9am-5:30pm. Branch at 30-31 Haymarket (☎7484 9610), ⊖Piccadilly Circus. Open M-F 9am-7pm, Sa 9am-6pm, Su 10am-5pm.

LOCAL SERVICES

Special Concerns: Artsline, 54 Chalton St. (☎7388 2227; www.artsline.org.uk), ⊖Euston, has info on disabled persons' access to entertainment venues. **Magic** (www.magicdeaf.org.uk) is an association of 14 museums in London that run events and facilities for deaf and hard-of-hearing visitors. **Transport for London: Access and Mobility** (☎7222 1234, Tube access 7941 4600, bus access 7918 4300; www.tfl.co.uk) provides info on public transportation accessibility within the city.

GLBT Resources: Gay London (www.gaylondon.co.uk) is an online community for gays and lesbians. A web portal for lesbian and bisexual women, **Gingerbeer** (www.gingerbeer.co.uk), lists clubs, bars, restaurants, and community resources. The **London Lesbian and Gay Switchboard** (☎7837 7324; www.llgs.org.uk) is a 24hr. helpline and info resource.

EMERGENCY AND COMMUNICATIONS

 London's phone code is **020.**

Emergency: ☎999 from any land line or 122 from a mobile phone.

Police: London is covered by 2 police forces: the **City of London Police** (☎7601 2222) for the City and the **Metropolitan Police** (☎7230 1212) for the rest. At least 1 station in each of the 32 boroughs is open 24hr. Call ☎7230 1212 to find the nearest station.

Hospitals: Charing Cross, Fulham Palace Rd. (☎8846 1234), entrance on St. Dunstan's Rd., ⊖Hammersmith. **Royal Free,** Pond St. (☎7794 0500), ⊖Belsize Park. **St. Thomas's,** Lambeth Palace Rd. (☎7188 7982), ⊖Waterloo. **University College London Hospital,** Grafton Way (☎7387 9300), ⊖Warren St.

Pharmacies: Most pharmacies are open M-Sa 9:30am-5:30pm; a "duty" chemist in each neighborhood opens Su, though hours may be limited. Late-night and 24hr. chemists are rare; one 24hr. option is **Zafash Pharmacy,** 233 Old Brompton Rd. (☎7373 2798), ⊖Earl's Ct. **Bliss,** 5-6 Marble Arch (☎7723 6116), ⊖Marble Arch, is open daily 9am-midnight.

Internet Access: If you're paying more than £2 per hour, you're paying too much. Try the ubiquitous **easyEverything** (☎ 7241 9000; www.easyeverything.com). Locations include 9-16 Tottenham Ct. Rd. (⊖Tottenham Ct. Rd.); 456-459 Strand (⊖Charing Cross); 358 Oxford St. (⊖Bond St.); 160-166 Kensington High St. (⊖High St. Kensington). Prices vary with demand, from £1 per 15min. during busy times; usually around £1.60 per hr. Min. 50p-£1. Generally open until 11pm.

Post Office: Post offices are on almost every major road. When sending mail to London, be sure to include the full post code. The largest office is the **Trafalgar Square Post Office,** 24-28 William IV St. (☎ 7484 9304), ⊖Charing Cross. Open M-F 8:30am-6:30pm, Sa 9am-5:30pm.

▚ ACCOMMODATIONS

Accommodations in London cost a good deal more than anywhere else in the UK. The area near **Victoria Station** (Westminster) is convenient for major sights and transportation. **Bloomsbury** is by far the budget traveler's best option. Competing for 2nd place, **Kensington** and **Earl's Court** have a number of mid-range, high-quality digs, while **Bayswater** has less expensive ones that are also a step down in quality. Book well in advance, especially in summer. Book YHAs online at www.yha.org.

BY PRICE

UNDER £20 (PRICE ICON ❶)	
▨ Ashlee House	BLOOM
▨ The Generator	BLOOM
Hyde Park Hostel	BAY
International Student House	M/RP
Leinster Inn	BAY
Pickwick Hall Int'l Backpackers	BLOOM
Quest Hostel	BAY
St. Christopher's Inn	NL
YHA Earl's Court	KEN/EC
▨ YHA Holland House	KEN/EC
▨ YHA Oxford Street	WEND

£20-34 (PRICE ICON ❷)	
Astor's Museum Hostel	BLOOM
Baden Powell House	KEN/EC
▨ City University Finsbury	CLERK

YHA St. Pancras International	BLOOM

£35-49 (PRICE ICON ❸)	
Admiral Hotel	BAY
Balmoral House Hotel	BAY
The Gate Hotel	NH
George Hotel	BLOOM
IES Chelsea Pointe	CHEL
Kandara Guesthouse	NL
Luna Simone Hotel	WEMIN
Morgan House	K/B
Oxford Hotel	KEN/EC
▨ Vicarage Hotel	KEN/EC

£50-75 (PRICE ICON ❹)	
Jenkins Hotel	BLOOM

BY NEIGHBORHOOD

BAYSWATER

Quest Hostel, 45 Queensborough Terr. (☎ 7229 7782; www.astorhostels.com). ⊖Bayswater. Night Bus N15, 94, 148. Chummy staff operates this simple backpacker hostel. Mostly co-ed dorms (2 female-only rooms); nearly all with bath. Otherwise, facilities on every other floor. Continental breakfast, linen, and lockers included. Laundry, luggage storage, Internet (50p per 15min.), and kitchen available. 4- to 9-bed dorms £14-18; twins £25. MC/V. ❶

Hyde Park Hostel, 2-6 Inverness Terr. (☎ 7229 5101; www.astorhostels.com). ⊖Bayswater. Night Bus N15, 94, 148. With a veritable theme park of diversions, this colorful and backpacker-friendly hostel is entertaining, though not fancy. Bar and dance space hosts DJs and parties (open W-Sa 8pm-3am). Ages 16-35 only. Kitchen, laundry, TV lounge, and secure luggage room. Continental breakfast and linen included. Internet access 50p per 7min. Reception 24hr. Reserve 2 weeks in advance for summer; 24hr. cancellation policy. Online booking with 10% non-refundable deposit. 4- to 18-bed dorms £11-18; twins £25; weekly rates available from £81-95 per person. MC/V. ❶

Leinster Inn, 7-12 Leinster Sq. (☎7729 9641; www.astorhostels.com). ⊖Bayswater. Night Bus N15, 94, 148. Mid-sized rooms are decent, and some come with bath. TV/pool room and small bar (open W-Sa until 3am). Safety deposit boxes, kitchen, luggage room, and laundry. Continental breakfast and linen included. Internet access (£1-1.60 per hr.). Key deposit £10. Reception 24hr. Dorms £14.50-17.50; singles £27.50-33; twins £44-55; triples £57. MC/V. ❶

Admiral Hotel, 143 Sussex Gardens (☎7723 7309; www.admiral-hotel.com). ⊖Paddington. Night Bus N15, 94, 148. Beautifully kept B&B; all rooms with shower, toilet, TV, and kettle. English breakfast included. 4-day cancellation policy. Singles £40-50; doubles £58-75; triples £75-90; quads £88-110; quints £100-130. Ask about winter and long-stay discounts. MC/V. ❸

Balmoral House Hotel, 156-157 Sussex Gardens (☎7723 7445; www.balmoralhouse-hotel.co.uk). ⊖Paddington. Night Bus N15, 94, 148. Spacious, well-kept rooms, each with smallish bathroom, satellite TV, kettle, and hairdryer. English breakfast included. Singles £45; doubles £70; triples £84; family suites for 5 £120. MC/V. ❸

BLOOMSBURY

▨ **The Generator,** Compton Pl. (☎7388 7666; www.generatorhostels.com), off 37 Tavistock Pl. ⊖Russell Sq. or King's Cross St. Pancras. Night Bus N19, N35, N38, N41, N55, N91, N243. The ultimate party hostel. 18+ unless part of a family. Co-ed and all-female dorms, a bar (6pm-2am), pints (£1 6-9pm), common rooms. Breakfast included. Lockers, free towels and linens, laundry, and kitchen. Internet 50p per 7min. Reception 24hr. Reserve 1 week in advance for Sa-Su. Credit card required with reservation. 12- to 14-bed dorms M-W and Su £12.50, Th-Sa £17.50; singles £35/56; twins £50/56; triples £60/69; quads £68/80. Discounts in winter and for longer stays. MC/V. ❶

▨ **Ashlee House,** 261-265 Gray's Inn Rd. (☎7833 9400; www.ashleehouse.co.uk). ⊖King's Cross St. Pancras. Night Bus N10, N63, N73, N91, 390. Retro-themed rooms and common areas feel like a trendy lounge bar. Co-ed (all-female available) dorms are small but bright, while private rooms include table, sink, kettle, luggage room, safe, laundry, and kitchen. New bathrooms, plus a small elevator and TV room. Continental breakfast included. Linen included; towels £1. Internet £1 per hr. 2-week max. stay. Reception 24hr. Apr.-Oct. 16-bed dorms £16; 8- to 10-bed £18; 4- to 6-bed £20; singles £37; doubles £50. Nov.-Mar. £1 less. MC/V. ❶

George Hotel, 58-60 Cartwright Gardens (☎7387 8777; www.georgehotel.com). ⊖Russell Sq. Night Bus N10, N73, N91, 390. Meticulous blue-and-yellow rooms with satellite TV, kettle, phone, alarm clock, and sink. English breakfast included. Free Internet available. Reserve 3 weeks in advance for summer; 48hr. cancellation policy. Singles £47.50, with shower £60; doubles £66.50/74, with bath £89; triples £79/89/99; basic quad £89. 15% discount for stays over 5 days. MC/V. ❸

Jenkins Hotel, 45 Cartwright Gardens (☎7387 2067; www.jenkinshotel.demon.co.uk), entry on Barton Pl. ⊖Euston or King's Cross St. Pancras. Night Bus N10, N73, N91, 390. Rooms are well-decorated and spotless, each with TV, kettle, phone, fridge, hairdryer, and safe. Free use of the tennis courts in Cartwright Gardens. English breakfast included. Reserve 1-2 months in advance for summer; 24hr. cancellation policy. Singles £52, with bath £72; doubles with bath £85; triples with bath £105. MC/V. ❹

Astor's Museum Hostel, 27 Montague St. (☎7580 5360). ⊖Tottenham Ct Rd., Russell Sq., or Goodge St. Night Bus N19, N35, N38, N41, N55, N91, N243. Bare-bones but friendly. Communal kitchen and free DVDs loans available. Caters to an 18- to 30-year-old set. English breakfast and linen included. Bring your own towel or buy one in a pinch (£5). Reservations recommended. 12-bed dorms £16; 10-bed £17; 8-bed £18; 6-bed £19; 4-bed £20; private double £50. AmEx/MC/V. ❷

YHA St. Pancras International, 79-81 Euston Rd. (☎7388 9998). ⊖King's Cross St. Pancras. Night Bus N10, N73, N91, 390. Caters to families and older adults. Family bunk rooms, single-sex dorms, basic doubles, and premium doubles (with bath and TV). Lockers (bring own lock). Lounge with video games. Laundry, kitchen, and elevators. English breakfast and linen included. Internet £1 per 15min. 10-day max. stay. Reserve 1 week in advance for Sa-Su or summer, 2 weeks for doubles. Dorms £24.60, under 18 £20.50; doubles £56, with bath £61.50. £3 discount with ISIC or NUS card. Non-HI members add £3 per night. MC/V. ❷

Pickwick Hall International Backpackers, 7 Bedford Pl. (☎7323 4958; www.pickwick-hall.co.uk). ⊖Russell Sq. or Holborn. Night Bus N7, N91. Most accommodations are in 3- to 4-bed single-sex "dorms" (one 6-bed dorm). Small, simple rooms are clean and include minifridge and microwave. No guests. Continental breakfast and linen included. Coin laundry, kitchen, TV lounge, Internet access, and lockers (bring your own lock). Triple with bath is a good deal. Reception approx. 8am-10pm. Book 2-3 days in advance, 3 weeks in advance for July-Aug. Singles £25, with bath £45; doubles £44/50; triples £60/66; quads £80/88. MC/V. ❶

KENSINGTON AND EARL'S COURT

▣ **YHA Holland House,** Holland Walk (☎7937 0748; www.hihostels.com). ⊖High St. Kensington or Holland Park. Night Bus #27, 94, 148. Half the rooms are in a gorgeous 17th-century mansion overlooking a large courtyard. Caters mostly to younger student groups. Internet access (50p per 7min.), TV room, laundry, kitchen. Full English breakfast included. Reception 24hr. Book dorms 2-3 weeks in advance for summer, although there are frequent last-minute vacancies. Dorms £21.60, under 18 £19.30; singles £30; doubles £50; triples £70; quads £90. £3 student discount. AmEx/MC/V. ❶

▣ **Vicarage Hotel,** 10 Vicarage Gate (☎7229 4030; www.londonvicaragehotel.com). ⊖High St. Kensington. Night Bus #27, N28, N31, N52. Walking on Kensington Church St. from Kensington High St., there are 2 streets marked Vicarage Gate; take the 2nd on your right. Immaculately maintained Victorian house with ornate hallways, TV lounge, and charming bedrooms. Full English breakfast included. Best to reserve 2 months in advance with 1 night's deposit. Singles £46, with private bathroom £75; doubles £78/102; triples £95/130; quads £102/140. Cash only. ❸

Oxford Hotel, 24 Penywern Rd. (☎7370 1161; www.the-oxford-hotel.com). ⊖Earl's Court. Night Bus N31, N74, N97. Mid-sized, bright rooms, all with shower and some with full bath. Rooms have comfortable beds, TV, kettle, and safe. Continental breakfast included. Reception 24hr. Reserve 2-3 weeks in advance for June. Singles with shower £40, with bath £55; doubles £60/70; triples with bath £82; quads £89/96; quints £110/120. Discount on stays over 7 days. MC/V. ❸

YHA Earl's Court, 38 Bolton Gardens (☎7373 7083; www.hihostels.com). ⊖Earl's Court. Night Bus N31, N74, N97. Victorian townhouse considerably better-equipped than most YHAs. Bright, tidy, single-sex dorms (4-10 people) have wooden bunks, lockers (bring own lock), and sink. Features a small garden, spacious communal kitchen, 2 TV lounges, and luggage storage. Breakfast included only for private rooms; otherwise £3.80. Linens included. Coin laundry and Internet access (5p per min.) available. 2-

week max. stay. 24hr. cancellation policy; £5 cancellation charge. Book private rooms at least 24hr. in advance. Dorms £19.50, under 18 £17.20; doubles £54; quads £78. Nonmembers £3 extra. MC/V. ❶

Baden Powell House/YHA South Kensington, 65-67 Queensgate (☎7584 7031; www.yha.org). ⊖Gloucester Rd. Night Bus N74, N97. Parties don't abound, but identically dressed 10-year-old Scouts do. Laundry, cafe, luggage storage, and a rooftop terrace. Full English breakfast included. Reception 24hr. Closed late Dec. to Jan. Wheelchair-accessible. 5- to 19-bed single-sex dorms £30.50 with YHA card, £32 without; under 18 £20 with YHA card, £21 without. AmEx/MC/V. ❷

OTHER NEIGHBORHOODS

▨ **YHA Oxford Street,** 14 Noel St. (☎0870 770 5984; www.yhalondon.org.uk), in the West End. ⊖Oxford Circus. More than 10 Night Buses run along Oxford St., including N7, N74, N159. Small, clean, sunny rooms with limited facilities but an unbeatable location for Soho nightlife. Double rooms have bunk beds, sink, mirror, and wardrobe. Some triple-decker bunk beds. Comfy TV and smoking lounge; toilets and showers on hallways. Pre-packed Continental breakfast £3.60. Towels £3.50. Internet and well-equipped kitchen available. Travelcards sold at reception. Reserve at least 1 month in advance. 3- to 4-bed dorms £22.60, under 18 £18.20; 2-bed dorms £24.60. ❶

▨ **City University Finsbury Residences,** 15 Bastwick St. (☎7040 8811; www.city.ac.uk/ems/accomm/fins.html), in Clerkenwell. ⊖Barbican. Night Bus N35 and N55 stop at the corner of Old St. and Goswell Rd. A grim 1970s tower block, but the inside is freshly renovated, and it's within walking distance of City sights, Islington restaurants, and Clerkenwell nightlife. Singles in the main building share shower, toilet, kitchen access, and laundry room. Dinner available at the City University cafeteria (£4.70). Book in advance. Open mid-June to mid-Sept. Wheelchair-accessible. Singles £21. MC/V. ❷

Luna Simone Hotel, 47-49 Belgrave Rd. (☎7834 5897; www.lunasimonehotel.com), in Westminster. ⊖Victoria or Pimlico. Night Bus N2, 24, N36. Sparkling and spacious showers, modern decor, and a staff that has thought of every last detail. Attractive yellow rooms with desk, big closet, TV, phone, kettle, safety deposit box, and hairdryer. Singles without bath are cramped, but doubles are bigger than average. No smoking. Full English breakfast included. Free Internet access. Reserve at least 2 weeks in advance. £10 cancellation fee; 1 night's charge if less than 48hr. notice. Singles £40, with bath £60; doubles with bath £80; triples with bath £100; quads with bath £120. 10-20% discount in low season. MC/V. ❸

IES Chelsea Pointe, corner of Manresa Rd. and King's Rd. (☎7808 9200; www.iesreshall.com), entrance on Manresa Rd.; in Chelsea. ⊖Sloane Sq., then bus #11, 19, 22, or 319, or ⊖South Kensington, then bus #49. Night Bus N11, N19, N22. Brand-new university residence hall offers clean and spacious dorm rooms year-round. In the heart of über-posh Chelsea. All rooms ensuite. Kitchen. Laundry. Free Internet access. 5 TV/DVD lounges. Reservations highly recommended. 72hr. cancellation policy. 20 rooms wheelchair-accessible. Singles £40; doubles £50. AmEx/MC/V. ❸

Morgan House, 120 Ebury St. (☎7730 2384; www.morganhouse.co.uk), in Knightsbridge and Belgravia. ⊖Victoria. A neighborhood standout. Stylish rooms, many with fireplaces, all with TV, kettle, and phone for incoming calls (pay phone downstairs). English breakfast included. Reserve 2-3 months in advance. 48hr. cancellation policy. Singles with sink £46; doubles with sink £66, with bath £86; triples £86/110; quad (1 double bed and bunk beds) with bath £122. MC/V. ❸

International Student House, 229 Great Portland St. (☎7631 8310; www.ish.org.uk), in Marylebone and Regent's Park. ⊖Great Portland St. Night Bus #18. Great location near Regent's Park with fantastic rates. Good selection of rooms during summer, limited options during school year. Some rooms ensuite. Facilities include a bar (open daily), nightclub, cafeteria, fitness center (£5 per day), and cinema (Su only). Continental breakfast included (except for dorms; £2); English breakfast £3. Laundry. Internet £2 per hr. Key deposit £10. 3-week max. stay. Advance booking recommended. Some rooms wheelchair-accessible. Dorms £12; singles £33.50; doubles £51; triples £61.50; quads £74. 10% discount on private rooms with ISIC. MC/V. ❶

The Gate Hotel, 6 Portobello Rd. (☎ 7221 0707; www.gatehotel.com), on the corner of Portobello Rd. in Notting Hill. ⊖Notting Hill Gate. Night Bus N52. Friendly staff makes staying here a pleasure. A great base for Notting Hill and West End exploits. Rooms have bath, TV/DVD, desk, and phone. Continental breakfast included. 1-week cancellation policy. Singles £55-77; doubles £75-90; triples £90-110. AmEx/MC/V. ❸

Kandara Guesthouse, 68 Ockendon Rd. (☎ 7226 5721; www.kandara.co.uk), in North London. From ⊖Angel, take bus #38, 56, 73, or 341 to the Ockendon Rd. stop. Night Bus N38, N73, 341. Far from the Tube but ample access to downtown. Classically decorated family-run B&B. Sparkling-clean rooms with plenty of privacy. 5 baths for 11 rooms. Breakfast included. Hairdryer and iron on request. No smoking. Reserve in advance; call for quad. 1-night deposit required with reservation; 1-week cancellation policy. Singles £42-49; doubles and twins £53-64; triples £64-74. MC/V. ❸

St. Christopher's Inn, 48-50 Camden High St. (☎ 7407 1856; www.st-christophers.co.uk), in North London. ⊖Mornington Crescent. Night Bus N5, N20, N253. The reception in Belushi's Bar downstairs serves as a fitting entrance to this party-friendly backpacker hostel. Location is perfect for hitting the Camden Town bars and Clerkenwell clubs. Most rooms have private bath; if not, showers are close by. Luggage room, safety deposit boxes, lockers, laundry, and common rooms. Linens and Continental breakfast included. Reception 24hr. Internet access. 10-bed dorms £15; 8-bed £16; 6-bed £17; doubles £23. Discount with online booking. ❶

🖸 FOOD

There is no getting around the culinary misstep that is stewed eel. Thankfully, Londoners have realized that food is not their specialty, abandoning medieval roots in favor of international chefs who know better. Head to **Whitechapel** for the region's best *Balti* food, to **Chinatown** for traditional dim sum, to **South Kensington** for French pastries, and to **Edgware Road** for a stunning assortment of Lebanese Shawarma. The cheapest places to get the ingredients for your own meal are local **street markets** (see **Shopping,** p. 128). For all your food under one roof, head to **supermarket chains** Tesco, Safeway, Sainsbury's, or Marks & Spencer.

BAYSWATER

🖾 **Mr. Jerk,** 19 Westbourne Grove (☎ 7221 4678; www.mrjerk.co.uk). ⊖Bayswater or Royal Oak. 2nd location at 189 Wardour St. (☎ 7287 2878), in the West End. Feast on the house specialty jerk chicken (£6.50), Trinidadian mutton *roti* (£5), or the traditional combo of ackee (a savory Caribbean fruit) and saltfish (£6). Sip a Guinness Punch or go fully local with Soursap (both £2.50). Takeaway available. Open M-Sa 10am-11pm, Su noon-8pm. AmEx/MC/V. ❷

Levantine, 26 London St. (☎ 7262 1111). ⊖Paddington. Enter to the faint aroma of incense and rose petals. A beautiful, elegant Lebanese restaurant. Indulge in the *maqueneq* (special Lebanese sausages; £5) or the affordable set lunch menu (£5). Loads of vegetarian options, featured nights of belly-dancing and *shisha* (water pipe), and even an ornate loo to boot. Open daily noon-midnight. MC/V. ❷

La Bottega del Gelato, 127 Bayswater Rd. (☎7243 2443). ⊖Bayswater. The handmade, creamy gelato is ideal after a hard day of sightseeing. Across the street from Kensington Gardens. 1-3 scoops £1.80-4. Open daily 10am-7pm, later in summer. ❶

BLOOMSBURY

🔲 **ICCo (Italiano Coffee Company),** 46 Goodge St. (☎7580 9688). ⊖Goodge St. Light-years ahead of its competition, ICCo serves delicious 11" pizzas for an eye-popping £3. Pre-packaged sandwiches and baguettes on fresh bread start at £1.50 (rolls 50p). Pasta from £2. Sandwiches and baguettes half-price after 4pm. Takeaway available. Pizzas available from noon. Open daily 7am-11pm. AmEx/MC/V. ❶

🔲 **Navarro's Tapas Bar,** 67 Charlotte St. (☎7637 7713; www.navarros.co.uk). ⊖Goodge St. Authenticity carries over to the excellent food—try the spicy and deliciously thick lentil stew. Tapas £3-6; 2-3 per person is plenty. £7.50 min. per person. Open M-F noon-3pm and 6-10pm, Sa 6-10pm. AmEx/MC/V. ❸

Newman Arms, 23 Rathbone St., entrance to pie room on Newman Passage (☎7636 1127). ⊖Tottenham Ct. Rd. or Goodge St. A pub whose real highlight is the famous upstairs pie room and restaurant. Seasonal game fillings are the most popular; vegetarian and fish options available. Pie with potatoes and veggies on the side £8.50. Pints from £3. Book in advance or face a hungry 45min. wait. Pub open M-F 11am-11pm. Restaurant open M-Th noon-3pm and 6-9pm, F noon-3pm. MC/V. ❷

Wagamama, 40 Streatham St. (☎7323 9223; www.wagamama.com). ⊖Tottenham Ct. Rd. or Russell Sq. The original branch of the London noodle dynasty. A chain, but cheap and tasty dishes make it a good dining option. Cafeteria-style seating. Ramen from £6. Wide vegetarian selection. Open M-Sa noon-11pm, Su 12:30-10pm. ❷

CHELSEA

🔲 **Buona sera, at the Jam,** 289a King's Rd. (☎7352 8827). ⊖Sloane Sq., then bus #19 or 319. "Bunk" tables stacked high into the air. Waiters climb small wooden ladders to deliver sizable pasta plates (£7.20-8.50) along with fish and steak dishes (£8-12). Open Tu-F noon-3pm and 6pm-midnight, Sa-Su noon-midnight. Reservations recommended F-Sa. AmEx/MC/V. ❸

🔲 **Chelsea Bun,** 9a Limerston St. (☎7352 3635). ⊖Sloane Sq., then bus #11 or 22. Spirited and casual Anglo-American diner. Extensive vegetarian and vegan options include faux sausages with a full English

THE BIG SPLURGE

TEA AT THE RITZ

For the ultimate afternoon tea, book a sitting at the Ritz. Long synonymous with luxury, high tea in the Palm Court allows you to play the part of nobility. (Don't forget to dress the part.) The easy listening piano tunes float in as the bespectacled maître d' in tails leads you to a table set, of course, with the finest (and very easily stained) linen. While you drink your tea, your eyes will inevitably wander about. Be sure to take in the elegant dress of the other patrons the gilded fountains. Relax, breathe easy, and realize that you may never feel this posh again.

Tea is not just tea at the Ritz. Alongside the obvious teacup and saucer is a full cast of goodies: homemade jam and preserves, sugar cubes, clotted cream, fresh butter, and finger sandwiches (with julienned cucumbers and no crusts) served on a three-tiered silver tray. Eager eaters will stock their plate with finger sandwiches, scones, and tarts until you force them to stop. If you are going to shell out, you may as well get your full money's worth. *(The Ritz, Piccadilly. ⊖Green Park. ☎7493 8181. Wheelchair accessible. Reserve 6 weeks in advance for M-F, 3 months for Sa-Su; there may be space closer to the date and earlier sittings are usually less full. Sittings at 11:30am, 1:30, 3:30, 5:30pm daily, with champagne tea at 7:30pm. Jacket and tie required for men. AmEx/MC/V.)*

breakfast. Pasta, salads, burgers, and omelettes £6-8. Early-bird specials available M-F 7am-noon (£2.20-3.20). Sandwiches (£2.80-7) and breakfasts (from £4) served until 6pm. £3.50 min. per person during lunch, £5.50 dinner. Open M-Sa 7am-11:30pm, Su 9am-7pm. MC/V. ❷

Chelsea Kitchen, 98 King's Rd. (☎7589 1330). ⊖Sloane Sq. Enjoy everything from avocado prawns to omelettes while sitting in charming, dimly lit booths. Soups, salads, and sandwiches £2-4; wine £1.60 per glass, £7.80 per bottle. Entrees with fries and salad £3.30-5.90. Min. £3.30 per person. Breakfast served until 11:30am. Open daily 7am-midnight. AmEx/MC/V with £10 minimum. ❶

Pizza Express, 152 King's Rd. (☎7351 5031; www.pizzaexpress.co.uk). ⊖Sloane Sq., then bus #11, 19, 22, 211, or 319. Perhaps the most impressive of Pizza Express's locations. A triumphal archway supported by caryatids and topped by a bronze chariot separates the large, charming courtyard from the sidewalk. A perfect sunny-day pizza spot. Open daily 11:30am-midnight. AmEx/MC/V. ❷

THE CITY OF LONDON

🍴**Café Spice Namaste,** 16 Prescot St. (☎7488 9242). ⊖Tower Hill or DLR: Tower Gateway. The extensive menu helpfully explains each Goan and Parsee specialty. Meat entrees are on the pricey side (from £10), but vegetarian meals (from £7) are affordable, especially for an establishment of this quality. Open M-F noon-3pm and 6:15-10:30pm, Sa 6:30-10:30pm. AmEx/MC/V. ❸

Futures, 8 Botolph Alley (☎7623 4529), between Botolph Ln. and Lovat Ln. ⊖Monument. Suits and their lackeys besiege this tiny takeaway joint during the lunch hour. Variety of vegetarian soups (from £2), salads (from £2), and hot dishes (from £4) change weekly. For breakfast, try pastries (from £1.25) or porridges and cereals (from £1). Wheelchair-accessible. Open M-F 7:30-10am and 11:30am-3pm. ❶

The Place Below, Cheapside (☎7329 0789), in the basement of St. Mary-le-Bow Church. ⊖St. Paul's or Mansion House. Climb down the winding steps from the foyer of St. Mary-le-Bow and you'll find yourself in a fantastic vegetarian restaurant. Fresh, elaborate sandwiches (from £4.50), yummy porridge (£1.50), and a constantly changing menu of entrees (from £5.70). Open M-F 7:30am-3pm. ❶

CLERKENWELL AND HOLBORN

🍴**Anexo,** 61 Turnmill St. (☎7250 3401; www.anexo.co.uk). ⊖Farringdon. Funky and laidback, this Spanish restaurant and bar serves up tasty Iberian dishes, including authentic *paella* (£7-9), fajitas (£7.50-11.50), and tapas (from £3.50). The lunch special is hard to beat (2 courses £6, 3 courses £8). M 2-for-1 tapas. Wheelchair-accessible. Takeaway available. Happy hour M-Sa 5-7pm. Open M-F 10am-10pm, Sa 6-11pm, Su 4:30-10pm. Bar open 11am-2am. AmEx/MC/V. ❷

🍴**Bleeding Heart Tavern,** corner of Greville St. and Bleeding Heart Yard (☎7404 0333). ⊖Farringdon. Highlights include the roast suckling pig with delicately spiced shards of apple (£12). Extraordinarily good service and fine ale round out your dining experience (entrees £8-13). Open M-F 7-10:30am, noon-2:30pm, and 6-10:30pm. Upstairs pub open M-F 11:30am-11pm. AmEx/MC/V. ❸

Aki, 182 Gray's Inn Rd. (☎7837 9281; www.akidemae.com). ⊖ Chancery Ln. The bambooified warmth of this smallish Japanese restaurant is brightened by its value-packed menu. Noodle dishes (from £4.30), chicken, fish, and meat entrees (£4.20-10), and sushi meals (from £5) are a bargain (set 3-course menus start at £6.50). Wheelchair-accessible. Open M-F noon-3pm and 6-11pm, Sa 6-10:30pm. AmEx/MC/V. ❶

St. John, 26 St. John St. (☎ 7251 0848; www.stjohnrestaurant.com). ✪Farringdon. Not a great place for vegetarians—menu is "nose to tail" eating. Menu changes daily; representative dishes include lamb tongue with turnips and anchovies (£14.70) and goat curd with roasted tomatoes (£13.50). Bar menu £8-12. Open M-F noon-3pm and 6-11pm, Sa 6-11pm. Bar open M-F 11am-11pm, Sa 6-11pm. AmEx/MC/V. ❹

KENSINGTON AND EARL'S COURT

▨ **Utsav,** 17 Kensington High St. (☎ 7368 0022; www.utsav-restaurant.co.uk). ✪High St. Kensington. Four regional chefs serve up artistically presented specialties from north, south, east, and west India. Try their creative twist on a vegetable *samosa* (£5) or the filling *masala dosa* (£6). The 2-course lunch (£5 veg, £6 non-veg) is a tasty steal. Open M-Sa 11am-11pm, Su 11am-10pm. AmEx/MC/V. ❷

Raison d'Être, 18 Bute St. (☎ 7584 5008). ✪South Kensington. Offers a bewildering range of filled baguettes and foccacia (£2.50-5.50). *Salades composées* (£3.20-5.20) and various other light dishes (yogurt with fruit £2.50) are all made-to-order. After your meal, enjoy a divine *café au lait* under the outside canopy. Open M-F 8am-6pm, Sa 9:30am-4pm. Cash only. ❶

The Orangery, Kensington Palace (☎ 7938 1406). ✪High St. Kensington. Built for Queen Anne's dinner parties and full of white, high-ceilinged stateliness. Popular with a tourist-heavy clientele for light gourmet lunches (£8-11) and set afternoon teas (from £7). Recently opened for light breakfasts as well (£2-5). Open daily 10am-noon for breakfast, noon-3pm for lunch, 3-6pm for tea. MC/V. ❷

MARYLEBONE AND REGENT'S PARK

▨ **Mandalay,** 444 Edgware Rd. (☎ 7258 3696). ✪Edgware Rd. With huge portions of wildly inexpensive food, this Burmese restaurant is justly plastered with awards. Lunch specials offer great value (curry and rice £4; 4 courses, including a banana fritter, £6). Entrees, including sizable vegetarian selection, £4-7.50. Open M-Sa noon-2:30pm and 6-10:30pm. Dinner reservations recommended. AmEx/MC/V. ❶

Patogh, 8 Crawford Pl. (☎ 7262 4015). ✪Edgware Rd. This tiny but charming Persian hole-in-the-wall serves generous portions of sesame-seed flatbread (£2) and freshly prepared starters (£2.50-5); flame-grilled entrees like *kebab koobideh* (minced lamb kebab) with bread, rice, or salad (£6-11) will feed you for days. Takeaway available. Open daily noon-midnight. ❷

The Golden Hind, 73 Marylebone Ln. (☎ 7486 3644). ✪Baker St. or Bond St. In operation since 1914, this no-nonsense "chippie" serves up fried cod and haddock (£3.40-£5.70) to a local clientele and a growing number of travelers in on the secret. Chips (£1.30) and mushy peas (you know you're curious; 90p) round out the bare-bones menu. Takeaway available. Open M-F noon-3pm and 6-10pm, Sa 6-10pm. Reservations recommended after 7pm. AmEx/MC/V. ❸

THE WEST END

▨ **Masala Zone,** 9 Marshall St. (☎ 7287 9966; www.realindianfood.com). ✪Oxford Circus The food is steeped in South Indian tradition, cooked in a kitchen visible from anywhere in the restaurant, and loaded with *masala* (spices). Menu has typical favorites (£6-8), as well as "street food," which comes in small bowls (£3.40-5.50), or the large *thali* (platter), which allows you to sample a variety of dishes (£7.50-11.50). Curries (£6-8) are particularly good. No smoking in main dining area. Open M-F noon-2:45pm and 5:30-11pm, Sa 12:30-11pm, Su 12:30-3:30pm and 6-10:30pm. MC/V. ❷

Rock and Sole Plaice, 47 Endell St. (☎7836 3785; www.rockandsoleplaice.com). ⊖Covent Garden. A self-proclaimed "master fryer" (qualifications unclear) turns out tasty haddock, cod, halibut, and sole filets (all with chips) for £8-11. Chicken and beef pies run from £4.50-7. Vegetarians can munch on samosas (£4.50). Open M-Sa 11:30am-11:30pm, Su 11:30am-10pm. MC/V. ❷

Cafe in the Crypt, Duncannon St. (☎7839 4342). ⊖Embankment or Charing Cross. In the basement of St.-Martin-in-the-Fields Church. An excellent fresh salad bar (£6.75), freshly made sandwiches (£4), and hearty warm puddings (£3) served cafeteria-style. Jazz some W nights. Open M-W 10am-7:30pm, Th-Sa 8am-10:30pm, Su noon-7:30pm. AmEx/MC/V with £5 minimum. ❶

Busaba Eathai, 106-110 Wardour St. (☎7255 8686). ⊖Tottenham Ct. Rd., Leicester Sq., or Piccadilly Circus. Students and locals line up for pad thai, curries, and wok creations (£6-8). No reservations, so be prepared to wait. Open M-Th noon-11pm, F-Sa noon-11:30pm, Su noon-10pm. AmEx/MC/V. ❷

Gerrard's Corner, 30 Wardour St. (☎7287 1878). ⊖Leicester Sq. Dim sum and shellfish specialties are straight out of Shanghai. Generous portions and a varied, group-friendly menu (5 or more courses; £9-15) will please the masses, while 80s love ballads will appeal to a smaller crowd. Vegetarian dishes £3.50-8; noodle dishes £4.60-7.50. Open M-Sa noon-11:45pm, Su 11:30am-11pm. AmEx/MC/V. ❷

Neal's Yard Salad Bar, 1, 2, 8-10 Neal's Yard (☎7836 3233). ⊖Covent Garden. 3-building complex of vegetarian and vegan fare. Order the takeaway lunch special at the counter (£5), including choice of filling main course (rotates daily), side of wheat- and gluten-free bread, and an excellent fruit juice smoothie. Open in summer daily 8:30am-11pm; in winter 8:30am-9pm. Cash only. ❶

NORTH LONDON

Gallipoli, 102 Upper St. (☎7359 0630), **Gallipoli Again,** 120 Upper St. (☎7359 1578), and the newest member of the family, **Gallipoli Bazaar,** 107 Upper St. ⊖Angel. After the success of the first restaurant, they opened another on the same block; Gallipoli Again has the added bonus of an outdoor patio. Spectacular Lebanese, North African, and Turkish delights like *Iskender kebab* (grilled lamb with yogurt and marinated pita bread in a top-secret sauce; £6) and the 2-course lunch (£6). Wheelchair-accessible. Open M-Th 10:30am-11pm, F-Sa 10:30am-midnight, Su 10:30am-11pm. Reservations recommended F-Sa. MC/V. ❷

Mango Room, 10-12 Kentish Town Rd. (☎7482 5065). ⊖Camden Town. The small Caribbean menu features fish, complemented with plenty of mango, avocado, and coconut sauces, and curry coconut chicken. Entrees from £9.50. Lunch from £5.50. A wide array of potent tropical drinks are served from the tiny bar, but only at night. Wheelchair-accessible. Reservations recommended Sa-Su. Open daily noon-11pm. MC/V. ❷

New Culture Revolution, 43 Parkway (☎017 1267 2700). ⊖Camden Town. Huge portions of noodles and steaming soups with meat or veggies. Choose from dumplings (£4.20), vegetable *chow mein* (£5), or chili and lemongrass seafood *lo mein* (£6). Open daily noon-11pm. AmEx/MC/V. ❶

Le Crêperie de Hampstead, 77 Hampstead High St. (www.hampsteadcreperie.com), metal stand on the side of the King William IV. ⊖Hampstead. French-speaking cooks take your order and leave you to wait and salivate while you watch them cook. Among many other varieties, try tasty mushrooms and garlic cheese (£3.30) or the famous "Cream Dream" (£2.10). Open M-Th 11:45am-11pm, F-Su 11:45am-11:30pm. ❶

Bloom's, 130 Golders Green Rd. (☎ 8455 1338). ⊖ Golders Green (zone 3). The entrees are simple and delicious, ranging from chopped liver sandwiches (£7) to chicken *schnitzel* (£11.50). Jewish favorites like *gefilte fish* (£3.50) and *latkes* (£2) served as side orders. Excellent soups. Extensive takeaway menu. Kosher. Parve available. Wheelchair-accessible. Open M-Th and Su noon-10:30pm, F 11am-2pm. ❷

EAST LONDON

▨ **Café 1001,** Dray Walk (☎ 7247 9679). ⊖ Aldgate East. In an alley just off Brick Ln. Dreadlocked twentysomethings lounge around the smoke-filled and spacious upstairs, while the staff doles out homemade food straight from casserole dishes downstairs. Freshly baked cakes (slices £1.80), pre-made salads, sandwiches (£2.50), and outdoor barbecue, weather-permitting. Nightly DJs or live bands 7pm-close. Open M-W and Su 7am-11pm, Th-Sa 7pm-midnight. ❶

▨ **Aladin,** 132 Brick Ln. (☎ 7247 8210). ⊖ Shoreditch. Serving up Pakistani, Bangladeshi, and Indian food, Aladin stands out among Brick Lane's overwhelming *Balti* options. Plenty of vegetarian dishes. Entrees £3-8.50. 3-course lunch £6. Daily lunch special noon-4:30pm. Open M-Th and Su noon-11:30pm, F-Sa noon-midnight. ❷

The Drunken Monkey, 222 Shoreditch High St. (☎ 7392 9606; www.the drunkenmonkey.co.uk). ⊖ Liverpool St. This dim sum restaurant and bar is hipper than most Shanghai nightclubs. Rice and noodle dishes £3.50-6.50; small dim sum plates £2.50-4.50. Takeaway available. Happy hour M-F 5-7pm, Sa 6-7:30pm, Su all day. Open M-F noon-midnight, Sa 6pm-midnight, Su noon-11pm. AmEx/MC/V. ❷

OTHER NEIGHBORHOODS

▨ **Jenny Lo's Teahouse,** 14 Eccleston St. (☎ 7259 0399), in Knightsbridge and Belgravia. ⊖ Victoria. The small, modern interior here bustles on weekdays, but the delicious *cha shao* (pork noodle soup; £5.75) and the broad selection of Asian noodles, from Vietnamese to Beijing style (£5.75-8), make it well worth the wait. Takeaway and delivery available. £5 per person min. Open M-F noon-3pm and 6-10pm. Cash only. ❷

▨ **George's Portobello Fish Bar,** 329 Portobello Rd. (☎ 8969 7895), in Notting Hill. ⊖ Ladbroke Grove. Fish like cod, rock, plaice, and skate come with a huge scoop of chunky chips (from £4.50). Burgers, kebabs, and falafel also available. Open M-F 11am-midnight, Sa 11am-9pm, Su noon-9:30pm. ❶

Lazy Daisy Café, 59a Portobello Rd. (☎ 7221 8417), in Notting Hill. ⊖ Notting Hill Gate. Tucked into an alley. Wide range of periodicals and a bin of toys keep customers of all ages happily occupied. All-day breakfast, including a lazy fry-up (£6) and eggs Florentine (£4.75). Lunches include nicoise salad (£6) and fish fingers (£5). Wheelchair-accessible. Open M-F 9:30am-5:30pm, Sa 9am-5pm, Su noon-2:30pm. ❶

Tas, 33 The Cut (☎ 7928 2111; www.tasrestaurant.com), in the South Bank. ⊖ Southwark. 2nd location at 72 Borough High St. (☎ 7928 3300). **Tas Cafe,** 76 Borough High St. (☎ 7403 8559). **Tas Pide,** 20-22 New Globe Walk (☎ 7928 3300). ⊖ London Bridge. A dynamic group of Turkish restaurants. Entrees from £6.75; 4 different 2-course menus starting at £8.25 and *meze* menus (selection of starters) starting at £7. Live music daily from 7:30pm. Wheelchair-accessible. Dinner reservations recommended at restaurants. Open M-Sa noon-11:30pm, Su noon-10:30pm. AmEx/MC/V. ❷

Cantina del Ponte, 36c Shad Thames, Butlers Wharf (☎ 7403 5403), in the South Bank. ⊖ Tower Hill or London Bridge. The busy Mediterranean mural can't hold a candle to the views of the Thames. Set lunch is a bargain at 2 courses for £11, 3 for £13.50 (available M-F noon-3pm). Pizzas from £5. Entrees from £10. Wheelchair-accessible. Open M-Sa noon-3pm and 6-10:45pm, Su noon-3pm and 6-9:45pm. AmEx/MC/V. ❸

Goya, 34 Lupus St. (☎7976 5309; www.goyarestaurant.co.uk), in Westminster. ⊖Pimlico. Join the local Spanish clientele for a post-siesta meal. Generous, diverse tapas (mostly £3-5), including plenty of vegetarian options; 2-3 per person is more than enough. Sangria £3; alcohol served only with food. Wheelchair-accessible. Open daily 11:30am-11:30pm. AmEx/MC/V with £10 minimum. ❸

⊙ SIGHTS

To walk from east to west is to watch the city unfold through time: from Christopher Wren's playground in the 2000-year-old City of London, along Holborn's Fleet St.—associated with the London press, the Royal Courts, and that nuisance "demon barber"—down to Westminster to hold court with the regents, royals, and ruffians who run this fair capital, and then up to Bloomsbury to mingle with the students and youth. Unlike London's museums, sights tend to be expensive. Sights aren't limited to ornate archways and piles of stones. From avant-garde architecture in Islington to the urban wilderness of Hampstead Heath, the best of London's sights are often those seen via excursions on foot.

MAJOR ATTRACTIONS

▨**WESTMINSTER ABBEY.** Founded as a Benedictine monastery, Westminster Abbey has become a house of kings and queens living and dead. Almost nothing remains of St. Edward's Abbey; Henry III's 13th-century Gothic reworking created most of the current grand structure. Britons buried or commemorated inside the Abbey include: **Henry VII, Bloody Mary, Elizabeth I** and the scholars and artists honored in the **"Poet's Corner"** (Chaucer, Dylan Thomas, the Brontë sisters, Jane Austen, Handel, and Shakespeare). A door off the east cloister leads to the octagonal **Chapter House,** the original meeting place of the House of Commons with a 13th-century tiled floor. Next door to the Abbey (through the cloisters), the lackluster **Abbey Museum** is housed in the Norman undercroft. The highlight of the collection is an array of fully dressed medieval royal **funeral effigies,** undergarments and all.

St. Margaret's Church, just north of the Abbey, enjoys a strange status: as a part of the Royal Peculiar it is not under the jurisdiction of the diocese of England or the archbishop of Canterbury. It was built for local residents by Abbey monks and has been beautifully restored in the past few years. Since 1614, it's been the official worshipping place of the House of Commons—the first few pews are cordoned off for the Speaker, Black Rod, and other dignitaries. *(Parliament Sq., in Westminster. Access Old Monastery, Cloister, and Garden from Dean's Yard, behind the Abbey. ⊖Westminster. Abbey ☎7654 4900, Chapter House 7222 5152, St. Margaret's 7654 4840; www.westminster-abbey.org. No photography. Partially wheelchair-accessible. Abbey open M-Tu and Th-F 9:30am-3:45pm, W 9:30am-7pm, Sa 9:30am-1:45pm, open Su for services only. Museum open daily 10:30am-4pm. Chapter House open daily 10:30am-4pm. Cloisters open daily 8am-6pm. Garden open Apr.-Sept. Tu-Th 10am-6pm; Oct.-Mar. daily 10am-4pm. St. Margaret's open M-F 9:30am-3:45pm, Sa 9:30am-1:45pm, Su 2-5pm. Hours subject to change, call first. Abbey and museum £8, concessions £6. Services free. Chapter House, Gardens, and St. Margaret's free. Audio guides available M-F 9:30am-3pm, Sa 9:30am-1pm; £3. 90min. tours M-F 10, 11am, 2, 3pm; Sa 10, 11am; Apr.-Oct. also M-F 10:30am and 2:30pm. £4. AmEx/MC/V.)*

THE TOWER OF LONDON. The turrets and towers of this multi-functional block—serving as palace, prison, royal mint, and living museum over the past 900 years—are impressive not only for their appearance but for their integral role in England's history. A popular way to get a feel for the Tower is to join one of the animated and theatrical ▨**Yeoman Warders' Tours.** Queen Anne Boleyn passed through **Traitor's**

Gate just before her death, but entering the Tower is no longer as perilous as it used to be. St. Thomas's Tower begins the self-guided tour of the **Medieval Palace.** At the end of the **Wall Walk**—a series of eight towers—is **Martin Tower,** which houses an exhibit that traces the history of the British Crown and is now home to a fascinating collection of retired crowns (*without* the gemstones that have been recycled into the current models); informative plaques are much better here than in the **Jewel House,** where the crown jewels are held. With the exception of the Coronation Spoon, everything dates from after 1660, since Cromwell melted down the original booty. The centerpiece of the fortress is **White Tower,** which begins with the first-floor ⚔**Chapel of St. John the Evangelist.** Outside, **Tower Green** is a lovely grassy area—not so lovely, though, for those once executed there. *(Tower Hill, next to Tower Bridge, in the City of London, within easy reach of the South Bank and the East End. ⊖Tower Hill or DLR: Tower Gateway. ☎08707 566 060, ticket sales 0870 756 7070; www.hrp.org.uk or www.tower-of-london.org.uk. Open Mar.-Oct. M 10am-6pm, Tu-Sa 9am-6pm, Su 10am-6pm; Nov.-Feb. M and Su 10am-5pm, Tu-Sa 9am-5pm. Buildings close at 5:45pm, last ticket sold 5pm and last entry 5:30pm. Tower Green open only by Yeoman tours, after 4:30pm, or for daily services. £13.50, concessions £10.50. Tickets also sold at Tube stations or by phone; buy them in advance to avoid long lines. "Yeoman Warder Tours" meet near entrance; 1hr., every 90min. M 10am-3:30pm, Tu-Sa 9:30am-3:30pm, Su 10am-3:30pm. Audio guides £3.)*

REAL DEAL. While the **Tower of London** is perennially popular, and is probably the most bang for your buck of the big-name sights, paying £13.50 (that's US$25 per person!) is absolutely absurd. For royal history, head to the **National Portrait Gallery** for free. –Yaran Noti

---

ST. PAUL'S CATHEDRAL. Majestic St. Paul's is a cornerstone of London's architectural and historical legacy and an obvious tourist magnet. Architect Christopher Wren's masterpiece is the 5th cathedral to occupy the site; the original was built in AD 604. In 1668, after Old St. Paul's had been swept away in the Great Fire, construction began on the current cathedral. Inside, the **nave** leads to the second-tallest freestanding dome in Europe (after St. Peter's in the Vatican), its height extended by the tricky perspective of the paintings on the inner surface. The first stop to scaling the heights yourself is the narrow **Whispering Gallery,** reached by 259 shallow wooden steps. None of the galleries are wheelchair-accessible, and the first climb is the only one that isn't steep, narrow, or slightly strenuous. Circling the base of the inner dome, the Whispering Gallery is a perfect resounding chamber: whisper into the wall, and your friend on the other side will hear you—or, theoretically, they could if everyone else weren't trying the same thing. Plumbing the depths, the **crypt** is packed wall-to-wall with plaques and tombs of great Britons (and the occasional foreigner). Nelson commands a prime location, with radiating galleries of gravestones and tributes honoring other military heroes, from Epstein's bust of T.E. Lawrence (of Arabia) to a plaque commemorating the casualties of the Gulf War. *(St. Paul's Churchyard, in the City of London. ⊖St. Paul's. ☎7246 8348; www.stpauls.co.uk. Partially wheelchair-accessible. Open M-Sa 8:30am-4:30pm. Last admission 4pm. Dome and galleries open M-Sa 9:30am-4pm. Open for worship daily 7:15am-6pm. Admission £8, concessions £7; worshippers free. Group of 10 or more 50p discount per ticket. Tours 90min. "Supertour" M-F 11, 11:30am, 1:30, 2pm; £2.50, concessions £2, children £1; English only. "Triforium" tour M-F 11:30am and 2:30pm; £5 per person; book in advance. Audio guide available in many languages daily 10am-3:30pm; £3.50, concessions £3.)*

ST. PAUL'S FOR POCKET CHANGE. To gain access to the Cathedral's nave for free, attend an Evensong service (M-Sa 5pm, 45min.). Arrive at 4:50pm to be admitted to seats in the quire.

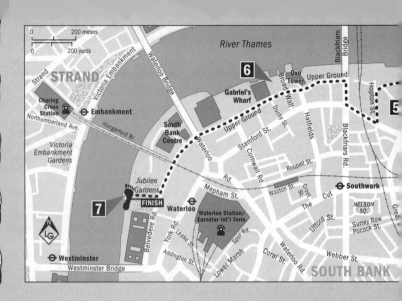

A stroll along the South Bank is a trip through history. Across the river you will pass the timeless monuments of London's past, like the Tower of London and St. Paul's Cathedral, while next to you the round glass sphere of City Hall and the converted power facility that houses Tate provide a stark and modern contrast. Whether you're searching for Shakespeare and Picasso or just hankering for a nice walk, no visit to the South Bank goes unrewarded.

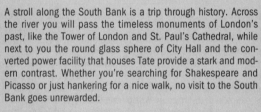

Time: 8-9hr.

Distance: 2.5 mi. (4km)

When To Go: Start early morning

Start: ⊖Tower Hill

Finish: ⊖Westminster

1 TOWER OF LONDON. Begin your trek to the Tower early to avoid the crowds. Tours given by the Yeomen Warders meet every 1½hr. near the entrance. Listen as they expertly recount tales of royal conspiracy, treason, and murder. See the **White Tower,** once both fortress and residence of kings. Shiver at the executioner's stone on the tower green and pay your respects at the Chapel of St. Peter ad Vinculum, which holds the remains of three queens. First get the dirt on the gemstones at **Martin Tower,** then wait in line to see the **Crown Jewels.** The jewels include such glittering lovelies as the First Star of Africa, the largest cut diamond in the world (p. 104). Time: 2hr.

2 TOWER BRIDGE. An engineering wonder that puts its plainer sibling, the London Bridge, to shame. Marvel at its beauty, but skip the Tower Bridge Experience. Or, better yet, call in advance to inquire what times the Tower drawbridge is lifted (p. 111). Time: no need to stop walking; take in the mechanics as you head to the next sight.

3 DESIGN MUSEUM. On Butler's Wharf, let the Design Museum introduce you to the latest innovations in contemporary design, from marketing to movements to haute couture. See what's to come in the forward-looking Review Gallery or hone in on individual designers and products in the Temporary Gallery (p. 122). From the museum, walk along the **Queen's Walk.** To your left you will find the **HMS Belfast,** which was launched in 1938 and led the landing for D-Day, 1944 (☎ 7940 6300; £7, concessions £5). Time: 1hr.

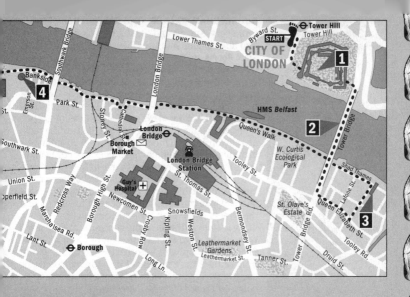

SHAKESPEARE'S GLOBE THEATRE. "I hope to see London once ere I die," says akespeare's Davy in *Henry IV*. In time, he may see it from the beautiful recreation of Will's ost famous theater. Excellent exhibits demonstrate the secrets of stage effects and how akespearean actors dressed, and tell of the painstaking process of rebuilding the theatre most 400 years after the original burned down (p. 114). You might be able to catch a mat-e performance if you time your visit right. Call in advance for tour and show times. Time: r. for tour; 3hr. for performance.

TATE MODERN. It's hard to imagine anything casting a shadow over the Globe Theatre, t the massive former Bankside Power Station does just that. One of the world's premier dern art museums, the Tate promises a new spin on well-known favorites and works by erging British artists. Be sure to catch one of the informative docent tours and don't forget ogle the rotating installation in the Turbine Room (p. 118). Time: 2hr.

GABRIEL'S WHARF. Check out the cafes, bars, and boutiques of colorful **Gabriel's narf.** If you missed the top floor of the Tate Modern, go to the public viewing gallery on the n floor of the **OXO Tower.** On your way to the London Eye, stop by the **South Bank Centre.** tablished as a primary cultural center in 1951, it now exhibits a range of music from Phil-rmonic extravaganzas to low-key jazz. You may even catch one of the free lunchtime or ernoon events. Call in advance for dates and times (☎ 7960 4242 or 08703 809 988). ne: 1½hr. for schmoozing and dinner.

LONDON EYE. Once known as the Millennium Wheel; given its "like-named" siblings—the sbehaving "Bridge" and bloated, egotistic "Dome"—it's no surprise that it shed its maiden me at the first possible chance. The London Eye has firmly established itself as one of ndon's top attractions, popular with locals and tourists. The Eye offers amazing 360° ws from its glass pods; you may be able to see all of London lit up at sunset. Book in vance to avoid the long queues, but be sure to check the weather (p. 114). Time: 1hr.

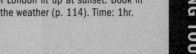

WALKING TOUR

THE LOCAL STORY

QUEEN'S GUARD

Let's Go got the scoop on a London icon, interviewing Corporal of Horse Simon Knowles, an 18-year veteran of the Queen's Guard.

LG: What sort of training did you undergo?
A: In addition to a year of basic military camp, which involves mainly training on tanks and armored cars, I was also trained as a gunner and radio operator. Then I joined the service regiment at 18 years of age.

LG: So it's not all glamor?
A: Not at all, that's a common misconception. After armored training, we go through mounted training on horseback in Windsor for 6 months where we learn the tools of horseback riding, beginning with bareback training. The final month is spent in London training in full state uniform.

LG: Do the horses ever act up?
A: Yes, but it's natural. During the Queen's Jubilee Parade, with three million people lining the Mall, to expect any animal to be fully relaxed is absurd. The horses rely on the rider to give them confidence. If the guard is riding the horses confidently and strongly, the horse will settle down.

LG: Your uniforms look pretty heavy. Are they comfortable?
A: They're not comfortable at all.

BUCKINGHAM PALACE. The Palace opens to visitors every August and September. Don't expect to find any insights into the Queen's personal life—the **State Rooms** are the only rooms on view, and they are used only for formal occasions. "God Save the Queen" is the rallying cry at the **Queens Gallery,** dedicated to changing exhibits of jaw-droppingly valuable items from the Royal Collection. Detached from the palace and tour, the **Royal Mews** acts as a museum, stable, riding school, and working carriage house. The main attraction is the Queen's collection of coaches, including the Cinderella-like "Glass Coach" used to carry royal brides, including Diana, to their weddings, and the State Coaches of Australia, Ireland, and Scotland. Another highlight is the four-ton **Gold State Coach,** which can occasionally be seen tooling around the streets in the early morning on practice runs for major events. To witness the spectacle of the Palace without the cost, attend a session of **Changing of the Guard.** Show up well before 11:30am and stand in front of the Palace in view of the morning guards, or use the steps of the Victoria Memorial as a vantage point. *(At the end of the Mall, between Westminster, Belgravia, and Mayfair. Enter State Rooms on Buckingham Palace Rd. ⊖St. James's Park, Victoria, Green Park, or Hyde Park Corner. ☎7766 7324, Queens Gallery 7766 7301, Royal Mews 7766 7302; www.the-royal-collection.com. Palace open daily early Aug.to late Sept. 9:30am-6:30pm (last admission 4:15pm). Purchase tickets by phone or online, or at the kiosk in Green Park. £13.50, students £11.50, children under 17 £7. Advance booking recommended; for disabled visitors, it is required. Queens Gallery open daily 10am-5:30pm, last admission 4:30pm. £7.50, concessions £6, families £19. Royal Mews open daily late July to late Sept. 10am-5pm, last admission 4:15pm; Mar.-July and late Sept. to late Oct. M-Th and Sa-Su 11am–4pm; last admission 3:15pm. £6, seniors £5, under 17 £3.50, families £15.50. Changing of the Guard daily Apr. to late July, every other day Aug.-Mar., provided the Queen is in residence, it's not raining hard, and there are no pressing state functions. Free. AmEx/MC/V.)*

THE HOUSES OF PARLIAMENT. The Palace of Westminster has been home to both the House of Lords and the House of Commons (together known as Parliament) since the 11th century, when Edward the Confessor established his court here. Standing guard on the northern side of the building, the **Clock Tower** is famously nicknamed **Big Ben,** after the robustly proportioned Benjamin Hall, a former Commissioner of Works. "Big Ben" actually refers only to the 14-ton bell that hangs inside the tower. **Victoria Tower,** at the south end of the palace building, was erected in 1834 to celebrate the emancipation of slaves in the British Empire. The tower contains copies of every Act of Parliament since 1497. A flag flown from the top indicates that Parliament is in session. When the Queen is in the building, a special royal banner is flown instead of the Union flag. Visitors with enough patience or luck to make it inside the chambers can hear the occasional debates between members of both the House of Lords and the House of Commons. *(Parliament Sq., in Westminster. Line for both Houses forms at St. Stephen's entrance, between Old and New Palace Yards. ⊖Westminster. ☎08709 063 773, Lords Info Office 7219 3107, Commons Info Office 7219 4272; www.parliament.uk/ visiting/visiting.cfm. "Line of Route" tour includes both houses. UK residents can contact their MPs for tours year-round, generally M-W mornings and F. Foreign visitors may tour Aug.-Oct. Book online, by phone, or in person at Abingdon Green ticket office (open in summer) across from the Palace of Westminster. Tours run Aug. M-Tu and F-Sa 9:15am-4pm, W-Th 1:15-4:30pm; Sept.-Oct. M and F-Sa 9:15am-4:30pm, Tu-Th 1:15-4:30pm. Tours depart every few min. £7. MC/V. House of Lords open during session M-Th 9am-6pm, F 9am-4:30pm; during recess M-F 10am-5pm. Chamber open Oct.-July M-W 2:30-10pm, Th 11am-7:30pm, and occasionally F from 11am onward. Wait for Lords generally shorter than for Commons, although it still may not be possible to enter until after "question time" (40min. M-W 2:30pm, Th-F 11am). House of Commons open during session M-Th 9am-6pm, F 9am-4:30pm; during recess M-F 10am-5pm. Chamber open Oct.-July M-Tu 2:30-10:30pm, W 11:30am-7:30pm, Th 10:30am-6:30pm, occasionally F 9:30am-3pm. Hours subject to change. Limited number of UK residents permitted in for "question time" during 1st hour of session. Foreign visitors must apply several weeks in advance for "question time" tickets through their embassy in London or wait until questions are finished for entrance. Arrive in afternoon to minimize waiting, which regularly exceeds 2hr. Normally possible to enter Gallery without waiting on F mornings when Parliament is sitting, which happens occasionally.)*

BY NEIGHBORHOOD

BLOOMSBURY

BRITISH LIBRARY. Castigated during its long construction by traditionalists for being too modern and by modernists for being too traditional, the new British Library building (opened in 1998) now impresses all doubters with its stunning interior. The heart of the library is underground, with 12 million books on 200 mi. of shelving; the above-ground brick building is home to cavernous reading rooms and an engrossing ▨**museum** (see p. 123). *(96 Euston Rd. ⊖Euston Sq. or King's Cross St. Pancras. ☎7412 7332; www.bl.uk. Wheel-*

They were designed way back in Queen Victoria's time, and the leather trousers and boots are very solid. The uniform weighs about 3 stone [about 45 lb.].

LG: How do you overcome the itches, sneezes, and bees?
A: Discipline is instilled in every British soldier during training. We know not to move a muscle while on parade no matter what the provocation or distraction—unless, of course, it is a security matter. But our helmets are akin to wearing a boiling kettle on your head; to relieve the pressure, sometimes we use the back of our sword blade to ease the back of the helmet forward.

LG: How do you make the time pass while on duty?
A: The days are long. At Whitehall the shift system is derived upon inspection in Barracks. Smarter men work on horseback in the boxes in shifts from 10am-4pm; less smart men work on foot from 7am-8pm. Some guys count the number of buses that drive past. Unofficially, there are lots of pretty girls around here, and we *are* allowed to move our eyeballs.

LG: What has been your funniest distraction attempt?
A: One day a taxi pulled up, and out hopped 4 Playboy bunnies, who then posed for a photo shoot right in front of us. You could call that a distraction if you like.

chair-accessible. All public spaces open M 9:30am-6pm, Tu 9:30am-8pm, W-F 9:30am-6pm, Sa 9:30am-5pm, Su 11am-5pm. Admission free. To use reading rooms, bring 2 forms of ID, one with a signature and one with a home address. Tours of public areas M, W, F 3pm, Sa 10:30am and 3pm; £6, concessions £4.50. Tours including one of the reading rooms Su and Bank Holidays 11:30am and 3pm. £7, concessions £5.50. Reservations recommended for all tours. Audio guides £3.50, concessions £2.50.)

OTHER BLOOMSBURY SIGHTS. A co-founder and key advisor of **University College London**—the first in Britain to ignore race, creed, and politics in admissions and, later, the first to allow women to sit for degrees—social philosopher Jeremy Bentham still watches over his old haunts; his body has sat on display in the South Cloister since 1850, wax head and all. *(Main entrance on Gower St. South Cloister entrance through the courtyard. ⊖Euston. www.ucl.ac.uk. Wheelchair-accessible. Quadrangle gates close at midnight; access to Jeremy Bentham ends at 6pm. Free.)* Next to the British Library are the soaring Gothic spires of **St. Pancras Station.** Formerly housing the Midland Grand Hotel, today Sir George Gilbert Scott's facade is a hollow shell awaiting redevelopment as a Marriott. *(Euston Rd. ⊖King's Cross or St. Pancras.)*

CHELSEA

THE ROYAL HOSPITAL. The environs of the Royal Hospital, including a monument, a garden park, and a retirement home, are home to the Chelsea Pensioners, who totter around the grounds as retirees have done since 1692. The main attraction is the once-ritzy **Ranelagh Gardens**—now a quiet oasis for picnics and parkplaying, except during the week of the **Chelsea Flower Show,** usually in late May. *(2 entrance gates on Royal Hospital Rd. ⊖Sloane Sq., then bus #137 or 360. ☎7881 5246. Wheelchair-accessible. Museum, Great Hall, and chapel open M-Sa 10am-noon and 2-4pm, Su 2-4pm; museum closed Su Oct.-Mar. Grounds open Apr. M-Sa 10am-7:30pm, Su 2-7:30pm; May-Aug. M-Sa 10am-8:30pm, Su 2-8:30pm; Sept. M-Sa 10am-7pm, Su 2-7pm; Nov.-Mar. M-Sa 10am-4:30pm, Su 2-4:30pm. Ranelagh Gardens have same hours as grounds but are closed 12:45-2pm. Free. Flower show: www.rhs.org.uk. Tickets must be purchased well in advance.)*

CHELSEA PHYSIC GARDEN. Founded in 1673 to provide medicinal herbs, the Physic Garden was the staging area from which tea was introduced to India and cotton to America. Today it remains a living repository of all manner of plants, from opium poppies to leeks. *(66 Royal Hospital Rd.; entrance on Swan Walk. ⊖Sloane Sq., then bus #137 or 360. ☎7352 5646; www.chelseaphysicgarden.co.uk. Call in advance for wheelchair access. Open early Apr. to Oct. W noon-5pm, Su 2-6pm; during Chelsea Flower Show (late May) and Chelsea Festival (mid-June) M-F noon-5pm. £6, concessions £3.50. Tea served daily 2-4:45pm, Su 2-5:45pm.)*

THE CITY OF LONDON

▦ALL HALLOWS-BY-THE-TOWER. Nearly hidden by redevelopment projects and nearby office buildings, All Hallows bears its longevity with pride. Just inside the entrance on the left stands the oldest part of the church, a Saxon arch dating from AD 675. The spectacular Lady Chapel is home to a magnificent altarpiece dating from 1500 and has been restored to look much as it did when it was built in 1489. *(Byward St. ⊖Tower Hill. ☎7481 2928; www.allhallowsbythetower.org.uk. Church open M-F 9am-5:45pm, Sa-Su 10am-5pm. Crypt and museum open daily 10:30am-4pm. Free.)*

▦GUILDHALL. Guildhall was once the administrative center of the Corporation of London. Before heading into the building itself, take a moment in the open stone **Guildhall Yard,** which is usually empty and feels strangely removed from the bustle of the City. Excavations in the 1990s revealed the remains of a Roman amphitheater below the Yard; its ruins are on display in the **Guildhall Art Gallery** (p. 120) on the Yard's eastern side. The towering Gothic building dates from 1440, though after repeated remodeling in the 17th and 18th centuries, little of the original remains. The downstairs crypt is only open by guided tour. Guildhall is often closed for events, but arrive early and you might be able to pop in for a look. The **Guildhall Library**, in the 1970s annex and accessed via Aldermanbury or the Yard, specializes in the history of London. It houses the **Guildhall Clockmaker's Museum** as well. *(Off Gresham St. Enter the Guildhall through the low, modern annex; entrance for library on Aldermanbury. ⊖St. Paul's, Moorgate, or Bank. Guildhall ☎ 7606 3030, for occasional tour information 7606 3030, ext. 1463. Open May-Sept. daily 10am-5pm; Sept. weekends are open-house; Oct.-Apr. M-Sa 10am-5pm. Last admission 4:30pm. Free. Library ☎ 7332 1854. Open M-Sa 9:30am-5pm. Free.)*

MONUMENT. The only non-ecclesiastical Wren building in the City, the Monument was built to commemorate the devastating Great Fire of 1666. A white Doric column, the colossal Monument can only be scaled by climbing the narrow spiral staircase inside. The enclosed platform at the top offers one of the best views of London, especially of the Tower Bridge. *(Monument St. ⊖Monument. ☎7626 2717. Open daily 9:30am-5pm. Last admission 4:40pm. £2. The Monument and the Tower Bridge Exhibition (see below) offer joint admission; £6.50, concessions £4.50.)*

TOWER BRIDGE. Not to be mistaken for its plainer sibling, **London Bridge**, Tower Bridge is the one you know from movies set in London. Historians and technophiles will appreciate the **Tower Bridge Exhibition,** which combines scenic 140 ft. glass-enclosed walkways with videos presenting a bell-and-whistle history of the bridge. *(Entrance to the Tower Bridge Exhibition is through the west side (upriver) of the North Tower. ⊖Tower Hill or London Bridge. ☎ 7940 3985, for lifting schedule 7940 3984; www.towerbridge.org.uk. Wheelchair-accessible. Open daily 10am-6pm. Last entry 5:30pm. £5.50, concessions £4.25.)*

OTHER CITY OF LONDON SIGHTS. The most famous modern structure in the City is **Lloyd's of London.** What looks like a towering post-modern factory is actually the home of the world's largest insurance market, built in 1986 with raw metal ducts, lifts, and chutes on the outside. *(Leadenhall St. ⊖Bank. Wheelchair-accessible.)* Only the tower and outer walls remain of Wren's ▓**St. Dunstan-in-the-East.** The Blitzed, mossy ruins have been converted into a stunning garden that is now a peaceful picnic spot. Vines cover the Gothic-style walls, and a bubbling fountain surrounded by benches makes it an oasis in the City. *(St. Dunstan's Hill. ⊖Monument or Tower Hill. Wheelchair-accessible.)* Government financial difficulties led to the founding of the **Bank of England** in 1694 as a way of raising money without taxes—the bank's Scottish and British creditors supplied £1.2 million, and the national debt was born. The 8 ft. windowless outer wall is the only remnant of Sir John Sloane's 1788 building; above it rises the current 1925 edifice. The ▓**Bank of England Museum** (see p. 120) provides the only way for lay people to get inside. *(Threadneedle. ⊖Bank.)*

CLERKENWELL AND HOLBORN

In Clerkenwell, many buildings are beautiful from the outside but inaccessible to tourists; walk the **Clerkenwell Historic Trail.** (Maps available at the 3 Things Coffee Room, 53 Clerkenwell Close. ☎7251 6311. ⊖Farringdon. Open M-Sa 11am-6pm.)

▓**THE TEMPLE.** South of Fleet St., this labyrinthine compound encompasses the inns of the **Middle Temple** to the west and the neighboring **Inner Temple** to the east—there was once an Outer Temple, but it's long gone. From 1185 until the order was dissolved in 1312, this land belonged to the crusading Knights Templar; the sole remnant of this time is the **Temple Church,** a Gothic nave, built in 1240, with an altar screen by Wren attached to the older round church. *(☎7353 3470. Hours vary depending on the week's services and are posted outside the door of the church for the coming week. Organ recitals W 1:15-1:45pm; no services Aug.-Sept. Free.)* According to Shakespeare's *Henry VI*, the red and white flowers that served as emblems in the Wars of the Roses were plucked in **Middle Temple Garden,** south of the hall. *(Garden open May-Sept. M-F noon-3pm. Free.)*

ROYAL COURTS OF JUSTICE. Straddling the official division between the City of Westminster and the City of London, this sprawling Neo-Gothic structure encloses courtrooms and the Great Hall (home to Europe's largest mosaic floor) amid labyrinthine passageways. All courtrooms are open to the public during trials. *(Where the Strand becomes Fleet St.; rear entrance on Carey St.* ⊖*Temple or Chancery Ln.* ☎*7947 6000. Wheelchair-accessible. Open M-F 9am-4:30pm; cases are heard 10am-1pm and 2-3:30pm. Be prepared to go through a metal-detector security checkpoint when you enter. Cameras are not permitted inside the building; 50p to check them at the door. Free.)*

OTHER CLERKENWELL AND HOLBORN SIGHTS. The mid-13th-century **Church of St. Etheldreda** is the last remaining vestige of the Bishop of Ely's palace and the only pre-Reformation Catholic church in the city. *(In Ely Place.* ☎*7405 1061. Church open daily 7:30am-7pm. Church open M-F noon-2:30pm. Free.)* The unusual spire of Wren's 1675 **St. Bride's Church** is the most imitated piece of architecture in the world: perhaps taking his cue from the church's name, a local baker used it as the model for the first multi-tiered wedding cake. *(St. Bride's Ave., just off Fleet St.* ⊖*Blackfriars.* ☎*7427 0133; www.stbrides.com. Open daily 8am-4:45pm. Lunchtime concerts and nighttime classical music; call for details. Free.)* Legend places **St. Clement Danes Church** over the tomb of Harold Harefoot, a Danish warlord who settled here in the 9th century. Its fame with Londoners derives from its opening role in the famous nursery rhyme—"Oranges and Lemons Say the Bells of St. Clement's"—and they still do, daily, at 9am, noon, 3, and 6pm. *(At the eastern junction of Aldwych and Strand.* ⊖*Temple.* ☎*7242 8282. Open M-F 9am-4pm, Sa-Su 9:30am-3:30pm. Free.)*

KENSINGTON AND EARL'S COURT

HYDE PARK AND KENSINGTON GARDENS. Surrounded by London's wealthiest neighborhoods, Hyde Park has served as the model for city parks around the world, including Central Park in New York and Paris's Bois de Boulogne. **Kensington Gardens,** contiguous with Hyde Park and originally part of it, was created in the late 17th century when William and Mary set up house in Kensington Palace. *(Framed by Kensington Rd., Knightsbridge, Park Ln., and Bayswater Rd.; bordered by Knightsbridge, Kensington, Bayswater, Marylebone, and Mayfair.* ⊖*Queensway, Lancaster Gate, Marble Arch, Hyde Park Corner, or High St. Kensington.* ☎*7298 2100; www.royalparks.gov.uk. Park open daily 5am-midnight. Gardens open 6am-dusk. Free for both. "Liberty Drive" rides available Tu-F for seniors and the disabled; call* ☎*07767 498 096. A full program of music, performances, and children's activities takes place during the summer; see park noticeboards for details.)* In the middle of the park is the **Serpentine,** officially known as the "Long Water West of the Serpentine Bridge." Dog-paddling tourists, rowers, and pedal boaters have made it London's busiest swimming hole. Nowhere near the water, the **Serpentine Gallery** holds contemporary art. *(*⊖*Hyde Park Corner. Boating* ☎*7262 1330. Open daily Apr.-Sept. 10am-5pm (6pm or later in fine weather). £4 per person for 30min., £6 per hr. Swimming at the Lido, south shore.* ☎*7706 3422. Open daily June to early Sept. 10am-5:30pm. Lockers and sun lounges available. £3.50, £2.80 after 4pm, students £2.50/1.60. Gallery open daily 10am-5pm. Free.)* At the northeast corner of the park, near **Marble Arch,** you can see free speech in action as proselytizers, politicos, and flat-out crazies dispense wisdom to bemused tourists at **Speaker's Corner** on Sundays, the only place in London where demonstrators can assemble without a permit.

KENSINGTON PALACE. In 1689, William and Mary commissioned Christopher Wren to remodel Nottingham House into a palace. Kensington remained the principal royal residence until George III decamped to Kew in 1760, but it is still in use—Princess Diana was the most famous recent inhabitant. Royalty fanatics can tour the rather underwhelming Hanoverian **State Apartments,** with *trompe l'oeil* paintings by William Kent. More impressive is the **Royal Ceremonial Dress Collection,** a magnifiscent spread of tailored and embroidered garments. *(Western edge of Kensington Gardens; enter through the park.* ⊖*High St. Kensington, Notting Hill Gate, or Queensway.*

☎ 7937 9561; www.royalresidences.com. Wheelchair-accessible. Open daily Mar.-Oct. 10am-6pm; Nov.-Feb. 10am-5pm; last admission 1hr. before closing. Admission £11, students £8.30; £1 discount online. Combo passes with Tower of London or Hampton Court available. MC/V.)

HOLLAND PARK. Smaller and less touristed than Kensington Gardens, Holland Park probably makes for a better picnic spot or quiet stroll than Hyde. Off Kensington High St. and full of shady paths, the grounds also offer open fields, popular soccer pitches, a golf bunker, cricket nets, tennis courts, and Japanese gardens. (Bordered by Kensington High St., Holland Walk, and Abbotsbury Rd. Enter at Commonwealth Institute. ⊖ High St. Kensington. ☎ 7471 9813, police 7441 9811, sport league and recreation info 7602 2226. Open daily 7:30am-dusk. Free.)

KNIGHTSBRIDGE AND BELGRAVIA

APSLEY HOUSE. Named for Baron Apsley, the house later known as "No. 1, London" was bought in 1817 by the Duke of Wellington. On display is Wellington's outstanding collection of art, mostly in the **Waterloo Gallery.** X-ray analysis revealed that the famous Goya portrait of Wellington on horseback—the model for many a pub sign—was originally of Napoleon's brother, Joseph Bonaparte. (Wellington himself disliked it for different reasons: he felt he looked "too heavy.") (Hyde Park Corner. ⊖ Hyde Park Corner. ☎ 7499 5676; www.english-heritage.org.uk/london. Wheelchair-accessible. Open Apr.-Oct. Tu-Su 10am-5pm; Nov.-Mar. Tu-Su 10am-4pm. £5, students £3.70, ages 5-18 £2.30. Joint ticket with Wellington Arch £6.30/4.70/3.20. Audio guide free. MC/V.)

WELLINGTON ARCH. Standing at the center of London's most infamous intersection, the Wellington Arch was ignored by tourists and Londoners alike until April 2001, when the completion of a restoration project revealed the interior to the public for the first time. Exhibits on the building's history and the changing nature of war memorials play second fiddle to the two spectacular observation platforms with a bird's-eye view of Buckingham Palace gardens, Green Park, and Hyde Park. (Hyde Park Corner. ⊖ Hyde Park Corner. ☎ 7930 2726; www.english-heritage.org.uk/london. Wheelchair-accessible. Open Apr.-Oct. W-Su 10am-5pm; Nov.-Mar. W-Su 10am-4pm. £3, students with ISIC card £2.30, ages 5-16 £1.50. Joint tickets with Apsley House available. MC/V.)

MARYLEBONE AND REGENT'S PARK

▧ REGENT'S PARK. When Crown Architect John Nash designed Regent's Park, he envisioned a residential development for the "wealthy and good." Fortunately for us commonfolk, Parliament opened the space to all in 1811, creating London's most popular and attractive recreation area. Most of the park's top attractions and activities lie near the **Inner Circle,** a road that separates the regal, meticulously maintained ▧ **Queen Mary's Gardens** from the rest of the grounds. While the few villas in the park—**The Holme** and **St. John's Lodge**—are private residences for the unimaginably rich and are not available for public viewing, the formal ▧ **Gardens of St. John's Lodge,** on the northern edge of the Inner Circle, provide a peek into the backyard of one such mansion. The climb up **Primrose Hill,** just north of Regent's Park proper, offers an impressive view of central London. (⊖ Baker St., Regent's Park, Great Portland St., or Camden Town. 500 acres of gardens stretching north from Marylebone Rd. to Camden Town. ☎ 7486 7905, police 7935 1259. Open daily 7am-dusk. Free.)

MADAME TUSSAUD'S. It may be one of London's top tourist attractions, but Madame Tussaud's is the most undeserving round-the-block queue. For those unwilling to pass up a photo-op with wax models of George Clooney and Tom Cruise, it is at least an indisputably unique 90min. experience. (Marylebone Rd. ⊖ Baker St. ☎ 08704 003 000; www.madame-tussauds.com. Wheelchair-accessible. Open Jan.-June and Sept.-Dec. M-F 9:30am-5:30pm, Sa-Su 9am-6pm; July-Aug. daily 9am-6pm. Prices depend on day of the week, entrance time, and season. Admission £14-23, under 16 £7-17. "Chamber Live" exhibit adds £2. Advance booking (by phone or online) £2 extra; groups (10+) approx. £1.50 less per person, but call in advance to ensure discount. AmEx/MC/V.)

THE SOUTH BANK

■**SHAKESPEARE'S GLOBE THEATRE.** This incarnation of the Globe is faithful to the original, thatched roof and all. The original burned down in 1613 after a 14-year run as the Bard's preferred playhouse. Today's reconstruction had its first full season in 1997 and now stands as the cornerstone of the International Shakespeare Globe Centre. For info on performances, see p. 127. *(Bankside, close to Bankside pier. ⊖Southwark or London Bridge. ☎7902 1500; www.shakespeares-globe.org. Wheelchair-accessible. Open daily May-Sept. 9am-noon (exhibit and tours) and 12:30-5pm (exhibit only); Oct.-Apr. 10am-5pm. Tours run daily every 30min. May-Sept. 9am-noon; Oct.-Apr. 10am-5pm, 10am-noon when for matinees. £9, concessions £7.50, ages 5-15 £6.50.)*

■**SOUTHWARK CATHEDRAL.** A site of worship since AD 606, the cathedral has undergone numerous transformations in the last 1400 years. Shakespeare's brother Edmund is buried here. In the rear of the nave, there are four smaller chapels; the northernmost Chapel of St. Andrew is dedicated to those living with and dying from HIV and AIDS. Near the center, the **archaeological gallery** is actually a small excavation by the cathedral wall, revealing a first-century Roman road. *(Montague Close. ⊖London Bridge. ☎7367 6700; www.dswark.org. Wheelchair-accessible. Open daily 8am-6pm. Free; £3.50 suggested donation. There is a group charge; book in advance. Audio guide £5; concessions £4, ages 5-15 £2.50. Camera permit £1.50; video permit £5.)*

LONDON EYE. Also known as the Millennium Wheel, at 135m (430 ft.) the British Airways London Eye is the biggest observational wheel in the world. The ellipsoidal glass "pods" give uninterrupted views from the top during each 30min. revolution. *(Jubilee Gardens, between County Hall and the Festival Hall. ⊖Waterloo. ☎08704 445 544; www.ba-londoneye.com. Wheelchair-accessible. Open daily late May-June and Sept. 9:30am-9pm; July-Aug. 9:30am-10pm; Feb.-Apr. and Oct.-Dec. 9:30am-8pm. Buy tickets from box office at the corner of County Hall before joining the line at the Eye; advance booking recommended, but check the weather. £12.50, concessions £10, children £6.50.)*

 THE REAL DEAL. While the **London Eye** does offer magnificent views, the queues are long and it's overpriced. For equally impressive sights in a quieter atmosphere, head to the **Monument** (p. 111), **Primrose Hill** (p. 113), or **Hampstead Heath** (p. 117). —Yaran Noti

THE WEST END

■**TRAFALGAR SQUARE.** John Nash first suggested laying out this square in 1820, but it took almost 50 years for London's largest traffic roundabout to take on its current appearance. The square is named in commemoration of the defeat of Napoleon's navy at Trafalgar, considered England's greatest naval victory. It has traditionally been a site for public rallies and protest movements. Towering over the square is the 51m granite **Nelson's Column**, which until recently was one of the world's tallest displays of decades-old pigeon droppings. Now, thanks to a deep-clean sponsored by the Mayor, this monument to naval hero Lord Nelson sparkles once again. *(⊖Charing Cross or Leicester Sq.)*

ST. MARTIN-IN-THE-FIELDS. The 4th church to stand here, James Gibbs's 1726 creation is instantly recognizable: the rectangular portico building supporting a soaring steeple made it the model for countless Georgian churches in Ireland and America. Handel and Mozart both performed here, and the church hosts frequent concerts. In order to support the cost of keeping the church open, a surprisingly extensive and delicious **cafe** (p. 102), bookshop, and art gallery dwell in the Crypt, and a tourist-oriented **daily market** is outside. *(St. Martin's Ln., northeast corner of Trafalgar Sq.; crypt entrance on Duncannon St. ⊖Leicester Sq. or Charing Cross. ☎7766 1100; www.stmartin-in-the-fields.org. Market open daily 11am-7pm. Open M-Sa 10am-7pm, Su noon-6pm. Tours Th 11:30am. Admission and tour free. Brass rubbing £2.90-15.)*

LONDON

MARYLEBONE

MAYFAIR

SOHO

COVENT GARDEN

ST. JAMES'S

River Thames

Newton St.

Drury Ln.

Bow St.

Endell St.

Neal St.

Eastman St.

Shelton St.

Long Acre

Garrick St.

Floral St.

New Row

Bedford St.

Bedfordbury

St. Martin's Ln.

Monmouth St.

St. Giles High St.

New Oxford St.

Great Russell St.

CAMBRIDGE CIRCUS

Charing Cross Rd.

Shaftesbury Ave.

Gerrard St.

Lisle St.

Cranbourn St.

Cross Rd.

Leicester Sq.

Irving St.

Orange St.

Whitcomb St.

TRAFALGAR SQ.

National Gallery

Pall Mall East

Coventry St.

Haymarket

Regent St.

Charles II St.

Pall Mall

Carlton House Terr.

Waterloo Pl.

Charing Cross

St. Martin-in-the-Fields

William IV St.

Strand

John Adam St.

Savoy Pl.

Victoria Embankment Gardens

Embankment

Craven

Northumberland St.

Whitehall

House Guards Parade

Admiralty Arch

The Mall

St. James's Park

Carting Ln.

Southampton St.

Tavistock St.

Wellington St.

Catherine St.

Covent Garden Plaza

St. Paul's Ch.

Transport Museum

Royal Opera House

Covent Garden

Tottenham Court Rd.

SOHO SQ.

Greek St.

Frith St.

Dean St.

Bateman St.

Great Chapel St.

D'Arblay St.

Berwick St.

Wardour St.

Poland St.

Marlborough St.

Duck Ln.

Brewer St.

Great Windmill St.

PICCADILLY CIRCUS

Piccadilly Circus

Glasshouse St.

Sackville St.

Vigo St.

Burlington Gdns.

Cork St.

Savile Row

Old Bond St.

New Bond St.

Clifford St.

Conduit St.

Royal Academy of Art

Piccadilly

Duke of York St.

ST. JAMES'S SQ.

Jermyn St.

Duke St.

Bury St.

King St.

St. James's St.

The Ritz

Green Park

Queen's Walk

Berkeley St.

Dover St.

Stratton St.

Bolton St.

Clarges St.

BERKELEY SQ.

Bruton St.

Mount St.

Mount Row

Bourdon St.

Bourdon Pl.

Davies St.

Dering St.

Brook's Mews

Avery Row

GROSVENOR SQ.

Grosvenor St.

St. George St.

HANOVER SQ.

Maddox St.

Heddon St.

Kingly St.

Carnaby St.

Newburgh St.

Marshall St.

GOLDEN SQ.

Lexington St.

Broadwick St.

Great Pulteney St.

Beak St.

Regent St.

Argyll St.

Oxford Circus

Gt. Castle St.

Margaret St.

Gt. Portland St.

Titchfield St.

Oxford St.

Berners St.

Newman St.

Wells St.

MANCHESTER SQ.

CAVENDISH SQ.

Margaret St.

Welbeck St.

Henrietta Pl.

Wigmore St.

James St.

Duke St.

Brook St.

S. Molton St.

N. Audley St.

Orchard St.

Bond St.

TO THE MARBLE ARCH (400yd)

Embankment

Victoria Embankment

Chinatown

Leicester Sq.

---

0   200 yards
0   200 meters

> **MUSIC FOR POCKET CHANGE.** St. Martin-in-the-Fields holds free lunchtime concerts M, Tu, and F at 1pm, and choral Evensong daily at 5pm.

ST. PAUL'S CHURCH. Not to be confused with St. Paul's Cathedral, this 1633 Inigo Jones church is now the sole remnant of the original square. Known as "the actors' church" for its long association with nearby theaters, the interior is festooned with plaques commemorating the achievements of Boris Karloff, Vivien Leigh, and Charlie Chaplin. *(On Covent Garden Piazza; enter via the Piazza, King St., Henrietta St., or Bedford St. ⊖Covent Garden. ☎7836 5221; www.actorschurch.org. Open M-F 8:30am-4:30pm. Morning services Su 11am. Evensong 2nd Su of month 4pm. Free.)*

ST. JAMES'S PALACE. Built in 1536 over the remains of a leper hospital, St. James's is London's only remaining palace built as such (Buckingham Palace was a rough-and-ready conversion of a Duke's house). As the official home of the Crown, royal proclamations are issued every Friday from the balcony in the interior Friary Court. Unless your name starts with HRH, the only part of the Palace you're likely to get into is the **Chapel Royal,** open for Sunday services from October to Easter at 8:30 and 11:30am. From Easter to July, services are held in Inigo Jones's **Queen's Chapel,** across Marlborough Rd. from the Palace, which was built in the 17th century for the marriage of then-prince Charles I. *(⊖Green Park.)*

SOHO. A conglomeration of squares and tourist capitalists, Soho is at least one of the most diverse areas in central London. **Old Compton Street** is the center of London's GLBT culture. In the 1950s, immigrants from Hong Kong started moving en masse to the few blocks just north of Leicester Sq., around **Gerrard Street** and grittier **Lisle Street,** which now form **Chinatown.** Gaudy, brash, and world-famous, **Piccadilly Circus** is made up of four of the West End's major arteries (Piccadilly, Regent St., Shaftesbury Ave., and the Haymarket). In the middle of all the glitz and neon stands the Gilbert's famous **Statue of Eros.** *(⊖Piccadilly Circus.)* Lined with tour buses, overpriced clubs, and generic cafes, **Leicester Square** is one destination that Londoners go out of their way to avoid. *(⊖Piccadilly Circus or Leicester Sq.)* A calm in the midst of the storm, **Soho Square** is a rather scruffy patch of green space popular with picnickers. Its removed location makes the square more hospitable and less trafficked than Leicester. *(⊖Tottenham Ct. Rd. Park open daily 10am-dusk.)*

WESTMINSTER

⊠ST. JAMES'S PARK AND GREEN PARK. The streets leading up to Buckingham Palace are flanked by two sprawling expanses of greenery: St. James's Park and Green Park. In the middle of St. James's Park is the placid **St. James's Park Lake**— the lake and the grassy area surrounding it make up an official waterfowl preserve. Across the Mall, the lush Green Park is the creation of Charles II, connecting Westminster and St. James. *(The Mall. ⊖St. James's Park or Green Park. Open daily 5am-midnight. Lawn chairs available Mar.-May and Sept.-Oct. 10am-6pm, weather permitting; June-Aug. 10am-10pm. £2 for 2hr., student deal £30 for the season. Last rental 2hr. before close. Summer walks in the park, 1hr., some M 1-2pm, including tour of Guard's Palace and Victoria Tower Gardens. Book in advance by calling ☎7930 1793.)*

WESTMINSTER CATHEDRAL. Following Henry VIII's divorce from the Catholic Church, London's Catholic community remained without a cathedral until 1884, when the Church purchased a derelict prison on what used to be a monastery site. The Neo-Byzantine church looks somewhat like a fortress and is now one of London's great religious landmarks. An elevator, well worth the minimal fee, carries visitors up the striped 273 ft. bell tower for an all-encompassing view of Westminster, the river, and Kensington. *(Cathedral Piazza, off Victoria St. ⊖Victoria. ☎7798 9055; www.westminstercathedral.org.uk. Open daily 8am-7pm. Suggested donation £2. Bell tower open Mar.-Nov. daily 9am-12:30pm and 1pm-5pm; Dec.-Feb. Tu-Sa 9am-12:30pm. £3, concessions £1.50. Organ recitals Su 4:45pm.)*

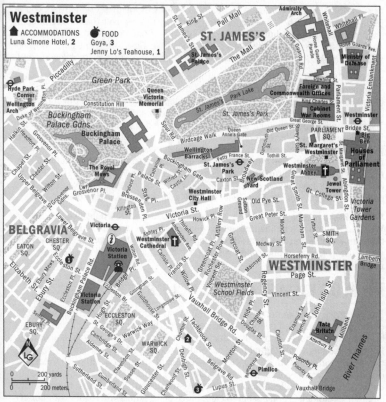

Westminster

🏠 ACCOMMODATIONS 🍴 FOOD
Luna Simone Hotel, **2** Goya, **3**
Jenny Lo's Teahouse, **1**

WHITEHALL. Whitehall refers to the stretch of road connecting Trafalgar Sq. with **Parliament Square** and is synonymous with the British civil service. Toward the north end of Whitehall, **Great Scotland Yard** marks the former headquarters of the Metropolitan Police. Nearer Parliament Square, heavily guarded steel gates mark the entrance to **Downing Street.** In 1735, No. 10 was made the official residence of the First Lord of the Treasury, a position that soon became permanently identified with the Prime Minister. The Chancellor of the Exchequer traditionally resides at No. 11, the Parliamentary Chief Whip at No. 12. Tony Blair's family, however, is too big for No. 10, so he swapped with Gordon Brown next door. The street is closed to visitors, but if you wait long enough you might see the PM going to or coming from work. The most photographed men in the area, the **Queen's Life Guards,** stand in the center of Whitehall. The guard changes Monday through Saturday at 11am and Sunday at 10am, with a dismount for inspection daily at 4pm—a 200-year tradition, broken only by WWII. *(Between Trafalgar Sq. and Parliament Sq.* ⊖*Westminster, Embankment, or Charing Cross.)*

NORTH LONDON

🏞**HAMPSTEAD HEATH.** Unlike so many other London parks, the Heath is not comprised of manicured gardens and paths, but wild, spontaneous growth tumbling over rolling pastures and forested groves. Dirt paths through the Heath are not well marked and are as random as the surrounding vegetation; travel in groups (for numerous eyes) to avoid getting lost. In the midst of the Heath is 🏞**Hill Gar-**

den—unless you're specifically on the lookout for this lovely secret garden, you're unlikely to find it. The flower-encrusted walkway passes over the former kitchen gardens of Lord Leverhulme's (founder of Lever Soap) mansion. *(⊖Hampstead. Train: Hampstead Heath. Bus #210. Wheelchair-accessible. Open 24hr. Hill Garden: In Hampstead Heath; take North End Way to Inverforth Close. Open daily 8:30am to 1hr. before sunset.)*

LORD'S CRICKET GROUND. The most famous cricket ground in England, Lord's is home to the local Marylebone Cricket Club (MCC) and hosts most of London's international matches. To see the **Lord's Museum,** home to the **Ashes Urn** and all the cricket-related memorabilia you could ever want to see, attend a match or take a 100min. tour led by a senior club member. On game days, tours after 10am skip the Long Room and media center, though visitors get a discount on game tickets (no tours during international test matches). Games take place on most days in summer. MCC games are £10 (students £4.50), but tickets to the rare international test matches are £45 and difficult to get. *(Enter at Grace Gate, on St. John's Wood Rd., a 10min. walk from ⊖St. John's Wood. ☎7432 1066; www.lords.org.uk. Wheelchair-accessible. Tours daily noon and 2pm, plus Apr.-Sept. 10am. Tours £8, concessions £5, under 16 £6.)*

ABBEY ROAD. Abbey Rd. itself is a long thoroughfare stretching from St. John's Wood to Kilburn; it's residential and tree-lined. Most people are only interested in the famous **zebra crossing** at its start, where it merges with Grove End Rd. The best way to stop traffic: a photo-op crossing the street a la John, Paul, George, and Ringo. *(⊖St. John's Wood.)*

🏛 MUSEUMS AND GALLERIES

For centuries, rich Londoners have exhibited a penchant for collecting. While not cheap, galleries of such collections offer some of the best art in the city, and many do have certain hours of free or reduced admission. On top of private collections, London also has a substantial national collection, helped in large part by its position in the 18th and 19th centuries as the capital of an empire. Although the methods by which various Syrian, Egyptian, and other ruins were obtained might seem dubious today, the collections are so impressive that art lovers, history buffs, and amateur ethnologists don't seem to care. Since 2002, admission to all major collections is free indefinitely in celebration of the Queen's Golden Jubilee.

MAJOR COLLECTIONS

▧**TATE MODERN.** Sir Giles Gilbert Scott's mammoth building, formerly the Bankside power station, houses the 2nd half of the national collection (the earlier set is held in the National Gallery). The Tate Modern is probably the most popular museum in London, as well as one of the most famous modern art museums in the world. The public galleries on the 3rd and 5th floors are divided into four themes. The collection is enormous while gallery space is limited—works rotate frequently. If you are dying to see a particular piece, head to the museum's computer station on the 5th floor to browse the entire collection. The 7th floor has unblemished views of the Thames and north and south of London. *(Main entrance on Bankside, on the South Bank; 2nd entrance on Queen's Walk. From Southwark Tube, turn left up Union then left on Great Suffolk, then left on Holland. ⊖Southwark or Blackfriars. ☎7887 8000; www.tate.org.uk. Wheelchair-accessible on Holland St. Open M-Th and Su 10am-6pm, F-Sa 10am-10pm. Free; special exhibits can be up to £10. Free tours meet on the gallery concourses: "History/Memory/Society" noon, Level 5; "Nude/Body/Action" 11am, Level 5; "Landscape/Matter/Environment" 3pm, Level 3; "Still Life/Object/Real Life" 2pm, Level 3. Audio guide: 5 types include highlights, collection, architecture, children's tour, and the visually impaired tour; £2. Talks M-F 1pm; meet at the concourse on the appropriate level; free.)*

■ **NATIONAL GALLERY.** The National Gallery was founded by an Act of Parliament in 1824, with 38 pictures displayed in a townhouse; over the years it's grown to hold an enormous collection. Numerous additions have been made, the most recent (and controversial) being the massive modern Sainsbury Wing—Prince Charles described it as "a monstrous carbuncle on the face of a much-loved and elegant friend." The Sainsbury Wing holds almost all of the museum's large exhibitions as well as restaurants and lecture halls. If pressed for time, head to **Art Start** in the Sainsbury Wing, where you can design and print out a personalized tour of the paintings you want to see. Themed audio guides and family routes also available from information desk. *(Main entrance on north side of Trafalgar Sq. ⊖Charing Cross or Leicester Sq. ☎7747 2885; www.nationalgallery.org.uk. Wheelchair-accessible at Sainsbury Wing on Pall Mall East, Orange St., and Getty Entrance. Open M-Tu and Th-Su 10am-6pm, W 10am-9pm. Special exhibitions in the Sainsbury Wing occasionally open until 10pm. Admission free; some temporary exhibitions £5-9, students and ages 12-18 £2-3. 1hr. tours start at Sainsbury Wing information desk. Tours daily 11:30am, 12:30, 2:30, 3:30pm, plus W 6, 6:30pm; free. Audio guides free, £4 suggested donation. AmEx/MC/V for ticketed events.)*

■ **NATIONAL PORTRAIT GALLERY.** This artistic Who's Who in Britain began in 1856 and has grown to be the place to see Britain's freshest new artwork as well as centuries-old portraiture. This portrait heaven was recently bolstered by the addition of the sleek Ondaatje Wing. New facilities include an IT Gallery, with computers allowing you to search for pictures and print out a personalized tour, and a 3rd-floor restaurant offering an aerial view of London—although the inflated prices (meals around £15) will limit most visitors to coffee. To see the paintings in historical order, take the escalator in the Ondaatje Wing to the top floor. *(St. Martin's Pl., at the start of Charing Cross Rd., Trafalgar Sq. ⊖Leicester Sq. or Charing Cross. ☎7312 2463; www.npg.org.uk. Wheelchair-accessible on Orange St. Open M-W and Sa-Su 10am-6pm, Th-F 10am-8:50pm. Admission free; special exhibitions up to £6. Audio guides £2. Lectures Tu, Th, and Sa-Su 1:10 and 3pm; free, but popular events require tickets, available from the information desk. Talks Th 7pm; free-£3. Live classical and jazz music every F 6:30pm; free.)*

BRITISH MUSEUM. With 50,000 items from all corners of the globe, the magnificent collection is undermined by a chaotic layout and poor labeling. Overall, the experience is an odd combination of Victorian-era exoticization of the foreign and more modern, PC multicultural reverence. That said, the building is magnificent, and the objects themselves are fascinating. Most people don't even make it past the main floor, but they should—the galleries upstairs and downstairs are some of the best. *(Great Russell St. ⊖Tottenham Ct. Rd., Russell Sq., or Holborn. ☎7323 8299; www.thebritishmuseum.ac.uk. Wheelchair-accessible. Great Court open M-W and Su 9am-6pm, Th-Sa 9am-11pm (9pm in winter); galleries open daily 10am-5:30pm, selected galleries open Th-F until 8pm. Free; £3 suggested donation. Temporary exhibitions around £5, concessions £3.50. Free tours daily 12:30pm from the Enlightenment Desk. 90min. "Highlights Tour" daily 10:30am, 1, 3pm. Advance booking recommended; £8, concessions £5. Various other themed tours run throughout the week; check website or info desk for details. Audio guide £3.50. MC/V.)*

VICTORIA AND ALBERT MUSEUM. As the largest museum of decorative (and not-so-decorative) arts in the world, the V&A rivals the British Museum for the sheer size and diversity of its holdings—befitting an institution dedicated to displaying "the fine and applied arts of all countries, all styles, all periods." Unlike the British Museum, the V&A's documentation is consistently excellent and thorough. Interactive displays, hi-tech touchpoints, and engaging activities ensure that the goodies won't become boring. Staff shortages can lead to the temporary closure of less-popular galleries without notice; it's best to call in advance. If you really want to see something in a cordoned-off gallery, try asking politely at the main entrance info desk; they may be convinced to send someone along to give you a private viewing. Themed itineraries available at the desk can help streamline your visit, and **Family Trail** cards suggest kid-friendly routes through the museum. *(Main entrance on Cromwell Rd., wheelchair-accessible entrance on Exhibition Rd. ❷South Kensington. ☎ 7942 2000; www.vam.ac.uk. Wheelchair-accessible. Open daily 10am-5:45pm, plus W and last F of month until 10pm. Admission free; additional charge for some special exhibits. Tours meet at rear of main entrance; free. Introductory tours daily 10:30, 11:30am, 1:30, 3:30pm, plus W 4:30pm. British gallery tours daily 12:30, 2:30pm. Focus tours W 7:30pm. Subjects change regularly. Talks and events meet at rear of main entrance. Gallery talks Th 1pm and Su 3pm, 45-60min.; free. Talks and tours W from 6:30pm; last F of month also draws a young artistic crowd with live performances, guest DJs, late-night exhibition openings, bar, and food.)*

TATE BRITAIN. Tate Britain is the foremost collection on British art from 1500 to the present, including pieces from foreign artists working in Britain and Brits working abroad. There are four Tate Galleries in England; this is the original Tate, opened in 1897 to house Sir Henry Tate's collection of "modern" British art and later expanded to include a gift from famed British painter J.M.W. Turner. Turner's modest donation of 282 oils and 19,000 watercolors can make the museum feel like one big tribute to the man. The annual and always controversial ◧ **Turner Prize** for contemporary visual art is still given here, the displays about which are worth a visit. Four contemporary British artists are nominated for the $40,000 prize; their shortlisted works go on show from late October through late January. *(Millbank, near Vauxhall Bridge, in Westminster. ❷Pimlico. Information ☎ 7887 8008, exhibition booking (M-F) 7887 8888; www.tate.org.uk. Wheelchair access via Clore Wing. Open daily 10am-5:50pm, last admission 5pm. Free; special exhibitions £3-9.50. Audio guide free. Tours: "Art from 1500-1800" 11am; "1800-1900" M-F noon; "Turner" M-F 2pm; "1900-2005" M-F 3pm; "1500-2005" Sa-Su noon and 3pm; all free. Regular events include "Painting of the Month Lectures" (15 min.) M 1:15pm and Sa 2:30pm; occasional "Friday Lectures" F 1pm; "Slide Lectures" Sa 1pm.)*

BY NEIGHBORHOOD

THE CITY OF LONDON

◧ **MUSEUM OF LONDON.** Located in the southwest corner of the Barbican complex, the Museum of London resembles an industrial fortress from the outside. Once inside, the engrossing collection traces the history of London from its Roman foundations to the present day, cleverly incorporating architectural history, including the adjacent ruins of the ancient **London Wall.** *(London Wall. Enter through the Barbican or from Aldersgate; wheelchair users take elevator at Aldersgate entrance. ❷Bank or Barbican. ☎ 08704 443 852; www.museumoflondon.org.uk. Open M-Sa 10am-5:50pm, Su noon-5:50pm. Last admission 5:30pm. Free. Audio guides £2. Frequent demonstrations, talks, and guided walks; free-£10.)*

BANK OF ENGLAND MUSEUM. The Bank itself is only available to those on business; to get to the museum, you will be shuttled by security attendants. The museum traces the history of the Bank from its foundation (1694) to the present day. Mini-displays showcase items like the Bank's official silver and German firebomb casings. *(Bartholomew Ln. ❷Bank. ☎ 7601 5545; www.bankofengland.co.uk. Wheelchair-accessible. Open M-F 10am-5pm. Free.)*

GUILDHALL ART GALLERY. Devoted to displaying the City's art collection, the walls are home to numerous portraits of former Lord Mayors. Downstairs is a fine collection of Victorian and pre-Raphaelite art that includes works by Stevens, Poynter, Rossetti, and Millais. *(Guildhall Yard, off Gresham St. ❷Moorgate or Bank. ☎ 7332 3700; www.guildhall-art-gallery.org.uk. Wheelchair-accessible. Open M-Sa 10am-5pm, last admission 4:30pm; Su noon-4pm, last admission 3:45pm. Free F all day, M-Th and Sa-Su after 3:30pm; otherwise £2.50, concessions £1, children free.)*

CLERKENWELL AND HOLBORN

■ **THE COURTAULD INSTITUTE GALLERIES.** The Courtauld's small but outstanding collection ranges from 14th-century Italian icons to 20th-century abstractions. Works are arranged by collector, not chronologically, so don't fret if you think you skipped a few hundred years. The undisputed gems of the collection are from the Impressionist and Post-Impressionist periods: Manet's *A Bar at the Follies Bergères*, van Gogh's *Self-Portrait with Bandaged Ear*, and a room devoted to Degas bronzes. *(In Somerset House. Strand, just east of Waterloo Bridge.* ⊖*Charing Cross or Temple.* ☎ *7420 9400; www.courtauld.ac.uk. Wheelchair-accessible. Open daily 10am-6pm. Last admission 5:15pm. 1hr. tours held Sa 2:30pm. £5, concession £4. Tours £6.50, concessions £6, including admission. Free M 10am-2pm. Lunchtime talks free with admission.)*

THE GILBERT COLLECTION. The Gilbert Collection of Decorative Arts opened in 2000 and houses some of the more exquisite objects in any London museum. The collection's 800 pieces fall into three categories: mosaics, gold- and silver-work, and snuffboxes. To fully appreciate the craftsmanship of these works, pick up a complimentary magnifying glass at the front desk, where you can also get a free audio guide. *(In Somerset House. Strand, just east of Waterloo Bridge.* ⊖*Charing Cross or Temple.* ☎ *7420 9400; www.gilbert-collection.org.uk. Wheelchair-accessible. Last admission 5:15pm. £5, concessions £4. 1hr. tours held Sa 2:30pm. £6.50, concessions £6, including admission.)*

SIR JOHN SOANE'S MUSEUM. Eccentric architect John Soane let his imagination run free when designing this intriguing museum for his own collection of art and antiquities. Framed by endlessly mirrored walls, items range from the mummified corpse of his wife's dog to an extraordinary sarcophagus of Seti I, for which Soane personally outbid the British Museum. *(13 Lincoln's Inn Fields.* ⊖*Holborn.* ☎ *1405 2107. Open Tu-Sa 10am-5pm, 1st Tu of month also 6-9pm. Free; £1 donation requested. Tours Sa 2:30pm, tickets sold from 2pm. £3, students free.)*

KENSINGTON AND EARL'S COURT

■ **SCIENCE MUSEUM.** Dedicated to the Victorian ideal of progress, the Science Museum focuses on the transformative power of technology in all its guises. Breeze through the entrance hall on your way to the **Welcome Wing.** Highlights include **Who am I?,** the **Flight Lab,** and the **Science of Art and Medicine.** *(Exhibition Rd.* ⊖*South Kensington.* ☎ *08708 704 868, IMAX 08708 704 771; www.sciencemuseum.org.uk. Wheelchair-accessible. Open daily 10am-6pm. Free. Audio guides cover Power, Space, and Making the Modern World; £3.50 each. IMAX shows usually every 75min., daily 10:45am-5pm; £7.50, concessions £6. Call to book and confirm showtimes. Online booking available. Daily demonstrations and workshops in the basement galleries and theater. MC/V.)*

NATURAL HISTORY MUSEUM. Architecturally the most impressive of the South Kensington trio, this cathedral-like Romanesque museum has been a favorite with Londoners since 1880. Shudder from **Creepy Crawlies** through to the **Dinosaur** galleries, making sure to swing by the **blue whale** at some point. *(Cromwell Rd.* ⊖*South Kensington.* ☎ *7942 5000; www.nhm.ac.uk. Wheelchair-accessible. Open M-Sa 10am-5:50pm, Su 11am-5:50pm; last admission 5:30pm. Closed Dec. 24 to Dec. 30. Admission free; special exhibits usually £5, concessions £3. MC/V.)*

THE SOUTH BANK

■ **SAATCHI GALLERY.** Charles Saatchi, famous for supporting provocative young artists, remains true to his mission in this space. County Hall's wood-paneled rooms showcase some of the most innovative contemporary Britart. Focused on Saatchi's own collection, the uncompromising gallery is not for the faint-hearted. *(County Hall.* ⊖*Waterloo or Westminster.* ☎ *7823 2363; www.saatchi-gallery.co.uk. Open M-Th and Su 10am-8pm, F-Sa 10am-10pm. £9, concessions £6.75.)*

LONDON

IMPERIAL WAR MUSEUM. Massive naval guns guard the entrance to the building, formerly the infamous asylum known as Bedlam. The best and most publicized display is on the 3rd floor: the **Holocaust Exhibition** provides an honest and poignant look at all the events surrounding the tragedy. (Not recommended for children under 14.) On the 4th floor, **Crimes Against Humanity** is a sobering interactive display with a 30min. film at the back. (Lambeth Rd., Lambeth. ⊖Lambeth North or Elephant & Castle. ☎7416 5320, recorded info 7416 5000; www.iwm.org.uk. Open daily 10am-6pm. Free. Audio guide £3, concessions £2.50.)

DESIGN MUSEUM. Housed in an arrestingly white Art Deco riverfront building, this contemporary museum's installations fit right into the cool surroundings. You might find anything from avante-garde furniture pieces to galleries on big-name graphic designers. (28 Shad Thames, Butlers Wharf. ⊖Tower Hill or London Bridge. ☎7403 6933; www.designmuseum.org. Wheelchair-accessible. Open daily 10am-5:45pm. Last entry 5:15pm. £6, concessions £4.)

THE WEST END

■ **ROYAL ACADEMY OF ARTS.** Housed in Burlington House, Piccadilly's only surviving aristocratic mansion, the Academy showcases tomorrow's contemporary stars. The Summer Exhibition (June-Aug.), held every year since 1769, is open-submission, providing an unparalleled range in every medium, much of which is available for purchase. On Friday nights, the museum stays open late with free jazz in the Friends Room after 6:30pm and candlelit suppers in the cafe. (Burlington House, Piccadilly. ⊖Piccadilly Cir. or Green Park. ☎7300 8000; www.royalacademy.org.uk. Wheelchair-accessible. Open M-Th and Sa-Su 10am-6pm, F 10am-10pm. Free.)

■ **THE PHOTOGRAPHERS' GALLERY.** This is one of London's only public galleries devoted entirely to camerawork. Two exhibitions run concurrently at the larger location (No. 5). Frequent gallery talks, book readings, and film screenings are free; occasional photographers' talks may charge admission. (5 and 8 Great Newport St. ⊖Leicester Sq. or Covent Garden. ☎7831 1772; www.photonet.org.uk. Partially wheelchair-accessible. Open M-Sa 11am-6pm, Su noon-6pm. Free.)

INSTITUTE OF CONTEMPORARY ARTS (ICA). In the grand Carlton House Terrace, the ICA is London's center for avant-garde art and hip contemporary artists. (The Mall. ⊖Charing Cross or Piccadilly Cir. ☎7930 0493; www.ica.org.uk. Open M noon-11pm, Tu-Sa noon-1am, Su noon-10:30pm; galleries close 7:30pm. "Day membership," giving access to galleries, cafe, and bar M-F £1.50, concessions £1; Sa-Su £2, concessions £1.50. Cinema £6.50, concessions £5.50; M-F before 5pm £5.50/4.50. No weekend concessions.)

THEATRE MUSEUM. The Theatre Museum is heaven for travelers interested in theater history and behind-the-scenes; the top floor covers the emergence of British dramatic and musical theater and has vintage props and 18th-century ticket stubs. The maze-like downstairs has costumes from famous shows like *Richard II* and shoes and costumes from the Russian Ballet. (Russell St. ⊖Covent Garden. ☎7943 4700; www.theatremuseum.org. Wheelchair-accessible. Open Tu-Sa 10am-6pm. Last admission 5:30pm. Free. Free guided tours noon, 2, 3:30pm. Make-up demos M-F 11:30am, 1, 2, 3:30pm; Sa noon, 4:30pm; Su 4:30pm.)

CHRISTIE'S. Like a museum but more crowded and with everything for sale, Christie's is the best of the auction houses. Open to the public on the days before an auction to display what's up for grabs, lots range from busts of Greek gods to Monets to sports memorabilia. Catalogues from £10. (8 King St. ⊖Green Park. There is a smaller branch at 85 Old Brompton St., in Kensington. ☎7839 9060; www.christies.com. Wheelchair-accessible. Open M-F 9am-5pm; during sales also Tu until 8pm and Su 2-5pm. Free.)

SOTHEBY'S. Before each auction, the items to be sold are displayed for viewing in the many galleries. Aristocratic Sotheby's is a busy place; auctions occur within days of each other. Each sale is accompanied by a glossy catalogue, from $10. *(34-35 New Bond St. ⊖Bond St. ☎7293 5000; www.sothebys.com. Wheelchair-accessible. Open for viewing M-F 9am-4:30pm, Sa and some Su noon-4pm. Free.)*

EAST LONDON

■ **WHITECHAPEL ART GALLERY.** Long the only artistic beacon in a culturally and materially impoverished area, Whitechapel is now at the forefront of a buzzing art scene. Its main purpose is to exhibit artists who live and work in the East End, but as emerging artists move to other areas of the city, such exhibitions are becoming less relevant. Thursday nights bring music, poetry readings, and film screenings, in addition to regular events and talks during the week. *(Whitechapel High St. ⊖Aldgate East. ☎7522 7888; www.whitechapel.org. Wheelchair-accessible. Open Tu-W and F-Su 11am-6pm, Th 11am-9pm. Gallery may close between installations; call in advance. Free.)*

■ **WHITE CUBE.** One of the gems of Hoxton Sq., this stark white building has showcased some of the biggest names in international contemporary art. White Cube has an impressive list of alums and featured exhibits, including heavyweights Chuck Close and Damien Hirst. *(48 Hoxton Sq. ⊖Old St. ☎7930 5373; www.whitecube.com. Wheelchair-accessible. Open Tu-Sa 10am-6pm. Sometimes closes for exhibit installation; call in advance. Free.)*

OTHER NEIGHBORHOODS

■ **CABINET WAR ROOMS.** From 1939 to 1945, what started as a government coal storage basement quickly became the bomb-proof nerve center of a nation at war. The day after the war ended in August 1945, the Cabinet War Rooms were abandoned, closed off, and left undisturbed for decades until their re-opening in 1984 by Margaret Thatcher. The display includes the ■**Churchill Museum,** with all sorts of Churchill's WWII artifacts. Generate all kinds of disruptive and noisy sound and graphics effects by selecting from the many dates along a giant interactive timeline. Check out August 6th, 1945, but don't say we didn't warn you. *(Clive Steps, far end of King Charles St., in Westminster. ⊖Westminster. ☎7930 6961; www.iwm.org.uk. Open daily 9:30am-6pm. Last admission 5pm. £10, students £8, under 16 free. MC/V.)*

■ **BRITISH LIBRARY GALLERIES.** Housed within the British Library (p. 109) is an appropriately stunning display of books, manuscripts, and related artifacts from around the world and throughout the ages. Displays are arranged by theme, and a rundown of highlights reads like some fantastic list of the most precious pages imaginable. Grab a free map at the main info desk. Highlights include the 2nd-century *Unknown Gospel,* the Beatles' hand-scrawled lyrics, a Gutenberg Bible, Joyce's handwritten draft of *Finnegan's Wake,* and pages from da Vinci's notebooks. *(96 Euston Rd., Bloomsbury. ⊖King's Cross St. Pancras. ☎7412 7332; www.bl.uk. Wheelchair-accessible. Open M and W-F 9:30am-6pm, Tu 9:30am-8pm, Sa 9:30am-5pm, Su 11am-5pm. Free. Audio guides £3.50, concessions £2.50.)*

■ **THE WALLACE COLLECTION.** Housed in palatial Hertford House, this stunning array of paintings, porcelain, and armor was bequeathed to the nation by the widow of Sir Richard Wallace in 1897. Excellent daily gallery tours will ensure that you see a good overview of the collection. *(Hertford House, Manchester Sq., in Marylebone and Regent's Park. ⊖Bond St. or Marble Arch. ☎7563 9500; www.the-wallace-collection.org.uk. Wheelchair-accessible. Open M-Sa 10am-5pm, Su noon-5pm. 1hr. tours daily at 1pm; W and Sa also 11:30am and 3pm, Su 1 pm and 3pm; free. Talks M-F 1pm and occasional Sa 11:30am; free. Free; £2 suggested donation. Audio guides £3.)*

THE IVEAGH BEQUEST. The impressive Iveagh collection in Kenwood House was bequeathed to the nation by the Earl of Iveagh, who purchased the estate in 1922. Highlights include *The Guitar Player*—one of 35 Vermeers in the world—and Rembrandt's compelling self-portraits. *(Kenwood House, in North London. Road access from Hampstead Ln. Walk or take bus #210 from North End Way or Spaniard's Rd., or from* ⊖*Archway or Golders Green (zone 3).* ☎ *8348 1286. Wheelchair-accessible. Open Apr.-Sept. M-Tu, Th, and Sa 10am-6pm; W and F 10:30am-6pm; Oct. closes 5pm; Nov.-Mar. closes 4pm. Free. Audio guide £3.50, concessions £2.60, children £1.75.)*

🎭 ENTERTAINMENT

Although West End ticket prices are through the roof and the quality of some shows is highly questionable, the city that brought the world Shakespeare, the Sex Pistols, and even Andrew Lloyd Webber still retains its originality and theatrical edge. London is a city of immense talent, full of student up-and-comers, experimental writers, and undergrounders who don't care about the neon lights.

CINEMA

The heart of the celluloid monster is Leicester Square, where releases premiere a day before hitting the city's chains. The dominant cinema chain is **Odeon** (☎ 0870 5050 007; www.odeon.co.uk). Tickets to West End cinemas cost £8-10+; weekday matinees are cheaper. For less mainstream offerings, try the ▨**Electric Cinema,** 191 Portobello Rd., for the combination of baroque stage splendor and the buzzing effects of a big screen. For an extra-special experience, choose a luxury armchair or two-seat sofa. (⊖Ladbroke Grove. ☎ 7908 9696; www.the-electric.co.uk. Front 3 rows M £5, Tu-Su £10; regular tickets M £7.50, Tu-Su £12.50; 2-seat sofa M £20, Tu-Su £30. Double bills Su 2pm £5/7.50/20. Wheelchair-accessible. MC/V.) ▨**Riverside Studios,** Crisp Rd., shows a wide range of excellent foreign and classic films. (⊖Hammersmith. ☎ 8237 1111; www.riversidestudios.co.uk. £6.50, concessions £5.50.) The ▨**National Film Theatre (NFT)** screens a mind-boggling array of films—six movies hit the three screens every evening, starting around 6pm (South Bank, underneath Waterloo Bridge. ⊖Waterloo, Embankment, or Temple. ☎ 7928 3232; www.bfi.org.uk/nft. £7.50, concessions £5.70.)

COMEDY

On any given night, you'll find at least ten comedy clubs in operation: check listings in *Time Out* or a newspaper. Summertime visitors should note that London empties of comedians in **August,** when most head to Edinburgh to take part in the annual festivals (p. 526); that means **July** provides plenty of comedians trying out material. ▨**Comedy Store,** 1a Oxendon St., is the UK's top comedy club and sower of the seeds that gave rise to *Ab Fab, Whose Line is it Anyway?,* and *Blackadder.* Tuesdays are "Cutting Edge" (current events-based satire), Wednesdays and Sundays *Comedy Store Players* improv, Thursdays through Saturdays standup. (⊖Piccadilly Circus. ☎ 7839 6642, tickets 08700 602 340; www.thecomedystore.biz. Shows Tu-Su 8pm, plus F-Sa midnight. 18+. Tu-W, F (midnight), and Su £13, concessions £8. Th-F early show and Sa £15. Box office open Tu-Su 6:30-9:30pm, F-Sa 6:30pm-1:30am. 100 seats always available at the door. AmEx/MC/V.) North London's ▨**Canal Cafe Theatre,** Delamere Terr., is one of the few comedy venues to specialize in sketch as opposed to stand-up. "Newsrevue" (Th-Sa 9:30pm and Su 9pm), is London's longest-running comedy sketch show, a hilarious satire of weekly current events. (Above the Bridge House pub. ⊖Warwick Ave. ☎ 7289 6054. Box office opens 30min. before performances. Weekly changing shows W-Sa 7:30 and 9:30pm; £5, concessions £4. Newsrevue £8, concessions £6. Both shows £12. £1 membership included in ticket price.)

DANCE

The **Barbican Theatre** at Barbican Hall (see below) hosts touring contemporary companies. The **Peacock Theatre,** Portugal St., in Holborn, has a program that leans toward contemporary dance, ballet, popular dance-troupe shows, and children- and family-geared productions. (⊖Holborn. ☎08707 370 337; www.sadler- swells.com. Some wheelchair-accessible seats can be booked 24hr. in advance; £9. Box office open M-Sa 10am-6:30pm, performance days 10am-8:30pm. £10-35; cheaper rates M-Th and Sa matinee. Standby tickets 1hr. before show £15; conces- sions available. Cheapest tickets at box office; fees for telephone and online book- ing. AmEx/MC/V.) Dancing within the Royal Opera House, the **Royal Ballet** is considered one of the world's premiere companies. (See Royal Opera, p. 125 for info.) Recently rebuilt, historic **Sadler's Wells**, Rosebery Ave., in Clerkwell, remains London's premier dance theater, with everything from classical ballet to contem- porary tap to the occasional opera. Recent performances have included Matthew Bourne's *Swan Lake*—which first premiered at Sadler's Wells in 1995. (⊖Angel. Exit left from the Tube, cross the road, and take the 2nd right on Rosebery Ave. Sadler's Wells Express (SWX) bus to Waterloo via Farringdon and Victoria leaves 8min. after the end of each mainstage evening show; £1.50, £1 with period Travel- card. Those arriving by regular bus can have their fare refunded (and get cash for the journey home) at the box office. ☎7863 8000; www.sadlerswells.com. Wheel- chair-accessible. Box office open M-Sa 9am-8:30pm. £6-45; stand-by concessions £15 1hr. before curtain; cash only. AmEx/MC/V.)

MUSIC

CLASSICAL

▨ **Barbican Hall,** Silk St. (☎0845 120 7500; www.barbican.org.uk), in City of London. ⊖Barbican or Moorgate. The resident **London Symphony Orchestra** plays here fre- quently; the hall also hosts concerts by international orchestras, jazz artists, and world musicians. Call in advance for tickets, especially for popular events. The online and phone box office sometimes have good last-minute options. Tickets £5-35.

English National Opera, London Coliseum, St. Martin's Ln. (☎7632 8300; www.eno.org), in Covent Garden. ⊖Charing Cross or Leicester Sq. All performances in English. Box office open M-Sa 10am-8pm. Purchase best-available, standby student tickets (£12.50) and balcony tickets (£8) 3hr. before show. Call to verify daily availabil- ity. Wheelchair-accessible. AmEx/MC/V.

Holland Park Theatre, Holland Park (box office ☎08452 309 769; www.rbkc.gov.uk/ hollandpark), in Kensington and Earl's Court. ⊖High St. Kensington or Holland Park. Open-air performance space in the atmospheric ruins of Holland House. Performances June to early Aug. Tu-Sa 7:30pm, occasional matinees Sa 2:30pm. Box office in the Old Stable Block just to the west of the opera; open from late Mar. M-Sa 10am-6pm or 30min. after curtain. Tickets £21, £38 (£35 for students during select performances), and £43. Special allocation of tickets for wheelchair users. AmEx/MC/V.

Royal Albert Hall, Kensington Gore (☎7589 8212; www.royalalberthall.com), in Kensington and Earl's Court. ⊖High St. Kensington. Best known for the ▨ **Proms,** the summer season of classical music (mid-July to mid-Sept.) Box office open daily 9am-9pm. MC/V.

Royal Opera, Bow St. (☎7304 4000; www.royaloperahouse.org), in Covent Garden. ⊖Covent Garden. Lavish, traditional productions with recent contemporary ventures. Prices for the best seats (orchestra stalls) top £75, but standing room and restricted-view seating in the upper balconies run for as little as £5. For some performances, 100 seats are available for £10; apply at least 2 weeks in advance at www.travelex.royalopera- house.org.uk. 67 seats available from 10am on day of performance, limit 1 per person. Box office open M-Sa 10am-8pm. AmEx/MC/V.

LONDON

JAZZ

▨ **Jazz Café,** 5 Parkway (☎ 7344 0044; www.jazzcafe.co.uk), in North London. ⊖Camden Town. Shows can be pricey at this night spot, but the top roster of jazz, hip-hop, funk, and Latin performers (£10-30) explains Jazz Café's popularity. Jazzy DJs spin on club nights following the show F-Sa until 2am. Partially wheelchair-accessible. Cover F-Sa £8-9, with flyer £5; Su £3, with musical instrument £1. Open M-Th 7pm-1am, F-Sa 7pm-2am, Su 7pm-midnight. MC/V.

Spitz, 109 Commercial St. (☎ 7392 9032; www.spitz.co.uk), in East London. ⊖Liverpool St. Fresh range of live music, from klezmer, jazz, and world music to indie, pop, and rap. All profits support worthy causes, from global refugee health to green-space preservation, through the Dandelion Trust. Free music in the bistro 4 nights per week. Cover free-£15. Upstairs doors open at 7pm most nights; venue open M-W 7pm-midnight, Th-Sa 7pm-1am, Su 4-10:30pm. MC/V.

606 Club, 90 Lots Rd. (☎ 7352 5953; www.606club.co.uk), in Chelsea. ⊖Sloane Sq., then bus #11 or 22. Look for the brick arch labeled 606 opposite the "Fire Access" garage across the street; ring the doorbell to be let in downstairs. The intrepid will be rewarded with brilliant British and European jazz in a smoky, candlelit basement venue. Reservations highly recommended. Cover (added to the food bill) M-Th £7-8, F-Sa £9, Su £8. M-W doors open 7:30pm, 1st band 8-10:30pm, 2nd 10:45pm-1:00am; Th-Sa doors open 8pm, music 9:30pm-1:30am; Su (vocalists) doors open 8pm, music 9pm-midnight. Music continues until the musicians don't want to play anymore. MC/V.

ROCK AND POP

▨ **The Water Rats,** 328 Grays Inn Rd, in Bloomsbury. (☎ 7837 7269). ⊖King's Cross St. Pancras. Pub-cafe by day, stomping ground for top new talent by night (from 8pm). Oasis was signed here after their first London gig. Cover £5-6, with band flyer £4-5. Music M-Sa 8pm to late (headliner 9:45pm). MC/V with £7 minimum.

Carling Academy, Brixton, 211 Stockwell Rd. (☎ 7771 3000; www.brixton-academy.co.uk), in South London. ⊖Brixton. Art Deco ex-cinema with a pitched floor. Named *Time Out's* "Live Venue of the Year" in 2004. Box office open only on performance evenings; order online or by telephone, or go to the Carling Academy, Islington box office. (16 Parkfield Street, Islington. Open M-Sa noon-4pm.) Tickets generally £20-30.

London Astoria (LA1), 157 Charing Cross Rd. (info ☎ 8963 0940, 24hr. ticket line ☎ 08701 500 044; www.londonastoria.com), in Soho. ⊖Tottenham Ct. Rd. Formerly a pickle factory, strip club, and music hal. Now a full-time rock venue. Now basking in an air of somewhat faded glory, the 2000-person venue is most popular for G-A-Y club night (p. 132). Box office open M-Sa 10am-6pm. AmEx/MC/V.

THEATER

LONG-RUNNING SHOWS (WEST END)

London's West End is dominated by musicals and plays that run for years, if not decades. For discount tickets, head to the **tkts** booth in Leicester Sq. (⊖Leicester Sq. www.tkts.co.uk. Most musicals around £23, plays £20-22; up to £2.50 booking fee per ticket. Open M-Sa 10am-7pm, Su noon-3pm. MC/V.) It is nearly always cheaper to go to the theater itself, especially for less popular shows; you are likely to get a better seat and pay less for same-day, rush, or concession tickets. **Billy Elliot: The Musical** is a new musical based on the movie, with music by Elton John. (Victoria Palace Theatre, Victoria St. ⊖Victoria. ☎ 08708 955 577. Shows M-Sa 7:30pm, plus Th and Sa 2:30pm. £17.50-50. Call about limited same-day student standby tickets. AmEx/MC/V.) **The Lion King** is the same old script, with gorgeous new puppets. (Lyceum Theatre, Wellington St. ⊖Covent Garden. ☎ 08702 439 000;

www.thelionking.co.uk. Shows Tu-Sa 7:30pm, plus W and Sa 2pm; Su 3pm. £20-47.50. Limited same-day seats and standing-room tickets released at noon. Ask about student discounts. Max. 2 tickets in person at box office. AmEx/MC/V.) **Mamma Mia!** is by far the best of the "pop's greatest hits"-style megashows. Nearly always sold out. (Prince of Wales Theatre, Coventry St. ✪Leicester Sq. Box office ☎08708 500 393, agents 0870 264 3333; www.mamma-mia.com. Shows M-Th 7:30pm; F 5, 8:30pm; Sa 3, 7:30pm. £25-49. Check the box office daily for returns. AmEx/MC/V.) New to the 2005 season, **Mary Poppins** has gotten rave reviews. (Prince Edward Theatre, Old Compton St. ✪Leicester Sq. ☎08708 509 191; www.marypoppinsthemusical.co.uk. Shows M-Sa 7:30pm, plus Th and Sa 2:30pm. £15-55. Same-day tickets released at noon; limit 2 per person. AmEx/MC/V.) With songs like "Springtime for Hitler," **The Producers** is as irreverent as it is entertaining. (Theatre Royal, Drury Ln. ✪Covent Garden. ☎08708 901 109. Shows M-Sa 7:30pm, plus W and Sa 2:30pm. £10-49. AmEx/MC/V.)

REPERTORY

■ **Shakespeare's Globe Theatre,** 21 New Globe Walk (☎7401 9919; www.shakespeares-globe.org), in the South Bank. ✪Southwark or London Bridge. Stages plays by Shakespeare and his contemporaries. Choose among 3 covered tiers of hard, backless wooden benches or stand as a "groundling"; come 30min. before the show to get a good place. Wheelchair-accessible. Performances mid-May to late Sept. Tu-Sa 7:30pm, Su 6:30pm; June-Sept. also Tu-Sa 2pm, Su 1pm. Box office open M-Sa 10am-6pm, 8pm on performance days. Seats from £12, concessions from £10; yard £5. Raingear £2.50.

■ **National Theatre,** South Bank (info ☎7452 3400, box office 7452 3000; www.nationaltheatre.org.uk), in the South Bank. ✪Waterloo or Embankment. Founded by Laurence Olivier, the National Theatre opened in 1976 and has been at the forefront of British theater ever since. Wheelchair-accessible. Box office open M-Sa 10am-8pm. Complicated pricing scheme that changes from show to show. Contact box office for details. Tickets typically start at £10. MC/V.

Royal Court Theatre, Sloane Sq. (☎7565 5000; www.royalcourttheatre.com), in Chelsea. ✪Sloane Sq. Recognized by *The New York Times* as a standout theater in Europe. Wheelchair-accessible. Main auditorium £7.50-27.50, concessions £9; standing room 10p from 1hr. before curtain. 2nd venue upstairs £12.50-16, concessions £9. M all seats £7.50. Advance-purchase and standby tickets available. Box office open M-Sa 10am-7:45pm, closes 6pm non-performance weeks. AmEx/MC/V.

"OFF-WEST END"

■ **The Almeida,** Almeida St. (☎7359 4404; www.almeida.co.uk), in North London. ✪Angel or Highbury and Islington. The top fringe theater in London, if not the world. Shows M-Sa 7:30pm, Sa matinees 3pm. Wheelchair-accessible. Tickets from £10. MC/V.

■ **Donmar Warehouse,** 41 Earlham St. (☎08700 606 624; www.donmarwarehouse.com), in Covent Garden. ✪Covent Garden. Artistic director Sam Mendes transformed this gritty space into one of the best theaters in the country. Tickets £13-29; students and under-18 standby 30min. before curtain £12; £5 standing-room tickets available once performance sells out. Box office open M-Sa 10am-7:30pm. AmEx/MC/V.

Royal Academy of Dramatic Arts (RADA), 62-64 Gower St.(☎7908 4800; www.rada.org), entrance on Malet St; in Bloomsbury. ✪Goodge St. A cheaper alternative to the West End, Britain's most famous drama school has 3 on-site theaters. Wheelchair-accessible. £3-10, concessions £2-7.50. Regular Foyer events during the academic year including plays, music, and readings M-Th 7 or 7:30pm (free-£4). Box office open M-F 10am-6pm, until 7:30pm performance nights. AmEx/MC/V.

Old Vic, Waterloo Rd. (☎ 7369 1722; www.oldvictheatre.com), in the South Bank. ⊖Waterloo. One of London's most historic and beautiful theaters. Box office M-Sa 10am-7:30pm. MC/V.

☐ SHOPPING

London has long been considered one of the fashion capitals of the world. Unfortunately, London features as many underwhelming chain stores as it does one-of-a-kind boutiques, as on **Oxford Street.** The truly budget-conscious should forget buying altogether and stick to window-shopping for ideas in **Knightsbridge** and **Regent Street.** Vintage shopping in **Notting Hill** is a viable alternative; however, steer clear, once again, of Oxford St., where so-called "vintage" clothing was probably made in 2002 and sells for twice as much as the regular line.

MAJOR CHAINS

As in any large city, London retail is dominated by chains. Fortunately, local shoppers are picky enough that buying from a chain doesn't mean abandoning the style for which Londoners are famed. Most chains have a flagship on or near **Oxford Street,** a second branch in **Covent Garden,** and another on **King's Road** or **Kensington High Street.** Branches often keep different hours, but usually stores are open 10am-7pm on days and noon-5pm on weekends. Popular London chains include **FCUK, Jigsaw, Karen Millen, Mango, Monsoon, Topshop/Topman,** and **Zara.** For books, head to **Waterstone's.**

Harrods, 87-135 Brompton Rd. (☎ 7730 1234; www.harrods.com), in Knightsbridge and Belgravia. ⊖Knightsbridge. The only thing bigger than the bewildering store is the mark-up on the goods—no wonder only tourists and oil sheikhs actually shop here. Wheelchair-accessible. Open M-Sa 10am-7pm, Su noon-6pm. AmEx/MC/V.

Harvey Nichols, 109-125 Knightsbridge (☎ 7235 5000; www.harveynichols.com), in Knightsbridge and Belgravia. ⊖Knightsbridge. Rue St-Honoré and Fifth Avenue all rolled up into 5 floors of fashion. Wheelchair-accessible. Open M-F 10am-8pm, Sa 10am-7pm, Su noon-6pm. AmEx/MC/V.

Selfridges, 400 Oxford St. (☎ 0870 837 7377; www.selfridges.com), in the West End. ⊖Bond St. The total department store covers everything from traditional tweeds to space-age clubwear. Massive Jan. and July sales. Wheelchair-accessible. Open M-F 10am-8pm, Sa 9:30am-8pm, Su noon-6pm. AmEx/MC/V.

Liberty, 210-220 Regent St. (☎ 7734 1234; www.liberty.co.uk), main entrance on Gt. Marlborough St., in the West End. ⊖Oxford Circus. The focus on top-quality design and handcrafts makes it more like a giant boutique than a full-blown department store. Famous for custom fabric prints. Wheelchair-accessible. Open M-W and F-Sa 10am-7pm, Th 10am-8pm, Su noon-6pm. AmEx/MC/V.

Fortnum & Mason, 181 Piccadilly (☎ 7734 8040; www.fortnumandmason.co.uk), in the West End. ⊖Green Park or Piccadilly Circus. Gourmet department store provides quality foodstuffs fit for a queen. Wheelchair-accessible. Open M-Sa 10am-6:30pm, Su noon-6pm (food hall and patio restaurant only). AmEx/MC/V.

STREET MARKETS

Better for people-watching than hardcore shopping, street markets may not bring you the big goods but are a much better alternative to a day on Oxford St. **Portobello Road Markets** include a general foods, antiques, and secondhand clothing. In order to see it all, come Friday or Saturday when everything is sure to be open. (⊖Notting Hill Gate; also Westbourne Park and Ladroke Grove. Stalls set their own times. General hours M-W and F-Sa 8am-6:30pm, Th 8am-1pm.) ■**Camden Pas-**

sage **Market** is more for looking than for buying—London's premier antique shops line these charming alleyways. (Islington High St., in North London. ⊖Angel. Turn right from the Tube; it's the alleyway that starts behind "The Mall" antiques gallery on Upper St. Stalls open W and Sa 8:30am-6pm; some stores open daily, but W is by far the best day to go.) Its overrun sibling **Camden Markets** mostly includes cheap club gear and tourist trinkets; avoid the canal areas. The best bet is to stick with the **Stables Market,** farthest north from the Tube station. (Make a sharp right out of the Tube station to reach Camden High St., where most of the markets start. All stores are accessible from ⊖Camden Town. Many stores open daily 10am-6pm; Stables open F-Su.) **Brixton Market** has London's best selection of Afro-Caribbean fruits, vegetables, spices, and fish. (Along Electric Ave., Pope's Rd., and Brixton Station Rd., and inside markets in Granville Arcade and Market Row; in South London. ⊖Brixton. Open daily 8am-6pm; closes W at 3pm.) Formerly a wholesale vegetable market, ▨**Spitalfields** has become the best of the East End markets. On Sundays, the food shares space with rows of clothing by local independent designers. (Commercial St., in East London. ⊖Shoreditch (during rush hour), Liverpool St., or Aldgate East. Crafts market open M-F 11am-3:30pm, Su 10am-5pm. Antiques market open Th 9am-5pm. Organic market open F and Su 10am-5pm.) Crowds can be overwhelming; head to the **Sunday (Up) Market** for similar items in a calmer environment. (Housed in a portion of the old Truman Brewery just off Hanbury St., in East London. ⊖Shoreditch or Aldgate East. Open Su 10am-5pm.)

▨ NIGHTLIFE

From pubs to taverns to bars to clubs, London has all the nightlife that a person could want. First-time visitors may initially head to the **West End,** drawn by the flashy lights and pumping music of Leicester Sq. For a more authentic experience, head to the **East End** or **Brixton.** Soho's **Old Compton Street** is still the center of GLBT nightlife. Before heading out for the evening, make sure to plan **Night Bus** travel. Listings open past 11pm include local Night Bus routes. Night Buses in the West End are ubiquitous—head to Trafalgar Sq., Oxford St., or Piccadilly Circus.

PUBS

▨ **Ye Olde Cheshire Cheese,** Wine Office Ct. (☎7353 6170; www.yeoldecheshirecheese.com), in Holborn. By 145 Fleet St., not to be confused with The Cheshire Cheese on the other side of Fleet St. ⊖Blackfriars or

SPITALFIELDS

Alternately claustrophobia-inducing and invigorating, this hugely popular, bustling market in East London is widely regarded as the best in the area. With an impressive array of organic fruits and vegetables, homemade baked goods, and ethnic food vendors, Spitalfields is an eater's paradise.

Growing beyond its humble, farmer's market roots, though, Spitalfields has become one of the best spots to find clothing, jewelry, housewares, and art from trendy independent designers. On Sunday mornings, the rows of over 200 stalls are packed with fashion-conscious shoppers trolling for good finds.

With so many people, it's best to come prepared. Wear comfy shoes. Bring a bottle of water. Stretch. And please, don't be that girl taking your shirt off in the middle of the aisle in order to try on a potential purchase. Most designers showcase their selections in other parts of the city and will be happy to schedule a private appointment with you. Alternatively, the nearby **Laden Showroom** and Sunday **(Up)Market** display many of the same excellent finds as Spitalfields, but without the maddening crowds. Then again, the bustling atmosphere is part of the Spitalfields experience. *(Shoreditch or Liverpool St. Crafts market open M-F 11am-3:30pm, Su 10am-5pm. Organic market open F and Su 10am-5pm.)*

St. Paul's. Once a haunt of Johnson, Dickens, Mark Twain, and Theodore Roosevelt. Front open M-Sa 11am-11pm, Su noon-3pm. Cellar Bar open M-F noon-2:30pm, M-Th and Sa also 5:30-11pm. Chop Room open M-F noon-9:30pm, Sa noon-2:30pm and 6-9:30pm, Su noon-2:30pm. Johnson Room open M-F noon-2:30pm and 7-9:30pm. AmEx/MC/V.

■ **Fitzroy Tavern,** 16 Charlotte St. (☎7580 3714), in Bloomsbury. ⊖Goodge St. Popular with artists and writers, this pub now oozes with good-looking students. Comedy every W 8:30pm (£5). Other special events regularly. Open M-Sa 11am-11pm, Su noon-10:30pm. MC/V.

The Jerusalem Tavern, 55 Britton St. (☎7490 4281; www.stpetersbrewery.co.uk), in Clerkenwell. ⊖Farringdon. Ideal for an evening of intense conversation. The broad selection of ales rewards the adventuresome. Specialty ales (£2.40) like grapefruit, cinnamon, and apple. Open M-F 11am-11pm, Sa 5-11pm, Su 11am-5pm. MC/V.

The Troubadour, 265 Old Brompton Rd. (☎7370 1434; www.troubadour.co.uk), in Kensington and Earl's Court. ⊖Earl's Court. A combination pub/cafe/deli. Once upon a time, the likes of Bob Dylan, Joni Mitchell, and Paul Simon played in the intimate basement club, and the place retains a bohemian appeal. Meals £5.50-10. 2-for-1 mixed drinks in the cafe weekdays 4:30-7:30pm. Open daily 9am-midnight. MC/V.

Dog and Duck, 18 Bateman St. (☎7494 0697), in the West End. ⊖Tottenham Ct. Rd. The smallest and oldest pub in Soho. Open M-Sa noon-11pm, Su noon-10:30pm. Food served daily noon-3pm and 5-9pm. MC/V.

BARS

■ **Vibe Bar,** 91-95 Brick Ln. (☎7377 2899; www.vibe-bar.co.uk), in East London. ⊖Aldgate East or Liverpool St. Night Bus: hub at Liverpool St. Station. Plop down on a sofa or get there early for an outside table. Free Internet access. The youngish crowd grooves to hip-hop, soul, acoustic, and jazz. DJs spin M-Sa from 7:30pm, Su from 7pm. Cover F-Sa after 8pm £3.50. Open M-Th and Su 11am-11:30pm, F-Sa 11am-1am.

■ **Lab,** 12 Old Compton St. (☎7437 7820), in the West End. ⊖Leicester Sq. or Tottenham Ct. Rd. With restrooms for "bitches" and "bastards," the only thing this funky cocktail bar takes seriously is its stellar drink menu. DJs spin house and funk from 8pm nightly. Open M-Sa 4pm-midnight, Su 4pm-10:30pm. AmEx/MC/V.

Filthy MacNasty's Whiskey Cafe, 68 Amwell St. (☎7837 6067), in North London. ⊖Angel or King's Cross. Night Bus N10, N63, N73, N91, 390. Shane MacGowan, U2, and the Libertines have all played in this laid-back Irish pub. Live music and occasional literary readings add to the bad-boy-cum-intellectual atmosphere. Open M-Sa noon-11pm, Su noon-10:30pm.

22 Below, 22 Great Marlborough St. (☎0871 223 5531), in the West End. ⊖Oxford St. In a basement next to Cafe Libre and opposite Carnaby St. Entertaining Old Rope comedy nights, oversized fresh fruit martinis (£6-7), and a friendly, casual crowd will make it hard to pull yourself off the comfy leather couches. M comedy (£3). Open M-F 5pm-midnight, Sa 7:30pm-midnight. MC/V.

Big Chill Bar, Dray Walk (☎7392 9180; www.bigchill.net), off Brick Ln., in East London. ⊖Liverpool St. Night Bus: hub at Liverpool St. Station. DJs spin an eclectic mix every night, while famously friendly crowds chat it up on big leather couches and on the outdoor patio. Open M-Sa noon-midnight, Su noon-10:30pm. MC/V.

Bar Kick, 127 Shoreditch High St. (☎7739 8700); in East London. ⊖Old St. Night Bus hub at Liverpool St. Station, and N55, N243. A dream come true for "table football" aficionados. Tasty mixed drinks (mojitos £5) and a Continental influence. Wheelchair-accessible. Open M-W noon-11pm, Th-Sa noon-midnight, Su noon-7pm. AmEx/MC/V.

Trap, 201 Wardour St. (☎ 7434 3820, www.traplondon.com), in the West End. ⊖Oxford Circus or Tottenham Ct. Rd. Downstairs bar and dance floor is one of the only places in the West End to groove to hip-hop. Tu-W R&B DJ; Th soul, funk, disco; F R&B club night; Sa *Sintillate* mix. Wheelchair-accessible. Cover £10 Th-F after 10pm; Sa before 10pm £7, after 10pm £15.

The Langley, 5 Langley St. (☎ 7836 5005; www.latenightlondon.co.uk), in the West End. ⊖Covent Garden. Twentysomethings file in for happy hour deals (daily 5-7pm; mixed drinks £3.25, margaritas and martinis £4.25) then head to the back room dance floor, where DJs play mainstream pop and R&B. DJs Th-Sa from 9pm. Cover Th after 10pm £3; F-Sa after 10pm £5. Open M-Sa 4:30pm-1am, Su 4-10:30pm. AmEx/MC/V.

NIGHTCLUBS

▨ **Fabric,** 77a Charterhouse St. (☎ 7336 8898; www.fabriclondon.com), in Clerkenwell. ⊖Farringdon. Night Bus #242. The rather young crowd is generally dressed down. F "Fabric Live" (hip-hop, breakbeat, bass and drum); Sa house, techno, electro; Su **"DTPM Polysexual Night"** (house; www.dtpm.net). Cover F £12; Sa before 10pm with flyer £11, after 11pm £15. Wheelchair-accessible. Open F 9:30pm-5am, Sa 10pm-7am, Su 10pm-5am. MC/V at bar with £15 minimum.

▨ **Notting Hill Arts Club,** 21 Notting Hill Gate (☎ 7460 4459), in Notting Hill. ⊖Notting Hill Gate. Night Bus #94, 148, N207, 390. Not at all touristy, due to its non-descript appearance from the outside, and very chill. As the night goes on, the doormen operate a 1-in, 1-out policy. Get there early to claim some space and avoid a wait. Cover M after 9pm £4; Tu-Th after 8pm £5; F after 8pm £6; Sa-Su after 6pm £5. Open M-W 6pm-1am, Th-F 6pm-2am, Sa 4pm-2am, Su 4pm-12:30am. MC/V.

▨ **Ministry of Sound,** 103 Gaunt St. (☎ 7378 6528; www.ministryofsound.co.uk), in the South Bank. ⊖Elephant and Castle; take the exit for South Bank University. Night Bus N35, N133, N343. Mecca for serious clubbers worldwide. Dress code generally casual, but famously unsmiling door staff makes it sensible to err on the side of smartness: no tracksuits or trainers, especially on weekends. R&B F 10:30pm-5am; vocal house Sa 11pm-7am. Cover F £12, Sa £15.

Tongue&Groove, 50 Atlantic Rd. (☎ 7274 8600; www.tongueandgroove.org), in South London. ⊖Brixton. Un-self-consciously trendy club and bar so popular and narrow that people dance on the speakers. W US house; Th special guests and Euro house; F house-based mix of African, Cuban, and Brazilian vibes; Sa soulful house, jazz breaks, some disco; Su funk and electronica. Cover Th after 11pm £2; F-Sa after 10:30pm £3. Open M-W and Su 7pm-3am, Th-Sa 7pm-5am. MC/V with £10 minimum.

Aquarium, 256 Old St. (☎ 7251 6136), in East London. ⊖Old St., exit 3. Night Bus hub at Liverpool St. Station. This club may be miles from the beach, but that doesn't mean you can't go swimming. With a pool and jacuzzi, along with 4 bars and 2 chill-out rooms, events here are hilarious, campy affairs. Sa world-famous "Carwash" (retro-glam-funk fashionfest) 10pm-3:30am; tickets ☎08702 461 966; www.carwash.co.uk. Cover Th men before midnight £5, after midnight with flyer £8, women after midnight with flyer £5; F men £15, women £10; Sa in advance £12.50, at door £15.

Bar Rumba, 36 Shaftesbury Ave. (☎ 7287 6933; www.barrumba.co.uk), in the West End. ⊖Piccadilly Circus. Rumba draws a young crowd that makes good use of the industrial-strength interior for dancing. M **"This! 2"** is the biggest night. Cover M after 9pm £5; W after 10pm £5, students £3 all night; Th before 10pm £4, after 10pm £7; F before 11pm £6, after 11pm £8; Sa 10-11pm £5, after 11pm £10; Su £5, women free before 10pm. Open M-Tu variable hours, W 9pm-3am, Th 8:30pm-3am, F 10pm-4am, Sa 9pm-4am, Su 8pm-1am. MC/V with £10 minimum.

LONDON

Ghetto, Falconberg Crt. (☎ 7287 3726; www.ghetto-london.co.uk), in the West End. ⊖Tottenham Ct. Rd. Behind the Astoria on Tottenham Ct. Road. Squeezes alternative nightlife into Soho's trendy culture. Mixed crowd. Popular nights W **"NagNagNag"** (alternative pop and rock); F **"The Cock"** (gay night). Cover: M-Tu £3, with flyer £2; W £5, concessions £3; Th £4, with flyer £2; F £7/5; Sa £7/6; Su £6/5. Open M-W 10:30pm-3am, Th-Sa 10:30pm-5am, Su 10pm-3am.

The End, 16a West Central St. (☎ 7419 9199; www.endclub.com), in the West End. ⊖Tottenham Ct. Rd. Cutting-edge clubber's paradise, full of hard house and pumping dancing. Th ▨ **"Discotec"** (popular mixed/gay clubbing with cosmopolitan crowd); Sa **As One.** Wheelchair-accessible. Cover M £6; W before 11:30pm £5, after 11:30pm £6; Th before midnight £6, after midnight £8; F £10-13; Sa £15. Open M 10pm-3am, W 10:30pm-3am, Th-F 10pm-4am, Sa 6pm-3am. AmEx/MC/V with £10 minimum.

GAY AND LESBIAN

Many venues have Gay and Lesbian nights on a rotating basis. Check *TimeOut* and look for flyers/magazines floating around Soho: *The Pink Paper* (free; available from newsagents) and *Boyz* (www.boyz.co.uk), the main gay listings magazine for London. As well as the listings below, try "The Cock" at **Ghetto,** "Polysexual Night" at **Fabric,** or ▨"Discotec" at **The End.**

▨ **The Edge,** 11 Soho Sq. (☎ 7439 1313; www.edge.uk.com), in the West End. ⊖Oxford Circus or Tottenham Ct. Rd. A friendly, laid-back gay and lesbian drinking spot. DJs spin Tu-Sa, piano bar Tu-F, and dancing F-Sa. Cover F-Sa after 11pm £2. Open M-Sa noon-1am, Su noon-10:30pm. MC/V.

▨ **The Black Cap,** 171 Camden High St. (☎ 7428 2721; www.theblackcap.com), in North London. ⊖Camden Town. North London's most popular gay bar and cabaret is always buzzing. Draws a mixed crowd. Partially wheelchair-accessible. Cover for downstairs M-Th and Su before 11pm £2, after 11pm £3; F-Sa before 11pm £3, after 11pm £4. Food served daily noon-6pm. Open M-Th noon-2am, F-Sa noon-3am, Su noon-12:30am.

▨ **Escape Dance Bar,** 10a Brewer St. (☎ 7731 2626; www.kudosgroup.com), in the West End. ⊖Leicester Sq. Dance with young, friendly folks to the latest pop hits in an enjoyably cramped and sweaty space. Cover Tu-Th after 11pm £3; F-Sa £4. Open M-Sa 5pm-3am, Su 5-10:30pm. AmEx/MC/V.

Candy Bar, 4 Carlisle St. (☎ 7494 4041; www.thecandybar.co.uk), in the West End. ⊖Tottenham Ct. Rd. or Oxford Circus. This estrogen-packed, pink-hued drinking spot is a one-stop shop for lesbian entertainment. Karaoke, striptease performances, DJs, and popular dance nights. W karaoke. Cover F-Sa after 9pm £5. Open M-Th and Su 5-11:30pm (music from 8:30pm), F-Sa 5pm-2am (music after 9pm). MC/V.

G-A-Y, 157 Charing Cross Rd. (☎ 7434 9592; www.g-a-y.co.uk), in the West End. ⊖Tottenham Ct. Rd. London's biggest gay and lesbian night, 4 nights a week. Sa G-A-Y big night out, rocking the capacity crowd with commercial-dance DJs and live pop performances. Wheelchair-accessible. Cover M and Th with flyer or ad (available at most gay bars) £1, students 50p; F with flyer or ad £2, after midnight £3; Sa £8-15 depending on performer. Open M and Th-F 11pm-4am, Sa 10:30pm-5am. Cash only.

G-A-Y Bar, 30 Old Compton St. (☎ 7494 2756; www.g-a-y.co.uk), in the West End. ⊖Leicester Sq. or Piccadilly Cir. A gay-and-lesbian feeder bar for the perennially popular G-A-Y Club. Lesbian-dominated bar downstairs. Plenty of straight folks tag along for the fluffy scene. Open M-Sa noon-midnight, Su noon-10:30pm. AmEx/MC/V.

Village Soho, 81 Wardour St. (☎ 7434 2124; www.village-soho.co.uk), in the West End. ⊖Piccadilly Circus. Enter at the main door on Wardour St. or at the slightly less-polished back door around the corner on Berwick St. Speedo-sporting superhero dancers, along with tourists and locals. Loud pop tunes. Cover F-Sa after 11pm £2. Open M-Sa noon-1am, Su noon-midnight. AmEx/MC/V.

Comptons of Soho, 53 Old Compton St. (☎7479 7961), in the West End. ⊖Leicester Sq. or Piccadilly Circus. Soho's oldest gay pub. Fills up early with a wonderfully friendly, predominantly male crowd of all ages. Wheelchair-accessible outside seating. Open M-Sa noon-11pm, Su noon-10:30pm. MC/V.

Ku Bar, 75 Charing Cross Rd. (☎7437 4303; www.ku-bar.co.uk). ⊖Leicester Sq. A fashionable gay hangout that offers a moderately dim interior and a loungy outdoor area. Happy hour noon-9pm offers discounted mixed drink jugs (£7) and beer refills (£1.50). Open M-Sa 1-11pm, Su 1-10:30pm. Cash only.

◪ DAYTRIPS FROM LONDON

GREENWICH. Maritime Greenwich was built as a Royal Palace, but after the Royal family vacated the premises, Greenwich became home to the Royal Navy, serving that role until 1997. It was in this capacity that it came to claim its other claim to fame: the **Prime Meridian.** The **Royal Observatory,** on the Prime Meridian line, was originally founded to produce accurate star charts for navigation. (*At the top of Greenwich Park, a short but steep climb from the National Maritime Museum; for an easier walk, take the Avenue from St. Mary's Gate at the top of King William Walk. There is also a tram that leaves from the back of the Museum every 30min. ☎8858 4422; www.nmm.ac.uk. Open daily 10am-5pm. Last admission 4:30pm. Summer open until 6pm, but call to confirm. Free.*) Its history of timekeeping led to Greenwich's being chosen as the site of Britain's most famous white elephant, the **Millennium Dome.** Situated some way from the historic sights in World Heritage Site Greenwich, it's soon to enter into a new incarnation as a 26,000-seat stadium. (*⊖North Greenwich.*) The ▧**National Maritime Museum** covers almost every aspect of seafaring history. Many of the galleries feel like a nautical theme park—the Explorers section recreates an Antarctic ice cave and a ship's foredeck. (*Romney Rd. between the Royal Naval College and Greenwich Park. DLR: Cutty Sark. ☎8858 4422; www.nmm.ac.uk. Open daily mid-July to early Sept. 10am-6pm; early Sept. to mid-July 10am-5pm. Last entry 30min. before close. Free.*) A former royal hunting ground, **Greenwich Park** sees young people and families come out in droves to sunbathe, strike up football games, and picnic. The remains of a first-century Roman settlement and Saxon **tumuli** (burial mounds) are down the hill from the observatory. (*Open daily 7am-dusk. Children's boating pool open June-Aug. daily 10:30am-5pm; Sept.-May Sa-Su 10:30am-5pm. 20min. paddleboat rental £2.50 per person.*)

Many people choose to make the **boat** trip (1hr.) from Westminster or Tower Hill; boats also run to the Thames Barrier. Travelcard holders get 33% off riverboat trips from a variety of companies. (*See Transport for London website for details; www.tfl.gov.uk/river/pdfdocs/river-services-guide-2005.pdf.*) **City Cruises** operates from Westminster Pier to Greenwich via the Tower of London. (*☎7740 0400; www.citycruises.com. Mar.-Nov. daily. Schedule changes constantly; call for details. Round-trip £8.60, DayRover ticket £9.*) **Thames River Services** boats also head from Westminster Pier to Greenwich via Embankment, with some boats going to the **Thames Barrier.** (*☎7930 4097. Late Mar. to Oct. daily every 30min. beginning at 10am. Last boat from Westminster 4:30pm (June-Aug. 5pm); last boat from Greenwich 5pm (July-Aug. 6pm). Same prices as above.*) The Greenwich **Tourist Information Centre** offers all the usual services as well as a slick exhibit on local history. Guided, yet somewhat uninspired, walking tours leave the center daily at 12:15pm for the town and observatory, and at 2:15pm for the Royal Naval College. (*Pepys House, 2 Cutty Sark Gardens. ☎08706 082 000. Tour £4, concessions £3, under 14 free. Open daily 10am-5pm.*)

ROYAL BOTANICAL GARDENS, KEW. In the summer of 2003, UNESCO announced the Royal Botanical Gardens as a World Heritage Site—a privilege shared by many of the historic sights in London. The 250-year-old Royal Botanical Gardens extend with a green English placidity in a 300-acre swath along the

Thames. The three conservatories are at the center of the collection. The steamy Victorian **Palm House** boasts *Encephalartos Altensteinii*, "The Oldest Pot Plant In The World," while the **Princess of Wales Conservatory** houses 10 different climate zones, from rainforest to desert, including two devoted entirely to orchids. Low-season visitors will not be disappointed—the **Woodland Glade** is renowned for displays of autumn color. Close to the Thames in the northern part of the gardens, **Kew Palace** (closed for renovations until mid-2006) is a modest red-brick affair used by royalty on Garden visits. On the hill behind and to the right of the palace, 17th-century medicinal plants flourish in the stunning **Queen's Garden;** small placards label one that cures back pain "caused by overmuch use of women." *(Kew, on the south bank of the Thames. The main entrance and Visitors Center is at Victoria Gate, nearest the Tube. ⊖Kew Gardens (zone 3). ☎8332 5000 for 24hr. recorded information; www.kew.org. Open Apr.-Aug. M-F 9:30am-6:30pm; Sa-Su 9:30am-7:30pm; Sept.-Oct. daily 9:30am-6pm; Nov.-Jan. daily 9:30am-4:15pm; Feb.-Mar. daily 9:30am-5:30pm. Last admission 30min. before close. Glasshouses close Feb.-Oct. 5:30pm; Nov.-Jan. 3:45pm. £10, concessions £7; after 4pm £4. 1hr. walking tours daily 11am and 2pm start at Victoria Gate Visitors Center; free. "Explorer" hop-on, hop-off shuttle makes 45min. rounds of the gardens; 1st shuttle daily 11am, last 4pm; £3.50, children £1. 1hr. buggy tours for mobility-impaired M-F 11am and 2pm; booking required; free.)*

HAMPTON COURT PALACE. Although a monarch hasn't lived here for 250 years, Hampton Court still exudes regal charm. Cardinal Wolsey built the first palace here in 1514, showing the young Henry VIII how to act the part of a powerful ruler. Henry learned the lesson all too well, confiscating Hampton in 1528 and embarking on a massive building program. In 1689, William and Mary employed Wren to bring the Court up to date, but less than 50 years later George II abandoned it for good. The **palace** is divided into six 45-60min. tour routes, all starting at **Clock Court,** where you can pick up a program of the day's events and an audio guide. In **Henry VIII's State Apartments,** only the massive Great Hall and exquisite Chapel Royal hint at past magnificence. Below, the **Tudor Kitchens** offer insight into how Henry ate himself to a 54 in. waist. Predating Henry's additions, the 16th-century **Wolsey Rooms** are complemented by Renaissance masterpieces. Wren's **King's Apartments** were restored to their original appearance after a 1986 fire. The **Queen's Apartments** weren't completed until 1734, postponed by Mary II's death. The **Georgian Rooms** were created by William Kent for George II's family. No less impressive are the **gardens,** with Mantegna's *Triumphs of Caesar* secreted away in the Lower Orangery. North of the palace, the **Wilderness,** a pseudo-natural area earmarked for picnickers, holds the ever-popular **maze,** planted in 1714. Its small size belies a devilish design. *(30min. from Waterloo by train; round-trip £5. 4hr. by boat Apr.-Oct.; daily 10:30, 11:15am, noon, 2pm; £13.50, round-trip £19.50. Westminster Passenger Cruises ☎7930 2062. Palace ☎08707 527 777; www.hrp.org.uk. Open late Mar. to late Oct. M 10:15am-6pm, Tu-Su 9:30am-6pm; late Oct. to late Mar. M 10:15am-4:30pm, Tu-Su 9:30am-4:30pm. Last admission 45min. before close. Palace and gardens £11.80, concessions £8.70. Admission free for worshippers at Chapel Royal; services Su 11am and 3:30pm. Audio guides and guided tours are included in ticket.)*

SOUTH ENGLAND

South England's history affirms both Britain's island heritage and its deep connection to the Continent. Early Britons who crossed the Channel settled the counties of Kent, Sussex, and Hampshire; William the Conqueror left his mark in the form of castles and cathedrals, many built around former Roman settlements. Today, Victorian mansions balance atop seaside cliffs and the masts of restored ships spike the skyline.

HIGHLIGHTS OF SOUTH ENGLAND

SHIMMY 'til the break of dawn at the nightclubs in Brighton (p. 152) after spending the day in the water in this tacky paradise.

DON'T LOOK DOWN over the famous chalk-white cliffs of Dover (p. 142)—look across to France instead.

FEEL INSPIRED while walking the South Downs Way (p. 148); it's the landscape that inspired the "Idea of England" and is strewn with Bronze Age burial mounds.

KENT

CANTERBURY
☎ 01227

And specially from every shires ende
Of Engelond to Caunterbury they wende.
　　—Geoffrey Chaucer, *The Canterbury Tales*

In 1170, three knights left Henry II's court in France, their motives unknown to history, and traveled to Canterbury to murder Archbishop Thomas à Becket beneath the massive columns of his own cathedral. Three centuries of innumerable pilgrims in search of miracles flowed to St. Thomas's shrine, creating the great medieval road between London and Canterbury. Chaucer caricatured this road and the society around it in the ribald *Canterbury Tales*, which have done more to enshrine the cathedral in perpetual memory than the now-vanished bones. In summer hordes of tourists descend upon the cobbled city center, while for the rest of the year Canterbury remains a lively college town.

◤ TRANSPORTATION

Trains: Canterbury has two central stations.

East Station, Station Rd. E, off Castle St., southwest of town. Open M-Sa 6:15am-8:20pm, Su 6:30am-9pm. South Eastern trains from **London Victoria** (1¾hr., 2 per hr., £17.80).

West Station, Station Rd. W, off St. Dunstan's St. Open M-Sa 6:15am-7:30pm, Su 9am-4:30pm. South Eastern from **London Charing Cross** and **London Waterloo** (1½hr., every hr., £14.90).

Buses: Bus station, St. George's Ln. (☎ 472 082). Open M-Sa 8:15am-5:15pm. **National Express** (☎ 08705 808 080) from **London** (2hr., 2 per hr., £11.40). Book tickets by 5pm. **Explorer** tickets allow 1-day unlimited bus travel in Kent (£7, concessions £5, families £14).

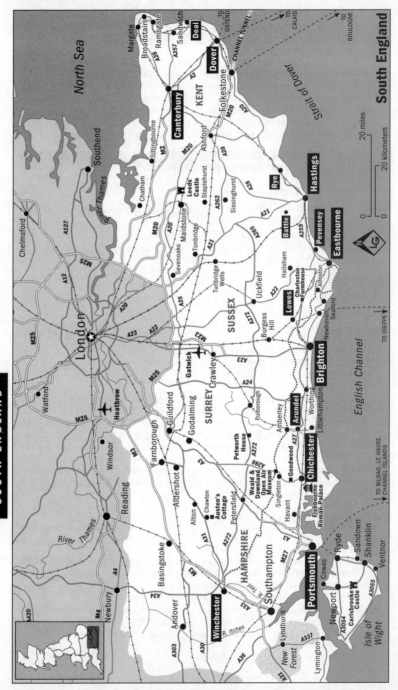

SOUTH ENGLAND

Taxis: Longport Cars Ltd. (☎458 885). Open daily 7am-2am.

Bike Rental: Downland Cycle Hire, West Station (☎479 643; www.downlandcycles.co.uk). £10 per day. Bike trailers £7 per day. £25 deposit. Open Tu-Sa 10am-5:30pm, Su 11am-4pm.

🔢 ORIENTATION AND PRACTICAL INFORMATION

Canterbury Center is roughly circular, defined by the eroding medieval city wall. An unbroken street crosses the city from northwest to southeast, changing names from **Saint Peter's Street** to **High Street** to **The Parade** to **Saint George's Street.** Butchery Ln. and Mercery Ln., each only a block long, run north to the **Cathedral Gates.**

Tourist Information Centre: The Buttermarket, 12-13 Sun St. (☎378 100). Books beds for a £2.50 charge plus a 10% deposit. Open Easter to Christmas M-Sa 9:30am-5pm, Su 10am-4pm; Christmas to Easter M-Sa 10am-4pm.

Tours: 1½hr. guided tours of the city from the TIC. Apr.-Oct. daily 2pm; July-Sept. M-Sa 11:30am and 2pm, Su 2pm. £4, concessions £3.50, children £2.80, families £12.

Financial Services: Banks on High St. **Thomas Cook,** 9 High St. (☎597 800). Open M-W and F-Sa 9am-5:30pm, Th 10am-5:30pm, Su 11am-4pm.

Launderette: Canterbury Clothes Care Company, 4 Nunnery Fields. (☎452 211). Open M-F 9am-6pm, Sa 9am-4pm, Su 9am-3pm. Last wash 30min. before close. £3.

Police: Old Dover Rd. (☎762 055), outside the eastern city wall.

Hospital: Kent and Canterbury Hospital, 28 Ethelbert Rd. (☎766 877).

Internet Access: Dot Cafe (☎478 778; www.ukdotcafe.com), at the corner of St. Dunstan's St. and Station Road. £2 per 30 min., £3 per hr. Wireless £2 per hr. Open daily 9am-9pm.

Post Office: 29 High St. (☎473 810), across from Best Ln. Bureau de change. Open M 8:30am-5:30pm, Tu-Sa 9am-5:30pm. **Post Code:** CT1 2BA.

🏠 ACCOMMODATIONS

Canterbury is busy and single rooms are scarce; always reserve ahead. **B&Bs** cluster around High St. and near West Station. The less-expensive ones (£18-20) on **New Dover Road,** half a mile from East Station, fill fast; turn right from the station and continue up the main artery, which becomes Upper Bridge St. At the second roundabout, turn right onto St. George's Pl., which becomes New Dover Rd.

🛏 **Kipps Independent Hostel,** 40 Nunnery Fields (☎786 121), 5-10min. from city center. Fully equipped self-catering kitchen, comfortable lounge, and a social atmosphere. Some dorms are ensuite. Laundry £3. Internet access £1 per 30min. Key deposit £10. Dorms £14; singles £19; doubles £33. MC/V with 50p surcharge. ❷

🛏 **Let's Stay,** 26 New Dover Rd. (☎463 628). One hostel-style room with four beds and a delightful staff. Ask about the origin of the name! Call ahead. Full breakfast included. Dorms £14. Cash only. ❷

Castle Court Guest House, 8 Castle St. (☎463 441). Quiet B&B a few minutes from Eastgate in the old town. Vegetarian breakfast available. Singles £25; doubles £46-50. Cash only. ❸

YHA Canterbury, 54 New Dover Rd. (☎462 911), in a lovely house ¾ mi. from East Station and ½ mi. southeast of the bus station. Relaxing lounge, kitchen facilities, and a bureau de change. Breakfast included. Lockers £1. Laundry £1.50. Internet £2.50 per 30min. Reception 7:30-10am and 3-11pm. Book ahead in summer. Dorms £16.40, under 18 £12.50. MC/V. ❷

Camping: Camping & Caravanning Club Site, Bekesbourne Ln. (☎463 216), off the A257, 1½ mi. east of the city center. Showers, laundry (£3), and facilities for the disabled. £5; non-member surcharge £5 per person. MC/V. ❶

🌓 FOOD

The Safeway **supermarket,** St. George's Center, St. George's Pl., is 4min. from the town center. (☎769 335. Open M-F 8am-9pm, Sa 8am-8pm, Su 11am-5pm.)

Azouma, 4 Church St. (☎760 076; www.azouma.co.uk). Generous portions of Middle Eastern and Mediterranean cuisine (£10-13). A belly dancer entertains Th nights and the lunchtime buffet is delicious and cheap (£7). Open daily noon-3pm and 5:30pm-midnight. MC/V. ❸

Marlowe's, 55 St. Peter's St. (☎462 194; www.marlowesrestaurant.co.uk). English food with Mexican flair, where colorful menus offset black-and-white photos of old Broadway. Choose from 8 toppings for 8 oz. burgers (£6.60) or a veggie dish (£6-9). Open M-Sa 9am-10:30pm, Su 10am-10:30pm. Cash only. ❷

Cafe des Amis du Mexique, St. Dunstan's St. (☎464 390), just outside the West Gate. Creative Mexican-inspired dishes in a funky, college-friendly atmosphere. Try the crispy duck confit with *mole* sauce (£10). AmEx/MC/V. ❷

C'est la Vie, 17b Burgate (☎457 525). Fresh, inventive takeaway sandwiches (£2.40-3.10). The "Smokey Mountain," with maple-smoked chicken, is the most popular baguette. 10% student discount. Open M-Sa 9:30am-3:30pm. Cash only. ❶

👁 SIGHTS

🏛**CANTERBURY CATHEDRAL.** Pilgrim contributions funded most of Canterbury Cathedral's architectural wonders, including the early Gothic **nave,** constructed mostly between the 13th and 15th centuries on a site allegedly consecrated by St. Augustine 700 years earlier. The site of **Saint Thomas à Becket's shrine,** destroyed by Henry VIII in 1538, is marked by a candle and protected by an impenetrable velvet rope. The **Altar of the Sword's Point** stands where Becket fell—the final murderer broke off the tip of his sword in the archbishop's skull. Henry IV, possibly uneasy after having usurped the throne, chose to have his body entombed near Becket's sacred shrine instead of in Westminster Abbey. Across from Henry lies Edward, the Black Prince, and the decorative armor he wore at his funeral adorns a nearby wall. The eerily silent **crypt,** billed as a site for quiet reflection, hosts both tourists and funerals. In a structure plagued by fire and rebuilt time and again, the **Norman crypt,** a huge 12th-century chapel, remains intact. The **Corona Tower** rises above the eastern apse but is not open to visitors. Under the **Bell Harry Tower,** at the crossing of the nave and transepts, perpendicular arches support intricate 15th-century fan vaulting. (☎762 862; www.canterbury-cathedral.org. Cathedral open Easter to Oct. M-Sa 9am-6pm, Su 12:30-2:30pm and 4:30-5:30pm; Oct. to Easter M-Sa 9am-5pm, Su 12:30-2:30pm and 4:30-5:30pm. 1¼hr. tours available, 3 per day M-Sa; check nave or welcome center for times. Evensong M-F 5:30pm, Sa-Su 3:15pm. £5, concessions £4. Tours £3.50, concessions £2.50. 40min. audio tour £3, concessions £2.)

SAINT AUGUSTINE'S ABBEY. The skeletons of once-magnificent arches and crumbling walls are all that remain of what was one of the greatest abbeys in Europe, built in AD 598 to house Augustine and the 40 monks he brought with him to convert England. Indoor exhibits and a free audio tour reveal the abbey's his-

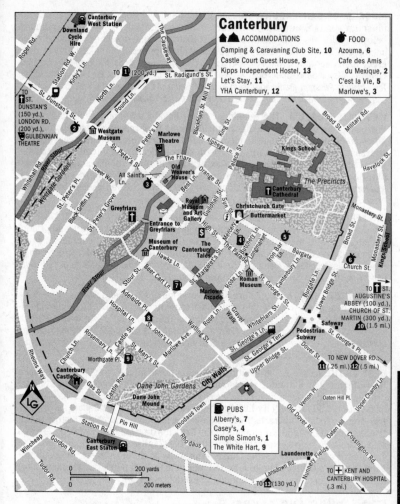

Canterbury

🏠🏠 ACCOMMODATIONS

Camping & Caravaning Club Site, **10**
Castle Court Guest House, **8**
Kipps Independent Hostel, **13**
Let's Stay, **11**
YHA Canterbury, **12**

🍴 FOOD

Azouma, **6**
Cafe des Amis
  du Mexique, **2**
C'est la Vie, **5**
Marlowe's, **3**

🍺 PUBS

Alberry's, **7**
Casey's, **4**
Simple Simon's, **1**
The White Hart, **9**

tory as burial place, royal palace, and pleasure garden. Don't miss St. Augustine's humble tomb under a pile of rocks. *(Outside the city wall near the cathedral. ☎ 767 345. Open Apr.-Sept. daily 10am-6pm; Oct.-Mar. W-Su 10am-4pm. £3.70, concessions £2.80.)*

CHURCH OF SAINT MARTIN. Surrounded by a peaceful graveyard, this small church sits just beyond Saint Augustine's Abbey. The oldest parish church in England still in use saw the marriage of pagan King Æthelbert to the French Christian Princess Bertha in AD 562, paving the way for England's conversion to Christianity. St. Augustine worshipped here before establishing his own monastery. Here, too, Joseph Conrad slumbers in darkness. *(North Holmes St. ☎ 463 469. Open Tu, Th, Su 10am-3pm. Free.)*

MUSEUM OF CANTERBURY. Housed in the medieval Poor Priests' Hospital, the museum spans Canterbury's history from St. Thomas to WWII bombings to beloved children's-book character Rupert Bear. A tongue-in-cheek animated video account of Becket and Henry II's relationship supplies the background to their grisly final encounter. (*Stour St.* ☎ *475 202. Open June-Sept. M-Sa 10:30am-5pm, Su 1:30-5pm; Nov.-May M-Sa 10:30am-5pm; last entry 4pm. £3.20, concessions £2.15, families £8.45. The Museum Passport grants admission to the Museum of Canterbury, the Westgate Museum, and the nearby Roman Museum. £5.90, concessions £3.50, families £14.15.*)

WESTGATE MUSEUM. The remainder of medieval Canterbury clusters near the Westgate, one of the few medieval fortifications to survive wartime blitzing. Pilgrims traditionally entered the city through this structure. Up the steep winding staircase, the museum—a former prison surrounded by well-tended gardens—keeps armor, old weapons, and a wax prisoner in three rooms, and offers commanding views of the city from atop the gate. (☎ *789 576; www.canterbury-museum.co.uk. Open M-Sa 11am-12:30pm and 1:30-3:30pm. Last admission 15min. before close. £1.15, concessions 70p, families £2.70.*)

GREYFRIARS. England's first Franciscan friary, Greyfriars was built over the River Stour in 1267. It was used briefly as a prison in the 19th century, and prisoners' etchings still mark the cell walls. Now the simple building contains a small museum devoted to the local order and a chapel. For a quiet break, walk through Greyfriars's **riverside gardens.** (*6a Stour St. Follow signs from the Westgate gardens or enter under Greyfriars Guesthouse.* ☎ *462 395. Open Easter to Sept. M-Sa 2-4pm. Free.*)

THE CANTERBURY TALES. Abbreviated versions of Chaucer's masterpiece echo through headphones while you walk past recreated scenes of the medieval pilgrims' road to Canterbury, complete with wax figures and the "authentic" stench of sweat, hay, and general grime. (*St. Margaret's St.* ☎ *479 227; www.canterburytales.org.uk. Open daily Mar.-June and Sept.-Oct. 10am-5pm; July-Aug. 9:30am-5pm; Nov.-Feb. 10am-4:30pm. £7, students £6.*)

BEST OF THE REST. A 15th-century Huguenot home on the river, the **Old Weaver's House** features an authentic witch-dunking stool. **Weaver's River Tours** runs 30min. cruises several times a day. (*1 St. Peter's St.* ☎ *07790 534 744; www.canterburyrivertours.co.uk. £5.50.*) In the city library, the **Royal Museum and Art Gallery** showcases paintings by locally born artists of earlier centuries and recounts the history of the "Buffs," one of the oldest regiments of the British Army. (*18 High St.* ☎ *475 221. Open M-Sa 10am-4:45pm. Free.*) Near the city walls to the southwest lie the remnants of the Conqueror's **Canterbury Castle.** Outside the walls to the northwest, the vaults of **Saint Dunstan's Church** contain a buried relic said to be the head of Thomas More; legend has it that his daughter bribed the executioner for it.

🍺🎭 PUBS AND CLUBS

Simple Simon's, 3-9 Church Ln. (☎ 762 355). This 14th-century alehouse is a popular local pub. Serves traditional English pub food (entrees £7) and often has live music. Open M-Sa 11am-11pm, Su noon-10:30pm. Food served daily noon-8pm.

Alberry's, 38 St. Margaret's St. (☎ 452 378). A stylish wine bar that pours late into the evening. Live music M, DJ Tu-Th. Happy hour 5:30-7pm. Open M-Sa 11am-2am.

Casey's, Butchery Ln. (☎ 463 252). A youthful pub on a side street near the cathedral, newly refurbished Casey's offers quasi-Irish ambience and traditional food (£6). Live Irish music Th-Sa. Open M-Th noon-11pm, F-Sa 11am-11pm, Su noon-10:30pm.

The White Hart, Worthgate Pl. (☎ 765 091), near East Station. Congenial pub with homemade lunch specials (£4-8), sweets (£3.50), and some of Canterbury's best bitters (£2.30-2.80). Enjoy the city's largest beer garden. Open M-Sa 11am-11pm.

🎵 🌿 ENTERTAINMENT AND FESTIVALS

For up-to-date entertainment listings, pick up *What, Where, When,* free at many pubs. **Buskers,** especially along St. Peter's St. and High St., play streetside Vivaldi while bands of impromptu players ramble from corner to corner, acting out the more absurd of Chaucer's scenes. **Marlowe Theatre,** The Friars, across from the Pilgrim Hotel, puts on touring London productions. (☎787 787. Box office open M and Sa 10am-9pm, Tu 10:30am-9pm, Su 2hr. before performances. Tickets £10-35, concessions available.) The **Gulbenkian Theatre,** at the University of Kent, University Rd., west of town on St. Dunstan's St., stages dance, drama, music, and comedy performances, and shows films. (☎769 075; www.kent.ac.uk/gulbenkian. Box office open during term time M-F 11am-5pm, Sa-Su 5:30-9pm. Tickets £5-21, £6 rush available from 7pm on performance nights.)

In the fall, the **Canterbury Festival** fills two weeks in mid-October with drama, opera, cabaret, chamber music, dance, talks, walks, and exhibitions. (☎452 853, box office 378 188; www.canterburyfestival.co.uk.) In Ashford, 5 mi. southwest of Canterbury, the popular **Stour Music Festival** celebrates Renaissance and baroque music for seven days in mid-June. The festival takes place at All Saint's Boughton Aluph Church, on the A28 and accessible by rail from West Station. Call the bookings office a month in advance. (☎812 740. Tickets £5-14.)

▣ DAYTRIPS FROM CANTERBURY

▨ SISSINGHURST CASTLE GARDEN

Trains run from Canterbury West to Staplehurst (round-trip £8.80), where buses #4 and 5 run to Sissinghurst. ☎01580 710 700; www.nationaltrust.org.uk/sissinghurst. Ticket is occasionally timed. Open mid-Mar. to Oct. M-Tu and F 11am-6:30pm, Sa-Su 10am-6:30pm; last admission 1hr. before close. £7.50.

A masterpiece of floral design by Bloomsbury Group stalwarts Vita Sackville-West and her husband, Harold Nicolson, Sissinghurst is the most popular garden in a garden-obsessed nation. Eight gardeners maintain the original design, a varied array of carved hedges, flower beds, and foliage. After savoring the serenity of the White Garden or the Cottage Garden, visitors may visit the property's large Elizabethan mansion or stroll along the moat to forested lakes and lose their way along one of many woodland walks. The staff encourages visitors to come after 4pm, when the sun's light reveals the garden's true beauty.

LEEDS CASTLE

Near Maidstone, 23 mi. west of Canterbury on the A20. Trains run from Canterbury West to Bearsted (1 per hr., £10); a shuttle goes from the station to the castle (£4). Shuttles leave the train station M-Sa 10:35am-2:35pm every hr., Su 10:55am-2:55pm every hr.; return shuttles leave the castle M-Sa 2-6pm on the hour, Su 2:15-6:15pm on the quarter hour. ☎01622 765 400 or 0870 600 8880. Castle open daily Mar.-Oct. 11am-7:30pm; Nov.-Feb. 10:15am-5:30pm. Grounds open daily Mar.-Oct. 10am-7pm; Nov.-Feb. 10am-5pm; last admission 2hr. before close. Castle and grounds £13, concessions £11. Call for combined transportation and admission tickets, available at train and bus stations.

Leeds was built immediately after the Norman Conquest and remained a favorite royal playground until Edward VI, Henry VIII's son, sold it for a song. The ground floor is a quintessential royal Tudor residence. It contrasts sharply with the modern second floor, which was impeccably outfitted by the same interior decorator responsible for Jackie Kennedy's White House overhaul. One wing displays an alarming collection of **medieval dog collars.** Outdoors, lose yourself in a **maze** of 2400 yew trees or the 500 acres of woodlands and gardens hosting black swans and other unusual waterfowl.

SOUTH ENGLAND

DOVER

☎ 01304

From the days of Celtic invaders to the age of the Chunnel, the white chalk cliffs of Dover have been many a traveler's first glimpse of England. They were the defiant face England presented to would-be invaders from the Romans to Napoleon to Hitler. Today, the tranquility of the cliffs is belied by the puttering of ferries and the hum of hoverspeeds. But a walk along the cliffs or an exploration of the magnificent castle will confirm any visitor's notions of British pageantry and pride.

⌨ TRANSPORTATION

Trains: Priory Station, Station Approach Rd. Ticket office open M-Sa 4:15am-11:20pm, Su 6:15am-11:20pm. Trains (☎08457 484 950) from **Canterbury** (20min., 2 per hr., £5.10) and several **London** stations (2hr., 4 per hr., £21.30).

Buses: Pencester Road Station (☎01304 240 024), between York St. and Maison Dieu Rd. Office open M-Tu and Th-F 8:45am-5:15pm, W 8:45am-4pm, Sa 8:30am-noon. The TIC sells National Express (☎08705 808 080) tickets. Buses run from **London,** continuing to the **Eastern Docks** (2¾hr., every hr., £10.80). Stagecoach (☎08702 433 711) from **Canterbury** (40min., every hr., £2.95) and **Deal** (40min., every hr., £2.45). A bus runs from **Folkestone,** a stop for Chunnel trains (30min., 2 per hr., £2.30).

Ferries: Eastern Docks sails to **Calais, France** and **Oostend, Belgium;** the TIC offers a booking service. P&O Stena (☎08706 202 020; www.posl.com) sails to **Calais** (35 per day, £15); as does SeaFrance (☎08705 711 711; www.seafrance.com. 17 per day, £10). The Seacat leaves the Hoverport at **Prince of Wales Pier** for Calais (£22). Bus service (£1) leaves Priory Station for the docks 45-60min. before sailing. (See **By Ferry,** p. 28.) The **Channel Tunnel** offers passenger service on Eurostar and car transport on Le Shuttle to and from the Continent. (See **By Chunnel,** p. 28.)

Taxis: Central Taxi Service (☎240 0441). 24hr.

🛈 PRACTICAL INFORMATION

Tourist Information Centre: The Old Town Gaol, (☎205 108; www.whitecliffscountry.org.uk), off High St. where it divides into Priory Rd. and Biggin St. Multilingual staff sells ferry, bus, and hoverspeed tickets and books accommodations for 10% deposit; after hours call for accommodations list. Open Apr.-May M-F 9am-5:30pm, Sa-Su 10am-4pm; June-Aug. daily 9am-5:30pm; Oct.-Mar. M-F 9am-5:30pm, Sa 10am-4pm.

Tours: White Cliffs Boat Tours (☎01303 271 388; www.whitecliffsboattours.co.uk) sails every hr. from the marina. £5.

Financial Services: Several **banks** are in Market Sq., including **Barclays** in the northwest corner. Open M-F 9:30am-4:30pm.

Launderette: Cherry Tree Launderette, 2 Cherry Tree Ave. (☎242 822), off London Rd., past the hostel. Full service available. Open daily 8am-8pm; last wash 7:15pm.

Police: Ladywell St. (☎240 055), off High St.

Pharmacy: Superdrug, 33-34 Biggin St. (☎211 477). Open M-Sa 8:30am-5:30pm, Su 10am-4pm.

Hospital: Buckland Hospital, Coomb Valley Rd. (☎201 624), northwest of town. Take bus #67 or 67A from the post office.

Post Office: 68-72 Pencester Rd. (☎241 747), inside Alldays. Open M-F 8:30am-5:30pm, Sa 8:30am-2pm. **Post Code:** CT16 1PW.

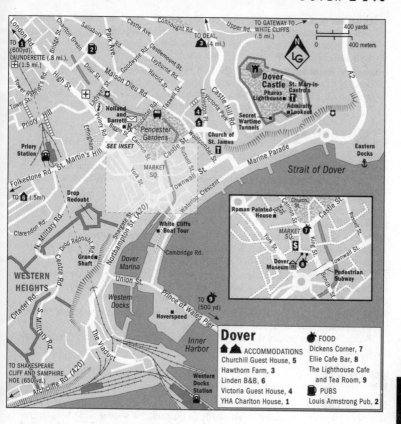

ACCOMMODATIONS

Rooms are scarce during the summer and the ferry terminal makes an unsafe campground. August is especially busy due to the influx of distance swimmers eager to try the Channel. Cheaper **B&Bs** congregate on **Folkestone Road,** a hike past the train station. Some reception desks stay open all night. Pricier B&Bs lie near the city center on **Castle Street,** and more can be found on **Maison Dieu Road.**

YHA Charlton House, 306 London Rd. (☎201 314). ½ mi. from Priory station; turn left on Folkestone Rd., then left at the roundabout on High St. Lounge, pool table, kitchen, full meal service, lockers, and Internet. Offers discounts on sights. Overflow at 14 Goodwyne Road (closer to town). Lockout 10am-1pm. Curfew 11pm. Dorms £16, under 18 £12.50. MC/V. ❷

Churchill Guest House, 6 Castle Hill Rd. (☎208 365). Large ensuite rooms, great views, big beds, and generous amenities. Full breakfast included. Singles £35; doubles £50-65. MC/V with 5% surcharge. ❹

Victoria Guest House, 1 Laureston Pl. (☎205 140). Well-traveled hosts extend a friendly welcome. Doubles £44-50. AmEx (with 5% surcharge)/MC/V. ❷

Linden Bed & Breakfast, 231 Folkestone Rd. (☎205 449). A ways off, but this plush B&B makes every effort to accommodate—ask about pickup from the train station or docks. Discount vouchers for local sights. Satellite TV. Singles £20-25; doubles and twins £40-55. MC/V. ❸

Camping: Hawthorn Farm (☎852 658), at Martin Mill Station off the A258 between Dover and Deal. 2min. walk from railway station; follow the signs. June-Aug. 2-person tent and car £13.50, with electricity £16; Mar.-May and Sept.-Oct. £11/13.50. Closed Nov.-Feb. Hikers and bikers £4; Mar.-May and Sept.-Oct. £3.50. Cash only. ❶

🅲🅼 FOOD AND PUBS

Despite (or perhaps because of) Dover's proximity to the Continent, its cuisine remains staunchly English. Chip shops line **London Road** and **Biggin Street.** Visit Holland & Barrett, 35 Biggin St., for **groceries.** (☎241 426. Open M-Sa 9am-5:30pm.)

Ellie Cafe Bar, Market Sq. (☎215 685). Have a meal (entrees £4.50-5.50) while watching the flat-screen TVs, or sip a martini (£3.50) in one of the lounge chairs looking onto Market Sq. Open M-Sa 9:30am-11:30pm, Su 11am-11pm. MC/V. ❷

Dickens Corner, 7 Market Sq. (☎206 692). The ground floor bustles with channelers wolfing baguettes and cakes (£2.10-3) or hot lunches (£4-5.50), while the upstairs tea room moves at a more refined pace. Open M-Sa 9am-4:30pm. MC/V. ❶

Louis Armstrong Pub, 58 Maison Dieu Rd. (☎204 759). Its presence is indicated only by a weather-beaten picture of Satchmo himself. Live music makes it worth the search. Open M-Sa 11am-11pm, Su noon-2pm and 7-11pm. Cash only. ❶

The Lighthouse Cafe and Tea Room, at the end of Prince of Wales Pier. Take in the castle, beaches, and white cliffs as you sip tea ½ mi. offshore, in the closest cafe to France. Worth the visit for the view alone. Open in summer daily 10am-5:30pm (check the sign at the start of the pier). Cash only. ❶

👁 SIGHTS

▧DOVER CASTLE. The view from Castle Hill Rd., on the east side of town, reveals why sprawling Dover Castle is famed for its magnificent setting and its impregnability. Overlooking the Pas de Calais, the castle was a natural focus of conflict from the Hundred Years' War to WWII, during which the castle trained its guns on German-occupied France. Hitler's missiles destroyed the **Church of St. James,** leaving the ruins crumbling at the base of the hill. Beside **St. Mary-in-Castro,** a tiled Saxon church, towers the **Pharos lighthouse**—the only extant Roman lighthouse and the tallest remaining Roman edifice in Britain. Climb to the platform of the **Admiralty Lookout** for unsurpassed views of the cliffs and harbor; 20p gets you a binocular look at France. A path along the battlements passes by big guns from the historical periods in which the castle was used. The (no longer) ▧**Secret Wartime Tunnels** constitute a 3½ mi. labyrinth only recently declassified. Begun in 1803, when Britain was under the threat of attack by Napoleon, the vast underground burrows served as the base for the WWII evacuation of Allied troops from Dunkirk and a shelter for Dover citizens during the air raids. The lowest of the five levels, not yet open to the public, was intended to house the government should the Cuban Missile Crisis have gone sour. Tours fill quickly and there is often a long wait; check in at the tunnels first. *(Buses from the town center run daily Apr.-Sept. every hr., 55p; otherwise, scale Castle Hill using the pedestrian ramp and stairs by the first castle sign to the left of Castle St. Open Apr.-June and Sept. daily 10am-6pm; July-Aug. daily 9:30am-6:30pm; Oct. daily 10am-5pm; Nov.-Jan. M and Th-Su 10am-4pm; Feb.-Mar. daily 10am-4pm. £9.)*

THE WHITE CLIFFS. Covering the surrounding coastline, the white cliffs make a beautiful backdrop for a stroll along the pebbly beach. A few miles west of Dover, the whitest, steepest, and most famous of them all is **Shakespeare Cliff,** tradition-ally identified as the site of blind Gloucester's battle with the brink in *King Lear.* *(25min. by foot along Snargate St. and Archcliffe Rd.)* To the east of Dover, past Dover Castle, the **Gateway to the White Cliffs** overlooks the Strait of Dover and serves as an informative starting point for exploration. *(Buses and Guide Friday go to Langdon Cliff at least once per hr. ☎202 756. Open daily Mar.-Oct. 10am-5pm; Nov.-Feb. 11am-4pm.)* Dozens of **cliff walks** lie a short distance from Dover; consult the TIC for trail information. **The Grand Shaft,** a 140 ft. triple-spiral staircase, was shot through the rock in Napo-leonic times to link the army on the Western Heights with the city center. *(Snargate St. ☎201 066. Open select days throughout year; call for dates.)*

DOVER MUSEUM. This museum depicts Dover's Roman days as the colonial out-post Dubras and houses a high-tech gallery with the remnants of the oldest ship yet discovered—at 3600-years-old. *(Market Sq. ☎201 066. Open Apr.-Sept. M-Sa 10am-5:30pm, Su noon-5pm; Oct.-Mar. M-Sa 10am-5:30pm. £2, concessions £1.25, families £5.50.)*

OTHER SIGHTS. Recent excavations have unearthed a remarkably well-preserved **Roman painted house.** It's the oldest Roman house in Britain, complete with under-ground central heating and indoor plumbing. *(New St., off Cannon St. near Market Sq. ☎203 279. Open Apr.-Sept. M-Sa 10am-5pm, Su 1-5pm. Last admission 4:30pm. £2, conces-sions 80p.)* For striking views, take the A20 toward Folkestone to **Samphire Hoe,** a well-groomed park planted in the summer of 1997 with material dug from the Channel Tunnel.The D2 bus to Aycliffe (£1) stops about a 10min. walk from the park, or walk the North Downs Way along the clifftop. *(Open daily 7am-dusk.)*

▶ DAYTRIP FROM DOVER

DEAL

Trains from Dover Priory arrive in Deal Station (15min., at least every hr., £3.40). The TIC in Deal Library on Broad St., books beds for a 10% deposit and provides the free Deal Historic Town Trails, which details 10 walks in the area. ☎369 576. Open M-Tu and Th-Su 9:30am-5pm, W 9:30am-1pm.

Julius Caesar landed here with an invasion force in 55 BC, and Deal's castles rep-resent Henry VIII's 16th-century attempt to prevent similar occurrences. **Deal Cas-tle,** south of town at the corner of Victoria Rd. and Deal Castle Rd., is one of Henry's largest Cinque Ports (anti-pirate establishments). A symmetrical maze of dark corridors and cells is guaranteed to entangle visitors. (☎01304 372 762. Open Apr.-Sept. daily 10am-6pm. £3.70.) **Walmer Castle,** ½ mi. south of Deal via the beachfront pedestrian path or the A258 (and 1 mi. from the Walmer train station), is the best-preserved and most elegant of Henry VIII's citadels. Walmer has been transformed into a country estate which, since the 1700s, has been the official res-idence of the Lords Warden of the Cinque Ports. Notable Wardens past include the Duke of Wellington, William Pitt, and Winston Churchill. The most recent warden was the Queen Mother; the beautiful gardens are planted with her favorite flowers. (☎01304 364 288. Open daily Mar. 10am-4pm, Apr.-Sept. 10am-6pm; Oct. W-Su 10am-4pm. Last admission 30min. before close. Closed when the Lord Warden is in resi-dence. £5.80. Free and worthwhile 30min. audio tour.) Perhaps the most famous res-taurant in Kent, **Dunkerley's Restaurant Bistro ❸,** 19 Beach St., overlooks the sea in Deal. Residents from all over the region flood in to dine on local fish for around £12. (☎375 016. Open M 7-9:30pm, Tu-Su noon-2:30pm and 7-9:30pm. AmEx/MC/V.)

SUSSEX

RYE
☎ 01797

Settled before the Roman invasion, today Rye's cobblestone streets and half-timbered houses are exceedingly beautiful to look at, but they don't hold much excitement. Most of this upscale town shuts down on Tuesday afternoons. Henry James wrote his later novels while living in **Lamb House,** at the corner of West St. and Mermaid St. (Open Apr.-Oct. W and Sa 2-6pm. Last admission 5:30pm. £2.90.) Check out **St. Mary's Church,** at the top of Lion St., a 12th-century parish church that houses one of Britain's oldest working clocks. (☎ 222 430. Open M-F 9am-6pm, Sa 9am-5:30pm, Su 11:40am-5:30pm. £2, concessions £1.) Around the corner from the church, **Ypres Tower,** built in 1350, was intended to fortify the town against invaders from the sea. The tower now contains the **Rye Museum,** displaying artifacts from Rye's past. (☎ 226 728. Open Apr.-Oct. M and Th-Su 10:30am-1pm and 2-5pm; Nov.-Mar. tower only Sa-Su 10:30am-3:30pm. Last admission 3pm. Tower and museum £2.90, concessions £2.) The area's only **YHA hostel** , Rye Rd., is in Guestling, 7 mi. south of Rye and 4 mi. north of Hastings. From Rye, head down the A259 past Winchelsea and Icklesham (look for the sign on the right). Alternatively, take bus #711 from Rye to the White Hart in Guestling (M-Sa 2 per hr. until 7:45pm; £1.85); from there, the hostel is downhill to the left. You can also take the train to Three Oaks (£2.90) and follow the signs 1½ mi. (☎ 01424 812 373. Laundry. Open July-Aug. daily; May-June and Sept.-Oct. Tu-Sa. Dorms £12.50, under 18 £9. **Camping** by booking only. Tents £5.30. MC/V.) Aside from the hostel, budget accommodations in the region are scarce. For **groceries,** visit Budgens, across from the train station in Rye. (☎ 226 044. Open M-Tu, Th-Sa 8am-8pm, W 8am-6pm, Su 10am-4pm.) At the bend of one of Rye's most antique streets, the **Olde Bell Inn** ❶, 33 The Mint, serves toasted sandwiches (£4-5) and other dainties in a cottage garden. (☎ 223 323. Open M, W, F-Sa 11am-10:30pm, Th 11am-11pm, Su noon-10pm.) If you get a sudden craving for sweets, pay a visit to the **Rye Chocolate Shop** ❶, 5a Market Rd., for some old-fashioned candy. (☎ 222 522. Open daily 9:30am-5pm.)

Use Rye as a pleasant base for exploring its historical neighbors. **Trains** (☎ 08457 484 950) arrive at the station off Cinque Port St. from: Brighton (2hr., every hr., £13); Dover (1½hr., every hr., £10.70); Eastbourne (1hr., every hr., £7.40); London (1¾hr., every hr., £19.80). Local **buses** (☎ 223 343) stop in front of the station. The oldest part of town is a 5min. hike up **Mermaid Street.** To get to the **Tourist Information Centre** from the station, walk down Cinque Port St. and turn right onto Wish St. and left onto the Strand Quay. The TIC, in the Heritage Centre, hands out self-guided audio tours and books rooms for free in person and for a £2 charge by phone. (☎ 226 696; www.visitrye.co.uk. Open daily 10am-5pm. Tours £2.50, concessions £1.50.) Get free **Internet access** at the library. (☎ 223 355. 1hr. max. Open M 9:30am-5:30pm, W 10am-5:30pm, Th 9:30am-12:30pm, F 9:30am-6pm, Sa 9:30am-5pm.) The **post office** is at 22-24 Cinque Port St. (☎ 229 711. Open M-F 8:30am-5:30pm, Sa 8:30am-1pm). **Post Code:** TN31 7AA.

◤ DAYTRIPS FROM RYE

PEVENSEY
Trains run every hr. from Rye and Hastings to Pevensey & Westham Station, half a mile from the castle (£7.10).

William I's march to Battle began from **Pevensey Castle,** a Roman fortress that was already 800 years old when the Norman forces landed. Considered one of the best examples of Roman building in England, the castle has since been reduced to only its original walls, 12 ft. thick and 30 ft. high. (☎01323 762 604. Open Apr.-Sept. daily 10am-6pm; Oct.-Mar. Sa-Su 10am-4pm. £3.70.) The most unusual aspect of Pevensey, however, owes its origins to commerce rather than conquest. The **Mint House,** on High St. just beyond the castle, was originally a Norman mint, connected to the castle by subterranean tunnels. Henry VIII's physician transformed it into a country retreat. Antiques for sale now fill the old oak-panelled rooms, and the ghost of one denizen's murdered mistress has been seen in the smallest room of the house. (☎01323 762 337. Open M-F 9am-5pm, Sa 10:30am-4:30pm. £1.50.)

HASTINGS

Trains arrive from Rye (20min., 2 per hr., £3.90). The TIC, at Queens Sq. and The Stade, signposted from the station, books accommodations for a £1 fee. ☎781 111; www.hastings.gov.uk. Open M-F 8:30am-6:15pm, Sa 9am-5pm, Su 10:30am-4:30pm.

Having surrendered its name and identity to a decisive battle (p. 64), the seaside resort town of Hastings still revels in its 1000-year-old claim to fame. Looming above the carousel and mini-golf-strewn promenade, the fragmentary remains of **Hastings Castle,** built by William the Conqueror, mark the spot where the Norman duke's troops camped before confronting Harold II and the Saxons. The castle met its functional demise in the 13th century, when part of the cliff collapsed and took half the fortifications with it. During WWII, homeward-bound Germans finished the job by dropping excess explosives on Hastings. Catch the **1066 Story,** a 17min. film on the famous spat between William and Harold (and Harald of Norway), and visit the castle's moldy dungeons. The castle's hilltop position offers some of the region's best views. (Take the West Hill Railway from George St. to the top of the hill. Round-trip £1, concessions 60p. ☎781 111; www.discoverhastings.co.uk. Open daily mid-July to Aug. 10am-5:30pm; Apr. to mid-July and Sept. 10am-5pm; mid-Feb. to Mar. and Oct. 11am-4pm; Nov. to mid-Feb. 11am-3:30pm. £3.50.) Before heading back to sea level, duck into St. Clements Caves for the **Smugglers Adventure.** Now more like a theme park, these miles of caves and tunnels were once the nerve center of the Sussex smuggling ring. A ghostly apparition of Hairy Jack is your guide through this spooky lair, full of eerie music and life-size figures that talk to you if you push their buttons. (☎422 964; www.smugglersadventure.co.uk. Open daily Apr.-Sept. 10am-5:30pm; Oct.-Mar. 11am-4:30pm. Last admission 4pm. £6.20.) Exhibits on the area's nautical past reside in several charity-run museums among the chippies on the seafront. The **Shipwreck Heritage Centre,** at the end of the parade on Rock-a-Nore Rd., is the largest and most notable. (☎437 452. Open daily Mar.-Sept. 10am-5pm; Nov.-Feb. 11am-4pm. Suggested donation £1.)

BATTLE

Trains run from Hastings (15min., 2 per hr., round-trip £2.60); Battle Abbey is in the center of town, signposted from the train station. The Battle Abbey TIC books accommodations for a 10% deposit. ☎773 721; www.battle-sussex.co.uk. Open Apr.-Sept. daily 10am-5pm; Oct.-Mar. M-Sa 10am-4pm.

The small town of Battle was named after the 1066 action between the Normans and Anglo-Saxons that took place here. To commemorate his victory in the Battle of Hastings, William built **Battle Abbey** in 1094, spitefully positioning its altar upon the very spot where Harold fell (p. 64). Little remains apart from the gate and a series of 13th-century common quarters. (☎773 792. Open daily Apr.-Sept. 10am-6pm; Oct.-Mar. 10am-4pm. £5.30, concessions £4.) The battlefield across which Duke William's cavalry charged is now marched across by sheep. A free audio tour of the abbey narrates the story of the battle from both Saxon and Norman perspectives as you walk the 1 mi. **battlefield trail** through the now-peaceful green fields.

SOUTH DOWNS WAY

The South Downs Way stretches 99 mi. from Eastbourne west toward Portsmouth and Winchester. It meanders through the rolling white chalk hills and livestock-laden greens that typify pastoral southern England, never far from coastal towns, yet rarely crossing into civilization. The Downs were initially cultivated by prehistoric populations; forts and settlements dot the former paths of Bronze- and Iron-Age tribes, who were followed by Romans, Saxons, and Normans. The Way is well marked from start to finish, and the walking is moderate enough even for novice hikers, making the South Downs—only recently designated a national park—one of the most accessible and rewarding outdoors experiences England has to offer.

▐ TRANSPORTATION

Trains (☎ 08457 484 950) run to Eastbourne from London Victoria (1½hr., 2 per hr., £18.90) and Petersfield from London Waterloo (1hr., 3 per hr., £16.20). From the west, take a train from Amberley (via Horsham), where the Way greets the River Arun. Eastbourne's helpful Bus Stop Shop, Arndale Centre, dispenses info on local **buses.** From the train station, turn left onto Terminus Rd.; Arndale Centre is on the left. (☎ 01323 416 416. Open M-Sa 9am-5pm.) Walking the path takes about ten days, but public transportation allows you to take it in segments. **Trains** connect Lewes to Southease (6min., 2 per hr., £1.80); County **Buses** #143 and 21 connect Eastbourne to Lewes (20min., 2 per day, £1.80). For details, call Eastbourne Buses (☎ 01323 416 416) or Traveline (☎ 870 608 2608).

Cycling has long been a popular means of seeing the downlands: D.H. Lawrence cycled the Way in 1909 to visit his friend Rudyard Kipling. Cyclists and **horses** have access to most of the trail, but in a number of places their routes diverge from those of the walkers. Cycling the Way takes 2-3 days. The Harvey map (£9 at the TIC or bookstores) shows all of the cycling paths in detail. If you're starting from Eastbourne, try Nevada Bikes, 324 Seaside (☎ 01323 411 549). At the other end of the trail, in Winchester, is Halford's, Moorside Rd. (☎ 01962 853 549). The Cyclists Touring Club (☎ 0870 873 0060; www.ctc.org.uk) answers cycling questions. Audiburn Riding Stables, Ashcombe Ln., Kingston, conducts guided 1hr. **horseback tours.** (☎ 01273 474 398. £18, under 16 £15.)

✦ ORIENTATION

Serious hikers will want to begin their exploration in **Eastbourne,** the official start of the Way. Eastbourne's **Beachy Head** (p. 150) is accessible by bus and well signposted from the train station. From the **Winchester** town center (p. 170), at the other end of the Way, head east on Bridge St., turn right on Chesil St., then left on East Hill. When East Hill splits, take the right fork onto Petersfield Rd. and head for the carpark—signs broadcasting "South Downs Way" should appear at this point. From the midpoint village of **Amberley,** just north of Arundel (p. 158), the Way runs north, parallel to the main road (B2139).

🛈 PRACTICAL INFORMATION

Eastbourne is the best place to arrange accommodations and find local services.

Tourist Information Centres:
Brighton: Bartholomew Sq.; see p. 152.

Eastbourne: Cornfield Rd. (☎09067 112 212; www.visiteastbourne.com). Provides basic but free maps and sells detailed 1:50,000 Ordnance Survey Landranger maps. Maps #185 and 197-99 are most useful (£5.50-7.50). Also sells a number of guides. Open Mar.-Oct. M-F 9:30am-5:30pm, Sa 9:30am-5pm; Nov.-Feb. M-F 9:30am-4pm, Sa 9:30-1pm.

Lewes: 187 High St. (☎01273 483 448). Books rooms and sells Ordnance Survey maps and guides. Open Apr.-Sept. M-F 9am-5pm, Sa 10am-5pm, Su 10am-2pm; Oct.-Mar. M-F 9am-5pm, Sa 10am-2pm.

Winchester: The Guildhall; see p. 170.

Guidebooks:

In Print: Paul Millmore's *South Downs Way* (£13) is the bible of the Downs. The Eastbourne and Lewes TICs sell *50 Walks in Sussex* (£8), useful for trekkers. *Millennium Cycle Rides* (£5) by Brian Smials explains good routes in 1066 country (East Sussex); the South Downs Way accommodation guide (£4.50) is helpful for finding places to stay.

Online: Two websites to try are the South Downs Way Virtual Information Centre (www.vic.org.uk) and the Southeast Walks site (www.southeastwalks.com).

Camping Supplies: Millets, The Outdoors Store, 146-148 Terminus Rd., Eastbourne (☎01323 728 340), stocks camping supplies and Ordnance Survey maps. Open M-Sa 9am-5:30pm, Su 10:30am-4:30pm. Brighton also has many outdoors shops.

Financial Services: All major **banks** are located in the **Eastbourne** town center. Be sure to pick up cash before hitting the trail. **Lloyd's TSB,** 104 Terminus Rd. (☎08453 000 000). Open M-Tu and Th-F 9am-5pm, W 10am-5pm, Sa 9am-2pm.

ACCOMMODATIONS

There are few towns along the Way, and **B&Bs** fill quickly. Consider making daytrips; **Brighton** (p. 152) makes a good base, as do **Lewes** (p. 157), **Arundel** (p. 158), and Southcliff Ave. in **Eastbourne.** For a relaxing night on the seafront before hitting the trail, take a room at **Alexandra Hotel ❸**, King Edward's Parade, in Eastbourne. (☎01323 720 131. Breakfast included. Open June-Sept., from £30 per person; Mar.-May and Oct.-Dec., from £28 per person. MC/V.) **Camping** on the Way is permitted with the landowner's permission.

The following three **YHA hostels** lie along or near the Way, each within a day's walk of the next, and each with a 11pm-8am lockout and 11pm curfew. Be sure to call at least two weeks ahead. For other hostels, check the accommodations sections in Brighton (p. 153) or Arundel (p. 158).

Alfriston: Frog Firle, Alfriston (☎01323 870 423). 1½ mi. from the Way and from Alfriston, 8 mi. from Eastbourne. Bus #126 passes the hostel; by foot from Alfriston, turn left from the market cross and pass the village green, then follow the overgrown riverside trail to Litlington footbridge and turn right along the path; the hostel is at the end in a stone house with bovine neighbors. Internet available. Open July-Aug. daily; Feb.-June and Sept.-Oct. M-Sa; Nov.-Dec. F-Sa. Dorms £12.50, under 18 £9. MC/V. ❷

Telescombe: Bank Cottages, Telescombe Village (☎01273 301 357). 2 mi. south of Rodmell, 2 mi. from the Way, 12 mi. west of Alfriston. From Rodmell (p. 151) follow signs directly to the hostel or take bus #123 or 14A and ask to be let off. 18th-century house and cheery staff. Open daily Apr.-Aug. Dorms £11, under 18 £8. MC/V. ❷

Truleigh Hill: Tottington Barn, Truleigh Hill, Shoreham-by-Sea (☎01903 813 419). 10 mi. from Brighton, 4 mi. from Shoreham station. Converted 1930s house with incredible views and modern facilities. Meals £3.75-5. Open daily July-Aug.; Mar.-June and Sept.-Oct. call 48hr. in advance. Dorms £12.50, under 18 £9. MC/V. ❷

🔣 HIKING THE SOUTH DOWNS WAY

EASTBOURNE TO ALFRISTON

The Victorian seaside city of **Eastbourne,** set in the shelter of **Beachy Head,** is the path's official starting point. The open-topped tour bus **Guide Friday** makes trips from Eastbourne's town center to the top of Beachy Head (Apr.-Sept. daily 2 per hr.; round-trip £6.50). Otherwise, walk west along the promenade following the signs until you reach the bottom of the cliffs; then make the strenuous ascent and follow the fields upward past wind-bent trees. The entire journey from the town center to the top of Beachy Head is approximately 4 mi. and a 1½hr. walk. Beware that at a sheer 543 ft. above the sea, Beachy Head can induce vertigo. Because the chalky cliffs are eroding, it is wise to stay far from the edge. From the top you can view the **Seven Sisters,** a series of chalk ridges carved by centuries of receding waters and surpassing the Head in majesty. The queenly sisters hold court about 4½ mi. away, over a series of hills. Far below, 19th-century red-and-white-striped lighthouse **Belle Tout** threatens to fall into the turquoise sea.

From Beachy Head, the path winds past a number of tumuli—Bronze-Age burial mounds dating to 1500 BC—but the overgrown brush makes most of them impossible to distinguish. The Way continues west to **Birling Gap,** the last undeveloped stretch of coast in south England. To reach **Alfriston,** a sleepy one-road village called "the last of the old towns," follow the Way 4 mi. inland over a path once used by smugglers between the Cinque Ports. Bus #126 comes from the railway station in Eastbourne (35min., 5 per day, £1.60).

Another option is the shorter **bridleway path** to Alfriston (8 mi.), which joins a trail just below East Dean Rd. The path passes through **Wilmington** and its famous **Long Man,** a 260 ft. earth sculpture of mysterious origins. Variously attributed to prehistoric peoples, Romans, 14th-century monks, and aliens, the Long Man is best viewed from a distance. It's rumored that Victorian prudes robbed him of male attributes that might have shed some light on his name. The **Giant's Rest ❷,** on The Street in Wilmington, serves home-cooked food (£5-12) and is a great starting

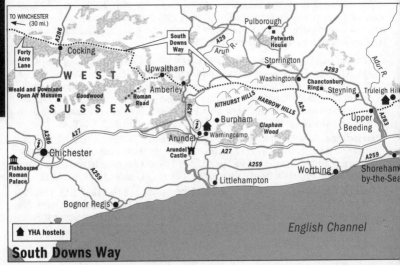

South Downs Way

point for walks. (☎01323 870 207. Open M-Sa 11:30am-3pm and 6-11pm, Su noon-10:30pm. Food served noon-2pm and 7-9pm. Cash only.) Going back through Long Man's gate, onto the South Downs Way over Windover Hill, leads to Alfriston.

ALFRISTON TO FORTY ACRE LANE

From Alfriston, join the Way behind the Star Inn, on High St. (the only street), and continue 7 mi. down gentle slopes to Southease. The Way crosses **Firle Beacon,** which has a mound at the top said to contain a giant's silver coffin. From Southease, proceed north ¾mi. to Rodmell. Rodmell's single street contains **Monk's House,** home of Leonard and Virginia Woolf from 1919 until their deaths. The house retains its intimacy and most of the original furnishings. The faithful can retrace the writer's last steps to the River Ouse (1 mi. away), where she committed "the one experience I shall never describe"; her ashes nourish a fig tree in the garden. (☎01892 890 651. Open Apr.-Oct. W and Sa 2-5:30pm. £2.90.) The **Abergavenny Arms ❷,** Newhaven Rd. (☎01273 472 416; food served M-Sa) in Rodmell is a good place to fuel up for the 2 mi. hike to the **YHA Telescombe** (p. 149).

The closest that the Way actually comes to **Lewes** (LEW-is) is at the village of **Kingston** to the southwest—where hikers from **Brighton** should pick up the trail. Fortifying pub grub (£7-10) is available at **Juggs Inn ❷** in Lewes. (☎01273 472 523. Open M-Sa 11am-11pm, Su noon-10:30pm. Food served noon-2:30pm and 6-9pm.) A stone at the parish boundary, called **Nan Kemp's Corner,** feeds one of the more macabre Downs legends: it is said that Nan, jealous of her husband's affection for their newborn, roasted it for him to eat and then killed herself here. Continue from Kingston for 8 mi. to **Pyecombe,** which brings you to **Ditchling Beacon,** the highest point in East Sussex's Downs. The hill was one in a series that relayed the news of the Spanish Armada's defeat to Elizabeth I. If you've come from Telescombe, **YHA Brighton** (p. 153), 2 mi. from Pyecombe, offers a night's rest.

Ambling from Pyecombe to **Upper Beeding** (8 mi.) takes you to **Devil's Dyke,** a dramatic chalk cliff. Local legend says that the dyke was built by Lucifer himself in a diabolical attempt to let the sea into the Weald and float away all the churches. Climb through fields overrun with crimson poppies to reach the **YHA Truleigh Hill**

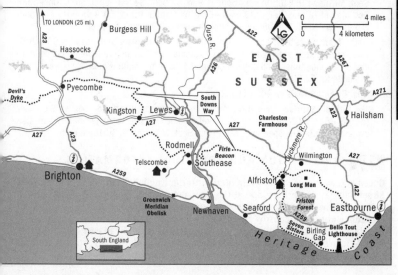

SOUTH ENGLAND

(p. 149), just 1½ mi. east of Upper Beeding. On the path from Upper Beeding to **Washington** (6¾ mi.) lies the grove of **Chanctonbury Ring**—trees planted in the 18th century around a 3rd-century Roman template, built on a previous Celtic layout.

The 6½ mi. trek from Washington to **Amberley** brings you to a path leading to **Burpham,** from which the **YHA Warningcamp** (p. 158) is 3 mi. away. The 19 mi. of orchids and spiked rampion fields from Amberley to **Buriton,** passing through **Cocking,** complete the Way to the northwest. Southward, across the River Arun to **Littleton Down,** are views of the Weald and the North Downs. The spire of Chichester Cathedral marks the beginning of **Forty Acre Lane,** the Way's final arm.

BRIGHTON   ☎01273

The home of the dirty weekend, Brighton (pop. 180,000) relishes its reputation for the risqué. According to legend, the future King George IV sidled into Brighton around 1784 for some hanky-panky. Having staged a wedding with a certain "Mrs. Jones" (Maria Fitzherbert), he headed off to the farmhouse that has since become the Royal Pavilion, and the regal rumpus began. Since then, Brighton has turned a blind eye to some of the more scandalous activities that occur along its shores, as holiday-goers and locals alike peel it off—all off—at England's first bathing beach. Kemp Town (jokingly known as Camp Town), among other areas, has a thriving gay and lesbian population. The huge student crowd, augmented by flocks of foreign youth, feeds the notorious clubbing scene of this "London-by-the-Sea."

▐ TRANSPORTATION

Trains: Brighton Station, uphill at the northern end of Queen's Rd. Ticket office open 24hr. Travel center open M-Sa 8:15am-6pm. Tickets and information also available at One Stop Travel (see below). Trains (☎08457 484 950) from: **Arundel** (1¼hr., every hr., £6.80); **London Victoria** (1hr., 2 per hr., £16.70); **Portsmouth** (1½hr., 2 per hr., £13.40); **Rye** (1¾hr., every hr., £13).

Buses: Tickets and info at **One Stop Travel** (☎700 406). Open June-Sept. M-Tu and Th-F 8:30am-5:45pm, W 9am-5:45pm, Sa 9am-5pm, Su 9:30am-3pm; Oct.-May M-Tu and Th-F 8:30am-5:45pm, W 9am-5:45pm, Sa 9am-5pm. National Express (☎08705 808 080) from **London Victoria** (2-2½hr., every hr., £9.30).

Public Transportation: Local buses operated by **Brighton** and **Hove** (☎886 200; www.buses.co.uk) congregate around Old Steine. The TIC can give route and price information for most buses; all carriers charge £1.40 in the central area. Daysaver tickets available for £2.60.

Taxis: Brighton Taxis (☎202 020). 24hr.

Bike Rental: Sunrise Cycle Hire, West Pier Promenade, Kings Rd., next to West Pier (☎748 881). £12 per day plus £20 refundable deposit. Weekly/monthly hire also available (£32/50). Open mid-Mar. to mid-Sept. M-Tu and Th-Su 10am-6pm.

✳ ▐ ORIENTATION AND PRACTICAL INFORMATION

Queen's Road connects the train station to the English Channel, becoming **West Street** halfway down the slope at the intersection with Western St. Funky stores and alternative restaurants cluster around **Trafalgar Street,** which runs east from the train station. The narrow streets of the **Lanes** constitute a pedestrian shopping area by day and the site of Brighton's carousing by night; head east onto North St. from Queen's Rd. to reach them. **Old Steine,** a road and a square, runs in front of the **Royal Pavilion,** while **King's Road** parallels the waterfront.

Tourist Information Centre: 10 Bartholomew Sq. (☎09067 112 255; www.visitbrighton.com). Enthusiastic staff vends materials on practically every subject, books National Express tickets, and reserves rooms for a £1.50 charge plus a 10% deposit. Open June-Sept. M-F 9am-5pm, Sa 10am-5pm, Su 10am-4pm; Oct.-May M-F 9am-5pm, Sa 10am-5pm.

Tours: CitySightseeing (☎880 123; www.city-sightseeing.com). 50min. bus tours leave from Brighton pier every 30min. Apr.-Oct., with stops at Royal Pavilion, the railway station, and Brighton Marina. £6.50.

Financial Services: Banks line North St., near Old Steine.

Special Concerns: Disability Advice Centre, 6 Hove Manor, Hove St., Hove (☎203 016). Open M and F 10am-4pm, Tu-Th 10am-1pm.

GLBT Resources: Lesbian and Gay Switchboard, (☎204 050). Open daily 5pm-11pm. The **TIC** also offers an extensive list of gay-friendly accommodations, clubs, and shops.

Launderette: Preston St. Launderette, 75 Preston St. (☎738 556). Open M-Sa 8am-9pm, last wash 7:45pm; Su 9am-7pm, last wash 5:45pm. Self-service wash and dry £4. **KJ,** 116 St. George's Rd. Open M-F and Su 8am-7pm, Sa 8am-6pm. Last wash 1hr. before close.

Police: John St. (☎0845 607 0999).

Hospital: Royal Sussex County, Eastern Rd. (☎696 955).

Pharmacy: Boots, 129 North St. (☎207 461). Open M-Sa 8am-7pm, Su 11am-5pm.

Internet Access: There are many small Internet cafes in the town center, especially along St. James St. Try **Starnet,** 94 St. James St. (80p per 30min., £1.20 per hr.).

Post Office: 51 Ship St. (☎08457 223 344). Bureau de change. Open M-Sa 9am-5:30pm. **Post Code:** BN1 1BA.

ACCOMMODATIONS

Brighton's best budget beds are in its **hostels**; the TIC has a complete list. The city's **B&Bs** and **hotels** begin at £25-30 and skyrocket from there, and many require two-night minimum stays on summer weekends. Many mid-range B&Bs line **Madeira Place;** shabbier establishments collect west of **West Pier** and east of **Palace Pier.** To the east, perpendicular to the sea, **Kemp Town** boasts a huge number of B&Bs. Rooms may be cheaper in the **Hove** area, just west of Brighton. Frequent conventions, especially in summer, make rooms scarce—book early or consult the TIC.

Baggies Backpackers, 33 Oriental Pl. (☎733 740). Oriental Pl. is on the right along King's Rd., past West Pier. Live music and spontaneous parties set the mood in this mellow hostel crowded with students. Co-ed bathrooms. Kitchen. Laundry £1.40. Key deposit £5. Dorms £13; doubles £35. Cash only. ❷

Hotel Pelirocco, 10 Regency Sq. (☎327 055; www.hotelpelirocco.co.uk). Wanna-be rock-stars will revel in the over-the-top, hip-to-be-camp atmosphere of Pelirocco. Each of 19 swanky individually themed rooms (try leopard-print "Betty's Boudoir") houses a PlayStation 2 and private bath. Singles £50-60; doubles £90-140. AmEx/MC/V. ❹

Brighton Backpackers Hostel, 75-76 Middle St. (☎777 717; www.brightonbackpackers.com). Lively, international flavor and great seaside location with clean rooms. Surround-sound speakers and pool table make the downstairs lounge an all-night party. The quieter annex faces the ocean. Dorms £15, weekly £80; doubles £25-30. MC/V. ❷

YHA Brighton, Patcham Pl. (☎556 196), 3 mi. north on the London Rd. Take Patcham bus #5 or 5A from Old Steine (stop E, £2) to the Black Lion Hotel. Georgian country house makes a good jumping-off point for the Way (p. 148). Breakfast included. Laundry. Reception closed 10am-1pm. Open Mar.-Oct. daily; Nov.-Feb. Th-Sa. Book ahead July-Aug. Dorms £16, under 18 £12.50. ❷

◗ FOOD

Competition keeps prices low, and many places offer student discounts. The Lanes area is full of trendy places waiting to gobble tourist cash. The chippers along the beachfront avenues or north of the Lanes offer better value. Get **groceries** at Somerfield, 6 St. James's St. (☎570 363. Open M-Sa 8am-10pm, Su 11am-5pm.) Satisfy sugar cravings with **Brighton rock candy,** available at any of the multitude of shops claiming to have invented it.

■ **The Hop Poles,** 13 Middle St. (☎710 444). This popular student hangout is also a bar. Menu offers very creative entrees, from red Thai seafood linguine to vegetarian lasagna. Entrees £6. Food served M-Th and Su 12:30-9pm, F-Sa 12:30-7pm. MC/V. ❷

■ **Food for Friends,** 17a-18a Prince Albert St. (☎202 310). A packed vegetarian joint with large portions and intense flavors. Inventive salads and entrees (£9-13) draw on Indian and East Asian cuisines, but traditional afternoon teas are offered as well. Open M-Th and Su noon-10pm, F-Sa noon-10:15pm. AmEx/MC/V. ❸

Nia Restaurant and Cafe, 87 Trafalgar St. (☎671 371). Very professional waitstaff serves elegantly prepared dishes (£10.50-14) in this cafe near the North Laine. The unique menu offers everything from Japanese cuisine to French pastries to Mediterranean dishes. Open M-Sa 9am-11pm, Su 9am-6pm. MC/V. ❸

Bombay Aloo, 39 Ship St. (☎776 038). Excellent Indian vegetarian cuisine draws faithful regulars. All-you-can-eat meals from 18 steaming and chilled vats (£5, £3.50 from 3:15-5:15pm). Entrees £3-7. Open daily noon-midnight. Sister restaurant (☎622 133), 11a St. James St., across from Somerfield, serves meat dishes. MC/V. ❶

◉ ◗ SIGHTS AND BEACHES

In 1792, Dr. Richard Russell wrote a treatise on the merits of drinking and bathing in seawater to treat glandular disease; thus began the transformation of the sleepy village of Brighthelmstone into a beach town with a decidedly hedonistic bent.

ROYAL PAVILION. Much of Brighton's present gaudiness may be traced to the construction of the proudly extravagant Royal Pavilion. George IV enlisted architect John Nash to turn an ordinary farm villa into a grandly ornate Chinese/Egyptian fantasy palace topped by Taj Mahal-style domes. Rumor has it that George wept tears of joy upon entering it, proving that wealth does not give one taste. After living there intermittently for several months, Queen Victoria decided to have it demolished—proving that wealth does not deny one taste—until the town offered to buy the royal playground. Tour the opulent rooms, complete with authentic furniture and decor, enjoy the pavilion from the surrounding parks by renting a deck chair (£1), or take in the view and a sandwich at **Queen Adelaide Tea Room** ❶. (☎292 880. Open daily Apr.-Sept. 9:30am-5:45pm; Oct.-Mar. 10am-5:15pm. Last admission 45min. before close. £6.10. Tours daily 11:30am and 2:30pm; £1.55. Queen Adelaide Tea room open daily Apr.-Sept. 10am-5pm; Oct.-Mar. 10:30am-4pm.)

THE PIERS. Brighton's unglamorous glitz hits the beach in the form of **Brighton Pier,** England's fourth most popular tourist attraction. It houses slot machines, video games, and condom dispensers, with a roller coaster and other mildly dizzying rides thrown in for good measure. **Volk's Railway,** Britain's first 3 ft. gauge electric train, shuttles along the waterfront. (☎681 061. Open Apr.-Sept. M-F 11am-5pm, Sa-Su 11am-6pm. £2.50.) The **Grand Hotel,** King's Rd., has been rebuilt since a 1984 IRA bombing that killed five but left Margaret Thatcher unscathed. A short walk along the coast past West Pier leads to the smaller residential community of **Hove.**

DOWN BY THE SEA. Brighton's original attraction is, of course, the beach, but those who associate the word "beach" with sand and sun may be sorely disappointed. The weather can be nippy even in June and July, and the closest thing to

SOUTH ENGLAND

Brighton

ACCOMMODATIONS
Baggies Backpackers, 6
Brighton Backpackers
Hostel, 12
Hotel Pelirocco, 7
YHA Brighton, 2

FOOD
Bombay Aloo, 5
Food for Friends, 10
The Hop Poles, 9
Nia Restaurant and Cafe, 1

PUBS
Fortune of War, 16
The Mash Tun, 4
Smugglers, 14
Ye Olde King and Queen, 3

CLUBS
The Beach, 15
Candy Bar, 13
Casablanca Jazz Club, 11
Event II, 8

To K9
LAUNDERETTE (.2 mi.)

Upper Bedford St.
Marine Parade
Charlotte St.
Wyndham St.
Grafton St.
Bristol Rd.
Lavender St.
Hereford St.
Park St.
West Dr.
Eastern Rd.

Upper Rock Gdns.
St. James's Ave.
Rock Pl.
New Steine
Madeira Dr.

Tarner Rd.
Elmore Rd.
Sussex St.
Devonshire Pl.
Chapel St.
Margaret St.
Madeira Pl.

Carlton Hill
Black St.
White St.
Mighell St.
High St.
George St.
Broad St.
Charles St.
Manchester St.

Edward St.
Dorset Gdns.
John St.

Marine Parade

Carlton Hill
William St.
Somerfield

St. James's St.
Steine St.
New Steine

Southover St.
Newhaven St.
Lewes St.
Jersey St.
Newark St.
Belgrave St.
Grove St.
Grove Hill
Albion Hill

Richmond St.
John St.
Ashton Rise
Morley St.
Ivory Pl.
Circus St.

Richmond Pl.
St. Peter's
St. George's Pl.
Grand Parade
Victoria Gardens
Prince's St.

London Rd.
Richmond Terr.
York Pl.
Cheapside
To 2 (3 mi.)
Pelham St.

One Stop Travel
Old Steine
DID
CASTLE SQ.
Castle St.
East St.

Whitecross St.
Trafalgar St.
Sydney St.
Blackman St.
Vine St.
North Cheltenham Pl.
Marlborough Pl.
Gloucester Pl.

The Dome
Brighton Museum & Art Gallery
Royal Pavilion

Station St.
Brighton Station
Terminus Rd.
Railway St.
Clifton St.

Kemp St.
Over St.
Frederick Pl.
Gloucester Rd.
Regent St.
Kensington Gdns.
Upper Gardener St.
Gardner St.
Tidy St.
Tichborne St.
Bond St.
New Rd.
Komedia
Theatre Royal

Guildford Rd.
Buckingham St.
Centurion Rd.
Guildford St.
Surrey St.
North Gardens
North Rd.
Spring Gdns.
Bread St.
Church St.
Kew St.
Windsor St.

THE LANES
Meeting House Ln.
Ship St.
Black Lion St.
King's Rd.
Prince Albert St.
Market St.
Town Hall
Bartholomew
Prince Albert St.

West Hill Rd.
Buckingham Rd.
St. Nicholas's Rd.
New Dorset St.
Queen's Rd.

Albert Rd.
Alfred Rd.
Dyke Rd.
Regent Hill
Regent Row
St. Nicholas's
Clock Tower
QUEEN SQ.
CHURCHILL SQ.

Compton Ave.
West Hill St.
Clifton Rd.
Vernon Terr.
Montpelier Cres.
Clifton Hill
Denmark Terr.
Powis Grove
Vine Pl.
Clifton Terr.
Upper North St.
Clifton Pl.
Montpelier Terr.
Victoria St.
Clarence Sq.
Russell Sq.
Cannon Pl.
Russell Rd.
Russell Pl.
CHURCHILL SQ.

Powis Rd.
POWIS SQ.
St. Michael's Pl.
Montpelier St.
Montpelier Villas
Victoria Rd.
Hampton Pl.
Crown St.
Western Rd.
Dean St.
Spring St.
Stone St.
Castle St.
Queensbury Mews
Regency Sq.
Regency Mews
Grand Hotel

Montpelier Pl.
Temple St.
Montpelier Rd.
Borough St.
Norfolk Rd.
Bedford Pl.
BEDFORD SQ.
Oriental Pl.
Sillwood St.
Sillwood Pl.
Sillwood Rd.
Montpelier Rd.
Little Preston St.
Preston St.

Sunrise Cycle Hire
Brighton Centre
Laundrette

Grand Junction Rd.
Beachfront
Arches
King's Rd.

West Pier

Brighton Pier

English Channel

500 yards
500 meters

sand here are fist-sized brown rocks. Fortunately, turquoise waters, hordes of bikini-clad beach-goers, and umbrella-adorned drinks allow delusions of the tropics to persist. To visit **Telescombe Beach,** 4½ mi. east of Palace Pier, follow the sign for "Telescombe Cliffs" at the Telescombe Tavern.

BRIGHTON MUSEUM AND ART GALLERY. More edifying than most of the town's attractions, this recently renovated gallery features English and international paintings, pottery, and Art Deco and Art Nouveau collections, as well as an extensive Brighton historical exhibit that fully explicates the phrase "dirty weekend." In the fine **Willett Collection of Pottery,** postmodern porcelains and Neolithic relics reflect the varied faces of this seaside escape. *(Church St., around the corner from the Pavilion.* ☎ *292 882. Open Tu 10am-7pm, W-Sa 10am-5pm, Su 2pm-5pm. Free.)*

LANES AND LAINES. Small fishermen's cottages once thrived in the Lanes, an intricate maze of 17th-century streets (some no wider than 3 ft.) south of North St. in the heart of Old Brighton. Now filled with overpriced jewelry shops and restaurants, the Lanes have lost some of their charm. Those looking for fresher shopping opportunities should head to **North Laines,** off Trafalgar St., where a variety of novelty shops and colorful cafes dominate. On Saturdays, the area is closed to traffic and cafe tables and street performers take over.

🎭🎵 NIGHTLIFE AND ENTERTAINMENT

For info on hot-and-happening nightspots, check free *Latest 7* or *The Source,* found at pubs, newsagents, and record stores, or *What's On,* a poster-sized flyer found at record stores and pubs. **Gay and lesbian** venues can be found in the latest free monthly issues of *G Scene* and *3Sixty,* available at newsstands; *What's On* also highlights gay-friendly events. The City Council spent £5 million installing surveillance equipment on the seafront and major streets to ensure safety during late-night partying, but still try to avoid walking alone late at night. The Lanes, in particular, can be too deserted for comfort. **Night buses** N69, 85, and 98-99 run infrequently but reliably in the early morning, picking up passengers at Old Steine, West St., Clock Tower, North St., the train station, and in front of many clubs, usually hitting each spot twice between 1 and 2:30am (£2.50).

PUBS

J.B. Priestley once noted that Brighton was "a fine place either to restore your health, or…to ruin it again." The city's sea of alcohol provides ample means to achieve the latter. The waterfront between West Pier and Brighton Pier is particularly good for reveling. This is a student town, and where there are students there are cheap drinks. Many pubs offer fantastic specials during the week.

Fortune of War, 157 King's Road Arches (☎205 065), beneath King's Rd. by the beach. Evening patrons can relax with their beverage of choice (pints £3.10) to watch the sun set over the Channel. Open M-Sa noon-11pm, Su noon-10:30pm.

Ye Olde King and Queen, Marlborough Pl. (☎607 207). This 1779 farmhouse offers football on TV, a groovy dance floor, a beautiful beer garden, and multiple bars. Live indie rock Sa nights. Open M-Th noon-11pm, F-Sa noon-midnight, Su noon-10:30pm. Food served noon-6pm, Su noon-5pm.

Smugglers, 10 Ship St. (☎328 439). A pirate's den with a dance beat and an adjoining jazz club. Bedsteads, 2 dance floors, velvet couches, and vodka-bottle chandeliers make this pub raucous, to say the least. Pints £2. Happy hour M-F noon-8pm. Open M-Sa noon-11pm, Su 7:30-10:30pm.

The Mash Tun, 1 Church St. (☎684 951). Alternative pub attracts a laid-back student crowd with good food, graffiti-adorned walls, and music ranging from hip-hop to rock to country. Happy hour M-Th and Su 3-9pm; £3.55 for a "double spirit and splash." Open M-F noon-11pm, Sa 11am-11pm. Food served daily noon-6pm.

CLUBS

Brighton is the hometown of Norman Cook, better known as Fatboy Slim, and major dance label Skint Records, so it's no surprise that Brightonians know a thing or two about dance music. Most clubs are open Monday through Saturday 9pm-2am; after 2am the party moves to the waterfront. Many clubs have student discounts on weeknights and higher covers (£4-10) on weekends.

The Beach, 171-181 King's Road Arches (☎722 272). Adds a monstrously big beat to the music on the shore. First F of every month is the swanky "red velvet" night; dress is modern casual. Drinks and snacks served noon-2pm. Cover £10, students £8. Club open M, W-Th 10pm-2am, F-Sa 10pm-3am.

Casablanca Jazz Club, 3 Middle St. (☎321 817; www.casablancajazzclub.com). One of few clubs in Brighton that regularly offers live jazz, funk, and Latin tunes to a mix of students and late-twentysomethings. Dance floor, DJ, and bar upstairs. Headbang, jig, mosh, and grind to bands in the basement. Cover Th-Sa £8. Open M-Sa 10pm-2am.

Event II, at the beach end of West St. (☎732 627). Regularly crammed with a down-from-London crowd looking for thrills. Experienced Brighton clubbers go for less conventional venues, but all agree it's great for a no-surprises good time. Cover from £5; Tu student nights £3. Open Tu and F-Sa 9:30pm-2am.

Candy Bar, 129 St. James's St. (☎662 424; www.thecandybar.co.uk). This new venue caters to lesbian clubbers with nightly entertainment. Check billing outside for the week's events. Cover F-Sa £5. Open M-Th 9pm-2am, F-Sa 9pm-3am, Su 9pm-12:30am.

MUSIC, THEATER, AND FESTIVALS

Brighton Centre, King's Rd. (☎0870 900 9100; www.brightoncentre.co.uk; box office open M-Sa 10am-5:30pm), and **The Dome,** 29 New Rd. (☎709 709; www.brighton-dome.org.uk; box office open 10am-6pm), host Brighton's biggest events, from Chippendales shows to concerts. Local plays and London productions take the stage at the **Theatre Royal** on New Rd., a Victorian beauty with a plush interior. (☎328 488; www.theatreroyalbrighton.co.uk. Tickets £8-25. Open M-Sa 10am-8pm.) **Komedia,** on Gardner St., houses a cafe, bar, theater, comedy club, and cabaret. (☎647 100; www.komedia.co.uk. Tickets £5-12; discounts available. Standby tickets 15min. before curtain. Box office open M-F 10am-10pm, Sa 10am-10:30pm, Su 1-10pm.) The **Brighton Festival** (box office ☎709 709), held each May, is the largest arts festival in England, celebrating music, film, and other art forms. Gays, lesbians, and supporters celebrate the concurrent **Brighton Pride Festival** (☎730 562; www.brightonpride.org) in early August. The famous Pride Parade is on the first Saturday of August, and there is a winter Pride Festival February 4-11 in 2006.

◪ DAYTRIPS FROM BRIGHTON

LEWES. Lewes has an appealing location in the Sussex chalklands and makes a perfect gateway for **South Downs Way** trails (p. 148). Consult the Lewes TIC (p. 149). The views from the ruins of the Norman **Lewes Castle,** High St., 5min. northwest of the train station, merit a visit, as do the small but rich collections of the **Museum of Sussex Archaeology** at the castle's base. (☎486 290. Open Tu-Sa

10am-5:30pm or dusk. £4.40. Admission to the museum comes with a castle ticket.) The 15th-century **Anne of Cleves House Museum,** Southover High St., 15min. from the castle, celebrates Henry VIII's Wife #4, the clever woman who not only managed to leave Henry with her head on her shoulders, but got to keep the house as well. (Trains from Brighton's Queen's Rd. station leave for Lewes every 15min.; £3.50. ☎ 474 610. Open Mar.-Oct. Tu-Sa 10am-5pm, Su-M 11am-5pm; Nov.-Feb. Tu-Sa 10am-5pm; £3. Castle and museum combination ticket £6.20/5.30/3.10/15.45.) Between Ann of Cleves's House and the castle lie the ruins of **Lewes Priory,** England's oldest Cluniac priory and the site where, after his loss at the battle of Lewes in 1264, Henry III signed the treaty that ended the struggle with his barons and provided for the nation's first representative parliament. (☎ 470 606. Entrance by guided tour only.) ▓**Bill's Produce Store ❶,** 56 Cliffe High St., in the town center, offers mouth-watering pizzas, quiches, and soups (£3-6) packed with farmstand-fresh produce (☎ 476 918; www.billsproducestore.co.uk).

THE CHARLESTON FARMHOUSE. Artist Vanessa Bell and her husband Duncan Grant moved here in 1916, transforming the farmhouse into the country retreat of the Bloomsbury group and a center for intellectual life in Britain. Italian frescoes and post-Impressionist paintings decorate the walls. On Fridays, visitors may sneak a peak at Vanessa Bell's studio and take longer guided tours. (East of Lewes, off the A27. Take bus #125 from the Lewes station (6 per day). ☎ 01323 811 265; www.charleston.org.uk. Open July-Aug. W-Sa 11:30am-6pm, Su 2-6pm; Apr.-June and Sept.-Oct. W-Su 2-6pm. Last admission 5pm. W-Sa entrance by guided tour only. £6; themed F £7. Garden only £2.50.)

ARUNDEL   ☎ 01903

The small town of Arundel sits in the shadow of towers and spires. Most visitors are drawn by the fairy-tale castle, but the village's beauty stems less from its architectural highlights, surrounded by wearisome antique shops and outlets, than from the River Arun and hillside location. Arundel provides a perfect place from which to explore the surrounding countryside and the **South Downs Way** (p. 148).

▐▀▐▓ TRANSPORTATION AND PRACTICAL INFORMATION

Trains (☎ 08457 484 950) arrive from: Brighton (1hr., every hr., £7.20); Chichester (20 min., 2 per hr., £4); London Victoria (1½hr., 2 per hr., £17.80); Portsmouth (1hr., every hr., £8.10). Many routes connect at Littlehampton to the south or Barnham to the west. Stagecoach Coastline **buses** (☎ 0845 121 0170) stop a on High St. and just on the town's side of the river, and come from Littlehampton (#702, 1-2 per hr.). South Downs Cycle Hire **rents bikes** 3 mi. east of Arundel on Blakehurst Farm. (☎ 889 562. £15 per day.) Call Castle Cars (☎ 884 444) for a **taxi.**

The **Tourist Information Centre,** 61 High St., dispenses the free *Town Guide* and information on the South Downs Way. (☎ 882 268. Open M-Sa 10am-5pm, Su 10am-4pm.) Other services include: a Lloyds **bank,** 14 High St. (☎ 717 221; open M-F 9:30am-4:30pm); **police** (☎ 0845 607 0999), on the Causeway; and the **post office,** 2-4 High St. (☎ 882 113; open M-F 9am-5:30pm, Sa 9am-12:30pm). **Post Code:** BN18 9AA.

▐▌ ACCOMMODATIONS

B&Bs (£25-30) uphold Arundel's elegance and are priced accordingly. Reserve ahead in summer. The TIC posts an up-to-date list of vacancies.

YHA Warningcamp (☎0870 770 5676), 1½ mi. out of town. Turn right out of the train station, cross the railroad tracks, turn left on the next road, and follow the signs. Family- and group-oriented accommodations. Two kitchens. Breakfast included. Other meals at reasonable prices. Laundry facilities. Internet access. Lockout 10am-5pm. Curfew 11pm. Open July-Aug. daily; Sept.-Oct. Tu-Sa; Nov.-Dec. F-Sa; Apr.-June M-Sa. Dorms £15, under 18 £11. Camping £8 per person. MC/V. ❷

Arden House, 4 Queens Ln. (☎882 544). 8 rosy rooms, some with wood-beam ceilings, close to the train station and town center. Full breakfast included. Singles £30-40; doubles £50, ensuite £55. Cash only. ❹

Camping: Ship and Anchor Marina, Ford Rd. (☎01243 551 262), 2 mi. from Arundel beside the River Arun. Well-kept site with pub and shops nearby. Open Mar.-Oct. Apr.- Sept. £7 per person; Mar. and Oct. £5 per person. £1.50 per vehicle. Showers 50p. ❶

🍴 FOOD

Arundel's pubs and tea shops are generally expensive and unremarkable. A few fruit and bread peddlers line High St. and Tarrant St. The Co-op, 17 Queen St., sells **groceries.** (Open M-Sa 6:30am-10pm, Su 7:30am-10pm.)

White Hart, 12 Queen St. (☎882 374). Pub grub and local ales in a wood-beamed interior. Homemade meals (£9-13) and veggie options. Open M-Sa noon-11pm, food served until 8:30pm; Su noon-10:30pm, food served until 7:30pm. ❷

Belinda's, 13 Tarrant St. (☎882 977). Locals frequent this 16th-century tea room for its large selection of traditional English fare. Linger over cream teas (tea and two scones £4.80), scones (£2.20), and Belinda's famous homemade jam in the cheerful outdoor tea garden. Open daily 9:30am-4:45pm. ❶

Castle Tandoori, 3 Mill Ln. (☎884 224). Dishes out spicy Indian cuisine in a buffet lunch (£9) and dinner (£13). Open daily noon-2:30pm and 6-11:30pm. ❸

Tudor Rose, 49 High St. (☎883 813), on the corner of High and Tarrant St. Order sandwiches (£3.25-5), roasts (£8), veggie dishes (£5-8), and homemade desserts (£2-5) while viewing the arms, armor, and other artifacts on the wall. Open daily 9am-6pm. ❷

👁 🎪 SIGHTS AND FESTIVALS

Poised above town like the backdrop of a Disney film, ◧**Arundel Castle** is lord of the skyline. The castle, the hereditary and current seat of the Duke of Norfolk, was built in the 11th century and restored piecemeal in the 18th and 19th centuries. Winding passages and 131 steps lead to the keep, which portrays life around 1190 with models and pictures and offers scenic vistas. Enjoy cream tea ($4) among the flowers in the castle's tea garden, near the carpark. (☎882 173. Open Apr.-Oct. M-F and Su noon-5pm; last entry 4pm. $11. Grounds only $6.)

Along the river across from the castle, a placard recounts the troubled past of the monks of **Blackfriars,** the Dominican priory whose ruins are nearby. Atop the same hill as Arundel Castle, the **Cathedral of Our Lady and St. Philip Howard** is more impressive for its French Gothic exterior than its standard interior. During the May holiday of **Corpus Christi,** thousands of flowers are laid in a pattern stretching 93 ft. down the center aisle, a tradition dating from 1877. (☎882 297; www.arundel-cathedral.org. Open daily in summer 9am-6pm; in winter 9am-dusk. Free.) At the **Wildfowl and Wetlands Trust Centre,** less than a mile past the castle Mill Rd., concealed paths through over 60 acres of wetlands permit visitors to watch over 1000 birds in a natural habitat. (☎ 883 355. Open daily in summer 9:30am-5:30pm; in winter 9:30am-4:30pm. Last admission 30min. before close. £6.)

Around the August bank holiday, the castle is the centerpiece of the **Arundel Festival,** 10 days of musical and Shakespearean shows. The **Festival Fringe** simultaneously offers free or inexpensive events. Tickets for both go on sale 6-8 weeks ahead of time. (☎ 883 690; www.arundelfestival.org.uk. Tickets up to £30.)

▶ DAYTRIP FROM ARUNDEL

PETWORTH HOUSE. Situated among acres of sculpted lawns and gardens designed by "Capability" Brown, Petworth House holds one of the UK's finest art collections. J.M.W. Turner often painted the house and landscape, and many of his works hang alongside canvases by masters Van Dyck, Bosch, Dahl, and Reynolds. Petworth is also famous for the **Petworth Chaucer,** an early 15th-century manuscript of The Canterbury Tales, and the intricate carvings in the legendary **Carving Room.** The 700-acre landscaped park hosts England's largest herd of fallow deer. *(Take the train 10min. to Pulborough and catch bus #1 to Petworth. ☎ 01798 342 207. House open Apr.-Oct. M-W and Sa-Su 11am-5pm. Last entry 4:30pm. Park open daily 8am-dusk. Tours of house 11am-1pm. House and grounds £7.50. Park only free.)*

CHICHESTER
☎ 01243

Confined for centuries within Roman walls, the the citizens of Chichester take pride in their town's position as a center of English culture. The settlement continues to thrive off its markets (cattle, corn, and others), and all roads still lead to the 16th-century Market Cross, but Chichester's tourist appeal relies on modern attractions. The town boasts an excellent theater, an arts festival, gallery exhibits, and a motor-racing spectacular. Timeless attractions, such as Chichester's cathedral and the nearby Fishbourne Roman Palace, provide permanent delight.

▐ TRANSPORTATION. Chichester is 45 mi. southwest of London and 15 mi. east of Portsmouth. **Trains** (☎ 08457 484 950) serve Southgate station from: Brighton (45min., 3 per hr., £8.70); London Victoria via Horsham (1¾hr., 2 per hr., £17.90); Portsmouth (30min., 3 per hr., £5.10). The **bus station** (☎ 01903 237 661) is opposite the train station. National Express (☎ 08705 808 080) **buses** come from London Victoria (3¾hr., 2 per day, £16). Stagecoach Coastline buses connect Chichester with Brighton (#700; 3hr., 2 per hr., £54.60) and Portsmouth (#700; 1hr., 2 per hr., £5.60). A **Day Goldrider** ticket grants a day's unlimited travel on buses in southern England from Kent to Salisbury (£5.70, concessions £4.20, families £11.40). For **taxis,** call Central Cars of Chichester (☎ 0800 789 432).

▐ ▐ ORIENTATION AND PRACTICAL INFORMATION. Four Roman streets named for their compass directions converge at **Market Cross,** and divide Chichester into quadrants. The **Tourist Information Centre,** 29a South St., books rooms for £2 plus a 10% deposit. (From the train station, exit left on Southgate, which becomes South St. ☎ 775 888; www.visitsussex.org. Open Apr.-Sept. M-Sa 9:15am-5:15pm, Su 11am-3:30pm; Oct.-Mar. M 10:30am-5:15pm, Tu-Sa 9:15am-5:15pm.) **Guided tours** depart from the TIC. (May-Sept. Tu 11am, Sa 2:30pm; Oct.-Apr. Sa 2:30pm. £2.50.) Other services include: HSBC **bank,** at the corner of South St. and East St. (open M-F 9am-5pm, Sa 9:30am-12:30pm); **police,** Kingsham Rd. (☎ 0845 607 0999); **Internet**

access at the Internet Junction, 2 Southgate (☎776 644; www.internetjunction.co.uk; £1 per 20min.; open M-Tu 9am-9pm, W-Sa 9am-8pm, Su 11am-8pm); and the **post office**, 10 West St., with a bureau de change (☎08457 223 344; open M and W-F 9am-5:30pm, Tu 9:30am-5:30pm, Sa 9am-3pm). **Post Code:** PO19 1AB.

⌐⌐ ACCOMMODATIONS AND FOOD. B&Bs abound, but cheap rooms are rare, especially on big racecourse weekends in nearby **Goodwood** (p. 162). Plan on paying at least £25 and expect a 15min. walk from the town center. ▓ **Bayleaf ❸**, 16 Whyke Rd., offers spacious, immaculate rooms, and fresh-squeezed orange juice as part of its delicious breakfast. (☎774 330. No smoking. Singles £26; doubles and twins £52. Cash only.) **University College Chichester ❸**, College Ln., rents out spacious single rooms as a B&B from June through August. (☎816 070. Singles £26.60, ensuite £33.) **Camp** at **Southern Leisure Centre ❶**, Vinnetrow Rd., a 15min. walk southeast of town. (☎787 715. Clean facilities with showers and laundry. Open Apr.-Oct. £12.50-14.50, with electricity £14.50-17.50.)

A **market** convenes on Wednesdays and Saturdays in the parking lot at Market Ave. and East St. Bakeries line North St., while **groceries** chill at Iceland, 55 South St. (Open M-F 9am-6:30pm, Sa 9am-5pm, Su 10am-4pm.) The **Pasta Factory ❷**, 5 South St., rolls out fresh pasta daily; its cannelloni inspire sweet dreams. (☎785 764. Entrees £7-10. Open M-F noon-3pm and 5-11pm, Sa noon-11pm, Su noon-9pm.) The Francophiles at **Maison Blanc Boulangerie and Patisserie ❶**, 56 South St., fill pastries from eclairs to *passionata* (*pain au chocolat* £1.15) and build sandwiches (*croque monsieur* £3.50) for dining in the rear cafe or as takeaway. (☎539 292. Open M-F 8:45am-5:30pm, Sa 8:45am-6pm, Su 9:30am-4pm.) The hip pre-theater set dresses to match the interior at **Woodies Wine Bar and Brasserie ❸**, 10 St. Pancras, the oldest wine bar in Sussex. (☎779 895. Entrees £7-15. Open M-F noon-2:30pm and 5:45-10:30pm, Sa noon-2:30pm and 5:45-11pm, Su noon-4pm and 5:45-11pm.) The town's best pubs also cluster around St. Pancras.

◘ SIGHTS. At **Chichester Cathedral,** just west of the Market Cross, Norman arches frame Reformation stained glass, Queen Elizabeth II and Prince Philip peer from the newly renovated West Front, and Chagall's stained-glass window depicts Psalm 150 with intense colors and detailed symbolism. Building began in 1091, and older items include two Romanesque sculptures and a Roman mosaic under a floor cutaway. The cathedral also holds an incredibly rare image of medieval handholding in the 14th-century effigies of Earl Fitzalan and his wife, which inspired Phillip Larkin's poem "An Arundel Tomb," displayed on a nearby pillar. (☎782 595; www.chichestercathedral.org.uk. Open daily in summer 7am-7pm; in winter 7am-6pm. Tours Apr.-Oct. M-Sa 11am and 2:15pm. Evensong M-Sa 5:30pm, Su 3:30pm. Free lunchtime concerts Tu. Requested donation £3, children £1.50.)

Chichester's other attractions include the **Pallants,** a quiet area with 18th- and 19th-century brick houses in the southeast quadrant. The **Pallant House,** 9 North Pallant, is a restored Queen Anne building attributed to Christopher Wren. Visitors come for its collection of 20th-century art, which includes works by Picasso and Cézanne. A packed schedule of temporary exhibits, concerts, and gallery talks ensures that something interesting happens daily. The museum will reopen in spring 2006, after the completion of renovations. (☎774 557; www.pallant.org.uk. Free tours Sa 3pm. Open Tu-Sa 10am-5pm; last admission 4pm. £4, students £2.50.)

◪▓ ENTERTAINMENT AND FESTIVALS. Located just north of town, the **Chichester Festival Theatre,** Oaklands Park, is the cultural center of Chichester. Founded by Sir Laurence Olivier, the internationally renowned venue has attracted such artists as Maggie Smith, Peter Ustinov, and Julie Christie. A newer part of the general theater, the **Minerva Studio Theatre** is a space for more intimate productions. The **Theatre Restaurant and Cafe** caters to theater-goers from noon on matinee days, and from 5:30pm for evening shows. (☎781 312. Box office open M-Sa 9am-8pm; until 6pm non-performance days. Tickets £15-20; rush seats £6-8, available at 10am day of show.) During the first two weeks in July, artists and musicians collaborate in a period of concentrated creativity for the **Chichester Festivities.** (The box office is at 45 East St. ☎780 192; www.chifest.co.uk. Tickets for talks £2-10, concerts £8-35. Open June until festival's end M-Sa 10am-5pm.)

⚡ DAYTRIPS FROM CHICHESTER

WEALD AND DOWNLAND OPEN AIR MUSEUM. The museum showcases 45 historical buildings that were saved from destruction by transplantion from the southeastern countryside to the site. The mostly medieval structures join exhibits on husbandry, forestry, geology, and society, and offer demonstrations on the function, structure, and decor of Tudor houses. A restored kitchen provides samples of Tudor bakery treats. Most houses have informative guides. *(7 mi. north of Chichester off the A286; take bus #60 to Singleton Horse and Groom (round-trip £4.90); ask the driver for a combination bus and admission ticket. ☎01243 811 363. Open Apr.-Oct. daily 10:30am-6pm, last admission 5pm; Nov.-Dec. and mid-Feb. to Mar. daily 10:30am-4pm; Jan. to mid-Feb. W and Sa-Su 10:30am-4pm. £7.70, seniors £6.70, children £4.10, families £21.)*

FISHBOURNE ROMAN PALACE. Built around AD 80, possibly by local ruler Togidubnus, the palace is the largest extant domestic Roman building in Britain. Historians believe the original residents possessed wealth of Pompeiian proportions, granted as a reward for their assistance in defeating the Boudiccan uprising. The remains include Britain's oldest mosaic floors and a formal garden replanted according to the original excavated Roman layout. *(About 2 mi. west of the town center; follow the signs from the end of Westgate Street or take bus #700 (round-trip £2.30). ☎785 859. Open Aug. daily 10am-6pm; Mar.-July and Sept.-Oct. daily 10am-5pm; Feb. and Nov.-Dec. daily 10am-4pm; Jan. Sa-Su 10am-4pm. Last admission 20min. before close. £5.40.)*

GOODWOOD. Three miles northeast of Chichester, splendid works by Canaletto, Reynolds, and Stubbs, and a world-famous sculpture collection vie for attention in the 18th-century seat of the Duke of Richmond. *(☎755 040; www.goodwood.co.uk. Open Aug. M-Th and Su 1-5pm; Apr.-July and Sept.-Oct. M and Su 1-5pm. 5 tours per day. The schedule is irregular; call ahead. £7.)* The rich and famous prefer **Racing at Goodwood,** a.k.a. 'Glorious Goodwood,' an equestrian tradition over 200 years old. *(☎755 022.)* The plebeian set choose the rumble of motorcars in late June or early July's famous **Festival of Speed** and September's **Motorcar Revival Race.** *(☎755 055.)*

HAMPSHIRE

PORTSMOUTH ☎023

Set Victorian seaside holidays against prostitutes, drunkards, and cursing sailors, and the 900-year history of Portsmouth (pop. 190,500) will emerge. Portsmouth's main source of pride is its harbor, whose turquoise waters are consistently choked with ferries, barges, and pleasure boats. Unfortunately, the city's incomparable naval prominence also served as the motive for its devastation during WWII, and today many of its buildings are victims of 1950s-era architecture. The historic dockyard, however, still harbors hundreds of years of British naval history.

▐ TRANSPORTATION

Trains: Portsmouth and Southsea Station, Commercial Rd., in the city center. Ticket office open M-Sa 5:40am-8:30pm, Su 6:40am-8:40pm. Travel center open M-F 8:40am-6pm, Sa 8:40am-4:30pm. **Portsmouth Harbour Station,** The Hard, ¾ mi. away, sends ferries to the Isle of Wight. Office open M-Sa 6am-7:15pm, Su 6:40am-7:45pm. Trains (☎08457 484 950) go to both stations from **Chichester** (30min., 2 per hr., £5.10) and **London Waterloo** (1¾hr., 4 per hour, £22.10).

Buses: The Hard Interchange, The Hard, next to Harbour Station. National Express (☎08705 808 080) buses arrive from **London Victoria** (2½hr.; every hour; £18.50) and **Salisbury** (1½hr., 1 per day, £12.50).

Ferries: Wightlink (☎08705 827 744) sails to the Isle of Wight from the harbor (15min.; 2-4 per hr.; round-trip £12-14). **Hovertravel** (☎9281 1000) departs from Clarence Esplanade for Ryde, Isle of Wight (9min., 2 per hr., round-trip £10). For services to the Continent, consult **By Ferry,** p. 28.

Public Transportation: A reliable and comprehensive bus system connects the city. **Local bus** companies First (☎08700 106 022) and Stagecoach (☎01903 237 661) run throughout. Daily pass £3, weekly pass £11.

Taxis: Aqua Cars (☎0800 666 666).

■✦ 𝟟 ORIENTATION AND PRACTICAL INFORMATION

Portsmouth sprawls along the coast for miles—**Portsmouth, Old Portsmouth** (near the Portsmouth and Southsea train station and Commercial Rd.), and the resort community of **Southsea** (stretching to the east) can seem like entirely different cities. Major sights cluster at Old Portsmouth, **The Hard,** and Southsea's **Esplanade.**

Tourist Information Centre: The Hard (☎9282 6722; www.visitportsmouth.co.uk), by the historic ships. Bursting with brochures; the map is worth the £1.50. Books accommodations for £2 fee plus a 10% deposit. Open daily Apr.-Sept. 9:30am-5:45pm, Oct.-Mar. 9:30am-5:15pm. Also **Southsea offices** in front of the Blue Reef Aquarium.

Tours: Waterbus (☎07889 408 137) offers 1hr. guided rides in Portsmouth Harbour, leaving from The Hard. Open 10:20am-4:30pm. £4.

Financial Services: Banks cluster around the Commercial Rd. shopping precinct, north of Portsmouth and Southsea Station. **Barclay's** can be found at the corner of Commercial and Edinburgh Rd. (☎9230 5858. Open M-F 9am-5pm, Sa 9:30am-4pm.)

Launderette: Laundrycare, 121 Elm Grove. (☎826 245.) Wash £2, dry £1.80. Open daily 8am-6pm. Last wash 4:45pm.

Police: Winston Churchill Ave. (☎0845 454 545).

Hospital: Queen Alexandra Hospital, Southwick Hill Rd. (☎9228 6000).

Pharmacy: Boots, 31-33 Palmerston Rd. (☎9282 1046). Open M-Sa 9am-5:30pm.

Internet Access: Free at the **library,** Civic Offices, Guildhall Sq. (☎9281 9311). Time may be limited to 30min. Open M-F 9am-7pm, Sa 9am-5pm, Su 12:30pm-4pm.

Post Office: Swindon St. (☎08457 223 344), opposite the train station. Open M and W-Sa 9am-5:30pm, Tu 9:30-5:30pm. **Post Code:** PO1 1AA.

▐ ACCOMMODATIONS

Moderately priced **B&Bs** ($25-30) clutter **Southsea.** Many are located along Waverley Rd., Clarendon Rd., Granada Rd., and South Parade. If you're arriving via the Portsmouth and Southsea Station, catch one of the frequent buses on Commercial Rd. (#40 and 1). From Portsmouth Harbour, hop aboard one of the buses (#5 and 6) that make the trek from The Hard to South Parade.

▓ **Portsmouth and Southsea Backpackers Lodge,** 4 Florence Rd. (☎9283 2495). Take any Southsea bus to The Strand and walk back up to the second road on the left. Immaculate rooms. Pan-European crowd and energetic owners. Comfy lounge, satellite TV, kitchen, grocery counter, laundry (£2), and Internet access (£1 per 30min.). Dorms £12; doubles £26, ensuite £29. Cash only. ❷

Britannia Guest House, 48 Granada Rd. (☎814 234). Colorful rooms and large dining room are decorated with the friendly owner's modern artwork. Full English breakfast included. Singles £25; doubles £45-50. MC/V. ❸

Birchwood Guest House, 44 Waverley Rd. (☎9281 1337). A touch of quiet elegance in a city of carnivals and sailors. 7 bright, spacious rooms have TVs, coffee, hair dryers, and alarm clocks. Personable hosts provide ample breakfasts. July-Aug. singles from £30; families £85. Sept.-June singles from £25; families £75. MC/V. ❸

Camping: Southsea Leisure Park, Melville Rd., Southsea (☎9273 5070). At the eastern end of the seafront, 5-6 mi. from The Hard. Site has toilets, showers, laundry facilities, shop, restaurant-bar, and pool. 1-person tent £9. 2-person tent £16. Electricity £2. ❶

▣▣ FOOD AND PUBS

Restaurants assemble along the waterfront, Palmerston Rd., Clarendon Rd.; between the shopping districts in Southsea; and on Commercial Rd. Pubs cluster near The Hard and along Palmerston. Ethnic eateries await on Albert Rd. near the University of Portsmouth's student houses. The Tesco **supermarket** is on Crasswell St. (☎839 222. Open M-F 7am-midnight, Sa 7am-10pm, Su 10am-4pm.)

Agora Cafe-Bar and Restaurant, 9 Clarendon Rd. (☎9282 2617). Serves English breakfasts (£3-5) and light fare by day and Turkish and Greek cuisine (£7.50-10) by night. Cafe open Tu-F 9am-4pm, Sa 9am-4:30pm, Su 10am-4pm. Restaurant open M-Sa 5:30pm-11:30pm, Su 5:30-10pm. Student discount. Cash only. ❷

Country Kitchen, 59a Marmion Rd. (☎9281 1425). Savory vegetarian and vegan dishes (£2-4) and guilt-free desserts please the taste buds and the wallet. Great service. Open daily M-F 8:30am-4pm, Sa 8:30-4:45pm. Hot food served until 2:30pm. Cash only. ❶

One Eyed Dog (☎9282 7188), corner of Elm Grove and Victoria Rd. South. This pub/trendy bar draws a steady flow of twentysomethings afternoon and night. The place to sate your thirst (drinks £2-3) but not your hunger (bar snacks only). Cheap beer M nights (£1.50). Open M-Th 4-11pm, F-Sa 1-11pm, Su 5-10:30pm. Cash only. ❶

◉ SIGHTS

The bulk of the sights worth seeing are near The Hard. The sail-shaped Spinnaker Tower, originally intended for millennium festivities, opened in summer of 2005, with three observation decks high above the Solent.

▓ PORTSMOUTH HISTORIC DOCKYARD

In the Naval Yard. Entrance next to the TIC; follow the signs. ☎9283 9766. Ships open daily Mar.-Oct. 9:45am-5:30pm, last entry 4:45pm; Nov.-Feb. 10am-5pm, last entry 4:15pm. Each sight £9.70. All-inclusive ticket allows one-time entrance to every sight and is valid for one year. £15.50.

Historians and armchair admirals alike will want to plunge head-first into the **Historic Dockyard,** which brings together a trio of Britain's most storied ships and a smorgasbord of nautical artifacts. Resurrect the past with these floating monuments to Britannia's mastery of the seas. The five galleries of the **Royal Naval Museum** fill in the temporal gaps between the three ships.

MARY ROSE. Henry VIII's *Mary Rose*, holding court in the harbor, is one of England's earliest warships. Henry was particularly fond of her, but, like many of his women, she died before her time, sunk by the French just after setting sail

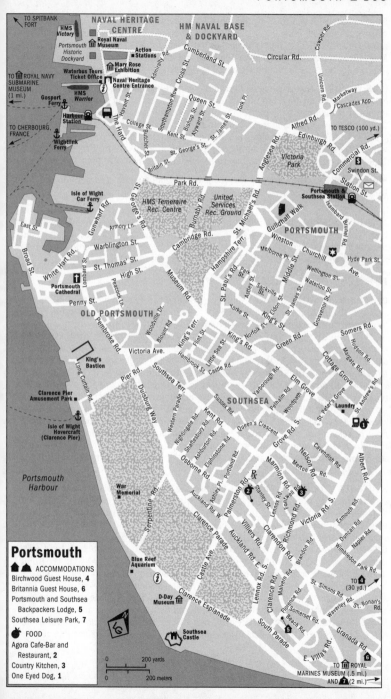

SOUTH ENGLAND

TO SPITBANK FORT

NAVAL HERITAGE CENTRE

HM NAVAL BASE & DOCKYARD

HMS Victory

Royal Naval Museum

Portsmouth Historic Dockyard

Action Stations

Mary Rose Exhibition

Waterbus Tours Ticket Office

Naval Heritage Centre Entrance

TO ROYAL NAVY SUBMARINE MUSEUM (1 mi.)

Gosport Ferry

HMS Warrior

Harbour Station

TO CHERBOURG, FRANCE

Wightlink Ferry

The Hard

College St.

Kent St.

Butcher St.

Havant Rd.

Southampton Row

Cross St.

Admiralty Rd.

Queen St.

Bishop St.

Alward St.

York Pl.

St. James's St.

St. George's St.

Britain St.

Cumberland St.

Circular Rd.

Cowper Rd.

Unicorn Rd.

Marketway

Cascades App.

Alfred Rd.

Edinburgh Rd.

TO TESCO (100 yd.)

Commercial Rd.

Station Rd.

Swindon St.

Anglesea Rd.

Victoria Park

Portsmouth & Southsea Station

Isambard Brunel Rd.

Isle of Wight Car Ferry

East St.

Broad St.

Gunwharf Rd.

Park Rd.

St. George's Rd.

HMS Temeraire Rec. Centre

United Services Rec. Ground

Burnaby Rd.

St. Michael's Rd.

Guildhall Walk

PORTSMOUTH

Armory Ln.

Warblington St.

White Hart Rd.

St. Thomas' St.

Lombard St.

High St.

Cambridge Rd.

Museum Rd.

Hampshire Terr.

St. Paul's Rd.

Park Rd.

Winston Churchill Ave.

Melborne Pl. St.

Middle St.

Hyde Park St.

Wellington St.

Waterloo St.

Astley St.

Sackville St.

Eldon St.

St. James's St.

Grosvenor St.

Portsmouth Cathedral

Penny St.

OLD PORTSMOUTH

Peacock Ln.

Woodville Dr.

Blount Rd.

King's Terr.

Flint St.

Yorke St.

Little Sea St.

King's St.

Norfolk St.

King's Rd.

Green Rd.

Somers Rd.

Hudson Rd.

Margate Rd.

Pembroke Rd.

Victoria Ave.

Hambrook St.

Castle Rd.

Cottage Grove

King's Bastion

Long Curtain Rd.

Pier Rd.

Southsea Terr.

Sussex Rd.

Yarborough Rd.

Pelham Rd.

Elm Grove

St. Peter's Grove

St. Andrew's Rd.

Laundry

Clarence Pier Amusement Park

Duisburg Way

Western Parade

Nightingale Rd.

Kent Rd.

Shaftesbury Rd.

Ashburton Rd.

Queen's Crescent

Woodpath

SOUTHSEA

Grove Rd. S.

Nelson Rd.

Merton Rd.

Cavendish Rd.

Albert Rd.

Isle of Wight Hovercraft (Clarence Pier)

Portsmouth Harbour

Serpentine Rd.

Osborne Rd.

Elphinstone Rd.

Portland Rd.

Marmion Rd.

Exmouth Rd.

War Memorial

Ashley Pl.

Auckland Rd. W.

Palmerston Rd.

Stanley St.

Lennox Rd. S.

Fawcett Rd.

Duncan Rd.

Napier Rd.

Wimbledon Park Rd.

Clarence Parade

Castle Ave.

Villiers Rd.

Auckland Rd. E. S.

Clarendon Rd.

Richmond Rd.

Victoria Rd. S.

TO 4 (30 yd.)

Blue Reef Aquarium

D-Day Museum

Clarence Esplanade

Lennox Rd.

Malvern Rd.

Florence Rd.

St. Simons Rd.

Brandon Rd.

Somerset Rd.

Beach Rd.

Waverley Rd.

St. Ronan's Rd.

Granada Rd.

Southsea Castle

South Parade

E. Villa Rd.

TO ROYAL MARINES MUSEUM (.5 mi.) AND 7 (2 mi.)

Portsmouth

▲ ACCOMMODATIONS
Birchwood Guest House, **4**
Britannia Guest House, **6**
Portsmouth and Southsea
Backpackers Lodge, **5**
Southsea Leisure Park, **7**

● FOOD
Agora Cafe-Bar and
Restaurant, **2**
Country Kitchen, **3**
One Eyed Dog, **1**

0   200 yards
0   200 meters

from Portsmouth in July 1545. Not until 1982 was Henry's flagship raised from her watery grave. The eerie, skeletal hulk will be sprayed with a waxen preservative mixture until 2009, a 15-year process that should make *Mary* live forever. The Mary Rose Museum displays over 19,000 artifacts discovered with the ship, including a collection of 168 longbows meant to be used as shipboard weapons.

HMS VICTORY. Napoleon must be rolling over in his spacious tomb knowing that Nelson's Trafalgar flagship is still afloat. This vessel holds the strongest sentiments of British nationalism, from the plaque on the spot where Nelson fell to the flag code display of his memorable statement, "England Expects That Every Man Will Do His Duty." The *Victory* is still a commissioned warship, the oldest in the world, so espionage laws prohibit taking photographs on board. From October to June, it can only be seen via guided tour—check your ticket for your time slot.

HMS WARRIOR. The *Warrior* was the pride of Queen Victoria's navy and the first iron-hulled warship in the world, but never saw battle. Visitors are free to wander about its four floors.

ACTION STATIONS. Pilot a helicopter or experience other simulated trials in this high-tech addition to the dockyards. The short Omni film *Command Approved* reveals a "typical" day aboard a Type 23 frigate: missiles fly as the ship engages in a war with modern-day pirates (June-Sept. every 30min; Oct.-May every hr.).

THE BEST OF THE REST

OTHER NAVAL SIGHTS. Portsmouth's museums rarely deal with more than the sea and its inhabitants. **Spitbank Fort,** a man-made island, protected Portsmouth through two World Wars. Today, it is a tour site by day and, oddly, a party venue by night. (☎9250 4207; www.spitbankfort.co.uk. 25min. crossing from the Dockyard. Tours Apr.-Oct. Su 2:45pm; call Solent Cruises at ☎01983 564 602. Tours £7, children £5. Pub nights W-Th 7:30-10:30pm, £16. Party Nights F-Sa 8pm-midnight, £22.50. Book tours in advance.) The **Royal Navy Submarine Museum** surfaces in Britain's only walk-on submarine, HMS *Alliance*. It also displays the Royal Navy's first submarine, *Holland I*. The Gosport ferry regularly crosses from the Harbour train station (£1.80); follow the signs or take bus #9 to Haslar Hospital. (☎9252 9217; www.rnsubmus.co.uk. Open daily Apr.-Oct. 10am-5:30pm; Nov.-Mar. 10am-4:30pm. Last admission 1hr. before close. £5.) The **Royal Marines Museum** chronicles the 400 years during which the British Empire was established, flourished, and was lost. (☎9281 9385; www.royalmarinesmuseum.co.uk. Open daily June-Aug. 10am-5pm; Sept.-May 10am-4:30pm. £4.75, students £2.25.)

SOUTHSEA. The ■D-Day Museum, Clarence Esplanade, leads visitors through life-size dioramas of the June 6, 1944, invasion, sharing perspectives from soldiers and the families they left behind. It also houses the Overlord Embroidery, a 272 ft. tapestry that chronologically provides an overview of events and scenes from the war surrounding the Overlord operation. (☎9282 7261. Open daily Apr.-Sept. 10am-5:30pm; Oct.-Mar. 10am-5pm. Last admission 30min. before close. £5.50, students £3.30. Audio guide to the embroidery 50p.) The imposing **Southsea Castle,** built by Henry VIII at the point of the Esplanade, was an active fortress until 1960. Don't miss the secret tunnels bordering the fortress. (Open Apr.-Sept. daily 10am-5:30pm; Oct. daily 10am-5pm. Last admission 30min. before close. £2.50, students £1.50.) The **Blue Reef Aquarium** features sting rays, sharks, displays of exotic coral and fish, anacondas, and poison dart frogs. Its quintet of otters makes the rest of the sea life jealous for attention. (☎9287 5222. Open daily Mar.-Oct. 10am-5pm; Nov.-Feb. 10am-4pm. £7, students £5.50.)

ISLE OF WIGHT   ☎01983

More tranquil and sun-splashed than its mother island to the north, the Isle of Wight offers travelers stunning scenery and sandy beaches. The Isle has softened the hardest of hearts, from Queen Victoria, who reportedly found much amusement here, to Karl Marx, who proclaimed the island "a little paradise."

▐▀ TRANSPORTATION

Ferries: Wightlink (☎08705 827 744; www.wightlink.co.uk) ferries frequently from: **Lymington** to **Yarmouth** (30min.; 2 per hr.; round-trip £9.40, children £4.70); **Portsmouth Harbour** to **Fishbourne** (car ferry; round-trip £10.40/5.20); **Portsmouth Harbour** to **Ryde** (15min., round-trip £10.40/5.20). Red Funnel ferries (☎08704 448 898; www.redfunnel.co.uk) steam from **Southampton** to **East Cowes** (every hr., round-trip £8). Hovertravel (☎811 000; www.hovertravel.co.uk) sails from **Southsea** to **Ryde** (9min., 2 per hr., round-trip £10.40/5.20).

Public Transportation: Train service on the Island Line (☎08457 484 950) is limited to the eastern end of the island, including Ryde, Brading, Sandown, Shanklin, and a few points between. Southern Vectis **buses** (☎532 373; www.svoc.co.uk) cover the entire island; TICs and travel centers (☎827 005) in Cowes, Shanklin, Ryde, and Newport sell the complete timetable (50p). Buy tickets on board. The **Island DayRover** ticket gives you unlimited bus travel (1-day £4, children £2).

Car Rental: South Wight Rentals, 10 Osborne Rd. (☎864 263), in Shanklin, offers free pickup and drop-off. From £22 per day. Open daily 8:30am-5:30pm. **Solent Self Drive,** 32 High St. (☎282 050), in Cowes. From £23 per day, £150 per week.

Bike Rental: Tav Cycles, 140 High St. (☎812 989; www.tavcycles.co.uk), in Ryde. £7 per half-day, £12 per day. Longer rentals available. £25 deposit per bike.

✳ ▐ ORIENTATION AND PRACTICAL INFORMATION

The Isle of Wight is 23 mi. by 13 mi. and shaped like a diamond, with towns clustered along the coasts. **Ryde** and **Cowes** are to the north, **Sandown, Shanklin,** and **Ventnor** lie along the east coast heading south, and **Yarmouth** is on the west coast. The capital, **Newport,** sits in the center, at the source of the River Medina.

Tourist Information Centres: Each supplies an individual town map and the free and thorough *Isle of Wight Official Pocket Guide.* A general inquiry service (☎813 800; www.islandbreaks.co.uk) directs questions to one of the seven regional offices listed below. In winter, TICs tend to close earlier than their posted hours. For accommodations, call the central booking line (☎813 813). Rooms are booked for a 10% deposit.

Cowes: Fountain Quay, in the alley next to the RedJet ferry terminal. Open M-Sa 9:30am-5:30pm, Su 10am-4pm; during Cowes Week (1st week in Aug.) daily 8am-8pm.

Newport: The Guildhall, High St., signposted from the bus station. Open M-Sa 9:30am-5:30pm, Su 10am-4pm.

Ryde: Western Esplanade, at the corner of Union St., opposite Ryde Pier and the bus station. Open M-Sa 9:30am-5:30pm, Su 10am-4pm.

Sandown: 8 High St., across from Boots Pharmacy. Open July-Aug. M-Sa 9:30am-5:30pm, Su 9:30am-4:30pm; Apr.-June and Sept.-Oct. M-Sa 9:30am-5:30pm, Su 10am-4pm. Call the central line for winter hours.

Shanklin: 67 High St. Open Apr.-Oct. M-Sa 9:30am-5:30pm, Su 10am-4pm. Call the central line for winter hours.

Ventnor: The Coastal Visitor's Centre, Salisbury Gardens, Dudley Rd. Open Apr.-Oct. M-Sa 9:30am-4.30pm. Call the central line for winter hours.

Yarmouth: The Quay, signposted from ferry. Open Apr.-Oct. M-Sa 9:30am-5:30pm, Su 10am-4pm. Call the central line for winter hours.

Financial Services: Banks can be found in all major town centers. Fill your pockets in the cities; ATMs are rare in small towns.

Police: Isle of Wight Police (☎0845 454 545).

Medical Services: St. Mary's Hospital (☎524 081), in Newport.

Specific Concerns: Disabled travelers can find help from **Dial Office** (☎522 823).

Internet Access: Ask the local TIC for the nearest location. **Internet Cafe,** 16-18 Melville St. (☎408 294), off High St. by the pier in Sandown, is your best bet for fast service. £1.50 per 15min. Open Tu-Sa 11am-6pm. **Ryde Library** (☎562 170) is free for members, and it only takes 5min. to become one. **Lord Louis Library,** Orchard St. (☎823 800), behind the bus station in Newport. Free. Book ahead.

Post Office: Post offices are in every town center. **Post Code:** PO30 1AB (Newport).

ACCOMMODATIONS

Accommodation prices on Wight range from decent to absurd, often depending on proximity to the shore. Budget travelers should try one of the YHA hostels at either end of the island, look into less-visited areas, or try their luck with the **Accommodation Booking Service** (☎813 813). Campsites are plentiful; check the free *Isle of Wight Camping and Touring Guide*, available from all TICs.

■ **YHA Totland Bay,** Hurst Hill, Totland Bay (☎752 165), on the west end of the island. Take Southern Vectis bus #7 or 7A to Totland War Memorial; turn left up Weston Rd., and take the 2nd left onto Hurst Hill. Hostel is on the top of the hill on the left. Comfortable lodgings in a fantastic cliffside location—a lucky few even get sea vistas. Kitchen. Lockout 10am-5pm. Curfew 11pm. Open May-Aug. daily; Mar.-Apr. and Sept.-Oct. Tu-Sa. Dorms £13, under 18 £10. AmEx/MC/V. ❷

■ **Claverton House,** 12 The Strand, Ryde (☎613 015). Lavishly appointed bedrooms and flower-scented private bathrooms with thick towels could tempt even the most ardent sightseer to spend the day in the tub, but the sea view from the dining room will lure you out again. Singles £60 for 2 nights; doubles £80 for 2 nights. Cash only. ❸

YHA Sandown, The Firs, Fitzroy St., Sandown (☎402 651). Signposted from town center; from the train station, take Station Ave. to Fitzroy St. on the right. Clean dorms, kitchen, and large lounge/dining room. Meals £3.60-5.20. Luggage storage and wet-weather shelter available during lockout (10am-5pm). No curfew. Open late Mar. to mid-Sept. daily; mid-Sept. to Dec. and Mar. W-Su. Dorms £13, under 18 £10. MC/V. ❷

Seaward Guest House, 14-16 George St., Ryde (☎563 168). Near the hovercraft, bus, and train stations. Friendly host offers 7 airy rooms. Hearty breakfasts with vegetarian options included. Singles £22; doubles and quads £20 per person, ensuite £24. MC/V. ❷

Camping: Beaper Farm Camping Site (☎615 210), between Ryde and Sandown; take bus #7. Showers and laundry facilities. Open May-Sept. May-June and Sept. £5 for 2 people; July-Aug. £8 for 2 people. Electricity £2. ❶

FOOD

Wanderers on Wight can find food on the local High St. or Esplanade. Local fish is a specialty. The *Official Eating Out Guide*, free and distributed by TICs, offers additional dining options. Most larger cities have supermarkets, and the island has nearly one pub per square mile. In Ryde, feast on exquisite gourmet baguettes and pastries (£1.40-4.70) from the **Baguette Factory ❶**, 24 Cross St. (☎611 115. Open M-Sa 8:30am-4pm.) **S. Fowler & Co. ❶**, 41-43 Union St., Ryde, buzzes with tourists and locals. Plenty of pub meals are under £5, including several vegetarian options. (☎812 112. Open daily 10am-midnight. Food served until 10pm. AmEx/MC/V.)

🎦 🌸 SIGHTS AND FESTIVALS

Wight's natural treasures are especially beautiful in the west, with hillsides, multi-colored **beaches**, and the famous Needles. Buses #7, 7A, and 7B to Alum Bay catch breathtaking views along cliff roads. **Zoos** specialize in everything from butterflies to dinosaurs, and one museum is dedicated to the fine art of **smuggling**. All these sights are listed in the *Official Pocket Guide* (p. 167) and are bound to delight.

▧ CARISBROOKE CASTLE. Carisbrooke includes one of England's most complete Norman shell-keeps, which has been sitting atop its motte for 900 years. The interiors contain detailed plaques; visitors can see where Charles I, a prisoner at Carisbrooke in 1647, got stuck in a window while trying to escape. A museum details the structure's history and includes the **Tennyson Room,** with the Victorian poet laureate's desk, cloak, and funeral pall. William the Conqueror's **Chapel of St. Nicholas** has been restored as a WWII memorial. *(From Newport, with the bus station on your left, follow Upper St. to James St., turn right on Trafalgar St., and bear left on Castle Rd., which becomes Castle Hill. ☎522 107. Open daily Apr.-Sept. 10am-5pm; Oct.-Mar. 10am-4pm. £5.30.)*

OSBORNE HOUSE. Despite its extravagance, with halls full of paintings and statues of Victoria, Albert, and family, this former royal residence showcases a personal side to Queen Victoria's life that isn't often seen. Victoria and Prince Albert commissioned it as a "modest" country home and refuge from affairs of state. After Albert died, it became Victoria's retreat, decorated with mementos and family photographs. The India Exhibit, featuring the elegant **Durbar Room,** is the most spectacular. In the Horn Room, nearly all of the furniture is made from antlers. **Horse-and-carriage rides** (£2.50) through the manicured grounds pass the children's Swiss Cottage; free minibuses follow the same route. *(Take Southern Vectis bus #4 or 5 from Ryde or Newport, respectively. ☎200 022. Open Apr.-Sept. daily 10am-5pm, last entry 4:30pm; Oct. M-Th and Su 10am-4pm; Nov.-Mar. by tour only. House and grounds £9, concessions £6.70, under 16 £4.50. Grounds only £5.30/4/2.70.)*

ALUM BAY AND THE NEEDLES. Some of Wight's most striking sights predate both Victorians and Normans. On the western tip of the island, the white chalk Needles jut into the sea. Alum's pleasure park distracts from the bay's natural beauty, but a **chairlift** runs down the cliffs to the famous colored beaches—used by resourceful Victorians for paint pigments. *(Take bus #7, 7A, 7B, or 42 to Alum Bay. ☎532 373. Needles Park (☎0870 458 0022; www.theneedles.co.uk) open daily Easter to Oct. 10am-5pm; later in Aug. Free. Car park £3. Chairlift round-trip £3.25, children £2.25.)*

WALKING, CYCLING, AND FESTIVALS. Walkers and cyclists enjoy the coastal path stretching from **Totland,** past lighthouses both modern and medieval at **St. Catherine's Point,** to **St. Lawrence** at the southern end of the island. Explore the island's 500 mi. of footpaths during the **Walking Festival** (☎813 800) in mid-May and **Cycling Festival** (☎823 347) in late September, when participants pace or race over scenic routes. Wight's **Garlic Festival,** which takes place on a weekend in late August, brings over 250 stalls selling garlic beer, garlic ice cream, and garlic prawns. *(☎863 566; www.garlicfestival.co.uk.)*

WINCHESTER   ☎ 01962

Though best known for its cathedral and as home to Jane Austen and John Keats, Winchester was a political and population center of early medieval England; both Alfred the Great and William the Conqueror deemed it the center of their kingdoms. Monks prepared the *Domesday Book* for William here (p. 64). During the Great Plague of 1665, the town was also a temporary court for Charles II.

▟ TRANSPORTATION

Winchester makes an excellent daytrip from **Salisbury** or **Portsmouth.**

Trains: Winchester Station, Station Hill, northwest of the city center. Ticket counter open M-F 6am-8:30pm, Sa 6am-7:30pm, Su 7am-8:30pm. Trains (☎ 08457 484 950) from: **Brighton** (1½hr., every hr., £19.40); **London Waterloo** (1hr., 3-4 per hr., £21); **Portsmouth** (1hr., every hr., £8); **Salisbury** (1hr., 2 per hr., £11.20). Be prepared to change trains at Basingstoke or Fareham.

Buses: Buses stop outside on Broadway near Alfred's statue, or inside the **bus station.** Open M-F 8:30am-5pm, Sa 8:30-noon. National Express (☎ 08705 808 080) runs from: **London** via **Heathrow** (1½hr., 7 per day, £11.80); **Oxford** (2½hr., 2 per day, £8.90); **Southampton** (30min., 12 per day, £2.30). Hampshire Stagecoach (☎ 08451 210 180) comes from **Salisbury** (#68; 1hr., 6 per day, £4.50). **Explorer** tickets are available for buses in Hampshire and Wiltshire (£6.50, children and seniors £5, families £13). **Local buses** (☎ 01256 464 501) stop by the bus and train stations. Day pass £2.60. Ask for a timetable of Winchester buses at the TIC.

Taxis: Francis Taxis (☎ 884 343), by the market.

✦ ❷ ORIENTATION AND PRACTICAL INFORMATION

Winchester's main (and commercial) axis, **High Street,** stretches from the statue of Alfred the Great at the east end to the arch of **Westgate** opposite. The city's bigger roads stem off High St., which transforms into **Broadway** as you approach Alfred.

Tourist Information Centre: The Guildhall, Broadway (☎ 840 500; www.visitwinchester.co.uk), across from the bus station. Stocks free maps, seasonal *What's On* guides, and city guides. **Walking tours** £3, children free. Helpful multilingual staff books accommodations for £3 in person or £5 by phone, plus a 10% deposit. Open May-Sept. M-Sa 9:30am-5:30pm, Su 11am-4pm; Oct.-Apr. M-Sa 10am-5pm.

Financial Services: Major **banks** cluster at the junction of Jewry St. and High St. Farther down is the **Royal Bank of Scotland,** 67-68 High St. (☎ 863 322). Open M-Tu and Th-F 9:15am-4:45pm, W 10am-4:45pm.

Launderette: 27 Garbett Rd., Winnall (☎ 840 658). Climb Magdalen Hill, turn left on Winnall Manor Rd., and follow until Garbett Rd. on your left. £2.50. Open M-F 8am-8pm, Sa 8am-6pm, Su 10am-6pm. Last wash 1hr. before close.

Police: North Walls (☎ 08450 454 545), near the intersection with Middle Brook St.

Hospital: Royal Hampshire County, Romsey Rd. (☎ 863 535), at St. James Ln.

Pharmacy: Boots, 35-39 High St. (☎ 852 2020). Open M-Sa 8:30am-6pm, Su 10:30am-4:30pm.

Internet Access: Winchester Library, Jewry St. (☎ 853 909). 8 terminals. Free. Open M-Tu and F 9:30am-7pm, W-Th and Sa 9:30am-5pm.

Post Office: Middlebrook St. Open M and W-Sa 9am-5:30pm, Tu 9:30am-5:30pm. **Post Code:** SO23 8UT.

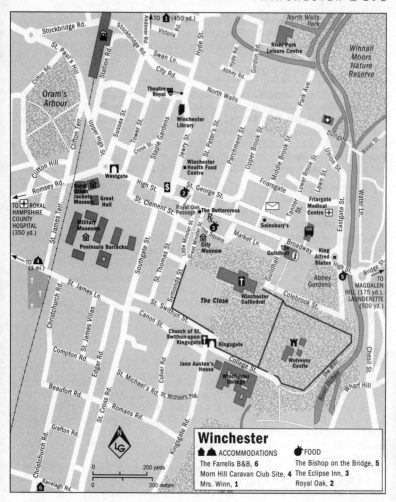

Winchester

▲▲ ACCOMMODATIONS   🍴 FOOD

The Farrells B&B, **6**   The Bishop on the Bridge, **5**
Morn Hill Caravan Club Site, **4** The Eclipse Inn, **3**
Mrs. Winn, **1**   Royal Oak, **2**

🔖 ACCOMMODATIONS

Winchester's **B&Bs** assemble half a mile southwest of the TIC, near **Ranelagh Road**, at the corner of Christchurch Rd. and St. Cross Rd. Buses #29 and 47 make the journey from the town center twice an hour; #69 runs the same route each hour. Many pubs also offer accommodations. A stream of Londoners drives up prices.

The Farrells B&B, 5 Ranelagh Rd. (☎869 555), off Christchurch Rd., a 10min. walk from town. This 19th-century house feels instantly welcoming, with decades of family photos and vintage Brit-abilia on the walls. Singles £30; doubles £46. Cash only. ❸

Mrs. Winn, 2 North Hill Close (☎864 926). Comfortable, cheap rooms up the road from the train station. Tended by hosts with an affection for backpackers and other budget travelers. £15 per person. Cash only. ❷

Morn Hill Caravan Club Site, Morn Hill (☎869 877), 3 mi. east of Winchester off A31, toward New Forest. Mainly for caravans, so extra facilities are limited. Open Mar.-Oct. Caravans £8.50-20.60. Tents at warden's discretion; call ahead. Cash only. ❶

🔸🔹 FOOD AND PUBS

High Street and **Saint George's Street** are home to food markets, fast-food joints, and tea houses. Restaurants serve more substantial fare on **Jewry Street,** where you'll find **Winchester Health Food Centre,** 41 Jewry St. (☎851 113. Open M-F 9:30am-5:45pm, Sa 9am-5:30pm.) For **groceries** and fresh food, go to Middle Brook St., off High St., where there is a Sainsbury's (☎861 792; open M-Sa 7am-8pm, Su 11am-5pm), an open-air **market** (open W-Sa 8am-6pm), and a farmers' market on the second and last Sunday of every month from May to September.

The Eclipse Inn, The Square (☎865 676). Winchester's smallest pub is in a 16th-century rectory the claustrophobic should avoid. Pub grub (£3-7) attracts regulars and, according to tales passed over pints, a ghost or two. Open M-Sa 11am-11pm, Su noon-11pm. Food served daily noon-3pm. ❶

The Bishop on the Bridge, 1 High St. (☎855 111), on the river. Enjoy a meal on the patio or lounge on leather chairs. Students flock here and stay late. Open M-Th noon-11pm, F-Sa noon-midnight, Su noon-10:30pm. Food served M-Sa until 9pm, Su until 8pm. ❷

Royal Oak, Royal Oak Passage (☎842 701), next to the Godbegot House off High St. Despite its refurbished gleam, this is yet another pub that claims to be the kingdom's oldest, tracing its origins back to 1390. Descend into the subterranean foundations and enjoy the locally brewed Greene King cask ale (£2.30) and pub grub (£4-8). Open daily 11am-11pm. Food served daily 11am-9pm. ❶

👁 SIGHTS

WINCHESTER CATHEDRAL. Winchester and Canterbury, housing the respective shrines of St. Swithun and St. Thomas à Becket, were the two spiritual capitals of medieval England. Winchester Cathedral's situation atop peat bogs has forced several reconstructions, rendering the modern structure a stylistic hybrid. Massive Gothic vaults dominate the nave of the longest cathedral in medieval Europe (556 ft.), but the original Norman stonework encloses the transept and accounts for the cathedral's squat and heavy appearance. The oddly Cubist stained glass window is courtesy of Cromwell's window-shattering soldiers. Jane Austen is entombed beneath a humble stone slab in the northern aisle. (*5 The Close. ☎857 200; www.winchester-cathedral.org.uk. Free 1hr. tours depart from the west end of the nave daily 10am-3pm on the hour. 1¼hr. tower tours (£3) also available W 2:15pm, Sa 11:30am and 2:15pm. Open M-Sa 8:30am-6pm, Su 8:30am-5:30pm. East End closes at 5pm. Suggested donation £4. Photography permit £2.*) At the south transept, the lavishly illuminated 12th-century Winchester Bible resides in the **Library,** and the Triforium Gallery contains several relics. (*Open in summer M 2-4:30pm, Tu-F 11am-4:30pm, Sa 10:30am-4:30pm; in winter W and Sa 11am-3:30pm. £1.*) Outside, to the south of the cathedral, is tiny **St. Swithun's Chapel,** rebuilt in the 16th century, nestled above **Kingsgate.** (*Always open. Free.*)

GREAT HALL. Henry III built a castle on the remains of a fortress of William the Conqueror; it became a favorite royal haunt. The Great Hall remains, a gloriously intact medieval structure containing a Round Table modeled after King Arthur's.

Henry VIII tried to pass the table off as authentic to Holy Roman Emperor Charles V, but the repainted "Arthur," resembling Henry himself, fooled no one. *(At the end of High St. atop Castle Hill. Open daily 10am-5pm. Free.)*

MILITARY MUSEUMS. Through Queen Eleanor's Garden, in the Peninsula Barracks, five military museums (the **Royal Hampshire Regiment Museum,** the **Light Infantry Museum,** the **Royal Greenjackets Museum,** the **Royal Hussars Museum,** and the **Gurkha Museum**) tell the stories of some of Britain's great military units. The Royal Greenjackets Museum is the best of the bunch. The highlight is a 276 sq. ft. diorama of the Battle of Waterloo containing 21,500 tiny soldiers and 9600 tiny steeds. *(Between St. James Terr. and Southgate St. ☎828 549. Open M-Sa 10am-1pm and 2-5pm, Su noon-4pm. £2, concessions £1, families £6. Hours for the other 4 museums are similar, but vary; the Gurkha museum is the only other to charge admission; £1.50, concessions 75p.)*

WOLVESEY CASTLE. The walk along the river to Wolvesey Castle, once home to the Norman bishop, may be more enjoyable than the site itself, since only the walls of the once-magnifiscent castle remain. *(The Close. Walk down The Weir on the river or down to the end of College St. ☎252 000. Open Apr.-Oct. daily 10am-5pm. Free.)*

CITY MUSEUM. Archaeological finds, photographs, and interactive exhibits explore the city's past. The Roman gallery includes a complete floor mosaic from the local ruins of a Roman villa, and the Anglo-Saxon room holds the 10th-century tomb. *(At Great Minster St. and The Square. ☎848 269. Open Apr.-Oct. M-Sa 10am-5pm, Su noon-5pm; Nov.-Mar. Tu-Sa 10am-4pm, Su noon-4pm. Free. 1hr. audio guide £2, under 16 free.)*

WALKS. The Buttercross, standing at 12 High St., is a good starting point for several walking routes through town. The statue derives its name from the shadow it cast over the 15th-century market, keeping the butter cool. An ideal walk is along the **River Itchen,** the same taken by poet John Keats; directions are available at the TIC (50p). For a view of the city, including the Wolvesey ruins, climb to **Saint Giles's Hill Viewpoint** at sunset. Pass the Mill, take Bridge St. to the gate marked Magdalen Hill, and follow the paths. *The Winchester Walk,* detailing various possible walking tours of Winchester, is available at the TIC (60p).

🎵 🌿 ENTERTAINMENT AND FESTIVALS

Weekends attract revelers to bars along **Broadway** and **High Street.** The **Theatre Royal,** Jewry St., hosts regional companies and concerts (☎840 440; www.theatre-royal-winchester.co.uk. Box office open M-F 10am-6pm, Sa 10am-5pm). The **Homelands Music Festival** takes place in late May. Though it can't compare with Glastonbury, it draws big names in rock every year. Buy tickets from the TIC. In early July, the **Hat Fair** (☎849 841; www.hatfair.co.uk), the longest-running street theater festival in Britain, fills a weekend with free theater and peculiar headgear.

🔅 DAYTRIPS FROM WINCHESTER

🏚 AUSTEN'S COTTAGE

Take Hampshire bus X64 (M-Sa 11 per day, round-trip £5.50) or London and Country bus #65 on Su, from Winchester. Ask to be let off at the Chawton roundabout and follow the brown signs. ☎01420 83262. Open Mar.-Nov. daily 11am-4pm.; Dec.-Feb. Sa-Su 11am-4pm. £4.50, students £3.50, children £1.

From 1809 to 1817, Jane Austen lived in the unassuming village of **Chawton,** 15 mi. northeast of Winchester. Visitors have come in droves since the recent cinematic fad for adaptations of her novels. It was here, at a tiny wooden table in the dining room of an ivy covered "cottage," that Lizzie Bennett, Emma Woodhouse, and their respective suitors were brought to life. You can still hear the creaking door that warned Austen to hide her writing amid her needlework. Personal letters, belongings, and first editions of her books adorn the walls and fill the bookcases.

THE NEW FOREST

20 mi. southwest of Winchester. Take bus #46 to Southampton (round-trip £5) and transfer to bus #56 or 56A to Lyndhurst (round-trip £5.40) or catch a train to Southampton and then a bus to Lyndhurst. ☎ 02380 283 444; www.thenewforest.co.uk. Museum open daily 10am-5pm. £3, concessions £2.50, families £9.

England's newest National Park was once William the Conqueror's 145 sq. mi. personal hunting ground. It remains, 1000 years later, an idyllic example of rural England. Wild ponies and deer wander freely, and the forest is dotted with villages. The **Rufus Stone** (near Brook and Cadnam) marks the spot where William's son was slain. For the young, pony rides are a popular activity; for the young at heart, try a 2hr. "western riding" tour at **Burley Villa Riding School** (☎ 01425 610 278) in New Milton. The **Museum and Visitor Centre** in Lyndhurst, the forest's largest town, has a list of campsites and other accommodations.

Refugee Immigration and the Channel Tunnel

When the $15 billion Channel Tunnel ("Chunnel") was completed in 1994, it was hailed as a tremendous advance in Europe's infrastructure. No longer would ferries or airplanes be needed to cross between England and France—the English Channel could be traversed in a mere 20 minutes. However, it turns out that the Chunnel serves as the most convenient route not only for cargo, but also for refugees who are desperate to find a way onto British soil.

Soon after its completion, refugees from Eastern Europe, the Middle East, and Central Asia began to mass on the French side of the Chunnel, hoping for passage to England. Britain has a well-deserved reputation for being the most hospitable nation in Europe to those fleeing their homes, providing shelter and food vouchers while considering applications for asylum. English is also the only foreign language many refugees know.

For many refugees, the journey begins by paying smugglers to secure passage to the tiny French town of Sangatte, unofficial waiting site for the men hoping to make the hazardous journey to England. (Those who attempt the crossing are almost all young males.) Often, they have forfeited their life savings to ride in the backs of trucks—or, if they are lucky, in private cars—across Europe to Sangatte. There they are greeted by Red Cross workers who supervise the camp, providing food and, more often than not, encouragement. Marc Gentilini, president of the French Red Cross, defends his organization's role: "These people have traveled thousands of miles to get here, and it is impossible to make them believe they can't go the last 32 miles."

Refugees pay smugglers for tips on the best ways of getting through the Chunnel—either by hitching rides on freight trains or, more dangerously, on the outside of the Eurostar, which can reach speeds up to 180 mph. They must sneak over fences and past security guards, then onto the trains by sprinting after them or leaping from an overpass. Hidden in the trucks carried on freight trains, on metal ledges under the body of the carriage, or on the sloping roofs of passenger cars, they wait for the train to arrive in England, where they can turn themselves over to the police and ask for asylum. Those who make it must face British social services and wait in limbo while they apply for asylum. If they are approved, they commonly face xenophobia during the search for positions for which they are overqualified. (Those who can afford a smugglers' passage are often successful professionals or students who end up working in restaurants or as manual labor.)

In November 2001, in an effort to stem the tide of refugees, the French rail service reduced by two-thirds the number of freight trains it sent through the Chunnel. A $9 million investment to improve security, including electric fences and more security personnel, has had some effect—50,000 would-be immigrants were apprehended in 2001. Nevertheless, there is still enough chance of success that people keep trying, occasionally planning mass invasions of the train-yards to overwhelm security forces. As long as the Chunnel affords some hope for a new life, refugees will continue to make their way across by whatever means possible. Despite all the difficulties, England provides a safe haven, far from the wars, political repression, and persecution many of them are fleeing. As Shewan, a migrant from northern Iraq who arrived in England a few years ago, plainly stated, "I feel safe in England. Here I am sure of my life. I know I'm going to stay alive."

Sarah Kerman holds a degree in Literature from Harvard University. She has done some freelance writing and has worked as a writing tutor at the Johns Hopkins Center for Talented Youth.

SOUTHWEST ENGLAND

England's southwest is a land of history and legend. King Arthur is said to have been born at Tintagel on Cornwall's northern coast and to have battled Mordred on Bodmin Moor. One village purports to be the site of Camelot, another the resting place of the Holy Grail, and no fewer than three small lakes are identified as the grave of Arthur's sword, Excalibur. In more modern myth, the ghost of Sherlock Holmes still pursues the Hound of the Baskervilles across Dartmoor. Since the Roman invasion, the isolated southwest has provided refuge for many clans and tribes, whose influence lingers everywhere from harbor towns to dusty hiking paths. Cornwall was the last stronghold of the Celts in England, and evidence of even older Neolithic communities remains, most famously at Stonehenge. Other eras have left their monuments as well, from Salisbury's medieval cathedral and Bath's Roman spas to the fossils on Dorset's Jurassic Coast.

HIGHLIGHTS OF SOUTHWEST ENGLAND

PUZZLE over one of history's most astounding engineering feats and one of the world's greatest mysteries at Stonehenge (p. 182).

DALLY in the world of 18th-century pleasure-seekers at Bath, a Roman spa town with elegant buildings and a history of improper behavior (p. 183).

STROLL on boardwalks on the Channel Islands; they're situated between Britain and France, beautiful, and VAT-free (p. 243).

TRANSPORTATION IN SOUTHWEST ENGLAND

It tends to be easier to get to Somerset, Avon, and Wiltshire than regions farther southwest. **Trains** (☎08457 484 950) offer fast service from London and the north. The region's primary east-west line from London Paddington passes through Taunton (£41), Exeter (£45), and Plymouth (£49), ending at Penzance (£57). Frequent trains from London Waterloo connect London to Bath, Bristol, and Salisbury. Branch lines connect St. Ives, Newquay, Falmouth, and Barnstaple to the network. A variety of Rail Rover passes can be used in the region: the **Freedom of the Southwest Rover** covers Cornwall, Devon, Somerset, and parts of Avon and Dorset (8 days out of 15 £61). The **Devon Rail Rover** is bounded by and includes travel on the Taunton-Exmouth line on the east and the Gunnislake-Plymouth line in the west (3 days out of 7 £24; 8 out of 15 £39.50). The **Cornish Rail Rover** is bounded by the Gunnislake-Plymouth line (£18/33).

Buses can be few and far between. National Express (☎08705 808 080) runs to major points along the north coast via Bristol and to points along the south coast (including Penzance) via Exeter and Plymouth. For journeys within the region, local buses routes are usually less expensive and farther-reaching than trains. First is the largest bus company in the area. The comprehensive Traveline service (☎0870 608 2608; open daily 7am-5pm) can help plan travel to any destination. **Explorer** and **Day Rambler** tickets (£6, concessions £4.25, families £12.50) allow unlimited travel on all buses within one region. The **Corridor Ticket** (£2.50; £1 surcharge before 8:45am)

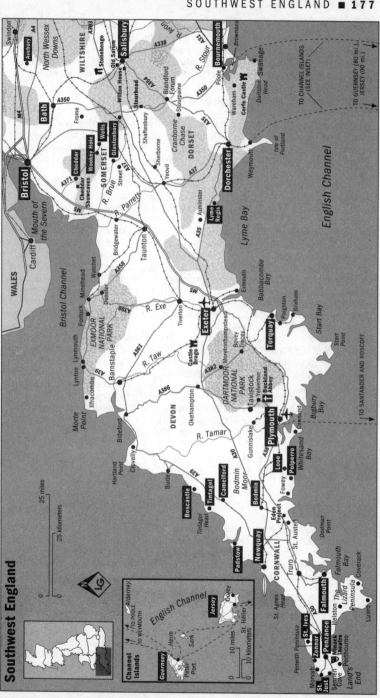

allows unlimited travel between two points on any route. When traveling to multiple destinations on one route, start at one end and ask the driver for a Corridor ticket to the end of the line, and for the day you'll have unlimited access to all the towns in between. Many tourist destinations are only served by trains and buses seasonally. For transport October to May, phone Traveline to check routes and schedules.

▨ ▨ HIKING AND OUTDOORS

Distances between towns in southwest England are so short that you can travel through the region on your own steam. The narrow roads and hilly landscape can make biking difficult, but hardy cyclists will find the quiet lanes and country paths rewarding. Bring along a large-scale Ordnance Survey map (£7; available at TICs) and a windbreaker.

The 630 mi. **South West Coast Path,** England's longest coastal path, originates in Somerset (at Minehead, in Exmoor National Park) and passes through North Devon, Cornwall, and South Devon, ending in Dorset (Poole). Winding past cliffs, caves, beaches, and resorts, it takes several weeks to walk in its entirety. However, as it passes through many towns, is accessible by bus, and features B&Bs and hostels at manageable intervals, it's perfect for shorter hikes. Many rivers intersect the path, some requiring ferries—check times carefully to avoid being stranded. Some sections of the trail are quite difficult, so consult with tourist offices before you begin. Most TICs sell guides and Ordnance Survey maps covering sections of the path, which is generally smooth enough to cover by **bike;** rental shops can often suggest three- to seven-day cycling routes. The path is divided into four parts. The **Somerset and North Devon Coastal Path** extends from Minehead through Exmoor National Park to Bude. The least arduous section, it features the highest cliffs in southwest England and passes the 100 ft. dunes of Saunton Sands and the steep cobbled streets of Clovelly on Hartland Point. The **Cornwall Coast Path,** with some of the most rugged stretches, starts in Bude, where magnificent Cornish cliffs harbor a vast range of birds and marine life, rounds the southwest tip of Britain, and continues along the coast to Plymouth. The **South Devon Coast Path** runs from Plymouth to Paignton, tracing spectacular cliffs, wide estuaries, and remote bays set off by lush vegetation and wildflowers. The final section, the **Dorset Coast Path,** picks up in Lyme Regis and runs to Poole Harbor. For more information, contact the **South West Coast Path Association** (☎01752 896 237) or any local TIC.

WILTSHIRE

SALISBURY ☎01722

A city of busy commercial avenues and winding back lanes, Salisbury itself is an attraction. Town life spirals outward from the market, overlooked by the towering cathedral spire, as it has for centuries. A quick glance down any street reveals facades from the Middle Ages to the industrial era. On a windy plain nearby, awe-inspiring Stonehenge stands its lonely vigil.

▣ TRANSPORTATION

Trains: Station on S. Western Rd., west of town across the River Avon. Ticket office open M-Sa 5:30am-8pm, Su 7:30am-8:45pm. Trains (☎08457 484 950) from most major towns, including: **London Waterloo** (1½hr., 2 per hr., £24.20); **Portsmouth** and **South-**

sea (1½hr., 2 per hr., £12); **Southampton** (40min., every hr., £6.20); **Winchester** (1hr., 2 per hr., £10.70).

Buses: Station at 8 Endless St. (☎336 855). Open M-F 8:15am-5:30pm, Sa 8:15am-5pm. National Express (☎08705 808 080) runs from **London** (3hr., 3 per day, £13.50). Buy tickets at the bus station travel office. Wilts and Dorset (☎336 855) runs from **Bath** (X4, every hr. M-Sa 8am-4pm, £4.20). An **Explorer** ticket is good for a day's worth of travel on Wilts and Dorset buses and some Hampshire, Provincial, Solent Blue, and Brighton & Hove buses (£6.50).

Taxis: Cabs cruise by the train station. **505050 Value Cars** (☎505 050) runs 24hr.

Bike Rental: Hayball Cycles Sport, 26-30 Winchester St. (☎411 378), across from Coaches and Horses. £10 per day, £5 overnight, £65 per week; deposit £25 per bike. Open M-Sa 9am-5:30pm; bikes due back at 5pm. For routes go to the TIC.

🛈 PRACTICAL INFORMATION

Tourist Information Centre: Fish Row (☎334 956; www.visitsalisbury.com), at the back of the Guildhall, in Market Sq. Books rooms for a 10% deposit. Open June-Sept. M-Sa 9:30am-6pm, Su 10:30am-4:30pm; Oct.-May M-Sa 9:30am-5pm. 1½hr. **Guided Walks** leave Apr.-Oct. daily 11am and F 8pm; June-Aug. daily 6pm; £2.50.

Financial Services: Banks are easily found. **Thomas Cook,** 18-19 Queen St. (☎08701 111 111). Open M-W and F-Sa 9am-5:30pm, Th 10am-5:30pm.

Launderette: Washing Well, 28 Chipper Ln. (☎421 874). Open daily 8am-9pm. Wash £3.40, dry £1.40.

Police: Wilton Rd. (☎411 444).

Pharmacy: Boots, 51 Silver St. (☎333 233). Open M-Tu and Th-Sa 8:30am-5:30pm, W 9am-5:30pm, Su 10:30am-4:30pm.

Internet Access: Salisbury Library, Market Place (☎324 145). Open M 10am-7pm, Tu-W and F 9am-7pm, Th and Sa 9am-5pm. Free with ID for 30min.

Post Office: 24 Castle St. (☎08457 223 344), at Chipper Ln. Bureau de change. Open M and W-Sa 9am-5:30pm, Tu 9:30am-5:30pm. **Post Code:** SP1 1AB.

🛏 ACCOMMODATIONS

Salisbury's proximity to a certain stone circle breeds numerous guest houses, most of them starting at around £35 per person—ask for an accommodations guide from the TIC. Accommodations tend to fill quickly in summer.

YHA Salisbury, Milford Hill House, Milford Hill (☎327 572). In a cedar grove on the edge of town. 70 beds, 4 kitchenettes, TV lounge, and cafeteria. Full breakfast included. Laundry £3 and Internet access 7p per min. Book well in advance, especially Easter to Oct. Dorms £16, under 18 £12.50. Camping available. MC/V. ❷

Matt and Tiggy's, 51 Salt Ln. (☎327 443), up the street from the bus station. A welcoming owner keeps spacious, hostel-style rooms. Kitchenette. £3 breakfast deal at Crosskeys restaurant. Book a few days in advance. Dorms £12. Cash only. ❷

Farthings B&B, 9 Swaynes Close (☎330 749; www.farthingsbandb.co.uk). A haven with a gorgeous garden, just a 10min. walk from the city center. May-Sept. singles £32; doubles £56. Oct.-Apr. singles £25; doubles £46. Discounts for long stays. Cash only. ❸

Camping: Hudson's Field, Castle Rd. (☎320 713). Between Salisbury and Stonehenge, 20min. from city center. Vehicle curfew 11pm. Open Mar.-Oct. £4-8. MC/V. ❶

🔲 🔳 FOOD AND PUBS

Even jaded pub dwellers can find a pleasant surprise among Salisbury's 60-odd watering holes. Most serve food (£4-6) and many have live music. **Market Square,** in the town center, fills on Tuesdays and Saturdays, with vendors hawking everything from peaches to posters (open 7am-4pm). A Sainsbury's **supermarket** is at The Maltings. (☎332 282. Open M-Sa 7am-10pm, Su 10am-4pm.)

▨ **Harper's "Upstairs Restaurant,"** 6-7 Ox Rd., Market Sq. (☎333 118). Inventive English and international dishes (£6-10). 2 course Early Bird dinner before 8pm. Open June-Sept. M-F noon-2pm and 6-9:30pm, Sa noon-2pm and 6-10pm, Su 6-9pm; Oct.-May M-F noon-2pm and 6-9:30pm, Sa noon-2pm and 6-10pm. AmEx/MC/V. ❷

▨ **Coach and Horses,** 39 Winchester St. (☎414 319). Salisbury's oldest pub, open since 1382. Traditional food (£7-14) and drinks (pint £2.70). Open M-Sa 11:30am-11pm, Su noon-10:30pm. Food served M-Sa 11:30am-9:30pm, Su noon-9pm. MC/V. ❶

The Old Mill Hotel, Town Path (☎327 517), atop the River Nadder at the end of a 10min. stroll along Town Path through the Harnem Water Meadows. The ideal setting for an outdoor drink or a long dinner (£12-16) in the 12th-century mill building. Open M-Sa 11am-11pm, Su noon-10:30pm. Food served noon-2pm and 7-9pm. AmEx/MC/V. ❸

Alchemy @ the Chough, Blue Bar Row (☎330 032). Has creative renditions of traditional meals, made from fresh ingredients. Entrees £7-9. Open M and W noon-11pm, Tu 11am-11pm, Th-F noon-midnight, Sa 11am-midnight, Su noon-10:30pm. MC/V. ❷

Wyndham Arms, 25 Estcourt Rd. (☎331 026), at the intersection with College St. This after-work pub is a perfect place to relax with locals and down pints of Hop Back (£2), the local ale. Open M-Th 4:30-11pm, F 3-11pm, Sa noon-11pm, Su noon-10:30pm. ❶

👁 SIGHTS

▨ SALISBURY CATHEDRAL

☎555 120. Cathedral open June-Aug. M-Sa 7:15am-8:15pm, Su 7:15am-6:15pm; Sept.-May daily 7:15am-6:15pm. Chapter House open June-Aug. M-Sa 9:30am-6:45pm, Su noon-5:30pm; Sept.-May daily 9:30am-5:30pm. Free tours every 30min. May-Oct. M-Sa 9:30am-4:45pm, Su 4-6:15pm; Nov.-Feb. M-Sa 10am-4pm. 1½hr. roof and tower tours May-Sept. M-Sa 11am, 2, 3pm; Su 4:30pm. June-Aug. M-Sa 11am, 2, 3, 6:30pm; Su 4:30pm; winter hours vary; call ahead. Evensong 5:30pm. Suggested donation £4, concessions £3.50. Roof and tower tour £3, concessions £2.

Salisbury Cathedral, built between 1220 and 1258, rises from its grassy close to a neck-breaking height of 404 ft., making it medieval England's highest spire. Its monumental size and ornamental intricacy make the overall visual effect stunning. The bases of the marble pillars bend inward under the strain of 6400 tons of limestone. Nearly 700 years have left the building in need of repair, and scaffolding shrouds parts of the outer walls, where the stone is disintegrating. The chapel houses the oldest functioning mechanical clock, a strange collection of wheels and ropes that has ticked 500 million times over the last 600 years. A tiny stone figure rests in the nave—legend has it that either a boy bishop is entombed on the spot or that it covers the heart of Richard Poore, founder of the cathedral. The incongruously abstract window at the eastern end is dedicated to prisoners of conscience. The best preserved of the four surviving copies of the Magna Carta rests in the **Chapter House** and is still legible, albeit in medieval Latin. Ask a guide for a complete list of the relief figures in the detailed friezes.

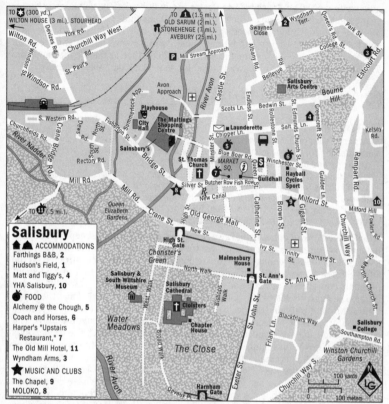

Salisbury

▲■ ▲▲ ACCOMMODATIONS
Farthings B&B, **2**
Hudson's Field, **1**
Matt and Tiggy's, **4**
YHA Salisbury, **10**

🍴 FOOD
Alchemy @ the Chough, **5**
Coach and Horses, **6**
Harper's "Upstairs
    Restaurant," **7**
The Old Mill Hotel, **11**
Wyndham Arms, **3**

★ MUSIC AND CLUBS
The Chapel, **9**
MOLOKO, **8**

SALISBURY AND SOUTH WILTSHIRE MUSEUM. The museum houses a mixture of artwork ranging from Turner's watercolors to articles of period fashion and doll houses. The worthwhile Stonehenge exhibit divulges an extensive amount of history. (*65 The Close, along the West Walk.* ☎ *332 151. Open July-Aug. M-Sa 10am-5pm, Su 2-5pm; Sept.-June M-Sa 10am-5pm. £4, concessions £3, under 16 £1.50, families £9.50.*)

🏛 🎭 NIGHTLIFE AND FESTIVALS

The sign outside **The Chapel,** 30 Milford St., states in clear mathematical terms that "no effort=no entry." Dress to impress, and you might be admitted to the three huge dance floors at a club that advertises itself as one of the UK's best. (☎ 504 255; www.thechapelnightclub.co.uk. Cover W £2; Th £4, ladies free; F £8; Sa £10. Open W 10:30pm-2:30am, Th 10:30pm-2:30am, F-Sa 10:30pm-3am.) **MOLOKO,** 5 Bridge St., is a chain bar, but still one of the most popular in town. Choose from an endless list of vodkas (£2.50-4.50), but try not to spill—the tiny space gets crowded on weekends. (☎ 507 050. M-Sa noon-midnight, Su 3-10:30pm.)

Salisbury's repertory theater company puts on shows at the **Playhouse,** Malthouse Ln., over the bridge off Fisherton St. (☎ 320 333. Box office open M-Sa 10am-8pm, non-performance days until 6pm. Tickets £8.50-17. Half-price tickets available same day.) The **Salisbury Arts Centre,** Bedwin St., offers music and theater year-round. (☎321 744. Box office open Tu-Sa 10am-4pm. Tickets from £5.) Summertime sees free Sunday **concerts** in various parks; call the TIC for info. The **Salisbury Festival** features dance exhibitions, music, and wine-tasting for two weeks in late May and early June. Contact the Festival Box Office at the Playhouse or the TIC for a program. (☎320 333; www.salisburyfestival.co.uk. Tickets from £2.50.)

⚡ DAYTRIPS FROM SALISBURY

▨ STONEHENGE

Wilts and Dorset (☎336 855) runs several buses, including daily service from the Salisbury train station (#3, 40min., round-trip £5.80). The first bus leaves Salisbury at 8:45am (Su 10:35am), and the last leaves Stonehenge at 6:20pm (Su 6:55pm). Check a schedule before you leave; intervals between drop-offs and pickups can be hours. An Explorer ticket (£6.50) allows travel all day on any bus, including those to Avebury, Stonehenge's less-crowded cousin (p. 183), and Old Sarum (p. 183). Wilts and Dorset also runs a tour bus from Salisbury (3 per day, £7.50-15). ☎01980 624 715. Open daily June-Aug. 9am-7pm; mid-Mar. to May and Sept. to mid-Oct. 9:30am-6pm; mid-Oct. to mid-Mar. 9:30am-4pm. £5.50.

A half-ruined ring of colossi amid swaying grass and indifferent sheep, Stonehenge has been battered for millennia by the winds whipping across the flat Salisbury plain. The 22 ft. high stones visible today mark the fifth temple constructed on the site—Stonehenge was already ancient in ancient times. The first arrangement probably consisted of an arch and circular earthwork furrowed in 3050 BC. Its relics are the **Aubrey Holes** (white patches in the earth) and the **Heel Stone** (the rough block standing outside the circle). The next monument used about 60 stones imported from Wales around 2100 BC and marked astronomical directions. The present shape, once a complete circle, dates from about 1500 BC. The tremendous effort and innovation required to transport and erect the 45-ton stones makes Stonehenge an incomparable monument to human endeavor. As a religious site, it has lain unused since the Bronze Age, and over the centuries some of the stones have been removed to other building projects. Celtic druids, whose ceremonies took place in forests, did not worship here, but in an era of religious freedom, modern druids claim the site for their own, and are permitted to enter Stonehenge on the summer Solstice to perform ceremonial exercises. In past years, however, new-age mystics have beaten them to the spot; in 1999 this led to conflict with the police and eventual arrests. Admission to Stonehenge includes a 30min. audio tour that uses handsets. The effect may be more haunting than the rocks themselves—a bizarre march of tourists appear engaged in phone calls. Nonetheless, the tour is helpful, and includes legends about the stones and the surrounding landscape. English Heritage also offers free guided tours (30min.). From the roadside or from Amesbury Hill, 1½ mi. up the A303, you can get a free, if distant, view of the stones. There are also many walks and trails that pass by; ask at the Salisbury TIC.

STOURHEAD. When peacocks casually cross your path, bits of classical sculpture dot the landscape, and the views are free of the signs of civilization, it is hard to believe you aren't dreaming. Once the estate of a wealthy English banking family, this 18th-century estate consists of proportioned natural and architectural beauty. The garden comes complete with lakes, waterfalls, and miniature reproductions of Greek temples. *(Trains run to Gillingham station from Salisbury; 25 min., every hr., £4. Bus #58A runs between Gillingham station and Stourhead, but service is infrequent. ☎01747 841 152. Open late Mar. to late Sept. M-Tu and F-Su 11am-5pm; Oct. M-Tu and F-Su 11am-4:30pm. Last admission 30min. before close. Garden and house £9.40.)*

WILTON HOUSE. Declared by James I to be "the finest house in the land," the home of the Earls of Pembroke is the quintessential aristocratic country home and setting for numerous films, including *Sense and Sensibility.* The impressive art collection includes the largest assortment of Van Dycks in the world and Rembrandt's celebrated portrait of his mother, which was stolen in 1994 and discovered two years later in the trunk of a car in London. Adjoining buildings provide exhibits on domestic arts and on D-Day—the house was an allied headquarters. *(3mi. west of Salisbury on the A30; take bus #60 or 61; M-Sa every 15min., Su every hr., round-trip £3. ☎ 746 720; www.wiltonhouse.com. Open daily late Mar.-Oct. 10:30am-5:30pm; last admission 4:30pm. House and grounds £9.75. Grounds and video only £4.50.)*

OLD SARUM. Old Sarum gets around. It evolved from a Bronze-Age gathering place into a Celtic fortress, which was won by the Romans, taken by the Anglo-Saxons, seized by the Normans, and eventually fell into the hands of the British Heritage Society. Civilization left Old Sarum in the 14th century when a new cathedral was built nearby, leaving stone ruins of the earlier castle strewn across the windswept hill. *(Off the A345, 2 mi. north of town. Buses #3 and 6-9 run every 15min. from Salisbury. ☎ 975 0700. Open daily Apr.-June 10am-5pm; July-Aug. 9am-6pm; Sept.-Oct. 10am-5pm; Nov.-Feb. 11am-3pm; Mar. 10am-4pm. £2.90, concessions £2.20.)*

AVEBURY ☎ 01672

The tiny village that has grown up by the **stone circle** at Avebury lends an intimate feel to this site, a far cry from the sightseeing mobs storming Stonehenge. Visitors can amble among the megaliths and even picnic in their midst. Dating from 2500 BC, Avebury's titans are older and larger than their favored cousins at Stonehenge. Built over the course of centuries, the circle has remained true to its original form and a mystery to archaeologists, mathematicians, and astronomers. Just outside the ring, curious and mysterious **Silbury Hill** rises from the ground. Europe's largest manmade mound has stumped researchers; its date of origin, 2660 BC, was only determined by the serendipitous excavation of a flying ant. Buses #5 and 6 (2 hr., 5 per day, round-trip £6.50) run from Salisbury. The **Alexander Keiller Museum** details the history of the stone circle and its environs. (☎ 539 250. Open daily Apr.-Oct. 10am-6pm; Nov.-Mar. 10am-4pm. £2.50.) The **Circle Restaurant ❷,** just beside the museum, serves sandwiches, soups, and desserts for £3-6. Locate the Avebury **Tourist Information Centre,** in the Avebury Chapel Center, next to the bus stop. (☎ 539 425. Open Apr.-Oct. Tu-Su 9:30am-5pm; Nov.-Mar. W-Su 9:30am-5pm.)

BEST DAY EVER. Early risers can see Stonehenge, Avebury, and Old Sarum (above) in one day. Head out to Stonehenge on the 8:45 or 9:45am bus (buy the Explorer ticket), then catch the 11:10am or 12:20pm bus to Amesbury and transfer to an Avebury bus. Take the 2 or 3pm bus back from Avebury and stop off in Old Sarum before you reach Salisbury.

SOMERSET AND AVON

BATH ☎ 01225

"Water is best" is Bath's unofficial motto, carved on everything from souvenir mugs to stones, and a quick glance into the city's history quickly shows why nothing is better. Bath has been a must-see for travelers since AD 43, when the Romans built an elaborate complex of baths to house the curative waters of the town they called *Aquae Sulis*. In the 18th and 19th centuries, Bath became a social capital second only to London, its scandalous scene immortalized by Jane Austen and Charles Dickens. Though damaged in WWII, the city is impeccably elegant, named a National Heritage city for its beautiful Georgian architecture.

▐ TRANSPORTATION

Trains: Bath Spa Station, Dorchester St., at the south end of Manvers St. Ticket office open M-Sa 5:45am-8:30pm, Su 8:45am-8:30pm. Travel center open M-F 8am-7pm, Sa 9am-6pm, Su 9:30am-6pm. Trains (☎08457 484 950) from: **Birmingham** (2hr., every hr., £29.50); **Bristol** (15min., 3 per hr., £4.80); **Exeter** (1¼hr., every hr., £24.40); **London Paddington** (1½hr., 2 per hr., £36); **London Waterloo** (2-2½hr., 2 per day, £34); **Plymouth** (2¼hr., every hr., £39.40); **Salisbury** (1hr., every hr., £10.80).

Buses: Manvers St. Station (☎08706 082 608). Ticket office open M-Sa 8am-5:30pm. National Express (☎08705 808 080) from **London** (3½hr., every 1½hr., £15) and **Oxford** (2¼hr., 1 per day, £8.40). First bus X39 runs from **Bristol** every 12min. M-Sa 6am-7pm. Badgerline sells a **Day Explorer** ticket, good for 1 day of unlimited bus travel in the region (£7, concessions £5).

Taxis: Abbey Radio (☎444 444).

Boat Rental: Bath Boating Station (☎312 900), at the end of Forester Rd. Punts and canoes £6 per person first hr., £2 each additional hr. Open daily Apr.-Oct. 10am-6pm.

✴ ▐ ORIENTATION AND PRACTICAL INFORMATION

The **Roman Baths**, the **Pump Room**, and **Bath Abbey** cluster in the city center, bounded by York St. and Cheap St. The River Avon flows just east of them, and wraps around the south part of town near the train and bus stations. Uphill to the northwest, historical buildings lie on **Royal Crescent** and **The Circus**.

Tourist Information Centre: Abbey Chambers (☎08704 446 442; www.visitbath.co.uk). Town map and mini-guide £1. The free *This Month in Bath* lists events. Books rooms for a £5 charge plus a 10% deposit. Open May-Sept. M-Sa 9:30am-6pm, Su 10am-4pm; Oct.-Apr. M-Sa 9:30am-5pm, Su 10am-4pm.

Tours: Several companies run tours of the city and surrounding sights.

The Mayor's Honorary Guides. Lead walking tours from the entrance to the Baths. Guides recount the history of the city and point out fascinating architectural features. Tours May-Sept. M, W-Th, Su 10:30am and 2pm; Tu and F-Sa 10:30am, 2, 7pm; Oct.-Mar. daily 10:30am and 2pm. Free.

Bizarre Bath (☎335 124; www.bizarrebath.co.uk). The hysterically funny guides impart few historical facts on this comedic walk through the city. 1½hr. tours begin at the Huntsman Inn at N. Parade Passage. Tours nightly Apr.-Sept. 8pm. £5, concessions £4.50.

The Great Bath Pub Crawl (☎310 364; www.greatbathpubcrawl.com). Meets at Lambretta's Bar on N. Parade, delves into Bath's illicit past, and stops for a few rounds. Tours Apr.-Sept. M-W and Su 8pm. £5.

Ghost Walk (☎350 512; www.ghostwalksofbath.co.uk). Tours leave from the Nash Bar of Garrick's Head, near Theatre Royal. 2hr. tours Apr.-Oct. M-Sa 8pm; Nov.-Mar. F 8pm. £6.

Mad Max Tours (☎464 323; www.madmaxtours.com). Tours begin at the Abbey and spin through Stonehenge, the Avebury Stone Circles, Castle Combe in the Cotswolds, and Lacock National Trust Village (the backdrop of *Harry Potter*). Full-day tours depart daily 8:45am, half-day tours depart daily 2pm. Tours half-day £12.50, full-day £22.50. Entrance to Stonehenge not included.

Financial Services: Banks open M-F 9:30am-5pm, Sa 9:30am-12:30pm. **Thomas Cook,** 20 New Bond St. (☎492 000). Open M-W and F-Sa 9am-5:30pm, Th 10am-5:30pm.

Launderette: Spruce Goose, Margaret's Buildings, off Brock St. (☎ 483 309). Wash £2-3, dry £1.20, soap 60p. Bring £1 coins for washers, 20p coins for dryers. Open M-F and Su 8am-9pm, Sa 8am-8pm. Last wash 1hr. before close.

Police: Manvers St. (☎ 01275 818 181), near the train and bus stations.

Hospital: Royal United Hospital, Coombe Park, in Weston (☎ 428 331). Take bus #14.

Pharmacy: Boots, 33-35 Westgate St. (☎ 482 069. Open daily 10am- 6pm.)

Internet Access: Central Library, Podium Shopping Centre (☎ 787 400). Free. Open M 10am-6pm, Tu-Th 9:30am-7pm, F-Sa 9:30am-5pm, Su 1-4pm. **Ret@iler Internet,** 12 Manvers St. (☎ 443 181). £1 per 20min. Open M-Sa 9am-9pm, Su 10am-9pm.

Post Office: 21-25 New Bond St. (☎ 08457 740 740), across from the Podium Shopping Centre. Bureau de change. Open M-Sa 9am-5:30pm. **Post Code:** BA1 1AJ.

ACCOMMODATIONS

Well-to-do visitors drive up prices in Bath, the second most expensive city in the UK, behind London. **B&Bs** cluster on **Pulteney Road** and **Pulteney Gardens. Marlborough Lane** and **Upper Bristol Road,** west of the city center, also offer options.

YHA Bath, Bathwick Hill (☎ 465 674). From N. Parade Rd., turn left on Pulteney Rd., right on Bathwick Hill, and climb the hill (40min.), or take bus #18 or 418 (every 20min., 80p). Secluded Italianate mansion is far away but beautiful. Reception 7am-11pm. Dorms £12.50, under 18 £9; doubles £32, ensuite £36. MC/V. ❷

YMCA, International House, Broad St. (☎ 325 900; www.bathymca.co.uk). From the train and bus stations, follow the signs to Bath Abbey. Follow High St. as it becomes Northgate St. and Broad St. Breakfast included. Internet access free. Dorms £12-14; singles £23.50-28; doubles £36-42; triples £47-54; quads £56-68. MC/V. ❷

Toad Hall Guest House, 6 Lime Grove (☎ 423 254). Make a left off Pulteney Rd. after passing under the overpass. Friendly B&B with 2 spacious doubles (1 can be let as single) and hearty breakfasts. Singles £25; doubles £45. Cash only. ❸

St. Christopher's Inn, 16 Green St. (☎ 481 444; www.st-christophers.co.uk). Convenient location. Downstairs bar offers an ideal hangout area for young crowd. Simple and clean bunks. Free luggage storage. Internet access £1 per 20min. Dorms £16-19.50; one double £50. Discounts available for online booking. MC/V. ❷

International Backpackers Hostel, 13 Pierrepont St. (☎ 446 787; www.hostels.co.uk/bath). 3 blocks from the baths. Laid-back backpacker's lair with music-themed suites. Kitchen available. Luggage storage £1 per bag. Laundry £2.50. Internet access £2 per hr. Reception 8am-midnight. Checkout 10:30am. Dorms M-Th and Su £13, F-Sa £14; doubles £35; triples £52.50. Book ahead in summer. MC/V. ❷

FOOD

Although restaurants in Bath tend to be expensive, reasonably priced eateries dot the city. For fruits and vegetables, visit the **Bath Guildhall Market** (☎ 477 945. Open M-Sa 9am-5:30pm). Next door to Green Park Station, a Sainsbury's **supermarket** will satisfy. (☎ 444 737. Open M-F 8am-10pm, Sa 7am-10pm, Su 10am-4pm.)

Demuths Restaurant, 2 N. Parade Passage (☎ 446 059; www.demuths.co.uk), off Abbey Green. Exotic vegetarian and vegan dishes like Andalusian tapas (£11.75). Superb chocolate fudge cake £4.75. Prix fixe lunch £7.50, dinner £11.75. Open M-F and Su 10am-5pm and 6-9pm, Sa 9:30am-5:30pm and 6-10pm. MC/V. ❷

Tilleys Bistro, 3 N. Parade Passage (☎484 200; www.tilleysbistro.co.uk). Savor Tilleys French and English creations while relaxing in the elegant and warm atmosphere. Ask to be seated downstairs if there's room. Thorough vegetarian menu available. Entrees £6.50-17. Open M-Sa noon-2:30pm and 6:30-11pm. MC/V. ❷

Sally Lunn's, 4 N. Parade Passage (☎461 634). 17th-century Bath resident Sally Lunn lived in the oldest house (built in 1482) and baked delicious buns. Takeaway buns in gift shop. Entrees £8.88-10.68. Open M-Sa 10am-6pm, Su 11am-6pm. MC/V. ❸

Mai Thai, 6 Pierrepont St. (☎445 557). Great Thai food at affordable prices. Served in a homey atmosphere. Entrees £4.50-8. Open daily noon-2pm and 6-10:30pm. £10 minimum. Make reservations on weekends. AmEx/MC/V. ❷

The Snack Bar, 1 Railway St. (☎461 705). Enjoy a full English breakfast (£2.90), a hot sandwich (£1.90), or a classic dessert. Conveniently located cafe near train and bus station. Open M-Sa 7am-5:15pm, Su 8:30am-5:15pm. Cash only. ❶

◉ SIGHTS

THE ROMAN BATHS. In 1880, sewer diggers inadvertently uncovered the first glimpse of an extravagant feat of Roman engineering. For 400 years, the Romans harnessed Bath's bubbling springs, which spew 264,000 gallons of 115° Farenheit (47° Celsius) water every day, with lead pipes. After excavation, the city became a mecca for Britain's elite. The ▨**museum** merits the entrance price with its displays on Roman excavation finds and building design. Make sure to see the Roman curses (politely referred to as offerings to Minerva), wishing eternal damnation upon naughty neighbors, the Roman coins, and the irrigation system. (*Stall St. ☎477 785; www.romanbaths.co.uk. Open daily July-Aug. 9am-10pm; Sept.-Oct. and Mar.-June 9am-6pm; Jan.-Feb. and Nov.-Dec. 9:30am-5:30pm. Last admission 1hr. before close. Guided tour included. £9.50, concessions £8.50. Joint ticket with Museum of Costume £12.50/11.*)

MUSEUM OF COSTUME AND ASSEMBLY ROOMS. The museum hosts a dazzling parade of 400 years of catwalk fashions, from 17th-century silver tissue garments to Jennifer Lopez's racy Versace jungle-print ensemble. Free audio tours dispel the myth of the Victorian 18-inch waist. (*Bennett St. ☎477 785; www.museumofcostume.co.uk. Open daily Mar.-Oct. 11am-5pm, Nov.-Feb. 11am-4pm. Last admission 30min. before close. £6.25, concessions £5.25.*) The museum is in the basement of the **Assembly Rooms,** which once held *fin de siecle* balls and concerts. Today's visitors, dressed somewhat less elegantly, can still take tea. Bombing during World War II ravaged the rooms, but a renovation has duplicated the originals. (*☎477 785. Open daily 11am-5pm. Free. Rooms are sometimes booked for private functions.*)

BATH ABBEY. Occupying the site where King Edgar was crowned the first king of all England in AD 973, the 140 ft. Abbey towers over its neighbors. In 1499, Bishop Oliver King commissioned the abbey to replace a Norman cathedral. Some years later, the Bishop heard an angel tell him to "let an Olive establish the Crown and a King restore the Church" in a dream. The olive tree (with a crown) and the magnificent ceiling stand as a testament to his belief. Also note the graphic, occasionally hilarious memorial plaques and the underlying Heritage Vaults, with a historical exhibit. (*Next to the Baths. ☎422 462; www.bathabbey.org. Open Apr.-Oct. M-Sa 9am-6pm, Su 1-2:30pm and 4:30-5:30pm; Nov.-Mar. M-Sa 9am-4pm, Su between services. Requested donation £2.50. Heritage Vaults open M-Sa 10am-4pm. Last admission 3:30pm. £1.*)

THE JANE AUSTEN CENTRE. Austen lived in Bath ("at 4 Sydney Pl., among other less fashionable addresses") from 1801 to 1806 and thought it a "dismal sight," although she still decided to set *Northanger Abbey* and *Persuasion* here. The Centre explicates Austen's references to Bath and depicts the city as it was when she lived here. (*40 Gay St. ☎443 000; www.janeausten.co.uk. Open M-Sa 10am-5:30pm, Su*

Bath

ACCOMMODATIONS
International Backpackers
Hostel, **13**
St. Christopher's Inn, **6**
Toad Hall Guest House, **16**
YHA Bath, **17**
YMCA, **5**

PUBS
The Bell, **1**
The Boater, **8**
Pig and Fiddle, **7**

FOOD
Demuths Restaurant, **11**
Mai Thai, **14**
Sally Lunn's, **12**
The Snack Bar, **15**
Tilleys Bistro, **10**

MUSIC AND CLUBS
Delfter Krug, **9**
Doolally's, **4**
Green Park Brasserie
and Bar, **14**
Moles, **2**

10:30am-5:30pm. Last entrance 5pm. £6, students £4.50.) Austen aficionados can also tour the sights in her novels, departing from the Abbey churchyard. *(Tours June-Sept. daily 11am; Oct.-May Sa-Su 11am. £4.50, concessions £3.50.)*

OTHER MUSEUMS AND GALLERIES. Next to Pulteney Bridge, the **Victoria Art Gallery**, Bridge St., holds a diverse collection of works by old masters and modern British artists. It houses Thomas Barker's "The Bride of Death"—Victorian melodrama at its sappiest. *(☎ 477 233; www.victoriagal.org.uk. Open Tu-F 10am-5:30pm, Sa 10am-5pm, Su 2-5pm. Free.)* The handsome **Holburne Museum**, Great Pulteney St., specializes in Georgian art and ceramics. The pride of its collection is Gainsborough's largest oil painting, "The Byam Family." *(☎ 466 669; www.bath.ac.uk/holburne. Open mid-Feb. to mid-Dec. Tu-Sa 11am-5pm, Su 11am-5pm. £4, concessions available.)* The **Museum of East Asian Art**, 12 Bennett St., displays objects dating back to 5000 BC, with a collection of jade and ceramics. *(☎ 464 640; www.meaa.org.uk. Open Tu-Sa 10am-5pm, Su noon-5pm. Last admission 4:30pm. £4, concessions £1-3, families £9.)* The **American Museum**, Claverton Manor, is worth visiting as much for its breathtaking landscape as for its exhibits. Climb 2 mi. up Bathwick Hill, or take bus #18 or 418 to Bath University. *(☎ 460 503; www.americanmuseum.org. Open late Mar.-Oct. Tu-Su 2-5:30pm (last entry at 5pm). Gardens and tea room open Tu-Su noon-5:30pm. £6.50.)*

HISTORIC BUILDINGS. Those interested in architectural history should visit the **Building of Bath Museum**, on the Paragon, which conveys a boggling wealth of information. Check out the model of the city; it took 10,000 hours to perfect its layout at a 1:500 scale. *(☎ 333 895. Open mid-Feb. to Nov. Tu-Su 10:30am-5pm. Last admission 4:30pm. £4.)* In the city's residential northwest corner, famed architects John Wood the elder and John Wood the younger built the **Georgian rowhouses. The Circus**, which has the same circumference as Stonehenge, has attracted illustrious inhabitants for two centuries; former residents include Thomas Gainsborough and William Pitt. Proceed up Brock St. to the **Royal Crescent**, a half-moon of 18th-century townhouses. The interior of **1 Royal Crescent** has been painstakingly restored to the way it was in 1770, down to the last butter knife. *(☎ 428 126. Open mid-Feb. to Oct. Tu-Su 10:30am-5pm; Nov. Tu-Su 10:30am-4pm. Last admission 30min. before close. £4.)* For stupendous views, climb the 154 steps of **Beckford's Tower**, Lansdown Rd., 2 mi. north of town. Take bus #2 or 702 to Ensleigh; otherwise, it's a 45min. walk. *(☎ 460 705. Open Easter to Oct. Sa-Su 10:30am-5pm. £3, concessions £2, families £7.)*

THERMAE BATH SPA. This state-of-the-art spa, housed in a complex near the Baths, hopes to revive the city's 2000-year-old tradition. The spa features thermal baths, a roof-top pool, yoga, massage, aroma therapy, and algae body wraps. The Romans never had it this good—or this expensive. *(Hot Bath St. ☎ 331 234. Baths £17 per 2hr., £35 per day. Advanced booking recommended. Open daily 9am-10pm.)*

GARDENS AND PARKS. Consult a map or the TIC's *Borders, Beds, and Shrubberies* brochure to locate the city's many stretches of cultivated green. Next to the Royal Crescent, **Royal Victoria Park** contains dozens of rare trees. For bird aficionados, there's also an aviary. *(Open 24hr. Free.)* **Henrietta Park**, laid in 1897 to celebrate Queen Victoria's Diamond Jubilee, was redesigned as a garden for the blind—only the most fragrant flowers and shrubs were chosen for its tranquil grounds. The **Parade Gardens**, at the base of North Parade Bridge, have lawn chairs, flower beds, and a pleasant green on the River Avon. The gardens won the Britain in Bloom competition so often that they were asked not to enter again. Check out the dedication plaques on the benches. *(☎ 391 041. Open daily June-Aug. 10am-8pm; Apr. and Sept. 10am-7pm; Nov.-Mar. 10am-4pm. Apr.-Sept. £1.50; Oct.-Mar. Free.)*

▼ ▶ PUBS AND CLUBS

Luring backpackers to its generous patio, the **Pig and Fiddle,** 2 Saracen St., off Broad St., is the first stop for many pub crawlers. (☎460 868. Open M-Sa 11am-11pm, Su noon-10:30pm.) Friendly and vibrant, **The Bell,** 103 Walcot St., challenges its clientele to talk over the live folk, jazz, blues, funk, salsa, and reggae. Pizzas are baked and served in the garden on weekend evenings. (☎460 426. Open M-Sa 11am-11pm, Su noon-10:30pm. Live music M and W evenings, Su lunch.) **The Boater,** 9 Argyle St., has a beer garden overlooking the river and the Pulteney Bridge. (☎464 211. Open M-Sa 11am-11pm, Su noon-10:30pm.) **Delfter Krug,** on Saw Close, draws a large weekend crowd with its outdoor seating and lively upstairs club, which plays hip-hop and pop. (☎443 352. Cover £2-5. Open M-Sa noon-2am, Su noon-10:30pm.) Underground **Moles,** 14 George St., pounds out soul, funk, and house, hosting frequent live acts in an intimate setting. (☎404 445. Cover £3-5. Open M-Th 9pm-2am, F-Sa 9pm-4am.) A cafe by day, **Doolally's,** 51 Walcot St., features mellow acts by night in its comfortable space. (☎444 122. Live music from 8pm. Open M-Sa 9am-11pm, Su 9am-6pm.) For jazz, locals favor **Green Park Brasserie and Bar,** a classy bistro in Green Park Station. (☎338 565. Open Tu-Su 10:30am-midnight. Live jazz W-Sa 8:30pm, Su 12:30pm.)

▶ ▓ ENTERTAINMENT AND FESTIVALS

In summer, buskers (street musicians) fill the streets with music, and a brass band often graces the Parade Gardens. The magnificent **Theatre Royal,** Saw Close, at the south end of Barton St., showcases opera and theater. (☎448 844. Box office open M-Sa 10am-8pm, Su noon-8pm. Tickets £5-27.) The **Little Theatre Cinema,** St. Michael's Place, Bath St., is Bath's local arthouse cinema, showing mostly independent and foreign films with a smattering of select blockbusters. (☎330 817. Box office open daily 1-8pm. Tickets £6, concessions £4-5.) Bath hosts several popular festivals; for information or reservations, call the **Bath Festivals Box Office,** 2 Church St., Abbey Green. (☎463 362; www.bathfestivals.org.uk. Open M-Sa 9:30am-5:30pm.) The renowned **Bath International Music Festival** (May 19-June 4 in 2006) features world-class symphony orchestras, choruses, and jazz bands. The overlapping **Fringe Festival** (☎480 079) celebrates the arts with 190 live performances (May 28-June 11 in 2006). The **Jane Austen Festival,** held at the end of September, features Austen-themed walks, meals, and movies. (Contact the Jane Austen Centre.) The **Literature Festival** will be held March 4-12 in 2006, the **Balloon Fiesta** in mid-May, and the **Film Festival** in late October. Stay abreast of the best events with the weekly *Venue* (£1.30), available at bookstores.

BRISTOL
☎0117

Well-cultured and surprisingly hip, Bristol is Britain's latest urban renewal success story. Ten years ago, you'd have been hard-pressed to find someone who wanted to visit Bristol, let alone live there. But today, the southwest's largest city (pop. 410,000) is one of England's fastest-growing communities, with expansive docks and a famed annual hot air balloon festival. A population of students and young professionals has reinvigorated the city. For now, this unpretentious city, with its rebuilt center and hopping nightlife, remains one of Britain's best-kept secrets.

SOUTHWEST ENGLAND

▐ TRANSPORTATION

Trains: Temple Meads Station. Ticket office open M-Sa 5:30am-9:30pm, Su 6:45am-9:30pm. Trains (☎08457 484 950) from: **Bath** (15min., 4 per hr., £5); **Cardiff** (50min., 2 per hr., £7.50); **London Paddington** (1¾hr.; 2 per hr.; £47 during rush hour, £34 other times); **Manchester** (3½hr., 2 per hr., £41.30). Another station, **Bristol Parkway,** is far, far away—make sure to get off at Temple Meads.

Buses: Marlborough Street Bus Station. Ticket office open M-Sa 7:20am-6pm, Su 9am-6pm. National Express (☎08705 808 080) buses arrive from **London** (2½hr., every hr., £15) and **Manchester** (5¾hr., 5-7 per day, £29) via **Birmingham** (2½hr., £15.80). National Express info shop open M-Sa 7am-8:10pm, Su 7am-9pm.

Public Transportation: First (☎08456 020 156) **buses** run in the city. Get bus and other travel information at the **Travel Bristol Info Centre,** Colston Ave. (☎08706 082 608). Open M-F 8:30am-5:30pm, Sa 8:30am-1pm, A **day pass** is £3 and an **Explorer** ticket, for 1-day unlimited travel in the southwest, £7.

Taxis: Trans Cabs (☎953 8638) or 24hr. **Streamline** (☎926 4001).

Ferries: Bristol Ferry Boat Co. (☎927 3416; www.bristolferryboat.co.uk). £12, students £10.

▟ ▐ ORIENTATION AND PRACTICAL INFORMATION

Bristol is a sprawling mass of neighborhoods. **Broadmead** is the shopping and commerce center, while restaurants and clubs fill the heart of the city along **Park Street** and **Park Row** in the **West End.** The student population to the northeast makes **Whiteladies Road** (follow Queen's Rd. north) another option for cafes and hip shopping.

Tourist Information Centre: Harbourside (information ☎09067 112 191, accommodations booking 0845 408 0474; www.visitbristol.co.uk), inside Wildwalk. From the train station, take bus #8 or 9 (£1) to the City Centre and follow the signs to Millenium Sq. Books accommodations for a £3 charge plus a 10% deposit. Open daily 10am-5pm.

Tours: CitySightseeing (☎01934 830 050; www.city-sightseeing.com). Bus tours every hr. 10am-4:30pm. £8, students £7. **Bristol Packet** (☎926 8157; www.bristolpacket.co.uk). Tours from Wapping Wharf near S.S. *Great Britain*. Also runs boat tours and daytrips to Avon Gorge and Bath. Aug. daily; Apr.-Sept. Sa-Su. £4-17.60, **Guided Walks of Bristol** (☎968 4638). Offers tours such as "Bristol Highlights," "Maritime Bristol," "Bristol Merchants and the Slave Trade," and "Bristol's Historic Wine Merchants." All start at the TIC. Tours Mar.-Sept. £3.50, children free.

Financial Services: HSBC, 11 Broadmead (☎08457 404 404). Open M-Sa 9am-5pm.

Police: Bridewell St. (☎927 7777)

Pharmacy: Superdrug, 39-43 Broadmead (☎927 9928). Open M-Sa 8:30am-5:30pm, Su 11am-5pm.

Hospital: Bristol Royal Infirmary, Upper Maudlin St. (☎923 0000). Frenchay (☎970 1212), in North Bristol near the M32.

Internet Access: BristolLife, 27-29 Baldwin St. (☎945 9926). £2 per hr. Open M-F 10am-8pm, Sa 11am-7pm. **Bristol Central Library,** College Green (☎903 7200). Free. Open M-Tu and Th 9:30am-7:30pm, W 10am-5pm, F-Sa 9:30am-5pm, Su 1-5pm.

Post Office: Mall Galleries, Union St. (☎08457 223 344), on the top floor of the shopping center. Open M-Sa 9am-5:30pm. **Post Code:** BS1 3XX.

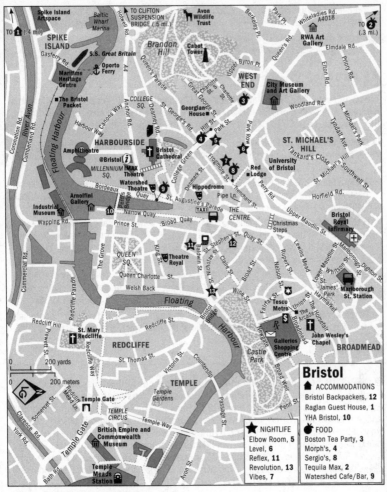

Bristol

⌂ ACCOMMODATIONS
Bristol Backpackers, **12**
Raglan Guest House, **1**
YHA Bristol, **10**

★ NIGHTLIFE
Elbow Room, **5**
Level, **6**
Reflex, **11**
Revolution, **13**
Vibes, **7**

🍎 FOOD
Boston Tea Party, **3**
Morph's, **4**
Sergio's, **8**
Tequila Max, **2**
Watershed Cafe/Bar, **9**

▚ ACCOMMODATIONS

A handful of comfortable, cheap, and convenient **B&Bs** lie south of the harbor on **Coronation Road.** Walk west along Cumberland Rd. for 15min., cross the red footbridge, turn right on Coronation Rd., and walk a few blocks past Deans Ln.

🏠 **Bristol Backpackers,** 17 St. Stephen's St. (☎925 7900; www.bristolbackpackers.co.uk). This former newspaper building right in the heart of Bristol is now a perfect place to park your pack. Laundry £1.50. Internet access £1 per hr. Reception 9am-11:30pm. Photo ID required. Book ahead for weekends. Dorms £14. MC/V. ❷

YHA Bristol, Hayman House, 14 Narrow Quay (☎08707 705 726). From City Center, across Pero's Bridge. Excellent city-center location, with cafe/bar. Breakfast included.

Kitchen. Luggage storage free. Laundry £4.50. Internet access £5 per hr. Reception 24hr. Dorms £18, under 18 £13. Book ahead, especially July-Sept. MC/V. ❷

Raglan Guest House, 132 Coronation Rd. (☎966 2129). Budget lodgings with comfy beds. Singles £25; doubles £40; triples £60. Cash only. ❸

🍴 FOOD

Plenty of restaurants line **Park Street** and **Whiteladies Road.** Wednesdays, a **farmer's market** takes over Corn St. (Open 9:30am- 2:30pm.) Tesco Metro, on Broadmead, has **groceries.** (☎948 7400. Open M-F 7am-10pm, Sa 7am-8pm, Su 11am-5pm.)

■ **Boston Tea Party,** 75 Park St. (☎929 8601). A collegiate favorite. Lunch includes soups and sandwiches. Relaxed coffee shop offers outdoor seating and funky lounge. Entrees £5-10. Open M 7am-6pm, Tu-Sa 7am-10pm, Su 9am-7pm. AmEx/MC/V. ❶

Tequila Max, 109 Whiteladies Rd. (☎466 144). Mexican restaurant by day, tequila bar by night. Festive decor. Enchiladas £10. Select entrees 2-for-1 for students on W. Open M-Th and Su noon-2:30pm and 5-11:30pm, F-Sa noon-12:30am. AmEx/MC/V. ❸

Watershed Cafe/Bar, 1 Canons Rd. (☎927 5101; www.watershed.co.uk). Great sandwiches by the river. "Light bites" £4.75, entrees £5.85-7. Free Internet access. Cafe/bar open M 11am-11pm, Tu-F 9:30am-11pm, Sa 10am-11pm, Su 10am-10:30pm. Food served M-Sa noon-9pm, Su noon-7pm. AmEx/MC/V. ❷

Sergio's, 1-3 Frogmore St. (☎929 1413; www.sergios.co.uk). Flavorful food awaits in this tiny, lively Italian eatery. Entrees £7-14. Bring your own beer. Takeaway pizza available. Open M-F noon-2:30pm and 5:30pm-late, Sa 5:30pm-late. AmEx/MC/V. ❷

Morph's, 55 Park St. (☎929 4888). Serves up traditional Greek fare in a modern setting. Features a full-sized tree in the middle of the restaurant. Entrees £8-15. MC/V. ❸

👁 SIGHTS

■ **@BRISTOL.** Opened in 2000 to herald Bristol's cultural renaissance, the three attractions of this modern science center will engross adults as much as kids. **Explore** features interactive exhibits in physics and biology, from a simulation of space flight to the virtual journey of an egg-bound sperm. **Wildwalk** traces the history of life on earth, complete with living specimens and a biodome. The four-story **IMAX,** housed near Wildwalk, shows 3-D films on the southwest's largest screen. *(Anchor Rd., Harbourside. ☎08453 451 235; www.at-bristol.org.uk. Explore and Wildwalk open daily 10am-5pm. IMAX shows every 1¼hr. plus evening shows Th-Su. 1 sight £6.50-8, concessions £5.50-6; 2 sights £11-12/9.25-9.70/; all 3 £17/12.)*

BRITISH EMPIRE AND COMMONWEALTH MUSEUM. In 1497, the explorer John Cabot set sail from Bristol Harbour for Newfoundland and inaugurated the most expansive empire in world history. Interactive exhibits bring museum-goers back to when "the sun never set on the British empire," offering perspectives on the political development of imperialism and the devastating effects of colonialism on indigenous civilizations. *(Station Approach, Temple Meads, in a former rail station. ☎925 4980; www.empiremuseum.co.uk. Open daily 10am-5pm. £6.50, concessions £5.50.)*

CLIFTON SUSPENSION BRIDGE. Isambard Kingdom Brunel, famed engineer of London's Paddington Station, built this scientific impossibility spanning the Avon Gorge. The refurbished Visitors Centre, due to reopen in spring 2006, explains just how Brunel did it; call ahead to check hours. *(Take bus #8 or 9. ☎974 4664; www.clifton-suspension-bridge.org.uk. Bridge open 24hr. Free guided tours daily June-Sept. 3pm. Free.)*

S.S. GREAT BRITAIN. Also a Brunel project, the *Great Britain* was the largest ship in the world when it was launched in 1843. The "world's first great ocean liner" traveled a million miles (no, really) and has just been spruced up with fresh paint and models of 19th-century passengers. Check out the sleeping quarters, sure to make your bunk feel king-sized. (☎926 0680; www.ss-great-britain.com. Open daily Apr.-Oct. 10am-4:30pm; Nov.-Mar. 10am-3:30pm. £7.50, students £4.50.)

OTHER MUSEUMS. The **City Museum and Art Gallery,** Queen's Rd., covers all the bases, from minerals to mummies, including a handsome collection of British ceramics. (☎922 3571; www.bristol-city.gov.uk/museums. Open daily 10am-5pm. Free.) The **Industrial Museum,** Princes Wharf, Wapping Rd., occupies a former transit shed. The ground floor exhibits antique rail and road vehicles manufactured in Bristol. The first floor displays a mock-up cockpit of a Concorde, used during the airliner's development, and a candid account of Bristol's role in the slave trade. (☎925 1470. Open Apr.-Oct. M-W and Sa-Su 10am-5pm; Nov.-Mar. Sa-Su 10am-5pm. Free.) From April to October, you can also visit the **Georgian House,** 7 Great George St., built in 1791, and the **Red Lodge,** Park Row, an Elizabethan home. (Georgian House ☎921 1326. Red Lodge ☎921 1360. Both open M-W and Sa-Su 10am-5pm. Free.) The **Arnolfini Gallery,** 16 Narrow Quay, exhibits contemporary art and hosts fringe artistic events. The gallery has been closed for refurbishment and is due to reopen in early 2006. (☎929 9191; www.arnolfini.org.uk. Open M-W and F-Sa 10am-5pm, Th 10am-9pm, Su noon-5pm. Free.)

CHURCHES. **John Wesley's Chapel,** 36 The Horsefair, Broadmead, in the midst of Bristol's shopping district, is the world's oldest Methodist building. Note the chair fashioned from an inverted elm trunk. (☎926 4740. Open M-Sa 10am-4pm. Free.) Founded in 1140, the **Bristol Cathedral** is known as a "hall church" because the nave, quire, and aisles are of equal height. The **Norman Chapter House** housed the monks' many books. (☎926 4879. Open daily 8am-6pm. Evensong M-F 5:15pm, Sa 3:30pm. Free guided tour Sa 11am.) **St. Mary Redcliffe,** Sir William Penn's father (of Pennsylvania fame) is buried in this gothic church. (☎953 7260; www.stmaryredcliffe.co.uk. Open May-Oct. M-Sa 9am-5pm, Su 8am-8pm; Nov.-Apr. M-Sa 9am-4pm, Su 8am-8pm. Free.)

BRANDON HILL. Just west of Park St. lies one of the most peaceful and secluded sights in Bristol. Pathways snake through flower beds to **Cabot Tower,** a monument commemorating the 400th anniversary of explorer John Cabot's arrival in North America. Ascend the 108 steps for a stunning view. (☎922 3719. Open daily until dusk. Free.)

BALLOON-STREWN: BRISTOL IN AUGUST

Tourist brochures all over the UK show Cornwall's famed rolling, green pastures and rocky coastline. Likewise, signs and posters never show Bristol without balloon-filled skies.

The city's favorite claim to fame is its world-famous International Balloon Fiesta, held every year since 1979. The first fiesta had 30 balloons. Today, hundreds of the brightly colored contraptions and a half-million people join in the festivities. In 2003, so many visitors crowded the massive Clifton Suspension Bridge that city officials have since closed the famous Brunel edifice during the fiesta to prevent structural damage.

Fiesta events include street performances by theater and improv comedy troupes, concerts, plenty of parties with local brew on the quay, exhibitions with giant cartoon-shaped inflatables, and dozens and dozens of traditional balloons. Shops, restaurants, and cafes stay open late and visitors crowd the lively streets.

At night, colored lights set the balloons aglow in the night sky. The balloons synchronize their lights with music to illuminate like a fireworks display.

In 2006, the International Balloon Fiesta will take place on August 10-13. For more information visit http://visitbristol.co.uk/site/whats_on/p_33681.

NIGHTLIFE

On weekend nights, virtually the entire city turns out in clubwear, with thousands of university students sustaining the energetic vibe. Bars and clubs cluster around Park St. and Park Row in the West End, and Baldwin St. and St. Nicholas St. in the Old City. A handful of gay clubs line Frogmore St.

Level, 24 Park Row (☎373 0473; www.levelnightclub.co.uk). A hot zone, this small subterranean club attracts a hip crowd for special events and R&B Sa. Its stunning interior is modeled on retro airport lounges. W student night. Cover £4. Open M-Sa 10pm-2am.

Revolution, St. Nicholas St. (☎930 4335). Any dissent in this completely packed, red-tinted bar drowns in the liquid goodness of exotic vodkas. Live DJs nightly. Open M-Th 11:30am-2am, F and Sa 11:30am-2am, Su 11:30am-12:30pm.

Elbow Room, 64 Park St. (☎930 0242; www.theelbowroom.co.uk). This bar features pool tables and moody purple and red lighting. Su live reggae. Open daily noon-2am.

Vibes, 3 Frog Ln., Frogmore St. (☎934 9076). A new gay venue with neon lights and modern decor. Different rooms play different music, from cheesy pop to hard house. Cover £1.50-4. Open M-Th 11:30pm-2am, F-Sa 10pm-3:30am.

Reflex, 18-24 Baldwin St. (☎945 8891). Throw yourself into a time warp at this popular 80s bar, complete with Rubik's cube disco lights and air guitar contests. W student night. Cover £1-5. Open M-Tu and Th-Sa 8pm-2am, W 9pm-2am, Su 8pm-12:30am.

ENTERTAINMENT AND FESTIVALS

Britain's oldest theater, the **Theatre Royal,** King St., was rebuked for debauchery until George III approved the actors' antics. (☎987 7877. Box office open M-Sa 10am-6pm. Tickets £7-20, £2 student discount.) The **Hippodrome,** St. Augustine's Parade, presents the latest touring productions and musicals. (Box office open M-Sa 10am-6pm, 8pm on evenings with performances.) The popular **Watershed,** 1 Canon's Rd. (☎927 5100; www.watershed.co.uk), a fantastic arthouse cinema on the quay, holds regular discussions on independent and foreign films and has a lively, well-priced cafe. (Box office open daily 10am until 15min. after the start of the day's final film.) **Bristol Harbour Festival** (☎903 1484) explodes with fireworks, raft races, street performances, live music, hundreds of boats, and a French market. During the **Bristol International Balloon Fiesta** (☎966 8716) in early August, hot-air balloons fill the sky while acrobats and motorcycle teams perform at ground level. **Bailey Balloons** takes visitors high, high above the gorge to sightsee. (☎01275 375 300; www.baileyballoons.co.uk. £145 per hr.). **GWR FM Big Balloon,** Castle Park, Castle St. offers a more affordable balloon riding opportunity. (www.gwrfmbigballoon.co.uk. £10, students £8. Open daily 10am to dusk, weather permitting.)

WELLS   ☎01749

Named for the natural springs at its center, Wells' (pop. 10,000) main feature is undoubtedly its magnificent cathedral. Charming, if self-consciously classy, this little town is lined with petite Tudor buildings and golden sandstone shops.

TRANSPORTATION

Trains leave Wells enough alone; the city has no train station. **Buses** stop at the **Princes Road Bus Park.** (☎673 084. Ticket office open M-F 9am-4:45pm, Sa 9am-12:45pm.) National Express (☎08705 808 080) buses arrive from London (3½hr., 1 per day, £17). First runs from Bath (#173; 1¼hr.; M-Sa every hr., Su 7 per day;

£4.50) and Bristol (#376; 1hr., every hr., £4.50). If you'll be skipping around in the area, buy a **Day Explorer Pass** (£7; concessions £5). For a **taxi**, call Wookey Taxis (☎678 039; 24hr.). **Rent bicycles** at Bike City, 31 Broad St. (☎671 711. £9 per day, 5 days £30. Deposit £50. Open M-Sa 9am-5:30pm.)

🛈 PRACTICAL INFORMATION

The **Tourist Information Centre**, Market Pl., at the end of High St., books rooms for £3 plus a 10% deposit and has bus timetables. Exit left from the bus station and turn left onto Priory Rd., which becomes Broad St. and eventually merges with High St. (☎672 552. Open daily Apr.-Oct. 9:30am-5:30pm; Nov.-Mar. 10am-4pm.) Other services include: Barclays **bank**, 9 Market Place (☎313 907; open M-F 9:30am-4:30pm) and Thomas Cook, 8 High St. (☎313 000; open M-W and F-Sa 9am-5:30pm, Th 10am-5:30pm); **work opportunities** at JobCentre, 46 Chamberlain St. (☎313 200; open M-Tu and Th-F 9am-5pm, W 10am-5pm); **police**, 18 Glastonbury Rd. (☎01275 818 181); a **pharmacy**, 17-21 High St. (☎01749 673 138; open M-Sa 9am-5:30pm, Su 10:30am-4:30pm); free **Internet access** at the **library** (open M-Th 9:30am-5:30pm, F 9:30am-7pm, Sa 9:30am-4pm); and the **post office**, Market Pl. (☎08457 223 344; open M-F 9am-5:30pm, Sa 9am-12:30pm), with a bureau de change. **Post Code:** BA5 2RA.

🏠 ACCOMMODATIONS

Most **B&Bs** offer only doubles, so making Wells a daytrip from Bristol or Bath may be a better option for solo travelers. The closest **YHA hostel** and **campground** are 2 and 10 mi. away, respectively, near Wookey Hole and Cheddar (p. 196). At **17 Priory Road ❸**, across the street from the bus station, Mrs. Winter offers warm and spacious rooms with volumes of books lining the shelves. (☎677 300; www.smoothhound.co.uk/hotels/brian.html. Singles £25; doubles £50; family rooms £25 per person. Cash only.) **Canon Grange ❸**, Cathedral Green (on Sadler St.), with the cathedral in its backyard, features inviting, rustic decor with hardwood floors and fluffy quilts. Follow the directions to the TIC, but from High St., turn left on Sadler. (☎671 800; www.canongrange.co.uk. Doubles £48, ensuite £58-62. MC/V.)

🍴 FOOD

Assemble a picnic at the **market** on High St., in front of the Bishop's Palace (open W and Sa), or purchase **groceries** at Tesco, across from the bus station on Tucker St. (☎08456 779 710; open M 8am-10pm, Tu-Sa 6am-10pm, Su 10am-4pm). At the **Good Earth ❶**, 4 Priory Rd., get great vegetarian soups (£2.65-3.25), quiches (£2.70), and homemade pizza (£2.50 per slice) for takeaway or enjoy them on the backyard patio. (☎678 600. Open M-Sa 9am-5:30pm. MC/V with £10 minimum.) A city jail in the 16th century, the **City Arms ❸**, 69 High St., now serves delicious meals, including a number of vegetarian options (entrees £7-16). Come nightfall, this is the hottest pub in town. (☎673 916. Restaurant open M-Sa 9am-10pm, Su 9am-9pm. Bar open M-Sa 10am-11pm, Su noon-10:30pm. AmEx/MC/V with £10 minimum.)

👁 SIGHTS

▓WELLS CATHEDRAL. The 12th-century church at the center of town is also the center of a well-preserved cathedral complex, with a bishop's palace, vicar's close, and chapter house. The facade comprises one of England's best collections of medieval statues: 293 figures in all. The 14th-century feat of engineering known as the **scissor arches** prevents the tower from sinking. The church's **astronomical clock**

(c. 1390) is the second-oldest working clock in the world. A group of jousting mechanical knights duke it out every 15min., and one frustrated knight has consistently lost for 600 years. The **Wells Cathedral School Choir,** an institution as old as the building itself, sings services from September to April. Pick up *Music in Wells Cathedral* at the cathedral or TIC. (☎674 483. Open daily Mar.-Sept. 7am-7pm; Oct.-Feb. 7am-6pm. Free tours 10, 11am, 1, 2, 3pm. Evensong M-Sa 5:15pm, Su 3pm. Suggested donation £5, students £2.) Beside the Cathedral, **Vicar's Close** is Europe's oldest continuously inhabited street; most houses date to 1363. (Open 24hr. Free.)

BISHOP'S PALACE. This palace has been the residence of the Bishop of Bath and Wells for 800 years. The suite of medieval buildings is centered around St. Andrew's Well and makes for great picnics. Bishop Beckynton channeled the flow in the 15th century, and the water still runs through the city streets today. The swans in the moat pull a bell-rope when they want to be fed—the first swans to learn lived here 150 years ago and their descendants have continued to teach their young. Visitors can feed them brown bread, not white—they get sick. (Near the cathedral. ☎678 691; www.bishopspalacewells.co.uk. Open Apr.-Oct. M-F 10:30am-6pm, Su noon-6pm; often open Sa, call ahead. Last admission 5pm. £4, students £1.50.)

WELLS AND MENDIP MUSEUM. This museum contains archaeological finds of the Mendip area and remnants of the cathedral's decor. Also on display are the milking pot, "crystal ball," and bones of the "Witch of Wookey Hole," a woman who, after mysteriously losing her beauty, retreated to a cave and occasionally spooked the locals. Recently, the owner of an attraction at Wookey Hole has sought the supposed remains of this infamous woman, but the owners of Wells and Mendip Museum are holding fast to the prized exhibit. (8 Cathedral Green. ☎673 477. Open Easter to Oct. daily 10am-5:30pm; Nov. to Easter M and W-Su 11am-4pm. £3.)

▓ DAYTRIPS FROM WELLS

CHEDDAR

From Wells, take bus #126 or 826 (25min.; M-Sa every hr. at 40min. past the hr., Su 7 per day; round-trip £4.35). Purchase tickets at the base of the hill near the bus stop or at Gough's Cave. ☎742 343; www.cheddarcaves.co.uk. Open daily May to mid-Sept. 10am-5pm; mid-Sept. to Apr. 10:30am-4:30pm. Caves, Jacob's Ladder, and open-top bus £10.90, students £7.90. Ladder only £3.50. Discounts at the Wells TIC. Cheddar's TIC is at the base. ☎01934 744 071. Open Mar.-Oct. daily 10am-5pm; Dec. to Easter M-Sa 10am-5pm, Su 11am-4pm.

A short journey from Wells brings you to a vale of cheese, in every sense of the word. The town of **Cheddar** lies near a large hill leading to the **Cheddar Gorge,** a miracle of nature/kitschy tourist attraction complete with colored lights and an audio tour "narrated by the Cheddar Man himself." Carved by the River Yeo (YO), the gorge is perforated by the **Cheddar Showcaves,** limestone hollows that extend deep into the earth. **Gough's Cave** houses a replica of **Cheddar Man,** a 9000-year-old skeleton (the original is now in the British Museum in London). More on Cheddar Man can be found at the new exhibition **Cheddar Man and the Cannibals,** at the base of the Gorge across from the TIC. The Exhibit warns that it is "not for the politically correct" and explains everything from theories of evolution to theories of cannibalistic human ancestors. Down the hill, **Cox's Cave,** the chosen honeymoon spot of J.R.R. Tolkien, features the mercilessly tacky "Crystal Quest," a "fantasy adventure" with wizards and hobgoblins. Admission to the caves includes a ride on an open-top **bus** that travels through the gorge and to the cave entrances in summer, and access to **Jacob's Ladder,** a 274-step climb to a lookout. At the top, a 3 mi. **cliff-top gorge walk** has views that outstrip the sights below. The **Cheddar Gorge Cheese Company,** at the hill's base, features cheese-making and cheese-tasting. (☎742 810.

Open daily 10am-5:30pm. Free.) Those who still feel the need for cheese can stay at the **YHA Cheddar ❷**, ½ mi. from Cheddar Gorge on a residential street. From the bus stop, walk up Tweentown Rd. away from the gorge, turn left on The Hayes, and right at Hillfield. (☎ 742 494. Kitchen. Laundry £1.50. Reception 8-10am and 5-11pm. Lockout 10am-5pm. Curfew at 11pm. Open July-Aug. daily; otherwise call 48hr. in advance. Dorms £12.50, under 18 £9. MC/V.)

WOOKEY HOLE. Two miles west of Cheddar, the **Wookey Hole Caves** (see right) are as beautiful as their neighbors. A 35min. tour takes visitors into the caves and ancient chambers discovered in 1935. Admission includes a visit to a working **papermill**, powered by the River Axe, and an old **amusement park** with gaudy carnival attractions, including a ghost tour. *From Wells, take bus #172 or 670 (15min., M-Sa 8 per day, round-trip £2). Caves ☎ 01749 672 243. Caves and papermill open daily Apr.-Oct. 10am-5pm; Nov.-Mar. 10am-4pm. £9.90. See www.wookey.co.uk for more info.*

GLASTONBURY   ☎ 01458

The reputed birthplace of Christianity in England, an Arthurian hotspot, and home to England's biggest summer music festival, Glastonbury (pop. 6900) is a quirky intersection of mysticism and pop culture. According to legend, King Arthur, Jesus, Joseph of Arimathea, and Saints Augustine and Patrick all came here. One myth claims Glastonbury Tor is the resting place of the Holy Grail and the spot to which the Messiah will return; another holds that it's the Isle of Avalon, where King Arthur eternally sleeps. Glastonbury's shops do their part to perpetuate the mystical vibe, peddling Celtic trinkets and healing crystals.

◪ TRANSPORTATION. Glastonbury has no train station; **buses** stop at the town hall in the town center. Consult the *Public Transport Timetable for the Mendip Area*, free at TICs, for schedules. First (☎ 08706 082 608, fare info 08456 064 446) buses run to Bristol (#376 or 377, 1hr., £4.30) via Wells. Travel to Yeovil (M-Sa #377, 1hr., 1 per day, departs at 9:24pm; Su #977, 1hr., every 2hr., £4) to connect to destinations in the south, including Lyme Regis and Dorchester. Travel a full day on all buses with the **Explorer Pass** (£7, concessions £5, families £15).

◪▮ ORIENTATION AND PRACTICAL INFORMATION. Glastonbury is 6 mi. southwest of Wells on the A39 and 22 mi. northeast of Taunton on the A361. The town is bounded by **High Street** in the north, **Bere**

LOCAL LEGEND

THE WITCH OF WOOKEY HOLE

Immortalized by lore and cloistered in the town's magnificent caves with only her sheep, the infamous "Witch of Wookey" inspired fear and loathing in locals from time immemorial. When a brave monk from nearby Glastonbury made the trek up the hill and into the cave to see if he could resolve—or perhaps absolve—the woman and the town of unfortunate situation, he was met by screams and curses. The woman ran away into the chambers of her cavern. As the monk followed her into the darkness, he heard running water and came upon an underground riverbed. Blessing the water, he threw some at the witch, who instantly turned to stone. Fueled by his success, the monk aimed a second volley at the witch's dog, freezing him beside her.

To this day, the witch and her mutt stand at watch over the expansive caves they once called home. Visit the caves and take a tour; knowledgeable (and eager) guides and an elaborate system of colored lights recreate the famous battle between witch and monk. Take note of the natural decor of the "rooms" in the witch's home, including its kitchen and parlor (one of the largest natural domes in Europe).

Tours ☎ 01749 672 243, or check out www.wookey.co.uk for information on daily tours, which run year-round.

Lane in the south, **Magdalene Street** in the west, and **Wells Road/Chilkwell Street** in the east. The **Tourist Information Centre,** The Tribunal, 9 High St., books rooms for a £3 charge plus a 10% deposit; after hours, find the B&B list behind the building in St. John's carpark. (☎832 954; www.glastonburytic.co.uk. Open Apr.-Sept. M-Th and Su 10am-5pm, F-Sa 10am-5:30pm; Oct.-Mar. M-Th and Su 10am-4pm, F-Sa 10am-4:30pm.) Other services include: a Barclays **bank,** 21-23 High St. (☎241 381; open M-F 9:30am-4:30pm) and a Thomas Cook, 42 High St. (☎831 809; open M-Sa 9am-5:30pm); **police,** 1 West End (☎01823 337 911); Moss **pharmacy,** 39 High St. (☎831 211; open M-F 9am-6pm, Sa 9am-5:30pm); **Internet access** at the library, 1 Orchard Ct., The Archer's Way, left off of High St. when heading up the hill (☎832 148; free; photo ID required; open M and Th-F 10am-5pm, Tu 10am-7pm, Sa 10am-4pm), at Cafe Galatea (see below), and at Glastonbury Backpackers' Pax Cafe (see below); and the **post office,** 35 High St. (☎831 536; open M-F 9am-5:30pm, Sa 9am-1pm). **Post Code:** BA6 9HG.

🏠 **ACCOMMODATIONS.** Single rooms are rare in Glastonbury. Buses stop by **Glastonbury Backpackers ❷,** 4 Market Pl., at the corner of Magdalene St. and High St. The bright blue building houses a friendly staff and a lively cafe-bar. (☎833 353; www.glastonburybackpackers.com. Kitchen. Internet access until 6pm. Reception 4:30-11pm. Dorms £12; doubles £30, ensuite £35. MC/V.) Right by the post office, **A. B&B ❸,** 52a High St., offers spacious rooms. Walk upstairs from the fruit and vegetable market to reception. (☎832 265. £25 per person. Cash only.) The nearest YHA hostel is the **YHA Street ❶,** The Chalet, Ivython Hill St., off the B3151 in Street. Take First bus #376 to Marshalls Elm, and follow the signs for about 1 mi. (☎442 961. Kitchen. Reception 8:30-10am and 5-10pm. Lockout 10am-5pm. Open July-Aug. daily; May-June Tu-Su; Sept.-Apr. call 48hr. in advance. Dorms £11.50, under 18 £8.50. MC/V.) At **Pilgrims ❷,** 12-13 Norbins Rd., unwind amidst Indian decor in large, cheery rooms near the heart of town. From High St., turn left on the footpath in front of St. John the Baptist Church and follow it as it wraps around the church and becomes Norbins Rd.; the house is down the street on the left. (☎834 722; www.pilgrimsbb.co.uk. Singles £35; doubles £55. Cash only.)

🍴🍸 **FOOD AND NIGHTLIFE.** A **farmer's market** takes place behind the TIC on the last Saturday of the month. Heritage Fine Foods, 32-34 High St., stocks **groceries.** (☎831 003. Open M-W 7am-9pm, Th-Sa 9am-10pm, Su 8am-9pm.) Find cheap baked goods and sandwiches (£1-5) at **Burns the Bread ❶,** 14 High St. (☎831 532. Open M-Sa 6am-5pm, Su 11am-4pm. Cash only.) The vegetarian and whole-food menu at **Rainbow's End ❶,** 17a High St., changes with the chef's whims, creating dishes such as Greek cheese pie with salad and garlic potatoes (£6). Soups, salads, and quiches run £3-7. (☎833 896. Open M-Sa 10am-4pm, Su 11am-4pm. Cash only.) **Cafe Galatea ❷,** 5a High St., is the best place for late-night veggie fare. Entrees (£7-8.50) play on Mexican, Indian, and Italian themes. (☎834 284. Internet access £3 per 30min., £5 per hr. Open W-Sa 11am-10pm, Su 10:30am-9pm. MC/V.) Carnivores should head to **Gigi's ❸,** 2-4 Magdalene St. Slightly forced Italian decor is forgiven in light of the sizable portions and late hours. The *pollo pizzaiola* is delicious. (☎834 612. Entrees £11.50-15. Open Tu-Th 6-10:45pm, F 6-11pm, Sa-Su noon-2:30pm and 6-11pm. MC/V.) Try a pint or some pub grub at **Ye Queens Head,** Skittle Alley, off High St., which shows local sports on a flatscreen TV in a classic pub atmosphere. (☎832 745. Frequent live music. Open M-Sa 11am-11pm, Su noon-10:30pm.)

👁️🎆 **SIGHTS AND FESTIVALS.** Legend holds that Joseph of Arimathea, the Virgin Mary's uncle, traveled with the young Jesus to do business in modern-day Somerset. Joseph later returned in AD 63 to found the massive 🔲**Glastonbury Abbey,** on Magdalene St. behind the Town Hall. Though the abbey was destroyed during the

English Reformation, the colossal pile of ruins that remains still evokes the grandeur of the original church. The **Lady Chapel, Abbot's Kitchen,** and museum recreate the grandeur and history vested in such sacred ground. Turn left and walk down what was formerly the nave (now a grassy plateau) to reach the **Tomb of Arthur and Guinevere.** After a fire damaged the abbey in 1184, the monks needed to raise some cash; fortunately, they "found" Arthur's grave on the south side of Lady Chapel in 1191 and reburied the bones here, inviting the King and Queen—and the royal treasurer—to attend the ceremony. Near the entrance to the abbey, the **Holy Glastonbury Thorn** blooms every Christmas and Easter. The original thorn, a short walk down Magdelene St. to **Wearyall Hill,** is said to have miraculously sprouted when Joseph of Arimathea drove his staff into the ground. (☎832 267; www.glastonburyabbey.com. Open daily June-Aug. 9am-6pm; Sept.-May 10am-dusk. £4.)

A 15min. hike from the base of the 526 ft. **Glastonbury Tor** brings visitors to a 6th-century pilgrimage site with stunning views. To get there, turn right at the top of High St. on Lambrook, which becomes Chilkwell St.; turn left at Wellhouse Ln. and walk uphill. The Tor is the site of the Isle of Avalon, where King Arthur sleeps until his country needs him again. The hill now features a simple tower, built in 1360 as a church. In summer, the **Glastonbury Tor Bus** takes pilgrims from the city center (St. Dunstan's carpark, next to the Abbey) to a shorter climb on the far side of the Tor, returning them to town via Chalice Well and the Rural Life Museum. (Tor open 24hr.; free. Hop-on, hop-off bus Apr.-Oct. every 30min. 9:30am-1pm and 2-5pm; £1.)

At the base of the Tor on Chilkwell St., **Chalice Well** is said to be where Joseph of Arimathea washed the holy grail. Legend once held that the well ran with Christ's blood; the red tint actually comes from rust deposits in the stream, but the revelation has not stopped modern-day mystics from making pilgrimages to prance barefoot in the waters. Ancient mystics interpreted the iron-red water's mingling with clear water from nearby **White Well** (which now runs through a cafe across the street) as a symbol of balance between feminine and masculine (Dan Brown take note). A tiered garden of climbing vines and "healing" pools now surrounds the fabled spring. (☎831 154. Open daily Apr.-Oct. 10am-5:30pm; Feb.-Mar. and Nov. 11am-5pm; Dec.-Jan. 11am-4pm. £2.85.) Down Chilkwell St. from the Chalice Well, the **Rural Life Museum** provides a mildly diverting account of what life was like for a poor Somerset farmer in the 19th century. (☎831 197. Open Apr.-Oct. Tu-F 10am-5pm, Sa-Su 2-6pm; Nov.-Mar. Tu-Sa 10am-5pm. Free.)

Glastonbury's greatest attraction is 5 mi. away in Pilton, the site of the annual ⚑**Glastonbury Festival,** undoubtedly the biggest and best of Britain's multitude of summer music festivals. Recent headliners include the White Stripes, David Bowie, Coldplay, Oasis, and Radiohead. The mud-covered three-day music love-in takes place at the end of June. Tickets are expensive—£125 in 2005—and sell out almost immediately every year. (Glastonbury Festival Office, 28 Northload St. ☎834 596; www.glastonburyfestivals.co.uk.)

THE DORSET COAST

BOURNEMOUTH   ☎01202

Only two centuries old, Bournemouth (pop. 150,000) is an infant among English cities. Once popular for its curative sea baths, today the seaside resort lures summer daytrippers with an expansive beach and boardwalk entertainment. The twin Central and Lower Gardens flank the square (where a "millennium flame" perpetually burns), giving a splash of color to the city center and paving visitors' way to the shore with lush lawns and the occasional palm tree.

⊑ TRANSPORTATION. The **train station** lies on Holdenhurst Rd., 15min. east of town center. (Travel center open M-F 9am-7pm, Sa 9am-6pm, Su 9am-5pm. Ticket office open M-Sa 5:40am-9pm.) **Trains** (☎ 08457 484 950) arrive from: Birmingham (3hr., every hr., £50); Dorchester (40min., every hr., £8); London Waterloo (2hr., 2 per hr., £33); Poole (10min., 2 per hr., £2.50). National Express (☎ 08705 808 080) **buses** queue behind the train station (ticket office open M-Sa 7:30am-6pm, Su 9am-6pm) and serve: Birmingham (5-6hr., 3 per day, £33.50); Bristol (3½hr., 1 per day, £13.50); London (3hr., every hr., £16; £1-5 Funfare available online); Poole (20min., 2-3 per hr., £1.50). Tickets are also sold at the TIC. Wilts and Dorset (☎ 673 555) runs local buses, including services to Poole and Southampton. An **Explorer** ticket (£6.50) provides unlimited travel. United **Taxi** (☎ 556 677) runs 24hr.

▓▐ ORIENTATION AND PRACTICAL INFORMATION. The downtown centers around **The Square**, which is flanked by the **Central Gardens** to the northwest and the **Lower Gardens** toward the water. The **Tourist Information Centre**, Westover Rd., sells a map (£1.50) and books rooms for a 10% deposit. From the train station, turn left on Holdenhurst Rd. and continue straight on Bath Rd., then follow the signs. (☎ 09068 020 234; www.bournemouth.co.uk. Open mid-July to Aug. M-Sa 9:30am-7pm, Su 10:30am-5pm; Sept. to mid-July M-Sa 9:30am-5:30pm.) Other services include: **American Express**, 95a Old Christchurch Rd. (☎ 780 752; open M, Tu, Th-F 9am-5pm, W 9:30am-5pm, Su 9:30am-3pm); **work opportunities**, especially seasonal work, at JobCentre, 181-187 Old Christchurch Rd. (☎ 08456 060 234; open M-Tu and Th-F 9am-5pm, W 10am-5pm); a **launderette**, 172 Commercial Rd. (☎ 551 850; wash £2.70, dry £1.50; open M-F 8am-9pm, Sa-Su 8am-8pm; last wash 1hr. before close); **police**, Madeira Rd. (☎ 552 099); Boots **pharmacy**, 18-20 Commercial Rd. (☎ 551 713; open M-Sa 9am-6pm, Su 10:30am-4:30pm); **Bournemouth Hospital**, Castle Land East, Littledown (☎ 303 626); **Internet access** at the Cyber Place, 25 St. Peter's Road (☎ 290 099; £1 per 20min.; open daily 9:30am-midnight) and at the library, 22 The Triangle, uphill from City Square (☎ 454 848; open M 10am-7pm, Tu and Th-F 9:30am-7pm, W 9:30am-5pm, Sa 10am-2pm; free for up to 1hr. per day; reservations requested); and the **post office**, 292 Holdenhurst Rd. (☎ 395 840; open daily 9am-5:30pm). **Post Code:** BH8 8BB.

▐▐ ACCOMMODATIONS AND FOOD. The **East Cliff** neighborhood, 5min. from the train station, bristles with **B&Bs**. Exit left from the station, cross Holdenhurst Rd. to St. Swithuns, and turn left on Frances Rd.; the route is signposted. **Bournemouth Backpackers ❶**, 3 Frances Rd., an independent hostel, fosters a homey environment with comfy lounges and a barbecue pit. (☎ 299 491; www.bournemouthbackpackers.co.uk. Kitchen. Reception 5-6pm; luggage storage £1 at the Travel Interchange. Dorms £15-17; doubles £36-40. Rates highest on Sa; discounts for longer stays. Cash only.) **Kantara ❸**, 8 Gardens View, provides guests with comfortable beds in bright rooms a short walk from the train and bus stations. (☎ 557 260; www.kantaraguesthouse.co.uk. £25 per person. MC/V.)

Christchurch Road has diverse eateries; **Charminster Road** is a center of Asian cuisine. **Eye of the Tiger ❸**, 207 Old Christchurch Rd., serves Bengali curries for £6-10, vegetarian options, and Tandoori specialties for £6.75-13. (☎ 780 900. Open daily noon-2pm and 6pm-midnight. 10% takeaway discount. MC/V.) **Shake Away ❶**, 7 Post Office Rd., has 150 flavors of milkshakes (£2.25-3.25), from marshmallow to rhubarb. (☎ 310 105. Open M-F 9am-5:30pm, Su 10am-4:30pm. Student discount. Cash only.) For an affordable upscale atmosphere, try **Bliss ❷**, 1-15 St. Peter's Rd., which offers a lunch buffet (£5). For dinner on weekends, call ahead. (☎ 297 149.

Free wireless Internet. Th karaoke 9pm. Buffet M-Sa noon-3pm. Open M-Th and Su noon-1am, F-Sa noon-4am. MC/V.) For coffee and a light lunch, stop at **Obscura Cafe ❶**, The Square. (☎314 231. Baguettes £4-5. Open daily 8am-dusk).

◐◢ SIGHTS AND BEACHES. The city center holds few interesting attractions. The Russell-Cotes Art Gallery and Museum, Russell-Cotes Rd., East Cliff, houses a collection of Victorian art, sculptures, and artifacts. (☎451 858. Open Tu-Su 10am-5pm. Free.) On the corner of Hilton Rd. and St. Peter's Rd., St. Peter's parish church holds the remains of Mary Shelley, author of *Frankenstein.* From the church to the waves you can't miss the Bournemouth Eye, a hot air balloon that gives visitors a bird's-eye view of the boardwalk. (☎314 539; www.bournemouthballoon.com. Open daily 10am-11pm. £10, students £7.50.) Visitors mostly come for Bournemouth Beach (☎451 781), a 7 mi. sliver of shoreline barely wide enough to hold its inflatable slides. Amusements and a theater can be found at Bournemouth Pier (50p; open July-Aug. 9am-11pm; Apr.-June and Sept.-Oct. 9am-5:30pm); a short walk leads to quieter spots.

Instead of staying in Bournemouth, travel the shore for stunning sights. A 95 mi. stretch of the Dorset and East Devon coast, or the **Jurassic Coast,** was recently named a World Heritage Site for its famous fossils and unique geology (www.jurassiccoast.com; see also **Lyme Regis,** p. 204). Beautiful **Studland Beach** sits across the harbor, reachable by bus #150 (50min., every hr., round-trip £3). A **nude beach** is just down the shore. Take bus #150 or 151 (25min., 2 per hr., £3) to reach the themed landscapes of **Compton Acres,** featuring an Italian garden with Roman statues and a sensory garden designed for the blind. (☎700 110. Open daily Mar.-Oct. 9am-6pm. £6.) The 1000-year-old **Corfe Castle** is no weathered pile of ruins: Parliamentarian engineers were ordered to destroy the castle during the English Civil War—what remains is a testament to its strength. Travel to Poole (bus #151) or Swanage (#150) to catch bus #142 (every hr., round-trip £5.75). (☎01929 481 294. Open daily Apr.-Sept. 10am-6pm; Mar. and Oct. 10am-5pm; Nov.-Feb. 10am-4pm. £5.)

▶▧ ENTERTAINMENT AND FESTIVALS. Students and vacationers fuel Bournemouth's bouncing nightlife. Most start at the roundabout up the hill from **Fir Vale Road,** working downhill through the numerous bars on **Christchurch Road.** Gay and gay-friendly nightlife options cluster where Commercial St. meets The Triangle. **FuFu,** at the top of Fir Vale Rd., is a good place to begin the night. (☎231 7069. Tu under-18. Open Tu-Th 8pm-midnight, F-Sa 8pm-2am.) Just next door, **Toko** is a sleek, sophisticated late bar with fish tanks, flat-screen TVs showing the latest music videos, and free wireless Internet. Monday night is giant games night; play giant Twister with the rest of town. (☎315 821. Open M-Th and Su 6pm-1am, F-Sa 3pm-4am.) **Circo** and downstairs club **Elements** attract crowds. (☎311 178. W student night. Cover £3-8; often free before 10pm. Open M and Th 9pm-2am, W 8pm-2am, F-Sa 8pm-3am.) A mile east of The Square, the **Opera House,** 570 Christchurch Rd., a former theater renovated into two dance floors, is one of the wildest (and cheapest) clubs in town. Take bus #22 from The Square. (☎399 922; www.slinky.co.uk. Most drinks £1-2. F "Slinky" with dance and trance music. Cover £1-15. Open Th-Su 9pm-4am.) In a tradition dating from 1896, 15,000 candles light up the Lower Gardens every Wednesday in summer during the **Flowers by Candlelight Festival.** In late June, Bournemouth's **Live! Music Festival** (☎451 702; www.bournemouth.co.uk) hosts free concerts by international performers.

DORCHESTER
☎ 01305

Stratford has Shakespeare, Swansea has Thomas, Haworth has the Brontës, and Dorchester has Thomas Hardy. Locals indulge his spirit to no end, from pub regulars sharing time-worn stories about the author to a somber statue overlooking the town's main street. Most businesses, from inns to shoe stores, manage to incorporate "Hardy" into their names. The inspiration for the fictional Casterbridge, Dorchester is a pleasant town best appreciated by those who know Hardy's work.

▟ TRANSPORTATION

Most **trains** (☎ 08457 484 950) come to **Dorchester South,** off Weymouth Ave. (Ticket office open M-F 6am-8pm, Sa 6:40am-8pm, Su 8:40am-7pm.) Trains run from Bournemouth (40min., every hr., £8) and London Waterloo (2½hr., every hr., £36.40). Some trains arrive at **Dorchester West,** also off Weymouth Ave., including those from Weymouth (15min., 8 per day, £2.80). Dorchester has no bus station, but **buses** stop at Dorchester South train station and on Trinity St. National Express (☎ 08705 808 080) serves Exeter (2hr., 1 per day, £9.70) and London (5hr., 3 per day, £18). Tickets are sold at the TIC. Wilts & Dorset (☎ 673 555) bus #184 goes to Salisbury via Blandford (2hr., 6 per day, £4.50). First bus #212 serves Yeovil (1½hr., every hr., £3.50), which connects south. Coach House Travel (☎ 267 644) provides local service. **Taxis** are available from Bob's Cars (☎ 269 500; 24hr.) and Dorset Cars (☎ 250 666). **Bike rental** is available from Dorchester Cycles, 31 Great Western Rd. (☎ 268 787. £10 per day. ID required. Open M-Sa 9am-5:30pm.)

✦▟ ORIENTATION AND PRACTICAL INFORMATION

The intersection of **High West** and **South Street** (which eventually becomes **Cornhill Street**) is the unofficial center of town. The main **shopping district** extends southward along South St. The **Tourist Information Centre,** 11 Antelope Walk, on Trinity St., stocks free town maps, books accommodations for a 10% deposit, and sells Explorer bus tickets. (☎ 267 992; www.westdorset.com. Open May-Sept. M-Sa 9am-5pm, Su 10am-3pm; Apr. and Oct. M-Sa 9am-5pm; Nov.-Mar. M-Sa 9am-4pm.) Other services include: Barclays **bank,** 10 South St. (☎ 326 730; open M-Tu and Th-F 9:30am-4:30pm, W 10am-4:30pm); a **launderette,** 16c High East St. (wash £2.60-3, dry 20p per 4min.; open daily 8am-8pm); **police,** Weymouth Ave. (☎ 251 212); Dorset County **Hospital,** Williams Ave. (☎ 251 150); Boots **pharmacy,** 12-13 Cornhill St. (☎ 264 340; open Aug. M-Sa 8:30am-5:30pm, Su 10am-4pm; Sept.-July M-Sa 8:30am-5:30pm); free **Internet access** at the **library,** Colliton Park, off The Grove (☎ 224 448; open M 10am-7pm, Tu-W and F 9:30am-7pm, Th 9:30am-5pm, Sa 9am-4pm) and at Amici, 7a Tudor Arcade, off South St. (☎ 261 700; £1 per 20min., wireless available; open daily 8am-6pm); and the **post office,** 43 South St., with a bureau de change (☎ 08457 223 344; open M-Sa 9am-5:30pm). **Post Code:** DT1 1DH.

▟ ACCOMMODATIONS

Plush suites await at **The White House ❸,** 9 Queens Ave., off Weymouth Ave. From the train station, exit left onto Station Approach and turn left onto Weymouth Ave.; Queen's Ave. is a few blocks up, past Lime Close. (☎ 266 714. Singles £27; doubles £44. Cash only.) **Maumbury Cottage ❷,** 9 Maumbury Rd., is close to both train stations. Kind Mrs. Wade lets one single, one double, and one twin and bakes bread for breakfast. (☎ 266 726. £20 per person. Cash only.) **The King's Arms ❷,** 30 High East St., is the most central accommodation in town, upstairs from a terrific pub. (☎ 265 353; www.kingsarmsdorchester.com. Full English breakfast £6, Continental £4. All rooms £47.50. MC/V.) Self-catering **YHA Litton Cheney ❶** is 10 mi. west of the city. Take bus #31 to Whiteway and follow the signs for 1½ mi. (☎01308 482 340. Reception 8-10am and 5-10pm. Lockout 10am-5pm. Curfew 10:30pm. Open Apr.-Aug. Dorms £11, under 18 £8. MC/V.) For camping, try **Giant's Head Caravan and Camping Park ❶**, Old Sherborne Rd., in Cerne Abbas, 8mi. north of Dorchester. Head out of town on The Grove and bear right onto Old Sherborne Rd., or take the #216 bus from Dorchester to Cerne Village and take the road to Buckland Newton. (☎01300 341 242; www.giants-head.co.uk. Showers, laundry, and electricity. Open Apr.-Sept. £11 for tent, car, and 2 adults. Cash only.)

⬛🅼 FOOD AND PUBS

The eateries along **High West Street** and **High East Street** provide a range of options. Get your **groceries** at the Dorchester Market, in the carpark near South Station (open W 8am-3pm), or at Waitrose, in the Tudor Arcade, off South St. (☎268 420; open M-W and Sa 8:30am-7pm, Th-F 8:30am-8pm, Su 10am-4pm). **6 North Square ❸** serves fresh Dorset seafood and other hearty meals in a hidden spot near the prison. (☎267 679. Lunch specials £5.35; dinner entrees £12.50. Open M-Sa 10:30am-2:30pm and 6:30-9:30pm. MC/V.) **The Celtic Kitchen ❶**, 17 Antelope Walk, near the TIC, serves delicious Cornish pasties (£1.70-2.10). (☎269 377. Open M-Sa 9am-4pm. Cash only.) For a spicier option, try **Thai Palace ❸**, 34 High West St., with an extensive menu including curries (£8-9) and seafood. (☎757 188. Open M-Th and Su noon-2pm and 5:30-11pm, F-Sa noon-2pm and 5:30-11:30pm. MC/V.)

Dorchester barely dabbles in nightlife, but find a good pint among the friendly, alternative crowd at the **Old George**, at the bottom of Trinity St. (☎263 534. DJs and live bands F-Sa. Open M-Th 11am-11pm, F-Sa 11am-midnight, Su noon-10:30pm.) Heed the warning to "duck or grouse" when entering the **King's Arms**, 30 High East St., and then drink and be merry at the historic inn, featured in Hardy's *Mayor of Casterbridge*. (☎265 353. Open M-Sa 11am-11pm, Su noon-10:30pm.) **Bojangles**, 33 Trinity St., is a new cocktail bar with flat-screen TVs and £2.50 drink specials. (☎263 404. Open M-W 11am-11pm, Th 11am-midnight, F-Sa 11am-1am, Su noon-midnight.) **Klimax**, 37-38 High West St., is the only "club" in town. Party on Thursday night and collect a £9 drink voucher for Friday or Saturday night. (☎269 151; www.klimaxbarandclub.co.uk. Open Th-F 10pm-2am, Sa 10pm-3am.)

LOCAL LEGEND

SPEAK SOFTLY AND CARRY A BIG STICK

The Cerne Giant (sometimes known as the "Rude Man o Cerne") is the most controversial and perhaps the most mysterious chalk hill figure in Britain. Laying prominently in Cerne Abbas, 9 miles from the town of Dorchester, the figure (measuring 180 ft from head to phallus to toe) resembles a huge cave drawing.

Some say he represents a Celtic warrior-god and is over 2000 years old; others claim he represents Hercules and is close to 1500 years old; while still a third group (citing that the figure has no historical documentation until 1694) argue he is a mere 300 years old and was created as a large-scale political cartoon mocking Oliver Cromwell.

Whomever he represents, he is a polarizing force. Some say his giant manhood brings good luck, and that any childless woman who lays prostrate before him will be granted the fulfillment of her desires. But others are uncomfortable with his manly presence. During WWII, the home guard covered his 30 ft appendage with camouflage supposedly to prevent enemy bombers from using it as an arrow to Bristol. A more believable version alleges that the embarrassed citizenry wanted the giant's giant privates to be covered as a matter of decency.

Take bus #216 from Dorchester and ask to be let off at the Cerne Viewing Point (£3.40).

👁 SIGHTS

Dorchester's attractions can't quite compete with the compelling sights in the surrounding hills. East of town, Hardy-related sites hint at the poet-novelist's inspiration for Wessex, a fictional region centered around Dorset. West of town, dramatic remnants of Iron Age and Roman Britain dominate the landscape. Negotiate both areas in a day with a bike or a bus schedule.

Here's the **Thomas Hardy** breakdown: he designed **Max Gate,** 1 mi. southwest of town off Arlington Rd., and lived there from 1885 until his death in 1928, penning *Tess of the D'Urbervilles* and *Jude the Obscure.* (☎262 538. Open Apr.-Sept. M, W, Su 2-5pm. £2.75.) He was christened in **Stinsford Church,** 2 mi. northeast of town in Stinsford Village, and the yard holds the family plot where his first and second wives are buried, though only his heart is buried here—his ashes lie in Westminster Abbey (p. 104). Take bus #184 (every 2hr., £1.30) from Trinity St. toward Puddletown; ask to be dropped off near the church. (Church admission free.) Finally, he was born in the aptly named **Hardy's Cottage,** Bockhampton Ln., deep in the woods 3 mi. northeast of Dorchester. Take bus #184 or 185 and ask to be let off at the cottage. (☎262 366. Open Apr.-Oct. M and Th-Su 11am-5pm or dusk. £3.20.) The **Dorset County Museum,** 66 High West St., explores Hardy history and then some, with a replica of Hardy's study and relics of the city's other keepers—Druids, Romans, and Saxons. (☎262 735. Open July-Sept. M-Sa 10am-5pm, Su 10am-5pm; Oct.-June M-Sa 10am-5pm. £5, concessions £4. Audio tour free.)

On the other side of town, scattered **ruins** recall Dorchester's status as a neolithic settlement, Celtic stronghold, and Roman city. The most significant of these is **Maiden Castle,** the largest Iron-Age fortification in Europe, dating to 3000 BC. The hillfort was protected by a tangle of walls and ditches until the Romans seized it in AD 43. Modern visitors can scale what little is left of the ancient ramparts, today patrolled by sheep. Take shuttle #2 (M-Sa 5 per day, £1) to Maiden Castle Rd., ¾ mi. from the hill. If it's nice out, opt to hike the scenic 2 mi. from the town center down Maiden Castle Rd. (Open 24hr. Free.) Roman sights within Dorchester are not impressive. Archaeologists have unearthed the foundation and mosaic floor of a first-century **Roman Town House** at the back of the County Hall complex. Walk north on The Grove until it intersects with Northernway, where stairs lead to the entrance. Just past the South Station entrance sprawls the **Maumbury Rings,** a Bronze-Age monument with a maw used as a Roman amphitheater.

⚡ DAYTRIP FROM DORCHESTER

LYME REGIS

From Dorchester, take First (☎01305 783 645) bus #31 from South Station (1¼hr., every hr., £3.20). The Tourist Information Centre, Guildhall Cottage, Church St., downhill from the bus stop, locates lodgings and stocks walking guides. ☎01297 442 138; www.lymeregistourism.com. Open Apr.-Oct. M-Sa 10am-5pm, Su 10am-4pm; Nov.-Mar M-Sa 10am-4pm, Su 10am-2pm. Historian Richard J. Fox conducts 1½hr. walking tours, which leave from Guildhall. ☎01297 443 568. Smugglers' tours Tu and Th 2:30pm. Ghost tours Tu and Th 7:30pm. £3. Numerous companies on the Cobb run boat tours.

Known as the "Pearl of Dorset," Lyme Regis (pop. 3500) surveys a majestic sweep of coastline. In 1811, a shopkeeper named Mary Anning discovered the first Ichthyosaurus fossil a mile west of Lyme Regis. Since then, fossil shops have sprung up throughout this coastal town. Paleontologist Steve Davies (see **Jurassic Park,** p. 205) has amassed an immense collection of local fossils, artfully displayed in the **Dinosaurland Fossil Museum,** Coombe St. (☎01297 443 541; www.dinosau-

rland.co.uk. Open daily 10am-5pm. £4, students £3.)
The museum has 200-million-year-old shells and a
100-million-year-old lobster fossil. Davies leads a 2hr.
dinosaur hunting walk (£5); contact Dinosaurland for
times; walks depend on the tides. Lyme Regis is also
known for the **Cobb,** a man-made sea wall that cradles the harbor. In Jane Austen's *Persuasion*, Louisa
Musgrove suffers an unfortunate fall on its steps. The
Marine Aquarium on the Cobb exhibits a small collection of local sea creatures, including a 5 ft. conger
eel. (☎01297 33106. Open daily Mar.-Oct. 10am-5pm.
£2, concessions £1.50.) The **Lyme Regis Museum,**
Bridge St., chronicles Lyme's history. (☎01297 443
370; www.lymeregismuseum.co.uk. Open Apr.-Oct.
M-Sa 10am-5pm, Su 11am-5pm; Nov.-Apr. Sa 10am-
5pm and Su 11am-5pm. £2.20.)

DEVON

EXETER   ☎01392

In 1068, the inhabitants of Exeter earned the respect
of William the Conqueror by holding their own
against his army for 18 days. When the city's wells
ran dry, the Exonians used wine for cooking, bathing, and drinking, which might explain the city's
eventual fall. Today, Exeter, a student center and
gateway to Devon and Cornwall, hums with vitality.
Restaurants, shops, and wine-bars surround the magnificent cathedral, which miraculously avoided bom-
bardment during WWII.

▐ TRANSPORTATION

Trains: Exeter has 2 stations.

St. David's Station, St. David's Hill, 1 mi. town. Ticket office
open M-F 5:45am-8:40pm, Sa 6:15am-8pm, Su 7:30am-
8:40pm. Trains (☎08457 484 950) from: **Bristol** (1hr.,
every hr., £16.90); **London Paddington** (2½hr., every hr.,
£46); **Salisbury** (2hr., every 2hr., £21.80).

Central Station, Queen St. Ticket office open M-Sa 7:50am-
6pm. From **London Waterloo** (3hr., 12 per day, £43.70).

Buses: Bus station, Paris St. (☎427 711). Ticket office
open M-F 8:45am-5:30pm, Sa 8:45am-1pm. **National
Express** (☎08705 808 080) buses from **Bristol** (2hr., 5
per day, £11) and **London** (4-5hr., 9 per day, £20.50).

Public Transportation: An **Exeter Freedom Ticket** (£3.50
per day, £9 per week) allows unlimited travel on city **minibuses.** The **Explorer Ticket** (£5 per day, £17 per week)
allows unlimited travel on **Stagecoach** (☎427 711) buses.

Taxis: Capital (☎433 433); **Club Cars** (☎213 030).

THE HIDDEN DEAL

JURASSIC PARK

Antiques can cost a pretty penny,
but one British collectible is absolutely free: fossils. The beaches
surrounding Lyme Regis are littered with specimens from 200 to
65 million years ago. How can
Wedgwood compete with a perfectly preserved prehistoric fish?

The best way to make a fossil
find is to join an expert-led tour.
Steve Davies, owner of Dinosaurland Fossil Museum, has decades
of experience, degrees in geology
and micro-paleontology, and the
fossils to prove it. Steve conducts
2hr. fossil-hunting excursions at
Black Ven, the mudflow 1 mi. east
of Lyme in which Mary Anning discovered her famous ichthyosaurus in 1811. Due to the erosion of
the cliffs, a new crop of fossils
arises every day, virtually guaran-
teeing a geological discovery.

The most common fossil-finds
are belemnites (squid-like mol-
lusks) and ammonites (beautiful
spiral-shelled cephalopods). The
fossils often striate the soft,
sandy rock into interesting
shapes. Some fossils are preserved in iron pyrite, or fool's
gold, which gives them a lustrous
appearance. Other common fossils include oysters, plant-like
crinoids, snails, fish, and even
ichthyosauri.

For tour times, contact Dinosau-
rland Fossil Museum, Coombe
St., Lyme Regis, ☎01297 443
541; or consult the chalk board
outside the museum doors. £4,
children £3.

⟨ PRACTICAL INFORMATION

Tourist Information Centre: Dix's Field (☎265 700). Books accommodations for a 10% deposit and sells National Express tickets. Open July-Aug. M-Sa 9am-5pm, Su 10am-4pm; Sept.-June M-Sa 9am-5pm.

Tours: The best way to explore is with the City Council's free 1½hr. **themed walking tours** (☎265 700), including "Murder and Mayhem," "Ghosts and Legends," and "Medieval Exeter." Most leave from the Royal Clarence Hotel off High St.; some depart from the Quay House Visitor Centre. Apr.-Oct. 4-5 per day; Nov.-Mar. 11am and 2pm.

Financial Services: Thomas Cook, 177 Sidwell St. (☎601 400). Open M-Sa 9am-5:30pm.

Work Opportunities: JobCentre, Clarendon House, Western Way (☎474 700), on the roundabout near the TIC. Open M-Tu and Th-F 9am-5pm, W 10am-5pm.

Launderette: Silverspin Cleaning Centre, 12 Blackboy Rd. (☎270 067). Wash £2.20, dry 50p per 8min. Open daily 8am-10pm.

Police: Heavitree Rd. (☎08705 777 444).

Hospital: Royal Devon and Exeter, Barrack Rd. (☎411 611).

Pharmacy: Boots, 251 High St. (☎432 244). Open M-W and F-Sa 8:15am-6pm, Th 8:15am-7pm, Su 10am-4:30pm.

Internet Access: Central Library, Castle St. (☎384 206). Free for the first 30min., £1.50 per 30min. thereafter. Open M-Tu and Th-F 9:30am-7pm, W 10am-5pm, Sa 9:30am-4pm, Su 11am-2:30pm.

Post Office: Sidwell St. (☎08457 223 344). Bureau de change. Open M-Sa 9am-5:30pm. **Post Code:** EX1 1AH.

⟨ ACCOMMODATIONS

A number of budget **B&Bs** lie near the **Clock Tower** roundabout north of Queen St., especially on **St. David's Hill,** between St. David's Station and the center of town.

▨ **Globe Backpackers,** 71 Holloway St. (☎215 521; www.exeterbackpackers.co.uk). Laid-back, clean hostel with friendly staff and kitchen. Luggage storage £1 per bag. Laundry service £3. Internet access 5p per min. Key deposit £5. Reception 8am-11pm. Check-out 11am. Book ahead. Dorms £12; doubles £32. MC/V with 50p surcharge. ❷

YHA Exeter, 47 Countess Wear Rd. (☎873 329), 2 mi. southeast of the city center. Take minibus K or T from High St. to the Countess Wear post office; follow signs to the spacious, cheery hostel (10min.). Internet access £5 per hr. Reception 8-10am and 5-10pm. Dorms £14, students and under 18 £11. MC/V. ❷

The University of Exeter (☎215 566). A range of options in the city. Open Apr. and July-Sept. Book ahead. Singles £14.50-17.75, ensuite £26.50; ensuite doubles £45.50. ❷

Telstar Hotel, 75-77 St. David's Hill (☎272 466; www.telstar-hotel.co.uk). Family-run B&B with comfortable floral-themed rooms, many newly renovated. Full breakfast included. Book 2 weeks ahead in summer. Singles £30-35; doubles £55-65. MC/V. ❸

⟨ FOOD

Get **groceries** at Sainsbury's, in the Guildhall Shopping Centre (☎432 741; open M-W 8am-6:30pm, Th-F 8am-7pm, Sa 7:30am-6:30pm, Su 10:30am-4:30pm).

Herbies, 15 North St. (☎258 473). A casual venue for exotic vegetarian delights. Entrees £6.25-8.25. Open M 11am-2:30pm, Tu-F 11am-2:30pm and 6-9:30 pm, Sa 10:30am-4pm and 6-9:30pm. MC/V. ❷

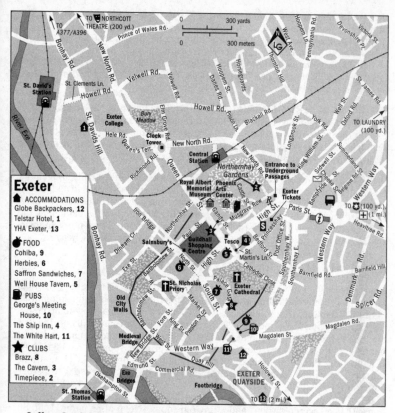

Exeter

🏠 ACCOMMODATIONS
Globe Backpackers, **12**
Telstar Hotel, **1**
YHA Exeter, **13**

🍴 FOOD
Cohiba, **9**
Herbies, **6**
Saffron Sandwiches, **7**
Well House Tavern, **5**

🍺 PUBS
George's Meeting
House, **10**
The Ship Inn, **4**
The White Hart, **11**

⭐ CLUBS
Brazz, **8**
The Cavern, **3**
Timepiece, **2**

Saffron Sandwiches, 6 South St. (☎670 599). Hearty sandwiches (£2.50-3.35) and jacket potatoes (£2.75-3.30) made to order. Open M-Sa 9am-4pm. Cash only. ❶

Cohiba, 36 South St. (☎678 445). Serves tapas (£4.50) and Mediterranean entrees (£9-15) with a mix of Latin tunes and exotic decor. Open M-Sa noon-11pm. MC/V. ❸

Well House Tavern, Cathedral Close (☎233 611). Good pub grub in an annex of the beautiful Royal Clarence Hotel. Entrees £8.50-13. Open M-Sa 11am-11pm, Su noon-10:30pm. Food served noon-2:30pm, bar menu served 2:30-5:30pm. AmEx/MC/V. ❷

🔍 SIGHTS

EXETER CATHEDRAL. Largely spared from the repeated bombings in Exeter during WWII, this cathedral is one of England's finest. Two massive Norman towers preside over the West Front, decorated with kings, saints, and a sculpture of St. Peter as a fisherman in his birthday suit. The interior features one of the longest uninterrupted vaults in Britain—a striking sight at over 300 ft. The 16th-century astronomical clock is reputed to be the source of the nursery rhyme "Hickory Dickory Dock." The grounds contain thousands of bodies, as all area natives were buried there until the 17th century. The cathedral is home to the 60 ft. **Bishop's Throne** (made without nails), disassembled and taken to the countryside in 1640 and again during WWII to save it from destruction. The Minstrels' Gallery contains carvings of angels playing 14th-century instruments. The Bishop's Palace library exhibits a collection of manuscripts known as the **Exeter Book,** the world's richest treasury of early Anglo-Saxon poetry. (☎ 285 983. *Cathedral open M-F and Su 9:30am-6pm, Sa 9:30am-4pm. Library open M-F 2-5pm. Evensong M-F 5:30pm, Sa-Su 3pm. Free guided tours Apr.-Oct. M-F 11am and 2:30pm, Sa 11am, Su 4pm. Requested donation £3.50.)*

THE ROYAL ALBERT MEMORIAL MUSEUM. This museum has 16 galleries of fascinating hodgepodge. The world culture galleries, amassed largely by local explorers (including Captain Cook), feature everything from totem poles and Egyptian tombs to Polynesian weaponry. The natural history exhibits include rare birds and a stuffed giraffe. *(Queen St. ☎ 665 858. Open M-Sa 10am-5pm. Free.)*

GARDENS. Upon penetrating the city, William the Conqueror built Rougemont Castle to keep the locals in check. Today only the castle walls remain and, due to security at the adjacent court building, tourists can only view the ruins from an awkward angle in the surrounding **Rougemont Gardens.** Follow the path along the castle walls through the impressive flowerbeds to reach the 17th-century **Northernhay Gardens** next door. *(Accessible from Castle St. Open daily dawn to dusk. Free.)*

🎭 🎵 NIGHTLIFE AND ENTERTAINMENT

Exeter boasts a growing nightlife, with bars and clubs in the alleys off **High Street,** near **Exeter Cathedral,** and on **Gandy Street.** Black lights and neon murals light up **Timepiece,** Little Castle St. (☎ 493 096; www.timepiecenightclub.co.uk. Cover £2-5. Open M-W 7pm-1am, Th-Sa 7pm-1:30am, Su 7pm-12:30am.) **The Cavern,** 83-84 Queen St., a tiny joint in a brick cellar, has live rock, punk, and local bands. (☎ 495 370; www.cavernclub.co.uk. Cover after 10pm £2-5. Open M-Th 8:30pm-1am, F-Sa 9pm-2am, Su 8pm-midnight. Cafe open M-Sa 11am-4pm.) **Brazz,** 10-12 Palace Gate, is a modern bar with a big-city feel and a two-story aquarium. (☎ 252 525; www.brazz.co.uk. Open M-F 11am-11pm, Sa 11am-midnight, Su noon-10:30pm.) The **White Hart,** 66 South St., a 14th-century free house, has a "secret garden" and a tiny tap room. (Open M-Sa noon-11pm, Su noon-10:30pm.) Over 700 years old, **The Ship Inn,** 1-3 St. Martin's Ln., was a favorite of Francis Drake, who wrote, "Next to mine own shippe I do love that Shippe in Exon." (☎ 272 040. Open M-Sa 11am-11pm, Su noon-10:30pm.) **George's Meeting House,** 38 South St., looks like the 18th-century nonconformist chapel it once was; patrons sip lager by a pulpit. (☎ 454 250. Open M-Sa 10am-11pm, Su 10am-10:30pm.)

The professional company at the **Northcott Theatre,** Stoker Rd., performs throughout the year. (☎ 493 493. Box office open M-Sa 10am-6pm, until 8pm on show nights. Tickets £11-18; student standby tickets £6.) In July and August, the Northcott company does Shakespeare in the park. Book tickets at at **Exeter Tickets,** High St., which supplies monthly listings of cultural events in the city. (☎ 211 080. Open M-Sa 9:30am-5:30pm.) The **Exeter Festival,** in late June and early July, features concerts, opera, dance lessons, stand-up comedy, and theater. For tickets, contact the **Festival Box Office,** Civic Centre, Paris St. (☎ 213 161; www.exeter.gov.uk/festival. Open M-Sa 10am-5pm. Tickets £8-20.) The **Exeter Phoenix Arts Center,** Gandy St. (☎ 667 080; www.exeterphoenix.org.uk), offers everything from dance classes to gallery talks and free summer public movie screenings in Northernhay Gardens.

EXMOOR NATIONAL PARK

Once a royal hunting preserve, Exmoor is among the smallest and most picturesque of Britain's national parks, covering 265 sq. mi. on the north coast of the
southwestern peninsula. Wild ponies still roam, and England's last herds of red
deer graze in woodlands. Although over 80% of Exmoor is privately owned, the territory is accommodating to respectful hikers and bikers.

▶ TRANSPORTATION

Exmoor's western gateway is **Barnstaple**; its eastern gateway is **Minehead**. Most
transportation into and within the park runs through one of these towns. Bus
service within the park is erratic. Western Exmoor lies in Devon, and bus routes
are detailed in *North Devon Bus Times;* eastern Exmoor occupies the western
part of Somerset and is covered by the *Public Transport Timetable for the
Exmoor and West Somerset Area.* Both guides are free at TICs. *Accessible
Exmoor,* free from National Park Information Centres (NPICs), provides a guide
for disabled visitors. Since single bus fares in the park are £3-4, it's wise to purchase **First Day Explorer** (£7) or **First Week Explorer** (£22) tickets, which allow
unlimited travel on all First buses. Plan ahead and call to check times. **Traveline**
(☎0870 608 2608) is the most helpful resource for planning public transport.

Trains: Barnstaple serves trains from Bristol (2½hr., 12 per day, £22.50); Exeter Central
and St. David's (1¼hr.; M-Sa 12 per day, Su 5 per day; £10.20); London Paddington
(4hr., 12 per day, £63). Minehead serves trains from Exeter St. David's (25min., every
hr., £11.90).

Buses: Barnstaple serves National Express (☎08705 808 080) buses from Bristol (3hr.,
1 per day, £16.80) and London Victoria (5½hr., 3-4 per day, £26). First DevonBus
(☎01752 402 060; open M-F 9am-4pm) #315 connects to Exeter (2¼hr.; M-Sa 4-5
per day, Su 2 per day; £4) and #82 to Plymouth (3¼hr.; M-Sa 6 per day, Su 2 per day;
£4). Minehead Station serves National Express buses from Exeter St. David's (25min.,
every hr., £11.90). First #28, 300, 928 (Su only) from Taunton (1¼hr.; M-Sa every hr.,
Su 9 per day; £4). Drivers sell combined bus and train tickets (£12).

Local Transportation: First Somerset bus #300 runs east to west along the coast, from
Taunton to Barnstaple via Dunster, Minehead, Porlock, Lynton, and Ilfracombe. Listed
prices are for off-peak hours (purchased after 8:45am). **Barnstaple** serves Devon
(☎01752 402 060) buses from **Ilfracombe** (#3 or 30; 40min.; M-Sa 4 per hr., Su every
hr.; £2.50); **Lynmouth** (#309-310, 1hr., M-Sa 3 per day, £2.20); **Lynton** (#309-310,
1hr., M-Sa every hr., £2.20). **Minehead** serves Somerset (☎01823 272 033) buses from:
Barnstaple (#300, 2¾hr., 1 per day, £4.30); **Dunster** (#15, 28, 39, 300, 398; 10min.;
1-2 per hr.; £1.25); **Ilfracombe** (#300, 2hr., 3 per day, £4.50); **Lynton** (#300, 1hr., 3 per
day, £2.80); **Porlock** (#38 or 300; 15min.; M-Sa 9 per day, Su 3 per day; £2).

✦ ℹ ORIENTATION AND PRACTICAL INFORMATION

Exmoor lies on 23 mi. of the Bristol Channel coastline between Barnstaple and Minehead. The park spans Somerset and Devon counties and sits north of Dartmoor
National Park. Both TICs and NPICs stock Ordnance Survey maps (£7.40), public
transport timetables, and the *Exmoor Visitor* newspaper, which lists events, accommodations, and walks, and has a useful map and articles on the area's geography.
This information can also be found at www.exmoor-nationalpark.gov.uk.

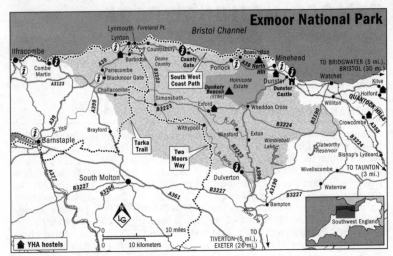

National Park Information Centres:

Blackmoor Gate: South Moulton Junction (☎01598 763 466), on the A399/A39. Open Apr.-Oct. daily 10am-5pm; Nov.-Mar. Sa-Su 11am-3pm.

Combe Martin: Seacot, Cross St. (☎01271 883 319), 3 mi. east of Ilfracombe. Open daily Apr.-Sept. 10am-5pm; Oct. 10am-4pm.

County Gate: (☎01598 741 321), on the A39, Countisbury, 5 mi. east of Lynton. Open daily Apr.-Oct. 10am-5pm.

Dulverton: Dulverton Heritage Centre, The Guildhall, Fore St. (☎01398 323 841). Open daily Apr.-Oct. 10am-1:15pm and 1:45-5pm; Nov.-Mar. 11am-3pm.

Dunster: Dunster Steep Car Park (☎01643 821 835), 2 mi. east of Minehead. Open daily Apr.-Oct. 10am-5pm; school holidays 11am-3pm.

Tourist Information Centres: All TICs book accommodations for a 10% deposit.

Barnstaple: The Square (☎01271 375 000), in the North Devon Museum. Open M-Sa 9:30am-5pm.

Ilfracombe: The Landmark Seafront (☎01271 863 001). Shares a building with the Landmark Theatre. Open Easter to Oct. daily 10am-5:30pm; Nov. to Easter M-F 10am-5pm, Sa 10am-4pm.

Lynton: Town Hall, Lee Rd. (☎0845 660 3232; www.lyntourism.co.uk). Open M-F 9:30am-5pm, Su 10am-4pm.

Minehead: 17 Friday St. (☎01643 702 624). Open July-Aug. M-Sa 9:30am-12:30pm and 1:30-5pm.

Porlock: West End High St. (☎01643 863 150). Open Easter to Oct. M-F 10am-1pm and 2-5pm, Sa 10am-5pm, Su 10am-1pm; Nov. to Easter M-F 10:15am-1pm, Sa 10am-2pm.

■ ACCOMMODATIONS

Hostels and **B&Bs** ($20-25) fill up quickly; check listings and the *Exmoor Visitor* at the TIC. At busy times, **camping** may be the easiest way to see the park. Most land is private; before pitching a tent, ask the owner's permission.

YHA Crowcombe (☎01984 667 249). A large house in the woods on the Taunton-Minehead Rd., ½ mi. from Crowcombe Village. Take bus #28 or 928 from Taunton toward Minehead, disembark at Red Post, and turn onto the road marked "Crowcombe Station"; the hostel is ¾ mi. down, on the right. Kitchen. Laundry £2.50. Lockout 10am-5pm. Sept.-June call 48hr. in advance. Dorms £11, under 18 £8. MC/V. ❷

YHA Elmscott (☎01237 441 367). Bus #319 or X19 from Barnstaple goes to Hartland; from the west end of Fore St. a footpath leads 2½ mi. through the Vale to the hostel. Kitchen. Laundry £3. Lockout 10am-5pm. Open Easter to Sept. Frequently closed on Su; call ahead. Dorms £11, under 18 £8. MC/V. ❶

YHA Exford, Withypoole Rd. (☎01643 831 288), Exe Mead. Take bus #178 (F), 285 (Su), or Red Bus #295 (June-Sept. only) from Minehead. The hostel is next to the River Exe bridge, in the center of the village. Kitchen and laundry. Lockout 10am-5pm. Curfew 11pm. Open July-Aug. daily; Sept.-June M-Sa. Dorms £12.50, under 18 £9. MC/V. ❷

YHA Lynton (☎01598 753 237), Lynbridge, Lynton. Take bus #309 or 310 from Barnstaple to Castle Hill Car Park or #300 from Minehead. From Lynton, pass the school and turn left up Sinai Hill; the hostel is signposted from there (10min. walk). Kitchen and laundry. Reception 8-10am and 5-10pm. Lockout 10am-5pm. Sept.-Mar. call 48hr. in advance. Dorms £11, under 18 £8. MC/V. ❶

YHA Minehead, Alcombe Combe (☎01643 702 595). Halfway between the town center and Dunster (2mi. from either), a 3hr. walk to Dunkery Beacon. From Minehead, follow Friday St. as it becomes Alcombe Rd., turn right on Church St. and follow to Manor Rd. (30min. walk). From Taunton, take bus #28 to Minehead or 928 to Alcombe; the bus stops 1 mi. from the hostel. Kitchen. Laundry £1.50. Lockout 10am-5pm. Open daily July-Aug.; call 48hr. in advance. Dorms £11, under 18 £8; doubles £29. MC/V. ❶

🔲 🏔 HIKING AND OUTDOORS

With wide-open moorland in the west and wooded valleys in the east, Exmoor has a varied landscape best toured on foot or bike. The **Exmoor National Park Rangers** lead nature and moorland **tours** (☎01398 323 665; £3 per person for 3hr.). **NPICs** offer 1½-10 mi. themed walks (£3-5, p. 210). The **National Trust** leads walks with various focuses, including summer birds, butterflies, deer, and archaeology. (☎01643 862 452. £1-8 per person.) More themed walks are listed in the *Exmoor Visitor*, free at NPICs and TICs. **Heritage Coach Tours** (☎01643 704 204) operates full-day, half-day, and evening bus tours. **Dulverton Visitors Center** is open year-round and offers information on all parts of the park (☎01398 323 841).

Barnstaple, just outside the park, isn't the only suitable hiking base, but it is the largest town in the region, a transport center, and the best place to get gear. Two good points to start woodland traipsings are **Blackmoor Gate,** 11 mi. northwest of Barnstaple, or **Parracombe,** 2 mi. farther northwest. Both are on the Barnstaple-Lynton bus route (#309). The **Tarka Trail** starts in Barnstaple and traces a 180 mi. figure-eight, 31 mi. of which are bicycle-friendly. **Tarka Trail Cycle Hire,** at the Barnstaple train station, is conveniently located at the trailhead. (☎01271 324 202. £9.50 per day. Open daily Apr.-Oct. 9am-5pm.) The *Coast Path* booklet (£2.75), available at any Exmoor TIC, details three walks from Minehead to Combe Martin, with color-coded paths and marked pit stops. Only 1 mi. from the park's eastern boundary, **Minehead** is also a good place to start hiking. The busy seaside resort provides plenty of lodging and an informative **nature trail,** beginning on Parkhouse Rd. Other well-marked paths weave through **North Hill.** The 630 mi. **South West Coast Path** (p. 178) starts in Minehead and ends in Poole; the 70 mi. portion running through Exmoor passes through Porlock, Lynmouth, Lynton, Ilfracombe, and Barnstaple. Contact the South West Coast Path Association for more information. (☎01752 896 237; www.swcp.org.uk.) The trailhead is on Quay St.—follow the signs for "Somerset and North Devon Coastal Path." Set in wooded valleys 9 mi.

along the South West Coast Path from Minehead, **Porlock** offers good hiking and horseback riding. The TIC sells *13 Narrated Walks around Porlock* (£2), which includes a 2 mi. hike to **Weir-Culborne Church**, England's smallest parish church, and an 8 mi. trek to Exmoor's highest point, **Dunkery Beacon.**

The TIC also has a list of local stables, including **Burrowhays Farm Riding Stables,** West Luccombe, 1 mi. east of Porlock off the A39. (☎01643 862 463. Open Easter to Oct. M-F and Su. Pony rides £12 per hr.) England's "Little Switzerland," the twin villages of **Lynton** and **Lynmouth,** sit atop the coast. The **Cliff Railway,** a Victorian-era water-powered lift, shuttles visitors between the two villages. (☎01598 753 486. Open daily late July to Aug. 10am-9pm; June and Sept. 10am-7pm; call ahead Oct.-May. £1.60, bikes £3.) **Exmoor Coast Boat Trips** leads drift-fishing trips and runs to Lee Bay and the Valley of Rocks. (☎01598 753 207. Both trips 1hr. £9.) Upstream from the harbor, **Glen Lyn Gorge,** Lynmouth Crossroads, showcases the benefits of hydroelectric power on its quirky ravine walk and recounts the 1952 flood that devastated Lynmouth. (☎01598 753 207. Open Easter to Oct. £3.50, concessions £2.) **Dunster,** a tiny village of cobblestone sidewalks 2½ mi. east of Minehead, is worth a visit for its 14th-century streets, thatched roofs, and **Dunster Castle.** The residence's elaborate interior includes what's reputed to be the oldest bathroom in Somerset. (☎01643 821 314. Open Mar.-Oct. M-W and Sa-Su 11am-5pm. Last admission 4:30pm. Gardens open daily 10am-5pm. £7.20. Gardens only £3.90.)

DARTMOOR NATIONAL PARK

Dartmoor National Park, south of Exmoor and west of Exeter, is a vast, granite-strewn landscape of lush woodlands and looming moors. The tiny towns in the pockets of the moors are filled with local and traveling hikers in every season. Granite tors and neolithic rock formations dot the forbidding uplands, while manor homes and country churches occupy gentler countryside below. The pure green 368 sq. mi. of the park is notorious for its rough terrain and harsh climate, mastered only by sheep and wild ponies.

▐ TRANSPORTATION

Transportation in Dartmoor can be erratic and shuts down almost completely on Sundays. Planning ahead is absolutely essential. Pick up the invaluable *Discovery Guide to Dartmoor by Bus and Train* (free at TICs), which has comprehensive transport schedules, a map, and hiking suggestions. **Disabled visitors** should also look for the *Access Guide to Dartmoor Towns and Villages*, available at TICs. Even locals rely on the free *Dartmoor Visitor* newspaper for activities and events listings. Travelers planning to use public transportation in Dartmoor should consider purchasing **Explorer** tickets, which allow unlimited travel. Stagecoach offers a one-day ticket on all buses for £6; First offers a one-day ticket on all buses for £5. **Sunday Rover** tickets allow unlimited travel on all buses and local trains (£5). The Sunday Rover Helpline (☎01837 54545) is (ironically) open from Monday to Friday (9am-6pm); be sure to plan your weekends ahead. For updated timetables, contact Traveline (☎08706 082 608).

Only one **train** services the park. The Dartmoor Line (☎01837 55637) runs from Okehampton to Exeter Central and Exeter St. David's from late May to mid-September (50min., Su 5 per day, £5). **Bus** service is more extensive. First DevonBus (☎0845 600 1420, fare inquiries 01752 402 060) #82, a.k.a. the "Transmoor Link," connects Plymouth to Exeter (late May to late Sept. M-Sa 3 per day, Su 5 per day; £4), via Yelverton, Princetown, Postbridge, Moretonhampstead, and Steps Bridge. Bus #359 also connects Exeter to Moretonhampstead (50min., M-Sa 7 per day, £2.80). To access

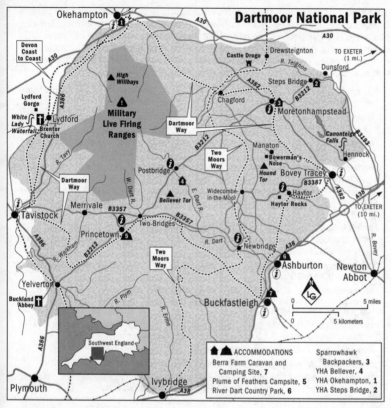

Dartmoor National Park

ACCOMMODATIONS
Berra Farm Caravan and Camping Site, **7**
Plume of Feathers Campsite, **5**
River Dart Country Park, **6**
Sparrowhawk Backpackers, **3**
YHA Bellever, **4**
YHA Okehampton, **1**
YHA Steps Bridge, **2**

the western and northern parts of the park, take a bus from Plymouth to Tavistock and Yelverton in the west (#83 or 86; 1hr., 4 per hr., £3.10) or Okehampton in the north (#86 or 118; 1½-2hr., 3 per day, £3.10). To reach Okehampton from Exeter take X9/10 (1hr.; M-Sa every 45min., Su 2 per day; £4). Once in Okehampton, it can be difficult to access the park by public transportation. Connect in Tavistock (#86 or 118; 1hr.; M-Sa every hr., Su 7 per day, £2). To reach the park's southern towns, try Stagecoach Devon (☎01392 427 711). Bus X38 runs from Plymouth to Exeter (M-Sa every hr.). First X80 also runs to Ivybridge (45min.; M-Sa 4 per day, Su 8 per day) from Plymouth and Torquay (1-1¼hr.; M-Sa 2 per hr., Su-8 per day).

Within the park, explore by foot or bike, since many sights are not accessible from the main roads. In winter, snow often renders the park impassable and brooks or small waterfalls can become dangerously slippery. Note that mobile phone service can be scarce in the park. **Hitchhikers** report that rides from sympathetic locals are easy to get, although Let's Go does not recommend hitchhiking

ORIENTATION AND PRACTICAL INFORMATION

Dartmoor National Park sits in Dartmoor county, 7 mi. inland from the windswept southern coast. Roughly diamond shaped, the park lies between the towns of Okehampton in the north, Tavistock in the west, Ivybridge in the south, and Bovey

Tracey and Ashburton in the east. Rivers and hiking paths criss-cross the park; a Range Danger Area (used by the military) occupies its northwest corner. The city of Exeter is 10 mi. east of the park; Plymouth is 5 mi. south. All NPICs and TICs stock the indispensable, free *Dartmoor Visitor*, which has a map and listings on events, accommodations, and guided walks (p. 211). As signs in TICs will often tell you, you can "learn moor" at www.dartmoor-npa.gov.uk.

National Park Information Centres: The Princetown NPIC serves as the main visitors center for the entire park, and has free exhibitions about the area.

Haytor: (☎01364 661 520), on the B3387, midway between Bovey Tracey and Whitticombe. Open Easter to Oct. daily 10am-5pm; Nov.-Dec. Sa-Su 10am-4pm.

Newbridge: (☎01364 631 303), in the Riverside carpark. Open Easter to Oct. daily 10am-5pm; Nov.-Dec. Sa-Su 10am-4pm.

Postbridge: Yelverton Rd., Moretonhampstead (☎01822 880 272), in a carpark off the B3212. Open Easter to Oct. daily 10am-5pm; Nov.-Dec. Sa-Su 10am-4pm.

Princetown (High Moorland Visitor Centre): The Square, Tavistock Rd. (☎01822 890 414), in the former Duchy Hotel. Stocks hiking supplies, like walking sticks and waterproof map cases. Open daily 10am-6pm.

Tourist Information Centres: The first three TICs listed below are gateways into Dartmoor; the last three are towns whose TICs work in conjunction with the National Park Authority and are staffed by volunteers.

Bovey Tracey: Lower Car Park, Station Rd. (☎01626 832 047). Open Easter to Sept. M-F 10am-4pm, Sa 9:30am-3:30pm.

Okehampton: 3 West St. (☎01837 53020), in the courtyard adjacent to the White Hart Hotel. Books accommodations for a 10% deposit. Open Easter to Oct. M-Sa 10am-5pm; Nov. to Easter M and F-Sa 10am-4:30pm.

Tavistock: Town Hall Building, Bedford Sq. (☎01822 612 938). Books accommodations for 10% deposit. Open daily Apr.-Oct. 9:30am-5pm; Nov.-Mar. 10am-4:30pm.

Ashburton: Town Hall, North St. (☎01364 653 426). Open M-Sa 9am-4:30pm.

Buckfastleigh: The Valiant Soldier (☎01364 644 522). Open Apr.-Oct. M-Sa 12:30-4:30pm.

Moretonhampstead: 11 The Square (☎01647 440 043). Books accommodations; donations requested. Open Apr.-Oct. daily 9:30am-5pm; Nov.-Mar. F-Su 10am-5pm.

ACCOMMODATIONS

B&B signs often appear on pubs and farmhouses along the roads. It's wise to book ahead. Try www.dartmooraccommodation.co.uk for more options. In **Okehampton,** a few B&Bs are on **Station Road** between the train station and the town center. **Tavistock,** the largest town in the area, has more expensive options near the bus station, but they fill up quickly and single rooms are scarce. Tavistock also has many services, like ATMs, not available in smaller towns. **Moretonhampstead,** a village in the heart of the park, is a charming place to stay, particularly for hikers.

HOSTELS

YHA Bellever (☎01822 880 227), 1 mi. southeast of Postbridge village. Bus #98 from Tavistock stops in front. #82 from Exeter or Plymouth (Oct. to Easter Sa-Su) stops in Postbridge; from there, walk west on the B3212 and turn left on Bellever (20-25min. walk). In the heart of the park and very popular. Friendly staff has plentiful local knowledge. Reception 7-10am and 5-10:30pm. Open Mar.-Oct. Dorms £12.50, under 18 £9; family rooms from £45. MC/V. ❷

YHA Okehampton, Klondyke Rd. (☎01837 53916). Behind the bus and train station, or a 15min. walk from the town center. From the TIC, turn right on George St., veer right onto Station Rd. just before Simmons Park, and continue uphill and under the bridge.

Modern hostel with TV, pool table, and kitchen. Mountain bike rental £10 per day. Reception July-Aug. 8am-8pm; Sept.-June 8-9am and 5-11pm. Open Feb.-Nov. Dorms £14, under 18 £10. Camping available Feb.-Nov. £14, under 18 £5. MC/V. ❷

YHA Steps Bridge (☎01647 252 435), 1 mi. southwest of Dunsford on the B3212, near the eastern edge of the park. Take bus #359 from Exeter (£2.40), get off at Steps Bridge, and hike up the steep drive. Volunteer-run. Kitchen. Reception 7-10am and 5-10pm. Curfew 11pm. Open Apr.-Sept. Dorms £10, under 18 £7. MC/V. ❶

Sparrowhawk Backpackers, 45 Ford St., Moretonhampstead (☎01647 440 318; www.sparrowhawk-backpackers.co.uk), 5min. from the village center. From the bus carpark, turn left and walk toward the church; at the fork, veer left and turn left onto Ford St. Crisp sheets cover bunks in the attic of a former stable. Environmentally conscious owners keep an all-vegetarian kitchen and sparkling facilities. Dorms £12. Cash only. ❷

CAMPING

Although official **campsites** and **camping barns** exist, many camp on the open moor. Most of Dartmoor is privately owned, so always ask permission. Camping is allowed on non-enclosed moorland more than three-quarters of a mile from the road or out of sight of inhabited areas; camping is prohibited within sight of any paved road, in common areas used for recreation, or on archaeological sites. Campers may only stay up to two nights in a single spot and are prohibited from building fires in the moors. Do not climb fences or walls unless signs permit it, do not feed the ponies, and keep domestic dogs in check lest they frighten the sheep. Check www.dartmoor-npa.gov.uk or www.discoverdartmoor.com before heading out, or consult the *Camping and Backpacking with Moor Care and Less Wear* (free at NPICs). When using official campsites, call ahead for reservations, especially in summer. **YHA Okehampton** ❶ also offers camping (see above).

Ashburton: River Dart Country Park, Holne Park (☎01364 652 511; www.ashburtoncaravan-park.co.uk.), ½ mi. off the A38. Follow signs. Lush surroundings and a boating lake. Laundry £2. Open Easter to Sept. Tent or caravan and 2 campers £10-17, with electricity £17-19.50. £4-6 surcharge for each extra camper. ❶

Buckfastleigh: Berra Farm Caravan and Camping Site, Colston Rd., (☎01364 642 234), 1½ mi. from town center. Follow the signs for the Otter Park, continue 200 yards past the entrance, and walk 1 mi. down Old Totnes Rd. 2-person tent £7.50. ❶

NO MOOR PONIES?

Ponies have roamed the region now contained within Dartmoor National Park since Roman times, but local conservationists are afraid that their numbers have declined to a dangerous low. In response, concerned pony-lovers have have started the Dartmoor Pony Heritage Trust (similar to Exmoor's "Moorland Mousie Trust") to ensure future foals.

Adapted to the harsh, rocky, and windy conditions of the moors, Dartmoor ponies look like a cross between low, shaggy Shetland ponies and bay horses. They stand no higher than 12 hands, are docile, and can be valuable when purebred.

Worried that "pony passports" (traceable tags for private horses) and low market value have led to negligence for the Dartmoor Pony breed, the Trust seeks to raise awareness about the importance of the ponies. They widely advertise that the ponies are good for riding (when tamed); the Trust also ensures that the ponies have adequate food and healthcare. In the summer of 2005, 300 brood mares and stallions of varying breeds were introduced into the land. With public support and increased attention on the wild ponies, the Trust hopes that their numbers will rise.

To find out more about the future of these UK natives, visit www.dartmoorponytrust.com.

Princetown: Plume of Feathers Campsite and Camping Barn (☎01822 890 240; www.plumeoffeathers-dartmoor.co.uk), behind the Plume of Feathers Inn, opposite the NPIC. Solid bunks with power showers and access to TV; book 2-3 months in advance. The "new bunk" has an indoor bathroom; the "old bunk" bathroom is outdoors. Bunks £6.25-7.50. Campsites £4.50. Showers included. ❶

HIKING AND OUTDOORS

The Dartmoor Commons Act of 1985 gives visitors free reign to trek the registered common land in Dartmoor, but visitors should not underestimate Dartmoor's moody **weather** and treacherous terrain. Ordnance Survey Explorer Map #28 (1:25,000; £7.45), a compass, sturdy boots, and waterproof garb are essential. There is no shelter away from the roads. The **Dartmoor Rescue Group** is on call at ☎999. The Devon Air Ambulance, for medical emergencies only, can be reached via ☎999 or directly on ☎466 666. (See **Wilderness Safety**, p. 46.)

The rugged terrain of Dartmoor, with remnants of the Bronze Age dotting its moorland, offers unparalleled **hiking**. The **National Park Authority** conducts guided walks (1-6hr.; £2-5, free if arriving at starting point by public transport), which are listed in the *Dartmoor Visitor* and by the events hotline (☎01822 890 414). NPICs and TICs have a wealth of information and advice as well as various guidebooks (under £10). The free *Dartmoor Walks* compiles eight of the most popular routes. A good option for short hikes is the free *Transmoor Link Bus Walks*, which details four hikes along the #82 Transmoor Link bus route (p. 212). **Dartmoor Way** is a 90 mi. circular route that hits the park's main towns, running through river valleys and skirting rural lakes. The 180 mi. **Tarka Trail** runs from Okehampton to Exmoor National Park in the north (p. 211). The 102 mi. **Two Moors Way** also connects the two parks, running from Lynmouth to Ivybridge.

The area is crowned by several peaks, the highest of which is **High Willhays** (2038 ft.). The peak is accessible only by foot; the peak is a hilly 4 mi. from Okehampton. Tiny **Brentor Church** crowns an extinct volcano near Lydford, accessible only by foot. A mile from Lydford, the 1½ mi. **Lydford Gorge** has a lush forest and a whirlpool known as the **Devil's Cauldron**. Walk along the top of the gorge to reach the fantastic 90 ft. **White Lady Waterfall.** (☎01822 820 320. Open daily Apr.-Sept. 10am-5:30pm; Oct. 10am-4pm; Nov.-Mar. 10:30am-3pm. Last admission 30min. before close. £4.50.) A wealth of **Bronze Age structures,** the remains of a Neolithic civilization, cluster near Merrivale. The knee-high stone circles, hut circles, burial chambers, and long stone rows date back 3500 years. Merrivale is on the #98 and 172 (summer only) bus routes. Haytor, near Bovey Tracey, features numerous tors, including the massive **Haytor Rocks** and the ruins at **Hound Tor**, where excavations unearthed the remains of 13th-century huts and longhouses. Venture north (1 mi. from Manaton) to discover the 40 ft. **Bowerman's Nose**, named after the man who first recognized the rock formation's resemblance to the human proboscis. Also near Bovey Tracey is the 220 ft. **Canonteign Falls**, England's highest waterfall; leave yourself plenty of travel time. (☎01647 252 434. Open daily 10am-6pm or dusk. Last admission 1hr. before close. £5.)

As you enjoy your hike, join in **letterboxing**. A treasure-hunt-like activity unique to the moors, letterboxing lets you see who has roamed the seemingly virgin territory before you. Letterboxes are hidden around the moors and contain a visitor's book and a rubber stamp. Bring your own inkpad to make your mark. Contact the Letterbox 100 Club (☎01392 832 768; www.walk.to/letterboxing) for more info.

Dartmoor's roads are good for **cycling**. Bookended by Ilfracombe and Plymouth, the 102 mi. **Devon Coast to Coast** winds along rivers and rural countryside. The 11 mi. portion between Okehampton and Lydford is known as the **Granite Way**, and offers traffic-free biking along a former railway line. **Okehampton Cycle Hire** rents bikes. From Fore St., go uphill on North St., which becomes North Rd., then bear left off the main road, continuing downhill to the T junction; follow signs for Garden Centre. (☎01837 53248. Open M-Sa 9am-5pm, Su 10am-4pm. £9.50 per day.) For **horseback riding,** NPICs can refer you to stables (rides £8-16 per hr.). **Dartmoor Safaris** operates **tours** through the moors in SUVs. Tours leave from Plymouth Bus Station, except for the Thursday tour, which leaves from The Strand, Torquay. (☎01752 500 567; www.dartmoorsafaris.co.uk. 8hr. tours depart 9:30am Apr.-Sept. "Taste of Dartmoor" tour Tu and F, "Hound of Baskervilles" tour W and Su. £36.)

WARNING. The Ministry of Defense uses parts of the northern moor for target practice and has done so since the 1880s. Consult the *Dartmoor Visitor* or an Ordnance Survey map for the boundaries of the danger area. Weekly firing schedules are available in NPICs, post offices, police stations, hostels, campsites, and pubs; in Friday's *Western Morning News;* by military freephone (☎0800 458 4868); and online at www.dartmoor-ranges.co.uk. Danger areas, marked by red flags by day and white lamps by night, change yearly, so be sure your information is up-to-date. Let's Go does not recommend handling any found military debris.

◉ SIGHTS

The Dartmoor landscape stretches across 368 sq. mi. of moorland, with Bronze-Age burial mounds and stone circles scattered throughout. Also prevalent are **tors,** granite towers which resulted from thousands of years of geological activity.

CASTLE DROGO. The "last castle in England" was built from 1910-30 for tea baron Julius Drewe, who believed himself to be a descendant of a William-the-Conqueror-era Norman and desired to live accordingly. From the castle, easy 3-4 mi. hikes go to the **River Teign** and its **Fingle Bridge;** there are croquet lawns open all summer with equipment for rent. *(Take bus #173 from Moretonhampstead or Exeter, 174 or 179 from Okehampton. ☎01647 433 306. Open Apr.-Nov. M and W-Su 11am-5:30pm. Last admission 4:30pm. Grounds open daily 10:30am-5:30pm. £6.50.)*

PRINCETOWN PRISON. Dartmoor's maximum-security prison in Princetown, the highest town in England, is still in use today and has a museum to showcase its eclectic past. The moorland surrounding the prison is the setting for Sherlock Holmes's famed escapade, *The Hound of the Baskervilles,* which emerged from an ancient Dartmoor legend of a black dog that stalked a scurrilous aristocrat. The interesting **Dartmoor Prison Heritage Centre** features a gallery of weapons made by inmates, including a knife made of matchsticks. Prisoner-made items are available at the prison shop. *(Tavistock Rd. ☎01822 892 130. Open daily 9:30am-12:30pm and 1:30pm-5pm. £2, concessions £1.)*

BUCKLAND ABBEY. A few miles south of Yelverton, the abbey was built by Cistercian monks in 1273 and later bought by Sir Francis Drake, who was born here and whose drum it still houses. It is said that if the drum is ever lost, England will go to ruins. While the interior is lackluster, the exterior and grounds make for pleasant strolls. *(Milton Combe Rd. Take Citybus #55 or 48 from Yelverton or 48 from Plymouth. ☎01822 853 607. Open mid-Mar. to Nov. M-W and F-Su 10:30am-5:30pm; Dec. to mid-Mar. Sa-Su 10:30am-5:30pm. Last admission 45min. before close. £6.)*

TORQUAY
☎01803

The largest city in the Torbay resort region and the self-proclaimed "English Riviera," Torquay isn't quite as glamorous as the French original. But the town Agatha Christie called home and in which Basil Fawlty ran his madcap hotel does have friendly beaches, abundant palm trees, and stimulating nightlife. A popular resort area for British city-dwellers, Torquay serves as a base for exploring the sunnier parts of the southwestern English coast.

⊞ 🛈 TRANSPORTATION AND PRACTICAL INFORMATION. Torquay's **train station** is off Rathmore Rd., near the Torre Abbey gardens. (Open M-F 7am-5:45pm, Sa 7am-4:45pm, Su 9:40am-5:10pm.) **Trains** (☎08457 484 950) arrive from: Bristol (2hr., 6 per day, £22.90); Exeter (45min., every hr., £7.10); London Paddington (3½hr., 1 per day, £48); London Waterloo (4hr., 1 per day, £48); Plymouth (1½hr.; every hr.; £8). **Buses** depart from The Pavilion, the roundabout where Torbay Rd. meets The Strand. The Stagecoach office, next to the TIC, provides information on its buses. (☎664 500. Open June-Aug. M-F 9am-5:30pm, Sa 9am-1pm; Sept.-May M-F 9am-5pm, Sa 9am-1pm.) Bus #85 runs to Exeter (1½hr.; May-Sept. M-Sa 2 per hr., Su 3 per day; Oct.-Apr. M-Sa 2 per hr., £5.20), as does the more direct X46 (1hr.; M-Sa every hr., Su 7 per day; £5.20). First buses X80 and X81 run to Plymouth (1¾hr., every hr., £6). Torbay Cab Co. **taxis** (☎292 292) are on call 24hr.

The **Tourist Information Centre**, Vaughan Parade, arranges theater bookings, offers discounted tickets for attractions, and books accommodations for a 10% deposit. The TIC also sells tickets for the **Eden Project** (p. 234). (☎08707 070 010; www.englishriviera.co.uk. Open June-Sept. daily 9:30am-6pm; Oct.-May M-Sa 9:30am-5pm.) Cruise Tours (1hr.; £5) offers **tours** from Princess Pier to Brixham (Western Lady Ferry Service, ☎297 292) and Paignton (Paignton Pleasure Cruises, ☎529 147). Buy tickets for both at the booth on Victoria Parade. (Open daily 9am-5pm.) Other services include: **banks** on Fleet St.; Thomas Cook **currency exchange**, 54 Union St. (☎352 100; open M and W-Sa 9am-5:30pm, Tu 10am-5:30pm); a **launderette**, 63 Princes Rd., off Market St. (☎293 217; wash £3-3.50, dry 20p per 4min.; open M-F 9am-7pm, Sa 9am-6pm, Su 10am-4pm); **police**, South St. (☎08705 777 444); a **pharmacy**, 2 Tor Hill Rd. (☎213 075; open M-F 9am-6pm, Sa 9am-5pm); **Torbay Hospital**, Newton Rd. (☎614 567); free **Internet access** at the library, Lymington Rd., beside the Town Hall (☎208 300; open M, W, F 9:30am-7pm; Tu 9:30am-5pm; Th 9:30am-1pm; Sa 9:30am-4pm) and at PC Bits, Market Shopping Court, Market St. (☎299 550; £1 per 20min.; open M-Sa 9:30am-4:30pm); and the **post office**, 25 Fleet St., with a bureau de change (open M-Sa 9am-5:30pm). **Post Code:** TQ1 1DB.

⌐🖪 ACCOMMODATIONS AND FOOD. Torquay's hotels and B&Bs get busy during summer, especially in August; book in advance. Find less-expensive beach **hotels** on **Babbacombe Road**, including **Torwood Gardens Hotel ❸**, 531 Babbacombe Rd., where feather pillows promise a good night's rest 5min. from the surf. (☎298 408. Apr.-Oct. singles £25; doubles £50; Nov.-Mar. singles £22.50; doubles and twins £45. MC/V.) Cheaper **B&Bs** line **Scarborough Road, Abbey Road,** and **Morgan Avenue.** Flower boxes and walls covered in chalk-scrawled poems foster a warm atmosphere at **Torquay Backpackers ❷**, 119 Abbey Rd. From the train station, turn left and walk down Torbay Rd., continuing straight uphill on Shedden Hill Rd., then turn left on Abbey Rd. (☎299 924; www.torquaybackpackers.co.uk. Laundry £3.50. Internet access £1 per 20min. Reception 9am-10pm. June-Sept. dorms £12; doubles £28. Oct.-May dorms £10; doubles £24. MC/V.) Walk up Abbey Rd. and turn right at the first street to find the **Rosemont Guest House ❷**, 5 Morgan Ave., offers comfortable rooms. (☎295 475. £15 per person, ensuite £16. Cash only.)

Buy **groceries** at Tesco, 25-26 Fleet St. (☎351 400. Open M-Sa 7am-10pm, Su 11am-5pm.) **No. 7 Fish Bistro ❸**, Inner Harbor, Beacon Terr., across from Living Coasts, is the place to splurge for dinner. The restaurant serves superb seafood (£11-17) in an amiable setting. (☎295 055; www.no7-fish.com. Open M-Tu 7-9pm, W 12:15-1:45pm and 6-9:45pm, Th-Sa 12:15-1:45pm and 6-9:45pm, Su 7pm-9pm. AmEx/MC/V.) Locals flock to **Hanbury's ❷**, Princes St., 2 mi. up Babbacombe Rd., for sit-down fish and chips (£7-11) and takeaway. Take bus #32H, 33, or 85 (8min., every 10-30min., £1.10) from The Strand to Princes St. (☎314 616. Open M-Sa noon-1:45pm and 5:30-9:30pm; takeaway open 4:30-9:30pm. MC/V.) **Blue Cargo ❷**, 8-9 Braddons Hill, off Fleet St., is a chic restaurant-bar with heaping portions and good prices. (☎203 390. Entrees from £4. Open daily 10:30am-11:30pm. MC/V.)

⬛⬛ SIGHTS AND BEACHES. Opened in 2003 with a spectacular view of the bay, **Living Coasts,** Beacon Quay, is an aviary that recreates the world's coastal environments, from Africa to the Antarctic. Watching the Auks swim is worth the trip. (☎202 470; www.livingcoasts.org.uk. Open daily Easter to Sept. 10am-6pm; Oct. 10am to dusk; Nov. to Easter 10am to dusk. Last admission 1hr. before close. £5.90, students £4.60.) To get out of the sun, head for the **Torquay Museum,** 529 Babbacombe Rd. (☎293 975; www.torquaymuseum.org. Open mid-July to Sept. M-Sa 9:30am-5:30pm, Su 1:30-5:30pm; Oct. to mid-July M-Sa 9:30am-5:30pm. £3, students £1.50.) **Princess Theatre,** Torbay Rd., offers another weatherproof option, presenting a wide range of live entertainment throughout the year. (☎08702 414 120. Tickets £10-30. Box office open M-Sa 10am-6pm, until 8pm on show nights.)

The weather in the "English Riviera" is not quite as ideal as in its more established French cousin. Yet on the precious sunny days, the beaches around Torquay are extremely popular, especially with local Brits. **Torre Abbey Sands** draws the hordes, but visitors can reach better beaches by bus. Just southeast of Torquay (bus #200, £1.15), **Meadfoot** features beach huts, deck chairs, and pebbly shores. Take bus #200 north to slightly rockier **Oddicombe,** hidden under a cove (every 10min., £1.15). Bus #34 heads farther north to peaceful **Watcombe** (15min., every 30min., £1.50) and nearly deserted **Maidencombe** (20min., £1.75).

⬛⬛ NIGHTLIFE AND FESTIVALS. When the sun dips and beaches empty, nightlife options come alive. **Mojo,** Palm Court Hotel, Torbay Rd., is a friendly seaside hangout with Torquay's latest bar hours and dancing after dark. Look for the bar with the huge outdoor murals as you head into town. (☎294 882. Live bands F. Open M-Th 11am-11pm, F-Sa 11am-1am, Su 11am-12:30am.) Nightclub **Claires,** Torwood St., lures London's top DJs for hardcore clubbing. (☎292 079. Cover £5. Open F-Su 9pm-2am.) The **Koko Lounge,** 50-54 Union St., a decadent, Romanesque club, grooves to rock, dance, and R&B. (☎212 414. Cover £2-5. Open M 8pm-1am, Th-Sa 9:30pm-2am, Su 9:30pm-12:30am.) During the last week of August, Torquay lives the high life during its annual Regatta; call the TIC for details.

PLYMOUTH
☎01752

Plymouth is best known not as a destination, but as a point of departure; Sir Francis Drake, Captain Cook, Lord Nelson, and the Pilgrims all departed from Plymouth. Massive air raids during WWII left the city a cracked shell, but among its rows of utilitarian buildings and awkward modern thoroughfares, find the cafe-lined Barbican and the meticulously manicured lawn of the Hoe.

▐ TRANSPORTATION

Plymouth lies on the southern coast between Dartmoor National Park and the Cornwall peninsula.

Trains: Plymouth Station, North Rd. Ticket office open M-F 5:20am-8:30pm, Sa 5:30am-7pm, Su 8am-8:30pm. Buses #5 and 6 run to the city center (35p). Trains (☎08457 484 950) arrive from **Bristol** (2hr., every 30min., £39), **London Paddington** (3½hr., every hr., £62), and **Penzance** (2hr., every 30min., £11).

Buses: Bretonside Station (☎254 542). Ticket office open M-Sa 8:30am-6pm, Su 9am-5pm. National Express (☎08705 808 080) from **Bristol** (3hr., 4 per day, £23.50) and **London** (5-6hr., 8 per day, £26). Stagecoach bus X38 runs to **Exeter** (1¼-1¾hr., 12-13 per day, £6).

Ferries: Brittany Ferries (☎08703 665 333; www.brittanyferries.com), at Millbay Docks. Follow signs to "Continental Ferries," 15min. from the town center. Taxi to the terminal £4. Buy tickets 24hr. ahead, though foot passengers may be able to purchase tickets upon arrival. Check in well before departure. To **Roscoff, France** (4-6hr., 12 per week, £58-65) and **Santander, Spain** (18hr., W and Su, £168).

Public Transportation: Citybus (☎222 221) **buses** from Royal Parade (from £1.10 round-trip; DayRover £2.80).

Taxis: Plymouth Taxis (☎606 060).

⚹🛈 ORIENTATION AND PRACTICAL INFORMATION

The commercial district formed by **Royal Parade, Armada Way,** and **New George Street** is Plymouth's city center. Directly south, the **Hoe** (or "High Place") is a large, seaside park. The **Royal Citadel,** home to many a man in uniform, is flanked by the Hoe to the west and, to the east, **The Barbican,** Plymouth's historic harbor.

Tourist Information Centres: 3-5 The Barbican, shares building with the Mayflower Museum (☎306 330; www.visitplymouth.co.uk). Books accommodations for a 10% deposit. Free map. Open Apr.-Oct. M-Sa 9am-5pm, Su 10am-4pm; Nov.-Mar. M-Sa 9am-5pm. Branch on Crabtree at the Plymouth Discovery Centre open M-Sa 9am-5pm.

Tours: Plymouth Boat Cruises (☎822 797) leave from Phoenix Wharf for short trips around Plymouth Sound (1½hr.; £5.50).

Financial Services: Banks line Old Town St., Royal Parade, and Armada Way. **Thomas Cook,** 9 Old Town St. (☎612 600). Open M-W and F-Sa 9am-5:30pm, Th 10am-5:30pm, Su 10:30am-4:30pm. **American Express,** 139 Armada Way (☎502 706). Open M and W-Sa 9am-5pm, Tu 9:30am-5pm.

Work Opportunities: JobCentre, Buckwell St. or Hoegate St. (both ☎616 100). Open M-Tu and Th-F 9am-5pm, W 10am-5pm.

Launderette: Hoegate Laundromat, 55 Notte St. (☎223 031). Service wash only. £6.50 per load. Open M-F 8am-6pm, Sa 9am-1pm.

Police: Charles Cross (☎08705 777 444), near the bus station.

Hospital: Derriford Hospital (☎777 111). In Derriford, about 5 mi. north of the city center. Take bus #42 or 50 from Royal Parade.

Pharmacy: Boots, 2-6 New George St. (☎266 271). Open M-W and F-Sa 8:30am-6:30pm, Th 8:30am-7pm, Su 10:30am-4:30pm.

Internet Access: Library (☎305 907), Northhill. Free. ID required. Open M and F 9am-7pm, Tu-Th 9am-6:30pm, Sa 9am-5pm. Computers close 30min. before library close.

Post Office: 5 St. Andrew's Cross (☎08457 740 740). Bureau de change. Open M-Sa 9am-5:30pm. **Post Code:** PL1 1AB.

🏠 ACCOMMODATIONS

B&Bs (£15-35) line **Citadel Road** and its side streets. Rooms tend to be small but cheap.

Globe Backpackers, 172 Citadel Rd. (☎225 158). The friendliest service you'll find in a hostel in a convenient location. Kitchen, smoking room, and cozy TV room. Laundry service upon request. Reception 8am-11pm. Dorms £12.50; doubles £30. MC/V. ❷

Seymour Guest House, 211 East Citadel Rd. (☎667 002), where Hoegate St. meets Lambhay Hill. Serviceable lodgings with a great location between The Barbican and The Hoe. Singles £20; doubles £36, ensuite £40. Cash only. ❷

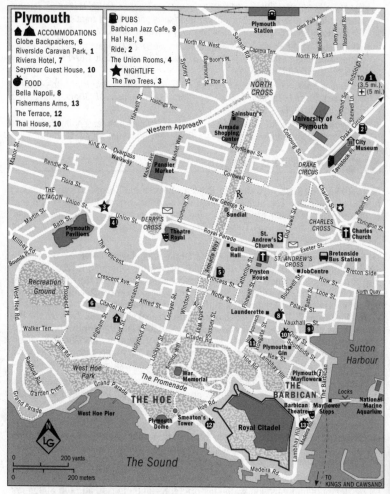

Plymouth

▲▲ ACCOMMODATIONS
Globe Backpackers, **6**
Riverside Caravan Park, **1**
Riviera Hotel, **7**
Seymour Guest House, **10**

🍴 FOOD
Bella Napoli, **8**
Fishermans Arms, **13**
The Terrace, **12**
Thai House, **10**

🍺 PUBS
Barbican Jazz Cafe, **9**
Ha! Ha!, **5**
Ride, **2**
The Union Rooms, **4**

⭐ NIGHTLIFE
The Two Trees, **3**

Riviera Hotel, 8 Elliot St. (☎667 379; www.rivieraplymouth.co.uk), a family-run hotel with numerous amenities, including direct-dial phones and hair dryers. Breakfast included. Singles £30-35; doubles from £53; family rooms from £57. MC/V. ❸

Camping: Riverside Caravan Park, Longbridge Rd., Marsh Mills (☎344 122; www.river-sidecaravanpark.com). Follow Longbridge Rd. 3½ mi. toward Plympton or catch the #50 bus. £8.75-10.25. MC/V. ❶

🏠🍴 FOOD AND PUBS

Tesco Metro, on the corner of New George St., sells **groceries** (☎617 400; open M-Sa 7am-8pm, Su 11am-5pm). **Pannier Market,** an indoor bazaar at the west end of New George St. has fruit and vegetable stands and knick-knacks. (☎304 904. Open M-Tu and Th-Sa 8am-5:30pm, W 8am-4:30pm.)

Thai House, 63 Notte St. (☎ 661 600; www.thethaihouse.com). Makes up for Plymouth's dearth of dining options with delicious spicy pad thai and great service. Entrees £6-18. Open Tu-Su 6-10:30pm. 15% takeaway discount. AmEx/MC/V. ❸

Bella Napoli, 41-42 Southside St., The Barbican (☎ 667 772). A family-run Italian establishment offering fresh fish from the quay. Pasta £9. Veal or fish £12-17. Open daily 6:30-10:30pm. AmEx/MC/V. ❸

Fishermans Arms, 31 Lambhay St. (☎ 661 457). Grab some grub at Plymouth's second-oldest pub. Open M-Th noon-11pm, F-Sa 11am-11pm, Su noon-10:30pm. Food served noon-3pm. MC/V. ❶

The Terrace, Madeira Rd. (☎ 603 533). A self-service cafe with reasonably priced light meals (salads and sandwiches £6.25-7). Open daily 8am-8pm. MC/V. ❶

👁 🌀 SIGHTS AND BEACHES

🟫**NATIONAL MARINE AQUARIUM.** Britain's largest and Europe's deepest tank is home to six sharks. The high-tech aquarium also features an immense coral reef tank and Britain's only giant squid. *(The Barbican. ☎ 600 301; www.national-aquarium.co.uk. Open daily Apr.-Oct. 10am-6pm; Nov.-Mar. 10am-5pm. Last admission 1hr. before close. £8.75, students £7.25.)*

THE HOE. Legend has it that Sir Francis Drake was playing bowls on the Hoe in 1588 when he heard that the Armada had entered the Channel. English through and through, he finished his game before hoisting sail to fend off the Spanish ships. Climb spiral steps and leaning ladders to the balcony of **Smeaton's Tower** for a magnificent view of Plymouth and the Royal Citadel. Originally a lighthouse 14 mi. offshore, the 72 ft. tower was moved to its present site in 1882. Nearby, the **Plymouth Dome** employs plastic dioramas and actors to relate Plymouth's past. *(☎ 603 300; www.plymouthdome.info. Tower open Apr.-Oct. daily 10am-4pm ; Nov.-Apr. Tu-Sa 10am-3pm. Dome open Apr.-Oct. daily 10am-5pm; Nov.-Apr. Tu-Sa 10am-4pm. Last entry 1hr. before close. Dome and Tower £6.50, concessions £5.50. Dome only £4.75/3.25. Tower only £2.25.)*

PLYMOUTH MAYFLOWER. The museum tells the tale of the *Mayflower* and everything you could possibly want to know about Pilgrims. *(3-5 The Barbican. ☎ 306 330. Open May-Oct. daily 10am-4pm; Nov.-Apr. M-Sa 10am-4pm. £2.)*

ST. ANDREW'S CHURCH. St. Andrew's has been a site of Christian meetings since 1087. Three days of bombing in 1941 left it virtually gutted; what visitors can see today is the product of rebuilding and renovation. *(Royal Parade. ☎ 661 414. Open M-F 9am-4pm, Sa 9am-1pm, Su for services only.)*

OTHER SIGHTS. The still-in-use **Royal Citadel** may be seen only via a guided tour of its battlements and garrison walls, historic guns, and church, all built 300 years ago by Charles II. *(Tours May-Sept. Tu 2:30pm. £3.)* At the **Mayflower Steps,** on The Barbican, a plaque and American flag mark the spot from which the Pilgrims set off in 1620. Subsequent departures have been marked as well, including Sir Humphrey Gilbert's journey to Newfoundland, Sir Walter Raleigh's attempt to colonize North Carolina, and Captain Cook's expedition. The blackened shell of **Charles Church,** destroyed by a bomb in 1941, now stands in the middle of the Charles Cross traffic circle as a memorial for victims of the Blitz. The **Plymouth Gin,** 60 Southside St., is England's oldest active gin distillery, at it since 1793. *(☎ 665 292; www.plymouthgin.com. 45min. tours. Open Mar.-Dec. daily 10:30am–4:30pm; Jan.-Feb. Sa 10:30am-3:30pm, Su 10:30am-4:30pm. £6.)*

BEACHES. Take a ferry to **Kingsand** and **Cawsand,** villages with small, pretty slips of sand. **Cawsand Ferry** leaves from the Mayflower Steps, but sometimes cancels trips due to unfavorable winds. *(☎ 07833 936 863. 30min.; 4 per day; £3.)*

ENTERTAINMENT AND FESTIVALS

Both young and old enjoy the view and atmosphere of the harbor at the traditional pubs along The Barbican. **Barbican Jazz Cafe**, 11 The Parade, strikes the right chord with moody decor and daily live jazz. (☎672 127; www.barbicanjazzcafe.com. 15% student discount. Open M-Sa 8pm-2am, Su 8pm-midnight.) Farther inland, Union St. offers a string of bars and clubs. The **Union Rooms,** 19 Union St., is a popular pre-club bar; selected pints and wines are £1.50-2.50. (☎254 520. Open M-W and Su 10am-midnight, Th-Sa 10am-2am.) Nearby, patrons rock out at the **The Two Trees,** 30 Union St. (Karaoke Tu and Su 10pm. Open M-Sa 7pm-2am, Su 7pm-2:30am.) **Ride,** 2 Sherwell Arcade, North Hill, beyond the City Museum, draws a hip student crowd and an after-work contingent. (☎669 749. Tu live music. Su "Cheese and Wine"; bottle of wine £5, cheese free. Happy hour daily 7-9pm. Open M-Th 4:30pm-2am, F-Sa 4:30pm-3am, Su 6pm-1am.) **Ha! Ha!,** 17-19 Princess St., in an old bank behind St. Andrew's Church has a chic interior and a chic clientele. (☎228 810; www.hahaonline.com. Th live music. F-Sa DJ. Su live jazz. Open M-W 10am-11pm, Th-Sa 10am-midnight, Su 10am-10:30pm.)

The **Theatre Royal,** on Royal Parade, has one of the West Country's best stages, featuring ballet, opera, and West End touring companies, including the Royal National Theatre. (☎267 222. Box office open M-Sa 10am-8pm; on non-performance days until 6pm. Tickets £16-44. Concessions available.) On the August Bank Holiday in even years (next in 2006), the public can explore the ships and submarines in the city's maximum-security naval base during **Plymouth Navy Days.** (☎553 941. Tickets on sale in late June.) The British **National Fireworks Championship** explodes in mid-August, while **Powerboat Championships** take place in mid-July.

DAYTRIPS FROM PLYMOUTH

LOOE. Long popular with tourists, the small coastal villages of Looe and Polperro are two of southern Cornwall's most picturesque. The larger of the two, **Looe** is split in half by a wide estuary. Far from the sandy shores and into the sea lies mile-wide **Looe Island,** until recently the only privately owned island in the UK, now under the care of the Cornish Wildlife Trust. **Boat tours** run around the coast and the bay, check for information at the quay. Those who would rather stay on land should visit the **Discovery Centre,** Millpool, on Looe's west side, which stocks the free *Looe Valley Line Trails from the Track,* a packet of 10 hiking trails. The **Tourist Information Centre,** Fore St., East Looe, books rooms for a £2 charge plus a 10% deposit. *(Reach Looe by train from Plymouth via Liskeard (1hr., £5.80). Discovery Centre ☎01503 262 777. Open daily Feb.-June and Oct. 10am-4pm; July-Sept. 10am-6pm; Nov.-Dec. 10am-3pm. TIC ☎01503 262 072; www.southeastcornwall.co.uk. Open daily Easter to May and Oct. to Christmas 10am-2pm; May-Sept. 10am-5pm.)*

POLPERRO. Polperro was once England's most notorious smuggling bay—its proximity to the Channel Islands made it perfect for illegal alcohol and tobacco transport. Visit the **Polperro Heritage Museum of Smuggling and Fishing,** which displays photos of smugglers, a smuggler's sword, and stories about smugglers. The **Visitors Information Centre,** Talland St., is at end of New St. *(From Looe, take Hamblys Coaches (☎01503 220 660) or First buses #80A and 81A (all 3 per day, £4.80). Heritage Museum ☎01503 273 005. Open daily Easter to Oct. 10am-6pm. Last admission 5:15pm. £1.60. Visitors Centre ☎01503 272 320. Open M-Sa 9:30am-5pm.)*

CLOVELLY. Picturesque Clovelly's steep main street has 170 treacherous cobbled steps. The Rous family has owned the entire town for 700 years. But time-capsule upkeep isn't cheap; visitors pay a town admission fee, after which most sights are free. Choose between the restored 1930s **Fisherman's Cottage** *(open 9am-4:45pm)* or making your own pottery at **Clovelly Pottery.** *(☎01237 431 042. £1.50 per pot. Open M-Sa 10am-6pm, Su 10am-5pm.)* In winter, a short walk east along the shore brings trekkers to a surging waterfall, which slows to a stream in warmer months. **Boat trips** from the harbor run to **Lundy Island,** a nature reserve. *(☎01237 431 042; www.lundyisland.co.uk. 2 per week. Day return £28; concessions available.)* Visitors pay admission to the village at the **Clovelly Visitor Centre,** in the carpark. *(First bus #319 connects Clovelly to Bideford (40min.; M-Sa 6 per day, Su 2 per day; £2.20) and Barnstaple (1hr., £2.10). Town admission £4.50. Visitor Centre ☎01237 431 781. Open daily July-Aug. 9am-5:30pm, Sept.-June 9am-6:30pm.)*

CORNWALL

Cornwall's version of England surprises most visitors. A rugged landscape of daunting cliffs that cradle sandy beaches, it's no wonder the Celts chose to flee here in the face of Saxon conquest. Today, the westward movement continues in the form of surfers, artists, and vacationers. The ports of Falmouth and Penzance celebrate England's maritime heritage, while stretches of sand around St. Ives and Newquay fulfill many a surfer's fantasies. Cornwall may have England's most precarious economy, visible in the derelict farmhouses and empty mine shafts that dot the countryside, but it's hard to tell in a region so rich in history and good humor, so proud of their past and of their pasty.

▐ TRANSPORTATION

Penzance is the southwestern terminus of Britain's **trains** (☎08457 484 950) and the best base from which to explore the region. The main rail line from **Plymouth** to **Penzance** bypasses coastal towns, but connecting rail service reaches **Newquay, Falmouth,** and **St. Ives.** A **Rail Rover** ticket may come in handy (3 days out of 7 £25.50, 8 of 15 £40.50). A **Cornish Railcard** costs £10 per year and saves a third off most fares.

The **First bus** network is thorough, although the interior of Cornwall is more often served by smaller companies. *The Public Transport Guide,* free at bus stations and TICs, compiles every route in the region and is essential reading for smooth travel. Buses run from **Penzance** to **Land's End** and **St. Ives** and from **St. Ives** to **Newquay,** stopping in the smaller towns along these routes. Many buses don't run on Sundays, and often operate only May through September. **Traveline** (☎0870 608 2608) can help you get anywhere you want to go. **Explorer** or **Rover tickets** allow unlimited travel on one company's buses and are of excellent value to those making long-distance trips or hopping from town to town. A **First Day South West Explorer** offers unlimited travel on First buses (£7), while a **First Week Explorer** offers a week's unlimited travel all day anywhere in Cornwall (£28). Cyclists may not relish the narrow roads, but the cliff paths, with their evenly spaced hostels, make for easy **hiking.** Serious trekkers can try the famous **Land's End-John O'Groats** route, running from Britain's tip to top.

BODMIN MOOR

Bodmin Moor is high country, containing Cornwall's loftiest points: Rough Tor (1312 ft.) and Brown Willy (1378 ft.). The region is rich with ancient remains, like the stone hut circles that litter the base of Rough Tor. Some maintain that Camelford, at the moor's northern edge, is the site of King Arthur's Camelot, and that Arthur and his illegitimate son Mordred fought each other at Slaughter Bridge, a mile north of town.

▐ TRANSPORTATION

The town of Bodmin sits at the southern edge of Bodmin Moor, which spreads north to coastal (but non-beachfront) Tintagel and Camelford. **Trains** (☎ 08457 484 950) arrive at **Bodmin Parkway** from: London Paddington (4hr., every hr., £66); Penzance (1¼hr., 15 per day, £9.80); Plymouth (40min., every hr., £7.30). The station is open M-F 6:10am-8pm, Sa 6:30am-8am, Su 10:35am-7:40pm. National Express **buses** (☎ 08705 808 080) arrive from Plymouth (1hr., 2 per day, £4.30). Western Greyhound (☎ 01637 871 871) #593 runs buses to Newquay (1hr., M-Sa 5 per day, £2.70). Access Camelford by first hopping the #555 to Wadebridge (30min., every hr., £2.20); from Wadebridge, take the #594 to Camelford (30min., M-Sa 5 per day, £2). To get to Camelford on weekends, or to reach Tintagel and Boscastle, take the #555 to Wadebridge (30min., every hr., £2.20) and transfer to #524 (M-Sa 4 per day, Su 3 per day, £2.40). **Hiking** is convenient from Camelford, and is the only way to reach the tors. **Bikes** can be hired in surrounding towns. **Hitchhiking** is dangerous; Let's Go does not recommend hitchhiking.

▟ ORIENTATION

Bodmin Moor, in central Cornwall, sits directly west of Dartmoor National Park. Bude Bay and the Irish Sea are to its north and west and the English Channel to its south. Its main city and transport hub is Bodmin, 10 mi. inland from the Channel. The moor stretches for thirty miles across.

▐ ACCOMMODATIONS

B&Bs can be booked through the Bodmin TIC (p. 226). **Jamaica Inn ❹**, Bolventor, Launceston, in the middle of the moor, is an 18th-century coaching inn that inspired the novel by Daphne du Maurier. Take First bus X10 (M-Sa 6 per day) from Wadebridge. (☎ 01566 86250; www.jamaicainn.co.uk. Singles £65; doubles £70-90. AmEx/MC/V.) Three miles away, **Barn End ❸**, Ninestones Farm, Common Moor, Liskeard, offers doubles. There's no direct bus, but the owners will pick you up from Bodmin or Liskeard if you call ahead. (☎ 01579 321 628. £22.50 per person. Cash only.) The nearest **YHA hostels** are in Boscastle (p. 227) and Tintagel (p. 226).

BODMIN ☎ 01208

The town of Bodmin, the ancient capital of Cornwall, is the last supply stop before the Arthurian stomping grounds. For hiking or cycling, the 17 mi. **Camel Trail** starts in Padstow and passes through Bodmin on the way to Poley's Bridge, with views of the River Camel, quarries, and tea shops. A former railway track, the trail is mostly smooth and level. In town, a few sights are of interest. The **Military Museum,** St. Nicholas St., behind Bodmin General Station, displays George Washington's Bible and account book (which reveals a missing $3000), pilfered by the Duke of Cornwall's infantry during the Revolutionary War. The infantry has fought in every major British war since 1702. (☎ 728 10. Open M-F 9am-5pm; July-Aug. also Su 10am-4pm. £2.50.) Built in 1779, the **Bodmin Jail,** Berrycombe Rd., was the safekeep for the crown jewels and Domesday Book during WWII. The museum depicts life in an 18th-century jail. (☎ 762 92. Open daily 10am to dusk. £4.75.) Hidden in Bodmin's forests, the stately 17th-century mansion **Lanhydrock,** was gutted by fire in 1881 and is now encompassed by gardens. Inside, plaster ceilings portraying scenes from the Old Testament overhang plush Victorian furnishings. From Bodmin, take Western Greyhound bus #555 (round-trip £2.20) or walk 2½ mi. southeast of Bodmin on the A38. (☎ 265 950. House open Apr.-Oct. Tu-Su 11am-5:pm. Gardens open daily mid-Feb. to Oct. 10am-6pm. £7.90.) The **Bodmin General Station,**

St. Nicholas St. (☎73666), serves Bodmin & Wenford Railway's private steam-hauled trains, which run to Bodmin Parkway and Boscarne Junction, 6 mi. away near Wadebridge. (Apr.-Sept. 4-7 per day. Full route £10; Bodmin General to Boscarne Junction £5.50/3.50/15.50; Bodmin General to Bodmin Parkway £7/£4/£18.)

Friendly Mr. Jeram offers agreeable rooms at **Elmsleigh ❷**, 52 St. Nicholas St., uphill from the TIC. (☎75976. £18 per person. Cash only.) A mile north of town, camp at the **Camping and Caravanning Club ❶**, Old Callywith Rd., with laundry and showers. Head north of town on Castle St., which becomes Old Callywith Rd. (☎73834. Open Mar.-Oct. £3-4.45 per person. Pitch £4.75. Electricity £2.30. Cash only.) To reach town from the **Bodmin Parkway Station**, 3 mi. away on the A38, take Western Greyhound **bus** #555 (every hr., £2.20) or call Chris Parnell **Taxis** (☎75000; £5 between station and town).For **car rental**, contact Bluebird Car Hire (☎07764 154 768), near St. Austell. The **Tourist Information Centre**, Shire Hall, Mount Folly, sells Ordnance Survey maps (£7.50). (☎766 16; www.bodminlive.com. Open Apr.-Oct. M-Sa 10am-5pm; Nov.-Apr. M-F 10am-5pm.) Other services include: **banks** on Fore St.; **police** (☎08705 777 444), up Priory Rd.; a **pharmacy**, 34 Fore St. (☎728 36; open M-Sa 9am-5:30pm); and the **post office**, 40 Fore St., in the back of Cost Cutters (☎08457 740 740; open M-F 9am-5:30pm, Sa 9am-12:30pm). **Post Code:** PL31 2HL.

TINTAGEL ☎01840

Tintagel is a tiny village proud of its connection to Arthurian lore. From Tintagel, visitors can explore sights associated with the legends of King Arthur and Merlin, particularly at the magnificent ruins of ◨**Tintagel Castle**, built by a 13th-century earl on the supposed site of Arthur's birth. Roman and medieval rubble piles atop a headland besieged by the Atlantic. Below, **Merlin's Cave** is worth the climb, but make sure to go at low tide and be careful on the steep cliffs. Even if you don't buy the legends, the views are spell-binding. (☎770 328. Open daily Apr.-Sept. 10am-6pm; Oct. 10am-5pm; Nov.-Mar. 10am-4pm. £4, concessions £3.) Inland, **King Arthur's Great Halls of Chivalry**, Fore St., allegedly held the round table of King Arthur. Millionaire Frederick Thomas Glasscock founded an Arthurian order following WWI, hoping to spread chivalry. Once boasting 17,000 supporters, membership has since fallen to 300. The Great Hall has two rooms: an antechamber with a 10min. video relating Arthur's story, and the great hall, which houses three(!) round tables. (☎770 526. Open daily in summer 10am-5pm; in winter 10am-dusk. £3, concessions £2.) Escape homages to Arthur on a 1½ mi. walk through ◨**St. Nectan's Glen** to a cascading 60 ft. waterfall, a spiritual healing center in times past. From the Visitor Centre, head toward Bossiney for about 1 mi., then follow signs along the footpath to your right; numerous paths lead to the glen. (☎770 760. Open Easter to Oct. daily 10:30am-6:30pm; Nov. to Easter F-Su 10:30am-6:30pm. £2.50.) On the way to Tintagel Castle from the TIC, indulge in homemade Cornish Fudge at **Granny Wobbly's Fudge Pantry.** Watch as the fudge is made in a 140-year-old pan in the pink dollhouse of a shop. Granny Wobbly's also serves Cornish ice cream. (☎770 595. Fudge £7 per box. Open daily 10:30am-5:30pm.)

The **Tintagel Visitor Centre**, Bossiney Rd., has a free exhibition that separates fact from fiction in Arthurian lore. The helpful staff also offers hiking and coastal walk suggestions. (☎779 084. Open daily Mar.-Oct. 10am-5pm; Nov.-Feb. 10:30am-4pm.) Western Greyhound **buses** #594 (M-Sa) and 524 (Su) come from **Camelford** (20min.; M-Sa 5 per day, Su 3 per day; £1.20). The **YHA Tintagel ❶**, at Dunderhole Point, is ¾ mi. from Tintagel. Head east out of town ¼ mi. past St. Materiana's Church, then follow the footpath to the shore. After 300 yards, look for the chimney. (☎770 6068. Kitchen. Laundry £2. Lockout 10am-5pm. Curfew 11pm. Open Easter to Oct. Dorms £10.60, under 18 £7.20. Cash only.)

BOSCASTLE

☎ 01840

Flanked by two grassy hills, tiny Boscastle is a scenic Cornish village divided by a sparkling river. High cliffs guard the harbor, and climbing the eastern cliff affords expansive sea views. The **National Trust Information Centre,** The Old Forge, Boscastle Harbour, offers hiking suggestions. (☎250 353. Open Apr.-Oct. 10:30am-5pm.) A **Visitor's Centre** in the Cobweb Car Park provides additional information and maps, as well as free Internet access. (☎250 010. Open daily Mar.-Oct. 10am-5pm; Nov.-Feb. 10:30am-4pm.) The Valency Valley above the village invites exploration, with scenic River Valency coursing through wooded vales. From the village car park, a 2½ mi. hike leads to **St. Juliot's Church.** Hikes along the headland cliffs provide spectacular views. In town, the **Museum of Witchcraft** is the largest of its kind. Its collection of artifacts, stories, and newspaper articles explain, chronicle, and defend the occult. Look for the weighing and docking chair used by witchhunters—if the accused weighed less than stacked bibles or floated in water they were considered guilty. (☎250 111. Open Easter to Halloween M-Sa 10:30am-5:30pm, Su 11:30am-5:30pm. £2.50, concessions £1.50.)

Western Greyhound buses #524 and 594 come to Boscastle from **Wadebridge** (1-1½hr.; M-Sa 9 per day, Su 3 per day; £2.40) via **Tintagel** (10min., £1), and from **Bude** (40min.; £2.20). The self-catering **YHA Boscastle Harbour ❶** has an incredible location in the town center, alongside the river. Call ahead, as recent flood damage has closed the hostel for an undetermined length of time. (☎0870 770 5710. Kitchen and laundry £2. Lockout 10am-1pm. Curfew 11pm. Open Apr.-Sept. Dorms £10.60, under 18 £7.20. MC/V.) **Riverside Hotel ❸,** The Bridge, has standard ensuite rooms. (☎250 216. Breakfast included. Singles £22.50-25. MC/V.)

PADSTOW

☎ 01841

Padstow, enchanting yet unassuming, is the prettiest of the north Cornwall fishing ports. The cobblestoned harbor, cluttered with sailboats and trawlers, overlooks an estuary and sandy beaches. It has also gained a national spotlight as the home of celebrity chef Rick Stein's array of eateries.

⚏🖪 TRANSPORTATION AND PRACTICAL INFORMATION. Western Greyhound **buses** #555 and 556 go to Bodmin from Padstow (45min., every hr., £3.90 round-trip) via Wadebridge and between Newquay and Padstow (2hr., 4-5 daily, round-trip £5). The **Tourist Information Centre,** Red Brick Bldg., North Quay, books rooms for a 10% deposit. (☎533 449. Internet access £1 per 15min. Open Apr.-Oct. M-Sa 9am-5pm, Su 10am-3pm; Nov.-Mar. M-F 9:30am-4:30pm.) **Rent bikes** at Padstow Cycle Hire, South Quay, in the carpark. (☎533 533. Open daily mid-July to Aug. 9am-9pm; Sept. to mid-July until 5pm. £10 per day. Helmets £1.) **Fishing** and **boating trips** depart from the harbor. Cornish Bird operates mackerel, reef, and wreck fishing trips (2-8hr.); anything you catch is yours. Book at Sport&Leisure, North Quay. (☎532 639; 532 053 after 6pm. Trips daily Easter to Oct. 9am-5pm. £8-20.) **Banks** cluster on Market Place and Duke St. Fill your prescriptions at Moss **pharmacy,** 8-10 Market St. (☎532 327; open M-F 9am-5:30pm, Sa 9am-5pm). **Post code:** PL28 8AA.

🖪🖸 ACCOMMODATIONS AND FOOD. Lodgings in Padstow are pleasant but pricey (from £30). A short uphill walk from the harbor, the suites at **North Point ❸,** Hill St., have delicate decor and harbor views. (☎532 355. Doubles £54-58. Cash only.) **Ms. Anne Humphrey ❸,** 1 Caswarth Terr., offers cozy rooms. (☎532 025. Singles £25; doubles £45. Cash only.) Find a wealth of knowledge at the home of **Peter**

and Jane Cullinan ❸, 4 Riverside, along the harbor as you walk into town. The top-floor double has a balcony overlooking the bay. (☎532 383. Doubles £50-64. Cash only.) The nearest hostel, the **YHA Treyarnon Bay ❶**, is 4½ mi. from Padstow, on Tregonnan in the small town of Treyarnon. It's off the B3276; take bus #56. (☎0870 770 6076. Open Apr.-Feb. Dorms £11.80, under 18 £8.50. MC/V.) **Trevean Farm Caravan and Camping Park ❶**, St. Merryn, is 3 mi. outside of town on the B3276. (☎520 772. Laundry. Open Apr.-Oct. 2-person tent site £8-9. Electricity £2. MC/V.) Splurge at **St. Petrocs Bistro ❹**, New St., which offers mouth-watering seafood for £14-20. (☎532 700. Open daily noon-2pm and 6-9:30pm. MC/V.) Take afternoon tea on 19th-century china at the tiny and intimate **Victorian Tea Room ❶**, 22 Duke St. (☎533 161. All-day breakfast £5. Open daily Apr.-Oct. 8am-7pm. Cash only.) Then grab a plate of fish and chips (£8) at **Stein's Fish & Chips ❷**, South Quay, the most affordable of British seafood chef Rick Stein's many Padstow eateries. (☎532 700; www.rickstein.com. Open M-Sa 11:30am-2:30pm and 5-9pm, Su noon-6pm. MC/V.)

◙ ♫ SIGHTS AND ENTERTAINMENT. Beyond the ferry point near the TIC, an easy **coastal walk** ascends the cliffs for ocean views; follow the path past the war memorial to reach expansive sands and an island-studded bay. Cyclists converge in Padstow for the start of the **Camel Trail** (p. 225) and the **Saints' Way,** which follows the route of the Celtic saints who landed here from Ireland and Wales. The **National Lobster Hatchery,** South Quay, across from the bus stop, was built to save the ailing lobster industry from overfishing. Expectant lobster moms are brought here to lay their eggs, and visitors can see the insect-like babies in various stages of development. (☎533 877; www.nationallobsterhatchery.com. Open May to mid-Sept. daily 10am-6pm; mid-Sept. to Apr. M-Sa 10am-4pm. £3, concessions £2.) Numerous nearby beaches are perfect for exploring, surfing, and sunbathing. Cave-pocked **Trevone Beach** is can be reached via bus #556 (5min.; M-Sa 7 per day, Su 5 per day). Bus #556 continues to remote **Constantine Bay** (15min.), with great surfing, and **Porthcothan Beach** (30min.), a good spot for tanning. The professionals at **Harlyn Surf School,** 16 Boyd Ave., teach to all levels at nearby Harlyn Bay. (☎533 076; www.harlynsurfschool.co.uk. Book in advance; meet at the school's trailer on Harlyn Beach. Open May-Oct. £25 per half-day, £50 per day.) **Ferries** chug across the bay to nearby **Rock,** where visitors will find sailing, waterskiing, windsurfing, and golfing. (☎532 239. 10-15min. Easter to Oct. daily; Nov. to Easter M-Sa. £2.)

NEWQUAY   ☎01637

Known as "the new California," Newquay (NEW-key; pop. 20,000) is an incongruous slice of surfer culture in the middle of Cornwall. The town has long attracted riders for its superior waves (by England's standards), and a steady stream of European partiers has transformed the once-quiet seaside resort into an English Ibiza, with wet t-shirt contests and dance parties late into the night. Though locals look forward to the end of August, when the tourist season ends, Newquay is keen to maintain its reputation as a favorite summer spot for England's youth.

▣ TRANSPORTATION

The train and bus information centers are at the **train station** on Cliff Rd. (Ticket office open M-F 9am-4pm, Sa 9am-1pm.) All **trains** (☎08457 484 950) come from Par (50min.; in summer M-F 8 per day, Sa-Su 5 per day; £4.50), where they connect to Penzance (1½hr., 12 per day, £11) and Plymouth (50min., 15 per day, £8.60). National Express (☎08705 808 080) **buses** arrive from London (7hr., 2-4 per day, £33). Buses travel to Manor Rd. from St. Austell (#21; 1hr., every hr., round-trip £3.60) and St. Ives (#301, 2¼hr., 4 per day, round-trip £5.30). Buses #89 and 90 come from Falmouth (1½hr.; M-Sa every hr.; round-trip £5). Get a **taxi** from Fleet Cabs (☎875 000; 24hr.).

🛈 PRACTICAL INFORMATION

A few blocks toward the city center from the train station, the **Tourist Information Centre**, Marcus Hill, has free maps and books accommodations for a £3.50 charge plus a 20% deposit. (☎854 020; www.newquay.co.uk. Open June-Sept. M-Sa 9:30am-5:30pm, Su 9:30am-12:30pm; Oct.-May M-F 9:30am-3:30pm, Sa 9:30am-12:30pm.) Western Greyhound, 14 East St., runs **bus tours** to the Eden Project (p. 234) and popular nearby coastal towns. (☎871 871. 5-8hr. daily tours. £8-15.) Tickets can be booked at the TIC. Other services include: **banks** on Bank St. (most open M-Tu and Th-F 9am-4:30pm, W 10am-4:30pm); **work opportunities** at a very busy Job-Centre, 32 East St. (☎894 900; open M-Tu and Th 9am-5pm, W 10am-5pm); **luggage storage** at Station Cafe (£1.50 per item; no overnight storage; open Apr.-Oct. daily 7am-3pm); a **launderette**, 1 Beach Parade, off Beach Rd. (☎875 901; wash £2.30-3, dry 20p per 4min., soap 45p; open M-F 10am-4pm, Sa 10am-3pm; last wash 1hr. before close); **police**, Tolcarne Rd. (☎08452 777 444); **Newquay Hospital**, St. Thomas Rd. (☎893 623); a Boots **pharmacy**, 15 Bank St. (☎872 014; open in summer M-F 8am-8pm, Sa 8am-6:30pm; in winter M-Sa 9am-5:30pm); **Internet access** at Cyber Surf @ Newquay, 2 Broad St., across from the Somerfield (☎875 497; 7p per min.; open in summer M-Sa 10am-10pm, Su noon-8pm; in winter M-Sa 11am-6pm, Su noon-5pm) and Tad and Nick's Cafe, 72-74 Fore St. (☎874 868; 5p per min.; open daily 10am-7pm); and the **post office**, 31-33 East St. (☎08457 223 344; open M 8:45am-5:30pm, Tu-F 9am-5:30pm, Sa 9am-12:30pm). **Post Code:** TR7 1BU.

🛏 ACCOMMODATIONS

B&Bs (£18-30) are near the TIC; numerous **hostels** (£12-16) gather on **Headland Road** and **Tower Road,** near Fistral Beach. Accommodations fill up weeks in advance when surfing competitions come to town; call ahead, especially in summer.

> **The Danes,** 4 Dane Rd. (☎878 130; www.thedanes.co.uk), on Fore St. Clean rooms and beautiful sea views. £27-32 per person. Cash only. ❸
>
> **Newquay International Backpackers,** 69-73 Tower Rd. (☎879 366; www.backpackers.co.uk). International crowd parties late into the night. Clean dorms and very friendly staff. Dorms £10-17; twins £11-17. July-Aug. 7-night min. MC/V. ❷
>
> **Original Backpackers,** 16 Beachfield Ave. (☎874 668), off Bank St., facing the beach. Kitchen. Laundry £3. Dorms £12-17, in winter £8-10. MC/V. ❷
>
> **Together Guest House,** 33 Trebarwith Crescent (☎871 996), a few blocks from the TIC toward the beach. Spacious black-and-white rooms. Singles £20-25. MC/V. ❸
>
> **Camping: Trenance Chalet and Caravan Park,** Edgcumbe Ave. (☎873 447). A campsite miraculously located in town. From the train station, turn right on Cliff Rd., then right on Edgcumbe and follow it for 10min. Laundry, restaurant, and cafe. Open Easter to Oct. £5-6.50 per person. Electricity 50p. AmEx/MC/V. ❶

🍴 ▥ FOOD AND PUBS

Restaurants in Newquay tend to be quick, bland, and costly. Pizza and kebab shops, catering to late-night stumblers, dot the town center. For cheap alternatives, head to pubs or Somerfield **supermarket,** at the end of Fore St. (☎876 006.

Open July-Aug. M-Th and Sa 8am-9pm, F 8am-10pm, Su 11am-4pm; Sept.-June M-Th and Sa 8am-8pm, F 8am-9pm, Su 11am-4pm.)

Ye Olde Dolphin, 39-47 Fore St. (☎874 262). Newquay's restaurant jewel. Meals can be expensive, but take advantage of the specials (6-8pm), including a 3-course meal for £12.45. Open M-Sa 6-11:30pm, Su noon-2pm and 6-11:30pm. MC/V. ❸

Prego Prego, 4 East St. (☎852 626). A variety of fresh panini (£3) and baguettes (£2.50) with fillings like sun-dried tomato and mozzarella or chicken pesto and peppers. Specialty coffees £1-1.65. Open daily 8am-4pm. Cash only. ❶

Cafe Irie, 38 Fore St. (☎859 200). Funky cafe serves creative dishes and takes requests; all-day breakfast options (full English £5). Great tunes and plenty of sofas. Acoustic jams M nights. Open July-Aug. daily 9am-midnight; Sept.-Nov. M-Th 10am-10pm, F-Sa 9am-midnight. Cash only. ❶

The Shack, 52 Bank St. (☎875 675). Friendly, family-oriented sit-down with a beach theme and tasty dishes (£4-11), from vegetarian and Caribbean plates to the popular lunchtime Shack Wraps (£3.75-4.75). Open in summer daily 10am-11pm; in winter M-F 10am-5pm, Sa 10am-11pm. MC/V. ❷

The Chy Bar & Kitchen, 12 Beach Rd. (☎873 415). Enjoy one of the best views in Newquay in this chic, brand-new upstairs eatery. Open M-Sa 10am-2am, Su 10am-12:30am. Food served until 11pm. MC/V. ❷

🌊 BEACHES

Atlantic winds descend on **Fistral Beach** with a vengeance, creating what most consider to be the best surfing in Europe. The shores are less cluttered than the sea, where throngs of wetsuited surfers pile in between the troughs and crests. Local surfers may say that ominous skies often forecast the liveliest surf, but as always, use caution. Lifeguards roam the white sands from May until September from 10am to 6pm. On the bay side, the sands are divided into four beaches: tamer waters at **Towan Beach** and **Great Western Beach** lure throngs of families, while enticing **Tolcarne Beach** and **Lusty Glaze Beach** attract beach-goers of all ages. **Sunset Surf Shop,** 106 Fore St., rents surf paraphernalia. (☎877 624. Boards £5-10 per day, £12-25 per 3 days, £25-40 per week. Wetsuits or bodyboards £4-5/10-12/20. Open Apr.-Oct. daily 9am-6pm.) **Fistral Surf,** with four branches in Newquay (main branch at 19 Cliff Rd.), also rents equipment; call for surf conditions. (☎850 808. Boards £7 per day, £18 per 3 days, £25 per week. Wetsuits £5/12-13/20. Open daily July-Aug. 8am-10pm; Sept.-June 9am-6pm.) Learn the ropes from **West Coast Surfari,** the oldest school in town. Meet at 27 Trebarwith Crescent, downhill from the TIC. (☎876 083 or book in surf shops. Lessons £25 per half-day, £35 per day.)

🎵 NIGHTLIFE

Newquay is teeming with large groups of sun-kissed surfers and visitors ready to drink up the club scene. Watch out for the ubiquitous stag and hen parties, and head toward the shore for some of the more relaxed nightlife venues. The trail of surfer bars begins on **North Quay Hill,** at the corner of Tower Rd. and Fore St. The sheer number of venues and size of the crowds guarantee a good time.

Central Inn, 11 Central Sq. (☎873 810), in the town center. Watch the busy bustle from the outdoor seating; always crowded. Open M-Th 11am-11pm, F-Sa 11am-midnight, Su 11am-10:30pm.

Sailors, 15 Fore St. (☎872 838). An elaborate lighting rig enhances the vibrant dance scene. Crowded downstairs pub. Tu "Unzipped" theme. W beach party. Open June-Sept. M-Sa 10pm-2am, Su 10pm-12:30am; Oct.-May Th-Sa 10pm-2am, Su 10pm-12:30am.

Tall Trees, Tolcarne Rd. Park (☎850 313; www.talltree-sclub.co.uk). From the train station, walk away from the town center, turn right at Tolcarne Rd., and veer right at what looks like the end. 2 floors and big crowds make the 10min. walk worth it. F-Sa R&B, chart, house, and trance. Cover £2-6. Open mid-Mar. to mid-Sept. M-Sa 9pm-2am; mid-Sept. to mid-Mar. F-Sa 9pm-2am.

Bertie's, East St. (☎870 369). Packs a crowd. Th and Su entry before 11pm and drinks £1; Sa ladies half-price. Cover £5-7. Bar open M-Sa 11am-11pm, Su 11am-10:30pm. Club open daily 9:30pm-2am.

The Koola, 8-10 Beach Road. (☎873 415). A pleasant and relaxed crowd, from barefoot surfers fresh from the waves to dolled-up locals out for a night on the town. 3 levels of dancing. Popular M drum 'n' bass night. Open daily 9pm-2am.

FALMOUTH ☎01326

With the third-deepest natural harbor in the world (after Rio de Janeiro and Sydney), Falmouth (pop. 23,000) has always owed its livelihood to the sea. At the confluence of seven rivers, the port was the perfect entry point into Cornwall for Spanish and French invaders; the 450-year-old twin fortresses of Pendennis and St. Mawes, built by Henry VIII, still eye each other from opposite sides of the bay. Today, the well-to-do port maintains a village-like charm. Hip restaurants and pubs promise a relaxed and enjoyable atmosphere, while the antique ships that often dock in the harbor bring Falmouth's seafaring history to life.

▄ TRANSPORTATION

Trains: Falmouth has 3 unmanned **train stations. Penmere Halt** is near Melvill Rd. and Killigrew St.; **Falmouth Town** is near the town center; and **Falmouth Docks** is near Pendennis Castle. Buy tickets at **Newell's Travel Agency,** 26 Killigrew St. (☎312 620), next to the TIC. Open M-F 9am-5:15pm, Sa 9am-3:45pm. Trains (☎08457 484 950) from: **Exeter** (3½hr., 8 per day, £20.70); **London Paddington** (5½hr., 5 per day, £68.50); **Plymouth** (2hr.; M-Sa 12 per day, Su 7 per day; £10.40); **Truro** (20min., every hr., £2.90).

Buses: All buses stop near the TIC. National Express (☎08705 808 080) from: **London** (8hr., 2 per day, £34) and **Plymouth** (2½hr., 2 per day, £6.10). Pick up schedules and tickets at Newell's Travel Agency. First bus #7 runs to **Penzance** (1¼hr., 6 per day, round-trip £4.50) via **Helston** (50min., every hr., £3.25), while #89 and 90 go to **Newquay** (1½hr., M-Sa 1 per 2hr., £5.70) via **Truro** (30min., £2.70). Truronian (☎01872 273 453) sends buses to the **Lizard Peninsula** (p. 234).

IN RECENT NEWS

CLUBBING WITH CAUTION

Further steps in a region-wide attempt to curb drink-spiking and date rape have been taken by one Newquay nightclub. **Sailors** (p. 230) became the first club in Cornwall to install a drink-dispensing machine—similar to a soda or candy dispenser—in July 2004. The machine allows clubbers looking for bottled drinks to avoid long lines at the bar, and alleviates stress on busy bartenders, as Newquay's beachgoers generally pack clubs to capacity.

The machine also promotes drink safety: patrons open drinks themselves, preventing any possibility of tampering. This coincides with the Spike Campaign, inaugurated by Cornish authorities in April 2004. The campaign is being carried by clubs like Sailors, who now use drink mats reminding customers to mind their drinks. Bartenders have also employed the help of "Spike," a green monster atop a bookmark containing contact information—if they pass an unattended drink twice, they will drop in the bookmark to remind patrons how easily someone could compromise their drinks.

Bars UK-wide have also begun selling "alcotops," brightly-colored reusable bottle tops (www.alcotop.co.uk). Clubbers can put the top on when they put down their drinks, dissuading potential spikers whose actions would take much longer and be much more conspicuous.

Ferries: Ferries leave from Prince of Wales Pier and Custom House Quay. St. Mawes Ferry Company (☎313 201; www.stmawesferry.co.uk) sails to **St. Mawes** (25min.; 2 per hr.; £4). Runs July-Aug. 8:30am-11pm; Sept.-June 8:30am-5:15pm. Newman's Cruises (☎01872 580 309) runs to **Smuggler's Cottage,** up the River Fal (45min.; M-Sa 2 per day; round-trip £6.50). Enterprise (☎374 241; www.enterprise-boats.co.uk) makes the idyllic trip to **Truro** (1hr.; May-Sept. M-Sa 5 per day; Oct.-Apr. call ahead; £6).

Taxis: Checkers (☎212 127; 24hr.); **Radio Taxis** (☎315 194).

✈ 🛈 ORIENTATION AND PRACTICAL INFORMATION

The rail line runs along the highest parts of Falmouth: streets from there to the sea and to B&Bs are steep and can make for a hard walk. **The Moor** is Falmouth's main square. The main street extends from there, changing names to **High Street, Market Street, Church Street, Arwenack Street,** and finally **Grove Place,** which leads to Discovery Quay, the dockside area home to the Maritime Museum and a number of shops and cafes.

The **Tourist Information Centre,** 11 Market Strand, Prince of Wales Pier, books beds for a 10% deposit. (☎312 300; www.go-cornwall.com. Open Apr.-June and Sept. M-Sa 9:30am-5:15pm; July-Aug. M-Sa 9:30am-5:15pm, Su 10:15am-1:15pm; Oct.-Mar. M-F 9:30am-5:15pm.) Many companies run **cruises** (1-2hr., £5-7) on River Fal to the north and Helford River to the southwest. K&S Cruises (☎211 056) offers fishing trips (2½ or 4hr.; M-F and Su 11am, 1, 2:35 pm; £8/16); book trips at the yellow kiosk on the Prince of Wales Pier. Other services include: **banks** on Market St.; Bubbles **launderette,** 99 Killigrew St. (☎311 291; open M-F 8am-7pm, Sa 9am-7pm, Su 10am-3pm); **police,** Dracaena Ave., (☎08452 777 444); **Falmouth Hospital,** Trescobeas Rd. (☎434 700); Superdrug **pharmacy,** 55 Market St. (☎318 140; open in summer M-Sa 8:30am-5:30pm, Su 10am-4pm; in winter M-Sa 8:30am-5:30pm) and Boots, 47 Market St. (312 373; open M-Sa 9am-5:30pm, Su 10:30am-4:30pm); **Internet access** at the **Falmouth Library,** The Moor (☎314 901; first 30min. free, 75p per 15min. thereafter; open M-Tu and Th-F 9:30am-6pm, Sa 9:30am-4pm), or at Quench Juice Cafe, a few doors from the TIC (☎210 634; 50p per 15min.; M-W 9am-6:30pm, Th-Sa 9am-11pm, Su 10:30am-4:30pm); and the **post office** with a bureau de change, The Moor (☎08457 740 740; open M-Tu 8:45am-5:30pm, W-F 9am-5:30pm, Sa 9am-12:30pm). **Post Code:** TR11 3RB.

🛏 ACCOMMODATIONS

Western Terrace has a wealth of B&Bs (£20-45 per person). **Avenue Road** and **Melvill Road** sport additional lodgings, while those on **Cliff Road** and **Castle Drive** promise great views for a pretty penny. Most fill up come summer, so be sure to book ahead, especially in summer. The friendly owners of **Boscovean ❷,** 3 Western Terr., offer lodgings for a good price. (☎212 539. Open Apr.-Oct. £20 per person. Cash only.) The proprietors are happy to meet requests, from veggie breakfasts to a spare umbrella, are the tiny, central **Castleton Guest House ❸,** 68 Killigrew St. (☎311 072. Singles £25; doubles £44; families £60. Cash only.) If you're **camping,** the nearest site is **Penance Mill Farm ❶,** 2 mi. away near Meinporth Beach. (☎312 431. Kitchen and laundry. 2-person tent £10.50-13. Electricity £2. Cash only.)

🍴 FOOD

Pick up **groceries** at Tesco, The Moor (☎0845 677 9267; open M-Sa 7am-8pm, Su 10am-4pm), at the foot of Killigrew St. Falmouth has many options for quality eats, from cheap pasties to outrageously priced lobsters. **Pipeline ❸,** 21 Church

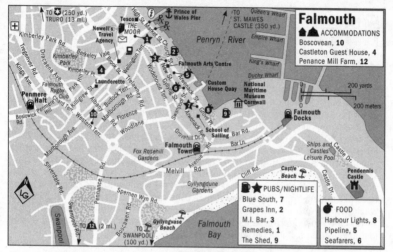

Falmouth

▲▲ ACCOMMODATIONS
Boscovean, **10**
Castleton Guest House, **4**
Penance Mill Farm, **12**

★ PUBS/NIGHTLIFE
Blue South, 7
Grapes Inn, 2
M.I. Bar, 3
Remedies, 1
The Shed, 9

♨ FOOD
Harbour Lights, 8
Pipeline, 5
Seafarers, 6

St., serves Mediterranean and Cajun fusion (£8.50-17) amidst playful decor. (☎312 774. Open July-Sept. Tu-Su noon-2pm and 6:30pm-10:30pm; Oct.-June W-Sa noon-2pm and 7-9:30pm, Su breakfast 10am-2pm. MC/V.) With the feel of a coastal cove, **Seafarers ❸**, 33 Arwenack St., serves mouth-watering seafood entrees from £12. (☎319 851. Open daily 10am-3pm and 6-10pm. Call ahead for reservations. MC/V.) Try the Moby Dick Giant Cod (£6.50) at the delicious fish-and-chip shop, **Harbour Lights ❶**, Arwenack St. (☎316 934. Takeaway open daily 11:30am-10pm; restaurant open daily 11:30am-9pm. Takeaway cash only; restaurant MC/V.)

👁 🌊 SIGHTS AND BEACHES

Opened in 2003, the **National Maritime Museum Cornwall**, Discovery Quay, houses a remarkable collection of boats, suspended mid-air in a state-of-the-art gallery. The museum includes an interactive exhibit on navigation, which allows you to prove your own nautical prowess in the radio-controlled sailing simulation. (☎313 388; www.nmmc.co.uk. Open daily 10am-5pm. £6.50, concessions £4.30, families £17.) **Pendennis Castle**, a tudor castle built by Henry VIII to guard the harbour at Pendennis Point, now features a walk-through diorama with waxen gunners and battle re-enactments in the summer. The battles and exhibit you can afford to skip, but don't miss the view of St. Mawes, a mirror image of Pendennis. (☎316 594. Open daily Apr.-June and Sept. 10am-5pm; July-Aug. 10am-6pm; Oct.-March 10am-4pm. £4.60, concessions £3.50.) A 25min. ferry across the channel (p. 232) ends among thatched roofs and aspiring tropical gardens in St. Mawes village. **St. Mawes Castle**, 10min. uphill from the ferry drop-off point, is actually a circular battlement built by Henry to blow holes through any ship spared by Pendennis's gunners. Though the tower is worth climbing, Pendennis wins the battle for superior views. (☎270 526. Open Apr.-June daily 10am-5pm; July-Sept. daily 10am-6pm; Oct. daily 10am-4pm; Nov.-March M and F-Su 10am-4pm. £3.60, concessions £2.70. Free 1hr. audio tour.) **Castle Beach**, on Pendennis Head, may be too pebbly for sunbathing, but is great for snorkeling. **Gyllyngvase Beach** and **Swanpool Beach**, just south of the center of town, are both sandy, and have areas suitable for windsurfing.

SOUTHWEST ENGLAND

🎵🎵 NIGHTLIFE AND ENTERTAINMENT

For a small town, Falmouth has a surprisingly vibrant social scene. At any time of day, enjoy a perfect harbor view with your pint at the **Grapes Inn,** 64 Church St. (☎314 704; open M-Sa 10:30am-11pm, Su 11am-10:30pm). The cocktails ($4) are delicious at **Blue South,** 35-37 Arwenack St., a sleek surf bar. (☎212 122. Happy hour 5-6pm, 2 cocktails $5. Open M-Sa 11am-11pm, Su 11am-10:30pm.) The town's hottest club, **Remedies,** The Moor, is best on weekends, when young crowds groove to hip-hop and Top 40 hits. (☎314 454. Cover F-Sa $5 after 10pm. Open M-Sa noon-2am, Su noon-1am.) Stop by the new cafe-bar, **The Shed,** Discovery Quay, for wine, coffee, and colorful, kitchy 50s decor (☎318 502; open M-Sa 10am-11pm, Su 10am-10pm). **M.I. Bar,** Church St., across from the Grapes Inn, has large leather couches and a sleek modern look. (☎316 909. Live music Su. Open M-Sa 11am-11pm, Su noon-10:30pm.) The **Falmouth Arts Centre,** 24 Church St., hosts exhibitions, concerts, theater, and films. (☎212 300; www.falmoutharts.com. Box office open M-Sa 10am-2pm. Exhibitions free. Theater and concert tickets $5-10.) **Regatta Week,** the second week of August, is Falmouth's main sailing event, with boat shows and music performances. The mid-October **Oyster Festival** features oyster tasting, craft fairs, and a parade. Contact the TIC for details.

📷 DAYTRIP FROM FALMOUTH

🏛 THE EDEN PROJECT

Bodelva, St. Austell. The St. Austell railway station is located on the Plymouth-Penzance line. From the station, Truronian (☎01872 273 453; www.truronian.com) bus T9 runs daily (20min., 11-13 per day, £2.70). Combined bus and Eden Project ticket £16.50, students £11.50. Bus T10 runs from Newquay (50min.; M-F 1 per day, Sa 2 per day, Su 1 per day; £4). From the north, take Western Greyhound bus #555 from Padstow (1½hr.; 8 per day; £3.50, round-trip £4), which passes through Wadebridge (1hr.) and Bodmin (40min.). Signposted from the A390, A30, and A391. ☎01726 811 972; www.eden-project.com. Open daily Apr.-Oct. 10am-6pm; Nov.-Mar. 10am-4:30pm. Last admission 1hr. before close. Buy advance tickets at any TIC. £12.50, students £6.

A "living theatre of plants and people," the Eden Project is one of England's most unique and fascinating sights. The steel geodesic domes, built for the millennium, welcomed four million visitors in their first two years. Once a clay mining quarry, the area is now home to three massive biodomes: one open and two covered. Enter the Mediterranean villas of the **Warm Temperate Biome** and breathe in the scent of olive groves and citrus trees. Brave the 82°F heat to enjoy the palm-tree laden **Humid Tropics Biome,** the world's largest greenhouse, which houses a living rainforest of over 1000 plants. The 30-acre **Roofless Biome** features hemp, sunflowers, tea, and a host of public art displays. A new education center opened in 2005; a dining area will open in spring 2006; the "Alchemy Centre" shows how to recycle trash into art. Don't miss the entertaining "Plant Takeaway" display, a representation of what would befall humans if all plants vanished. Exhibits change with the seasons, from summer gardens to a winter skating park. Walking through the grounds and the domes takes at least 3 hours.

THE LIZARD PENINSULA   ☎01326

The Lizard Peninsula is one of England's least touristed corners. Though its name has nothing to do with reptiles—"Lizard" is a corruption of Old Cornish "Lys ardh," meaning "the high place"—the peninsula does possess a significant outcrop of serpentine rock, so described because of its uncanny resemblance to snake skin. **South West Coastal Path** (p. 178) traces the Lizard around Britain's most southerly point, through dramatic seascapes and lonely fishing villages. The tiny village of **Lizard** receives somewhat more attention thanks to **Lizard Point,** the southernmost tip of Britain. A short, signposted walk from the village, this windy outcrop remains surprisingly undeveloped save for a 300-year-old lighthouse and the **National Trust Information Centre.** (☎290 604. Open Apr.-Oct. 10am-4pm; mid-June to mid-Sept. until 5pm.) ▧**Kynance Cove,** 3 mi. northwest of Lizard Point along the coast, is an enchanting sight. Its sandy beach is studded by great masses of rock that create a lively surf. The National Trust has just completed a "green" visitor facility, with a self-contained "biobubble" for sewage treatment. Escape the summer hordes by trekking 3hr. farther northwest to rocky **Mullion Cove,** where steep but climbable cliffs await. **Mullion Island,** 250 yards off the cove, is home to more seabirds than officials can count. The cove is also accessible from Mullion village, 1½ mi. inland. Seven miles from Helston in the middle of the peninsula, over 60 satellite dishes make up **Goonhilly Satellite Earth Station Experience,** the world's largest satellite station. The site covers an area equivalent to 160 soccer fields. Interactive exhibits allow you to see your head in 3-D and send emails to outer space. (☎0800 679 593; www.goonhilly.bt.com. Open daily June-Sept. 10am-6pm; last admission 5pm. Call ahead in winter. £6, concessions £4.50.) The **National Seal Sanctuary,** Europe's leading marine mammal rescue center and home to sea lions, otters, and seal pups, is 6 mi. from Helston, in the town of Gweek. (☎221 361; www.sealsanctuary.co.uk. Open daily 10am-4pm. £10.50, concessions £7-8.)

Truronian **buses** run from Helston to Goonhilly (T2; 20min. M-Sa every 2hr.; T3, Su 20min., 2 per day, round-trip £2.50) and Gweek (T2; 30min.; 2 per day; round-trip £2.30). The ▧**YHA Lizard ❷,** a refurbished Victorian villa and former hotel, boasts a stunning view of the tempestuous Lizard Point waters, and comfortable lodgings. (☎291 145. Kitchen and laundry. Reception 8:30-10am and 5-10pm. Open Apr.-Oct. Dorms £14, under 18 £10. MC/V.) For **campsites,** consult the numerous listings in the free *Go West Guide to Cornwall* and the *Map and Guide to the Lizard Peninsula,* both available at TICs. The **Tourist Information Centre,** 79 Meneage St., Helston, books accommodations for a 10% deposit. (☎565 431; www.go-cornwall.com. Open Aug. M-Sa 10am-4:30pm; Sept.-July M-F 10am-4:30pm, Sa 10am-1pm.) Stock up on cash in Helston—elsewhere, **banks and ATMs are rare.**

PENZANCE
☎01736

Penzance is the very model of an ancient English pirate town, water-logged and swashbuckling. The city's armada of antique shops wages countless raids on tourists, luring them with troves of trinkets. But with glorious sunsets and mildly bawdy pubs, it's difficult not to enjoy such an irreverent, fun-loving town.

▗ TRANSPORTATION

Trains: Station on Wharf Rd., at the head of Albert Pier. Ticket office open M-F 6:05am-8:10pm, Sa 6am-6:10pm, Su 8:15am-5:30pm. Trains (☎08457 484 950) from: **Exeter** (3¼hr., every hr., £20.70); **London** (5½hr., 7 per day, £67.50); **Newquay** (3hr., 8 per day, £10.70); **Plymouth** (2hr., every hr., £11); **St. Ives** (via St. Erth: 40-60min., every hr., £4.20).

Buses: Station on Wharf Rd. (☎0845 600 1420), at the head of Albert Pier. Ticket office open M-F 8:30am-4:45pm, Sa 8:30am-3pm. National Express (☎08705 808 080) from: **London** (8½hr., 7 per day, £34) and **Plymouth** (3hr., 7 per day, £6.10).

Taxis: Nippy Cabs (☎366 666) and **A Cars** (☎333 222).

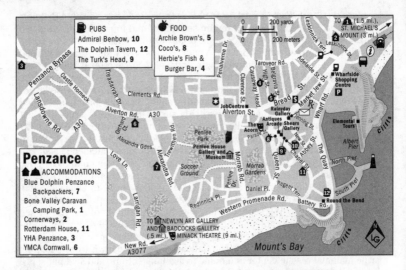

PUBS
Admiral Benbow, **10**
The Dolphin Tavern, **12**
The Turk's Head, **9**

FOOD
Archie Brown's, **5**
Coco's, **8**
Herbie's Fish &
Burger Bar, **4**

Penzance
▲▲ ACCOMMODATIONS
Blue Dolphin Penzance
  Backpackers, **7**
Bone Valley Caravan
  Camping Park, **1**
Cornerways, **2**
Rotterdam House, **11**
YHA Penzance, **3**
YMCA Cornwall, **6**

✦ ❓ ORIENTATION AND PRACTICAL INFORMATION

Penzance's train station, bus station, and TIC cluster on **Wharf Road. Market Jew Street** (a corruption of the Cornish "Marghas Yow," meaning "Market Thursday") is laden with pasty shops and bargain stores. It becomes **Alverton Street,** then **Alverton Road,** before turning into the **A30,** the road to Land's End.

Tourist Information Centre: Station Rd. (☎362 207; www.go-cornwall.com), between the train and bus stations. Books beds for a £3 fee plus 10% deposit. Free map. Open May-Sept. M-Sa 9am-5:30pm, Su 9am-1pm; Oct.-Apr. M-F 9am-5pm, Sa 10am-1pm.

Tours: Anyone interested in riotous jokes about Neolithic man should try ▓ **Harry Safari** (☎08456 445 940; www.harrysafari.co.uk.), a corny trip through the Cornish wilds. 4hr. M-F and Su leaves Penzance at 9:30am. £20.

Financial Services: Barclays, 8-9 Market Jew St. Open M-Tu and Th-F 9am-4:30pm, W 10am-4:30pm, Sa 9am-1:30pm.

Launderette: Polyclean, 4 East Terr. (☎364 815), opposite the train station. Wash £2.20-4, dry 20p per 3min., soap 30p. Open daily 8am-8pm; last wash 7pm.

Police: Penalverne Dr. (☎08705 777 444), off Alverton St.

Hospital: West Cornwall Hospital, St. Clare St. (☎874 000).

Pharmacy: Boots, 100-102 Market Jew St. (☎362 135). Open M-Sa 9am-5:30pm, Su 10am-4pm.

Internet Access: Penzance Public Library, Morrab Rd. (☎363 954). First 30min. free, then 75p per 15min. Open M-F 9:30am-6pm, Sa 9:30am-4pm. Also at **Penzance Computer Centre,** 36b Market Jew St. (☎333 391), opposite the Wharfside Centre. 70p per 15min.

Post Office: 113 Market Jew St. Open M-F 9am-5:30pm, Sa 9am-12:30pm. Bureau de change. **Post Code:** TR18 2LB.

▐ ACCOMMODATIONS

Penzance's fleet of **B&Bs** ($20-30) mostly gather on **Alexandra Road,** a 10min. walk from the town center. Several buses run from the station to Alexandra Rd. (50p).

▨ **YHA Penzance,** Castle Horneck (☎362 666). Walk 20min. from the train or bus station or take Sunset Coach #5 or 6 from the bus station to the Pirate Pub, and walk straight up Castle Horneck Road. 18th-century mansion with spacious dorms and amazing staff. Tickets reserved for every Minack Theatre show (p. 239). Internet access. Lockout 10am-noon. Dorms £14, under 18 £10; twins £28. Camping £5.50. MC/V. ❷

▨ **Cornerways,** 5 Leskinnick St. (☎364 645; www.penzance.co.uk/cornerways), behind the train station. Friendly and cozy, with ensuite single, double, and triple rooms. Veggie breakfasts available. Book months ahead for summer. £25 per person. AmEx/MC/V. ❸

Blue Dolphin Penzance Backpackers, Alexandra Rd. (☎363 836; www.pzbackpack.com). Relaxed and clean, with ensuite dorms. Dorms £13; doubles £28. MC/V. ❷

YMCA Cornwall, The Orchard, Alverton (☎365 016; www.cornwall.ymca.org.uk). Bar and lounge. Breakfast £3.60. Internet £1.20 per 30min. Reception M-F 10am-8:30pm. Dorms from £14.50; singles £19.30; twins £34.40. Cash Only. ❷

Rotterdam House, 27 Chapel St. (☎332 362). 1 twin, 1 double, and 2 singles in this quaint house, thought to have been built by the grandfather of the Brontë sisters in 1760. Book well ahead, especially in summer. £17-20 per person. Cash only. ❷

Camping: Bone Valley Caravan Camping Park, Heamoor, Penzance (☎360 313). Take bus #11 or 17, disembark at the Sportsman's Arms pub, and walk ¼ mi. Family-run site, 1½ mi. from the city center. Kitchen and laundry. Call ahead in July and Aug. Open Mar.-Dec. From £6.50 per pitch. AmEx/MC/V. ❶

🄵 FOOD

Expect to pay around £10-15 to dine at one of Penzance's excellent seafood spots along The Quay. The best buys are in coffee shops and local eateries on smaller streets and alleys near Market Jew Street. **Groceries** can be purchased at Iceland, on the lower floor of the shopping center (☎361 130. Open M-W 8:30am-6:30pm, Th-F 8:30am-8pm, Sa 8am-6:30pm, Su 10am-4pm.).

Coco's, 12-13 Chapel St. (☎350 222). Relaxed tapas bar with Matissean decor. Tapas £5-9. Mediterranean entrees £9.50-13. Open M-Sa 9:30am-11pm, Su 10:30am-9:30pm. Food served M-Sa 10:30am-2:30pm and 6:30-10pm, Su 10:30am-2:30pm and 6:30-9pm. MC/V. ❷

Archie Brown's, Bread St. (☎362 828), above Richard's Health Food Store. Sunny and artsy, this veggie cafe makes creative meals, like mushroom burgers in pitas (£5) and homity pie (£2). Open M-Th and Sa 9am-5:30pm, F 9am-5:30pm and 7-9pm. MC/V. ❷

Herbie's Fish and Burger Bar, 56 Causeway Head (☎362 850). An unassuming little joint. Fish made to order and deep-fried to perfection. Cod and chips £3.15; try the 40oz. "Millennium Burger" (with 8 slices of cheese!) at your own risk. Open in summer M-Sa 11:30am-2:30pm and 4:15-7pm. Cash only. ❶

🄶 SIGHTS

Penzance features an impressive number of **art galleries,** which crop up every other block. The *Cornwall Gallery Guide* booklet (£1), available at galleries and the TIC, lists the best galleries in Penzance and nearby cities. Archangel St. Michael is said to have appeared to some fishermen on Marazion, just offshore from Penzance, in AD 495—reason enough to build a Benedictine monastery on the spot. Today, **St. Michael's Mount** has a church and castle at its peak and a village at its base; at low tide, visitors can stroll there via a lumpy, seaweed-strewn causeway, but at high tide, the ferry is the only way to go. The castle's

BARGAIN BOOTY

If one man's trash is another man's treasure, then Penzance's **Antiques Arcade** is both a landfill and a goldmine. Two levels of nameless shops sell antique (and not-so-antique) bric-a-brac. And among the markets of the Cotswolds and London, the quiet mall has established itself as a premier venue for inexpensive and authentic antiques, making it popular with dealers for decades.

Upstairs, straining eyes will discover eclectic goods. Common items include Wedgwood dinnerware and display pieces (from £20), Victorian dressing gowns (£10-40), Newlyn copper, and terra cotta pottery. More exotic pieces include rococo perfume bottles, porcelain merry-go-round horses, and art deco lamps. Upstairs, the devoted staff are helpful and unpretentious, as attentive to neophytes as to bona fide collectors. (☎338 121. Open M-Sa 9:30am-5pm.)

Venture downstairs for an even bigger smorgasbord of odds and ends at the **Flea Market.** There's a large stock of retro surf gear for a trek to the Cornish coast, paintings and drawings (£5), porcelain plates (20p-£7), costume jewelry (£2-10), and small furniture. After you've hoarded your treasure, pick up a guide to the other antique markets. They abound: Cornwall is one of England's best-kept artistic secrets. *(61-62 Chapel St. ☎363 267. Open Tu-Sa 9am-5pm.)*

interior is modest (look for a model of the castle made entirely from the corks of champagne bottles), but the grounds are attractive, and the thirty-story views captivating. Sturdy walking shoes are a must. Walk 3 mi. from the TIC to Marazion Sq. or take bus #2, 2A, 2B, 7, 16B, 17B, 300, or 301 (round-trip £1.40). The Mount is accessible by ferry (£1) and sometimes by foot. (☎710 507, ferry and tide info 710 265. Open Apr.-Oct. M-F, Su 10:30am-5:30pm; Nov.-Mar. M, W, F by tour only, appointment necessary. Last admission 4:45pm. £5.50. Private gardens £3.)

The **Penlee House Gallery and Museum,** Morrab Rd., is internationally known for its impressive collection of Newlyn School art, while the museum upstairs has an eclectic collection of historical artifacts. Look for the 18th-century Scold's Bridle, a menacing warning against loose lips. (☎363 625; www.penleehouse.org.uk. Open May-Sept. M-Sa 10am-5pm; Oct.-Apr. 10:30am-4:30pm. £2, concessions £1, children free. Sa free.) The curator of the **Rainyday Gallery,** 116 Market Jew St., compiles the Cornwall Gallery Guide. (☎366 077. Open M-Sa 10am-5pm.) Another gallery worth a visit is **Badcocks Gallery,** The Strand, Newlyn, for contemporary art, crafts and jewelry (☎366 159; open Tu-F 10:30am-5:30pm, Sa 11am-5:30pm). **Round the Bend,** The Barbican, Battery Rd., is England's only permanent exhibition of contemporary automata. These quirky, often ingenious machines range from the daring to the droll—and most are for sale. (☎332 211. Open daily Easter to Sept. 11am-5pm. £2.50, children £1.50.) The brand-new **Elemental Tours,** Albert Pier, provide marine wildlife tours in the waters of Cornwall. (☎811 200; www.elementaltours.co.uk. Tours held year-round; times depend upon weather and conditions. Call ahead.)

NIGHTLIFE AND ENTERTAINMENT

The true character of Penzance emerges in its excellent pubs, most of which line Chapel St. **Admiral Benbow,** 46 Chapel St., is decorated entirely with paraphernalia culled from local shipwrecks, including a Captain's headboard that dates to the 16th century. (☎363 448. Pints £2.80 Open M-Sa 11am-11pm, Su noon-10:30pm.) **The Turk's Head,** 49 Chapel St., dating from the 13th century, is Penzance's oldest pub and was sacked by Spanish pirates in 1595. (☎363 093. Open M-Sa 11am-3pm and 5:30-11pm, Su noon-3pm and 5:30-10:30pm.) **The Dolphin Tavern,** The Quay, has the dubious distinction of the being the first place tobacco was smoked in Britain upon Sir Walter Raleigh's return from Virginia. The pub is said to be haunted by at least three ghosts. (☎364 106. Pint £2-2.80. Open M-Sa 11am-11pm, Su noon-10pm.) **The Acorn,** Parade St., hosts a variety of performances, from jazz bands to comedy clubs to the productions of the **Kneehigh Theatre.** (☎365 520. Box office open Tu-Sa 11am-3pm. Tickets £5-20.) The week of June 26 brings the pagan **Golowan Festival,** featuring fireworks, and the election of the mock Mayor of the Quay.

▓ DAYTRIP FROM PENZANCE

▓ MINACK THEATRE

9 mi. southwest of Penzance, in the town of Porthcurno. Take First bus #1A from the bus station (30min.; M-Sa 6-9 per day, Su 2 per day; round-trip £4), or Sunset Coaches #345 or 346 from YHA Penzance or the TIC (1hr.; M-F 2 per day, Sa 1 per day). Car access is via the B3283. ☎810 181; www.minack.com. Open daily Apr.-Sept. 9:30am-5:30pm; Oct.-Mar. 10am-4pm. £3, under 16 £1.20. Open mid-May to Sept. M-F 9:30am-8pm, Sa-Su 9:30am-5:30pm. Performances M-F 8pm, also W and F 2pm. Tickets £6-7.50, children £3-4. £2 surcharge for phone booking. MC/V.

In summer, patrons flock to the spectacularly situtated open-air ▓**Minack Theatre,** a breathtaking space hacked into a cliffside at Porthcurno, Minack. The theater hosts performances of everything from classic Shakespearean drama to modern comedies to ballet. As legend has it, a woman named Rowena Cade constructed the surreal amphitheater with her own hands. The theater's 750 stone seats have afforded patrons stunning views of the surrounding waters since 1932. On a clear day, visitors can see the Lizard Peninsula, 20 mi. to the southeast. Bring a picnic and warm clothing for chilly summer evenings.

ST. IVES ☎01736

As I was going to St. Ives, I met a man with seven wives.
Each wife had seven sacks, each sack had seven cats,
Each cat had seven kits. Kittens, cats, sacks, and wives,
How many were going to St. Ives?

Only one, of course. But medieval St. Ives (pop. 11,400), edged by pastel beaches and azure waters, has attracted visitors for centuries. The cobbled alleyways, colored by overflowing flowerpots, drew a colony of painters and sculptors in the 1920s; today, their legacy fills the windows of countless local art galleries, including a branch of the Tate. Virginia Woolf, too, was bewitched by the energy of the Atlantic at St. Ives: her masterpiece *To the Lighthouse* is thought to refer to the distant Godrevy Lighthouse, disappearing and reappearing in the morning fog.

▐ ▓ TRANSPORTATION AND PRACTICAL INFORMATION. Trains (☎08457 484 950) to St. Ives pass through or change at St. Erth (15min., every hr., £1.70), though direct service is sometimes available. National Express (☎08705 808 080) **buses** stop in St. Ives (4 per day) between Plymouth (3hr., £6.10) and Penzance (25min., £2.80). From Penzance, there are also frequent First buses (#16, 16B, 17B; 40min.; 2 per hr.; round-trip £3). Bus #301 runs in July and August from Newquay (1¾hr., 4 per day, £4.70). First **DayRover** tickets allow unlimited travel on First buses for £7.

St. Ives is a jumble of alleys and tiny streets. The **Tourist Information Centre,** in the Guildhall, books accommodations for a £3 charge plus a 10% deposit and sells maps (20p). From the bus or train station, walk to the foot of Tregenna Hill and turn right on Street-an-Pol. (☎796 297. Open Easter to Sept. M-Sa 9am-5:30pm, Su

10am-4pm; Oct. to Easter M-F 9am-5pm, Sa 10am-4pm.) **Columbus Walks** leads 4-8 mi. hikes through the area. (☎07980 149 243. M-Th. $3-7.50; F-Sa walks available upon request with 2 days notice.)

Other services include: **banks** along High St., including Barclays (☎08457 555 555; open M-Tu and Th-F 9:30am-4:30pm, W 10am-4:30pm); **work opportunities** at JobCentre, Royal Sq. (☎575 200; open M and W-F 9am-12:30pm and 1:30-4pm, Tu 10am-12:30pm and 1:30-4pm), across from International Backpackers; Boots **pharmacy**, High St. (☎795 072; open M-Sa 8:30am-8:30pm, Su 9am-4:30pm); **Internet access** at the **library**, Andrews St., near the TIC (☎795 377. First 30min. free, then $3 per hr. Open Tu-F 9:30am-6pm, Sa 9:30am-12:30pm); and the **post office**, Tregenna Pl. (☎795 004; open M-F 9am-5:30pm, Sa 9am-12:30pm), with a bureau de change. **Post Code:** TR26 1AA.

⌐ ACCOMMODATIONS. Expensive **B&Bs** ($25-35) are near the town center on **Parc Avenue** and **Tregenna Terrace;** walk uphill on West Pl., which becomes **Clodgy View** and **Belmont Terrace** (10min.), where cheaper B&Bs offer fine sea views. **St. Ives International Backpackers ❶,** The Stennack, a few blocks uphill from the library, is covered with bright murals and reception is at a tiki-hut desk. (☎799 444; www.backpackers.co.uk. Internet access $1 per 15min. Dorms $11-16; twins $13-18 per person. July-Aug. 7 night min. MC/V.) **Hobblers House ❸,** on the corner of The Wharf and Court Cocking, near Dive St. Ives, has spacious rooms practically on the beach. (☎796 439. Open Mar.-Sept. No single rooms. Doubles $50. MC/V.) **Sunrise ❸,** 22 The Warren, downhill from the train and bus station and away from the town centre, has bright, sunny rooms and superb breakfasts with pancakes and kippers. (☎795 407. Breakfast included. Singles $27-30. MC/V.) For camping or caravanning, **Ayr Holiday Park ❶** is the closest site. Make the 10min. walk to Bullan's Ln. (off The Stennack), then turn right on Bullan Hill and left on Ayr Terr. at the top of the road. (☎795 855; www.ayrholidaypark.co.uk. Laundry $5. $9. MC/V.)

⌂▥ FOOD AND PUBS. Get **groceries** at the Co-op, Royal Sq., two blocks uphill from the TIC. (☎796 494. Open daily M-Sa 8am-11pm, Su 8am-10:30pm.) For local seafood at reasonable prices, the trendy **Seafood Cafe ❸,** 45 Fore St., can't be beat. Choose your fish raw from the display area ($8.50-17) and select garnishes. (☎794 004. Open daily noon-3pm and 5:30-11pm. MC/V.) The **Porthminster Cafe ❸,** at the end of Porthminster Beach, offers a heavenly view in a relaxed atmosphere. Enjoy local seafood at tables on the sand. (☎795 352. Entrees $4.50-16. Open daily 9-11am, noon-4pm, and 6-10pm. MC/V.) Back in the town center, **Tides Café ❸,** 4-6 The Digey, serves fusion dishes. (☎799 600. Lunch $5-10. Dinner $12-16. Open M-Sa noon-3pm and 7-10pm. AmEx/MC/V.) Miniscule **Ferrell & Son Bakery ❶,** at the corner of Fore St. and Bunkers Hill, sells pasties ($2-3) touted as Cornwall's best. (☎797 703. Open M-Sa 9am-5:30pm. Cash only.) Perhaps the best view in Cornwall can be enjoyed at the **Tate Cafe ❶,** on the roof of the Tate. Enjoy modern cuisine in a postmodern atmosphere, with very friendly service. (☎791 122. Sandwiches $5-7. Open daily 11:30am-4:30pm.)

▥ GALLERIES AND MUSEUMS. Renowned for its superb light, St. Ives was once an artists' pilgrimage site, and the town's art community is still strong. *Cornwall Galleries Guide* ($1) navigates the dozens of galleries littered throughout St. Ives' maze-like alleys. A special ticket offers same-day admission to the Tate and the Barbara Hepworth Museum ($8.50, concessions $4.25). Like its sister, the Tate Modern in London (p. 118), the **Tate Gallery,** on Porthmeor Beach, focuses on modern and abstract art. Exhibits rotate every three months and feature local and international artists. (☎796 226; www.tate.org.uk. Open Mar.-Oct. daily 10am-

5:30pm, last admission 5pm; Nov.-Feb. Tu-Su 10am-4:30pm. Free 1hr. tours M-F 2:30pm. £5.50.) Under the wing of the Tate, the **Barbara Hepworth Museum and Sculpture Garden,** on nearby Ayr Ln., allows visitors to view the famed 20th-century sculptor's former home, studio, and garden. (Open Mar-Oct. daily 10am-5:30pm, last admission 5pm; Nov.-Feb. Tu-Su 10am-4:30pm. £4.25, students £2.25.) To view works in the St. Ives-school style, try the **Belgrave Gallery,** 22 Fore St., associated with the Belgrave Gallery London (☎794 888; open M-Sa 10am-1pm and 2-6pm), or **Wills Lane Gallery,** Wills Ln. (☎795 723; open 11am-1pm and 2-5pm.; call ahead.)

◪ BEACHES. St. Ives's ▨beaches are among England's finest. Expansive stretches of sand slowly descend into the sea, with shallow shores perfect for romantic strolls. Follow the hill down from the train station to **Porthminster Beach,** a magnificent stretch of golden sand and tame waves. To escape the crowds of toasting flesh, head for quieter **Porthgwidden Beach. Porthmeor Beach,** below the Tate, attracts surfers but has less-appealing sands. Farther east, **Carbis Bay,** 1¼ mi. from very similar Porthminster, is less crowded and easily accessible. Take the train one stop toward St. Erth or bus #17 (M-Sa) or 17B (Su).

Beach activities in St. Ives are numerous. **Wind An' Sea Surf Shop,** 25 Fore St., rents surfboards and wetsuits. (☎794 830. £5 per day, £25 per week. £5 deposit. Wetsuit £5. Open daily Easter to Oct. 10am-10pm; Nov. to Easter 10am-6pm.) Beginners can start with a lesson at **St. Ives Surf School,** on Porthmeor Beach. (☎07792 261 278. £25 per 2hr., £100 per week. Price includes equipment. Open daily May-Sept. 9am-6pm.) **Dive St. Ives,** 25 The Wharf, offers diving lessons among shipwrecks, reefs, sea anemones, and sometimes even dolphins and sharks. (☎799 229. 3-day course July-Aug. £250; Sept. and June £200. Open daily July-Aug. 9am-10pm, Sept.-June 9am-6pm.) The less athletically inclined may prefer **boat trips,** which leave from the harbor. **Pleasure Boat Trips** heads to **Seal Island,** a permanent seal colony, and around the bay. (☎797 328. 1¼-2hr. £8.) Many boat companies head to the famous **Godrevy Lighthouse** (£7). Rent a motor boat from **Mercury Self-Drive** at the harbor. (☎07830 173 878. £8 per 15min., £12 per 30min., £18 per hr. All for 5 to 6 people. Open daily Easter to Sept. 9am-dusk.)

◪ NIGHTLIFE. Beer has flowed at **The Sloop,** by far St. Ives's best-known watering hole, on the corner of Fish St. and The Wharf, since 1312. (☎796 584. Open daily 9am-11pm, Su 9am-10:30pm.) Nearby, the **Lifeboat Inn,** Wharf Rd., hosts bands on Wednesdays and Sundays and karaoke on Fridays and every other Saturday. (☎794 123. Open M-Sa 11am-11pm, Su noon-10:30pm.) The Irish **Craic Bar,** The Stennack, inside the Western Hotel, offers acoustic, folk, jazz, and blues with the adjoining **Kettle 'n' Wink,** named for when ale houses hid smuggled brandy in a kettle and customers placed their order by looking at the kettle and winking. (☎795 227. Craic Bar open M-Sa 6-11pm. Kettle 'n' Wink open M-Sa 11am-11pm, Su noon-10:30pm.) **Isobar,** at the corner of Street-an-Pol and Tregenna Pl., is St. Ives's busiest club. On Wednesdays, all drinks are half price. (☎799 199. Cover W and F £5, Sa £6. Open M-Tu and Th 8pm-1am, W and F-Sa 8pm-2am, Su 8pm-12:30am.)

PENWITH PENINSULA ☎01736

A largely untouched region of windswept cliffs and sandy shores, Penwith was once the center of Cornwall's mining industry. Copper mines and abandoned tin chimneys are all that remain; today, the stunning views over the jagged shores from green pastures attract mostly beach-goers and hikers. From June to September, First **bus** #300 runs a loop from Penzance, passing through Land's End, Sennen, St. Just, Pendeen, Zennor, and St. Ives (5 per day; £5.50).

SOUTHWEST ENGLAND

ZENNOR. Legend holds that a mermaid drawn by the singing of a young man in this village returned to the sea with him in tow. On misty evenings, locals claim to see and hear the pair. The immaculate **Old Chapel Backpackers Hostel ❷** is close to gorgeous hiking and 4 mi. from the beaches at St. Ives. (☎ 798 307; www.backpackers.co.uk/zennor. Cafe. Continental breakfast £3, English £4.50. Showers 20p per 6min. Laundry wash £1.50, dry £1. Dorms £12; family rooms £50. MC/V.) Sunset Coach bus #343 comes from St. Ives en route to Penzance (20min., M-Sa 6 per day); bus #300 runs a similar route from June to September (5 per day).

LAND'S END. Six kitschy tourist attractions capitalize on England's westernmost point, but none merits the admission fee as views are free. On Tuesdays and Thursdays in August, there are fireworks over the water. First **buses** #1 and 1A go to Land's End from Penzance (1hr., every hr., £4) and #300 comes from St. Ives (35min., 5 per day, £4.30 round-trip). For those unafraid of hills and hell-bent drivers, biking affords glimpses of coastlines. The **Visitor Centre** sells tickets for local attractions and dispenses local history. (☎ 08704 580 044. Open daily July-Aug. 10am-6pm; Sept.-June 10am-5pm.)

ST. JUST. On Cape Cornwall, 4 mi. north of Land's End, the coast of St. Just (pop. 4000) remains untainted by tourism and is a good base for visiting ancient menhirs and quoits. One mile from the TIC, **Cape Cornwall** was thought to mark the intersection of the Atlantic Ocean and the English Channel. The cape's promontory, crowned by a chimney, offers superior views. From the Cape, Land's End is a tough 6 mi. walk south along the **South West Coastal Path.** Three miles northeast of St. Just in Pendeen, **Geevor Tin Mine** functioned until 1990. The site now houses a museum dedicated to the history of mining. (☎ 788 662; www.geevor.com. Open Easter to Oct. M-F and Su 10am-5pm; Nov. to Easter M-F and Su 10am-4pm. Last admission 1hr. before close. £6.50. 50% discount with bus ticket.)

The **YHA Land's End ❷**, Letcha Vean, in Cot Valley, occupies three pristine acres. From the bus station's rear exit, turn left and follow the road as it becomes a footpath leading to the hostel (25 min.); a map is posted at the St. Just library. (☎ 788 437. Breakfast £3.80. Reception 8:30-10am and 5-10pm. Open May-Sept. daily; mid-Feb. to Apr. and Oct. Tu-Sa. Dorms £12.50, under 18 £9. MC/V.) Most routes to Land's End pass through Pendeen and St. Just. **Buses** #17, 17A, and 17B come from Penzance (45min., every hr., round-trip £2.90). Bus #300 (whose open upper deck offers a fantastic view) runs from St. Ives (1hr., 5 per day, £3.50). The **Tourist Information Centre,** at the library opposite the bus park, books local rooms and carries *Ancient Sites in West Penwith* (£4), outlining walks from St. Just. (☎ 788 669. Open June-Sept. M-W 10am-1pm and 2-5pm, F 10am-1pm and 2-6pm, Sa 10am-1pm. **Internet access** available, first 30min. free, 75p per 15min. thereafter.)

■ **SENNEN COVE.** Just 2 mi. from Land's End along the coast, Sennen Cove is a gorgeous mile-long beach, inviting even to those who find the Cornish coastline austere. Find ensuite lodgings with enviable views at the **Old Success Inn ❹**, on the cove. From bar snacks (£7-9) to elaborate seafood dishes (£10-12), the adjoining restaurant serves a full menu. (☎ 871 232; www.oldsuccess.com. £44 per person. Restaurant open noon-9:30pm, bar M-Sa 11am-11pm, Su noon-10:30pm. MC/V.) First **buses** #1, 1A, and 300 and Sunset Coaches #345 come from Penzance (40min.; M-Sa 7 per day, Su 5per day; £3.20).

ANCIENT MONUMENTS. Inland on the Penwith Peninsula, some of the least-spoiled Stone- and Iron-Age monuments in England lie along the Land's End-St. Ives bus route. Once covered by mounds of earth, the quoits (also called cromlechs or dolmens) are thought to be burial chambers from 2500 BC. The **Zennor Quoit** is named for the village. The **Lanyon Quoit,** off the Morvah-Penzance road about 3 mi. from each town, is one of the area's most impressive megaliths. The famous stone near Morvah, on the Land's End-St. Ives bus route, has the Cornish name **Mên-an-Tol,** or "stone with a hole through the middle." The donut is allegedly endowed with curative powers. The best-preserved Iron-Age village in Britain is at **Chysauster,** about 4 mi. from both Penzance and Zennor; there's a 2½ mi. footpath off the B3311 near Gulval.

THE CHANNEL ISLANDS

Situated in the waters between England and France, tiny Jersey and Guernsey (and even tinier Alderney, Sark, and Herm) comprise the Anglo-French holiday spot, the Channel Islands. Eighty miles south of England and thirty miles west of France, the Islands provide visitors with a fusion of cultures and a touch of elegance. The Channel Islands declared their loyalty to the British Crown in 1204, but Jersey and Guernsey still consider themselves to be autonomous, with Guernsey overseeing the smaller islands. Among the rocky coves lie fortifications built during the islands' occupation by the Germans during World War II. With an idiosyncratic system of government, a unique language, and stellar shopping and seafood, the islands are fascinating (if expensive) to visit.

⚑ GETTING THERE

From England, **ferries** are your best bet for getting to the Islands. Condor Ferries (☎01202 207 216; www.condorferries.com) run one early and one late ferry per day to Saint Helier, Jersey, and Saint Peter Port, Guernsey from the mainland cities of Weymouth, Poole, and Portsmouth (£45-67, round-trip £56-109). Trips to Guernsey take 2hr., to Jersey 3½-3¾hr. Departing from Portsmouth is cheapest, but the ferries are slower (7hr. to Guernsey, 10½hr. to Jersey). The tides and the season affect frequency and ticket prices. Check the website for up-to-date scheduling or call the reservation hotline (☎0845 124 2003). Arrive for all ferries 45min. prior to departure time. ISIC holders (p. 14) receive a 20% discount.

 A WHOLE NEW WORLD. Though part of the UK, Jersey and Guernsey are self-governing; in some senses, you're in foreign territory. The British pound is the official currency, but ATMs dish out Jersey or Guernsey pounds. These pounds have equal value to British pounds, but are not accepted outside the Channel Islands. Change your money as few times as possible to avoid exchange commissions. Toward the end of your stay, ask local merchants and restaurants to give your change in British pounds. Also keep in mind that your mobile may think you're in France, affecting your rate. Some mobiles may not work at all, and pay-as-you-go phones from the mainland usually cannot be topped up here. Your best bet is to purchase an international "Speedial" phone card from a post office or newsagent.

JERSEY   ☎01534

The largest of the Channel Islands, Jersey offers the bustling city center of St. Helier, a smattering of palm trees, rocky coastlines, and a gorgeous countryside. The same oscillating tides that make ferry schedules erratic also transfigure the island's coastline into an otherworldly landscape of jagged rocks at low tide.

█ TRANSPORTATION. An efficient system of **buses** makes local travel painless. Connex (☎877 772; www.mybus.je) buses are based at the station on Weighbridge, St. Helier and travel all over the island. The public buses have conspicuous "Out of the Blue" signs. (Office open M-F 8am-6pm, Sa-Su 9am-5pm. Tickets 90p-£1.60, all fares £1 after 7pm. Unlimited travel passes 1-day £6, 3-day £15.30, 5-day £22.50, 7-day £31.50.) Easylink offers a hop-on, hop-off tour service (☎876 418; M-F and Su from Weighbridge Terminal). **Explorer** tickets are best if your plans take you all over the island (1-day £7, 3-day £16.50, 5-day £21, one person under 16 free with every ticket). Easylink also offers direct service to sites on any of its four links (single £2-3.70). For **taxis,** try Arrow Luxicabs (☎887 000) or Yellow Cabs (☎888 888), both 24hr. **Rent bicycles** at Zebra Car and Cycle Hire, 9 The Esplanade. (☎736 556; www.zebrahire.com. Bicycles £10 per day. Open daily 8am-5pm.)

█ █ ORIENTATION AND PRACTICAL INFORMATION. The ferry drops travelers at **Elizabeth Harbor, Saint Helier,** a transport hub, shopping district, and nightspot. Exit the Harbor, head left, and follow signs to the Esplanade, then make a right to find the **Tourist Information Centre,** Liberation Square, St. Helier. (☎500 700; www.jersey.com. Open M-Sa 8:30am-5:30pm, Su 8:30am-2:15pm.) The TIC is stocked with useful pamphlets, maps, and tide tables. Pick up *Walking in Jersey* and *Cycle Jersey,* both free. Les Petits Trains runs **tours** with English or French commentary from the TIC (Train-Hopper all-day ticket £8.50). Also try Tantivy Blue Coach Tours (☎706 706; www.jerseycoaches.com; all-day island tour £16). Other services include: **banks** at the intersection of Conway, New, and Broad St., and a Thomas Cook, 14 Charing Cross (☎506 900; open M-Tu and Th-Sa 9am-5:30pm, W 10am-5:30pm); **police,** Rougebouillon St. (☎612 612); Jersey General **Hospital,** Gloucester St. (☎622 000) and a **visitors' doctor** (☎616 833); Roseville **pharmacy,** 7 Roseville St. (☎734 698; open daily 9am-9:30pm); **Internet access** at usetheinternet, 9 Charing Cross (☎733 665; £1 per 15min.; open M-F 10am-7pm, Sa 10am-5:30pm, Su noon-4pm) and at Jersey Library, Halkett Pl. (☎759 991; £1 per 15min.; open M and W-F 9:30am-5:30pm, Tu 9:30am-7:30pm, Sa 9:30am-4pm); and the **post office,** Broad St. (☎616 616; open M-F 8:30am-5pm, Sa 8:30am-2pm) with a bureau de change. **Post Code:** JE1 1AA.

█ █ ACCOMMODATIONS AND FOOD. With tourism their biggest industry, the islands are teeming with accommodation options. Pick up *Out of the Blue,* an accommodations guide (free at the TIC) or contact the **Jersey Hospitality Association** (☎721 421; www.jerseyhols.com). Book ahead, as accommodations fill quickly in summer. In St. Helier, pretty (and pricey) **B&Bs** line the Havre des Pas, by the beach. Travelers looking for a cheaper night's rest should head east to the coastal St. Martin area. The only hostel on the island is the beautiful, new, 105-bed **YHA Jersey ❷,** Haut de la Garenne, La Rue de la Pouclée des Quatre Chemis, St. Martin. To reach the hostel, take bus #3a from St. Helier (20min., every hr.); after 5:45pm take #1 to Gorey (last bus 11pm) and walk ½ mi. up the steep hill behind the row of restaurants on the pier, cross the road, turn left, and walk up the hill. (☎840 100. Breakfast included. Reception 7-10am and 5-11pm. Open Feb.-Nov. daily; Dec.-Jan. F-Sa. Dorms £18, under 18 £13. MC/V.) For beautiful views, try the **Seascale Hotel ❸,** Gorey Pier, which can be reached via bus #1/1a/1b (25min., 2 per hr.) from St. Helier. (☎854 395; www.seascalehotel.com. June-Sept. £32 per person; Oct.-May £24-27 per person. AmEx/MC/V.)

Rozel Camping Park ❶, St. Martin, offers a view of the French coast. (☎855 200; www.jerseyisland.com/country/rozelcamping. Tents only. Toilets, showers, pool, and laundry. £8.20 per person. MC/V.)

Jersey offers a range of excellent restaurants. Peer at mosaics and a fountain (and that's just the bathroom) at the **Beach House ❷**, Gorey Pier. Enjoy an extensive menu, from tortilla wraps (£6) to salmon (£9). Call ahead to reserve an outdoor table. (☎859 902. Open M 11am-6pm, Tu-Su 12:30-3:30pm and 6:30-9:30pm. Food served until 30min. before close. MC/V.) **City Bar and Brasserie ❸**, 75-77 Halkett Pl., offers sizable portions and free Internet access from wall-mounted computers. (☎510 096; www.cityjersey.com. Sandwiches £4.50-6.25; entrees £7-14.50. Open M-Sa 10am-11pm. AmEx/MC/V.) Grab coffee, a milk-shake, or cake at the **Curiosity Coffee Shop ❹**, 14 Sand St., while browsing the Internet on your laptop. This homey local joint is chock-full of mismatched furniture and well-loved board games. (☎510 075. Free wireless Internet with purchase. Open M-F 7am-7pm, Sa 7am-6pm.)

◪ SIGHTS. Jersey's sights celebrate the island's ever-changing role in the world beyond its waters. The **Jersey Heritage Trust** oversees many of the museums; check out www.jerseyheritagetrust.org. The gigantic ▧**Mont Orgueil Castle,** on Gorey Pier, was built in the 13th century to protect the island from the French. Climb to the top for a spectacular vista, though the views from below are impressive enough. (☎853 292. Open daily Apr.-Oct. 10am-6pm; Nov.-Mar. 10am-dusk. Last admission 1hr. before close. £5.25, concessions £4.40.) Across from Liberation Sq. by the St. Helier marina, the **Maritime Museum and Occupation Tapestry Gallery** features hands-on exhibits. Enter the "Elements Gallery" to learn about tides, currents, and winds; choose a sail combination so your small wooden boat will outpace its opponents. Downstairs, see tapestries woven to commemorate the 50th anniversary of Jersey's liberation from German occupation during WWII. (☎811 043. Open daily Apr.-Oct. 10am-5pm; Nov.-Mar. 10am-4pm. £6, concessions £5.) The **Jersey War Tunnels,** Les Charrieres Malorey, St. Lawrence, provide a somber history lesson about life in Jersey under Nazi occupation; one exhibit is housed in a former German military hospital. (☎860 808; www.jerseywartunnels.com. Open mid-Feb. to mid-Dec. daily 10am-6pm. Last admission 4:30pm. £8.60, students £6.40.) The **Jersey Zoo** is run by a conservation trust and features endangered species on its 30 acres of land. The zoo has an organic garden where it grows food for the animals. Take bus #3a or 3b or get off at the Easylink stop. (☎860 000. Open daily July-Aug. 9am-6pm; Sept.-June 10am-5pm. £11.50, students £8.50.)

◪ ▧ ENTERTAINMENT AND FESTIVALS. Jersey offers a variety of venues for entertainment. The **Opera House,** Gloucester St., presents the latest in theater. (☎511 115; www.jerseyoperahouse.co.uk. Open M-Sa 10am-6pm; also open until 8pm on performance nights and from 1hr. before performances on Su.) Various pubs and clubs offer nightlife options. Locals endorse the island's largest night-club, **Liquid Club,** at the Waterfront Centre, which has views of St. Aubin's Bay (☎789 356; cover £3-10; open W-Su 10pm-2am), and **The Cosmopolitan,** on The Esplanade, which offers drag musical revues. (☎720 289. Shows W 9:15pm, Th-Sa 10pm, Su 6pm. Nightclub cover £6. Open F-Sa 11:30pm-2:30am.) If visiting during October, take a bite of **Tennerfest** (also in Guernsey), which challenges local restaurants to come up with the best £10 menu. Check out www.jersey.com for more on all festivals musical, floral, and otherwise.

GUERNSEY ☎ 01481

TRANSPORTATION. Island Coachways **buses** (☎720 210; www.buses.gg) operate island-wide, with frequent service to tourist favorites. The bus terminal is on the waterfront, where Quay and South Esplanade converge. Buses #7 and 7a (every hr., 50p) circle the coast. Island Coachways also offers themed **tours** (like "Guernsey in a Day" and "Fairy Princesses of Pleinmony") from May to September. Tours usually begin and end at the bus terminal and depart at 10am. Call for fares and information. For a **taxi,** call PTR Taxis (☎07781 133 233) or Island Taxis (☎07781 129 090; 24hr.).

ORIENTATION AND PRACTICAL INFORMATION. A **Tourist Information Centre** awaits visitors immediately upon exiting the ferry; its larger office is across the harbor on North Esplanade. The TIC has maps and the helpful *Naturally Guernsey*, which provides information on the attractions of the island as well as nearby Herm, Sark, and Alderney. The center also books accommodations for a £2 charge plus a 10% deposit. (☎723 552; www.guernseytouristboard.com. Open in summer M-Sa 9am-6pm, Su 9am-1pm; in winter M-F 9am-5pm, Sa 9am-4pm.) Other services include: **banks** on High St. and a Thomas Cook, 22 Le Pollet (☎724 111; open M-Sa 9am-5:30pm); the **police,** Hospital Ln. (☎725 111); Princess Elizabeth **Hospital,** Le Vauquiedor, St. Martin (☎725 241); Boots **pharmacy,** 26-27 High St. (☎726 565; open M-Sa 8:30am-5:30pm); **Internet access** at Guille-Alles Library, The Market, St. Peter Port (☎720 392; £1 per 30min.; open M and Th-Sa 9:15am-4:45pm, Tu 10am-4:45pm, W 9:15am-7:45pm; reservations required) and at Allsorts, 32 Mill St., St. Peter Port (☎726 832; 75p per 15min.; open M-Th 10am-8pm, F-Sa 10am-7pm); and the **post office,** Smith St. (☎711 720; open M-F 8:30am-5pm, Sa 8:30am-noon). **Post Code:** GY1 2JG.

ACCOMMODATIONS AND FOOD. Hotels fill quickly. For lodgings near town with views of Sark and Herm, try **St. George's Hotel ❹,** St. George's Esplanade, St. Peter Port. (☎721 027. Breakfast included. Aug. £35 per person; Sept.-July £33 per person. MC/V.) Farther down the road, **La Piette Hotel ❹,** is a good deal for those traveling in pairs. (☎710 885; www.visit-guernsey.co.uk. Breakfast included. Mid-May to mid-Oct. singles £57; doubles £96; Nov.-Apr. £55/92. MC/V.)

Guernsey will easily satisfy your seafood-tooth. Get fresh fruit and veggies at the **market,** appropriately located on Market St. (open M-Sa 7:30am-5pm). **La Cucina ❷,** North Plantation, above Yugo's Take-Out, serves sandwiches (£5) with a Mediterranean influence. (☎715 166. Open Tu-Sa noon-2pm and 5:30-9:30pm. Cash only.) **Christie's ❸,** Le Pollet, has an airy French-bistro feel. Try the sandwiches or seasonally available local seafood. (☎726 624. Lunch entrees £4.50-15. Open daily noon-2:30pm and 6-10:30pm. MC/V.) For a casual bite, the best possible view of the harbor, and yummy crepes (£2.70-6.50), try the **Boathouse ❷,** on Victoria Pier. (☎700 061. Open daily Apr.-Oct. 9am-9:30pm.) **Isabel's Bar and Brasserie ❸,** 35 Le Pollet, is a sleek new restaurant with four stories and a sophisticated after-hours bar scene. (☎721 121. Entrees £5.25-12. Open M-Sa 8am-11pm, Su 10am-9pm.)

SIGHTS. Pull yourself away from Guernsey's wildflowers and beaches long enough to tour ◙**Hauteville House,** St. Peter Port. Victor Hugo's home during his exile from France remains virtually unaltered since the days when he wrote *Les Miserables* here. The house is full of secret passages, hidden inscriptions, and furnishings supposedly made by Hugo himself. (☎721 911. Open Apr.-Oct. M-Sa 10am-4pm. £4, concessions £2.) The **Castle Cornet,** St. Peter Port, and its views are worth a look, its museums less so. Built in 1204, the Castle has changed hands often, most recently when Britain gave it back to Guernsey in 1947 in thanks for the island's loyalty during WWII. (☎721 657. Open daily Apr.-Oct. 10am-5pm. Last admission 4:15pm. £6, students free.) A "Venue" ticket (£9) may be purchased for entrance into the castle, the **Fort Grey Shipwreck Museum** (☎265 036; open daily Easter to Oct. 10am-5pm), and the **Guernsey Museum and Art Gallery** (☎726 518; open daily 10am-5pm).

Island RIB Voyages takes visitors on a 34 ft. commercial boat into the waters surrounding Guernsey to see puffins, seals, and other wildlife in their natural habitats while learning about their environment from the onboard marine zoologist. (☎713 031; www.islandribvoyages. 1hr. tour £18, children £12.) Nearby **Herm** (www.herm-island.com) and **Sark** (www.sark.info) are worthwhile daytrips. Pristine beaches await travelers at Herm, while Sark retains its feudal inheritance laws from the 16th century. Uncorrupted by cars (transport on the island is left to foot, bicycle, or horse-drawn carriage), Sark's timeless quality is unmatched. If traveling in early July, be sure to check out the annual **Sheep Racing** competition.

▣▒ ENTERTAINMENT AND FESTIVALS. Shopping in Guernsey is particularly popular due to the absence of Britain's staggering 17.5% Value-Added Tax (VAT; p. 18). After finding your bargains, plop down for a pint at one of the bars that line the waterfront. **Ship & Crown,** North Esplanade, is a local favorite (☎721 368; pints £2-2.50; open M-Sa 10am-midnight, Su noon-midnight), and the **Albion House Tavern,** Church Sq., is a historic experience in its own right—it's the closest tavern to a church in the British Isles, thanks to a protruding gargoyle. (☎723 518. Pints £1.75-2.50. Open daily 10:30am-midnight.) Along with **Tennerfest** in October (p. 245), Guernsey hosts many other competitions and celebrations year-round. Don't miss the **Battle of Flowers** in August, when locals duke it out for the honor of best floral float. (☎254 473.)

THE HEART OF ENGLAND

The pastures and half-timbered houses that characterize the country-side west of London are the stuff of stereotype. The Heart of England contains many of England's most famous attractions: Oxford, Britain's oldest university town; Stratford-upon-Avon, Shakespeare's home; and the impossibly picturesque villages of the Cotswolds. It takes a resourceful traveler to avoid the touring hordes here, but the region is so rich in history and beauty that the task is far from impossible.

HIGHLIGHTS OF THE HEART OF ENGLAND

ADMIRE the gargoyles in Oxford, a stunning university town, rich in architecture and bizarre student traditions (p. 253).

PLAY PRINCESS at Windsor, one of the world's most sumptuous royal residences, which has housed 40 reigning monarchs (p. 251).

BE OR NOT BE in Stratford-upon-Avon, where tourist trails honor the Bard's footsteps and the Royal Shakespeare Company venerates his every syllable (p. 264).

ST. ALBANS   ☎01727

From the Catuvellauni tribe to the Roman legions, from Norman conquerors to warring royal houses, each new ruling class has wanted to either set St. Albans on fire or make it a magnificent capital. The Roman soldier Alban was beheaded here for sheltering a priest, making him England's first Christian martyr.

⌖ TRANSPORTATION. St. Albans has two **train stations;** City Station, the main one, and Abbey Station, which runs local service. **Trains** (☎08457 484 950) enter City Station from London King's Cross Thameslink (25min., 4 per hr., round-trip ₤7.80). To get to the town center, turn right out of the station on Victoria Rd., follow the curve and continue straight for about 10min. Avoid the uphill hike by hopping any "Into Town" bus (65p). Sovereign (☎854 732) **buses** usually stop at City Station and along St. Peter's St. From London, take #797 to Hatfield (37min.) and then UniversityBus (☎01707 255 764) #602 to St. Albans (25min.).

⛫🛈 ORIENTATION AND PRACTICAL INFORMATION. Leaving City Station, **Hatfield Road** to the left and **Victoria Street** to the right both lead to town; the two streets are intersected by the main drag, which changes from **St. Peter's Street** to **Chequer Street** to **Holywell Hill** down the slope. The **Tourist Information Centre,** Market Place, St. Peter's St., has a free map and sight-filled miniguide, and books accommodations for ₤3 plus a 10% deposit. (☎864 511; www.stalbans.gov.uk. Open Easter to Oct. M-Sa 9:30am-5:30pm; Nov. to Easter M-Sa 10am-4pm.) Other services include: **banks** at the beginning of Chequer St.; **police,** on Victoria St. (☎796 000); Maltings **pharmacy,** 6 Victoria St. (☎839 335; open M-F 9am-6:30pm, Sa 9am-5pm); **Internet** at the library in The Maltings, across from the TIC (☎860 000; open M and W 9:30am-7:30pm, Tu 9:30am-5:30pm, Th 9:30am-1pm, F 10:30am-7:30pm, Sa 9am-4pm); and the **post office,** 2 Beaconsfield Rd. (☎860 110). **Post Code:** AL1 3RA.

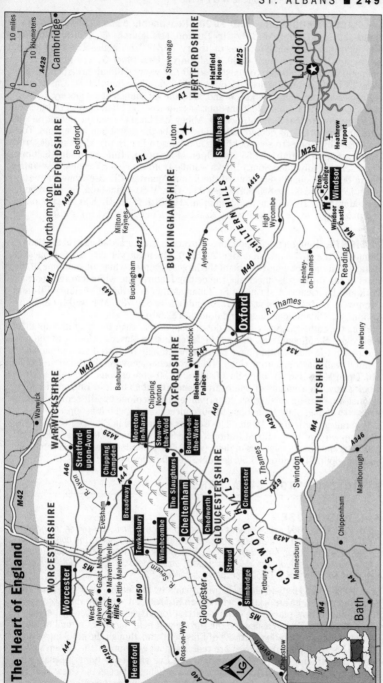

The Heart of England

ᴦᴄ ACCOMMODATIONS AND FOOD. Reasonable **B&Bs** (₤20-40) are scattered and often unmarked. By City Station, **Mrs. Murphy ❸**, 478 Hatfield Rd., adorns rooms with small touches of luxury. (☎842 216. Singles ₤25-35; doubles, twins, and family rooms ₤40-60. Cash only.) **Mrs. Nicol ❹**, 178 London Rd., opens her beautiful home to guests. (☎846 726; www.178londonroad.co.uk. Satellite TV in all rooms. Singles ₤35; doubles ₤50; family rooms ₤50-80. Cash only.)

Veggies abound at the **market** (W and Sa by the TIC) and Iceland **grocery**, 144 Victoria St. (☎833 908. Open M-F 9am-8pm, Sa 9am-7pm, Su 11am-5pm.) For lunch or curiosity, visit **Ye Olde Fighting Cocks ❶**, Abbey Mill Ln., between the Cathedral and Verulamium park. This octagonal building may be the oldest pub in England. Tunnels, used by monks to see cockfights and later to flee Henry VIII's cronies, run from cathedral to pub. (☎865 830. Open M-Sa noon-11pm, Su noon-10:30pm. Food served daily noon-8pm.) Ducks waddle from the River Ver near the **Waffle House ❷**, St. Michael's St., toward the Roman quarter. Choose from many toppings for ₤2.40-6.50. (☎853 502. Open Apr.-Oct. M-Sa 10am-6pm, Su 11am-6pm; Nov.-Mar. M-Sa 10am-5pm, Su 11am-5pm.) Hip **Zizzi ❷**, 26 High St., serves pasta and pizza for ₤5-8. (☎850 200; www.zizzi.co.uk. Open daily noon-11pm.)

ᴳ SIGHTS. Built on the foundations of a Saxon church, ▓**Cathedral of St. Alban** is defined by the 1077 Norman design. At 227 ft., the medieval nave is the longest in Britain, and the wooden roof one of the largest. Painted while the outcome of the Wars of the Roses was uncertain, the ceiling features the white and red roses of York and Lancaster. A shrine to St. Alban stands in defiance of Henry VIII and Cromwell, its fragments at last reassembled. (☎860 780. M-F and Su 8:30am-5:45pm, Sa 8:30am-9pm. Suggested donation ₤2.50.)

From the cathedral, walk 10min. down Fishpool St., over the river and uphill as it becomes St. Michael's St. to visit the ▓**Verulamium Museum.** Homes of the rich and poor of Roman Britain have been painstakingly recreated around mosaics, painted wall plasters, and various other artifacts discovered in the area. (☎751 810. Open M-Sa 10am-5:30pm, Su 2-5:30pm. ₤3.30, concessions ₤2, families ₤8.) A block away, the remains of one of five **Roman theaters** built in England huddles against a backdrop of English countryside; archaeologists still scour the site. (☎835 035. Open daily 10am-5pm. ₤1.50, concessions ₤1, children 50p.)

Two miles south of St. Albans, The **Gardens of the Rose** in Chiswell Green is the "flagship garden" of the Royal National Rose Society. Over 30,000 roses scale tall buildings and conquer sweeps of field. (☎850 461. Open June-Sept. M-Sa 9am-5pm, Su 10am-6pm. ₤4, children ₤1.50, seniors ₤3.50, families ₤10.)

ᴾ DAYTRIP FROM ST. ALBANS

HATFIELD HOUSE

Buses #300 and 301 link St. Albans and Hatfield House (20min., 1-3 per hr., round-trip £3.30). The Hatfield train station, across from the main gate, makes the house easily accessible from other towns. ☎01707 262 823. House open daily Easter to Sept. noon-4pm. Hour-long guided tours M-F. House, park, and gardens £8, children £4. Park and gardens £4.50, children £3.50. Park only £2, children £1.

Stately 225-room Hatfield House is now owned by the Marquess of Salisbury, but is best-known for its association with **Queen Elizabeth I.** It was here that Lizzy spent her childhood, was placed under house arrest for suspected treason by her sister, **Queen Mary** (p. 65), and ascended the throne and held her first Council of State. Hatfield holds two famous portraits of Elizabeth, and, though the stockings attributed to her are fakes, the gloves are real. Keep an eye out for the Queen's 22 ft. family tree, tracing her lineage to Adam and Eve via Noah, Julius Caesar, King Arthur, and King Lear. All that remains of her original palace is the Great Hall; the rest was razed to make way for the mansion that dominates the estate today.

WINDSOR AND ETON ☎ 01753

The town of Windsor and the attached village of Eton center entirely on Windsor Castle and Eton College, two famed symbols of the British upper crust. In the Middle Ages, residential Windsor fanned out from the castle perimeters, and it is now thick with specialty shops, tea houses, and pubs, all of which wear a certain charm but cater mostly to the throngs of day-trippers from nearby London.

█ TRANSPORTATION

Two train stations lie near the castle; signs point into town. **Trains** (☎ 08457 484 950) pull into Windsor and Eton **Central Station** from London Paddington via Slough (40min., 2 per hr., round-trip £7). Trains arrive at Windsor and Eton **Riverside** from London Waterloo (50min., 2 per hr., round-trip £7). Green Line **buses** #702 arrive at Central from London Victoria (1¼hr., every hr., round-trip £5-10).

▄▄ █ ORIENTATION AND PRACTICAL INFORMATION

Windsor village slopes from the foot of the castle. **High Street** spans the hilltop, then becomes **Thames Street** at the statue of Queen Victoria and continues to the river, at which point it reverts to High St.; the main shopping area, **Peascod Street**, meets High St. at the statue. The **Tourist Information Centre**, 24 High St., near Queen Victoria, has free brochures and an accommodation guide. (☎ 743 900; www.windsor.gov.uk. Open May-Sept. M-Sa 10am-5pm, Su 10am-4pm; Oct.-Apr. M-F and Su 10am-4pm, Sa 10am-5pm. Other services include: **police**, on the corner of St. Marks Rd. and Alma Rd. (☎ 50600); **Internet** in the bureau de change in Central Station (open M-Sa 9:30am-5:30pm, Su 10am-5pm) or McDonald's, 13-14 Thames St. (£2 per hr.; open daily 6:30am-10pm); and the **post office**, 38-39 Peascod St. (open M and W-Sa 9am-5:30 pm, Tu 9:30am-5:30pm). **Post Code:** SL4 1LH.

█ █ ACCOMMODATIONS AND FOOD

Windsor lacks budget accommodations. If you decide to stay, the TIC will locate **B&Bs** for a £5 fee plus a 10% deposit; call ☎ 743 907. The **Clarence Hotel ❹**, 9 Clarence Rd., includes a lounge area with cable TV and spacious rooms. (☎ 864 436; www.clarence-hotel.co.uk. Full breakfast included. Singles £49-63; doubles £52-74; family rooms £60-91.) **Alma House ❹**, 56 Alma Rd., is in a quiet neighborhood a few minutes from town. (☎ 862 983. Singles £50; doubles £65; family rooms £85-90.)

Chain joints dominate Thames St. The **Waterman's Arms ❶**, Brocas St., is over the bridge to Eton, next to the boat house. Founded in 1542, it's still a local favorite, offering pub classics for £4-7. (☎ 861 001. Food served M-F noon-2pm and 6-9pm, Sa noon-9pm, Su noon-4:30pm.) **Gran Panini ❶**, 49 Thames St. (☎ 859 331), has sandwiches (£2.40), pasties (£2), potatoes (£4), and specials.

◉ SIGHTS

WINDSOR CASTLE

☎ 831 118. Open daily Mar.-Oct. 9:45am-5:30pm; Nov.-Feb. 9:45am-4pm. Last admission 1¼hr. before close. £12.50, under 17 £6.50. Audio tours £3.50. Guides £5.

The largest and oldest continuously inhabited castle in the world, Windsor features some of the most sumptuous rooms in Europe and some of the rarest artwork in the Western tradition. It was built high above the Thames by William the Conqueror as a fortress rather than as a residence, and 40 reigning monarchs have since left their marks. Today, members of the royal family often stay here for weekends and special ceremonies. The Queen is officially in residence for the

TOP TEN LIST

ETON-SPEAK

The elite prep school Eton College has educated philosophers, princes, and Prime Ministers for over 500 years and has a vernacular to describe the school's many ranks, quirks, and rituals. Common words (with example sentences) include:

1. Stick-ups: collars worn with the school's black morning suit. "With a stiff upper lip and bruised neck, Ansel regretted over-starching his stick-ups."

2. Colleger: one of 70 student scholars selected by examination. "Truant Kevin was no colleger."

3. Wet bob: a boy who rows crew in summer. "David, a wet bob, suffered from tan lines."

4. Dry bob: a boy who plays cricket in summer. "Dustin, a dry bob, suffered from shin splints."

5. Half: a school term. "Studious Seth hated the end of half."

6. Division: a form, class, or grade. "Silly Stuart failed sixth division."

7. Tutor: a faculty member responsible for supervising studies. "The tutor advised that Jeremy repeat maths."

8. The Block: a stool-shaped bench where students were flogged. "Michael, and his buttocks, shivered as he passed the Block."

9. Pop, popper: one of 25 self-elected student prefects. "Owen abused his power as a popper."

10. Montem: a procession made by the students from the school to Salt Hill in Slough, stopped due to rowdy behavior. "The sixth division rioted gleefully during Montem."

month of April and one week in June—more than any other building, this is her home. During royal stays, large areas of the castle are unavailable to visitors. The admission prices are lowered on these occasions, but it is wise to call ahead. Visitors can watch the **Changing of the Guard** in front of the Guard Room at 11am (in summer M-Sa; in winter alternate days M-Sa). The Guards can also be seen at 10:50am and 11:30am as they march to and from the ceremony through the streets.

UPPER WARD. Reach the upper ward through the Norman tower and gate. Stand in the left line to enter the ward past **Queen Mary's Doll House,** a replica of a grand home on a 1:12 scale, with tiny handwritten classics in its library and functional plumbing and electrical systems. The opulent **state apartments** are used for ceremonial events and official entertainment. The rooms are ornamented with art from the prodigious **Royal Collection,** including works by Holbein, Reubens, Rembrandt, van Dyck, and Queen Victoria herself. The **Queen's Drawing Room** features portraits of Henry VIII, Elizabeth I, and Mary I, but don't miss smaller embellishments, like the silver dragon doorknobs. A fire in 1992 destroyed the **Lantern Room,** the **Grand Reception Room,** and the stunning **St. George's Hall,** but they are now fully restored.

MIDDLE AND LOWER WARD. The **Round Tower** dominates the middle ward. A stroll downhill to the lower ward brings you to **St. George's Chapel,** a 15th-century structure with delicate vaulting and an exquisite wall of stained glass dedicated to the Order of the Garter, England's most elite knighthood. Used for the marriage of Sophie and Prince Edward, the chapel houses the tombs of the Queen Mother and George III. Ask a guide to explain the accident of history that placed the bones of Charles I and Henry VIII under the same stone until the early 19th century.

OTHER SIGHTS

ETON COLLEGE. Eton College, founded by Henry VI in 1440 as a college for paupers, has ironically evolved into England's preeminent public—which is to say, private—school. Despite its position at the apex of the British class system, Eton has shaped some notable dissident thinkers, including Aldous Huxley, George Orwell, and former Liberal Party leader Jeremy Thorpe. The boys still practice many of the old traditions, including wearing tailcoats to class. The 25 houses that surround the quad act as residences for the approximately 1250 students. King's Scholars, selected for scholarships based on exam scores, live in the house known as "College" in the courtyard of College Chapel. The **Museum of Eton Life** displays relics and stories of the school's extensive past. *(10-15min. walk down Thames St., across Windsor Bridge, and along Eton High St. ☎671 177. Open daily late Mar. to mid-Apr. and July-Aug. 10:30am-4:30pm; Sept.-June 2-4:30pm; schedule depends on academic calendar. Tours daily 2:15 and 3:15pm. £3.80, under 16 and seniors £3. Tours £5, under 16 £4.)*

LEGOLAND WINDSOR. A whimsical addition to the town, this imaginative amusement park will wow the 11-and-under set with its rides, playgrounds, and circuses. Its Miniland took 100 workers, three years, and 25 million blocks to craft. The replica of the City of London includes a 6 ft. St. Paul's and dozens of other city landmarks. *(Tickets available at the Windsor TIC. ☎08705 040 404; www.legoland.co.uk. Open daily mid-July to Aug. 10am-7pm; Apr.-June and Sept.-Oct. 10am-5pm or 6pm. £24, children and seniors £22. Shuttle from town center £3, children £1.50.)*

OXFORD ☎01865

Oxford has been home to nearly a millennium of scholarship—25 British prime ministers and numerous other world leaders have been educated here. In 1167, Henry II founded Britain's first university, whose distinguished spires have since struck the imaginations of such luminaries as Lewis Carroll and C.S. Lewis. Today, trucks barrel, buses screech, and bicycles scrape past the pedestrians choking the streets. Despite the touring crowds, Oxford has an irrepressible grandeur and spirit: visit the basement room of Blackwell's Bookshop, the impeccable galleries of the Ashmolean, the serene lily ponds of the Botanic Garden, and the perfectly maintained quadrangles of Oxford's 39 colleges.

TRANSPORTATION

Trains: Station on Botley Rd., down Park End. Ticket office open M-F 5:45am-8pm, Sa 6:15am-8pm, Su 7:10am-8pm. Trains (☎08457 484 950) from: **Birmingham** (1¼hr., 2 per hr., £19); **Glasgow** (5-7hr., every hr., £65-75); **London Paddington** (1hr., 2-4 per hr., £9.50-18.10); **Manchester** (3hr., 1-2 per hr., £21-42).

Buses: Bus station on Gloucester Green. **Stagecoach** (☎772 250; www.stagecoach-bus.com) runs from **Cambridge** (3hr., 2 per hr., £6) and operates the **Oxford Tube** (☎772 250) from **London** (1¾hr.; 3-5 per hr.; £10, students £8). The **Oxford Bus Company** (☎785 400; www.oxfordbus.co.uk) runs from: **London** (1¾hr.; 3-5 per hr.; £10, students £8); **Gatwick** (2hr.; every hr. 8am-9pm; £20, concessions £10); **Heathrow** (1¼hr.; 3 per hr.; £15, concessions £7.50).

Public Transportation: The **Oxford Bus Company Cityline** (☎785 400) and **Stagecoach Oxford** (☎772 250) offer swift and frequent service to: Iffley Rd. (#3, 4, 4A, 4B, 4C, 16B), Banbury Rd. (#2, 2A, 2B, 2D), Abingdon Rd. (X3, X13, #4, 16, 16A, 35, 35A), Cowley Rd. (#5, 5A, 5B, 5C), and elsewhere. Fares are low (most 60p-£1.40). Stagecoach offers a **DayRider ticket** and the Oxford Bus Company a **Freedom ticket**, which give unlimited travel on local routes (£3-4.50 for 24hr., £10-17 for 5 days). A **PLUS+PASS** allows for unlimited travel on all Oxford Bus Company, Stagecoach, and Thames Travel buses (☎785 410; 1 day £5, 1 week £14).

Taxis: Radio Taxis (☎242 424). **ABC** (☎770 077). **City Taxis** (☎201 201). All 24hr.

ORIENTATION AND PRACTICAL INFORMATION

Queen Street becomes **High Street**, and **Cornmarket Street** becomes **St. Aldate's** at **Carfax Tower,** the center of the original city. The colleges are all within a mile of one another, mainly east of Carfax along High St. and Broad St.

Tourist Information Centre: 15-16 Broad St. (☎ 726 871; www.visitoxford.org). A pamphleteer's paradise. The busy staff books rooms for a £4 charge plus a 10% deposit. Visitors' guide and map £1.25, monthly *In Oxford* guide free, restaurant guide free, accommodations list £1. Job listings, long-term accommodation listings, and entertainment news posted daily at the TIC and at www.dailyinfo.co.uk. Open M-Sa 9:30am-5pm; Easter to June and Aug.-Oct. also Su 10am-3:30pm; June-July also Su 10am-4pm. Last room booking 4:30pm.

Tours: The 2hr. official Oxford University **walking tour** (☎ 726 871) leaves from the TIC and provides access to some colleges otherwise closed to visitors. Daily 11am and 2pm; in summer also 10:30am and 1pm. £6.50, children £3. **Blackwell's** (☎ 333 606) offers walking tours. General tours Tu 2pm, Th 11am, Sa noon. £6, concessions £5.50. Literary tour of Oxford Tu 2pm, Th 11am; "Inklings" tours about C.S. Lewis, J.R.R. Tolkien and circle of friends W 11:45am; Historic Oxford Tour F 2pm. All tours 1½hr. £6, concessions £5. **Guided Tours** (☎ 07810 402 757), 1½hr., depart from outside Trinity College on Broad St. and offer access to some colleges and other university buildings. Daily every hr. 11am-4pm. £6, children £3. The same company runs evening **Ghost Tours,** also leaving from Trinity. 1¼hr. In summer daily 8pm. £5, children £3. **Bus tour** companies allow hop-on, hop-off access. **Guide Friday** (☎ 790 522) departs from the train station every 15min. 9:30am-6pm for a 1hr. tour. £9, concessions £6, children £4.

Budget Travel: STA Travel, 36 George St. (☎ 792 800). Open M-W and F 9:30am-6pm, Th 10am-6pm, Sa 10am-5pm, Su 11am-4pm.

Financial Services: Banks line Cornmarket St. **Marks & Spencer,** 13-18 Queen St. (☎ 248 075), has a bureau de change with no commission. Open M-W and F 8:30am-6:30pm, Th 8:30am-7:30pm, Sa 8:30am-6:30pm, Su 11am-4:30pm. **Thomas Cook,** 5 Queen St. (☎ 447 000). Open M-Sa 9am-5:30pm. The **TIC** also has a bureau de change with no commission.

Work Opportunities: JobCentre, 7 Worcester St. (☎ 445 000). Open M-Th 9am-5pm, F 10am-5pm.

Launderette: 127 Cowley Rd. Wash £2.60-3.90, dry £2.60. Also 66 Abingdon Rd. Wash £2-3, dryers take 20p and £1 coins. Soap 70p-£1. Open 7am-10pm, last wash 9pm.

Police: St. Aldate's and Speedwell St. (☎ 266 000).

Hospital: John Radcliffe Hospital, Headley Way (☎ 741 166). Take bus #13 or 14.

Pharmacy: Boswell's, 1-4 Broad St. (☎ 241 244). Open M-F 9:30am-6pm, Sa 9am-6pm, Su 11am-5pm.

Internet Access: Oxford Central Library, Queen St. (☎ 815 549), near Westgate Shopping Center. Free. Open M-Th 9:15am-7pm, F-Sa 9:15am-5pm. **Mices,** 118 High St. (☎ 726 364). Open daily 10am-6pm. Branch at 91 Gloucester Green; open M-Sa 9am-11pm, Su 10am-11pm. Both branches £1 per 20min.

Post Office: 102-104 St. Aldate's (☎ 08457 223 344). Bureau de change. Open M-Sa 9am-5:30pm. **Post Code:** OX1 1ZZ.

▌ ACCOMMODATIONS

Book at least a week ahead from June to September, especially for singles. **B&Bs** (from £25) line the main roads out of town and are reachable by bus or a 15-45min. walk. Try www.stayoxford.com for options. The 300s on **Banbury Road,** north of town, are accessible by buses #2, 2A, 2B, and 2D. Cheaper B&Bs lie in the 200s and 300s on **Iffley Road** (bus #4, 4A, 4B, 4C, and 16B to Rose Hill) and on **Abingdon Road** in South Oxford (bus #16 and 16A). If it's late, call the **Oxford Association of Hotels and Guest Houses** (East Oxford ☎ 721 561, West Oxford 862 138, North Oxford 244 691, South Oxford 244 268).

YHA Oxford, 2a Botley Rd. (☎727 275). An immediate right from the train station onto Botley Rd. Superb location and bright surroundings. All rooms ensuite. Facilities include TV room, kitchen, library, and lockable wardrobes. Full English breakfast included. Lockers £1. Towels 50p. Laundry £3. Internet access 7p per min. 4- and 6-bed dorms £20.50 per person, under 18 £15.40; twins £46. £3 student discount. MC/V. ❷

Oxford Backpackers Hostel, 9a Hythe Bridge St. (☎721 761), between the bus and train stations. Advertised as a "funky hostel." Inexpensive bar, pool table, music, and colorful murals. Passport required. Luggage storage £1 per item. Laundry (wash and dry) £2.50. Internet £1 per 30min. Dorms £13-14; quads £16 per person. MC/V. ❷

Heather House, 192 Iffley Rd. (☎249 757). A 10min. walk from Magdalen Bridge, or take the bus marked Rose Hill from the bus or train station or Carfax Tower. Sparkling, modern rooms. Singles £35-40; doubles £60-75. MC/V. ❹

Newton House, 82-84 Abingdon Rd. (☎240 561), ½ mi. from town. Take any Abingdon bus across Folly Bridge. Affable staff and beautiful furnishings. Recently renovated; all rooms have TV and phone. Singles £38, ensuite £48; twins and doubles £52, ensuite £64. AmEx/MC/V. ❹

Old Mitre Rooms, 4b Turl St. (☎279 821), between Mahogany hair salon and Past Times Stationery. Look for the blue door. Especially packed during weekends, so book ahead. Open July-Sept. Singles £30; twins £56; triples £72. MC/V. ❸

Falcon Private Hotel, 88-90 Abingdon Rd. (☎511 122). A great place to nest while exploring Oxford. All rooms ensuite, impressive conveniences—TV, phone, hair dryer, alarm clock, and guest lounge. Singles from £42; doubles and twins from £76; triples from £90. Occasional winter price reductions. AmEx/MC/V. ❹

Camping: Oxford Camping and Caravanning, 426 Abingdon Rd. (☎244 088), behind Touchwoods camping store. Toilet and laundry facilities. £4.10-5.80 per person. Electricity £2.30. MC/V. ❶

◘ FOOD

A bevy of budget options seduce tourists and students fed up with college food. **Gloucester Green Market,** behind the bus station, abounds with tasty treats. (Open W 8am-3:30pm.) The **Covered Market,** between Market St. and Carfax, has produce and deli goods. (Open M-Sa 8am-5pm.) Get **groceries** at Sainsbury's, in the Westgate Shopping Center. (Open M-Sa 7am-8pm, Su 11am-5pm.) Across Magdalen Bridge, cheap restaurants along the first four blocks of **Cowley Road** serve Chinese, Lebanese, Indian, and Polish food, as well as fish and chips. Try a sandwich from the **kebab vans,** usually found on Broad St., High St., Queen St., and St. Aldate's.

Kazbar, 25-27 Cowley Rd. (☎202 920). Mediterranean tapas bar just outside of town. Posh atmosphere, with Spanish-style decor and mood lighting. Tasty tapas (£2.20-4.75) like *patatas con chorizo.* Open daily noon-11pm. AmEx/MC/V. ❶

Pierre Victoire Bistrot, 9 Little Clarendon St. (☎316 616). French cuisine in a cozy country-style spot. Lunch £5-7; dinner £9-14. Pre-theater menu of 2 courses and coffee £9.90 M-Th and Su 7-9pm. 3 courses, wine, and coffee £17.50 M-Th and Su. Open M-Sa noon-2:30pm and 7-11pm, Su noon-3:30pm and 6-10pm. MC/V. ❸

The Nosebag, 6-8 St. Michael's St. (☎721 033). Cafeteria-style service in a 15th-century stone building. Eclectic menu includes great vegan and vegetarian options and tasty homemade soups for under £8. Indulge in a scrumptious dessert such as walnut brownies or double fudge cake (£1.35-2.75). Open M-Th 9:30am-10pm, F-Sa 9:30am-10:30pm, Su 9:30am-9pm. AmEx/MC/V. ❷

TO BLENHEIM PALACE, WOODSTOCK (8 mi.), STRATFORD-UPON-AVON (60 mi.)., A34 AND A44

Oxford

▲ ACCOMMODATIONS
Falcon Private Hotel, 27
Heather House, 23
Newton House, 26
Old Mitre Rooms, 17
Oxford Backpackers Hostel, 11
Oxford Camping & Caravanning, 28
YHA Oxford, 10

🍴 FOOD
Aquavitae, 25
Chiang Mai, 18
G&D's Cafe, 4
Kazbar, 21
Makan La, 9
The Nosebag, 8
Pierre Victoire Bistrot, 3
Queen's Lane Coffee House, 20

🍺 PUBS
The Bear, 19
Castle Tavern, 16
The Eagle and Child, 5
The Head of the River, 24
The Jolly Farmers, 15
The King's Arms, 6
Turf's Tavern, 7

★ CLUBS
The Bridge, 12
Duke of Cambridge, 2
Freud, 1
KISS, 14
Thirst, 13
The Zodiac, 22

Oxford University Press

Beaumont Buildings

Ashmolean Museum

Martyr's Memorial

Oxford Playhouse

Oxford Story

Gloucester Green

JobCentre

STA Travel

Apollo Theatre

Oxford Union

Oxford Canal

Castle Mill Stream

Chain Alley

Remains of Oxford Castle

Quaking Bridge

Painted Room

Carfax Tower

Town Hall

Marks & Spencer

Modern Art Oxford

Sainsbury's

Westgate Shopping Centre

Pembroke St.

Brewer St.

Rose Pl.

Ice Rink

River Thames

Bulstake Stream

Friars Wharf

HEART OF ENGLAND

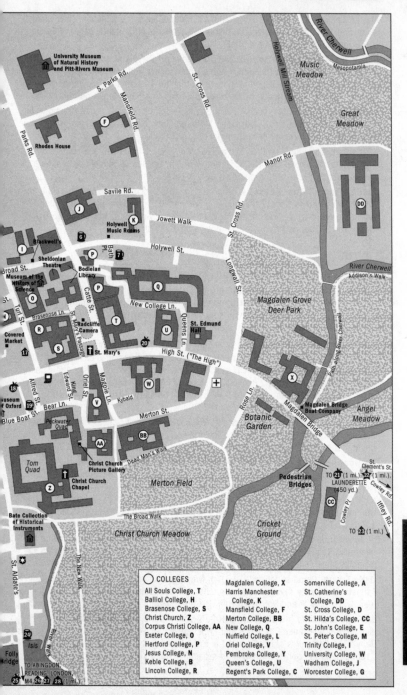

University Museum of Natural History and Pitt-Rivers Museum

S. Parks Rd.

St. Cross Rd.

River Cherwell

Mesopotamia

Music Meadow

Great Meadow

Mansfield Rd.

Parks Rd.

Rhodes House

Manor Rd.

St. Cross Rd.

Holywell Mill Stream

F

Savile Rd.

J

K

Holywell Music Rooms

Jowett Walk

DD

Blackwell's

6

Bath Pl.

I

Sheldonian Theatre

P

7

Holywell St.

River Cherwell

Addison's Walk

Broad St.

Museum of the History of Science

Bodleian Library

P

P

New College Ln.

Q

Longwall St.

Magdalen Grove Deer Park

Catte St.

St. Mary's Passage

O

Turl St.

Brasenose Ln.

R

Radcliffe Camera

T

St. Edmund Hall

St. Cross Rd.

Queens Ln.

U

20

St. Mary's

High St. ("The High")

Covered Market

17

S

Path along River Cherwell

Alfred St.

King Edward St.

Oriel St.

Magpie Ln.

W

Magdalen Bridge Boat Company

Museum of Oxford

18

19

Kybald

Bear Ln.

V

Merton St.

Rose Ln.

Magdalen Bridge

X

Angel Meadow

Blue Boar St.

Packwater Quad

AA

BB

Dead Man's Walk

Botanic Garden

Tom Quad

Christ Church Picture Gallery

T

Christ Church Chapel

Z

Merton Field

Pedestrian Bridges

St. Clement's St.

TO **21** (1 mi.), **22** (1 mi.), LAUNDERETTE (450 yd.)

Cowley Rd.

CC

Cowley Pl.

Iffley Rd.

Bate Collection of Historical Instruments

The Broad Walk

Cricket Ground

TO **23** (1 mi.)

St. Aldate's

The New Walk

Christ Church Meadow

River Thames

Isis

24

Folly Bridge

TO ABINGDON, READING, LONDON, M4, 26, 27, 28 (1 mi.)

25

○ COLLEGES

All Souls College, **T**	Magdalen College, **X**	Somerville College, **A**
Balliol College, **H**	Harris Manchester	St. Catherine's
Brasenose College, **S**	College, **K**	College, **DD**
Christ Church, **Z**	Mansfield College, **F**	St. Cross College, **D**
Corpus Christi College, **AA**	Merton College, **BB**	St. Hilda's College, **CC**
Exeter College, **O**	New College, **Q**	St. John's College, **E**
Hertford College, **P**	Nuffield College, **L**	St. Peter's College, **M**
Jesus College, **N**	Oriel College, **V**	Trinity College, **I**
Keble College, **B**	Pembroke College, **Y**	University College, **W**
Lincoln College, **R**	Queen's College, **U**	Wadham College, **J**
	Regent's Park College, **C**	Worcester College, **G**

Makan La, 6-8 St. Michael's St. (☎203 222), underneath The Nosebag, serves Malaysian and European food. Noodle dishes £5. Open M-Th 9:30am-10pm, F-Sa 9am-10:30pm, Su 9:30am-9:30pm. AmEx/MC/V. ❶

Chiang Mai, 130a High St. (☎202 233), tucked in an alley; look for the small blue sign. Thai menu served in a 14th-century home. Try the curry with venison (£8.50). Appetizers £5-7. Entrees £7-10. Open M-Th noon-2pm and 6-10:15pm, F-Sa noon-2pm and 6-10:30pm, Su noon-2pm and 6-10pm. Reservations recommended. AmEx/MC/V. ❷

Aquavitae, 1 Folly Bridge (☎247 775). Super-sleek Italian eatery with fantastic waterside seating. Entrees £9-17.50. Open M-F noon-3pm, Sa-Su noon-11pm. Hours may vary, call ahead. Reservations recommended. MC/V. ❹

G&D's Cafe, 55 Little Clarendon St. (☎516 652). Superb ice cream and sorbet (£1.75-4), tasty pizza bagels (£3.45-4.15), and a bright, boisterous student atmosphere. A favorite in the Jericho area. Open daily 8am-midnight. Cash only. ❶

Queen's Lane Coffee House, 40 High St. (☎240 082). Established in 1654, the Queen's Lane is the oldest coffeehouse in Europe. Mingle with university students while sampling full English breakfasts (£4.50-6) or freshly-made sandwiches (£3-4.75). Open daily 7:30am-8pm, summer until 9:30pm. Cash only. ❶

PUBS

In Oxford, pubs far outnumber colleges; some even consider them the city's prime attraction. Most open by noon, begin to fill around 5pm, and close at 11pm (10:30pm on Sundays). Be ready to pub crawl—many pubs are so small that a single band of celebrating students will squeeze out other patrons, while just around the corner others will have several spacious rooms.

Turf's Tavern, 4 Bath Pl. (☎243 235), hidden off Holywell St. Arguably the most popular student bar in Oxford (they call it "the Turf"), this 13th-century pub is tucked in an alley off an alley, against ruins of the city wall. Bob Hawke, former prime minister of Australia, downed a yard of ale (over 2½ pints) in the record time of 11 seconds here while studying at the university. Choose from 11 ales. Open M-Sa 11am-11pm, Su noon-10:30pm. Hot food served in back room daily noon-7:30pm.

The King's Arms, 40 Holywell St. (☎242 369). Oxford's unofficial student union. Merry masses head to the back rooms and local ladies and gents sip tea and coffee in the bright, non-smoking tea room. Open M-Sa 10:30am-11pm, Su 10:30am-10:30pm.

The Bear, 6 Alfred St. (☎728 164). Famous patrons and Oxford students once exchanged their neckties for a free pint at this oldest and tiniest of Oxford's many pubs. Now over 4500 adorn the walls and ceiling of the pub, established in 1242. Unfortunately, the deal no longer applies. During the day, the clients are older than the neckwear, and the young sit out back with 2-pint pitchers of Pimm's (£9). Open M-Sa noon-11pm, Su noon-10:30pm.

The Jolly Farmers, 20 Paradise St. (☎793 759). One of Oxfordshire's first gay and lesbian pubs. Crowded with students and twentysomethings, especially on weekends; significantly more sedate in summer. Open M-Sa noon-11pm, Su noon-10:30pm.

Castle Tavern, Paradise St. (☎201 510). Now under the same ownership as The Jolly Farmers, the Castle Tavern has a traditional pub atmosphere and is gay- and lesbian-friendly. Open M-W and Su noon-11pm, Th-Sa noon-2am.

The Eagle and Child, 49 St. Giles (☎302 925). A historic pub, this archipelago of paneled alcoves welcomed C.S. Lewis and J.R.R. Tolkien, who referred to it as the "Bird and Baby." *The Chronicles of Narnia* and *The Hobbit* were first read aloud here. Open M-Sa 11am-11pm, Su noon-10:30pm. Food served M-F noon-10pm, Sa-Su noon-9pm.

The Head of the River, Folly Bridge, St. Aldate's (☎ 721 600). This aptly named pub has the best location in Oxford to view the Thames, known locally as the Isis. Watch the rowboats pass while enjoying a pint on the spacious deck, heated when the chill sets in. Open M-Sa 11:30am-11pm, Su noon-10:30pm. Food served daily until 9pm.

◎ SIGHTS

The TIC sells a map (£1.25) and the *Welcome to Oxford* guide (£1), which lists the colleges' visiting hours. Note that those hours can be rescinded without explanation or notice. Some colleges charge admission. Don't bother trying to sneak into Christ Church outside opening hours, even after hiding your backpack and copy of *Let's Go*—bouncers, affectionately known as "bulldogs," in bowler hats and stationed 50 ft. apart, will squint their eyes and kick you out.

CHRIST CHURCH

Just down St. Aldate's from Carfax. ☎ 286 573; www.chch.ox.ac.uk. Open M-Sa 9am-5:30pm, Su 1-5:30pm; last admission 4pm. Chapel services M-F 6pm; Su 8, 10, 11:15am, 6pm. £4, concessions £3, families £9.

"The House" has Oxford's grandest quad and its most socially distinguished students, counting 13 past Prime Ministers among its alumni. Charles I made Christ Church his capital for three and a half years during the Civil Wars and escaped dressed as a servant when the city was besieged. Lewis Carroll first met Alice, the dean's daughter, here. Today, the dining hall and Tom Quad serve as shooting locations for *Harry Potter* films. In June, be respectful of irritable undergrads prepping for exams as you navigate the narrow strip open to tourists.

CHRIST CHURCH CHAPEL. The only church in England to serve as both a cathedral and college chapel, it was originally founded in AD 730 by Oxford's patron saint, St. Frideswide, who built a nunnery here in honor of two miracles: the blinding of her troublesome suitor and his subsequent recovery. A stained-glass window (c. 1320) depicts St. Thomas à Becket kneeling moments before his gory death in Canterbury Cathedral. Look for the strange depiction of a floating toilet in the bottom right of a window showing St. Frideswide's death and the White Rabbit frets in the windows in the hall.

TOM QUAD. The site of undergraduate lily-pond dunking, Tom Quad adjoins the chapel grounds. The quad takes its name from Great Tom, the seven-ton bell that has rung 101 (the original number of students) times at 9:05pm (the original undergraduate curfew) every evening since 1682. (The bell rings at 9:05 because technically Oxford should be 5min. past Greenwich Mean Time. Christ Church keeps this time within its gates.) Nearby, the fan-vaulted college hall displays portraits of some of Christ Church's famous alums—Sir Philip Sidney, William Penn, John Ruskin, John Locke, and a bored-looking W.H. Auden in a corner by the kitchen.

OTHER SIGHTS. Through an archway (to your left as you face the cathedral) lie **Peckwater Quad** and the most elegant Palladian building in Oxford. Look here for faded rowing standings chalked on the walls and for Christ Church's library, which is closed to visitors. Spreading east and south from the main entrance, **Christ Church Meadow** compensates for Oxford's lack of "backs" (the riverside gardens in Cambridge). Housed in the Canterbury Quad, the **Christ Church Picture Gallery** has a noteworthy collection of works by Tintoretto, Vermeer, and da Vinci, among others. *(Entrances on Oriel Sq. and at Canterbury Gate; visitors to the gallery should enter through Canterbury Gate. ☎ 276 172. Open Apr.-Sept. M-Sa 10:30am-1pm and 2-5:30pm, Su 2-5pm; Oct.-Mar. closes at 4:30pm. £2, concessions £1.)*

OTHER COLLEGES

MERTON COLLEGE. Merton's library houses the first printed Welsh Bible. Tolkien lectured here, inventing the Elven language in his spare time. The college's 14th-century **Mob Quad** is Oxford's oldest and least impressive, but nearby **St. Alban's Quad** has some of the university's best gargoyles. Japanese Crown Prince Narahito lived here during his university days. *(Merton St. ☎ 276 310; www.merton.ox.ac.uk. Open M-F 2-4pm, Sa-Su 10am-4pm. Free.)*

UNIVERSITY COLLEGE. Built in 1249, this soot-blackened college vies with Merton for the title of oldest, claiming Alfred the Great as its founder. Percy Bysshe Shelley was expelled for writing the pamphlet *The Necessity of Atheism*, but was later immortalized in a prominent monument, on the right as you enter. Bill Clinton spent his Rhodes days here; his rooms at 46 Leckford Rd. are a tour guide's endless source of smoked-but-didn't-inhale jokes. *(High St. ☎ 276 602; www.univ.ox.ac.uk. Open to tours only.)*

ORIEL COLLEGE. Formally known as the "House of the Blessed Mary the Virgin in Oxford," Oriel is wedged between High St. and Merton St. and was once the turf of Sir Walter Raleigh. *(☎ 276 555; www.oriel.ox.ac.uk. Open to tours only, daily 1-4pm. Free.)*

CORPUS CHRISTI COLLEGE. The smallest of Oxford's colleges, Corpus Christi surrounds a sundialed quad. The garden wall reveals a gate built for visits between Charles I and his queen, who were residents at adjacent Christ Church and Merton colleges during the Civil Wars. *(☎ 276 700; www.ccc.ox.ac.uk. Open 2-5pm.)*

ALL SOULS COLLEGE. Only the best are admitted to this prestigious graduate college. Candidates who survive the admission exams are invited to dinner, where the dons confirm that they are "well-born, well-bred, and only moderately learned." All Souls is also reported to have the most heavenly wine cellar in the city. The Great Quad, with its fastidiously kept lawn and two spare spires, may be Oxford's most serene, as hardly a living soul passes over. *(Corner of High St. and Catte St. ☎ 279 379; www.all-souls.ox.ac.uk. Open Sept.-July M-F 2-4pm. Free.)*

THE QUEEN'S COLLEGE. Though the college dates back to 1341, Queen's was rebuilt by Wren and Hawksmoor in the 17th and 18th centuries in the distinctive Queen Anne style. A trumpet call summons students to dinner, where a boar's head graces the table at Christmas. That tradition supposedly commemorates a student who, attacked by a boar on the outskirts of Oxford, choked the animal to death with a volume of Aristotle. Alumni include Edmund Halley, Jeremy Bentham, and Rowan Atkinson, the celebrated Mr. Bean. *(High St. ☎ 279 120; www.queens.ox.ac.uk. Open to blue badge tours only.)*

MAGDALEN COLLEGE. With extensive grounds and flower-laced quads, Magdalen (MAUD-lin) is considered Oxford's handsomest college. The college boasts a deer park flanked by the river Cherwell and Addison's Walk, a circular path that touches the river's opposite bank. Though Dudley Moore attended, the college's (world's?) most decadent wit is alumnus Oscar Wilde. *(On High St., near the Cherwell. ☎ 276 000; www.magd.ox.ac.uk. Open daily Oct.-Mar. 1pm to dusk; Apr.-June 1-6pm; July-Sept. noon-6pm. £3, concessions £2.)*

TRINITY COLLEGE. Founded in 1555, Trinity has a splendid baroque chapel with a limewood altarpiece, cedar latticework, and cherubim-spotted pediments. The college's series of eccentric presidents includes Ralph Kettell, who would come to dinner with a pair of scissors and chop anyone's hair that he deemed too long. *(Broad St. ☎ 279 900; www.trinity.ox.ac.uk. Open M-F 10am-noon and 2-4pm, Sa-Su 2-4pm; during vacations also Sa-Su 10am-noon. £1, concessions 50p.)*

BALLIOL COLLEGE. Students at Balliol preserve some semblance of tradition by hurling abuse over the wall at their conservative Trinity College rivals. Matthew Arnold, Gerard Manley Hopkins, Aldous Huxley, and Adam Smith were all sons of Balliol's mismatched spires. The interior gates of the college bear lingering scorch marks from the executions of 16th-century Protestant martyrs, and a mulberry tree planted by Elizabeth I still shades slumbering students. *(Broad St. ☎277 777; www.balliol.ox.ac.uk. Open daily 2-5pm. £1, students and children free.)*

NEW COLLEGE. This is the self-proclaimed first *real* college of Oxford; it was here, in 1379, that William of Wykeham dreamed up an institution that would offer a comprehensive undergraduate education under one roof. The bell tower has gargoyles of the Seven Deadly Sins on one side and the Seven Virtues on the other—all equally grotesque. New College claims Kate Beckinsale and Hugh Grant as two attractive alums. *(New College Ln. Use the Holywell St. gate. ☎279 555; www.new.ox.ac.uk. Open daily Easter to mid-Oct. 11am-5pm; Nov. to Easter 2-4pm. £2, students and children £1.)*

SOMERVILLE COLLEGE. With alumnae including Indira Gandhi and Margaret Thatcher, Somerville is Oxford's most famous once-women's college. Women were not actually granted degrees until 1920—Cambridge held out until 1948. Today, all of Oxford's colleges are co-ed except St. Hilda's, which remains women-only. *(Woodstock Rd. From Carfax, head down Cornmarket St., which becomes Magdalen St., St. Giles, and finally Woodstock Rd. ☎270 600; www.some.ox.ac.uk. Open daily 9am-5pm. Free.)*

EXETER COLLEGE. Exeter was established by the bishop of Exeter in 1314; he set a 14-year limit on schooling for the students, whom he wanted to become priests but not bishops. Richard Burton matriculated here and a bust of esteemed alum J.R.R. Tolkien overlooks the back of the chapel. *(Turl St. ☎279 600; www.exeter.ox.ac.uk. Open daily 2-5pm. Free.)*

OTHER SIGHTS

◼ASHMOLEAN MUSEUM. The grand Ashmolean—Britain's finest collection of arts and antiquities outside London and Britain's oldest public museum—opened in 1683. It showcases sketches by Michelangelo and Raphael, the gold coin of Constantine, and the Alfred Jewel, as well as works by da Vinci, Monet, Manet, van Gogh, Rodin, and Matisse. Check out the stunning Greek pottery, Roman jewelry, and Egyptian artifacts. *(Beaumont St. ☎278 000. Tours £2. Open Tu-Sa 10am-5pm, Su noon-5pm; in summer open Th until 7pm. Free.)*

THE BIG SPLURGE

PINTS AND PUNTS

Venice has richly dressed gondoliers; Oxford has tipsy punters. Navigating the River Thames's tributaries, which snake through Oxford's grounds, is a traditional pasttime at the university. Today's students combine punting with another local favorite (beer) to create a sport marked more by carousing and leisure than exertion.

Before venturing out, punters receive a tall pole, a small oar, and an advisory against falling into the river (though many an undergrad has cheerfully ignored the warning and taken a plunge).

You can take part in this Oxford tradition and try punting (and relaxing) for yourself at **Magdalen Bridge Boat Company,** just under Magdalen Bridge. For a leisurely ride down the river, you can hire a chauffeured punt (£20 per 30min.; fee includes a complimentary bottle of wine). The more athletic, adventurous, or sauced can try for themselves. (M-F £10 per hr., Sa-Su £12 per hr. £30 deposit. 5 person max. Bring your own wine.) The punts head south on the River Cherwell or north along the Isis. Be sure to look aside should you pass Parson's Pleasure, a field by the river used for sunbathing in the buff.

Magdalen Bridge. ☎202 643. Open daily Mar.-Oct. 9:30am-9pm. Cash only.

BODLEIAN LIBRARY. Oxford's principal reading and research library has over five million books and 50,000 manuscripts. It receives a copy of every book printed in Great Britain. Sir Thomas Bodley endowed the library's first wing in 1602—the institution has since grown to fill the immense **Old Library** complex, the **Radcliffe Camera** next door, and two newer buildings on Broad St. Admission to the reading rooms is by ticket only. The Admissions Office will issue you a two-day pass (£3) if you are able to prove your research requires the use of the library's books and present a letter of recommendation and ID. No one has ever been permitted to take out a book, not even Cromwell. Well, especially not Cromwell. *(Broad St. ☎ 277 000. Library open M-F 9am-10pm, Sa 9am-1pm; summer M-F 9am-7pm, Sa 9am-1pm. Tours leave from the Divinity School in the main quadrangle; in summer M-Sa 4 per day, in winter 2 per day, in the afternoon. Tours £4, audio guide £2.)*

BLACKWELL'S BOOKSTORE. With six miles of bookshelves, Blackwell's is by far the largest bookshop in Oxford and is a famed national favorite. *(53 Broad St. ☎ 792 792. Open M and W-Sa 9am-6pm, Tu 9:30am-6pm, Su 11am-5pm.)*

SHELDONIAN THEATRE. This Roman-style auditorium was designed by a teenage Christopher Wren. Graduation ceremonies, conducted in Latin, take place in the Sheldonian, as do everything from student recitals to world-class opera performances. *The Red Violin* and *Quills*, as well as numerous other movies, were filmed here. Climb up to the cupola for an excellent view of Oxford's scattered quads. The ivy-crowned stone heads on the fence behind the Sheldonian do not represent emperors; they are a 20th-century study of beards. *(Broad St. ☎ 277 299. Open M-Sa 10am-12:30pm and 2-4:30pm; in winter until 3:30pm. £1.50, under 15 £1. Purchase tickets for shows from Oxford Playhouse, ☎ 305 305. Box office open M-Tu and Th-Sa 9:30am-6:30pm or until 30min. before last showing, W 10am-6:30pm. Shows £15.)*

CARFAX TOWER. The tower marks the center of the original city. A hike up its 99 (very narrow) spiral stairs affords a superb overlook from the only present-day remnant of medieval St. Martin's Church. "Carfax" originally gets its name from the Norman French *quatre vois* ("four ways"), which refers to the intersection of the city's North, South, East, and West gates. Then and now, Carfax has served as the landmark of the city centre and as a meeting place for locals and travelers alike. *(Corner of Queen St. and Cornmarket St. ☎ 792 653. Open daily Apr.-Oct. 10am-5pm; Oct.-March 10am-3:30pm, weather permitting. £1.60, under 16 80p.)*

THE BOTANIC GARDEN. Green and growing things have flourished for three centuries in the oldest botanic garden in the British Isles. The path connecting the garden to Christ Church Meadow provides a view of the Thames and the cricket grounds on the opposite bank. *(From Carfax, head down High St.; the Garden is at the intersection of High St. and Rose Ln. ☎ 286 690. Open daily May-Sept. 9am-6pm, last admission 5:15pm; Mar.-Apr. and Oct. 9am-5pm, last admission 4:15pm; Nov.-Feb. 9am-4:30pm, last admission 4:15pm. Glass houses open daily 10am-4pm. £2.50, concessions £2, children free.)*

THE MUSEUM OF OXFORD. From hands-on exhibits to a murderer's skeleton, the museum provides an in-depth look at Oxford's 800-year history. *(St. Aldate's. Enter at corner of St. Aldate's and Blue Boar St. ☎ 252 761. Open Tu-F 10am-4:30pm, Sa 10am-5pm, Su noon-4pm. Last admission 30 min. before close. £2, concessions £1.50, children 50p, under 5 free, families £4.)*

BEST OF THE REST. At **The Oxford Story**, 6 Broad St., a well-advertised, painfully slow-moving ride hauls visitors through dioramas that chronicle Oxford's past. *(☎ 728 822. Open July-Aug. daily 9:30am-5pm; Sept.-June M-Sa 10am-4:30pm, Su 11am-4:30pm. 45min. ride. £7, students £6, seniors £5.75, children £5.25, families £22.50.)* Behind the **University Museum of Natural History**, Parks Rd., the **Pitt-Rivers Museum** has an eclectic archaeological and anthropological collection, including shrunken heads, rare butterflies, and bong-like artifacts. *(Natural History Museum ☎272 950. Open daily noon-5pm. Free. Pitt-Rivers Museum ☎270 927; www.prm.ox.ac.uk. Open M-Sa noon-4:30pm, Su 2-4:30pm. Free.)* The **Museum of the History of Science,** Broad St., features clocks, astrolabes, and Einstein's blackboard. *(☎277 280. Open Tu-Sa noon-4pm, Su 2-5pm. Free. Tours £1.50.)* The **Modern Art Oxford,** 30 Pembroke St., hosts international shows. *(☎722 733. Tu-Sa 10am-5pm. Su noon-5pm. Free.)* The **Bate Collection of Musical Instruments,** St. Aldate's St., rests in the Faculty of Music. *(Before Folly Bridge. ☎276 139. Open M-F 2-5pm, also Sa 10am-noon during term time. Free.)*

█ CLUBS

After happy hour at the pubs, head up **Walton Street** or down **Cowley Road** for late-night clubs.

Freud, 119 Walton St. (☎311 171). Formerly St. Paul's Church. Impressive, bizarre decoration: part cathedral, part circus, part modern art installation gone wrong. Cafe by day, collegiate cocktail bar by night. Open M and Su 11am-midnight, Tu 11am-1am, W 11am-1:30am, Th-Sa 11am-2am.

The Bridge, 6-9 Hythe Bridge St. (☎342 526; www.bridgeoxford.co.uk). Dance to R&B, hip-hop, dance, and pop on 2 floors. Erratically frequented by big student crowds. Cover £3-7. Open M-Sa 9pm-2am, closed M in summer.

KISS, 36-39 Park End St. (☎200 555; www.kissbar.co.uk). Intimate bar conveniently located near several clubs for some pre-dancing cocktails. 2-for-1 drink specials during daily happy hour (7-9:30pm). No cover. Open M-Sa 7pm-2am.

Thirst, 7-8 Park End St. (☎242 044). Lounge bar with a DJ and backdoor garden. Across from KISS, Thirst serves up cheap cocktails (£1.50) until 1am M-W. Budget drinks also during "happy hour" and "stupid hour." Open M-Sa 6:30pm-2am. Cover £3-10.

Duke of Cambridge, 5-6 Little Clarendon St. (☎558 173). Oxford's choice cocktail lounge, with sophisticated decor and half-price cocktails during happy hour (M-Th and Su 5-8:30pm, F-Sa 5-7:30pm). Cocktails £5.50-6.50; the Thai cosmo is excellent. Smart casual dress. Open M-Sa 5-11pm, Su 5-10:30pm.

The Zodiac, 190 Cowley Rd. (☎420 042; www.the-zodiac.co.uk). Big dance floor with theme nights and the city's best live gigs. Radiohead filmed the video for "Creep" here. Cover £5-15. Club open W-Th 10:30pm-2am, F 10:30pm-4am, Sa 10:30pm-3am. Box office open Sept.-June M-Sa 1-6pm; July-Aug. Th-Sa 1-6pm. Phone booking £1.

Bar Risa, 3-5 Hythe Bridge St. (☎722 437). Prepare for long lines when the pubs close at 11pm. Enjoy 2 dance floors, frequent comedy nights, and cozy lounge booths right off the dance floor. Gay night M 11pm-2am. Open daily noon-2am.

█ ENTERTAINMENT

Check *This Month in Oxford*, free at the TIC, or *Daily Information*, posted all over town and online (www.dailyinfo.co.uk), for event listings.

MUSIC. Centuries of tradition give Oxford a quality music scene. Colleges offer concerts and Evensong services; **New College** has an excellent boys' choir. Performances at the **Holywell Music Rooms,** on Holywell St., are worth checking out; **Oxford Coffee Concerts** feature famous musicians and ensembles every Sunday. (☎305 305. Tickets £8.) The **City of Oxford Orchestra,** a professional symphony orchestra, plays a subscription series at the Sheldonian and in college chapels during the summer. (☎744 457. Tickets £14-25.) The **New Theatre,** George St., features performances from lounge-lizard jazz to musicals to the Welsh National Opera. (☎320 760. Tickets £10-50. Student, senior, and child discounts available.) As for modern music, The Beatles have Liverpool and Radiohead have Oxford; any number of pubs and music stores claim band lore. And with its proximity to Manchester and London and large student population, Oxford is on an excellent circuit for smaller British bands at clubs like the Zodiac and large venues like South Park.

THEATER. The **Oxford Playhouse,** 11-12 Beaumont St., hosts amateur and professional plays as well as music and dance performances. The playhouse also sells discounted tickets for venues city-wide. (☎305 305; www.oxfordplayhouse.com, www.ticketsoxford.com. Box office open M-Tu and Th-F 9:30am-6:30pm, W 10am-6:30pm.) The university itself offers marvelous entertainment; college theater groups often stage productions in gardens or cloisters.

FESTIVALS. The university celebrates **Eights Week** at the end of May, when the colleges enter crews in bumping races and beautiful people sip Pimm's on the banks. In early September, **St. Giles Fair** invades one of Oxford's main streets with an old-fashioned English fun fair. Daybreak on **May Day** (May 1) cues one of Oxford's most celebratory moments: the Magdalen College Choir sings madrigals from the top of the tower beginning at 6am, and the town indulges in Morris dancing, beating the bounds, and other age-old rituals of merry men—pubs open at 7am.

▶ DAYTRIP FROM OXFORD

BLENHEIM PALACE

In the town of Woodstock, 8 mi. north of Oxford. Stagecoach (☎772 250) bus #20 runs to Blenheim Palace from Gloucester Green bus station (30-40min., every hr. 8am-5pm, round-trip £4). ☎01993 811 091. House open daily mid-Feb. to mid-Dec. 10:30am-5:30pm. Last admission 4:45pm. Grounds open daily 9am-9pm. £13, concessions £10.50, children £7.50, families £35. Free tours every 5-10min.

The largest private home in England (and one of the loveliest), Blenheim Palace (BLEN-em) was built in honor of the Duke of Marlborough's victory over Louis XIV at the 1704 Battle of Blenheim. The 11th Duke of Marlborough now calls the palace home. His rent is a flag from the estate, payable each year to the Crown—not a bad deal for 187 furnished rooms. High archways and marble floors accentuate the artwork inside, including wall-size tapestries of 17th- and 18th-century battle scenes. Winston Churchill, a member of the Marlborough family, spent his early years here before being shipped off to boarding school; he returned to propose to his wife, and now rests in a nearby churchyard. The grounds consist of 2100 glorious acres, all designed by landscaper "Capability" Brown.

STRATFORD-UPON-AVON ☎01789

Shakespeare was born here. This fluke of fate has made Stratford-upon-Avon a major stop on the tourist superhighway. Proprietors tout the dozen-odd properties linked, however remotely, to the Bard and his extended family; shops and restaurants devotedly stencil his prose and poetry on their windows and walls. But, behind the sound and fury of rumbling tour buses and chaotic swarms of daytrippers there lies a town worthwhile for the beauty of the Avon and for the riveting performances in the Royal Shakespeare Theatre.

☐ HENCE, AWAY!

Trains: Station Rd., off Alcester Rd. Office open M-Sa 6:20am-8:20pm, Su 9:45am-6:30pm. Trains (☎08457 484 950) from: **Birmingham** (50min., every hr., £5.20); **London Paddington** (2¼hr., every 2hr., £36.50); **Warwick** (25min., 9 per day, £3.70).

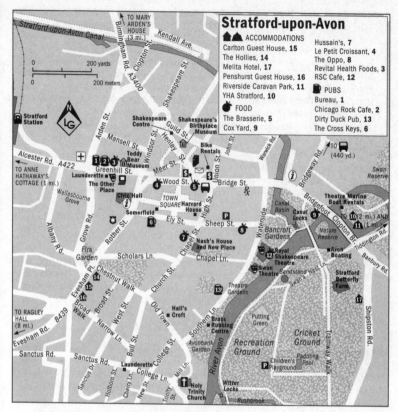

Stratford-upon-Avon

▲▲▲ ACCOMMODATIONS
Carlton Guest House, **15**
The Hollies, **14**
Melita Hotel, **17**
Penshurst Guest House, **16**
Riverside Caravan Park, **11**
YHA Stratford, **10**

🍎 FOOD
The Brasserie, **5**
Cox Yard, **9**

Hussain's, **7**
Le Petit Croissant, **4**
The Oppo, **8**
Revital Health Foods, **3**
RSC Cafe, **12**

🍺 PUBS
Bureau, **1**
Chicago Rock Cafe, **2**
Dirty Duck Pub, **13**
The Cross Keys, **6**

Buses: Riverside Coach Park, off Bridgeway Rd. near the Leisure Centre. National Express (☎08705 808 080) from **London** (3hr., 3 per day, £14). Tickets at the TIC.

Public Transportation: Local Stratford Blue **bus** X20 stops on Wood St. and Bridge St. from **Birmingham** (1¼hr.; M-Sa every hr., Su every 1½hr.; £4). Stagecoach #1618 services **Coventry** (2hr., every hr., £3.50) via **Warwick** (20-40min., every hr., £3).

Taxis: Taxi Line (☎266 100). **Shakespeare Tours** (☎204 083).

Bike Rental: Clarkes, Guild St. (☎205 057). Mountain bikes £10 per day, £5 per half-day. Open Tu-F 9am-5pm, Sa 10am-4pm.

Boat Rental: Avon Boating, Swan's Nest Ln. (☎01789 267 073), by Clopton Bridge. Rents rowboats (£2.50 per hr., children £1.50) and motorboats (£10 per 30min., £16 per hr.). Open daily Apr.-Oct. 9am-dusk, weather permitting.

🛈 WHO IS'T THAT CAN INFORM ME?

Tourist Information Centre: Bridgefoot (☎0870 160 7930). Provides maps, guidebooks, tickets, and accommodations lists. Books rooms for a £3 charge and a 10% deposit. Open Apr.-Sept. M-Sa 9am-5:30pm, Su 10:30am-4:30pm; Oct.-Mar. M-Sa 9am-5pm. Another Information Centre in the Civic Hall, 14 Rother St. (☎299 866). Open daily 9am-5:30pm.

Tours: 2hr. **walking tours** led by Shakespearean actors start at the Royal Shakespeare Theatre (☎403 405). Apr.-June Th and Sa 10:30am; July-Sept. Th and Sa-Su 10:30am; Oct.-Mar. Sa 10:30am. £6, concessions £5. **Guide Friday City Sightseeing,** Civic Hall, 14 Rother St. (☎299 866) heads to Bard-related houses every 15-20min. from Civic Hall. £8, concessions £6, children £3.50. Offers bus ticket and admission to any of the Shakespeare Houses (£15/12/7) and tours to the **Cotswolds** (£17.50/15/8) and **Warwick Castle** (£19.50/14.50/11; includes castle admission). Office open daily 9am-5:30pm. **Ghost Walks** (☎292 478) depart from the Swan fountain, near the Royal Shakespeare Theatre, Th 7:30pm. £4. Advanced booking required.

Financial Services: Barclays, (☎08457 555 555), at the intersection of Henley and Wood St. Open M-Tu and Th-F 9am-5pm, W 10am-4:30pm. **Thomas Cook,** 37 Wood St. (☎293 582). Open M and W-Sa 9am-5:30pm, Tu 10am-5:30pm.

Launderette: Greenhill, Greenhill St. Across from Revital Health Foods. Bring change. Wash £3-5.60; dry 20p; soap £1. Open daily 8am-8pm, last wash 7pm. Also **Sparklean Launderette,** 74 Bull Street (☎269 075). Open daily 8am-9pm.

Police: Rother St. (☎414 111).

Hospital: Stratford-upon-Avon Hospital, Arden St. (☎205 831), off Alcester Rd.

Pharmacy: Boots, 11 Bridge St. (☎292 173). Open M-Sa 8:30am-5:30pm, Su 10:30am-4:30pm.

Internet Access: Central Library, 12 Henley St. (☎292 209). Free. Open M and W-F 9am-5:30pm, Tu 10am-5:30pm, Sa 9:30am-5pm, Su noon-4pm. **Cyber Junction,** 28 Greenhill St. (☎263 400). £2.50 per 30min., £4 per hr.; concessions £2-3.50. Open M-F 10am-6pm, Sa 10:30am-5:30pm, Su 11am-5pm.

Post Office: 2-3 Henley St. (☎08457 223 344). Bureau de change. Open M-Tu 8:45am-5:30pm, W-F 9am-5:30pm, Sa 9am-6pm. **Post Code:** CV37 6PU.

🏰 TO SLEEP, PERCHANCE TO DREAM

B&Bs abound, but singles can be hard to find. Accommodations in the £20-26 range line **Evesham Place, Evesham Road,** and **Grove Road.** Or try **Shipston Road** across the river, a 15-20min. walk from the station.

■ **Carlton Guest House,** 22 Evesham Pl. (☎293 548). Spacious rooms and spectacular service make this B&B a great value. Attentive staff learns the guests' names. Singles £20-26; doubles and twins £40-52; triples £60-78. Cash only. ❸

YHA Stratford, Wellesbourne Rd., Alveston (☎297 093), 2 mi. from Clopton Bridge. Follow B4086 from town center (35min.), or take bus X18 or X77 (#618 in the evening) from Bridge St. (10min., every 30min., £1.60). Attractive grounds. 200-year-old building. Breakfast included. Internet 7p per min. Dorms £17, under 18 £12.30. MC/V. ❷

Melita Hotel, 37 Shipston Rd. (☎292 432). Upscale B&B with gorgeous garden, retreat-like atmosphere, and excellent breakfasts. Guests relax on the sunny patio with less-than-intimidating guard dog Harvey and his accomplice Daisy. Singles from £52; doubles £79; triples £106; quads £125. AmEx/MC/V. ❹

Penshurst Guest House, 34 Evesham Pl. (☎205 259; www.penshurst.net). Vegetarian breakfasts and evening hot chocolate available. Singles £25; doubles, triples, and quads £22-25 per person. Cash only. ❸

The Hollies, 16 Evesham Pl. (☎266 857). Hosted by a warm proprietor and her daughter. Large rooms, comfortable beds, and a quiet atmosphere make for a relaxing stay. Doubles £40, ensuite £45. MC/V. ❸

Camping: Riverside Caravan Park, Tiddington Rd. (☎292 312), 30min. east of town on the B4086. Sunset views on the Avon, but often crowded. Village pub is a 3-4min. walk. Showers. Open Easter to Oct. Tent sites for up to 4 people £11. AmEx/MC/V. ●

◪ FOOD OF LOVE

Baguette stores and bakeries are scattered throughout the town center; a Somerfield **supermarket** is in Town Square. (☎292 604. Open M-W 8am-7pm, Th-Sa 8am-8pm, Su 10am-4pm.) The first and third Saturdays of every month, the River Avon's banks welcome a **farmer's market.**

The Oppo, 13 Sheep St. (☎269 980). Receives rave reviews from locals. Low 1500s-style ceilings and candles make for a classy-yet-cozy ambience. Try the lasagne (£9), lamb kleftico (£13.50), or grilled goat cheese and tomato salad (£10). Open daily noon-2pm and M-Th 5:30-9:30pm, F-Sa 5-11pm, and Su 6-9:30pm. MC/V. ❸

Hussain's, 6a Chapel St. (☎267 506). Stratford's best Indian menu and a favorite of Ben Kingsley. Tandoori prepared as you like it; fabulous chicken tikka masala. 3-course lunch £6. Entrees from £6.75. 10% discount for takeaway and pre-theater dining. Open daily 12:30-2:30pm and 5pm-midnight. AmEx/MC/V. ❷

Le Petit Croissant, 17 Wood St. (☎292 333). Delicious tarts, baguettes, croissants, pasties, and quiches (from 50p). Sandwiches £1.80-2.50. Open M-Sa 8:30am-6pm. Cash only. ●

The Brasserie, 59-60 Henley St. (☎262 189). Serves food cafeteria-style, so you can choose from freshly prepared hot and cold selections and a myriad of irresistible baked goods. Outdoor seating in good weather. Open daily 7:30am-5:30pm. MC/V. ❷

Revital Health Foods, 8 Greenhill St. (☎292 353). The "Whole Food Takeaway" includes vegan sage and mushroom rolls; potato, cheese, and tomato flan; and "healthy" organic vegan chocolate cake (£1-2). Open M-Sa 9am-5:30pm. MC/V. ●

RCS Cafe Bar, (☎403 415) inside the Royal Shakespeare Theatre, off Waterside St. There is no better view of the Avon. Summer specials for lunch run from £3.50-8.50. Also a perfect spot for a drink during matinee intermission. Full menu served M-Sa noon-10:30pm, Su noon-4pm. ❷

Cox's Yard, Bridgefoot (☎404 600; www.coxsyard.co.uk), next to Bancroft Gardens. A great pub/restaurant/coffee shop directly on the Avon. Watch swans and enjoy the pool table, comfy couches, and pub grub. Wireless Internet available upon request. Late night upstairs bar with "tribute" bands. Coffee shop open M-F 10am-4:30pm, Sa-Su 10am-5:30pm. Pub open in summer M-Tu and Su noon-11pm, W-Th noon-12:30am, F-Sa noon-1:30am. ❷

◪ DRINK DEEP ERE YOU DEPART

Bureau, 1 Arden St. (☎297 641). This pub's silvered staircase leads to a dance area at night. Various promotions, like £1 drinks M and 2-for-1 drink specials Th. Open M and Th noon-1am, Tu-W and Su noon-midnight, F-Sa noon-2am. Cover M and W-Sa £2-5.

Dirty Duck Pub, 66 Waterside (☎297 312). Originally called "The Black Swan," rechristened by alliterative Americans during WWII. River view outside, huge bust of Shakespeare within. Theater crowds abound. Actors themselves make entrances almost nightly, as the pub has a special license to serve RSC members past 11pm. Dame Judy Dench got engaged here and has her own table in the back room. Open M-Sa 11am-11pm, Su noon-10:30pm.

The Cross Keys, Ely St. (☎293 909). Pub on the outside and trendy lounge within, "The Keys" is the perfect locale for a quiet drink beside the comfy fireplace. Happy hour daily 5-8pm; free pool M-Th 5-7pm. Open M-Sa noon-11pm, Su 11am-10:30pm. Food served noon-2:30pm and 6-9pm.

Chicago Rock Cafe, 8 Greenhill St. (☎293 344). Popular with locals. W cover bands, Th karaoke, W-Su DJs. Try the "feast for a fiver" (unsurprisingly, £5) Tu-Su 5-7pm. Open M-Sa noon-1am, Su noon-12:30am.

👁 THE GILDED MONUMENTS

TO BARD...

Stratford's Will-centered sights are best seen before 11am, when the daytrippers arrive, or after 4pm, when the crowds disperse. The five official **Shakespeare properties** are Shakespeare's Birthplace, Mary Arden's House, Nash's House and New Place, Hall's Croft, and Anne Hathaway's Cottage. Opening hours are listed by season: summer (June-Aug.); mid-season (Apr.-May and Sept.-Oct.); and winter (Nov.-Mar.). Diehards should get the **All Five Houses** ticket, which also includes entrance to Harvard House. (☎204 016. £13, concessions £12, children £6.50, families £29.) Those who don't want to visit every shrine can get a **Three In-Town Houses** pass, covering the Birthplace, Hall's Croft, and Nash's House and New Place (£10/8/5/20).

SHAKESPEARE'S BIRTHPLACE. The only in-town sight directly associated with Him includes an exhibit on his father's glove-making, a peaceful garden, and the requisite celebration of his life and works. Join such distinguished pilgrims as Charles Dickens by signing the guestbook. *(Henley St. ☎201 823. Open in winter M-Sa 10am-4pm, Su 10:30am-4pm; mid-season daily 10am-5pm; in summer M-Sa 9am-5pm, Su 9:30am-5pm. £6.70, concessions £5.50, children £2.60, families £15.)*

SHAKESPEARE'S GRAVE. The least-crowded and most-authentic way to pay homage to the Bard is to visit his grave inside the quiet Holy Trinity Church— though groups pack the arched door at peak hours. Rumor has it that Shakespeare was buried 17 ft. underground by request, so that he would sleep undisturbed. A curse on the epitaph (said to be written by the man himself) ensures skeletal safety. The church also harbors the graves of wife Anne and daughter Susanna. *(Trinity St. ☎266 316. Entrance to church free; requested donation to see grave £1, students and children 50p. Open Apr.-Sept. M-Sa 8:30am-6pm, Su noon-5pm; Mar. and Oct. M-Sa 9am-5pm, Su noon-5pm; Nov.-Feb. M-Sa 9am-4pm, Su noon-5pm. Last admission 20min. before close.)*

MARY ARDEN'S HOUSE. This farmhouse in Wilmcote, 3 mi. from Stratford, was only recently determined to be the childhood home of Mary Arden (Shakespeare's mother). Historians thought she grew up in the stately building next door. A history recounts how Mary fell in love with Shakespeare, Sr. *(Connected by footpath to Anne Hathaway's Cottage. ☎293 455. Open in summer M-Sa 9:30am-5pm, Su 10am-5pm; mid-season daily 10am-5pm; winter daily 10am-4pm. £5.70, concessions £5, children £2.50.)*

NASH'S HOUSE AND NEW PLACE. Tourists flock to the home of the first husband of Shakespeare's granddaughter Elizabeth, his last descendant. **Nash's House** holds a fascinating local history collection, but most want to see **New Place**— Shakespeare's retirement home and at the time Stratford's finest house. Today only the foundations remain (now surrounded by a manicured garden) due to a disgruntled 19th-century owner named Gastrell who razed the building, even cutting down Shakespeare's mulberry tree, to spite Bard tourists. Gastrell was run out of town, and to this day Gastrells are not allowed in Stratford. *(Chapel St. ☎292 325. Open in summer M-Sa 9:30am-5pm and Su 10am-5pm; in mid-season daily 11am-5pm; in winter*

M-Sa 11am-4pm. £3.50, concessions £3, children £1.70, families £9.) Down Chapel St. from Nash's House, the sculpted hedges, manicured lawn, and abundant flowers of the **Great Garden of New Place** offer a peaceful respite from the mobbed streets and hold a mulberry tree said to be grown from the one Gastrell chopped down. *(Open M-Sa 9am to dusk, Su 10am-5pm. Free.)*

HALL'S CROFT. Dr. John Hall married Shakespeare's oldest daughter Susanna and garnered fame in his own right as one of the first doctors to keep detailed records of his patients. The Croft features an exhibit on Hall, a grand garden featuring flowers mentioned in Shakespeare's works, and artifacts from Shakespeare's time, when spider's webs were used to guard against scurvy. *(Old Town. ☎ 292 107. Open in summer M-Sa 9:30am-5pm, Su 10am-5pm; in mid-season daily 11am-5pm; in winter daily 11am-4pm. £3.50, concessions £3, children £1.70, families £9.)*

ANNE HATHAWAY'S COTTAGE. The birthplace of Shakespeare's wife, about a mile from Stratford in **Shottery,** is a fairy-tale, thatched-roof cottage. It boasts (very old) original Hathaway furniture and a hedge maze. Entrance entitles you to sit on a bench He may or may not also have sat on. *(Take the hop-on, hop-off Guide Friday tour bus or brave the poorly marked footpaths north. ☎ 292 100. Open in summer M-Sa 9am-5pm, Su 9:30am-5pm; in mid-season M-Sa 9:30am-5pm, Su 10am-5pm; in winter daily 10am-4pm. £5.20, concessions £4, children £2, families £12.)*

...OR NOT TO BARD
Non-Shakespearean sights are available.

STRATFORD BUTTERFLY FARM. Europe's largest collection of butterflies flutters through tropical surroundings. Less appealing creepy-crawlies—like the Goliath Bird-Eating Spider—dwell in glass boxes nearby. *(Off Swan's Nest Ln. at Tramway Walk, across the river from the TIC. ☎ 299 288. Open daily in summer 10am-6pm; in winter 10am-5pm. Last admission 30min. before close. £4.50, concessions £4.25, children £3.75.)*

HARVARD HOUSE. Period pieces and pewter punctuate this Tudor building. Once inhabited by the mother of the founder of that university in Boston, the house is now owned by the Shakespeare Birthright Trust. *(High St. ☎ 204 507. Open July-Sept. W-Su noon-5pm; May-June and Oct. W and Sa-Su noon-5pm. £2.50, children free.)*

RAGLEY HALL. Eight miles from Stratford on Evesham Rd. (A435), Ragley Hall houses the Earl and Countess of Yarmouth. Set in a stunning 400-acre park, the estate has an art collection and a sculpture park. *(Bus #246 (M-Sa 5 per day) runs to Alcester Police Station. Walk 1 mi. to the gates, then ½ mi. up the drive. ☎ 762 090. House open Apr.-Sept. Su, M-Th 10am-6pm; last entry 4:30pm. £7.50, concessions £6.50, children £4.50.)*

TEDDY BEAR MUSEUM. The miniscule, musty museum in the middle of town boasts thousands of stuffed, ceramic, and painted bears, from 12 of the "Diana bears" (left in front of Kensington Palace) to the original Fozzie, a gift from Jim Henson. Despite the extensive advertising for the collection about town and the half dozen town signs pointing you toward the collection, this is a sight you can definitely bear to miss. *(19 Greenhill St. ☎ 293 160. Open daily 9:30am-5:30pm. £3, concessions £2.45, children £2, families £9.50.)*

♫ THE PLAY'S THE THING

THE ROYAL SHAKESPEARE COMPANY
The box office in the foyer of the Royal Shakespeare Theatre handles the ticketing for all theaters. Ticket hotline ☎ 08706 091 110; www.rsc.org.uk. Open M-Sa 9:30am-8pm. Tickets £5-40. Both the RST and the Swan theaters have £5 standing room tickets. Stu-

dents and under 25 receive tickets half-price; call in advance for M-W performances. Standby tickets in summer £15; in winter £12. Disabled travelers should call in advance to advise the box office of their needs; some performances feature sign language interpretation or audio description. RSC ☎403 405. Tours 45min. M-F 2 per day starting from the RSC foyer, Sa-Su 2 per day from the Swan Theatre. Call ahead as times are based on theater schedules. £5, concessions £4.

One of the world's most acclaimed repertories, the Royal Shakespeare Company sells well over one million tickets each year and claims Kenneth Branagh and Ralph Fiennes as recent members. In Stratford, the RSC performs in three connected theaters. The **Royal Shakespeare Theatre** sits on the Avon, across from Chapel Lane. Next door, the RSC took the shell of burnt-out Memorial Theatre and renovated it as the **Swan Theatre.** A smaller and more intimate space than the attached RST, it resembles Shakespeare's Globe and stages plays by other wordsmiths. Down the road lies the company's black box theater, the **Other Place,** which hosts modern shows and invites Abbot and Costello routines. (Which theater? The Other Place. No, what's the name of the theater? The Other Place...) The RSC conducts backstage tours.

❄ OUR RUSTIC REVELRY

A **traditional town market** is held on Rother St. in Market Place on the second and fourth Saturdays of every month. On Sundays from June to August, a **craft market** takes place along the river. (☎267 000. Both open 9am-5pm.) Stratford's biggest festival begins on the weekend nearest April 23, **Shakespeare's birthday.** The modern, well-respected **Shakespeare Birthplace Trust,** Henley St., hosts a **Poetry Festival** every Sunday evening in July and August; past participants include Seamus Heaney, Ted Hughes, and Derek Walcott. (☎292 176. Tickets £7-10.)

WORCESTER   ☎01905

Worcester (WUH-ster) sits between Cheltenham and Birmingham, along the Severn. But Worcester lacks the former city's gentility and the latter's size and bustle. Worcester has certain claims to fame—Worcester Cathedral, gorgeous Royal Worcester Porcelain, and tasty Worcestershire sauce—but those uninspired by dishware may want to make this small city a daytrip.

⬛ TRANSPORTATION. Foregate St. Station, at the edge of the town center on Foregate St., is the city's main train station. (Ticket window open M-Sa 6:10am-7pm, Su 9:10am-4:30pm. Travel center open M-Sa 9:30am-4pm.) **Shrub Hill Station,** just outside of town, serves Cheltenham and has less frequent service to London and Birmingham. (Ticket window open M-Sa 5:10am-9pm, Su 7:10am-9:30pm.) **Trains** (☎08457 484 950) travel to Worcester from: Birmingham (1hr., every hr., £5.30); Cheltenham (30min., every 2hr., £5.40); London Paddington (2½hr., every 1½hr., £27.40). The **bus station** is at Angel Pl., near the Crowngate Shopping Centre. National Express buses (☎08705 808 080) run from Birmingham (1½hr., 1 per day, £3.50); Bristol (5hr., 1 per day, £9.50); London (4hr., 2 per day, £16.50). First (☎359 393) is the regional bus company; its **FirstWorcester City** ticket allows for one day of unlimited travel within Worcester (£2.50). Associated Radio **taxis** (☎763 939) run 24hr. **Bike rental** is available from Peddlers, 46-48 Barbourne Rd. (☎24 238. £8 per day, £30 per week. Deposit £50. Open M-Sa 9:30am-5:30pm.)

⬛⬛ ORIENTATION AND PRACTICAL INFORMATION. The city center is bounded by the train station to the north and the cathedral to the south. The main street runs between the two, switching names from **Barbourne Road** to **The Tything** to **Foregate Street** to **The Foregate** to **The Cross** to **High Street.**

The **Tourist Information Center,** The Guildhall, High St., sells the *Worcester Visitor Guide* (75p) and books beds (10% deposit). From Foregate St. Station, turn left on Foregate St. and walk 15min.; the TIC is on the ground floor of The Guildhall, the Queen Anne-style building on High St. (☎726 311. Open M-Sa 9:30am-5pm.) "Worcester Walks" **tours** leave from the TIC. (☎222 117; www.worcester-walks.co.uk. 1½hr. M-Tu and Th-F 11am, W 11am and 2:30pm. Ghost tours also available.) Other services include: a Barclays **bank,** 54 High St. (☎08457 555 555; open M-F 9am-5pm, Sa 9am-3pm); a bureau de change at Barclays (open M-F 9am-3pm); Severn Laun-Dri **launderette,** 22 Barbourne Rd. (wash £4.20, dry £1, soap 70p; open daily 9am-8pm; last wash 7pm); **police,** Castle St. (☎08457 444 888), off Foregate; a Boots **pharmacy,** 72-74 High St. (☎726 868; open M-F 8:30am-5:30pm, Sa 8:30am-6pm, Su 10am-4pm); **Worcestershire Royal Hospital,** Newtown Rd., Charles Hastings Way (☎763 333; bus #31); **Internet** at the library, in the City Museum (☎765 312; free; open M and F 9:30am-7pm, Tu-Th 9:30am-5:30pm, Sa 9:30am-4pm) and at Coffee Republic, 31 High St. (£1 per 20min., £3 per hr.; open M-F 7:30am-6pm, Sa 8:30am-6pm, Su 9am-6pm); and the **post office,** 8 Foregate St., with a bureau de change (☎08457 223 344; open M-Sa 9am-5:30pm). **Post Code:** WR1 1XX.

▐ ACCOMMODATIONS. B&B prices in Worcester are high, as proprietors cater to businesspeople or to Londoners weekending in the country. Try your luck on **Barbourne Road,** a 15-20min. walk north on Foregate from the city center or a short ride on bus #144 or 303. The nearest **YHA hostel** is 7 mi. away in Malvern, 12min. by train (p. 272). The comfortable **Osborne House ❸,** 17 Chestnut Walk, has TV in every ensuite room and brilliant marmalade. (☎22 296. Singles £25-40; doubles £45, ensuite £50. MC/V.) At **The Barbourne ❸,** 42 Barbourne Rd., many of the pink rooms are ensuite; some even have bathtubs. (☎27 507. Singles £30; twins and doubles £45; families £60. AmEx/MC/V.) Its blue counterpart, the nearby **City Guest House ❸,** 36 Barbourne Rd., features comfy beds and friendly service. (☎24 695. Singles £25. MC/V.) Riverside **Ketch Caravan Park ❶,** Bath Rd., has camping with toilets and showers. Take the A38 2 mi. south of Worcester or local bus #32; it stops across the road. Walk across the street from the Harvester Pub. (☎820 430. Open Apr.-Oct. £9 per tent or caravan. Electricity £1.75. Showers 20p. Cash only.)

▐▌ FOOD AND PUBS. A Sainsbury's **supermarket** is tucked into the Lynchgate Shopping Centre, 26-27 Cathedral Plaza. (☎21 731. Open M-Sa 8am-6pm, Su 10:30am-4pm.) Look for Indian restaurants and cheap sandwich shops near **The Tything,** at the north end of the city center. **Monsoon ❷,** 35 Forgate St., delivers well-priced entrees (£6-9.50), excellent service, and a pleasant atmosphere. (☎726 333. Takeaway discount 20%. Open M-Th and Su 6pm-midnight, F-Sa 6pm-1am. AmEx/MC/V.) At **Clockwatchers ❶,** 20 Mealcheapen St., sandwiches and homemade soups live up to the address, starting at £1.40 for takeaway. (☎611 662. Open M-Sa 8:30am-5pm. AmEx/MC/V.) **Falmouth Pasty Company ❶,** St. Swithin St., serves fresh pasties (£1.25 for a generous small, £2.35 for an enormous large) in every variety. (☎724 393. Open M-Sa 9am-5pm. Cash only.) For pint-sized entertainment, the pub scene on **Friar Street** is popular. **The Conservatory,** 34 Friar St., has a lively crowd and ales from £2. (☎26 929. Open M-Sa 11am-11pm.) Later in the night, check out **RSVP,** The Cross, a church-turned-bar filled with students and stained glass. (☎729 211. Open M-W 10am-11pm, Th-Sa 10am-1am, Su noon-12:30am.)

◙ SIGHTS. Worcester Cathedral, founded in AD 680, towers by the River Severn at the southern end of High St. Over the years, the buttresses supporting the nave have deteriorated, and the central tower is in danger of collapsing. Renovation attempts are perpetual; even steel rods set in the tower's base don't detract from the building's Norman detail. The **choir** contains intricate 14th-century misericords and King John's tomb; copies of the *Magna Carta* are displayed outside. **Wulston's Crypt** is an entire underground level, with a display of the boot remnants from a skeleton found during construction. (☎28 854; www.worcestercathedral.org.uk. Open daily 7:30am-6pm. Tower open daily 10:30am-4pm. Evensong M-Th and Sa 5:30pm, Su 4pm. Tours late July M-F and Sa; Jan. to mid-July and Aug.-Dec. Sa only. Suggested donation £3. Guided tours £5; book ahead. Tower tours £2, students £1.50, children £1, families £5.) Relive the 1651 Battle of Worcester at the **Commandery,** Sidbury Rd., where visitors can sit in on the trial of Charles I. Historians hope to find Civil War paraphernalia in the Commandery's garden. (☎361 821; www.worcestercitymuseums.org.uk. Open M-Sa 10am-5pm, Su 1:30-5pm. £4.10, concessions £3.10, families £10.60.) The **Royal Worcester Porcelain Company,** southeast of the cathedral on Severn St., makes the bone china on which the royal family has been served since George III reigned. Crockery junkies can visit the adjacent **Worcester Museum of Porcelain,** which holds England's largest collection. (☎746 000; www.worcesterporcelainmuseum.org. Open M-Sa 9am-5:30pm, Su 11am-5pm. £4.50, concessions £3.70, under 5 free, families £10. Guided tours M-Th 10:30, 11:30am, 1:30, 2:30pm; F 10:30, 11:30am, 1:30pm. Tours £6, families £19. Call ahead to book.) The highlight of the **Worcester City Museum and Art Gallery,** Foregate St., near the post office, is Hitler's clock, found in his office in 1945 by the Worcester Regiment. (☎25 371. Open M-F 9:30am-5:30pm, Sa 9:30am-5pm. Free.) Three miles south of the train station, **Elgar's Birthplace Museum,** Lower Broadheath, is filled with the manuscripts and memorabilia of Sir Edward Elgar, the composer responsible for the *Pomp and Circumstance March No. 1* (of graduation-ceremony fame). Midland Red West bus #419/420 stops 1 mi. away at Crown East Church (10min., 2 per day, round-trip £2.50). Otherwise, walk 6 mi. along the Elgar trail. (☎333 224; www.elgarmuseum.org. Open Feb. to late Dec. daily 11am-5pm. Last admission 4:15pm. £5, seniors £4.50, students £3.50, children £2.)

▶ DAYTRIP FROM WORCESTER

MALVERN

The Worcestershire Way winds through the Malverns for 45 mi. to Kingsford County Park in the north. Trains (15min., every 30min., £2.90) and First buses (40min., 1-2 per hr., £2.75) come from Worcester. The Tourist Information Centre, 21 Church St., by the post office in the town center, assists with advice and pamphlets and books accommodations for a 10% deposit. (☎892 289. Open Easter to Oct. daily 10am-5pm; Nov. to Easter M-Sa 10am-5pm, Su 10am-4pm.)

The name Malvern refers collectively to the adjacent towns of Great Malvern, West Malvern, Malvern Link, Malvern Wells, and Little Malvern, all of which hug the base and the east side of the Malvern Hills. The tops of the Malvern Hills peek over the A4108 southwest of Worcester and offer 8 mi. of trails and quasi-divine visions of greenery. **Great Malvern,** a Victorian spa town, was built around the 11th-century **Malvern Priory** on Abbey Rd. Benedictine monks rebuilt the structure in the 15th century. (Suggested donation £1.) On the hillside a 20min. hike above town, **St. Ann's Well** supplies the restorative "Malvern waters" that fueled Great Malvern's halcyon days. The waters are forced up under great pressure and are purified by rocks. Today, the water is further purified by more modern means. The beautifully renovated **Malvern Theatres** on Grange Rd., 10min. from the Great Malvern train station, host plays, dances, and music events, including theater from London's West End. (☎892 277. Box office open M-Sa 9:30am-8pm. Tickets £16-26.)

The **YHA Hatherly ❶,** 18 Peachfield Rd., Malvern Wells, has a TV lounge, game room, and members' kitchen. Take bus #675 from Great Malvern or walk 20min. from the TIC; follow Wells Rd. (☎569 131. Lockout 10am-5pm. Curfew 11pm. Open daily mid-Feb. to Oct.; Nov.-Dec. F-Sa. £11, under 18 £8. AmEx/MC/V.)

CHELTENHAM ☎01242

Despite growing up in Bath's shadow, Cheltenham (pop. 110,000) remains a small but well-to-do city. Ever since George III sampled its waters in 1788, the town has flourished; Cheltenham's reputation as a fashionable place of leisure is evident in its upscale restaurants, spacious gardens, and trendy boutiques. On weekends, students from the University of Gloucestershire pack the pubs and clubs, energizing the city center. Though it has few important sights, Cheltenham continues to draw visitors as the most convenient base for visiting the Cotswolds.

▐ TRANSPORTATION

Cheltenham is 43 mi. south of Birmingham. *Getting There* (free from the TIC) details bus services.

Trains: Cheltenham Spa Station, Queen's Rd., at Gloucester Rd. Ticket office open M-F 5:45am-8:15pm, Sa 5:45am-7pm, Su 8:15am-8:15pm. Trains (☎08457 484 950) from: **Bath** (1½hr., 2 per hr., £12); **Birmingham** (45min., 2 per hr., £11); **London** (2½hr., every hr., £33-56.50); **Worcester** (25min., every 2hr., £5.40).

Buses: Royal Well Coach Station, Royal Well Rd. National Express office open M-Sa 9am-4:45pm. Also shares an office with Stagecoach (229 High St.; ☎544 120). Open M-Sa 9am-5pm. National Express (☎08705 808 080) from: **Bristol** (1¼hr., 3 per day, £6.10); **Exeter** (4-5hr., 2 per day, £19.40); **London** (3hr., 4 per day, £15.50). Stagecoach (☎01452 523 928) serves **Gloucester** (40min., every 10min., £1.70). Swanbrook Coaches (☎01452 712 386) runs from **Oxford** (1½hr., 3 per day, £6.50).

Taxis: Taxi stands by the Royal Well Coach Station or on the Promenade. Freephone in train station. Try **Central Taxis** (☎228 877), **Starline Taxi** (☎250 250), **Handycars** (☎262 611; 24hr.), or **AtoB** (☎580 580; 24hr.).

▐ ▐ ORIENTATION AND PRACTICAL INFORMATION

The heart of Cheltenham is the intersection of pedestrian-only **High Street** and the **Promenade,** the town's central boulevard. The train station is at the western edge of town; walk 30min. or catch bus D or E (5min., every 10min., £1.25).

Tourist Information Centre: Municipal Offices, 77 The Promenade (☎522 878, accommodations booking 517 110; www.visitcheltenham.info). Books accommodations (10% deposit) and posts B&B vacancies. Open M-Tu and Th-Sa 9:30am-5:15pm, W 10am-5:15pm.

Financial Services: Banks are along High St. Most are open M-F 9am-4:30pm, W 10am-4:30pm, Sa 9am-12:30pm. **Thomas Cook,** 159 High St. (☎847 900. Open M-Tu and Th-Sa 9am-5:30pm, W 10am-5:30pm, Su 11am-5pm.)

Library: Central Library, Clarence St. (☎532 685). Open M, W, F 9:30am-7pm; Tu and Th 9:30am-5:30pm; Sa 9:30am-4pm.

Launderette: Soap-n-Suds, 312 High St. (☎512 107). Wash £2-3, dry 20p per 3min. Open daily 7:30am-8pm. Last wash 7pm.

Police: Holland House, 840 Lansdown Rd. (☎08450 901 234).

Hospital: Cheltenham General, Sandford Rd. (☎08454 222 222). Follow Bath Rd. southwest from town and turn left onto Sandford Rd.

Internet Access: Smart Space, Regent St. (☎512 515), upstairs from the Everyman Theatre. Free with purchase of food or drink from the cafe (sandwiches £4.75). Open M-Sa 9:30am-9:30pm; closes 6pm in Aug. and on non-performance nights.

Post Office: 225-227 High St. (☎08457 223 344). Bureau de change. Open M-Sa 9am-5:30pm. **Post Code:** GL50 1AA.

ACCOMMODATIONS

Standards and prices tend to be high (£30-40) at Cheltenham's **B&Bs.** They cluster in the **Montpellier** area and along **Bath Road,** a 5min. walk from the town center.

Bentons Guest House, 71 Bath Rd. (☎517 417). English countryside decor and generous comforts, from hair dryers to towel warmers. Platter-size plates can barely hold the breakfast. £28 per person. Cash only. ❸

YMCA, Vittoria Walk (☎524 024; www.cheltenhamymca.com). Well-kept facilities and a comfortable lounge. Men and women accepted. 24hr. security. Very central. Use of the adjacent gym available. Breakfast included. Laundry £1.90. Reception M-F 7:30am-10pm, Sa-Su 9am-10pm. Dorms £15.50; singles £21. Book ahead. MC/V. ❷

Lonsdale House, 16 Montpellier Dr. (☎232 379). Classic bedrooms and a classy dining room. Top-floor rooms are smaller; ask to stay on the ground or first floor. Singles £28, ensuite £39; doubles £54/59. AmEx/MC/V. ❸

Cross Ways, 57 Bath Rd. (☎527 683). The proprietor's experience as an interior designer is apparent in this Regency home's sumptuous furnishings. Rooms as comfortable as they are lavish. Book a few weeks in advance. AmEx/MC/V. ❹

FOOD

Fruit stands, butchers, and bakeries dot **High Street,** while posh restaurants and cafe-bars line **Montpellier Street** across from Montpellier Gardens. A Tesco Metro **supermarket,** is at 233 High St. (☎847 400. Open M 8am-midnight, Tu-F 6am-midnight, Sa 6am-10pm, Su 11am-5pm.) A **farmers market** is held the second and last Friday of the month outside the TIC (9am-3pm). A Thursday morning **market,** in the parking lot near Henrietta St., sells fruits, meats, and other wares.

Gianni, 1 Royal Well Pl. (☎221 101), just south of the bus stop on Royal Well Rd. Huge portions of modern Italian food in a fun, lively atmosphere. Try the *penne alla gianni* (£7). Appetizers £1.50-7. Pastas £6-8. Entrees £10-14. Open M-Th and Su noon-3pm and 6:30-10:30pm, F-Sa noon-3pm and 6:30-11pm. AmEx/MC/V. ❸

Flynn's Bar and Brasserie, 16-17 The Courtyard, Montpellier St. (☎252 752). Walk down the stairs and peek left to find Flynn's. Locals swear by it. Appetizers, like the delicious deep-fried goat cheese in phyllo dough (£5), are small; entrees (£9-13) are not. Outdoor seating. Open M-F noon-2:30pm and 6-10:30pm, Sa noon-3pm and 6-10:30pm, Su 1-9pm. AmEx/MC/V. ❷

Jazz and Blues Cafe, 288 High St. (☎582 346; www.thejazzandbluescafe.com). Relaxed cafe serves up a specialty seafood gumbo (£10.50). Live music Th-Sa. Open M-Sa 9am-5pm and 7-10pm, Su 11am-4pm and 7-10pm. AmEx/MC/V. ❷

Shake's, 216 High St. Look for the bright pink sign and the cartoon cow. Shake's has over 100 flavors of ice cream and makes freshly blended frozen yogurt smoothies. Open M-F 11am-6pm, Sa 10am-6pm, Su 11am-5pm. Cash only. ❶

SIGHTS AND FESTIVALS

Cheltenham possesses the only naturally **alkaline water** in Britain. You can enjoy its diuretic and laxative effects—if "enjoy" is the right word—at the town hall, Imperial Sq. (☎521 621. Open M-Sa 9:30am-5:30pm.) The **Pittville Pump Room,** 10min. north of High St., presides over a park designed in its honor. Opened in 1830, the former spa is Cheltenham's finest Regency building. (☎523 852. Open M and W-Su

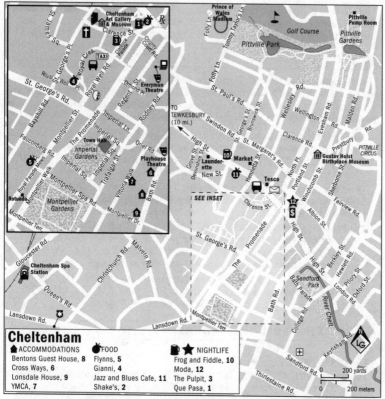

Cheltenham

🔺 ACCOMMODATIONS
Bentons Guest House, **8**
Cross Ways, **6**
Lonsdale House, **9**
YMCA, **7**

🍎 FOOD
Flynns, **5**
Gianni, **4**
Jazz and Blues Cafe, **11**
Shake's, **2**

🍸⭐ NIGHTLIFE
Frog and Fiddle, **10**
Moda, **12**
The Pulpit, **3**
Que Pasa, **1**

10am-4pm.) Treatment of the well system periodically interrupts free tastings; improvements should let the well run regularly starting September 2006. On your way back to town, stop by the **Gustav Holst Birthplace Museum,** 4 Clarence Rd., to relive the composer's early life in his impeccably restored home. (☎524 846; www.holstmuseum.org.uk. Open Feb.-Dec. Tu-Sa 10am-4pm. £2.50, children and concessions £2, families £7.) The **Cheltenham Art Gallery and Museum,** Clarence St., showcases a horde of English miscellany from the Arts and Crafts movement. Items include stuffed pheasants and Victorian tiaras. (☎237 431; www.artsand-craftsmuseum.org.uk. Open M-Sa 10am-5:20pm. Free.) Down the Promenade, downtowners sunbathe among blooms at the **Imperial Gardens.**

The indispensable *What's On* poster, displayed on kiosks and at the TIC, lists concerts, plays, tours, sporting events, and hot spots. The **Cheltenham International Festival of Music** (three weeks in July) celebrates modern classical works. The concurrent **Fringe Festival** organizes jazz, big band, and rock performances. The **International Jazz Festival** takes place at the end of April and the beginning of May, while October heralds the **Cheltenham Festival of Literature.** Full details on these festivals are available from the box office. (Town Hall, Imperial Sq. ☎227 979; www.cheltenhamfestivals.co.uk.) The **National Hunt,** a horseracing event, starts in the winter and will culminate March 14-17 in 2006, causing the population of Cheltenham to nearly double at its peak. (☎513 014, bookings 226 226; www.cheltenham.co.uk.

Tickets sold Sept.-Feb.; tickets sell out quickly. Tickets £20-70.) The **Cheltenham Cricket Festival,** the oldest in the country, starts in August. Inquire about match times at the TIC, or call ☎0117 910 8000. Purchase tickets (£12-15) at the gate.

■ NIGHTLIFE

On weekends, Cheltenham springs to life as students and twentysomethings invade its nightspots. Numerous pubs, bars, and clubs line **High Street** east of the Promenade. Popular venues also cluster around **Clarence Street** and the top of **Bath Road.** Many offer drink specials and reduced covers for students.

Frog and Fiddle, 315 High St. (☎701 156). Chill on the big leather couches or outdoor seating in the courtyard, or play pool and arcade games upstairs. Students make for a laid-back scene. Tu curry and a pint £5. F live music and open mic 9pm. Open M-Sa noon-11pm, Su noon-10:30pm.

Que Pasa, 15-21 Clarence St. (☎230 099; www.quepasa.co.uk). Students make this new bar a regular stop for weekend pub crawls. The fiesta is best on Sa nights. Promotions every night; M 2-for-1 cocktails. Open M-Sa 11am-midnight, Su noon-10:30pm.

The Pulpit, Clarence Parade (☎269 057). Look for yellow signs proclaiming "Scream." This huge converted church fills with a younger crowd on weekends and has a lounge-like feel during the day. Comfortable couches, pool tables, pub grub, and an ornate wooden pulpit. Open M-Th and Su noon-11pm, F-Sa noon-midnight.

Moda, 33-35 Albion St. (☎570 583; www.clubmoda.co.uk). Enter from High St. Cheltenham's most stylish nighttime option; 3 floors of funky house, R&B, 70s, and 80s music. Cover £2-5. Free before 10pm M and Th-Sa. Open M, W, Th-Sa 9pm-2am.

▶ DAYTRIP FROM CHELTENHAM

TEWKESBURY

Stagecoach (☎01242 575 606) bus #41 departs from High St., across from the Tesco Metro, in Cheltenham (25min.; M-Sa every 20-30min., Su every 2hr.; round-trip £3.40). The Tourist Information Centre, in the Town Museum, sells pamphlets (20p) outlining walks through the famous battlegrounds of 1471, the 18th-century alleys, and the heritage trail (40p). ☎01684 295 027. Open Easter to Oct. M-Sa 9:30am-5pm, Su 10am-4pm; Nov. to Easter M-Sa 9:30am-5pm.

Ten miles northwest of Cheltenham, Tewkesbury is a quiet medieval town with a trove of half-timbered houses. Its most celebrated structure is the stately **Tewksbury Abbey,** whose Norman tower is the largest in England. Massive round pillars support the vaulted nave and panels of 14th-century stained glass. First consecrated in 1121, the abbey was reconsecrated after the 1471 Battle of Tewkesbury, when Yorks killed the abbey's monks for attempting to protect refuge-seeking Lancastrians in the Wars of the Roses; the townspeople later bought the Cathedral from Henry VIII. The Cathedral houses three organs, including the recently rebuilt "Milton Organ." (☎01684 850 959; www.tewkesburyabbey.org.uk. Open Apr.-Oct. M-Sa 7:30am-6pm, Su 7:30am-7pm; Nov.-Mar. M-Sa 7:30am-5:30pm, Su 7:30am-7pm. Services Su 8, 9:15, 11am, 6pm. Requested donation £3.) Beside the abbey, the **John Moore Countryside Museum,** 45 Church St., is in a merchant's cottage built in 1450. The museum displays exhibits of native 15th-century woodland and wetland wildlife and live animal shows. (☎01684 297 174; www.gloster.demon.co.uk/JMCM. Open Apr.-Oct. Tu-Sa 10am-1pm and 2-5pm; Nov.-Mar. Sa and bank holidays 10am-1pm and 2-5pm. £1.25, concessions £1, children 75p, families £3.25.) In the opposite direction, the **Tewkesbury Borough Museum,** 64 Barton St., in the same building as the TIC, includes an exhibit on the 1471 battle that ended the Wars of the Roses. (☎01684 292 901; www.tewkesburymuseum.org. Open W-Sa 10am-1pm and 2-4:30pm. £1, concessions 75p, children 50p, families £2.50.)

THE COTSWOLDS

The Cotswolds have deviated little from their etymological roots—"Cotswolds" means "sheep enclosure in rolling hillsides." Grazing livestock roams 800 sq. mi. of English hillside strung together by sleepy towns. Saxon villages and Roman settlements, hewn from Cotswold stone, link a series of trails accessible to walkers and cyclists. Hardcore hikers abound, but the Cotswolds are not just for outdoors enthusiasts; any traveler looking for the British countryside will find it here.

▐ TRANSPORTATION

Public transport to and in the Cotswolds is scarce; planning ahead is a must. The villages of the "Northern" Cotswolds (Stow-on-the-Wold, Bourton-on-the-Water, Moreton-in-Marsh) are more easily reached via Cheltenham, while Gloucester serves the more remote "Southern" Cotswolds (Slimbridge and Painswick).

Train stations in the Cotswolds are few and far between. **Trains** from London (1½hr., every 1-2hr., £21.20) via Oxford (30min., £8.20) come to **Moreton-in-Marsh Station** (open M-Sa 6:30am-1pm). In the Southern Cotswolds, trains run to **Cam and Dursley Station** (3 mi. from Slimbridge) from Gloucester (15min., every hr., £3.40) and London Paddington (2½hr., 7 per day, £27.80).

It's easier to reach the Cotswolds by **bus**. The Cheltenham TIC's free *Getting There* details service between the town and 27 popular destinations. The free *Explore the Cotswolds by Public Transport*, available at most TICs, lists bus timetables. Schedules vary depending on the day of the week. Pulham's Coaches P1 (☎01451 820 369) runs from Cheltenham to Moreton-in-Marsh (1hr., M-Sa 7 per day, £1.75) via Bourton-on-the-Water (35min., £1.65) and Stow-on-the-Wold (50min., £1.70). For Lower and Upper Slaughter, ask the driver to drop you at Slaughter Pike, between Bourton-on-the-Water and Stow-on-the-Wold; the villages are ½ mi. from the road. Castleway's Coaches (☎01242 602 949) go from Cheltenham to Broadway (50min., M-Sa 4 per day, £2.10) via Winchcombe (20min., £1.90). First (☎08706 082 608) buses M21 and M22 run to Chipping Campden from Moreton-in-Marsh (20min., M-Sa 9 per day, £1.60) via Broadway (5min., M-Sa 5 per day) before ending in Stratford (1hr., M-Sa 8 per day, £2.60).

In the Southern Cotswolds, Stagecoach bus #51 runs from Cheltenham to Cirencester (40min., M-Sa every hr., £2.25). Beaumont Travel (☎01452 309 770) bus #55 runs to Cirencester from Moreton-in-Marsh (1hr., M-Sa 8 per day, £1.50) via Stow-on-the-Wold (40min., £1.30) and Bourton-on-the-Water (20min., £1.20). Both buses are covered by a **Cotswold Rover ticket,** which may be purchased from the driver (£4, children £2). Service from Cheltenham to Gloucester is frequent on Stagecoach bus #94 (30min.; M-F every 10min., Su every 20min.; £2.10). From Gloucester bus station, Stagecoach bus #91 (35min., every hr., £2.50) and Beaumont Travel B7 (30min., 5 per day, £1.80) run to Slimbridge Crossroads.

The easiest way to explore is by car, but the best way to experience the Cotswolds is on foot or by bike. The Toy Shop, on High St. in Moreton-in-Marsh, offers **bike rentals** with a lock, map, and route suggestions. (☎01608 650 756. £12 per half-day, £14 per day. Credit card deposit. Open M and W-Sa 9am-1pm and 2-5pm.) **Taxis** are a convenient, if expensive, way of getting to areas inaccessible by public transportation. TICs have lists of companies serving their area: 'K' Cars (☎01451 822 578 or 07929 360 712) is based in Bourton-on-the-Water and Cotswold

Taxis (☎07710 117 471) operates from Moreton-in-Marsh. **Coach tours** cover the Cotswolds from Cheltenham, Gloucester, Oxford, Stratford-upon-Avon, Tewkesbury, and other cities. Try the **Cotswold Discovery Tour,** a full-day bus tour that starts in Bath and visits five of the most scenic and touristed villages. (☎09067 112 000; www.madmax.abel.co.uk. Tours Apr.-Oct. Tu, Th, Su 9am-5:15pm. £25.)

✈🔢 ORIENTATION AND PRACTICAL INFORMATION

The Cotswolds lie mostly in Gloucestershire, bounded by Stratford-upon-Avon in the north, Oxford in the east, Cheltenham in the west, and Bath in the south. The range hardly towers—the average Cotswold hill reaches only 600 ft.—but the rolling hills can make hiking and biking strenuous. The best bases from which to explore are Cheltenham, Cirencester, Stow-on-the-Wold, and Moreton-in-Marsh.

Tourist Information Centres: All provide maps, bus schedules, and pamphlets on area walks, and book beds, usually for a £2 charge plus a 10% deposit.

Bath: See p. 265.

Bourton-on-the-Water: Victoria St. (☎01451 820 211). Open Apr.-Oct. M-Sa 10am-5pm; Nov.-Mar. M-Sa 9:30am-4:30pm.

Broadway: 1 Cotswold Ct. (☎01386 852 937). Open M-Sa 10am-1pm and 2-5pm.

Cheltenham: See p. 273.

Chipping Campden: Old Police Station, High St. (☎01386 841 206). Open daily Apr.-Oct. 10am-5:30pm; Nov.-Mar. 10am-5pm.

Cirencester: Corn Hall, Market Pl. (☎01285 654 180). Open Apr.-Dec. M 9:45am-5:30pm, Tu-Sa 9:30am-5:30pm; Jan.-Mar. M 9:45am-5pm, Tu-Sa 9:30am-5pm.

Gloucester: 28 Southgate St. (☎01452 396 572). Open July-Aug. M-Sa 10am-5pm, Su 11am-3pm; Sept.-June M-Sa 10am-5pm.

Moreton-in-Marsh: District Council Building, High St. (☎01608 650 881). Open in summer M 8:45am-4pm, Tu-Th 8:45am-5:15pm, F 8:45am-4:45pm, Sa 10am-1pm; in winter M 8:45am-4pm, Tu-Th 8:45am-5:15pm, F 8:45am-4:45pm, Sa 10am-12:30pm.

Stow-on-the-Wold: Hollis House, The Square (☎01451 831 082). Open Easter to Oct. M-Sa 9:30am-5:30pm; Nov. to Easter M-Sa 9:30am-4:30pm.

Winchcombe: High St. (☎01242 602 925), next to Town Hall. Open Apr.-Oct. M-Sa 10am-1pm and 2-5pm, Su 10am-1pm and 2-4pm; Nov.-Mar. Sa-Su 10am-1pm and 2-4pm.

🏠 ACCOMMODATIONS

The *Cotswold Way Handbook and Accommodation List* (£2) details **B&Bs,** which usually lie on convenient roads a short walk from small villages. The *Cotswolds Accommodation Guide* (50p) lists B&Bs in or near larger towns. Expect to pay £30 per night unless you stay at one of the YHA hostels. **YHA Stow-on-the-Wold ❷**, The Square, is a 16th-century building beside the TIC. The hostel offers bright, ensuite rooms with wood bunks and village views. (☎01451 830 497. Kitchen, lounge, and family room with toys. Laundry £3. Reception 8-10am and 5-10pm. Lockout 10am-5pm. Curfew 11pm. Book a month in advance. Open mid-Feb. to Oct. daily; Nov.-Dec. F-Sa. Dorms £14, under 18 £10; families £55-70. MC/V.) The 56-bed **YHA Slimbridge ❶**, Shepherd's Patch, off the A38 and the M5, is 4 mi. from the Cotswold Way. The nearest train station (Cam and Dursley) is 3 mi. away; it's easier to take bus #91 or B7 from Gloucester to the Slimbridge Crossroads roundabout and walk 2 mi. (☎08707 706 036. Laundry £2.60. Reception 7:15-10am and 5-11pm. Curfew 11pm. Open mid-July to early Sept. daily; Oct.-Nov. and Jan. to mid-July F-Sa. Dorms £11, under 18 £8; twins £26; families £37.50-69. MC/V.)

Campsites cluster close to Cheltenham, but there are also convenient places to rough it within the Cotswolds. Try **Fosseway Farm ❶**, Stow Rd., 5min. out of More-

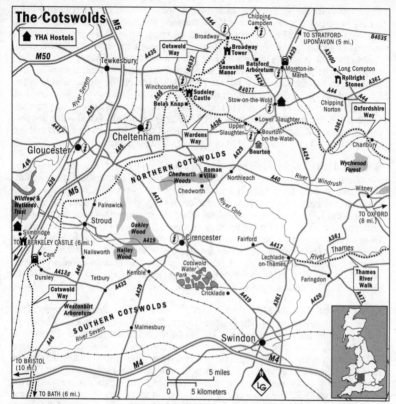

The Cotswolds

YHA Hostels

M50
Tewkesbury
M5
A438
River Severn
Gloucester
A417
A48
A38
M5
Painswick
Stroud
Slimbridge
TO BERKELEY CASTLE (6 mi.)
Cam
Dursley
Nailsworth
A4135
A46
Tetbury
Kemble
A433
A429
Westonbirt Arboretum
River Severn
SOUTHERN COTSWOLDS
Malmesbury
TO BRISTOL (10 mi.)
TO BATH (6 mi.)
M4
Swindon
M4

A44
Broadway
Cotswold Way
A435
B4632
Broadway Tower
Snowshill Manor
Batsford Arboretum
Winchcombe
A46
Sudeley Castle
Bela's Knap
B4077
Stow-on-the-Wold
Cheltenham
Wardens Way
A436
Upper Slaughter
Lower Slaughter
Bourton-on-the-Water
Bourton
A429
NORTHERN COTSWOLDS
Chedworth Woods
Roman Villa
Chedworth
Northleach
A40
River Coln
A417
Cirencester
Fairford
A417
Cotswold Water Park
Oakley Wood
Halley Wood
A419
Cricklade
A419
A361

Chipping Campden
TO STRATFORD-UPON-AVON (5 mi.)
B4035
A429
A3400
A44
Moreton-in-Marsh
Long Compton
Rollright Stones
A361
Chipping Norton
Oxfordshire Way
A44
A361
River Windrush
Wychwood Forest
Charlbury
A424
Witney
TO OXFORD (8 mi.)
A361
Lechlade-on-Thames
River Thames
Faringdon
A420
Thames River Walk
A471

0   5 miles
0   5 kilometers

ton-in-Marsh toward Stow-on-the-Wold. (☎01608 650 503. Campers' breakfast £3.50. Caravans and tents £12. Electricity £2. MC/V.) *Camping and Caravaning in Gloucestershire and the Cotswolds* (free at local TICs) lists more options.

🥾 HIKING

For centuries, travelers in the Cotswolds have walked the well-worn footpaths from village to village. The gentle hills, thatched roofs, and docile sheep make moving at a pace beyond three or four villages per day inadvisable. The free *Cotswold Events* booklet, available at TICs, lists music festivals, antique markets, woolsack races, and cheese-rolling opportunities.

The TIC stocks a variety of **walking** and **cycling guides.** The *Cotswold Map and Guidebook in One* (£5) is good to plan bike routes and short hikes. For more intense hiking or biking, the Ordnance Survey Outdoor Leisure Map #45 shows altitudes and more obscure trails (1:25,000; £7). The Cotswolds Voluntary Warden Service (☎01451 862 000) leads free **guided walks,** some with themes (1½-7½hr.). All walks are listed on its website (www.cotswoldsaonb.com) and in the Programme Guide section of the bi-annual *Cotswold LION* (free at the TIC).

Long-distance hikers can choose from a handful of trails. The extensive **Cotswold Way** spans just over 100 mi. from Bath to Chipping Campden, has few steep climbs, and can be done in a week. The trail passes through pasture lands and the remains of ancient settlements. Pockmarks and gravel make certain sections unsuitable for biking or horseback riding. Consult the **Cotswold Way National Trail Office** (☎01453 827 004) for details. The **Oxfordshire Way** (65 mi.) runs between the popular hyphen-havens Bourton-on-the-Water and Henley-on-Thames, site of the famed regatta. Amble through pastures while wending from Bourton-on-the-Water to Lower and Upper Slaughter along the **Warden's Way,** a half-day hike. Adventurous souls can continue to Winchcombe. The **Thames Path Walk** starts on the western edge of the Cotswolds in Lechlade and follows the Thames 184 mi. to Kingston, near London. The section from the Cotswolds to Oxford is low-impact and particularly peaceful. Contact the **National Trails Office** (☎01865 810 224) for details. Local roads are perfect for **biking**; rolling hills welcome both casual and hardy cyclers. Parts of the Oxfordshire Way are hospitable to cyclists, if slightly rut-riddled.

WINCHCOMBE. Convenient as a starting point for a hike through the Cotswolds, Winchcombe sits 6 mi. north of Cheltenham on the A46 and features **Sudeley Castle,** a 10min. walk from the town center. Once the estate of King Æthelred the Unready, the castle was a prized possession in the Middle Ages. Today, it is home to Lord and Lady Ashcombe, who have filled the castle with Tudor memorabilia and maintain 14 acres of prize-winning gardens. The chapel contains the tomb of Henry VIII's Queen #6, Katherine Parr. In summer, Sudeley also holds jousting tournaments and Shakespeare under the stars. (☎01242 602 308; www.sudeleycastle.co.uk. Castle open daily Mar.-Oct. 11am-5pm. Last admission 4:30pm. Gardens open daily Mar.-Oct. 10:30am-5:30pm. Castle and gardens £7.20, concessions £6.20, children £4.20. Gardens only £5.50/4.50/3.25. £1 surcharge Su May-Aug.)

BOURTON-ON-THE-WATER. Touted as the "Venice of the Cotswolds," this village is a popular stop for hikers. The Oxford Way trailhead is here, as is a confluence of other trails, including the Warden's, Heart of England, Windrush, and Gloucestershire Ways. Follow signs to the **scale model of Bourton,** a miniature labor of love (£2.75; open daily 10am-5:15pm). Between rose-laden gates and dung-strewn fields, the **Cotswold Perfumery,** on Victoria St., features fragrant flowers and a theater equipped with "Smelly Vision," which releases scents as they're mentioned on screen. (☎01451 820 698; www.cotswold-perfumery.co.uk. Open M-Sa 9:30am-5pm, Su 10:30am-5pm. £2, concessions £1.75.) **Birdland,** on Rissington Road, has a motley crew of winged creatures from neon pink flamingos to penguins. (☎820 480; www.birdland.co.uk. Open daily Apr.-Oct. 10am-6pm; Nov.-Mar. 10am-4pm. Last admission 1hr. before close. £5, seniors £4, children £3, families £14.50.)

STOW-ON-THE-WOLD. Inns and taverns crowd the Market Square of this self-proclaimed "Heart of the Cotswolds." Despite chain stores, like the Tesco **supermarket** on Fosse Way (☎01451 807 400; open M-F 6am-midnight, Sa 6am-10pm, Su 10am-4pm), Stow still exudes bucolic Cotswold charm. A traditional **farmers' market** is held the second Thursday of every month in the Market Square (☎01453 758 060; open 9am-2pm). Three miles downhill, off the A424, **Donnington Trout Farm** lets visitors fish, feed (20p), or eat the trout (from £2). The staff can smoke just about anything, even pigeons. (☎01451 830 873. Open Apr.-Oct. daily 10am-5:30pm; Nov.-Mar. Tu-Su 10am-5pm.) The **YHA hostel** (p. 278) is in the center of town. Ensuite rooms are a perk at the **Pear Tree Cottage ❹,** an old stone house on High St. (☎01451 831 210. Singles £35; doubles £45-50. Cash only.)

THE SLAUGHTERS. No need to fear; the Slaughters got their names from the Old English word *slough*, meaning "stream." The towns, complete with bubbling brooks, are a few miles southwest of Stow. The less-touristed and more charming Lower Slaughter is connected to its sister village, Upper Slaughter, by the Warden's Way. In Lower Slaughter, the **Old Mill,** on Mill Ln., scoops water from the river that flows past; a mill has stood on the spot for 1000 years. (☎01451 820 052. Open daily in summer 10am-6pm; in winter 10am to dusk. £1.25, children 75p.)

MORETON-IN-MARSH. With a train station, frequent bus service, and a bike shop, Moreton is a convenient base from which to explore the north. Little else in the town is of interest. A mile up the road is **Batsford Arboretum,** 55 acres of waterfalls, a Japanese rest house, and trees. (☎01386 701 441; www.batsarb.co.uk. Open Feb. to mid-Nov. daily 10am-5pm; mid-Nov. to Jan. Sa-Su 10am-4pm. £5, concessions £4, children £1.) A Tesco Express **market** is on High St. in the center of town, next to the bus stop. (☎01608 652 287. Open M-Sa 6am-11pm, Su 7am-11pm.) **Warwick House B&B ❸,** London Rd., offers amazing value, with comfortable rooms, a garden, and free access to a leisure center. (☎01608 650 773; www.snoozeandsizzle.com. Free pickup from station. £21-25 per person. Cash only.) **Blue Cedar House ❸,** Stow Rd., a 5min. walk on High St. toward Stow, has welcoming rooms and an airy breakfast area. (☎01608 650 299. Book ahead. Free pick-up from train station. £25 per person. 10% discount for 4 or more nights. Cash only.)

BROADWAY. Only 4 mi. southwest of Chipping Campden, restored Tudor, Jacobean, and Georgian buildings with traditional tile roofs rise high on each side of Broadway's main street, giving the town a genteel air. **Broadway Tower,** a 20-40min. uphill hike, enchanted the likes of poet Dante Gabriel Rossetti and affords a view of 12 counties. Call ahead, as opening hours and days change often. (☎01386 852 390. Open daily Apr.-Oct. 10:30am-5pm; Nov.-Mar. 10:30am-3pm. £3.50, concessions £3, children £2, families £10.) **Snowshill Manor,** 2½ mi. southwest of Broadway, was once home to a collector of everything and anything; it now houses about 20,000 random knicknacks. (☎01386 852 410. Open late Mar. to Apr. M-Th and Su noon-5pm; May-Oct. M-W and Su noon-5pm. £7, children £3.50.)

CHIPPING CAMPDEN. Years ago, quiet Chipping Campden was the capital of the Cotswold wool trade ("chipping" means "market"). **Market Hall,** in the middle of the main street, attests to a 400-year history of commerce. The Gothic **Church of St. James,** a signposted 5min. walk from High St., is one of the region's prettiest churches. (☎01386 840 671; www.stjameschurchcampden.co.uk. Open Mar.-Oct. M-Sa 10am-5pm, Su 2-6pm; Nov. and Feb. M-Sa 11am-4pm, Su 2-4pm; Dec.-Jan. M-Sa 11am-5pm. Suggested donation £1.) Currently, the town is famous for its

OLYMPICKS OF AULD

Chipping Campden's scenic Dover Hill has hosted the Cotswold Olympicks for almost 400 years. The games were founded by local landowner Robert Dover in 1612. Although occasionally suspended, the games in their 1963 revival have adapted to modern times. The light-hearted nature of the activities—wrestling, Chinese boxing, backsword fighting (exhibition only), and the time-honored purring (shin-kicking; participants pad their trousers with hay)—still draws fans in droves.

Early participants sought escape from oppressive Puritan social norms; today's "athletes" find the tradition, camaraderie, and general mayhem to be the real attraction. The thrill of competition and the ensuing debauchery attracts young and old, respected and riff-raf alike, and have been chronicled by the likes of Ben Jonson and Shakespeare (in *The Merry Wives of Windsor*). Held the Friday after the April Bank Holiday, the games commence at the command of a "Robert Dover" and continue until dusk. At night, participants and revelers sing, dance, and generally dawn-delay in the town square. Bonfires and fireworks give way to Saturday's Scuttlebrook Wake festivities, which include a parade with bagpipers in tartan, the crowning of the May Queen, Morris dancing, and a street fair.

For more information, visit www.stratford-upon-avon.co.uk or ask at a Cotswold or Stratford TIC.

Cotswold Olympic Games, held in the first week of June (p. 281). The games take place on **Dovers Hill.** From St. Catherine's on High St., turn right onto West End Terr., take the first left, and follow the public footpath 1 mi. uphill.

CIRENCESTER. One of the larger towns, and sometimes regarded as the capital of the region, Cirencester (SI-ruhn-ses-ter) is the site of Corinium, a Roman town founded in AD 49. Although only scraps of the amphitheater remain, the **Corinium Museum,** Park St., has a formidable collection of Roman paraphernalia. Check out the statues or get dolled up as a Roman soldier. (☎01285 655 611. Open M-Sa 10am-5pm, Su 2pm-5pm. £3.70, concessions £2-3.) Cirencester's **Parish Church of St. John the Baptist** is Gloucestershire's largest "wool church." The Church is home to a cup made for Anne Boleyn in 1535. (☎01285 659 317. Open M-Sa 9:30am-5pm, Su 2:15-5pm. 3 services per day. Grounds close 9pm. Donation requested.) The **world's highest yew hedge** bounds Lord Bathurst's mansion at the top of Park St.; bear right and make a left on Cecily Hill to enter the 3000-acre **Cirencester Park,** whose stately central aisle was designed by Alexander Pope. **Westonbirt Arboretum,** the National Arboretum, stationed 3½ mi. south of nearby Tetbury, features 17 mi. of tree-lined paths. (☎01666 880 220. Open daily 10am-8pm or until dusk. £6.50, concessions £5.50, children £1, families £13.) Alexcars (☎01285 653 985) bus A1 runs to the arboretum from Cirencester on Saturdays in summer (40min., Apr.-Sept. Sa 2 per day, £2.90 round-trip). Otherwise, take the A1 to Tetbury (45min., M-F 7 per day, £1.70) and transfer to Stagecoach bus #620 or 628 (7min., M-Sa 5 per day, £1.30). An **antique market** is on Fridays in Corn Hall, near the TIC (☎0171 263 6010; open 10am-4:30pm). A cattle market takes place every Tuesday on Tetbury Rd. and a **country market** is every Friday at Brewery Arts, off Castle St. (open 8:30-11:30am).

CHEDWORTH. Tucked in the hills southeast of Cheltenham, Chedworth contains a well-preserved **Roman villa,** equidistant from Cirencester and Northleach off A429. The villa's famed mosaics came to light in 1864 when a gamekeeper noticed tile fragments revealed by clever rabbits. (☎01242 890 256. Open Tu-Su 10am-5pm. £5, children £2.50.) From Cirencester, Beaumont Travel buses reach the villa on weekends, but make a same-day return trip to avoid being stranded overnight. The **Cotswold Lion** (☎01451 862 000), a bus run by the National Trust, serves the villa from Cirencester, but only on summer weekends (15min., £4).

SLIMBRIDGE. Slimbridge, 12½ mi. southwest of Gloucester off the A38, is a dull village with two draws: a pleasant hostel (**YHA Slimbridge,** p. 278) and the largest of seven **Wildfowl & Wetlands Trust** centers in Britain. Sir Peter Scott has developed the world's biggest collection of wildfowl here, with over 180 different species, including all six varieties of flamingos. Unfortunately, it is too far out of the way to be feasible for travelers without a car. (☎01453 891 900; www.wwt.org.uk. Open daily 9:30am-5:30pm. Last admission 30min. before close. £6.75, concessions £5.50, children £4, families £17.50.) Six miles southwest of Slimbridge, off the A38 between Bristol and Gloucester, lies massive **Berkeley Castle** (BARK-lay). The stone fortress boasts impressive towers, a dungeon, the cell where King Edward II was murdered, Queen Elizabeth I's bowling green, and a timber-vaulted Great Hall, where barons of the West Country met before forcing King John to sign the *Magna Carta.* (☎01453 810 332. Open Apr.-Sept. Tu-Sa 11am-4pm, Su 2-5pm; Oct. Su 2-5pm. £7.50, seniors £6, children £3.50, families £18.50. Tours free and frequent.)

PREHISTORIC REMAINS. Archaeologists have unearthed some 70 ancient habitation sites in the Cotswolds. Belas Knap, a 4000-year-old burial mound, stands 1½ mi. southwest of Sudeley Castle. It is accessible from the Cotswold Way or via a scenic 2½hr. walk from Winchcombe; the Winchcombe TIC has a free pamphlet with directions. The Rollright Stones, off the A34 between Chipping Norton and Long Compton (a 4½ mi. walk from Chipping Norton), is a 100 ft. wide ring of 11 stones. Consult Ordnance Survey maps (£4-7) or ask at TICs for other sites.

HEREFORD ☎01432

Near the Welsh border and the scenic River Wye, Hereford (HAIR-eh-fuhd; pop. 60,000) boasts a centuries-long history as the agricultural hub of the Wye Valley. Once known for its "whiteface" cattle, Hereford's modern commercial manifestations are found in the upscale stores of High Town, a pedestrian agora that hosts both farmers' markets and local entertainment. Meanwhile, good bus and rail connections provide a springboard for travel to the Wye Valley.

▮ TRANSPORTATION. The **train** and **bus stations** are on Commercial Rd. **Trains** (☎08457 484 950) arrive from: Abergavenny (25min., every hr., £6); Cardiff (1¼hr., every hr., £12.70); Chepstow via Newport (1½hr., every hr., £14.20); London Paddington via Evesham (3hr., every hr., £32.10); and Shrewsbury (1hr., 2 per hr., £12.20). National Express (☎08705 808 080) runs **buses** from Birmingham (2hr., 1 per day, £6.90) and London (4¼hr., 3 per day, £17). A convenient bus stop is on Broad St., a few stops past the TIC. Stagecoach Red and White buses come from Cardiff via Abergavenny (X4, 2½ hr., every 2hr., £4.50) and Brecon via Hay-on-Wye (#39, 1¾hr., M-Sa 6 per day, £5). On Sundays, Yeoman's bus #40 takes over the Brecon route (4 per day). For bus info, pick up the *Herefordshire Public Transport Map and Guide* (40p) or the free *Monmouthshire County Council Local Transport Guide* at the TIC. **Rent bikes** from Phill Prothero Cycles, Bastion Mews, off Union St. (☎359 478. £10; includes lock, helmet, and repair kit. Open M-W and F 8:30am-5:30pm, Th 8:30am-1pm, Sa 9am-5:30pm.)

▮ PRACTICAL INFORMATION. The **Tourist Information Centre**, 1 King St., books beds for a £1.50 charge plus a 10% deposit. (☎268 430. Open M-Sa 9am-5pm.) **Walking tours** leave from the TIC. (1½hr. Mid-May to mid-Sept. M-Sa 11am, Su 2:30pm. £2.) Other services include: Barclays **bank**, King St. (☎422 000; open M-F 9am-5pm, Sa 9am-3pm); a **launderette**, 136 Eign St. (☎269 610; wash £2, soap 20p, dry 20p per 5min.; open M-Sa 8am-6pm, Su 8:30am-6pm; last wash 1hr. before close); **police** on Bath St. (☎08457 444 888); free **Internet** at the library, Broad St. (open Tu-W and F 9am-7:30pm; Th 9am-5:30pm; Sa 9:30am-4pm); Garrick House, Widemarsh St. (☎260 500; open M-W 8:45am-5pm, Th-F 8:45am-3:30pm); and the **post office**, 14-15 St. Peter's St. (☎275 221; open M-F 9am-5:30pm, Sa 9am-4pm). **Post Code:** HR1 2LE.

▮▮ ACCOMMODATIONS AND FOOD. Cheap lodgings in Hereford are scarce; your best bet is to walk to the **B&Bs** (from £25) near the end of **Bodenham Road**. **Bouvrie House ❸**, 26 Victoria St., offers a good location and cheery rooms. (☎266 265. Singles £25; doubles £42. Cash only.) The **Holly Tree ❸**, 19-21 Barton Rd., has reasonable prices a little farther from the town center. (☎357 845. No smoking. Doubles £40-44. Cash only.) **Westfields ❷**, 235 Whitecroft Rd., has low prices a 10-15 min. walk from town. Rooms are clean and bathrooms spacious. (☎267 712. £20 per person. Cash only.) Tesco **supermarket**, Newmarket St., has your picnic needs covered. (Open 24hr. from M 8am to Sa 10pm.) Stop by the **Market Hall Buttermarket** for produce and sweets. (Open M-Sa 9am-5:30pm.) At **Cafe@All Saints ❶**, in All Saints Church on High St., try the open-face focaccia sandwich with salad for £4.25. (☎370 415. Open M-Sa 8:30am-5:30pm. MC/V.) Locals and tourists relax on couches amid Victorian trinkets at the **Antique Teashop ❶**, 5a St. Peter's St. Pastries (£3) and teas (£2) allow for dignified nibbling and sipping. (☎342 172. Open M-Sa

9:45am-5pm, Su 10:15am-5pm. Cash only.) Sweet and sour pork ($6) complements sweet and sudsy beer at the **Black Lion Inn ❷**, 31 Bridge St. (☎343 535. Open M-Sa 11am-11pm, Su noon-10:30pm. Food served noon-2:30pm and 6-9pm. MC/V.)

◖◗ ☐ SIGHTS AND SHOPPING. The immense pillars of **Hereford Cathedral** make even skeptics gasp as painted vines and elaborate Romanesque stonework loom hundreds of feet above churchgoers. In the cathedral is the 13th-century **Mappa Mundi** ("cloth of the world"), which dates from back when the earth was flat. In the **Chained Library,** 1500 volumes are linked to the shelf by slender chains; the practice was common in the 17th century, when books were as valuable as small parcels of land. (☎374 200. Cathedral open daily until Evensong. Mappa Mundi and library open May-Sept. M-Sa 10am-4:15pm, Su 11am-3:15pm; Oct.-Apr. M-Sa 11am-3:15pm. Cathedral free. Mappa Mundi and library $4.50, concessions $3.50.) The slew of cider facts (and vats) housed by the **Cider Museum,** off Pomona Pl., is fascinating. Don't let their "What Went Wrong with the Brew" display deter you from the free brandy-tasting. (☎354 207; www.cidermuseum.co.uk. Open Apr.-Oct. M-Sa 10am-5pm; Nov.-Mar. Tu-Sa noon-4pm. $3, students $2.) The 17th-century **Old House,** High Town, aptly labeled "the black and white house" on signs around town, is a carefully preserved incarnation of Britain's bourgeois past. (☎260 694. Open Apr.-Sept. Tu-Sa 10am-5pm, Su 10am-4pm; Oct.-Mar. Tu-Sa 10am-4pm. Free.) Hereford's **High Town** area is a network of shop-lined walkways featuring a generic parade of chain stores. Thrifty shoppers may prefer **Chapters,** 17 Union St., where used books go for mere pence. (☎311 302. Open M-Sa 9:30am-4:30pm.) ◙**The Dinosaw Market,** 16-17 Bastion Mews, off Union St., promises "things that are not normal" and delivers; an entertaining array of vintage garb, wooden turtles, pink boas, and assorted bric-a-brac fills the store. (☎353 655. Open M-Sa 10am-5:30pm.)

▧ NIGHTLIFE. Old and young come out to play on weekends in Hereford, but options are few and crowded. **Play,** 51-55 Blueschool St., is a smoky, fabric-draped haunt meant for avid clubbers. Ladies drink free on Monday nights. (☎270 009. Cover $3-5. Open M, Th, Su 9:30pm-1:30am; F-Sa 9pm-2am). **Booth Hall,** East St., is a pub that cranks up its music inside while customers sip drinks in the courtyard. (☎344 487. Open M-Sa 11am-11pm, Su 7-10:30pm. Food served M-Sa noon-3pm.)

THE MIDLANDS

Mention "the Midlands," and you'll evoke images grim, urban, and decidedly sunless. But go to the Midlands and you may be surprised by the quiet grandeur of this smokestacked pocket. Warwick's storybook castle and Lincoln's breathtaking cathedral are two of Britain's stand-out attractions; Shrewsbury and Stamford are architectural wonders. Even Birmingham, the region's oft-maligned center, has its saving graces, among them lively nightlife and the Cadbury chocolate empire. Deep in the Severn Valley, gorgeous Ironbridge was named a World Heritage Site.

HIGHLIGHTS OF THE MIDLANDS

ADMIRE the world's first cast-iron bridge in Ironbridge and explore living museums at this monument to Britain's Industrial Revolution (p. 291).

CLIMB your way to Lincoln's cathedral, once Europe's tallest building and now the stunning centerpiece of this city-on-a-hill (p. 302).

STROLL past the stone buildings of Stamford on your way to Burghley House, one of Britain's most lavish homes (p. 297).

WARWICK
☎ 01926

Modest Warwick (WAR-ick) is right to be fiercely proud of its famous castle. Locals boast that the castle is the UK's biggest tourist attraction, and a walk through its grandiose grounds reveals why. The town also sports unique architecture due to damage from the Great Fire of 1694. Warwick is best suited for a daytrip from Birmingham or Stratford-Upon-Avon.

TRANSPORTATION AND PRACTICAL INFORMATION. The Warwick **train station** is on Coventry Rd. (Ticket office open M-Sa 5:50am-7:50pm, Su 9:30am-5:40pm.) **Trains** (☎08457 484 950) run daily from: Birmingham (40min., 2 per hr.,

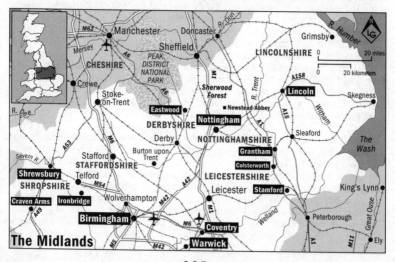

The Midlands

£4.40); London Marylebone (2hr., every hr., £21.90); Stratford-Upon-Avon (25min., every 2hr., £3.40). National Express (☎08705 808 080) **buses** stop in Old Square from London (3hr., 3 per day, £13.50). Flightlink (☎08705 757 747) buses go to Warwick rail station from Birmingham (1hr., 1 per day, £6.50) and Heathrow (5hr., 3 per day, £23.50) airports; buy tickets at **Co-op Travel,** 15 Market St. (☎410 709. Open M and W-F 9am-5:30pm, Tu 9:30am-5:30pm, Sa 9am-5pm.) **Local buses** #16 and 18 (3-4 per hr., £2.55-2.85) both stop at Market Pl. from Coventry (55min.) and Stratford (20min.). Warwickshire Traveline (☎414 140) has local bus info. For a **taxi,** try **B&R Cars** (☎771 771). The **Tourist Information Centre,** Court House, Jury St., books rooms for a £2.50 charge plus a 10% deposit and stocks a 50p guided trail map and a free town map. (☎492 212; www.warwick-uk.co.uk. Open daily 9:30am-4:30pm.) **Tours** leave from the TIC (Su 11am, £3). Other services include: **Barclays,** 5 High St. (☎303 000; open M-Tu and Th-F 9:30am-4:30pm, W 10am-4:30pm); a Boots **pharmacy,** 6-8 Cornmarket St. (☎247 461; open M-Th 8:30am-7pm, F-Sa 8:30am-6pm, Su 11am-5pm); Warwick **Hospital,** Lakin Rd. (☎495 321); the **police,** Priory Rd. (☎410 111); and the **post office,** Westgate House, 45 Brook St. (☎491 061; open M-F 9am-5:30pm, Sa 9am-4pm). **Post Code:** CV34 4BL.

▐▌ACCOMMODATIONS AND FOOD. A stay near the castle can be pricey, but **Emscote Road** (bus X17 runs from Market St. to Emscote frequently) has quality affordable options. From the train station, turn right on Coventry Rd. and left at the Crown & Castle Inn on Coten End, which becomes Emscote Rd. The humorous young proprietor maintains a laid-back atmosphere at **Westham Guest House ❸,** 76 Emscote Rd., 10min. from the Crown & Castle. (☎491 756. Singles £20-22; doubles and twins £38-40, ensuite £40-45; triples and quads from £55. Cash only.) A friendly young couple runs the lovely and bright **Avon Guest House ❸,** 7 Emscote Rd. (☎491 367; www.avonguesthouse.com. Singles £25-30; doubles and twins £48; family rooms £50-80. Cash only.) Find **Chesterfields ❷,** 84 Emscote Rd., by looking for the sign with the cartoon elephant. This B&B, right near the X17 bus stop, offers another cozy option. (☎774 864. Singles from £22; doubles and twins from £44, ensuite from £46; family rooms from £45. Cash only.) **Agincourt Lodge Hotel ❹,** 36 Coten End, features huge rooms, some with four-post beds and fireplaces. (☎499 399. Singles £40-55; doubles £55-75; family rooms £90. MC/V.)

For **groceries,** try Tesco on Emscote Rd. (☎307 600. Open continuously from M 8am to Sa 10pm, Su 10am-4pm. AmEx/MC/V.) **Fanshawe's ❹,** 22 Market Pl., serves mouth-watering meals, from oven-baked lamb to pan-fried duck. Top it off with gourmet desserts like crème brûlée. The set menu (one course £18, two £20, three £22.50) offers good value. (☎410 590. Open M-Sa 6pm-10pm. AmEx/MC/V.) The **Crown & Castle Inn ❶,** 2-4 Coventry Rd., has sandwich-and-chips lunch specials (£3.50 for a baguette, £4.50 for a main course) and an all-you-can-eat carvery (£4) in a traditional pub. (☎492 087. Open M-Sa 11am-11pm, Su 11am-10:30pm. AmEx/MC/V.) Warwick Castle hosts a five-course **medieval banquet ❺,** with unlimited wine and ale and ongoing entertainment, every night from 8 to 11pm. (☎406 602. Call for reservations. Jan.-Oct. £42.50; Nov.-Dec. £49.50.)

◪ SIGHTS. Many medievalists regard 14th-century ◪**Warwick Castle** as England's finest. Today, it exists as a study in marketing by the people who brought you Madame Tussaud's. The dungeons are manned by life-size wax soldiers preparing for battle, while student-actor types dressed as "knights" and "craftsmen" discuss their trades in the festival village (and encourage you to shell out £2.50 to play the carnival games on the grounds). You'll also find medieval games, storytelling by the Red Knight, and events like summer jousting tournaments, birds of prey and bowman shows, and live concerts (past artists include Meatloaf). Climb 530 steps to the top of the towers and see the countryside unfold like a fairy-tale kingdom, or stop for a photo at one of the many gardens planned by "Capability" Brown, including one peacock-populated park. (☎495 421, 24hr. recording 0870 442 2000. Open daily Apr.-Sept. 10am-6pm; Oct.-Mar. 10am-5pm. £14.50, children £8.75, seniors £10.50, families £39; weekends and bank holidays 50p-£1 more; mid-Sept. to Apr. £1-2 less. Audio tours £2.95.) Warwick Ghosts-Alive, a feature best enjoyed by grade-school tour groups, brings to life the murder of Sir Fulke Greville (£2.50).

Other sights include **St. Mary's Church,** Church St., which has a 12th-century Norman crypt containing one of only two surviving ducking stools (for witches) in England. The church **tower** offers fantastic views. (☎403 940. Open daily summer 10am-5pm; winter 10am-4:30pm. Requested donation £1. Tower admission £1.50, children 50p, families £3.50.) In 1571, Elizabeth I gave Lord Leycester the **Lord Leycester Hospital,** 60 High St., to house 12 old soldiers who had fought with him in the Netherlands; today, veterans live inside. The building's **Regimental Museum** and **Brethren's Kitchen** are interesting. (☎491 422. Open Easter to Oct. Tu-Su 10am-5pm; Nov. to Easter 10am-4pm. £5, includes entrance to the Master's Garden during the summer.) The **Warwickshire Museum,** Market Hall, has displays on natural history. (☎412 501. Open Oct.-Apr. Tu-Sa 10am-5pm; May-Sept. Su 11:30am-5pm. Free.)

⚡ DAYTRIP FROM WARWICK

COVENTRY. Coventry sits 12 mi. northeast of Warwick and has magnificent **twin cathedrals.** The juxtaposition of the old and new cathedrals—the destroyed and the resurrected—is breathtaking; the modern cathedral towers over the stained-glass and stone skeleton of the old. (☎7652 1200. Open daily 9am-5:30pm. Requested donation £3. Camera charge £2.) The tourist season commences the first weekend of June during the **Lady Godiva Festival,** which honors Countess Godgifu (who would buy chocolates with a name like that?) of Coventry. Lady Godiva's renowned nude ride through the town is celebrated in an annual parade. A statue of the lady lies near the cathedrals. The **Coventry Transport Museum,** Hales St. displays the largest collection of British cars in the world. (☎7683 2425. Open daily 10am-5pm; last admission 4:30pm. Free.) The **Tourist Information Centre,** Bayley Ln. stocks brochures and gives travel advice. (☎02476 227 264. Open M-F 9:30am-5pm, Sa 10am-4:30pm, Su 11am-5pm.)

BIRMINGHAM ☎0121

Many outside busy Birmingham grimace at the mention of this industrial city, a transport hub and a mecca for convention-goers. But a walk through Britain's second most populous city (pop. 1 million) reveals the fruits of focused efforts to overcome an ugly reputation. The architecturally stunning shopping area, the Bullring, is Europe's largest retail project, and Birmingham boasts more canals than Venice. The Dalí-esque department store Selfridges sports a wave-like, bubbled facade of 15,000 aluminum discs. Fashionable boutiques, restaurants, and bars line the waterside. Though offering little in the way of histori-cal interest, the city is quickly defended by loyal "Brummies," masses of merchandise-toters to cliques of nighttime clubbers to the thousands of stu-dents at the city's university.

⬛ TRANSPORTATION

Birmingham is situated along several train and bus lines running between London, central Wales, southwest England, and points north.

Flights: Birmingham International Airport (☎08707 335 511). Free transfer to the Birmingham International train station for connections to New St. Station and London.

Trains: New Street Station serves trains (☎08457 484 950) from: **Liverpool Lime Street** (1½hr., every hr., £19.80); **London Euston** (2hr., 2 per hr., £27.40); **Manchester Piccadilly** (2hr., every hr., £21); **Nottingham** (1¼hr., 3 per hr., £10.10); **Oxford** (1¼hr., 2 per hr., £19). Others pull into **Moor Street, Jewellery Quarter,** and **Snow Hill** stations. Follow signs to get from New St. to Moor St. Station (10min. walk).

Buses: Digbeth Station, Digbeth High St. National Express (☎08705 808 080; office open M-Sa 7:15am-7pm, Su 8:15am-7pm) from: **Cardiff** (2½hr., 3 per day, £19.40); **Liverpool** (3hr., 4 per day, £13); **London** (3hr., every hr., £14); **Manchester** (2½hr., 1 per 2hr., £10.50).

Public Transportation: Information at **Centro** (☎200 2700 or 200 2787; www.centro.org.uk), in New St. Station. Stocks transit maps and bus schedules. Call ahead. Bus and train day pass £5; bus £2.80, children £1.70. Open M-Tu and F 8:30am-5:30pm, W-Th and Sa 9am-5pm.

Taxis: Blue Arrow (☎0121 622 1000), **A2B** (☎733 3000), **TOA** (☎427 8888), **Go 2 Cars** (☎705 2222), **M&M** (☎242 1222), **Ambassador Cars** (☎444 1000).

◪ PRACTICAL INFORMATION

Tourist Information Centre: The Rotunda, 150 New St. (☎202 5099). Books rooms for a 10% deposit and sells theater and National Express tickets. Open M-Sa 9:30am-5:30pm, Su 10:30am-4:30pm. Also a small information center in Central Library (see below).

Financial Services: Banks in the city center. **American Express,** Bank House, 8 Cherry St. (☎644 5533). Open M-Tu and Th-F 8:30am-5:30pm, W 9:30am-5:30pm, Sa 9am-5pm. **Thomas Cook,** 99 New St. (☎255 2600). Open M-W and F-Sa 9am-5:30pm, Th 10am-5:30pm.

Police: Steelhouse Ln. (☎0845 113 5000).

Pharmacy: Boots, The Bullring (☎632 6418), across from New St. station. Open M-F 8am-8pm, Sa 9am-8pm, Su 11am-5pm.

Internet Access: Central Library, Chamberlain Sq. (☎303 4511), has free access on its 100 computers, but there's usually a wait. Call ahead to book a 1hr. slot. Open M-F 9am-8pm, Sa 9am-5pm. **Ready to Surf,** Corporation St. (☎236 2523). £1 per hr. Open M-Sa 9am-6pm, Su 11-5pm.

Post Office: Big Top, 19 Union Passage (☎643 7051). Bureau de change. Open M-Sa 9am-1pm. **Post Code:** B2 4TU.

┏ ACCOMMODATIONS

Despite its size, Birmingham has no hostels; the TIC does, however, have good **B&B** listings. Take bus #9, 109, 126, or 139 to busy **Hagley Road** for more options.

Cook House, 425 Hagley Rd. (☎429 1916). Take bus #9 or 139 from Colmore Row (20min.) and ask to stop before The King's Head pub, then walk back a few minutes. Many rooms in this Victorian home have fireplaces and original furnishings. Singles £20-22, ensuite £28; doubles and twins £38, ensuite £46. Cash only. ❸

Wentworth Hotel, 103 Wentworth Rd. (☎427 2839). From Harborne swimming bath, turn right on Lonsdale Rd. then left on Wentworth Rd. Spacious rooms and a warm atmosphere. Singles £35; doubles £58; family room £65. MC/V. ❹

Fountain Court, 339-343 Hagley Rd. (☎429 1754). Family-run hotel offers ensuite rooms and lounges. Singles M-Th £38.50, F-Su £35; doubles £65. AmEx/MC/V. ❹

Birmingham

🏠 ACCOMMODATIONS
Cook House, **7**
Fountain Court, **8**
Wentworth Hotel, **9**

🍴 FOOD
Del Villaggio, **5**
The Old Joint Stock, **1**

Thai Edge, **3**
Warehouse Cafe, **4**

⭐ NIGHTLIFE
9 Bar, **6**
Birmingham
Academy, **2**
Nightingale, **10**

🔃 FOOD

Birmingham is most proud of **balti**, a Kashmiri-Pakistani cuisine invented by immigrants and cooked in a special pan. Brochures at the TIC map out the city's *balti* restaurants; the best are southeast of the city center in the *"Balti* Triangle." **Groceries** can be purchased from Sainsbury's, Martineau Pl., 17 Union St. (☎ 236 6496. Open M-Sa 7am-8pm, Su 11am-5pm.) An indoor **market** on Edgbaston St. offers fresh produce. (☎ 622 5449. Open M-Sa 9am-5:30pm.)

The Old Joint Stock, 4 Temple Row (☎ 200 1892), directly behind St. Philip's Cathedral. This gorgeous gastropub, with sweeping curtains and an ornate domed ceiling, has a relaxed clientele and reasonable prices (sandwiches £6.50-7.50). The building was once the Birmingham Joint Stock Bank. ❸

Thai Edge, 7 Oozells Sq. (☎ 643 3993), off Broad St., next to Ikon Gallery. Bamboo poles and minimalist furniture give this popular Thai restaurant a stylish look. Delicious pad thai. Entrees £6-15. Open M-Th noon-2:30pm and 5:30-11:30pm, F-Sa noon-2:30pm and 5:30-midnight, Su noon-3pm and 5:30-11pm. AmEx/MC/V. ❸

Warehouse Cafe, 54 Allison St. (☎ 633 0261), off Digbeth, above the Friends of the Earth office. Look for the brick building with the mural on the side. Birmingham's only vegetarian and vegan establishment. A creative organic menu, daily specials, and lunchtime veggie burgers (£3-5). Open M-Sa noon-3pm, F-Sa also 6-9pm. Cash only. ❶

THE MIDLANDS

Del Villaggio, 245 Broad St. (☎643 4224). Romantic petal-covered tables, cushioned benches, and dim lighting in a modern Italian restaurant. Lunch promotion offers a free glass of the house red or white with any pizza or pasta. Dinner can be pricey; try **Cafe Villaggio,** next door, for affordable takeaway and eat-in options. Open daily noon-2:30pm and 5-11pm. Food served until 10pm. AmEx/MC/V. ❸

⚙ SIGHTS

Birmingham's most significant attraction may be its regenerated shopping districts: **The Mailbox,** Wharfside St., is home to Harvey Nichols, Emporio Armani, and other shops and cafes. Look for the giant red building, which used to be a mailsorting factory. (☎632 1000; www.mailboxlife.com. Open M-W 10am-6pm, Th-Sa 10am-7pm, Su noon-6pm. Times may vary.) The sprawling **Bullring,** The Bullring, recognizable by the wavy, scaled Selfridges, has over 140 retail shops, plus restaurants and cafes. (☎632 1500; www.bullring.co.uk. Open M-F 9:30am-8pm, Sa 9am-8pm, Su 11am-5pm.) **Brindleyplace,** 2 Brunswick St., along the canals, has fewer shops. (☎643 6866; www.brindleyplace.com. Hours set by stores.)
Ikon Gallery, 1 Oozells Sq., in Brindleyplace, shows cutting-edge multimedia art and Turner Prize-winning exhibitions. The beautiful neo-gothic 1877 building hides a postpostmodern white cube interior. (☎248 0708; www.ikon-gallery.co.uk. Open Tu-Su 11am-6pm. Free.) **St. Martin's in the Bull Ring,** the site of Birmingham's first parish church, lies in stunning contrast to the futuristic architecture of Selfridges. The church is the city's unofficial icon and worth a stop. (☎643 5428. Open Tu-Su noon-6pm). The **Birmingham Museum and Art Gallery,** Chamberlain Sq. off Colmore Row, houses costumes, pre-Raphaelite paintings, William Blake's illustrations of Dante's "Inferno," and a new gallery for modern art. (☎303 2834; www.bmag.org.uk. Open M-Th and Sa 10am-5pm, F 10:30am-5pm, Su 12:30-5pm. Free.) Hop onto **The Wheel of Birmingham,** Centenary Square, to see Birmingham's latest architecture from high above Symphony Hall, the International Convention Center, and the Birmingham Repertory Theatre. (☎055 6080. Open daily 11am-11pm. £5.50, children £3.50.) The **Barber Institute of Fine Arts,** in the University of Birmingham on Edgbaston Park Rd., displays works by Rubens, Renoir, Matisse, Gauguin, and Degas. (Bus #61, 62, or 63 from the city center. ☎414 7333. Open M-Sa 10am-5pm, Su 2-5pm. Free.)
The **National Sea Life Centre,** The Water's Edge, Brindleyplace, is home to over 3000 creatures and has the world's first fully transparent 360° underwater tunnel. (☎643 6777. Open daily 10am-5pm. £10, students £8, seniors £7.50, children £7.) **Thinktank at Millennium Point,** Curzon St., Digbeth, offers an interactive science experience, including the kid-friendly LEGOLab. An IMAX theater is in the same complex. (☎202 2222. Open daily 11am-5pm. £7, concessions £5.50, children £5, families £18.) Signs point northwest to over 100 shops lining the **Jewellery Quarter,** which hammers out almost all the jewelry in Britain. **Birmingham City Walks** offers private and public tours along the canals and through the Bullring and the City Center to view the Victorian and modern architecture. (☎427 2555 or through the TIC; www.birmingham-tours.co.uk. Public tours £3-6, private tours vary.) Alternatively, hire a boat around Sherborne Wharf and float through the canals.
Twelve minutes south of town by rail or bus lies ▣**Cadbury World,** a cavity-inducing celebration of the chocolate empire. Sniff your way through the story of chocolate's birth in the Mayan rainforests, watch the factory at work, indulge in free samples of chocolate, and take a trippy Willy Wonka-esque train ride through a land of animatronic cacao beans. Be prepared to fight sugar-high schoolchildren. (By train from New St. to Bournville (every 10 min.) or bus #84 from the city center

(runs less regularly). ☎451 4159; www.cadburyworld.co.uk. Open Mar.-Oct. daily 10am-3pm; Nov.-Feb. Tu-Th and Sa-Su 10am-3pm. £10.50, concessions £8.30, children £8, families £28-33, oompa-loompas free.)

NIGHTLIFE AND ENTERTAINMENT

Birmingham's student population fuels its excellent nightlife venues. Streets beyond the central district can be dangerous. As always, take care at night.

BARS AND CLUBS

Broad Street teems with trendy cafe-bars and clubs. A thriving gay-friendly scene centers on **Essex Street.** Pick up the bimonthly *What's On* to discover the latest hotspots. Clubbers on a budget should grab a guide to public transport's Night Network from the Centro office in New St. Station; **night buses** generally run hourly until 3:30am on Friday and Saturday nights.

9 Bar, 192 Broad St. (☎643 5100). The alluringly dark decor of this futuristic warehouse inspires much drinking and posturing, as well as occasional dancing. Dress smart casual. Cover F £1, Sa £3-5. Open W-Sa 8pm-2am, Su 8pm-1am; 2:30-5am for occasional afterparties.

Nightingale, Essex House, Kent St. (☎622 1718; www.nightingaleclub.co.uk). 2 frenzied dance floors, 5 bars, jazz lounge, and billiard room attract a mostly gay and lesbian crowd from all over. Cover (around £3) varies. Dress smart casual. Open M-Th and Su 5pm-2am, F 5pm-4am, Sa 5pm-7am.

Birmingham Academy (officially Carling Academy Birmingham), 52-54 Dale End (☎262 3000; www.birmingham-academy.co.uk). Birmingham offshoot of monolithic Brixton music venue. Best live venue in Birmingham, with popular club nights. Hours and ticket prices vary. Box office open M-F 11am-5pm, Sa 11am-3:30pm.

MUSIC AND THEATER

The City of Birmingham Symphony Orchestra, at the ICC on Broad St. (☎780 3333; www.cbso.co.uk), plays in the stunning, glass Symphony Hall, opened by the Queen in 1991. Box office open M-Sa 10am-8pm, 10am-6pm if no performance. Su hours depend on concert times. Tickets £5-80, concessions and group discounts available, student standby tickets 1hr. before concerts £3-5.

Hippodrome Theatre, Hurst St. (☎08707 301 234; www.birminghamhippodrome.com). Once a music hall featuring vaudeville artists, the theater now hosts West End musicals and ballet. M-F 10am-9pm, Sa 9:30am-9pm. Tickets £8.50-34, concessions available.

Birmingham Repertory Theatre, Centenary Sq. (☎236 4455), on Broad St. A less grandiose but still celebrated theater hosting dramas, comedies, and new plays. Open M-Sa 9:30am-6pm. Tickets £10-21, discount standby tickets for students and seniors.

The Birmingham International Jazz Festival (☎454 7020) brings over 200 jazz bands, singers, and instrumentalists to town during the first 2 weeks of July. Most events are free; get information on events from the TIC or www.birminghamjazzfestival.com.

IRONBRIDGE   ☎01952

Pretty towns shouldn't have deceptively ugly names, though this one could hardly be more apt: the center of Ironbridge is a grand 18th-century iron bridge arching 55 ft. above the Severn. The bridge owes its existence to Abraham Darby III, who reigned over the iron industry that transformed this scenic riverside settlement into the self-proclaimed birthplace of the Industrial Revolution. Ironbridge's 10 museums cluster around a charming tree-lined village whose horizon juxtaposes lingering industrial infrastructure and stunning natural beauty.

▐ TRANSPORTATION. The nearest **train station** is at Telford, 20min. from Shrewsbury on the Birmingham-Shrewsbury-Chester line (M-Sa 1-4 per hr., Su every hr.). The only way to reach Ironbridge directly is by **bus.** It is essential to call ahead, as the patchy timetables available at TICs often don't agree with schedules posted at bus stops. For bus information, call the TIC, Telford Travelink (☎200 005), or Traveline (☎0870 608 2608). Arriva Midlands North (☎08457 056 005) #96 goes to Ironbridge from Telford (15min., M-Sa 6 per day) and Shrewsbury (40min., M-Sa 6 per day). Most buses to and from Ironbridge do not run past 5 or 6pm. Arriva (☎08456 015 395) runs #99 on the Wellington-Bridgnorth route, stopping at Ironbridge and Coalbrookdale from Telford (25min., M-Sa 16 per day). Arriva #76 (20min., M-Sa 5 per day) and #77 (20min., M-Sa 3 per day) provide service between Coalbrookdale and Coalport (both home to YHA hostels), stopping at the Iron-bridge Museum of the Gorge en route. On weekends and bank holidays, two Gorge Connect services (WH1 and WH2, both 1-2 per hr.) shuttle between the Ironbridge museums; **DayRover** tickets are a good idea (£3, children £1.50) for all-day travel.

▐▐ ORIENTATION AND PRACTICAL INFORMATION. Ironbridge is the name of both the river gorge and the village at the gorge's center. The 10 **Ironbridge Gorge Museums** huddle on the banks of the Severn Valley in an area of 6 sq. mi. Some are difficult to reach without a car—buses run infrequently and stop only at selected points, and bike rental shops are conspicuously absent in town. Central Ironbridge is home to the Iron Bridge and Tollhouse. The Museum of the Gorge is half a mile to the west of the village. North of the Museum of the Gorge, in **Coalbrookdale,** are the Coalbrookdale Museum of Iron, the Darby Houses, and Enginuity. Past the Jackfield bridge, 1½ mi. east of Ironbridge village, **Coalport** is home to the Coalport China Museum and the Tar Tunnel. The Blists Hill Victorian Town is half a mile north of Coalport. The staff at the **TIC,** on the ground floor of the Tollhouse across the Iron Bridge, provides the free *Ironbridge Gorge Visitor Guide* and books accommodations for a 10% deposit. (☎884 391; www.ironbridge.org.uk. Open M-F 9am-5pm, Sa-Su 10am-5pm.) The only **ATM** in town is in Walker's Newsagent on Tontine Hill, and there is a surcharge to use the machine. (Open M-Su 7:30am-5:30pm.) Lloyd's **pharmacy** is located on The Square. (Open M-F 9am-6pm and Sa 9am-1pm.) The **post office** is also on The Square. (☎433 201. Open M-Tu and Th-F 9am-1pm and 2-5:30pm, W 9am-1pm, Sa 9am-12:30pm.) **Post Code:** TF8 7AQ.

▐▐ ACCOMMODATIONS AND FOOD. The two buildings of the **YHA Ironbridge Gorge ❷** grace the valley's opposite ends, 3 mi. apart. One is in **Coalport,** next to the Coalport China Museum, in a renovated china factory, and is equipped with laundry facilities, Internet access (50p per 6min.), and a licensed restaurant. (☎588 755. Reception closes 10:30pm. Open Easter to Oct. daily; Nov. to Easter F-Sa. MC/V. Dorms £14, under 18 £10; ensuite doubles £36.) The more basic hostel in **Coalbrookdale** inhabits a huge remodeled schoolhouse on a hill, 1 mi. from the bridge and TIC. Walk past the Museum of the Gorge and turn right at the roundabout in Coalbrookdale. It has a lounge, games room, kitchen, and laundry. (☎588 755. Reception closes 10:30pm. Open daily Easter to Oct.; winter weekends. MC/V. Lockout 10am-5pm. Dorms £12.50, under 18 £9.) Arriva bus #76 reaches both; Coalbrookdale is also a stop on #77. From Shrewsbury or Telford, #96 passes within half a mile of each.

Other budget accommodations are scarce. Area **B&Bs** charge upwards of £25 per person, and solo travelers can expect to pay at least £35 for a single room. **Coalbrookdale Villa ❹**, 17 Paradise St., is a stunning Gothic house 10min. from Ironbridge village and only a few steps from the Coalbrookdale museum cluster. Its grassy gardens are home to pet sheep that the owners refer to as their "eco-friendly lawn-mowers." The kind proprietor provides welcome trays and full breakfasts. (☎433 450. Singles £48; doubles £62-65. Cash only.) Built in the center of Ironbridge village in 1784, **The Tontine Hotel ❸**, The Square, was constructed by the same men responsible for the bridge, in order to accommodate the growing crowds of tourists. Rooms come with color TVs, telephones, and views of the bridge. Singles are rarely available. (☎432 127. Singles £25; doubles £40-56. MC/V.) The nearest campsite is the **Severn Gorge Caravan Park ❶**, Bridgnorth Rd., in Tweedale, 3 mi. from Ironbridge and 1 mi. north of Blists Hill. (☎684 789. 2-person tent sites £12. Electricity £4. Showers free.)

At **Peacock's Pantry ❷**, 2-4 The Wharfage, menus feature a huge selection of meals like the "Ironmaster" ploughman's lunch (£5), complete with iron-rich black pudding. (☎433 993. Open daily 11am-5pm. Cash only.) Try the warm sausage rolls (£1.20) or the world-famous pork pies at **Eley's ❶** on Tontine Hill; they've been around so long that the shop is recreated in the Victorian village of Blists Hill. (☎432 504. Open M-F 8am-5:30pm and Sa-Su 9am-6pm. Cash only.) Walk 5-10min. uphill toward Madeley for steak-and-kidney pie (£6.50) at the **Horse and Jockey ❶**, 15 Jockey Bank, called the best in England by *Britain Meat*. (☎433 798. Open daily noon-2:30pm and 7-9:30pm. MC/V.)

🏛 **MUSEUMS.** The Ironbridge Gorge Museums are the area's pride and joy, and with good reason: you'd be hard pressed to find a better portrayal of Britain's unique industrial heritage. Spend at least two days to cover them well. If visiting all 10 (or even a significant fraction), buy an **Ironbridge Passport** from any of them, which admits you once to each of the museums (£13.25, seniors £11.50, students and children £8.75, families £42). The major museums are open daily 10am-5pm, while smaller collections such as the Darby Houses have limited hours.

The famous **Iron Bridge,** built in 1779 by Abraham Darby III, spans the River Severn with eye-catching black trusses. A small sign posted on the side of the **Tollhouse** at its southern end lists the fares for every carriage, mule, or child that crosses; even royalty isn't exempt. The TIC occupies the ground floor while the second level houses an exhibit about the

THE LOCAL STORY

VICTORIANA

The recreated Victorian village of **Blists Hill** is authentic to its Victorian roots, not only down to the last teaspoon, but to the smoke from the factory fires. Part of the Museums of the Gorge, Blists Hill stands on a real village site. Coke goes into the 1790 coke mine; charcoal fires a 1850 steam engine; and there's traditional bitter cask ale in Bank's Pub. "Shop owners" and "factory workers" dress in detailed period costume and eagerly share information on their crafts.

On Wednesdays at 11am, two factory wokers demonstrate iron casting, handling red-hot liquid iron with no modern equipment or protection. After throwing large blocks of coke and charcoal into the foundry, the workers release the liquid iron into a bucket, pour it into a mold, and set it to cool.

The pharmacy sports an original dentist's chair and pain-inducing instruments from the 1800s. The chemist demonstrates her ability to cut pills from a large roll of medicinal putty and set them to harden. All of the candy at the confectionary and other period goods can be purchased with original Victorian currency; the town bank changes pence into shillings, farthings, and pennies.

Take bus #39 from Ironbridge to the Madeley Bridge stop. Walk back to the roundabout and then walk up Legges Way; Blists Hill is 5-10min. down the road.

bridge's history, including a brief biography of one of its more eccentric funders, John "Iron Mad" Wilkinson, who minted iron coins stamped with his own image. (☎884 391. Open Easter to Oct. M-F 9am-5pm, Sa-Su 10am-5pm. Free.) A 10min. walk from Ironbridge, the **Museum of the Gorge** provides an introduction to the area's history and is a good place to begin a day's exploration. (☎432 405. £2.25, students £1.20.)

In Coalbrookdale to the northwest, the **Coalbrookdale Museum of Iron** traces the history of the Darby family iron saga. The top floor Great Exhibition recreates the 1851 extravaganza that saw its craft glorified. The massive furnace where Abraham Darby first smelted iron with coke is also on-site. (☎435 960. £5.45, students £3.50.) Just up the hill, the **Darby Houses** model the quarters of the multiple generations of ironmasters who dwelt there. (☎432 551. £3.20/1.75.) **Enginuity,** just across the courtyard from the Museum of Iron, houses child-friendly hands-on displays that will even teach adults a thing or two. (☎435 905. £5.45/3.80.)

In Coalport to the west, the **Coalport China Museum** and the recently reopened **Jackfield Tile Museum** show the products of their industries; both offer demonstrations and workshops. (Both museums ☎580 650. £4.65, students £3.) Don a hard hat at the eerie **Tar Tunnel,** where surprised workers first discovered smudgy natural bitumen dripping from the walls. (☎580 827. £1.25/1.) Across the river from the village are the **Broseley Pipeworks,** located in a town of the same name. Here, clay pipe-making workshops have been preserved in a state of decrepit authenticity. This is the farthest museum (about 30min. by foot), but one of the most interesting. (☎884 391. Open June-Sept. daily 1-5pm. £3.20/1.75.) At the **Blists Hill Victorian Town,** half a mile uphill from Coalport, over 40 recreated buildings deliver kitschy antiquity through local craft. Visitors can exchange modern money for Victorian farthings at the local bank, or chat with actors going about their make-believe business. (☎582 050. £8.75/5.85.) Though it's not part of the Ironbridge Passport deal, the **Ironbridge Open Air Museum of Steel Sculpture** is worth a look. Over 60 modern steel sculptures are installed on 10 acres on Cherry Tree Hill, just uphill from the Museum of Iron. (☎433 152. Open Mar.-Nov. Tu-Su 10am-5pm. £2/1.50.)

SHREWSBURY   ☎01743

Brightly arrayed hatters' windows, hole-in-the-wall boutiques, and a crooked network of ancient roads make Shrewsbury (SHROWS-bree; pop. 60,000) a haven for those with a weakness for stereotypically English streetscapes. The Severn, the longest river in England, nearly encircles the whole of Shrewsbury, which was located here for this natural defense. Roger de Montegomery, second-in-command to William the Conqueror, claimed the area during the 11th century. Immortalized in Shakespeare's *Henry IV,* the Battle of Shrewsbury—between antagonists Prince Hal and Harry Hotspur—reputedly occurred nearby.

▛ TRANSPORTATION

The **train station,** is at the end of Castle St. (Ticket office open M-Sa 5:30am-10pm.) **Trains** (☎08457 484 950) run from: Aberystwyth (1¾hr.; M-Sa 8 per day, Su 5 per day; £15.30); London (3hr.; 1-3 per hr.; £62 peak times, £37.50 off-peak); Swansea (3½-4hr.; M-Sa 3 per day, Su 2 per day; £16.40); Wolverhampton (40min., 2-3 per hr., £7.20); and most of North Wales via Wrexham General and Chester (1hr.; M-Sa every hr., Su 6 per day; £6.90). The **bus station** is on Raven Meadows, which runs parallel to Pride Hill. (☎231 010. Ticket office open M-F 8:30am-5:30pm, Sa 8:30am-4pm.) **National Express** (☎08705 808 080) arrives from: Birmingham (1½hr., 2 per day, £4.80); Llangollen (1hr., 1 per day, £3.60); London (4½hr., 2 per day, £20.50). **Arriva Midlands** #96 runs from Telford via Ironbridge (1hr., M-Sa 6 per day). **Taxis** queue in front of the train station; or call Access Taxis (☎ 360 606. 24hr.).

🌼 ORIENTATION

The **River Severn** circles Shrewsbury's town center in a horseshoe shape, with the curve pointing south. The town's central axis runs from the train station in the northeast to Quarry Park in the southwest: beginning as **Castle Gates**, the road becomes **Castle Street**, then pedestrian-only **Pride Hill**, then **Shoplatch, Mardol Head**, and **St. John's Hill**. **St. Mary's Street** and **High Street** branch off from either end of Pride Hill at the center of town, converging to become Wyle Cop. This road turns into the English Bridge, crosses the river, and reaches the Abbey. The accessible A5 nearly circles the city at a distance of 10 mi.

🔳 PRACTICAL INFORMATION

The Tourist Information Centre, Music Hall, The Square, across from the Market Building, books accommodations for £1.50 (£2 over the phone) plus a 10% deposit. (☎ 281 200; www.shropshiretourism.info. Open May-Sept. M-Sa 9:30am-5:30pm, Su 10am-4pm; Oct.-Apr. M-Sa 10am-5pm.) Historic 1½hr. **walking tours** from the TIC pass through Shrewsbury's medieval "shutts" (closeable alleys). Special Wednesday summer tours feature tea with the mayor. (☎ 281 200. May-Sept. daily 2:30pm; Oct. M-Sa 2:30pm; Nov.-Apr. Sa 2:30pm. £3, children £1.50.) Other services include: Barclays **bank,** 44-46 Castle St., off St. Mary's St. (open M-F 9am-5pm and Sa 9:30pm-3:30pm); a **launderette,** 55 Monkmoor Rd., off Abbey Foregate (☎ 355 151; self-service Sa only; wash £3, dry 20p per 3min., service £9 per load; open M-F 8am-5pm, Sa 10am-4pm, and Su 10am-2pm; last wash 1hr. before close); **police,** Clive Rd. in Monkmoor (☎ 08457 444 888); Royal Shrewsbury **hospital,** Mytton Oak Rd. (☎ 261 138); free **Internet** access at the library (Shropshire Reference and Information Service), 1A Castle Gates, just downhill from the main library (☎ 255 380; open M, W, F 9:30am-5pm; Tu and Th 9:30am-8pm; Sa 9am-5pm; Su 1pm-4pm; photo ID required); Boots **pharmacy,** 9-11 Pride Hill (☎ 351 111; open M-Sa 9am-5:30pm and Su 10:30am-4:30pm); and a **post office,** St. Mary's St., just off Pride Hill, with a bureau de change (☎ 08457 740 740; open M-Sa 9am-5:30pm). **Post Code:** SY1 1DE.

🛏️ 🍴 ACCOMMODATIONS AND FOOD

Singles are hard to find, so reserve several weeks ahead in summer. Several **B&Bs** (£20-30) lie between **Abbey Foregate** and **Monkmoor Road.** A taxi (from £3.20) lets you skip the considerable hike from the bus and train stations. A charming brick townhouse, **Allandale ❸** hides behind the abbey on Abbey Foregate, and hangs its porch with flower baskets and its walls with prints. (☎ 240 173. £25 per person. Cash only.) Comely **Glyndene ❸,** Park Terr., has an elaborate bell-pull and tasteful rooms with TVs. From the bridge, follow the road left of the abbey. (☎ 352 488; www.glyndene.co.uk. £25 per person. Cash only.) The beautifully decorated **Trevellion House ❸,** 1 Bradford St., off Monkmoor Rd., features elegant ensuite rooms with wrought-iron beds. (☎ 249 582. Singles £30; doubles from £50. Cash only.)

Shrewsbury hosts an indoor "Market under the Clock" at the corner of Shoplatch and Bellstone. (☎ 351 067. Open Tu-W and F-Sa, roughly 9am-4pm.) Somerfield **market** is at the Riverside Mall, on Raven Meadows near the bus station. (Open M-W and Sa 8am-6pm, Th-F 8am-7pm, Su 10:30am-4:30pm.) Tucked in St.

Alkmund's Sq., by Butcher Row, the ☒**Bear Steps Coffee House ❶** has patio seating next to a shaded park and warns its taller guests to watch their heads when dining indoors, as timbers are lower than 6 ft. The delicious quiche with bread and butter is £5. (☎244 355. Open roughly M-Sa 10am-4pm. Cash only.) Despite its playful name, **Jesters Restaurant ❸**, 14-15 St. Mary's St., keeps it cool with leather armchairs and an inviting bar inside. Light lunches include wraps (crispy duck with green onion, £5) while dinner entrees start at £11. (☎358 870. Open M-Sa 11am-late. Food served until 9pm. AmEx/MC/V.) **The Good Life Wholefood Restaurant ❶**, Barracks Passage, off Wyle Cop, serves vegetarian cuisine cheap. The nut-loaves (£2.70) are wonderful. (☎350 455. Open Tu-F 9:30am-3pm and Sa 9:30am-4pm.)

⊙ SIGHTS

Aside from its annual flower show, Shrewsbury's biggest attraction is its architecture. Tudoresque houses dot the shopping district and rally in full force at the **Bear Steps**, which start in the alley on High St. across from the Square. **Churches,** many on Saxon foundations, cluster in the town center. At the end of Castle St., the riverside acres of **Quarry Park** are filled with expansive grassy lawns along the oft-flooded Severn. At the center of the park, **Dingle Garden** explodes with bright flowers. Shrewsbury also honors its native sons; check out **Darwin's statue** opposite the castle, the colossal **Lord Hill Column** at the end of Abbey Foregate on the tallest Doric column in Europe, and MP **Robert Clive of India** outside Market Sq.

Vivid red sandstone makes **Shrewsbury Castle,** near the train station, stand out. Built out of wood in 1083, the castle has since been replaced by the Great Hall, which now holds the **Shropshire Regimental Museum** and displays arms from as early as the 18th century. For great views, climb to nearby **Laura's Tower,** a summer garden house built in the 1780s as a 21st-birthday present. (☎358 516. Museum and tower open Easter to May Tu-Sa 10am-5pm; June-Sept. daily 10am-5pm; Oct. to Easter Tu-Sa 10am-4pm. Grounds open Easter to Sept. daily 9am-5pm; Oct. to Easter M-Sa. £2, seniors £1, students and children free. Grounds free.) The **Shrewsbury Museum and Art Gallery,** Barker St., off Shoplatch, displays Iron-Age log boats and a silver mirror from AD 130, as well as exhibits from later history; try on a Tudor frill collar. (☎361 196. Open June-Sept. M-Sa 10am-5pm, Su 10am-4pm; Oct.-Mar. Tu-Sa 10am-4pm; Apr.-May Tu-Sa 10am-5pm. Free.) Beyond the English Bridge, **Shrewsbury Abbey,** a Benedictine abbey founded in 1083, holds the remains of a shrine to St. Winefride, a 7th-century princess who was beheaded and then miraculously recapitated to become an abbot and patron of North Wales and Shrewsbury. A memorial to local WWI poet Wilfred Owen lies in the garden. (☎232 723. Open daily Easter to Oct. 10am-4:45pm; Nov. to Easter 10:30am-3pm. Free.) Shrewsbury hosts an annual **Art Festival** (☎07817 167 772) during July, but the mid-August **Flower Show** sees Shrewsbury's population burgeon to 100,000 over two days to ogle at the world's longest-running horticultural show. (☎234 050; www.shrewsburyflowershow.org.uk. £14.)

▶ DAYTRIP FROM SHREWSBURY

CRAVEN ARMS
Craven Arms is located 20 mi. south of Shrewsbury on the A49. Easiest access is by bus #435 from Shrewsbury (1 hr., 7 per day.)

Twenty miles south of Shrewsbury in Craven Arms, the ☒**Land of Lost Content,** at the corner of Dale St. and Market St., offers a fascinating collection of nostalgic Brit-pop cultural relics. Named after A.E. Housman's "A Shropshire Lad," the museum holds over 30 displays, including a clip-on "Roy Roger" tie, lace-trimmed diapers, cod liver oil, and all the childhood belongings you wish you hadn't left behind. (☎01588 676 176; www.lolc.org.uk. Open Feb.-Nov. daily 11am-5pm; Dec.-Jan. by appointment. £5, children £2.50.) A few blocks away at the **Secret Hills Shropshire Discovery Centre,** on the corner of School Rd. and the A49, visitors explore exhibits on local history, including a replica of the local mammoth skeleton. (☎01588 676 000. Open daily Apr.-Oct. 10am-5:30pm; Nov.-Mar. 10am-4:30pm. Last admission 1hr. before close. £4.25, concessions £3.75, children £2.75.)

STAMFORD ☎01780

William the Conqueror built a castle at Stamford that was destroyed in a string of nasty sieges and is now the site of a small bus station. Long a stopping point for royalty on their way north and a playground for nobility, this tiny city lures travelers with its high spires, crooked alleys, and Norman arches, earning Stamford its reputation as one of the most impressive stone towns in England.

🖥🚌 TRANSPORTATION AND PRACTICAL INFORMATION. Stamford sits at the edge of Lincolnshire, with Cambridgeshire to the south. **Trains** (☎08457 484 950) stop at **Stamford Station,** south of town, from: Cambridge (1hr., every hr., £13.80); Lincoln (2½ hr., 2 per hr., £17.80); London King's Cross (1hr., every hr., £29.80). **Buses** pass through Sheepmarket, off All Saints' St. National Express (☎08705 808 080) makes the trip from London (5½hr., 1 per day, £22.50). To reach the **Tourist Information Centre,** in the Stamford Arts Centre on St. Mary's St., walk straight out of the train station, follow the road as it curves to the right, then take a left on High St. St. Martin's, cross the River Welland, and take a right on St. Mary's St. The TIC gives away a town map, sells the *Town Trail* guide (75p), and books beds for free. (☎755 611. Open Oct.-Mar. M-Sa 9:30am-5pm; Apr.-Sept. M-Sa 9:30am-5pm, Su 10:30am-3:30pm.) Other services include: **banks** along High St.: **Lloyd's TSB,** 65 High St. (☎0845 072 3333; open M-Tu and Th-F 9am-5pm, W 10am-5pm, Sa 9am-12:30pm); **police,** North St. (☎752 222; open daily 8:30am-6:30pm); free **Internet** at the library, on High St. (☎763 442; book in advance; open M and W 9am-8pm, Tu and Th-F 9am-5:30pm, Sa 9am-1pm); and the **post office,** 9 All Saints' Pl. (☎08457 223 344; open M-F 9am-5:30pm, Sa 9am-12:30pm). **Post Code:** PE9 2EY.

🛏🍴 ACCOMMODATIONS AND FOOD. Consider daytripping from Cambridge or Lincoln to avoid Stamford's high prices. **B&Bs** stay on the outskirts; call ahead to get a lift. Try **Gwynne House ❹,** 13 King's Rd., which has large rooms and bathrooms and serves a full English breakfast (☎762 210; www.gwynnehouse.co.uk. Singles £35; doubles and twins £55; family room £75. Cash only). The **Candlesticks Hotel ❹,** 1 Church Ln., convenient to the city center, has a gourmet restaurant and ensuite rooms. (☎764 033. Singles £45; doubles and twins £60. AmEx/MC/V.)

For **groceries** hit Tesco, 46-51 High St. (☎683 000. Open M-W and Sa 7:30am-6pm, Th-F 7:30am-7pm, Su 10am-4pm.) With delicious baguette sandwiches (£5.50), pastries (£1.50), and hot lunches (£6.75-7.25), the **Central Restaurant ❶,** 7 Red Lion Sq., is the best place to get freshly-prepared food at low prices during the day. Includes a restaurant, tea rooms, and an uncannily good bakery. (☎763 217. Open M-Th 9:30am-5pm, F-Sa 8am-5pm. AmEx/MC/V with £5 minimum.) Once the Midlands's premier coaching inn, the **George Hotel ❷,** High St. St. Martin's, is now an upscale hotel and restaurant. Eat in the moderately-priced garden lounge for the atmosphere and Continental fare. (☎750 750. Entrees £10-15. Food served noon-10:30pm. AmEx/MC/V.) Savor a pot of tea (£1.20) and warm your stomach with omelettes and jacket potatoes (£3-6) at **Paddington ❶,** 12a Ironmonger St. (☎751 110. Open M-Th and Sa 9:15am-5pm, F 9:15am-4:30pm. Cash only.)

◧♫ SIGHTS AND ENTERTAINMENT. Stamford's main attraction is ⊠**Burghley House**, England's largest Elizabethan mansion. A 1 mi. walk from Stamford's town center through Burghley Park, it is signposted from High St. St. Martin's. Ringed with gardens designed by "Capability" Brown, the house was the prized creation of William Cecil, Queen Elizabeth I's High Treasurer, and is still occupied by his descendents today. The famous **Heaven Room** and infamous **Hell Staircase** display fantastic works by Antonio Verrio—look for where he's painted himself into the scene. Don't miss Burghley's newest addition, a 12-acre **Sculpture Garden** showcasing rare flowers and modern sculpture. (☎752 451; www.burghley.co.uk. House open Apr.-Oct. M-Th and Sa-Su 11am-5pm. Last admission 4:30pm. Sculpture Garden open daily 11am-5pm. Park open daily Apr.-Oct. 7am-6pm; Nov.-Mar. 7am-8pm. £8.20, concessions £7.20, children £3.70. Sculpture garden June-Aug. Sa-Su £3, children 50p. Park free.) The **Stamford Arts Centre**, St. Mary's St., hosts local productions and national touring companies. (☎763 203. Box office open M-Sa 9:30-8pm and 1hr. before Su shows.) Begun in 1968, the **Stamford Shakespeare Festival** is based at Elizabethan **Tolethorpe Hall** and attracts over 35,000 each year. (☎756 133; www.stamfordshakespeare.co.uk. June-Aug. Tickets £8-16.)

NOTTINGHAM ☎0115

Nottingham (or Snottingham, as the early Anglo-Saxon chronicle has it; pop. 270,000) maintains its age-old tradition, begun by the mythical Robin Hood, of taking from the rich. The modern city uses its favorite rogue to lure tourists to its fluffy attractions; everything, from the streets to the bus lines to the Indian restaurants, manages to exploit Nottingham's fabled hero's name. Despite all this, Nottingham has begun to promote itself as a center of commerce and non-fictional history. Today, Victorian architecture mingles with modern metallic shopping centers, while ordinary streets burst with fashionable shops and trendy bar-cafes.

▐ TRANSPORTATION

Trains: Nottingham Station, Carrington St., south of the city, across the canal. Trains (☎08457 484 950) from: **Lincoln** (1hr., 2 per hr., £6.20); **London St. Pancras** (1¾hr., 2 per hr., £41); **Sheffield** (1hr., every hr., £7.60).

Buses: Broad Marsh Bus Station (☎950 3665), between Collin St. and Canal St. Ticket and info booth open M-F 9am-5:30pm. **National Express** (☎08705 808 080) from **London** (3hr., 8 per day, £15) and **Sheffield** (1½hr., 9 per day, £5.75). **Victoria Bus Station** is at the corner of York St. and Cairn St. **Nottinghamshire County Council Buses** link points throughout the county.

Public Transportation: For short urban journeys, hop on a **Nottingham City Transport** bus (40-90p). All-day local bus pass £2. For public transit info, call the **Nottinghamshire Buses Hotline** (☎0870 608 2608; www.nctx.co.uk). Open daily 7am-8pm. The city is currently in the process of expanding a **tram** system (☎942 7777; www.thetram.net) as well, which now mostly connects downtown with the suburbs of Nottinghamshire, but will soon serve as a major source of intercity transportation. The first phase runs from the Nottingham train station to Hucknall, stopping along the way.

▉ ⓘ ORIENTATION AND PRACTICAL INFORMATION

Nottingham is a busy city and its streets are often confusing and scantily labeled. Its hub is **Old Market Square,** the plaza that spreads before the domed Council House (beware the low-flying pigeons). The canal cuts across the south of the city.

Nottingham

ACCOMMODATIONS
Bentinck Hotel, **8**
Igloo, **2**
Lindum House, **1**

FOOD
Alley Cafe, **4**
Bellini, **6**

PUBS
Ye Olde Trip to
Jerusalem, **7**

NIGHTLIFE
Rock City, **3**
The Social, **5**

Tourist Information Centre: 1-4 Smithy Row (☎915 5330; www.experiencenottingham-shire.com), off Old Market Sq. Many reference guides, tour and **job listings,** a free city map, and free entertainment listings. Books rooms (before 4:30pm) for an additional fee plus a 10% deposit. Open M-F 9am-5:30pm, Sa 9am-5pm, Su 10am-4pm.

Tours: Nottingham Experience (☎911 5005) leads 30min. tours, leaving from the castle gatehouse. Book in advance by phone. Office open daily Apr.-Oct. 10am-4pm. £4, concessions £2.50.

Financial Services: American Express, 2 Victoria St. (☎924 7705). Open M-Tu and Th-F 9am-5:30pm, W 9:30am-5:30pm, Sa 9am-5pm.

Launderette: Brights, 150 Mansfield Rd. (☎948 3670), near the Igloo hostel. Open M-Tu and Th-F 9:15am-7pm, W and Sa 9:15am-6pm, Su 9:30am-5pm; last wash 1hr. before close on weekdays, 1.5hr. on weekends.

Police: North Church St. (☎967 0999).

Hospital: Queen's Medical Center, Derby Rd. (☎924 9924).

Internet Access: Nottingham Central Library, Angel Row (☎915 2841). Free. Open M-F 9:30am-7pm, Sa 9am-1pm. **Combat Strike,** The Cornerhouse, on Burton St. (☎988 1880; www.combatstrike.com). £4 per hour. Open M-Th 11am-10pm, F-Su 10am-late.

Post Office: Queen St. Open M-Sa 10am-5:30pm. **Post Code:** NG1 2BN.

ACCOMMODATIONS

Moderately priced **guest houses** (£30-35) cluster on **Goldsmith Street,** near Nottingham Trent University.

Igloo, 110 Mansfield Rd. (☎947 5250), on the north side of town, across from the Golden Fleece. Convenient, if a bit lackluster. TV lounge and kitchen. Curfew 3am. Dorms £13.50. Discounts for extended stays. MC/V with 50p surcharge. ❷

Bentinck Hotel, Station St. (☎958 0285), directly across from the train station. Great location. Clean rooms with TVs, and a bar downstairs open until 11:30pm. Singles £19.50, ensuite £23.50. MC/V. ❸

Lindum House, 1 Burns St. (☎847 1089). Take the tram to the High School station, near the Arboretum. TVs and plants in sunny rooms off an impressive wooden staircase in a friendly Victorian guest house. Breakfast included. No smoking. Singles £40; doubles and twins £50-60. Cash only. ❹

FOOD AND PUBS

Quick, inexpensive bites abound on **Milton Street** and **Mansfield Road.** Gaggles of sandwich shops, trendy cafes, and ethnic eateries line **Goosegate.** There is a Tesco **supermarket** in the Victoria Shopping Centre. (☎980 7500. Open M-Tu and Th-Sa 8am-7pm, W 8am-8pm, Su 11am-5pm.)

The Alley Cafe, 1a Cannon Ct. (☎955 1013), off Long Row West. Low prices and high-quality smoothies and sandwiches (£3.10) in a friendly, comfortable vegetarian hideaway. Check for specials and lower prices at off-peak meal times. The bar is a hotspot after dinner ends at 9pm. Open M-Tu 11am-6pm, W-Sa 11am-11pm. MC/V. ❶

Ye Olde Trip to Jerusalem, 1 Brewhouse Yard (☎947 3171; www.triptojerusalem.com). This popular pub, claimant to the title of "Oldest Inn in England," served its first pot of ale in 1189 and was a staging point for soldiers setting off on the Crusades. Known as "The Trip," the pub is carved into the castle's base. Open M-Sa 11am-11pm, Su noon-10:30pm. Food served M-Sa 11am-6pm, Su noon-6pm. MC/V with £5 minimum. ❶

Bellini, 62-64 Maid Marian Way (☎941 1117). Creative Continental cuisine plus Iranian specialties. Entrees £5-9. 10% student discount. Open M-Sa noon-2pm and 6-11pm, Su 6-10pm. MC/V. ❷

SIGHTS

GALLERIES OF JUSTICE. This interactive museum occupies five subterranean levels below the old Shire Hall. Visitors can explore special exhibitions, like evidence from the 1963 **Great Train Robbery,** before being submitted to the worst of historical English "justice" in the **Crime and Punishment Galleries** (you'll be convicted of trumped-up charges before a merciless judge). Learn about Britain's history of punishment, such as the practice of "ducking," or repeatedly dunking an offender into a body of water, while viewing authentic punishment devices like stocks and gallows in Nottingham's historic "county gaol." Tours last approximately 1¼hr. *(Shire Hall, High Pavement. ☎952 0555; www.galleriesofjustice.org.uk. Open mid-July to Aug. daily 10am-5pm; Sept. to mid-July Tu-Su 10am-3pm. Last admission 1hr. before close. £8, concessions and children £6, families £23.)*

NOTTINGHAM CASTLE. William the Conqueror put up the original timber structure in 1068, and Henry III had the whole thing redone in stylish gray stone. The ruins of the castle now top a sandstone rise south of the city center. In 1642,

Charles I raised his standard against Parliament here, kicking off the Civil War. For its pernicious part in the affair, the castle was destroyed by Parliamentarians. What's left now houses the **Castle Museum and Art Gallery,** a collection of historical exhibits on Nottinghamshire's past, Victorian art, silver, and the regimental memorabilia of the Sherwood Foresters, the regional militia. (☎ 915 3700. Open daily 10am-5pm. Last entry 4:30pm. £3, concessions £1.50, families £7.) While you're there, check out **Mortimer's Hole,** the underground passageway leading from the base of the cliff to the castle. (☎ 915 3700. 50min. tours leave from museum entrance Oct.-Mar. M-Sa 11am, 2, 3pm; Apr.-Sept. Su noon, 2pm. £2, concessions £1.)

CITY OF CAVES. Nottingham is riddled with hundreds of caves. As early as the 10th century, Anglo-Saxon dwellers dug homes out of the soft and porous "Sherwood sandstones" on which the city rests. In medieval times, the caves were often preferred to more conventional housing—they required no building materials and incurred lower taxes. During WWII, many caves were converted to air-raid shelters. Visitors can take a guided tour of one cave complex, surreally situated beneath (and accessed through) the second floor of Broad Marsh Shopping Centre. (☎ 952 0555; www.cityofcaves.com. Open daily 10:30-4:30pm. Last tour 4pm. 40min. guided tour £4.25, concessions £3.50, families £14. 40min. audio tour £3.75/2.75/11.50.)

TALES OF ROBIN HOOD. Cable cars transport visitors through an amusement-park version of Sherwood Forest. Release your inner outlaw at a medieval banquet (£35 per person for costume, 4 courses, and lots of beer) or at a **medieval murder mystery** (£23.50 per person for three courses) where you can figure out who killed the Sheriff's bride-to-be. (30-38 Maid Marian Way. ☎ 948 3284. Open daily 10am-5:30pm. Last admission 4:30pm. £7, concessions £6, children £5, families £20.)

🎵 NIGHTLIFE AND ENTERTAINMENT

Students crowd the city's more than thirty clubs and pubs. Live bands, primarily of the punk and indie variety, play to a young crowd on the two floors at **The Social,** 23 Pelham St., where theme nights and special events abound. (☎ 950 5078; www.the-social.com. Open M-Tu 5pm-12:30am, W-F 5pm-2am, Sa noon-2am.) **Rock City,** 8 Talbot St., hosts local bands and has enough theme nights to accommodate musical tastes from punk to techno. "Loveshack" Fridays bop to three decades of pop, while Saturdays are alternative. (☎ 941 2544; www.rock-city.co.uk. Cover £5-25. Open Tu and Th-Sa 10pm-2am.) Traditional theater can be found at the **Theatre Royal,** Theatre Sq. (☎ 989 5555; www.royalcentre-nottingham.co.uk.) The **Nottingham Playhouse,** Wellington Circus, features more offbeat productions, though it offers its share of Shakespeare as well. (☎ 941 9419; www.nottinghhamplay-house.co.uk. Box office open M-Sa 10am-8pm. Tickets £7-35.)

🏛 DAYTRIPS FROM NOTTINGHAM

NEWSTEAD ABBEY. The ancestral estate of **Lord Byron** stands north of Nottingham in the village of Linby. The sprawling, stately home is built around the remnants of a medieval abbey. Byron moved in as a child and remained here until he was forced to sell the abode. Many personal effects remain, including a replica of Byron's "skull cup"—an ancient human cranium the poet coated with silver, inscribed with verse, and filled with wine. The original was reinterred in 1863. Raucous peacocks hold court in the gardens; a sign warns that shiny cars are vulnerable during mating season. (Buses #737, 747, and 757 travel from Nottingham Victoria Station to the abbey gates (30min., 3 per hr., round-trip £3.50), 1 mi. from the house and grounds. Additional buses on Su and bank holidays stop directly at the house. ☎01623 455

900; www.newsteadabbey.org.uk. House open Apr.-Sept. daily noon-5pm. Last entry 4pm. Grounds open 9am-6pm; last admission 5pm. House and grounds £6, concessions £4, under 16 £2.50. Grounds only £3, concessions £2.50, families £8.50.)

SHERWOOD FOREST. To the north of Nottingham spreads famed Sherwood Forest, considerably thinned since the 13th century. The **Sherwood Forest Visitor Centre** has a small museum; beware the legions of children armed with mini-archery sets. To escape the crowds, take the signposted 3½ mi. walk, making sure to stop at the "Major Oak," which, at 33 ft. in girth, allegedly served as Robin's hideout. In early August, the medieval **Robin Hood Festival** includes a jousting tournament. Check with the TIC for exact dates. *(Buses #33 and 36 leave Nottingham Victoria Station (40min., 1 per 1½hr., £5.80). ☎01623 823 202. Forest and centre open daily 10am-5pm. Free.)*

EASTWOOD. Eastwood native and teacher D. H. Lawrence had his novels banned from the bookshelves; now he's buried in Westminster Abbey. The **D.H. Lawrence Birthplace Museum** celebrates his fame from a house where he spent his first two years. *(8a Victoria St., near Mansfield Rd. ☎01773 717 353. Open daily Apr.-Oct. 10am-5pm; Nov.-Mar. 10am-4pm. M-F free; Sa-Su £2, children and concessions £1.20, families £5.80.)* The **Sons and Lovers Cottage,** where young D.H. lived from 1887 to 1891, is free and open by appointment. *(28 Garden Rd. ☎01773 712 132. Eastwood is 6 mi. west of Nottingham. Rainbow bus #1 (40min., £4.20) leaves often from Nottingham Victoria Station.)*

LINCOLN   ☎01522

Medieval streets climb their cobbled way past half-timbered homes to Lincoln's dominating 12th-century cathedral, a relative newcomer in a town built for retired Roman legionnaires in the 1st century AD. Lincoln does not draw many tourists, but those who do make it will find a bustling marketplace and (after a steep uphill climb to the city's peak) sweeping views of the dusky Lincolnshire Wolds (especially from along Yarborough Rd.). Lincolnshire is also renowned for its sausage, excellent examples of which may be found in the market.

▐ TRANSPORTATION

Lincoln's **Central Station** is on St. Mary's St. (Office open M-Sa 5:45am-7:30pm, Su 10:30am-9:20pm. Travel center open M-Sa 9am-5pm.) **Trains** arrive from: Leeds (2hr., 2 per hr., £19.80); London King's Cross (2hr., every hr., £46); Nottingham (1hr.; M-Sa 2 per hr., Su 7 per day; £6.90). Opposite Central Station is **City Bus Station,** Melville St. (Open M-F 8:30am-5pm, Sa 9am-1:45pm.) National Express **buses** come from London (5hr., 1 per day, £19-20) and Birmingham (3hr., 1 per day, £12.20). For info on Lincolnshire bus services, contact the Lincolnshire Roadcar station on Deacon Rd. (☎522 255; www.roadcar.co.uk. Open M-F 8:30am-5pm.)

✈ ▐ ORIENTATION AND PRACTICAL INFORMATION

Lincoln has an affluent acropolis on **Castle Hill** and a cottage-filled lower town near the tracks. The TIC and major sights lie at the junction of **Steep Hill** and Castle Hill. The University of Lincoln campus is to the northwest.

Tourist Information Centre: 9 Castle Hill (☎873 213; www.lincoln.gov.uk). Books rooms for a £2 charge plus a 10% deposit. Pick up a miniguide with map (50p). Open M-Th 9:30am-5:30pm, F 9:30am-5pm, Sa 10am-5pm. Also at The Cornhill (☎873 256). Offers same services. Open M-Th 9:30am-5:30pm, F 9am-5pm, Sa 10am-5pm.

Tours: 1hr. tours depart from the TIC July-Aug. daily 11am and 2:15pm; Sept.-Oct. and Apr.-June Sa-Su only. £3.

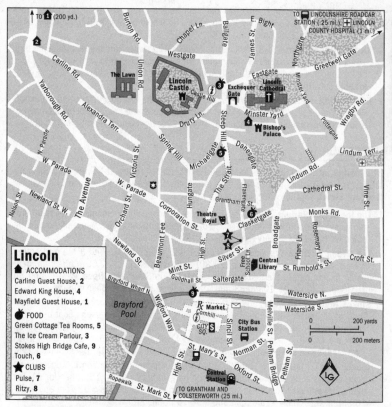

Lincoln

⛺ ACCOMMODATIONS
Carline Guest House, **2**
Edward King House, **4**
Mayfield Guest House, **1**

🍎 FOOD
Green Cottage Tea Rooms, **5**
The Ice Cream Parlour, **3**
Stokes High Bridge Cafe, **9**
Touch, **6**

★ CLUBS
Pulse, **7**
Ritzy, **8**

Financial Services: Major **banks** line High St. and Cornhill Pavement. **Thomas Cook,** 4 Cornhill Pavement (☎346 400). Open M-Tu and Th-Sa 9am-5:30pm, W 10am-5:30pm.

Pharmacy: Boots, 311-312 High St. (☎524 303). Open M-Sa 8:30am-6pm, Su 10:15am-4:45pm.

Police: West Parade (☎882 222), near the town hall.

Hospital: Lincoln County Hospital, Greetwell Rd., off Greetwell Gate. (☎512 512).

Internet Access: Central Library, Free School Ln. (☎510 800). Free. Open M-F 9:30am-7pm, Sa 9:30am-4pm. **Sun Cafe,** St. Mary's St. (☎569 292). £2 per hr. Open M-Sa 9am-6pm, Su noon-5pm.

Post Office: City Sq., Sincil St. (☎513 004), just off High St. Bureau de change. Open M-Tu and Th 8:30am-5:30pm, W and F 9am-5:30pm. **Post Code:** LN5 7XX.

🏠 ACCOMMODATIONS

B&Bs (most £17-20) dot **Carline Road** and **Yarborough Road,** west of the castle. Consult the accommodations list in the window of the TIC on Cornhill.

Mayfield Guest House, 213 Yarborough Rd. (☎533 732). Entrance behind house on Mill Rd., off Long Leys Rd., a 20min. walk northwest from the station (or take bus #7 or 8 to Yarborough Rd.). Victorian mansion near a windmill with large rooms, most ensuite, and fluffy quilts. Mind the cockatiel. No smoking. Singles £25; doubles £46; twins £48; triple £60. AmEx/MC/V. ❸

Carline Guest House, 1-3 Carline Rd. (☎530 422; www.carlineguesthouse.co.uk). 15min. walk northwest of the train station (or take bus #7 or 8 to Yarborough Rd.). Big beds, spacious ensuite rooms, tasty breakfasts, and friendly owners make for a comfortable stay. Doubles £48. AmEx/MC/V. ❸

Edward King House, Minster Yard (☎528 778), near the Bishop's Palace and cathedral. Run by the diocese. Views are divine, building immaculate, and central location miraculous. Continental breakfast included. Singles £25; doubles £48. AmEx/MC/V. ❸

🍴 FOOD

The **market,** at Sincil St., sells local food and oddities (open M-F 9am-4pm, Sa 9am-4:30pm). Restaurants, tea rooms, and takeaways grace **High Street,** while pubs line **Bailgate Street,** on the other side of the hill.

🍴 **The Ice Cream Parlour,** 3 Bailgate. This tiny shop scoops out homemade ice cream, frozen yogurt, and sorbet. A double scoop of orange brandy is £1.90. Descend the winding staircase to a 14th-century tea room. Open daily 10am-dusk. Cash only. ❶

The Green Cottage Tea Rooms, 18 Steep Hill (☎537 909). With 3 tea and coffee menus, a selection of baguettes (£4.80) and pastries (£1.20-2.50), this is an ideal place to rest before the last leg of your ascent up Steep Hill. Open M, W-F, and Su 10:30am-4:30pm, Sa 10am-5:30pm. Lunch served noon-3pm. Cash only. ❶

Stokes High Bridge Cafe, 207 High St. (☎513 825). Busy tea room in a century-old Tudor-style house/bridge, displayed on many a postcard. Watch swans float by on the green canal, or look down on the High St. bustle from 3 floors above while nibbling steak pie (£5.40). 2-course lunch special (£4.50) served 11:45am-2pm. Open M-Sa 9am-5pm; stops serving at 4:30pm. Tea served 2-5pm. MC/V with £10 minimum. ❶

Touch, 43-47 Clasketgate (☎522 221; www.touchrestaurantbar.com). Modern European cuisine in an sleek atmosphere, with bargain buffet lunch: 15 dishes for £4. For dinner, try entrees like lime-scented tuna (£12.50). £1 discounts 5:30-7pm and 9:30-10:30pm. Open daily 11am-3pm and 5:30-10:30pm. MC/V. ❸

👁 SIGHTS

🏛 **LINCOLN CATHEDRAL.** While the rest of Lincoln endured a millennium of rumblings in which Roman barricades, bishops' palaces, and conquerors' castles were erected and destroyed, the magnificent cathedral remained king of the hill. Begun in 1072 but not completed for three centuries, it was the continent's tallest building until the spire toppled. The shimmering Lincolnshire limestone and broad front overwhelm the castle across the street. Its many endearing features include the imp in the **Angel Choir,** who turned to stone while attempting to chat with seraphim. A treasury room displays sacred silver and a shrine to child martyr Sir Hugh. Rotating exhibits reside in the first library designed by **Christopher Wren.** (☎544 544; www.lincolncathedral.com. Open June-Aug. M-Sa 7:15am-8pm, Su 7:15am-6pm; Sept.-May M-Sa 7:15am-6pm, Su 7:15am-5pm. Evensong M-Sa 5:30pm, Su 3:45pm. Tours M-Sa 11am, 1, 3pm; free roof tours M, W, F 2pm; Tu, Th, Sa 11am and 2pm. Tour required to enter. Library open during exhibitions and by appointment. Cathedral £4, concessions £3, children £1.)

LINCOLN CASTLE. Home to one of four surviving copies of the *Magna Carta,* this 1068 castle was also the house of pain and solitude for inmates of the Victorian Castle Prison. A cheerful guide leads the "Prison Experience," among other tours. Visit the dungeon in Cobb Hall, where shackles still protrude from the stone walls. (☎511 068. Open Apr.-Oct. M-Sa 9:30am-5:30pm, Su 11am-5:30pm; Nov.-Mar. M-Sa 9:30am-4:30pm, Su 11am-4:30pm. Last admission 1hr. before close. Tours daily Sa-Su 11am and 2pm. £3.70, concessions £2.15, families £9.60.)

BISHOP'S PALACE. The medieval Bishop's Palace was originally wedged between the walls of the upper and lower Roman cities. Thanks to 12th-century Bishop Chesney, a passageway through the upper city wall links the palatial remains to the cathedral. The palace itself—in Chesney's time the seat of England's largest diocese—is now peacefully ruined, surrounded by vineyards and views. (☎527 468. Open Apr.-June and Sept.-Oct. daily 10am-5pm; July-Aug. daily 10am-6pm; Nov.-Mar. M and Th-Su 10am-4pm. £3.60, concessions £2.70, children £1.80, families £9.)

⬛ 🌼 NIGHTLIFE AND FESTIVALS

On the corner of Silver St. and Flaxengate, **Ritzy** (☎522 314) draws long lines, while upstairs, **Pulse** (☎522 314) has a range of theme nights. (Both clubs open M-F 10pm-2am, Sa 10pm-2:30am, Su 9pm-12:30am. Last admission 1hr. before close. £5 cover.) The monthly *What's On*, at the TIC, has the latest nightlife listings. The **Theatre Royal,** Clasketgate, near the corner of High St., stages drama, concerts, and musicals. (☎525 555. Box office open M-F 10am-2pm and 3-6pm, Sa 10am-2pm and 5-6pm. Tickets £7-22, concessions available M-Th.) Lincoln offers one of Europe's largest **Christmas Markets,** 4 days of Victorian banqueting and fairs in the marketplace in early December. July brings the **Waterfront Festival,** with street theater, acrobats, and jet ski displays, and the **Lincoln Early Music Festival** is in August.

⬛ DAYTRIPS FROM LINCOLN

GRANTHAM. Young Sir Isaac Newton attended the **King's School** in Grantham and left his signature carved in a windowsill. (Brook St. ☎01476 563 180. By appointment only. Free; donations accepted.) The **Grantham Museum** has exhibits on Newton and another of Grantham's own, Margaret Thatcher. (Museum on St. Peter's Hill, by the TIC. ☎01476 568 783. Open M-Sa 10am-5pm; last admission 4:30pm. Free. Grantham is 25 mi. south of Lincoln; 45min. by train (round-trip £8.80). Lincolnshire Roadcar (☎522 255) bus #1 (1¼hr.; M-Sa 2 per hr., Su less frequent; round-trip £4) runs from St. Mark St. Station.)

COLSTERWORTH. Seven miles from Grantham stands **Woolsthorpe Manor,** Newton's birthplace. Young Isaac scribbled his early musings on the farmhouse wall, and visitors can still peep at his genius-graffiti. Whether he was actually bonked by one of the apple tree's inspirational fruits is debatable, but this is the site of his "what goes up, must come down" deliberations. The barn contains the **Sir Isaac Newton Science Discovery Centre,** a fantastic hands-on exhibit that clarifies Newtonian ideas for the mathematically-disinclined. (Lincolnshire Roadcar, ☎522 255, runs from Grantham (18min., every 2-3hr., round-trip £2.60). ☎01476 860 338. Open Apr.-Oct. W-Su 1-5pm; Mar. and Oct. Sa-Su 1-5pm. Manor £3.60, children £1.80. Discovery Centre free.)

EAST ANGLIA

Once swampy marshland, the Fens were drained in the 1820s, yielding new fertile farmland. Continental-style windmills helped maintain the drained fens and some still mark the marshes. From Norwich east to the English Channel, the water that once drenched enormous medieval peat bogs was channeled into the maze of waterways known as the Norfolk Broads, now a popular national park. Farther inland, Norman invaders made their way to Ely, building a cathedral from stone transported by boat across then-flooded fenland; and in a village to the south, renegade scholars from Oxford set up shop along the River Cam in the 15th century.

HIGHLIGHTS OF EAST ANGLIA

STROLL among Cambridge's colleges or punt down the river in this picturesque university town, one of the world's oldest and best-known reserves of scholarship (p. 307).

GAZE skyward at Ely Cathedral, a medieval masterwork, still breathtaking as it towers over former fenland (p. 316).

MIND your map in Norwich, a twisting, wool-trading town, once the largest in Anglo-Saxon England, where markets and festivals have endured for centuries (p. 326).

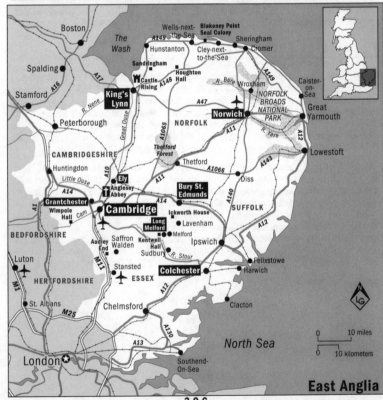

East Anglia

▐ TRANSPORTATION IN EAST ANGLIA

The major rail operator is **One Railway** (☎0845 600 7245; www.onerailway.com). A combined **Plus Pass** (£60), available at stations within East Anglia, entitles you to a week's unlimited travel on all **train** routes in the region. A **regular Plus Pass** allows a week of unlimited travel in either Norfolk or Suffolk (£29). Both zones are covered by their own one- and three-day passes (£10 and £20). Plus Passes also grant free travel on various lines of the Norwich, Ipswich, and Great Yarmouth **bus** services.

East Anglia's flat terrain and dry climate (relative to the rest of England) pleases **cyclists** and **hikers,** though bike rental shops are rare outside of Cambridge and Norwich. The area's most popular walking trail is **Peddar's Way,** which runs from Knettishall Heath to Holme and includes the **Norfolk Coast Path** and **Weaver's Way.** TICs in Norwich, Bury St. Edmunds, and several Suffolk villages issue *Peddar's Way and Norfolk Coast Path* and other walking guides.

Harwich (HAR-idge) is a ferry depot for Holland, Germany, and Scandinavia, and **Felixstowe** has ferries to Belgium. (See **By Ferry,** p. 28). Call the Harwich Tourist Information Centre, Iconfield Park, Parkeston, for details. (☎01255 506 139. Open Apr.-Sept. M-F 9am-5pm, Sa-Su 9am-4pm; Oct.-Mar. M-F 9am-5pm, Sa 9am-4pm.) The Felixstowe TIC is on the seafront. (☎01394 276 770. Open daily 9am-5:30pm.)

CAMBRIDGESHIRE

CAMBRIDGE ☎01223

In contrast to museum-oriented, metropolitan Oxford, Cambridge is determined to retain its pastoral academic robes—the city manages, rather than encourages, visitors. No longer the exclusive preserve of upper-class sons, the university has opened its doors to women and state school pupils. Some old upper-crust traditions are slipping, too: now students only bedeck themselves in gown and cravat once a week. At exams' end, Cambridge explodes in Pimm's-soaked glee, and May Week (two weeks in mid-June, naturally) launches a swirl of parties and balls.

▐ TRANSPORTATION

Bicycles are the primary mode of transportation in Cambridge, a city which claims more bikes per person than any other place in Britain. On bike or on foot, watch out for confused drivers: one-way streets and countless foreign youths used to riding on the wrong side of the road complicate summer transport. If driving to Cambridge, take advantage of its efficient park-and-ride system.

Trains: Station on Station Rd. Ticket office open daily 5am-11pm. Trains (☎08457 484 950) arrive from **London King's Cross** (45min., 3 per hr., £16.40) and **London Liverpool Street** (1¼hr., 5 per hr., £16.40).

Buses: Drummer St. Station. Ticket booth open daily 8:45am-5:30pm; tickets also often available onboard. National Express (☎08705 808 080) comes from **London** (2hr., 2 per hr., £9.30), and runs shuttles from: **Gatwick** (4hr., every hr., £28); **Heathrow** (2½hr., every hr., £24); **Stansted** (1hr., every hr., £8.80). Stagecoach Express (☎01604 676 060) runs from **Oxford** (3hr., every hr., from £6). Buy tickets from the Bus and Coach office opposite the station.

Public Transportation: Stagecoach (☎423 578) runs from the train station to the city center and around town (£1-2). Whippet Coaches (☎01480 463 792) offers daytrips.

Taxis: Cabco (☎312 444) and **Camtax** (☎313 131). Both 24hr.

Bike Rental: Mike's Bikes, 28 Mill Rd. (☎312 591). £10 per day. £35 deposit. Lock and light included. Open M-Sa 9am-6pm, Su 10am-4pm. MC/V.

Cambridge has two main avenues; the main shopping street starts at **Magdalene Bridge** and becomes **Bridge Street, Sidney Street, Saint Andrew's Street, Regent Street,** and **Hills Road.** The other main thoroughfare starts as **Saint John's Street,** becoming **Trinity Street, King's Parade,** and **Trumpington Street.** From the **Drummer Street** bus station, **Emmanuel Street** leads to the shopping district near the TIC. To get to the center from the train station, turn right onto Hills Rd. and follow it for ¾ mi.

Tourist Information Centre: Wheeler St. (☎09065 862 526; www.visitcambridge.org), 1 block south of Market Sq. Pack of 5 cycling map routes £2.75. Books rooms for £3 plus a 10% deposit. A Cambridge Visitors Card gives city-wide discounts (£2.50). Advance booking hotline (at least 5 days; ☎457 581; calls charged at 60p; open M-F 9am-5pm). Open M-F 10am-5:30pm, Sa 10am-5pm, Su 11am-4pm.

Tours: 2hr. walking tours of the city and a college or two (usually King's) leave from the TIC. Call for times and tickets (☎457 574). £8.50, children £4. **City Sightseeing** (☎01353 663 659) runs 1hr. hop-on, hop-off bus tours every 15-30min. Apr.-Oct. £8, concessions £6, children £3.50.

Budget Travel: STA Travel, 38 Sidney St. (☎366 966; www.statravel.co.uk). Open M-Th 9:30am-6:30pm, F 10am-5:30pm, Sa 11am-5pm.

Financial Services: Banks on Market Sq. **Thomas Cook,** 8 St. Andrew's St. (☎543 100). Open M-Tu and Th-Sa 9am-5:30pm, W 10am-5:30pm. **American Express,** 25 Sidney St. (☎08706 001 060). Open M-F 9am-5:30pm, Sa 9am-5pm.

Work Opportunities: Blue Arrow, 40 St. Andrews St. (☎323 272; www.bluearrow.co.uk). Year-round temp work. Arrange early for summer. Open M-F 8am-5:30pm.

Pharmacy: Boots, 65-67 Sidney St. (☎350 213). Open M 9am-6pm, Tu 8:30am-6pm, W 8:30am-7pm, Th-Sa 8:30am-6pm, Su 11am-5pm.

Launderette: Clean Machine, 22 Burleigh St. (☎566 677). £3 per small load. Open M-F 9am-8:30pm, Sa-Su 9am-4pm. Last wash 1hr. before close.

Police: Parkside (☎358 966).

Hospital: Addenbrookes, Long Rd. (☎245 151). Take Cambus C1 or C2 from Emmanuel St. (£1), and get off where Hills Rd. intersects Long Rd.

Internet Access: International Telecom Centre, 2 Wheeler St. (☎357 358), across from the TIC. £1 for first 30min., then 3-4p per min. Open M-Sa 9am-11pm, Su 10am-11pm. **Jaffa Net Cafe,** 22 Mill Rd. (☎308 380). £2 per hr., £5 for 5hr. 10% student discount. Open daily 10am-10pm.

Post Office: 9-11 St. Andrew's St. (☎08457 223 344). **Bureau de change.** Open M-Sa 9am-5:30pm. **Post Code:** CB2 3AA.

⚑ ACCOMMODATIONS

Rooms are scarce, which drives up prices. Most **B&Bs** aren't in the town center, but some around **Portugal Street** and **Tenison Road** house students during the academic year and are open to visitors in July and August.

▧ **Tenison Towers Guest House,** 148 Tenison Rd. (☎363 924; www.cambridgecitytenisontowers.com). Fresh flowers grace airy rooms in this impeccable Victorian house 2 blocks from the train station. No smoking. Breakfast includes homemade muffins. Singles £28-30; doubles £55. Cash only. ❸

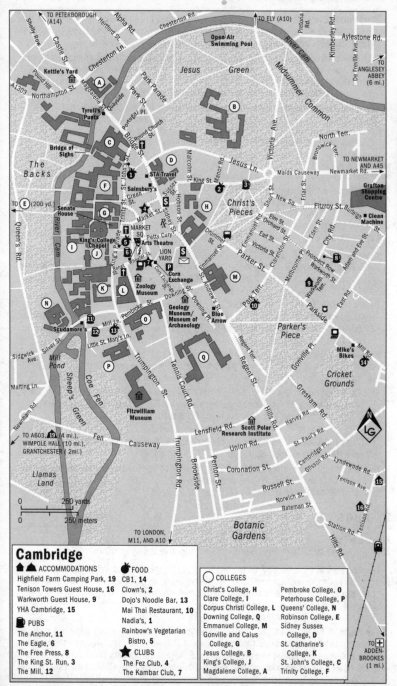

Cambridge

▲ ACCOMMODATIONS
Highfield Farm Camping Park, **19**
Tenison Towers Guest House, **16**
Warkworth Guest House, **9**
YHA Cambridge, **15**

■ PUBS
The Anchor, **11**
The Eagle, **6**
The Free Press, **8**
The King St. Run, **3**
The Mill, **12**

● FOOD
CB1, **14**
Clown's, **2**
Dojo's Noodle Bar, **13**
Mai Thai Restaurant, **10**
Nadia's, **1**
Rainbow's Vegetarian
Bistro, **5**

★ CLUBS
The Fez Club, **4**
The Kambar Club, **7**

○ COLLEGES
Christ's College, **H**
Clare College, **I**
Corpus Christi College, **L**
Downing College, **Q**
Emmanuel College, **M**
Gonville and Caius
College, **G**
Jesus College, **B**
King's College, **J**
Magdalene College, **A**

Pembroke College, **O**
Peterhouse College, **P**
Queens' College, **N**
Robinson College, **E**
Sidney Sussex
College, **D**
St. Catharine's
College, **K**
St. John's College, **C**
Trinity College, **F**

Warkworth Guest House, Warkworth Terr. (☎363 682). Sunny ensuite rooms near the bus station for those wishing to skip the walk to the city center. Breakfast included. Singles £45; twins and doubles £65; triples £75; families £85. MC/V. ❹

YHA Cambridge, 97 Tenison Rd. (☎354 601). A relaxed, welcoming atmosphere close to the train station. 103 beds. Well-equipped kitchen, laundry, luggage storage, TV lounge, and bureau de change. English breakfast included. Lockers £1. Internet 50p per 7min. Reception 24hr. £17, under 18 £13. MC/V. ❷

Highfield Farm Camping Park, Long Rd., Comberton (☎262 308; www.highfieldfarm-touringpark.co.uk). Take Cambus #118 (every 45min.) from Drummer St. Flush toilets and laundry. July-Aug. £8.25-10.25; May-June and Sept. £7.75-9.25; Apr. and Oct. £7.25-8.50. Electricity £2. Cash only. ❶

◖ FOOD

Market Square has bright pyramids of cheap fruit and vegetables (open M-Sa 9:30am-4:30pm). Get **groceries** at Sainsbury's, 44 Sidney St. (☎366 891. Open M-Sa 8am-10pm, Su 11am-5pm.) Cheap Indian and Greek fare sates hearty appetites on the edges of the city center. South of town, **Hills Road** and **Mill Road** brim with budget restaurants popular with the college crowd.

Clown's, 54 King St. (☎355 711). Cheerful staff adds the final dash of color to this humming spot—children's renderings of clowns plaster the orange walls. Serves a variety of pastas and Italian desserts (£2.50-6.50). Set menu of a drink, salad, small pasta dish, and cake £6.50. Open M-Sa 8am-midnight, Su 8am-11pm. Cash only. ❶

Dojo's Noodle Bar, 1-2 Mill Ln. (☎363 471; www.dojonoodlebar.co.uk). Whips out comically enormous plates of noodles, some vegetarian, at warp speed. Everything under £6.50. Open M-Th noon-2:30pm and 5:30-11pm, F noon-4pm and 5:30-11pm, Sa-Su noon-11pm. Cash only. ❶

Rainbow's Vegetarian Bistro, 9a King's Parade (☎321 551; www.rainbowcafe.co.uk). Duck under the rainbow sign. A tiny burrow featuring creative vegan and vegetarian fare, all for £7.25. Open Tu-Sa 10am-10pm. Food served until 9:30pm. Cash only. ❷

Mai Thai Restaurant, Park Terr. (☎367 480; www.mai-thai-restaurant.com). A stylishly colorful restaurant with great views across Parker's Piece. Entrees £6-17. Open daily June-Sept. noon-11pm; Oct.-May noon-3pm and 6-11pm. AmEx/MC/V. ❸

CB1, 32 Mill Rd. (☎576 306). A student hangout coffee shop where all of the drinks (£1-1.50) are made right on the counter and the walls are crammed with used books. Internet 4p per min. Open daily 10am-8pm. Cash only. ❶

Nadia's, 11 St. John's St. (☎568 336). An uncommonly good bakery with a divine aroma. Flapjacks (£1 each) and sandwiches (£2.25-2.45) are a brunch unto themselves. Takeaway only. Branch at 16 Silver St. Open daily 8am-5pm. Cash only. ❶

◪ PUBS

King Street has a diverse collection of pubs. Most stay open 11am-11pm (Su noon-10:30pm). The local brewery, Greene King, supplies many of them.

The Mill, 14 Mill Ln. (☎357 026), off Silver St. Bridge. Patrons infiltrate the riverside pub on spring nights for punt- and people-watching. In summer, clientele include the odd student and hordes of international youths. Features a rotating selection of ales. Open M-Sa 11am-11pm, Su noon-10:30pm. Food served M-Th noon-3pm and 6-7pm, F-Sa noon-7pm, Su noon-4pm.

The Eagle, 8 Benet St. (☎505 020). Cambridge's oldest pub. Watson and Crick rushed in breathlessly to announce their discovery of DNA—the barmaid insisted they settle their 4-shilling tab before she'd serve them. British and American WWII pilots stood on each other's shoulders to burn their initials into the ceiling of the RAF room. Open M-Sa 11am-11pm, Su noon-10:30pm.

The Anchor, Silver St. (☎353 554). Another undergrad watering hole that's crowded day and night. Savor a pint while watching amateur punters collide under Silver St. Bridge. Open M-Sa 10am-11pm, Su 11am-10:30pm.

The King St. Run, 86 King St. (☎328 900). The quintessential college pub packs in the student crowd amid university kitsch. Open M-Sa 11am-11pm, Su noon-10:30pm.

The Free Press, Prospect Row (☎368 337), behind the police station. Named after an abolitionist rag, now popular with locals. No smoking and no cell phones. Open M-F noon-2:30pm and 6-11pm, Sa noon-3pm and 6-11pm, Su noon-3pm and 7-10:30pm.

🌀 SIGHTS

Cambridge is an architect's fantasia, packing some of England's most breathtaking monuments into less than a single square mile. The soaring **King's College Chapel** and St. John's postcard-familiar **Bridge of Sighs** are sightseeing staples, while more obscure college quads open onto ornate courtyards and gardens. Most historic buildings are on the **east bank** of the Cam between Magdalene Bridge and Silver St. The gardens, meadows, and cows of the **Backs** lend a pastoral air to the **west bank.**

The **University of Cambridge** has three eight-week terms: Michaelmas (Oct.-Dec.), Lent (Jan.-Mar.), and Easter (Apr.-June). Visitors can gain access to most colleges daily, though times vary; call the TIC for hours. Many are closed to sightseers during Easter term, virtually all are closed during exams (mid-May to mid-June), and visiting hours are limited during May Ball festivities. **King's, Trinity, Queens',** and **Saint John's** should top your list. Porters (bowler-wearing ex-servicemen) maintain security. The fastest way to blow your cover is to trample the sacred **grass** of the courtyards, a privilege reserved for the elite. In July and August, most undergrads skip town, leaving it to PhD students and mobs of tourists.

COLLEGES

KING'S COLLEGE. King's College was founded by Henry VI in 1441 as a partner school to Eton; it wasn't until 1861 that students from other schools were allowed to compete for scholarships. Ironically, King's is now the most socially liberal of the Cambridge colleges, drawing more of its students from state schools than any other; the college was also the site of student riots in 1968. Its most stunning attraction is the Gothic King's College Chapel. From the south-west corner of the courtyard, you can see where Henry's master mason left off and the Tudors began work—the earlier stone is off-white. The elaborate wall that separates the college grounds from King's Parade was a 19th-century addition; originally the chapel and grounds were hidden behind a row of shops and houses. The interior is a single chamber divided by a carved choir screen. Heralding angels hover against the world's largest fan-vaulted ceiling, described by Wordsworth as a "branching roof self-poised, and scooped into ten thousand cells where light and shade repose." Look for the 15th-century graffiti to the right of the altar and the devilish portrait of a craftsman's estranged wife on the choir screen. Behind the altar hangs Rubens's "Adoration of the Magi" (1639). The canvas has been protected by an electronic alarm since an attack by a crazed chisel-wielder several years ago. There are often free music recitals; schedules are kept at the entrance. As you picnic by the riverbank, think of those who have gone before you: John Maynard Keynes, E. M. Forster, and Salman Rushdie all felt the college's grounds beneath their feet. In mid-June, university degree ceremonies are held in the Georgian Senate House. *(King's Parade. ☎331 100. Chapel and grounds open M-Sa 9:30am-4:30pm, Su 10am-5pm. Contact TIC for tours. Listing of services and musical events £1; available at porter's lodge. Choral services 10:30am and 5:30pm most nights. £4.50, concessions £3, under 12 free.)*

TRINITY COLLEGE. Henry VIII intended the College of the Holy and Undivided Trinity (founded 1546) to be the largest and richest in Cambridge. Currently Britain's third largest landowner (after the Queen and the Church of England), the college has amply fulfilled his wish. Legend holds that it is possible to walk from Cambridge to Oxford without stepping off Trinity land. The alma mater of Sir Isaac Newton, who lived in E staircase for 30 years, the college has a host of illustrious alumni: literati Dryden, Byron, Tennyson, and Nabokov; atom-splitter Ernest Rutherford; philosopher Ludwig Wittgenstein; and Indian statesman Jawaharlal Nehru. The **Great Court,** is the world's largest enclosed courtyard, reached from Trinity St. through **Great Gate.** Look for the apple tree near the gate: it is supposedly descended from the tree that gave Newton the idea for his formulation of gravity. The castle-like gateway is fronted by a statue of Henry VIII grasping a wooden chair leg—the original scepter was stolen so frequently that the college administration removed it. On the west side of the court stand the dour **chapel** and the **King's Gate tower.** Lord Byron used to bathe nude in the **fountain,** the only one in Cambridge. The poet also kept a bear as a pet (college rules only forbade cats and dogs). The south side of the court is home to the palatial **Master's Lodge** and the cathedral-like **Great Hall,** where students and deans dine under hundreds of grotesque carved faces. On the other side of the Hall is the exquisite Renaissance facade of **Nevile's Court.** Newton measured the speed of sound by timing the echo in the cloisters by **Wren Library.** The building houses alumnus **A. A. Milne's** original handwritten copies of *Winnie the Pooh* and Newton's personal copy of his *Principia.* Pass through the drab, neo-Gothic **New Court** (Prince Charles's former residence), adjacent to Nevile's Court, to get to the Backs, where you can rent **punts** or enjoy the view from **Trinity Bridge.** *(Trinity St. ☎ 338 400. Chapel and courtyard open daily 10am-5pm. Wren Library open M-F noon-2pm. Dining hall open daily 3-5pm. Easter to Oct. £2.20, concessions £1.30, families £4.40. Nov. to Easter free.)*

SAINT JOHN'S COLLEGE. Established in 1511 by Lady Margaret Beaufort, mother of Henry VIII, St. John's centers around a paved plaza rather than a grassy courtyard. The **Bridge of Sighs,** named after the Venetian original, connects the older part of the college with the towering neo-Gothic extravagance of **New Court,** whose silhouette has been likened to a wedding cake. The **School of Pythagoras,** a 12th-century pile of wood and stone thought to be the oldest complete building in Cambridge, hides in St. John's Gardens. No one knows how it got its name. The college also boasts the longest room in the city—the Fellows' Room in Second Court spans 93 ft. and was the site of D-Day planning. *(St. John's St. ☎ 338 600. Open daily 10am-5:30pm. Evensong 6:30pm most nights. £2, concessions £1.20, families £4.)*

QUEENS' COLLEGE. Founded not once, but twice—by Queen Margaret of Anjou in 1448 and Elizabeth Woodville in 1465—Queens' College has the only unaltered Tudor courtyard in Cambridge. Though rumored to be built on principle alone, the **Mathematical Bridge** has always included screws and bolts. *(Silver St. ☎ 335 511. Open daily Mar.-Oct. 10am-4:30pm. £1.30.)*

CLARE COLLEGE. Clare's coat of arms—golden teardrops ringing a black border—recalls the college's founding in 1326 by thrice-widowed, 29-year-old Lady Elizabeth de Clare. Misery has not laid permanent claim to the college, however: Clare has some of the most cheerful **gardens** in Cambridge. They lie across elegant Clare Bridge. Walk through Wren's **Old Court** for a view of the University Library, where 82 mi. of shelves hold books arranged by size rather than subject. *(Trinity Ln. ☎ 333 200. Open daily 10am-4:30pm. £3, under 10 free.)*

CHRIST'S COLLEGE. Founded as "God's house" in 1448 and renamed in 1505, Christ's has since won fame for its **gardens** and its association with John Milton and Charles Darwin. Darwin's rooms (unmarked and closed to visitors) were on G staircase in First Court. **New Court,** on King St., is one of Cambridge's most modern structures, with symmetrical concrete walls and dark windows. Bowing to pressure from aesthetically offended Cantabrigians, a wall was built to block the view of the building from all sides except the inner courtyard. *(St. Andrews St.* ☎ *334 900. Gardens open daily term-time 9am-4:30pm; in summer 9:30am-noon. Fellows' garden open term-time M-F 9:30am-noon and 2-4pm; in summer M-F 9:30am-noon. Free.)*

JESUS COLLEGE. Jesus has preserved an enormous amount of medieval work on its spacious grounds. Beyond the high-walled walk called the "Chimney" lies a three-sided court fringed with colorful flowerbeds. Through the arch on the right sit the remains of a gloomy medieval nunnery. *(Jesus Ln.* ☎ *339 339. Courtyard open daily 9am-8pm; open during exams to groups of 3 or fewer.)*

MAGDALENE COLLEGE. Located within a 15th-century Benedictine hostel, Magdalene (MAUD-lin), sometime home of Christian allegorist and Oxford man C.S. Lewis, has retained its religious emphasis. It also retained men-only status until 1988. **Pepys Library,** in the second court, displays the noted statesman and prolific diarist's collections. *(Magdalene St.* ☎ *332 100. Library open Easter to Aug. M-Sa 11:30am-12:30pm and 2:30-3:30pm; Sept. to Easter M-Sa 2:30-3:30pm. Free.)*

SMALLER COLLEGES. Thomas Gray wrote his *Elegy in a Country Churchyard* while staying in **Peterhouse College,** the smallest college, founded in 1294. *(Trumpington St.* ☎ *338 200.)* The modern medieval brick pastiche of **Robinson College** is the newest. In 1977, local self-made man David Robinson founded it for the bargain price of £17 million, the largest single gift ever received by the university. *(Across the river on Grange Rd.* ☎ *339 100.)* **Corpus Christi College,** founded in 1352 by the townspeople, contains the oldest courtyard in Cambridge, aptly named Old Court and unaltered since its enclosure. The library, however, maintains the snazziest collection of Anglo-Saxon manuscripts in England. Alums include Sir Francis Drake and Christopher Marlowe. *(Trumpington St.* ☎ *338 000.)* The 1347 **Pembroke College** harbors the earliest work of Sir Christopher Wren and counts Edmund Spenser, Ted Hughes, and Eric Idle among its grads. *(Next to Corpus Christi.* ☎ *338 100.)* A chapel designed by Wren dominates the front court of **Emmanuel College,** known as "Emma." John Harvard, benefactor of his own university, studied here, as did John Cleese. *(St. Andrews St.* ☎ *334 200.)* **Gonville and Caius** (KEYS) **College** was founded twice, once in 1348 by Edmund Gonville and again in 1557 by John Keys, who chose to take the Latin form of his name. *(Trinity St.* ☎ *332 400.)*

MUSEUMS AND CHURCHES

■**FITZWILLIAM MUSEUM.** A welcome break from academia, the museum fills an immense Neoclassical building, built in 1875 to house Viscount Fitzwilliam's immense and varied collections. Egyptian, Chinese, Japanese, Middle Eastern, and Greek antiquities downstairs are joined by a muster of 16th-century German armor. Upstairs, five galleries feature works by Reubens, Monet, and Brueghel. The **Founder's Library** is a must-see, housing an intimate collection of French Impressionists. The drawing room shows William Blake's books and woodcuts. *(Trumpington St.* ☎ *332 900. Open Tu-Sa 10am-5pm, Su noon-5pm. Call about lunchtime and evening concerts. Suggested donation £3.)*

OTHER MUSEUMS. Kettle's Yard, at the corner of Castle and Northampton St., displays early 20th-century art. Tate curator Jim Ede founded the museum in 1956 to be a "a refuge of peace and order." Visitors can wander the house as if it were their own. *(*☎ *352 124; www.kettlesyard.org.uk. House open Apr.-Sept. Tu-Su 1:30-4:30pm; Oct.-Mar. Tu-Su 2-4pm. Gallery open Tu-Su 11:30am-5pm. Free.)* The **Scott Polar Research Institute,** Lensfield Rd., commemorates arctic expeditions with photographic and artistic memorabilia. *(*☎ *336 540; www.spri.cam.ac.uk. Open Tu-Sa 2:30-4pm. Free.)*

EAST ANGLIA

CHURCHES. The **Round Church (Holy Sepulchre),** where Bridge St. meets St. John's St., is one of five surviving circular churches in England and the second oldest building in Cambridge, built in 1130 (and later rebuilt) on the pattern of the Holy Sepulchre in Jerusalem. (☎311 602. *Open M and Su 1-5pm, Tu-Sa 10am-5pm. £1, students and children free. Tours W 11am, Su 2:30pm. £3.)* **St. Benet's,** a rough Saxon church on Benet St. built in 1025, is the oldest structure in Cambridgeshire. (☎353 903. *Open daily 8am-6pm. Free.)* The tower of **Great St. Mary's Church,** off King's Parade, affords the best view of the broad greens and the colleges. Pray that the 12 bells don't ring while you're ascending the 123 tightly packed spiral steps. *(Tower open M-Sa 9:30am-5:30pm, Su 12:30-5pm. £2, children £1, families £5. Church free.)*

♪ ※ ENTERTAINMENT AND FESTIVALS

PUNTING

Punting on the Cam is a favored form of hands-on entertainment. Punters take two routes—from Magdalene Bridge to Silver St. or from Silver St. to Grantchester. On the shorter, busier, and more interesting first route, you'll pass the colleges and the Backs. To propel your boat, thrust the pole behind the boat into the riverbed and rotate the pole in your hands as you push forward. Be aware that punt-bombing—jumping from bridges into the river alongside a punt, thereby tipping its occupants—is an art form. You can rent at **Tyrell's,** Magdalene Bridge, Quayside (☎07989 394 941; £14 per hr. plus £60 deposit), or **Scudamore's,** Silver St. Bridge (☎359 750; www.scudamores.com; M-F £14 per hr. plus a £70 deposit, Sa-Su £16 per hr. plus a £70 deposit; MC/V). Student-punted **tours** (about £12 per person) are another option. Inquire at the TIC for a complete list of companies.

THEATER

The Arts Box Office (☎503 333; open M-Sa noon-8pm) handles ticket sales for the **Arts Theatre,** around the corner from the TIC on Pea's Hill. The **ADC Theatre** (Amateur Dramatic Club), Park St. (☎359 547), offers student-produced plays, term-time movies, and a folk festival. You can get an earful at the **Corn Exchange,** at the corner of Wheeler St. and Corn Exchange St. across from the TIC, a venue for band, jazz, and classical concerts. (☎357 851. Box office open M-Sa 10am-6pm, until 9pm on performance evenings; Su 6-9pm on performance days only. £7.50-24, concessions available.) The **Cambridge Shakespeare Festival** (www.cambridge-shakespeare.com), in association with the festival at Oxford, features plays through July and August. Tickets (£12, concessions £9) are available at the Corn Exchange or from the City Centre Box Office (☎357 856).

NIGHTLIFE

At dusk, **evensong** begins in sonorous King's College Chapel, a breathtaking treat for day-worn spirits—not to mention a good way to view the college grounds for free. (M-Sa 5:30pm, Su 3:30pm. Don't forget evensong at other colleges, notably St. John's, Caius, and Clare.) **Pubs** are the core of Cambridge nightlife (p. 310) but clubs are also on the curriculum. Students, bartenders, TIC brochures, and the latest issue of the term-time *Varsity* (20p) are always good sources of information. Small and dim, **The Kambar Club,** 1 Wheeler St., opposite the Corn Exchange box office, hosts the only indie night in town on Friday, as well as garage, goth, and electronica during the week. (☎842 725. Open M-Sa 10pm-2:30am. Cover £5, students £3.) **The Fez Club,** 15 Market Passage, offers everything from Latin to trance, complete with comfy floor cushions in a lush Moroccan setting. (☎519 224. Show up early to avoid £2-8 cover. Open M-Th 9pm-2:30am, F-Sa 9pm-3am, Su 9pm-2am. Cover M-Th £2-5, F-Sa £6-8, students half price M and W.)

MAY WEEK

For two weeks in June, students celebrate the end of the term with May Week, crammed full of concerts, plays, and balls followed by recuperative riverside breakfasts. The boat clubs compete in a series of races known as the **bumps.** Crews line up along the river and attempt to ram the boat in front before being bumped from behind, an event open to the public. The celebration includes **Footlights Revue,** a series of comedy skits; performers have included then-undergrads, and future *Monty Python* stars, John Cleese, Eric Idle, and Graham Chapman.

FESTIVALS

Midsummer Fair, dating from the 16th century, appropriates the Midsummer Common for five days in the third week of June (call the TIC for exact dates). The free **Strawberry Fair** (www.strawberry-fair.org), on the first Saturday in June, attracts a crowd with food (yes, including strawberries), music, and body piercing. **Summer in the City** (www.cambridge-summer.co.uk) brightens the summer with a series of concerts and special exhibits culminating in a huge weekend celebration, the **Cambridge Folk Festival** (☎357 851) in late July. Book tickets well in advance (about £38); camping on the grounds is £5-18 extra.

DAYTRIPS FROM CAMBRIDGE

GRANTCHESTER

To reach Grantchester Meadows from Cambridge, take the path following the river. Grantchester village lies 1 mi. from the meadows; ask the way or follow the blue bike path signs (1½hr. by foot from Cambridge). If you have the energy to paddle your way, rent a punt or canoe. Or hop on Stagecoach Cambus #118 (9-11 per day, round-trip £1.25).

In 1912, poet Rupert Brooke wrote "Grantchester! Ah Grantchester! There's peace and holy quiet there." His words hold true today, as Grantchester is still a mecca for Cambridge literary types. The peaceful walk along the Cam is a refreshing break from the university's intensity. Brooke's home at the **Old Vicarage** is now owned by bad-boy novelist Lord Jeffrey Archer and is closed to the public. The weathered and intimate 14th-century **Parish Church of St. Andrew and St. Mary,** on Millway, is not to be missed. Wend your way to the idyllic ▓**Orchard Tea Gardens ❶,** 45 Mill Way, once a haunt of the "neo-Pagans," a Grantchester offshoot of the famous Bloomsbury Group. Stop by for mouthwatering scones (£2). The main village pub, the **Rupert Brooke ❷,** 2 Broadway, is a nice place to sit down after a long hike. Boasting a new chef, the pub is striving to improve the reputation of British cuisine. (☎840 295; www.therupertbrooke.com. Open daily 11:30am-3pm and 5:30-11pm.) Outdoor plays are occasionally performed on summer evenings; ask at the Cambridge TIC. (☎845 788. Light lunches £4-8. Open daily Apr.-June 9:30am-6pm; Nov.-Mar. 9:30am-5:30pm; July-Oct. 9:30am-7pm.)

ANGLESEY ABBEY

6 mi. northeast of Cambridge on the B1102 (signposted from A14). Buses #111 and 122 run from Drummer St. (25min., 1 per hr.); ask to be let off at Lode Crossroads. ☎811 200. House open Apr.-Oct. W-Su and bank holidays 1-5pm. Gardens open July-Aug. daily 10:30am-5:30pm; Apr.-Oct. W-Su 10:30am-5:30pm; last admission 4:30pm. £7.

Northeast of Cambridge, 12th-century Anglesey Abbey has been remodeled to house the priceless exotica of the first Lord Fairhaven. One of the niftiest clocks in the known universe sits inconspicuously on the bookcase beyond the library's fireplace, but don't worry if you miss it—there are 55 other timepieces to enjoy along with a multitude of bizarre tokens and trifles. In the 100-acre gardens, trees punctuate lines of clipped hedges and manicured lawns.

WIMPOLE HALL

Bus #175 from Drummer St. (35min., £2). Hall ☎ 206 000. Open Apr.-Nov. Tu-Th and Sa-Su 1-5pm. £6.60, children £3.20. Farm ☎ 207 257. Open Mar.-July and Sept.-Oct. M-W and Sa-Su 1-5pm; Aug. M-Th and Sa-Su 1-5pm; Nov. Su 1-4pm. Gardens open dawn to dusk. Farm £6.90, children £3.40. Hall and farm £10.20/5.50, families £26.

Cambridgeshire's most elegant mansion lies 10 mi. southwest of Cambridge. The hall holds works by Gibbs, Flitcroft, and Joane; outside, an intricate Chinese bridge crosses a lake set in 60 acres of **gardens** designed by "Capability" Brown. **Wimpole's Home Farm** brims with longhorn cattle, Soay sheep, and Tamworth pigs.

AUDLEY END AND SAFFRON WALDEN

Trains leave Cambridge every hr. for Audley End. ☎ 01799 522 399. House open Apr.-Sept. M and W-Su noon-5pm; Mar. and Oct. W-Su 11am-4pm. Grounds open Apr.-Sept. daily 10am-6pm; Mar. and Oct. M and Th-Su 10am-5pm; last admission 1hr. before close. £9, concessions £6.70. Grounds only £4.60/3.50. Free 1hr. guided tours, 10 per day. TIC ☎ 01799 510 444. Open Apr.-Oct. M-Sa 9:30am-5:30pm; June-Aug. also Su 10:30am-1pm; Nov.-Mar. M-Sa 9:30am-5pm.

The house "too big for a king" proves that even the monarchy has its limits. The magnificent Jacobean hall is but a quarter of Audley End's former size—it once extended down to the river, where part of the Cam was rerouted by "Capability" Brown. The grand halls display case after case of stuffed critters, including some extinct species. One signposted mile east of Audley End is the old market town **Saffron Walden,** best known for the "pargetting" (plaster molding) of its Tudor buildings and its two mazes, a Victorian hedge maze and an ancient earthen maze. The **Tourist Information Centre** is on Market Sq. Rest at the **YHA hostel ❶,** 1 Myddylton Pl. (☎ 0870 770 6014. Lockout 10am-5pm. Curfew 11pm. Open July-Aug. daily; Apr.-June and Sept.-Oct. Tu-Sa; Mar. F-Sa. £11, under 18 £8. MC/V.)

ELY   ☎ 01353

The prosperous town of Ely (EEL-ee) was an island until steam power drained the surrounding fenlands in the early 19th century, creating a flat, reed-covered region of rich farmland. Legend has it that the city got its name when St. Dunstan transformed local monks into eels for their lack of piety. A more likely story is that "Elig" (Eel Island) was named for the slitherers that infest the surrounding waters. Today Ely remains proud of its eel-inspired heritage, offering the delicacy fresh from the Great River Ouse in many of its local restaurants and creating an "Eel Heritage Walk" that covers all the city's major sights. Ely Cathedral is the town's most prominent attraction and the city center can be covered in an afternoon.

🖪🖬 TRANSPORTATION AND PRACTICAL INFORMATION. Ely is the junction for **trains** (☎ 08457 484 950) between London (1¼hr., 2 per hr., £18.80) and various points in East Anglia, including Cambridge (15min., 3 per hr., round-trip £3.90) and Norwich (1hr., 2 per hr., £10). Cambus **bus** (☎ 01223 423 554) X9 arrives at Market St. from Cambridge (30min., 1 per hr., £3.40). **Walking** from Cambridge to Ely is also possible, a beautiful, easy 17 mi. trek through the flat fens. Ask at the TIC in Cambridge or Ely for a copy of *The Fen Rivers Way* (£3).

Ely's two major streets—**High Street** and **Market Street**—run parallel to the length of the cathedral; the Cromwell House and some shops are on **St. Mary's Street.** To reach the cathedral from the train station, walk up Station Rd. and continue up Back Hill. Just past the Cathedral, the **Tourist Information Centre,** 29 St. Mary's St., in the Oliver Cromwell Museum, books rooms for £2 plus a 10% deposit; call at least two days ahead. (☎ 662 062. Open Apr.-Oct. daily 10am-5:30pm; Nov.-Mar. M-F and Su 11am-4pm, Sa 10am-5pm.) They also sell a combination ticket, the **Passport to Ely,** that lets you into Ely Cathedral, Cromwell House, Ely Museum, and the Stained Glass Museum (£11, concessions £8.70, children free). Other services include: **police,** Nutholt Ln. (☎01223 358 966); **Prince of Wales Hospital,** Lynn Rd. (☎652 000); **Internet access** at the library, 6 The Cloisters, just off Market Pl. (☎08450 455 225; free to search the web, 50p per 10min. for email; open Tu-W and F 10am-5pm, Th 9:30am-8pm, Sa 9:30am-4pm); and the **post office,** 19-21 High St. (☎669 946; open M-F 9am-5:30pm, Sa 9am-1pm). **Post Code:** CB7 4LQ.

▛▟ ACCOMMODATIONS AND FOOD. Close to the train station and river and with 16th-century architecture, **Mr. and Mrs. Friend-Smith's ❸,** 31 Egremont St., lets doubles with views of the garden and the cathedral. (☎663 118. Doubles £52. Cash only.) Other options include **The Post House ❸,** 12a Egremont St., with moderate-sized rooms close to the city center. (☎667 184. Singles £25; doubles £50, ensuite £55. Cash only.) Camp among spuds and sugar beets with a cathedral view at **Braham Farm ❶,** Cambridge Rd., off the A10, 1 mi. from the city center. (☎662 386. Caravan and Camping Club members only. £3.50. Electricity £2. Cash only.)

Most shops close on Tuesday afternoons in winter as they have for centuries. Stock up on provisions at the **market** in Market Pl. (Open Th and Sa 8am-3pm.) Waitrose **supermarket,** Brays Ln., is hidden behind a Georgian brick facade. (☎668 800. Open M-Tu and Sa 8:30am-6pm, W-Th 8:30am-8pm, F 8:30am-9pm, Su 10am-4pm. AmEx/MC/V.) The **Almonry ❷,** just off the corner of High St. and Brays Ln., serves basics (£6-7) to the well-heeled in a garden right beneath the cathedral. (☎666 360. Open M-Sa 10am-5pm, Su 11am-5pm. MC/V.) The **Old Fire Engine House ❸,** 25 St. Mary's St., has a menu that changes twice daily and features local produce and game. Appropriately enough, smoking is not allowed. (☎662 582. Entrees £15. Open M-Sa 10:30am-5:30pm and 7:30-9pm, Su 12:30-5:30pm. MC/V.) The **Steeplegate ❶,** 16-18 High St., serves calorific snacks and tea (£2-7) in two rooms built over a medieval undercroft next to the cathedral. (☎664 731. Open June-Oct. M-Sa 10am-5pm; Nov.-May M-F 10am-4:30pm and Sa 10am-5pm. MC/V.) The **Minster Tavern ❶,** Minster Pl., opposite the cathedral, is popular for lunch. (☎652 901. Entrees £5-7. Open M-Sa 11am-11pm, Su noon-10:30pm. AmEx/MC/V.)

◪ SIGHTS. The towers of massive **◪Ely Cathedral** are impossible to miss. The Saxon princess St. Etheldreda founded a monastery on the site in AD 673, early Norman masons took a century to construct the nave, and Victorian artists painted the ceiling and completed the stained glass. The present **Octagon,** an altar topped by the lantern tower, replaced the original tower, which collapsed in 1322. The eight-sided cupola shoots up vertically from the domed ceiling's center, supported by eight stone pillars. Don't overlook the 215 ft. tiled **floor maze.** (☎667 735. Open Apr.-Sept. daily 7am-7pm; Oct.-Apr. M-F 7:30am-6pm, Su 7:30am-5pm. Cathedral admission £4.80, concessions £4.20. Free guided tours; in summer 10:45am, 1, 2:15, 3:15pm; in winter 10:45am, 1, 2:45pm. Octagon tours Apr.-Oct. 4 per day; £4, concessions £3.50; with cathedral entry, £3/2.50. West Tower tours Apr.-Oct. Tu, Th, F 1 per day; £3.50/2.50; call ahead. Evensong M-Sa 5:30pm, Su 3:45pm.)

At the **brass rubbing center** in the cathedral, visitors can use chalk and paper to rub out the brass engravings from surrounding churches. Materials cost £2-6.50. (☎660 345. Open M-Sa 10:30am-4pm, Su noon-3pm.) The beautiful monastic buildings around the cathedral are still in use: the **infirmary** houses one of the resident canons, and the **bishop's palace** is a home for the terminally ill. The other buildings are used by the **King's School,** one of England's older public (read: private) schools.

The brilliant **◪Stained Glass Museum,** within the Cathedral, details the history of the art form and displays over 100 of its finest examples. (☎660 347; www.stainedglassmuseum.com. Open Easter to Oct. M-F 10:30am-5pm, Sa

10:30am-5:30pm, Su noon-6pm; Nov. to Easter M-F 10:30am-4:30pm, Sa 10:30am-5pm, Su noon-4:30pm. Last admission 30min. before close. £3.50, concessions £2.50, families £7.)

For an architectural tour of Ely, follow the path outlined in the TIC's free *Eel Trail* pamphlet, which also notes artwork related to the eel. **Ely Museum,** at the Bishop's Gaol on the corner of Market St. and Lynn Rd., tells the story of the fenland city. (☎ 666 655. Open in summer M-Sa 10:30am-5pm, Su 1-5pm; in winter M-Sa 10:30am-4pm. £3, concessions £2.) **Oliver Cromwell's House,** 29 St. Mary's St., holds wax figures, 17th-century decor, and Cromwell's "haunted" bedroom. Fish and chips will look positively gourmet after a perusal of Lady Cromwell's recipe for eel pie with oysters. (☎ 662 062. Open Apr.-Oct. daily 10am-5:30pm; Nov.-Mar. M-Sa 10am-5pm, Su 11am-4pm. £3.85, concessions £3.35, children £2.60.)

NORFOLK

KING'S LYNN   ☎ 01553

King's Lynn was one of England's foremost 16th-century ports. Five hundred years later, the once mighty current of the Great Ouse (OOZE; as in slime) River has slowed to a leisurely flow, as has the pace of the town. The dockside city borrows its Germanic look from trading partners such as Hamburg and Bremen; the earth tones of the flat East Anglian countryside meet with somber red-brick facades and modern warehouses. The sights can be uninspiring, but the town makes a perfect stopover for hikers exploring the region.

█▊ TRANSPORTATION AND PRACTICAL INFORMATION. Trains (☎ 08457 484 950) come to the station on Blackfriars Rd. from: Cambridge (50min., 1 per hr., £8.50); London King's Cross (1½hr., 1 per hr., £23.40); Peterborough (1¾hr., 2 per hr., £7.90). **Buses** arrive at the Vancouver Centre (office open M-F 9am-5pm.) First Eastern Counties (☎ 01603 660 553) buses travel from Norwich (1½hr., 2 per hr., round trip £7.20) and Peterborough (1¼hr., 2 per hr., round-trip £6.30). National Express (☎ 08705 808 080) runs daily from London (4hr., 1 per day, £13.00).

The **Tourist Information Centre,** in the Custom House on the corner of King St. and Purfleet Quay, 10min. from the train station, books rooms for a 10% deposit; take a left out of the station and a right onto Blackfriars St., which becomes New Conduit St. and then Purfleet St. (☎ 763 044. Open Apr.-Sept. M-Sa 10am-5pm, Su noon-5pm; Oct.-Mar. M-Sa 10am-4pm, Su noon-4pm.) Buy National Express tickets at the station or from **West Norfolk Travel,** 2 King St. (☎ 772 910. Open M-Sa 8am-6pm. AmEx/MC/V.) Other services include: **police,** at the corner of St. James and London Rd. (☎ 691 211); the **hospital,** on Gayton Rd. (☎ 613 613); free **Internet access** at the **library,** on London Rd. across from The Walks (☎ 772 568; open M, W, and F 9am-8pm; Tu, Th, and Sa 9am-5pm); and the **post office** (☎ 08457 223 344) at Baxter's Plain on the corner of Broad St. and New Conduit St. (Open M-F 9am-5:30pm, Sa 9am-12:30pm.) **Post Code:** PE30HB.

▐ ACCOMMODATIONS AND FOOD. The quayside ◙**YHA King's Lynn ❶,** a short walk from the train and bus stations (keep your eyes peeled—it's easy to miss), occupies part of 16th-century Thoresby College, on College Ln. near the Old Gaol House. The river view and friendly staff make this your best bet. (☎ 0870 770 5902. Curfew 11pm. Open Easter to June M-Tu and F-Su; July-Aug. daily; Sept. Su-Tu. Call ahead for availability. Dorms and singles £11, under 18 £8. MC/V.) **B&Bs** are a hike from city center; the less expensive ones span Gaywood Road and Tennyson Avenue. Eight dainty rooms comprise the Victorian **Fairlight Lodge ❸**, 79 Goodwins Rd. (☎762 234; www.fairlightlodge-online.co.uk. Full breakfast included. Singles £24-29; doubles and twins £40-46. Cash only.) Super-soft beds dominate the (nearly all ensuite) rooms at **Maranatha Guest House ❸**, 115-117 Gaywood Rd., and a pool table livens up the lounge. (☎774 596. Singles £30; doubles £50. MC/V.)

King's Lynn restaurants operate on their own time; many close on Sundays. Several supermarkets congregate around the Vancouver Centre. For fresh fruit, visit the markets held at the larger **Tuesday Market Place,** on the north end of High St., or at **Saturday Market Place** on the south end. The **Thai Orchid ❸**, 33-39 St. James St., offers aromatic Thai dishes for £6-9. (☎767 013. Open M-Th noon-2pm and 6-11:30pm, F-Sa noon-2pm and 6pm-midnight, Su noon-2pm and 6-11pm. MC/V.) Inexpensive Italian meals (£5-7.50) await at **Antonio's Wine Bar ❷**, Baxter's Plain, off Tower St. (☎772 324. Open Tu-Sa noon-3pm and 6:30-11pm. Food served until 9:30pm. MC/V.) Quiet **Archers ❶**, on Purfleet St. near the TIC, serves varied lunches (£3-6) and teas. (☎764 411. Open M-Tu 9am-4pm, W-Sa 9am-4:30pm. Cash only.)

◙ ♫ SIGHTS AND ENTERTAINMENT. The sights of King's Lynn are modest, but a **walking tour** is still rewarding. The *King's Lynn Town Walk* guide (50p) is sold at the TIC. The Gaol House is the starting point for 1½hr. guided walks of the town (2pm, 4 days per week; £3, concessions £2.50, children £1). At the **Tales of the Old Gaol House,** Saturday Market Pl., try out the stocks for a taste of 17th-century justice. The Regalia Room displays treasures in the undercroft. (☎774 297. Open Apr.-Oct. M-Sa 10am-5pm; Nov.-Mar. Tu-Sa 10am-4pm. £2.60, concessions £2.25, children £1.85.) **St. Margaret's Church,** also on Saturday Market Pl., was built in 1101. Peaceful **Tower Gardens** ensconce Greyfriars Tower on one side of St. James' St., while the **Walks** stretch away on the other side. The **Town House Museum of Lynn Life,** 46 Queen St., leads through medieval, Tudor, Victorian, and 1950s reconstructions. (☎773 450. Open May-Sept. M-Sa 10am-5pm; Oct.-Apr. M-Sa 10am-4pm. £2.60, concessions £2.20, children £1.50, families £6.)

The **Corn Exchange** at Tuesday Market Pl. sells tickets for music, dance, and theater events. (☎764 864. Open M-Sa 10am-6pm; on performance nights also Su 1hr. prior to show. Shows usually 7:30 or 8pm.) Near Tuesday Market Pl., the 15th-century **Guildhall of St. George,** 27-29 King St., is said to be the last surviving building where Shakespeare appeared in one of his own plays. It now hosts the **King's Lynn Arts Centre.** (☎764 864. Open M-F 10am-2pm. Free.) The Guildhall brings the **King's Lynn Festival** to town in the last two weeks of July, offering classical and jazz music, opera, ballet, puppet shows, and films. Get schedules at the TIC or the Festival Office, 5 Thoresby College, Queen St. (Info ☎767 557, tickets 764 864. Box office open M-Sa 10am-6pm. Tickets £3-30. MC/V with £1 surcharge.) The simultaneous free **Festival Too** offers a wide range of bands performing in Tuesday Market Place. Find further information at the TIC or the Corn Exchange.

▶ DAYTRIPS FROM KING'S LYNN

SANDRINGHAM. Sandringham has been a royal country retreat since 1862; the final version was built in 1870 and has been home to four generations of monarchs. The Edwardian interior houses halls of weaponry and Spanish tapestries, while the grounds feature orderly gardens and a man-made lake. The museum touts the big-game trophies of King George V and cars owned by Edward VII in 1900, Prince Charles in 1990, and Princes William and Harry today. Its manicured 60 acres are open to the public when not in use by the royals. It closes for one week in July; ask at the King's Lynn TIC or call for exact dates. *(10 mi. north of King's Lynn. First Eastern*

Counties bus #411 arrives from King's Lynn; 25 min.; M-Sa 9 per day, Su 1 per hr.; round-trip £3.80. ☎01553 612 908; www.sandringhamestate.co.uk. Open daily Apr.-Sept. 11am-4:45pm, Oct. 11am-3pm; museum and gardens open daily Apr.-Sept. 11am-5pm; Oct. 11am-4pm. £7.50, concessions £6, children £4.50, families £19.50. Museum and gardens only £5/4/3/13.)

CASTLE RISING. This solid keep, built around 1140 atop a giant mound and ringed by an earthwork bank, sheltered Queen Isabella, the "She-Wolf of France," after she plotted the murder of her husband, Edward II. The beautiful view and informative tour make for a worthwhile trip. *(First Eastern Counties buses run from King's Lynn; #411-413, 15min., M-Sa 17 per day; #415, 15min., Su 11 per day; round-trip £3.50. ☎01553 631 330; www.castlerising.com. Open Apr.-Sept. daily 10am-6pm; Oct. daily 10am-6pm or dusk; Nov.-Mar. W-Su 10am-4pm. Admission and audio tour £3.85, concessions £3.10, children £2.20, families £11.50.)*

HOUGHTON HALL. Built in the mid-18th century for Robert Walpole, England's first prime minister, Houghton Hall is a magnificent example of Palladian architecture. Its rooms were intended to reflect the grandeur of Walpole's office and include original tapestries and "the most sublime bed ever designed." The hall includes one of the world's largest model soldier museums. White fallow deer roam the grounds. *(13 mi. northeast of King's Lynn, off the A148 toward Cromer. Easily reached by car; otherwise take the X98 bus and ask the driver to stop at Fakenham, then follow signs for 1 mi. ☎01485 528 569; www.houghtonhall.com. Grounds and museum open Apr.-Sept. W-Th and Su 11am-5:30pm; house open Apr.-Sept. W-Th and Su 1:30-5pm. Last entry 4:30pm. £7, children £3, families £16.)*

THE NORTHERN NORFOLK COAST

The northern Norfolk Coast is a tranquil expanse of British seashore where only the occasional windmill or mansion punctuates untamed beaches, salt marshes, and boggy bays. Those with eight to twelve days to spare can traverse the linked 93 mi. of the **Norfolk Coast Path** and **Peddar's Way** (p. 307), two relatively easy treks. The Peddar's Way, an old Roman road to the coast, begins in **Knettishall Heath Country Park,** extending through **Little Cressingham, North Peckenham,** and the medieval ruins of **Castle Acre,** meeting the Norfolk Coast Path between Hunstanton and Brancaster. The Norfolk Coast Path begins 16 mi. north of King's Lynn at Hunstanton, stretches east to **Wells-next-the-Sea** and then **Sheringham** and the **Norfolk Broads** (p. 325), finishing in **Cromer.** The trail and its villages are also fine daytrips from both Norwich and King's Lynn. The Norfolk Coast Hopper, Norfolk Green Service #36 (☎0870 608 2608), makes daily stops between Hunstanton and Sheringham (1½hr.; every hr. in summer, fewer in winter; all-day ticket £6). **Coastal Voyager** runs sea trips from Southwold (☎07887 525 082; book in advance; £16 per half hour, children £9), and **Skyride Balloons** at Clarkes Lane in King's Lynn (☎07000 110 210; £120 per person) offers the best sea views of all.

The highlight of the coast is ◾**Blakeney Point Seal Colony.** Though accessible by a 4 mi. footpath from Cley-next-the-Sea, the seals would rather their admirers visit by boat; **Bishop's Boats** runs trips from March to October from Blakeney Quay. (☎01263 740 753; www.bishopsboats.co.uk. £7, children £4). In Hunstanton, on the Southern Promenade, the **Hunstanton Sea Life Sanctuary and Aquarium** rehabilitates injured and abandoned seals. (☎01485 533 576; www.sealsanctuary.co.uk. Open daily July-Aug. 10am-5pm; Apr.-June and Sept.-Oct. 10am-4pm; Jan.-Mar. and Nov.-Dec. 10am-3pm. £9, concessions £6.)

For a taste of luxury, visit **Holkham Hall**, 2 mi. west of Wells-next-the-Sea, the home of the Earl of Leicester. Marvel at the marble hall before admiring the amusing **Bygones Museum**, with over 4000 knickknacks from the family's past. (☎ 01328 710 227. Open May-Sept. M and Th-Su noon-5pm. Hall and museum £10, children £5, families £25. Hall only £6.50, children £3.25. Museum only £5/2.50.)

The Norfolk Coast is an easy daytrip from King's Lynn, though Hunstanton, at the western edge, is a more intimate touring base. **Buses** #410-413 run from Vancouver Centre in King's Lynn to Hunstanton (45min.; M-Sa 2 per hr., Su every hr.; round-trip £5.50). For details on the Northern Norfolk Coast, maps, and bus schedules, consult the Hunstanton **Tourist Information Centre**, Town Hall, The Green. (24hr. ☎ 01485 532 610. Open daily Apr.-Sept. 10am-5pm; Oct.-Mar. 10:30am-4pm.) *Walking the Peddar's Way and Norfolk Coast Path with Weavers Way* (£2.70) is a guide and accommodations list. On the coast, Hunstanton's **YHA hostel ❶**, 15 Avenue Rd., is a 5min. walk from the bus station—take Sandringham Rd. south, then turn right on Avenue Rd. TV lounge, laundry, and patio await. (☎ 01485 532 061. No secure storage. Open Apr.-Oct. W-Sa. Dorms £12.50, under 18 £9. MC/V.)

NORWICH   ☎ 01603

The dizzying streets of Norwich (NOR-idge) wind outward from the Norman castle, past the cathedral, and to the scattered fragments of the 14th-century city wall. Though Norwich retains the hallmarks of an ancient city, a university and active art community ensure that it is also thoroughly modern. Clearly, the hum of "England's city in the country" has not yet abated, with a daily market almost a millennium old still thriving alongside busy art galleries and nightlife.

▐ TRANSPORTATION

Easily accessible by bus, coach, or train, Norwich makes a logical base for touring both urban and rural East Anglia, particularly the Norfolk Broads.

Trains: Station at the corner of Riverside and Thorpe Rd., 15min. from the city center (bus 40p). Ticket window open M-Sa 4:45am-8:45pm, Su 6:45am-8:30pm. One Anglia (☎ 08457 484 950) from: **Great Yarmouth** (30min., every hr., £4.40); **London Liverpool Street** (2½hr., 2 per hr., £35.80); **Peterborough** (1½hr., every hr., £16.40).

Buses: Station (☎ 660 553) on Surrey St., off St. Stephen St. Open M-F 8am-5:30pm, Sa 9am-5:15pm. National Express (☎ 08705 808 080) from **London** (3hr., 5 per day, £14). First Eastern Counties (☎ 08456 020 121) travels from **King's Lynn, Peterborough,** and other Norfolk towns; **Ranger tickets** give 1 day of unlimited travel on First Eastern Counties (£10, children £6, seniors £4.50, families £20).

Taxis: Five Star (☎ 0800 575 575). 24hr.

▐▐ ORIENTATION AND PRACTICAL INFORMATION

Although the sights are fairly close together, twisting streets are bound to confuse.

Tourist Information Centre: The Forum, Millennium Plain, Bethel St. (☎ 727 927; www.visitnorwich.co.uk). Sells mini-guides (50p) and books rooms for a £3 charge plus a 10% deposit. Open Apr.-Oct. M-Sa 9:30am-5:30pm, Su 10:30am-4:30pm; Nov.-Mar M-Sa 9:30am-5:30pm. Offers 1½hr. **walking tours** Apr.-Oct. £2.50, children £1.

Financial Services: Thomas Cook, 14 London St. (☎ 241 100). Open M-Sa 9am-5:30pm.

Launderette: Wash-In, 31b Thorpe Rd. (☎762 602), just after Stracey Rd. Wash £3, dry £2. Detergent 20p. Open M-F 9am-8pm, Sa 9am-7pm, Su 9am-6pm. Last wash 1hr. before close.

Pharmacy: Boots, Riverside Retail Park (☎662 894). Open M-F 8:30am-8:30pm, Sa 8:30am-6pm, Su 10:30am-4:30pm.

Police: Bethel St. (☎0845 456 4567). Open daily 8am-midnight.

Hospital: Norfolk and Norwich University Hospital, Colney Ln., (☎286 286), at the corner of Brunswick Rd. and St. Stephen's Rd.

Internet Access: Library (☎774 774), next to Origins in the Forum. Register for a simple "Internet-only" user card and get free access on 20+ computers upstairs or at 6 "Express Terminals" downstairs. Open M and W-F 9am-8pm, Tu 10am-8pm, Sa 9am-5pm. Express open M and W-F 9am-9:30pm, Tu 10am-9:30pm, Sa 9am-8:30pm, and Su 10:30am-4:30pm.

Post Office: Castle Mall (☎08457 223 344). Bureau de change. Open M-Sa 9am-5:30pm. **Post Code:** NR1 3DD.

ACCOMMODATIONS

Lodgings (from £24) are located on **Stracey Road,** a 5min. walk from the train station. Turn left onto Thorpe Rd., walk two blocks from the bridge, and go right onto Stracey Rd. Many **B&Bs** (from £26) line **Earlham Road** and **Unthank Road,** but they're at least 20min. west of downtown and farther from the train station. More B&Bs are on **Dereham Road;** follow St. Benedict's St., which becomes Dereham.

The Abbey Hotel, 16 Stracey Rd. (☎612 915), 5min. from the train station up Thorpe Rd. A TV, wash basin, cocoa, and biscuits await in every room of this clean building. Full breakfast included. Singles £24-34; doubles and twins £44-58. Cash only. ❸

Earlham Guest House, 147 Earlham Rd. (☎454 169; www.earlhamguesthouse.co.uk). Take bus #26 or 27 from city center to The Mitre pub or walk 15min. across town. Tasteful and clean rooms with TVs. Full breakfast included. Singles £25-28; ensuite doubles £52. AmEx/MC/V. ❸

Stracey Hotel, 2 Stracey Rd. (☎628 093). Lace decor in an old Victorian building. Convenient location. Cocktail bar, snooker room, and TV lounge. Full English breakfast included. Singles £25; twins £42; ensuite doubles £45. Cash only. ❸

FOOD AND PUBS

In the heart of the city, just a stone's throw from the castle, is one of England's largest and oldest **open-air markets,** with a wide variety of fresh and organic produce. (Open M-Sa roughly 8:30am-4:30pm.) Tesco Metro **supermarket,** on St. Giles St., is in the city center. (Open M-Sa 7:30am-8pm, Su 11am-5pm.)

■ **The Treehouse,** 14-16 Dove St. (☎763 258). Check the chalkboard menu for the day's creative vegetarian specials in meal (£8.40) or deceptively large "snack" (£6.40) sizes. For dessert, try a vegetarian or vegan milkshake (£3). 10% student discount. Open M-W 10am-4pm, Th-Sa 10am-9pm. Food served from 11:30am. Cash only. ❷

Italia Nostra, 52 St. Giles St. (☎617 199; www.italianostra.co.uk). Authentic Italian entrees (£7-10) are served by friendly Sicilian owners. Save room for the homemade tiramisu (£4.50). Open M-Sa 11:30am-1:30pm and 6pm-midnight. MC/V. ❷

The Waffle House, 39 St. Giles St. (☎612 790; www.wafflehouse.co.uk), serves Belgian waffles smothered in everything from chocolate mousse to spinach and potato curry. 2-courses M-F 11am-4pm £5.75. Open M-Sa 10am-10pm, Su 11am-10pm. MC/V. ❷

The Orgasmic Cafe, 6 Queen St. (☎760 650; www.orgasmic-cafe.com). Go ahead, gasp stylishly as you polish off a meal of freshly baked bread stuffed with salmon, spinach, and *crème fraiche* (£5.50) or one of many inventive pizzas (£5-8). Open M-Sa 10:30am-11pm, Su 11am-11pm. Food served until 10:30pm. MC/V. ❷

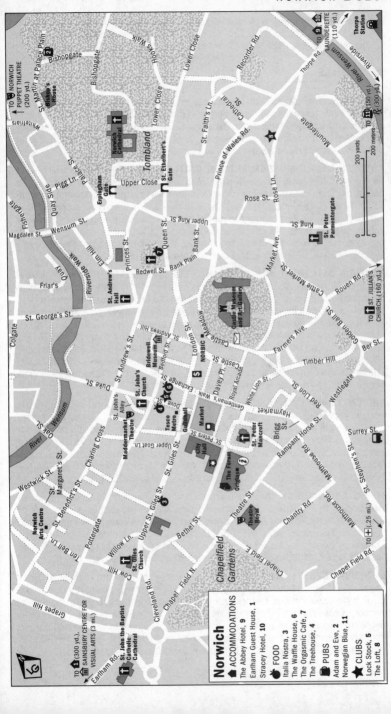

EAST ANGLIA

Norwich

▲ ACCOMMODATIONS
The Abbey Hotel, **9**
Eartham Guest House, **1**
Stracey Hotel, **10**

☆ FOOD
Italia Nostra, **3**
The Waffle House, **6**
The Orgasmic Cafe, **7**
The Treehouse, **4**

🍺 PUBS
Adam and Eve, **2**
Norwegian Blue, **11**

★ CLUBS
Lock Stock, **5**
The Loft, **8**

Adam and Eve, Bishopgate (☎667 423), at the end of Riverside Walk behind the cathedral. Norwich's first pub (est. 1249) is now its most tranquil, hugging the wall around the cathedral yard. Open M-Sa 11am-11pm, Su noon-10:30pm. Cash only. ❶

👁 SIGHTS

▨ ORIGINS. This ultra-interactive history complex, with three floors of exhibits and consoles, fascinates all ages. Settlers from the Vikings to American soldiers are treated with equal measures of humor and hard fact. An 18min. film shows the hidden sights of Norfolk on a 180-degree panoramic screen. *(In the Forum, next to the TIC. ☎727 922. Open M-Sa 10am-5:15pm, Su 11am-4:45pm; £5, concessions £4.)*

NORWICH CASTLE MUSEUM AND ART GALLERY. The original castle was built in the early 12th century by the Norman monarch Henry I, intent on subduing the Saxon city. Its current exterior dates from an 1830s restoration, though a recent £12 million refurbishment was the largest in the castle's history. The **Norman Keep** has multimedia displays about the medieval lives of nobility, and the archaeology gallery displays relics of Celtic Queen Boudicca. The art gallery contains oil paintings and watercolors. *(☎493 645. Open July-Aug. M-Sa 10am-5:30pm, Su 1-5pm; Sept.-June M-F 10am-4:30pm, Sa 10am-5pm, Su 1-5pm. £6, concessions £5, children £4.45.)*

NORWICH CATHEDRAL AND TOMBLAND. The castle and the Norman cathedral dominate Norwich's skyline. The cathedral, built by an 11th-century bishop as penance for having bought his position, features the largest monastic cloisters in England and flying buttresses that support the second-tallest spire in the country (315 ft.). Use the magnifying mirror in the nave to examine the intricately carved overhead bosses. In summer, the cathedral hosts orchestral concerts. *(☎218 300. Open daily mid-May to mid-Sept. 7:30am-7pm; mid-Sept. to mid-May 7:30am-6pm. Evensong M-F 5:15pm, Sa-Su 3:30pm. Suggested donation £4. Tours M-F 10:45am, noon, 2:15pm; £2.50.)* Like a macabre amusement park, **Tombland,** in front of the Cathedral Park, was once a Plague burial site and is now a nightclub hotspot.

BRIDEWELL MUSEUM. This museum displays the history of local industry, recreating an early 19th-century pharmacy, public bar, and tap room, among other common locales of the past. There is also an exhibit on a current Norwich favorite, its football team the Canaries. The enchanting medieval building has its own storied history, having served at various times as a merchant's house, mayor's mansion, factory, and prison. *(Bridewell Alley, off St. Andrew's St. ☎615 975. Open Apr.-Oct. Tu-F 10am-4:30pm, Sa 10am-5pm. £2.90, concessions £2.40, children £1.50, families £6.40.)*

ST. JULIAN'S CHURCH. Julian of Norwich, a 14th-century nun, took up a cell attached to the church and became the first-known woman to pen a book in English— *Revelations of Divine Love*, based on her visions. This small church, first erected in Saxon times and one of the 29 Norwich churches mentioned in the Domesday Book, was bombed during WWII and later rebuilt. *(St. Julian's Alley off Rouen Rd. ☎767 380. Open daily May-Sept. 8am-5:30pm; Oct.-Apr. 8am-4pm. Free.)*

SAINSBURY CENTRE FOR VISUAL ARTS. Located at the University of East Anglia, 3 mi. west of town on Earlham Rd., this center was destroyed during the English Reformation and restored after WWII. Sir Sainsbury, Lord of the Supermarket, donated his superb modern art collection, including works by Picasso and Bacon, to the university in 1973. The building was designed by Sir Norman Foster. *(Take any university-bound bus, such as #26, and ask for the Constable Terr. stop. ☎593 199; www.scva.org.uk. Open Tu and Th-Su 11am-5pm, W 11am-8pm. £2, concessions £1.)*

NIGHTLIFE

Many Norwichian pubs and clubs offer live music. On **Prince of Wales Road,** near the city center, five clubs within two blocks jockey for social position. **The Loft,** on Rose St., is a relaxed, gay-friendly club with live music and dancing downstairs on Friday and soul and funk wafting from the loft for the student-age clientele. Thursday and Saturday have mostly gay partiers, while Friday and Sunday are mixed. (☎623 559; www.loftnightclub.co.uk. Cover Th and Su £2, F £4, Sa £5. Open Th-F 10pm-2am, Sa 10pm-3am, Su 10pm-1am.) **Lock Stock,** 15 Dove St., with its Sunday night "Exclusive Chilled-out Zone," is another hotspot. (☎629 060. Open F-Sa 9pm-4am, Su 9pm-2am.) The Riverside has several clubs and bars to choose from, notably, **Norwegian Blue,** in the Riverside Leisure complex, with decor inspired by fjords and IKEA's minimalist style. A 30 ft. waterfall behind the bar splashes over 27 different vodkas. (☎618 082. Open M-Sa noon-11pm, Su noon-10:30pm. Food served until 10pm.) The **City Rail Link** (☎08456 020 121) bus #25 transfers partiers between the university and the train station, stopping close to most venues (every 30min. after 11pm; all night Tu-Sa; last bus Su 11:15pm, M 11:45pm. £1.50-2.50).

♫ 🎋 ENTERTAINMENT AND FESTIVALS

The TIC, cafes, and B&Bs have information on all things entertaining. Next to the Assembly House on Theatre St., the Art Deco **Theatre Royal** hosts opera and ballet companies and London-based theater troupes such as the Royal Shakespeare Company and Royal National Theatre. (☎630 000; www.theatreroyalenorwich.co.uk. Box office open M-Sa 9:30am-8pm, non-performance days until 6pm. £3-44, concessions available.) The home of the Norwich Players, **Maddermarket Theatre,** St. John's Alley, stages high-quality drama in an Elizabethan-style theater. Adhering to tradition, all actors remain anonymous. (☎620 917; www.maddermarket.co.uk. Box office open M-Sa 10am-9pm; non-performance days M-F 10am-5pm, Sa 10am-1pm. Tickets £7-9.) The **Norwich Arts Centre,** between Reeves Yard St. and Benedicts St., hosts world music, ballet, and comedy. (☎660 352. Box office open M-Sa 10am-10pm. Tickets £3-18.) The **Norwich Puppet Theatre,** St. James, Whitefriars, in a restored medieval church, presents shows for all ages. (☎629 921. Box office open M-F 9:30am-5pm, Sa 1hr. prior to show. £6, concessions £4.20, children £3.75.) Ask the TIC about free summer **Theatre in the Parks** (☎212 137).

The **Norfolk and Norwich Festival**—an extravaganza of theater, dance, music, and visual arts—explodes for ten days in early May. **Open Studios,** in late May, offers two weeks of open artists' studios around the county. July welcomes the **Lord Mayor's Celebration,** with a raucous parade. Check at the TIC for festival details.

▶ DAYTRIP FROM NORWICH

NORFOLK BROADS NATIONAL PARK

To reach the Broads, take a train from Norwich, Lowestoft, or Great Yarmouth to Beccles, Cantley, Lingwood, Oulton Broad, Salhouse, or Wroxham. From Norwich, First Eastern Counties buses go to: Brundell (#17, 17a; 30min.; 2 per hr.; round-trip £3); Horning (#54; 30min., every hr., round-trip £4.40); Strumpshaw (#17a; 30min., every hr., round-trip £3); Wroxham (#54; 40min., every hr., round-trip £3.60); limited service to other Broads towns (#705; M-F every hr.).

Birds and beasts flock to the Norfolk Broads, a soggy maze of marshlands, where traffic in hidden waterways conjures the surreal image of sailboats floating through fields. The landscape was formed in medieval times when peat was dug out to use for fuel. Over the centuries, water levels rose and the shallow lakes, or "broads," were born. Travel with care, as floods are frequent. Among the many **nature trails** that pass through the Broads, **Cockshoot Broad** lets you birdwatch, a circular walk around **Ranworth** identifies the various flora, and **Upton Fen** is popular for its bugs. Hikers can challenge themselves with the 56 mi. **Weaver's Way** between Cromer and Great Yarmouth. The village of **Strumpshaw** has a popular bird reserve. (☎ 715 191. Open daily dawn to dusk. £2.50, families £5.)

The best way to see the Broads is by boat, and many companies around the bridge in Wroxham rent day launches (£10-17 per hr.). Numerous companies also offer **cruises** around the Broads. **Broads Tours** of Wroxham, on the right before the town bridge, runs river trips and rents day boats. (☎ 782 207. Boat rentals £11-13 per hr. Open daily 9am-5:30pm. 1½-2hr. tours July-Aug. 7 per day, £10-12; Sept.-June 11:30am and 2pm. £6-7, children £4.80-5.20.) Certain areas of the Broads are accessible only by car or bike; the pamphlet *Broads Bike Hire*, available at the Wroxham TIC, lists rental shops. A convenient place to **rent bikes** is Broadland Cycle Hire in Wroxham. Follow Station Rd. to the river and take a left onto The Rhond. (☎ 783 096; www.broadlandcyclehire.co.uk. Book in advance in summer. £7 per half-day, £10 per day, £45 per week. Open daily 9am-5pm.)

Wroxham, 10min. from Norwich by train, is the best base for information-gathering and preliminary exploration of some of the area's wetlands. To reach the **Wroxham and Hoveton Broads Information Centre** from the train station and bus stop, turn right on Station Rd. and walk about 90 yd. Knowledgeable Broads rangers answer questions and supply maps, guides, and contact information. The office also lists boat rental establishments and campsites throughout the area and books rooms around the park. (☎ 782 281. Open Easter to Oct. M-Sa 9am-1pm and 2-5pm.)

SUFFOLK AND ESSEX

BURY ST. EDMUNDS   ☎ 01284

In AD 869, Viking invaders tied the Saxon monarch King Edmund to a tree, used him for target practice, and then beheaded him. Approximately 350 years later, 25 barons met in the Abbey of St. Edmund to swear to force King John to sign the *Magna Carta*, sowing the seeds of democracy in Western Europe. From these two defining moments comes Bury's motto: "shrine of a king, cradle of the law."

Along Crown St. lies 🏠**Abbey Gardens,** a park containing the ruins of the 11th-century **Abbey of St. Edmund,** one of the few abbey ruins where the rubble core of the walls (and not the cut stones they were once covered with) is exposed. The 25 *Magna Carta* barons met here in 1214. (Open until sunset. Free.) Next door, the interior of 16th-century **St. Edmundsbury Cathedral** is strikingly colorful; look heavenward and admire the painted wooden ceiling and the shields of the *Magna Carta* barons above the High Altar. (☎ 754 933. Open daily June-Aug. 8:30am-8pm; Sept.-May 8:30am-6pm. Evensong W-Sa 5:30pm, Su 3:30pm. Suggested donation £2. 1hr. guided tours M-Sa 11am, £3.) The **Manor House Museum,** bordering the abbey garden, has an eclectic collection of clocks, antique women's clothing, and fine arts, all housed in a 18th-century mansion. (☎ 757 076. Open W-Su 11am-4pm. £2.60, concessions £2.10, families £8.20.) **Moyse's Hall Museum,** Corn Hill in the marketplace, is devoted to town history. (☎ 706 183. Open M-F 10:30am-4:30pm, Sa-Su 11am-4pm. £2.60, concessions £2.10, families £8.20.) In late May, the two-week **festival** brings music, street entertainment, and fireworks.

Accommodations are hard to come by in Bury. The TIC books **B&Bs** in town or on nearby farms (£20-30). Beside Abbey Gardens, **Park House ❸**, 22a Mustow St., lets one ensuite room in the best location in town. (☎703 432. Continental breakfast included. Reserve in advance. 1 person £25; 2 people £38. Cash only.) The hosts at **Hilltop Guest House ❷**, 22 Bronyon Cir., will pick you up from the bus station. (☎767 066; www.hilltop22br.freeserve.co.uk. Singles £18-25; twins £40; family rooms £45.) Bury bustles on **market** days (W and Sa 9am-4pm). Inexpensive Indian restaurants crowd along Risbygate St. The pint-sized **Nutshell,** Abbeygate at the Traverse, might be Europe's smallest pub; ask about its entry in the *Guinness Book of World Records.* (☎764 867. Open M-Sa 11am-11pm, Su noon-10:30pm.)

Bury makes a good daytrip from Norwich or Cambridge, especially if you include a jaunt to Lavenham, Sudbury, or Long Melford. **Trains** (☎08457 484 950) arrive from: Cambridge (40min., every hr., round-trip £10.80); Felixstowe (1½hr., every hr., £5.90); London (2¼hr., 2 per hr., £29). A National Express **bus** (☎08705 808 080) comes from London (2¼hr., 2 per day, £12.50). Cambus #X11 (☎0870 608 2608) runs from Drummer St. in Cambridge (1hr.; M-Sa every hr., Su 6 per day; £4). The **Tourist Information Centre** is on 6 Angel Hill opposite Abbey Gate. (☎764 667. Open Easter to Oct. M-Sa 9:30am-5:30pm, Su 10am-3pm; Nov. to Easter M-Sa 10am-4pm.) Find **Internet access** at Computer Magic, at 51 St. Andrews St. (☎0871 717 7296; £3 per hr.; open M-F 9am-5:30pm, Sa 9am-4pm). The **post office** is at 17-18 Cornhill St. and has a bureau de change. (☎08457 223 344; open M-F 9am-5:30pm, Sa 9am-12:30pm.) **Post Code:** IP33 1AA.

▶ DAYTRIPS FROM BURY ST. EDMUNDS

ICKWORTH HOUSE. Three miles southwest of Bury, in the village of Horringer, the capacious home of the Marquis of Bristol is a Neoclassical oddity. Dominated by a 106 ft. rotunda, the opulent staterooms are filled with 18th-century French furniture and numerous portraits, including works by Titian, Velasquez, and Gainsborough. The classical Italian garden is splendid. *(First Eastern Counties buses #141-144 leave Bury's St. Andrew's Station; 15min., M-Sa 10 per day, round-trip £3.10. ☎01284 735 270. House open late Mar. to Oct. M-Tu, F-Su, and bank holidays 1-5pm. Last admission 4:30pm. Gardens open daily 10am-5pm. Last admission 4:30pm. Park open daily dawn to dusk. £6.70, children £3. Gardens and park only £3.10/90p.)*

LONG MELFORD. Two Tudor mansions, complete with turrets and moats, grace the village of Long Melford. **Melford Hall,** the more impressive, has retained much of its original Elizabethan exterior and its paneled banquet hall. Peek at the Victorian bedrooms before exploring the colorful gardens. *(☎01787 379 228. Open May-Sept. M and W-Su 2-5:30pm; Apr. and Oct. Sa-Su 2-5:30pm. £4.70, children £2.35.)* More entertaining than stately, 500-year-old **Kentwell Hall** is filled with authentically costumed guides. It also does occasional WWII recreations and hosts an open-air theater in the summer, featuring opera, Shakespeare, and bands. *(☎01787 310 207; www.longmelford.com. Open July-Aug. daily noon-5pm; Mar.-May and Sept.-Oct. Su noon-5pm. £7.15, children £4.60, seniors £6.10.)* Stop by the 1484 **Long Melford Church,** between the two mansions, built with funding from rich wool merchants. *(Long Melford is 14 mi. from Bury, accessible by H.C. Chambers bus #753. 50min., 11 per day, round-trip £4.20.)*

COLCHESTER ☎01206

England's oldest recorded town, Colchester (pop. 98,000) has seen its share of violence. The first Roman capital in Britain, it was also the first town to fall to Celtic Queen Boudicca's revolt. Romans recaptured the place and built what is now the oldest surviving city wall in Britain. It is the site of one of William the Conqueror's first castles, which King John successfully beseiged in 1216. Colchester's half-timber buildings now make up a pedestrian-only town center.

Completed in 1125, **Colchester Castle** now houses the dynamic and morbid **Castle Museum,** with extensive displays of Roman artifacts found in the area, including skeletons, coffins, and weapons from the period of the Boudiccan revolt. The castle was also used as a jail from 1226; several of the cells are still on display, with graphic descriptions of the punishments employed until just a century ago. A tour takes you from the depths of the Roman foundations to the heights of the Norman towers. (☎282 939. Open M-Sa 10am-5pm, Su 11am-5pm. Last admission 4:30pm. Tours noon-4pm on the hour. Castle £4.70, concessions £3. Tours £1.80, children £1.) Pass the time viewing the fine collection of 18th-century Colchester grandfather clocks in **Tymperleys Clock Museum,** off Trinity St. (Open Apr.-Oct. Tu-Sa 10am-1pm and 2-5pm. Free.) Colchester also has several smaller free museums; visit www.colchestermuseums.org.uk.

Colchester has few offerings for the budget traveler. The cheapest place to stay is in one of the large rooms at the **Scheregate Hotel ❸,** 36 Osborne St. (☎573 034. Breakfast included. £5 key deposit. Singles £26-34; doubles £42-48. MC/V.) Sainsbury's **market** is at 9-14 Priory Walk, off Queen St. (Open M-Sa 8am-6:30pm, Su 10am-4pm.) At the **Thai Dragon ❷,** 35 East Hill, costumed waitresses serve a three-course lunch (£8), as well as a variety of well-presented dinners for £5-8. (☎863 414. Open M-Sa noon-2:30pm and 6-11pm, Su noon-2:30pm and 6-10:30pm. MC/V.)

Colchester is best visited as a daytrip from London or nearby East Anglian towns. **Trains** (☎08457 484 950) pull into **North Station** from Cambridge (2½hr., 5 per hr., £15.90) and London Liverpool St. (1hr., 12 per hr., £17.50). Regional trains arrive at North Station, 2 mi. from town; take a connecting train to Colchester Town Station. **Buses** from Cambridge (2½hr., 1 per day, £7.50) and London (2½hr., 3 per day, £12) arrive at the **Bus Authority,** Queen St. (☎282 645), around the corner from the TIC. For regional bus transportation inquiries, call ☎01787 227 233, M-Sa 6am-4pm. The **Tourist Information Centre,** 1 Queen St., across from the castle, books rooms for a 10% deposit and leads 2hr. city **tours.** (☎282 920; www.visitcolchester.com. Open Easter to Oct. M-Tu and Th-Sa 9:30am-6pm, W 10am-6pm, Su 11am-4pm; Oct. to Easter M-Sa 10am-5pm. Tours Mar.-Oct.; call ahead for dates. £2.75, children £1.50.) **Internet access** is available at Compuccino, 17 Priory Walk, three blocks south of the TIC. (☎519 090; £2.50 per hr.) The **post office** is at 68-70 North Hill. (☎08457 223 344. Open M-Sa 9am-5:30pm.) **Post Code:** CO1 1AA.

NORTHWEST ENGLAND

In the 19th century, coal clouds and sprawling mills revolutionized quiet village life. Prosperity followed the smokestacks, making the cities of the northwest the world's wool and linen workshops. The decline of heavy industry hit these cities especially hard, but in the past few decades they have enthusiastically embraced post-industrial hipness. Today their innovative music and arts scenes are world-famous—Liverpool and Manchester alone produced four of *Q* magazine's ten biggest rock stars of the century—and a large student population feeds through-the-roof nightlife. Travelers can find respite from the frenetic urbanity in the Peak District to the east or Cumbria to the north, where the stunning crags and waters of the Lake District are sure to send poets into pensive meditation.

HIGHLIGHTS OF NORTHWEST ENGLAND

EXPLORE Liverpool, Beatles fans: virtually every pub, restaurant, and corner claims some connection to the Fab Four (p. 335).

REVEL in Manchester's nightlife, where trendy cafe-bars morph into late-night venues for dancing and drinking (p. 343).

ROAM the hills, groughs, and moors of the Peak District (p. 352), then explore the dramatic mountains and sparkling waters of the Lake District (p. 360).

NORTHWEST CITIES

CHESTER   ☎01244

With fashionable stores behind mock-medieval facades, tour guides in Roman armor, and a town crier in full uniform, Chester feels like a medley of the quintessentially English. Built by Romans, the city was later a base for Plantagenet campaigns against the Welsh; old town law stated that Welshmen wandering the streets after 9pm could be beheaded. Though it once had trading connections throughout continental Europe, Chester was left to turn its archaism into a selling point after silt blocked the River Dee in the 17th century.

◳ TRANSPORTATION

Chester serves as a rail gateway to Wales via the North Wales line. The train stops 10min. northeast of the city proper, off Hoole Rd., but showing your ticket gets a free ride into downtown. Buses converge between Northgate St. and Inner Ring Rd. near Town Hall.

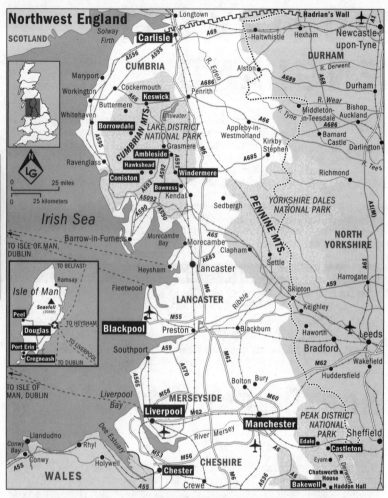

Trains: Station on City Rd. (☎08457 484 950.) Ticket office open M-Sa 5:30am-12:30am, Su 8am-midnight. Trains from: **Birmingham** (1¾hr.; 1-2 per hr., most indirect; £11.50); **Holyhead** (1½hr., 1-2 per hour, £18.60); **London Euston** (2½hr.; 1-2 per hr.; £76 before 9am, £54 after 9am); **Manchester Piccadilly** (1hr., 1-2 per hr., £9.90). Frequent **Merseyrail** service makes Chester an easy daytrip from **Liverpool** (45min., 2 per hr., £4.15).

Buses: The new station is near Town Hall off Northgate St. An information stand helps travelers during the day. **National Express** (☎08705 808 080) from: **Birmingham** (3hr., 6 per day, £9.70); **Blackpool** (3-5hr., 4 per day, £8.40); **London** (6-8hr., 7 per day, £20.50); **Manchester** (1½-2hr., 5 per day, £5.40). **Huxley Coaches** (☎01948 770 661) bus C56 to Foregate St. from **Wrexham** (1hr., M-Sa every hr.). **First** buses connect from **Liverpool** (1½hr., every 20min., £2.20).

Public Transportation: Call ☎0870 608 2608 for local bus info (daily 8am-8pm). Routes can be found in 15 *Bus Times* booklets, available free at the TIC. The **Chester Women's Safe Transport Service** (☎310 585) operates a women-only bus M-Sa.

Taxis: Radio Taxis (☎372 372), **Abbey Taxis** (☎318 318), and **King Cabs** (☎343 343). All 24hr.

⬛ 🛈 ORIENTATION AND PRACTICAL INFORMATION

Chester's center is bounded by a **city wall** with seven gates. **Chester Cross** is at the intersection of **Eastgate Street, Northgate Street, Watergate Street,** and **Bridge Street,** which comprise the heart of the downtown commercial and pedestrian district. From just outside the southern walls, a tree-lined path, **The Groves,** follows a mile of the River Dee. North of the walled city lie the bus stop and **Liverpool Road,** which heads toward the hospital and the zoo. The train station is on the northwestern edge of town and the **Roodee** (Chester Racecourse) occupies the southwest edge.

Tourist Information Centre: Town Hall, Northgate St. (☎402 385; www.chestertourism.com), at the corner of Princess St. Bureau de change. Branch at the **Chester Visitor Centre,** Vicar's Ln. (☎402 111), opposite the Roman amphitheater. Both book accommodations for a £3 charge, book National Express tickets, and sell city maps and a city guide with accommodations listings. Pick up *What's On in Chester and Cheshire* (free) for information on upcoming events. Both open May-Oct. M-Sa 9:30am-5:30pm, Su 10am-4pm; Nov.-Apr. M-Sa 9:30am-5pm, Su 10am-4pm. On Su in winter, only the Visitor Centre is open.

Tours: A legionnaire in full armor leads the **Roman Soldier Wall Patrol.** June-Aug. Th-Sa 1:45pm from the Visitor Centre, 2pm from the TIC. £3.50, concessions £3. Ghouls lurk on the **Ghost Hunter Trail.** After 5:30pm, buy tickets at the Dublin Packet pub on Northgate St. June-Oct. Th-Sa 7:30pm from the TIC; Nov. Sa only. £3.50. A similar self-guided tour is detailed in *Haunted Chester,* a £1.50 pamphlet sold in bookstores and the TIC. For a run-down of Chester's history, try the **History Hunter.** May-Oct. daily 10:30am and 2:15pm from the Visitor Centre; Nov.-Apr. Sa-Su only. £4. The **Secret Chester** tour, which also departs from the Visitor Centre (Tu, Th, Su 2pm; Sa 10am and 2pm), reveals the secrets of Chester's past by affording access to historic buildings. £4.50. Inquiries for the above at ☎402 445. The open-top **Guide Friday** (☎01789 294 466) buses offer hop-on, hop-off service. 4 per hr. £7. A more general **Busybus** (☎0870 874 1800; www.busybus.co.uk) tour covers Chester and surrounding Cheshire for a half day and visits many stately manor homes in the area.

Financial Services: NatWest is on the corner of Eastgate St. and Werburgh St. Open M-Tu and Th-F 9am-5pm, W 9:30am-5pm, Sa 9:30am-3:30pm. **Thomas Cook** (☎583 500) has a commission-free bureau de change near Chester's Cross on Bridge St. Open M-Tu and Th-Sa 9am-5:30pm, W 10am-5:30pm, Su 11am-4pm.

Launderette: Garden Lane Launderette, 56 Garden Ln. (☎382 694). Wash £2.50, dry 20p per 3min., soap 50p, required service charge 50p. Open M-Sa 9:30am-6:30pm.

Police: In the Town Hall (☎350 000).

Pharmacy: Boots, adjacent to the TIC in the Forum Center (☎342 852). Open M-F 8am-6pm, Sa 9am-6pm. The Foregate St. branch is open Su 11am-5pm.

Hospital: Countess of Chester (West Chester) Hospital, Liverpool Rd. (☎365 000). Take bus #40A from the station or #3 from the Bus Exchange.

Internet Access: Library, Northgate St. (☎312 935), beside the Town Hall. Free. Open M and Th 9:30am-7pm, Tu-W and F 9:30am-5pm, Sa 9:30am-4pm. **i-station,** 4 Rufus Ct. (☎351 888). £2 per 30min. Open M-Su 8:30am-9:30pm.

Post Office: 2 St. John St. (☎348 315), off Foregate St. Bureau de change. Open M-Sa 9am-5:30pm. Branch at 122 Northgate St. (☎326 754). Open M-F 9am-5:30pm, Sa 9am-12:30pm. **Post Code:** CH1 2HT.

ACCOMMODATIONS

B&Bs (from £25) are concentrated on **Hoole Road,** a 5min. walk from the train station (turn right from the exit, climb the steps to Hoole Rd., and turn right over the train tracks), and **Brook Street** (right from the train station exit, then the first left). Bus #53 (6 per hr.) runs to the area from the city center.

■ **Chester Backpackers,** 67 Boughton St. (☎400 185; www.chesterbackpakers.co.uk). Convenient location within a 5-10min. walk from both the train station and the city center. Feels like a laid-back student flat, including a lounge with video and book collection. The patio is a nice place for an afternoon read. Kitchen, luggage storage, laundry, and Internet access. Dorms £13; singles £18.50; doubles £30. MC/V. ❷

YHA Chester, 40 Hough Green (☎680 056), 1½ mi. from the city center. Cross the river on Grosvenor Rd. and turn right at the roundabout (40min. walk), following the signs pointing toward North Wales. Buses #7 and 16 arrive from the bus station, #4 from the train station. Renovated Victorian with breakfast included. Internet access. YHA membership required (£12-14). Reception 7am-10:30pm. Open mid-Jan. to mid-Dec. Dorms £16, under 18 £12.50; twin £29, ensuite £38. MC/V. ❷

Laburnum Guest House, 2 St. Anne St. (☎ 380 313). 4 large, ensuite rooms close to town. Singles £26; doubles £50. Cash only. ❸

FOOD

A Tesco **supermarket** hides at the end of an alley off Frodsham St. (Open M-Sa 7am-9pm, Su 11am-5pm.) The **market,** 6 Princess St., in Market Hall, has excellent, cheap fruits and vegetables. (☎402 340. Open M-Sa 8am-5pm.) On Sundays the town hosts an outdoor **Farmers' Market.** (Open 9:30am-4pm.)

■ **Philpott's,** 2 Goss St. (☎345 123), off Watergate St. Philpott's has cheery service, a pristine counter, and fabulous hand-crafted sandwiches (from £1.60). Takeaway only. Open M-Sa 7:30am-2:30pm. Cash only. ❶

La Tasca, 6/12 Cuppin St. (☎400 887). Friendly and lively atmosphere make this tapas bar and restaurant a great weekend spot. A variety of meat and vegetarian tapas available, as well as plenty of sangria. Cash only. ❷

The Blue Bell, 65 Northgate St. (☎317 758). Its name comes from the "curfew bell" that once rang at 8pm each night to demand that strangers leave the city. Entrees from £11.50, lunch from £5.95, and an award-winning cheese plate for £5.50. Open daily from 11am. Food served noon-2pm and 6:30-9:30pm. MC/V. ❸

Gabby's Creperie, Music Hall Passage (☎07811 352 847), just off Northgate St. Design your own savory crepe (from £2.50) or sample one of Gabby's ingenious offerings. Open M-F 11am-5pm, Sa 10am-5pm, Su 11am-4:30pm. Cash only. ❶

Hattie's Tea Shop, 5 Rufus Ct. (☎345 173), off Northgate St. A bustling teashop with friendly service and great homemade cakes. "Bumper salad" (with ham, tuna, cheese, and egg) £6.25. Open M-Sa 9am-5pm, Su 11am-4pm. Cash only. ❷

SIGHTS

ARCHITECTURE. Chester's faux-antiquated architecture is the most striking feature of its city center, though the self-consciously droll buildings mostly house chain stores and fast-food cafes. Some of the structures do date from the

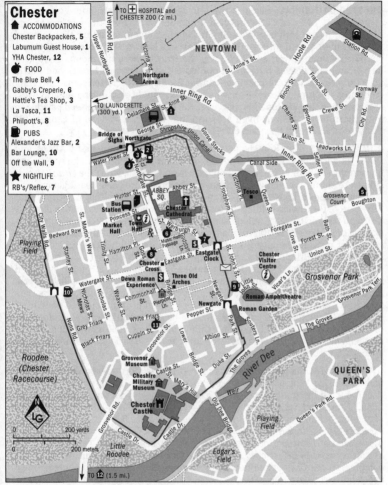

Chester

ACCOMMODATIONS
Chester Backpackers, **5**
Laburnum Guest House, **1**
YHA Chester, **12**

FOOD
The Blue Bell, **4**
Gabby's Creperie, **6**
Hattie's Tea Shop, **3**
La Tasca, **11**
Philpott's, **8**

PUBS
Alexander's Jazz Bar, **2**
Bar Lounge, **10**
Off the Wall, **9**

NIGHTLIFE
RB's/Reflex, **7**

medieval or Tudor eras, however, most notably the 13th-century **"3 Old Arches"** on Bridge St., which are believed to make up the oldest storefront in England. Charming black-and-white painted facades characterize the later **"Magpie"** style, a Victorian phenomenon. Occasional street performers (like classical string septets) grace this much-trafficked area, and the town crier performs from May to August Tuesday through Saturday at noon. Climb the famous **city walls** or the 13th-century **rows** of Bridge St., Watergate St., and Eastgate St., where walkways provide access to another tier of storefronts. Some historians theorize that Edward I imported the tiered design from Constantinople, which he visited while crusading. **Northgate,** which offers a fine view of Welsh hills, was rebuilt in 1808 to house the city's jail. The **Bridge of Sighs** is outside the gate; it carried doomed convicts from jail to chapel for their last mass, although a good number attempted escape by jumping into the canal before railings were installed. Cameras click before **Eastgate Clock,** the second-most-photographed timepiece in the world—behind London's Big Ben.

CHESTER CATHEDRAL. Begun in the 11th century, the construction (and reconstruction) of Chester Cathedral had a number of stages—the last major one concluded in the 16th century and left the magnificent structure that remains today. One-of-a-kind intersecting stone arches known as **"the crown of stone"** support its main tower, and a choir at the front (where the monks once kept devotions) showcases intricate woodwork full of strange beasts and battle scenes. More elaborate carvings can be found on the **misericords**—literally translated as "mercy seats"—on which monks would rest during lengthy worship sessions. Art aficionados marvel at the two-century-old **Cobweb painting** in a northern niche, a short-lived art form that used silk instead of canvas. *(Off Northgate St.* ☎ *324 756. Open daily 8am-6pm. £4. Audio guide included.)*

ROMAN SIGHTS. The Romans had conquered most of Britannia by AD 43, and Deva (modern-day Chester) was an important strategic outpost. The walled city housed the soldiers' barracks and military headquarters, while the *canabae* outside were set up for wicked indulgences like prostitutes and board games. The **Grosvenor Museum** houses a display of artifacts and models that illustrate what life was like for Roman soldiers-in-residence. A connected period house displays 3-D vignettes of 400 years of high society. *(27 Grosvenor St.* ☎ *402 008; www.grosvenor-museum.co.uk. Open M-Sa 10:30am-5pm, Su 1-4pm. Free.)* At the edge of Grosvenor Park, just outside the city wall, specialists are unearthing the largest **Roman amphitheater** in Britain. Lions were shipped in for the bloody gladiatorial bouts. *(Open 24hr. Free.)* Nearby, the **Roman Garden** provides a great picnic space on shaded grass lined with stunted Roman columns. Off Bridge St., the **Dewa Roman Experience,** Pierpoint Ln., affords a full-immersion encounter with Chester's classical past. Visitors board an old galley vessel bound for a recreated version of Britannia. The museum also chronicles the layered archaeological exploration of the town and contains hands-on exhibits that allow visitors to touch Roman artifacts. *(*☎ *343 407. Open Feb.-Nov. M-Sa 9am-5pm, Su 10am-5pm; Dec.-Jan. daily 10am-4pm. £4.25, concessions £3.75.)*

OTHER SIGHTS. Chester Zoo, one of Europe's largest, houses everything from jaguars to lions, as well as human-sized prairie dog tunnels and a "monkey kitchen." Watch out for the free-roaming peacocks as you make your way to the "Twilight Zone," Europe's largest free-flight bat cave. Check the posted signs to witness action-packed animal feedings. *(Take First bus #1 from the Bus Exchange (every 20min., round-trip £2). On Sundays, catch Arriva #411 or 412.* ☎ *380 280; www.chesterzoo.org. Open daily in summer 10am-6pm; otherwise, 10am-4:30pm. Last admission 1-1½ hr. before close. £13.50, concessions £12, families £45.50.)* The **Chester Military Museum,** in the castle complex, traces Chester's armed forces from medieval archers to contemporary special forces. Learn how 18th-century recruiting sergeants "enlisted" unsuspecting beer-guzzlers with a well-placed shilling. *(*☎ *327 617; www.chester.ac.uk/militarymuseum. Open daily 10am-4:30pm. Last admission 4pm. £2, concessions £1.)*

🎭 🎵 NIGHTLIFE AND ENTERTAINMENT

Many of the city's 30-odd pubs parrot Olde English decor, and almost all are open from noon to 11pm Monday through Saturday and from noon to 10:30pm on Sunday. Watering holes group on **Eastgate Street** and **Foregate Street** and throughout the town center. Jazz and blues waft into the outdoor courtyard of **Alexander's Jazz Bar,** Rufus Ct., Wednesdays and Thursdays in summer. *(*☎ *340 005. Tu unplugged acoustic; F soul and funk; Sa live comedy. Cover £2-20. Open M-Sa 10:30am-2am, Su noon-12:30am.)* Situated on what was once a Roman defense ditch, **Off the Wall,** 12 St. John's St., offers two-meal deals for £6.50 and inexpensive wine for £5.10 per bottle. *(*☎ *348 964. Food served daily noon-5pm and from 8pm.)* Put on your dancing shoes and head to **RB's/Reflex,** 12-16 Northgate St., Chester's only traditional nightclub. The trendy and fun-loving come here nightly to explore the club's three floors, each with different music and a distinct vibe. (☎327 141. Cover £2-7. Open M-W 10pm-2am, Th-Sa 7am-2am, Su 7pm-12:30am.) Winner of the Best Bar Award in Chester for the last two years, **Bar Lounge**, 75 Watergate St., knows how to create a good vibe. The bar caters to a twentysomething, champagne-cocktail crowd, while the expansive beer garden is a bit more low-key. (Open M-Th noon-11pm, F-Sa 11am-11pm, Su 11pm-10:30pm.) On sporadic spring and summer weekends, England's oldest **horse races** are held on the **Roodee**, attracting huge and boisterous crowds. If you plan to visit over a race weekend, book far in advance. (☎304 600. Tickets from £6, average is £20.) The **Chester Summer Music Festival** draws classical musicians to the cathedral in July. (☎320 700. Ticket prices vary but usually start at £7.) Check the TIC's free *What's On in Chester* for other events.

LIVERPOOL ☎0151

Much of Britain is quick to belittle once-industrial Liverpool, but Scousers—as Liverpudlians are colloquially known—don't seem to mind much. Their good humor has stood the test of hard knocks and big bombs, and an energized metropolis has emerged. With over 65,000 students and the construction of many free museums and public projects, Liverpool is in the process of a cultural face-lift. Scousers proudly demonstrate their love for Liverpool: crazed fans sport jerseys for the area's two near-deified football squads and the streets bustle with vibrant nightlife. Named the European Capital of Culture 2008 by the European Commission, Liverpool's rapid development shows no signs of slowing anytime soon. Oh, yeah—and some fuss is made over the Beatles.

▐ TICKET TO RIDE

Trains: Lime Street Station, Lime St. and St. John's Ln. Ticket office open M-Sa 5:15am-11:35pm, Su 7:15am-10:30pm. Trains (☎08457 484 950) from: **Birmingham** (1¾hr., M-Sa every hr., Su 6 per day; £19.80); **London Euston** (3hr., every hr., £54); **Manchester Piccadilly** (1hr., 2-4 per hr., £8). **The Moorfields, James Street,** and **Central** stations serve mainly as transfer points to local Merseyrail trains, including to **Chester** (45min., 2 per hr., £4.15).

Buses: Norton Street Station receives National Express (☎08705 808 080) from: **Birmingham** (3hr., 5 per day, £9.50); **London** (4½-5½hr., 5-6 per day, £20); **Manchester** (1hr., 1-3 per hr., £5.25). Other buses stop at **Queen Square** and **Paradise Street** stations. The 1-day **Mersey Saveaway** (Sa-Su £2.10, children £1.60) works on area buses and is unrestricted during off-peak hours. Also valid on ferry and rail.

Ferries: Liverpool Sea Terminal, Pier Head, north of Albert Dock. Open daily 9am-5pm. The Isle of Man Steam Packet Company (☎08705 523 523; www.steam-packet.com) runs ferries from Princess Dock to the **Isle of Man** and **Dublin** (see **By Ferry**, p. 376).

Local Transportation: Private buses cover the city and the Merseyside area. Consult the transport experts at **Mersey Travel** (☎08706 082 608; www.merseytravel.gov.uk) in the TIC. Open M and W-Sa 9am-5:30pm, Tu 10am-5:30pm, Su 10:30am-4:30pm.

Taxis: Mersey Cabs (☎207 2222). 24hr.

▐▐ HELP!

Liverpool's central district is surprisingly pedestrian-friendly. There are two clusters of museums: on **William Brown Street,** near Lime St. Station and the lovely urban oasis of St. John's Garden, and at **Albert Dock,** on the river. These flank the central shopping district, whose central axis comprises **Bold Street, Church Street,** and **Lord Street** and is largely composed of pedestrian-only walkways and plazas.

Tourist Information Centre: Queen Square Centre, Queen Sq. (☎0906 680 6886; www.visitliverpool.com). Gives away the handy *Visitor Guide to Liverpool, Merseyside, and England's Northwest* as well as a huge stock of pamphlets and local events schedules. Books beds for a 10% deposit. Open M and W-Sa 9am-5:30pm, Tu 10am-5:30pm, Su 10:30am-4:30pm. Branch at **Albert Dock Centre,** Albert Dock, inside the Maritime Museum (☎0906 680 6886). Open daily 10am-5pm.

Tours: In addition to those listed below, numerous **bus tours** (from £5) and **walking tours** (£4, concessions £3) run in summer; ask the TIC. The TIC also offers guided 2hr. expeditions around and inside **John and Paul's Liverpool homes** through the National Trust. Apr.-Oct. W-Sa. Book in advance. £12.

Phil Hughes (☎228 4565, mobile 07961 511 223). If you are lucky enough to get a seat in Phil's van, you will be treated to the most comprehensive Beatles tour in Liverpool. This expert guide runs personalized 3-4hr. tours with Liverpool highlights. Passengers alight at Strawberry Fields and Eleanor Rigby's grave. 1 per day—book in advance. £12; private tours £65.

Magical Mystery Tour (☎709 3285; www.caverncitytours.com). A yellow-and-blue bus takes 40 fans to Fab Four sights, leaving the Queens Sq. TIC. The 2hr. tour is interesting but feels packaged. Purchase tickets in advance at either of the TICs or at the Beatles Story. M-F 2:10pm, Sa-Su 11:40am and 2:10pm. £12, small souvenir included.

Financial Services: Banks flood the shopping districts, and ATMs seem to sprout from every alleyway. **Lloyd's TSB,** 53 Great Charlotte St. (open M-W and F 9am-5pm, Th 10am-5pm), and **HSBC,** 4 Dale St. (open M-F 9:30am-5pm), are two options. **American Express,** 54 Lord St. (☎702 4505) has a bureau de change. Open M and W-F 9am-5:30pm, Tu 9:30am-5:30pm, Sa 9am-5pm.

Work Opportunities: JobCentrePlus, 20 Williamson Sq. (☎801 5700). Open M-Tu and Th-F 9am-5pm, W 10am-5pm.

Launderette: The **YMCA** (56-60 Mount Pleasant) offers washing and drying for £2 each from 2pm to 10pm. The **YHA Liverpool** (p. 338) allows non-residents to use its facilities.

Luggage Storage: Inside Lime Street Station. Open M-Th 7am-9pm; F-Su 7am-11pm. £5 per item per 24hr.

Police: Canning Pl. (☎709 6010) and 70 Church St. (☎777 4147).

Pharmacy: Boots, 18-20 Great Charlotte St. (☎709 4711). Open M-Sa 8:15am-6:15pm, Su 8:30am-5pm.

Internet Access: Central Library, William Brown St. (☎233 5835). Free access on the 2nd fl. Open M-F 9am-6pm, Sa 9am-5pm, Su noon-4pm. Free access in the **Merseyside Youth Association Ltd,** 65-67 Hanover St. (☎702 0700). Open daily 8am-9pm.

Post Office: 42-44 Houghton Way (☎08457 740 740), in St. John's Shopping Centre below the Radio City Tower. ATM and bureau de change. Open M-Sa 9am-5:30pm. **Post Code:** L1 1AA.

⚑ A HARD DAY'S NIGHT

Cheap accommodations lie east of the city center. **Lord Nelson Street** is lined with modest hotels, as is **Mount Pleasant,** one block from Brownlow Hill and Central Station. Stay only at places approved by the TIC, and if you need a good night's sleep, consider springing for a single—some hostels host herds of clubbing teens on weekend nights. Demand for beds is highest in early April for the Grand National Race and during the Beatles Convention at the end of August.

▨ **International Inn,** 4 S. Hunter St. (☎709 8135; www.internationalinn.co.uk), off Hardman St. Clean and fun, this hostel welcomes visitors from all over the world with style and 2-, 4-, 6-, 8-, and 10-person ensuite rooms. Pool table, lounge, and kitchen. Bedding is provided as well as coffee, tea, and toast. Internet access £1 per 30min. in the adjoining **Cafe Latténet.** Cafe open M-F 8am-9pm, Sa-Su 9am-5:30pm. Dorms £15, weekends £16; twins £36. AmEx/MC/V. ❷

Liverpool

♦ ACCOMMODATIONS
Embassie Backpackers, 20
International Inn, 13
University of Liverpool, 19
YHA Liverpool, 16
YMCA Liverpool, 6

🍴 FOOD
Everyman Bistro, 15
Country Basket Sandwich Bar, 2
Hole in the Wall, 4
Kimos, 5
Tabac, 11
Tavern Company, 1

🍺 PUBS
Hannah's, 12
Modo, 7
The Philharmonic, 14
The Pilgrim Pub, 18
Slaters Bar, 9

★ CLUBS
BaaBar, 8
The Blue Angel, 17
The Cavern Club, 3
Society, 10

■ **Embassie Backpackers,** 1 Falkner Sq. (☎707 1089; www.embassie.com). A first-rate hostel in a nice neighborhood. The friendly staff is eager to acquaint you with its numerous amenities (pool table, kitchen, and satellite TV lounge) or chat over free toast and tea. Busy on weekends. Arranges for the Phil Hughes Beatles tour to pick up from the hostel doors. Laundry. Reception 24hr. Dorms £14.50 for the 1st night, £13.50 each additional night. Cash only. ❷

YHA Liverpool, 25 Tabley St. (☎08707 705 924). Pristine, upscale digs on 3 Beatles-themed floors, near Albert Dock. Suitable rooms for families. Kitchen, currency exchange, and Big Apple Diner. Breakfast included. Laundry and Internet access available. Membership required. Dorms £15-19, under 18 £12.50-14. MC/V. ❷

University of Liverpool. The conference office (☎794 6440, bookings 794 6453) has information for travelers. Breakfast £2. Available mid-June to mid-Sept. Singles £17. Cash only. ❷

YMCA Liverpool, 56-60 Mount Pleasant (☎709 9516). All rates at the YMCA include breakfast. Rooms are satisfactory and clean. Singles £19; doubles £36; triples £48. ❷

◖ SAVOY TRUFFLE

Cafes and budget-friendly kebab stands line **Bold Street, Hardman Street,** and **Leece Street,** while takeaways crowd near late-night venues and around **Berry Street.** Cheap all-you-can-eat deals can be found in both trendy and dodgy neighborhoods. A glittering arch over Nelson St., imported from Shanghai as a recent gift from the People's Republic, marks the entrance to the oldest **Chinatown** in the world. Upscale restaurants cluster around **Queen Square** and downtown. A Tesco Metro **supermarket** with great sandwiches is in Clayton Sq., across from St. John's Shopping Centre. (Open M-F 6am-midnight, Sa 6am-10pm, Su 11am-5pm.)

■ **Tabac,** 126 Bold St. (☎709 9502). Sleek, trendy decor hides the fact that the food is actually quite cheap. Sandwiches on freshly baked focaccia bread (melted brie and bacon £4) are served all day. Dinner specials £6.50-9.50. Breakfast from £2. Wine bar opens early. Open M-F 8:30am-11pm, Sa 9am-12am, Su 10am-11pm. MC/V. ❷

Country Basket Sandwich Bar, Drury Ln. (☎236 0509), between Brunswick St. and Water St. Breakfast, lunch, and snack foods line the walls, with outrageously low prices advertised on every leftover surface. Try the toasties or lunchtime roasts. Hours vary. ❶

Hole in the Wall, 37 School Ln. (☎709 7733). Considerably larger and brighter than its name would suggest. Serves a huge variety of barms and quiches (from £4). Takeaway available. Open M-Sa 8:30am-4pm. Cash only. ❶

Tavern Company, 4 Queen Sq. (☎709 1070), near the TIC. Mexican BBQ meets upscale bar. Burritos (£8.50) and spirits. Open M-Sa noon-11pm, Su noon-9:30pm. Food served M-Th noon-10pm, F-Sa noon-10:30pm, Su noon-9:30pm. MC/V. ❷

Kimos, 46 Mt. Pleasant (☎709 2355). A large menu of Mediterranean and North African cuisine with lots of vegetarian options. All tapas, salads, burgers, pizzas, soups, and sandwiches are under £5, and dinner specials like lamb couscous (£7.70) are also available. Breakfast served until 6pm. Open daily 10am-11pm. Cash only. ❷

Everyman Bistro, 5-9 Hope St. (☎708 9545) in the basement. Generous portions of a myriad of tasty dishes. The menu is always changing. Creamy desserts tempt Everyman and woman. Open M-W noon-midnight, Th noon-1am, F-Sa noon-2am. MC/V. ❷

◪ COME TOGETHER

Two of the Liverpool's most notable products—football fans and rock musicians—were born of pub culture, and the city has continued to incorporate these traditions into its pub scene. There's not a spot in Liverpool that's far from a good selection of watering holes; those catering to the younger set cluster between **Slater Street** and **Berry Street,** where cheap drink specials are in plentiful supply.

Hannah's, 2 Leece St. (☎708 5959). Offers great live music on weekdays and a DJ on weekends. The huge beer garden adjacent to the downstairs bar bustles with activity in nice weather. Open M-Sa 11:30am-2am, Su noon-12:30am.

The Philharmonic, 36 Hope St. (☎707 2837). John Lennon once said the worst thing about being famous was "not being able to get a quiet pint at the Phil." Non-celebrities can still enjoy a mellow beer in this gorgeous old lounge, where the clientele and the decor are reminiscent of an old boys' club. Don't miss the famous mosaic tiling in the men's bathroom, though women should ask at the bar before checking for themselves. Open M-Sa noon-11pm, Su noon-10:30pm.

Modo, 23-25 Fleet St. (☎709 8832). Bubbling with young professional folks (or with students posing as professionals), Modo's lounge blasts techno and its couches provide ample space for putting out the vibe. The expansive urban beer garden allows for conversation and makes Modo exceedingly popular. Most drink here, but a club hides downstairs. Open M-Sa 11:30am-2am, Su noon-12:30am.

The Pilgrim Pub, 34 Pilgrim St. (☎709 2302). Frequented by drama and art types, the Pilgrim provides a relaxed and friendly atmosphere in its two bars and beer garden. Cheap drinks and live music weekends. Open M-Sa 10am-11pm, Su 10am-10:30pm.

Slaters Bar, 26 Slater St. (☎708 6990). Youthful queues form outside. Cheap drinks, with pints from £1.10. Open M-Sa 11am-2am, Su noon-10:30pm.

◉ MAGICAL MYSTERY TOUR

With first-rate museums, two dazzling cathedrals, and the twin religions of football and the Beatles, Liverpool's attractions are endowed with spirited heritage and modern vitality. The city center oozes with theaters and cultural centers, while **Hope Street** to the southeast connects Liverpool's two 20th-century cathedrals. Most other sights are located on or near **Albert Dock,** an open rectangle of Victorian warehouses now stocked with offices, restaurants, and museums.

THE BEATLES STORY. Walk-through recreations of Hamburg, the Cavern Club, and a shiny Yellow Submarine. Trace the rise and—sigh—fall of the band from their beginnings in the Cavern Club, to Beatlemania, to dabblings in transcendental meditation, to solo careers. The audio guide (included with admission) is narrated by Paul McCartney, Alan Williams (the Beatles' first manager), and numerous family members and friends. Audio-taped screeches of real fans and (of course) recordings of the foursome accompany your tour. Crowded on weekends. *(Albert Dock. ☎709 1963; www.beatlesstory.com. Open daily 10am-6pm. Last admission 1hr. before close. £9.)*

TATE GALLERY. The Liverpool branch of this legendary institution boasts a collection of favorites (Warhol, Pollock, Picasso) and lesser-knowns from the 20th century. International artists dominate the ground floor and the next level shows a rotating collection from the gallery's archives. By prior arrangement, the staff will fit the visually impaired with special gloves and allow them to touch some of the art. The helpful and knowledgeable staff roams the galleries. Fascinating special exhibits. *(Albert Dock. ☎702 7400; www.tate.org.uk/liverpool. Open Tu-Su 10am-5:50pm. Free. Suggested donation £2. Special exhibits £5, concessions £4.)*

LIVERPOOL CATHEDRAL. Begun in 1904 and completed in 1978, this Anglican cathedral makes up for what it lacks in age with sheer size. Its walls claim a number of superlatives, featuring the highest Gothic-style arches ever built (107 ft.), the highest and heaviest (31 tons) bells in existence, and an organ with 9765 pipes, second in size only to the one in Royal Albert Hall in London. Take two lifts and climb

MEET THE BEATLES

Let's Go *interviewed Allan Williams, owner of the Jacaranda Coffee Bar in Liverpool and the first manager of the world's favorite mop-heads. Williams regaled us with tales of a simpler time...when the Beatles were coffee shop bums, skipping lectures to hang out at the Jac, eating their beloved "bacon-butty" sandwiches, and listening to the music they would come to dominate...when Pete Best kept the beat (not that Ringo interloper) and the group had to be smuggled into Hamburg as "students" (and then deported when a 17-year-old George Harrison was busted for hanging out at 18+ clubs). Here are just a few of his memories.*

LG: So tell me how you first met the Beatles.
A: My wife and I had a coffee bar club... because I was a rock 'n' roll promoter, all the groups used to come to my place, mainly because I let them rehearse for free in the basement... I only knew [the Beatles] as coffee bar layabouts—they were always bumming coffee off of *anybody*... I had complaints about the obscene graffiti that the girls were writing about the groups, and here these lads were from the art school and they could paint. I said, "Will you decorate the ladies' toilets for me?" And the way they decorated them, I'd have preferred the graffiti, to be

108 stairs for awe-inspiring views or wait below for haunting minor chords capable of rattling windows, heads, and disbelievers. *(Upper Duke St. ☎ 709 6271; www.liverpoolcathedral.org.uk. Cathedral open daily 8am-6pm. Tower open daily Mar.-Sept. 11am-5pm, Oct.-Feb. 11am-4pm. Tower £3.25, children £1.50. Cathedral only free.)*

MORE BEATLES. For other Beatles-themed locales, get the **Beatles Map** (£3) at the TIC. To reach **Penny Lane,** take bus #86A, 33, or 35 from Queen's Sq.; for **Strawberry Fields,** take #176 from Paradise St. Souvenir hunters can raid the **Beatles Shop,** 31 Matthew St., canopied with shirts and the best Beatles posters in town. Doors are open "8 Days a Week." *(☎ 236 8066; www.thebeatlesshop.co.uk. Open M-Sa 9:30am-5:30pm, Su 10:30am-4:30pm.)*

FACT. Housed in a shimmering metallic building, FACT stands for Film, Art, and Creative Technology. Built to showcase the digital arts, most of the exhibits revolve around film and video. Don't miss the digital remixing studio on the first floor, where you can learn to spin like a DJ. Blockbuster films are occasionally shown, but most patrons come for the artsy and foreign. A new special exhibition opens every six weeks and is always the work of a "time-based" artist or a demonstration of new media. *(Wood St. ☎ 707 4450; www.fact.co.uk. Open M-Sa 11am-11pm, Su noon-10:30pm. Entrance and all exhibits free. Film screenings about £5, W £3.50.)*

MERSEYSIDE MARITIME MUSEUM. Liverpool's heyday as a major port has passed, but the six floors of this impressive museum allow you to explore the legacies of Scouser history. On the bottom floor is the phenomenal **H.M. Customs and Excise Museum** (set to close in summer 2006), with an intriguing array of confiscated goods from would-be smugglers, including a tortoise-turned-mandolin and a teddy bear full of cocaine. In the basement, the **Transatlantic Slavery Gallery** allows visitors to walk through the darkened hull of a recreated slave ship and learn how many (answer: a lot) of Liverpool's street names are connected to the slave trade. *(Albert Dock. ☎ 478 4499. Open daily 10am-5pm. Free.)*

METROPOLITAN CATHEDRAL OF CHRIST THE KING. Controversially "modern," some would sooner call this oddity of the skyline ugly. A crown of crosses tops its reinforced-concrete "Lantern Tower" (resembling an upside-down funnel), while inside, bright slivers of stained glass bathe the chapel alcoves in sparkling jewel tones. The bronze Stations of the Cross by sculptor Sean Rice are dramatic, and the circular chapel is immense. *(Mt. Pleasant. ☎ 709 9222. Open in summer M-Sa 8am-6pm, Su 8am-5pm; closes earlier in winter, depending on demand. Free.)*

LIVERPOOL AND EVERTON FOOTBALL CLUBS. If you're not here for the Beatles, you're probably here for the football. The rivalry between the city's two main teams, **Liverpool** and **Everton,** is deep and passionate. Both offer tours of their grounds (Anfield and Goodison Park, respectively), which may be booked in advance. *(Bus #26 from the city center to Anfield. Bus #19 from the city center to Goodison Park. Liverpool ☎260 6677. Everton ☎330 2277. Liverpool tour, including entrance to their museum £9, concessions £5.50. Everton tour £8.50/5. Match tickets usually £29-32.)*

THE WILLIAMSON TUNNELS HERITAGE CENTRE. Called "The King of Edge Hill" by some (and the "Mole of Edge Hill" by those more skeptical of his vision), William Josephson kept hundreds of local laborers employed during a post-war depression building huge, multi-level tunnels to nowhere. What little has been excavated can now be toured by visitors with 30min. to spare. *(The Old Stableyard, Smithdown Ln. ☎709 6868. Open in summer Tu-Su 10am-6pm; in winter Th-Su 10am-5pm. Last admission 1hr. before close. £3.50, concessions £3, families £10.)*

WALKER ART GALLERY. The massive collection in this stately gallery centers on British art from the 18th and 19th centuries, but features a wide range of pieces, including medieval and classical works and a variety of impressive post-Impressionist paintings. *(William Brown St. ☎478 4199. Open daily 10am-5pm. Free.)*

OTHER SIGHTS. A small museum below the conservation studios for the National Museum and Galleries of Merseyside, the **Conservation Centre,** Whitechapel, provides insight into the processes of art restoration and preservation. Hands-on exhibits are particularly engaging for children. *(☎478 4999. Open M-Sa 10am-5pm, Su noon-5pm. Tours W and Sa 2 and 3pm. Free.)* The newly renovated **World Museum** houses everything from pteradactyl bones to totem poles. It contains a "Treasure House" of prized objects from around the world, a World Cultures Gallery, an extensive Egyptian collection, and a planetarium. *(William Brown St. Open daily 10am-5pm. Free.)*

🎵 AND YOUR BIRD CAN SING

As recent accolades have shown, Liverpool is a city of burgeoning culture, from theater to live music. Liverpool is gearing up for the honor of European Capital of Culture 2008 with countless one-time festivals and events in the coming years. Check www.liverpool08.com or contact the TIC close to the time of your visit. The **International Street Theatre Festival** (late July to early Aug.; ☎709 3334; www.brou-

honest with you. They were just *throwing* paint on them as if they were Picassos.

LG: Sort of Pollock-style...
A: Heh. Yeah...

LG: And how did you become their manager?
A: I put this big rock 'n' roll show on. They came and saw me the next day and said, "Hey Al? When are you going to do something for us like?" And I said to them, "Look, there's no more painting to be done." And they said, "No, we've got a *group.*" I said, "I didn't know that." And they said, "Well, will you manage us?" By then I had got to know them, and they were quite nice personalities—very witty. And I go, "Oh yeah, this could be fun." And then I managed them.

Williams told us how it was their stint in Hamburg, and not Liverpool, that made the Beatles. He then described his falling out with the group, over (what else?) contract disputes and general rock star ingratitude.

A: I wrote them a letter saying that they appeared to be getting more than a little swell-headed, and, remember, "I managed you when nobody else wanted to know you. But I'll fix it now so that you'll never ever work again."
LG: Uh-oh.

A: Heh-heh. So that's my big mistake, yeah. Heh. And on that note, we'll finish.

haha.uk.com) brings international performances to the city. At the end of August, a week-long **Beatles Convention** draws Fab Four devotees (☎236 9091; www.caverncitytours.com). The TIC stocks a comprehensive festival list.

Philharmonic Hall, Hope St. (☎709 3789; www.liverpoolphil.com). The **Royal Liverpool Philharmonic,** one of England's better orchestras, performs here along with many others, including jazz and funk bands. Office open for telephone bookings M-Sa 10am-5:30pm, Su noon-5pm; on concert nights, counter is open from 5:30pm until 15min. after the performance begins. Tickets average £20, same-day concessions £5.

Liverpool Empire Theatre, Lime St. (☎08706 063 536; www.liverpool-empire.co.uk). A variety of dramatic performances, including famed troupes such as the Royal Shakespeare Company. Box office open M-Sa 10am-6pm, longer on performance days, Su from 2hr. prior to performances. Tickets £6-50, concessions available.

Everyman Theatre, 13 Hope St. (☎709 4776; www.everymanplayhouse.com). The nontraditional counterpart to its urban partner, Liverpool Playhouse. Box office open M-Sa 10am-6pm, 8pm on performance nights. Tickets £5-18.

Unity Theatre, 1 Hope Pl. (☎709 4988; www.unitytheatreliverpool.co.uk). This socially conscious theater was established in 1937 to support Spanish citizens fighting Franco. Box office open M 1-6pm, Tu-Sa 10:30am-6pm; 10:30am-8:30pm on show dates.

Bluecoat Arts Centre (☎709 5297), off School Ln. Closed until early 2007 for restoration that will enhance the cohesiveness of the functions of the building—from performance and exhibit space to retail outlets and meeting places.

▧ HIPPY HIPPY SHAKE

The *Liverpool Echo* (35p), sold daily by street vendors, has up-to-date information, especially in the *What's On* section of Friday editions. *Itchy Liverpool* (£3 at TICs) is another useful guide to the nightlife scene. Generally, however, you need only wander near the Ropewalks to find something your style.

Quiggins, 12-16 School Ln. (☎709 2462; open M-Sa 10am-6pm) and the **Gostin Shopping Arcade,** 32-36 Hanover St. (☎709 4142; open M-Sa 10am-6pm) sell crazy hipster paraphernalia in a collection of stores and have tons of flyers detailing the club scene. Check out posted bills, inquire about gay and lesbian events, and pick up the *Gay Guide to Liverpool* at **News From Nowhere,** 96 Bold St., a feminist bookshop run by a women's cooperative. (☎708 7270. Open M-Sa 10am-5:45pm.)

On weekend nights, the downtown area overflows with young pubbers and clubbers, especially **Matthew Street, Church Street,** and the area known as the **Ropewalks,** bounded by Hanover St., Bold St., Duke St., and Berry St. Window-shop venues to find what you like and dress smartly (no trainers) to avoid provoking an army of bouncers. Avoid wandering into dark alleys. The pricier bars and clubs clustered around **Albert Dock** tend to appeal to well-groomed twentysomethings.

Society, 64 Duke St. (☎707 3575; www.society.co.uk). Recently revamped with a plush Temple Room and exclusive VIP lounge above a steamy dance floor. Decked-out crowds make theme nights notorious, and Tu student nights are known as "Mischief." Cover F and Su £5, Sa £10. Open F 10:30pm-2am, Sa 10:30pm-4am, Su 10:30pm-1am.

The Cavern Club, 10 Mathew St. (☎236 9091). The restored incarnation of this legendary underground Beatles venue still has many of its original brick archways in place. Talented up-and-coming musicians play here, hoping that history will repeat itself. F and Sa live music. Cover £2-4 after 11pm. Pub open M-Sa from 11am, Su noon-11:30pm. Club open M-W 11am-7pm, Th-Sa 11am-2:30am, Su 11am-12:30am.

The Blue Angel, 108 Seel St. (☎709 1535). This local dive, better known as the Raz, has an appeal that's less about style and more about good times. M live music. M sees 70p pints, Tu everything £1, Th 3-for-2 deals. Cover £1-1.50. Open M-Sa 10pm-2am.

BaaBar, 43-45 Fleet St. (☎708 8673). Admire the disco balls that cover the ceiling while deciding among 35 varieties of shooters. Drinks are cheap and there are specials nearly every night. Student-oriented. Open M-Sa 11am-2am, Su 4pm-midnight. MC/V.

MANCHESTER ☎0161

The Industrial Revolution transformed the unremarkable village of Manchester into Britain's second-largest urban area. A center of manufacturing in the 19th century, the city became a hotbed of liberal politics, its deplorable working-class conditions arousing the indignation of everyone from Frederic Engels (who called it "hell on earth") to John Ruskin ("devil's darkness"). Since a 1996 bombing by the IRA, Manchester has regenerated, with fantastic modern architecture and new public spaces; cranes punctuate the skyline and Manchester's unofficial city symbol is the bee (to represent a hive of urban activity). "Madchester" played an instrumental role in the evolution of pop and punk, especially the New Wave of the 80s. Manchester's nightclubs welcome droves of partiers, and though dodgy in parts, the city is undergoing a rapid gentrification and is accessible to the street smart. Manchester now savors a reputation as one of the hippest spots in England.

█ TRANSPORTATION

Flights: Manchester International Airport (☎489 3000; arrival information ☎090 1010 1000, 50p per call). Trains (15-20min., 4-6 per hr., £3) and buses #44 and 105 run to Piccadilly Station.

Trains: Two main stations, connected by Metrolink (see below), serve Manchester. Additional service to local areas available at the **Deansgate** and **Oxford Road** stations.

> **Manchester Piccadilly,** London Rd. Travel center open M-Sa 8am-8:30pm, Su 11am-7pm. Trains (☎08457 484 950) from: **Birmingham** (1¾hr., every hr., £21); **Chester** (1hr., every hr., £9.90); **Edinburgh** (4hr., 5 per day, £49); **London Euston** (2½-3hr., every hr., £54); **York** (40min., 2 per hr., £16.20).
>
> **Manchester Victoria,** Victoria St., mostly serves trains from the west and north. Ticket office open M-Sa 6:30am-10pm, Su 8am-10:15pm. From **Liverpool** (50min., 2 per hr., £8).

Buses: Chorlton Street Coach Station, Chorlton St. Office open M-Th and Sa 7:30am-7pm, F and Su 7:30am-8pm. National Express (☎08705 808 080) from: **Birmingham** (2½hr., every hr., £10.50); **Leeds** (1¼hr., every hr., £7.30); **Liverpool** (55min., every hr., £5.50); **London** (4-6hr., 7-12 per day, £19.50); **Sheffield** (1½hr., roughly every hr., £6.50).

Public Transportation: Piccadilly Gardens is home to about 50 bus stops. Pick up a free route map from the TIC. Buses generally run until 11:30pm, some lines until 2:30am on weekends. Office open M-Sa 7am-6pm, Su 10am-6pm. Fare 80p-£2.20. All-day ticket £3.30, £3 if purchased before 9:30am.

Metrolink trams (☎205 2000, service information 08706 082 608; www.gmpte.com) link 8 stops in the city center with **Altrincham** in the southwest, **Bury** in the northeast, and **Eccles** in the west (4 per hr., 60p-£4.60). Combined bus and tram ticket £4.60. **Metroshuttle** bus service runs from the City Centre to main attractions and shopping areas. Buses every 10 min., M-Sa 7am-7pm, Su 10am-6pm. Free.

Taxis: Mantax (☎230 3333), **Radio Cars** (☎236 8033), **Hastings** (☎226 1066), **Taxiphone** (☎236 2322).

✦ ▌ ORIENTATION AND PRACTICAL INFORMATION

The city center is an odd polygon formed by **Victoria Station** to the north, **Piccadilly Station** to the east, the canals to the south, and the **River Irwell** to the west. The many byways can be tricky to navigate, but the area is fairly compact, and Mancunians are generally helpful.

NORTHWEST ENGLAND

Tourist Information Centre: Manchester Visitor Centre, Town Hall Extension, Lloyd St. (☎234 3157; www.visitmanchester.com). Books accommodations for a £2.50 charge plus a 10% deposit. Distributes the *Manchester Pocket Guide* and the *Greater Manchester Network Map.* Open M-Sa 10am-5:30pm, Su 10:30am-4:30pm. Guided walks and private **tours** available from the TIC.

Tours: City Sightseeing (☎0871 666 0000; www.city-sightseeing.com). Runs hop-on, hop-off bus tours, departing from St. Peter's Sq. Tours May-Sept. daily 10am-4:30pm, every 30-60min.

Budget Travel: STA Travel, 75 Deansgate (☎839 3253). Open M-F 10am-6pm, Sa 10am-5pm.

Manchester	★ NIGHTLIFE
▲ ACCOMMODATIONS	ATTIC, **24**
Burton Arms, **1**	Churchills, **13**
Hatters Tourist Hostel, **8**	Cord, **3**
The Millstone Hotel, **2**	Cruz 101, **12**
University of Manchester, **27**	Dry Bar, **6**
YHA Manchester, **22**	Essential, **10**
	Fab Cafe, **16**
	The Lass O'Gowrie, **25**
◖ FOOD	Matt and Phred's, **4**
Camel One, **28**	Mtwo, **11**
Cornerhouse Cafe, **23**	Music Box, **20**
Dimitri's, **19**	Night and Day Cafe, **7**
Eden, **14**	Queer, **15**
Gaia, **17**	Revolution, **26**
Tampopo Noodle House, **9**	Simple Bar & Restaurant, **5**
	The Temple, **22**
	Tribeca, **20**

Financial Services: Many banks in city center. **Thomas Cook,** 23 Market St. (☎910 8787). Branch at 22 Cross St. Both open M-F 10am-6pm, Sa 9am-5:30pm, Su 11am-5pm. **American Express,** 10-12 St. Mary's Gate (☎833 7303). Open M-Tu and Th-F 9am-5:30pm, W 9:30am-5:30pm, Sa 9am-4pm.

Work Opportunities: Visa holders can contact **Manpower,** 87-89 Mosley St. (☎236 8891), for work placement.

Police: Bootle St. (☎872 5050).

Crisis Line: Samaritans, 72-74 Oxford St. (☎236 8000, 24hr. 08457 909 090).

Pharmacy: Boots, 32 Market St. (☎832 6533). Open M-W 8am-6pm, Th 8am-8pm, F 8am-6:30pm, Sa 9am-6:30pm, Su 11am-5pm. Many branches, including 116 Portland St. and 20 St. Ann St.

Hospital: Manchester Royal Infirmary, Oxford Rd. (☎276 1234).

Internet Access: Central Library, St. Peter's Sq. (☎234 1982). Free. Library card required. Call ahead to book a 2hr. slot or expect a long wait. Open M-Tu and Th 10am-7:45pm, W 1-7:45pm, F-Sa 10am-4:45pm. **easyInternet Cafe,** 8-10 Exchange St., (☎839 3500), in St. Ann's Sq. £2.50 per hr., £3 per day, £7 per week, 25 days £20. Open M-Sa 7am-11pm, Su 9am-11pm.

Post Office: 26 Spring Gardens (☎839 0687). Open M-Tu and Th-Sa 8:30am-6pm, W 9am-6pm. Poste Restante (☎834 8605) has a separate entrance. Open M-F 6am-1pm, Sa 6am-8:50am. **Post Code:** M2 1BB.

▶ ACCOMMODATIONS

Cheap stays in the city center are hard to find, though summer offers the possibility of decently priced student housing. The highest concentration of budget lodgings is 2-3 mi. south in the suburbs of **Fallowfield, Withington,** and **Didsbury;** take bus #40, 42, or 157. Browse the free *Where to Stay* (at the TIC) for listings.

YHA Manchester, Potato Wharf, Castlefield (☎08707 705 950; www.yhamanchester.org.uk). Take the metro to G-Mex Station or bus #33 from Piccadilly Gardens toward Wigan to Deansgate. Clean, spacious rooms at the scenic confluence of the city's canals. Friendly staff, good security. Breakfast included. Lockers £1-2; free lockable cupboards in rooms. Laundry £1.50. Internet access 7p per min. Hair dryers, irons, and towels free with £2-5 deposit. Reception 24hr. Dorms £20.50; doubles £45. MC/V. ❷

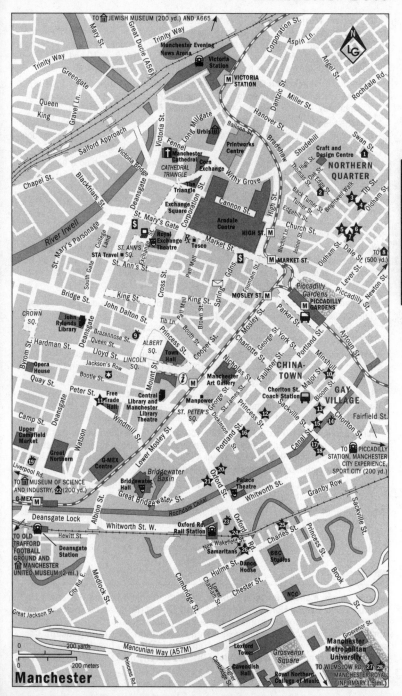

Manchester

The Hatters Tourist Hostel, 50 Newton St. (☎236 9500; www.hattersgroup.com). A clean bed at a cheap price in exchange for crowded rooms in a renovated hat factory. Young attendants with the inside scoop on the city. Light breakfast included. Reception 24hr. Co-ed and single-sex dorms. 12- or 16-bed dorm £14; 8- or 10-bed £15; 4-bed dorm £17.50; triple £20 per person; twin or double £45. AmEx/MC/V. ❷

University of Manchester: Call the **University Accommodation Office** (☎275 2888) to find out which dorms are open for lodging during summer (mid-June to mid-Sept.). 3-7 day min. stay. Reserve a week or more in advance. From £60 per week. MC/V. ❶

The Millstone Hotel, 67 Thomas St. (☎839 0213). Simple but comfortable ensuite rooms conveniently located near Northern Quarter nightlife. Singles £35; twins and doubles £45; triples £60. Book ahead on weekdays. AmEx/MC/V. ❹

Burton Arms, 31 Swan St. (☎834 3455). Basic rooms above a pub on a busy street. A 15min. walk from both train stations and St. Peter's Sq. Singles £19.50, ensuite £30. AmEx/MC/V. ❸

▶ FOOD

Outwit the pricey **Chinatown** restaurants by eating the multi-course "Businessman's Lunch" offered by most (M-F noon-2pm, $4-8). Better yet, visit **Curry Mile**, a stretch of Asian restaurants on Wilmslow Rd., for quality cuisine. Come evening, hip youths wine and dine in the cafe-bars. A Tesco **supermarket** is at 58-66 Market St. (☎911 9400. Open M-F 6am-midnight, Sa 6am-10pm, Su 11am-5pm.)

▨ **Tampopo Noodle House,** 16 Albert Sq. (☎819 1966; www.tampopo.co.uk). This spartan noodle house is one of Manchester's favorites. Noodles (£6-11) with influences from Thailand, Malaysia, Indonesia, Vietnam and Japan are quick and delicious. Try the Pad Krapow with prawns and chilis. Open daily noon-11pm. AmEx/MC/V. ❷

Dimitri's, Campfield Arcade, Tonman St. (☎839 3319). Greek delicacies in a bright space; eat in the outdoor arcade area. TEntrees £11-14. Live music F and Sa nights. Open daily 11am-midnight. AmEx/MC/V. ❸

Gaia, 46 Sackville St. (☎228 1002). Renaissance decor features velvet curtains, paintings, and candlelight. Daytime sandwiches and pizzas £4-7. Entrees £9-15. Open M-Th and Su noon-midnight, F-Sa noon-2am. Food served until 9:30pm. AmEx/MC/V. ❸

Cornerhouse Cafe, 70 Oxford St. (☎200 1508). Part of the Cornerhouse Arts Centre; features 1 bar, 3 galleries, and 3 arthouse cinemas. Offerings include gourmet pizza and cajun chicken. Entrees £6-8. Open M-Sa 11am-11pm, Su 11:30am-10:30pm. Food served until 10pm. Bar open M-Sa 9:30am-11pm, Su 12:30-10:30pm. MC/V. ❷

Camel One, 107 Wilmslow Rd. (☎257 2282). Simple eatery with extensive Indian menu (£2-5.50). Made-to-order kebab sandwiches. Open daily 10am-7pm. Cash only. ❶

Eden, 3 Brazil St. (☎237 9852). Adams and Eves enjoy Italian and Continental dishes at this canalside restaurant in the Gay Village. Dine on "the barge" (a boat-shaped deck on the water) and enjoy the pizza special (2 pizzas and 2 bottles of beer £12, M-Sa noon-5pm). Open M-F 11am-11pm and Sa-Su 11am-2am. ❸

◀ SIGHTS

Be sure to see **Manchester Town Hall,** at Albert St. Tucked behind the Town Hall Extension, the **Central Library** is the city's jewel. One of the largest municipal libraries in Europe, the domed building has a music and theater library, a literature library, and the UK's second-largest Judaica collection. The **Library Theatre Company** (☎236 7110; www.librarytheatre.com), located in the basement of Central Library, puts on modern plays. The **John Rylands Library,** 150 Deansgate, keeps rare books; its most famous holding is the St. John Fragment, a piece of New Testament writing from the 2nd century. The museum is closed for renovations until summer 2006. (☎275 3751; http://rylibweb.man.ac.uk/spcoll. Call for hours. Free.)

Reopened in June 2002 after a three-year, £35 million renovation, the **Manchester Art Gallery,** on Nicholas St., holds Rossetti's stunning *Astarte Syriaca* among its gigantic collection. (☎235 8888; www.manchestergalleries.org. Open Tu-Su and bank holidays 10am-5pm. Free; admission for special exhibitions varies.) In the **Museum of Science and Industry,** Liverpool Rd., in Castlefield, working steam engines and looms provide a dramatic illustration of Britain's industrialization. Excellent for children. (☎832 2244. Open daily 10am-5pm. Free. Special exhibits £3-5.) The Spanish and Portuguese synagogue-turned-**Jewish Museum,** 190 Cheetham Hill Rd., traces the history of the city's sizable Jewish community and offers city tours. (☎834 9879. Open M-Th 10:30am-4pm, Su 10:30am-5pm. Closed on Jewish holidays. £3.95, concessions £2.95, families £9.50.) The **Manchester Craft@Design Centre,** 17 Oak St., showcases crafts, from specialty stationary to handmade jewellery, in a glass-roofed atrium that used to be a Victorian fish market. (☎832 4274; www.craftanddesign.com. Open M-Sa 10am-5:30pm. Free.) The fantastic new **Urbis** museum, Cathedral Gardens, between Victoria Station and Exchange Sq., explores modern urban culture and art. The awe-inspiring museum is a sculpture itself, clad in 2200 handmade plates of glass and with a "ski-slope" copper roof. Recent shows include an exploration of British punk culture. (☎605 8205; www.urbis.org.uk. Open Tu-Su 10am-6pm. Free.)

Loved and reviled, **Manchester United** is England's reigning football team. The **Manchester United Museum and Tour Centre,** Sir Matt Busby Way, at the Old Trafford football stadium, displays memorabilia from the club's inception in 1878 to its recent successes. Follow signs from the Old Trafford Salford Quays Metrolink stop. (☎08704 421 994. Open daily 9:30am-5pm. Tours every 10min., 9:40am-4:30pm. Pre-booking encouraged. No tours on match days. £9, seniors £6, children free, families £25. Special rates available for groups.) Manchester's less-infamous team, Manchester City, offers the **Manchester City Experience,** with a tour of the new museum and stadium. Sport City, in the ReebokCity Building, is a 20 min. walk from Piccadilly Station to Ashton New Road. (☎062 1894. Open M 11:30am-4:30pm, Tu-Sa 9:30am-4:30pm, Su 11am-3pm. £7.50, concessions £4.50.)

■ NIGHTLIFE

CAFE-BARS AND CLUBS

Many of Manchester's excellent lunchtime spots morph into pre-club drinking venues or even become clubs themselves. Manchester's clubbing and live music scene remains a national trendsetter. Centered on **Oldham Street,** the **Northern Quarter** is the city's youthful outlet for live music, its alternative vibe and underground shops attracting a hip crowd. Partiers flock to **Oxford Street** for late-night clubbing and reveling. Don't forget to collect fliers—they'll often score you a discount. **Afflecks Palace,** 52 Church St., supplies paraphernalia from punk to funk; the walls of the stairway are postered with event notices. (☎839 6392. Open M-F 10am-5:30pm, Sa 10am-6pm.) **Fat City,** 20 Oldham St., sells hip-hop, reggae, funk, and jazz records as well as passes to clubbing events. (☎237 1181. Open M-Sa 10am-6pm, Su noon-5pm.) At night, streets in the Northern Quarter are dimly lit. If you're crossing from Piccadilly to Swan St. or Great Ancoats St., use Oldham St., where the neon-lit clubs (and their supersized bouncers) provide reassurance.

Simple Bar & Restaurant, 44 Tib St. (☎835 2526). Fuel up before heading out to the clubs. 2 course lunch £6. Open M-Th and Su noon-11pm, F-Sa noon-midnight.

MADCHESTER

1. Start the night at the traditional pub **Lass O'Gowrie**, 36 Charles St. (☎273 6932). Open M-Sa 11am-11pm, Su noon-10:30pm (food served M-Sa noon-7:30pm, Su noon-5pm).

2. The upstairs **ATTIC**, 50 New Wakefield St. (☎236 6071), grooves to live music. Open M-Sa noon-2am, Su 6pm-midnight. Cover £3-7.

3. Squeeze into **The Temple** (☎278 1610), on Bridgewater St. (literally), for a smoky, intimate drink. Open M-Sa noon-10:30pm, Su 5-10:30pm.

4. Stop by relaxed **Revolution**, 88-94 Oxford St. (☎237 5377), for a vodka specialty. Open M-Th 11:30am-1am, W-Sa 11:30am-2am, Su noon-midnight.

5. Loud music and a committed crowd await at the **Music Box**, Oxford Rd. (☎273 3435). Open Th-Sa from 10pm. Cover £5-8.

6. Mtwo, Peter St. (☎839 1112) hosts trendy dressers and dancers. Open W-Th 10pm-2am, Sa 9pm-3am. Cover £3-6.

7. The crowd at **Fab Cafe**, 11 Portland St. (☎236 2019) is boisterous. Open M-Th 5pm-2am, F-Sa 3pm-2am, Su 6-10:30pm.

8. Start to unwind at the chill **Night and Day Cafe**, 26 Oldham St. (☎236 1822). Open M-Sa 11am-2am, Su 11am-11pm. Cover £3-7.

9. Close out the night with some relaxing jazz tunes at **Matt and Phred's**, 65 Tib St. (☎831 7002). Live jazz sets every night. Open M-Sa 5pm-2am.

Cord, 8 Dorsey St. (☎832 9494). Where corduroy meets chic. No, really. Well-dressed crowd and elaborate drinks. Open M-Sa noon-11pm.

Dry Bar, 28-30 Oldham St. (☎236 9840). Used to be called Dry 201, in reference to Factory Records catalogue system. Cavorting clubbers fill this sultry spot, which locals will tell you is the longest bar in Manchester. Open M, W, Su 11am-midnight, Tu and Th 11-2am, F-Sa 11-3am.

Tribeca, 50 Sackville St. (☎236 8300), serves a wide variety of cuisines and a wider variety of cocktails. Take your food and drinks onto one of the seductively decorated beds downstairs. Open M and Su noon-12:30am, Tu-Sa noon-2am.

THE GAY VILLAGE

In the 1990s the **Gay Village** developed along **Canal Street,** once a run-down part of the city, and has since become one of the premier "going-out" neighborhoods. Northeast of Princess St., the Gay Village fills with crowds that dance by night and mingle by day. When the weather cooperates, morning patrons can be found flooding the many sidewalk tables lining the canal.

Essential, 8 Minshull St. (☎236 0077; www.essential-manchester.com), at the corner of Bloom St., off Portland St. One of the Gay Village's more popular clubs. Dress smart casual. Cover £3-8. Open F 10:30pm-5am, Sa 10:30pm-6am, Su 10:30pm-3am.

Cruz 101, 101 Princess St. (☎950 0101, info line 237 1554; www.cruz101.com). Fun and sexy cruisers teach a lesson in attitude. 2 floors with 6 bars. Dress smart casual. Cover M, W, Th £2; F £3; Sa £5. Open M and W-Sa 10pm-2am.

Churchills, 37 Chorlton St. (☎236 5529; www.churchillsmanchester.com). This pub-club in the heart of the Gay Village hosts M Old School-themed nights, W drag disco, Tu and Th karaoke nights, and F-Sa disco dance parties. No cover. Open M-Sa noon-2am, Su noon-12:30am.

Queer, 4 Canal St. (☎228 1360; www.queer-manchester.com). Huge booths, flat-screen TVs, and sweeping drapes create a great atmosphere at new bar in the middle of Canal. Open M-Sa 11-2am, Su 11-12:30am.

🎵 ENTERTAINMENT

Manchester's many entertainment venues accommodate diverse interests. The **Manchester Evening News (MEN) Arena** (☎930 8000; www.men-arena.com), behind Victoria Station, hosts concerts and sporting events. The **Manchester Festival** (☎234 3157; www.the-manchester-festival.org.uk) runs all summer with dramatic and musical events. The Gay Village hosts a number of festivals, most notably late August's **Mardi Gras** (☎238 4548), which raises money for AIDS relief. **Manchester Pride** (☎230 2624; www.manchesterpride.com), held on the August bank holiday weekend, has live entertainment, sporting events, and a parade.

Royal Exchange Theatre (☎833 9833; www.royalexchange.co.uk) has returned to St. Ann's Sq. after a 1996 IRA bomb destroyed the original building. The theater stages traditional and Shakespearean plays and premieres original works. Box office open M-Sa 9:30am-7:30pm. Tickets £7.25-25.50. Other concessions available.

Bridgewater Hall, Lower Mosley St. (☎907 9000; www.bridgewater-hall.co.uk). Manchester's foremost venue for orchestral concerts and home of Manchester's own Hallé Orchestra. Open M-Sa 10am-8pm, Su noon-6pm. Tickets £5-30.

Palace Theatre, Oxford St. (☎245 6600). Caters to classical tastes in theater, opera, and ballet. Box office open M-Sa 10am-6pm and before performances.

BLACKPOOL   ☎01253

Recent proposals to clear Blackpool's brassy boulevards of tacky souvenirs just don't seem to get it: tourists flock here for bright lights, simple joys, and cheap thrills, and Blackpool delivers. Penny arcades, 24hr. snooker tables, donkey rides, exotic dancers, tattoo parlors—such frivolities cater to 6.8 million visitors every year. Its urbane 19th-century resort status was lost long ago, and those who can forgive the gaudy hedonism partake in nights of uninhibited fun.

NORTHWEST ENGLAND

▐ TRANSPORTATION

Buses and trains are regular, but drivers should be warned: it's not uncommon to see two or more traffic cops on a single street dispensing fines.

Trains: Blackpool North Station (☎620 385), 4 blocks down Talbot Rd. from North Pier. Booking office open M-F 6:30am-9pm, Sa 6:40am-8:40pm, Su 9:10am-4:40pm. Trains (☎08457 484 950) arrive from: **Birmingham** via **Preston** (2½hr., 1-2 per hr., £31); **Leeds** (2hr., every hr., £14.80); **Liverpool** (1½hr., every 2hr., £11.90); **London Euston** via **Preston** (4hr., every hr., £58); **Manchester** (1¼hr., 2 per hr., £10.75).

Buses: Station on Talbot Rd. Ticket office open M-Sa 9am-1:15pm and 2-5pm, Su 9:30am-1pm and 1:30pm-3:30pm. National Express (☎08705 808 080) buses from **Birmingham** (3-4hr., 5 per day, £16.40); **London** (6½-8hr., 4 per day, £24); **Manchester** (2hr., 4 per day, £5.90).

Public Transportation: Local trains use Blackpool South and Pleasure Beach stations. **Local bus** info is available at the local transportation center at 22-24 Market St. (☎473 302). Open M-Sa 8:15am-6pm and Su 10am-3pm. Bus #1 covers the Promenade from North Pier to Pleasure Beach every 20min.; on weekends, **vintage trams** run this route more frequently. A 1-day **Travelcard** (£5.25, concessions £4.75) buys unlimited travel on trams and local buses; otherwise, one ride costs £1.10. 3-day pass £13.

Taxi: Sea Cabs (☎626 262). 24hr.

▐ PRACTICAL INFORMATION

Tourist Information Centre: 1 Clifton St. (☎478 222). Arranges accommodations for £3 plus a 10% deposit, books local shows for £1.50, and sells street maps for £1. (Find the same map in their free accommodations listings.) Open May-Oct. M-Sa 9am-5pm; Nov.-Apr. M-Sa 9am-4:30pm. Branch (☎478 222) on the Promenade. Open M-

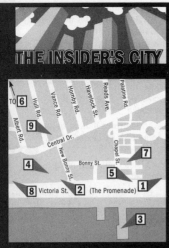

THE INSIDER'S CITY

TO 6
Hull Rd.
Albert Rd.
Vance Rd.
Hornby Rd.
Havelock St.
Reads Rd.
Palatine Rd.
9
Central Dr.
New Bonny St.
Chapel St.
4
Bonny St.
7
5
8 Victoria St.   2   (The Promenade) 1
3

HEN, STAG, BLACKPOOL

Every weekend, thousands of Brits flock to Blackpool to partake in the sacred ritual of the stag (bachelor) or hen (bachelorette) party. Alcohol is imbibed, dancing is done, and no prisoners are taken. With this tour, navigate Blackpool's Promenade like you own the place, or at least plan to drink it dry.

1 Dressing the part is a necessity. Go to **Scottie's Got It,** 161 The Promenade, for wigs, rasta garb, sequined cowboy hats, and pimp apparel. Open F 9:30am-11:30pm, Sa 9:30am-12:30am.

2 Head to **Gypsy Petulengo's** booth under the Coral Island awning on the Promenade. For £10 she will use her 60 years of experience to predict how the hen night will end.

3 For £3, ride hundreds of feet above the beach on the **Central Pier Ferriswheel.** Bring your

Sa 9:30am-5pm, Su 10am-4:30pm. A few iPlus **kiosks** scattered throughout town offer up 24hr. computerized information.

Financial Services: Banks are easy to find, especially along Corporation St. and Birley St. Most are open M-F 9am-4:30pm.

Launderette: Albert Road Launderette, Regent Rd. Open M-F 9am-7pm, Sa 9am-5pm, Su 10am-3pm. Last wash 1hr. before close. Wash £2, dry 20p per 5min.

Police: Bonny St. (☎293 933).

Hospital: Victoria Hospitals, Whinney Heys Rd. (☎300 000).

Pharmacy: Boots (☎622 276), at Bank Hey St. and Victoria St. Open M-F 9am-5:30pm, Sa 9am-6pm, Su 10am-4:30pm.

Internet Access: Blackpool Public Library, Queen St. (☎478 080). Free. Open M and F 9am-5pm, Tu and Th 9am-7pm, W and Sa 10am-5pm. **Cafe@Claremont,** Dickson Rd. (☎299 306). Open M-F 9am-4pm.

Post Office: 26-30 Abingdon St. (☎08457 223 344). Bureau de change. Open M-F 9am-5:30pm, Sa 9am-12:30pm. **Post Code:** FY1 1AA.

🏠 ACCOMMODATIONS

With over 2600 guest houses holding 96,000 beds, you won't have trouble finding a room, except on weekends during the Illuminations (p. 352), when prices skyrocket. Budget-friendly **B&Bs** dominate the blocks behind the Promenade between the North and Central Piers (£15-30). Pick up the free *Blackpool: Where Great Holidays are Made* guide at the TIC for an impressive list.

Silver Birch Hotel, 39 Hull Rd. (☎622 125). From either station, head down Talbot Rd. to the ocean, take a left on Market St., pass the Tower, and turn left onto Hull Rd. The proprietor provides pleasant rooms and warm Irish hospitality. Most rooms are ensuite with TVs. Breakfast £2. Singles £13; doubles £26. Cash only. ❷

Summerville Guest House, corner of South King St. and Albert Rd (☎621 300). Follow the directions to Raffles, but turn onto South King St. after the left on Church St. TVs in all rooms but tokens are required. Breakfast included. £16 per person. ❷

Manor Grove Hotel, 24 Leopold Grove (☎625 577). Follow the Raffles directions, but turn right at Church St., left onto Leopold Grove, and walk 1 block. Spacious rooms with Internet jacks, TV, phone, and bath. Hearty English breakfast included. Doubles £50, more on weekends. MC/V. ❸

Raffles Hotel, 73-77 Hornby Rd. (☎294 713; www.raffleshotelblackpool.co.uk). From the train or bus station, head toward the ocean along Talbot Rd., turn left on Topping St., left on Church St., right on Regent Rd., and right onto Hornby Rd. Spacious rooms. Breakfast included. Twins, doubles, and family rooms £26-32 per person. MC/V. ❸

FOOD

Because waterfront cuisine consists mostly of candy floss and fish and chips, heading off the Promenade should yield some more appetizing alternatives. The Iceland **supermarket,** 8-10 Topping St., is on the same block as the bus station. (☎751 575. Open M-Sa 8:30am-10pm, Su 10:30am-4pm.) ◪**Henry's Wine Bar and Bistro ❸,** Queen St., is an enclave of refinement amidst the hedonism that is Blackpool. Henry's offers a three-course dinner (including steak) for £11. Sip your wine in this former theater, with curtains still intact and chandeliers draped in Christmas lights. (☎752 997. AmEx/MC/V.) The cozy **Coffee Pot ❶,** 12 Birley St., serves big portions; try the roast beef dinner (£5), which comes with Yorkshire pudding, boiled potatoes, and two vegetables. (☎751 610. Open daily June-Nov. 8am-6pm; Dec.-May 8am-4:30pm. Cash only.) **Robert's Oyster Bar ❶,** 90 Promenade, on the Central Beach, is stocked full of prawns (£1.40) and fresh oysters (£1 each) for takeaway. (Open roughly 9:45am-6pm weekdays, until 9pm weekends. Cash only.)

SIGHTS AND ENTERTAINMENT

36 nightclubs, 38,000 theater seats, several circuses, and a tangle of roller coasters line the **Promenade,** which is traversed by Britain's first electric tram line. Even the three 19th-century piers are stacked with ferris wheels and chip shops. The only thing the hedonistic hordes don't come for is the ocean.

BLACKPOOL TOWER. A London businessman returned from the 1890 Paris World Exposition determined to erect Eiffel Tower imitations throughout Britain. Only Blackpool embraced his enthusiasm, and in 1894 the 560 ft. tower graced the city's skyline. Unfortunately, it looks more like a rusty junkheap find than France's sleek symbol of modernity. The five-story **Towerworld** in its base is a bizarre microcosm of Blackpool's eclectic kitsch, with a neon-blue aquarium, motorized dinosaur ride, sprawling jungle gym, arcade games, and casino. An overly ornate ballroom hosts sedately dancing senior citizens during the day and live swing band performances at night (8pm). Towerworld's circus, named the UK's best, runs up to four shows per day and features mesmerizing tightrope walking, dance, and stunt acts in a rather gaudy performance arena. Mooky the Clown

own on board and toast the sunset. Open daily until 10pm.

4 Try your luck at **Coral Island,** a theme park, arcade, and casino. Tonight could be your lucky night. Open M-F 10am-11pm, Sa-Su 9am-1am.

5 "It's not sinful, it's sinless," or so says the sign at **Sinless,** Blackpool's premier lapdancing club. The moving and shaking happens directly across from Central Promenade.

6 Next, head to **Mardi Gras,** on the corner of Dickson and Talbot Rd. This male strip club and risque drag cabaret show plays host to a mostly gay crowd and numerous boisterous hen parties. Open M-Sa noon-2am, Su noon 12:30am.

7 To cool off from Sinless and Mardi Gras, try your hand at snooker, a game like pool, at **Ardwick,** by Coral Island. If you're feeling lucky, make a bet. Open daily noon 11pm.

8 Hit the dance floor at **Palace Discoteque** (☎626 281). This steamy dance floor girates until 2am on Friday and Saturday.

9 You've done a stag or hen weekend—commemorate your adventure with a tattoo, the true sign of a Blackpool weekender. Head to **Body Creation Tattoos,** Hull St. (☎622 933), directly behind Coral Island.

was voted Britain's best. Admission covers all activities. (☎ 292 029; www.blackpool-tower.co.uk. Open daily May-Oct. 10am-11pm; Nov.-Apr. 10am-6pm. £12, concessions £10. Tickets allow all-day admission.)

PLEASURE BEACH. Around 6.8 million people visit this sprawling amusement park annually, second in Europe only to EuroDisney. Pleasure Beach is known for its wooden roller coasters—the twin-track **Grand National** (c. 1935) is a mecca for coaster enthusiasts. Thrill-seekers line up for the aptly named **Big One** and aren't disappointed as the 235 ft. steel behemoth sends them down a heartstopping 65° slope at 87 mph. Admission to the park is free, and the pay-as-you-ride system keeps queues fairly short. By night, Pleasure Beach features illusion shows. (Across from South Pier. ☎ 0870 444 5566. Opening times vary with month and day, but generally 10:30am-9:30pm in summer months. £2-7 per ride. 1-day pass £30, 2-day £45.)

THE ILLUMINATIONS. Blackpool, the first electric town in Britain, consummates its love affair with bright lights in the orgiastic Illuminations. The annual display takes place over 5 mi. of the Promenade from September to early November. In a colossal waste of electricity, 72 mi. of cables light up the tower, the Promenade, star-encased faces of Hollywood actors, corporate emblems, and garish placards. Check with the TIC for more information.

THE GRUNDY ART GALLERY. Once satiated with the attractions of the Promenade, go to the Grundy, which chronicles Blackpool's rise, fall, and, er, resurgence. The special exhibitions on the first floor rotate historical, modern, and contemporary art showcases. The permanent exhibit includes Viking artifacts found around Blackpool's beaches. (Queen St. ☎ 478 170. M-Sa 10am-5pm. Free.)

■ NIGHTLIFE

Between North and Central Piers, Blackpool's famous **Golden Mile** shines with more neon than gold, hosting scores of sultry theaters, cabaret bars, and bingo halls. Rowdy **Syndicate** brings droves to Church St. (☎ 753 222). Blackpool's most frequented clubs are on the Promenade. **Heaven & Hell,** on Bank Hey St., is one block south of the Tower (☎ 625 118), and **Sanuk,** 167-170 Promenade, is farther north at the corner of Springfield Rd. (☎ 292 900). Most clubs charge from £2-5 for cover, and are open 10pm-2am. **O'Neill's Pub,** at the corner of Talbot Rd. and Abingdon St., provides moderately-priced beer and a plethora of pool tables. Come join the guys watching football and getting ready for a big night out. Open daily 12pm-11pm. **Funny Girls,** 5 Dickson Rd., a drag show, has been rated the UK's #1 Burlesque Show Bar. (Booking office ☎ 624 901, information 291 144. Tickets from £5.)

PEAK DISTRICT NATIONAL PARK

Though no actual mountains or peaks exist in the Peak District, the region lays claim to a great diversity of landscape. In the more touristed southern region, known as the White Peak, green hills cradle idyllic country villages and walkers enjoy the extensive network of public trails. The more rugged northern region, the Dark Peak, is the playground of ramblers who wander among its moors, groughs, and peat bottoms. Nestled between industrial leviathans Manchester, Nottingham, and Sheffield, the Peak District is one of the most visited National Parks in the world—over 20 million visit each year. Yet it's only been popular since 1951, when it was made Britain's first national park; long ago, the entire area was fenced off in bucolic isolation as a royal hunting ground. Transport is best in the south and near outlying cities, but hikers should veer north for a more isolated escape.

TRANSPORTATION

Trains (☎ 08457 484 950) are scarce in the district: three lines enter its boundaries, but only one crosses the park itself. One line travels from Derby to Matlock, on the park's southeastern edge (30min.; M-Sa 13-14 per day, Su 9 per day; £3.50). Another runs from Manchester to Buxton (1hr., every hr., £5.70). The **Hope Valley line** (M-F 11 per day, Sa 16 per day, Su 12 per day) goes from Manchester across the park via Edale (55min., £6.90), Hope (1hr., £7.20), and Hathersage (1¼hr., £7.20), terminating in Sheffield (1½hr., £11.20). Both lines from Manchester enter the park at New Mills—the Buxton line at Newtown Station and the Hope Valley line at Central Station. A 20min. signposted walk separates the stations.

A sturdy pair of legs is more than sufficient for inter-village journeys, but the Derbyshire County Council's *Peak District Timetables* (60p) is invaluable for those in search of comprehensive bus information. The timetable includes all routes as well as a large map and information on day-long bus tickets, cycle hire, hostels, TICs, campgrounds, market days, and hospitals. A helpful resource for planning regional travel can be found at www.derbysbus.net.

Buses make a noble effort to connect the scattered Peak towns, and Traveline (☎ 0870 608 2608) is a comprehensive and centralized resource. Coverage of many routes actually improves on Sundays, especially in summer. National Express buses run from London once a day to Bakewell (4¾hr., £19), Buxton (5hr., £19), and Matlock (4½hr., £19). The "Transpeak" makes the journey between Manchester and Derby, stopping at Buxton, Bakewell, Matlock, and other towns in between (3hr., 6 per day). Bus X18 (5 per day) runs from Sheffield to Bakewell (45min.), Buxton (1¼hr.), and Leek (1¾hr.) en route to Hanley (2¼hr.). Buses #272, 273, and 274 reach Castleton from Sheffield (40-55min., 15 per day, Su 12 per day). Buses #65-66 run between Sheffield and Buxton via Eyam (1¼hr.; M-Sa 5 per day, Su 3 per day) and bus #173 runs from Bakewell to Castleton (50min.; M-Sa 5 per day, Su 3 per day). Bus #200 runs from Castleton to Edale (20 min., M-F 3-7 per day), sometimes continuing to Chapel-en-le-Frith. On weekends it runs as #260 and stops at the Castleton caverns (7 per day). Ride is free with proof of railway transport.

If you're going to use public transport, pick one of the half-dozen bargain day tickets available; they're clearly explained in the *Timetables* booklet, and several have their own brochures at the TIC. The best deal is the **Derbyshire Wayfarer** (£7.50, concessions £3.75, families £12), which allows one day of train and bus travel throughout the Peak District north to Sheffield and south to Derby. Day passes are sold at the Manchester train stations and at National Park Information Centres (NPICs), as well as at local rail stations and on most buses.

PRACTICAL INFORMATION

Daytime facilities in the Peak District generally stay open all winter because of the proximity to cities. Some B&Bs and hostels welcome travelers until December; YHA Edale is open year-round. Most TICs book accommodations for a 10% deposit or £2. The **Peak District National Park Office**, Aldern House, Baslow Rd., Bakewell, Derbyshire (☎ 01629 816 200; www.peakdistrict-npa.gov.uk) is a useful contact.

National Park Information Centres: All NPICs carry detailed walking guides and provide fun facts on the park.

Bakewell: Old Market Hall (☎ 0870 444 7275), at Bridge St. From the bus stop, walk a block down Bridge St. with Bath Gardens on your left. Doubles as the TIC, with accommodations booking. Upstairs exhibit on the town's history. Open daily Mar.-Oct. 9:30am-5:30pm; Nov.-Feb. 10am-5pm.

Castleton: Buxton Rd. (☎0870 444 7275). From the bus stop, follow the road past the post office into town and head right; the NPIC is along the road that leads to the caverns. Great geological and cultural display in annex. Open daily Apr.-Oct. 9:30am-5:30pm; Nov.-Mar. 10am-5pm.

Edale: Fieldhead (☎01433 670 207), between the rail station and village; signs point the way from both directions. Open Apr.-Oct. daily 9am-1pm and 2-5:30pm; Nov.-Mar. Sa-Su 9am-1pm and 2-5pm.

Fairholmes: Upper Derwent Valley (☎01433 650 953), near Derwent Dam. Open Apr.-Oct. daily 9:30am-1pm and 2-5pm; Nov.-Mar. Sa-Su 9:30am-4:30pm.

Tourist Information Centres:

Ashbourne: 13 Market Pl. (☎01335 343 666). Open Mar.-Oct. M-Sa 9:30am-5pm, Su 10am-4pm; Nov.-Feb. M-Sa 10am-4pm.

Buxton: The Crescent (☎01298 25106). Open daily Mar.-Sept. 9:30am-5pm; Oct.-Feb. 10am-4pm.

Matlock: Crown Sq. (☎01629 583 388). Open daily Mar.-Oct. 9:30am-5pm; Nov.-Feb. 10am-4pm.

Matlock Bath: The Pavilion (☎01629 55082), along the main road. Open Mar.-Oct. daily 9:30am-5pm; Nov.-Feb. Sa-Su 10am-4pm. Hours vary.

ACCOMMODATIONS

NPICs and TICs both distribute the park-wide *Peak District Camping and Caravanning Guide*, which lists all campsites and caravanning (RV) sites. The *Peak District Visitor's Guide*, with a list of accommodations and attractions, is free from TICs and NPICs. **B&Bs** are plentiful and moderately-priced (singles £20-25) in the countryside and more expensive (£30-35) in towns. YHA hostels (around £10-15) usually fill far in advance. Expect to pay higher rates in more touristed towns. **Bakewell** and **Matlock Bath** are well-stocked with B&Bs. Most hostels are not open every day of the week. Many farmers allow **camping** on their land, sometimes for a small fee; remember to ask first and leave the site as you found it.

The 11 YHA-operated, farmer-owned **camping barns ❶** are simple shelters, providing a sleeping platform, water tap, and toilet; bring a sleeping bag and camping equipment. If you're lucky, you will find a shower and/or hot water. You must book and pay ahead through the **Camping Barns Reservation Office**, 6 King St., Clitheroe, Lancashire BB7 2EP (☎0870 770 8868). You can pay over the phone with a credit card, or they'll hold your reservation for five days while you mail a booking form; forms are available in camping barn booklets, distributed at NPICs and TICs, and are available online at www.yha.org.uk. Barns can be found in: **Abney,** between Eyam and Castleton; **Alstonefield,** between Dovedale and Manifold Valley; **Birchover,** near Matlock off the B5056; **Butterton** (two barns), near the southern end of the park, along the Manifold track; **Edale** village; **Losehill,** near Castleton; **Middleton-by-Youlgreave; Nab End,** in Hollinsclough; **Taddington,** on Main Rd.; and **Underbank,** in Wildboarclough. All charge £5 per person per night.

The Peak District has almost 20 **YHA hostels,** some of which are listed below, but don't let numbers fool you—most fill quickly with school groups, so call ahead to reserve a space. The hostels generally lie within a day's hike of one another and sell maps detailing routes to neighboring hostels. Alternatively, *Peak District Timetables* (60p at TICs) lists both YHAs and the bus services to them. Most hostels serve meals and are phasing out 10am-5pm lockouts, but 11pm curfews are still generally in place. Many offer a £1 **student discount.** Three of the smaller ones (Bretton, Langsett, and Shining Cliff) book through the central **YHA Diary** office (☎01142 884 541); only call the hostels directly for general information or for lodging within the following week, and remember that most require booking 48hr. in advance. Membership is generally required and can be purchased in installments.

Bakewell: Fly Hill (☎01629 812 313), a 5min. walk from the town center. From the bus stop at Rutland Sq., walk up N. Church Street and follow it as it curves right at the top. Follow the signs and take the 2nd right. 28 beds, a kind staff, board games, and huge meals. Lockout 10am-5pm. Curfew 11pm. Open July-Aug. daily; Nov.-Dec. F-Sa; all other times open for group bookings only. Dorms £11, under 18 £8. MC/V. ❶

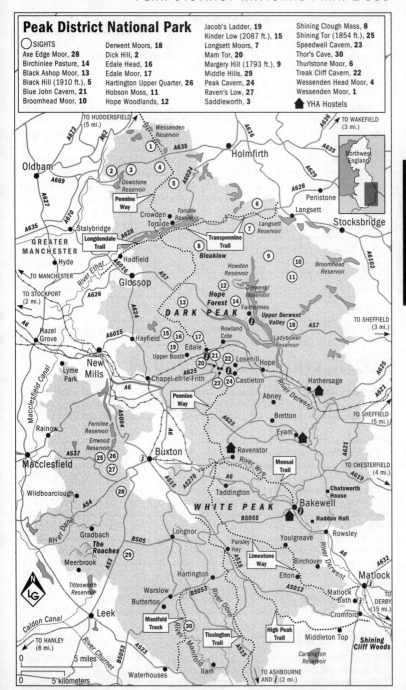

Peak District National Park

◯ SIGHTS

Axe Edge Moor, **28**
Birchinlee Pasture, **14**
Black Ashop Moor, **13**
Black Hill (1910 ft.), **5**
Blue John Cavern, **21**
Broomhead Moor, **10**

Derwent Moors, **18**
Dick Hill, **2**
Edale Head, **16**
Edale Moor, **17**
Hartington Upper Quarter, **26**
Hobson Moss, **11**
Hope Woodlands, **12**

Jacob's Ladder, **19**
Kinder Low (2087 ft.), **15**
Longsett Moors, **7**
Mam Tor, **20**
Margery Hill (1793 ft.), **9**
Middle Hills, **29**
Peak Cavern, **24**
Raven's Low, **27**
Saddleworth, **3**

Shining Clough Mass, **8**
Shining Tor (1854 ft.), **25**
Speedwell Cavern, **23**
Thurlstone Moor, **6**
Thor's Cave, **30**
Treak Cliff Cavern, **22**
Wessenden Head Moor, **4**
Wessenden Moor, **1**

🔺 YHA Hostels

Castleton: Castleton Hall (☎01433 620 235). Pretty country house and attached vicarage in the heart of town. The vicarage has nicer rooms with baths and no curfew or lockout. Free coffee and tea. Spacious self-catering kitchen, several lounges, and Internet access. Very popular—book at least 2-3 weeks ahead. Curfew 11pm. Open Feb.-Dec. daily. Dorms £12.50, under 18 £9. MC/V. ❷

Edale: (☎01433 670 302), Rowland Cote, Nether Booth, 2 mi. east of Edale village. From the train station, turn right and then left onto the main road; follow it to Nether Booth, where a sign points the way. Buses also stop within ½ mi. of the hostel. Includes a climbing tower. Curfew 11pm. Dorms £12.50, under 18 £9. MC/V. ❷

Eyam: (☎01433 630 335), Hawkhill Rd. Walk down the main road from the square, pass the church, and look right for the sign. With a turret and an oaken door, it's more castle than hostel. Internet access. Lockout 10am-5pm. Curfew 11pm. Open Feb.-Oct. M-Sa; late Oct. to Nov. F-Sa; call otherwise. Dorms £12.50, under 18 £9. MC/V. ❷

Hathersage: Castleton Rd. (☎01433 650 493). Stone building with white-framed windows and creeping ivy. Lockout noon-5pm. Curfew 11pm. Open Apr.-Aug. M-Sa; Sept.-Oct. Tu-Sa; otherwise rentable. Dorms £11, under 18 £8. MC/V. ❶

Matlock: 40 Bank Rd. (☎01629 582 983). Conveniently located in a regional train and bus hub. Laundry and Internet access. Curfew 11pm. Open mid-Feb. to Sept. daily; Nov. to mid-Feb. F-Sa. Dorms £12.50, under 18 £9. MC/V. ❷

Ravenstor: (☎01298 871 826), ½ mi. from Millers Dale. Buses #65 and 66 will stop here (both M-Sa 10 per day, Su 7 per day). Bar, TV, game room, and Internet access. Curfew 11pm. Open Feb.-Oct. Sa-Su. Dorms £12.50, under 18 £9. MC/V. ❷

Youlgreave: Fountain Sq. (☎01629 636 518). Buses #171 and 172 from Bakewell stop nearby. The building was once used as a village co-operative department store, and men still sleep in a room labeled "Women's Underwear." Curfew 11pm. Open Feb.-Mar. F-Sa; Apr.-Oct. M-Sa; Nov.-Dec. F-Sa. Dorms £12.50, under 18 £9. MC/V. ❷

🖼🎿 HIKING AND OUTDOORS

With over 5000 mi. of public footpaths, the central park is marvelous territory for rambling. Settlement is sparser and buses fewer north of Edale in the land of the **Kinder Scout plateau,** the great **Derwent reservoirs,** and the gritty cliffs and peat moorlands. From Edale, the **Pennine Way** (p. 391) runs north to Kirk Yetholm, across the Scottish border. Be advised that warm clothing and the customary supplies and precautions should be taken (see **Wilderness Safety,** p. 46). Be respectful as there are many acres of private land close to the trails. Guidebooks and a variety of walking and hiking maps (from £2) are available at TICs and NPICs (p. 353).

The park authority offers **bike rental** at seven Cycle Hire Centres, all of which are listed in the *Peak District Timetables.* They can be found in Ashbourne (☎01335 343 156), on Mapleton Ln.; Derwent (☎01433 651 261), near the Fairholmes NPIC; Hayfield (☎01663 746 222), at Station Picnic Site on Sett Valley Road; Middleton Top (☎01629 823 204), at the visitors' center; Parsley Hay (☎01298 84493), in Buxton; Waterhouses (☎01538 308 609), in the Old Station Car Park between Ashbourne and Leek on the A523; and Carsington Water (☎01629 540 478), near Matlock off Ashbourne-Wirksworth Rd. (Bikes £9 per 3hr., £13 per day; £20 deposit. Tandem bikes £22 per 3hr., £30 per day; £100 deposit. Helmet included. Most open Apr.-Sept. daily 9:30am-6pm; Oct.-Mar. call for hours.) *Cycle Derbyshire,* available at NPICs, includes opening hours, locations, and a trail map.

CASTLETON   ☎01433

The small town of Castleton (pop. 705) lays claim to a tremendous amount of natural beauty and has succeeded in earning itself a fairly predictable level of tourist traffic. Its postcard-perfect streets are lined with ivy-covered stone buildings and hedged gardens. The beauty of the hillsides conceals still more, as the semi-precious purple mineral Blue John (banded fluorspar) is found only in the local bedrock and for ridiculous prices in main street shops. These hills are also home to the area's main attraction: four caverns.

TRANSPORTATION AND PRACTICAL INFORMATION. Castleton lies 2 mi. west of the **Hope** train station (don't ask for Castleton Station, or you'll end up in a suburb of Manchester), and bus #272 runs from Hope to Castleton. **Buses** arrive from Sheffield, Buxton, and Bakewell (p. 353). Hikers looking for a challenge can set off southward from town on the 26 mi. **Limestone Way Trail** to Matlock. Castleton's **NPIC** (p. 354) stocks maps and brochures (most under £1) on local walks. Particularly useful is *Walks around Castleton* (30p), which outlines 2½-9½ mi. hikes. Ramblers preparing for the moors should visit the **Peveril Outdoor Shop**, in the center of town off the marketplace by the hostel, or one of the town's numerous other outdoors shops. (☎620 320. Open M-F 9:30am-5pm, Sa-Su 9:30am-6pm.) The nearest **bank** is 6 mi. east in Hathersage; the Cheshire Cheese Hotel, How Ln., and the Peaks Inn, How Ln., both have **ATMs.** The **post office,** How Ln., is in a convenience store close to the bus stop. (☎620 241. Open M-Tu and Th-F 9am-1pm and 2-5:30pm, W and Sa 9am-12:30pm.) **Post Code:** S33 8WJ.

ACCOMMODATIONS AND FOOD. Castleton is home to many B&Bs, but expect to pay at least £35 for a single. The **YHA Castleton ❶,** Castle St., with a cluster of old stone buildings around a quiet courtyard, is as comfortable as it is comely. It sits in the center of town, next to the castle entrance (p. 356). Those seeking the luxury of a B&B can try ivy-walled **Cryer House ❸,** Castle St., where the proprietors keep two lovely double rooms and a skylit tea shop. (☎620 244. Doubles £49. Cash only.) Attractive patios and traditional pubs line Castle St. All serve food for reasonable prices. "Families, ramblers, and pets all welcome" at **The George ❷,** Castle St. (☎620 238. Food served noon-2pm and 6pm-9pm. Cash only.)

SIGHTS. Buses don't serve the caves on weekdays, but on weekends #260 makes a loop between Edale and Castleton (Sa-Su and bank holidays 6-7 per day), stopping at Blue John, Speedwell, and Treak Cliff. The lack of weekday buses should not discourage, since all caves are within walking distance. Peak Cavern is 5min. from town; Speedwell and Treak Cliff are about 20min. outside the city; and Blue John is within a 45min. walk. All caves are in the same direction; as you leave Castleton on Cross St. (which becomes Buxton Rd.), formerly the A625, you'll pass a large sign for Peak Cavern. Road signs for the others appear within 10min.

Although it's not the first cave on the road out of Castleton, **Treak Cliff Cavern** is the one most worth visiting, with engaging 40min. tours that accentuate the amazing natural features of its interiors—deep purple seams of Blue John and frozen cascades of rigid flowstone. The "sculpted" mineral shapes in the stunning **Dream Cave** are reminiscent of melted candle wax. (☎620 571; www.bluejohnstone.com. Open Easter to Oct. daily 10am-4:20pm; Nov.-Feb. 10am-3:20pm; Mar. to Easter 10am-4:20pm. Tours every 15-30min. £6.) Just outside Castleton, in the gorge beneath the castle ruins, **Peak Cavern** features the largest aperture in Britain. Known in the 18th century as the "Devil's Arse," the cavern features 1hr. tours led by wry-humored guides; Christmastime sees mincemeat pies and live brass bands for subterranean merrymaking. (☎620 285; www.devilsarse.com. Open Easter to Oct. daily 10am-5pm; Nov. to Easter Sa-Su 10am-5pm. 2 to 3 tours per weekday; call for times. Last tour 4pm. £6, concessions £5, children £4.) A joint pass (£10.50, concessions £9, children £7) is sold for Peak Cavern and **Speedwell;** the latter offers boat tours through the underground canals of an old lead mine that culminate at "The Bottomless Pit," a huge subterranean lake. (☎620 512; www.speedwellcavern.co.uk. Tours daily in summer 9:30am-5pm; in winter 10am-3:30pm.) **Blue John** is the only cave besides Treak Cliff to offer visitors views of the mineral veins from which it takes its name. (☎620 638. Open daily in summer 9:30am-5:30pm; in winter 9:30am-dusk.) The caverns are all quite cold (so dress warmly) and screeching school groups convene midday (so go early).

William Peveril, the illegitimate son of William the Conqueror, built 11th-century **Peveril Castle** atop a hill with far-reaching views to survey possible threats to local lead mines. The climb may be daunting, but the view of Hope Valley is worth the effort. (☎620 613. Open early Mar. to Apr. daily 10am-5pm; May-Aug. daily 10am-6pm; Sept.-Oct. daily 10am-5pm; Nov. to early March M and Th-Su 10am-4pm. £3.)

EDALE AND THE NORTHERN DARK PEAK AREA ☎01433

The deep dale of the River Noe contains a collection of villages known as **Edale.** The area offers little besides a church, rail stop, cafe, pub, school, and hostel, but its environs are among the most spectacular in northern England. The northern **Dark Peak** area is wild hill country, with vast moors like **Kinder Scout** and **Bleaklow,** undisturbed by motor traffic. In these mazes, paths are scarce and weather-worn; be careful going through the peat bogs. The rare town huddles in the crook of a valley, with provisions and shelter for weary walkers. Less experienced hikers should stick to Edale and southern paths.

On summer weekends Edale brims with hikers and campers preparing to tackle the **Pennine Way** (which begins with a 3- to 4-day stretch through the Peaks; p. 352), or to trek one of the shorter (1½-8½ mi.) trails detailed in the National Park Authority's *8 Walks Around Edale* (£1.40). The 3½ mi. path to **Castleton** begins 70 yards down the road from the TIC and affords a breathtaking view of both the Edale Valley (Dark Peak) and the Hope Valley (White Peak), but requires a good 25min. of uphill walking. A favorite for those returning to Edale for the night is the hike to **Mam Tor,** a decaying Iron-Age fort once home to Celtic worshippers of Brigantia, a fertility goddess. The hill is known as the "shivering mountain" for its shale sides. A round-trip hike from Edale takes about 3hr. Cliffs in the area beckon fearless hang-gliders from near and far.

YHA Edale (p. 356) is far from town (just over 1 mi.) but not unmanageable for hearty backpackers, though the less athletic can opt for the few B&Bs that line Edale's only real road. Campers can try **Fieldhead ❶,** behind the TIC. (☎670 386. £3.50-4 per person, children £2.50-2.75. Cars £1.50. Showers 20p. Cash only.) Edale lies on the Hope Valley rail line and is served by trains every 1-2hr. from Manchester Piccadilly (50min.) and Sheffield (35min.). Stop at the huge **NPIC** (p. 354) near the train station for weather forecasts and map and compass training.

BAKEWELL ☎01629

Light-hued stone homes, a gentle river, and a sophisticated rural feel make Bakewell the quintessential country getaway. Located near several scenic walks through the **White Peaks,** the town is best known as the birthplace of **Bakewell pudding,** allegedly created in the 1860s when a flustered cook at the Rutland Arms Hotel tried to make a tart by pouring an egg mixture over strawberry jam instead of mixing it into the dough. Bakewell's stone buildings line a network of crooked streets and hidden courtyards that converge on a park at central **Rutland Square.** The River Wye curls around the town edging Riverside Gardens (open 24hr.), overhung with willows and spanned by the five graceful arches of a **medieval bridge** (c. 1300). On the hill above town, **All Saints Church** is surrounded by tilting gravestones, many of which have decayed from centuries of exposure to the elements. Nearby on Cunningham Pl., a 16th-century timber-frame house shelters the **Old House Museum,** which displays regional heritage in the form of a Tudor lavatory, blueprints for a Peak house made of cow dung, and other, less excrementitious items. (☎813 642; www.oldhousemuseum.org.uk. Open Apr.-Oct. daily 11am-4pm. £2.50, children £1, under 5 free.)

The comfy **YHA Bakewell,** on Fly Hill, is a short walk from the TIC (p. 353). **B&Bs** are plentiful given the village's size, but expect to pay about £30 per person and even more for a single; the *Peak District Visitor Guide*, free at the TIC, lists B&Bs in the area. Truly elegant stays await at the **Rutland Arms Hotel ❹,** The Square, which has lodged famous Peak-country pilgrims like Byron, Coleridge, Wordsworth, and Turner. Individually decorated rooms feature luxurious beds and satellite TVs. (☎812 812; www.bakewell.demon.co.uk. Full breakfast included. June-Oct. singles £55-64; doubles £94-104. Nov.-May £53-62/85-93. AmEx/MC/V.) The Bakewell Breakfast that will keep you running all day at **The Garden Room ❹,** 1 Park Rd., a 5min. walk from the town center. (☎814 299. Singles £35. Cash only.) Entire villages pour into Bakewell's **market,** held since 1330, off Bridge St. (open M 9am-4pm). The Midlands Co-Op peddles **groceries** at the corner of Granby Rd. and Market St. (open M-Sa 8am-10pm, Su 10am-4pm). Bakewell has a dense population of cafes, though only a few of them have names that don't include the word "pudding." With lemon-yellow walls and giant cloth sunflowers blooming out of earthenware vases, **JC's ❷,** Kings Ct., delivers superior bistro fare in its cozy dining room and adjoining courtyard. Indulgences include smoked Scottish salmon with lemon and rye bread (£9), smoked salmon and black pepper panini (£5), and French lemon tarts with raspberry *coulis* for £2.90. (☎810 022. Open M-Th and Su 10:30am-5pm, F 10:30am-7pm, Sa 10am-5:30pm. MC/V.) Located off a courtyard in the center of town, **The Treeline Cafe ❷,** Diamond Ct., has an outside courtyard draped with grapevines. The cafe serves an array of sandwich rolls, panini, soups, and salads from £4. (☎813 749. Open Easter to Oct. M-Sa 10am-5pm, Su 11am-5pm; Nov. to Easter M-W and F-Su 10am-5:30pm. MC/V.)

Buses arrive in Rutland Sq. from: Manchester via Buxton (1¾hr, 6 per day); Matlock, site of the nearest train station (#172, R61; 20-50min.; 1-3 per hr.); Sheffield (X18 or 240; 1hr.; M-Sa 13-14 per day, Su 10-12 per day). Bakewell's **NPIC,** at the intersection of Bridge St. and Market St., doubles as a **TIC** (p. 353). Other services include: an **HSBC,** Rutland Sq. (open M-F 9:30am-4:30pm); **camping supplies** at Yeoman's, 1 Royal Oak Pl., off Matlock St. (☎815 371; open M-Sa 9am-5:30pm, Su 10am-5pm); **police,** Granby Rd. (☎812 504); free **Internet** access at Bakewell Public Library, Orme Ct. (☎812 267; open M-Tu and Th 9:30am-5pm, W and F 9:30am-7pm, Sa 9:30am-4pm); and a **post office,** in the Spar on Granby Rd. (☎815 112; open M 8:30am-5:30pm, Tu-F 9am-5:30pm, Sa 9am-1pm). **Post Code:** DE45 1ET.

NORTHWEST ENGLAND

▶ DAYTRIPS FROM BAKEWELL

▧ CHATSWORTH HOUSE

Take bus #179 (2 per day) directly to the house or ask the TIC about other buses that stop close by. ☎01246 582 204; www.chatsworth.org. 1½hr. audio tour £2.50. Guidebooks for house and garden £3 each. Open daily mid-Mar. to late Dec. 11am-5:30pm; last admission 4:30pm. Gardens open daily June-Aug. 10:30am-6pm; Sept.-May 11am-6pm. Last admission 5pm. Mar.-Oct. £9.50, concessions £7.50, children £3.50, families £22.50; Nov.-Dec. £10.50/10/4.50/28. Gardens only £5.75/4.25/2.50/14.

When the 6th Duke of Devonshire ordered a new set of marble carvings for the fireplaces of his (third) dining room at Chatsworth, he was a bit disappointed with the results; he had "wanted more abandon and joyous expression." Only in a house as magnificent as this one could his complaint seem anything but ridiculous. Once called "the National Gallery of the North," this palatial estate is as much museum as residence, displaying works by Van Dyck, Rembrandt, and Tintoretto. Entrance to the **Queen of Scots Rooms,** where Mary stayed from 1560 to 1581, costs an additional £1.50. Get lost in the hedge maze but don't miss the rock garden, which looks a bit like a miniature golf course. Green lawns and sequestered paths will (and should) keep you all day in this "Palace of the Peaks."

HADDON HALL

Haddon Hall is 2 mi. from Bakewell; from town, walk down Matlock St. as it becomes Haddon Rd. and then the A6; a nicer path along the river covers half the distance. Several buses, including #171-172, 179, and TP, stop outside the gate; ask the TIC for details. ☎812 855; www.haddonhall.co.uk. Open Apr.-Sept. daily 10:30am-4:30pm; Oct. Th-Su 10:30am-4pm. £7.25, concessions £6.25, children £3.75, families £19.

"The most perfect English house to survive from the Middle Ages" remains intact thanks to neglect during the Victorian renovations that altered so many other estates. The house stands in contrast to Chatsworth; without the ornamentation and extravagance of so many other homes and castles, Haddon retains its original Elizabethan ambience. Its stone walls seem at home in the scenic sheep-studded countryside, and visitors can admire the winding Wye River from Haddon's award-winning gardens. Numerous filmmakers have been charmed by the building's striking crenellated facade and terraced rose gardens; visitors may recognize it as the setting for *The Princess Bride*, Franco Zeffereli's *Jane Eyre*, and *Elizabeth*. The house museum includes numerous artifacts, some dating back to the 16th century, found during the renovation of the house in the 1920s. Inadequate wall text makes the £2.50 guide a sound investment.

CUMBRIA

LAKE DISTRICT NATIONAL PARK

With some of the most stunning scenery in England, the Lake District owes its beauty to a thorough glacier-gouging during the Ice Age. Here, jagged peaks and windswept fells stand in desolate splendor as water pools in serene mountain lakes. The shores are busy, but less packed than one would expect for a region where tourism employs 85% of the population. Though summertime hikers, bikers, and boaters almost equal sheep in number, there is always some lonely upland fell or quiet cove where your footprints will seem the first for generations.

▐ TRANSPORTATION

Trains: By train, **Oxenholme,** on the West Coast Mainline, is the primary gateway to the lakes. Trains (☎08457 484 950) run to Oxenholme from: **Birmingham** (2hr., every 2 hr., £39.50); **Edinburgh** (2hr., 6 per day, £29); **London Euston** (3½hr.; M-Sa 16 per day, Su 11 per day; £62); **Manchester Piccadilly** (1½hr.; M-Sa 10 per day, Su 9 per day; £12.50). A branch line covers the 10 mi. to **Windermere** from Oxenholme (20min., every hr., £3.25). Direct service runs to Windermere from **Manchester Piccadilly** (1¾hr., every hr., £12.55).

Buses: National Express (☎08705 808 080) arrives in **Windermere** from **Birmingham** (4½hr., 1 per day, £29) and **London** (7½hr., 1 per day, £27), continuing through **Ambleside** and **Grasmere** to **Keswick.** Stagecoach connects **Keswick** with **Carlisle** (1¼hr.; 2-3 per day). Stagecoach in Cumbria is the primary operator in the region. A complete timetable *(The Lakeland Explorer)* is available free from TICs and onboard each bus. Major routes include: "Lakeslink" bus #555 from **Lancaster** to **Carlisle,** stopping at **Kendal, Windermere, Ambleside, Grasmere,** and **Keswick** (M-Sa 14 per day, Su 7 per day), and the open-top Lakeland Experience bus #599 between **Bowness** and **Grasmere** (50min., Apr.-Aug. 2-3 per hr.). An **Explorer** ticket offers unlimited travel on all area Stagecoach buses. The 4- and 7-day passes save money, even for shorter stays. 1-day £8, children £5; 4-day £18/13; 7-day £25/17. Explorer tickets may be purchased on buses and at TICs. Also try *Getting Around Cumbria and the Lake District* (free from TICs) or call Traveline (☎08706 082 608).

National Trust Shuttles: On Sundays in summer, the National Trust operates free buses between popular sights, some of which are not ordinarily accessible by public transport. Call ☎01768 773 780 for more information.

YHA Shuttle: The **YHA Ambleside** provides a minibus service (☎01539 432 304) for hikers (or just their packs) between hostels in **Coniston Holly How, Elterwater, Grasmere, Hawkshead, Langdale,** and **Windermere** (2 per day, £3; schedules available at hostels), plus a daily service to **Patterdale.** Trips from Windermere train station to Windermere and Ambleside hostels are free, but not the return. For worn-out hikers who still want to see the lakes, for £4 you can enjoy the scenery from the bus's circular route. Runs Easter to Oct.

Tours: For those who wish to explore, **Mountain Goat** (☎01539 445 161), downhill from the TIC in Windermere, does the climbing for you in off-the-beaten-track, partial- and full-day themed bus tours. £17.50-27.50. Across the street, **Lakes Supertours,** 1 High St. (☎01539 442 751), in the Lakes Hotel, runs similar half- and full-day tours. £17-27.50.

◢✻ ⁊ ORIENTATION AND PRACTICAL INFORMATION

The Lake District National Park occupies a vast tract of land that fills the heart of Cumbria. The major lakes radiate out from the small town of Grasmere, which lies roughly in the park's center. The A591 runs along the north-south axis of the park, joining the towns of **Windermere, Bowness, Ambleside, Grasmere,** and **Keswick.** From these towns smaller thoroughfares radiate out into the rest of the park. **Derwentwater** is one of the most beautiful lakes, Windermere is the largest and most developed, and western lakes like **Buttermere** and **Crummock Water** are the most wild.

National Park Information Centres: All dispense information and maps, secure fishing licenses, book accommodations (10% deposit for accommodation in town; £3 surcharge for non-local accommodation) and offer guided walks. Often, they exchange currency. More information at www.lake-district.gov.uk.

Ambleside Waterhead: (☎01539 442 895), on the pier. From town, walk south on Lake Rd. or Borrans Rd. or get off at Waterhead Hotel bus stop. Open daily Easter to Oct. 9:30am-5:30pm.

Bowness Bay: Glebe Rd. (☎01539 442 895). Open July to Aug. daily 9:30am-6pm; Apr.-June and Sept.-Oct. daily 9am-5:30pm; Nov.-Mar. F-Su 10am-4pm.**Coniston:** Ruskin Ave. (☎01539 441 533), behind the Tilberthwaite Ave. bus stop. Open Easter to Oct. daily 9:30am-5:30pm; Nov. to Easter F-Su 10am-3:30pm.

Brockhole: (☎01539 446 601). Between Windermere and Ambleside. Most buses stop here. Has exhibits, talks, films, and special events. Open daily Apr.-Oct. 10am-5pm.

Glenridding: Main Carpark (☎01768 482 414). Open daily Easter to Oct. 9:30am-5:30pm; Nov. to Easter 9:30am-3:30pm.

Grasmere: Redbank Rd. (☎01539 435 245). Open Easter to Oct. daily 9:30am-5:30pm; Nov. to Easter F-Su 10am-4pm.

Hawkshead: Main Carpark (☎01539 436 525). Open July-Aug. daily 9:30am-5:30pm; Easter to June and Sept.-Oct. daily 9:30am-5:30pm; Nov. to Easter Sa-Su 10am-3:30pm.

Keswick: Moot Hall, Market Sq. (☎01768 772 645). From the bus station, turn right onto Main St. and continue to Markey Sq. Open daily 9:30am-5:30pm.

Pooley Bridge: The Square (☎01768 482 414). Open daily Easter to Oct. 10am-5pm.

Seatoller Barn: Borrowdale (☎01768 777 294), at the foot of Honister Pass. Open daily Apr.-Oct. 10am-5pm.

ACCOMMODATIONS

Though **B&Bs** line the streets in many towns and there's a hostel around nearly every bend, lodgings in the Lake District fill up quickly June through August; reserve well in advance, especially for weekend stays. Hostels, in particular, can be full all summer long; call ahead. TICs and NPICs book rooms. Twenty-six **YHA hostels** provide accommodations in the park, but can differ substantially in facilities and style. Reception is often closed 10am-5pm, though public areas and restrooms are usually accessible throughout the day. The **YHA shuttle** travels between the bigger hostels (p. 361). YHA also operates 14 wilderness **camping barns** in the Lakes; for information or reservations call the Keswick NPIC (☎01768 772 645). **Campgrounds** are scattered throughout the park. The Lake District YHAs also run a convenient reservation service (☎01539 431 117).

Ambleside: Waterhead, Ambleside (☎01539 432 304), 1 mi. south of Ambleside on the Windermere Rd. (A591), 3 mi. north of Windermere. Bus #555 stops in front of this mother of all hostels. 254 beds in a refurbished hotel with an amazing view of the water. Books tours, rents mountain bikes (£6.50 half-day, £8.50 full day), and serves great meals. Breakfast included. Dorms £19, under 18 £14.50. MC/V. ❷

Black Sail: Black Sail Hut, Ennerdale, Cleator (☎07711 108 450). Set in splendid remote hills, 3½ mi. from Seatoller. 16 beds. Call in advance. Reception 8:30-10am and 5-10pm. Open daily May-Sept. Dorms £11-14, under 18 £8-11. MC/V. ❶

Borrowdale: Longthwaite, Borrowdale (☎01768 777 257). Take bus #79 from Keswick and then follow signs from Rosthwaite Village. Comfortable riverside hostel with 88 beds. Internet £2.50 per 30min. Reception 7:30am-noon and 1-11pm. Open Mar.-Dec. Dorms £14-17, under 18 £10-13. MC/V. ❷

Buttermere: King George VI Memorial Hostel, Buttermere (☎01768 770 245). Turn right at Bridge Hotel from the bus stop and walk ¼ mi. south on the B5289. Lounges and kitchen. 70 beds. Breakfast included. Packed lunch £3.40-4.30; dinner from £4.50. Lockout 10am-1pm. Open Mar.-Oct. Dorms £16-19, under 18 £12.50-14. MC/V. ❷

Cockermouth: Double Mills, Cockermouth (☎01900 822 561), in the town center, off Fern Bank at Parkside Ave. Converted 17th-century water mill. 26 beds. Open Apr.-Oct. Dorms £9.30, under 18 £7. MC/V. ❶

Coniston Coppermines: Coppermines House (☎01539 441 261), 1¼ mi. northwest of Coniston along the Churchbeck River. The rugged journey to the hostel is a scenic challenge. 26 beds in a former mine manager's house. Breakfast £2.80, packed lunch £3.40-4.30, dinner from £5.50. Laundry £1.50. Reception 8-10am and 5-11pm. Open Easter to Oct. Dorms £11-14, under 18 £8-11. MC/V. ❷

Coniston Holly How: Far End, Coniston (☎01539 441 323), just north of the village at the junction of Hawkshead Rd. and Ambleside Rd. Modernized country house is a good base for walking. 61 beds. Breakfast £3.80. Free laundry. Curfew 11pm. Open Jan.-Sept.; call in advance. Dorms £12.50-15.50, under 18 £9-12. MC/V. ❷

Derwentwater: Barrow House, Borrowdale (☎01768 777 246), 2 mi. south of Keswick on the B5289. Take bus #79, also a Keswick Launch stop. 88-bed, 200-year-old house with its own waterfall. Breakfast £3.80, packed lunch £3.40-4.30, dinner from £7.50.

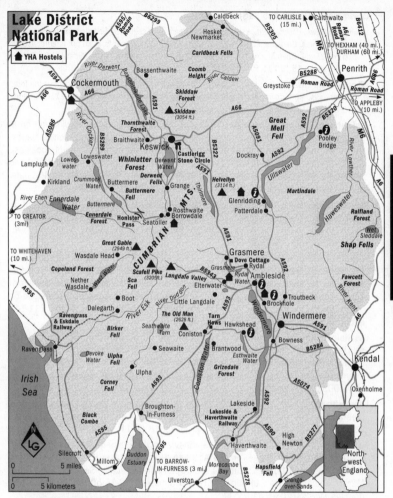

Internet access £2.50 for 30min. Curfew 11:30pm. Open Mar.-Oct. daily; Nov.-Feb. F-Sa. Dorms £12.50-15.50, under 18 £9-10.50. MC/V. ❷

Elterwater: (☎01539 437 245). 43 beds on a Great Langdale Valley farm; popular with walkers. Take bus #516 to Elterwater, turn left and follow the road over a stone bridge. Breakfast £3.80, packed lunch £3.40, dinner from £5.50. Internet access £2 per hr. Reception 5-11pm. Open Apr.-Sept. daily; Feb.-Mar. and Oct.-Dec. Tu-Sa; Jan. F-Sa. Dorms £11-14, under 18 £8-11. MC/V. ❶

Eskdale: (☎01946 723 219). In a quiet valley 1½ mi. east of Boot on the Ravenglass-Eskdale railway, adjacent to Hardknot Pass. 50 beds. Breakfast £3.80, packed lunch £4.30, dinner from £5. Reception 7:30-10am and 5-10:30pm. Open Apr.-Oct. Dorms £11-14, under 18 £8-11; doubles £26. MC/V. ❶

Grasmere: (☎01539 435 316). 2 hostels.

Butharlyp Howe: Easedale Rd., 150 yd. from Grasmere town center. 81-bed Victorian house with 2- to 9-bed rooms. Breakfast £3.80, packed lunch £3.40-4.30, dinner from £6.50. Internet access 50p per 15min. Open Mar.-Oct. daily; Nov.-Feb. F-Sa. Reception 5-11pm. Curfew 11pm. Dorms £14-17, under 18 £10-11.50. MC/V. ❷

Thorney How: Easedale Rd.; from Butharlyp Howe walk another ½ mi. and turn right at the fork; the hostel is ¼ mi. down on the left. 51-bed, 350-year-old farmhouse. Dorms £11-14, under 18 £8-9.50. MC/V. ❶

Hawkshead: Esthwaite Lodge (☎01539 436 293), 1 mi. south of Hawkshead on a posted route. Bus #505 from Ambleside stops at the village center. Follow Newby Bridge Rd. to this Regency mansion overlooking Esthwaite Water. 109 beds. Breakfast £3.80, packed lunch £3.40-4.30, 3-course dinner £7.50. Laundry. Internet £2.50 per 30min. Curfew 11:30pm. Open Feb.-Oct. daily; Nov.-Dec. F-Sa. Reception 7:30-10am and 1-10:30pm. Dorms £12.50-15.50, under 18 £9-10.50. MC/V. ❷

Helvellyn: Greenside, Glenridding (☎01768 482 269), 1½ mi. from Glenridding on a route toward Helvellyn. 60 beds in 2- to 6-bed rooms. Reception 8-11am, 5-10:30pm. Open July-Aug. daily; call 48hr. in advance year-round for availability. Dorms £11-14, under 18 £8-9.50. MC/V. ❶

Honister House: (☎01768 777 267), near Seatoller. Gray building at the summit of Honister Pass, 9 mi. south of Keswick. Bus #77 from Keswick (May-Oct.); #79 stops within 1½ mi. Continue along Honister Pass and follow the signs. 29 beds. Breakfast £3.80, packed lunch £3.40-4.30, 3-course dinner £7.50. Reception 7:30-10am and 5-11pm. Open June-Aug. daily; Apr.-May and Sept.-Oct. M-Tu and F-Su. Dorms £11-14, under 18 £8-9.50; twins £27.50. MC/V. ❶

Keswick: Station Rd. (☎01768 772 484). From the TIC, bear left down Station Rd.; YHA sign on the left. 91 beds in a former hotel with balconies, clean rooms, and pool in the common room. Breakfast £3.80, packed lunch £3.40-4.30, 3-course dinner £7.50. Internet access £2.50 per 30min. Curfew 11:30pm. Closed for renovations; reopens May 2006. Call in advance. Dorms £12.50-15.50, under 18 £9-10.50. MC/V. ❷

Langdale: High Close, 1 mi. from Elterwater village. Bookings through Ambleside YHA (see above). Old Victorian lodge in a beautiful setting. Laundry. Reception 5-11pm. Open daily Mar.-Oct. Dorms £11.50-14.40, under 18 £8-11. MC/V. ❶

Patterdale: (☎01768 482 394). Scandinavian-style, grass-roofed building ¼ mi. south of Patterdale village, on the A592 to Kirkstone Pass. 82 beds. Reception 8:30am-noon and 1-10pm. Curfew 11pm. Open Apr.-Aug. daily; Sept.-Oct. and Feb.-Mar. M and Th-Su; Nov. to mid-Feb. F-Sa. Dorms £12.50-15.50, under 18 £9-12; doubles £27-33/20-26. MC/V. ❷

Wastwater: Wasdale Hall, Wasdale (☎01946 726 222), ½ mi. east of Nether Wasdale. A climber's paradise; 48 beds in a half-timbered house on the water. Breakfast £3.80, packed lunch £3.40-4.30, 3-course dinner £7.50. Reception 8-10am and 5-11pm. Open Apr.-Oct. daily; Nov.-Dec. F-Sa; mid-Feb. to Mar. M and Th-Su. Dorms £11-14, under 18 £8-11. MC/V. ❶

Windermere: Bridge Ln. (☎01539 443 543), 2 mi. north of Windermere off the A591. Catch the YHA shuttle from the train station. Spacious, 70-bed house with panoramic views of the lake below. Mountain bikes for rent. Breakfast £3.80, packed lunch £3.40-4.30, 3-course dinner £7.50. Laundry. Internet access £2.50 per 30min. Open Feb.-Nov. daily; early Dec. F-Sa. Dorms £12.50-15.50, under 18 £9-10.50. MC/V. ❷

HIKING AND OUTDOORS

Outdoor enthusiasts run (and walk and climb) rampant in the Lakes. NPICs have guidebooks for mountain-bike trails, pleasant family walks, tough climbs, and hikes ending at pubs. Most also offer guided walks throughout the summer. Hostels are another excellent source of information, with large maps on the walls and free advice from experienced staff.

> **TIP** **TAKE A LOAD OFF.** If you're hiking the Lake District but don't want to cart your pack, make use of the YHA shuttle (p. 361), which runs between major hostels in the area and costs just £3.

The Lake District offers some of the best **hiking** in Britain. While there are many trails, be aware that they can be hard to follow at times—even on popular routes. If you plan to go on a long or difficult outing, check with the Park Service, call **weather information** (☎01768 775 757; 24hr; YHAs also post daily forecasts), and leave a plan of your route with your B&B proprietor or hostel warden before setting out. Steep slopes and unreliable weather can quickly reduce visibility to only a few feet. A good map and compass are necessities. The Ordnance Survey Explorer Maps #4-7 detail the four quadrants of the Lake District (1:25,000; £7), while Landranger Maps #89-91 and 96-98 chart every hillock and bend in the road for those planning overland or especially difficult routes (1:50,000; £12). The Lakes are also fine **cycling** country. Several long-distance routes (part of the National Cycling Network; ☎01179 290 888) traverse the park. There are excellent short routes as well; *Ordnance Survey One Day Cycle Rides in Cumbria* (£10) is a helpful guide. Bike rental is available in many towns, and staffers can often suggest routes. Any cyclist planning an extensive stay should grab the *Ordnance Survey Cycle Tours* (£9), which provides detailed maps of on- and off-trail routes. The circular **Cumbria Cycle Way** tours some of Cumbria's less-traveled areas via a 259 mi. route from Carlisle in the north around the park's outskirts. Pick up *The Cumbria Way Cycle Route* (£4) from a TIC for details. For all travelers in the Lakes but for cyclists especially, beware the narrow and stonewalled roads off the A591: cars and large buses generally tear around on the winding lanes.

The Lake District is popular for **rock climbing.** Two good sources for climbing information are Rock & Run, 3-4 Cheapside, Ambleside (☎01539 433 660; open M-Sa 9am-5:30pm, Su 10am-5pm) and the Keswick Indoor Climbing Wall (p. 371).

WINDERMERE AND BOWNESS ☎015394

The largest tourist center in the Lake District, Windermere, and its lakeside sidekick, Bowness-on-Windermere (combined pop. 11,000), fill to the gills with vacationers in July and August, when sailboats and water-skiers swarm the lake. As transportation hubs and gateways to the rest of the park's natural playgrounds, the two towns offer a tamer take on the region.

TRANSPORTATION AND PRACTICAL INFORMATION. The **train station** and **bus depot** are in Windermere; Bowness, flanking the lake, is an easy 1½ mi. walk south. From the station, turn left onto Victoria Rd.; staying to the left, follow Crescent Rd. through town to New Rd., which becomes Lake Rd. and leads to the pier. **Bus** #599 runs from the station to Bowness (3 per hr., £1). For information on getting to Windermere, see p. 360. Try Windermere **Taxis** (☎ 42 355) for a cab, or **rent bikes** from Country Lanes Cycle Hire at the station. (☎ 44 544. £10 per half-day, £15 per day; discounts with train ticket. Open daily Easter to Oct. 9am-5pm.)

The Windermere **Tourist Information Centre,** near the train station, stocks walking guides (from 40p), books National Express and Stagecoach tickets, arranges accommodations, and has a bureau de change. (☎ 46 499. Open daily July-Aug. 9am-6:30pm; Easter to June and Sept.-Oct. 9am-6pm; Nov. to Easter 9am-5pm.) Both towns have **banks.** Windermere services include: **luggage storage** at Darryl's Cafe, 14 Church St. (☎ 42 894; £1.50 per item; open M and Th-Su 8am-6pm); a **launderette** on Main Rd. (☎ 42 326; wash £3, dry 20p per 4min.; open M-F 8:30am-5:30pm, Sa 9am-5pm); **police,** Lake Rd. (☎ 01768 891 999); **Internet** access at Tri-Arom, Birch St. (☎ 44 639; www.triarom.co.uk; £1 per 10min., £5 per hr.; open M-F 9:30am-5:30pm, Sa 9:30am-5pm); and the **post office,** 21 Crescent Rd. (☎ 43 245; open M-F 9am-5:30pm, Sa 9am-12:30pm). **Post Code:** LA23 1AA.

🛏🍴 **ACCOMMODATIONS AND FOOD.** Windermere and Bowness have a number of **B&Bs,** but booking ahead is advisable during peak periods. The best values among Windermere's B&Bs include the motorcyclist- and family-friendly **Brendan Chase B&B ❷,** 1-3 College Rd., with large rooms in two Edwardian townhouses (☎ 45 638; singles £25; doubles from £40; cash only); the warm and well-appointed **Ashleigh Guest House ❸,** 11 College Rd. (☎ 42 292; www.ashleighhouse.com; singles £30; doubles £42-60; MC/V); and the quiet and homey **Greenriggs ❷,** 8 Upper Oak St. (☎ 42 265; singles £17-27; doubles £34-60; cash only). In Bowness, **Laurel Cottage ❸,** St. Martins Pl., is a 400-year-old stone building off the main thoroughfare, near the pier. (☎ 45 594; www.laurelcottage-bnb.co.uk. Singles £27; doubles £58-72. MC/V.) Find **camping** at lovely **Park Cliffe ❷,** Birks Rd., 4½ mi. south of Bowness. Take bus #618 from Windermere station. (☎ 01539 531 344. Open early Mar. to early Nov. £11-12 per tent. AmEx/MC/V.) A smaller option is the **Orrest Head ❶** campsite above Windermere. (☎ 01539 542 619. No vehicles. £4 per person. Cash only.)

In Windermere, stock up on supplies at Booth's **grocery,** next to the station. (☎ 46 114. Open M-F 8:30am-8pm, Sa 8:30am-7pm, Su 10am-4pm.) For fresh fruit, **Valerie Ann's,** 27b Crescent Rd., vends produce outside its door. (☎ 42 068. Open M-F 9am-5:30pm, Sa 9am-4:30pm.) **The Light House ❷,** at the top of Main Rd., sells light fare throughout the day (sandwiches £4), but stays open late as a bar and bistro. (☎ 88 260; www.lighthousecafebar.co.uk. Open Apr.-Oct. M-Sa 8:30am-11pm, Su 8:30am-10:30pm, food served until 10pm; Nov.-Mar. M-Sa 8:30am-9pm, Su 8:30am-9pm. MC/V.) **Jackson's ❸,** St. Martins Pl., serves modern British cuisine; a 3-course meal costs £13. (☎ 46 264. Open M-F 6-11pm, Sa-Su 5:30-11pm. MC/V.) During the day, the **Bowness Kitchen Cafe ❶,** Lake Rd., is great place to grab a quick bite of lunch. (☎ 45 529. Sandwiches and soups £3-5. Open daily 9am-5pm. MC/V.)

📷🏞 **SIGHTS AND OUTDOORS.** Sample the natural beauty of Windermere's surroundings on a **lake cruise.** A number of sightseeing boats depart from Bowness pier. **Windermere Lake Cruises** (☎ 43 360) is the main operator, with trips north to Waterhead Pier in Ambleside (30min.; round-trip £6.65) and south to Lakeside (40min., £7/3.55). Nonstop sightseeing cruises are also available (45min., £5/2.50). On all routes, departures are frequent from April to October, reduced the rest of the year. The **Freedom of the Lake** pass allows unlimited one-day travel (£12). A cruise to **Lakeside,** at Windermere's southern tip, lets you visit the freshwater **Aquarium of the Lakes.** (☎ 01539 530 153; www.aquariumofthelakes.co.uk. Open daily Apr.-Sept. 9am-6pm; Oct.-Mar. 9am-5pm. Last admission 1hr. before close. £6.25.) Take a ride on the 4 mi. steam-powered **Lakeside and Haverthwaite Railway.**

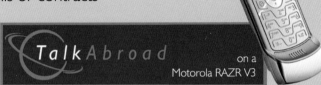

(☎01539 531 594. Easter to Oct. ₤4.50.) Booths at the Bowness and Ambleside piers sell tickets that combine the lake cruise with one or both of these attractions. Motorboat and **rowboat rentals** are available at Bowness Pier. (☎40 347. Motorboats ₤12 per hr., rowboats ₤3 per hr.)

In-town sights are less remarkable than the lake's offerings, but children and Jemima Puddleduck fans will enjoy **The World of Beatrix Potter,** an indoor recreation of scenes from the author's stories. (☎88 444; www.hop-skip-jump.com. Open daily Apr.-Oct. 10am-5:30pm; Feb.-Mar. 10am-4:30pm. ₤4.) The **Windermere Steamboat Museum,** 1 mi. north of Bowness on Rayrigg Rd., displays the world's oldest mechanically powered boat next to full and scale models. The museum also runs a steamboat cruise around the lake. (☎45 565. Open Apr.-Oct. daily 10am-5pm. Museum ₤4.25. Cruises ₤5.50.

The short but steep climb to **Orrest Head** (1½ mi. round-trip) is moderately difficult, but affords one of the best views in the Lake District; it begins opposite the the TIC on the other side of A591.

AMBLESIDE ☎ 015394

Set in a valley 1 mile north of Windermere's waters, Ambleside is an attractive village with convenient access to the southern lakes. It's popular with hikers, who are drawn by its location—or perhaps by its absurd number of outdoors shops. Lake cruises depart from the Waterhead Pier, where you can also rent boats. As in Windermere, most non-lake sights lack excitement. At tiny **Bridge House,** off Rydal Rd., bridge and house are one and the same. It shelters a (cramped) **National Trust Information Centre.** (☎32617. Open Apr.-Oct. M and Th-Su 10am-5pm. Free.) **Trails** extend in all directions from Ambleside. Splendid views of higher fells can be had from the top of **Loughrigg** (a moderately difficult 7 mi. round-trip). The **Stockghyll Force** waterfall is concealed in a wooded area an easy mile from town. Area TICs have guides to these and other walks.

Ambleside's ◩**YHA hostel** (p. 362) is near the steamer pier at Waterhead, a pleasant 1 mi. walk from the town center. **Ambleside Backpackers ❷,** Old Lake Rd., offers 72 bunks in a comfortable, clean, and airy house. (☎32 340. Well-equipped self-catering kitchen. Breakfast included. Laundry and Internet access available. Reception 8:30am-1pm and 4-8:30pm. Dorms ₤14. MC/V.) **B&Bs** cluster on **Church Street** and **Compston Road,** while others line the busier **Lake Road** leading in from Windermere. **Linda's B&B and Bunkhouse ❷,** Compston Rd., has four rooms with TVs and can also be rented out entirely as a private, hostel-style bunkhouse. (☎32 999. Dorms ₤12, with breakfast ₤15. Singles ₤15, with breakfast ₤20. No smoking. Cash only.) **Compston House American Style B&B ❹,** Compston Rd., is a more upscale choice. Transplanted New Yorkers welcome you to their well-furnished and appealing home. Excellent pancakes are served at breakfast. (☎32 305; www.compstonhouse.co.uk. Singles ₤26-66. AmEx/MC/V.) Forage for trail snacks at the **market** on Kelsick Rd. (open W 10am-3:30pm) or at Granny Smith's **grocery,** Market Pl., where you will find organic fruits and vegetables and other natural foods (☎33 145; open M-F 8am-5pm, Sa 8am-6pm, Su 9am-4pm; cash only). **Pippin's ❶,** 10 Lake Rd., serves great sandwiches, all-day breakfasts, and pizza—plus it's open late. (☎31 338. Meals ₤3-5. Open M-Th and Su 8:30am-10pm, F-Sa 8:30am-11pm. AmEx/MC/V.) At **Lucy's ❸,** Church St., a gourmet grocery, restaurant, and wine bar make for large evening crowds. (☎31 191. Entrees ₤13-15. Open daily 9am-10pm. MC/V.) The **Glass House ❸,** Ryndal Rd., serves Mediterranean and modern British cuisine, and is decorated with blown glass. (☎32 137. Lunch ₤6.50-8. Dinner ₤11-15. Early-bird special 6:30-7:30pm. Open M-F noon-2:30pm and 6:30-9:30pm, Sa noon-5pm and 6:30-10pm, Su noon-5pm and

6:30-9:30pm. Reserve ahead. MC/V.) One good turn deserves a stop at the **Golden Rule**, on Smithy Brow, a good local pub that taps local beer. (☎33 363. Open M-Sa 11am-11pm, Su noon-11pm. Cash only.)

Buses stop on Kelsick Rd. Bus #555 runs within the park to Grasmere, Windermere, and Keswick (every hr.). Bus #505 joins Hawkshead and Coniston (M-Sa every hr.). **Rent bikes** from Ghyllside Cycles, The Slack. (☎33 592. £10 per half-day, £14 per day. Open May-Oct. daily 9:30am-5:30pm; Nov.-Apr. M-Tu and Th-Su 9:30am-5:30pm.) The **Tourist Information Centre** is in the Central Building on Market Cross. It offers services identical to those of the TIC in Windermere (p. 365) and doubles as an NPIC. (☎32 582; www.amblesideonline.co.uk. Open daily 9am-5pm.) There's also a **NPIC** at Waterhead (p. 361). Other services include: **banks** on Market Pl.; a **launderette,** across from the bus station on Kelsick Rd. (☎34 943 open M-W and F-Sa 10am-1pm and 2-6pm; last wash 5pm); the **police** (☎32 218); and the **post office,** Market Pl. (☎32 267; open M-F 9am-5:30pm, Sa 9am-12:30pm). **Post Code:** LA22 9BU.

GREAT LANGDALE VALLEY ☎015394

The spectacular and often mist-filled **Great Langdale** valley, a horseshoe-shaped glacial scar dominated by the towering Langdale Pikes, begins 3 mi. west of Ambleside. In a grove of trees at the center of the valley, the tiny town of **Elterwater,** half a mile from its namesake lake, is happily overwhelmed by its surroundings. This is great **hiking** country—one possibility is the terrific and only moderately difficult walk connecting Elterwater with Grasmere (4 mi.). Another option is a circuit of the valley beginning from Elterwater village (6 mi.). Hard-core trekkers won't be able to resist the siren song of the **Pikes.** Several popular ascents begin from the Old Dungeon Ghyll Hotel (see below), 6 mi. from Ambleside. The path to the summit of the **Pike of Blisco** is only 2½ mi. (but about 2000 ft. up). **Bus** #516 travels from Ambleside to the Old Dungeon Ghyll Hotel via Elterwater (M-Sa 6 per day, Su 5 per day). There are two **YHA hostels** in the area: **Elterwater** (p. 364), in town, and **Langdale** (p. 364), beautifully set 1 mi. away. The **Britannia Inn ④,** in Elterwater village, has comfortable accommodations by the bus stop. (☎37 210. Doubles in summer £76, in winter £74. AmEx/MC/V.) Where the road from Ambleside ends, the **Old Dungeon Ghyll Hotel ④** sits encircled by wilderness. The O.D.G., as the locals say, is an excellent base for hiking and offers a cozy sanctuary for weary walkers. (☎37 272. £42-44 per person, with dinner £60. AmEx/MC/V.)

CONISTON ☎015394

Less touristed than its nearby counterparts, Coniston retains the rustic feel of the region's past. Fells to the north and **Coniston Water** to the south make it popular with hikers and cyclists. The town is also known for its former resident, Victorian artist-writer-critic John Ruskin. The **John Ruskin Museum,** on Yewdale Rd., displays a collection of his sketches and photographs, as well as general exhibits on the history and geology of Coniston. (☎41 164. Open Mar.-Nov. daily 10am-5:30pm; Dec.-Feb. W-Su 10am-3:30pm. Last admission 40min. before close. £3.75.) Ruskin's **gravestone** is in St. Andrew's Churchyard. Pretty **Brantwood,** Ruskin's 250-acre 1872 manor, looks across the lake at Coniston and the Old Man (p. 368); it holds Ruskin's art and prose collections. (☎41 396. Open mid-Mar. to mid-Nov. daily 11am-5:30pm; mid-Nov. to mid-Mar. W-Su 11am-4:30pm. £5.50, students £4.)

The easiest way to reach Brantwood is by water: the National Trust offers trips on the elegant Victorian **steam yacht** *Gondola*. (☎41 288. Apr.-Oct. 5 per day, departs Coniston Pier every hr. 11am-4pm. Round-trip £5.80.) The Coniston Launch also cruises to Brantwood and offers other excursions. (☎36 216;

www.conistonlaunch.co.uk. Apr.-Oct. 10 per day, fewer in winter. North Lake Cruise £9.60, South Lake Cruise £11.80.) Hikers can explore the nearby abandoned **Coppermines** area (4½ mi.) in search of the "American's stope"—an old copper mine shaft named in honor of a Yankee who leapt over it twice successfully and survived a 160 ft. fall the third time. Another popular walk is to **Tarn Hows** (from Coniston 5 mi. round-trip; p. 369). The ambitious can take on the surprisingly feisty 2633 ft. **Old Man** just to the north of town (5 mi. round-trip). The TIC has more information on these and other walks in the area.

Coniston has two **YHA hostels**. The **Beech Tree Guest House ❸**, Yewdale Rd., is a comfortable **B&B** at a decent price. (☎41 717. Doubles £44-46, ensuite £54. Cash only.) Cozy and close to the bus stop, **Emma's B&B ❷**, Tilberthwaite Ave., boasts large rooms. (☎41 231. £25 per person. AmEx/MC/V.) **Bus** #505 travels between Ambleside and Coniston, with some trips originating in Windermere (50min. from Windermere; M-Sa 12 per day, Su 6 per day). Buses stop at the corner of Tilberthwaite and Ruskin Ave. Coniston's **Tourist Information Centre** and **NPIC** are on Ruskin Ave. The town has no ATM but **banks** are available. Find **bike rentals** at Summitreks, 14 Yewdale Rd. (☎41 212. £14 per day. Open daily 9am-5pm.) The **post office**, is on Yewdale Rd. (☎41 259. Open June-Aug. M-F 9am-12:30pm and 1:30-6pm, Sa 9am-noon; Sept.-May M-F 9am-12:30pm and 1:30-5pm, Sa 9am-noon.) **Post Code:** LA218DU.

HAWKSHEAD ☎015394

In the village of **Hawkshead**, 4 mi. east of Coniston, you can imagine yourself pulling Wordsworth's hair and passing him notes at the **Hawkshead Grammar School**, Main St., where the poet studied from 1779 to 1787. (☎35 647. Open Easter to Oct. M-W and F-Sa 10am-12:30pm and 1:30-5pm, Su 10am-12:30pm and 1-5pm. £1.) Also on Hawkshead's main street is the **Beatrix Potter Gallery.** Housed in offices once used by her husband, the gallery displays the original sketches and watercolors from her beloved children's stories. (☎36 355. Open late Mar. to Oct. M-W and Sa-Su 10:30am-4:30pm. Last admission 4pm. £3.50.) Potter lived 2 mi. from Hawkshead on her farm at **Hill Top.** The house, which was featured in many of her stories, remains exactly as she left it. Here you can make like Peter Rabbit and cavort in Mr. McGregor's garden, but be prepared to wait, as lines can be long. Clever bunnies book ahead. (☎36 269. Open late Mar. to Oct. M-W and Sa-Su 10:30am-4:30pm Last admission 4pm. £5.) **Tarn Hows,** a pond surrounded by a pine grove, is a peaceful (though popular) picnic spot.

In summer, **bus** #505 stops in Hawkshead on its way between Ambleside and Coniston (M-Sa 12 per day, Su 6 per day). **Mountain Goat** offers a combined boat and bus shuttle to Hill Top from Bowness, as well as a bus from Hawkshead. (☎45 164. Apr.-Sept. 8 per day. Round-trip from Bowness £6, children £4.) On summer Sundays, the National Trust (☎01768 773 780) offers a **shuttle** to Tarn Hows from Coniston and Hawkshead. Get trail advice at the Hawkshead **NPIC** (p. 361).

GRASMERE ☎015394

With a lake and a canonized poet all to itself, the attractive village of Grasmere receives more than its fair share of camera-clicking tourists. The sightseers crowd in at midday to visit sights pertaining to William Wordsworth's life and death, but the mornings and evenings are refreshingly peaceful. Guides provide 30min. tours of the early 17th-century **Dove Cottage**, where Wordsworth lived with his wife Mary and his sister Dorothy from 1799 to 1808, and which is almost exactly as he left it. Next door, the outstanding **Wordsworth Museum** includes pages of his handwritten poetry and opinions on his Romantic contemporaries. The cottage is 10min. from the center of Grasmere down Stock Ln. (☎35 544; www.wordsworth.org.uk. Open mid-Feb. to mid-Jan. daily 9:30am-5pm. Cottage and museum ₤6, students ₤4.60. Museum only ₤4.) **Wordsworth's grave** is in town at St. Oswald's churchyard.

Another 1½ mi. southeast of Grasmere is **Rydal Mount,** the wordsmith's home from 1813 until his death in 1850. The small hut in which he frequently composed verse lies across the garden terrace facing the water. Bus #599 stops here. (☎33 002. Open daily Mar.-Oct. 9:30am-5pm; Nov.-Dec. and Feb. M and W-Su 10am-4pm. ₤4.50, seniors ₤3.75, students ₤3.50, children ₤1.50, families ₤10. Garden only ₤2.) Closer to town along Redbank Rd., **Faeryland Grasmere** offers an idyllic spot to get a pot of tea and gaze across the water at the fells, or hire **rowboats** and strike out onto the deep green lake. (₤6-15 per person; ₤20 deposit. Open daily Apr.-Oct. 10am-5:30pm; Nov.-Mar. 10:30am-4:30pm.)

Grasmere is a good place for daffodil-seeking Wordsworthians to begin their rambles. A steep, strenuous scramble (4 mi. round-trip) leads to the top of **Helm Cragg.** The 6 mi. **Wordsworth Walk** circumnavigates the two lakes of the Rothay River, passing the poet's grave. The combined **TIC/NPIC** is on Redbank Rd. There are two Grasmere **YHA hostel** buildings within a 15min. walk: Butharlyp How and Thorney How. The **Glenthorne Quaker Guest House ❸,** 5 mi. up Easedale Rd., across from the main bus stop, provides lovely views of nearby Silver Howe from clean and spacious rooms. (☎35 389; www.glenthorne.org. Singles from ₤28, full board from ₤44. Cash only.) **The Harwood ❸,** Red Lion Sq., offers convenient accommodations in the center of town. (☎35 248. 2-night min. stay on weekends. ₤30-35 per person; ₤28-30 weeknights. MC/V.) **Sara Arundales ❷,** Broadgate, serves baguettes by day (₤4) and transforms into a bistro by night. (☎35 266. Dinner ₤10-12. Open mid-Feb. to Dec. daily 10:30am-4pm and 6-9pm. MC/V.) The cozy and secluded **Jumble Room ❸,** Langdale Rd., prepares a number of organic vegetarian and seafood plates. (☎35 188. Open Easter to Oct. W-Su 10:30am-4:30pm and 6pm until food runs out; Oct. to Easter F-Su 10:30am-4:30pm and 6pm until food runs out. MC/V.) The famous gingerbread at **Sarah Nelson's Grasmere Gingerbread Shop ❶,** a staple since 1854, is a bargain at 30p a piece in the tiny Church Cottage, outside St. Oswald's Church. (☎35 428. Open Easter to Nov. M-Sa 9:15am-5:30pm, Su 12:30-5:30pm; closes earlier in winter. Cash only.)

KESWICK   ☎017687

Sandwiched between towering Skiddaw peak and the northern edge of Derwentwater, Keswick (KEZ-ick) rivals Windermere as the Lake District's tourist capital, with tranquil charms, an appealing town center, and beautiful lakes.

🛈 PRACTICAL INFORMATION. For information on how to get to Keswick, see p. 360. The **NPIC** is behind the clock tower in Market Pl. Keswick Mountain Bikes, off Main St., in the Southey Hill Industrial Estate, **rents bikes.** (☎75 202; www.keswickbike.co.uk. ₤12 per half-day, ₤17 per day. Open M-Sa 9am-5:30pm, Su 10am-5:30pm.) Other services include: **banks** on Main St.; a **launderette,** Main St., at the mini-roundabout (wash ₤2.50, dry ₤1.25; open daily 7:30am-7pm); **police,** 8 Bank St. (☎75 448); **Internet access** at U-Compute Cyber Cafe, above the post office (☎75 127; ₤2 per 30min., ₤3 per hr.; open M-Sa 9am-5:30pm, Su 9:30am-4:30pm); and the **post office,** 48 Main St. (☎72 269; open M-F 9am-5:30pm, Sa 9am-1pm). **Post Code:** C84 599.

🛏🍴 ACCOMMODATIONS AND FOOD. The **Keswick** and **Derwentwater YHA hostels** grace the town. The area between Station St., St. John St. (Ambleside Rd.), and Penrith Rd. abounds with **B&Bs.** Better options lie on the far side of the town center, away from the hubbub and closer to the bus station. With a stunning view of the lake and mountains, **Appletrees ❸**, The Heads, makes for a good stay. (☎80 400; www.appletreeskeswick.com. Singles £30; doubles £56-58.) Just down the road, **Berkeley Guest House ❸**, The Heads, also has nice views. (☎74 222; www.berkeley-keswick.com. Singles £29; doubles from £40.) Away from the lake but still a good bet, **Badgers Wood ❸**, 30 Stanger St., is vegetarian-friendly, with rooms named after trees. Ask Mr. Paylor about the best hiking and walking routes. (☎72 621; www.badgerswood.co.uk. Singles £28; doubles £52. Cash only.)

Buy **groceries** at the enormous Co-op on Main St., next to the launderette. (☎72 688. Open M-Sa 8am-8pm, Su 10am-5pm.) For some meatless treats and generally tasty fare, grab sandwiches and wraps (£3-5) at **Lakeland Pedlar ❶**, off Main St. (☎74 492. Open May-June M-F 10am-4pm, Sa-Su 9am-5pm; July-Sept. M-Th 9am-5pm, F-Sa 9am-9pm; Oct.-Apr. daily 10am-4pm.) **Brysons ❶**, 42 Main St., is an excellent bakery with an upstairs tea room. (Open M-Sa 9am-5:30pm, Su 9am-5pm.) **The Rembrandt Restaurant ❷**, 25 Station St., serves freshly baked scones and traditional meals in a homey setting. (☎72 008. 2 courses £9, 3 courses £10. Open May-Oct. daily 9am-10pm; Nov.-Apr. M-Th and Su 10am-5:30pm, F-Sa 10am-9pm.) **Ye Olde Queen's Head ❷**, beside the Lakeland Pedlar, is perfect for unwinding over a pint and playing a game of pool. (☎73 333. Happy hour daily 5:30-6:30pm. Open M-Sa 11am-11pm, Su noon-10:30pm.)

◎ ♫ SIGHTS AND ENTERTAINMENT. The best sight in Keswick is **Derwentwater**, undoubtedly one of the prettiest in this land of lakes. The lapping waves are only a 5min. walk south of the town center along Lake Rd. The **Keswick Launch** sends cruises to other points on the lake, has rowboats and motor boats for hire at the marina (2-person rowboats £8 per hr., 2-person motor boats £20 per hr.), and lands at the start of a handful of trails around the shore. (☎72 263. 50min. Mid-Mar. to Nov. 6-11 cruises per day; Dec. to mid-Mar. 3 per day. £6, under 16 £3, families £13.50.) Right beside the factory where the No. 2 was invented, the **Cumberland Pencil Museum** displays the world's longest pencil and features on the industry's history. The museum lies just out of the town center along Main St. (☎73 626; www.pencils.co.uk. Open daily 9:30am-4pm. £2.50, students £1.75.) The **Keswick Museum and Art Gallery**, in Fitz Park on Station Rd., has an interesting grab bag of Victorian artifacts. (☎73 263. Open Easter to Oct. Tu-Sa 10am-4pm. Free.) For a break from indoor pursuits, the **Theatre by the Lake** (by the, er, lake) features a year-round program of repertory theater, music, and dance and makes for a nice evening's entertainment. (☎74 411. Box office open daily 9:30am-8pm.)

◪ HIKING. A standout 4 mi. amble from Keswick crosses slopeside pastures and visits the **Castlerigg Stone Circle,** a neolithic henge dating back nearly 5000 years. Archaeologists believe it may have been used as a place of worship, astronomical observatory, or trading center. Another short walk hits the beautiful **Friar's Crag**, on the shore of Derwentwater, and **Castlehead**, a viewpoint encompassing town, lakes, and peaks beyond. Both of these walks are relatively easy on the legs, with only a few moderately tough moments. The more strenuous **Catbells and Newlands** hike runs 8½ mi. and includes a short passage on the Keswick Launch. Maps and information on these and other walks are available at the NPIC (guides 60p). Climbing enthusiasts can get in a bit of practice before heading for the hills at the **Keswick Indoor Climbing Wall,** a 5min. walk from town along Main St. The keen staff also leads outdoor tours for groups of five or more, spanning such pursuits as cycling, climbing, and ghyll scrambling. (☎72 000. Open daily 10am-9pm. Climbing wall £4.25, instruction available. Reservations required for outdoor guided tours.)

NORTHWEST ENGLAND

BORROWDALE ☎017687

One of Lakeland's most beautiful spots, the valley of Borrowdale gracefully winds its way south from the tip of Derwentwater. There are relatively few settlements in this serpentine, tree-filled valley, adding to its appeal. **Ashness Bridge,** in the north, is worth a look, but lies some distance from the main road (and thus from public transportation, though small van tours do tend to stop here). The tiny village of **Rosthwaite** has a few hotels and B&Bs. Towering over all is **Scafell Pike** (3210 ft.), the highest mountain in England, which, along with nearby and similarly lofty **Scafell** and **Great Gable,** forms an imposing triumvirate with some of the toughest and most rewarding hiking in the lakes. Treks up these peaks begin from **Seatoller,** at the head of the valley, which is home to an **NPIC.** Walks to the summits are very strenuous and not to be taken lightly—Scafell Pike is 4 mi. to the top and a 3100 ft. climb; Great Gable is also 4 mi., though not as steep.

Accommodations are scattered throughout the valley. **YHA Borrowdale** (p. 362) is in the valley itself, and **Derwentwater** (p. 362) and **Honister House** (p. 364) are nearby. In Rosthwaite, the **Yew Tree Farm ❸** lies just along a small lane opposite the general store. (☎77 675. Breakfast included. Ensuite rooms from £30 per person.) Wanderers with deeper pockets might try the elegant yet laid-back **Scafell Hotel ❹,** which also runs a pub with passable grub. (☎77 208; www.scafell.co.uk. £45-70 per person. MC/V.) The nearby **Flock-In Tea Room** is the valley's best bet for a bite to eat, serving up tasty soups and stews. (☎77 675. Open M-Tu and Th-Su 10am-5pm.) **Bus** #79 runs from Keswick to Seatoller via Rosthwaite (30min., 10-20 per day).

BUTTERMERE VALLEY ☎017687

A genuine sense of isolation and a harsh, wild beauty pervade Lake Buttermere and Crummock Water. Stark mountains descend right into the water. Miniscule **Buttermere** village consists of only a handful of buildings and lies between the two waters, each just a few minutes' walk away. **Hikes** range from relatively flat circular walks around Crummock Water (10½ mi.) and Buttermere (5 mi.) to a more challenging trek over the fells, which brings you to the neighboring YHA Black Sail and eventually YHA Wastwater (14½ mi.; p. 361). Information on good routes is available at the YHA Buttermere. The drive in and out of Buttermere Valley is beautiful on its own; southbound, it passes the striking Honister Pass, a big green half-pipe filled with scattered rocks. YHA Buttermere is a mere quarter-mile south of the village, while the uniquely situated Honister Hause sits atop Honister Pass.

Among the few structures in the village itself, the well-appointed and upscale **Bridge Hotel ❺** is the lone accommodation option, though a fine one, with antique rooms, four-poster beds, and lace curtains. (☎70 252; www.bridge-hotel.com. All rooms ensuite. Singles from £75, Nov.-Mar. £65. MC/V.) Just up the hill, **Skye Farm ❶** provides basic camping. (☎70 222. £5 per person. Cash only.) Bus #77/77A (55min., Apr.-Oct. 8 per day) serves Buttermere from Keswick. #77A reaches Buttermere via the Honister Pass and, though slower, it is far more scenic.

ULLSWATER ☎017684

In Ullswater, around each rocky outcrop or grassy bank a new corner of the lake is visible. The main settlements, **Glenridding** and **Patterdale,** are on the southern tip of the water, and either one can be a departure point for the popular climb up **Helvellyn** (3118 ft.). One possible ascent begins in Glenridding and follows four steep miles to the peak. Departing from the Glenridding Pier, the **Ullswater Steamers** cut across the lake with stops at Howtown and Pooley Bridge. (☎82 229; www.ullswater-steamers.co.uk. 15 per day in summer, 3 per day in winter; round-trip from £6.40.) An outstanding, less-strenuous route runs along the lake's eastern shore from Glenridding to Howtown, where you can then catch the steamer for a pleasant ride back. Another Ullswater attraction is **Aira Force,** one of the most accessible waterfalls in the Lakes, just off the A5091 toward Keswick. While Windermere is the place for motorized water sports, Ullswater is great for sailing and paddling around. The **Glenridding Sailing Centre** rents sailboats, canoes, kayaks, and windsurfers. (☎82 541; www.lakesail.co.uk. Canoes £45 per day, kayaks £30, sailboats £85, windsurfers £10. Lessons from £20. Open mid-Mar. to mid-Oct. daily 10am-5pm; mid-Oct. to mid-Dec. and mid-Feb. to mid-Mar. F-Su 10:30am-3:30pm.)

B&Bs include comfortable **Mosscrag ❸,** across the stream from the NPIC (☎82500; www.mosscrag.co.uk. Singles £26, ensuite £30; doubles £40, ensuite £45. MC/V.) **Beech House ❷** is on the main road (☎82 037; from £20 per person; MC/V). **YHA Helvellyn** is 1½ mi. from Glenridding on the way up the peak (p. 363). **YHA Patterdale** is a basic hostel, and Patterdale village has several guest houses, including **Old Water View ❸.** (☎82 175. Singles from £25. AmEx/MC/V.) Upscale hotels dot the lake.

Public transport to Ullswater is limited. The only year-round **bus** service is #108 from Penrith, which follows a scenic route along the lake and connects to Keswick. Sit on the left side for the best views (5 per day, 40 min., £3.80). Two more services operate seasonal schedules: #517 from Bowness/Windermere to Glenridding (55min.; Apr.-July Sa-Su 3 per day; Aug. daily) and #208 from Keswick to Patterdale via Aira Force and Glenridding (35min.; June-July Sa-Su 5 per day, Aug. daily). The **YHA shuttle** (p. 361) goes once daily from the southern lakes to Patterdale. A **NPIC** camps out in the main carpark in Glenridding (p. 361), and you'll find plenty of options for resting your head in town.

CARLISLE
☎01228

Cumbria's principal (that is, only) city, Carlisle was once nicknamed "The Key of England" for its strategic position in the Borderlands between England and Scotland. Roman Emperor Hadrian, Mary, Queen of Scots, Robert the Bruce, and Bonnie Prince Charlie have all played lord of the land from here. Today, Carlisle remains an ideal stopover for more peaceful border crossings, as well as a good base for examining Hadrian's Wall (p. 429).

▐ **TRANSPORTATION.** Carlisle's **train station** is on Botchergate, across from the castle. (Ticket office open M-Sa 4:45am-11:30pm, Su 9am-11:30pm.) **Trains** arrive from: Edinburgh (1½hr., every hr., £27); Glasgow (1½hr., every hr., £27); London Euston (4hr., every hr., £90); Newcastle (1½hr.; M-Sa every hr., Su 9 per day; £10.80). The **bus station** is on Lonsdale St. (Open M-Sa 8:30am-6:30pm, Su 9:45am-5:30pm.) National Express (☎08705 808 080) arrives from London (6½hr., 3 per day, £28.50). Stagecoach in Cumbria **bus** #555 travels from Keswick in the Lake District (1¼hr., 3 per day, £5). **Bike rental** is available at Scotby Cycles, Church St., on the roundabout. (☎546 931. £12 per day. £20 deposit. Open M-Sa 9am-5:30pm.)

▐▐ **ORIENTATION AND PRACTICAL INFORMATION.** Carlisle's city center is a pedestrian zone formed by the intersection of **English Street** and **Scotch Street.** The **Tourist Information Centre** lies in the town center at the Old Town Hall. To get there from the train station, turn left, going between the massive gatehouses, and walk three blocks and across Old Town Square. To get to the TIC from the bus station, turn left, cross Lowther St., and walk through the shopping center. The TIC exchanges currency and books rooms. (☎625 600. Open June M-Sa 9:30am-5:30pm; July-Aug. M-Sa 9:30am-5:30pm, Su 9:30am-5:30pm; Mar.-May and Sept.-Oct. M-Sa 9:30am-5pm; Nov.-Feb. M-Sa 10am-4pm.) Other services include: **banks** on English

St.; **police** (☎528 191); **Internet access** at @CyberCafe, 8-10 Devonshire St. (☎512 308; open M-Sa 8am-10pm, Su 10am-10pm; £3 per hr.) and the library, in the Lanes shopping center, across from the TIC (☎607 310; £2 per hr.; open M-F 9:30am-7pm, Sa 9:30am-4pm, Su noon-4pm); and the **post office,** 20-34 Warwick Rd., with a bureau de change (☎512 410; open M-Sa 9am-5:30pm). **Post Code:** CA1 1AB.

⌂ ACCOMMODATIONS AND FOOD. While Carlisle has no hostels, **Old Brewery Residences ❷,** Bridge Ln., offers inexpensive college dormitory accommodations in July and August. (☎597 352. Free wireless Internet. £16, under 18 £11. MC/V.) Running east out of the city, **Warwick Road** and its side streets are scattered with a few **B&Bs.** Top picks include: the relatively large and welcoming **Cornerways Guest House ❷,** 107 Warwick Rd. (☎521 733; www.cornerwaysbandb.co.uk; singles £25-30; doubles £45-55; MC/V); **Langleigh House ❸,** 6 Howard Pl. (☎530 440; all rooms ensuite; singles £25; doubles £47.50; cash only); and the comfortable **Howard Lodge Guest House ❸,** 90 Warwick Rd. (☎529 842; all rooms ensuite; singles £25-30; doubles £40-50; cash only).

The fairground interior of **The Market Hall,** off Scotch St., holds fresh fruit, veggies, and baked goods (open M-Sa 8am-5pm). **Casa Romana ❷,** 44 Warwick Rd., has tasty Italian fare. Entrees start at £3.20 on the happy hour menu (daily until 7pm); big pasta dishes are around £10. (☎591 969. Open M-Sa noon-2pm and 5:30pm-10pm.) **The Lemon Lounge ❺,** 18 Fisher St., has won a following in town with creative cuisine like strawberry and parma ham salad or sea bass with peaches. (☎546 363. 3-course meal with wine £45-50. Open M-Sa noon-3pm and 5-10pm. Call ahead for reservations. AmEx/MC/V.)

☕ NIGHTLIFE. At night, the Botchergate area gets rowdy; **Bar Code,** 17 Botchergate, is a popular stop. (☎530 460. Live DJ F-Sa. Open M-Th 11am-11pm, F-Sa 11am-2am, Su noon-11pm. Food served noon-3pm. Cash only.) Students tend to stay on the far side of the city center; one student favorite is **The Boardroom,** which was once lodging for monks visiting the cathedral. Jukebox tunes and karaoke (Th 8pm) create an upbeat atmosphere. (☎527 695. Open M-Sa 11am-11pm, Su noon-10:30pm. Food served noon-2pm.)

◉ SIGHTS. Built by William II with stones from Hadrian's Wall, **Carlisle Castle** looms in the northwest corner of the city. Mary, Queen of Scots, was once imprisoned here. Hundreds of Scots incarcerated in the dungeons after the 1745 Jacobite rebellion stayed alive by slurping water that collected in the trenches of the dark stone walls. Discover these "licking stones" as you learn about forms of torture used on the Scots. Admission grants access to **Cumbria's Military Museum,** which pays tribute to more modern warriors. (☎591 922. Open daily Apr.-Sept. 9:30am-6pm; Oct.-Mar. 10am-4pm. Guided tours June-Sept. 2 per day. £4. Tours £1.60.) The **Tullie House** museum and gallery on Castle St. has exhibits on the Borders Reivers, ancient Roman tweezers, and a rare 16th-century violin. (☎534 781. Open Apr.-June and Sept.-Oct. M-Sa 10am-5pm, Su noon-5pm; July-Aug. M-Sa 10am-5pm, Su 11am-5pm; Nov.-Mar. M-Sa 10am-4pm, Su noon-4pm. £5.20.)

The **Carlisle Cathedral,** Castle St., founded in 1122, contains some fine 14th-century stained glass and the Brougham Triptych, a beautifully carved Flemish altarpiece. Also noteworthy are the carved wooden misericords, seats used by the clergymen so they could rest while standing at prayer. Sir Walter Scott married his sweetheart on Christmas Eve, 1797, in what is now called the Border Regiment Chapel. (☎548 151. Open M-Sa 7:45am-6:15pm, Su 7:45am-5pm. Evensong M-F 5:30pm. Suggested donation £2.)

ISLE OF MAN ☎ 01624

Nearly every inch of this 33-by-13 mi. islet in the middle of the Irish Sea shows its fierce pride by waving, sporting, even tattooing the wheel-like emblem of independence: the Three Legs of Man. Its accompanying motto, which translates to "Whichever Way You Throw Me I Stand," speaks aptly to the predicament of the island over the last few millennia, during which it's been thrown around quite a bit. Vikings conquered the island in the 9th century, and the English and Scottish began struggling for control in 1266. The English monarchy prevailed and granted dominion over the island to Lord John Stanley in 1405 for a tribute of two falcons a year. Self-government was not restored until 1828.

Today, Man controls its own internal affairs while remaining a crown possession. However compromised its version of independence might be, the Tynwald Court, established by the Vikings, is the longest-running Parliament in the world. It is still called to session each year on July 5th, in a ceremony held completely in Manx (a cousin of Irish and Scottish Gaelic) on Tynwald Hill, site of the original Norse governmental structure. Man takes pride in its unique tailless Manx cats and multi-horned Manx Loghtan sheep, as well as its famed local delicacy, the kipper (herring smoked over oak chips). The island might be best known for its T.T. Races, which draw motorcyclists for a fortnight of adrenaline-junkie festivities.

✈ GETTING THERE

Ronaldsway Airport (☎ 821 600) is 10 mi. southwest of Douglas on the coast road. Buses #1, 1C, 2A, and 2 connect to Douglas (25min., 1-3 per hr.), while others stop at points around the island. Manx Airlines has been purchased by **British Airways** (☎ 0845 773 3377; www.britishairways.com). Flights come from Birmingham, Glasgow, London Gatwick, Manchester, and other airports in Britain. **British European** (☎ 01232 824 354; www.british-european.com) also serves the Isle.

Ferries dock at the **Douglas Sea Terminal.** (Travel shop open M-Sa 6:30am-8pm.) The Isle of Man Steam Packet Company (☎ 661 661 or 08705 523 523; www.steam-packet.com) runs the only ferries to the isle from: Belfast (2¾hr.; Apr.-Oct. 2 per week, usually W and Su); Heysham, Lancashire (3½hr., 2 per day); and Liverpool (2½hr.; Apr.-Oct. 1-4 per day, Nov.-Mar. 3-4 per week). Fares are highest in summer and on weekends (£15-32, children from £9, round-trip £30-64.) Book early on the website for the cheapest fares.

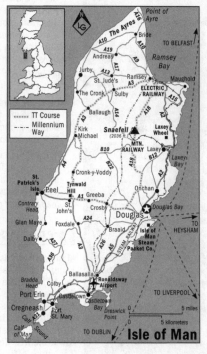

Isle of Man

RUMPIES OR STUMPIES?

Like most visitors, Mother Nature seems to have had just a little more fun on the Isle of Man. Loghtan sheep sprout four coiled horns, summer orchids spring from over 17 natural glens, and local scallops, called "queenies," are eminently tasty.

The Isle's most famed natural asset, however, is the Manx cat—normal but for its pathetic stump of a tail. How the species lost its rearmost appendage is still debated in delightfully erroneous folklore. One story holds that 9th-century Viking invaders planned to decorate their helmets with cat tails; mother cats, knowing (in their infinite feline wisdom) of the plan, bit off the tails of their infant kittens to foil the covetous soldiers. Popular local wisdom points even further in the past to Noah's Ark. One frisky cat nearly missed last call for the ark, and when the vessel's doors began to close his tail was caught in the jamb and lost forever.

Three varieties of the Manx puss exist: "rumpies" are completely tail-less, "stumpies" have the suggestion of a tail-like nub, and "rumpy risers" have a bit of bone or cartilage where the tail should be. Keep an eye peeled for one, or you can visit the Mann Cat Sanctuary, which hosts a few Manx felines.

Ash Villa, Main Rd., Santon. 824 195; www.manncat.com. Open W and Su 2pm-5pm.)

ⓒ LOCAL TRANSPORTATION

The Isle of Man may have more cars per person than anywhere else in the world except Los Angeles, but it also has an extensive system of public transportation, run by **Isle of Man Transport** (☎663 366; www.iombusandrail.info) in Douglas. The **Travel Shop,** on Lord St. next to the bus station, has free bus maps and schedules. (☎662 525. Open M 8am-12:30pm and 1:30-5:45pm, Tu-F 8am-5:45pm, Sa 8am-12:30pm and 1:30-3:30pm.) The Travel Shop and the Douglas TIC sell **Island Explorer tickets,** which provide unlimited travel on most Isle of Man Transport buses and trains, as well as on horse trams (1-day £10, 3-day £20, 5-day £30).

Trains: Isle of Man Railways (☎663 366) runs along the east coast from Port Erin to Ramsey (Easter to Oct.; limited service in winter). The 1874 **Steam Railway** runs from Douglas to Port Erin via Castletown. The 1899 **Electric Railway** runs from Douglas to Ramsey. **Groudle Glen Railway** is a 2 ft. narrow-gauge railway carrying passengers out to Sea Lion Rocks. The **Snaefell Mountain Railway** runs to Snaefell, the island's highest peak (2036 ft.); trains #1 and 2 are the oldest in the world. Stations are marked on the transportation map.

Buses: Frequent buses connect every village. **Douglas** is the hub, with a main station on Lord Street.

Tours: Protours, Summer Hill (☎674 301), buses travelers around for full (£16.50) and half days (£7-8), departing from Douglas W and Su. Office on Central Promenade open 45min. before tour departures.

Bicycling: The island's small size makes it easy to navigate by bike. The southern three-quarters of the Isle are covered in challenging hills—manageable, but worthy of Man's reputation as professional terrain. TICs provide a map of 1-day cycle trails.

🛈 PRACTICAL INFORMATION

Manx currency is equivalent in value to British currency but not accepted outside the Isle; if you use an ATM on the island, make sure to plan for the fact that it will give you all of your bills in Manx currency. Notes and coins from England, Scotland, and Northern Ireland can be used in Man. Manx coins are reissued each year with different and often bizarre designs, which can be viewed at the Treasury office on Bucks Rd. in Douglas. When preparing to leave the island, you can ask for your change in UK tender and usually get it. **Manx**

stamps are also unusual: the eagle-eyed will notice that the Queen's head bears no crown. Post offices and newsstands sell Manx Telecom **phonecards,** but mobile phone users on plans from elsewhere in Britain will likely incur surcharges. The Isle shares Britain's **international dialing code,** ☎44. In an **emergency,** dial ☎999 or 112.

The island-wide **Story of Mann** is a collection of museums and exhibits focused on the island's heritage, including sites in once-capital Castletown, Peel, Ballasalla, and Ramsey. The town of Laxey celebrates the Laxey Wheel, nicknamed Lady Isabella, a 72 ft. sesquicentennial waterwheel (the largest in the world), while Cregneash Folk Village recreates Manx crofting life, and the Manx Museum in Douglas institutionalizes the whole affair. You can save money by purchasing a 4-site **Heritage Pass** (£10), available from any of the museums (☎648 000; www.storyofmann.com).

█ HIKING

In 2004, the first ever **Isle of Man Walking Festival** (☎661 177) brought a five-day walking extravaganza to the island, expected to be repeated in June 2006. Diehards trek 31 mi. and climb 8000 ft. between Ramsey and Port Erin in the **Manx Mountain Marathon,** Britain's longest one-day race, in early April.

Raad ny Foillan ("Road of the Gull") is a 95 mi. path around the island marked with blue seagull signs. The spectacular ◙**Port Erin to Castletown route** (12 mi.) offers the best of the island's south: beaches, cliffs, splashing surf, and wildlife. **Bayr ny Skeddan** ("The Herring Road"), once used by Manx fishermen, covers the less thrilling 14 mi. land route between Peel in the west and Castletown in the east. It overlaps the **Millennium Way,** which runs 28 mi. from Castletown to Ramsey along the 14th-century Royal Highway, ending 1 mi. from Ramsey's Parliament Sq. *Walks on the Isle of Man* (£2.25), available at the TIC, gives a cursory description of 11 long or short walks, and another pamphlet gives tips on reaching numerous glens. Twelve campsites, listed at the TIC, dot the isle.

✿ EVENTS

The island's economy relies heavily on tourism, so frequent festivals celebrate everything from jazz to angling. TICs stock a calendar of events; ask for *What's On the Isle of Man* or check out www.isleofman.com. The first two weeks of June turn Man into a merry motorcycling beast for the **T.T. (Tourist Trophy)**

FROM THE ROAD

THE T.T. AND ME

Setting out for a stroll on the Isle of Man, I was soon distracted by a buzzing sound. As I had been stung by a large bumble bee when I was 5, I became alert. The buzzing was getting louder; maybe a swarm of them was after me. I thought, I hoped, that killer bees were still contained in South America.

Suddenly the buzz grew incredibly loud. I turned my head in a panic. A pack of blurred objects flashed past me on the road. They weren't killer bees, but motorcycles. I was witnessing the Isle's most famed event, the T.T. motorcycle races, a tradition since 1904.

The event (officially called the Manx Grand Prix) has grown dramatically over the years; today over 40,000 enthusiasts come to the Isle to watch in the last week of May and first week of June. On race days most of the Isle's roads close down to create a 37-mile track. Competitors enter in the breakneck singles race or the sidecar competition, in which a second person rides in an attached cab. The treacherous path weaves through small villages, often with stone walls on either side of the road. 180 bikers have been killed since the races began. There were no accidents that I saw, only blurs as the motorcycles reached speeds of more than 180 miles per hour. Next time I'm on the Isle of Man, that might just be me.

—John Arthur Epley

Races (www.iomtt.com). The population doubles, the Steam Packet Co. schedules extra ferries at special rates, and Manx Radio is replaced by "Radio T.T." The races were first held on Man in 1907, because restrictions on vehicle speed were less severe (read: nonexistent) on the island. The circuit consists of 38 mi.of hairpin turns and mountain climbs that top racers navigate at speeds over 120 miles per hour. The winner's name and make of motorcycle are engraved on the same silver "tourist trophy" that has been used since 1907.

Southern "100" Motorcycle Races (☎822 546; July 10-14 in 2006) take place over three days in mid-July, bringing more bikers and general good times to the Isle. July also sees the annual **Manx National Week,** during which new legislation is proclaimed at **Tynwald Fair** (☎685 500). Though this ritual relies on fiercely honored traditions (representatives don wigs and traditional robes), other summer activities are a bit looser in execution. The **World Tin Bath Championships,** a race across the harbor in tin tubs in August, a **Baton Twirling Competition,** also in August, an **International Chess Tournament** in September, and a **Darts Festival** in April invite Manx natives and visitors alike to revel in idiosyncrasy.

DOUGLAS
☎01624

Grand hotels, a buzzing concrete promenade, and a string of teashops and classy venues remind travelers they aren't too far from the mainland. In fact, for such a quirky land, the isle's capital is rather dull, despite its glamorous history as a smuggling and summering hub for much of northwest England. Its buses, trains, ferries, and horse-drawn carts, however, easily shuttle tourists to those attractions only Man can provide, and Douglas acts as a useful gateway from which to explore the Isle's more scenic corners. Most travelers return to Douglas each evening to enjoy its energetic and affordable nightlife.

TRANSPORTATION. Ferries arrive at the Sea Terminal, at the southern end of town, where North Quay and the Promenade converge near the bus station. Isle of Man Transport (☎663 366), on Lord St., runs local trains and buses (see Local Transportation, p. 376). Slow-but-inexpensive horse-drawn **trams** clip-clop down the Promenade between the bus and Electric Railway stations in summer. Stops are posted every 200 yards (☎663 366. Open daily June-Aug. 9:10am-8:50pm; Sept.-May until 6:30pm.) Motorized **buses** (60p) also run along the Promenade, connecting the bus and Steam Railway stations with the Electric Railway. For **taxis,** call 24hr. A-1 Radio Cabs (☎674 488) or Telecabs (☎0800 123). Several **car rental** companies are based in Douglas; try Athol, on Peel Rd. (☎623 232), or Mylchreests (☎823 533), which operates at the Sea Terminal. Eurocycles, 8a Victoria Rd., off Broadway, rents **bikes.** (☎624 909. Call ahead in summer. £12 per day. ID deposit. Open M-Sa 9am-5pm.)

ORIENTATION AND PRACTICAL INFORMATION. Douglas stretches for 2 mi. along the seafront, from **Douglas Head** to the **Electric Railway** terminal. Douglas Head is separated from town by the **River Douglas.** The ferry and bus terminals lie just north of the river. The **Promenade** curves from ferry terminal to the Electric Railway terminal along the beach, dividing the coastline from the shopping district with a line of Victorian row houses. Shops and cafes line the **Strand,** a pedestrian thoroughfare that begins near the bus station and runs parallel to the Promenade, turning into Castle St. before terminating at a taxi queue near the Gaiety Theatre.

The **Tourist Information Centre,** Sea Terminal Building, provides transportation timetables and the worthwhile *What's On* guide. (☎686 766; www.visitisleofman.com. Open Easter to Sept. daily 9:15am-7pm; Oct. to Easter M-F 9:15am-

5:30pm.) Other services include: Lloyds TSB **bank,** 78 Strand St. (☎ 08457 301 280; open M-F 9:30am-4:30pm, Sa 9:30am-12:30pm); Thomas Cook, 7/8A Strand St. (☎ 626 288; open M-W and F-Sa 9am-5:30pm, Th 10am-5:30pm); a **launderette,** 24 Broadway (☎ 621 511; open M, W, F-Sa 8:30am-5pm, Tu 8:30am-4:30pm, Su 11am-4pm; wash £3.50, dry 20p per 4 min.); **police,** Glencrutchery Rd. (☎ 631 212); **Nobles Isle of Man Hospital,** in Bradden (☎ 650 000); **Internet access** at Feegan's Lounge, 8 Victoria St. (☎ 679 280; £1 per 20min.; open M-Sa 9am-6pm, Su 1pm-5pm), the library, 10-12 Victoria St. (☎ 696 461; open M-Sa 9:15am-5:30pm; 75p per 15min., free for students after 4pm), or noisy Leisure Amusement Centre, 68-72 Strand St. (☎ 676 670; open M-Su roughly 9am-9pm); Boots **pharmacy,** 14-22 Strand St. (☎ 616 120; open M-Sa 8:30am-5:30pm, Su 1-4:30pm); and the **post office,** at the corner of Regent St. and The Strand (☎ 686 141; open M and W-F 9am-5:30pm, Tu 9:30am-5:30pm, Sa 9am-12:30pm). **Post Code:** IM1 2EA.

⌂⌂ ACCOMMODATIONS AND FOOD. Douglas is awash with **B&Bs** and **hotels.** For T.T. Races weeks, they fill a year in advance and raise their rates. The **Devonian Hotel ❷,** 4 Sherwood Terr., on Broadway, is a Victorian-style townhouse conveniently located just off the Promenade. Friendly proprietors accommodate those leaving on early ferries. (☎ 674 676.; www.thedevonian.co.uk. All rooms with TVs. Singles £20; doubles £36. Cash only.) Just next door, the unmarked **Athol House Hotel ❸,** 3 Sherwood Terr. on Broadway, features elegant ensuite rooms with classy pine furniture and TV. (☎ 629 356. From £25. Cash only.) The recently refurbished **Glen Mona ❹,** 6 Mona Dr., offers 12 luxurious ensuite rooms with TVs, some with jacuzzis. (☎ 676 755; www.glenmona-iom.co.uk. Singles £40-70; doubles £60-90. MC/V.) **Grandstand Campsite ❶** is behind the T.T. Races' start and finish line. (☎ 696 330. Showers £1. Laundry £2. Reception M-F 9am-5pm. Open mid-June to Sept., closed the last two weeks of Aug. £8.50-10 per person.) TICs list 11 other campsites. During the T.T. fortnight, seven makeshift sites open in football fields and public parks.

Grill and chip shops line **Duke Street, Strand Street,** and **Castle Street,** while many of the hotels along the **Promenade** feature classier restaurants. The Food For Less **grocery** is on Chester St., behind The Strand. (Open M-W and Sa 8am-8pm, Th-F 8am-9pm, Su 9am-6pm.) At the **Bay Room Restaurant ❶,** in the Manx Museum, diners enjoy hot lunches like Manx mutton broth (£4.25) and Manx seafood medley (£7) amidst sculptures from the gallery collection. (☎ 612 211. Open M-Sa 10am-4:30pm. Cash only.) The dining rooms in **Copperfield's Olde Tea Shoppe and Restaurant ❸,** 24 Castle St., strive for historical ambience. Viking Feasts (£6.75-11.95), Edwardian Extravaganzas (£8.95), and Naughty Nancy's Fancies (95p-£3.75) complete the theme. (☎ 613 650. Open in summer M-Sa 11am-6pm; in winter M-Sa 10am-4pm. Cash only.) At **Brendann O'Donnell's ❶,** 16-18 Strand St., Guinness posters and traditional music remind patrons of the Isle's proximity to Ireland. (☎ 621 566. Open M-Th and Su noon-11pm, F-Sa noon-midnight. Cash only.)

◨◫ SIGHTS AND ENTERTAINMENT. From the shopping district, signs point to the Chester St. parking garage next to Food For Less, where an elevator ride to the 8th floor roof leads visitors across a footbridge to the entrance of the **Manx Museum.** Displays include a 20min. film on the history of the island as well as the **Manx National Gallery of Art.** Particularly lively are sections about the island's days as a Victorian holiday mecca, when it was unofficially known as the Isle of Woman due to its attractive seasonal population. The museum also traces the history of Jewish refugees interned on the island during WWII and displays many Celtic artifacts from the Isle's early years. (☎ 648 000. Open M-Sa 10am-5pm. Free.) Past the

Villa Marina Gardens on Harris Promenade sits the **Gaiety Theatre,** designed in 1900 and recently restored to something like its former glory. Take a 1½hr. tour to see a Victorian trap system under the stage and other antique machinery. (☎694 555. The box office, three doors down from the theater, inside the theater office, is open M-Sa 10am-4:30pm; the box office inside the theater opens 1hr. before curtain. Tours Apr.-Sept. Sa 10:15am. Tickets £10-20, concessions available. Tours £6, children £3.) The distant, sandcastle-like structure in Douglas Bay is the **Tower of Refuge,** built as a hope for shipwreck survivors, but closed to the general public.

Pubs on the island are numerous and grow boisterous, especially during the T.T. fortnight. At **Quids Inn,** on the Promenade, once you insert £1 into the subway-like turnstile, almost all of your drinks will cost £1. Some of the **clubs** in Douglas are 21+ and some are free until 10 or 11pm, with a £2-5 cover thereafter. Put in a long day (and night) at **The Office,** off the Promenade by Castle Mona, which has a small dance floor and an ample bar. (☎610 763. Open M-Th and Su noon-midnight, F-Sa noon-1am. Food served noon-8pm.) **Paramount City,** Queen's Promenade, houses two nightclubs: the Director's Bar plays favorites from the 50s to the 90s, while the Dark Room pumps chart and dance. (☎622 447. Open F-Sa 10pm-3:30am.)

▶ DAYTRIP FROM DOUGLAS

The oldest village on the island, Cregneash is worth a daytrip from Douglas or Peel, and is a beautiful 1½-4hr. walk from Port Erin. It is known for the open-air **Cregneash Village Folk Museum,** which has carefully preserved (and partially recreated) a traditional Manx crofting town with thatched-roof cottages and live demonstrations of blacksmithing and wool dying. Visitors pick their way between roosters as they wander between buildings like the **Karran Farm,** where old women work on gorgeous silk patchwork as they cook rice pudding over a fire. *(Bus #1 runs to Cregneash from Douglas (1¼hr., M-Sa 2 per day) and Port Erin (20min., M-Sa 5 per day).* ☎648 000. Open daily Apr.-Oct. 10am-5pm. £3, children £1.50).

PEEL   ☎01624

Long ago, this "cradle of Manx heritage" played host to the Vikings, whose Nordic pedigree lives on still in Manx blood. The Quayside maintains a rough-and-tumble sailor's edge, while ▓ruins across the harbor loom dark against western sunsets. The most prominent of these relics are the stone towers of **Peel Castle,** which share the skyline of **St. Patrick's Isle** with the stone arches of **St. German's Cathedral** and the excavated tomb of a well-to-do Viking woman nicknamed "The Pagan Lady." The audio tour, included in the admission price, informs visitors about the history and significance of the various ruins, which are located on a scenic cliff overlooking the village of Peel. The site is reached by a pedestrian causeway from the Quay. (Open Easter to Oct. daily 10am-5pm. Last admission 1hr. before close. £3.) Across the harbor on the Quay, the comprehensive **House of Manannan** showcases a panorama of audiovisual displays that usher visitors from a fire-lit Celtic roundhouse to a 30-foot Viking war ship shored on a recreated indoor beach, culminating at a (fake) blood-splattered fish-gutting table. (☎648 000. Open daily 10am-5pm. Last admission 3:30pm. £5.) **Moore's Traditional Curers,** Mill Rd., is purportedly the only kipper factory of its kind left in the world. Informal tours let visitors watch kippering in action and even climb up the interior of one of the massive smoking chimneys. You can also sample a fresh kipper sandwich in their shop. (☎843 622; www.manxkippers.com. Shop open M-Sa 10am-5pm. Tours Apr.-Oct. M-Sa 3:30pm. £2, children £1.) Just down the Quay, the **Leece Museum** exhibits relics from Peel's past. Downstairs is the site of the "Black Hole" prison cell, which now only locks up unfortunate wax figures. (☎845 366. Open Oct. to Easter Tu-Sa noon-4pm; Easter to Sept. W-Su 10am-4pm. Free.) Outside of Peel at Ballacraine Farm, **Ballacraine Quad Bike Trails** leads 1½hr. trail rides, including training and refreshments. (☎801 219. £40 per person.)

The **Peel Camping Park ❶**, Derby Rd., is run through the local Town Hall office and has laundry facilities and showers. (☎842 341. Open Easter to Sept. £4 per person.) Shoprite **grocery**, 13 Michael St., is in the center of town. (Open M-Sa 8:30am-8pm, Su 10am-6pm.) The **Harbour Lights Cafe and Tearoom ❷**, Shore Rd. on the Promenade, offers Manx kipper teas—tea, kippers, bread, and teacake. (☎495 197. Kipper tea £7. 3-course supper £25. Lighter lunch options also available. Open Tu-Su 10am-5pm. Cash only.) "Often licked but never beaten," **Davison's Manx Dairy Ice Cream ❶**, on Shore Rd. next to the tea room, boasts a huge flavor selection, including Turkish Delight and butterscotch honeycomb. (☎844 761. Open daily Apr.-Sept. 10am-9pm; Oct.-Mar. 10am-5pm. Cash only.)

Buses (☎662 525) arrive and depart across the street from the Town Hall on Derby Rd., coming from Douglas (#4, 4B, 5A, 6, 6B, X5; 35min.; M-Sa 1-2 per hr., Su 11 per day; £2.80) and Port Erin (#8, 55min., M-Sa 3 per day, £3). The **TIC** is a window in the Town Hall, Derby Rd. (☎842 341. Open M-Th 8:45am-4:45pm, F 8:45am-4:30pm.) The **post office** is on Douglas St. (☎842 282. Open M-F 9am-12:30pm and 1:30-5:30pm, Sa 9am-12:30pm.) **Post Code:** IM5 1AA.

PORT ERIN   ☎01624

A quiet city set in a spectacular locale, Port Erin's beauty is all natural. A number of hikes start from the town of Port Erin itself. One of the nicest is the 30min. trail out to **Bradda Head**, which hugs the bay before giving way to a rocky uphill scramble. At the top of the hill, climbers arrive at **Milner's Tower**, a curious structure designed to look like a key. Views of the sea and nearby Calf of Man compensate for the climb up the dimly lit spiral staircase. The trail begins at the Bradda Glen gates off the Promenade, or from the carpark 100 yards down the road. The **Coronation Footpath**, which begins from the same spots, offers a gentler ascent. Trips to the **Calf of Man** depart daily from Port Erin pier. (☎832 339 or 496 793. Trips depart daily 10:15, 11:30am, 1:45pm in summer, weather permitting; fewer during low season. Book ahead.)

Anchorage Guest House ❸, Athol Park, has superb the views of the town. (☎832 355; www.anchorageguesthouse.com. Open Feb.-Nov. £22.50-26 per person. AmEx/MC/V.) Returning hikers can treat themselves at **Graingers at Bradda Glen ❸**, at the end of Bradda Close. This cliffside cottage offers local seafood and vegetarian specials. (☎833 166. Open M-Sa 11am-4pm and 5:30-8pm, Su noon-4pm. Entrees from £9. Cash only.) In town, try **Shore Cafe ❶**, Shore Rd., which offers hearty sandwiches from £2.25 and freshly baked sweets; an ice cream bar is adjacent. Port Erin is easily accessible as a daytrip from Douglas or Peel. **Buses** #1 and X2 run to Port Erin from **Douglas** (50min., 2 per hr.) and two per day continue all the way to **Cregneash**. Hiking pamphlets are available from the **Tourist Information Centre**, on Station Rd. (☎832 298). The **post office** is at 8 Church Rd. (Open M-F 9:30am-12:30pm and 1:30-5:30pm.)

NORTHEAST ENGLAND

Framed by Scotland and the North Sea, this corner of England has always been border country. Hadrian's Wall marks a history of skirmishes with fierce northern neighbors, and the area's three national parks, some of the most remote countryside in England, retain their frontier ruggedness. No trail tests hikers like the Pennine Way, Britain's first and longest official long-distance path. The isolation of the northeast testifies to its agricultural bent; even the main industry (textile manufacturing) sprang from the abundance of sheep. But while the principal urban areas of Yorkshire and Tyne and Wear grew out of the wool and coal industries and bear their scars, today the refurbished city centers welcome visitors.

HIGHLIGHTS OF NORTHEAST ENGLAND

GAWK at York's colossal Gothic cathedral, which contains the largest medieval glass window in the world (p. 388).

SAMPLE the the nightlife and the famed brown ale of Newcastle, home to crowded dance floors, lively locals, and legendary nightlife (p. 417).

ADMIRE the remains of Hadrian's Wall, which once delineated the northernmost border of the Roman Empire (p. 429).

YORKSHIRE

SHEFFIELD ☎ 0114

While Manchester was clothing the world, Sheffield (pop. 550,000) was setting its table, first with hand-crafted flatware, and eventually stainless steel (invented here). As 20th-century industry moved elsewhere, economic depression, made familiar by *The Full Monty*, set in. Today, Sheffield is ambitiously attempting an urban transformation, billing itself as a revitalized cultural and commercial center. Sheffield is the last bastion of urbanity and nightlife before the Peak District.

⚏🛈 TRANSPORTATION AND PRACTICAL INFORMATION. Sheffield lies on the M1 motorway, about 30 mi. east of Manchester and 25 mi. south of Leeds. **Midland Station** is on Sheaf St., near Sheaf Sq. **Trains** (☎ 08457 484 950) arrive from Birmingham (1¼hr., 2 per hr., £21), London St. Pancras (2¼hr., every hr., £48), Manchester (1hr., 2 per hr., £11.40), and York (1hr., 2 per hr., £12.20). The major **bus station** in town is the **Interchange,** between Pond St. and Sheaf St. (☎ 275 4905. Lockers £1-2. Open M-F 8am-5:30pm.) National Express (☎ 08705 808 080) **buses** travel from: Birmingham (2½hr., 6 per day, £14.50); London (4hr., 8 per day, £14.50); Nottingham (1½-2hr., 9 per day., £5.75). The **Supertram** covers the city. (☎ 272 8282; www.supertram.com. Daily pass £2.50, weekly £8.)

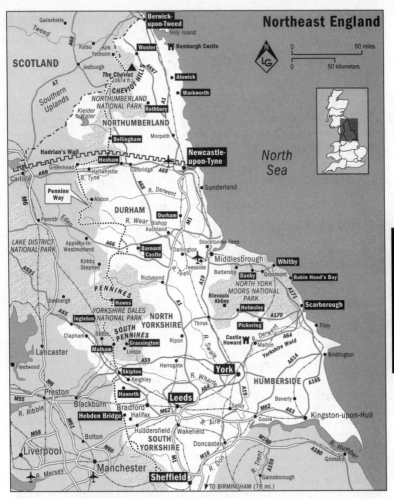

Sheffield's **Tourist Information Centre,** 1 Tudor Sq., off Surrey St., distributes the free *Visit Sheffield* brochure. (☎221 1900, bookings 08707 000 121; www.sheffieldtourism.co.uk. Open M-Sa 10am-1pm and 2:15-4pm.) Other services include: **banks** on Pinstone St., Fargate, and Church St.; **Thomas Cook,** 119 Pinstone St. (☎260 7600; open M-W and F-Sa 9am-5:30pm, Th 10am-5:30pm); **police,** West Bar Green (☎220 2020); Northern General **hospital,** Herries Rd. (☎243 4343); **Internet access** with free wireless at Matrix, 4 Charter Sq. (☎275 4100; £1.50 per 30min.; open M-Sa noon-10pm), wireless at the Showroom (see below), and at **Central Library,** Surrey St. (☎273 4727; free; open M 10am-8pm, Tu and Th-Sa 9:30am-5:30pm, W 9:30am-8pm); and the **post office,** 9 Norfolk Row (☎281 4713; open M-Tu and Th-F 8:30am-5:30pm, W 9am-5:30pm, Sa 8:30am-3pm). **Post Code:** S1 2PA.

Sheffield

🏠 ACCOMMODATIONS
Rutland Arms, 4
York Villa, 7

🍎 FOOD
Blue Moon Cafe, 1
Showroom Cafe-Bar, 3

⭐ CLUBS
The Casbah, 4
The Leadmill, 6
Gatecrasher One, 5

▌▐ ACCOMMODATIONS AND FOOD. Budget accommodations are scarce in Sheffield. If you don't mind the 30min. commute by train, try the **YHA hostel** in **Hathersage** (p. 356). **B&Bs** in Sheffield cost at least £19 per night. **York Villa ❷**, 63 Norfolk Rd., keeps guests in elegant floral rooms in a manse only 5min. from the train station. (☎272 4566. Singles £19; doubles £30. Cash only.) **Rutland Arms ❸**, 86 Brown St., near the train and bus stations, offers tidy rooms above a lively pub. (☎272 9003. Singles £21; doubles £30; twins £32; family room £42. AmEx/MC/V.)

Cheap eats in the city center are hard to come by; head for the student haunts on **Ecclesall Road** or the cafe-bars on **Division Street** and **Devonshire Street.** The Spar **supermarket** is at the intersection of Division St. and Backfields Alley. (☎275 2900. Open 24hr.) The minimalist **Showroom Cafe-Bar ❷**, 7 Paternoster Row, draws a trendy, wine-sipping crowd. Lounge on the couch over great chicken dishes, burgers, and stir-fry (£6.50-12) before watching films next door. (☎249 5479; www.showroom.org.uk. Film ticket, entree, and wine £14.50. Open M-W 11am-11pm, Th 11am-1am, F-Sa 11am-2am, Su 11am-10:30pm. Food served until 9pm. MC/V.) **Blue Moon Cafe ❶**, 2 St. James St., 3 blocks up the hill from Castle Sq., after the Cathedral Church of St. Peter and St. Paul, offers a selection of veggie entrees from £5.40. (☎276 3443. Takeaway available. Open M-Sa 8am-8pm. AmEx/MC/V.)

⬛ SIGHTS. The opening of the ⬛**Millennium Galleries,** Arundel Gate, linked to Tudor Sq. by the impressive indoor **Winter Garden,** has brought vitality to Sheffield's arts scene. Two of the galleries host small national and international exhibitions. The excellent **Ruskin Gallery** was established in 1875 by Victorian critic John Ruskin, who intended to show that "life without industry is guilt, and industry without art is brutality." A gallery celebrates metalwork; stifle that groan of boredom and take a closer look. (☎278 2600; www.sheffieldgalleries.org.uk. Open M-Sa 10am-5pm, Su 11am-5pm. Free. Special exhibits usually £4, concessions £3.) The ⬛**Graves Gallery,** on Surrey St. above the public library, displays post-war British art, Romantic and Impressionist paintings, and traveling exhibits. (☎278 2600. Open M-Sa 10am-5pm. Free.) The **Site Gallery,** 1 Brown St., showcases contemporary works of media art and photography. (☎281 2077. Open Tu-F and Su 11am-6pm, Sa 11am-5:30pm. Free.) The **Kelham Island Industrial Museum,** Alma St., studies Sheffield's industrial movement. Take bus #53 from the Interchange to Nursery St., turn left on Corporation St., right on Alma St., and wind 200 yards through an industrial park. (☎272 2106; www.simt.co.uk. Open M-Th 10am-4pm, Su 11am-4:45pm. Last admission 1hr. before close. £3.50, concessions £2.50.)

⬛⬛ NIGHTLIFE AND ENTERTAINMENT. Most clubs are in the southeastern section of the city, around **Matilda Street;** *Visit Sheffield* has current nightlife listings. **The Leadmill,** 6 Leadmill Rd., plays to almost every taste in three student-packed rooms. (☎221 2828. Cover £2-5. Open M-F 10pm-2am, Sa 10pm-2:30am.) **The Casbah,** 1 Wellington St., at the corner of Cambridge St., has live bands throughout the week, while the DJ and bar upstairs are open on weekends. (☎275 6077. Cover £2-5. Open M-Sa 8pm-2am.) **Gatecrasher One,** 112 Arundel St., hosts Sheffield's largest party on Saturdays. (☎276 6777. Cover M and Th £2-3, F £3-5, Sa £10-15 after 10:30pm. Open M and Th-F 10pm-2am, Sa 10pm-6am.) For nightlife without a hangover, visit the **Crucible** and **Lyceum Theatres,** both in Tudor Sq. with a shared box office on 55 Norfolk St. Staging musicals, plays, and dance shows, they comprise the largest theater complex in England outside London. (☎249 6000. £10-36, same-day tickets £7.50.)

YORK ☎01904

With a pace suitable for ambling and its tallest building a cathedral, England's York bears little resemblance to the new American version. In AD 71, the Romans founded Eboracum as a military and administrative base; the town remained important as Anglo-Saxon "Eoforwic" and Viking "Jorvik." York's history of murder, massacre, and mass-suicide has prompted the title of "most haunted city in the world." Tourists brandishing zoom lenses come in search of the ample remnants of York's history, from a mammoth cathedral to tiny medieval alleyways—and York manages to put itself on display without sacrificing authenticity.

▐ TRANSPORTATION

Trains: York Station, Station Rd. Luggage storage £4 per item; open daily 8am-8:30pm. Travel center open M-Sa 8am-7:45pm, Su 9am-7:45pm. Ticket office (tickets sold for same-day travel only) open M-F 5:30am-10:15pm, Sa 5:45am-9:40pm, Su 7:30am-9:40pm. Trains (☎08457 484 950) from: **Edinburgh** (2½hr., 2 per hr., £59.50); **London King's Cross** (2hr., 2 per hr., £68.30); **Manchester Piccadilly** (1½hr., 2 per hr., £17.10-21.10); **Newcastle** (1hr., 4 per hr., £19-28); **Scarborough** (45min., every hr., £13.70-14.90).

Buses: Stations at 20 Rougier St., Exhibition Sq., the train station, and on Piccadilly. Major bus stop along The Stonebow. (Information ☎551 400.) National Express (☎08705 808 080) from **Edinburgh** (5½hr., daily 10:55am, £29), **London** (5hr., 4 per day, £23), and **Manchester** (3hr., daily 5pm, £7.90).

Public Transportation: First York (☎ 622 992, timetables 551 400) has a ticket office at 20 Rougier St. Open M-F 9am-5pm. **Yorkshire Coastliner** (☎ 0113 244 8976 or 01653 692 556; www.coastliner.co.uk) runs buses from the train station to **Castle Howard** (p. 391) and other towns toward the coast. Timetables available at TICs.

Taxis: Station Taxis (☎ 623 332). 24hr. Wheelchair-accessible service available with advance booking.

Bike Rental: Bob Trotter, 13 Lord Mayor's Walk (☎ 622 868). From £10 per day. £50 deposit. Open M-W and F-Sa 9am-5:30pm, Th 9:30am-5:30pm, Su 10am-4pm.

✦ 🛈 ORIENTATION AND PRACTICAL INFORMATION

York's streets are winding, short, rarely labeled, and prone to name changes. Fortunately, most attractions lie within the **city walls,** so you can't get too lost, and the towers of the **Minster,** visible from nearly everywhere, provide easy orientation. The **River Ouse** (rhymes with "muse") cuts through the city, curving west to south. The city center lies between the Ouse and the Minster; **Coney Street, Parliament Street,** and **Stonegate** are the main thoroughfares. The **Shambles,** York's quasi-medieval shopping district, lies between Parliament St. and Colliergate.

Tourist Information Centre: Exhibition Sq. (☎ 621 756; www.visityork.org). Books rooms for a £4 charge plus a 10% deposit. *The York Visitor Guide* (£1) has a detailed map. Also sells *Snickelways of York* (£6), a handwritten booklet of walks through York's alleyways. Open Apr.-Oct. M-Sa 9am-6pm, Su 10am-5pm; Nov.-May M-Sa 9am-5pm, Su 10am-4pm. Branch in the train station. Open Easter to Oct. M-Sa 9am-6pm, Su 10am-5pm; Nov. to Easter M-Sa 9am-5pm, Su 10am-4pm.

Tours: A free 2hr. **walking tour** is offered by the Association of Voluntary Guides (☎ 630 284). Tours depart in summer 10:15am, 2:15, and 6:45pm; in winter 10:15am. Meet in front of the York City Art Gallery. The 1¼hr. **Ghost Hunt of York** (☎ 608 700) meets at the Shambles daily at 7:30pm. £4. **Guide Friday/City Sightseeing** (☎ 655 585) leads hop-on, hop-off bus tours. £8, concessions £6. Several companies along the **River Ouse** near Lendal, Ouse, and Skeldergate Bridges offer 1hr. **boat cruises,** including **YorkBoat,** Lendal Bridge (☎ 628 324). Office open M-F 9am-5:30pm. At least 4 trips per day; call ahead. £6.50.

Financial Services: Banks abound on Parliament St. and Coney St. **Thomas Cook,** 4 Nessgate (☎ 881 400). Open M, W, and F-Sa 9am-5:30pm, Tu 10am-5:30pm.

Pharmacy: Boots, 48 Coney St. (☎ 653-657). Open M-W and F-Sa 8:30am-6pm, Th 8:30am-7pm.

Police: Fulford Rd. (☎ 631 321).

Hospital: York District Hospital (☎ 631 313), off Wigginton Rd. Take bus #1 or 18 from Exhibition Sq. and ask for the hospital stop.

Internet Access: Cafe of the Evil Eye, 42 Stonegate (☎ 640 002). Wireless also available. £2 per hr. Open M-Sa 10am-11pm, Su 11am-10:30pm. **York Central Library,** Museum St. (☎ 655 631), has 25 Internet terminals, free to members for 2hr. per day (anyone can apply for membership with 2 forms of ID; one ID must have an address); otherwise £2 per hr. Booking is open to members and is advisable. Open M-W and F 9am-8pm, Th 9am-5:30pm, Sa 9am-4pm.

Post Office: 22 Lendal St. (☎ 0845 722 3344) with a **bureau de change.** Open M-Sa 9am-5:30pm. **Post Code:** YO1 8DA.

ACCOMMODATIONS

B&Bs (from £18) are concentrated on the side streets along **Bootham** and **Clifton**, in the Mount area down **Blossom Street**, and on **Bishopthorpe Road**, south of town. Most offer vegetarian breakfast options. Book weeks ahead in summer, when competition for inexpensive beds is fierce; the TICs can help.

York Backpackers, 88-90 Micklegate (☎627 720; www.yorkbackpackers.co.uk). Backpackers, school trips, and tourists converge in this 18th-century mansion. Kitchen, laundry (£3 per load), and TV lounge. "Dungeon Bar" open 5 nights per week, always F-Sa, until late. Continental breakfast included. Ask about working in exchange for accommodation. Large dorms £13-14; doubles £35. MC/V. ❷

Foss Bank Guest House, 16 Huntington Rd. (☎635 548). Walk or take bus #13 from the train station; 200 yards up Huntington Rd. Offers comfortable beds in clean rooms just a 5min. walk from the city walls. Spacious rooms with shower and sink. Doubles are particularly swanky. No smoking. Singles £27; doubles £48, ensuite £56. Cash only. ❸

York Youth Hotel, 11-13 Bishophill Senior (☎625 904; www.yorkyouthhotel.com). Well-located hostel catering primarily to groups. Laundry and Internet. Key deposit £3. Reception 24hr. No smoking. Dorms £12; singles £25; twins £38. AmEx/MC/V. ❷

YHA York International, Water End (☎653 147), Clifton, 2 mi. from train station. From the train station, follow the river path "Dame Judi Dench" (connects to Water End). TV lounge, giant Connect-4 game set, and kitchen. 150 beds. Breakfast included. Bike rental from £1.50 per hr. Reserve in advance in summer. Dorms £18, under 18 £13; singles £25; doubles £45. £3 discount for students and single parents. MC/V. ❷

Camping: Riverside Caravan and Camping Park, Ferry Ln. (☎705 812), Bishopthorpe, 2 mi. south of York off the A64. Take bus #11 or 11Y (2 per hr., round-trip £1.20), and ask to be let off at the campsite. July-Aug. and early Sept. £11 per 2-person tent and 1 car; Apr.-June and mid-Sept. to Oct. £10 per 2-person tent. Cash only. ❶

FOOD AND PUBS

Greengrocers peddle at **Newgate Market,** between Parliament St. and the Shambles. (Open Apr.-Dec. M-Sa 9am-5pm, Su 9am-4:30pm; Jan.-Mar. M-Sa 9am-5pm.) There are more pubs in the center of York than gargoyles on the Minster's east wall. Find cheap eats at the many Indian restaurants lying just outside the city gates. **Groceries** available at Sainsbury's, at the intersection of Foss Bank and Heworth Green. (☎643 801. Open M-Sa 8am-8pm, Su 11am-5pm.)

Oscar's Wine Bar and Bistro, 8 Little Stonegate (☎652 002), off Stonegate. Find huge portions of tasty grub (£6-8), like cajun chicken, lasagna, and a spicy bean burger, in a historic pub with a lively, ivy-covered courtyard. Happy hour M 4-11pm, Tu-F 5-7pm, Su 4-10:30pm. Open M-Sa 11:30am-11pm, Su noon-10:30pm. MC/V. ❷

The Fudge Kitchen, 58 Low Petergate (☎645 596). Over 20 flavors of gooey fudge, from Vintage Vanilla to Banoffee (slices £3.50-4), are made before your eyes by chefs in traditional dress. Free samples. Open M-Sa 10am-6pm, Su 10am-5:30pm. MC/V. ❶

El Piano, 15 Grape Ln. (☎610 676). Hispanic flavors infuse veggie dishes in this laid-back, colorful establishment in a corner of the city center. Dishes served in 3 sizes: chica £2.45, tapas £4, entree £6. Also serves breakfast. Open M-Sa 10am-midnight, Su noon-5pm. MC/V. ❷

Victor J's Artbar, 1 Finklestreet (541 771; www.vjsartbar.com). A casual, colorful bistro with a convenient location, VJ's serves huge portions of tasty sandwiches (brie, roasted veggies, and pesto ciabatta £6) and burgers (£5-6) that will please your belly and your budget. Open M-Sa 10am-11pm, Su 11am-7pm. MC/V. ❷

👁 SIGHTS

The best introduction to York is a walk along its **medieval walls** (2½ mi.), especially the northeast section and behind the cathedral. The walls are accessible up stairways by the gates. Beware the tourist stampede, which only wanes in early morning and just before the walls close at dusk.

⬛ YORK MINSTER

☎ *557 216 639 347; www.yorkminster.org. Open daily 7:30am-6:30pm. Evensong M-Sa 5pm, Su 4pm. Free 1hr. guided tours leave near the entrance every 30min., daily 9:30am-3:30pm. £5, concessions £3.50. Combined ticket with Undercroft £7, concessions £5.*

Tourists, priests, and worshippers converge at the Minster, the largest Gothic cathedral in cubic footage this side of Italy (where they don't even measure things in feet). The cathedral displays an estimated half of all the medieval stained glass in England. The 15th-century **Great East Window,** which depicts the beginning and end of the world in more than a hundred small scenes, is the world's largest medieval stained-glass window. Look for the statue of Archbishop Lamplugn toward the East Window—he has two right feet. The main chamber of the vast church, with its ornate stained glass windows and domed ceilings, is generally mobbed by tourists, but the tombs and stonework are less appreciated and equally impressive.

CHAPTER HOUSE AND LIBRARY. If you fancy something a bit less holy, turn to the Chapter House's grotesque medieval carvings. Every figure is unique, from mischievous demons to a three-faced woman. Keep an eye out for the tiny Virgin Mary on the right upon entering, so small she went unnoticed by Cromwell's idol-smashing thugs. **Minster Library** was designed by Christopher Wren. *(Chapter House open daily 9am-6pm. Library open M-Th 9am-5pm, F 9am-noon. Both free.)*

CENTRAL TOWER. It's a mere 275 steps up to the top of the tower, but ascents are only allowed during a 5min. period every 30min. because the narrow staircase won't allow passing traffic. *(Open daily 9:30am-5pm. £2.50.)*

UNDERCROFT, TREASURY, AND CRYPT. Displays narrate how the foundation of the Minster's central tower began to crack in 1967. Visitors can tour the huge concrete and steel foundations inserted by engineers and remnants of the previously unearthed buildings. Explore the remains of the Roman legionary headquarters on the **Roman level,** including the site where Constantine was proclaimed emperor. Duck into the **crypt,** not a crypt at all but the altar of the Saxon-Norman church, with a shrine of **St. William of York** and the 12th-century **Doomstone** upon which the cathedral was built. The **treasury** displays the material wealth of the old archbishops, including Yorkshire silver vessels and the Horn of Ulph. Those not paying the entrance fee can have a look inside the crypt through the gate in the East Wing. *(Open daily 9:30am-5pm. £3.50, concessions £3. 45min. audio tour included.)*

OTHER SIGHTS

⬛ **YORK CASTLE MUSEUM.** Housed in a former debtor's prison, the huge York Castle Museum lives up to its billing as Britain's premier museum of everyday life. The comprehensive exhibits were the brainchild of the eccentric Dr. John Kirk, who began collecting household items—from Victorian wedding dresses to old-fashioned hard candies to antique vacuum cleaners—during his house calls from the 1890s to the 1920s. The many themed rooms include **Kirkgate,** an intricately

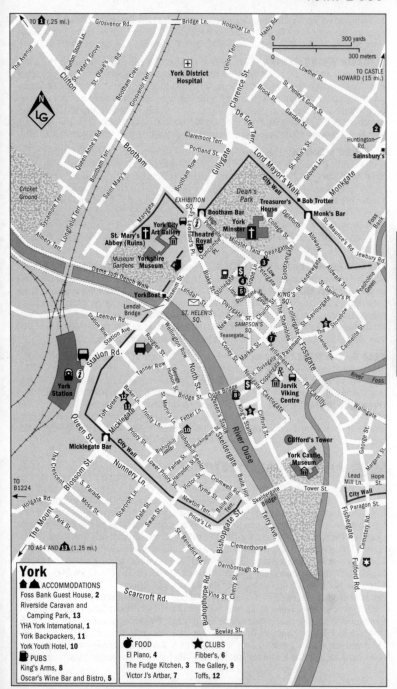

TO ▲1 (.25 mi.)
Grosvenor Rd.
Bridge Ln.
Hospital Ln.
Haxby Rd.

The Avenue
Burton Stone Ln.
St. Peter's Grove
St. Olave's Rd.
Bootham Cres.
Grosvenor Terr.
Union Terr.
Clarence St.
Lowther St.
St. Penley's Grove St.
Brook St.
Garden St.

N
LG

York District Hospital

TO CASTLE
HOWARD (15 mi.)

300 yards
300 meters

Queen Anne's Rd.
Bootham Terr.
Saint Mary's
Bootham
Claremont Terr.
Portland St.
Bootham Row
De Grey Terr.
Gillygate
Lord Mayor's Walk
St. John's St.
Groves Ln.
Monkgate

2 Huntington Rd.
Sainsbury's

Cricket Ground

Sycamore Terr.
Longfield Terr.
Almery Terr.
Dame Judi Dench Walk

EXHIBITION SQ.
Marygate
York City Art Gallery
St. Mary's Abbey (Ruins)
Museum Gardens
Yorkshire Museum

Dean's Park
City Wall
Treasurer's House
Bob Trotter
Monk's Bar

Bootham Bar
York Minster
Ogleforth
College St.
Minster Yard
Deangate
Low Petergate
Goodramgate
St. Maurice's Rd.
Jewbury Rd.
Aldwark
St. Saviour's Pl.
Peasholme Green
Foss Bank

Theatre Royal
High Petergate
Blake St.
Stonegate
Davygate
Swinegate
Church St.
St. Andrewgate
St. Saviour's St.

YorkBoat
Lendal Bridge
Museum St.
Lendal
ST. HELEN'S SQ.
New St.
Coney St.
SAMPSON'S SQ.
Feasegate
Market St.
Parliament St.
The Shambles
KING'S SQ.
Colliergate
Fossgate
6 Stonebow
The Garden Terr.
Carmelite St.

Leeman Rd.
Station Rise
Station Ave.
Station Rd.
Tanner Row
Rougier St.
Wellington Row
George Hudson St.
North St.
Bridge St.
Ouse Bridge
Queen's Staith
King's Staith
Nessgate
Coppergate
Castlegate
Jorvik Viking Centre
Piccadilly
River Foss
Walmgate

York Station

Toft Green
Barker Ln.
Micklegate
St. Martin's Ln.
Trinity Ln.
Priory St.
Fetter Ln.
Bishophill Junior
Bishophill Senior
Buckingham St.
Clifford St.
Clifford's Tower
York Castle Museum
George St.
Margaret St.
Hope St.

TO
B1224
The Crescent
Blossom St.
Micklegate Bar
City Wall
Nunnery Ln.
Fairfax St.
Lower Priory St.
Hampden St.
Victor St.
Kyme St.
Cromwell Rd.
Skeldergate
River Ouse
Baile Hill Terr.
Skeldergate Bridge
Lead Mill Ln.
City Wall
Tower St.
Paragon St.

TO
The Mount
Holgate Rd.
S. Parade
Park St.
Moss St.
Scarcroft Ln.
Dale St.
Swan St.
St. Benedict's Rd.
Newton Terr.
Price's Ln.
Baile Hill
Clementhorpe
Terry Ave.
Fishergate
Paragon St.
Cemetery Rd.
Fulford Rd.

TO A64 AND ▲13 (1.25 mi.)
Scarcroft Rd.
Bishopthorpe Rd.
Darnborough St.
Vine St.
Cherry St.
Bewlay St.

York

▲▲ ACCOMMODATIONS
Foss Bank Guest House, 2
Riverside Caravan and
  Camping Park, 13
YHA York International, 1
York Backpackers, 11
York Youth Hotel, 10

🍺 PUBS
King's Arms, 8
Oscar's Wine Bar and Bistro, 5

🍎 FOOD
El Piano, 4
The Fudge Kitchen, 3
Victor J's Artbar, 7

★ CLUBS
Fibber's, 6
The Gallery, 9
Toffs, 12

reconstructed Victorian shopping street, and **Half Moon Court,** its Edwardian counterpart. *(Between Tower St. and Piccadilly. ☎ 650 335. Open mid-July to August daily 9:30am-5pm; Sept. to mid-July M-Th and Sa-Su 9:30am-5pm, F 10am-5pm. £6, concessions £4.50.)*

■ **JORVIK VIKING CENTRE.** This is one of the busiest attractions in the city; arrive early or late to avoid lines, or book at least a day ahead, especially in summer. Visitors ride through the York of AD 948 in floating "time cars," past artifacts, painfully accurate smells, and animatronic mannequins. Built atop a major archaeological site, the museum contains unusually well-preserved Viking artifacts. *(Coppergate. ☎ 643 211, advance bookings 543 403; www.vikingjorvik.com. Open daily Apr.-Oct. 9am-6pm; Nov.-Mar. 10am-5pm. Last admission 1hr. before close. £7.45, concessions £6.30.)*

CLIFFORD'S TOWER. This tower is one of the last remaining pieces of York Castle and a chilling reminder of one of the worst outbreaks of anti-Jewish violence in English history. In 1190, Christian merchants tried to erase their debts to Jewish bankers by annihilating York's Jewish community. On the last Sabbath before Passover, 150 Jews took refuge in a tower that previously stood on this site and, faced with the prospect of starvation or butchery, committed suicide. Those who did not were massacred. The present tower also provides long views towards the Minster. *(Tower St. ☎ 646 940. Open daily Apr.-Sept. 10am-6pm, Oct. 10am-5pm, Nov.-Mar. 10am-4pm. £2.80, concessions £2.10.)*

YORKSHIRE MUSEUM AND GARDENS. Hidden in 10 gorgeous acres of gardens, the Yorkshire Museum presents Roman, Anglo-Saxon, and Viking artifacts, as well as the priceless **Middleham Jewel** (c. 1450), an enormous sapphire set in a gold amulet engraved with the Trinity and the Nativity. In the gardens, children chase pigeons among the ruins of **St. Mary's Abbey,** once the most influential Benedictine monastery in northern England. *(Enter from Museum St. or Marygate. ☎ 687 687. Open daily 10am-5pm. £4, concessions £3, families £11. Gardens and ruins free.)*

BEST OF THE REST. The **York City Art Gallery,** Exhibition Sq., across from the TIC, shows continental work, a better selection of English painters (including William Etty, York native and pioneer of the English painted nude), and a spattering of pottery. *(☎ 551 861. Open daily 10am-5pm; last admission 4:30pm. £2, concessions £1.50.)* The **Treasurer's House,** Chapter House St. next to the Minster, built on the site of the Minster's treasurer's residence, holds the collection of antique furnishings amassed by Edwardian connoisseur Frank Green. *(☎ 624 427. Open Apr.-Oct. M-Th and Su 11am-4:30pm. £4.50. Tours of the haunted cellar £2. Gardens free.)*

■ ❀ NIGHTLIFE AND FESTIVALS

To discover the best of after-hours, consult *What's On* and *Artscene,* available at the TIC, for listings of live music, theater, cinema, and exhibitions. Twilight activities take place in **King's Square** and on **Stonegate,** where barbershop quartets share the pavement with jugglers, magicians, and soapboxers. Next to the TIC, the 250-year-old **Theatre Royal,** St. Leonards Pl., offers stage fare. *(☎ 623 568. Box office open M 10am-6pm, Tu-Sa 10am-8pm. £8.50-18, students and those under 25 £3.50.)* The ever-packed **King's Arms,** King's Staith, has outdoor seating along the Ouse. Highwater markers inside the pub glorify past floods. *(☎ 659 435. Open M-Sa 11am-11pm, Su noon-10:30pm. Cash only.)* **The Gallery,** 12 Clifford St., has two hot dance floors and six bars. *(☎ 647 947. Smart casual, no trainers or sportswear on weekends. Cover £3.50-8. Open M-Th and Su 10pm-2am, F-Sa 10pm-3am.)* **Toffs,** 3-5 Toft Green, plays mainly dance and house. *(☎ 620 203. Weekly student nights; discount with student ID. No trainers or sportswear on weekends. Cover £3.50-7. Open M-Sa 10pm-2am.)* As York's main music venue, **Fibber's,** Stonebow House, the Stonebow, doesn't lie about the quality (usually high) of live music playing nightly.

F-Sa become club nights with a DJ and dancing after live music ends. (☎651 250; www.fibbers.co.uk. Live music 8-10:30pm.) The Minster and local churches host a series of **summer concerts,** including July's **York Early Music Festival** (☎658 338). The city recently revived a centuries-old tradition of performing the medieval **York Mystery Plays** (☎635 444) in the nave of the Minster during June and July.

▶ DAYTRIP FROM YORK

▨ CASTLE HOWARD

15 mi. northeast of York. Yorkshire Coastliner bus #840 runs to the castle, 842 runs from the castle (40min., May-Oct. 2 per day in each direction, round-trip £5); reduced admission with bus ticket (ask for a heritage voucher). Take the morning bus from York to catch the bus back in the afternoon. Bring small bills for bus. ☎01653 648 333; www.castle-howard.co.uk. Open Mar.-Oct. daily 11am-4:30pm; gardens 10am-6:30pm. Last admission 4pm. £9.50, concessions £8.50. Gardens only £6.50/6.

The domed Castle Howard, still inhabited by the Howard family but open to visitors, inspired Evelyn Waugh to write *Brideshead Revisited* and was the scene for the BBC's film adaptation. Roman busts and portraits of Howard ancestors in full regalia clutter the halls. The **long gallery** is a promenade between enormous windows and shelves stuffed with books. Head to the **chapel** for kaleidoscopic pre-Raphaelite stained glass. More stunning than the castle are its 999 acres of luxurious rose gardens, fountains, and lakes, all roamed by raucous peacocks. From its hilltop, the **Temple of the Four Winds** offers views of the rolling hills.

PENNINE WAY

The Pennine Peaks arch up the center of Britain from the Peak District to Scotland. Britain's first long-distance trail, the 268 mi. Pennine Way begins at Edale, crosses the plateau of Kinder Scout, passes into the Yorkshire Dales at Malham, and reemerges at the peak of Pen-y-ghent. The northern section crosses the High Pennines, terminating at Kirk Yetholm in Scotland. The rebellious population of this region have erected chapels in defiance of Canterbury, embraced socialism in the face of textile barons, and won public right-of-way access for these very trails.

◪ HIKING THE PENNINE WAY

Hikers have completed the Way in as few as ten days, but most spend three weeks on the trail. Brief but rewarding forays on well-traveled walkways leave from major towns. The unusual limestone formations in the Yorkshire Dales and the lonely moor of Kinder Scout are Way highlights. The Pennines do not, however, coddle hikers. Sudden storms can reduce visibility, leave paths swampy, and sink you knee-deep in peat. All save the most hardcore hikers stay away from the Pennines in the winter. Bring a map and compass and know how to use them. Rain gear, warm clothing, and extra food are also essential. (See **Wilderness Safety,** p. 46.) Wainwright's *Pennine Way Companion* (£10), a pocket-sized volume available from bookstores, is a good supplement to Ordnance Survey maps (£6-8), all available at National Park Information Centres and TICs. Comprehensive coverage of the route comes in the form of two National Trail Guides, *Pennine Way North* and *Pennine Way South*, each £12. Those wishing to see some of the Way without hoofing the whole thing should get hold of the *Pennine Way Public Transport Guide*, free at NPICs. For £5-10 per bag, the **Pennine Way/Dales Way Baggage Courier** (☎01729 830 463, 07713 118 862) will cart your pack as you hike.

🏠 ACCOMMODATIONS

YHA hostels are spaced within a day's hike (7-29 mi.) of each other. Book online at www.yha.org.uk. Any NPIC or TIC can supply details on trails and alternate accommodations; pick up the *Pennine Way Accommodations Guide* (90p).

YHA HOSTELS

The following hostels are arranged from south to north, with the distance from the nearest southerly hostel listed. Unless otherwise noted, reception is open from 5pm, and breakfast and evening meals are served.

Edale: In the Peak District. See p. 354.

Mankinholes: 2 mi. outside Todmorden (☎01706 812 340). 2-, 4-, and 6-person rooms. Dorms £10.60, under 18 £7.20. MC/V. ❷

Haworth: Just outside the town. 18 mi. from Mankinholes. See p. 394.

Earby: 13 Birch Hall Ln., Earby (☎01282 842 349), 12 mi. from Haworth. Self-catering. Open Apr.-Oct. Dorms £10.60, under 18 £7.20. MC/V. ❶

Malham: 15 mi. from Earby in the Yorkshire Dales. See p. 401.

Hawes: 19 mi. from Stainforth in the Yorkshire Dales. See p. 400.

Keld: 9 mi. from Hawes in the Yorkshire Dales. See p. 400.

Baldersdale: Blackton, Baldersdale (☎0870 770 5684), 15 mi. from Keld in a converted stone farmhouse overlooking Blackton Reservoir. Open daily July-Aug.; Apr.-June and Sept.-Oct. M-F, call ahead to confirm. Dorms £10.60, under 18 £7.20. MC/V. ❶

Langdon Beck: Forest-in-Teesdale (☎01833 622 228), 15 mi. from Baldersdale. Open year-round; call to confirm. Dorms £10.60, under 18 £7.20. MC/V. ❷

Dufton: Redstones, Dufton, Appleby (☎0870 770 5800), 12 mi. from Langdon Beck. Has a small shop. Open daily Apr.-Oct. Dorms £10.60, under 18 £7.20. MC/V. ❶

Alston: The Firs, Alston (☎01434 381 509), 20 mi. from Dufton. Open daily Apr.-Oct.; Sept.-Oct. M-Tu, F-Su. Dorms £10.60, under 18 £7.20. MC/V. ❶

Greenhead: 17 mi. from Alston. See p. 430.

Once Brewed: 7 mi. east of Greenhead. See p. 430.

Bellingham: 14 mi. from Once Brewed in Northumberland. See p. 424.

Byrness: 15 mi. from Bellingham in Northumberland. See p. 424.

CAMPING BARNS

In the High Pennines, the YHA operates six **camping barns,** hollow stone buildings on private farms. Available amenities—electricity, hot water, heating, showers and so on—vary from farm to farm. The telephone numbers below are for confirming arrival times only; to book, call ☎0870 770 6113 or e-mail campbarnsyha@enterprise.net. You can also get information on the YHA website (www.yha.org.uk) and in the free *Camping Barns in England*, available at TICs.

Holwick Barn: Mr. and Mrs. Scott, Low Way Farm, Holwick (☎01833 640 506), 3 mi. north of Middleton-in-Teesdale. Sleeps 20. £6 per person. MC/V. ❶

Witton Barn: Witton Estate, Witton-le-Wear (☎01388 488 322), just off the Weardale Way. Sleeps 15. £5 per person. MC/V. ❶

SOUTH PENNINES

The South Pennines offer hikes along the dramatic hills known as "the moors." Visitors to the picturesque villages of Hebden Bridge and Haworth can look forward to an eyeful of green, a host of sheep, and the refreshing feel of country life.

TRANSPORTATION

The proximity of the South Pennines to Leeds and Bradford makes **train** transport (☎08457 484 950) fairly easy. Arriva's Transpennine Express (☎0870 602 3322) reaches Hebden Bridge directly from Blackpool and Leeds (several per hr. M-Sa 7am-9pm, every hr. on Su). Metro's Airedale Line, from Leeds, stops at Keighley (KEETH-lee), 5 mi. north of Haworth. From there, reach Haworth by the **Keighley & Worth Valley Railway's** private volunteer-operated steam trains (☎01535 645 214). **Bus** travel will take you through smaller cities. Travel to Halifax to get to Hebden Bridge, and Keighley to get to Haworth; both cities are convenient destinations from **Leeds.** Local buses make the 30min. journey from these cities to Hebden Bridge and Haworth; for more information, see below or call **Metroline** (☎0113 245 7676). TICs have a wide selection of trail guides. The **Worth Way** traces a 5½ mi. route from Keighley to Oxenhope; ride the steam train or Metroline bus back to your starting point. From Haworth to Hebden Bridge, choose a trail from the TIC's *Two Walks Linking Haworth and Hebden Bridge* (50p), which guides visitors along the dark and verdant paths that inspired the Brontë sisters.

HEBDEN BRIDGE   ☎01422

A historic stone village sandwiched between two hills, Hebden Bridge lies close to the **Pennine Way** and the circular 50 mi. **Calderdale Way.** The medieval village expanded modestly in the booming textile years of the 18th and 19th centuries, and many of the trademark "double-decker" stone houses of this period are still standing. Today, Hebden Bridge's narrow canals, small bridges, friendly locals, and slow pace of life give the town an allure all its own. The streets of Hebden Bridge are lively, particularly in the summer. One of the most popular hiking destinations is the National Trust's **Harcastle Crags** (☎844 518), a ravine-crossed wooded valley of greenery known locally as Little Switzerland, 1½ mi. northwest along the A6033; pick up a free guide from the TIC. You can also take day hikes to the villages of **Blackshaw Head, Cragg Vale,** or **Hepstonstall.** Hepstonstall holds the remains of Sylvia Plath and the ruins of the oldest Methodist house of worship in the world. **Brontë Boats Canal Cruising** gives boat trips along the Rochdale Canal. (☎845 557; www.bronteboats.co.uk. 1hr. cruises Feb.-Dec. Sa-Su 2pm and 3:30pm. £5.50, concessions £3.50. On alternate F, 3hr. cruise with dinner £17.50.)

At **1 Primrose Terrace ❷**, 1 Primrose Terr., find simple but bright rooms. From the train station, walk through the park and follow the canal to the stairs on your left. (☎844 747. Breakfast included. Singles £18. Cash only.) **Angeldale Guest House ❹**, a large Victorian house at the north end of Hangingroyd Ln. (not Hangingroyd Rd. or Grove), has lovely, spacious rooms. (☎847 321; www.angeldale.co.uk. Singles £35-59; doubles and twins £47-58; family rooms from £46. MC/V.) Purchase **groceries** at the Co-op, 41 Market St. (☎842 452. Open M-Sa 8am-9pm, Su 10am-4pm.) For award-winning scones (£1.30-1.75), visit the **Watergate Tearooms ❶**, 9 Bridge Gate. (☎842 978. Open daily 10:30am-4:30pm. MC/V.) Satisfying pizzas and pastas (£5-8) are served up at local favorite **Hebdens Pizza & Italian Cuisine ❷**, on Hangingroyd Ln., just across the bridge from St. George Sq. (☎843 745. Takeaway also available. Open W-Th 4:30-10pm, F-Sa 5:30-10:30pm, Su 4:30-9:30pm. AmEx/MC/V.) **Mooch ❶**, is at 24 Market St. Enjoy a sandwich or salad (£2.50-7) while listening to jazz. (☎846 954. M 9am-8pm, W-Sa 9am-8pm, Su 10am-7pm. Last order 1hr. before close. Cash only.) For another trendy bistro, visit **Organic House ❶**, just up the block from Mooch on Market St. Try one of the reasonably priced (from £4.25) vegetarian or vegan dishes. (☎843 429. Open Tu-Sa 9am-6pm, Su 10am-5pm.)

Hebden Bridge lies halfway along the Manchester-Leeds rail line. **Trains** pass through at least hourly and sometimes more frequently. Call ahead. (☎845 476. Manchester £7, Leeds £3.20.) **Buses** stop at the train station and on New Rd. The **Hebden Bridge Visitor & Canal Center (TIC)** offers the popular *Walks Around Heb-*

den Bridge (40p) and a mass of other walking guides. (☎843 831; www.hebden-bridge.co.uk. Open M-F 9:30am-5:30pm, Sa-Su 10:30am-5:30pm.) **Internet access** is free at the library, at the corner of Cheetham and Hope St. (☎842 151. Open M and Th 9:30am-7:30pm, Tu 9:30am-1pm, W and F 9:30am-5pm, Sa 9:30am-4pm.) The **post office** is on Holme St., off New Rd. (☎842 366. Open M-F 9am-5:30pm, Sa 9am-12:30pm.) **Post Code:** HX7 8AA.

HAWORTH ☎01535

Haworth's (HAH-wuth) *raison d'être* stands at the top of its hill—the parsonage that overlooks Brontëland. A cobbled main street milks all association with the ill-fated literary siblings, with tearooms and shops lining the climb to the Brontë home. The village today wants for wandering heroines, but the moors remain.

■☑ TRANSPORTATION AND PRACTICAL INFORMATION. The **train station** (☎645 214) only serves the **Keighley and Worth Valley Railway's** private steam trains, which run to and from Keighley on weekends and bank holidays all year, and daily during July and August (25min.; call ahead for times; £7). **Metroline** (☎603 284) buses #663-665 and 720 also reach Haworth from Keighley (15min., every 15-30min., £1.20-1.40). Bus #500 will take you to and from Hebden Bridge (30min., 4-5 per day, £1.30). Or you can pick up a guide from the TIC (50p) and hike there yourself, though at roughly 8 mi. of moor, it's quite a trek. The **Tourist Information Centre,** 2-4 West Ln., at Main St.'s summit, provides the useful Four Walks from the Centre of Haworth (40p) and the town's mini-guide (35p), and books beds for a 10% deposit. (☎642 329. Open May-Aug. daily 9:30am-5:30pm; Sept.-Apr. 9:30am-5pm.) **Tours,** including a graveyard tour, are available from Heart of Haworth Village Walks. Tickets are also sold at the TIC. (☎642 329; www.bronteguide.com. Tours daily; call ahead. Open Apr.-Dec. £5.50, concessions £3.50.) The **post office,** 98 Main St., is the only place to exchange currency. (☎644 589. Open M-F 9am-1pm and 1:30-5:30pm, Sa 9am-12:30pm.) **Post Code:** BD22 8DP.

▟◳ ACCOMMODATIONS AND FOOD. Once the home of the doctor who attended Charlotte Brontë's death, ▨**Ashmount ❸,** 5min. from the TIC on Mytholmes Ln., has sweeping views and an original neo-gothic-style interior. (☎645 726. Singles £32; doubles £47; triples £60; families £70. MC/V.) ▨**The Old Registry ❸,** 2-4 Main St., has gorgeous themed double rooms. (☎646 503. Singles from £40; doubles and twins £60; triples £75. MC/V.) Housed in a Victorian mansion, the elegant **YHA Haworth ❶** (also known as Haworth Youth Hostel) is a 15min. hike from the train station; turn left out of the train station, up Lees Ln., then left on Longlands Dr. It offers a TV lounge and pleasant garden. (☎642 234. Meals £3-5.25. Open mid-Feb. to Oct. daily; Nov. to mid-Dec. F-Sa. Dorms £9-12.50; twins and families £29. MC/V.) For **groceries,** try Spar on Station Rd. (☎647 662. Open daily 7:30am-10:30pm.) One of Haworth's most popular pubs, **The Fleece Inn ❶,** 67 Main St., has a classic pub atmosphere that draws crowds of locals. (☎642 172. Open M-Sa 11am-11pm, Su noon-10:30pm. MC/V.) **The Black Bull ❶,** once frequented by the errant Branwell Brontë, is a stone's throw from the TIC and the Brontë house that Branwell called home. (☎642 249. Open M-Sa 11am-11pm, Su noon-10:30pm. MC/V.) Restaurants line **Mill Hey,** just east of the train station. **Haworth Tandoori ❷,** 41 Mill Hey, a neighborhood favorite, serves a wide selection of curries, biryanis, and vegetarian dishes. (☎644 726. Open daily 5:30pm-midnight. MC/V.)

◪ SIGHTS. Down a tiny lane behind the village church lies the home where England's most famous literary siblings, the Brontës, spent their isolated child-hoods. The tasteful ▨**Brontë Parsonage** details the lives of Charlotte, Emily, Anne, Branwell, and their ill-tempered father. The quiet rooms, including the dining room where the sisters penned Wuthering Heights and Jane Eyre, contain original furnishings and mementos. Displays include the sofa on which Emily died, Charlotte's wedding bonnet, locks of the sisters' hair, and the toy figures that inspired their early stories (☎642 323; www.bronte.info. Open daily Apr.-Sept. 10am-5pm; Oct.-Mar. 11am-5pm. £4.90, concessions £3.60.) A footpath behind the church leads uphill toward the pleasant (if untempestuous) **Brontë Falls,** a 2 mi. hike.

LEEDS
☎ **0113**

Victorian Leeds (pop. 750,000) was famous for one thing: the finest wools in England. Although most textile jobs have moved overseas, Britain's fourth-largest city has experienced an economic revival. The birthplace of Marks & Spencer now sports swanky shops, a dynamic arts scene, popular restaurants, and numerous nightlife venues, making this young professionals' hub worthy of exploration.

TRANSPORTATION AND PRACTICAL INFORMATION

Trains: City Station, City Sq. Ticket office open 24hr. Trains (☎08457 484 950) from **London King's Cross** (2½hr., every hr., £67.90), **Manchester** (1½hr., 4 per hr., £14.50), and **York** (30min., 3-4 per hr., £8.50).

Buses: Station on New York St., next to Kirkgate Market. Office open M-W and F 8:30am-5:30pm, Th 9:30am-5:30pm, Sa 9am-4:30pm. Luggage storage £2. **National Express** (☎08705 808 080) serves Leeds from most major cities, including: **Birmingham**

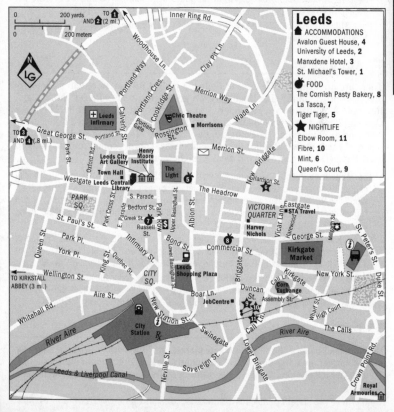

Leeds

🏠 ACCOMMODATIONS
Avalon Guest House, **4**
University of Leeds, **2**
Manxdene Hotel, **3**
St. Michael's Tower, **1**

🍴 FOOD
The Cornish Pasty Bakery, **8**
La Tasca, **7**
Tiger Tiger, **5**

⭐ NIGHTLIFE
Elbow Room, **11**
Fibre, **10**
Mint, **6**
Queen's Court, **9**

(3¼hr., 4-6 per day, £20.40); **Edinburgh** (7½hr., 2 per day, £34); **Glasgow** (6hr., 1 per day, £34); **Liverpool** (2hr., every hr., £9.90); **London** (5hr., every hr., £19); **Manchester** (1hr., every hr., £7.30); **York** (45min.; M-Sa every 30min., Su every hr.; £4.30). **Metroline** (☎245 7676, www.metroline.co.uk) runs local buses to **Bradford** (1hr., every 30min., £1.30) and **Hull** (1¾hr., 7 per day, £4).

Taxis: City Cabs (☎246 9999), **Streamline Taxis** (☎244 3322), **Telecabs** (☎263 7777).

Tourist Information Centre: Gateway Yorkshire (☎242 5242, bookings 0800 808 050), in the train station, books rooms for a £2 charge and a 10% deposit. Open M 10am-5:30pm, Tu-Sa 9am-5:30pm, Su 10am-4pm.

Budget Travel: STA Travel, 88 Vicar Ln. (☎0870 168 6878). Open M-Sa 10am-6pm.

Financial Services: Every conceivable **bank** lies on Park Row. Most open roughly M-F 9am-5:30pm, Sa 9am-1:30pm.

Work Opportunities: JobCentre, 12-14 Briggate (☎215 5382). Open M-Tu and Th-F 9am-4pm, W 10am-4pm.

Police: Millgarth St. (☎241 3059), north of the bus station.

Pharmacy: Boots, in Leeds City Station (☎242 1713). Open M-F 6am-midnight, Sa 8am-midnight, Su 9am-midnight.

Internet Access: Leeds Central Library, the Headrow (☎247 8911), across the street from Town Hall. Free. ID required. Fills quickly, call ahead to schedule a session. Open M-W 9am-8pm, Th 9:30am-5:30pm, F 9am-5pm, Sa 10am-5pm, Su noon-4pm. Last session 30min. before close. **Virgin Megastore,** Albion St. (☎243 8117). £1 per 25min. Open M 8am-6pm, Tu-W and F-Sa 9am-6pm, Th 9am-7pm, Su 11am-5pm.

Post Office: 116 Albion St. (☎08457 223 344). **Bureau de change.** Open M-Sa 9am-5:30pm. **Post Code:** LS2 8LP.

🏠 ACCOMMODATIONS

There are no hostels in Leeds, and finding a budget **B&B** often requires a lengthy bus ride into a suburb like Headingly. To get to Headingly's B&B-rich Cardigan Rd., take any bus toward Headingly from Infirmary St., get off at St. Michael's Church (20min.), and walk 5min. down St. Michael's Ln. Well-located hotels offer weekend discounts; find the listings in the TIC's free *Visit Leeds* booklet. The **University of Leeds** ❸ (☎242 4996) offers ensuite single dorm rooms from mid-July to early Sept. (Dorms £20, £115 per week. 2-night min. MC/V.)

The Manxdene Hotel, 154 Woodsley Rd. (☎243 2586), a 15min. walk from the city center. Head east on Great George St., which becomes Clarendon Rd., and turn left on Woodsley Rd. More easily accessible by bus (#56, 63, or 74A from Infirmary St.) or cab (£5). Affordable rooms with standard amenities. Singles £30-50, ensuite £40-60; twins and doubles £40-60. AmEx/MC/V. ❸

St. Michael's Tower Hotel, 5-6 St. Michael's Villa, Cardigan Rd. (☎275 5557). One of the least extravagant Cardigan Rd. options, with a lounge and TVs. Singles £27, ensuite £33; twins and doubles £40-43; ensuite family rooms £20 per person. MC/V. ❸

Avalon Guest House, 132 Woodsley Rd. (☎243 2545; www.avalonguesthouseleeds.co.uk). Family-run B&B with basic facilities. Take bus #56 from Infirmary St. Singles £25-40; doubles £36-50; twins £38-50; family rooms £50-70. Call ahead; prices vary. MC/V. ❸

🍴 FOOD

Butchers and bakers abound at **Kirkgate Market,** off New York St., Europe's largest indoor market, in a majestic Victorian building. (☎214 5162. Indoor stalls open M-Tu and Th-Sa 9am-5pm, W 9am-2pm; outdoor stalls close 30min. earlier. Farmer's

Market on first Su of every month.) **Vicar Lane,** north of The Headrow, offers less expensive restaurants. Get **groceries** at Morrisons, Woodhouse Ln., Merrion Centre. (☎242 2575. Open M-Tu and Sa 8am-7pm, W-F 8am-8pm, Su 11am-5pm.)

> **Tiger Tiger,** 117 Albion St. (☎236 6999; www.tigertiger-leeds.co.uk). Huge restaurant with an open terrace and comfy alcoves that make for a chic dining experience. "Famous" lunch deals offer 1 course for £3. Drinks half-price during happy hour (5-7:30pm). Open M-Sa noon-2am, Su noon-midnight. AmEx/MC/V. ❶
>
> **La Tasca,** 4 Russell St. (☎244 2205). Warm and inviting, with a tasteful Spanish theme. Serves tasty tapas (£2.35-3.75) and paella (£9.95) by romantic candlelight. Ideal for sharing. Open M-Th and Su noon-11pm, F-Sa noon-11:30pm. AmEx/MC/V. ❷
>
> **The Cornish Pasty Bakery,** 23 Albion Pl. (☎246 8044). Hot pockets with assorted fillings (£1.25-2.75), fresh panini (£2), and pizza (£2.20). Open M-Sa 9am-5pm, Su 9am-4pm. Cash only. ❶

🔆 📋 SIGHTS AND SHOPPING

The 🔲**Royal Armouries,** Armouries Dr., has one of the world's best collections of arms and armor. The museum features every kind of armor imaginable, from a 16th Century "horned helmut" complete with metal beard stubble (the museum's trademark) to Mughal elephant armor. Demonstrations by actors in period dress and outdoor horse events, including a joust, are held regularly. From the bus station, walk south under the overpass, veer left at the traffic circle, turn right at Crow Bridge, left at Armouries Way, and look for a modern gray building. With construction taking place along the canal, the museum can be especially difficult to find. (☎220 1999; www.royalarmouries.org. Open daily 10am-5pm. Free.)

Leeds's massive **library** and two art museums are clustered adjacent to the Victorian **Town Hall.** The **Leeds City Art Gallery,** The Headrow, features one the best collections of 20th-century British art outside London. (☎247 8248; www.leeds.gov.uk/artgallery. Open M-Tu and Th-Sa 10am-5pm, W 10am-8pm, Su 1-5pm. Free.) The adjacent **Henry Moore Institute,** holds excellent modern sculpture exhibitions. (☎246 7476; www.henry-moore-fdn.co.uk. Open M-Tu and Th-Su 10am-5:30pm, W 10am-9pm. Free.) The well-maintained ruins of 12th-century **Kirkstall Abbey,** 3 mi. west of the city center on Kirkstall Rd., inspired artist J.M.W. Turner. Take bus #33 or 33A, and get off when you see the abbey on your left. (☎230 5492. Open daily from dawn until dusk. Free.) Leeds is known for its shopping, and some of its malls and stores are sights in their own right. For the best in town, see **Leeding Fashions,** right.

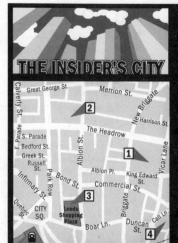

LEEDING FASHIONS

1 Start out at the **Victoria Quarter** (open M-Sa 9am-6pm, Su 11am-5pm; www.vqleeds.com), recently renovated and home of the first Harvey Nichols outside London.

2 Next head to **The Light,** The Headrow (open M-W and F-Sa 9am-6pm, Th 9am-7pm, Su 11am-5pm). Dine, drink, catch a movie on one of 13 screens, and pop into the trendy stores, including JOY, which caters to younger shoppers.

3 Bargain-hunting shoppers should head down Park Row to **Leeds Shopping Plaza,** Grosvenor Mall, which has a T.K. (yes, T.K.) Maxx. (Open M-Th 8am-5:45pm, F-Sa 8am-6pm, Su 11am-5pm.)

4 The **Corn Exchange,** just off Boar Ln., is a domed building with everything from vintage to cutting edge clothing. "Strut" is devoted to Leeds' independent labels. (Open M-F 10am-5:30pm, Sa 9:30am-6pm, Su 10:30am-5pm.)

NIGHTLIFE

Clubbers flock to Leeds to partake in neon nights of commercial dance, house, indie-rock, and hip-hop music. Find up-to-date club listings in the monthly *Absolute Leeds* (£1.90), available at the TIC.

Mint, 8 Harrison St. (☎244 3168; www.mintclubleeds.co.uk). Funky house and an inviting dance floor make this club ultra-popular. Open Th-Su 10pm-late. Cover £6-12.

Elbow Room, 64 Call Ln., 3rd/4th fl. (☎245 7011; www.elbow-room.co.uk). Purple pool hall and neon-lit bar, with both crowds to get lost in and corner couches to escape to. Pool £7-8 per hr. 2-for-1 cocktails daily 5-8pm. Cover F-Sa £3-5, free before 9pm. Open M-Th noon-2am, F-Sa noon-3am, Su noon-midnight.

Queen's Court, 167-168 Lower Briggate (☎245 9449; www.queens-court.co.uk). Leeds's premier gay club. M "Pink Pounder" 2 floors, 2 DJs, all drinks £1. Cover varies, usually around £3. Bar open M-Sa noon-2am, Su noon-midnight; club open M 9:30pm-2am, Th-Sa 10:30pm-2am. Food served noon-6pm. MC/V.

Fibre, (☎08701 200 888; www.barfibre.com), next door to Queen's Court, draws a trendy crowd in a chic gay-friendly club. Look for summer "courtyard" parties between Queen's Court and Fibre, call ahead for dates and times. Weekday 2-for-1 drink specials 5-8pm. Open M-W and Su 11am-midnight, Th 11-1am, F-Sa 11-2am.

YORKSHIRE DALES

The traces of earlier residents enhance the beauty of the Yorkshire Dales (valleys formed by swift rivers and lazy glacial flows). Abandoned castles and stone farmhouses are scattered among the pastures and one-pub villages of the region. Bronze- and Iron-Age tribes blazed "green lanes," footpaths that remain on the high moorland, Romans built roads and stout forts, and 18th-century workers pieced together countless stone walls. As with most British national parks, 99% of the land is privately owned, but property owners allow hikers to cross their land.

TRANSPORTATION

Skipton (p. 402) is the most convenient place to enter the park. **Trains** (☎08457 484 950) run to Skipton from Bradford (35min., 4 per hr., £4.50), Carlisle (2hr., every hr., £13.50), and Leeds (40min., 2 per hr., £5.40). The Settle-Carlisle Railway (☎01729 822 007), one of England's most scenic routes, slices through Skipton, Garsdale, and Kirkby Stephen (1¾hr., 3-4 per day, £13.40). National Express (☎08705 808 080) **buses** run to Skipton's bus station on Keighley St. from London (6hr., 1 per day, £20) and Leeds (#537, 1½hr., 2 per day, £4.75).

For non-hikers, getting around the Dales without a car is a challenge. The seasonal *Dales Connection* timetable (free at TICs and NPICs) helps clarify public transport. Traveline (☎0870 608 2608) also answers transportation questions. Many inter-village **buses** run only a few times per week and tend to hibernate in winter. There are more buses on weekends and bank holidays; weekday transportation is sporadic. Pride of the Dales (☎01756 753 123) connects Skipton to Grassington (#72, 30min., every hr., £2.40), sometimes continuing to Kettlewell (#72, 1¼hr., every 2hr., £2.70). Pennine Bus (☎01756 749 215) connects Skipton to Malham (#210, 45min., 2 per day, £3.40) and Settle (#580, 40min., every hr., £3.70). Other villages are served less regularly, and, although **postbuses** run once per day to scheduled towns, they depart very early and stop frequently.

7 PRACTICAL INFORMATION

Sampling the Dales requires several days, a pair of sturdy shoes, and careful planning. In the south of the park, **Skipton** (p. 402) serves as a transport hub and provides services not available in the smaller villages. **Grassington** (p. 402) and **Linton**, just north, are scenic bases for exploring southern Wharfedale. **Malham** (p. 403) is a sensible starting point for forays into western Wharfedale and eastern Ribblesdale. To explore Wensleydale and Swaledale in the north, begin from **Hawes** (p. 403) or **Leyburn** (p. 403). In addition to the National Park Information Centres listed below, most towns have TICs.

> **National Park Information Centres:** Pick up the invaluable annual park guides, *The Visitor* and *The Yorkshire Dales Official Guide* (both free), along with numerous maps and walking guides. All NPICs book accommodations for a 10% deposit.
>
> **Aysgarth Falls:** (☎01969 663 424), in Wensleydale, 1 mi. east of the village. Open Apr.-Oct. daily 10am-5pm; Nov.-Mar. W and F-Su 10am-4pm.
>
> **Grassington:** Hebden Rd., Wharfedale (☎08701 666 333). Open Apr.-Oct. daily 10am-5pm; Nov.-Mar. F-Su 10am-4pm. 24hr. info terminal outside.
>
> **Hawes:** Station Yard, Wensleydale (☎01969 667 450). Open daily 10am-5pm; 24hr. info terminal outside.
>
> **Malham:** Malhamdale (☎01729 830 363), at the southern end of the village. Open Apr.-Oct. daily 10am-5pm; Nov.-Mar. F-Su 10am-4pm.
>
> **Reeth:** (☎01748 850 252), in the Green. Open daily Apr.-Oct. 9am-5pm; Nov.-Mar. 9:30am-4pm.
>
> **Sedbergh:** 72 Main St. (☎01539 620 125). Open Apr.-Oct. daily 10am-5pm; Nov.-Mar. Sa-Su 10am-4pm.

┌ ACCOMMODATIONS AND CAMPING

The free *Yorkshire Dales Accommodation Guide* is available at NPICs and TICs. As in all of England, park officials discourage wild (unofficial) camping; organized campsites abound.

YHA HOSTELS

The Yorkshire Dales area hosts nine **YHA hostels.** Hawes, Keld, and Malham lie on the Pennine Way (p. 391), while Stainforth, Kettlewell, Dentdale, and Grinton Lodge sit a few miles off it. Ingleton, on the western edge of the park, is a good jumping-off point for the Lake District. Kirkby Stephen, north of Hawes, is served by rail, but set a little farther from the hiking trail. All fill up weeks in advance, especially in summer, but hostel employees will call other YHAs.

TOP TEN LIST

DO IT IN THE DALES

The Yorkshire Dales are England's agricultural heart. Take advantage of the bucolic setting and take in some bovine sights and treats. The milk, cheese, and produce are excellent; the emerald green hills freckled with fat cows are perfect for walking or biking.

1. Chow down on some fresh cheese from a creamery in **Wensleydale** (p. 403).

2. Ride over the **Ribblehead Viaduct,** an ancient bridge built by the Romans, on the **Settle-Carlisle Railway** (p. 398).

3. Take a hike from one town to another through the miles of pastures.

4. Visit towering **Malham Cove** (p. 403), an enormous outcropping of limestone.

5. Watch rope being made in **Hawes** (p. 403), as it has been for over a century in several of the town's shops.

6. Rehash a long day at one of the region's pubs over a local ale like Dent Bitter.

7. Wander through the stone corridors of the impressive **Skipton Castle** (p. 402).

8. Check out **Buttertubs Pass;** the road is lined with limestone cylinders into which farmers used to dip butter to cool on the way to market.

9. Rent a bike and take a daytrip through old cattle paths between the many farms.

10. Hike a portion of the 268 mi. **Pennine Way** (p. 401), passing through Hawes or Keld.

Dentdale: Cowgill, on Dentdale Rd. (☎0870 770 5790), 6 mi. east of Dent, 2 mi. from the Hawes-Ingleton road. A former shooting lodge on the River Dee. Open mid-Mar. to Aug. M-Sa; Sept. to late Oct. Tu-Sa; Feb. to mid-Mar. and late Oct. to late Nov. F-Sa. Dorms £12.50, under 18 £9. MC/V. ❷

Grinton: Grinton Lodge (☎01748 884 206), ¾ mi. south of town on the Reeth-Leyburn road. Kitchen and laundry. Reception 7:30-10am and 5-10pm. Curfew 11:30pm. Open Apr.-Oct. daily; Feb.-Mar. M-Sa; Nov.-Dec. F-Sa. Dorms £12.50, under 18 £9. MC/V. ❷

Hawes: Lancaster Terr. (☎0870 770 5854), west of Hawes on Ingleton Rd., uphill from town. 54 beds. Curfew 11pm. Open Apr.-Sept. daily; Mar. and Sept.-Oct. Tu-Sa; late Jan. to Feb. and Nov.-Dec. F-Sa. Dorms £11, under 18 £8. MC/V. ❶

Ingleton: Greta Tower (☎0870 770 5880), near Market Sq. Kitchen and laundry. Reception closed noon-5pm. Curfew 11pm. Open Mar.-Sept. and late Dec. daily; Sept.-Oct. M-Sa; Feb. Tu-Sa; Nov. to mid-Dec. F-Su. Dorms £12.50, under 18 £9. MC/V. ❷

Keld: Keld Lodge (☎0870 770 5888), Upper Swaledale, west of Keld village. 38 beds. No smoking. Curfew 11pm. Open July-Aug. daily; Apr.-June and Sept.-Oct. Tu-Sa. Dorms £11, under 18 £8. MC/V. ❶

Kettlewell: Whernside House (☎0870 770 5896), in the village center. 43 beds. No smoking. Occasional curfew 11pm. Open July-Aug. daily; June and Sept.-Oct. Tu-Sa; Feb.-Mar. and late Oct. to mid-Sept. W-Sa. Dorms £12.50, under 18 £9. MC/V.❶

Kirkby Stephen: Market St. (☎0870 770 5904). In a former chapel, complete with pews and stained glass. 44 beds. Kitchen and laundry. Lockout 10am-5pm. Curfew

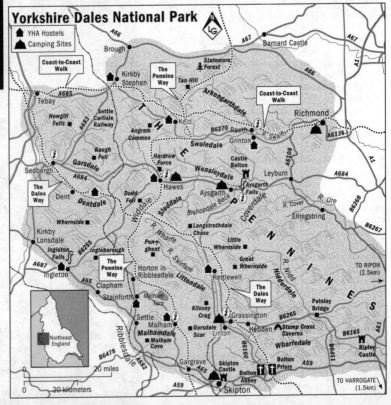

Yorkshire Dales National Park

11pm. Open July-Aug. daily; Apr.-June and mid-Sept. to Oct. M-Sa; Feb.-Mar. and late Oct. to mid-Sept. W-Sa. Dorms £11, under 18 £8. MC/V. ❶

Malham: John Dower Memorial Hostel (☎0870 770 5946). Well-equipped and hiker-friendly. 82 beds. Kitchen and laundry. Reception 7-11am and 5-11pm. Lockout 11am-5pm. Curfew 11pm. Open Feb.-Oct. daily; late Jan. and Nov. to mid-Dec. Th-Sa. Dorms £12.50, under 18 £9. MC/V. ❷

Stainforth: Taitlands (☎0870 770 6046), 2 mi. north of Settle, ¼ mi. south of Stainforth. Georgian house with a walled garden. Small kitchen and laundry. Open daily during school holidays; F-Sa otherwise. Dorms £12.50, under 18 £9. MC/V. ❷

DALES BARNS AND CAMPING

Numerous **Dales Barns,** converted barns split up into hostel-style bunk rooms, cost £5-10 per night. Most have showers and kitchens. Book weeks ahead and get specific directions along the trails. **Campgrounds** are difficult to reach on foot, but farmers may let you use their stretches of dale. Ask TICs for a full list of both.

Skirfare Bridge Dales Barn (☎01756 761 028; www.skirfaredalesbarn.co.uk). Sleeps 25. £10. Cash only. ❶

Grange Farm Barn (☎01756 760 259). £10, under 18 £8. Cash only. ❶

Hill Top Farm, Malham (☎01729 830 320). £8. Cash only. ❶

Craken House Farm, Leyburn (☎01969 622 204), ½ mi. south of town center. £6, rooms £18-20, camping £4, 2-person tent £7. Cash only. ❶

Howarth Farm Camping and Caravan Site, Skipton (☎01756 720 226). Discounts for extended stays. £4 per person. Cash only. ❶

Wood Nook, Grassington (☎01756 752 412). £8.50 per adult with tent and car. Electricity £1. MC/V. ❶

Bainbridge Ings, Haws (☎01969 667 354; www.bainbridgeings.co.uk), ½ mi. from Haws on the Old Gale Rd. Open Apr.-Oct. 2-person tent and car £9, £1 per extra person. Electricity £1.50. Cash only. ❶

Brompton-on-Swale Caravan Park, Richmond (☎01748 824 629). Open Apr.-Oct. £12 per 2-person tent. Extra person £2.50. No teenagers without an adult. MC/V. ❶

Street Head Caravan Park, Aysgarth (☎01969 663 472). 2-person tent and car £9. Electricity £2. Cash only. ❶

🔲 🏔 HIKING AND OUTDOORS

Since buses are infrequent and the scenery breathtaking, hiking remains the best way to see the Dales. The park's seven NPICs can help you prepare for a trek along one of three long-distance footpaths. The challenging 268 mi. **Pennine Way** (p. 391) curls from Gargrave in the south to Tan Hill in the north, passing Malham, Pen-y-ghent, Hawes, Keld, and most of the major attractions of the Dales. The more manageable, 84 mi. **Dales Way** runs from Bradford and Leeds past Ilkley, through Wharfedale via Grassington and Whernside, and by Sedbergh on its way to the Lake District; it crosses the Pennine Way near Dodd Fell. The 190 mi. **Coast-to-Coast Walk** stretches from Richmond to Kirkby Stephen.

Take a **map** and **trail guide;** stone walls and hills look similar after a while. Don't forget to leave gates as you found them; there is livestock in the area. **Ordnance Survey** maps (£7.50) are available for most paths and can be purchased at any NPIC or outdoors supply store. Outdoor Leisure #2, 30, and Landranger #91 and 98 are good for specific regions; *Touring Map and Guide #6* (£5) covers the Dales in general. NPICs sell leaflets (£1-2.20) covering over 30 short routes. YHA produces its own leaflets (30p) on day hikes between hostels. Cyclists can ask at NPICs about rental stores and buy route cards plotting the **Yorkshire Dales Cycleway,** six interconnected 20 mi. routes though the Dales (£2.50). Bicycles are forbidden on footpaths, but not on bridleways (trails for horses). The **Pennine Way/Dales Way Baggage Courier** will cart your pack. (☎01729 830 463, mobile 07713 118 862. £5-10 per bag.) If you'd rather not walk at all, ⬛**Cumbria Classic Coaches** runs various trips in 1950s-era double decker buses, generally on Tuesdays, from Kirby Steven to Hawes. (☎01539 623 254; www.cumbriaclassiccoaches.co.uk. £9 per person.)

> **WARNING.** The Dales are filled with **shake holes:** small, often unmarked depressions, similar to grassy potholes, that indicate underground caverns. They can give way with lethal consequences. Ordnance Survey maps and a compass are essential, especially on unmarked trails. See **Wilderness Safety,** p. 46.

SKIPTON   ☎01756

Skipton is most useful as a transfer point or rest stop; once you've gathered your gear, skip town and strike out for the Dales. Vacant **Skipton Castle** is the main sight and one of the most complete medieval castles in England. The last surviving Royalist bastion in the north, the castle surrendered to Cromwell's army after a three-year siege. (☎792 442. Open Mar.-Sept. M-Sa 10am-6pm, Su noon-6pm; Oct.-Feb. M-Sa 10am-4pm, Su noon-4pm. £5.20, concessions £4.60.)

B&Bs are moderately priced and easy to find—just look along **Keighley Road.** Find luxurious canopy beds at **Carlton House ❸,** 46 Keighley Rd. (☎700 921. Singles £25; doubles £50. Cash only.) Nearby, **Westfield Guest House ❷,** 50 Keighley Rd., delivers huge breakfasts and huge beds for small prices. (☎790 849. Doubles £48-50. Cash only.) Load up on fresh gooseberries and cheese at the **market,** which floods High St. (Open M, W, F-Sa.) **Healthy Life,** 10 High St., near the church, stocks soy haggis and more traditional veggie favorites, while upstairs **Wild Oats Cafe ❶** serves daily vegan specials (£1-3.50), along with cream tea and sandwiches. (☎790 619. Store open M-Sa 9am-5:30pm. Cafe open M-Sa 9:30am-4:30pm. MC/V.) **Bizzie Lizzies ❷,** 36 Swadford St., delivers exceptional fish and chips for £5-7. (☎701 131; www.bizzielizzies.net. Open daily 11:30am-9pm. Cash only.)

Skipton's **train station** is ¼ mi. west of the city center on Broughton Rd. **Buses** stop at the bus station between Swadford St. and Keighley Rd., behind Sunwin House. **Rent cars** from Skipton Self Drive, Otley Rd. Garage. (☎792 911; www.skiptonselfdriveltd.co.uk. From £29 per day; discounts for longer rentals.) Admire the Dales from the water with Pennine Cruisers of Skipton, The Boat Shop, 19 Coach St., which **rents dayboats** on the Leeds and Liverpool Canal. (☎795 478. £75-185 per day; from £430 per week.) Airborne Adventures sends **hot-air balloons** over the Dales from Skipton and Settle twice daily. (☎730 166. £150 per person; 2 person min.) The **Tourist Information Centre,** 35 Coach St., books rooms for a 10% deposit. (☎792 809. Open Apr.-Oct. M-Sa 10am-5pm, Su 11am-3pm; Nov.-Mar. M-Sa 10am-4pm.) Other services include: HSBC **bank,** 61 High St. (☎0845 740 4404; open M-F 9:30am-4:30pm), and the **post office** at Sunwin House, 8 Swadford St. (☎792 724; open M-F 9am-5:30pm, Sa 9am-1pm; supermarket open M-F 9am-5:30pm, Sa 8:30am-5:30pm). **Post Code:** BD23 1UR.

WHARFEDALE AND GRASSINGTON   ☎01756

The valley of Wharfedale, created by the River Wharfe, is best explored using cobbled **Grassington** as a base. Spectacular **Kilnsey Crag** lies 3½ mi. from Grassington toward Kettlewell, through a deep gorge and Bronze-Age burial mounds. The **Stump Cross Caverns,** 5 mi. east of Grassington, are adorned with stalagmites and glistening rock curtains. (☎752 780. Open Mar.-Oct. daily 10am-6pm; Nov.-Feb. Sa-Su 10am-4pm. Last admission 1hr. before close. £5. Dress warmly.)

Close to the center of Grassington, **Raines Close ❸,** 13 Station Rd., lets comfortable ensuite rooms, some with spectacular views. (☎752 678; www.rainesclose.co.uk. Doubles £56-64. Cash only.) Across the street, **Springroyd House ❸,** 8A Station Rd., offers three clean rooms in the village center. (☎752 473. Doubles £46-52. Cash only.) Pubs and cafes pack Main Street, including **Lucy Fold Tea Room ❶,** 1 Garr's Ln., off Main St., whose offerings include omelettes, sandwiches, and jacket potatoes, all for £2.75-5. (☎752 414. Open W-Su 10:30am-5pm. Cash only.)

Pride of the Dales **bus** #72 arrives in Grassington from Skipton (M-Sa, every hr., £2.50). The **NPIC,** Hebden Rd. (p. 399), stocks the useful *Grassington Footpath Map* (£1.60) and standard park trail guides (£1) and leads occasional guided walks from March to October (£2). Other services include: **outdoor gear** at The Mountaineer, Pletts Barn Centre, at the top of Main St. (☎752 266; open daily 9am-5pm); Barclays **bank,** at the corner of Main St. and Hebden Rd. (☎296 3000; open M-F 9:30am-3:30pm); and the **post office,** 15 Main St. (☎752 226; open M-F 9am-5:30pm, Sa 9am-12:30pm). **Post Code:** BD23 5AD.

MALHAMDALE AND INGLETON

Limestone cliffs and gorges slice the pastoral valley of Malhamdale, creating spectacular natural beauties within easy walking distance of one another. A 3hr. hike from the **NPIC** (p. 399) passes the stunning, stony swath of **Malham Cove,** a massive limestone cliff and the placid water of **Malham Tarn.** Shuttle buses (15min.; 2 per hr.; 50p) run from the NPIC to the cove and the tarn. Two miles from Malham village is the equally impressive **Gordale Scar,** cut in the last Ice Age by a glacier. For more info, pick up *A Walk in Malhamdale #1* (£1.20) from Malham's NPIC. The **YHA Malham** (p. 401) is popular with Pennine Way hikers.

North of Malham, the high peaks and cliffs of Ingleborough, Pen-y-ghent, and Whernside form the **Alpes Penninae.** The 24 mi. **Three Peaks Walk,** which connects the Alpes, begins and ends in **Horton in Ribblesdale** at the clock of the **Pen-y-ghent Cafe,** a hiker's haunt that serves as the local TIC. (☎01729 860 333. Open Apr.-Oct. M and W-Su 8am-6pm; Nov.-Mar. W-Su 9am-5pm.) **Ingleton** is near the middle of the trek. The village's **TIC,** in the community center carpark, books rooms for a 10% deposit. (☎015242 41049. Open Apr.-Oct. daily 10am-4:30pm.) The 4½ mi. walk through the **Ingleton Waterfalls** is one of the park's most popular routes. (☎01524 241 930; www.ingletonwaterfallswalk.co.uk. 2½-4 hrs. £3.50. Open 9am-dusk.) Pick up a leaflet from the TIC or read the Ingleton town trail sign in the town center. The **YHA Ingleton** (p. 400) and several **B&Bs** (around £18) on Main St. are good budget options. A 1 mi. walk brings you to **Stacksteads Farm ❶,** Tatterthorne Rd., which offers a bunk barn with 22 beds. (☎01524 241 386. Cash only.)

WENSLEYDALE AND HAWES   ☎01969

The northern Wensleydale landscape transforms into fertile dairyland. Base your ventures in **Hawes,** which has an **NPIC** (p. 399) that books accommodations for a 10% deposit. Pay 40p at the **Green Dragon Pub** to access the trail to the **Hardrow Force waterfall,** 1 mi. north on the Pennine Way. The **Dales Countryside Museum,** in the same building as the NPIC, chronicles the history of the farmers and villagers who have populated the Dales for centuries. (☎667 494. Open daily 10am-5pm. £3, concessions £2.) The silhouette of **Castle Bolton** graces Wensleydale, and visitors can explore the dungeon and battlements. (☎623 981. Open daily Mar.-Nov. 10am-5pm. £5.) **B&Bs** (£17-21) line Main St. for those not content with the **YHA Hawes** (p. 400); check the list outside town hall each afternoon. Pubs, takeaways, and a Barclays **bank** (open M-F 9:30am-3:30pm) are also along Main St. Farther north, **Swaledale** is known for picturesque barns and meadows. Also worthwhile are the tiered **Aysgarth Falls** to the east and the natural terrace of the **Shawl of Leyburn.** Aysgarth and Leyburn are served by Pride of the Dales **buses** #156-157 from Hawes to Northallerton (2 hr., every hr., round-trip £2.50). Aysgarth's **NPIC** is in the carpark above the falls (p. 399), and Leyburn has a **TIC.** (☎623 069. Open Easter to Sept. daily 9:30am-5:30pm; Oct. to Easter M-Sa 9:30am-4:30pm.)

NORTH YORK MOORS

The hilly, heather-clad expanses and cliff-lined coast of the North York Moors have changed little since inspiring Emily Brontë and Bram Stoker. Bleak ridges are cheered in summer by large swaths of purple heather, and deep-sided valleys supply the path for superb scenic railways. The region's stunning landscape, from pastoral towns to an impossibly dramatic coastline, makes the North York Moors one of Britain's most visually exciting national parks.

▐ TRANSPORTATION

The primary gateways to the North York Moors are York to the south and Middlesbrough to the north. Middlesbrough is a short train ride from Darlington (30min., every hr., £3.40) on the main London-Edinburgh rail line. The *Moors Explorer* pamphlet, free at TICs and NPICs, covers bus and rail service in glorious detail—service varies by season and is significantly reduced in winter. Traveline also provides timetables (☎08706 082 608).

Three **train** lines serve the park. There is frequent service between York and Scarborough (45min., 1-2 per hr., £9.30). The scenic Esk Valley Line runs from Middlesbrough to Whitby via Danby and Grosmont (1½hr., 5 per day, £7.30). The tourist-oriented North Yorkshire Moors Railway (reservations ☎01751 472 508, timetables 01751 473 535) links the north and south, chugging from Pickering to Grosmont (1hr.; 3-7 per day, no service during some low-season times; see p. 410).

Buses run more frequently than trains. To save cash, always ask the driver for a day or week pass rather than a single. Yorkshire Coastliner (☎01653 692 556) bus #840 travels between Leeds, York, Pickering, and Whitby (3hr., 5 per day), while #843 runs between Leeds, York, and Scarborough (3hr., every hr.). Arriva bus #93/93A journeys between Middlesbrough, Whitby, Robin Hood's Bay (#93 only), and Scarborough (2hr., every hr.). Scarborough and District (☎01723 503 020) bus #128 covers Scarborough, Pickering, and Helmsley (1½hr., every hr.). The national park operates the Moorsbus, with seasonal routes through the park; schedules are available at all TICs. The Moorsbus runs only on certain days, so make sure to plan ahead. (☎07980 737 589; www.moorsbus.net. Apr.-Oct. Su; daily late July-Aug. All-day pass £2.50.)

✦ ORIENTATION

North York Moors National Park is 30 mi. north of York. Toward the park's southwest corner, appealing **Helmsley** has several excellent sights and good access to hiking, particularly when the Moorsbus shuttle is operating (see above). To the east, centrally located **Pickering** is the starting point for the scenic **North Yorkshire Moors Railway,** as well as a sweatless way to take in the views. The **Esk Valley,** cutting across the north of the park and served by another beautiful railway, the **Esk Valley Line,** is good terrain for hikers. The seaside resort towns **Whitby** and **Scarborough** are often flooded with summer vacationers and feel distant from the park. **Robin Hood's Bay,** just south of Whitby, is a small and atmospheric coastal village.

▐ PRACTICAL INFORMATION

The *Moors & Coast* visitor guide (50p), available at any TIC or NPIC, is particularly useful, highlighting the region's events and attractions.

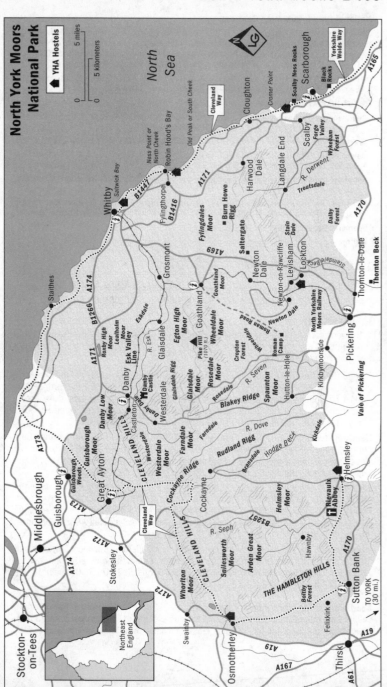

North York Moors National Park

▲ YHA Hostels

0   5 miles
0   5 kilometers

North Sea

NORTHEAST ENGLAND

National Park Information Centres:

Danby: The Moors Centre (☎01439 772 737; www.visitthemoors.co.uk). From the Danby train station, turn left after you pass the gate and right at the crossroads before the Duke of Wellington Inn; the center is ½ mi. ahead on the right. The larger NPIC and an invaluable source. Open Apr.-Oct. daily 10am-5pm; Mar. and Nov.-Dec. daily 11am-4pm; Jan.-Feb. Sa-Su 11am-4pm.

Sutton Bank: (☎01845 597 426), 6 mi. east of Thirsk on the A170. Open Apr.-Oct. daily 10am-5pm; Mar. and Nov.-Dec. daily 11am-4pm; Jan.-Feb. Sa-Su 11am-4pm.

Tourist Information Centres:

Goathland: The Village Store and Outdoor Centre (☎01947 896 207). Open Easter to Oct. daily 10am-5pm; Nov. to Easter M-W and F-Su 10am-4pm.

Great Ayton: High Green Car Park (☎01642 722 835). Open Apr.-Oct. M-Sa 10am-4pm, Su 1-4pm.

Guisborough: Priory Grounds, Church St. (☎01287 633 801). Open Apr.-Sept. Tu-Su 9am-5pm; Oct.-Mar. W-Su 9am-5pm.

Helmsley: (☎01439 770 173), at the entrance to the castle. Open Mar.-Oct. daily 9:30am-5pm; Nov.-Feb. F-Su 10am-4pm.

Pickering: The Ropery (☎01751 473 791), beside the library, just down the road from the train station. Open Mar.-Oct. M-Sa 9:30am-5pm, Su 9:30am-4pm; Nov.-Feb. M-Sa 10am-4:30pm.

Scarborough: see p. 409.

Whitby: see p. 410.

▛ ACCOMMODATIONS

Local TICs book beds for a small fee and a 10% deposit. **B&Bs, hotels,** and **caravan parks** in or near the national park are listed under the appropriate towns.

YHA HOSTELS

The following YHA hostels provide lodging in the Moors. Reservations are highly recommended, especially in summer. Clearly named bus stops are rare; tell drivers where you're headed.

Boggle Hole: (☎01947 880 352), Mill Beck, Fylingthorpe. Easy access to the Cleveland Way and Coast to Coast trails. 80 beds in 2- to 10-bed dorms. A seaside 19th-century mill, 1 mi. south of Robin Hood's Bay along the beach or, during high tide, cliffs. Breakfast, packed lunch, and dinner available. Reception 1pm until late. Open Feb.-Oct. daily; Nov. F-Sa. Dorms £12.50-15.50, under 18 £9-10.50. MC/V. ❷

Helmsley: (☎01439 770 433). From Market Pl. take Bondgate Rd., turn left onto Carlton Rd., and left again at Carlton Ln.; hostel is on the left. Breakfast £3.80, packed lunch from £3.40, dinner from £5.50. Lockout 10am-5pm. Open Apr.-Oct. daily; Sept.-Nov. call ahead. Dorms £10.60, under 18 £7.20, under 5 free. MC/V. ❶

Lockton: Old School (☎01751 460 376), off the Pickering-Whitby Rd. 2 mi. from the North Yorkshire Moors Railway Station at Levisham. 4 mi. north of Pickering; take Coastliner bus #840 toward Whitby. Self-catering. 21 beds in 3- to 8-bed rooms. Reception 8-10am and 5-10pm. Open July-Aug. daily; Apr.-May and Sept. call 48hr. in advance. Dorms £12.50-15.50, under 18 £9-10.50. MC/V. ❶

Osmotherley: (☎01609 883 575), Cote Ghyll, Northallerton. Between Stockton and Thirsk, just northeast of Osmotherley. Reception 8am-noon and 1-11pm. Lockout 11:30pm-7am. Open Mar.-Nov. daily; Feb. F-Sa. Dorms £12.50-15.50, under 18 £9-10.50. Full board £23.50/19.20. MC/V. ❷

Scarborough: The White House, Burniston Rd. (☎01298 871 826), 2 mi. from Scarborough. Take bus #3 from the train station to Scholes Park Rd., then follow Burniston Rd. away from town and turn left just after crossing a small river. In a former mill on a river,

15min. from the sea. 85 beds in 2- to 20-bed dorms. Lockout 10am-5pm. Open Mar.-Aug. daily; Sept.-Oct. call ahead. Dorms £12.50-15.50, under 18 £9-10.50. MC/V. ❷

Whitby: (☎01947 602 878). 12th-century stone building near the abbey, atop 199 stone steps. Family rooms available. Reception open 8-10am and 5-11pm. Curfew 11pm. Open Apr.-Aug. daily; Sept.-Oct. M-Sa; Jan.-Mar. and Nov. F-Sa. Dorms £12.50-15.50, under 18 £9-10.50. MC/V. ❶

CAMPING

The YHA operates four **camping barns** (p. 392) in the Moors: in **Farndale,** Oakhouse farmyard; **Kildale,** on the Cleveland Way; **Sinnington,** on the edge of the park between Pickering and Helmsley; and **Westerdale,** in Broadgate Farm. Make reservations in advance; call ☎08707 708 868. All barns are £5 per person or less.

◨ ◪ HIKING AND OUTDOORS

Coastal towns aside, hiking is the best way to travel these vast tracts of moor. Wrapping fully around the national park, the 93 mi. **Cleveland Way** is the yellow brick road of the North York Moors. A particularly well-marked and breathtaking portion of the Way is the 20 mi. trail between Whitby and Scarborough (the less eager might go as far as Robin Hood's Bay, 5½ mi. from Whitby)—hills on one side, tranquil sea on the other, and miles of shoreline cliffs ahead. Ambitious hikers might consider tackling the 79 mi. **Wolds Way,** a stunning coastal hike that extends from Scarborough to the sandstone cliffs of Filey, or the shorter and unofficial **White Rose** (37 mi.). The popular **Coast to Coast Walk** (192 mi.) begins in St. Bees and terminates in Robin Hood's Bay (at a pub, of course). Excellent day hikes begin at stations on the park's two scenic **railways,** the Esk Valley Line (p. 404) and the North Yorkshire Moors Railway (p. 410). Trails are not always marked or even visible; hikers should carry a map and compass (see **Wilderness Safety,** p. 46).

The Moors are steep, and **cycling** around them is a challenge, but the paths along the plateaus are less strenuous. The **Whitby to Scarborough Coastal Railtrail,** with sea views, refreshment stops, and sections for all skill levels, is especially popular. There are also many sections of the **National Cycle Network** that pass through the area; these are well-signed and avoid busy roads. Check out www.sustrans.org.uk for more info. You can **rent bikes** at Trailways, Old Railway Station, in Hawsker, 2 mi. south of Whitby on the A171. (☎01947 820 207; www.trailways.fsnet.co.uk. From £7.80 per day. Open Easter to Nov. daily 10am-6pm; Dec. to Easter call ahead.) TICs and NPICs offer lists of other bike rental stores in the region.

The Moors can be either horribly hot or bitterly cold in the summer. Call the Danby NPIC (☎02187 660 654; see p. 406) for the **weather forecast** before setting out, but conditions can vary dramatically within the park, and it *is* England—bring raingear. The National Park Authority produces a number of guides on the Moors such as the *Walks Around* booklets (£2), which detail popular short walks. Before hitting the trails, consult more in-depth books (£3-6) and get advice from tourist officials. The Ordnance Survey Explorer Maps (£7.50) include guides to the eastern and western sides of the park. **Disabled travelers** should pick up the *Easy Going North York Moors Guide* (£4.50) or call ☎01439 770 657 for guidance.

HELMSLEY ☎01439

Tourist-oriented shops notwithstanding, picturesque Helmsley seems to revel in the past. The town centers around the cobbled **Market Place,** site of a Friday market. Built in 1120 to strengthen the Scottish border, **Helmsley Castle** acquired its shattered profile during the Civil War, when Cromwell blew the place in half.

(☎770 442. Open daily Apr.-Sept. 10am-6pm; Oct.-Mar. 10am-4pm. ₤4, concessions ₤3.) The **Walled Garden** behind the castle contains over 50 varieties of Yorkshire apple and showcases orchids in winter. (☎771 427; www.helmsleywalledgarden.co.uk. Open Apr.-Oct. daily 10:30am-5pm; Nov.-Mar. M-F 10:30am-4pm, Sa-Su noon-4pm. ₤3, concessions ₤2.) **Duncombe Park,** ¾ mi. south of Market Pl. on Buckingham Sq., is a large park and nature reserve home to the 18th-century villa of Lord and Lady Feversham. Informative guides point out family portraits, but you may spot the noble twosome in person. (☎770 213. Gardens open Easter to Oct. M-Th and Su 11am-5:30pm. House open by hourly tour only noon-3:30pm. ₤6.50, concessions ₤5. Gardens only ₤3.60.) An enjoyable 3½ mi. walk out of town along the beginning of the Cleveland Way leads to the stunning 12th-century ⬛**Rievaulx Abbey** (REE-vo). Established by monks from Burgundy, the abbey was an aesthetic masterpiece until Thomas Mannus, first Earl of Rutland, initiated a swift decay, stripping it of valuables. It is now one of the most spectacular ruins in the country. (Moorsbus M8 stops here. ☎798 288. Open Apr.-Sept. daily 10am-6pm; Oct.-Mar. M and Th-Su 10am-4pm. ₤4, concessions ₤3.) A steep half-mile uphill, the **Rievaulx Terrace & Temples** is a small park above the abbey with 17th-century faux-classical temples at either end. (☎798 340. Open Mar.-Sept. daily 10:30am-5pm. ₤3.80.)

Helmsley has a comfortable **YHA hostel** (see p. 406) and **B&Bs. Stilworth House ❸**, 1 Church St., lets attractive, large, ensuite rooms in a Georgian townhouse near the main square. (☎771 072; www.stilworth.co.uk. ₤35 per person.) **Nice Things Cafe ❶**, 10 Market Pl., serves up tasty toasted sandwiches for ₤4. (☎771 997. Open M-F 9am-5pm, Sa-Su 9am-5:30pm. Hot food served until 3:30pm.)

Buses stop on Market Pl., where you'll find Helmsley's **Tourist Information Centre** (p. 406). Auto-less, footsore travelers might choose to catch a **taxi** to the nearby sights. (☎770 923; about ₤5 to Rievaulx.) Other services include: **banks,** on Market Pl.; **police,** Ashdale Rd. (☎01653 692 424; open daily 9am-10am and 6pm-7pm); free **Internet access** at the library, in the Town Hall (open Tu 10am-12:30pm; Th 10am-12:30pm and 2-5pm; F 10am-12:30pm, 2-5pm, and 5:30-7pm; Sa 10am-1pm); and the **post office,** Bridge St., just off Market Pl. (open M-Tu and Th-F 9am-12:30pm and 1:30-5:30pm, W and Sa 9am-12:30pm.) **Post Code:** YO62 5BG.

PICKERING   ☎01751

The attractive market town of Pickering is best known as an endpoint of the popular **North Yorkshire Moors Railway,** though it can also serve as a convenient base for exploring the national park. **Pickering Castle** soon became a favorite royal hunting spot. Though not much to look at today, Pickering is a great example of a Norman motte-and-bailey castle (p. 75). Remnants of the keep command an excellent view of the countryside. (☎474 989. Open Apr.-Sept. daily 10am-6pm; Oct. M and Th-Su 10am-4pm. ₤3, concessions ₤2.30.) The **Parish Church of St. Peter and St. Paul** is a squat Norman building with a 15th-century Gothic spire. Its medieval frescoes are in surprisingly good condition. (Open dawn-dusk. Suggested donation ₤1.)

The nearest hostel to Pickering is the **YHA Old School** in Lockton (p. 406). Among B&Bs, **Bridge House ❸**, 8 Bridge St., is close to the train station and has a pleasant rear garden beside a stream. (☎477 234; www.pickering.uk.net/bridgehouse. ₤35-40 per person.) For a friendly welcome and ensuite rooms, try **Grindale House ❸**, 123 Eastgate. (☎476 636; www.grindale-house.co.uk. Singles ₤35; doubles ₤50. MC/V.) **Wayside Caravan Park ❷**, Wrelton, 2½ mi. down the Pickering-Helmsley road, is well-maintained with beautiful park views. (☎472 608. Open Apr.-Oct. ₤13 per tent.) Pickering's **Tourist Information Centre** is at The Ropery (p. 406). Other services include: **banks,** on Market Pl.; **Internet access** at the library, next to the TIC (open M-Tu and Th 9:30am-5pm, F 9:30am-7:30pm, Sa 9:30am-4:30pm); and the **post office,** 7 Market Pl., inside Morland's Newsagents, with a bureau de change (☎472 256; open M-F 9am-5:30pm, Sa 9am-1pm). **Post Code:** YO18 7AA.

SCARBOROUGH   ☎01723

Situated on a hilly peninsula separating two long beaches and dominated by a castle-topped crag, Scarborough has been a popular destination since the mid-1600s. Although it can be tacky, Scarborough is still a major attraction for English families, especially in summer. The town has the distinct feel of a seaside resort, with numerous fish-and-chip stalls, a lively boardwalk, and ever-present seagulls.

▐ TRANSPORTATION. The **train station** is on Westborough, the main shopping street. Regional **buses** arrive and depart from several locations on Westborough; National Express services stop behind the train station, and Arriva buses in front.

▓▊ ORIENTATION AND PRACTICAL INFORMATION. A cliff crowned by Scarborough Castle divides **North Bay** and **South Bay,** both fronted by a long stretch of beach. The **Tourist Information Centre** is located on Sandside, by the South Bay. (☎383 636. Open M-Sa 9:30am-5:30pm, Su 11am-5pm.) Other services include: **banks** (with ATMs), along Westborough; **police** (☎500 300) on the corner of Northway and Victoria Rd.; **Internet access** at Cyberi @, 5 Columbus Ravine (☎341 880; £1 per hr.; open M-F 9am-5pm, Sa 9am-noon) and at the public library on Vernon Rd. (£1 per hr.); a **launderette,** 48 North Marine Rd. (☎375 763; wash £2-3, dry 20p per 4min.); and the **post office,** 11-15 Aberdeen Walk (☎08457 223 344; open Tu, W, F 9am-5:30pm; M and Th 8:45am-5:30pm; Sa 9am-12:30pm). **Post Code:** YO11 1AB.

▐▐ ACCOMMODATIONS AND FOOD. YHA **Scarborough** is 2 mi. from town (p. 406). Reasonable **B&Bs** (£17-20) can be found along Blenheim Terr., Rutland Terr., and Trafalgar Sq. **Kerry Lee Hotel ❷,** 60 Trafalgar Sq., is welcoming, spotless, and well-priced. (☎363 845. From £15 per person, ensuite £17. MC/V.) Nearby, **Whiteley Hotel ❸,** 99-101 Queen's Parade, offers attentive service and well-kept ensuite rooms, some overlooking the North Bay. (☎373 514. June-Sept. £23.50 per person, £27.50 for sea view; Oct.-May £21.50. MC/V.) Old-fashioned **Parmelia Hotel ❷,** 17 West St., has family-friendly accommodations just south of the town center. (☎361 914. Singles £20; doubles £23. Cash only.) The friendly **Terrace Hotel ❷,** 69 Westborough, welcomes the fatigued just two blocks from the train station. (☎374 937. Singles £22; doubles £38. £2 discount on additional nights. Cash only.)

For the cheapest eats, head down Westborough and turn left at St. Helen's Sq. to reach the Public Market Hall for an **outdoor market.** (☎373 579. Open M-Sa about 8am-5:30pm.) You haven't truly been to Scarborough until you've sampled its fish and chips. Many locals swear by **Mother Hubbards ❶,** 43 Westborough, where haddock with chips, bread and butter, and tea or coffee is £5. (☎376 109; www.mother-hubbards.co.uk. Open M-Sa 11:30am-6:30pm.) The **Golden Grid ❷,** 4 Sandside, in an airy dining room along the boardwalk, serves a wide range of daily specials and fresh grilled fish that goes well beyond the simple battered haddock. (☎360 922. Cod and chips £5.25. Grilled fish specials £9-16. Open daily 11am-9pm.)

▊▐ SIGHTS AND ENTERTAINMENT. While Scarborough's beach and boardwalk occupy most visitors, its other attractions are also worthwhile. Dominating the horizon atop the city's dividing headland, ▓**Scarborough Castle** was built by Henry II in 1158. A longtime strategic stronghold, the site also served as home to

Bronze-Age warriors, a Roman signal station, and a Viking fort. Its fascinating history of stubborn sieges is more than matched by tremendous views over town and sea. (☎372 451. Open Apr.-Sept. daily 10am-6pm; Oct. daily 10am-5pm; Nov.-Mar. W-Su 10am-4pm. £3, concessions £2.30; includes 1hr. audio tour.) Just down the hill, the cemetery of 12th-century **St. Mary's Parish Church,** across Church Ln., holds the grave of Anne Brontë. (☎500 541. Open May-Sept. M-F 10am-4pm, Su 1-4pm.) The **Stephen Joseph Theatre,** at the corner of Westborough and Northway right across from the train station, stages a wide range of productions and shows films. (☎370 541; www.sjt.uk.com. Box office open M-Sa 10am-8pm and before curtain.)

NORTH YORKSHIRE MOORS RAILWAY

The steam-pulled North Yorkshire Moors Railway (NYMR) chugs 18 mi. through the heart of the national park. A heritage railway, it has brilliantly restored steam engines and old-fashioned tickets. Although the whole production is in some ways a tourist trap, it's hard to avoid melting into childish excitement as the train hisses and lurches from station to station. Most visitors make a round-trip of it to savor the views, but stations along the way open up some good **hiking;** pick up *Twelve Scenic Walks from the North York Moors Railway* (£2) at any TIC. Traveling north from **Pickering,** the railway soon reaches **Levisham,** a pretty village 1½ mi. east of the station. Nearby Lockton has a self-catering **YHA hostel** (p. 406). Another stop (by request only), **Newton Dale,** is near many backcountry walks. The most popular stop is **Goathland,** largely because it was the village featured in the British TV series *Heartbeat*. The train also appeared as the "Hogwarts Express" in the first *Harry Potter* film, so be prepared for aspiring wizards in search of Platform 9¾. The NYMR terminates at **Grosmont,** also a stop on the Whitby-Middlesbrough-Esk Valley Line. *(NYMR information: ☎01751 472 508, timetable 473 535; www.northyorkshiremoorsrailway.com. 3-7 round-trips late Mar. to Oct. daily.; Nov.-Dec. most weekends; Jan.-Feb. select holidays. Grosmont to Pickering £10. All-day rover tickets £12, concessions £10.50.)*

WHITBY   ☎01947

Straddling a harbor between two desolate headlands, this beautiful seaside resort town has been the muse for history-makers and literary greats. Here Caedmon sang the first English hymns and Lewis Carroll wrote *The Walrus and the Carpenter* while eating oysters. A former whaling outpost and one of two English ports with midsummer sunrises and sunsets over the water, Whitby also inspired Captain James Cook to set sail for Australia in the 18th century. Though it has all of the diversions found in most English beach towns—fish-and-chip huts, waterfront amusements, and the like—the natural allure of the town and harbor manage to shine through, and the breathtaking ruins of Whitby Abbey loom above it all.

█+█ ORIENTATION AND PRACTICAL INFORMATION. Whitby populates the west and east banks of the River Esk, with the North Sea bordering the town to the north. The remnants of Whitby Abbey stands atop 199 steps on the east bank of the river. **Trains** and most **buses** stop at **Station Square,** Endeavour Wharf, on the west side of the river. You can also flag Scarborough-bound buses along Langborne Rd. (☎602 146. Station open M-Sa 8:15am-3:45pm.) Whitby's **Tourist Information Centre,** Station Sq., across Langborne Rd., books rooms for £1 plus a 10% deposit. (☎01723 383 636. Open daily May-Sept. 9:30am-6pm; Oct.-Apr. 10am-12:30pm and 1-4:30pm.) Other services include: **banks,** on Baxter's near the bridge; a **launderette,** 71 Church St. (☎603 957; wash £2.70-£3.50, dry 20p per 5min.; open M-Tu and Th-Sa 8:30am-5pm, W 8:30am-1pm); **police,** Spring Hill (☎603 443); **Internet access** at the library, Windsor Terr. (☎602 554; 50p per 30min.; open M and Th-F 9:30am-

5:30pm, Tu 9:30am-7pm, Sa 9:30am-4pm); and the **post office,** Langborne Rd., inside the North Eastern Co-op next to the train station (☎602 327; open M-F 8:30am-5:30pm, Sa 9am-3pm). **Post Code:** YO21 1DN.

▉▉ ACCOMMODATIONS AND FOOD. The **YHA Whitby** (p. 407), located on a hilltop right before Whitby Abbey, has incredible views. Another hostel, **Whitby Backpackers Harbour Grange ❶,** Church St., has a dockside patio, kitchen, and tidy rooms for a great price. It's 15min. from the TIC—cross the bridge to the east side of the river, walk south on Church St., and look right just after Green Ln. (☎600 817. Linen £1. Curfew 11:30pm. Dorms £10. Cash only.) **B&Bs** gather on **West Cliff,** along Royal Crescent, Crescent Ave., Abbey Terr., and nearby streets. The **Ashford Guest House ❸,** 8 Royal Crescent, is well-furnished, with ensuite rooms and sea views. (☎602 138. £24.50-£26.50 per person. Cash only.) **Camp** at the **Northcliffe Caravan Park ❶,** Bottoms Lane, 4 mi. south of town in High Hawkser. Take bus #93 from the bus station (£1), or head south on the A171 and turn onto the B1447. (☎880 477. Laundry. Mar.-Oct. £8-12; closed Nov.-Feb. Showers free. Cash only.)

The town has a twice-weekly **market** just off Church St. near the Abbey, and a giant Co-op **grocery** between the train station and the TIC. (☎600 710. Open M-F 8am-10pm, Sa 8am-8pm, Su 10:30am-4:30pm.) **The Magpie Cafe ❷,** 14 Pier Rd., serves great fish and chips. (☎602 058. Entrees £7-14. Open daily 11:30am-9pm. Cash only.) On the east side of the river, **Sanders Yard Restaurant ❶,** 95 Church St., set in a charming courtyard just off the main road, serves tasty vegetarian morsels (sandwiches £3.50) in a funky cafe and tea garden. (☎825 010; www.sandersyard.co.uk. Open daily Apr.-Oct. 9am-7pm; Nov.-Mar. 9am-5:30pm.)

◸◿ SIGHTS AND ENTERTAINMENT. Enjoying marvelous views of the bay below, the splendid ruins of ◪**Whitby Abbey** sit atop a towering hill. Bram Stoker was a frequent visitor to Whitby, and the abbey and graveyard may have inspired *Dracula.* The abbey's nonfictional history commenced in AD 675, but the present structure dates to the 14th century. (☎603 568. Open Mar.-Sept. daily 10am-6pm; Oct. daily 10am-5pm; Nov.-Feb. M and Th-Su 10am-4pm. £4, concessions £3. Free audio tour.) Next to the Abbey, the medieval **St. Mary's Church** has a triple-decker pulpit and a maze of box pews. (☎603 421. Open daily July-Aug. 10am-4:30pm; in winter 11am-2pm. Suggested donation £1.) On Bagdale, **Pannett Art Gallery and Whitby Museum,** in Pannett Park, has model ships, domestic bygones, and a fossil collection. (☎821 310; www.whitbygalleries.com. Open May-Sept. Tu-Su 9:30am-4:30pm; Oct.-Apr. Tu 10am-1pm, W-Sa 10am-4pm, Su 2-4pm. Museum £3, concessions £2.50. Gallery free.) The **Captain Cook Memorial Museum** is at Grape Ln., on the east side of the river. Occupying a historic home where Cook once stayed, the museum contains original letters, drawings, navigational instruments, and Captain Cook wax figures. (☎601 900; www.cookmuseumwhitby.co.uk. Open Apr.-Oct. daily 9:45am-5pm; Mar. Sa-Su 11am-3pm. £3, seniors £2.50, students £2.)

Whitby has a small **live music** scene; pubs like **Tab & Spile,** New Quay Rd. (☎603 937), across from the train station, have performances most nights starting at 9pm. The town takes particular pride in its **Folk Festival** (☎708 424), which brings dance, concerts, and workshops during the last full week in August. The *What's On* brochure at the TIC and the *Whitby Gazette* (published Tu and F) list events.

ROBIN HOOD'S BAY   ☎01947

Robin Hood's Bay lies in a valley that plunges down to the sea. The local population gets around by foot through the maze-like stepped alleys that snake between stone cottages. Though this enchanting town can get touristy during the summer, if you stay overnight a sense of tranquility descends. The popular **YHA Boggle Hole**

(p. 406) is 1 mi. from town. Though the town can be a daytrip, hotels and B&Bs are available. For comfortable ensuite rooms in an old sea captain's villa, try **Birtley House** ❸, Station Rd., overlooking both village and sea. (☎880 566. Singles £37.50; doubles £55. Cash only.) At the upper edge of town on the main road, **Candy's Coffee Bar** ❶, Bank Top Rd., serves up scrumptious sandwiches (£2) and more substantial lunches (£3-5). (☎07960 250 960. Open daily mid-Mar. to Oct. 9:30am-5pm; Nov. to mid-Mar. 9:30am-4:30pm.) Robin Hood's Bay is 6 mi. south of Whitby; Arriva **bus** #93 stops here en route from Scarborough (40 min.) to Whitby (20 min.).

DANBY AND THE ESK VALLEY   ☎ 01287

The gorgeous Esk Valley cuts across the northern reaches of North York Moors National Park. Outstanding views can be had without leaving the railcars of the **Esk Valley Line** (p. 404) as they travel between Whitby and Middlesbrough. It's well worth stopping off, however—this is a splendid spot for **hiking,** and marked trails leave from almost every station along the rail route. TICs and NPICs can provide further details and literature, such as *Walks in the Esk Valley* (£1.90). At the small town of **Grosmont,** the Esk Valley Line connects with another scenic train line, the **North Yorkshire Moors Railway** (p. 410). Farther west in the valley, rolling hills give way to some of the national park's finest moorland. Danby is blessed with a scenic setting snuggled in the moors. **The Moors Centre** NPIC (p. 406) is the best place to research possible routes. *Walks from the Moors Centre* (£2) lists excellent nearby walks, among them an easy 30min. jaunt to **Danby Castle,** a roofless jumble of 14th-century stones attached to a working farm. In good weather, an ascent of the 981 ft. **Danby Beacon** affords outstanding views. **The Duke of Wellington Inn** ❹ has convenient accommodations near the train station. (☎01287 660 351. Singles £35; doubles £66. MC/V.) Another option is the **Danby Mill Farm** ❷, which offers simple, riverside B&B accommodations. Turn right on the main road after leaving the train station. The farm is on the right just after the first bridge (☎01287 660 330; singles from £16; cash only). The village of **Castleton** is one stop beyond Danby, and from here the **Esk Valley Walk** (35 mi.) begins winding its way back to the coast. A lovely walk follows its first 2 mi. and ends in Danby.

COUNTY DURHAM

DURHAM   ☎ 0191

The commanding presence of England's greatest Norman Romanesque cathedral lends grandeur to the small city of Durham (pop. 90,000). For 800 years, the Bishops of Durham had absolute authority over the surrounding county, with their own currency, army, and courts. In the 1830s, new rulers—Durham University students—took over the hilltop city. Though the stream of students dries during the summer, hordes of tourists and revelers flow steadily through the narrow streets.

▟ TRANSPORTATION

Durham lies 20 mi. south of Newcastle on the A167 and an equal distance north of Darlington. The **train station** is on a steep hill west of town. (☎232 6262. Ticket office open M-F 6am-9pm, Sa 6am-8pm, Su 7:30am-9pm.) **Trains** (☎08457 484 950) arrive from: Edinburgh (2hr., 2-3 per hr., £37); London King's Cross (3hr., 2 per hr., £88); Newcastle (15min., 3 per hr., £4.10); York (45min., 3 per hr., £17). The **bus station** is on North Rd., across Framwellgate Bridge from the city center. (☎384 3323.

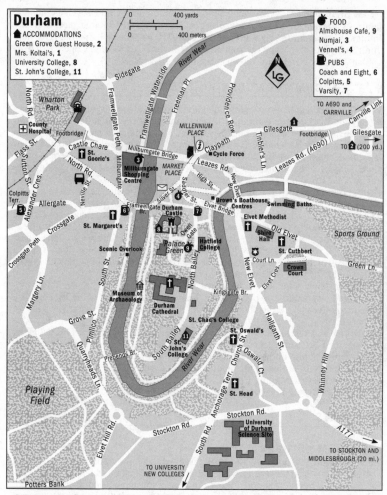

Durham

▲ ACCOMMODATIONS
Green Grove Guest House, **2**
Mrs. Koltai's, **1**
University College, **8**
St. John's College, **11**

🍎 FOOD
Almshouse Cafe, **9**
Numjai, **3**
Vennel's, **4**

🍺 PUBS
Coach and Eight, **6**
Colpitts, **5**
Varsity, **7**

NORTHEAST
ENGLAND

Office open M-F 9am-5pm, Sa 9am-4pm.) National Express (☎ 08705 808 080) runs from: Edinburgh (4½hr., 1 per day, £20); Leeds (2½hr., 4 per day, £12.75); London (6-7hr., 4 per day, £25). Go Northern and Arriva run a joint service from the Eldon Sq. station in Newcastle (#723; 1hr., 2 per hr., £4). Arriva buses serve most local routes. **Rent bikes** at Cycle Force, 29 Claypath. (☎ 384 0319. £12 per day. £35 deposit. Open M-F 9am-5:30pm, Sa 9am-5pm, Su 11am-3pm.)

🔧 🔋 ORIENTATION AND PRACTICAL INFORMATION

The **River Wear** coils around Durham, creating a partial moat crossed by a handful of footbridges. With its cobbled medieval streets, Durham is pedestrian-friendly, though travelers burdened with heavy packs will find its hills challenging. The **Tourist Information Centre**, 2 Millennium Pl., lies just east of the Millburngate Bridge.

(☎384 3720. Open M-Sa 9:30am-5:30pm, Su 11am-4pm.) Other services include: **banks** in Market Pl.; **police,** New Elvet (☎386 4222); free **Internet access** at the library, Millennium Pl., right across from the TIC (☎386 4003; open M-F 9:30am-7pm, Sa 9:30am-5pm); and the **post office,** 33 Silver St. (☎386 0839; open M and W-Sa 9am-5:30pm, Tu 9:30am-5:30pm). **Post Code:** DH1 3RE.

▮▯ ACCOMMODATIONS AND FOOD

Durham's accommodations can fill quickly; reserve ahead (especially during university graduation in late June) or take advantage of the TIC's free booking service. Durham lacks hostels, but the number of inexpensive **dormitory rooms** is a boon for summer travelers. Others merely tour it, but you can pretend to be lord or lady of Durham Castle in the ▨**University College ❸** dorms. The castle also has a small number of luxurious ensuite rooms. (☎334 4106 or 334 4108; www.durhamcastle.com. Breakfast included. Singles from £25, ensuite £35; doubles £45/65.) Behind Durham Cathedral, **St. John's College ❸,** 3 South Bailey, also offers accommodations. (☎334 3877. Breakfast included. From £23 per person, ensuite £33.) The dorms are available July-Sept. and around Easter and Christmas; contact the Durham University Conference and Tourism Office (☎334 2000). There are inexpensive **B&Bs** along Gilesgate. Among the most appealing are **Green Grove Guest House ❸,** 99 Gilesgate (☎384 4361; from £20 per person) and **Mrs. Koltai's ❸,** 10 Gilesgate, which is closer to the town center (☎386 2026; £20 per person). **Camping** is free along the river during festival weekends; call the TIC for details.

Fresh produce abounds at the **Indoor Market,** off Market Pl. (Open M-Sa 9am-5pm.) Students congregate over sandwiches or pastas (£2.50-4) in the 16th-century courtyard of **Vennel's ❶,** Saddler St., a cool bohemian alcove up a narrow passage from the street. (Open daily 9:30am-5pm. Bar open 7:30-11pm.) The busy **Almshouse Cafe and Restaurant ❷,** 10 Palace Green, near the cathedral, serves delicious specials for £4-6. Sandwiches £2. (☎361 1054. Open daily in summer 9am-8pm; in winter 9am-5:30pm. Food served noon-2:30pm and 5:30-8pm.) Dine on excellent Thai cuisine (£10) at **Numjai ❷,** 19 Millburngate Centre, at the northeast corner of the Millburngate Shopping Centre, right on the river. (☎386 2020; www.numjai.co.uk. Open daily 11:30am-2:30pm and 6-10pm.)

◉ SIGHTS

▨ DURHAM CATHEDRAL

Built between 1093 and 1133 (and still largely intact), the extraordinary Durham Cathedral stands, in the words of Sir Walter Scott, as "half church of God, half castle 'gainst the Scot." It is considered the finest Norman cathedral in the world. Explanatory panels are sprinkled throughout the cathedral, though a more detailed pamphlet (£1) is also available. The stunning **nave** was the first in England to incorporate pointed arches. At the end of the nave, the beautiful **Galilee Chapel** features 12th-century wall paintings. Nearby is the simple tomb of the Venerable Bede, author of the 8th-century Ecclesiastical History of the English People, the first history of England. Behind the choir is the **tomb of Saint Cuthbert,** who died in AD 687 and was buried on Holy Island. When 9th-century Danish raiders sent the island's monks packing, the brothers brought along the saint's body as they fled. After wandering for 120 years, a vision led the monks to Durham, where they built White Church (later the cathedral) to shelter the saint's shrine. Next to the choir, the **Bishop's throne** stands nearly three inches higher than the Pope's throne at the Vatican. (*Crowning the hill in the middle of the city.* ☎386 4266; www.durhamcathedral.co.uk. *Open June-Sept. M-Sa 9:30am-8pm, Su 12:30-8pm; Oct.-May M-Sa 9:30am-6pm, Su 12:30-5pm. Tours available June-Sept. Suggested donation £4.*) The cathedral's central **tower** reaches 218 ft. and is supported by intricately carved stone pillars. The spectacular view from the top is well worth the 325-step climb it takes to get there. *(Open mid-Apr. to Sept. M-Sa 10am-4pm; Oct. to mid-Apr. M-Sa 10am-3pm, weather permitting. £2, under 16. £1, families £5.)* The **Monks' Dormitory** off the cloister houses pre-Conquest stones and casts of crosses under an enormous 600-year-old timber roof. *(Open Apr.-Sept. M-Sa 10am-3:30pm, Su 12:30-3:15pm. 80p.)* The **Treasures of St. Cuthbert,** also off the cloister, holds saintly relics, holy manuscripts dating back 1300 years, and rings and seals of the Bishops. *(Open M-Sa 10am-4:30pm, Su 2-4:30pm. £2, concessions £1.50.)*

DURHAM CASTLE. Begun in 1072, this fortress was for centuries a key bastion of the county's Prince Bishops (top brass religious royalty). Today it's a splendid residence for university students or summer sojourners. *(Across from the Cathedral. ☎ 334 3800. Admission by guided tour only. Open daily Mar.-Sept. 10am-12:30pm and 2-4pm; Oct.-Feb. M, W, Sa-Su 2-4pm. £5.)*

BEST OF THE REST. A pleasant afternoon can be spent wandering the horseshoe bend of the River Wear. Along the bank between Framwellgate Bridge and Prebends Bridge, the **Museum of Archaeology** showcases an extensive collection of Roman stone altars alongside finds from the prehistoric period to the present. *(☎ 334 1823. Open Apr.-Oct. daily 11am-4pm; Nov.-Mar. M and F-Su 11:30am-3:30pm. £1, concessions 50p.)* **Brown's Boathouse Centres,** Elvet Bridge, rents rowboats. *(☎ 386 3779. £3 per hr. per person. £5 deposit.)* For a less arduous journey, the center runs a 1hr. cruise on the **Prince Bishop River Cruiser.** *(☎ 386 9525. Easter to Sept. daily; times depend on weather and university boating events. £4.50, concessions £4.)*

◪ ▓ NIGHTLIFE AND FESTIVALS

Don't let Durham's historic majesty fool you: in the evening a rollicking crowd of students and locals enlivens the scene. After-hours entertainment is closely tied to university life, and when students depart for the holidays, most nightlife follows suit. The intersection of **Elvet Bridge** and **Saddler Street,** right in the city center, is a good place to be at 10pm. A young crowd fills the popular **Varsity** pub, 46 Saddler St. *(☎ 384 6704. Open M-Sa 11am-11pm, Su noon-10:30pm.)* Serving a mostly local crowd, the sporty riverside **Coach and Eight,** Bridge House, Framwellgate Bridge, is enormous and has a giant-screen TV to match. *(☎ 386 0056. Discotheque Th-Su. Open M-W 10am-11pm, Th and Su 10am-midnight, F-Sa 10am-1pm.)* **Colpitts,** Colpitts Terr., is well suited to live music and offers a more low-key setting. *(☎ 386 9913. Open M-Sa noon-11pm, Su noon-10:30pm.)*

The TIC stocks the free pamphlet *What's On,* a great source of information on festivals and local events. Durham holds its **Summer Festival** in the first weekend of July, showcasing folk music, craftsmaking, and other amusements, including a town crier competition *(☎ 384 3720).* Other major events include the June **Durham Regatta,** England's foremost amateur rowing competition since 1834.

▶ DAYTRIP FROM DURHAM

BEAMISH OPEN-AIR MUSEUM. Perhaps the area's most famous attraction outside of Durham, Beamish is a re-creation of 18th- and early 19th-century life in North England, featuring villages with costumed actors, a farmhouse, a manor house, an 1825 replica railway, and a tour into the depths of a former **drift mine.** There's quite a lot to see; plan on spending two to four hours, depending on the season—some attractions only operate in high season. *(8 mi. northwest of Durham on the A693. Go Northern bus #720 travels from Durham to the museum gates (30min., every hr.). ☎ 370 4000. Open daily Apr.-Oct. 10am-5pm; Nov.-Mar. Tu-Th and Sa-Su 10am-4pm, last admission 3pm. Closed late Dec. £15, concessions £12; all visitors £5 in winter.)*

BARNARD CASTLE ☎ 01833

Twenty miles southwest of Durham along the River Tees, Barnard Castle—the name of both a peaceful market town and its Norman ruins—is the best base for exploring the castles of Teesdale and the peaks of the North Pennine Hills. It also hosts a collection of European masters at the impressive Bowes Museum.

🖂❼ TRANSPORTATION AND PRACTICAL INFORMATION. To reach Barnard Castle from Durham, take Go North East **bus** #723 to Darlington (50min., 2 per hr., £2.60), and then change to Arriva bus #75 to Barnard Castle (40min., 2-3 per hr., £3). Just down the road from the main bus stop lies the well-stocked **Tourist Information Centre,** Woodleigh, Flatts Rd. (☎ 690 909. Open Apr.-Oct. M-Sa 9:30am-5pm, Su 11am-5pm; Nov.-Mar. M-Sa 11am-4pm.) Other services include: **banks** on Market Pl.; **police,** Harmire Rd. (☎ 637 328); and the **post office,** 2 Galgate, with a bureau de change (☎ 638 247; open M-Sa 9am-5:30pm). **Post Code:** DL12 8BE.

▐▌❂ ACCOMMODATIONS AND FOOD. Barnard Castle has no hostel, but is blessed with superb **B&Bs,** many of which line Galgate. **Marwood House ❸,** 98 Galgate, offers TV, an exercise room, and a sauna. (☎ 637 493. Singles from £25, ensuite £28-30.) Across the street, the **Homelands ❸,** 85 Galgate, has upscale rooms and a lovely garden. (☎ 638 757. Singles £28, ensuite £35; doubles £56-60. Cash only.) The **Hayloft,** 27 Horsemarket, is an indoor market jammed with antiques and bric-a-brac, a cafe, and produce (open W and F-Sa 9:30am-5pm). **Stables Restaurant ❶,** in the Hayloft, provides sandwiches and salads (£3), along with other meals for under £4. (☎ 690 670. Open M-Sa 9am-4:30pm, Su 10am-3:30pm. Cash only.)

◐ SIGHTS. Perched above the River Tees, the remains of **Barnard Castle,** including a well-preserved inner keep, sprawl across six acres. (☎ 638 212. Enter between the TIC and a church. Open Apr.-Sept. daily 10am-6pm; Oct. daily 10am-4pm; Nov.-Mar. M and Th-Su 10am-4pm. £3.30, concessions £2.50. Free audio tour.) In the 19th century, John and Josephine Bowes built the remarkable **▧Bowes Museum** along Newgate to bring Continental culture to England. The gallery now houses the couple's extensive private collection. Among its many treasures is the largest gathering of Spanish paintings in Britain—El Greco's magnificent *Tears of St. Peter,* among others—and a mechanized silver swan (activated every day at 12:30 and 3:30pm) fancied by Mark Twain. (☎ 690 606; www.bowesmuseum.org.uk. Open daily 11am-5pm. Tours May-Aug. Tu-Th 2 per day, Sa-Su 1 per day. £6, concessions £5, families £15, under 16 free.) Dickens fans can follow the **Dickens Drive,** a 25 mi. route that traces the path the famed author took in 1838 while researching for Nicholas Nickleby. Pick up *In the Footsteps of Charles Dickens,* free from the TIC. Overlooking the River Tees, the ruins of 12th-century **Egglestone Abbey** are a pleasant 3 mi. circular walk along the river to the southeast of town. Arriva bus #79 from Barnard Castle will also drop you there. (Open dawn-dusk. Free.) Northeast of Barnard Castle on the A688, **Raby Castle** (RAY-bee) is a palatial 14th-century fortress with a deer park. Take bus #75 (20min., 2 per hr., £1.50) toward Darlington. (☎ 660 202; www.rabycastle.com. Castle open June-Aug. M-F and Su 1-5pm; May and Sept. W and Su 1-5pm. Park and gardens open same days 11am-5:30pm. £9, concessions £8. Park and gardens only £4/3.50.)

TYNE AND WEAR

NEWCASTLE-UPON-TYNE ☎ 0191

The largest city in the northeast, Newcastle (pop. 278,000) has all but shed its image as a faded capital of industry. Ambitious building efforts—from a restoration of the historical district to a world-class music hall and a museum of modern art—have lent the city energy and even pockets of beauty. Things heat up at night, when locals, students, and tourists head to Newcastle's (in)famous pubs and clubs. Best of all, perhaps, are the people: Newcastle Geordies are proud of their accent, very proud of their football club, and very, very proud of their brown ale.

▛ TRANSPORTATION

Newcastle lies 1½hr. north of York on the A19 and 1½hr. east of Carlisle on the A69. Edinburgh is 2½hr. north of Newcastle on the A1, which follows the North Sea coast, or the A68, which cuts inland.

Trains: Central Station, Neville St. Travel center sells same-day tickets M-Sa 4:30am-9:20pm, Su 7:10am-10pm and advance tickets M-F 7am-8pm, Sa 7am-7pm, Su 8:40am-8pm. Luggage storage £4 per bag. Trains (☎08457 484 950) from: **Carlisle** (1½hr., frequent, £11.10); **Durham** (15min., 4 per hr., £4.30); **Edinburgh** (1½hr., frequent, £36); **London King's Cross** (3½hr., every hr., £83).

Buses: Newcastle has two main bus stations.

St. James Station, St. James Blvd., serves National Express (☎08705 808 080) buses from **Edinburgh** (3hr., 4 per day, £13.50) and **London** (7hr., 4 per day, £24).

Haymarket Station, by the Metro stop, and adjunct **Eldon Square Station,** Percy St., are the gateways for local and regional service by Arriva (☎261 1779). Ticket office open M-F 7am-5pm, Sa 9am-4pm.

Ferries: International Ferry Terminal, Royal Quays, 7 mi. east of Newcastle. Fjord Line (☎296 1313; www.fjordline.no) and DFDS Seaways (☎08750 333 000; www.dfdsseaways.co.uk) offer ferry service to **Norway, Sweden,** and the **Netherlands** (see **By Ferry,** p. 28). Bus #327 serves all departures, leaving Central Station and stopping at YHA Newcastle 2½hr. and 1¼hr., respectively, before each sailing. From the Percy Main Metro stop, the quay is a 20 min. walk.

Public Transportation: Call Traveline (☎08706 082 608) for complete details. The Metro **subway** system runs from the city center to the coast and the airport, as well as to neighboring towns like Gateshead and Sunderland. Tickets (£1-2.40) are purchased beforehand and checked onboard. The **DaySaver** allows 1 day of unlimited travel (£3.20). Trains run 6am-11:30pm. Local **buses** stop throughout the city, with main terminals at the Haymarket Metro and the Eldon Square Shopping Centre. A **DayRover,** available at TICs and Metro and bus offices, offers unlimited travel on all Tyne & Wear public transport (£4.50, under 18 £2.30).

Taxis: Taxis are easy to find in the city center. **ABC Taxi** (☎232 3636); **Biker Taxi** (☎276 1192).

✶ ORIENTATION

The free map of Newcastle available at the TIC is essential; streets change in direction and name, especially near the river. **Grey's Monument** is in the center of the city and is useful for orientation. Dedicated to Charles, Earl of Grey, the man responsi-

GEORDIE (AN PROU')

What exactly is a Geordie (JOR-dee)? Anyone born in the regions of Northumberland, Durham, or Tyne and Wear can claim Geordie status. But possessive as these Northerners are of their nickname, its precise origins are debatable.

All agree that the name "Geordie" is a diminutive of "George." During the Jacobite Rebellion of 1745, Newcastle's denizens supported the Hanoverian King George and were deemed "for George" by the Jacobites. In 1815, George Stephenson, renowned as the principal inventor of the railroad locomotive, invented the miner's lamp. It quickly gained favor among Northumberland miners, who became known as Geordies. In 1826, Stephenson spoke before the Parliamentary Commission of Railways, and his dialect amused the snooty southerners, who began to call all keelmen carrying coal down the Thames "Geordies."

The Geordie accent, which renders English indecipherable to many ears, stretches vowel sounds. If you hear a Geordie remark "Eez adaft-ay, an eez on tha booze," he's telling you, "That man is silly and has had too much to drink." This singular dialect does not always mask such polite commentary, however. "Aa'll pay ye heed sk a byestin," is translated "I may hurt you," but the Geordie slang may convey a more accurate sentiment.

ble for the 1832 Reform Bill and for mixing bergamot into tea, this 80 ft. pillar in **Monument Mall** sits opposite **Eldon Square.** The main shopping drag, **Northumberland Street,** is nearby. The city of **Gateshead** sits across the Tyne (rhymes with "mine") from Newcastle and is home to many of the area's attractions.

▌ PRACTICAL INFORMATION

Tourist Information Centre: Central Arcade, 132 Grainger St. (☎277 8000). Books rooms for a 10% deposit. Open June-Sept. M-F 9:30am-5:30pm, Sa 9am-5:30pm, Su 10am-4pm; Oct.-May M-F 9:30am-5:30pm, Sa 9am-5:30pm. Branch at Central Station open M-F 9:30am-5pm, Sa 9am-5pm.

Tours: The TIC offers various walking and coach tours June-Sept. (£2-6.50). **Citysightseeing Newcastle Gateshead** (☎08716 660 000; www.city-sightseeing.com) operates a popular hop-on, hop-off tour. Departures every 30-60min. from Central Station.

Financial Services: Halifax, 11 New Bridge St. W (☎08706 005 000). Open M-Tu and F-Sa 9am-5:30pm, W 10am-5:30pm, Th 9am-8pm.

Police: (☎214 6555), at the corner of Market St. and Pilgrim St.

Hospital: Royal Victoria Infirmary, Queen Victoria Rd. (☎232 5131).

Pharmacy: There are numerous pharmacies along Northumberland St., near the library.

Internet Access: City Library, Princess Sq. (☎277 4100), Northumberland Pl. Free. 2hr. max. Open M-Th 9am-8pm, F-Sa 9am-5pm, Su noon-4pm.

Post Office: 9 Clayton St. (☎281 3882), inside the shopping center entrance. **Post Code:** NE2 4RP.

▌ ACCOMMODATIONS

Inexpensive lodgings are scarce in Newcastle; call ahead. Pickings are slim in the city center, but the YHA hostel and several guest houses are within reasonable walking distance or a short Metro ride. Guest houses and small hotels cluster in residential **Jesmond,** 1 mi. from the city center and serviced by the Metro.

YHA Newcastle, 107 Jesmond Rd. (☎08707 705 972). Metro: Jesmond. A 20min. walk from the city center. 50 beds in a comfortable townhouse. Often full; call well in advance. Internet access £2.50 per 30min. Reception 7-11pm. Curfew 11pm. Open mid-Jan. to mid-Dec. Dorms £16-19, under 18 £12.50-15.50. AmEx/MC/V. ❷

University of Northumbria, Sandyford Rd. (☎227 3215; www.unn.ac.uk). Metro: Haymarket. Check in at Claude Gibb Hall. Standard dorm bed-basin-desk com-

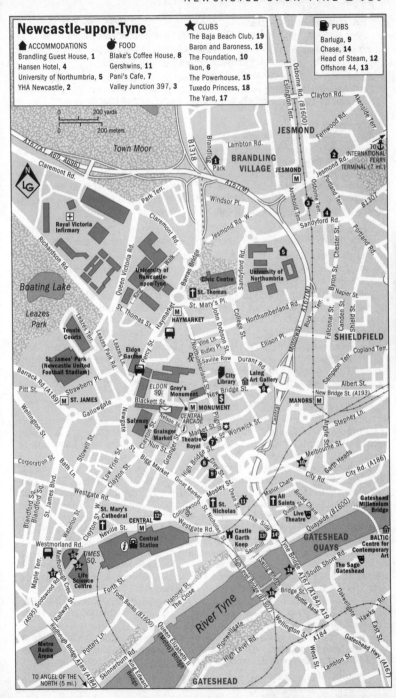

Newcastle-upon-Tyne

ACCOMMODATIONS
Brandling Guest House, 1
Hansen Hotel, 4
University of Northumbria, 5
YHA Newcastle, 2

FOOD
Blake's Coffee House, 8
Gershwins, 11
Pani's Cafe, 7
Valley Junction 397, 3

CLUBS
The Baja Beach Club, 19
Baron and Baroness, 16
The Foundation, 10
Ikon, 6
The Powerhouse, 15
Tuxedo Princess, 18
The Yard, 17

PUBS
Barluga, 9
Chase, 14
Head of Steam, 12
Offshore 44, 13

bos, some with partial kitchen, in close proximity to the city center. Breakfast included. Open June-Aug. Singles M-Th and Su from £23.25, F-Sa from £30.50. MC/V. ❸

Brandling Guest House, 4 Brandling Park (☎281 3175). Metro: Jesmond. 9 spacious rooms on a quiet block. Singles from £29; doubles from £46. MC/V. ❸

Hansen Hotel, 131 Sandyford Rd. (☎281 0289). Metro: Jesmond. Small hotel a 15min. walk from the city center. Internet access in hotel cafe 7am-4:30pm £1. Singles £23-28; doubles £46-56. Discounts for groups of 4 or more. AmEx/MC/V. ❸

🍴 FOOD

Newcastle has tons of inexpensive food. Chinese eateries form a small Chinatown along **Stowell Street** near St. James Blvd.; all-you-can-eat specials for £6 are common. Many of the restaurants lining **Dean Street** serve cheap lunch specials. Safeway **supermarket,** Clayton St., is located in the city center. (☎261 2805. Open M-Sa 8am-7pm, Su 11am-5pm.) The **Grainger Indoor Market** is on Grainger St., near the monument. (Open M and W 8am-5pm, Tu and Th-Su 8am-5:30pm.)

Pani's Cafe, 61 High Bridge St. (☎232 4366. www.pani.net). Italian eatery steps from Grey St. with £7-10 dishes and a bustling vibe. Open M-Sa 10am-10pm. Cash only. ❷

Blake's Coffee House, 53 Grey St. (☎261 5463). A popular, central hangout with a range of lunch fare (£4-5) and good sandwiches (£2-3). Open M-F 7am-5:30pm, Sa-Su 7am-4pm. Cash only. ❶

Valley Junction 397, Archbold Terr. (☎281 6397), in an old train station near the Jesmond Metro terminal. Bengali-influenced cuisine served in an antique railway car. The Indian lager Kingfisher (£3.25) blends well with spinach-based paneers (£6-7). Vegan fare available. Open Tu-Sa noon-2pm and 6-11:30pm, Su 6-11:30pm. MC/V. ❷

Gershwins, 54 Dean St. (☎261 8100; www.gershwinsrestaurant.co.uk). Cool underground restaurant with overhead star lighting. Runs special theater menus and serves Continental cuisine (£10-15). Reservations recommended on theater nights. Open M-F 11:30am-2:30pm and 5:30-11pm, Sa 11:30am-11pm. MC/V. ❸

👁 SIGHTS

The largely intact **Castle Garth Keep,** at the foot of St. Nicholas St., is all that remains of the 12th-century New Castle, which was built on the site of the castle of Robert Curthose, William the Conqueror's illegitimate son. Oddly enough, the "New Castle" for which the city is named is the original Curthose structure. (☎232 7938. Open daily Apr.-Sept. 9:30am-5:30pm; Oct.-Mar. 9:30am-4:30pm. £1.50, concessions 50p.) Just uphill at the corner of Mosley St., the **Cathedral Church of St. Nicholas** is topped with an elegant set of small towers around a double arch, meant to resemble Jesus's crown of thorns. (Open M-F 7am-6pm, Sa 8am-4pm, Su 7am-noon and 4-7pm. Free.) The **Laing Art Gallery,** New Bridge St., displays a striking array of watercolors and sculptures and pieces by pre-Raphaelite masters. The galleries also host frequent exhibitions, recently featuring the works of Van Gogh. (☎232 7734. Open M-Sa 10am-5pm, Su 2-5pm. Free.) Newcastle has spearheaded its recent urban renewal with projects showcasing science, technology, and the arts. The **Life Science Centre,** Times Sq., on Scotswood Rd. by the train station, is a family-friendly, hands-on science museum with a motion simulator and 3-D movies. (☎243 8210; www.lifesciencecenter.org.uk. Open M-Sa 10am-6pm, Su 11am-6pm. Last admission 3:30pm. £7, concessions £5.50.)

Newcastle's recent cultural renaissance manifests itself most clearly along the **Gateshead Quays,** the site of major new development in the city. The **Gateshead Millennium Bridge** is the world's only rotating bridge, opening like a giant eyelid to allow ships to pass. Colored spotlights illuminate its footbridge every evening. Best reached by the bridge, the ⬛BALTIC Centre for Contemporary Art, housed in a renovated mid-century warehouse, is the largest center for contemporary visual art outside London. (☎478 1810; www.balticmill.com. Open M-W and F-Sa 10am-7pm, Th 10am-10pm, Su 10am-5pm. Free.) Nearby, the Sage Gateshead, a glass and steel structure that resembles a giant glass beetle, dominates the riverbank. Completed in 2005, the massive world-class complex of concert halls is home to the Northern Sinfonia, the Northumberland regional orchestra. (☎443 4661; www.thesagegateshead.org. Box office open M-Sa 10am-8pm, Su 10am-6pm. Tours Sa-Su noon and 5:30pm. £6. Tickets £6-21. MC/V.) Heading south from Newcastle by rail or road, you can't miss the ponderous Angel of the North, 5 mi. from the city off the A1. Admired by an estimated 33 million people per year, the striking 200-ton steel sculpture is 66 ft. tall and wider than a jumbo jet.

▣ NIGHTLIFE

Home of the nectar known as brown ale, Newcastle has a legendary party scene. Rowdy Geordie havens line Bigg Market, which features one of England's highest concentrations of bars. Be cautious in this area—stocky footballer Paul "Gazza" Gascoigne was beaten up twice here for deserting Newcastle. Beside the river, Quayside (KEY-side) and Gateshead (across the Tyne) attract a slightly younger crowd. For a less heart-stopping, bass-thumping night out, Osborne Road, in Jesmond, 1 mi. north of the city center, is increasingly popular with students and locals for traditional bar-hopping. *The Crack* (monthly; free at record stores) is the best source for music and club listings in Newcastle.

PUBS

Pubs are generally open Monday to Saturday 11am-11pm and Sunday noon-10:30pm; some are only open evenings. Most offer happy hours until 8pm.

Chase, 10-15 Sandhill (☎245 0055), Quayside. Neon lights and a fluorescent bar give this hopping pub a trendy rep. The outdoor garden is the place to see and be seen. Open daily 6-11pm.

The Head of Steam, 2 Neville St. (☎230 4236). Across from Central Station. This split-level venue features the best in live soul, funk, and reggae; occasionally local DJs go head to head in special mixing contests. DJs F-Sa 9pm. Live bands M-Th and Su 8pm. Open M-Sa 11am-11pm, Su noon-10:30pm.

Offshore 44, 40 Sandhill (☎261 0921), Quayside. Bearing an uncanny resemblance to a pirate's lair, this riverside pub blasts rock classics amidst treasure chests, candles, and palm trees. Packed by 10pm and popular with the student crowd. Open M-Sa 11am-11pm, Su noon-10:30pm.

Barluga, 35 Grey St. (☎230 2306). A posh pub with serious class, offering a selection of oysters, mussels, and caviar. Perfect for an afternoon cocktail or a pre-theater swig. Laid-back all-day jazz brunch Su £10. Open M-Sa 11am-11pm, Su noon-10:30pm.

CLUBS

Opening hours and special events vary with season. Most clubs expect sharp streetwear; leave the sneakers at home.

Tuxedo Princess, Hillgate Quay (☎477 8899), Gateshead. Perhaps the city's hottest dance club, located on a decommissioned ship under Tyne Bridge and complete with a rotating dance floor. Call for tickets in advance to avoid a ridiculous wait at the door. £2 drinks for students F-Sa until 11:30pm. Cover £4-10. Open M, Th, and Sa 9pm-2am; F 9:30pm-2am.

The Foundation, 57 Melbourne St. (☎261 8985; www.foundation-club.co.uk). With a dark and smoky interior, this gutted factory warehouse attracts a flashy crowd. Sa night "Shindig" attracts the country's top DJs. Cover £5-10. Open M and Th 10pm-2am, F and Sa 9pm-4am, Su 10pm-3am.

Ikon, 49 New Bridge St. (☎261 2526). Lined with bars, this club has a crowded dance floor every night. Cover £3-7. Open Th-Sa 10pm-2am.

The Baja Beach Club, Pipewellgate (☎477 6205), Gateshead. Churning out hip-hop hits and pop anthems, this club maintains a huge following thanks in large part to its bikini-clad staff. Cover £2-6. Open M-Sa 9pm-2:15am.

GAY- AND LESBIAN-FRIENDLY NIGHTLIFE

The Powerhouse, Westmorland Rd. (☎261 9755). Uber-popular gay-friendly club. Ultra-chic black decor. The Purple Lounge upstairs offers views of the talent below. Cover £5-8. Open M-F 10:30pm-3am, Sa 10am-4am, Su 10:30am-1am.

Baron and Baroness, Times Sq. (☎233 0414). Rustic wood decor contrasts with its neighbors. 2 levels are filled with alcoves. Open M, Th, and Su 11am-midnight; Tu-W 11am-11pm; F-Sa 11am-1am.

The Yard, 2 Scotswood Rd. (☎232 2037). An attractive bar that eschews the clubby atmosphere of its neighbors. Uproarious drag shows M and Su. Karaoke Su 5-11pm. Cover £5-10. Open M-Th 1pm-1am, F-Sa noon-1am, Su 1pm-12:30am.

♫ ENTERTAINMENT

For more refined entertainment, treat yourself to an evening at the lush, gilt-and-velvet **Theatre Royal,** 100 Grey St. (☎0870 905 5060; www.theatreroyal.co.uk. Booking office open M-Tu and Th-Sa 9am-8pm, W 10am-8pm.) The **Royal Shakespeare Company** makes a month-long stop at the Theatre Royal each fall, complementing the top-notch array of musicals with Shakespeare and contemporary plays. The **Live Theatre,** 27 Broad Chare, Quayside, showcases local writers and new talent with dance, music, and theater nightly. (☎232 1232; www.live.org.uk. Ticket office open M-F 10am-6pm and Sa-Su from 2hr. before shows. Cafe open 10am-11pm.)

St. James' Park, home of the **Newcastle United Football Club,** is a prominent feature of the city skyline. Tickets can be hard to come by; book in advance. (☎201 8400, ticket office 261 1571; www.nufc.co.uk.) The **Newcastle Racecourse,** in the enormous High Gosforth Park, holds a number of top horse-racing events each year and makes for a great day at the track. (☎236 2020.)

NORTHUMBERLAND

NORTHUMBERLAND NATIONAL PARK

Northumberland National Park stretches south from the Cheviot Hills to Hadrian's Wall, marking the site of many skirmishes involving territorial Romans. Great coniferous forests, heathered moorlands, hills, and bogs cover this idyllic region. This roughest-edged of England's national parks is blissfully free of tourists.

▐ TRANSPORTATION

Public transportation is limited and requires planning. **Bus** routes radiate outward from Berwick-upon-Tweed in the north and Newcastle in the south. Getting to the area by bus is tricky; getting around the area by bus is nearly impossible. Bus #880 runs from Hexham to Bellingham (45min.; M-Sa 10 per day, Su 3 per day). Bus #416/516 runs from Newcastle to Rothbury via Morpeth

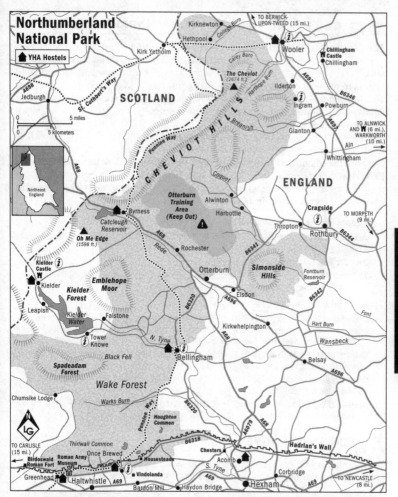

Northumberland National Park

🏠 YHA Hostels

(1¼hr.; M-Sa 7 per day, Su 3 per day) and bus 508 goes via Belsay (1½hr., Su only, 2 per day). Change at Morpeth if traveling to Rothbury from Alnwick. From Wooler, bus #470/473 heads to Alnwick (50min.; M-Sa 14 per day, Su 2 per day) and #267/464 to Berwick (1hr.; M-Sa 10 per day, Su 3 per day). Bus #710 connects Wooler with Newcastle and the Scottish Borders (W and Sa 1 per day). National Express's (☎08705 808 080) Newcastle-Jedburgh-Edinburgh bus cuts through the park and stops at Byrness (#383, 1 per day). Bus #714 travels from Gateshead (across the river from Newcastle) via Bellingham to Kielder/Kielder Water (2hr.; June-Oct. Su 1 per day). Year-round, **Postbus** #815 journeys from Hexham to Kielder via Bellingham (2½hr., M-Sa 2 per day). For schedules, call Traveline (☎08706 082 608), grab the extremely helpful 256-page *Northumberland Public Transport Guide* (£1.20), or opt for the more manageable (and free) *Experience Northumberland by Bus*, available at TICs and bus stations. Though not valid on every service in the area, a single-day **Northeast Explorer ticket** (£6), available on participating buses, is a good buy.

▰ ❓ ORIENTATION AND PRACTICAL INFORMATION

The park runs from **Hadrian's Wall** (p. 429) in the south up along the Scottish border as far north as the Cheviot foothills. **Bellingham, Rothbury,** and **Wooler** are small towns near the park's eastern edge that offer accommodations and good access to walking routes. In the southwest, just outside the park, the large reservoir of **Kielder Water** is surrounded by England's largest pine forest (the **Kielder Forest**) and is popular for a variety of outdoor pursuits. The A69 marks the park's southern border while the A68 cuts right through its heart toward Scotland. The Ministry of Defense operates a **live firing range** in the middle of the park south of the Cheviot Hills; walkers should heed the warning signs.

Northumberland National Park operates three **National Park Information Centres (NPICs),** which can advise on hikes and activities and make accommodation bookings. During the warmer months, they offer ranger-led talks and walks. There are also several **Tourist Information Centres** in the area.

National Park Information Centres:

Ingram: Visitor Centre (☎01665 578 890). Open daily June-Aug. 10am-6pm; Apr.-May and Sept.-Oct. 10am-5pm.

Once Brewed: For Hadrian's Wall; see p. 430.

Rothbury: Church St. (☎01669 620 887). Open June-Aug. daily 10am-6pm; Apr.-May and Sept.-Oct. daily 10am-5pm; Nov.-Mar. Sa-Su 10am-3pm.

Tourist Information Centres:

Bellingham: Main St. (☎01434 220 616). Open Easter to mid-May M-Sa 9:30am-1pm and 2-5pm, Su 1-5pm; mid-May to Sept. M-Sa 9:30am-1pm and 2-5pm, Su 1-5pm; Oct. M-Sa 9:30am-1pm and 2-5pm, Su 1-5pm; Nov. to Easter M-F 2-5pm.

Kielder Forest: Visitor Centre (☎01434 250 209), off the C200 in Kielder Castle. Open Apr.-Oct. daily 10am-5pm; Nov.-Dec. Sa-Su 11am-4pm.

Tower Knowe (Kielder): Visitor Centre (☎01434 240 436), off the C200. Open Apr.-Oct. daily 10am-6pm; Nov.-Mar. Sa-Su 10am-4pm.

Wooler: Cheviot Centre, 12 Padgepool Pl. (☎01668 282 123). Open Easter to June and Oct. M-Sa 10am-4pm, Su 10am-3pm; Jul.-Aug. M-Sa 10am-5pm, Su 10am-4pm.; Nov.-Mar. Sa-Su 10am-3pm.

▰ ACCOMMODATIONS

Bellingham, Rothbury, Wooler, and Kielder Water have **B&Bs** and **hotels.** The following **YHA hostels** offer accommodations in or near the park.

Bellingham: Woodburn Rd. (☎08707 705 694). Self-catering cedar cabin along the Pennine Way. Reception 5-11pm. Open July-Aug. daily; Apr.-June and Sept.-Oct. Tu-Sa. Dorms £10-13, under 18 £7-10. MC/V. ❶

Byrness: 7 Otterburn Green (☎08707 705 740). National Express bus #383 (Newcastle-Edinburgh via Jedburgh) will stop here. Basic, self-catering hostel along the Pennine Way. Reception 5-11pm. Open Apr.-Sept. Dorms £10-13, under 18 £7-10. MC/V. ❶

Kielder: Butteryhaugh, Kielder Village (☎08707 705 898), off the C200. Spacious, modern facility. Open daily Jan.-Oct. Dorms £12.50-13.50, under 18 £9-10. MC/V. ❶

Wooler: 30 Cheviot St. (☎08707 706 100). A 5min. walk up Cheviot St. from the bus station. Comfortable hostel with self-catering kitchen and laundry. Reception 8:30-10:30am and 5-10:30pm. Open Apr.-Oct. Dorms £11-14, under 18 £8-11. MC/V. ❶

HIKING

The **Pennine Way** (p. 391) traverses the park, entering at Hadrian's Wall, passing through Bellingham and the Cheviot Hills, and terminating at Kirk Yetholm, Scotland. **St. Cuthbert's Way** runs through the Cheviot Hills and Wooler on its way between Melrose, Scotland, and Holy Island. Shorter options abound, including walks in the **Simonside Hills,** near Rothbury, and the **Cheviot foothills,** near Wooler. Ordnance Survey produces two Explorer maps, which together cover the entire park and are available at local NPICs and TICs (£13). Many books, including *Walking the Cheviots* (£8), describe walks in depth. The area's isolation is a good reason to walk here—but maps and proper equipment are essential (see **Wilderness Safety,** p. 46). NPICs and TICs can provide hiking suggestions.

BELLINGHAM AND KIELDER WATER ☎ 01434

Modest Bellingham (BELL-in-jum) is a convenient gateway. The Pennine Way passes through; one fine section heads 18 mi. south to Once Brewed, along Hadrian's Wall. Also leaving from town is the easy 3 mi. round-trip walk to **Hareshaw Linn,** a beautiful waterfall in a rocky gorge that has attracted picnickers since Victorian times. Guides (20p) are available at the **TIC** on Main St. (p. 424). In town, the 12th-century **Church of St. Cuthbert** was built with a rare stone-vaulted roof so that raiding Border Reivers couldn't burn it down.

Another 10 mi. beyond Bellingham and just outside the park lies **Kielder Water,** a man-made reservoir that today provides northeast England with much of its drinking water. Two visitor centers, **Tower Knowe** and **Kielder Castle,** serve the area and are joined by the C200, which runs along the reservoir's western shore. The densely packed **Kielder Forest** surrounds the water and promises great hiking and cycling along its many timber-hauling roads, including the popular 26 mi. **Kielder Water Circuit. Kielder Bikes,** just past Kielder Castle on the way up from town, provides good advice on the extensive network of on- and off-road routes. (☎ 250 392. Open daily dawn-dusk. Bikes £7.50 per half-day, £8.75 per day.) The **Kielder Water Ferry Osprey** departs from Tower Knowe and tours the reservoir, also stopping at the Leaplish Waterside Park, a popular spot for campers, lodgers, and caravans. (☎ 250 312. 1¼hr. Apr.-Oct. 5 per day. £5.50, concessions £5.) The **Hawkhirst Adventure Camp** (☎ 250 217) offers a variety of activities, including canoeing, archery, and climbing, although availability varies significantly, so call ahead. The reservoir also offers great **trout fishing;** be sure to consult the *Northumbrian Waters Angling Guide,* available at TICs, for rules and regulations.

Bellingham and Kielder Water each have YHA hostels (p. 424). The friendly and all-ensuite **Lyndale Guest House ❸,** West View, also boasts a jacuzzi. (☎ 220 361. Singles £28; doubles £56. MC/V.) There are a number of B&Bs in Kielder Village and Falstone Village, at the northern and southern tips of the water respectively. At the Leaplish Waterside Park the **Reiver's Rest ❷** offers clean dorms and private lodging beside the C200. (☎ 250 312. Dorms £15; doubles £35. MC/V.)

ROTHBURY ☎ 01669

Rothbury, a market town along the River Coquet, is a popular starting point for excursions into the nearby **Simonside Hills.** Rothbury's **NPIC** (p. 424) gives advice on local trails. Among them, the **Sacred Mountain Walk** (9 mi.) rewards those who complete its strenuous climb with some of the finest views in the park. Another popular choice, the **Rothbury Terraces** (2 mi.) follows an old carriage path and passes near Cragside, the 19th-century creation of the first Lord Armstrong. (¾ mi.

For detailed information on local walks, pick up the free *Rothbury and Coquet-dale: Northumberland National Park* at the NPIC.) One mile north of Rothbury on the B6341, **Cragside** was one of the most advanced houses of its day, with luxuries like electric lighting (powered by its own hydroelectric generator) and a house-wide heating system. The interior is particularly well-preserved, with costumed National Trust guides. Bus #508 (5min., June-Sept. Su 2 per day, 70p) connects Newcastle and Cragside via Rothbury. (☎620 150. Open Apr.-Oct. House open Tu-Su 1-5:30pm; last admission 4:30pm. Estate open 10:30am-7pm; last admission 5pm. House and estate £8.50. Estate only £5.70.) Among the **B&Bs** clustered on Rothbury's High Street is the **Orchard Guest House ❹**. (☎620 684; www.orchardguesthouse.co.uk. Doubles from £68. AmEx/MC/V.) Alternatively, **Katerina's Guest House ❸** has four-post, quilt-covered beds. (☎620 691. Doubles £50-60. Cash only.) The Coop, High St., sells **groceries.** (☎620 456. Open daily 8am-10pm.) Find **Internet access** at Rothbury Computers, Town Foot. (☎620 070. £2 per 30-min. Open M-F 9am-5pm, Sa 10am-4pm.)

WOOLER ☎01668

The town of Wooler makes a good base for exploring the northern part of the park, such as the nearby **Cheviot Hills.** A number of short walks include the popular routes to **Humbleton Hill** and a self-guided trail to the Iron-Age **Yeavering Bell** hill fort. More ambitious hikers will want to take on the challenging 7 mi. trek to **The Cheviot** (2674 ft.), whose summit view stretches from the Scottish border to the North Sea. The long-distance **St. Cuthbert's Way** also pays Wooler a visit (p. 425). Six miles southeast of Wooler, **Chillingham Castle** once played host to King Edward I. English eccentricity is now on full display here—the castle is crammed with a variety of bizarre objects collected by current owner Sir Humphry Wakefield. The castle also offers a few self-catering **apartments ❹;** call for rates. (☎215 359. Open July-Aug. daily noon-5pm; May-June and Sept. M and W-Su noon-5pm. £6, concessions £5.50.) In a park beside the castle graze the sixty-odd **wild cattle,** the only entirely purebred cattle in the world. Originally enclosed in 1235, the cattle have been inbred for over seven centuries. They resemble other cows, but cannot be herded, are potentially dangerous, and even kill one of their own if he or she is touched by human hands. (☎215 250. Open Apr.-Oct. M and W-Sa 10am-noon and 2-5pm, Su 2-5pm; by warden-led 1-1½hr. tours only. £4.50, concessions £3.) Wooler also has a **TIC** (p. 424). There's a good **YHA hostel** (p. 424) and several **B&Bs,** including **Winton House ❸**, 39 Glendale Rd. (☎281 362. Singles £25; doubles from £40. Cash only.) The Co-op at 14-18 High St. sells **groceries** (☎281 528. Open M-Sa 8am-6pm.) **Bus** #470 stops in Chillingham en route to Alnwick (20min., 5 per day).

ALNWICK AND WARKWORTH ☎01665

About 31 mi. north of Newcastle off the A1, the small town of **Alnwick** (AHN-ick) bows before the magnificent ⬛**Alnwick Castle,** a former Percy family stronghold now home to the Duke and Duchess of Northumberland. The manicured grounds and stately home appeared in the films *Elizabeth* and *Harry Potter.* Inside, tour some of the richly ornamented rooms, which display an array of the family's heirlooms and artwork. (☎605 847. Open daily Apr.-Oct. 10am-5pm. Last admission 4:15pm. £8, concessions £7.50.) A short walk from the castle brings you to the **Alnwick Garden,** which, in addition to the cascading fountains, beautiful rose gardens, and ivy-enclosed walks, boasts a giant treehouse restaurant, a hedge labyrinth, and a poison garden. (☎511 350; www.alnwickgarden.com. Open daily in summer 10am-6pm; in winter 10am-4pm. £6, concessions £5.75, under 16 free. Castle and garden £12, concessions £11.) Seven miles southeast of Alnwick, the ruins of 12th-century **Warkworth Castle** guard the mouth of the River Coquet. Shakespeare set much of *Henry IV* at this Percy bastion. (☎711 423. Open Apr.-Sept. daily 10am-6pm; Oct. daily 10am-4pm; Nov.-Mar. M and Sa-Su 10am-4pm. £3, concessions £2.30.) Carved from the Coquet cliffs, the 14th-century **hermitage** lies a short walk down the river; the castle staff will ferry you over and a fleet of rowboats is available for rental. (Open Apr.-Sept. W and Su 11am-5pm. £2, concessions £1-1.50.)

The Tea Pot ❸, 8 Bondgate Without, is a good place to rest. (☎604 473. £20-22 per person, no singles; £1 off with *Let's Go*. Cash only.) For a place closer to the gardens of the castle, try the **Lindisfarne B&B ❸**, 6 Bondgate Without. (☎603 430. From £21 per person. Cash only.) Across from the bus station, **Grapevine ❶**, 1 Market Sq., offers toasted panini from £3. (☎604 872. Open Apr.-Sept. M-F 8am-10pm, Sa 8am-7pm, Su 10am-4pm; Oct.-Mar. M-Tu 8am-7pm, W-F 8am-10pm, Sa 8am-7pm, Su 10am-4pm. Food served M-F until 9pm, Sa 6pm, Su 4pm. AmEx/MC/V.)

The **bus station** is at 10 Clayport St. Buses #505, 515, and 525 connect Alnwick with Berwick (1hr.; M-Sa 8 per day, Su 5 per day) and Newcastle (1¼hr.; M-Sa 14 per day, Su 5 per day). Buses #420, 422, and 518 make frequent trips between Alnwick and Warkworth (25min.). The **Tourist Information Centre** is at 2 The Shambles, Market Pl. (☎510 665. Open July-Aug. M-F 9am-6pm, Sa-Su 9am-5pm; Sept.-June M-Sa 9am-5pm, Su 10am-4pm.) Along Bondgate Without (yes, that's a street name), Barter Books, housed in a disused Victorian railway station, provides **Internet access**, but the secondhand bookshop alone is worth visiting. (☎604 888. Open daily May-Oct. 9am-7pm; Nov.-Apr. 9am-5pm. £2 per 30min.) Rent **bikes** at Alnwick Cycles, 24 Narrowgate. (☎606 738; www.alnwickcycles.co.uk. Open M-Sa 10am-5pm, Su 12:30-4pm. £15 per day, £8 per half-day.) The **post office** is at 19 Market St. (☎602 141. Open M-F 8:45am-5:30pm, Sa 8:45am-12:30pm.) **Post Code:** NE66 1SS.

BERWICK-UPON-TWEED   ☎01289

Just south of the Scottish border, Berwick-upon-Tweed (BARE-ick) has changed hands more often than any town in Britain—13 times between 1296 and 1482 alone. The town's history of strife has helped propagate the local legend that Berwick is still at war with Russia (see **A Really Cold War,** right). Most of the original **Berwick Castle** is buried beneath the train station, although some of the 13th-century

LOCAL LEGEND

A REALLY COLD WAR

Despite the perpetual and divisive intra-Continental conflicts of the twentieth century, Europe has unified. Today, Icelanders and Greeks and everyone in between live in economic and political cooperation. Everyone, that is, except for the citizens of Russia and the small English village of Berwick-upon-Tweed.

Due to an unfortunate semantic accident, Berwick-upon-Tweed has been at war with Russia for 153 years. In a 1502 treaty, Berwick was described as being "of" the Kingdom of England, rather than "in" it; Berwick received special mention in every ensuing royal proclamation. Nothing came of this inconvenience until 1853, when Queen Victoria signed a declaration of war on Russia, in the name of "Victoria, Queen of Great Britain, Ireland, Berwick-upon-Tweed, and the British Dominions beyond the sea." In the peace treaty ending the war, no mention of Berwick appeared.

Sources vary on what happened next. Some say the matter was cleared up by Tsarist Russia in 1914. Others assert a Soviet official signed a peace treaty in 1966 with the mayor of Berwick, who then said, "please tell the Russian people that they can sleep peacefully in their beds." Either way, no official documents have surfaced that can resolve the debate. Berwick, for its part, appears to have no intention of backing down.

fortress still stands beside the river. The town's most substantial sight is the tongue-twisting **Berwick Barracks,** which contains the regimental museum of the King's Own Scottish Borderers. (☎304 493. At the corner of Parade and Ravensdowne. Open Apr.-Sept. daily 10am-6pm; Oct. daily 10am-4pm; Nov.-Mar. M and Th-Su 10am-4pm. £3.30, concessions £2.50.)

   Berwick Backpackers ❶, 56-58 Bridge St., is a comfy 20-bed hostel in the middle of town that provides bagged breakfasts at no extra cost. (☎331 481; www.berwickbackpackers.co.uk. Kitchen, laundry, and Internet. Reception M-Sa 9am-noon and 4-9pm. Dorms £15-20. MC/V.) For **B&Bs,** a good choice is the luxurious **Clovelly House ❸,** 58 West St., right in the town center. (☎302 337. £22 per person. Cash only.) Friendly **Four North Road ❸,** 4 North Rd., just left up the road, a few minutes from the train station, is a good option. (☎306 146; www.fournorthroad.co.uk. From £20 per person. Cash only.) Stock up on **groceries** at Somerfield, Castlegate. (☎308 911. Open M-Sa 8am-8pm, Su 10am-4pm.) At **Foxton's ❸,** 26 Hide Hill, survey an exhibition of local art with your meal. (☎308 448. Entrees £9-12. Open June-Aug. M-Sa 9am-11pm, Su 11am-2pm; Sept.-May M-Sa 9am-11pm. MC/V.)

   Berwick is a good transport hub. The **train station** (open M-Sa 6:30am-7:50pm, Su 10:15am-7:30pm) has frequent rail service from Edinburgh (45min., £14.60), London King's Cross (4hr., £51), and Newcastle (50min., £13.40). From the train station, it's a 5min. walk down Castlegate to the town center. Most **buses** stop at the train station and at the corner of Castlegate and Marygate, on Golden Sq. Bus #505/515/525 travels from Newcastle (2¼hr.; M-Sa 6 per day, Su 5 per day; £12.20) via Alnwick (1hr.). The **Tourist Information Centre,** 106 Marygate, books rooms for a 10% deposit. (☎330 733. Open June-Sept. M-Sa 10am-6pm, Su 11am-3pm; Oct.-May M-Sa 10am-3pm, Su 11am-3pm.) Get free **Internet access** at the Berwick Library, Walkergate. (☎334 051. Open M-Tu 10am-5:30pm, W and F 10am-7pm, Sa 9:30am-12:30pm.) Tweed Cycles, 17a Bridge St., provides **bike rental** and good trail advice. (☎331 476. £12 per day. Open M-Sa 9am-5:30pm.) The **post office** is on West St. (☎307 596. Open M-Sa 9am-5:30pm.) **Post Code:** TD15 1BH.

HOLY ISLAND AND BAMBURGH CASTLE ☎01289

Ten miles from Berwick-upon-Tweed, wind-swept ⬛**Holy Island,** at low tide connected to the mainland by a causeway, rises just off the coast. Seven years after Northumberland's King Edwin converted to Christianity in AD 627, the missionary Aidan arrived from the Scottish island of Iona to found England's first monastery. While his wooden structure is long gone, the sandstone ruins of the later **Lindisfarne Priory** still stand in the island's tiny village. (☎389 200. Open Apr.-Sept. daily 9:30am-5pm; Oct. daily 9:30am-4pm; Nov.-Jan. M and Sa-Su 10am-2pm; Feb.-Mar. M and Sa-Su 10am-4pm. £3.60, concessions £2.70.) The hill beyond the priory provides a good view of the ruins and will save you a few quid. Tiny **Saint Cuthbert's Isle,** marked by a wooden cross 220 yd. off the coast of the priory, is where the hermit-saint took refuge when even the monastery proved too distracting. A mile's walk from the Priory, **Lindisfarne Castle** is a 16th-century fort that sits dramatically atop a hill, with a crowded and less-inspiring interior of 19th-century furnishings. (☎389 244. Open Apr.-Oct. M-Th and Sa-Su 10:30am-4:30pm; times vary with tide; call ahead. £5.) Paths lead beyond the castle and snake along the island's North Sea shore. After returning to the village, try the blend of fermented honey and white wine known as **Lindisfarne Mead,** a syrupy-sweet concoction brewed since ancient times, free samples of which are available at **Landisfarne Limited,** across from the Priory (☎389

230. Opens 30min. before low-tide and closes 30min. after.) Crossing the 4 mi. seaweed-strewn causeway is possible only at low tide; check the tide tables at a TIC before you go. Bus #477 runs from Berwick to Holy Island (daily in Aug.; Sept.-July W and Sa). **Border Cabs** drive over the causeway before the tide sweeps in. (☎07769 515 915. £14 round-trip.) If the waves trap you, there are a few accommodations, but they fill quickly. **The Bungalow ❸**, Chaire Ends, is your best bet, offering real comfort. (☎389 308. Doubles £60. MC/V.)

Bamburgh Castle, a stunning Northumbrian landmark, straddles a rocky outcropping 25 mi. south of Berwick. The castle's renovation began in the 1890s when it was acquired by the first Baron Armstrong, whose family still resides in its sumptuous interior. The public tour offers a look at one of the largest armories outside London and the ornate, vaulted ceilings of the **King's Hall.** Below the castle and beyond the dunes, sandy beaches make for excellent walks with views of the castle. (☎01668 214 515. Open Apr.-Oct. daily 11am-5pm. Last admission 4:30pm. £5, concessions £3.50.) Reach Bamburgh by **bus** (#411 from Berwick; 45 min.; M-Sa 8 per day, Su 4 per day). Holy Island and Bamburgh Castle can be seen in a single day, though the tides can make scheduling tight.

HADRIAN'S WALL

In AD 122, when Emperor Hadrian ordered the construction of a wall to guard Rome's farthest borders, he undoubtedly wanted to prevent those uncouth blue-tattooed warriors to the north from infiltrating his civilized empire. Hadrian's unease created a permanent monument on the Roman frontier—first a V-shaped ditch 27 ft. wide, then a stone barrier 15 ft. high and 9 ft. thick. Eight years, 17 milecastles (forts), 5500 cavalrymen, and 13,000 infantrymen later, Hadrian's Wall stretched unbroken for 73 mi., from beyond modern-day Carlisle to Newcastle. The years have not been kind to the emperor's massive undertaking. Most of the stones have been carted off and reused in surrounding structures, and the portions of wall that do remain either stand at half their original height or are buried under a modern highway. The best-preserved ruins are along the western part of the wall, at the southern edge of Northumberland National Park (p. 422).

◪ TRANSPORTATION. Traveling by car is definitely the best way to see the wall; failing that, **buses** are available. Stagecoach in Cumbria sends the Hadrian's Wall Bus, a.k.a. AD122 (who knew public transport had a sense of humor?) from Carlisle to Hexham, stopping at all the wall's major sights and offering a guided commentary. (2¼hr., June to mid-Sept. 6 per day, 85p-£5.20; guides July-Aug. M and Su 3 per day.) One daily bus extends to Newcastle. Bus #685 runs year-round between Newcastle and Carlisle via Hexham, Haltwhistle, Greenhead, and other wall towns (2hr.; M-Sa 12 per day, Su 4 per day). A **Hadrian's Wall Bus DayRover ticket,** available from TICs or bus drivers, is a good idea for those planning to make several stops in one day (£6). Another option is the **Hadrian's Wall Rail Rover,** a ticket valid 2 out of 3 days on the Tyne Valley train line and the Tyne & Wear Metro (£12.50).

Trains (☎08457 484 950) run frequently between Carlisle and Newcastle (1½hr., every hr., £10.20), but stations lie at least 1½ mi. from the wall; be prepared to hike to the nearest stones. Trains depart about every hour and stop at: Brampton (1hr., £8.70), 2 mi. from Lanercost and 5 mi. from Birdoswald; Haltwhistle (55min., £8), 2 mi. from Cawfields; Bardon Mill (40min., £7.10), 2 mi. from Vindolanda and 4½ mi. from Housesteads; Hexham (25min., £4.40), and Corbridge (30min., £4.10).

GIVING BACK

BURIED TREASURE

Near Hadrian's Wall, the archaeological site of Vindolanda contains a wealth of artifacts from a Roman settlement predating the wall. Archaeologists believe that Roman soldiers created an early defensive garrison at Vindolanda and that eventually a small town developed there. Workers at the site have recently found a series of 2000-year-old inscribed wooden tablets, including a birthday invitation and a household inventory of socks and underwear. Some of the writing was done in rare ink and several appear to have been burned.

Six months per year, the excavations are open to any enthusiastic digger who doesn't mind getting his or her hands dirty. Archaeologists predict that it will take another 200 years to unearth all of the site's secrets, so they need all the help they can get. Volunteers usually stay for one or two weeks, but longer stays can be arranged.

A typical day involves 4½ hours of digging, with breaks and meals in between. Volunteers can stay in the nearby YHA Once Brewed hostel, only 1½ miles from the site. The program costs £50 and applicants must be physically fit and at least 16 years old.

For more information visit www.vindolanda.com or call Andrew Birley at ☎01434 345 277.

Make sure to pick up the free and invaluable *Hadrian's Wall Bus and Summer Days Out* brochure. Available at any area TIC or bus, it has timetables and information on accessing the wall using all forms of transportation.

⚏🛈 ORIENTATION AND PRACTICAL INFORMATION. Hadrian's Wall runs 73 mi. between Carlisle in the west and Newcastle in the east, spanning Cumbria, Northumberland, and Tyne and Wear. The towns of **Greenhead, Haltwhistle, Once Brewed, Bardon Mill, Haydon Bridge, Hexham** (the hub of Wall transportation), and **Corbridge** lie somewhat parallel to the wall from west to east. For general information, check the **Hadrian's Wall Information Line** (☎01434 322 002; www.hadrians-wall.org). Useful publications and accommodation bookings are available at the Hexham **Tourist Information Centre,** at the bottom of the hill across from the abbey on Hallgate Rd. (p. 431), and the **National Park Information Centre** in Once Brewed, on Military Rd. (☎01434 344 396 or 344 777. Open June-Aug. daily 9:30am-5:30pm; Apr.-May and Sept.-Oct. daily 9:30am-5pm; Nov.-Mar Sa-Su 10am-3pm.)

🛏 ACCOMMODATIONS. Both Carlisle and Hexham have many B&Bs and make good bases for daytrips to the wall. Other towns near the wall, such as Corbridge and Haltwhistle, also have accommodations. Two hostels lie along the Hadrian's Wall Bus route. **YHA Greenhead ❶,** 16 mi. east of Carlisle, is in a converted chapel a short walk from the wall. (☎08707 705 842. Breakfast £3.80, packed lunch £3.40-4.30, dinner from £5.50. Reception 7:30-10am and 5-10:30pm. Open Easter to Nov. Dorms £11-14, under 18 £8-9.50. MC/V.) **YHA Once Brewed ❷,** Military Rd., Bardon Mill, has a central location 2½ mi. northwest of the Bardon Mill train station, 3 mi. from Housesteads Fort, 1½ mi. from Vindolanda, and half a mile from the wall itself. (☎08707 705 980. Breakfast £3.80, packed lunch £3.40-4.30, dinner from £5.50. Laundry. Internet access £2.50 per 30min. Reception 8-10am and 2-10pm. Open Feb.-Nov. Dorms £12.50-£15.50, under 18 £9-10.50. MC/V.) The isolated **Hadrian Lodge ❷** makes a good base for serious walkers; take a train to Haydon Bridge, then follow the main road uphill 2½ mi. (☎01434 684 867. Kitchen and laundry. Book in advance. Dorms £18; singles £39.50; doubles £59.50. AmEx/MC/V.)

◙ **SIGHTS.** All sights listed below are accessible by the Hadrian's Wall Bus. If you have limited money or time, visit ▧**Housesteads**, the most complete Roman fort in Britain, 5 mi. northeast of Bardon Mill on the B6318. Half a mile from the road, the well-preserved ruins are set high on a ridge and adjoin one of the best-preserved sections of the wall. (☎01434 344 363. Open daily Apr.-Sept. 10am-6pm; Oct.-Mar. 10am-4pm. £3.50, concessions £2.60.) Milecastles and bridges dot the area between Greenhead and **Birdoswald Roman Fort.** The fort itself, 15 mi. east of Carlisle, offers views of walls, turrets, and milecastles. The interactive **Visitors Centre** introduces the wall and traces Birdoswald's 2000-year history. (☎01697 747 602. Open daily Mar.-Oct. 10am-5:30pm. Museum and wall £3, concessions £2.50.)

Constructed of stones "borrowed" from the wall, the **Roman Army Museum** sits at Carvoran, 1 mi. northeast of Greenhead. It presents impressive stockpiles of artifacts, interactive stations, and a faux Roman Army recruiting video. (☎01697 747 485. Open daily Apr.-Sept. 10am-6pm; Feb.-Mar. and Oct.-Nov. 10am-5pm. Last admission 30min. before close. £3.30, concessions £2.90. Joint Saver tickets with Vindolanda £6.50, concessions £5.50.) ▧ **Vindolanda,** 1½ mi. north of Bardon Mill and 1 mi. southeast of Once Brewed, is a fort and civilian settlement predating the wall. Ongoing excavations have revealed hundreds of inscribed wooden tablets that illuminate many details of Roman life. (☎01434 344 277; www.vindolanda.com. Open daily Apr.-Sept. 10am-6pm; Feb.-Mar. and Oct.-Nov. 10am-5pm. £4.50, concessions £3.80; for Joint Saver ticket, see above.) Dramatically situated on the cliffs of Maryport next to the fort, the **Senhouse Museum** houses Britain's oldest antiquarian collection, with exhibits on Roman religion and warfare. (☎01900 816 168. Open Apr.-June Tu and Th-Su 10am-5pm; July-Oct. daily 10am-5pm; Nov.-Mar. F-Su 10:30am-4pm. £2.50.) From Chollerford, 3 mi. north of Hexham, Britain's best-preserved cavalry fort, **Chesters,** can be reached by a footpath leading ¼ mi. west. The extensive remains of a bath house dot the fort's riverside setting; a museum houses altars and sculptures from the wall. (☎01434 681 379. Open daily Apr.-Sept. 9:30am-6pm; Oct.-Mar. 10am-4pm. £3.50, concessions £2.60.) In 2003 the **Hadrian's Wall National Trail** opened, providing a continuous route for long treks and day walks. Alternatively, the recently opened **Hadrian's Cycleway** provides two-wheeled access to all the wall's main attractions without following the actual course of the wall.

HEXHAM
☎01434

West of Newcastle on the A69, the town of Hexham makes a fine base for exploring Hadrian's Wall. The cobbled town center encircles the impressive **Hexham Abbey.** Founded by St. Wilfrid in AD 637, the Abbey was the first in England to follow the rule of St. Benedict. (☎602 031. Open daily May-Sept. 9:30am-7pm; Oct.-Apr. 9:30am-5pm. Free guided tours June-Sept. Su, Tu, Th 2pm. Suggested donation £2.) Facing the abbey, the substantial 14th-century **Gatehouse Tower** recalls Hexham's turbulent past. More tangible evidence of these troubles can be found in the 14th-century dungeon of the **Hexham Old Gaol,** behind Market Pl. (☎652 357. Open daily 10am-4:30pm. Last admission 4pm. £4, concessions £2.)

The **West Close House ❸,** Hextol Terr., off Allendale Rd., offers homemade jam, friendly service, lovely rooms, and a well-tended garden. (☎603 307. From £21 per person. Cash only.) The equally friendly **Laburnum House ❷,** 23 Leazes Crescent, has spacious rooms 15 min. from the center of town. (☎601 828. From £20 per person. Cash only). The **YHA Acomb ❷,** 3 mi. from Hexham, tucks backpackers into a converted stable. Take bus #880, 881, or 882 from the Hexham railway station. (☎08707 705 664. Open Apr.-June and Sept.-Oct. W-Su; July-Aug. daily; Jan.-Mar. F-Sa. Dorms £11-14, under 18 £9-10.50. MC/V.)

Hexham's **train station** is a 10 min. walk from the Abbey and the center of town (see **Transportation**, p. 429). The **Tourist Information Centre** stands between the train station and town center, in the carpark facing Safeway. (☎652 220. Open May-Sept. M-Sa 9am-6pm, Su 10am-5pm; Oct.-Apr. M-Sa 9am-5pm.) Other services include: **banks** along Priestpopple Rd.; **police,** Shaftoe Leagues (☎604 111); **General Hospital,** Corbridge Rd. (☎655 655); free **Internet access** at the **library,** Beaumont St., inside Queens Hall (☎652 488; open M and F 9:30am-7pm, Tu-W 9:30am-5pm, Sa 9:30am-12:30pm); **bike rental** at the Bike Shop, 16-17 St. Mary's Chase (☎601 032; £15 per day; open M-Sa 10am-5pm; MC/V); and the **post office,** Priestpopple Rd., in Robbs of Hexham department store (☎602 001; open M-Tu, Th, and Sa 8:30am-5:30pm, W 9am-5:30pm, F 8:30am-6pm). **Post Code:** NE46 1NA.

WALES (CYMRU)

Known to early Anglo-Saxon settlers as foreigners ("waleas"), but self-identified compatriots ("cymry"), the people of Wales have always had a fraught relationship with their neighbors to the east. Though inhabitants of the same isle as the English, if many of the nearly 3 million Welsh people had their druthers, they would be floating miles away. Wales clings steadfastly to its Celtic heritage and the Welsh language endures in conversation, commerce, and literature. When heavy industry became unprofitable in the 1970s, Wales turned its economic focus to tourism. Travelers today are lured by miles of dramatic beaches, cliffs, mountains, and brooding castles, remnants of the long battle with England. Against this striking backdrop, the Welsh express their nationalism in the voting booths and in celebrations of their distinctive culture and language.

TRANSPORTATION

GETTING THERE

Most travelers reach Wales through London. **Flights** to Cardiff International Airport originate within the UK and from a few European destinations. The new airline **Air Wales** (☎08707 773 131; www.airwales.co.uk) connects Cardiff to Dublin, Liverpool, Plymouth, Newcastle, Jersey, and Paris. **Ferries** cross the Irish Sea, shuttling travelers between Ireland and Holyhead, Pembroke, Fishguard, and Swansea (see **By Ferry,** p. 28). Frequent **trains** leave London for Cardiff (2hr.); call **National Rail** (☎08457 484 950; www.nationalrail.co.uk) or **Arriva Wales** (☎08456 061 660; www.arrivatrainswales.co.uk) for schedules and prices. **National Express buses** (☎08705 808 080; www.nationalexpress.co.uk) are a slightly slower, cheaper way to get to Wales: a trip from London to Cardiff takes just over 3hr. and costs £18-33.

GETTING AROUND

BY TRAIN. BritRail (US ☎1-877-677-1066; www.britrail.net) passes are accepted on all trains, except narrow-gauge railways, throughout Wales. The **Freedom of Wales Flexipass,** which allows limited rail travel and daily bus travel (4 rail trips in 8 days £45; 8 rail trips in 15 days £75), is valid on the entire rail network and for most major buses. Pass holders also receive discounts on some narrow-gauge trains, bus tours, and tourist attractions. Call **Arriva Trains** (☎08456 061 660) for information. **Narrow-gauge railways** tend to be tourist attractions rather than actual means of transport, but trainspotters can purchase a **Great Little Trains of Wales Passport** ticket (round-trip £55; ☎01286 870 549; www.greatlittle-trainsofwales.co.uk), which allows travel on any of the eight member rail lines.

BY BUS. The overlapping routes of Wales's numerous bus operators are difficult to navigate. Most are local services; almost every region is dominated by one or two companies. **Traveline** has updated bus information for all services (☎08706 082 608; www.traveline-cymru.org.uk); regional carriers, unless noted, use Traveline for ticket booking and customer service. **Cardiff Bus** (www.cardiffbus.com) blankets the area around the capital. **TrawsCambria** #701, the main north-south bus route, runs from Cardiff and Swansea to Machynlleth, Bangor, and Llandudno. **Stagecoach** (www.stagecoachbus.com) buses serve routes from Gloucester and Hereford in England; the routes cover the Wye Valley, Abergavenny, and Brecon. **First Cymru** (☎01792 582 233; www.firstgroup.com/ukbus/wales/swwales/home) covers the Gower peninsula and southwest Wales, including Pembrokeshire Coast National Park. **Arriva Cymru** (☎01492 592 111; www.arriva.co.uk) provides service in North Wales. Regional public transport guides, available free at Tourist Information Centres (TICs), exist for many areas, but for some you'll have to consult an array of small brochures. The very useful *Wales Bus, Rail, and Tourist Map and Guide* provides information on routes, but not timetables. **Local buses often don't run on Sunday;** some special tourist buses, however, run *only* on Sundays in summer. Bus schedules and prices change often; confirm them in advance.

BY FOOT, BICYCLE, AND THUMB. Wales has numerous beautiful and well-marked footpaths and cycling trails; the **Offa's Dyke Path** (p. 450) and the **Pembrokeshire Coast Path** (p. 450) are particularly popular. The **Wales Tourist Board** (☎0871 211 251; www.visitwales.com) maintains the websites **Walking Wales** (www.walking.visitwales.com) and **Cycling Wales** (www.cycling.visitwales.com), provides links to tour operators and other useful sites, and publishes print guides of the same names. The **Countryside Council for Wales** (☎01248 385 500; www.ccw.gov.uk) may also be helpful. *Let's Go* does not recommend **hitchhiking,** but many people choose this form of transport, especially in the summer and in cases of bungled bus schedules.

LIFE AND TIMES

HISTORY

CELTS, ROMANS, AND NORMANS. As the western terminus of many waves of emigration, Wales has been influenced by a wide array of peoples since prehistoric times. Stone, Bronze, and Iron Age inhabitants dotted the Welsh landscape with stone villages, earth-covered forts, *cromlechs* (standing stones also known as menhirs and dolmens), and partially subterranean burial chambers. It was the early **Celts,** however, who established themselves in the way most apparent today. During the 4th and 3rd centuries BC, two waves of Celts, the first from northern Europe and the second from the Iberian peninsula, immigrated to Wales. By AD 59, the Romans had invaded and established a fortress at Segontium (present-day **Caernarfon,** p. 502), across the Menai Straits from **Ynys Môn (Isle of Anglesey,** p. 506), the center of druidic, bardic, and warrior life in northern Wales. Although the Romans had achieved a symbolic conquest, wily Celtic resistance compelled them to station two of their four legions in Britain along the modern-day Welsh border.

When the Romans departed from Britannia in the early 5th century AD, they left not only towns, amphitheaters, roads, and mines, but also the Latin language and the seeds of Christianity, both of which heavily influenced the development of Welsh society. For the next 700 years, the Celts (possibly ruled by **King Arthur**) ruled themselves, doing their best to hold back invading Saxons, Irish, and Vikings. They were not, in the end, successful; in the 8th century, Anglo-Saxon **King Offa** and his troops pushed what Celts remained in England into Wales and other corners of the island (including Cornwall and Scotland). To make sure they stayed put, Offa built **Offa's Dyke** (p. 450), a 150 mi. earthwork that marked the first official border between England and Wales. Though Wales consisted of a collection of Celtic kingdoms united by language, customary law, a kinship-based social system, and an aristocracy, the kingdoms did not achieve political unity until the 13th-century reign of **Llywelyn ap Gruffydd,** the only Welsh ruler recognized by the English as the Prince of Wales.

Wales

TO DÚN LAOGHAIRE, DUBLIN

ENGLAND

Isle of Anglesey

Irish Sea

Amlwch

Llanallgo

Holyhead

A5025

A5105

Conwy Bay

Llandudno

Birkenhead

Liverpool

Prestatyh

R. Mersey

M53

Penmon

Beaumaris

Conwy

Rhyl

A55

M56

Holy Island

Llanfair P.G.

Bangor

A55

A470

A55

Chester

Menai Strait

Caernarfon

Trefriw

Llanrwst

Ruthin

A525

Caernarfon Bay

Llanberis

Capel Curig

Betws-y-Coed

Corwen

Wrexham

Snowdon Mountain Railway

Mt. Snowdon (3560 ft.)

Blaenau Ffestiniog

Llangollen

A5

Tre'r Ceiri

Porthmadog

A487

Ffestiniog Railway

Dee

Cerriog

Oswestry

Tanat

Llanystumdwy

A497

Criccieth

Portmeirion

A494

Lake Bala

Severn

Llŷn Peninsula

A499

Pwllheli

Harlech

SNOWDONIA NATIONAL PARK

Lake Vyrnwy

Shrewsbury

Aberdaron

Abersoch

Barmouth

Dolgellau

Welshpool

A483

Cader Idris

Dovey

Newtown

Cardigan Bay

Aberdyfi

Machynlleth

Severn

A49

Borth

CAMBRIAN MOUNTAINS

A483

Ludlow

Aberystwyth

A44

Knighton

Rhayader

Wye

Aberaeron

Llandrindod Wells

Tregaron

Teifi

Hereford

Aberporth

Lampeter

Builth Wells

A487

Llanwrtyd Wells

A483

Wye

A470

Cardigan

Llandovery

Hay-on-Wye

A49

PEMBROKESHIRE COAST NATIONAL PARK

Newcastle Emlyn

Brecon

A479

BLACK MTS.

Fishguard

Llandeilo

BRECON BEACONS NATIONAL PARK

Abergavenny

Monmouth

A40

St. David's

Carmarthen

A40

Merthyr Tydfil

Tintern

St. Bride's Bay

Haverfordwest

Shrewsbury

A4A

Tawe

Aberdare

Pontypool

Wye Valley

A449

Pembroke

Tenby

Llanelli

Cwmbran

Chepstow

PEMBROKESHIRE COAST NATIONAL PARK

Carmarthen Bay

Swansea

Port Talbot

Newport

M4

A470

Gower Peninsula

Mumbles

Bridgend

Cardiff

TO CORK

Swansea Bay

Barry

Mouth of the Severn

R. Severn

Bristol

TO ROSSLARE

N

LG

0   20 miles

0   20 kilometers

Bristol Channel

ENGLAND

THE ENGLISH CONQUEST. Within 50 years of William the Conqueror's invasion of England in 1066, the **Normans** had subjugated a quarter of Wales. The new-comers built a series of castles and market towns, established the feudal system, and introduced a variety of continental monastic orders. The English **Plantagenet Kings** invaded Wales throughout the 13th century, and killed Prince Llywelyn ap Gruffydd in 1282. **Edward I** appointed his son the "Prince of Wales," and in 1284 dubbed the Welsh English subjects. To keep these perennially unruly "subjects" in check, Edward constructed a series of massive castles at strategic spots throughout Wales. The magnificent surviving fortresses at **Conwy** (p. 485), **Caernarfon** (p. 502), **Caerphilly** (p. 448), **Harlech** (p. 497), and **Beaumaris** (p. 508) stand as testament to his efforts.

In the early 15th century, the bold insurgent warfare of **Owain Glyndŵr** (Owen Glendower) temporarily freed Wales from English rule. Reigniting Welsh national-ism and rousing his compatriots to arms, Glyndŵr and his followers captured the castles at Conwy and Harlech, threatened the stronghold of Caernarfon, and con-vened a national parliament at Machynlleth. Glyndŵr created the ideal of a **unified Wales** that has captured the country's collective imagination ever since. Despite support from Ireland, Scotland, and France, the rebellion soon waned under the stresses of poverty, war, and the plague. By 1417 Glyndŵr had disappeared into the mountains, leaving only legend to guide his people. Wales placed its hope in Welsh-born **Henry VII**, who emerged victorious from the Wars of the Roses and ascended the English throne in 1485 (p. 65).

The 1536 **Act of Union** granted the Welsh the same rights as English citizens and returned the administration of Wales to the local gentry. The act officially "united and annexed" the country and gave Wales parliamentary representation. **The Courts of Great Session** were established in 1543 and remained the law of the land until 1830. Increased equality came at the price of increased assimilation, and English quickly became the language of the Welsh courts, government, and gentry.

Throughout the 17th century, the consolidation of land into large **gentry estates** stratified Welsh society and demonstrated the difficulty of sustaining the booming population. Though certain prominent noblemen supported the parliamentary cause, many Welsh harbored sympathy for the monarchy at the onset of the Civil War. Pockets of religious resistance also proliferated as the result of the efforts of Puritan missionaries; Nonconformists, Baptists, and Quakers all gained footholds during this period.

METHODISM AND THE INDUSTRIAL REVOLUTION. Profound religious shifts changed Welsh society in the 18th and 19th centuries. As the church became more Anglicized and tithes grew more burdensome, the Welsh grew more receptive to new Protestant sects. The **Methodist revolution** claimed 80% of the population by 1851. Life centered on the chapel, which housed tight local communities of shared religion, heritage, and language. **Chapel life** remains one of the most distinctive fea-tures of Welsh society; the Sunday closure of stores in much of Wales (particularly in the north) is but one lasting effect.

The **Industrial Revolution** swept the Isles in the 19th century; industrialists exploited coal veins in the south of Wales and iron and slate deposits in the north. New roads, canals, and most importantly, **steam railways,** were built to transport these raw materials, and the Welsh population grew from 450,000 to 1.2 million between 1750 and 1851. Especially in the south, pastoral landscapes were transformed into grim mining wastelands, and those who braved these dangerous workplaces faced taxing labor, poverty, and despair. Early attempts at unionism failed, and workers turned to violence in order to improve condi-tions. The discontent was channeled into the **Chartist Movement,** which demanded political representation for all men; its high point was an uprising in Newport in 1839. Welsh society became characterized by two forces: a strongly

leftist political consciousness—aided by the rise of organized labor—and large-scale **emigration**. Welsh miners and religious groups replanted themselves in America (particularly in Pennsylvania), and in 1865 a group founded **Y Wladfa** (The Colony) in the Patagonia region of Argentina. Welsh tenant farmers led the **Rebecca Riots** against the government and wealthy landowners from 1839 to 1843. Attempts to secure an independent autonomy reached a peak in the Home Rule movement of 1886-96 but fizzled due to internal dissent.

The strength of the Liberal Party in Wales bolstered the career of **David Lloyd George**, who rose from being a homegrown rabble-rouser to Britain's Prime Minister (1916-22). But by 1922, the Labour Party had become dominant in industrial communities. Numerous Welshmen went to fight **World War I**; over 35,000 never returned. Continued emigration and the **economic depression** of the 1930s compounded this loss.

WALES TODAY

Long home to a distinct culture and people, Wales now faces the challenges and opportunities of its new role as a more distinct political entity. The unsteady Welsh economy resists any sort of quick fix; the coal and steel industries that fashioned the country during the Industrial Revolution have sharply declined in recent decades, resulting in poverty and unemployment more severe than that endured by the rest of Britain. **Economic rebuilding** is particularly difficult for a nation that has never had diversified industries, especially as it seeks to avoid basing its new economy on low-paying jobs. A recent upsurge in **tourism** is promising, however, and visitors are discovering a Wales that outshines its grimy, industrial past. **Cardiff** (p. 442), the Welsh capital since only 1955, is in the process of reinventing itself as a center of art and culture.

MODERN POLITICS. Nationalism and a vigorous campaign to retain one of Europe's oldest languages have dominated Welsh politics in the late 20th century. In 1967 the **Welsh Language Act** established the use of Welsh and English in the courts, while the 1988 **Education Reform Act** ensured that all children would be introduced to the language. The government and other concerned parties have established Welsh language classes, publications, radio stations, and even a Welsh television channel (known as Sianel Pedwar Cymru, "Channel 4 Wales," or S4C for short). The 1993 **Welsh Language Act** stipulated that Welsh and English should be regarded as equal in public business.

Nationalist movements emerged in other political arenas as well. Although **Plaid Cymru,** the Welsh Nationalist Party, did not capture a parliamentary seat until 1966, it has since repeatedly demonstrated its political potency. In the 1950s, a **Minister for Welsh Affairs** was made part of the national Cabinet, but Tory rule in the 1980s brought the legitimacy of governing from London into question.

On September 18, 1997, the Welsh voted in favor of **devolution,** but unlike their Scottish counterparts, support for the idea was tepid, with only 50.3% voting "yes" despite major governmental backing. This was still enough to lead to elections for the 60-seat **Welsh Assembly** in May 1999; Labour won a strong plurality in both the 1999 and 2003 elections. (Elections are held every four years.) Devolution has given Wales a taste of its long-sought self-governance. But Wales retains intimate bonds with Westminster; unlike Scotland, Wales shares its educational and legal system with England.

CULTURE AND CUSTOMS

Though Cardiff's cosmopolitan bustle rivals that of other European cities, the real Wales lies in the rural towns and villages, where pleasantries are exchanged across garden hedges, locals swap gossip over post office counters, and a visitor can expect to remain anonymous for all of about three minutes. Welsh **friendliness** and **hospitality**

BLACK PUDDING

Black pudding is not a pudding (a British word for dessert). It is an iron-rich protein treat and Welsh B&B proprietors' most gruesome secret. The queasy should beware, as black pudding's signature ingredient is blood.

Butchers and carveries make the delicacy by heating pig's blood and then adding offal and fat to thicken the mix. Then, the substance is molded into links and allowed to cool and congeal. When cooked, the pudding has the consistency of sausage and is black. Black puddings, which can be as large as hams, are customarily eaten with potatoes or at breakfast.

While the main ingredient is pig's blood, the meats composing the pudding vary. Some butchers prefer beef, while others use pork or poultry. In Wales, the most common meat used is lamb or mutton. Other fillers include bread, barley, and oatmeal.

The origins of black pudding are unknown, but some attribute its invention to two Bavarians, drunk on absinthe, who made a bet about the uses of offal. Black pudding (or a Greek prototype) is mentioned in Homer's *Odyssey*. Other names for the substance are blood pudding or blood sausage. In Spain, the specialty is called *morcilla*.

Try your black pudding, which can be very tasty, with breakfast and sop up your plate with toast. When in Wales...

seem unfailing; long conversations and cheerful attention tend to be the rule. The **Welsh language** (see below) is an increasingly important part of everyday life, and visitors can expect to find road signs, pamphlets, and timetables written both in English and in Welsh. **Nationalism** runs deep in Wales and may surface at unexpected moments. Above all, never call a Welshman "English" or his country "England."

Wales has long been a country defined by its customs, and **folk culture** has always been at its core. Chances to partake in the distinctly and uniquely Welsh—witnessing an **eisteddfod** (p. 440), listening to a traditional male choir, or tasting homemade baked goods—should not be passed by. Welsh national symbols are the **red dragon**, the **leek**, and the **daffodil**. **St. David's Day**, in honor of Wales's patron saint, is celebrated March 1 and is one opportunity to see the Welsh **national costume**—a long red cloak and tall black hat. **All Hallow's Eve** (Oct. 31) has traditional significance for the Welsh as the start of the Celtic New Year.

LANGUAGE

> Let me not understand you, then; speak it in Welsh.
> —William Shakespeare, *Henry IV*

Though modern Welsh borrows from English, as a member of the **Celtic family** of languages, *Cymraeg* is based on an entirely different grammatical system. After a sharp decline since 1900 (when about 50% of the population spoke Welsh), the language is undergoing a powerful resurgence. Today, more than one quarter of the country speaks Welsh, and half of them speak it as a first language. Welsh-speaking communities are particularly strong in the rural north and west.

Though English suffices nearly everywhere in Wales, it's a good idea to familiarize yourself with the language in order to avoid the laughter of bus drivers when you garble the name of your destination. Welsh shares with German the deep, guttural **ch** heard in "Bach" or "loch." **Ll**—the oddest Welsh consonant—is produced by placing your tongue against the top of your mouth, as if you were going to say "l" and blowing. If this technique proves baffling, try saying "hl" (hlan-GO-hlen for "Llangollen"). **Dd** is said either like the "th" in "there" or the "th" in "think" (hence the county of 'Gwynedd' is pronounced the same way as 'Gwyneth' Paltrow). **C** and **g** are always hard, as in "cat" and "golly." **W** is generally used as a vowel and sounds either like the "oo" in "drool" or "good." **U** is pronounced like the "e" in "he." Tricky **Y** changes its sound with its placement in the word, sounding either like the "u" in "ugly" or the "i" in "ignoramus." **F** is spoken as a "v," as in "vertigo," and **ff** sounds exactly like the English "f." Emphasis nearly always falls on the penultimate syllable, and there are (happily) no silent letters.

Most Welsh place names are derived from prominent features of the landscape. *Afon* means river, *betws* or *llan* church or enclosure, *caer* fort, *llyn* lake, *mynydd* mountain, and *ynys* island. The Welsh call their land *Cymru* (KUM-ree) and themselves *Cymry* ("compatriots"). Because of the Welsh system of letter mutation, many of these words will appear in usage with different initial consonants. *Let's Go* provides a delicious mouthful of **Welsh Words and Phrases** on p. 704.

THE ARTS

LITERATURE

In Wales, as in other Celtic countries, much of the national literature stems from a vibrant **bardic tradition.** The earliest extant poetry in Welsh comes from 6th-century northern England, where the **cynfeirdd** (early poets), including the influential poet **Taliesin,** composed oral verse for their patron lords. The *Gododdin,* a series of lays attributed to the poet **Aneirin,** is a celebration of valor and heroism from this period. The 9th-11th centuries brought sagas focusing on pseudo-historical figures, including **King Arthur** and **Myrddin (Merlin).** Documenting the most prolific period in Welsh literature, 12th-century monastic scribes compiled Middle Welsh manuscripts. Most notable is the **Mabinogion,** a collection of eleven prose tales drawing on mythology and heroic legend. In the 14th century, **Dafydd ap Gwilym** developed the flexible poetic form *cywydd.* Often called the greatest Welsh poet, he turned to love and nature as subjects and influenced the work of later poets such as **Dafydd Nanmor** and **Iolo Goch** well through the 17th century. A growing Anglicization of the Welsh gentry in the 18th century led to a decline in the tradition of courtly bards.

In 1588, Bishop William Morgan wrote the **Welsh translation of the Bible,** which helped standardize the language and provided the foundation for literacy throughout Wales. A circle of popular Welsh romantic poets, **Y Beridd Newydd** (the New Poets), including T. Gwynn Jones and W.J. Gruffydd, wrote in the 19th century. The horrors of WWI produced an anti-romantic poetic voice typified in the work of **Hedd Wyn.** The work of 20th-century Welsh writers (in both Welsh and English) features a compelling self-consciousness in addressing questions of identity and national ideals. The incisive poetry of **R.S. Thomas** alternates between a fierce defense of his proud heritage and a bitter rant against its claustrophobic provincialism, while **Kate Roberts's** short stories and novels, such as *Feet in Chains,* dramatize fortitude in the face of dire poverty. The best-known Welsh writer is Swansea's **Dylan Thomas,** whose emotionally powerful poetry, as well as popular works like *A Child's Christmas in Wales* and the radio play *Under Milk Wood,* describe his homeland with nostalgia, humor, and a bit of bitterness. **Roald Dahl** emerged from Cardiff to spin tales of fantasy for children (and other types of fantasy for adults). Wales's literary heritage is preserved in the **National Library of Wales** in Aberystwyth (p. 477), which receives a copy of every Welsh-language book published in the UK.

MUSIC

The Welsh word **canu** means both "to sing" and "to recite poetry," suggesting an intimate historical connection between the sung and the spoken word. Though little Welsh music from before the 17th century has survived, three traditional medieval instruments are known: the **harp,** the **pipe** (hornpipe or bagpipe), and the **crwth,** a six-stringed bowed instrument. The indigenous musical tradition began to disappear in the 16th century, and traditional playing died out by the 17th century. The 18th-century rise of chapels led to a lasting tradition of church music; composers adapted Welsh folk tunes into sacred songs and and the hymns of composers such as **Ann Griffiths** became popular. The homophonic religious music of the 18th century became the basis for the famed harmonic **choral singing** of the 19th and 20th centuries. While

WELSH RABBIT

Switzerland has gooey fondue, Italy hot pizza, and Mexico steaming quesadillas, but none of these are quite as delicious as Wales' contribution to the culinary pantheon of carbohydrates and cheese. Take a piece of bread, smear it with a thick concoction of beer, mustard, spices, and, of course, cheese, and then melt it all under high heat until brown and bubbly, and you have a traditional Welsh rabbit.

Erroneously spelled and pronounced "rarebit" by some, rabbit has a contested etymology. Some claim it was coined by patronizing Englishmen, who considered the Welsh so hopeless that they couldn't even catch a hare for supper—and instead were forced to eat bread and cheese. Another story contends that St. Peter lured the Welsh people out of heaven using a "rabbit" of sorts—a bait of roasted cheese ("caws pobi") to get them outside the pearly gates.

The Welsh don't have an Isle-wide monopoly on the tasty dish; older cookbooks contain Scottish and English rabbit recipes. The instructions for these often call for a "salamander," a large iron slab on a stick (it looks much like a pizza wheel) that was heated and then rested just inches above the bread as a rudimentary broiler. Now toaster ovens do the trick, and rabbit is common throughout Wales in local cafes and vegetarian hangouts.

many associate the all-male choir with Wales, both single-sex and mixed choirs are an integral part of social life, and choral festivals like the **cymanfa ganu** (singing meeting) occur throughout Wales.

Cardiff's **St. David's Hall** regularly hosts both Welsh and international orchestras. The **Welsh National Opera,** featuring renowned tenor **Bryn Terfel,** has established a worldwide reputation. Modern Welsh composers, including **Alun Hoddinott** and **William Mathias,** have won respect in the classical genre. Soprano **Charlotte Church** earned international attention with her 1998 debut, *Voice of an Angel.* **Rock music** is the voice of youth, although the most famous Welsh pop music exports are **Tom Jones** and **Shirley Bassey.** Current popular Welsh bands, like the **Manic Street Preachers, Catatonia, Stereophonics,** and the **Super Furry Animals,** combine Britpop and a (sometimes fierce) nationalism.

FOOD

Traditional Welsh cooking relies on leeks, potatoes, onions, dairy products, lamb (considered the best in the world), pork, fish, and seaweed. Soups and stews are ubiquitous. **Cawl** is a complex broth, generally accompanied by bread. Wales produces a wide range of dairy products, including the soft, white cheese **Caerphilly. Welsh rarebit** (also called "Welsh Rabbit"; see left) is buttered toast topped with a thick, cheesy, mustard-beer sauce. Most visitors are drawn to the distinctive, tasty **breads. Welsh cakes** are buttery, scone-like treats, studded with currants and golden raisins and traditionally cooked on a bakestone or griddle. The adventurous should sample **laverbread,** a cake-like slab made of seaweed, while the sweet-toothed will love **bara brith** (a fruit and nut bread served with butter), and **teisennau hufen** (fluffy, doughnut-like cakes filled with whipped cream). **Cwrw** (beer) is another Welsh staple; **Brains S.A.** is the major brewer in Wales.

FESTIVALS

The most significant of Welsh festivals is the **eisteddfod** (ice-TETH-vod), a competition of Welsh literature (chiefly poetry), music, and arts and crafts. Hundreds of local *eisteddfodau* are held each year, generally lasting one to three days. The most important of these is the **National Eisteddfod** (Eisteddfod Genedlaethol Cymru; see sidebar). The **International Musical Eisteddfod,** held in Llangollen (p. 491) in July and August, draws folk dancers, singers, and choirs from around the world for performances and competitions.

SOUTH WALES

The ragged mountains and stunning coastlines of South Wales have witnessed countless epics of invasion and oppression. The scarred mining fields of its central hills, the pastoral scenes of its river valleys, and the grit and hum of its major ports refuse any common denominator. Today the land seems caught between its rural charms and its growing urban savvy, its English influence and its Welsh heritage.

HIGHLIGHTS OF SOUTH WALES

HIKE the Wye Valley for a fine view of Tintern Abbey (p. 451) and proceed north to the stark peaks of Brecon Beacons National Park (p. 454).

BROWSE the shelves of Hay-on-Wye's literary wonderland, which boasts the largest secondhand bookstore in the world (p. 452).

EXPLORE the rugged coastline of Pembrokeshire National Park (p. 466), home to the holiday town of Tenby (p. 469) and the majestic Cathedral of St. David's (p. 474).

CARDIFF (CAERDYDD) ☎02920

Cardiff calls itself "Europe's Youngest Capital" and seems eager to meet the demands of this title, presenting its rich history along with a spruced-up set of modern sensibilities. Alongside its impressive traditional monuments are landmarks of a different tenor: a towering new stadium by the river and a glitzy cluster of cosmopolitan dining and entertainment venues. At the same time, tradition and local pride, made manifest in the red dragons emblazoned upon flags and store windows, remain as strong as ever.

▐ TRANSPORTATION

Trains: Central Station, Central Sq., south of the city center, behind the bus station. Ticket office open M-Sa 5:45am-9:30pm, Su 6:45am-9:30pm. Trains (☎08457 484 950) from: **Bath** (1-1½hr., 1-3 per hr., £12.40); **Birmingham** (2hr., 2 per hr., £21.70); **Bristol** (45min., 3 per hr., £9.70); **Edinburgh** (7-7½hr., 3 per day, £91); **London Paddington** (2hr., 2 per hr., £58.50); **Swansea** (1hr., 2 per hr., £8.40).

Buses: Central Station, on Wood St. National Express booking office and travel center. Show up at least 15min. before close to book a ticket. Open M-Sa 7am-5:45pm, Su 9am-5:45pm. National Express (☎08705 808 080) from: **Birmingham** (2½hr., 8 per day, £20.40); **London** (3½hr., 9 per day, £18.45); **London Gatwick** (5hr., 11 per day, £37); **London Heathrow** (3½hr., 11 per day, £33.50); **Manchester** (6hr., 8 per day, £30.90). Avoid confusion by picking up timetables at the bus station and a free *Wales Bus, Rail, and Tourist Map and Guide* at the TIC.

Local Transportation: Cardiff **Bus** (Bws Caerdydd) St. David's House, Wood St. (☎666 444). Office open M-F 8:30am-5pm, Sa 9am-4:30pm. Runs a 4-zone network of green and orange buses in Cardiff and surrounding areas. Stops are often shared with Stagecoach and other carriers. Show up at the stop 5-10min. early; schedules can be unreliable, especially on Sundays. Service ends M-Sa 11:20pm, Su 11pm. Fares 65p-£1.55; reduced fares for seniors and children. Week-long **Multiride Passes** available (£12, children £6). **City Rider** tickets allow 1 day of unlimited travel in the greater Cardiff area and can be purchased from drivers (£3.50, children £2.30, families £6.75). Pick up the free *Guide to Bus Fares* in Cardiff from the bus station or TIC.

Taxis: Castle (☎344 344) and **Dragon** (☎333 333).

South Wales

SOUTH WALES

Cardigan Bay

Bristol Channel

ENGLAND

BRECON BEACONS NATIONAL PARK

BLACK MTS.

CAMBRIAN MTS.

Severn Estuary

Bristol

Cardiff

Penarth

Barry

Swansea

Newport

Chepstow

Tintern

Abergavenny

Monmouth

Hay-on-Wye

Brecon

Tenby

Fishguard

St. David's

Pembroke

Llanthony Priory

Tintern Abbey

Wye Valley

Raglan Castle

Caerphilly Castle

Castell Coch

Manorbier Castle

Carew Castle

Pembroke Castle

St. David's Cathedral

Hereford

Leominster

Llandrindod Wells

Builth Wells

Rhayader

Aberaeron

New Quay

Aberporth

Cardigan

Newcastle Emlyn

Newport

Treviné

St. David's Head

Broad Haven

Milford Haven

Pembroke Dock

Haverfordwest

Whitland

Carmarthen

Laugharne

Saundersfoot

Caldey Island

Llandovery

Llandeilo

Llanybydder

Lampeter

Ammanford

Llanelli

Cross Hands

Neath

Talbot

Porthcawl

Bridgend

Cowbridge

Llantwit Major

Caerphilly

Tongwynlais

Merthyr Tydfil

Aberdare

Blaenavon

Pontypool

Cwmbran

Mumbles Bay

Oxwich

Port Eynon

Rhossili

Gower Peninsula

Fforest Fawr

Black Mountain

Brycheiniog Forest

Crychan Forest

Tywi Forest

Caeo Forest

Brechfa Forest

Mynydd Bach

Carmarthen Bay

BRECON BEACONS

PEMBROKESHIRE COAST NATIONAL PARK

TO ROSSLARE

TO CORK

10 miles

10 kilometers

🔳🔢 ORIENTATION AND PRACTICAL INFORMATION

Cardiff Castle is the historical center of the city, though the shops lining Queen St. and The Hayes see much of Cardiff's foot traffic. Farther east, the River Taff bounds Bute Park Arboretum, separating residential neighborhoods from downtown and flowing into Cardiff Bay. The **Civic Centre,** university, and **National Gallery** are north of the castle. The arcades and narrow streets south of the castle provide much of the city's cultural fare.

> **Tourist Information Centre:** The Hayes (☎227 281; www.visitcardiff.com), in the newly renovated Old Library. Books rooms for a £2 charge plus a 10% deposit. Open M-Sa 10am-6pm, Su 10am-4pm. Offers **luggage storage,** £3 per item.

> **Tours: City Sightseeing Cardiff** offers a hop-on, hop-off bus tour that departs from the main gate of Cardiff Castle every 30min. Purchase tickets from the driver, the TIC, or at www.city-sightseeing.com. £7, concessions £5, children £2.50, families £16.50. **Cardiff Waterbus** (☎07940 142 409; www.cardiffwaterbus.com.) Every hr. in summer. £4, children £2. Vehicles tour Cardiff Bay, starting in Penarth and passing Mermaid Quay.

> **Financial Services: Banks** line Queen St. and St. Mary St. **American Express,** 3 Queen St. (☎0870 6001 0601). Open M-F 9am-5:30pm, Sa 9am-5pm. **Thomas Cook,** 16 Queen St. (☎422 500), offers commission-free currency exchange. Open M-Th and Sa 9am-5:30pm, F 10am-5:30pm, Su 11am-6pm.

> **Work Opportunities:** During tourist seasons and especially in rugby season, local establishments look for part-time workers. Signs appear in many windows and the occasional temp agency. Try **Job Centre Plus,** 64 Charles St. (☎428 400). Open M-Tu and Th-F 9am-5pm, W 10am-5pm. Visit the TIC for more information. Employers sometimes post notices on the bulletin board at the Cardiff International Backpacker (p. 444).

> **Launderette: Drift In,** 104 Salisbury Rd. (☎01222 239 257), northeast of Cardiff Castle. Wash £3, dry 20p per 3min. Open M-F 9am-9pm, Sa 9am-6pm, Su 10am-6pm.

> **Police:** King Edward VIII Ave. (☎222 111). Open 24hr.

> **Hospital: University Hospital of Wales,** Heath Park, North Cardiff (☎747 747), 3½ mi. from the city center.

> **Pharmacy: Boots,** 36 Queens St. (☎231 291). Open M-Sa 8:30am-6pm, Su 11am-5pm.

> **Internet Access:** The **public library,** at Frederick St. and Bridge St. (☎382 116), offers free access in 30min. slots. Open M-W and F 9am-6pm, Th 9am-7pm, Sa 9am-5:30pm. Sign up in advance. The **TIC** provides computers for checking email at £1.50 per 20min. **McDonald's,** 12-14 Queen St. (☎222 604), has 4 kiosks. £1 per 30min. Open M-Th 7:30am-11pm, F-Sa 7:30am-midnight, Su 7:30am-9pm. BT public telephones are sometimes accompanied by Internet booths, starting at 10p per min.

> **Post Office:** 2-4 Hill's St. (☎227 305), off The Hayes. Open M-Sa 9am-5:30pm. Bureau de change. Offers MoneyGram wiring service. **Post Code:** CF10 2SJ.

🏠 ACCOMMODATIONS

Budget accommodations are tough to find in the city center, but the TIC lists reasonable **B&Bs** (£18-20) on the outskirts. B&Bs (from £25) lie on **Cathedral Road,** a short ride on bus #32 or a 15min. walk; better bargains await on side streets. Hotels near the castle are pricey; cheaper ones (around £20) cluster further out. Between June and September, **Cardiff University Student Housing** lets dorm rooms to documented students (☎874 864. From £8.50-10 per person, depending on length of stay. Book in advance.) Pick up a free accommodations guide at the TIC.

> 🛏 **Cardiff International Backpacker,** 98 Neville St. (☎345 577). From Central Station, go west on Wood St., turn right onto Fitzhamon Embankment just across the river and left onto Despenser St. (not Place). Lounge (kitchen and bar within) and happy hour (M-Th

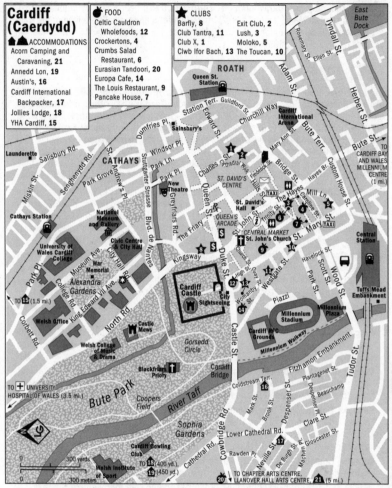

Cardiff (Caerdydd)

▲▲ ACCOMMODATIONS
Acorn Camping and Caravaning, **21**
Annedd Lon, **19**
Austin's, **16**
Cardiff International Backpacker, **17**
Jollies Lodge, **18**
YHA Cardiff, **15**

🍎 FOOD
Celtic Cauldron Wholefoods, **12**
Crockertons, **4**
Crumbs Salad Restaurant, **6**
Eurasian Tandoori, **20**
Europa Cafe, **14**
The Louis Restaurant, **9**
Pancake House, **7**

★ CLUBS
Barfly, **8**
Club Tantra, **11**
Club X, **1**
Clwb Ifor Bach, **13**
Exit Club, **2**
Lush, **3**
Moloko, **5**
The Toucan, **10**

and Su 7pm-9pm). Pop up to the rooftop for views of Cardiff and a hammock. Free toast and coffee for breakfast; free lockers with deposit. Internet access £1 per 30min. M-F curfew 2:30am. Dorms £16.50; doubles £38; triples £48; quads £60. ❷

Jollies Lodge, 109 Cathedral Road (☎221 495). Jolly good price for a private room within walking distance of the city center. £20 per person. Cash only. ❷

Austin's, 11 Coldstream Terr. (☎377 148; www.hotelcardiff.com). Views of the giant Millennium Stadium from this B&B perched on the River Taff, 3min. from the castle. Singles £28; doubles £45. AmEx/MC/V. ❸

YHA Cardiff, 2 Wedal Rd., Roath Park (☎462 303). Take bus #28 or 29 from Central Station (20min., 4-5 per hr., 95p) and get off at Shirley Rd.; Wedal Rd. is across the roundabout. Adjacent gardens offer streamside walks and wildflowers. Breakfast included. Internet access 50p per 5min. Reception 7:30am-11pm. Dorms £17.50, under 18 £14. MC/V. ❷

Annedd Lon, 157 Cathedral Rd. (☎223 349). This 19th-century Victorian house provides a peaceful respite 20min. from the castle. All rooms ensuite. Breakfast included. Singles £30; doubles £55; quads £85. MC/V. ❸

Acorn Camping and Caravaning (☎01446 794 024), near Rosedew Farm, Ham Ln. South, Llantwit Major. 1hr. by bus X91 from Central Station, 15min. walk from the Ham Ln. stop. £6.50 for one person, £8.50 for two people, group discounts available. Electricity £2.75. AmEx/MC/V. ❶

🔥🍴 FOOD AND PUBS

Pubs, chains, and British fare dominate popular locations like **Mill Lane**. The **Old Brewery Quarter**, at the corner of St. Mary St. and Caroline St., offers mid-range and higher-end restaurants. Caroline St. is a post-club hotspot, with curried and fried goodies and late hours (most open M-W until 3am and Th-Sa until 4am). Corner stalls and local bakeries are everywhere, though more creative and expensive restaurants (£10-20) await in the narrow streets south of the castle. Greek, Indian, and kebab takeaways congregate on **Salisbury Street** near the university. Skylit **Central Market** provides produce, bread, and lots of raw meat (open daily 10am-4pm).

■ **Europa Cafe,** 25 Castle St. (☎667 776), across from the castle, toward the river. Black stone walls hung with abstract art combine with worn floors and a red plush couch to give this coffee shop a trendy yet comfortable feel. Upcoming performers and theme nights are chalked on the wall, and big mochas (£2.40) accompany eclectic books, which you can read for free. Open daily 10:30am-5:30pm. Cash only. ❶

■ **Celtic Cauldron Wholefoods,** 47-49 Castle Arcade (☎387 185). A synthesis of Welsh cuisine and assorted ethnic traditions. Try the Glamorganshire sausage or seaweed-based laverbread (each £5). Open M-Sa 8:30am-5pm, Su 11am-4pm. MC/V. ❶

The Louis Restaurant, 32 St. Mary St. (☎225 722). The "Special Louis 9 Breakfast" (£2.50) can sate the most biting hunger. Plenty of seating in clean, bright locale. M-Sa 9am-8pm, Su 10:30am-4:30pm. MC/V. ❶

Crockertons, 10 Caroline St. (☎220 088; www.crockertons.co.uk). Its "urban food" uses local Welsh ingredients. Streetside patio. Lots of vegetarian and vegan options. Antipasto £5 and sandwiches £3.50. Open M-Sa 7am-7pm, Su 11am-5pm. MC/V. ❶

Crumbs Salad Restaurant, 33 Morgan Arcade (☎395 007). This vegetarian restaurant has a homey charm. Mixed salad (£4) and homemade soup (£3.50). Takeaway available for discount. Open M-F 10am-3pm, Sa 10am-4pm. Cash only. ❶

Pancake House, Old Brewery Quarter (☎644 954). Overlooking the bustle, Pancake House offers enough crepes and gourmet pancakes to satisfy any hunger. Try the bacon, avocado, and sour cream (£3.50) or the apple and cinnamon (£3). Newspapers provided. Open M-Th 10am-10pm, F-Sa 10am-11pm, Su 9am-10pm. MC/V. ❶

Eurasian Tandoori, 68 Cowbridge Rd. (☎398 748). You'll find contemporary Indian and Indonesian cuisine at this hideaway, close to Cardiff Backpacker. Free delivery for orders over £10.50. Open M-Th and Su 6pm-12:30am, F-Sa 6pm-2am. ❷

🔘 SIGHTS

■ **CARDIFF CASTLE.** Two thousand years have drastically changed these grounds, but the peacocks still wear crowns (of sorts) suited for the royalty that inspired the castle's extravagance. The Keep or "White Tower," built in 1081 as shelter for the ruling lord in tumultuous times, is an anachronism even within stone fortress walls. A Victorian mansion, designed by William Burges for the 3rd Marquess of Bute, mimics medieval styles. Lord Bute wanted the Arab Room to resemble a mosque in order to educate the people of Cardiff about other cultures. Watch for the owls during falconry shows. (*Castle St. ☎878 100. Open daily Mar.-Oct. 9:30am-6pm; Nov.-Feb. 9:30am-5pm. Last admission 1hr. before close. Free tours leave every 20min. £6.50, students £5, children and seniors £4, family £21.*)

NATIONAL MUSEUM AND GALLERY. Popular impressionist paintings do impress, but don't miss the diverse local exhibits, like a room full of carved Celtic crosses and a walk-through display of Wales's indigenous flora and fauna. *(Cathays Park, next to City Hall. ☎ 397 951. Open Tu-Su 10am-5pm. Free audio tours. Donation requested.)*

CIVIC CENTRE. The Centre is composed of the white Portland stone City Hall and the National Museum, along with the courts and police building. These buildings, constructed during Cardiff's steel and coal boom, stand guard around the stately green expanse of Alexandra Gardens. *(Cathays Park. Free. Always open.)*

🏙 🎵 NIGHTLIFE AND ENTERTAINMENT

CLUBS
After 11pm, most of Cardiff's downtown pubs stop serving alcohol, and the action migrates to nearby clubs—most located around **St. Mary Street.** Cardiff's dress code is trendy, but you'll get in anywhere if you look well-kept. After dark, hail a cab, particularly if you are alone. For nightlife listings, pick up the *Itchy Cardiff* guide (£3.50) or the free *Buzz* magazine from the TIC.

The Toucan, 95-97 St. Mary St. (☎ 372 212). Named the "Best Night Out in Cardiff Bar None" by the *Guardian*, the Toucan's low couches and multicolored walls harbor old and young alike, from experienced musicians to clubbing newbies. Music and dancing on the 2nd floor; food and comfy seating on the ground level. Open Tu 7pm-12:30am, W 7pm-1am, Th-Sa 7pm-2am, Su 8pm-12:30am. Food served until 11pm.

Clwb Ifor Bach (The Welsh Club), 11 Womanby St. (☎ 232 199). 3 worlds collide in the Clwb: the ground floor plays cheesy pop and oldies, especially on W student nights; the middle floor—also the bar—lets you chill to softer music; the top, with low ceilings, rocks out to live bands or hardcore trance. There are drink specials every night, but the cover can be hefty (£3-10) for renowned bands. Open M-Th until 2am, F-Sa until 3am.

Barfly, The Kingsway (☎ 667 658). At the center of Cardiff's alternative rock scene, Barfly hosts live music most nights in its dark, underground complex. Cover £3-7. Open M-Tu and Th 7:30-11:30pm, W and F-Sa 7:30pm-2am, Su 7:30pm-midnight.

Moloko, 7 Mill Ln. (☎ 225 592). Enjoy the huge teletrons and posh atmosphere while listening to bumping house music spun by live DJs. Open daily noon-2am.

Club Tantra, 31 Westgate St. (☎ 399 400). This Middle-East-influenced club spins world music for an international feel in an intimate venue. Open Tu 10:30am-11pm, W-Sa 10:30am-2am. Food served until 4pm.

GAY NIGHTLIFE
Cardiff's gay scene is centered on Charles St., where clubbers and bar-goers spill out into the streets.

Club X, 35 Charles St. (☎ 400 876). All sorts of trendy clubbers flood in and start dancing after 1am, when other places begin to close. W open bar with cover. Cover £3-7. Open W 9pm-2am, F-Sa 10pm-6am.

Lush, 22 Caroline St. (☎ 359 123). A "mixed venue," Lush welcomes all to its comfortable leather couches. An extensive cocktail menu (£5.50), vaulted ceilings, and chandeliers create a decadent feel. Urban house music gets pre-clubbers in the mood. 2-for-1 drinks W. Open M-Th and Su 6:30pm-midnight, F-Sa 6:30pm-1am.

Exit Club, 48 Charles St. (☎ 640 102). Where Cardiff's gay crowd dances to chart faves. Su night features live entertainment, often drag shows. Cover £2-3, free before 9:30pm. Open M-Th 8pm-2am, F-Sa 8pm-3am, Su 8pm-1am.

SOUTH WALES

ARTS

Cardiff is experiencing an a renewed interest in Welsh vocal, theatrical, and artistic traditions. The TIC offers free brochures for local art events.

New Theatre, Park Pl. (☎878 889; www.newtheatrecardiff.co.uk), off Queen St. Formerly the home of the Welsh National Opera, this theater now hosts musicals, ballets, and comedies. Box office open M-Sa 10am-8pm; closes at 6pm on non-performance nights. Tickets £8-50. Student standby tickets available M-F after 6pm on night of show for £5.

St. David's Hall, The Hayes (☎878 444). One of Britain's top concert halls; hosts the **BBC National Orchestra of Wales,** in addition to various bands and comedians. Box office open M-Sa 10am-6pm. Tickets £6-60; some concessions available.

Chapter Arts Centre, Market Rd., Canton (☎304 400). Accessible by the #17 or 18 bus. This red brick building acts as a gallery and a venue for film, dance, and drama. Box office open M-F 10am-9pm, Sa 1:30-9pm, Su 2-9pm.

Wales Millennium Centre, in Cardiff Bay (☎08700 402 000; www.wmc.org.uk). Built in 2004, the Centre is the crown jewel of the Cardiff arts scene. It hosts a variety of Broadway-style shows, ballets, and traditional music events. Tickets from £5.

SPORTS

Rugby matches are played at the gargantuan **Millennium Stadium,** a 73,000-seater with retractable roof. (☎822 228; www.millenniumstadium.com. Open M-Sa 10am-5pm, Su 10am-4pm. Tours £5.50, children £3. Book in advance.) Tours leave from the **Millennium Stadium Shop,** at Entrance 3, Westgate St. (Open M-Sa 10am-5:30pm, Su 10am-4pm.) In the fall (rugby season), tickets are available at the shop or from the **Welsh Rugby Union** (☎08700 138 600; www.wru.co.uk). Football fans can find all manner of gear at **Football Mad** on St. Mary St. (☎664 567; www.footballmadshop.co.uk), or join a 5-a-side league (☎389 999; £20 per team per game.)

◢ DAYTRIPS FROM CARDIFF

The fairgrounds and sandy beaches of **Barry Island** attract travelers all year. The beaches are open year-round; take the train (25 min., 4 per hr., £2). **Taff Trail** winds from Cardiff Bay through the Taff Valley to the heart of Brecon Beacons (p. 454).

■ **CAERPHILLY CASTLE.** Visitors might find this 30-acre castle site easy to navigate, but attacking 13th-century warriors had to contend with trebuchets and crossbows (now unloaded and on display). The Great Hall (70 ft. by 35 ft.) stands in the center; a moat, two parapets, and a "Chinese Box" system of concentric fortifications surround it. A nearby park offers stunning views of the castle against the surrounding countryside. *(Take the train (20min., M-Sa 2 per hr., £3), or bus #26. ☎883 143. Open June-Sept. daily 9:30am-6pm; Apr.-May daily 9:30am-5pm; Oct.-Mar. M-Sa 9:30am-4pm, Su 11am-4pm. Last admission 30min. before close. £3, concessions £2.50, families £8.50. Audio tour £1.)*

MUSEUM OF WELSH LIFE (AMGUEDDFA WERIN CYMRU). Four miles west of Cardiff in **St. Fagan's Park,** this open-air museum occupies more than 100 acres with over 40 buildings—some nearly 500 years old. The Celtic Village and Welsh peasant cottage in particular are full of strokes of authenticity, like interiors that smell like smoke, a horse-and-cart ride (£1, children 50p), and even a miniature stone pig-house (with pigs in summer). Since no tours are offered, take advantage of the guides and craftsmen stationed around the park. The recently restored Italian Garden had been "lost" for almost a century, and the video display documenting the restoration is interesting. *(Buses #32 and 320 run to the museum from Central Station (20min., 1-2 per hr., £2.60). ☎573 500. Open daily 10am-5pm. Free. Guidebook £2.)*

LLANDAFF CATHEDRAL. A Celtic cross, one of the oldest Christian relics in Britain, stands outside this 12th-century cathedral. Inside, the ancient arch over the altar contrasts with a 20th-century concrete version, topped by "Christ in Majesty" forged from aluminum. St. Dyfrig and St. Teilo are entombed here, and Dante Gabriel Rossetti's triptych *Seed of David* stands in one corner. The ivy-covered ruins of the **Castle of the Bishops of Llandaff** lie nearby. Though its luster is somewhat faded—800 years have seen the cathedral turned into a "hog trough" by Cromwell and gutted by a German bomb—Llandaff's grounds still emanate grace and history. *(Take bus #60 or 62 from Central Station to the Black Lion Pub (15min.) and walk up High St., or walk down Cathedral Rd., through Llandaff Fields, and straight on the small, scenic path behind the rugby club. ☎564 554. Open daily 7:30am-7pm. Evensong daily 6pm. Free.)*

CASTELL COCH. Lord Bute and architect William Burges—whose shared appetite for restoration was left unsatisfied by their work at Cardiff Castle—rebuilt the ruins of this 13th-century castle in the late 1800s. Their attempt to resurrect a medieval style ultimately looks like something from a fairy tale, with spires, latticed gables, and whimsical decor. String-pulling Fates look down upon would-be guests in the two-story parlor, and monkeys frolic overhead in the Lady's top-floor bedroom while miniature golden castles flank her sink. Unlike many of the other castles near Cardiff, Castell Coch occupies a secluded forest hillside, offering hikers connections to the Taff Trail. *(Take bus #26 or 26a (25min., 1-2 per hr.) from Central Station to Tongwynlais, get off across from the post office, and walk 15min. up Mill St. ☎810 101. Open Apr.-May daily 9:30am-5pm; June-Sept. daily 9:30am-6pm; Oct.-Dec. and mid-Feb. to Mar. M-Sa 9:30am-4pm, Su 11am-4pm. £3, concessions £2.50, families £8.50. Audio tour £1.)*

WYE VALLEY

It's no wonder Wordsworth mused on tranquility and pastoral majesty in this once-troubled Welsh-English border territory. It seems untouched by human encroachment and the passage of time. Sheep farms are set among forests, and walking trails flow past storied castles and abbeys as aimlessly as the meandering Wye moves through its own valley.

▐ TRANSPORTATION

Chepstow provides the easiest entrance to the valley. **Trains** (☎08457 484 950) run to Chepstow from Cardiff (45min., 1-2 per hr., £5.40) and Newport (20min., every 2hr., £4.20). National Express (☎08705 808 080) **buses** go to Chepstow from: Cardiff (50min., 13 per day, £4.30); London (2½hr., 7 per day, £17); Newport (25min., every hr., £2.80). Stagecoach Red and White buses #65 and 69 loop between Chepstow and Monmouth (8-9 per day); bus #69 stops in Tintern. Stagecoach sells 1-day **Network Rider** passes (£4.50, concessions £2, families £9), good for travel on all Stagecoach Red and White, Phil Anslow, and Cardiff buses. Few buses run on Sunday in the valley. TICs offer the free *Monmouthshire Local Transport Guide* for timetables and *Discover the Wye Valley by Foot and by Bus* (50p) for information on walking trails accessible by bus. **Hitchhikers** try their luck on the A466 in the summer; some stand near the entrance to Tintern Abbey or by the Wye Bridge in Monmouth. Let's Go does not recommend hitchhiking.

HIKING

The hills near the Wye offer wooded trails, open meadows, and vistas of the valley. Two main trails, the Wye Valley Walk and Offa's Dyke Path, follow the river on either side and are accessible from many different points. TICs disperse pamphlets and sell Ordnance Survey maps (1:25,000; £8.50). Campsites are scattered throughout the area; ask at the Chepstow, Tintern, Hereford, and Powys TICs.

Wye Valley Walk (136 mi.). West of the river, this walk heads north from Chepstow via Hay-on-Wye to Prestatyn along wooded cliffs and farmland, eventually ending in Rhayader. From **Eagle's Nest Lookout,** 3 mi. north of Chepstow, 365 steps descend steeply to the riverbank. At **Symond's Yat Rock,** 15½ mi. north of Chepstow, the hills drop away to a panorama of the Wye's horseshoe bends, 7 counties, and a cliff where peregrine falcons nest every spring. Legend has it Mordiford was once home to a dragon. A popular walk from Chepstow follows the Wye Valley Walk up the Welsh side of the river to Tintern and the Offa's Dyke Path (see below) back. The Chepstow TIC offers a guide to this 12 mi. hike for 80p. For more information, consult www.wyevalleywalk.org.

Offa's Dyke Path (177 mi.). East of the river, this path starts in Sedbury's Cliffs and winds along the Welsh-English border, ending at Prestatyn on Wales' northern coast. Built by Saxon King Offa to keep the Welsh at bay, it is Britain's longest archaeological monument, and some of the earthwork (20 ft. high) still stands. Join at Chepstow, Monmouth, Bisweir or Redbrook, and follow the yellow arrows and acorn signs. Check trail maps (available at TICs) before starting; some paths change grade suddenly. Consult the **Offa's Dyke Association,** halfway up the trail in Knighton (☎01547 528 753).

Royal Forest of Dean. This 27,000-acre forest, once the hunting ground of Edward the Confessor and Williams I and II, lies across the English border. Known as the "Queen of Forests," its ancient woods and farmlands provide pleasant hikes. Contact the **Forest Service,** Bank St., in Coleford, England, across the river from Monmouth (☎01594 833 057; open M-Th 8:30am-5pm, F 8:30am-4pm) or the **Coleford Tourist Information Centre,** High St. (☎01594 812 388; open M-Sa 10am-5pm). **Forest of Dean Tour Guides** (☎01594 529 358; www.forestofdeantours.org; £5-18) offers guided tours.

CHEPSTOW (CAS-GWENT) ☎01291

Established a year after the Battle of Hastings, this town (originally Ceap-stowe, or "marketplace") seems to have forgotten its industrial, ship-building past. Though its shopping area offers a pleasant afternoon's diversion, Chepstow's best attraction is **Castell Casgwent,** Britain's oldest datable stone castle. Ferns spring from its cliffside ruins, which offer stunning views. Look for the "murder holes" above the gate. (☎624 065. Open daily 9:30am-6pm. Last admission 5:30pm. £3, students £2.50, families £8.50.) Chepstow celebrates its history in the **Chepstow Festival** (www.chepstowfestival.co.uk; normally the last two weeks of July and the first week of August), a three-week spectacular featuring a light show, mock armed battles, music, and theater. The festival takes place in even years, with smaller exhibitions in odd years. Book accommodations in advance.

Though Chepstow is a more convenient transportation base, nearby Tintern offers cheaper **B&B** accommodations in prettier surroundings. The nearest **YHA hostel** is at St. Briavel's Castle, in England (see **Tintern,** p. 451). The **First Hurdle Guest House ❸,** 9-10 Upper Church St., offers comfortable rooms near the castle. (☎622 189. Singles £35; doubles £50. AmEx/MC/V.) The Tesco **market** on Station Rd. is open 24hr. but closes Sa 10pm-Su 10am and Su 4pm-M 8am.

Chepstow's **train station** is on Station Rd., and **buses** stop above the town gate in front of the Somerfield. Buy train and bus tickets onboard, except those for buses to major cities, which must be purchased at the Travel House, 9 Moor St. (☎623 031. Open M-Sa 9am-5:30pm.) A **Tourist Information Centre,** on Bridge St., faces the castle. Book accommodations or pick up the free *What's On Chepstow*. (☎623 772; www.chepstow.co.uk. Open daily Apr.-Oct. 10am-5:30pm; Nov.-Mar. 10am-3:30pm.) Other services include: Barclays **bank,** Beaufort Sq. (☎01633 205 000; open M-F 9am-4:30pm); a launderette, 36 Moor St., near the bus station (☎626 372; wash £2.80, dry £1-2, soap 50p; open M-F 8:30am-7pm, Sa 9:15am-5:30pm, Su 9am-7pm); **police,** Moor St. (☎623 993), across from the post office; the **Community Hospital** (☎636 636), west of town on St. Lawrence Rd.; free **Internet access** at the library on Manor Way in the town center (☎635 730; open M, W, F 9am-5:30pm; Tu 10am-5:30pm; Th 9am-8pm; Sa 9:30am-4pm); and the **post office,** Albion Sq. (☎622 607; open M-F 9am-5:30pm, Sa 9am-12:30pm). **Post Code:** NP16 5DA.

TINTERN   ☎01291

The A466 follows the Wye and weaves its way past the small stone houses of Tintern. The village, located 5 mi. north of Chepstow, thrives on the tourism brought by ▓**Tintern Abbey,** the center of a 12th-century society of Cistercian monks. The roof opens to the clouds, arches point skyward, and grass sprouts in the transepts; the abbey's tranquility seems even to match that of the countryside. And while William Wordsworth once famously drew ascetic inspiration from this "wild secluded scene," the nearby gift shops and tour buses suggest that Tintern is not quite as "secluded" as it once was. (☎689 251. Open June-Sept. daily 9:30am-6pm; Apr.-May and Oct. daily 9:30am-5pm; Nov.-Mar. M-Sa 9:30am-4pm, Su 11am-4pm. £3.25, concessions £2.75, families £9.25. 45min. audio tour £1, plus £5 deposit. Last admission 30min. before close. Last audio guides 1hr. before close.) Those interested in the view from "a few miles above" should ask gift shop employees for directions to **Monk's Trail,** a wooded path that winds through the hills across the river. An uphill hike (2 mi.) leads to **Devil's Pulpit,** a huge stone from which Satan is said to have tempted the monks as they worked in the fields.

Tintern's **Old Station** lies a mile north of the abbey on the A466, though the Wye River Path is a more scenic and safe route, as the road narrows and sidewalks vanish. The out-of-service train station holds a series of railway carriages, one of which houses the **Tourist Information Centre.** The TIC books accommodations for a £1 charge. (☎689 566. Open daily Apr.-Oct. 10:30am-5:30pm.) There are several sights of interest between the abbey and the Old Station on A466. At the **Anchor Tintern** (☎689 207), sample the fruits of a cider mill once used by the monks themselves—supposedly the oldest in existence. **Stella's Books,** on Monmouth Rd., in the middle of the village proper, stores over 50,000 obscure old volumes behind its unassuming storefront, including a particularly entertaining array of antiquated children's books. (☎689 755; www.stellabooks.com. Open daily 9:30am-5:30pm.) **Parva Farm Vineyard,** just past the Wye Valley Hotel on the A466, produces nearly 4,000 bottles of wine and honey mead a year. The owners let visitors tour the hillside for £1, tasting included. (☎689 636. Open daily 10:30am-6:30pm.)

The nearest **YHA hostel** is **St. Briavel's Castle ❷,** 4 mi. northeast of Tintern across the English border. Once King John's hunting lodge and later a fortress against the Welsh, this 12th-century castle's offers a hostel experience unlike any other. Don't miss the 17th-century graffiti on one dorm wall. From the A466 (bus #69 from Chepstow; ask to be let off at Bigsweir Bridge) or Offa's Dyke, follow signs for a 2 mi. uphill hike from the edge of the bridge. On Wednesdays, bus L12 runs from Monmouth to St. Briavel's. (☎01594 530 272. Lockout 10am-5pm. Curfew 11:15pm. Dorms £12.50, under 18 £9. MC/V.) **B&Bs,** many with river views, lie along the A466 in the village. At the edge of Tintern, **Holmleigh B&B ❷** has cozy rooms in a stone house with gables and a cliff at its back. Take bus #69 from Chepstow and ask to be let off at the Wye Valley Hotel; it is a 2min. walk back. (☎689 521. Singles from £19. Cash only.) **Campers** can use the **field ❶** next to the old train station (£2 per

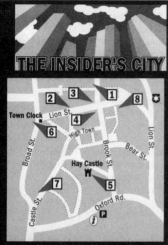

THE INSIDER'S CITY

NEVER JUDGE A BOOK BY...

Second-hand books changed Hay-on-Wye from a hillside shire into a book-selling epicenter. Here's a rough guide to the best shops.

1 **Poetry Bookshop,** The Ice House, Brook St. (☎821 812), is the only bookstore in the UK devoted entirely to poetry. Open M-Sa 10am-6pm, Su 11am-5pm.

2 With 500,000 volumes, **Richard Booth's Books,** 44 Lion St. (☎820 322), is the largest second-hand bookshop in the world. Rifle through the drawers of old postcards—a century's worth of handwritten notes. Open M-Th 9am-5:30pm, F-Sa 9am-7pm, Su 11:30am-5:30pm.

3 "When an old book is published, read a new one," demands a sign in front of **Addyman Books,** 39 Lion St. (☎821 136). Relax at one of its upstairs couches or rockers to peruse its various genres. Open daily 10am-5pm.

person). Near St. Briavel's Castle hostel is the **George Inn Pub ❶,** a 16th-century local favorite with original timber, low ceilings, and dim lighting straight out of a medieval tale. (☎01594 530 228. Open M-Sa 11am-11pm, Su noon-10:30pm. Cash only.) The **Moon and Sixpence ❶,** High St., next to the Holmleigh B&B, serves an array of country foods in a pub atmosphere. (☎689 284. Open daily noon-11pm. Food served noon-2:30pm and 6:30-9:30pm. Cash only.)

HAY-ON-WYE (Y GELLI) ☎01497

Put simply, Hay-on-Wye is a town defined by its 34 bookstores. The little village, with cobbled alleys and small-town charm, owes its reputation as the world's foremost "Town of Books" (and its world-famous annual Guardian Hay Festival) mainly to Richard Booth, who founded Booth's Books, now the largest second-hand bookstore in the world. And while the winding Wye and 2,227 ft. Hay Bluff may astound visitors, Hay's literary charm is even more seductive.

TRANSPORTATION AND PRACTICAL INFORMATION. The closest **train station** is in Hereford, England (p. 283). Stagecoach Red and White (☎01633 838 856) **bus** #39 stops at Hay between Hereford and Brecon (1hr. from Hereford, 45min. from Brecon; M-Sa 7 per day; £4.40). Yeoman's (☎01432 356 202) bus #40 runs the same route (Su 3 per day; £3.05). The **Tourist Information Centre,** Oxford Rd., in the small shopping center by the bus stop, offers Internet access (75p per 15min.) and books beds for a £2 charge. (☎820 144; www.hay-on-wye.co.uk. Open daily Apr.-Oct. 10am-1pm and 2-5pm; Nov.-Mar. 11am-1pm and 2-4pm.) Other services include: Barclays **bank,** on Broad St. (open M-F 10am-4pm); free **Internet access** at the library, Chancery Ln. (☎820 847; open M 10am-1pm, 2-4:30pm, and 5-7pm; Th-F 10am-1pm and 2-5pm, Sa 9:30am-1pm); a **launderette** behind the castle on Castle Ln. (£2, soap 20p; open M-Sa 7am-8pm); and the **post office,** 3 High Town (☎820 536; open M, W, F 9am-1pm and 2-5:30pm, Tu 9am-1pm, Th 9am-5:30pm, Sa 9am-12:30pm). **Post Code:** HR3 5AE.

ACCOMMODATIONS AND FOOD. The nearest **YHA hostel** is 8 mi. away in Capel-y-Ffin (p. 456). Numerous **B&Bs** occupy the center of town. Delightful stays await at **The Bear ❸,** Bear St., a 16th-century coaching inn with low-timbered ceilings, poofy beds, and inviting fireplaces, several of which are filled with books. (☎821 302; www.the-bear-hay-on-wye.co.uk. Singles £26; twins £50; doubles £61. MC/V.) **Oxford Cottage ❷,** Oxford Rd., provides cozy, sunlit rooms and free run of the kitchen. (☎820 008; www.oxfordcottage.co.uk. £22 per person. Cash only.) **Camp** along the Wye Valley Walk or Offa's Dyke (p. 450); **Radnor's End Campsite** ❶ is closest to town; cross the river via Bridge St. and walk 500 yd. to the right, then turn left into the camp. (☎820 780. £4 per person. Cash only.)

Get **groceries** at Spar, 26 Castle St. (☎820 582; open M-Sa 8am-10pm, Su 8am-7:30pm.) **The Granary** ❷, Broad St., has extravagant salads (£8), "toasties" (£4), and patio seating. (☎820 790. Open daily Sept.-June 10am-5:30pm; July-Aug. 10am-10pm. AmEx/MC/ V.) **Oscars** ❷, 17 High Town, offers scones and pastries (£1-1.50) as well as tasty meals and lunch staples, like filled baguettes. (☎821 193. Open daily 10:30am-4:30pm. MC/V.) Families are welcome at the **Wheatsheaf Inn** ❶, Lion St., where locals hang out at the bar and game room. (☎820 186. Open M-Sa 11am-11pm, Su noon-10:30pm. Food served M-F noon-2:30pm and 6-8pm, Sa-Su noon-2:30pm. MC/V.) Cheaper eats await at **Xtreme Organix** ❶, 10 Castle St., a burger/kebab joint that uses only local organic meat. (☎821 921. Open daily 9:30am-11pm. Cash only.) Finish up by digging into confections from the **Fudge Shop** ❶, Oxford Rd., by the bus station. (☎821 529. Open daily 10am-5:30pm. MC/V.)

◰ ※ SIGHTS AND FESTIVALS. Hay's 13th-century **Norman castle**, scarred by wars, fires, and neglect, no longer houses traditional royalty. Rather, Richard Booth, the self-proclaimed King of Hay, stores just a fraction of his unfathomable number of second-hand books on the first floor. The castle is only part of Booth's huge network of stores (many of them **"honesty bookshops,"** where a paybox sits atop outdoor shelves of 30p books), which shaped Hay into a bibliophile's dream. Other independent stores offer equally delightful selections; some shops specialize, like the Poetry Bookshop, while others *specialize*, like B&K Books, dedicated to beekeeping. To find your dream book, check out our **Insider's City** (see left), pick up the TIC's free *Secondhand & Antiquarian Booksellers & Printsellers* map and brochure, or search over a million titles at www.haybooks.com. The world-renowned, annual 10-day **literary festival** brings the glitterati (recently, Bill Clinton, John Updike, and Richard Starkey—a.k.a. Ringo Starr) to town to give readings. (May 26-Jun. 4 in 2006. Book accommodations early. Tickets £6-16.) For those interested in less cerebral pursuits, **Paddles & Pedals**, 15 Castle St., rents canoes and kayaks. (☎820 604. £20 per half-day (5 mi.), £30 per day (14 mi.). Book ahead. Free pickup.)

4 Created as an annex for Addyman's, **Murder and Mayhem**, 5 Lion St. (☎821 613), specializes in detective fiction, true crime, and horror; painted pistols, menacing daggers, and a hanging gnome complement the theme. Open July-Aug. daily 10:30am-5:30pm; Sept.-June M-Sa 10:30am-5:30pm.

5 **Hay Castle** (☎821 503), the centerpiece of Richard Booth's empire houses books, photography, and artwork. A 24hr. self-service "honesty bookstore" lines the street-level courtyard (books 30-50p). Open daily Apr.-Oct. 9:30am-6pm; Nov.-Mar 9am-5:30pm.

6 Children will revel in the wide selection of **Rose's Books** (☎820 031), which specializes in out-of-print children's books. Roald Dahl's lesser-known works and an illustrated Tolkien's *Bestiary* are sure to tickle your tot. Open daily 9:30am-5pm.

7 **Bookends,** Castle St. (☎821 341) sells all of its volumes for £1 or less. It's a great place to discover new authors or old classics. Open Apr.-Oct. M-W and Su 11am-5:30pm, Th-Sa 9am-8pm; Nov.-Mar. daily 9am-5:30pm.

8 Find your inner sportsman at the **Lion St. Bookshop** (☎820 121), owned by a boxing aficionado. The number and array of books about boxing is, frankly, alarming. Open M-Sa 10am-5pm.

BRECON BEACONS

Brecon Beacons National Park *(Parc Cenedlaethol Bannau Brycheiniog)* encompasses 520 sq. mi. of varied landscape. The park divides into four regions: the mist-cloaked farms and peaks of Brecon Beacons, a possible location for King Arthur's mountain fortress; the lush woods of Fforest Fawr, with the spectacular waterfalls of Ystradfellte; the Black Mountains to the east, often described as "Tolkeinesque"; and the remote western ridges of Black Mountain (singular), above Upper Swansea Valley. The park, founded in 1957, is nearly all owned by farmers, so take care when trekking. The market towns on the fringe of the park, particularly Brecon and Abergavenny, make pleasant touring bases, but hostels allow easier access to the park's inner regions.

▐ TRANSPORTATION

Getting around Brecon Beacons isn't too difficult; it's getting in with public transport that proves a challenge. The **train** line (☎08457 484 950) from London Paddington to South Wales runs via Cardiff to Abergavenny at the park's southeastern corner and to Merthyr Tydfil on the southern edge. The Heart of Wales rail line passes through Llandeilo and Llandovery in the isolated Black Mountain region, eventually terminating in Swansea. National Express (☎08705 808 080) **bus** #509 runs once a day to Brecon, on the northern side of the park, from London (£21) and Cardiff (£3.30). Stagecoach Red and White (☎01685 388 216) buses cross the park en route to Brecon from: Abergavenny (X43, 50min., 7 per day, £4.50); Hay-on-Wye (#39 or 40; 45min.; M-Sa 8 per day, Su 2 per day; £2.80-4.10); Swansea (#63, 1½hr., 3 per day, £4.50). Bus B8 runs between Brecon and Abergavenny once on Sundays. The free *Brecon Beacons: A Visitor's Guide*, available at most TICs, details some bus coverage and describes walks accessible by public transport. The indispensable *Powys City Council Travel Guide*, available only at TICs, has over 100 pages of bus listings. For travel throughout Brecon Beacons on Sundays and bank holidays in July and August, use Beacons Buses (☎01873 853 254; www.visitbreconbeacons.com), which caters to tourists and will drop you off almost anywhere. **Brecon Cycle Centre** (p. 460), among others, rents mountain bikes. **Hitchhikers** say the going is a bit easier on major roads as minor roads see very little traffic. Let's Go does not recommend hitchhiking.

▐ PRACTICAL INFORMATION

Stop at a **National Park Information Centre (NPIC)** for before venturing forth. Free maps are available, but Ordnance Survey Outdoor Leisure Maps #12 and 13 (£7.50) are indispensable for serious exploring and for reaching safety in bad weather. The park staff conducts guided walks between April and November; call ahead.

National Park Information Centres:

Mountain Centre (National Park Visitor Centre in Libanus): (☎01874 623 366; www.breconbea-cons.org), in Libanus. Walk to A470 or take bus X43 to Libanus (7min., M-Sa 6 per day), 5 mi. southwest of Brecon, then walk 1½ mi. uphill; on Su in July-Aug., take a shuttle to the front door (15min., 6 per day) or bus B6 (15min., 2 per day) from Brecon. Open daily July-Aug. 9:30am-6pm; Nov.-Feb. 9:30am-4:30pm; Mar.-June and Sept.-Oct. 9:30am-5pm.

Abergavenny: see p. 458.

Craig-y-nos: (☎01639 730 395), at the Craig-y-nos Country Park. Stagecoach Bus #63, the Swansea-Brecon route (30min. from Brecon, M-Sa 3 per day); ask to be dropped at Craig-y-nos. Open Easter to Sept. M-F 10am-5pm, Sa-Su 10am-5:30pm; Oct. to Easter M-F 10am-4pm, Sa-Su 10am-4:30pm.

Llandovery: Kings Rd. (☎01550 720 693). Near Black Mountain; take Heart of Wales train or bus #280 from Carmarthen. Open daily Easter to Sept. 10am-1pm and 1:45-5:30pm; Oct. to Easter M-Sa 10am-1pm and 1:45-4pm, Su 10am-noon.

Brecon Beacons National Park

ACCOMMODATIONS

YHA Capel-y-Ffin, 5
YHA Llanddeusant, 1
YHA Llwyn-y-Celyn, 3
YHA Tyn-y-Caeau, 4
YHA Ystradfellte, 2

SOUTH WALES

HEART OF WALES RAILWAY

ENGLAND

TO HEREFORD (21 mi.)

TO CARDIFF (25 mi.)

TO SWANSEA (10 mi.)

TO CARMARTHEN (15 mi.)

Wales

▐ ACCOMMODATIONS

The few Brecon B&Bs and hotels are listed in *Mid Wales and the Brecon Beacons Guide*. The most comprehensive listing is at www.brecon-beacons.com, which lists guest houses, hostels, cottages, caravans, farms, and campsites.

Campsites ($4-10 per tent) are plentiful, but often difficult to reach without a car. Many offer laundry and grocery facilities, and all have parking and showers. Nearly all are on working farms. Other farmers may let you camp on their land if you ask first and leave the site as you found it; be prepared to make a donation toward feeding the sheep. The *Stay on a Farm* guide, available at the TIC, lists over 100 such farms across Wales. NPICs in the region also give out *Camping on Farms*, which lists many options in the park.

Scattered across the part are five YHA hostels, including **Ty'n-y-Caeau**, near Brecon (p. 462). The other four are:

Capel-y-Ffin: (kap-EL-uh-fin; ☎01873 890 650), near River Honddu at the eastern edge of the Black Mountains. 1¼mi. from Offa's Dyke Path, 8 mi. from Hay-on-Wye. Take bus #39 or 40 from Hereford to Brecon and stop at Hay. The road to the hostel climbs Gospel Pass past Hay Bluff. From Abergavenny, turn off A465 at Llanfihangel Crucorney to Llanthony; follow signs to Capel-y-Ffin. Horseback-riding trips by Black Mountain Holidays leave from here (☎01873 890 650; ask for Howard). Lockout 10am-5pm, daytime access to toilets and weather shelter. Curfew 11pm. Open mid-Apr. to Sept., but call 48hr. in advance. Dorms £10, under 18 £7. Camping £5 per tent. MC/V. ❶

Llanddeusant: (HLAN-thew-sont; ☎01550 740 218), at the foot of Black Mountain near Llangadog village; take the Trecastle-Llangadog road for 9 mi. off the A40. Restricted daytime access 10am-5pm. Curfew 11pm. Open mid-Apr. to Aug.; Sept. to mid-Apr., call 48hr. in advance. Dorms £10.60, under 18 £7.60. MC/V. ❶

Llwyn-y-Celyn: (HLEWN-uh-kel-in; ☎01874 624 261), 7 mi. south of Brecon, 2 mi. north from Storey Arms carpark on the A470. Take Sixty Sixty Bus #43 from Brecon or Merthyr Tydfil (M-Sa every 2hr., Su 3 per day). Close to Pen-y-Fan and the Beacons range. Farmhouse near a nature trail. Lockout 10am-noon; access to lounge and toilets. Curfew 11pm. Open Easter to Aug. daily; Sept.-Oct. Th-M; Nov. and Feb. to Easter F-Su. Book 2-3 weeks in advance. Dorms £12.50, under 18 £9. MC/V. ❶

Ystradfellte: (uh-strahd-FELTH-tuh; ☎01639 720 301), south of the woods and waterfall district, 3 mi. from the A4059 on a paved road; 4 mi. from the village of Penderyn; a 5min. walk from the Porth-yr-Ogof cave. Hard to reach by public transport (bus X5 stops 5 mi. away). Small 17th-century cottages. Kitchen. Open Apr. to late September; flexible, call 48hr. in advance. Dorms £10.60, under 18 £7.60. Cash only. ❶

▐ HIKING

WARNING. The mountains are unprotected and often difficult to scale. Cloud banks breed storms in minutes. In violent weather, do not take shelter in caves or under isolated trees, which tend to draw lightning. A compass is essential; much of the park is trackless, and landmarks get lost in sudden mists. Never hike alone, and consider registering with the police. See **Wilderness Safety**, p. 46.

THE BRECON BEACONS

Llangorse Lake, 8 mi. from Brecon, is the highest natural lake in South Wales and is home to a crannog (Iron-Age dwelling) on a man-made island. To the south, the Mountain Centre NPIC outside Libanus (p. 454) houses an exhibit on its history and wildlife. Pamphlets on walks around the center start at £1; these strolls weave through fields of sheep and occasionally stop at churches, ancient monoliths aligned with celestial bodies, and even an Iron-Age fort. The most popular path to the top of **Pen-y-Fan** (pen-uh-VAN; 2907 ft.), the highest mountain in South Wales, begins at **Storey Arms** (a carpark and bus stop 5 mi. south of Libanus on the A470) and offers views of **Llyn Cwm Llwch** (HLIN-koom-hlooch), a 2000 ft. glacial pool in the shadow of neighboring **Corn Du** (CORN-dee) peak. The summit also hosts the remains of an ancient burial cairn. Many hikers complain about overcrowding and litter on the trail. The easiest route begins behind a carpark and public toilets called Pont ar Daf, just past Storey Arms on the A470 coming from Brecon. The paved path continues most of the way. Most other paths are unmarked—consult NPICs (in Brecon, or the Mountain Centre) for recommendations and directions. An arduous ridge path leads from Pen-y-Fan to other peaks in the Beacons.

The touristy **Brecon Mountain Railway,** which departs from Pant Station in Merthyr Tydfil, allows a glimpse of the south side of the Beacons as the narrow-gauge train runs along the Taf Fechan Reservoir north to Pontsticill. (☎01685 722 988. Runs daily late Mar. to late Oct. 11am-4pm. £8.50, children £4.25, seniors £7.75.)

THE WATERFALL DISTRICT (FOREST FAWR)

Near the southern edge of the park on a limestone outcrop, a well-watered forest erupts with mosses and ferns. The triangle defined by **Hirwaun, Ystradfellte,** and **Pontneeddfechan** delineates the forest boundaries, within which rivers tumble through rapids, gorges, and spectacular falls near **Ystradfellte,** 7 mi. southwest of the Beacons. At **Porth-yr-Ogof** ("Mouth of the Cave"), the River Mellte ducks into a cave at the base of the cliff and emerges as an icy pool. Swimming is ill-advised—the stones are slippery and the pool deepens alarmingly. Exploring any grottoes beyond the main cave without a guide can also be dangerous. Erosion makes the paths narrow and hard to navigate. Remote but worth the sweat is the **Sgwd yr Eira** waterfall (which means "Fall of Snow" but is also called "Lady's Fall" after one of the 26 daughters of King Brychan) on the River Hepste, half a mile from its confluence with the Mellte. You can stand behind thundering water in the hollow of a cliff face and remain dry as a bone. Follow the marked paths to the falls from Gwaun Hepste. Hikers reach the waterfall district from the Beacons by crossing the A470 near the YHA Llwyn-y-Celyn, climbing Craig Cerrig-gleisiad cliff and Fan Frynych peak, and descending along a rocky Roman road. The route crosses a nature reserve and trackless heath.

Between Swansea and Brecon, off the A4067, the **Dan-yr-Ogof Showcaves** are the park's most highly promoted attractions. Though their stalagmites and eerie rock formations are quite impressive, their "showcase" status has left them commercial and heavily trafficked, most notably the grotesque but award-winning Dinosaur Park—complete with a "fearsome T-Rex." (☎01639 730 284, 24hr. info 730 801. Open daily Apr.-Oct. 10am-3pm. £9.50, children £6.) From YHA Ystradfellte, 10 mi. of trails pass **Fforest Fawr** on their way to the caves. A **campsite ❶** is nearby. After turning off the A406 for the Showcaves, turn right at the T-junction. (Camping £4 per person. Caravans £10. Electricity free.) Relax at **Craig-y-nos Country Park,** half a mile away. (☎01639 730 395. Open May-Aug. M-F 10am-6pm, Sa-Su 10am-7pm; Mar.-Apr. and Sept.-Oct. M-F 10am-5pm; Sa-Su 10am-6pm; Nov.-Feb. M-F 10am-4pm, Sa-Su 10am-4:30pm. Free.) Stagecoach **bus** #63 (1½hr, 3 per day, £3-4) stops at the hostel, caves, and campsite en route from Brecon to Swansea.

THE BLACK MOUNTAINS

Located in the easternmost section of the park, the Black Mountains are a group of lofty ridges offering 80 sq. mi. of solitude. Summits like **Waun Fach** (2660 ft.), the highest point, may seem dull and boggy, but the ridge walks offer views unsurpassed in Wales. Ordnance Survey Outdoor Leisure Map #13 (1:25,000; £7.50) is essential. **Crickhowell,** on the A40 and Roy Brown's coaches route between Abergavenny and Builth Wells (#82, 25min., 1 every Tu), is one of the best starting points for forays into the area, though hikers staying overnight might want to base themselves in Abergavenny. You can also explore by **bus:** Stagecoach Red and White #39 between Brecon and Hay-on-Wye (p. 452) descends the north side of the Black Mountains. **Gospel Pass,** the park's highest mountain pass, often sees sun above the cloud cover. Nearby, **Offa's Dyke Path** (p. 450) traces the park's eastern boundary. The ridge valleys are studded with churches, castles, and ruins. On Sundays and bank holidays in July and August, Offa's Dyke Flyer **bus** runs from Hay-on-Wye to Llanfihangel Crucorney and stops at access points to the Black Mountains on the way (☎01873 853 254; 3 per day, £2.75). The Flyer aside, there is almost no public transportation along valley routes.

ABERGAVENNY (Y FENNI) ☎01873

On the eastern edge of Brecon Beacons National Park, Abergavenny (pop. 10,000) trumpets itself as the "Gateway to Wales." While shop-lined pedestrian areas offer all the charms of Welsh village life, the region's real charm lies outside city limits: Abergavenny is the starting point of countless hikes through the Black Mountains.

◪ TRANSPORTATION. Trains (☎08457 484 950) run from: Bristol (1hr., 1-2 per hr., £8.20); Cardiff (40min., every hr., £7.90); Chepstow (1¼hr, every 2hr., £8.60); Hereford (25min., 2 per hr., £6); London (2¼hr., every hr., £59); Newport (25min., 1-2 per hr., £5). To get to town, turn right at the end of Station Rd. and walk 5min. along Monmouth Rd. The **bus station** is on Monmouth Rd., by the TIC. Stagecoach Red and White (☎01633 838 856) **buses** roll in from: Brecon (X43, 1hr., M-Sa 7 per day, £3.50); Cardiff (X3, 1½hr., every hr., £4.50); Hereford (X4, 1hr., 5 per day, £4.50). Call **Lewis Taxis** (☎854 140) for inexpensive door-to-door service.

◪ PRACTICAL INFORMATION. The well-stocked **Tourist Information Centre,** Monmouth Rd., across from the bus station, arranges local theater bookings and reserves beds for £2. (☎857 588; www.abergavenny.co.uk. Open daily Apr.-Oct. 10am-5:30pm; Nov.-Mar. 10am-4pm.) It shares space with the **National Park Information Centre,** which has helpful maps and useful guidance for hikers. (☎853 254. Open daily Apr.-Oct. 9:30am-5:30pm.) Other services include: **banks** along Brecon Rd. and Frogmore St.; **police,** Tudor St. (☎852 273), between Nevill St. and Baker St.; the **hospital** (☎732 732), Nevill Hall, on the A40; free **Internet access** at the Public Library, Library Sq., Baker St. (☎735 980; open M, W, F 9:30am-5:30pm; Tu 10am-5:30pm; Th 9:30am-8pm; Sa 9:30am-4pm), or Celtic Computer Systems, 39 Cross St. (☎858 111; £2.50 per 30min.; open M-Sa 9:30am-5:30pm); and the **post office,** St. John's Sq., where Tudor St. turns into Castle St., with a bureau de change (☎08457 223 344; open M-F 9am-5:30pm, Sa 9am-12:30pm). **Post Code:** NP7 5EB.

◪◪ ACCOMMODATIONS AND FOOD. B&Bs lie on **Monmouth Road,** past the TIC, and **Hereford Road,** 15min. from town. **Black Sheep Backpackers ❷,** 24 Station Rd., is located across from the train station and offers a colorful basement lounge with a kitchen and a full bar upstairs. (☎859 125; www.blacksheepbackpackers.com. Internet access £1 per 30min. Dorms £13.50; doubles £30. Cash only.)

The **market** in Market Hall on Cross St. has fresh fruit, vegetables, and baked goods (open Tu, F, and Sa 9am-5pm; largest on Tu). A massive flea market assembles once a week (W 9am-5pm). **Harry's Carvery ❶,** St. John's St., just off High St., has a formidable slew of edibles (£2-3). Try a *ciabatta* (£2.55) or defy sandwich conventions with a Brie and cranberry foccaccia. (☎852 766. Open daily 8:30am-4pm. Cash only.) **Mad Hatters Cafe ❶**, 58 Cross St., serves pastries (£1-2) and savories (sandwiches from £3) in a pantry-style dining room with a collection of teapots. (☎859 839. Open M-Sa 9:30am-5:30pm, Su 10am-5pm. Cash only.) The elegant restaurant at **The Angel Hotel ❹**, 15 Cross St., delivers inventive dishes crafted from local ingredients. Entrees like beef with bernaise (£15) barely leave room for the sumptuous desserts. (☎857 121. Open daily noon-2:30pm and 7-10pm. MC/V.)

◨▨ SIGHTS AND OUTDOORS. Site of many a medieval intrigue, Abergavenny's **castle** is now reduced to a picturesque, though unremarkable, ruin. A 19th-century hunting lodge on the grounds houses the **Abergavenny Museum.** (☎854 282. Open Mar.-Oct. M-Sa 11am-1pm and 2-5pm, Su 2-5pm; Nov.-Feb. M-Sa 11am-1pm and 2-4pm. Grounds open daily 8am-dusk. Free.) The **Borough Theatre,** Cross St., puts on a variety of shows in the center of town. (☎850 805. Box office open Tu-Sa 9:30am-5pm. Tickets from £5, concessions available.)

Abergavenny's real attractions are the surrounding hills; pick up *Walks from Abergavenny* (£2) from the NPIC for details on hikes. Because almost all of the Black Mountain trails are unmarked, it's crucial to get detailed directions and an Ordnance Survey Map (£6.50-7.50) from the NPIC. Three major summits are accessible from Abergavenny by foot, though all require fairly long hikes. **Blorenge** (1833 ft.) is 2½ mi. southwest of town. A path begins off the B4246 or from the TIC, traversing woodlands to the uplands; it ascends the remaining 1500 ft. in 4½ mi. (6hr. and 12 mi. round-trip). The trail to the top of **Sugar Loaf** (1955 ft.), 2½ mi. northwest, starts half a mile west of town on the A40. Many report that it's easy to hitch a ride to the carpark and start hikes from there, though Let's Go does not recommend hitchhiking. The path to **Skirrid Fawr** (the "Holy Mountain"; 1595 ft.) lies northeast of town and starts 2 mi. down the B4521. **Pony trekking** can be enjoyable. Try Grange Trekking Centre (☎890 215; £19 per half-day, £29 per day) and Llanthony Riding and Trekking (☎890 359; £18 per half-day, £35 per day).

▧ DAYTRIPS FROM ABERGAVENNY

If traveling to the sights near Abergavenny by bus, a **Network Rider** pass (p. 449) is usually cheaper than round-trip tickets.

BIG PIT NATIONAL MINING MUSEUM FOR WALES. Recently named a World Heritage Site, the hillsides of Blaenavon, 9 mi. southwest of Abergavenny, bear the scars of years spent at the center of the South Wales coal-mining and iron-production industries. The museum allows hard-hatted visitors to descend a 300 ft. shaft and experience the cramped, dark working conditions to which men, women, and children as young as 10 were subjected. Ex-miners share stories and industrial history in the subterranean workshops. Dress warmly and wear sensible shoes. *(Bus X3 (20min., 13 per day) to Pontypool, then #30 (20min., every 2hr.) to Blaenavon. ☎01495 790 311. Open mid-Feb. to Nov. daily 9:30am-5pm. Underground tours 10am-3:30pm. Free. Those under 3 ft. 3 in. not admitted underground. Under 16 not admitted without a guardian.)*

LLANTHONY PRIORY. All the megaliths in the Black Mountains are said to point toward ruined and relatively untouristed Llanthony Priory. In the 12th century, founder William de Lacy doffed his hunting gear and aristocratic title, rebuilding ancient ruins left at this site so that he could live a more contemplative hermetic life. *(Take Stagecoach Red and White bus X4 (M-Sa 6 per day) or follow the A465 to Llanfihangel Crucorney, where the B4423 begins. Some hitch the last 6 mi. to the priory, but Let's Go does not recommend hitchhiking. Always open. Free.)*

RAGLAN CASTLE. A mere 569 years old, Raglan was the last medieval castle built in Wales. Sir William Thomas constructed it for aesthetic rather than military purposes. Still, the castle withstood an English Civil War siege with admirable fortitude before finally falling to Cromwell's troops in 1646. The remaining ruins comprise an impressive network of open-air towers and crumbling staircases that cut striking profiles against the hills beyond. *(Take bus #83 from Abergavenny or Monmouth (20min., 6 per day, £4.50) or #60 from Monmouth or Newport (40min. from Newport, 2 per hr., £3-4.20). From the bus stop in Raglan, follow Castle Rd. to the highway and cross over the pedestrian path to the road up to the castle. ☎01291 690 228. Open June-Sept. daily 9:30am-6pm; Apr.-May and Oct. daily 9:30am-5pm; Nov.-Mar. M-Sa 9:30am-4pm, Su 11am-4pm. Last admission 30min. before close. £2.75, concessions £2.25, families £7.75.)*

BRECON (ABERHONDDU)   ☎01874

Just north of the mountains, Brecon (pop. 8000) is the best base for exploring the dramatic northern region of Brecon Beacons National Park. Georgian architecture looms over tiny side streets where residents and backpackers sip tea and plan hikes through neighboring forests. A motley bunch alights in Brecon in August, when the exceptional Jazz Festival fills every bed and street corner.

⊏ TRANSPORTATION. Brecon has no bus or train station, but **buses** arrive regularly at the Bulwark in the central square. Ask for schedules at the TIC. National Express (☎08705 808 080) bus #509 runs from London (6hr., 1 per day, £21) via Cardiff (1¼hr., 1 per day, £3.30). Stagecoach Red and White (☎01633 838 856) buses arrive from Abergavenny (X43, 50min., 7 per day, £4.50) and Swansea (#63, 1½hr., M-Sa 3 per day, £4-5). Buses #39 and 40 come from Hereford via Hay-on-Wye (M-Sa 8 per day, £4.50); on Sundays, Yeomans (☎01432 356 202) follows the same route (#40, Su 3 per day, £4.50). Brecon Cycle Centre, 10 Ship St., **rents mountain bikes** and gives advice on maintenance and trails. (☎622 651. £15 per day, £25 per weekend. Open M-Sa 9am-5pm, Su by appointment.) Bikes and Hikes (p. 460) also rents equipment and organizes climbing, caving, and other expeditions. (☎610 071. Bike rental £16, assorted activities £25-35 per day.)

⚠ PRACTICAL INFORMATION. The **Tourist Information Centre** is located in the Cattle Market carpark, across from Safeway; walk through Bethel Sq. off Lion St. (☎622 485. Open M-F 9:30am-5:30pm, Sa 9:30am-5pm, Su 9:30am-4pm.) Other services include: Barclays **bank,** at the corner of St. Mary's St. and High St. (☎01633 205 000; open M-F 9am-4:30pm); a **launderette,** St. Mary's St. (☎07960 979 625; £6-9; open M-Sa 9am-5:30pm); **police,** Lion St. (☎622 331); Boots **pharmacy,** Bethyl Sq. (☎622 917; open M-Sa 9am-5:30pm); free **Internet access** at Brecon Branch Library, Ship St. (☎623 346; open M and W-F 9:30am-5pm, Tu 9:30am-7pm, Sa 9:30am-1pm) and at Brecon Cyber Cafe, 10 Lion St. (☎624 942; £1.25 per 15min., students £1; open M-Sa 10am-5pm); and the **post office,** in the Cooperative Pioneer, off Lion St. (☎623 735; open M-F 8:30am-5:30pm, Sa 8:30am-4:30pm). **Post Code:** LD3 7HY.

⌂ ACCOMMODATIONS. Book far in advance for mid-August—the Jazz Festival claims every pillow in town. **Bikes and Hikes ❷,** 10 The Struet, at the Elms, near the TIC, lives up to its name: the outdoors-enthusiast owners rent equipment and lead trips. Their hostel has nice facilities, including a pool room and large kitchen. (☎610 071. Dorms £12.50. Cash only.) Delightful **Mrs. J. Thomas ❸,** 13 Alexandra Rd., behind the TIC, has traveled to 27 countries, lived in 18, and displays exotic memorabilia in her sparkling dining room. Watch out for the tiger rug, head still attached. (☎624 551. TV, tea service, and breakfast included. £22 per person. Cash only.) **Mulberry House ❷,** 3 Priory Hill, offers comfortable rooms with TVs across from the cathedral. (☎ 624 461. £19 per person. Cash only.) The nearest **YHA hostel** is **Ty'n-y-Caeau** (tin-uh-KAY-uh) ❶, 3 mi. from Brecon. From the town center, walk down The Watton to the A40-A470 roundabout. Follow the Abergavenny branch of the A40. After the roundabout, take the footpath to the left of Groesffordd (grohs-FORTH), turn left on the main road, and continue 10-15min., bearing left at the fork; the hostel is on the right. Or take the longer and more scenic canal path to Brynich, taking a left to Groesffordd. The X43 bus stops in Groesffordd (7 per day), but a 1½ mi. walk remains. The Victorian townhouse has gardens, a TV room, and Internet access. (☎ 665 270. Dorms £12.50, under 18 £9. MC/V.) **Camp** at **Brynich Caravan Park** ❶, 1½ mi. east of town on the A40, signposted from the A40-A470 roundabout. The canal path provides a prettier walk. (☎ 623 325; www.brynich.co.uk. Open Easter to Oct. £5, £11 for 2 people and car. Prices vary. MC/V.) During the Jazz Festival, campsites open on farms.

◘ FOOD. Buy **groceries** at the Cooperative Pioneer, off Lion St. (☎ 625 257. Open M-Sa 8am-9pm, Su 10am-4pm.) **Cegin Cymru** ❶ ("Welsh Food Centre"), in the George Inn courtyard, stocks a selection of tinned laverbread and clotted cream fudge. (☎ 620 020. Open Easter to Christmas M-Sa 9am-5pm, Su 10am-4pm. MC/V.) **St. Mary's Bakery** ❶, 4 St. Mary St., sells baked goods (35p-£1) and warm pork baps. (☎ 624 311. Open M-F 6:30am-5pm, Sa 7am-2pm. Cash only.) **The Café** ❷, 39 High St., serves sandwiches (from £3), mouth-watering cheesecake (£2.20), "Welsh Black" in a relaxed atmosphere. (☎ 611 191. Open M-Sa 10am-5pm. Cash only.) **Pilgrim's Tea Rooms and Restaurant** ❶, attached to the cathedral, makes you feel like high society: sip your cream tea with scones (£2.60) or try the cheesy cauliflower (£5.50) in the cathedral gardens. (☎ 610 610. Open daily 10am-5pm. Cash only.)

◙ ※ SIGHTS AND FESTIVALS. As much a museum as a place of worship, **Brecon Cathedral** holds the standards of the Welsh 24th Regiment and impressive examples of craftsmanship. History is literally carved into the stone columns; "mason's marks" were the small designs (crosses, clovers) that illiterate stoneworkers used to label their work. The **Heritage Centre,** in the same hilly grove, details the art of bell-ringing and the history of the cathedral. Look for the gargoyle on the center's streetside wall; the phallus attached makes it a rare specimen. (Cathedral ☎ 623 857, center 625 222. Cathedral open daily 8:30am-6pm. Center open Mar.-Dec. M-Sa 10:30am-4:30pm, Su noon-3pm.) **Brecknock Museum and Art Gallery,** in the Assize Courthouse near The Bulwark, features artifacts from rural Wales: walking sticks, milk churns, and a smithy. Don't miss the life-size Victorian Court, complete with barristers and judge. (☎ 624 121. Open Oct.-Mar. M-F 10am-5pm, Sa 10am-1pm and 2-5pm; Apr.-Sept. M-F 10am-5pm, Sa 10am-1pm and 2-5pm, Su noon-5pm. £1, concessions 50p.) At the **Royal Regiment of Wales Museum Brecon,** The Barracks, military paraphernalia commands all available space. (☎ 613 310; www.rrw.org.uk. Open Apr.-Sept. daily 10am-5pm; Oct.-Mar. M-F 10am-5pm. Last admission 4:30pm. £3.) For the August **Brecon Jazz Festival** (☎ 611 622; www.breconjazz.co.uk) the streets are blocked off as thousands converge to appreciate jazz and local brews. Other events include **antique fairs** (last Sa of the month) and **crafts fairs** in Market Hall (Easter to Nov. each 3rd Sa of the month).

THE GOWER PENINSULA

The 18 mi. Gower Peninsula is rife with unexpected finds. Ancient burial sites, castles, and churches dot the land and expansive white beaches connect border flower-covered limestone cliffs. Mumbles, its largest city, entrances wide-eyed visitors with beaches, nightlife, and a seaside demeanor as unassuming as its name.

⌨ TRANSPORTATION. Buses to the peninsula leave from Swansea's Quadrant Station. First Cymru (☎08706 082 608) buses #2 and 2A leave Swansea for Oystermouth Sq. in Mumbles (20min., 4 per hr., £1.70) and continue to Langland Bay and Caswell Bay. Buses #117 and 118 run to Oxwich (40min., 2 per day, £3.10) and to Rhossili via Port Eynon (1hr., every 2hr., £3.10). Bus #14 shuttles to Pennard (35min., every hr., £3.10). On Sundays, bus travel is difficult, though buses #48 and 49 run 3 times. The **First Cymru Day Saver** is valid through the Gower and Swansea (£5.50, under 18 £4), while the **Gower & City Rider** allows a week's unlimited travel around the Peninsula (£20). A.A. **Taxis** (☎360 600) provides cabs. The Swansea **Bikepath** and **Promenade** traces the coast from Swansea Bay to Mumbles pier.

⯀ PRACTICAL INFORMATION. Mumbles, the largest city on Gower, has the most helpful services. The **Tourist Information Centre** shares space with Mumbles Methodist Church on Mumbles Rd. (☎361 302. Open Sept.-June M-Sa 10am-5pm; July-Aug. M-Sa 10am-5pm, Su noon-4:30pm.) Other services include: Barclays **bank**, 16 Newton Rd. (☎492 600; open M-F 9am-4:30pm); Wales' first "virtual **police** station" on Newton Rd., near Castle St.; free **Internet access** at Oystermouth Library, Dunns Ln., a block from the TIC (☎368 380; photo ID required; open M-Th 9am-6pm, F 9am-8pm, Sa 9:30am-5pm); and the **post office,** 522 Mumbles Rd. (☎366 821; open M-Sa 9am-5:30pm). **Post Code:** SA3 4DH.

⌨⌂ ACCOMMODATIONS AND FOOD. West Gower has less touristy and cheaper accommodations than Mumbles. **B&Bs** charge upwards of £25 for singles and cluster on **Mumbles Road** and in the **South End** area (a 10min. walk from the TIC); singles are hard to find. With large bay windows, the gabled **Coast House ❸,** 708 Mumbles Rd., lets you watch schooners over breakfast scones. (☎368 702. Most rooms with TV and bath. Singles £30, doubles from £55.) Behind it, **Rock Villa ❸,** 1 George Bank, offers comparable views, comfortable nooks, and familial hospitality. (☎366 794. Singles £28; doubles and twins £56-60. MC/V.) **Glenview Guest House ❹,** 140 Langland Rd., a 10min. walk uphill from the TIC, is a Victorian belle with luxurious ensuite rooms, views of Underhill Park, and a log fire for wintry nights. (☎367 933. Open Dec.-Oct. Singles £55; doubles £60-70; twins £65-75; family rooms £75-90; family suite £95-120. MC/V.) Take bus #14 to reach accommodations in nearby **Bishopston.** To camp at **Three Cliffs Bay Caravan Park ❶,** North Hills Farm, Penmaen, take bus #18 from Swansea. (☎371 218. £6 per person; electricity £1.50. Cash only.) Bus #18A runs from Swansea to Port Enyon, west of Mumbles and home to the great **⯀YHA Port Eynon ❶.** This former lifeboat house on the beach offers nice rooms, a clean kitchen, and a cozy common area. (☎390 706. Reception 8-10am and 5-10pm. Check-in after 5pm. Open Easter to Nov. £12.50, under 18 £9. MC/V.) Beachside **camping** is also possible in Port Eynon.

In Mumbles, the Somerfield **supermarket** is at 512 Mumbles Rd. (Open daily 8am-8pm.) **The Choice is Yours,** 7 Newton Rd., sells freshly harvested produce. (☎367 255. Open M-Sa 8:30am-5:30pm. MC/V.) On a wooden pier, busy **Verdi's ❶,** Knab Rock, at the southern end of Mumbles Rd., scoops out a variety of traditional (cookies 'n' cream) and distinctive (honeycomb, apple cobbler) flavors. Verdi's restaurant next door serves bistro cuisine. (☎369 135. Single scoop £1.20. Open daily 9am-9:30pm. MC/V.) **Claude's Restaurant ❷,** 93 Newton Rd., promises "food with flair" and delivers with concoctions like onion- and goat- cheese tartlets and monkfish with a saffron pancetta infusion. (☎366 006; www.claudes.org.uk. Open Tu-Sa noon-2:30pm and 6:30pm-9:30pm, Su noon-2:30pm. AmEx/MC/V.) **Madisons ❶,** 620 Mumbles Rd., is a small coffee shop with a big view of the bay that serves favorites like omelettes and Welsh rarebit (£2.75). If given a day's notice, they will pack picnic lunches for hikes. (☎368 484. Open daily 8am-5pm. Cash only.)

⚅◪ **SIGHTS AND BEACHES.** Perched high above Mumbles, the ramparts of 13th-century **Oystermouth Castle**, on Castle Ave. off Newton Rd., offer a bird's eye view of the labyrinthine streets. (☎ 368 732. Open Apr. to mid-Sept. daily 11am-5pm. £1.) Farther down the peninsula, the 56-acre **Mumbles Hill Nature Reserve** is a steep but worthwhile excursion; hikers find sweeping vistas of Swansea's coastal flats between patches of scrub and natural arbors. The path begins with a staircase by the George Hotel, 10min. from the TIC. Examining the small collection at the **Lovespoon Gallery**, 492 Mumbles Rd., will yield a rich understanding of the heritage behind these traditional Welsh signs of affection. (☎ 360 132; www.lovespoons.co.uk. Spoons £5; engraving £6. Open M-Sa 10am-5:30pm. AmEx/MC/V.)

The Gower Peninsula is strewn with gorgeous beaches, some more friendly to swimmers than others. From Southgate and Pennard, a 30min. walk along the Coast Path brings you to **Three Cliffs**, a cave-ridden area almost completely submerged at high tide. **Langland Bay, Caswell Bay, Oxwich Bay,** and **Port Eynon Bay** are all popular and clean, with superb views. To reach Langland, walk 45min. along the Bays Footpath that begins around the point of Mumbles Head. Caswell is another 45min., and Oxwich and Port Eynon are several miles beyond; buses #117 and 118 from Swansea will stop here. On the peninsula's western tip, cliffs hug the sweeping curve of ◪**Rhossili Beach**, whose wide expanse and seclusion make overcrowding unlikely; take bus #118 from Swansea. Within 2½hr. of low tide, a causeway provides access to the seabird haven **Worm's Head,** a series of crags that looks like a "wurm" (Welsh for dragon) lumbering out to sea. Call ☎ 306 534 for information on tides. **Llangennith Beach,** north of Rhossili, draws surfers from all over Wales.

◪▩ **NIGHTLIFE AND FESTIVALS.** A fishing hole by day, **Mumbles** becomes a watering hole at night. The stretch of **Mumbles Road** at Mumbles Head is lined with pubs, some of them former haunts of Dylan Thomas. In University of Swansea lingo, to hang out on Mumbles Rd. is to "go mumbling"; to start at one end and have a pint at each pub is to "do the Mumbles Mile." Flower's, Usher's, Buckley's, and Felin Foel are local ales. The **Gower Festival** fills the peninsula's churches with string quartets and Bach chorales during the last two weeks of July (booking ☎ 475 715; tickets £8-12). The *What's On* guide, free at the Mumbles TIC, has details.

SWANSEA (ABERTAWE)   ☎ 01792

Native son Dylan Thomas's paradoxical assessment of Swansea (pop. 230,000) as "this ugly lovely town," is remarkably resonant. The "ugly" bit is obvious: slab concrete buildings line urban roads, industrial equipment borders the coast, and box houses cover the hillsides in well-defined grids. Yet Swansea is an active city; it hosts colorful cafes and free museums and embodies a utilitarian charm. Farther west, an expanse of sandy beaches extends onto the nearby Gower Peninsula.

◪ **TRANSPORTATION.** Swansea has direct connections to most major cities in Britain. At the **train station,** 35 High St., **trains** (☎ 08457 484 950) arrive from: Birmingham (3½hr., 2 per hr., £35.40); Cardiff (1hr., 1-2 per hr., £8.40); London (3hr.; every hr.; M-Th and Su £46, F-Sa £58). The **Quadrant Bus Station** (☎ 0870 608 2608) is near the Quadrant Shopping Centre and the TIC. National Express (☎ 08705 808 080) runs **buses** from: Birmingham (3½hr., 2 per day, £24.50); Cardiff (1¼hr., 11 per day, £5.90); London (4½hr., 3 per day, £20.50). First Cymru (☎ 08706 082 608) buses cover the Gower Peninsula and the rest of southwest Wales; a shuttle runs to Cardiff (1hr., M-Sa 2-4 per hr., £7.50). A **First Cymru DaySaver** ticket (£3.10, concessions £1.90, families £5) allows unlimited travel for a day in Swansea; a £1.40 pass will get you unlimited travel M-Th nights after 7pm. The **Swansea Bay Pass,** purchased on the bus, covers a week of travel on the Peninsula (£12.50, concessions

SOUTH WALES

£8.40). Stagecoach Buses arrive from smaller towns around Wales, including Brecon (1½hr., 3 per day, £4.50). Data Cabs (☎474 747) and Yellow Cab (☎652 244) offer **taxi** services. From late July to September, **cruises** set sail from Swansea to Ilfracombe and other spots on the Bristol Channel (☎01412 432 224; £20-35).

◪ PRACTICAL INFORMATION. On the north side of the bus station, the **Tourist Information Centre** books rooms for a £2 charge plus a 10% deposit and stocks events calendars and a helpful city map. (☎468 321; www.visitswanseabay.com. Open in summer M-Sa 9:30am-5:30pm, Su 10am-4pm; in winter M-Sa 9:30am-5:30pm.) Other services include: Barclays **bank** (☎01633 205 000), The Kingsway (open M-F 9am-5pm, Sa 9:30am-3pm); American Express, 28 The Kingsway (☎455 188; open M-F 9am-5pm, Sa 9am-4pm); **police**, Grove Pl. (☎456 999), at the bottom of Mt. Pleasant Hill; **Singleton Hospital,** Sketty Park Ln. (☎205 666); Co-op **pharmacy,** 13 Orchard St. (☎643 527; open M-F 9am-5:30pm, Sa 9am-1pm); free **Internet access** at the Swansea Public Library, Alexandra Rd. (☎516 750; book ahead; photo ID required; open M-Tu and Th 9am-6pm, W and F 9am-8pm, Sa 9am-5pm) and on the ground floor of Debenham's in the Quadrant Shopping Centre (£1.50 per 30min.; open M-F 9:30am-6pm, Sa 9am-6pm); and the **post office,** 35 The Kingsway, with bureau de change (open M-Sa 9am-5:30pm). **Post Code:** SA1 5LF.

◪◪ ACCOMMODATIONS AND FOOD. The closest hostel is the popular **YHA Port Eynon,** an hour out of town by bus (p. 462). Inexpensive **B&Bs** and guest houses line **Oystermouth Road,** along the bay. Frequent buses make downtown access easy. **Ael-y-Bryn House ❷,** 88 Bryn Rd., has bay views and small but well-furnished rooms with TV and tea. (☎466 707. £23-30 per person. MC/V.) **Harlton Guest House ❷,** 89 King Edward Rd., offers adequate rooms with bright color schemes. (☎466 938; www.harltonguesthouse.co.uk. £15 per person. MC/V.) In summer, many travelers **camp** at sites along the Gower Peninsula.

Indian and Chinese takeaways line **St. Helen's Road.** Small cafes, bistros, and trendy restaurants dominate **Oxford Street** and **Wind Street.** The city convenes at the **Swansea Market,** the largest indoor market in Wales, on the side of the Quadrant Shopping Centre opposite the bus station (open M-Sa 8:30am-5:30pm). **Govinda's Vegetarian Restaurant ❶,** 8 Cradock St., is a small shrine to tranquility nestled just off The Kingway. Try a salad with a freshly baked roll (£1.35) or an huge platter of vegetables (£6) "prepared in every way imaginable." (☎468 469. Open M-Th and Su noon-3pm, F-Sa noon-6pm. Cash only.) Self-described as "hotter than a chili pepper, smoother than a Latin lover," **¡Mambo! ❷,** 46 The Kingsway, serves tasty Caribbean fare (lunch £6) in a dining room lit by purple lanterns and becomes a trendy watering hole in the evening. (☎456 620. Open 10am-11pm. AmEx/MC/V.) The **Cross Keys ❶,** 12 St. Mary's St., is a sprawling pub, with a menu as large as its beer garden, a full bar to satisfy the barfly, and flashy games to occupy the bar-shy. (☎630 921. Open M-Sa 11am-11:20pm, Su noon-10:30pm. Food served M-Th 11am-8pm, F-Sa 8am-5:30pm, Su noon-6pm. MC/V.)

◪ SIGHTS. The bronze, hollowed eyes of **Dylan Thomas** gaze seaward at the end of Swansea's marina. The late poet, a demi-god of local culture and national literature, inspires many tours, which shepherd iambic junkies along the **Dylan Thomas Uplands Trail** and **City Centre Trail,** past the poet's favorite haunts. Detailed guidebooks to the trails (from £1.50) are available at the **Dylan Thomas Centre,** Somerset Pl., which venerates Thomas and his "craft of sullen art." Visitors can listen as Thomas breathlessly recites five of his poems; famous portraits hang alongside his notoriously sizeable bar tabs (£8, in 1953). The center also presents dramatic, cinematic, and literary performances. (☎463 980, box office 463 892. Open Tu-Su 10:30am-4:30pm. Free.) The **Swansea**

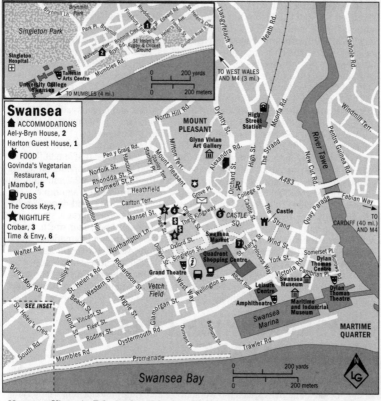

Swansea

🏠 ACCOMMODATIONS
Ael-y-Bryn House, **2**
Harlton Guest House, **1**

🍴 FOOD
Govinda's Vegetarian
Restaurant, **4**
¡Mambo!, **5**

🍺 PUBS
The Cross Keys, **7**

★ NIGHTLIFE
Crobar, **3**
Time & Envy, **6**

Museum, Victoria Rd., is the oldest in Wales and features the body of Hor, a gilded and mummified Egyptian priest, and the "Cabinet of Curiosities," an institutionalized celebration of randomness. (☎ 653 763. Open Tu-Su 10am-5pm; last admission 4pm. Free.) The collection at the **Glynn Vivian Art Gallery,** Alexandra Rd., reflects the eclectic tastes of its largest donor, Richard Glynn Vivian, a wealthy prodigal son who fled Victorian society for the pleasures of travel and art acquisition, amassing an impressive array of china and paperweights along the way. Seasonal shows feature local artists. (☎ 516 900. Open Tu-Su 10am-5pm. Free). The **castle,** reduced to unmemorable ruins by rebel-hero Owain Glyndŵr, lies between Wind St. and The Strand and goes unnoticed by most; cars whiz by feet from its walls, and office buildings usurp its spot in the skyline. It overlooks **Castle Square,** a circular plaza around a fountain. As in Cardiff, recent rebuilding has transformed the **maritime quarter** from a decaying dockland to a land of upscale apartment blocks and outdoor cafes. In the **Maritime and Industrial Museum,** just behind a Leisure Centre, a fully refurbished tram commemorates the world's first passenger railway, which chugged from Swansea to Oystermouth in 1807, powered first by workhorse, then by sails, then finally conventional methods. The museum is expected to reopen in 2006 after renovations. (☎ 653 763. Open Tu-Su 10am-5pm. Free. The passenger railway exhibit is open next door.)

NIGHTLIFE AND ENTERTAINMENT. The young folk of Swansea do not go gentle on weekend nights; rather, festivities begin at pre-club bars as early as 7pm and rage, rage until 3am. Or at least they rage term-time; most clubs see a sharp downturn during summer vacation. Nightlife centers around **The Kingsway,** where swarms of students club-hop on weekend nights. **Time & Envy,** 72 The Kingsway, is the most prestigious club because of its sheer size. Time aficionados gyrate under 20 ft. katanas and a Chinese dragon while those who elect Envy leer from the second floor balcony. (☎653 142. All-inclusive members night F £12. Cover £5-7. Open W-Th 10pm-2am, F-Sa 10pm-3am.) A short walk away, **Crobar,** Northampton Ln., offers a low-key alternative with white leather booths and a smoky, dimly lit second floor. (☎470 074. Cover from £5. Open F 10pm-3am, Sa 10pm-4am.) About 5 mi. away, pubs on Gower's **Mumbles Road** are a barfly's magnet.

The bimonthly *What's On,* free at the TIC, lists events around town. The **Dylan Thomas Theatre,** along the marina, stages dramas and musicals. (☎473 238. Tickets from £6, concessions from £5.) The **Grand Theatre,** on Singleton St., puts on opera, ballet, concerts, and comedy. (☎475 715. Box office open M-Sa 9:30am-8pm, Su 1hr. before show. Tickets £10-35; same-day concessions often available.) The **Taliesin Arts Centre,** University College, hosts films, art shows, and dance. (☎296 883. Box office open M-F 10am-6pm, Sa noon-6pm, and before curtain. Brochures available on campus.) In mid-August, the village of Pontardawe, 8 mi. north, floods with international folk and rock musicians for the **Pontardawe International Music Festival** (☎830 200; www.pontardawefestival.com; weekend ticket £30). The **Swansea Festival** (☎411 570, bookings 475 715), in October, hosts shows, concerts, and family activities. Revelry continues with the **Dylan Thomas Celebration** (☎463 980; www.dylanthomasfestival.com), which includes readings, shows, and lectures that run from Dylan's birthday to the date of his death (Oct. 27-Nov. 9).

PEMBROKESHIRE COAST NATIONAL PARK

The 225 sq. mi. of Pembrokeshire Coast National Park *(Parc Cenedlaethol Arfordir Penfro)* are spread between long oceanside stretches and scattered inland pockets. The park spans the wooded Gwaun Valley and ancient Celtic ruins in the Preseli Hills, but the coastline remains its most compelling draw. The coves and towering sea cliffs lure serious backpackers and day hikers along 186 mi. of coastal trail. While oil refineries and working harbors dot the path as reminders of man's encroachments, sand dunes and wildflowers still dominate the scene.

TRANSPORTATION

The best place to enter the region is **Haverfordwest.** Buses radiate from here to the various coastal regions, which offer a wider variety of accommodations and prettier surroundings. The rail system is less useful for travelers seeking to make connections around the coast, as lines end at Pembroke Docks and Milford Haven. While Let's Go does not recommend hitchhiking, hitchers frequent the area. Mountain bikes are an excellent means of transport on the one-lane roads. Do not ride on the coastal path itself; it is illegal and dangerous.

Trains: (☎08457 484 950) arrive from **Cardiff** (3hr., 8-10 per day, £15.10) and **London Paddington** (4½hr., 7-9 per day, £51). Also to **Fishguard** on the north coast and **Tenby** and **Pembroke Dock** on the south (change at **Whitland**).

Buses: The free *Pembrokeshire Bus Timetables* and *Pembrokeshire Coastal Bus Services Timetables* list comprehensive and standardized bus information for the summer and are available at local TICs. Richards Brothers (☎02139 613 756) #411 runs from **Haver-**

fordwest to **Fishguard** (1½hr., 5 per day) and **St. David's** (45min., 7 per day, £2.15). First Cymru (☎01792 580 580) runs from **Haverfordwest** to **Milford Haven** (#302; 30min.; M-Sa 1-2 per hr., Su 7 per day) and **Tenby** via **Pembroke** (#349; 1½hr., 12 per day). Silcox Coaches (☎01646 683 143) and Taf Valley Coaches (☎01994 240 908) run from **Haverfordwest** to **Broad Haven** (#311; 20min., M-Sa 7 per day). The Puffin Shuttle #400 runs between **St. David's** and **Milford Haven** (2hr., 3 per day), and the Strumble Shuttle #404 connects **St. David's** and **Fishguard** (1½hr., 3 per day). First Cymru's **FirstDay Pass** (£4) will get you unlimited bus transport within Pembrokeshire on their buses, while the more useful West Wales Rover Ticket (£5) works all day on any bus service.

Bike Rental: Voyages of Discovery, Cross Sq. (☎01437 721 911), opposite Lloyd's Bank in St. David's. £10 per half-day, £15 per day. Open daily 8am-7pm.

Outdoor Equipment: A number of **outdoor activity centers** rent canoes, kayaks, ponies, bikes, fishing poles, horses, golf clubs, SCUBA and snorkeling gear, etc.; check *Explore Pembrokeshire*, available at NPICs, for locations. Among the most popular outdoor activity centers is the excellent **TYF Adventure** (see **Crazy, or Just Coasteering?**, right) in Tenby and St. David's (☎01437 721 611 or 0800 132 588; www.tyf.com).

☑ PRACTICAL INFORMATION

The **National Park Information Centers (NPICs)** below sell annotated maps (from 40p) of the coastal path. The indispensable trail guide is pricey ($13) but detailed and includes color maps. Ask about guided walks offered by the park. For **weather information,** call any NPIC; in an emergency, contact **rescue rangers** at ☎999 or 112.

National Park Information Centres:

Newport: 2 Bank Cottages, Long St. (☎01239 820 912). Open Apr.-Oct. M-Sa 10am-5:30pm; June-Aug. M-Sa 10am-5:30pm, Su 10am-1:15pm.

St. David's: The Grove (☎01437 720 392; www.stdavids.co.uk). Doubles as the town TIC. Open Apr.-Oct. daily 9:30am-5:30pm; Nov. to Easter M-Sa 10am-4pm. Closed 2 weeks in Jan.

Tourist Information Centres:

Fishguard: see p. 475.

Haverfordwest: 19 Old Bridge (☎01437 763 110), adjacent to bus stop. Open Apr.-Sept. M-Sa 9:30am-5:30pm; Oct.-Mar. M-Sa 10am-4pm.

Milford Haven: 94 Charles St. (☎01646 690 866). Open Apr.-Oct. M-Sa 10am-1pm and 1:30-5pm.

Saundersfoot: The Barbecue, Harbour Car Park (☎01834 813 672). Open Apr.-Oct. daily 10am-5:30pm; Nov.-March M and F-Sa 10am-4pm.

Tenby: see p. 469.

THE BIG SPLURGE

CRAZY, OR JUST COASTEERING?

You swim from the beach to an isolated islet; huffing all the way, you scramble up a pebbly rock-face, and peer off a 50 ft. crag into the roaring blue breakers below. And then you jump.

No, you're not crazy, you're coasteering, a sport pioneered on the Pembrokeshire coast in the 1980s. It combines several things your-mother told you never to do at the beach—rock scrambling, cliff diving, running. and swimming. With a heart-pounding feat to contemplate (and hopefully execute) every next minute, it's sure to tickle your inner adventurer. And, as you explore isolated caves and inlets, you catch the best views of untouched stretches of coast.

TYF in St. David's (see right) specializes in the sport; TYF's owner pioneered coasteering (his company owns the trademark for the name). Courses are graded on three levels, from beginner to advanced. Enthusiasts of all abilities are encouraged to participate, but be prepared for 3hr. of sustained activity.

The half-day pricetag with TYF is £42, but for the ultimate experience, try the all-inclusive £200 weekend. TYF provides two nights' B&B accommodation and plenty of watersports.

(Booking office on High St. in St. David. ☎01347 721 611; www.tyf.com. Open daily 9am-5:30pm, longer in summer. AmEx/MC/V.)

ACCOMMODATIONS

Many farmers convert fallow fields into summer **campsites** (about £4 per tent); inquire before pitching. Some hostels allow camping but will only accommodate a few campers. Roads between Tenby, Pembroke, and St. David's are home to plenty of **B&Bs** (£15-30), but they fill quickly in summer, and buses come only every few hours. Spaced along the coastal path, the park's **YHA hostels,** listed below, are all within a day's walk of one another. If you plan at least 14 days ahead, you can book these hostels by calling ☎08702 412 314 or visiting www.yha.org.uk.

Broad Haven (☎01437 781 688), on St. Bride's Bay off the B4341. Take bus #311 from Haverfordwest to Broad Haven (20min., 4-6 per day) or #400 from St. David's (35min., 3 per day) or Milford Haven (1¼hr., 3 per day). 77 beds. Lockout 10am-1pm. Curfew 11pm. Call 48hr. in advance. Dorms £12.50, under 18 £9. MC/V. ❷

Manorbier Skrinkle Haven (☎01834 871 803). From the train station, walk past the A4139 to the castle, turn left onto the B4585, right to the army camp, and follow the signs. A modern building near Manorbier Castle (p. 472). Laundry. Lockout 10am-5pm. Curfew 10:30pm. Open daily Mar.-Oct. Dorms £12.50, under 18 £9. MC/V. ❷

Marloes Sands (☎01646 636 667), near the Dale Peninsula. Take Puffin bus #400 (1¼hr., 3 per day) from St. David's or Milford Haven—ask to be let off at the hostel. A cluster of farm buildings on National Trust property, with access to a huge and unspoiled beach. A good site for watersports. Lockout 10am-5pm. Curfew 11pm. Open Apr.-Oct. Dorms £8.50, under 18 £6. MC/V. ❶

Pen Y Cym (☎08707 705 988), near Solvo. Located close to Newgale Beach. Showers and laundry provided. Rated one of the best in Britain. Lockout 10am-4pm. Curfew 11pm. Dorms £14, under 18 £10. MC/V. ❷

Pwll Deri (☎08707 706 004). On breathtaking 300 ft. cliffs around Strumble Head near Fishguard. Lockout 10am-5pm. Curfew 11pm. Open mid-July to Aug. daily; Sept.-Oct. and Apr.-June M and Th-Su. Dorms £10, under 18 £7. MC/V. ❶

St. David's (☎01437 720 345), near St. David's Head. From the A487 (Fishguard Rd.), turn onto the B4583 and follow signs from the golf club. Men stay in the cowshed, women in the stables. Daytime access to self-catering kitchen. Open mid-July to Aug. daily; Sept.-Oct. and Apr. to mid-July W-Su. Dorms £10, under 18 £7. MC/V. ❶

Trefin (☎01348 831 414). A schoolhouse in Trefin, between St. David's and Fishguard. Bus #411 stops upon request. Just ½ mi. from the coast, near pretty walks. Lockout 10am-5pm. Curfew 11pm. Open daily July-Aug.; Sept.-Oct. and Apr.-June Tu-Sa. Except from mid-July to Aug., advance booking is required. Dorms £10, under 18 £7. MC/V. ❶

HIKING AND OUTDOORS

For short hikes, stick to accessible **St. David's Peninsula** in the northwest. Otherwise, set out on the 186 mi. **Pembrokeshire Coast Path,** marked with acorn symbols along manageable terrain, which begins in the southeast at Amroth and continues west across sandstone through Tenby. Bosherton's Lily Ponds, manmade inlets that bloom in early summer, cut inland and circle around to St. Govan's Head, where worn steps lead to **St. Govan's Chapel.** One myth has it that Sir Gawain retreated here after the fall of Camelot. The waters of the well are said to heal ills and grant wishes, and supposedly no mortal can count the steps. From here to the impressive **Elegug Stacks**—offshore pinnacles of rock with the largest seabird colonies of the entire coastline—the path passes natural sea arches (the famous 80 ft. Green Bridge is particularly striking) and limestone stacks. Unfortunately, the stretch from St. Govan's Head to the Stacks (6 mi.) is sometimes used as an artillery range and closed to hikers. Call the **Castemartin Range Office** (☎01646 662 367) or the **Pembroke National Visitor Centre** (☎01646 622 388) for openings or check at the Tenby TIC. For 10 mi. west of the Stacks the coast is permanently off-limits, and the path veers inland to **Freshwater West,** crossing industrial areas. Here it passes **Stack Fort,** an imposing circular fortress built to defend against the French.

From Freshwater West to **Angle Bay,** the coastline walk covers mild terrain. At Milford Haven the path is cut by a large channel. Geologists call it a "ria," or drowned river valley. From the Dale Peninsula, the path passes by the long, clean beaches of **St. Bride's Bay,** where **Marloes Sands** provides a stretch of sand and the **Three Chimneys,** columns of stone shaped by erosion, tower. The path curves to Newgale and arrives at **St. David's Head,** the site of many Iron-Age hill settlements. The ocean has carved caves and secluded inlets, leaving a stretch of jagged and awe-inspiring terrain. Past St. David's at Abereiddi, the sea has refilled an old slate quarry to create the beautiful "Blue Lagoon." The final stretch of the Coastal Path, between Newport and the village of St. Dogmaels, is quite strenuous (its total ascent is equal to that of Mt. Snowdon) and breathtaking. The free *Explore Pembrokeshire,* available at TICs, gives trail tips and provides bus information. To explore Pembrokeshire by horseback, contact **Heathertown Riding Centre** (near Tenby; ☎01646 651 025; open Easter to Oct.; £13.50 per hr.) or **Maesgwynne Riding Stables** (near Fishguard; ☎01348 872 659; open all year; £12 per hr.).

■ ISLANDS OFF THE PEMBROKESHIRE COAST

GRASSHOLM AND SKOMER. On Grassholm, the most distant island, 35,000 pairs of gannets raise their young each year. **Dale Sailing Company** runs tours around, but not to, the island. The boats leave from Martin's Haven on the Dale Peninsula and often encounter Manx shearwaters and storm petrels. (☎01646 603 110. Tours F noon; call ahead. £25.) The company sails more often to Skomer, a marine reserve and breeding ground for auks, seals, and puffins. (Tours Apr.-Oct. Tu-Su; call ahead for times. £8 boat fee, £6 landing fee; children £5 boat fee, no landing fee.)

RAMSEY ISLAND. Owned by the Royal Society for the Protection of Birds, Ramsey Island hosts the largest gray seal colony in Wales and many rare seabirds off St. David's Peninsula. On the east side of the island lurk the **Bitches,** a rock chain that has brought countless sailors to their doom. **Thousand Islands Expeditions,** Cross Sq., in St. David's, sails around the island from St. Justinian's lifeboat station. (☎01437 721 686. 1½hr. Easter to Nov. daily 9am-6pm. £14, children £7; more extensive journeys from £18, children £14.) The adventurous can journey between the Bitches and through sea caves, the longest in Wales, on an inflatable vessel (2hr. tour £30, children £15). **Voyages of Discovery and Ramsey Island Cruises,** Cross Sq., in St. David's, runs tours and trips through rock gorges on specially designed rubber craft. (☎0800 854 367. Tours from £18, concessions £16.20, children £10.)

SOUTH WALES

TENBY (DINBYCH-Y-PYSGOD) ☎01834

Called "the Welsh Riviera," Tenby is neither archetypal Welsh town nor polished seaside resort. The city balances its history as "the little fort of the fishes"—the literal translation of Dinbych-y-Pysgood—with new tourist appeal. And although the novelty shops, chip dives, and penny arcades threaten to debase its charm, its coastline and multicolored seaside houses reinforce the Tenby's allure. In July and August, half of Britain, their children, and their dogs descend upon the town. But the warm beaches and maritime legacy should attract visitors all year.

E TRANSPORTATION. The unstaffed **train station** is at the bottom of Warren St. Activity Wales, Tudor Sq., offers travel services. (☎844 000. Open M-Sa 9am-5pm.) **Trains** (☎08457 484 950) arrive from: Cardiff (2½hr., 4 per day, £15); Carmarthen (45min., 3 per day, £5.60); Pembroke (30min., M-Sa 3 per day, Su 2 per day, £3.20); Swansea (1½hr., 3 per day, £8.80).

Buses leave from the multi-story carpark on Upper Park Rd., next to Somerfield market. First Cymru (☎01792 580 580) arrives from Haverfordwest via Pembroke (#349; M-Sa every hr. until 5:40pm, Su 3 per day). Or head from Swansea to Carmarthen (X11; M-Sa 2 per hr., £3.70) and transfer to Silcox Coaches (☎842 189; www.silcoxcoaches.co.uk) bus #333 (1hr.; M and W-F 1 per day, Tu and Sa 2 per day). A Silcox Coaches office is in the Town Hall Arcade between South Parade and Upper Frog St. National Express (☎08705 808 080) also runs from Swansea (#508; 1½hr., 3 per day, £6.40). First Cymru FirstDay Saver (£4) and FirstWeek Saver (£12) buy unlimited daily or weekly travel within Pembrokeshire on First buses, while the West Wales Rover Ticket (£5) works on all bus lines. **Taxis** congregate near pubs on F and Sa nights; call Tenby's Taxis (☎843 678).

■ ☷ ORIENTATION AND PRACTICAL INFORMATION. The old town is in the shape of a triangle, with its sides formed by the train station, **North Beach,** and **South Beach** (which becomes **Castle Beach**), with the beaches coming to a point at **Castle Hill.** From the station, **Warren Street** approaches town, becoming **White Lion Street** and continuing to the promenade over North Beach. Off White Lion, **South Parade** and **Upper Frog Street** lead toward South Beach, while **High Street** and **Crackwell Street** veer toward the castle and eventually converge at the harbor. **The Croft** runs along North Beach, and the **Old Wall** runs along South Parade.

Overlooking North Beach, the **Tourist Information Centre,** on Upper Croft Rd. by the Somerfield, has a free accommodations list. (☎842 404. Free town maps. Bookings £2 plus a 10% deposit. Open June to mid-July daily 10am-6pm; mid-July to Aug. daily 10am-6pm; Sept.-May M-Sa 10am-4pm.) Other services include: Barclays **bank,** 18 High St. (the ATM is hidden on Frog St.; open M-F 9am-4:30pm); Washeteria **launderette,** Lower Frog St. (☎842 484; wash £1.70-2.60, dry 20p per 5min., soap 20p; open daily 8:30am-9pm; last wash 8:30pm); **police,** Warren St. (☎0845 330 2000), near the church off White Lion St.; **Tenby Cottage Hospital,** Church Park Rd. near Trafalgar Rd. (☎842 040); **Internet access** at Tenby County Library, Greenhill Ave. (☎843 934; free; book in advance; open M and W-F 9:30am-1pm and 2-5pm, Tu 9:30am-1pm and 2-6pm, Sa 9:30am-12:30pm), or at Webb-Computers, 17 Warren St. (☎844 101; £1 per 30min.; open M-F 9am-5pm, Sa 9am-4pm); Boots **pharmacy,** High St. (☎842 120; open M-Sa 9-5:30pm, Su 10am-4pm); and the **post office,** Warren St., at South Parade (☎843 213; open M-F 8:30am-5:30pm, Sa 8:30am-12:30pm). **Post Code:** SA70 7JR.

♖ ACCOMMODATIONS. On **Warren Street,** outside the town wall near the train station, **B&Bs** (£20-26) line the sidewalks; the side streets of **Greenhill Avenue** and those off the Esplanade and Trafalgar Rd. have almost as many. You can also take a bus to **Saundersfoot** (#352; M-Sa every hr., Su 1-2 per hr. in summer). Overlooking North Beach, **Gwynne House ❸,** Bridge St., offers a relaxed, beach house-like ambience. (☎843 450. Doubles £55, all ensuite. MC/V.) Comfortable rooms near South Beach await in the **Blue Dolphin Hotel ❷,** St. Mary's St. (☎842 590. Rooms £19-21 per person, ensuite £25-29. MC/V.) The bright ensuite rooms at **Lyndale ❸,** Warren St., may have you spending more time in bed than on the beach. (☎842 836. Singles £23-30. Cash only.) Campers can head to **Meadow Farm ❶,** at the top of The Croft, overlooking the town. (☎844 829. Open Easter-Sept. £6. Free showers. Cash only.)

SOUTH WALES

❏ FOOD. Most of Tenby's restaurants are aimed at vacationers and charge accordingly. Lunch specials can soften the blow at nicer eateries, and packing a picnic is an appealing and inexpensive option. **Tenby Market Hall,** between High St. and Upper Frog St., sells deli goods and baked treats. (Open July-Sept. daily 8:30am-5:30pm; Oct.-June M-Sa 8:30am-5:30pm.) A Somerfield **supermarket** is located on Upper Park Rd. (Open M-Th and Sa 8am-8pm, F 8am-9pm, Su 10am-4pm.) The sandwich crafters at **The Country Kitchen ❶,** Upper Frog St., have turned the filled baguette into a science, with delicious fillings and great prices. (☎843 539. Baguettes from ₤1.90, sandwiches from ₤1.40. Open daily in summer 9:30am-5pm; in winter M-Sa 9:30am-5pm. Cash only.) **Pam Pam ❸,** 2 Tudor Sq., tucked away from the bustle of Tudor Sq., offers great food and a hefty vegetarian selection for steep dinner prices (entrees ₤7-19). Their "light meals menu," however, which runs until 5pm, will get you excellent fare for ₤4-8. (☎842 946. Open daily 11am-10pm. MC/V.) In an alley connecting Bridge St. and St. Julian's St., a jungle of flowers marks **Plantagenet House ❹,** Quay Hill. Inside, diners feast by candlelight on organic collops of Welsh pork with cheddar and chives (₤8) or local sea bass (₤21) in the hearth of the oldest and tallest (39 ft.) medieval Flemish chimney in Wales. This fine establishment specializes in seafoods as rich as its architectural history. (☎842 350. Starters from ₤6, entrees from ₤17. Open Easter to Oct. daily noon-3pm and 6pm-late; Nov. to Easter F-Sa 6pm-late and Su noon-3pm. MC/V.) **The Ceramic Cafe ❷,** St. George's St., tempts with tasty lunch foods (from ₤3) as you decorate pottery pieces. (☎845 968. Open M-Sa 10am-5pm. MC/V.)

◧◪ SIGHTS AND BEACHES. A sun-bleached **Prince Albert the Good** stands atop Castle Hill, overlooking the ruins of the castle and colorful Tenby. On clear days the views reach across Carmarthen Bay, Rhossili Beach's Worm's Head, and the Devon coast. In a renovated section of the castle itself, the **Tenby Museum and Art Gallery** presents Tenby's heritage, including a wax recreation of "Leekie Porridge," a Tenby pirate. (☎842 809. Open Easter to Nov. daily 10am-5pm; Dec. to Easter M-F 10am-5pm. ₤2.50, concessions ₤2, children ₤1.25.) The three floors of the **Tudor Merchant's House,** on Quay Hill off Bridge St., detail life in a 16th-century Welsh household. The furniture and herb garden reveal much about upper-class living, but so does the garderobe, a three-story latrine whose contents were excavated in 1984 to find out what really fueled Tudor Tenby's merchant class. (☎842 279. Open daily Apr.-Sept. 10am-5pm; Oct. 10am-3pm. ₤2, children ₤1, families ₤5.) At night, Tenby's ghouls share the streets with resort revelers; the 1½hr. **Walks of Tenby** and **Ghost Walk of Tenby** depart from the Lifeboat Tavern in Tudor Sq. at 8pm. (☎845 841. Mid-June to mid-Sept. daily; mid-Sept. to mid-May M-Sa. Advance booking required. ₤3.75, concessions ₤3.50, children ₤2.75, families ₤13.)

Promenades and clifftop benches afford marvelous views, but most visitors zip straight to the sand. On sunny days, **North Beach,** below the Croft, and **South Beach,** beyond the Esplanade, swarm with pensioners and naked toddlers. At the eastern tip of Tenby, **Castle Beach** reaches into caves that lure the curious explorer, but only more remote beaches consistently offer escape from oceanside throngs. A variety of inventive **boat excursions** leave from the harbor; check the kiosks at Castle Beach (☎07973 280 651) for the "Seal Safari"—a one-hour jet boat ride to St. Margaret's Island and Cathedral Caves (₤10, children ₤6.50)—or the Sunset Cruise, a 2hr. excursion held only in July and Aug. (₤9.50, children ₤5.50).

▶ DAYTRIPS FROM TENBY

CALDEY ISLAND. Three miles south of Tenby, this largely unspoiled island hosts a diverse community of seabirds, seals, and 20 Cistercian monks, who produce perfume from indigenous lavender and gorse in their gorgeous Italianate monastery. The **chocolate factory** inspired by the monks' Belgian roots turns out over 12 tons of sweets a year (bars from £1). Though the monastery is closed to visitors, the island provides other pleasant explorations through woods and uncrowded coastline. *(Caldey Boats sails from Tenby Harbor. ☎ 844 453. Cruises 20min. Easter to Oct. 3 per hr. M-Sa 10am-3pm; last round-trip 5pm. Round-trip £9, children £4, seniors £8.)*

DYLAN THOMAS BOATHOUSE. Dylan Thomas spent his last four years in the boat house in **Laugharne** (LAN), about 15 mi. northeast of Tenby, happily claiming that he "got off the bus, and forgot to get on again." Today, the boathouse contains original furniture (including toys dug up from the garden) and a recreated version of Thomas' writing shed—his "house on stilts high among beaks." Though quite a trek from Tenby by public transport, it's a rewarding pilgrimage for Thomas aficionados or anyone who likes herons. *(Take First Cymru bus #351 to Pendine (50min., every 2hr.) and then transfer to #222, which goes from Pendine to Laugharne (12min., M-Sa 10 per day). ☎ 01994 427 420; www.dylanthomasboathouse.com. Open daily May-Oct. 10am-5pm; Nov.-Apr. 10:30am-3pm. £3, concessions £2.25, children £1.50.)*

MANORBIER CASTLE. Gerald of Wales, a noted 12th-century transcriber of rural life, was a champion of this castle—his birthplace. He referred to it as "the pleasantest spot in Wales," and it's still a contender today. Aside from stunning views (up a dank staircase), the castle offers a dovecote for harvesting pigeons (to eat) and wax figurines that stand guard throughout the castle. *(First Cymru bus #349 shuttles between Tenby, Manorbier, Pembroke, and Haverfordwest (M-Sa every hr., Su 3 per day in summer). ☎ 01834 871 394. Open daily Easter to Sept. 9:30am-5:30pm. £3.50, children £1.50, seniors £2.50.)* Manorbier has a **YHA hostel** (p. 468) and numerous **B&Bs**.

CAREW CASTLE. Strange and handsome Carew Castle, 5 mi. northwest of Tenby, is an odd mixture of Norman fortress and Elizabethan manor, where mighty stone towers flank the delicate sills of the somewhat out-of-place windows. Check *Coast to Coast*, free at most TICs, for events at the castle. *(Take Silcox bus #361 from Tenby to the castle (45min., M-Sa 3-4 per day). ☎ 01646 651 782. Open daily Mar.-Oct. 10am-4:30pm. Tours at 2:30pm. Castle and mill £3, concessions £2, families £8.)*

PEMBROKE (PENFRO) ☎ 01646

In the heart of a county known as "Little England beyond Wales," Pembroke no longer feels like the fierce military stronghold its Norman occupants designed. Battlements that once formed a bastion of anti-Cromwell resistance now offer shade to historical reenactments and hungry picnickers, and the waters which once served to protect the castle on three sides now harbor swans.

▢ TRANSPORTATION. Pembroke's unstaffed **train station** is on Lower Lamphey Rd. at the opposite end of Main St. from the castle. **Trains** (☎ 08457 484 950) run from Pembroke and Pembroke Dock to Tenby (20min., 7 per day, £3.10), Swansea (2hr.; M-F 6 per day, Sa 7 per day, Su 3 per day; £8.50), and points farther east. In Pembroke, **buses** going east stop outside the Somerfield supermarket; those going north stop at the castle. National Express (☎ 08705 808 080) goes to Cardiff via

Swansea (3¾hr., 3 per day, £12.80) and London (6hr., 2 per day, £24). First Cymru (☎01792 580 580) stops in Pembroke and at Pembroke Dock between Tenby (#349; 40-50min.; M-Sa 11 per day, Su 4 per day; £2.10) and Haverfordwest (35-40min.; M-Sa 13 per day, Su 4 per day).

⚷ 🛈 ORIENTATION AND PRACTICAL INFORMATION. Pembroke Castle lies up the hill on the western end of **Main Street;** the street's other end (at the train station) fans into five roads from a roundabout. Across the river and to the north is Pembroke Docks. Downhill from Pembroke's town center, the **Tourist Information Centre,** Commons Rd., occupies a former slaughterhouse and has displays on town history and the Pembrokeshire Coastal Path. The staff books accommodations for a £2 charge plus a 10% deposit, sells ferry tickets, and gives out free town maps. (☎622 388. Open Easter to June daily 10am-5pm; July-Oct. daily 10am-5:30pm.) Other services include: Barclays **bank,** 35 Main St., in Pembroke (open M-F 9am-4:30pm); Pembroke Dock **police,** 4 Water St. (☎682 121); the Pembroke Dock **hospital,** Fort Rd. (☎682 114); Mendus **pharmacy,** 31 Main St. (☎682 370; open M-F 9am-6pm, Sa 9am-1pm); free **Internet access** at the Pembroke library, 38 Main St., (☎682 973; open Tu and F 10am-1pm and 2pm-5pm, W and Sa 10am-1pm, Th 10am-1pm and 2-7pm) and at Dragon Alley, 63 Main St. (☎621 456; £1 per 15min., £3 per hr.; open M-Tu 10am-7pm, W-Th 10am-9pm, F-Sa 10am-6pm); and the **post office,** 49 Main St. (☎682 737; open M-F 9am-5:30pm, Sa 9am-1pm). **Post Code:** SA71 4JT.

🛏 🍴 ACCOMMODATIONS AND FOOD. The nearest **YHA hostel** is in Manorbier on the bus line between Tenby and Pembroke (p. 468). The few **B&Bs** in Pembroke are scattered, though some reasonable options are on Main St. Singles are scarce; book ahead. Mrs. Willis fosters an elegant atmosphere at her bright blue ◨**Beech House ❷,** 78 Main St. In these stately, pristine rooms with crystal chandeliers, you'll be amazed you aren't spending more. The billiards room is comfortable and the breakfast, delicious. (☎683 740. £17.50 per person. Cash only.) A few doors down, **Woodbine ❸,** 84 Main St., pampers with huge ensuite rooms, big wardrobes, TVs, and flowers on the windowsills. (☎686 338. £22.50 per person. Cash only.)

Stock up at Somerfield **supermarket,** 6-10 Main St. (Open M-Sa 8am-8pm, Su 10am-4pm). Wisebuys **grocery,** 19 Main St., offers an olive bar and assortment of local jams. (☎687 046. Open M-Sa 7am-5:30pm.) **Henry's Gift Shop and Cafe ❶,** 5 Main St., a block from the castle, serves tasty pies, scones, and cakes (from £1) in a lovely tea room. (☎622 293. Shop open M-Sa 10am-5pm. Food served M-Sa 10am-4pm. AmEx/MC/V.) Across the Northgate St. bridge is the **Watermans Arms ❷,** 2 The Green, where patrons choose from an extensive curry menu. The deck provides great views of the castle and the swans that float on Mill Pond. (☎682 718. Open daily Easter to Oct. noon-11pm; winter hours vary. Food served noon-10pm.)

◨ SIGHTS. Austere ◨**Pembroke Castle** shadows Pembroke's Main St. and overshadows much of the town's history. Today, the castle's stone chambers invite hours of exploration. Henry VII, founder of the Tudor dynasty, was born in one of the seven massive towers. The Great Keep rises 75 ft. and visitors ascend more than 100 twisted, slippery steps to reach its domed top. The underground gloom of Wogan's Cavern provided shelter for Stone-Age cave-dwellers, who left primitive tools. (☎684 585; www.pembrokecastle.co.uk. Open daily Apr.-Sept. 9:30am-6pm; Mar. and Oct. 10am-5pm; Nov.-Feb. 10am-4pm. Tours May-Aug. M-F and Su 4 per day. £3.50, concessions £2.50, families £10. Tours £1.) The **Pembroke Glassblowing Studio,** The Commons, is hot—1250°C, to be precise, but only inside the ovens. Watch craftspeople blow souvenirs. (☎682 482. Open Easter to Oct. M-F 10am-

4pm. Glassblowing M-F 11am-3pm.) Located in a beautifully converted Methodist Church, **The Pembroke Antiques Centre,** Wesley Chapel, on Main St., will engross browsers and determined purchasers alike. (☎687 017. Open M-Sa 10am-5pm.)

ST. DAVID'S (TYDDEWI)   ☎01437

St. David's is the smallest city in Britain, with the largest cathedral. This enchanting place is little more than a few streets curled around a central village green, but it has been a favored destination among pilgrims for almost a millennium; in the Middle Ages, two pilgrimages to St. David's were considered equivalent to one trip to Rome. Now the village is filled with outdoors outfitters and adventure options.

🖪🔽 TRANSPORTATION AND PRACTICAL INFORMATION. Pick up the *Pembrokeshire Bus Timetables,* free at any Pembrokeshire TIC. The Richards Brothers (☎01239 613 756) Haverfordwest-Fishguard **bus** hugs the coast, heading from both towns to St. David's (#411; 50min. from both; M-Sa 6-7 per day from Fishguard, 12 per day from Haverford, Su 2 per day; £2.15). Other buses terminate at St. David's during the week. For a cab, call Tony's **taxis** (☎720 931).

The **National Park Information Center,** The Grove, doubles as the TIC and lies at the east end of High St. The stone in the middle of the courtyard is positioned to be illuminated by sunlight on St. David's Day each year. (☎720 392; www.stdavids.co.uk. Open Easter to Oct. daily 9:30am-5:30pm; Nov. to Easter M-Sa 10am-4pm.) Other services include: Barclays **bank,** at High St. and New St. (open M-F 9:30am-4pm); **police,** High St. (☎0845 330 2000); the nearest **hospital** (☎764 545), in Haverfordwest; St. David's **pharmacy,** 13-14 Cross Sq. (☎720 243; open M-F 9am-6:30pm, Sa 9am-4:30pm); free **Internet access** at the library, in City Hall, on High St. (open Tu and F 10am-1pm and 2pm-5:30pm); and the **post office,** 13 New St. (☎720 283; open M-F 9am-5:30pm, Sa 9am-1pm). **Post Code:** SA62 6SW.

🖪🖸 ACCOMMODATIONS AND FOOD. The **YHA St. David's** (p. 468) lies 2 mi. northwest of town at the foot of a rocky outcrop near St. David's Head. Beautiful **Alandale ❸,** 43 Nun St., is run by hosts whose warmth is even more memorable than their lovely rooms with cathedral views. (☎720 404. £30 per person.) In the center of town, **The Coach House ❷,** 15 High St., has a cozy lounge and a wide range of simple, clean lodgings, all with TV and most ensuite. The breakfast menu caters to special dietary needs and vegetarians using local, organic items. (☎720 632. £25 per person, children £12.50. £10 deposit. MC/V.)

Pebbles Yard Gallery and Expresso Bar ❶, Cross Sq., has a cafe that serves pitas, salads, and coffee in a trendy loft. (☎720 122. Open daily 10am-5:30pm. Cash only.) Across the street is **Chapel Chocolates ❶,** The Pebbles, whose ice cream is so popular that the cathedral has prohibited its consumption inside. Try something wild like Christmas Pudding (cones £1.20), or stick to an impressive array of truffles. (☎720 023; www.chapelchocolates.com. Open daily 10am-5:30pm. AmEx/MC/V.) **Cartref ❷,** 23 Cross Sq., serves up sandwiches, baguettes, light meals from £4, and classic pub fare in the evening. (☎720 422. Open daily Mar.-May 11am-2:30pm and 6:30-8:30pm; June-Aug. 11am-10pm. MC/V.)

🖸 SIGHTS. St. David's Cathedral, perhaps the finest in Wales, stands below the village. It dates from the 6th century, when David and his followers lived ascetic lives in picturesque isolation. Pilgrims flocked to the site; now, modern-day "pilgrims" file past the **reliquary** reputed to hold the bones of St. David, patron saint of Wales, and his comrade St. Justinian. The latter was killed on nearby Ramsey Island but, in saintly conscientiousness, carried his own head back to the mainland. In the St. Thomas à Becket chapel, a stained-glass window portrays three surly knights jabbing swords at the martyr. The ceilings are dazzlingly intricate, made of inlaid wood in an elaborate painted design. (☎720 060; www.stdavidsca-thedral.org.uk. Open M-Sa 8:30am-6pm, Su 12:45-5:45pm, and for evening services. Suggested donation £2.50, children £1.) Those with a love for pealing bells are wel-come to sit in on a ringer's practice session in the tower. (Su 5:30-6pm, W and F 7:45-9pm. Suggested donation £1.) The **Bishop's Palace,** across a stream from the cathedral, was built by Bishop Henry Gower in the 14th century, when it was acceptable for a bishop to have the largest palace in Wales. Now in ruins, the dis-tinctive arched parapets connote the lavishness of the medieval bishopric. (☎720 517. Open June-Sept. daily 9:30am-6pm; Oct. and Apr.-May daily 9:30am-5pm; Nov.-Mar. M-Sa 9:30am-4pm, Su 11am-4pm. £2.50, concessions £2, families £7.) A mile south of town, the walls of **St. Non's Chapel** mark St. David's birthplace. Water from the nearby well supposedly cures all ills; take Goat St. downhill and follow the signs. Tours run to **Ramsey Island,** off the coast (p. 469).

FISHGUARD ☎01348

Buses radiate from Fishguard to smaller villages on the Pembrokeshire Coast, making the town a convenient hub. The immediate area offers many scenic walks and short hikes. Deeply enamored with their maritime history, Fishguard's friendly pubs play host to local legends of smugglers' caves and pirate attacks.

▐ **TRANSPORTATION. Trains** (☎08457 484 950) pull into Fishguard Harbour, Goodwick, from London via Bristol, Newport, Cardiff, Swansea, and Whitland (4½hr., 2 per day, £78.50). **Buses** stop at Fishguard Sq., the town center. Ask at the TIC for a free bus and train timetable. From the north, take Richards Brothers (☎01239 613 756) buses from Aberystwyth to Cardigan (#550 or 551; 2hr., M-Sa 10 per day) and then on to Fishguard (#412; 45min., M-Sa 12 per day, £3-4). Take First Cymru (☎01792 580 580) buses from Tenby or Pembroke to Haverfordwest (#349; 1hr.; M-Sa every hr., Su 4 per day; £2.40) and from Haverfordwest to Fishguard (#412; 45min., 1-2 per hr.). Town bus #410 shuttles between Fishguard Harbour and Fishguard Sq. (5min., 2 per hr., 45p). Merv's **taxis** (☎875 129) are on call 24hr.

▌ **PRACTICAL INFORMATION.** The **Tourist Information Centre,** Town Hall, Main St., books buses and ferries, and rooms for a £2 charge plus a 10% deposit. (☎873 484. Open Easter to Oct. daily 10am-5pm.; Nov. to Easter M-Sa 10am-4pm.) Other services include: Barclays **bank,** across from the TIC (open M-F 9am-4:30pm); **police,** Brodog Terr. (☎0845 330 2000); a **launderette,** Brodog Terr. (☎872 140; wash £1.95, dry 60p; open M-Sa 8:30am-5:30pm; last wash 4:30pm); free **Internet access** at the library on High St., one block from Market Sq. (☎872 694; open M-Tu and F 9:30am-1pm and 2pm-5pm, W and Sa 9:30am-1pm, Th 9:30am-1pm and 2pm-6:30pm), or £2 per 30min. at Ocean Lab (p. 476); Boots **pharmacy,** Market Sq. (☎872 856; open M-F 9am-5:30pm, Sa 9am-5pm); and the **post office,** 57 West St. (☎873 863; open M-F 9am-5:30pm, Sa 9am-12:30pm). **Post Code:** SA65 9NG.

▐▐ **ACCOMMODATIONS AND FOOD. B&Bs** (from £20) are on High St. in Upper Fishguard and Vergam Terr. **Hamilton Guest House and Backpackers Lodge ❷,** 21-23 Hamilton St., is well-kept, with a book-lined TV lounge, toast-and-tea break-fasts, and a sauna. (☎874 797; www.fishguard-backpackers.com. Kitchen, laundry, and Internet access. Dorms £13; doubles £30; triples £42; quads £52. Cash only.) The rooms at **Avon House ❷,** 76 High St., are almost as cheery as the hosts. (☎874 476; www.avon-house.co.uk. Singles from £20. Cash only.) **Deep Well B&B ❷,** 74 High St., provides spacious rooms. (☎872 559. £20 per person. Cash only.)

SOUTH WALES

Y Pantri ❶, 31 West St., rolls sandwiches, fills baguettes (£1.50), and sells various pasties for 95p. (☎872 637. Open M-Sa 9am-5:30pm. Cash only.) **The Taj Mahal ❷**, 22 High St., serves a huge variety of quality curries. (☎874 593. Entrees from £5. Restaurant open daily 6-11:30pm. Takeaway open 6pm-midnight. MC/V.) **The Old Coach House ❷**, High St., has a vast menu of traditional British pub grub (£4-10) and draws a youthful crowd. (☎875 429. Live music Sa night. Open M-F 11am-11pm, Sa 11am-1am, Su noon-10:30pm. Food served noon-2:30pm and 6-9pm. AmEx/MC/V.)

◼◼ SIGHTS AND NIGHTLIFE. The **Marine Walk,** a paved path that follows the coastline through woods and along grassy cliffs, has exquisite overlooks of town and sea and plaques with historical trivia. Ramblers can also see **Goodwick Harbor,** where the ill-fated flagship *Lusitania* began its journey to America. **Preseli Venture** offers half- and full-day adventures that include sea kayaking, surfing, and awesome coasteering. (☎837 709. 18+. £39 per half-day. All-inclusive weekend £169.) During the day, sun gluttons dot pebbly **Goodwick Beach.** Inquire at the TIC about hikes into the **Preseli Hills,** ancient grounds speckled with stone circles and a mysterious **standing stone.** If indoor pursuits are more your style, check out the shops near **Upper Fishguard Square.**

Weekend nightlife erupts into a pub scene of festival proportions. **The Old Coach House** (see above) is the place to be, but all the pubs along **High Street** see some action until 11pm. **The Royal Oak,** West St. at Market Sq., is a pub proud of its history; the infamous "last invasion" surrender treaty was signed here in 1797. The pub keeps the original table and other artifacts on display and serves up Welsh specialties in huge portions from £7. (☎872 514. Live music F-Sa. Open M-Sa 11am-11pm and Su noon-10:30pm.)

NORTH WALES

The mountains of the north have long harbored the most fervent Welsh nationalism. In the 14th century, Welsh insurgents plotted against the English from deep within Snowdonia. English King Edward I designed a ring of spectacular fortresses to keep the rebels in the mountains. Welsh pride never wavered and remains strong despite centuries of union with England. Today, this pride shows itself at weekend football matches or on signs and menus written only in Welsh. To escape the crowds swarming the coastal castles, head to the mountain footpaths, lakes, and hamlets of Snowdonia National Park, which spans most of northwest Wales. To the west, the Llŷn Peninsula beckons with sandy beaches; to the northwest, the Isle of Anglesey is rich in prehistoric remains; and to the east, quiet villages sleep in the Vale of Conwy.

HIGHLIGHTS OF NORTH WALES

SCALE one of many craggy peaks at **Snowdonia National Park** (p. 492), land of high moors, dark pine forests, and deep glacial lakes.

ENJOY the refreshing streams and unspoiled surroundings of villages like **Betws-y-Coed** (p. 488) in the **Vale of Conwy.**

ADMIRE the fine castles at **Beaumaris** (p. 508), **Caernarfon** (p. 504), **Conwy** (p. 483), and **Harlech** (p. 497).

ABERYSTWYTH   ☎01970

Host to the largest university in Wales, Aberystwyth (ah-ber-RIST-with) thrives on youthful vigor. Where 19th-century vacationers once enjoyed the frivolities of resort living, bars now buzz with spirited academics during the school year. The summer months see the Georgian boardwalk awash with activity as locals thread through shopping districts and take in bayside breezes.

TRANSPORTATION

A transport hub for all of Wales, Aberystwyth sits at the end of a rail line running from Birmingham, England.

Trains: Station on Alexandra Rd. Office open M-F 6:20am-5:25pm, Sa 6:20am-3:20pm. Trains (☎08457 484 950) from **Machynlleth** (30min.; M-Sa 9 per day, Su 6 per day; £3.70) and **Shrewsbury** (1¾hr.; M-Sa 7 per day, Su 4-5 per day; £12.40). Machynlleth is the southern terminus of the Cambrian Coaster line, which runs from **Pwllheli**. Its **Day Ranger** ticket covers travel on the line (£7, children £3.50, families £13.20). The Vale of Rheidol Railway (☎625 819) arrives from a few mountain sites (p. 481).

Buses: Station on Alexandra Rd., beside the train station. National Express (☎08705 808 080) from **London** (8hr., daily at noon, £25.50) via **Birmingham** (7hr., daily 1pm, £25). TrawsCambria bus #701 from **Cardiff** via **Swansea** (4hr., 2 per day). Arriva Cymru (☎08706 082 608) to **Bangor** via **Porthmadog** (X32; 3½hr., M-Sa 5 per day), and **Machynlleth** (#32; 45min., M-Sa 8 per day, £2.80). Richard Brothers (☎01239 613 756) to **Cardigan** via **Synod Inn** (#550/551; 1hr., M-Sa 6 per day). Arriva Cymru/ Summerdale Coaches (☎01348 840 270) runs the same route twice on Su. **Day Rover**

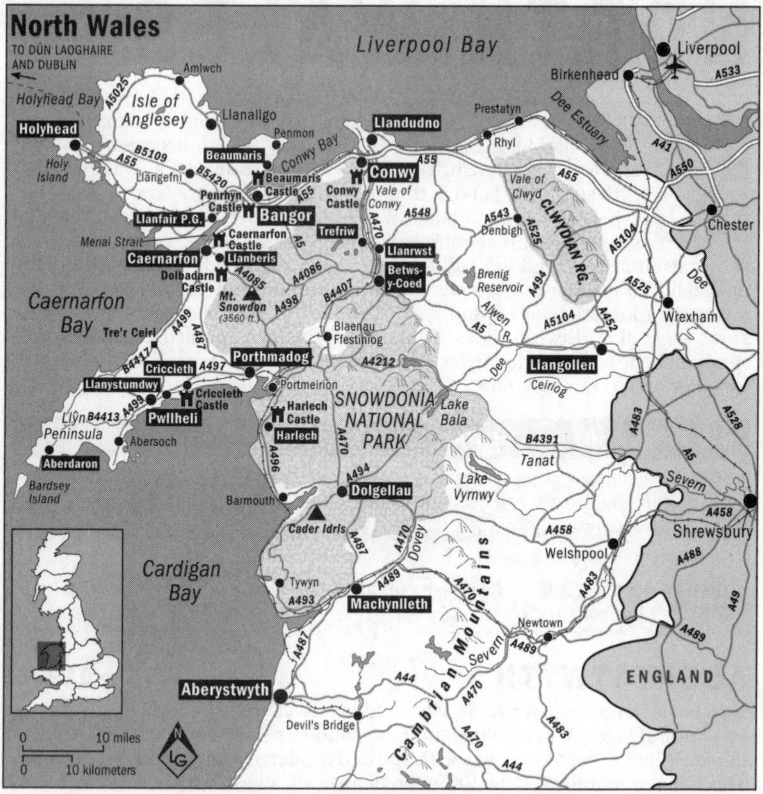

tickets (£5, children £3.70 or £2.50 with paying adult) are valid on most buses in the Ceredigion, Carmarthenshire, and Pembrokeshire areas. The **North and Mid-Wales Rover** is valid on buses and trains on the North Wales main line, the Conway Valley, and the Cambrian Line (1-day £20, 3-day £30, 7-day £44).

Taxis: Express (☎612 319).

PRACTICAL INFORMATION

Tourist Information Centre: Lisburn House, Terrace Rd. (☎612 125). Books rooms for £2 plus a 10% deposit. Open daily July-Aug. 10am-6pm; Sept.-June M-Sa 10am-5pm.

Launderette: Wash 'n' Spin 'n' Dry, 16 Bridge St. (☎820 891). Wash £2.20, dry 20p per cycle, soap 10p. Bring change. Open daily 7am-9pm. Last wash 8:30pm.

Banks: Barclays, 26 Terrace Rd. (☎653 353). Open M-F 9am-5pm.

Police: Blvd. St. Brieuc (☎0845 330 2000), at the end of Park Ave.

Hospital: Bronglais General Hospital, Caradog Rd., off Penglais Rd. (☎623 131).

Pharmacy: Boots, Terrace Rd. Open M-F 9am-6pm, Sa 9am-5:30pm, Su 10am-4pm.

Internet Access: Library, Corporation St. (☎633 703), at the corner of Baker St. Free. Book ahead. Open M-F 9:30am-8pm, Sa 9:30am-5pm. **Biognosis,** 21 Pier St. (☎636

953). £3.50 per hr., £1.50 minimum. Open M-F 9:30am-5:30pm, Sa 10am-4pm.
Daton Computers, Bridge St. (☎610 050) £1 per 30min. Open M-F 9am-5:30pm.

Post Office: 8 Great Darkgate St. (☎632 630). Bureau de change. Open M-F 9am-5:30pm, Sa 9am-12:30pm. **Post Code:** SY23 1DE.

■ ACCOMMODATIONS

Aberystwyth's streets overflow with B&Bs (from £20) and more upscale seaside hotels, especially near the beachfront and on **Bridge Street.**

Maes-y-Môr, 25 Bath St. (☎639 270). Cheap accommodations in a prime location just a block away from the ocean. Rooms have access to a common kitchen. Linens and towels provided. Launderette on ground floor. Singles £17. Cash only. ❷

The Cambria, Marine Terr. (☎626 350; www.thecambria.co.uk), across from the pier. Enjoy clean and cheap rooms, some with ocean views, in a convenient location. Singles £15; twins £25. Cash only. ❷

Sunnymead, 34 Bridge St. (☎617 273). Warm yellow-trimmed house with warm hospitality. £22 per person. MC/V. ❷

YHA Borth (☎871 498), 8 mi. north of Aberystwyth, in an Edwardian house overlooking the ocean. Take the train to Borth, or ride Crosville bus #511 or 512 and ask to stop at the hostel. From the train station, turn right onto the main road and walk 5 min. Near beautiful beaches and often full. Kitchen. Open daily Mar.-Oct. with 48hr. notice; Nov.-Feb. call further in advance. Dorms £13, under 18 £10. MC/V. ❷

Midfield Caravan Park (☎612 542), 1½ mi. from town on the A4120, 200 yd. uphill from the A487 junction. From Alexandra Rd., take any bus to Southgate. Turn left for Devil's Bridge and walk 200 yd. uphill. Lovely site, with a view of town and hills. £6 per person. Electricity £2.50. Cash only. ❶

◖ FOOD

Pier Street takeaways are cheap and open Sunday, as are beachside shacks and some sit-down restaurants. Spar **market,** 32 Terrace Rd., is open 24hr.

The Treehouse Cafe, 14 Baker St. (☎615 791). Feel wholesome eating your veggie burger (£5.75), your steakburger (£6.20), or your baked peppers stuffed with lamb (£7.50)—it's all organic. So are the crisp veggies and local fruits sold on the ground floor. Cafe open noon-3:30pm. Food store open M-Sa 9am-5pm. MC/V. ❷

Sunclouds, 25 North Parade (☎617 750). Baguettes and baps usually rule the day, but you'll be glad for the hot, homemade soup with crusty bread (£3) when it's chilly. Open M-Sa 10am-4:30pm. Cash only. ❶

Cambria Tea Rooms and Restaurant, Marine Terr. (☎626 350), across from the pier, serves jacket potatoes (£3.60), panini (from £4.25), and light meals, like tagliatelle with smoked salmon (£5.75). Pleasant dining room with ocean views. Cash only. ❶

Spartacus, Terrace Rd. (☎627 799). Offers basic panini and baguettes (from £2) and a salad bar in a small seating area. Open M-Sa 8am-6pm, Su 9am-5:30pm. Cash only. ❶

◎ SIGHTS

NATIONAL LIBRARY OF WALES. Occupying a grand classical building that overlooks the sea, town, and surrounding cliffs, this library houses almost every Welsh book or manuscript ever printed. The **Gregynog Gallery** rotates dis-

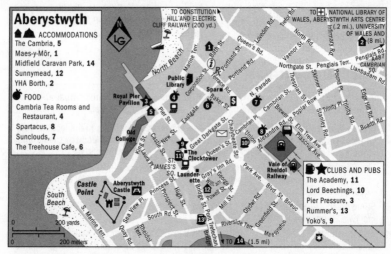

Aberystwyth

▲▲ ACCOMMODATIONS

The Cambria, **5**
Maes-y-Môr, **1**
Midfield Caravan Park, **14**
Sunnymead, **12**
YHA Borth, **2**

🍎 FOOD

Cambria Tea Rooms and
    Restaurant, **4**
Spartacus, **8**
Sunclouds, **7**
The Treehouse Cafe, **6**

⭐ CLUBS AND PUBS

The Academy, **11**
Lord Beechings, **10**
Pier Pressure, **3**
Rummer's, **13**
Yoko's, **9**

plays of various firsts in Welsh printing with exhibits of Welsh art. *(Off Penglais Rd., past the hospital. ☎632 800; www.llgc.org.uk. Reading room open M-F 9:30am-6pm, Sa 9:30am-5pm. Exhibitions open M-Sa 10am-5pm. Free.)*

ELECTRIC CLIFF RAILWAY. At the northern end of the promenade, an electric railcar has been creaking up the steep 430 ft. slope of Constitution Hill since 1896. The top brings the world's largest camera obscura—a contraption that affords a stunning view of the coastline. *(☎617 642. Runs daily July-Aug. 10am-6:30pm; mid-Mar. to June and Sept.-Oct. 10am-5:30pm. 6 per hr. Round-trip £2.50, concessions £2, children £1. Camera obscura free with rail ride.)*

ABERYSTWYTH CASTLE. Castle Point, south of the Old College and the site of one of Edward I's many now-decrepit castles, offers one of the best views in Aberystwyth. Henry, Prince of Wales, took this castle with cannons, but today picnickers peacefully overtake what's left of the fortress. The grounds are graced with flowers and, oddly, a miniature golf course. *(Always open. Free.)*

PIER. The once-famous Victorian Pier is now overrun with an arcade, pizza parlor, pub, and nightclub. At the south end of the promenade, the university's **Old College** is a neo-Gothic structure restored in 1885 as Wales's first university. Prince Charles was drilled in Welsh here before being crowned Prince of Wales. *(Arcade open daily Mar.-Sept. 10am-11pm; Oct.-Feb. 10am-10pm.)*

OTHER SIGHTS. Above the TIC, the well-maintained **Ceredigion Museum** fills a grand old theater, the Coliseum, and houses two floors on Welsh history. *(☎633 088. Open M-Sa 10am-5pm. Free.)* Up Penglais Rd., on the University of Wales campus, the **Aberystwyth Arts Centre** sponsors drama and films in Welsh and English. *(☎623 232. www.aber.ac.uk/artscentre. Box office open M-Sa 10am-8pm and Su 2-5:30pm. Films every weeknight. Tickets from £4.50. Concessions available.)*

🎤🍺 PUBS AND CLUBS

Aberystwyth has more than 50 pubs, and student crowds keep them buzzing.

🍺 **The Academy,** St. James Sq. *(☎636 852).* This cavernous converted chapel piles bottles of absinthe (£3 per shot) on the organ in the game room; barflies grasping Stellas flank the pulpit, watching the 16 ft. telescreen. M-Th and Su drink specials. Open M-F noon-11pm, Sa 11am-11pm, Su noon-10:30pm. Food served noon-3pm and 6-8:30pm.

Rummer's, Pont Trefechan Bridge (☎625 177). A vine-covered riverside beer garden packed with students. DJ W. Live music of all types Th-Sa. Open M-Tu 7pm-midnight, W-Sa 7pm-1am, Su 7-10:30pm.

Lord Beechings, Alexandra Rd. (☎625 069). Comfortable atmosphere and an enormous array of comfort foods to match (most under £5). Open M-Sa 11am-11pm, Su noon-10:30pm. Food served W-F and Su noon-3pm, Sa noon-7pm.

Pier Pressure, The Royal Pier, Marine Terr. (☎636 100). Mirrors quake and smashed clubbers shake. Th rocks to 60s-80s; F-Sa "Cheese Factory" pulls a young crowd. Cover Th-F £4, Sa £6. Open M-W 10pm-1am, Th-Sa 10pm-2am, Su 10pm-midnight.

Yoko's, 12 Pier St. (623 963). Young clubbers crowd the comfy couches and the steamy dance floor at this mainstream dance venue. Cover after 10:30pm F £4, Sa £5. Open M-W and Su 9:30pm-1am, Th-Sa 9:30pm-2am.

◤ DAYTRIP FROM ABERYSTWYTH

DEVIL'S BRIDGE
The scenic narrow-rail Vale of Rheidol train runs from Aberystwyth. Mid-July to Aug. M-Th 4 per day, F-Su 2 per day; Easter to mid-July and Sept.-Oct. 2 per day. £12, children £3. The area is not accessible by public transport.

Originally built to serve lead mines, the **Vale of Rheidol Railway** (☎625 819) winds through farmland and gorgeous hills. An hour's ride leads to Devil's Bridge (built by the evil one himself), which is actually three bridges of varying ages built atop one another. The lowest bridge was probably built in the 12th century by monks from the nearby **Strata Florida Abbey.** (☎01974 831 261. Abbey open Apr.-Sept. W-Su 10am-5pm. Last admission 30min. before close. Grounds open daily Apr.-Sept. 10am-5pm; Oct.-Mar. 10am-4pm. £2.25, concessions £1.75, families £6.25; Oct.-Apr. grounds free, but exhibits closed.) Catch great views of the bridge with a 10min. walk down **Jacob's Ladder** and see the **Devil's Punchbowl** in the stream. (☎890 233. Jacob's Ladder £2.50, concessions £2, children £1.25. Punchbowl £1.) From there an easy 30min. walk through woods and mossy hills affords views of the 300 ft. waterfall and more of the bridge.

MACHYNLLETH   ☎01654

Machynlleth (mach-HUN-hleth) is best known for its brief stint as the capital of Wales. Freedom-fighter Owain Glyndwr set up a parliament here back in the 15th century, summoning delegates from across the country and even signing an alliance with France against the British. Though the rebellion unraveled, the Celtic pride behind it lives on in Machynlleth's appealing city center (little more than two streets) in museums, eateries, and even street signs.

◤ **TRANSPORTATION.** The train station (☎702 887), Doll St., receives **trains** (☎08457 484 950) from: Aberystwyth (30min., 11 per day, £3.70); Birmingham (2¼hr.; M-F 10 per day, Sa 11 per day, Su 6 per day; £22.10); Shrewsbury (1¼hr.; M-F 10 per day, Sa 11 per day, Su 6 per day; £11.40). The Cambrian Coaster Day Ranger covers routes from Aberystwyth (£6.60, children £3.30, families £13.20, after 4:30pm £3.70). **Buses** stop by the clock tower. Arriva Cymru (☎08706 082 608) buses #32 and X32 pass through Machynlleth as they shuttle between Aberystwyth and Dolgellau on a north-south route (30min. from both; M-F 9 per day, Sa 8 per day, Su 2 per day). #28 and 33 provide east-west transport to and from smaller towns.

⬛⁉ ORIENTATION AND PRACTICAL INFORMATION. Pentrehedyn Street, Penrallt Street, and **Maengwyn Street** converge at the **clock tower,** which oversees most of Machynlleth's hustle and bustle. From the train station, turn left onto Doll St., veer right at the church onto Penrallt St., and continue until you see the tower. The **Tourist Information Centre,** in the Owain Glyndwr Centre, Maengwyn St., books rooms for a £2 charge plus a 10% deposit. (☎702 401. Open in summer M-Sa 9:30am-5pm, Su 9:30am-4:30pm; in winter M-Sa 9:30am-5pm, Su 9:30am-4:30pm.) Other services include: Barclays **bank,** on Penrallt St. beneath the clock tower (open M-F 9am-4:30pm); a **launderette,** New St. around the corner from the Spar (wash £2.50, dry 20p; open M-Sa 8:30am-8pm, Su 9am-8pm; last wash 7:15pm); **police,** Doll St. (☎0845 330 2000); the **hospital,** off Maengwyn St. (☎702 266); Rowland's **pharmacy,** 8 Pentrehedyn St., near the clock tower (☎702 237; open M-W and F 9am-5:30pm, Th 9am-12:30pm, Sa 9am-4:30pm); **Internet access** at the library, Maengwyn St. (☎702 322; free; open M and F 9:30am-1pm and 2-7pm, Tu-W 9:30am-1pm and 2-5pm, Sa 9:30am-1pm), or at Celtica (☎702 702; open daily 10am-6pm; £1 per hr.) on Aberystwyth Rd.; and the **post office,** 51-53 Maengwyn St., inside Spar (☎702 323; office open M-Th 8:30am-5:30pm, F 9am-5:30pm, Sa 9am-1pm). **Post Code:** SY20 8AF.

⬛⬛ ACCOMMODATIONS AND FOOD. Machynlleth lacks hostels, but nearby Corris has a bunkhouse and a hostel. Take the X32 or #32 bus (10min.; M-F 9 per day, Sa 8 per day, Su 2 per day). **Braich Goch Bunkhouse ❷,** across from the bus stop, offers cheap rooms in a convenient location. (☎761 229; www.braichgoch.co.uk. Dorms £12.50.) **Corris Youth Hostel ❷,** on Corris Rd., is an old schoolhouse a 5-10min. walk from the bus stop. Go into town and turn left up the hill after the creek. (☎761 686. Breakfast included. Laundry. Lockout 10am-5pm. Dorms £15. Cash only.) **B&Bs** are expensive and hard to find. **Gwelfryn ❸,** 6 Greenfields Rd., has a flowery front porch and basic rooms. (☎702 532; www.gwelfryn.co.uk. £21 per person. Cash only.) Campers can seek out riverside **Llwyngwern Farm ❶,** off the A487 next to the Centre for Alternative Technology. (☎702 492. Open Apr.-Sept. £8 for two people. Cash only.)

A Spar **supermarket** is at 51-53 Maengwyn St. (open M-Sa 7am-11pm, Su 7am-10:30pm). An impressive **market,** which dates from 1291, runs along Maengwyn St., Pentrehedyn St., and Penrallt St. (open W 9:30am-4pm). The **Quarry Cafe and Shop ❶,** 13 Maengwyn St., part of the Centre for Alternative Technology, serves delicious vegan soups, salads (under £3), and rotating daily entrees (from £5) with tasty fruit trifle for dessert. (☎702 339. Open July-Aug. M-Sa 9am-5pm, Th 9am-2pm, Su 10am-4pm; Sept.-June M-Sa 9am-5pm, Th 9am-2pm. Cash only.) Enjoy mouth-watering freshly-baked pastries, quiches, and sandwiches at **BJ's Bistro ❶,** Maengwyn St. The full Welsh breakfast (£4) comes with black pudding. (☎703 679. Open M 7:30am-3pm, Tu-Sa 7:30am-4pm and 6pm-9:30pm, Su noon-2pm. Cash only.) Machynlleth pubs don't offer diverse dining options, but tasty dishes are served beside a massive hearth at the **Skinners Arms ❷,** 14 Penrallt St., near the clock tower. Entrees in the lounge are £5-10; lighter meals are £3-7 at the bar. Come nightfall, the pub welcomes locals with tempting brews. (☎702 354. Open M-Tu noon-11pm, W-Sa 11am-11pm, Su noon-10:30pm. Food served daily noon-2pm and 6-8pm. Cash only.)

⬛ SIGHTS. On a former slate quarry 3 mi. north of town along the A487, the staff of the **Centre for Alternative Technology** has been developing, promoting, and living environmentally-sound lifestyles since 1974. Chug up the 200 ft. cliff via a funicular powered by water imbalances and learn about wave, wind, and solar power sources in fascinating outdoor displays. Don't miss the "Mole

Hole" (a kiddie favorite) or the "Compost Sampler" which encourages you to touch—and smell—various types of natural fertilizer. Take Arriva bus #34 (5-10min., M-Sa 11 per day, £2.40) to the entrance or #32 (5min., M-Sa 10 per day) to Pantperthog and walk 200 yd. north across the bridge. (☎705 950; www.cat.org.uk. Open daily Sept.-June 10am-5:30pm; July-Aug. 9:30am-6pm. Last admission 1hr. before close. Funicular open Easter to Oct. £8, concessions £7.20, children £5.20. Free audio tour.) Farther up the A487, the passages of another old slate mine lure tourists to **King Arthur's Labyrinth**—a surreal celebration of the Arthurian legend on a subterranean boat tour. From Machynlleth take bus #32 or 35 toward Dolgellau and ask to get off at the Corris Craft Centre. (☎761 584; www.kingarthurslabyrinth.com. Dress warmly. Open daily Apr.-Oct. 10am-5pm. £5.15, concessions £4.60, children £3.60.) From the clock tower, a 2min. downhill walk along Aberystwyth Rd. (A487) brings you to **Celtica,** which sports a gift shop and glitzy light and fog. (☎702 702; www.celticawales.com. Open daily 10am-6pm. Last admission 4:20pm. £5, concessions £4.40, children £4.) In Y Tabernacl on Penrallt St., the **Museum of Modern Art, Wales** features Welsh art. Some evenings, the neighboring performance hall fills with music. (☎703 355; www.momawales.org.uk. Open M-Sa 10am-4pm. Free.) The museum and theater are the center of the late August **Machynlleth Festival,** featuring musical performances and lectures. (☎703 355; www.momawales.org.uk. Tickets £3-15.)

VALE OF CONWY

Much of the Vale of Conwy lies within Snowdonia National Park, but the lush swales, tall conifers, and streams suggest an ecosystem far gentler than Snowdon's desolate peaks. Cyclists favor the scenic terrain because views are glorious and gear-changes infrequent. The excellent *Gwydyr Forest Guide* (£2) details 14 walks past the mossy glens and waterfalls.

▐▀ TRANSPORTATION

The single-track, 27 mi. Conwy Valley line (☎08457 484 950) offers unparalleled views. **Trains** run between Llandudno and Blaenau Ffestiniog, stopping at Llandudno Junction, Llanrwst, and Betws-y-Coed (1hr.; M-Sa 5 per day, Su 3 per day). The **North and Mid-Wales Rover** ticket is good for nearly unlimited bus and train travel as far south as Aberystwyth (1-day £20, 3-day £30, 7-day £44). Most area **buses** stop at Llanrwst, some also at Betws-y-Coed. The main bus along the Conwy River is Arriva Cymru (☎08706 082 608) #19, which runs from Llandudno and Conwy to Llanrwst (M-Sa 1-2 per hr., Su 10 per day). Sherpa bus S2 runs from Llanrwst to Pen-y-Pass via Betws-y-Coed (30min.; M-Sa 7 trips per day, Su 8 per day). Bus #97A connects Betws-y-Coed with Porthmadog (1hr., 3 per day). Routes constantly change; consult the *Gwynedd* or *Conwy County* transport booklet, free at local TICs. Arriva's **Explorer Pass** allows unlimited travel on Arriva buses (one day £5; one week £12.50).

CONWY   ☎01492

Conwy's impressive stone walls remain from Edward I's attempt to keep the native Welsh out of his 13th-century castle. The town plays the obligatory role of tourist mecca, so it is both crowded and convenient. Conwy's elegant, narrow streets and quayside hold an assortment of eclectic attractions.

TRANSPORTATION

Trains: Conwy Station, off Rosehill St. Trains (☎08457 484 950) stop only by request. The station lies on the North Wales line, between **Holyhead** and **Chester.** Trains stop at nearby **Llandudno Junction,** which connects to the Conwy Valley line. Ticket office open M-Sa 5:30am-6:30pm, Su 11:30am-6:30pm. Not to be confused with Llandudno proper (a resort town 1 mi. north; p. 486), Llandudno Junction is a 20min. walk from Conwy. Turn left on a side road after exiting the station, walk under a bridge, and climb the stairs to another bridge across the estuary.

Buses: Buses are the best way to get directly to Conwy, with two main stops on Lancaster Sq. and on Castle St. before the corner of Rosehill St. National Express (☎08705 808 080) buses come from: **Liverpool** (2¾hr., 1 per day, £8.40); **Manchester** (4½hr., 1 per day, £13.20); and **Newcastle** (10hr., 1 per day, £45). Arriva Cymru (☎0870 608 2608) buses #5 and 5X stop in Conwy as they climb the northern coast from **Caernarfon** via **Bangor** to **Llandudno** (1¼hr.; M-Sa 2 per hr., Su every hr.). Bus #9 leaves from Holyhead and passes through Conwy on the way to Llandudno (1½hr., M-Sa every hr.). Bus #19 crosses Conwy on its **Llandudno-Llanrwst** journey down the Vale of Conwy (15min. from Llandudno, 40min. from Llanrwst; M-Sa 1-2 per hr., Su 10 per day). The free *Conwy Public Transport Information* booklet is available at the TIC.

Taxis: Castle Cars (☎593 398).

ORIENTATION AND PRACTICAL INFORMATION

Old Conwy is roughly triangular in shape. The castle lies in one corner; **Castle Street,** which becomes **Berry Street,** runs from the castle parallel to the **Quay** and the river beyond it. **High Street** stretches from the Quay's edge to **Lancaster Square,** from which **Rosehill Street** circles back to the castle. In the opposite direction, **Bangor Road** heads north past the wall.

Tourist Information Centre: (☎592 248) in the same building as the castle entrance. Stocks street maps and books beds for a £2 charge plus a 10% deposit. Open daily June-Sept. 9:30am-6pm; Oct.-Nov. and May 9:30am-5pm; Dec.-Apr. 9:30am-4pm.

Financial Services: Barclays, 23 High St. (☎616 616). Open M-F 10am-4pm.

Police: Lancaster Sq. (☎517 171 ext. 48091).

Hospital: (☎860 066) off Maesdu Rd. in Llahdudno.

Internet Access: Library, Town Hall, Castle St. (☎596 242). Free. Open M and Th-F 10am-5:30pm, Tu 10am-7pm, W and Sa 10am-1pm.

Pharmacy: 24 High St. (☎592 418). Open M-Sa 9am-5:30pm.

Post Office: 7 Lancaster Sq. (☎573 990). Open M-Tu 8:30am-5:30pm, W-F 9am-5:30pm, Sa 9am-1:30pm. **Post Code:** LL32 8HT.

ACCOMMODATIONS

Swan Cottage, 18 Berry St. (☎596 840; www.swancottage.btinternet.co.uk), in a 16th-century building near the center of town. One of few B&Bs within the town wall. Cozy rooms with timber ceilings and TVs. Singles £19; doubles £38. Cash only. ❷

Bryn B&B (☎592 449), just outside the gates at the corner of St. Agnes Rd. and Synchant Pass, flanked by a colorful garden and bounded on one side by the city wall. Singles £35; doubles £50. Cash only. ❹

YHA Conwy, Larkhill, Sychnant Pass Rd. (☎593 571), a 10min. uphill walk from the town walls. From Lancaster Sq., head down Bangor Rd., turn left on Mt. Pleasant and right at the top of the hill; it's up a driveway on the left. Self-catering kitchen and TV room. Free lockers. Laundry (wash £2, dry £1 per 20min.). Internet access 50p per 6min. Bike rental £6.50 per half-day. Dorms £14, under 18 £10. MC/V. ❷

Glan Heulog, Llanrwst Rd., Woodlands (☎593 845), a 10min. walk from the castle. Go under the arch near the TIC on Rosehill St., down the steps, and across the carpark. Turn right and walk 5min. down Llanrwst Rd. With TVs, ensuite rooms, and "healthy option" breakfasts. Singles from £29; doubles from £46. MC/V. ❷

Camping: Conwy Touring Park, Llanrwst Rd. (☎592 856; www.conwytouringpark.com), 1 mi. from town. Follow Llanrwst Rd. and signs. Open Easter to Sept. £4-10 per tent. Electricity £3. MC/V. ❶

◖ FOOD

Although fair Conwy fries fish and curries favor with curry flavor, High Street is lined with a number of classier (and pricier) restaurants. Spar sells inexpensive **groceries** (open daily 8am-10pm). A weekly market fills the train station parking lot in summer. (☎581 924. Open Tu 8:30am-5pm.)

Bistro Conwy, Chapel St. (☎596 326), near the wall close to Bangor Rd. Inspired Welsh fare amidst dried bouquets. Entrees from £14. Open Tu-Sa 6:30-9pm. MC/V. ❸

Edward's Butchery, 18 High St. (☎592 443; www.edwardsofconwy.co.uk). Well-deserved accolades hang from the huge meat counter; hearty pies (from £1.25) are the specialty. Open M-Sa 7am-5:30pm. AmEx/MC/V. ❶

Shakespeare Restaurant, High St. (☎582 800), in the Castle Hotel. This award-winning venue uses local foods in exquisite daily specials. It's decorated with panels of Shakespeare canvases by Victorian-era artist John Dawson-Watson, who supposedly painted for his keep while here. Open M-Sa 7-9:30pm, Su 12:30-2:30pm and 7-9pm. MC/V. ❹

Pen-y-Bryn Tea Rooms, High St. (☎596 445). Caters to those with a fondness for good tea (high tea £4.50) and 16th-century timbered nooks. Assortment of sandwiches from £3.50. Open M-F 10am-5pm, Sa-Su 10am-5:30pm. Cash only. ❶

◉ SIGHTS

▨ **CONWY CASTLE.** Conwy, one of Edward I's 13th-century fortresses, is magnificent. This ominous castle needed no concentric fortifications; parapets joining eight rugged towers sit imposingly atop natural rock. Untold Normans wasted away in the prison and Richard II was betrayed in the chapel and deposed in 1399. The £1 guided tour is worth it; try to get on "celebrity" guide Neville Hortop's tour—his ferocious approach to history is ultimately more entertaining than unsettling, and his zeal brings the history of the castle alive. (☎592 358. Open June-Sept. daily 9:30am-6pm; Apr.-May and Oct. daily 9:30am-5pm; Nov.-Mar. M-Sa 9:30am-4pm, Su 11am-4pm. £4, concessions £3.50, families £11.50.)

PLAS MAWR. The National Trust has lovingly restored this 16th-century mansion to recall its days as home to merchant Robert Wynn, down to the exquisite furnishings and plasterwork. Don't miss the display on Tudor-era hygiene and its discussion of so-called "pisse prophets." The entrance price includes a free 1hr. audio tour that attempts to psychoanalyze Wynn according to his architectural choices. (☎580 167. Open June-Aug. Tu-Su 9:30am-6pm; Apr.-May and Sept. Tu-Su 9:30am-5pm; Oct. Tu-Su 9:30am-4pm. £4.50, concessions £3.50, families £12.50.)

NORTH WALES

THE SMALLEST HOUSE. When this 380-year-old house was finally condemned in 1900, its owner (a strapping 6'3" fisherman) spent years measuring other tiny homes to prove that this one was the smallest in Britain. With a frontage of 6 ft., you can question his taste in housing all you like, but you can't question the legitimacy of his claim. There's (obviously) not much to see here beyond its two floors and a small gift stand. *(Head down High St. and onto the Quay. ☎ 593 484. Open daily Aug. 10am-9pm; Easter to July and Sept.-Oct. 10am-6pm. 75p, children 50p.)*

CONWY MUSSEL CENTRE. Learn about the history of mussel raking in Conwy. The waters surrounding Conwy are some of the most mussel-fertile waters in the world. Watch demonstrations about cleaning and processing of the "poor man's shellfish." *(☎ 592 689. Open in summer daily 10am-5pm; call ahead in winter. Free.)*

OTHER SIGHTS AND ENTERTAINMENT. Almost a mile long, the **town wall** was built at the same time as the castle and bristles with its 22 towers and 480 arrow slits. Follow the signs around town to its three entry points. *(Always open. Free.)* A historian involved in the restoration of 14th-century **Aberconwy House,** Castle St., the oldest home in Conwy, once called it "remarkable simply because it is still standing." While the house has some nice antique pieces, the place is as unexciting as his summation implies. *(☎ 592 246. Open mid-Mar. to Oct. M and W-Su 11am-5pm. Last admission 4:30pm. £2.60, children £1.30.)* Preserving a bit of tranquility in the town center, **St. Mary's Church** is noteworthy for its stained glass and its cemetery, which holds the grave that inspired Wordsworth's "We are Seven." *(Hours vary; if the doors aren't open, keys are available from the rectory M-F 10am-5pm.)* During the first week of July, the **North Wales Bluegrass Festival** *(☎ 580 454; www.northwalesbluegrass.co.uk)* brings a bit of Appalachia to Conwy.

LLANDUDNO ☎ 01492

Around 1850, the Mostyn family envisioned the bucolic village of Llandudno (hlan-DID-no) as a resort town; accordingly, they constructed a city with wide avenues open to sea and sky. Today, Victorian hotels and shores dappled with sunbathers prove the family's foresight. The Great Orme, a massive tor on its own peninsula, lures many to its slopes.

▐ TRANSPORTATION. Llandudno is the northern terminus of several transport lines. The train station is at the end of Augusta Rd. (Ticket office open July-Aug. M-Sa 8:40am-3:30pm, Su 10:15am-5:45pm; Sept.-June M-Sa 8:40am-3:30pm.) **Trains** *(☎ 08457 484 950)* arrive on the Conwy Valley line from Blaenau Ffestiniog via Llanrwst and Betws-y-Coed (1¼hr.; M-Sa 6 per day, Su 2 per day; £5.30). On the North Wales line, trains enter Llandudno Junction, 1 mi. south of town, from: Bangor (20min., 1-3 per hr., £4.20); Chester (1hr., 1-4 per hr., £11.20); Holyhead (50min., 19 per day, £8.60). Trains sometimes stop at Llandudno by request. National Express *(☎ 08705 808 080)* **buses** hit Mostyn Broadway daily from: Chester (1¾hr., £8.25) and London (8hr., £24); and twice per day from Manchester (4¼hr., £10.75). Arriva Cymru *(☎ 0870 608 2608)* buses #5, 5A, and 5X come from: Bangor (1hr., 1-3 per hr.); Caernarfon (1½hr., 1-3 per hr.); Conwy (20min.; M-Sa 2-3 per hr., Su every hr.; £1.10). Bus #19 arrives from Llanrwst, passing through Conwy (1hr.; M-Sa 8 per day, Su 10 per day). Snowdon Sherpa S2 runs from Betws-y-Coed (50min., 3 per day). Kings Cabs *(☎ 878 156; last cab M-W and Su 1:30am, F-Sa 3-4am)* runs **taxis. Rent bikes** at West End Cycles, 22 Augusta St., near the train station. *(☎ 876 891. From £7 per day. £25 deposit. Open M-Tu and Su and Th-Sa 9am-5:30pm.)*

⚠️ 🔢 ORIENTATION AND PRACTICAL INFORMATION. Llandudno is flanked by two **beaches** with pretty boardwalks; the West Shore is less built up than the North, which has Victorian promenades and a long pier. Mostyn St. is the main drag. A left on Augusta St. as you exit the train station leads to the **Tourist Information Centre,** 1-2 Chapel St., which books rooms for a £2 charge plus a 10% deposit. (☎876 413. Open Easter to Oct. M-Sa 9am-5:30pm, Su 9:30am-4:30pm; Nov. to Easter M-Sa 9am-5pm.) Other services include: Barclays **bank,** at the corner of Mostyn St. and Market St. (open M-F 9:30am-4:30pm, Sa 9:30am-12:30pm); **police,** Oxford Rd. (☎517 171); **General Hospital,** near the Maesdu Golf Course on the West Shore (☎860 066); free **Internet access** at the library, on Mostyn St. between Lloyd St. and Trinity Sq. (☎876 826; open M-Tu and F 9am-6pm, W 10am-5pm, Th 9am-7pm, Sa 9:30am-1pm) and at Le Moulin Rouge, (see below); and the **post office,** 14 Vaughn St., with a **bureau de change** (☎876 125; open M-F 9am-5:30pm, Sa 9am-12:30pm). **Post Code:** LL30 1AA.

🔢 📇 ACCOMMODATIONS AND FOOD. Lodging is easy to find in Llandudno, though the town becomes crowded in summer. Budget travelers should seek out **B&Bs** (£15-19) on **Chapel Street, Deganwy Avenue,** and **St. David's Road.** Conveniently located next to the TIC, **Walsall House ❷,** 4 Chapel St., has cozy rooms with TVs. (☎875 279; www.walsallhouse.co.uk. Breakfast £2. £15-18 per person. MC/V.) Nearby **Merrydale Hotel ❷,** 6 Chapel St., has simple, cheery rooms. (☎860 911. £20 per person. Cash only.) **Burleigh House ❷,** 74 Church Walks, is close to the beach. (☎875 946. Singles £18; doubles £40, ensuite £50; suites £28 per person. Cash only.) **Beach Cove ❷,** 8 Church Walks, offers clean rooms in an excellent location. (☎879 638. Singles £19; doubles £37. MC/V.)

The **Fat Cat Cafe-Bar ❶,** 149 Mostyn St., offers non-traditional dishes. (☎871 844. Open M-Sa 10am-11pm, Su 10am-10:30pm. AmEx/MC/V.) Down a set of stairs off an alley, **The Cocoa House ❷,** George St., provided the social atmosphere of a pub while serving cocoa instead of alcohol during the temperance movement. These days, it is fully licensed and offers creative lunch specials from £3. (☎876 601. Open M-Sa 10am-4:30pm. Cash only.) **Le Moulin Rouge ❶,** 104 Mostyn St., serves crisp panini with fillings like bacon, tomato, Stilton, and pears. (☎874 111. Panini £3. 20min. Free Internet access with £3 purchase. Open M-Su 8am-5:30pm. Cash only.) **The Cottage Loaf ❷,** Market St., maintains a tavern atmosphere with a beer garden and serves good pub grub. (☎870 762. Entrees from £6. Open M-Sa 11am-11pm, Su noon-10:30pm. Food served noon-8pm. Cash only.) Hundreds of other options line main streets, including an enormous ASDA **grocery** store, between Mostyn Blvd. and Conway Rd. (☎860 068. Open M-F 8am-10pm, Sa 8am-8pm, Su 10:30am-4:30pm.)

🔢 SIGHTS. Llandudno's pleasant beaches, the Victorian **North Shore** and the quieter **West Shore,** are both outdone by the looming **Great Orme,** a huge nature reserve full of caves, pastures, and some 200 feral Kashmir goats (a resident species since the 1890s). At the 679 ft. summit, even gift shops and coin-op arcades cannot dull the wonder of the flowered hillside. Pick up the free *Walks to the Summit* brochure from the TIC. The **Great Orme Tramway,** which departs from Church Walks, offers a quicker trip. (☎879 306. 20min. Apr.-Oct. 3 per hr. 10am-6pm. Round-trip £4.50, children £3.20.) Perhaps the most exciting way to reach the summit, however, is on the **Llandudno Cable Cars,** which depart from the Happy Valley Gardens. (☎877 205. 20min. round-trip. Open 10am-5pm, weather permitting. Round-trip £5.50, children £2.85.) Halfway up the side of the Great Orme, stop for an engrossing tour of the **Bronze-Age Copper Mines.** Visitors explore narrow underground passages where miners exposed the ore veins with rocks and animal bones 4000 years ago. With just primitive tools, the miners dug the "Vivian Shaft" more than 470 ft. down to sea level. (☎870 447. Open daily Feb.-Oct. 10am-5pm. £5, children £3.50, families £15.)

Occupying an old warehouse near the TIC, the **Homefront Experience,** New St., off Chapel St., walks visitors through torch-lit corridors and a full-size bomb shelter, relating the hardscrabble existence of blackout and blitz on the British homefront. (☎871 032. Open Mar.-Nov. M-Sa 10am-4:30pm, Su 11am-3pm. £3, children £2.) Alice Liddell, muse to Lewis Carroll, spent her childhood summers in Llandudno, and the town has used this connection to justify a low-budget fantasy recreation at the **Alice in Wonderland Centre,** 3-4 Trinity Sq. Dramatic readings accompany mechanized characters and stuffed animals in formal attire. (☎860 062; www.wonderland.co.uk. Open Easter to Oct. M-Sa 10am-5pm, Su 10am-4pm; Nov. to Easter M-Sa 10am-5pm. £3, children £2.50.)

Eight miles south of Llandudno, twisting pathways cross the lawns and carp-filled ponds of **Bodnant Gardens.** The upper terraces give way to a river glen downhill. The gardens host plays on summer evenings. (From Llandudno, take Arriva bus #25 (45min., M-Sa 11 per day) to the gates or the Conwy Valley train (M-Sa 6 per day, Su 3 per day) to the Tal-y-Cafn stop, 2 mi. away. ☎650 460. Open daily mid-Mar. to Oct. 10am-5pm. Last admission 4:30pm. £5.50, children £2.75.)

▨ ▨ NIGHTLIFE AND ENTERTAINMENT. Llandudno's two clubs are a 10min. walk from the town center down Mostyn St. **Broadway Boulevard,** Mostyn Broadway next to the North Wales Theatre, is a versatile venue with cheap drinks and a solid mix of chart favorites. (☎879 614. No trainers. Cover £2-6.50. Open W and F-Sa 9pm-2am, Su 9:30pm-12:30am. Last admission midnight.) A bit farther down Mostyn Broadway and left on Clarence Rd. is **Washington,** a complex with two venues, **Capitol** on the first floor and **Buzz Club** on the second. Capitol is lined with portraits of US presidents and caters to an older set; Buzz is a more traditional dance club. (☎877 974. No trainers. Cover £2-4. Th gay night. Open Th-Sa 9pm-1:30am.) **North Wales Theatre,** sandwiched between Mostyn Broadway and the Promenade, hosts plays and concerts. (☎872 000; www.nwtheatre.co.uk. Schedules at the TIC. Box office open M-Sa 9:30am-8:30pm, Su noon-4pm. Tickets £6-47, concessions available.)

BETWS-Y-COED   ☎01690

At the southern tip of the Vale of Conwy and the eastern edge of the Snowdonia mountains, picturesque Betws-y-Coed (BET-oos uh COYD) has evolved from art colony into tourist haven. Its main street is crammed with novelty shops, hotels, and outdoor supply stores that coach-tour travelers move through like migratory birds. Yet the town retains its friendliness, and its stunning surroundings overcome this commercialization. Dark green hills rise from the banks of two coursing rivers to frame the town.

▣ TRANSPORTATION. Trains (☎08457 484 950) stop in Betws-y-Coed on the Conwy Valley line (p. 483). Sherpa **bus** S2, operated by Arriva Cymru, connects Betws-y-Coed with Pen-y-Pass, stopping at some area hostels (20min., M-Sa 1-2 per day) and Llanrwst (10min., 1-2 per hr.), continuing to Llandudno with #19 (1¼hr., 8 per day). Sherpa #97A shuttles between Porthmadog and Betws-y-Coed (1hr., 3 per day). On Saturdays, Arriva bus #70 runs from Corwen, Wrecsam, and Llangollen in one direction and Llanrwst and Llandudno in the other. Rent **bicycles** from Beics Betws, up the street behind the post office. (☎710 766; www.bikewales.co.uk. From £16 per day. Open daily 9:30am-5pm.)

✱ 🛈 ORIENTATION AND PRACTICAL INFORMATION. The main street is **Holyhead Road** (A5). It runs northwest from the River Conwy, slants past the park at the town center (where Station Rd. branches toward the train station), and makes a turn west toward Swallow Falls. Possibly the busiest **Tourist Information Centre** in North Wales (also a Snowdonia NPIC), the Betws TIC is at the Old Stables, between the train station and Holyhead Rd. A spirited staff provides timetables and information on sights and books rooms for ₤2 plus a 10% deposit. (☎ 710 426; www.eryri-npa.gov.uk. Open daily Easter to Oct. 9:30am-5:30pm; Nov. to Easter 9:30am-4:30pm.) From April to September, **guided walks** around Betws are available. (☎ 01514 880 052 or 07790 851 333. 6-8 mi. and 5-6hr. By appointment. ₤5.) A number of **outdoor stores** line Holyhead Rd. Two Cotswold outlets are among them, one (☎ 710 710) next to the Royal Oak Hotel, the other (☎ 710 234) south of town. (Both open M-Tu, Th, and Su 9am-6pm, W 10am-6pm, F-Sa 9am-7pm.) The latter houses the upstairs Cafe Active which provides **Internet access** for 50p per 15min. (☎ 710 999. 10p per printout. Cash only. Open M-Tu, Th, and Su 9am-6pm, W 10am-6pm, F-Sa 9am-7pm.) Other services include: an HSBC **bank** at the southern edge of Holyhead Rd. near the train station (open M 9:15am-2:30pm, Tu-F 9:15am-1pm); **police** (☎ 710 222); and the **post office,** with a commission-free bureau de change, inside the Londis, at the T-junction of Holyhead and Station Rd. (☎ 710 565; open M-F 9am-5:30pm, Sa 9am-12:30pm). **Post Code:** LL24 0AA.

🛏 🍴 ACCOMMODATIONS AND FOOD. The best deal amidst Betws's expensive, centrally located accommodations is the **Bunkhouse ❷** at the Glan Aber Hotel. The price and location make up for the spartan amenities and decor. (☎ 710 325. Dorms from ₤13.) Two hostels are located conveniently near town: **YHA Capel Curig** (p. 494) and **YHA Betws-y-Coed ❷,** at the Swallow Falls Complex 2 mi. west of town on the A5. (☎ 710 796; www.swallowfallshotel.co.uk. Kitchen. Laundry ₤1.50. Reception 8am-9pm. Call 48hr. ahead. ₤12.50, under 18 ₤9. Cash only.) Most **B&Bs** (from ₤18) cluster along Holyhead Rd. For a lounge and fine views of riverside lambs, head for **Glan Llugwy ❷,** on the western edge of town, about 10min. from the park. Walk along Holyhead Rd. toward Swallow Falls, or call the owners for a lift. They provide packed lunches or laundry service on request. (☎ 710 592. From ₤22 per person. Cash only.) **Bryn Llewelyn ❸** is a bit closer to the town center on Holyhead Rd., with large, clean rooms. (☎ 710 601; www.bryn-llewelyn.co.uk. Singles from ₤25; doubles ₤40-52. Cash only.) **Riverside Caravan Park ❶** sits behind the train station. (☎ 710 310. Open mid-Mar. to Oct. ₤5.50 per person. Electricity ₤2. Cash only.)

Spar **market,** at the northern bend of Holyhead Rd., houses a large bakery and sandwich bar. (☎ 710 324. Open daily 8am-10pm.) A small cafe with hand-painted tables and corkboard art, **Caban-y-Pair ❷,** Holyhead Rd., serves affordable home-cooked food. Soups and sandwiches start at ₤2.70. (☎ 710 505. Open daily June-Oct. 9am-5:30pm; Nov.-May 10am-5pm. Cash only.) A knight guards the door at **Three Gables ❷,** Holyhead Rd., keeping watch over the kitschy treasures that adorn its walls. Try the pizzas, from ₤9. (☎ 710 328. Open Easter to Oct. daily noon-9:30pm; Nov. to Easter F-Su noon-9:30pm. AmEx/MC/V.)

◪ SIGHTS. Betws is known for its eight bridges. The first bridge was built in 1475. Inigo Jones may have contributed to building the second, which consists of 11 stone arches hopping from rock to rock. Of particular note is Telford's 1815 cast-iron **Waterloo Bridge,** situated at the village's southern end and built the year that battle ensured Napoleon's political demise. A miniature **suspen-**

sion bridge spans the Conwy, while **Pont-y-Pair Bridge,** "the bridge of the cauldron," crosses the Llugwy to the north. Behind the train station, weathered gravestones surround humble 14th-century **St. Michael's Church.**

Two miles west, signposted off the A5, the waters of the Llugwy froth at **Swallow Falls.** Local lore claims that the soul of an evil 17th-century sheriff is trapped below. (Always open. £1.) Bus S2 between Betws and Snowdon stops at the falls, as do most #97A buses to Porthmadog (4min., 1-3 per hr.). Half a mile farther along the A5, "the Ugly House," **Tŷ Hyll** ("tih-hih"), is named for its rough facade, which consists of boulders stacked without much delicacy. Now the house serves as the Snowdonia Society headquarters and houses a display and shop area. (☎720 287. Open daily Apr.-Sept. 9am-5pm. £1.)

A large portion of Betws-y-Coed's appeal lies in its prime location, and visitors should take advantage of the stunning scenery. Many of the outdoor stores on Holyhead Rd. can arrange excursions. The **National Whitewater Centre,** headquartered in nearby Bala, offers river expeditions. (☎01678 521 083; www.ukrafting.co.uk. £25-100, wetsuit rental £2-5.)

TREFRIW   ☎01492

To the south, Trefriw curves alongside the River Crafnant. **Lake Crafnant,** 3 mi. uphill from town (along the road, opposite the Fairy Hotel), is surrounded by some of Snowdonia's highest peaks. North of town, 1½ mi. along the A470, a spring spews medicinal water at the **Trefriw Wells Spa,** purportedly discovered by Roman soldiers. A self-guided tour takes visitors into a rust-toned grotto where voiceovers offer a bit of geology and local history. Reach through stalactites to sample the iron-rich water. In the store on the premises, a month's supply goes for £6.50. (☎640 057. Open Easter to Sept. daily 10am-5:30pm; Oct. to Easter M-Sa 10am-dusk, Su noon-dusk. £3, children £2, families £8.50.)

B&Bs (from £15) line Trefriw's main street. The rustic **YHA Rowen ❶,** a farmhouse halfway between Trefriw and Conwy, is a superb place to rest after the treacherous mile hike from the road; bus #19 (20min., every hr.) will take you a quarter mile from the beginning of the ascent. (☎650 089. Lockout 10am-5pm. Curfew 11pm. Open May-Aug., rentable during other times. Dorms £10, under 18 £7.50. Cash only.) To reach Trefriw, take Arriva **bus** #19 from Betws-y-Coed, Conwy, Llandudno, or Llandudno Junction (M-Sa 1-2 per hr., Su 10 per day).

LLANRWST   ☎01492

A short walk toward Trefriw leads to **Gwydir Castle,** the 16th-century manor of Sir John Wynne placed "two bowshots above the river Conwy." Peacocks strut the many paths through gardens and fountains. The manor itself (it earned the title "castle" unofficially) is surprisingly opulent, with strings attached—it claims to be one of the most haunted houses in Wales. When the home was auctioned in 1921, American newspaper giant William Randolph Hearst acquired Lot 88: the wall panels, doorframe, fireplace, and leather frieze of Gwydir's dining room. In 1994, the castle's new owners traced the lot to a storage box in a New York museum, purchased it, and restored the room. (☎641 687. Open daily Easter to Oct. 10am-4:30pm, often closed Sa for weddings. £3.50, children £1.50.) Stock up on **groceries** at the local Spar (open daily 7am-11pm), or at the Tuesday **market.** Connected to town by a 1636 bridge built by Inigo Jones, the 15th-century stone **Tu-Hwnt-i'r-Bont ❶** served once as the court house, but now serves cream teas on the second floor. (Sandwiches from £2.50. Open Easter to Oct. Tu-Su 10:30am-5pm.) Llanrwst has several **banks** with ATMs that cluster around Lancaster Sq., marked by the large clocktower.

LLANGOLLEN ☎ 01978

Set in a hollow in the hills near the English border, Llangollen (hlan-GOTH-hlen) hosts the annual International Musical Eisteddfod, an extravaganza that has drawn over 400,000 performers and competitors since it began in 1947. The town also boasts surrounding natural attractions; hikers head to Horseshoe Pass, and whitewater enthusiasts take in the Dee and its tributaries.

⌗⁊ TRANSPORTATION AND PRACTICAL INFORMATION. For a tourist town, Llangollen can be difficult to reach by public transport. **Trains** (☎ 08457 484 950) come to Wrexham, 30min. away, from Chester, London, and Shrewsbury. A closer train station is Ruabon, from which B&B owners occasionally fetch travelers. To get to Llangollen from Wrexham, take Bryn Melyn (☎ 860 701) bus #X5 (30min., M-Sa 4 per hr., £2.20). Direct service to Llangollen is possible on some **buses;** Arriva Cymru (☎ 0870 608 2608) bus #94 comes from Barmouth (3hr.; M-Sa 7 per day, Su 4 per day; £4.90) and Dolgellau (2hr.; M-Sa 8 per day, Su 4 per day; £3.30). Arriva Cymru's bus #19 runs once per day on weekends from Llandudno and 5 times per day on weekdays (2¼ hr.). Lloyd's Coaches (☎ 01654 702 100) runs #694, which stops at Llangollen between Chester and Machynlleth, on the first and third Saturdays of the month.

The **Tourist Information Centre,** on Castle St. in The Chapel, books rooms for a £2 charge plus a 10% deposit. (☎ 860 828. Open daily Easter to Oct. 9:30am-5:30pm; Nov. to Easter 9:30am-5pm.) Activity weekends are available from **Pro Adventure,** 23 Castle St. (☎ 861 912; www.adventureholiday.com. Open Tu and Th-Sa 9am-5pm. Kayaking £38 per half-day. Bike rental £3.50 per hr.) Other services include: Barclays **bank,** 9 Castle St., opposite the TIC (☎ 202 700; open M-Tu and Th-F 10am-4pm, W 10:30am-4pm); a **Launderette,** 3 Regent St. (wash £2.20, dry 20p per 5min.; open M-Sa 9am-6pm); **police** (☎ 01492 517 171, ext. 54940); free **Internet access** at the library, upstairs from the TIC (☎ 869 600; open M 9:30am-7pm, Tu-W 9:30am-5:30pm, F 9:30am-5:30pm, Sa 9:30am-12:30pm); and the **post office,** 41 Castle St., with a bureau de change. (☎ 862 812; open M-F 9am-5:30pm, Sa 9am-12:30pm). **Post Code:** LL20 8RU.

⌂⌗ ACCOMMODATIONS AND FOOD. The **YHA Llangollen ❶,** Tyndwr Hall, Tyndwr Rd., is a manse 1½ mi. out of town. Follow the A5 toward Shrewsbury, bear right up Birch Hill, and after a half mile take a right at the junction. (☎ 860 330. Internet access £1 per 20min. Open mid-Feb. to Oct., rentable other months. Dorms £10.60, under 18 £7.20. MC/V.) **B&Bs** (£20-25) are numerous, especially along **Regent Street.** Once an 18th-century inn, **Poplar House ❸,** 39-41 Regent St., offers satellite TV and lavish breakfasts. (☎ 861 772. Singles from £25. Cash only.) The gardens and all-weather tennis court of **Oakmere ❹,** Regent St., promise relaxing evenings. (☎ 861 126; www.oakmere.llangollen.co.uk. Singles from £45; doubles £55. Cash only.) **Campsites** abound; ask at the TIC or try **Eirianfa Riverside Holiday Park ❶,** 1 mi. from town on the A5 toward Corwen. (☎ 860 919. £8-12 per tent. MC/V.)

Spar, 26-30 Castle St., in the center of town, sells **groceries.** (☎ 860 275. Open M-Sa 7am-11pm, Su 8am-10:30pm.) Classy cuisine has found a home in comfortable pub-like quarters at ▧**Corn Mill ❸,** Dee Ln., where the patio hangs low over the Dee River. If the entrees are too expensive (£8-13.25), spend a few pounds on a pint and watch the waterwheel spinning outside. (☎ 869 555. Open M-Sa noon-11pm, Su noon-10:30pm. Food served noon-9pm. AmEx/MC/V.) At **Maxine's Cafe and Books ❶,** 17 Castle St., thumb through thousands of volumes in the warehouse upstairs, and grab a meal below. The all-day breakfast is £4.25. (☎ 860 334. Open M-Sa 9am-

5pm, Su 10am-5pm. Cash only.) At **Ecclestons Bakers and Confectioners ❶**, Castle St., find cheap and freshly-baked takeout pasties, sandwiches, and salads. (☎861 005. Open M-Sa 9am-4pm. Cash only.)

🔲 **SIGHTS.** The ruins of 🔳**Castell Dinas Brân** (Crow Castle) lie on a hilltop above town, "to the winds abandoned and the prying stars," as Wordsworth once mused. The view spans from Snowdonia to the English Midlands, and the grassy mounds of the summit are scattered with crumbling archways and walls. Two main paths lead to the castle: a 40min. gravel trail zig-zags up the side, while a 1hr. walk follows a pastoral road before ascending gradually from the other side. Both are reached by an unmarked trail that begins where Wharf Rd. hits Dinbren Rd., uphill from the canal bridge. When you reach the intersection of dirt roads, continue straight up the hill following the sign for Offa's Dyke Path. Up Hill St. from the town center, **Plas Newydd** is the former *ferme ornee* (estate in miniature) of two noblewomen who fled Ireland in 1778. While their elopement was dramatic, their life in Llangollen was defined by peaceful companionship. As "two of the most celebrated virgins in Europe," they appealed to the era's intellectuals; Wellington and Sir Walter Scott visited, as did Wordsworth, who penned a poem in their honor. (☎861 314. Open daily Easter to Oct. 10am-5pm. Last admission 4:15pm. Includes audio tour. £3, concessions £2, families £8. Gardens open year-round 8am-6pm. Free.) The ruins of 13th-century **Valle Crucis Abbey** grace a valley 30-45min. from Llangollen along Abbey Rd. Its empty arches frame trees, sky, and an unfortunate cluster of caravans. (☎860 326. Open daily Apr.-Sept. 10am-5pm; Oct.-Mar. 10am-4pm. £2, concessions £1.50, families £5.50; free in winter.) Both are important landmarks for those interested in the history behind Arthurian legend. Other sites in the area include **Croes Gwenhwyfar** (Guinevere's Cross) and **Eliseg's Pillar.**

Views of the gently sloping Dee River Valley greet passengers on the **Llangollen Railway,** with a convenient station where Castle St. hits highway A593/A452. The engine stops at Carrog and Berwyn, among other stations, to provide an afternoon's entertainment. (☎860 951. Runs Apr.-Oct. daily 3-7 per day; Nov.-Mar. Sa-Su 3 per day. Times vary; call ahead.)

🎭 **FESTIVALS.** Every summer, the town's population of 3000 swells to 80,000 for the **International Musical Eisteddfod** (ice-TETH-vod). From July 4-9, 2006, the hills (and fields, and streets) will be alive with the singing and dancing of competitors from 50 countries. Book tickets and rooms far in advance through the **Eisteddfod Box Office,** Royal International Pavilion, Abbey Rd. (☎862 000, bookings 862 001; www.international-eisteddfod.co.uk. Open mid-Mar. through the festival M-F 10am-5pm. Tickets £7-50. Unreserved seats and admission to grounds on day of show can be purchased on the fields. £6, children £4.)

SNOWDONIA NATIONAL PARK

The impressive battlements of Edward I lie within the 840 sq. mi. natural fortress of Snowdonia National Park. Known in Welsh as Eryri ("Place of Eagles"), Snowdonia yields diverse terrain—mountain lakes mark grassland with glittering blue, and the cliff-faces of abandoned slate quarries slope into wooded hills. Rock climbing attracts many to Snowdonia; Sir Edmund Hillary trained here before attempting Everest. Though Snowdonia lies largely in private hands—only 0.3% belongs to the National Park Authority—endless public footpaths accommodate visitors. Snowdonia is also a stronghold of national pride: 65% of its inhabitants speak Welsh as their native tongue.

▐ TRANSPORTATION

Trains (☎ 08457 484 950) stop at larger towns on the park's outskirts, including Bangor and Conwy. The Cambrian Coaster line hits Harlech and Dolgellau in the south. The Conwy Valley Line runs across the park from Llandudno through Betws-y-Coed to Blaenau Ffestiniog (1hr. from Llandudno to Blaenau Ffestiniog; M-Sa 6 per day, Su 2-3 per day). **Buses** serve the interior from towns near the edge of the park. *The Gwynedd Public Transport Maps and Timetables* and *Conwy Public Transport Information* booklets, indispensable for travel in the two counties that constitute the park, are both available for free in the region's TICs. Snowdon Sherpa buses, usually painted blue, maneuver between the park's towns and trailheads with helpful but irregular service, and will stop at any safe point in the park on request. A **Gwynedd Red Rover** ticket (£5, children £2.45) buys unlimited travel for a day on all buses in Gwynedd and Anglesey; a Snowdon

Sherpa Day Ticket secures a day's worth of rides on Sherpa buses (£3, children £1.50). Most routes run every 1-2hr., but Sunday service is sporadic at best.

Narrow-gauge railway lines let you enjoy the countryside in a select locations without a hike, though they tend to be pricey. The Ffestiniog Railway (p. 511) weaves from Porthmadog to Blaenau Ffestiniog, where mountain views give way to the raw cliffs of slate quarries. You can travel part of its route to Minffordd, Penrhyndeudraeth, or Tan-y-bwlch. At Porthmadog, the narrow-gauge rail meets the Cambrian Coaster service from Pwllheli to Aberystwyth; at Blaenau Ffestiniog, it connects with the Conwy Valley Line. (☎ 01766 516 000; 3hr.; 4-8 per day; £16, concessions £12.80.) The Snowdon Mountain Railway and the Llanberis Lake Railway make trips from Llanberis (p. 499).

▐ PRACTICAL INFORMATION

TICs and National Park Information Centres (NPICs) stock leaflets on walks, drives, and accommodations, as well as Ordnance Survey maps (£6.50-7.50). For details, contact the **Snowdonia National Park Information Headquarters** (☎ 01766 770 274). The semi-annual booklet put out by the Snowdonia National Park Authority, free at TICs across North Wales, is a good source of information on the park and accommodations. You can also check out www.eryri-npa.gov.uk or www.gwynedd.gov.uk.

National Park Information Centres:

Aberdyfi: Wharf Gardens (☎ 01654 767 321), in the center of town. Open daily Apr.-Oct. 9:30am-12:30pm and 1:30-5pm.

Betws-y-Coed: The busiest and best stocked. See p. 488.

Blaenau Ffestiniog: Isallt Church St. (☎01766 830 360). Open Apr.-Oct. daily 9:30am-12:30pm and 1:30-5:30pm.

Dolgellau: see p. 495.

Harlech: see p. 497.

ACCOMMODATIONS

In the mountains, **camping** is permitted as long as you leave no mess, but the Park Service discourages it because of recent disastrous erosion. In the valleys, the landowner's consent is required. Public campsites dot the roads in summer; check listings below and inquire at NPICs. This section lists **YHA hostels** in Snowdonia; **B&Bs** are listed under individual towns. The seven hostels in the mountain area are some of the best in Wales and are marked on the Snowdonia map. All have kitchens, and most offer meals. Keep in mind that YHA now strongly advises you book hostels 48hr. in advance, as many now have unpredictable opening dates in winter. Book online at www.yha.org.uk.

Bryn Gwynant (☎08707 705 732), above Llyn Gwynant and along the Penygwryd-Beddgelert Rd., ¾ mi. from the Watkin path. On Su and bank holidays, take Snowdon Sherpa bus S4 from Caernarfon (40min., 5 per day) or Pen-y-Pass (10min., 9 per day). Sherpa summer express #97A comes from Porthmadog or Betws-y-Coed (30min. each way, 3 per day). An old Victorian residence built in the heart of the park. Lockout 10am-5pm. Curfew 11pm. Open Mar.-Oct. Dorms £12.50, under 18 £9. MC/V. ❶

Capel Curig (☎08707 705 746), 5 mi. from Betws-y-Coed on the A5. Sherpa buses S2 and S3 stop nearby from Llandudno, Betws-y-Coed, and Pen-y-Pass. At the crossroads of many mountain paths; favored by climbers and school kids. Spectacular view of Mt. Snowdon across a lake. Breakfast included. Lockout 10am-5pm. Open mid-Feb. to Oct. daily; Nov.-Jan. F-Sa. Dorms £16, under 18 £12.50. MC/V. ❷

Idwal Cottage (☎08707 705 874), just off the A5 at the foot of Llyn Ogwen in northern Snowdonia, 4 mi. from Bethesda. Take Sherpa bus #66 from Bangor (20min., every hr.), changing to S3 at Bethesda (10min.; M-Sa 6 per day, Su 10 per day), which goes to the hostel. On Su, #7 from Bangor stops at the hostel (30min., 2 per day). Lockout 10am-5pm. Curfew 11pm. Open Mar.-Nov. daily; Dec.-Feb. F-Sa. Dorms £12.50, under 18 £9. MC/V. ❷

Kings (Dolgellau) (☎08707 705 900), Penmaenpool, 4 mi. from Dolgellau. Arriva bus #28 from Dolgellau (5min.; M-Sa 9 per day, Su 3 per day); the hostel is 1 mi. uphill from the stop. A country house in the Vale of Ffestiniog. Open mid-Apr. to Aug. daily; Sept.-Oct. and Mar.-Apr. F-Sa; rentable Nov.-Mar. Dorms £11, under 18 £8. MC/V. ❶

Llanberis (☎01286 870 280), ½ mi. up Capel Goch Rd., with views of Llyn Peris, Llyn Padarn, and Mt. Snowdon; follow signs from High St. Open Apr.-Oct. daily; Nov.-Dec. F-Sa; Jan.-Feb. rentable; Mar. flexible opening. Fills up with school groups much of July and Aug. Dorms £14, under 18 £10. MC/V. ❷

Pen-y-Pass (☎08707 705 990), in Nant Gwynant, 6 mi. from Llanberis and 4 mi. from Nant Peris. Take Sherpa bus S1 from Llanberis (20min.; late May to Sept. every hr.; Oct. to late May M-Sa 6 per day, Su 9 per day). At the head of Llanberis Pass, 1170 ft. above sea level, it has the highest elevation of any hostel in Wales. Doors open onto a track to the Snowdon summit. Outdoors shop sells supplies and rents hiking boots, waterproofs, and ice axes. Dorms £12.50, under 18 £9. MC/V. ❷

Snowdon Ranger (☎08707 706 038), Llyn Cwellyn. The base for the Ranger Path, one of the grandest Snowdon ascents. Take Sherpa bus S4 from Caernarfon (20min.; M-Sa 8 per day, Su 6 per day). Lockout 10am-5pm. Open Easter to Aug. daily; Sept.-Oct. Tu-Su; Nov. to Easter F-Su. Dorms £11, under 18 £8. MC/V. ❶

⚠ OUTDOOR ACTIVITIES

Weather on Snowdonia's mountains shifts quickly, unpredictably, and with a vengeance. No matter how beautiful the weather is below, it will be cold and wet in the high mountains; bring a waterproof jacket and pants, gloves, a hat, and a wool sweater. Peel off layers as you descend. The free *Stay Safe in Snowdonia* is available at NPICs and offers advice and information on hiking and climbing. (See **Wilderness Safety**, p. 46.) Pick up the Ordnance Survey Landranger Map #115 (1:50,000; ₤6.50), Outdoor Leisure Map #17 (1:25,000; ₤7.50), and path guides (40p) at TICs and NPICs. Call **Mountaincall Snowdonia** (☎09068 500 449) for a local three- to five-day forecast.

Snowdonia National Park Study Centre, Plâs Tan-y-Bwlch, Maentwrog, Blaenau Ffestiniog, conducts two- to seven-day courses on naturalist topics, such as botanical painting. (☎01766 590 324. Courses ₤140-450, includes accommodation.) **YHA Pen-y-Pass**, Nant Gwynant (p. 494) puts groups in touch with guides for mountaineering, climbing, and water sports. **Beics Eryri Cycle Tours**, 44 Tyddyn Llwydyn, offer trips from Caernarfon for multi-night forays into the park, supplying maps, bikes, accommodation, and luggage transport. (☎01286 676 637. From ₤60 per night.) **Dolbadarn Trekking** operates out of Llanberis (p. 499).p. 499 Ask park rangers about guided **day-walks**. The brave can paraglide off the peaks of Snowdonia with the help of **Snowdon Gliders**. (☎01248 600 330; www.snowdongliders.co.uk. Call ahead.) The less brave can climb indoors at the **Beacon Climbing Centre**. (☎01286 650 045. 1½hr. session ₤45. Open M-F 11am-10pm, Sa-Su 10am-10pm.) **Llyn Tegid**, Bala, Wales' largest natural lake, has excellent windsurfing. Other adventures are detailed in *The Snowdon Peninsula: North Wales Activities* brochure, available in TICs and NPICs.

DOLGELLAU ☎01341

Set in a deep river valley, Dolgellau (dol-GECTH-lai) is a refuge from the formidable mountains above. Low clouds drift overhead, often shrouding the nearby peaks. The majestic views and extensive paths attract hikers of all skill levels to the town, whose stone and slate houses are hewn from local rock.

⌐ TRANSPORTATION. Buses stop in Eldon Sq. near the TIC, which details all local services in *Gwynedd Public Transport Maps and Timetables*. Arriva (☎0870 608 2608) bus #X94 (M-Sa 10 per day, Su 6 per day) heads to: Barmouth (20min.); Llangollen (1½hr.); Wrexham (2hr.). Bus #2 heads through the mountains to Bangor via Caernarfon and Porthmadog (2¾hr., Su only, 2 per day.). Buses #32 and X32 pass through Dolgellau on their way to Porthmadog, Machynlleth (40min.; M-Sa 10 per day, Su 2 per day; ₤2.80), and Aberystwyth (1¼hr., M-Sa 6 per day, Su 2 per day). Bus #28 goes to Machynlleth (1½hr., M-Sa 9 per day). **Rent bikes** at Greenstiles Cycles, Smithfield Rd. (☎423 332. ₤10 per half day; ₤15 per full day. Open M-Sa 9:15am-5pm, Su 10am-4pm. MC/V.)

🛈 PRACTICAL INFORMATION. The **Tourist Information Centre**, Eldon Sq., by the bus stop, books rooms for a ₤2 charge plus a 10% deposit. It doubles as a **Snowdonia National Park Information Centre**, with an exhibit on local mountains and trails. (☎422 888. Open July-Aug. daily 9:30am-5:30pm; Easter to May and Sept.-Oct. daily 9:30am-12:30pm and 1:30-5:30pm; Nov. to Easter Th-M 9:30am-12:30pm and 1-4:30pm.) Equip yourself with camping and hiking gear and Ordnance Survey maps (₤6.50-7.50) at **Cader Idris Outdoor Gear**, Eldon Sq., across from the bus stop. (☎422 195; www.cader-idris.co.uk. Open June-Sept. M-Sa

NORTH WALES

9am-5:30pm, Su 10am-4pm; Oct.-May M-Sa 9am-5:30pm.) Other services include: HSBC **bank**, Eldon Sq. (☎525 400; open M-F 9:30am-4:30pm); a **launderette**, Smithfield St., across from Aber Cottage Tea Room (wash £2.20-3.40, dry £1; no soap; open M and W-Su 9am-7pm; last wash 6:30pm); **police**, Old Barmouth Rd. (☎0845 607 1002); Dolgellau and Barmouth District **hospital**, off Penbrynglas (☎422 479); Rowland's **pharmacy**, 3 Eldon Row near the TIC, (☎422 404; open M-Sa 9am-5:30pm); free **Internet access** at the library, Bala Rd. (☎422 771; open M and F 10am-7pm, Tu and Th 10am-5pm, W 10am-1pm, and Sa 10am-noon); and the **post office**, inside Spar at Plas yn Dre St. (☎422 466; open M-F 9am-5:30pm, Sa 9am-12:30pm). **Post Code:** LL40 1AD.

⊓⊏ ACCOMMODATIONS AND FOOD. The **YHA Kings** (p. 494) is 4 mi. away. In Dolgellau itself, lodging is scarce and expensive, starting around £22-25. The refurbished (and 350-year-old) **Aber Cottage ❸**, on Smithfield St. near the bridge, has pristine and elegant bedrooms. (☎422 460. Breakfast included; al fresco dining available. Singles £35; doubles £55. Cash only.) Two **B&Bs** with lower rates and spectacular views of the Idris range cling to the hills just north of town. **Aros-fyr ❷**, Pen y Cefn, is a working farm with bright, airy rooms. From the bus stop, cross Smithfield St. bridge, turn left, then right at the school, and follow the steep road until a sign on the right directs you past farm sheds. (☎422 355. Singles £20. Cash only.) Comfortable **Dwy Olwyn ❸** keeps horses and serves big breakfasts. Cross the Smithfield St. bridge, turn right, then left onto the unmarked road after the Somerfield, and follow the signs 5min. uphill. (☎422 822; www.dwyolwyn.co.uk. Singles £25; doubles £40. Cash only.) **Camping** is available at the deluxe **Tanyfron Caravan and Camping Park ❶**, a 10min. walk south on Arron Rd. onto the A470. (☎422 638. From £11 per tent; car £2 extra. Electricity £2. Free showers. Cash only.)

Spar **market** is on Plas yn Dre St. (☎422 200. Open daily 8am-10pm.) Rustic charm and Welsh home cooking await at the **Aber Cottage Tea Room ❷**, Smithfield St., part of the B&B. Patrons unwind in plush chairs and sample a variety of gourmet soups (from £3.50) and pastries. (Open daily 10am-5pm. Cash only.) **Popty'r Dref ❶** bakery and delicatessen, Upper Smithfield St., just off Eldon Sq., tempts passers-by with bready aromas and foodstuffs packed to the ceiling. Try the homemade honey buns. (☎422 507. Pastries £1-2. Open M-F 8am-5pm, Sa 8am-4pm. Cash only.) Duck under the low portal at **Y Sospan ❷**, Queen's Sq., behind the TIC, for sandwiches (from £2.50) and minty lamb steak (£9.15). The venue turns into an upscale bistro and wine bar in the evening. (☎423 174. Open M-F 9am-9pm, Sa-Su 9am-9:30pm. AmEx/MC/V.)

◙ SIGHTS. The famous **Precipice Walk** (4 mi., 2hr.) follows an easy path revealing vistas of Mawddach Estuary and the huge Idris range. Once restricted to the well-to-do guests of the nearby Caeynwch estate, the **Torrent Walk** (2½ mi., 1½hr.) circles along an ancient Roman pathway through woodlands and past waterfalls. Walks after heavy rains are graced with gushing torrents. The **Llyn Cau, Cader Idris and Tal-y-Llyn Walk** (7 mi., 5½hr.) is a strenuous excursion that should only be attempted in good weather. The hard work pays off in panoramas of a glacial lake and native birds from 2617 ft. Mynydd Pencoed. Pick up pamphlets (40p) or *Local Walks Around Dolgellau* (£4) at the TIC; the latter contains 15 hikes for all levels. The entrances to most of the footpaths are not in the town itself; ask directions at the TIC.

CADER IDRIS

Visitors who descend into nearby cities from the misty overpasses near Cader Idris will appreciate its allure. This dark mountain offers spectacular trails and desolate, stunning terrain. This portion of Snowdonia offers scenic walks that are less crowded than those of Mt. Snowdon. All paths cross privately owned farm and grazing land; be courteous and leave all gates as you found them. The 5 mi. pony track from **Llanfihangel y Pennant** is the longest but easiest path to the summit. After a relatively level section, the path climbs steadily through wind-sculpted rocks overlooking the Mawddach estuary and continues over the mountain. The trail from Tŷ Nant is not particularly strenuous and begins at **Tŷ Nant farm**, 3 mi. from Dolgellau. As you ascend, the environs change from hazels and hawthorns to the craggy precipice. Avoid Fox's Path, which ascends Idris from the same place: many accidents occur on its steep scree slope. The **Minffordd Path** (about 3 mi.) is the shortest but steepest ascent. On its way to the summit, it crosses an 8000-year-old oak wood and rises above the lake of **Llyn Cau**, tracing boulders and cairns left by glaciers. Watch out for the Cwn Annwn (Hounds of the Underworld), said to fly around the range's peaks. Allow 5hr. for any of these walks. Booklets (40p) charting each are available at the NPIC. For longer treks, the Ordnance Survey Outdoor Leisure #23 or Landranger #124 map (£6.50-7.50) is essential.

The 9000-acre **Coed-Y-Brenin Forest Park** covers the peaks and valleys around the Mawddach and Eden rivers and is known for its world-class mountain biking trails. Roaming hikers are rewarded with fallow deer sightings and a landscape of mosses, ferns, and rare lichen. The **Karrimor Mountain Bike Trail** features a number of steep climbs and sweeping descents as it traverses 61 mi. of forest roads. The **Red Bull Mountain Biking Trail** labels its rough roads and tumble tracks with daunting names like "Rocky Horror Show" and "Root of all Evil"—challenges meant for experienced riders only. The forest also has trails reserved for hikers and is best entered 7 mi. north of Dolgellau off the A470, near the **Coed-Y-Brenin Visitor Centre**. (☎440 666. Open Apr.-Oct. daily 9am-5pm; Nov.-Mar. Sa-Su 10am-5pm.) Mountaineers and sportsmen will find the town of **Dolgellau** (p. 495) and the **YHA Corris** (p. 482) convenient spots to rest.

HARLECH   ☎01766

Reputedly from the Welsh "harddlech," meaning "beautiful slope," Harlech's name says it all. The steep paved ascent rises above sand dunes and below green ridges, passes the tea rooms and inns of High Street (Stryd Fawr) before leading to Harlech's castle, perched over the sea. From the castle, clear days allow views of Snowdonia's serrated skyline and Llŷn's town lights at dusk.

▐ TRANSPORTATION. Harlech lies midway on the Cambrian Coaster line. The uphill walk to town from the unstaffed train station is a challenge; follow the signs until you arrive at a striking sculpture of "Two Kings" from the Mabinogion. **Trains** (08457 484 950) arrive from Machynlleth (1¼-1½hr.; M-Sa 7 per day, Su 3 per day; £6.20); Porthmadog (20min.; M-F 9 per day, Sa 7 per day, Su 3 per day); Pwllheli (45min.; M-F 9 per day, Sa 7 per day, Su 3 per day); and other towns on the Llŷn Peninsula. The **Cambrian Coaster Day Ranger** (£6.60, children £3.30, families £13.20) allows unlimited travel on the Coaster line for a day and is barely more than the single fare from Machynlleth. Arriva Cymru (☎0870 608

2608) **bus** #38 links Harlech to southern Barmouth (M-Sa 11 per day £2.15) and northern Blaenau Ffestiniog (M-Sa 9 per day), stopping at the carpark on Stryd Fawr and the train station.

ORIENTATION AND PRACTICAL INFORMATION. The castle opens out onto **Twtil;** slightly uphill is the town's major street, **Stryd Fawr** (often called High St.). Near the castle, the **Tourist Information Centre,** Stryd Fawr, doubles as a **National Park Information Centre.** The staff stocks hiking pamphlets and Ordnance Survey maps (£6.50-7.50), and books accommodations for a £2 charge plus a 10% deposit. (☎780 658. Open Easter to Oct. daily 9:30am-12:30pm and 1:30-5:30pm.) Other services include: HSBC **bank,** Stryd Fawr (open M-F 9:30-11:30am); **police** (☎01492 517 171); free **Internet access** at the library, which is up the hill on Stryd Fawr past the Spar (☎780 565; open M and F 4:30-7pm, W 10am-1pm); and the **post office,** Stryd Fawr (☎780 231; open M-Tu and Th-F 9:30am-5:30pm, W 9am-12:30pm, Sa 9am-5pm). **Post Code:** LL46 2YA.

ACCOMMODATIONS AND FOOD. Revel in spacious rooms at ⚑**Arundel ❷,** Stryd Fawr, where breakfast is served in a conservatory with views of the ocean and castle. Walk past the TIC and take a right before the Yr Ogof Bistro. The proprietor will happily pick you up if the climb from the train station isn't appealing. (☎780 637. Singles £16. Cash only.) The closest hostel is **YHA Llanbedr ❶,** originally built as a country guest house and located 4 mi. south of town. Take the train to the Llanbedr stop (10min.) or ride bus #38 and ask to be let off at the hostel. (☎0870 770 5926. Open Apr.-Nov. Dorms £11, under 18 £9.50. MC/V.) The **Byrdir Guest House ❷,** a former hotel on Stryd Fawr near the bus stop, offers a ground floor bar and comfortable rooms with TVs and washbasins. (☎780 316. Singles from £19.50. Cash only.) **Camp** at **Min-y-Don Park ❶,** Beach Rd., between the train station and the beach. (☎780 286. Laundry £1. Open Mar.-Oct. £10-12 per tent. Free showers. Cash only.)

Spar **market** is near the edge of Stryd Fawr's main drag, right before the road curves. (☎780 592. Open daily 8am-8pm.) At ⚑**Plâs Cafe ❷,** guests linger over afternoon cream teas (£3.50) and sunset dinners (from £8) while enjoying sweeping ocean views. (☎780 204. Open daily Mar.-Oct. 10am-8:30pm; Nov.-Feb. 10am-5:30pm. AmEx/MC/V.) **Yr Ogof Bistro ❸,** Stryd Fawr, has fantastic meat dishes made with lamb and cattle raised on the proprietor's farm. Try the "Boozy Pork" (£10) or go for more traditional £12 steaks. (☎780 888. Open M-Sa 6:30-9pm; opens earlier in summer. MC/V.) The bar at the **Lion Hotel ❷,** off Stryd Fawr above the castle, provides pints in this virtually publess town. Bar snacks are 70p to £4, while meals run £6-10. (☎780 731. Open M-F noon-11pm, Sa 11am-11pm, Su noon-10:30pm. Food served until 8:30pm. MC/V.)

SIGHTS AND ENTERTAINMENT. Harlech Castle's walls, once lapped by the now receded oceans, seem to spring naturally from their craggy perch. One of the "iron ring" fortresses built by Edward I to watch over the spirited Welsh troublemakers, it still affords awesome views of forests, coastlines, and mountains, along with a golf course and caravan parks. Spiral scaffolding and rounded windows hint at Harlech's Savoy-inspired design, and rebel Owain Glyndwr's brief occupancy and parliament here suggest a Welsh mettle. (☎780 552. Open June-Sept. daily 9:30am-6pm; Apr.-May and Oct. daily 9:30am-5pm; Nov.-Mar. M-Sa 9:30am-4pm, Su 11am-4pm. Last admission 30min. before close. £3, concessions £2.50, families £8.50. Audio guides £1.) Public **footpaths** run from Harlech's grassy dunes to the forested hilltops above the town; get recommendations and directions at the TIC. **Theatr Ardudwy** (☎780 667; www.theatrardudwy.co.uk), on the A496, hosts a variety of performances, including operas, comedies, concerts of every sort, and even dancing Buddhist monks (tickets £7-20). Sun worshippers will appreciate the white sand **beach,** a 20min. walk from town. Walk down the road by the Castle, turn right on the A496, and then turn left through the golf course, following the signs.

MOUNT SNOWDON AND VICINITY ☎01286

By far the most popular destination in the park, **Mount Snowdon** is the highest peak in both England and Wales, at 3560 ft. The Welsh name for the peak, Yr Wyddfa (ur-WITH-va; "burial place") comes from a legend that Rhita Gawr, a giant cloaked with the beards of the kings he slaughtered, is buried here. Over half a million hikers tread the mountain each year. In fair weather, the steep green slopes and shimmering lakes tucked beneath the mountain's ragged cliffs are stunning. Future hikes were in peril in 1998 when a plot of land that included Snowdon's summit was put up for sale, but celebrated Welsh actor Sir Anthony Hopkins sprang to the rescue, contributing a vast sum to the National Trust to save the pristine peak. Park officers request that hikers stick to the six well-marked trails to avoid damage to Snowdon's ecosystem. The most popular route is the **Llanberis Path** (5 mi.), which begins right outside of Llanberis. It is the longest and easiest of the trails, but other paths, like the **Miner's Track,** offer far superior views and criss-cross numerous valleys. **The Pyg Track,** which begins in nearby Pen-y-Pass, is a less-frequented gem. Start climbing early in the day to avoid crowds. Dress warmly on misty days. Trains run up to the summit on the **Snowdon Mountain Railway** (p. 499); a mail box at the top allows you to send postcards from above it all with a special stamp.

Though Mt. Snowdon is the main attraction in the northern part of the park, experienced climbers cart pick-axes and ropes to the **Ogwen Valley.** There, climbs to **Devil's Kitchen** (Twll Du), the **Glyders** (Glyder Fawr and Glyder Fach), and **Tryfan** all begin from **Llyn Ogwen.** Tryfan's unusual peak has been immortalized in countless National Park posters. Though its elevation has been set at 3010 ft., nobody's quite sure which of two adjacent rocks (nicknamed Adam and Eve) is the summit. No trip to the top is complete without performing the famed "jump" (about 3 ft.) between the two crags. Climbers should pick up the appropriate Ordnance Survey maps and get advice on equipment at **Joe Brown's Store** (p. 499). Horseback riding is available at the **Dolbadarn Trekking Centre,** High St., Llanberis. (☎870 277; www.dolbadarnhotel.co.uk. £15 per hr.)

LLANBERIS ☎01286

Beyond its mountain-town veneer, Llanberis offers an exciting atmosphere, blending youthful energy, local pride, and rugged outdoorsmanship. The town's perpetually shifting community of climbers, cyclists, and hikers keeps it lively seven days a week (and most nights as well), while its lake and imposing mountain ranges make for numerous forays for the outdoor adventurers.

🖃🔢 TRANSPORTATION AND PRACTICAL INFORMATION. Situated on the western edge of the park, Llanberis is a short ride from Caernarfon on the A4086. Catch KMP (☎870 880) **bus** #88 from Caernarfon (25min.; £1.50, round-trip £2; M-Sa 1-2 per hr., Su every hr. until 7:20pm). KMP #85/86 arrives frequently from Bangor (35-50min.; M-Sa 1-2 per hr., Su 7 per day).

The **Tourist Information Centre,** 41b High St., doles out hiking tips and books beds for a £2 charge plus a 10% deposit. It stocks a number of brochures on hikes in Snowdonia, including pamphlets (40p) on the six routes up Mt. Snowdon. (☎870 765. Open Easter to Oct. daily 9:30am-5pm; Nov. to Easter M and F-Su 11am-4pm.) Pick up gear, maps, coffee, and advice at **Joe Brown's Store,** Menai

ASS THE ELDERBERRY

Celtic winemaking is unique in hat no grapes are used—only other fruits, berries, and honey. Authentic Celtic wines are rare, and the best can be found in Llanberis. Deryl Jones is a third-generation winemaker.

G: How many wines do you make?

A: About 30.

G: Do you have a favorite?

A: Parsnip, because it's so unusual. It's got this earthy pea-chiness that's very fascinating to me, but it's the least popular. I thoroughly enjoy it.

G: What sort of training do you have?

A: None, it's just something that's been handed down for generations and it's also just experimenting. It's fun. One time one comes out sweet, the next time sharper.

G: Where does all of your fruit and honey come from?

A: We have our own bees, and they're all local berries. One is illegal to pick, but I can't tell you which one. It makes an interesting wine, obviously.

G: How do you avoid bee stings?

A: I just keep away from them. I'm allergic.

G: What makes Celtic wine so good?

A: The excitement of something totally different. We try to make

Hall, High St. (☎870 327. Open in summer M-Sa 9am-6pm, Su 9am-5pm; in winter M-Sa 9am-5:30pm, Su 9am-5pm.) Other services include: HSBC **bank,** 29 High St. (open M and W 9:30am-11:30pm, Tu and Th-F 1:30-3:30pm) and the bankless Barclays ATM, at the entrance to Electric Mountain on the A4086; Rowlands **pharmacy,** High St. (☎870 264. Open M-F 9am-1pm and 2pm-5:30pm, Sa 9am-1pm.); **Internet access** at Pete's Eats (p. 500) and at Castle Gift Shop, High St. (☎870 379; 5p per min., min. £1; open daily 7am-6pm); and the **post office,** 36 High St. (☎870 201; open M-Tu and Th-F 9am-5:30pm, W and Sa 9am-7:30pm). **Post Code:** LL55 4EU.

⌂◘ ACCOMMODATIONS AND FOOD. During summer weekends, this tiny town is booked full, so book ahead. The pleasant outskirts of Llanberis harbor tiny **▨Snowdon Cottage ❸.** From the bus station, walk up the hill past the railway station and the Victoria Hotel. The Cottage is around the bend on your right. With a castle-view garden, sweet-smelling and cozy rooms, an "Egyptian" bathroom, a welcoming hearth, and a gracious host, staying in may be preferable to the outdoors. (☎872 015. £22 per person. Discounts for multiple nights. Cash only.) Plenty of sheep and cows keep hostelers company at the **YHA Llanberis** (p. 494), while the **Heights Hotel ❷,** 74 High St., draws a youthful clientele with 21 bunk beds packed into three co-ed dorms. On weekends, half the town crowds into its two ground-floor bars, glass-walled "conservatory" (smoking lounge), and pool room. (☎871 179. Dorms £14, with breakfast £19; doubles £50; 3- to 6-person rooms £22.50 per person. AmEx/MC/V.) **Pete's Eats** (see below) has dorm-style accommodations from £12. Enjoy comfortable, mostly ensuite rooms at the grand **Plas Coch Guest House ❸,** High St. (☎872 122; www.plas-coch.co.uk. Singles from £35; doubles £50-62. Cash only.)

Spar **market** is at the corner of High St. and Capel Goch Rd. (Open M-Sa 7am-11pm, Su 7am-10:30pm.) **Snowdon Honey Farm ❶,** High St., sells a huge selection of its own meads and Celtic wines, as well as honey, tea, sandwiches, cakes, and ice cream. Samples are given with much cheer. (☎870 218. Open daily 7am-6pm. Cash only.) Lively **Pete's Eats ❶,** 40 High St., opposite the TIC, is the place to refuel after a day outdoors. Sample a walnut cheeseburger (£2.40) or chili (£5.20) with mugs of tea (£1) as you enjoy the culture collision of high chair-bound tots and grungy-hip hikers. (☎870 117. Internet access 5p per min.; 50p min. Open daily July-Aug. 8am-9pm; Nov.-June 8am-8pm. MC/V.)

☉ SIGHTS. Llanberis brims with attractions. Most lie near the fork where the A4086 meets High St. Part self-promotion, part journey to the center of the earth, **Electric Mountain** takes visitors on an informative (and occasionally exciting) underground tour of the Dinorwig power station. Located deep in the heart of a mountain formerly quarried for slate, the station occupies the largest man-made cavern in Europe—St. Paul's Cathedral could fit inside. (☎870 636. Open June-Aug. daily 9:30am-5:30pm; Apr.-May and Sept.-Oct. daily 10:30am-4:30pm; Nov.-Mar. W-Su 10:40am-4:30pm. £6.50, concessions £4.75, families £16.) The immensely popular and pricey **Snowdon Mountain Railway** has been letting visitors "climb" Snowdon's summit since 1896, winding along narrow tracks that start from its base station on the A4086. The 2½hr. round-trip allows 30min. at the peak, but one-way tickets are available for those who would like to hike up or down. (☎08704 580 033; www.snowdonrailway.co.uk. Runs daily Mar. to early Nov. 9am-5pm; Mar.-May trains stop half-way up. Weather permitting. Single £14, children £11; round-trip £20/14.)

In nearby **Parc Padarn,** accessed by a footpath next to the bus stop on the A4086, the **Welsh Slate Museum** explores the history and state of the mining industry with a 3D film, impressively recreated miners' dwellings from various eras, and live displays of slate splitting and finishing. Don't miss the largest waterwheel in Britain. (☎870 630; www.nmgw.ac.uk. Open Easter to Oct. daily 10am-5pm; Nov. to Easter M-F and Su 10am-4pm. Last admission 1hr. before close. Free.) A short uphill walk takes you to the **Quarry Hospital Visitor Centre.** This old hospital, built by the owner of the mines to deal with health issues "privately," now houses a morbidly fascinating array of factoids, sinister medical implements, and a morgue with slate tables. (☎870 892. Open Apr. to early Sept. daily 11am-5pm. £1.) The park is also home to the **Llanberis Lake Railway,** which runs a scenic route from Gilfach Ddu station at Llanberis through the woods along the lake. (☎870 549; www.lake-railway.co.uk. 40min. round-trip. Open Apr.-June and Sept.-Oct. M-F and Su; July-Aug. daily. £6, children £4.) The **Woodland and Wildlife Centre,** at the halfway point, is a nice picnic spot.

Follow the road into the park until a footbridge to the right leads to **Dolbadarn Castle,** where Prince Llywelyn of North Wales is said to have imprisoned his brother for 23 years. Only a single, ragged tower remains. The area affords a view of the Lady of

one for each month or time of the year. So, you get something like rhubarb which is refreshing for summer. It's a progression. Gooseberry is lovely in front of the fire in winter; it's very aromatic. And dandelion can go all over the place.

LG: No grapes? And it's still wine?
A: The Romans were the first to bring the grapes. This argument still goes on today. I don't care what people think. My argument is to taste it and enjoy it. I want to get rid of this snobbish side of wine.

LG: What's the biggest challenge?
A: Keeping sales to a manageable level. To keep on enjoying life. I've met you today. Life is good.

LG: Have you ever had anyone come in and try to sample each wine?
A: Oh yes! There's one! She was in here one September and she sat on a stool and started drinking from the beginning of the row of bottles. Once she got about halfway through she started entertaining everyone.

LG: Any secrets to making a good Celtic wine?
A: It would fail to be a secret! It's all a secret. Come here and find out for yourself.

Snowdon, a rock formation that resembles Elizabeth II. (Always open. Free.) For an eye-level view of the waterfall **Ceunant Mawr,** follow the well-marked footpath from Victoria Terr. by the Victoria Hotel (¾ mi.).

CAERNARFON ☎ 01286

Occupied since pre-Roman times and once the center of English government in northern Wales, Caernarfon has witnessed countless struggles for regional political control. It was originally built for English settlers, a legacy that remains visible in a magnificent castle (one of many) built by Edward I. The Welsh have always been eager to claim it for themselves, by violence if necessary. During a 1294 tax revolt, they managed to break in, sack the town, and massacre its English inhabitants. Though its streets are lined with modern shops and cafes, Caernarfon embraces its traditional Welsh character; visitors can hear the town's own dialect used in its streets and pubs. Caernarfon's preserved fortress is one of the most spectacular of Edward I's ring of castles.

▐ TRANSPORTATION. The nearest train station is in Bangor (p. 504), though numerous **buses** pass through Caernarfon on their way north to Bangor and Anglesey. The central stop is on Penllyn in the city center. Arriva Cymru (☎ 0870 608 2608) buses #5 and 5X come from Conwy and Llandudno via Bangor (1¾hr. from Llandudno; M-Sa 3 per hr., Su every hr.). Express Motors (☎ 881 108) bus #1 arrives from Porthmadog (45-60min., M-Sa every hr., £2.60) as does Arriva bus #32 (Su 6 per day). Clynnog & Trefor (☎ 660 208) and Berwyn (☎ 660 315) run bus #12 from Pwllheli (45min.; M-Sa every hr., Su 3 per day). KMP (☎ 870 880) bus #88 runs from Llanberis (25min.; M-Sa 1-2 per hr., Su every hr. until 6:50pm). Arriva's TrawsCambria bus #701 arrives daily from Cardiff (7½hr.). National Express (☎ 08705 808 080) bus #545 arrives from London via Chester (9hr., every day, £26) or with a change in Birmingham (9½hr., every day, £26). A **Gwynedd Red Rover ticket** provides unlimited bus travel in the county for one day (£5, children £2.45). *Gwynedd Public Transport Maps and Timetables* gives comprehensive info on bus and train routes. Castle Sq. shelters a **taxi** stand or try Tacsi Aindows (☎ 677 391).

◨ ◪ ORIENTATION AND PRACTICAL INFORMATION. The heart of Caernarfon lies within and just outside the town walls, though the city spreads far beyond. From the castle entrance, the TIC is across **Castle Ditch Road,** which runs past **Castle Square** in one direction and down to the waterfront Promenade in the other. **Castle Street** intersects Castle Ditch Rd. at the castle entrance and leads to **High Street. Bridge Street** runs north from Castle Square and turns into the heavily trafficked **Bangor Street.**

The **Tourist Information Centre,** Castle St., facing the castle entrance, stocks the free *Visitor's Guide to Caernarfon* and books accommodations for a £2 charge plus a 10% deposit. (☎ 672 232. Open Apr.-Oct. daily 9:30am-5:30pm; Nov.-Mar. M-Sa 10am-4:30pm.) Get **camping supplies** at 14th Peak, 9 Palace St. (☎ 675 124. 10% student discount. Open M-Sa 9am-5:30pm, Su 1-4pm.) Other services include: **banks** in Castle Sq. and down Bridge St.; a **launderette,** Skinner St., off Bridge St. (☎ 678 395; open M-Th 9am-6pm, F-Sa 9am-5:30pm, Su 11am-5:30pm; last wash 1hr. before close; £5); **police,** Maesincla Ln. (☎ 673 333, ext. 5242); **Internet access** at the library, at the corner of Bangor St. and Lon Pafiliwn (☎ 675 944; free; open M-Tu and Th-F 10am-7pm, W 10am-1pm, Sa 9am-1pm) or at the Dylan Thomas Internet Café, 4 Bangor St. (☎ 678 777; £3 per hr.; wireless available; open M-Sa 9am-6pm; cash only); a **pharmacy,** 1A Castle

Sq. (☎672 352; open M-Sa 8:30am-6:30pm, Su 11:30am-2pm); and the **post office** with a bureau de change, Castle Sq. (☎08457 223 344; open M-F 9am-5:30pm, Sa 9am-12:30pm). **Post Code:** LL55 2ND.

⌂ ACCOMMODATIONS. Rooms abound, but cheap ones don't. **⧉Totter's Hostel ❷,** 2 High St. provides spacious rooms with comfortable wooden bunks; the basement is equipped with a full kitchen, a hand-crafted banquet table, and medieval stone arches. (☎672 963; www.applemaps.co.uk/totters. Dorms £13. MC/V.) **B&Bs** (£23-25) line **Church Street** inside the old town wall; those on **St. David's Road,** a 10min. walk from the castle and uphill off the Bangor St. roundabout, are sometimes cheaper. **Tegfan ❸,** 4 Church St., offers an excellent location with clean rooms and TVs. (☎673 703. £22 per person. Cash only.) At **Bryn Hyfryd ❸,** St. David's Rd., travelers can sink into flowery bedspreads; one room sports a sun deck, another coast views, and all bath facilities. (☎673 840. Singles £27.50; doubles £55; family rooms £70. Cash only.) **Marianfa ❸,** St. David's Rd., has a variety of spacious ensuite rooms with stunning views of the Menai. Ask about motorbike and sight-seeing packages. (☎674 815; www.ukworld.net/marianfa. Singles £25; doubles £50. Cash only.) **Camp** at **Cadnant Valley ❶,** Cwm Cadnant Rd. (☎673 196; www.cwmcadnantvalley.co.uk. 2-person tent £6-8.50, with car £8-12, more in summer. Showers and laundry. MC/V.)

◨⊠ FOOD AND PUBS. A Safeway **supermarket** sits on North Road (A487). Take Bangor St. past the roundabout. (Open M-Th 8:30am-10pm, F 8am-10pm, Sa 8am-8pm, Su 10am-4pm.) Spar, 29-31 Castle Sq. stocks a much smaller selection closer to the center of town. (☎676 805. Open M-Sa 7am-11pm, Su 7am-10:30pm.) On Saturdays and some Mondays, a **market** takes over Castle Sq. (Open 9am-4pm.) **Hole-in-the-Wall Street** is a narrow alleyway known for its dense collection of eateries. **Stones Bistro ❸,** 4 Hole-in-the-Wall St., near Eastgate, has candlelit tables and local art adorning its walls. The Welsh lamb (£13) is served with your choice of a mint, honey, yogurt, pepper, or tomato-garlic sauce. (☎671 152. Open Tu-Sa 6-11pm. AmEx/MC/V.) The stout wooden doors of the **Anglesey Arms ❶** open onto the Promenade just below the castle. Relax outdoors with a pint as the sun dips into the shimmering Menai. (☎672 158. Live entertainment F. Open M-Sa 11am-11pm, Su noon-10:30pm. MC/V.) Younger crowds flock to **Cofi Roc,** on Castle Sq., for tribute bands every Friday. (☎673 100; www.cofiroc.com. Open M-Tu and Th 9:30am-5pm, W 9:30am-midnight, F 9:30am-1am, Sa 9:30am-2am, and Su 9pm-12am. MC/V.) Relax within the stone walls of **Bwyty Oyof Y Odraig's (The Dragon's Cave) ❸,** 26 Hole-in-the-Wall St., which serves up innovative Welsh fare. A variety of meat, vegetarian, and fish options, such as salmon and spinach encased in a puff pastry (£11), await in the cozy dining room. (☎677 322. Open M and W-Su 6pm-late. MC/V.)

◨⊡ SIGHTS AND ENTERTAINMENT. Built by Edward I to resemble Roman battlements, **⧉Caernarfon Castle** has been called by one resentful Welshman a "magnificent badge of our subjection." Its eagle-crowned turrets, colorfully banded stones, and polygonal towers cost Edward the equivalent of the Crown's annual budget and nearly 17% of his skilled labor force. Its walls withstood a rebel siege in 1404 with only 28 defenders. Summer sees a variety of performances, including scenes from the Welsh epic *The Mabinogi*. Wisecracking docents run tours every hour for £1.50, and a free 20min. video recounts the castle's history every 30min. The **regimental museum** of the Royal Welsh Fusiliers, inside the castle, is huge and worthwhile. Medals, uniforms, and helmets accompany rich historical exhibits. Don't miss the Regimental "Goat Major" (each brigade was required to have one), whose gilded horns and

NORTH WALES

headplate have inspired generations of Fusiliers. (☎677 617. Open June-Sept. daily 9:30am-6pm; Apr.-May and Oct. daily 9:30am-5pm; Nov.-Mar. M-Sa 9:30am-4pm, Su 11am-4pm. £4.75, concessions £3.75, families £13.25.) Most of Caernarfon's 13th-century **town wall** survives, and a stretch between Church St. and Northgate St. is open for climbing during the same hours as the castle.

The remains of a Celtic settlement scatter atop **Twt Hill,** alongside the Bangor St. roundabout; the jutting peak offers an excellent overlook above town and castle. For views of Menai Strait and its surroundings, call **Menai Strait Pleasure Cruises** (☎672 772), which runs 40min. from May to October (11:30am-4:30pm, weather and tides permitting; £4.50, children £3). Hilltop **Segontium Roman Fort** was once the center for military activity in North Wales. Plundered by the builders of Caernarfon Castle, the fort is now reduced to rubble, though a museum houses a display of archaeological excavations. From Castle Sq., follow signs uphill along Ffordd Cwstenin. (☎675 625; www.segontium.org.uk. Museum open Tu-Su 12:30-4:00pm, grounds open daily 10am-4:30pm. Free.)

Six miles south of Caernarfon, peaceful **Parc Glynllifon** is bordered by the remains of a log fence built to "keep the peasants out and the pheasants in," but visitors are now welcome to wander the lawns and exotic trees. The 19th-century manor and ornate fountain in the forest make the grounds a great spot for a picnic. Take bus #12 (15min., every hr., £1.70 round-trip) south from Caernarfon to the Parc Glynllifon stop. (☎830 222. Open daily 9am-5pm. £3, children £1, families £6.) **K2,** St. Helen's Rd., is a huge nightclub off Castle St.; descend the stairs next to the post office. (☎673 100. No sportswear or trainers. Cover £2-6. Open F-Sa 10pm-1:30am.) **Medi,** Palace St., is a diverse venue with a cocktail bar, disco, and lounge on three floors. (☎674 383. No sportswear. £2 cover on Sa between 11:30pm and 12:30am. Open F-Sa 9am-2am, Su 9am-11pm. MC/V.)

BANGOR ☎01248

A stronghold of Welsh princes turned university town, Bangor seems neither regal nor academic, but rather a pleasant coastal hub, the most convenient base from which to explore the Isle of Anglesey. Bangor offers shopping and bars crammed until the early hours with University of Wales students.

▐ TRANSPORTATION. Bangor is the transport depot for the Isle of Anglesey to the west and Snowdonia to the southeast. The **train station** is on Holyhead Rd., at the end of Deiniol Rd. (Ticket office open in summer M-Sa 5:30am-6:30pm, Su 7:15am-6:30pm; in winter M-Sa 5:30am-6:30pm, Su 9am-6:30pm.) **Trains** (☎08457 484 950) arrive from: Chester (1¼hr., 1-2 per hr., £13); Holyhead (30min.; M-Sa 15 per day, Su 10 per day; £5.80); Llandudno Junction (20min.; M-Sa 1-2 per hr., Su 10 per day; £4.10). The **bus station** is on Garth Rd., downhill from the town clock. Arriva Cymru (☎08706 082 608) **bus** #4 arrives from Holyhead via Llangefni and Llanfair P.G. (1¼-1½hr., M-Sa 2 per hr., £3.20), while on Sunday #44 makes the trip six times. Buses #53, 57, and 58 come from Beaumaris (30min.; M-Sa 2-3 per hr., Su 8 per day; £2.10). Arriva buses #5, 5A, 5B, and 5X journey from Caernarfon (25min.; M-Sa every 10-20min., Su every hr.; £1.10); #5 and 5X continue east to Conwy (40min.; M-Sa 2-3 per hr., Su every hr.; £1.60) and Llandudno (1hr.; M-Sa 2-3 per hr., Su every hr.; £1.90). Transfer at Caernarfon for the Llŷn Peninsula, including Pwllheli and Porthmadog. National Express (☎08705 808 080) buses come from London (8½hr., 1 per day, £26.50). For **taxis,** call Ace Taxi (☎351 324) or Chubb's Cabs (☎353 535; 24hr.).

⚡️❼ ORIENTATION AND PRACTICAL INFORMATION. Bangor's age-old street plan and unmarked roads might leave visitors vulnerable to confusion, but the essential corridor is bounded by **Deiniol Road** and **High Street,** which run parallel to each other and sandwich the city. **Garth Road** starts from the town clock on High St. and winds past the bus station, merging with Deiniol Rd. **Holyhead Road** begins its winding ascent at the train station. The **University of Wales at Bangor** straddles both sides of **College Road.**

The **Tourist Information Centre,** Town Hall, Deiniol Rd., by the bus station, books rooms for a £2 charge plus a 10% deposit. (☎352 786. Open May-Sept. M, W, and F 9:30am-4pm; Tu, Th, and Sa 9:30am-5pm.) Other services include: **banks** on High St. near the clocktower; **police** (☎370 333), behind the Town Hall on Deiniol Rd.; the **hospital** (☎384 384), Penthosgarnedd; a **pharmacy,** 276 High St. (☎362 822; open M-Sa 9am-5:30pm); **Internet access** free at the library, across from the TIC (☎353 479; open M-Tu and Th-F 9:30am-7pm, W and Sa 9:30am-1pm); and the **post office,** 60 Deiniol Rd., with a bureau de change (☎377 301; open M-F 9am-5:30pm, Sa 9am-12:30pm). **Post Code:** LL57 1AA.

🛏🍴 ACCOMMODATIONS AND FOOD. Finding a room in Bangor during graduation festivities (the second week of July) is difficult; book months ahead. The **YHA Bangor ❷,** Tan-y-Bryn, is half a mile from the town center. Follow High St. to the water and turn right onto the A5122 (Beach Rd.), then right at the sign. Buses #5 and 5X (to Llandudno; 2 per hr.) pass the hostel; ask to be let off. This 19th-century country estate on the former grounds of Penrhyn Castle once housed Vivien Leigh and Sir Laurence Olivier. (☎353 516. Foosball and laundry. Internet access 7p per min. Open Apr.-Sept. daily; Oct. and Mar. Tu-Sa; Nov. and Jan.-Feb. F-Sa. Dorms £13, under 18 £8.50. MC/V.) **B&B** options (from £17) in Bangor are solid if not particularly exciting; the most agreeable occupy the townhouses on **Garth Road** and its extensions. **Mrs. S. Roberts ❷,** 32 Glynne Rd., between Garth Rd. and High St., has TVs and 13 choices for breakfast. (☎352 113. Singles £17. Cash only.) Comfortable **Dilfam ❷** is 10min. from the TIC down Garth Rd. (☎353 030. Singles £20; doubles £40, ensuite £46. Cash only.) **Dinas Farm ❶,** 3 mi. from Bangor on the banks of the River Ogwan, offers camping. Follow the A5 past Penrhyn Castle and turn left off the A5122. (☎364 227. Open Easter to Oct. £4 per person. Electricity £2. Cash only.)

High Street has a surprisingly varied selection of bakeries, pubs, and eateries, as well as a Kwik Save **supermarket.** (Open M-Sa 8am-10pm, Su 10am-4pm.) Vegetarian-friendly **Herbs ❷,** 162 High St., has a salad bar (£3.25), cheap lunches (from £3), and interesting combinations like mackerel salad and cranberry with brie (£4) in a dining room decorated with mosaics and potted plants. (☎351 249; www.herbsrestaurant.co.uk. Open M-Th 10am-3pm, F-Sa 10am-9pm. AmEx/MC/V.) **Gerrards ❶,** 251 High St., at the clock tower, has bakery fare (2 lunches for £6) in a spacious venue. Don't miss the caramel fudge. (☎371 351. Open M-Sa 9am-5pm. Sandwiches served until 4:30pm. Cash only.) Choose between "East" or "West" on the menu at the ultra-mellow **Java Restaurant ❷,** up an alley off of High St., near Abbey St. Specials include a burger with salad, chips, and a pint for £7. (☎361 652. Open M-Tu 10am-6pm, W-Sa 10am-10pm. Hot food served 10am-3pm and 6-9pm. MC/V.)

📷🎭 SIGHTS AND ENTERTAINMENT. George Hay Dawkins-Pennant's 19th-century **Penrhyn Castle** pegs itself as the pinnacle of the short-lived neo-Norman school. The intricate main staircase is full of carved faces and took over 10 years to complete. The house is also home to the second-largest art collection in

NORTH WALES

Wales, after the National Gallery. Its slate-baron owner was on a mission to prove that the material has numerous uses; elaborate slate dressers, a slate billiard table, even a slate canopy bed testify to his quest. Walk up High St. toward the bay, then turn right on the A5122 and go north 1 mi., or catch bus #5 or 5X from town to the grounds entrance (10min.; M-Sa 2 per hr., Su every hr.; 60p); the castle is another mile. (☎353 084. Castle open daily July-Aug. 11am-5pm; late Mar. to June and Sept.-Oct. noon-5pm. Grounds open daily July-Aug. 10am-5:30pm; late Mar. to June and Sept.-Oct. 11am-5:30pm. Last admission 30min. before close. £7, children £3.50, families £17.50.)

St. Deiniol's Cathedral, Gwynedd Rd., off High St., has been the ecclesiastical center of this corner of Wales for 1400 years, yet it sits humbly amidst the commercial district. (☎353 983. Open M-F 8am-6pm, Sa 10am-1pm, Su for services.) The **Bangor Museum and Art Gallery,** also on Gwynedd Rd., houses an authentic man-trap—a snare-like contraption used as an anti-poaching device by insidious landowners—and a collection of regional crafts and artifacts. (☎353 368. Open Tu-F 12:30-4:30pm, Sa 10:30am-4:30pm. Free.) Watch tides ebb and flow at the long, onion-domed Victorian **pier** at the end of Garth Rd.

The modern **Theatre Gwynedd,** Deiniol Rd., at the base of the hill, houses a thriving troupe that performs in Welsh and English. (☎351 708. Box office open M-F 9:30am-5pm, Sa 10am-5pm, and before performances. Tickets £5-26; concessions available.) Bangor's students keep clubs buoyant, and many pubs along **High Street** pump up the volume on weekends. Dance your way to happiness (or buy it in liquid form) at **Bliss,** Dean St., off High St. (☎354 977. Cover £2-6. Open W 8:30pm-1am, Th-Sa 9pm-1am.) At cover-free **Joop's,** 358-360 High St., a younger crowd parties. (☎372 040. Open F-Sa 9pm-1am.)

ISLE OF ANGLESEY (YNYS MÔN)

Anglesey's old name, Môn mam Cymru ("Anglesey, mother of Wales"), indicates roots embedded deeply in its Celtic past; although you won't find spectacular castles or cathedrals, telltale druidic burial sites and tiny chapels dot the farmlands whose granaries have long supported Wales. Anglesey's sense of Welsh heritage, however, is hardly confined to this history: six of every ten islanders speak Welsh as a first language.

▐ TRANSPORTATION

Apart from major towns, Anglesey is difficult to explore without a car. Bangor, on the mainland, is the best hub for the island. **Trains** (☎08457 484 950) run on the North Wales line to Holyhead from Bangor (30min.; M-F 1-2 per hr., Su 13 per day; £5.80); some stop at Llanfair P.G. The main **bus** company is Arriva Cymru (☎0870 608 2608), whose buses radiate out to most of the island's major towns from the Menai and Britannia bridges. Smaller bus companies fill the gaps. Buses are reliable, albeit bumpy. Arriva bus #4 travels north from Bangor to Holyhead via Llanfair P.G. and Llangefni (1½hr., M-Sa 2 per hr., £3.20); on Sundays, #44 follows a similar route (6 per day). Buses #53, 57, and 58 hug the southeast coast from Bangor to Beaumaris (30min.; M-Sa 2 per hr., Su 8 per day; £2.10); some continue to Penmon (40min.; M-Sa 12 per day, Su 4 per day). Bus #62 goes to Amlwch, on the northern coast, from Bangor (1hr.; M-Sa 1-2 per hr., Su 5 per day; £1.75). Bus #42 from Bangor curves along the southwest coast to Aberffraw before continuing north to Llangefni (50min. to Aberffraw, 1¼hr. to Llangefni; M-Sa 9 per day, Su 3 per day). Lewis y Llan (☎01407 832 181) bus #61 travels from Amlwch to Holyhead (50min.; M-Sa 7 per day, Su 4 per day). Bus #32 shuttles north from Llangefni to Amlwch (40min.; M-Sa 8 per day, Su 4 per day). The **Gwynedd Red Rover** ticket (£4.95, children £2.45) covers a day's travel in Anglesey and Gwynedd. Pick up the free *Isle of Anglesey Public Transport Timetable* at TICs.

◉ SIGHTS

Various peoples have inhabited Anglesey since prehistoric times. Burial chambers, cairns, and other remains are scattered on Holyhead and along the eastern and western coasts. Most ancient monuments now lie on farmers' fields, so a map detailing exactly how to reach them is helpful. TICs sell Ordnance Survey Landranger Map #114 (1:50,000; £6) and the more detailed Explorer #262 and 263, each of which covers half of the island (1:25,000; £7). The *Guide to Ancient Monuments* (£3) details the history of various prehistoric relics, while the pamphlet *Rural Cycling on Anglesey* is a must for bikers (free at TICs). Bus drivers will drop you off as close to sights as possible if you let them know which sights you want to see.

PLAS NEWYDD. The 19th-century country home of the Marquess of Anglesey, 2 mi. south of Llanfair P.G., is filled with ornate decor. The 58 ft. Rex Whistler *trompe l'oeil* mural in the dining room is a whimsically imagined Mediterranean cityscape (with visions of Wales slipped in); it's the largest painted canvas in Britain. Don't miss the painter's trick: the mountains and footprints seem to move as you walk across the dining room. *(Take bus #42 from Bangor to the house 30min.; M-Sa 11 per day, Su 6 per day, or catch #4 to Llanfair P.G. 25min., M-Sa 2 per hr. ☎01248 714 795. House open mid-Mar. to Oct. M-W and Sa-Su noon-5pm. Garden open daily 11am-5:30pm. Last admission 4:30pm. £5, children £2.50. Garden only £3/1.50.)*

BRYN CELLI DDU. The most famous of Anglesey's remains, Bryn Celli Ddu (bryn kay-HLEE thee; "The Mound in the Dark Grove") is a burial chamber dating from the late Neolithic period. From the outside, this 4000-year-old construction looks like any old mound of earth in the middle of a sheep pasture, but a flashlight (bring your own) helps illuminate the etchings on the walls inside. The spiral rock outside of the chamber is a reproduction—the original is at the National Gallery in Cardiff. *(Bangor-Holyhead bus #4 stops at Llandaniel (M-Sa 14 per day); walk 1 mi. from there. Site is signposted off the A4080. Bus #42 to Plas Newydd also comes within 1 mi. of Bryn. Free.)*

LLANALLGO. Three sets of remains cluster near the town of Llanallgo. Follow the minor road (to the left of the Moelfre road) to the ancient **Lligwy Burial Chamber.** Between 15 and 30 people are entombed in this squat enclosure, covered with a 25-ton capstone. Farther on stand the ruins of the 12th-century chapel **Hen Capel Lligwy** and the **Din Lligwy Hut Group,** the remains of a fortified village lived in by the natives of Anglesey during Roman occupation. *(Arriva bus #62 hits Llanallgo on its Bangor-Cemaes route (40min.; M-Sa 1-2 per hr., Su 5 per day). Ask the driver to stop at the roundabout heading to Moelfre.)*

PENMON PRIORY. The late medieval priory of Penmon houses two ruined buildings and Europe's largest dovecote (a cylinder of nesting holes for pigeons). From the parking lot, a path leads to sixth-century **St. Seiriol's Well,** reputed to have healing qualities. *(Take Arriva Cymru bus #57 or 58 from Bangor or Beaumaris to Penmon (40min. from Bangor, 20min. from Beaumaris; M-Sa 11 per day, Su 5 per day) and follow the sign to Penmon Point; the priory is a 25min. walk on the same road. Free.)*

LLANFAIRPWLL...   ☎01248

Llanfairpwllgwyngyllgogerychwyrndrobwllllantysiliogogogoch (HLAN-vire-poohl-gwin-gihl—ah, never mind) prides itself on having the longest name of any village in the world. Give or take a controversial adjective, the name translates to: "Saint Mary's Church in the hollow of white hazel near the rapid whirlpool and the Church of Saint Tysillio near the red cave." Sights in both New Zealand and Thailand claim longer titles—at 92 and 163 letters, respectively—though these names (one of them packed with extensive reference to "the man with the big knees...known as land eater") bear the tell-tale signs of publicity-seeking embellishment. For more information on this otherwise nondescript village's claim to fame, visit the **Tourist Information Centre**, which conveniently adjoins a network of shops selling heaps of commemorative trinkets. (☎713 177. Books accommodations for £2 plus a 10% deposit. Open Apr.-Oct. M-Sa 9:30am-5:30pm, Su 10am-5pm; Nov.-Mar. M-Sa 9:30am-5pm, Su 10am-5pm.) Mercifully, the town is known locally as "Llanfairpwll" or "Llanfair P.G."

BEAUMARIS   ☎01248

Four miles northeast of the Menai Bridge on the A545, the town of Beaumaris manages to exude quiet charm without intruding on the surrounding country. Nearby Bangor seems as if it belongs to another distant world entirely. Tall trees and moat-dwelling ducklings now guard **Beaumaris Castle,** the last and largest of Edward I's Welsh fortresses, which sits in marshland, a location uncharacteristic of Edward I's "iron ring" castles. It was to be his masterpiece and, though unfinished, is regarded as one of the most well-designed castles in Britain. (☎810 361. Open June-Sept. daily 9:30am-6pm; Apr.-May and Oct. daily 9:30am-5pm; Nov.-Mar. M-Sa 9:30am-4pm, Su 11am-4pm. Last admission 30min. before close. £3, concessions £2.50, families £8.50.)

Beaumaris Gaol, on Bunkers Hill, presents a fascinating and chilling view of incarceration in Victorian Angelsey. Individual cells feature histories of past occupants and house grim relics from their daily lives, including a system of ropes that allowed female inmates to rock their babies from the working rooms below. Out back, visitors can see Britain's only remaining treadwheel, which demanded hours of grueling labor from inmates to supply the prison with water. (☎810 921. Open daily Easter to Sept. 10:30am-5pm. Last admission 4:30pm. £3, concessions £2.25, families £10.) More charming distractions can be found at the **Museum of Childhood Memories,** 1 Castle St., which displays legions of tin wind-ups, round-eyed dolls, and pea-shooting piggy banks. (☎810 448. Open Easter to Oct. M-Sa 10:30am-5:30pm, Su noon-5pm; Nov. to Easter Sa-Su 10:30am-5pm. Last admission 45min. before close. £4, concessions £3.25, children £2.25, families £11.) Inexpensive **catamaran cruises** (1¼hr.) down the Menai Strait and around **Puffin Island** leave from the Starida booth on the pier. (☎810 379 or 810 251. Weather permitting; call ahead. £5, children £4.)

The closest hostel is the **YHA Bangor** (p. 505). Few of the town's **B&Bs** offer singles; consider sleeping in Bangor or Caernarfon. Summers are extremely busy. Camping is best at **Kingsbridge Caravan Park ❶**, 1½ mi. from town, toward Llangoed. At the end of Beaumaris's main street, follow the road past the castle to the crossroads, turn left toward Llanfaes, and continue 400 yd. Arriva buses #57 and 58 running from Bangor will stop nearby if you ask. (☎490 636. Open Mar.-Oct. £4-5, children £1.50-2. Electricity £2. Cash only.) Buy **groceries** at Spar, 11 Castle St. (Open M-Su 7am-11pm.) Tea shops cluster around the castle; one of the nicest is **Beau's Tea Shop ❶**, 30 Castle St., where stained-glass lamps lend an amber glow. (☎811 010. Open M-Sa 10am-4:30pm, Su 11am-4:30pm. Cash only.) **Sarah's Delicatessen ❶**, 11 Church St., sells gourmet vittles and local cheeses. (☎811 534. Open M-Th 9am-5pm and F-Sa 9am-5:30pm. MC/V.)

Buses stop on Castle St. The **Tourist Information Centre**, located in Town Hall, on Castle St., provides a free town map and accommodations information. (☎810 040. Open Easter to Oct. M-Th and Sa 10am-4:45pm.) HSBC **bank** is also on Castle St. (Open M-F 11am-3:30pm.) The **post office** is at 10 Church St. (☎810 320. Open M-Tu and Th-F 9am-5:30pm, W and Sa 9am-12:30pm.) **Post Code:** LL58 8AB.

HOLYHEAD (CAERGYBI)   ☎01407

An unattractive town attached to Anglesey by a causeway and a bridge, Holyhead is primarily known as a port for ferries headed to Ireland. **Irish Ferries** (☎08705 171 717) and **Stena Line** (☎08705 421 170) operate ferries and catamarans to **Dublin** and its suburb, **Dún Laoghaire.** Foot passengers check in at the terminal adjoining the train station; cars proceed along the asphalt. A walkway, expected by 2006, will provide access to both stations from the town. Arrive 30min. early and remember your passport. (See **By Ferry,** p. 46.)

St. Cybi's Church, in the center of town between Stanley St. and Victoria Rd., has lovely stained-glass windows and a huge, decorated wood organ. Cromwell used the building as a military headquarters and subsequently wrecked it; it was largely rebuilt in the 17th century. The **Caer Cybi,** a fourth-century Roman defense from sea raiders, surrounds the grounds. (☎763 001. Open daily May-Sept. 11am-3pm. Call ahead in low season. Free.) The **Maritime Museum,** Beach Rd., occupies the oldest lifeboat house in Wales and details Holyhead's nautical history. Highlights include surprisingly evocative busts of Hitler and Mussolini carved from whales' ears. (☎764 374. Open Apr.-Oct. Tu-Su 1-5pm. £2, concessions £1.50, children 50p, families £5.) The many paths of **Holyhead Mountain's** north and south stacks are good for bird-watching, and the lighthouse overlooks the Irish Sea. **Caer y Tŵr** and **Holyhead Mountain Hut Group** sit at the mountain's base. The former is an Iron-Age hill fort, the latter a settlement inhabited from 500 BC until Roman times.

Holyhead **B&Bs** are plentiful and accommodating to passengers at the mercy of boat schedules. Owners may arrange to greet you at unusual times if you call ahead, and "B&B" here often translates to B&PL (beds and packed lunches). To reach **Orotavia ❷**, 66 Walthew Ave., go up Thomas St., which becomes Porth-y-Felin Rd., and turn right onto Walthew Ave. (not nearby Walthew St. or Walthew Ln.); call for a ride from the station if bogged down with bags. (☎760 259; www.orotavia.co.uk. Singles £20; doubles £45. Cash only.) Down the road from Orotavia, **Witchingham ❸**, 20 Walthew Ave., offers rides from the station. (☎762 426. £22.50 per person. Cash only.) **Roselea ❷**, 26 Holborn Rd., is the closest B&B to the station and ferries. (☎764 391. Singles £25; doubles and twins £40. Cash only.) Few Holyhead dining options are noteworthy, but **Market Street** is lined with the typical slew of chippers and bakeries, as well as a Kwik Save **supermarket** (open M-Sa 8am-8pm, Su 10am-4pm).

Reach Holyhead every hour (Su every 2hr.) by **train** from: Bangor (30min., £5.80); Chester (1½hr., £15.80); and London (4½-6hr.; two weeks in advance £15, same day £63). Arriva Cymru (☎0870 608 2608) **bus** #4 comes from Bangor via Llanfair P.G. and Llangefni (1½hr., M-Sa 2 per hr., £3.20); on Sundays #44 journeys from Bangor, sometimes stopping in Ysbyty Gwynedd (1½hr., 8 per day). Eurolines/Bus Éireann #861/871 comes from London (7½hr., 2 per day, £29) via Birmingham (4hr.) and #880 comes from Leeds (6hr., daily, £29) through Manchester (4¾hr.) and Liverpool (2½hr.). For a **taxi,** call Alphacab (☎765 000).

The **Tourist Information Centre,** accessible through Terminal One of the train and ferry station, sells ferry tickets and books rooms for a £2 charge plus a 10% deposit. (☎762 622. Open daily 8:30am-6pm.) Other services include: **banks** on Market St.; **police,** at the top of Stanley St. by the library (☎762 323); free **Internet access** at the library, Newry Fields (☎762 917; open M 10am-5pm, Tu and Th-F 10am-7pm, W 10am-1pm, Sa 9:30am-12:30pm); and the **post office,** 13a Stryd Boston, with a **bureau de change** (☎08457 223 344; open M-F 9am-5:30pm, Sa 9am-12:30pm). **Post Code:** LL65 1BP.

LLŶN PENINSULA

With jagged mountains to the east, quiet Anglesey to the north, and choppy seas on three sides, the pastoral scenes and dramatic cliffs of the Llŷn Peninsula seem perfectly out of place. They have humbled visitors since the Middle Ages, when pilgrims traversed the peninsula on their way to Bardsey Island. The serenity these travelers sought can still be found in Iron-Age settlements high on mountains. The golden beaches are dotted with weekenders—Hell's Mouth is famous for surfing, and Black Sands, near Porthmadog, is a convenient favorite for everything else. The farther west you venture, the more unsullied the Llŷn becomes, and some of its smallest villages have managed to retain some of the serenity that its larger (and less comely) towns have lost.

▐ TRANSPORTATION

The northern end of the Cambrian Coaster (☎08457 489 450) **train** line runs through Porthmadog and Criccieth to Pwllheli, stopping at smaller towns in between. Trains begin at Aberystwyth or Birmingham and require a change at Machynlleth for Porthmadog (2hr. from Machynlleth; M-Sa 5-7 per day, Su 3 per day) and Pwllheli (2hr. from Machynlleth). The Cambrian Coaster Day Ranger offers unlimited travel along the line (£7 per day, children £3.50).

National Express (☎08705 808 080) **bus** #545 arrives in Pwllheli from London via Bangor, Birmingham, Caernarfon, and Porthmadog (10-10½hr., 1 per day, £26.50.) Bus #380 arrives in Pwllheli from Newcastle-upon-Tyne via Manchester, Liverpool, and Bangor (12-14hr., 3 per day, £44.50.) TrawsCambria bus #701 stops in Porthmadog once a day from Aberystwyth (2hr.), Swansea (6hr.), and Cardiff (7hr.). In the other direction, #701 travels from Porthmadog to Bangor (1hr.). Express Motors (☎01286 881 108) bus #1 stops in Porthmadog on its winding route between Blaenau Ffestiniog (30min.; M-Sa every hr.; in summer M-Sa every hr., Su 5 per day) and Caernarfon (45-60min.), continuing to Bangor (1-1¼hr.; M-Sa 6 per day, Su 3 per day). Berwyn (☎01286 660 315) and Clynnog & Trefor (☎01286 660 208) run bus #12 between Pwllheli and Caernarfon (45min.; M-Sa every hr., Su less frequent).

Several bus companies, primarily Arriva Cymru (☎0870 608 2608), serve most spots on the peninsula for about £2. Check schedules in the essential *Gwynedd Public Transport Maps and Timetables*, available from TICs and on some buses. Arriva and Caelloi (☎01758 612 719) run bus #3 from Porthmadog to Pwllheli via Criccieth (30-40min.; M-Sa 1-2 per hr., Su 6 per day). Leaving from Pwllheli, buses #8, 17, 17B, and 18 weave around the western tip of the peninsula. A **Gwynedd Red Rover ticket,** available on buses, secures a day of travel throughout the peninsula and further afield (£4.95, children £2.45).

PORTHMADOG
☎ 01766

Buses, trains, and cars converge on bustling Porthmadog (port-MA-dock), making it a hub for hikers and beach-bound weekenders. Its principal attraction is the **Ffestiniog Railway**, a narrow-gauge line that departs from Harbour Station on High St. The train is only three seats (and a tiny aisle) wide, but it offers spectacular views and a bumpy 13½ mi. ride into scenic Snowdonia. (☎ 516 000; www.festrail.co.uk. 3hr. round-trip. June-Aug. 4-10 per day; Apr.-May and Sept.-Oct. 2-4 per day; Nov.-Mar. call for timetables. £16, concessions £12.80, families £32.) At the **Llechwedd Slate Caverns**, outside of Blaenau Ffestiniog, visitors can venture into the hollow leftovers of the "other" Welsh mining industry. The site features two underground tours, a cluster of exhibits, and a recreated Victorian-era mining village (complete with the former residence of the blind harpist of Meirionydd). Though the **Deep Mine Tour**, with a Victorian ghost as your guide, offers a perilous descent on Britain's steepest passenger railway and views of an underground lake, the **Miner's Tramway Tour** is more stimulating, guiding visitors through expansive cathedral-like caves to witness mining demonstrations. John's #142 bus connects the slate mines to the Blaenau Ffestiniog railway station (5min.) and coordinates well with train arrivals and departures (5 per day round-trip). The mines are accessible by car just off the A70, 10 mi. south of Betws-y-Coed. Book well in advance (☎ 830 306. Open daily from 10am. Last tours leave Mar.-Sept. at 5:15pm; Oct.-Feb. 4:15pm. Tours £8.75, concessions £7.25, children £6.50.)

At the other end of Porthmadog, across from the train station, the modest **Welsh Highland Railway** (along with Russell, its dogged 1906 locomotive) tries to recapture the glory days of rail travel, reconstructing the atmosphere of a 1920s steam line. Once the longest narrow-gauge line in Wales, the track runs to **Pen-y-Mount**. (☎ 513 402; www.whr.co.uk. Timetables available at Tremadog Rd. Station. Easter to Sept. 6 per day; Oct. and Feb. 5 per day. Call for exact schedules. £5, children £3, families £14.) For a bigger adrenaline rush, try flying a Hovercraft over land or water with **Llŷn Hovercrafts,** just outside of Abersoch. (☎ 01758 713 527. £45 per 30min. Open Easter to Sept. daily 10am-5pm; in winter by arrangement.)

The best places to stay are 10-15min. down High St. (past the railway station, where it becomes Church St.) in neighboring **Tremadog**. National Express #545 and #380 and local bus Arriva #3 stop in Tremadog. The first house on the right on Church St., best known as Lawrence of Arabia's birthplace, now houses **Snowdon Lodge ❷**, with a TV, fireplace lounge, and kitchen. During the day, the front dining room moonlights as an upscale cafe. The owners impress with local lore and expert hiking advice. (☎ 515 354; www.snowdonlodge.co.uk. Continental breakfast included. Laundry £2. Internet access. Apr.-Oct. dorms £13.50; Nov.-Mar. £12.50. Twins and doubles £29-33; triples £44-50. AmEx/MC/V.) Signs on **High Street** and **Snowdon Street** in Porthmadog mark hotels and **B&Bs**. A cheaper option is run by **Mrs. G. Williams ❸**, 30 Snowdon St., whose double rooms are bright and cheery. (☎ 513 968. Doubles £40. Cash only.)

Castle Bakery ❶, 105 High St., stocks savory pasties (from 70p), *bara brith* (a Welsh bread; £2), sandwiches (£1.60-3) and a simple salad bar. (☎ 514 982. Open daily 8:30am-5pm. Cash only.) At **Jessie's ❶**, 75 High St., chose from a huge range of cheap sandwiches. (☎ 512 814. Open M-Sa 9am-5pm, Su 10am-4pm. Cash only.) **The Australia ❶**, 31-33 High St., has good grub (£3-7) and a wide-screen TV. Lore holds that a crew of sailors from Porthmadog abandoned their vessel in Australia, and the Aussies who replaced them frequented this bar once in Wales. (☎ 510 930. Open M-Sa 11am-11pm, Su noon-10:30pm. Food served M-F noon-3pm and 6-8:30pm, Sa-Su noon-3pm. MC/V.)

From the train station, a right turn on High St. leads to town. **Buses** stop on High St. For travel to the rest of the peninsula, they pick up outside the park. Arriving back, they stop across the street outside the Australia pub (p. 511). Dukes **Taxis** (☎514 799) helps out if you need a lift. K.K. Cycles, 141 High St., **rents bikes.** (☎512 310. £8 per day. Open M-Sa 9am-6pm.) The **Tourist Information Centre,** High St., by the harbor, books rooms for a £2 charge plus a 10% deposit. (☎512 981. Open daily Easter to Oct. 9:30am-5:30pm; Nov. to Easter 10am-5pm.) Other services include: Barclays **bank,** 79 High St. (☎08456 000 651; open M and W-F 9:30am-4:30pm, Tu 10am-4:30pm); **Internet access** at the I.T. Centre, 156 High St. (☎514 944; £1.50 for the first 15min., then 50p per 15min.; open M-F 9:30am-5:30pm, Sa 10am-2pm) or free at the library, Chapel St. (☎514 091; open M 10am-noon and 2-6:30pm, Tu and F 10am-noon and 4-7pm, W 10am-noon and 2-4:30pm, Th and Sa 10am-noon) or the TIC; a **launderette,** 34 Snowdon St. (wash £2.50, dry £1; open M-Su 8am-7pm); Rowland **pharmacy,** 68 High St. (☎513 921; open M-F 9am-5:30pm, Sa 9am-12:30pm); and the **post office,** at the corner of High St. and Bank Pl., with a bureau de change (☎512 010; open M-F 9am-5:30pm, Sa 9am-12:30pm). **Post Code:** LL49 9AD.

CRICCIETH   ☎01766

Above coastal Criccieth (KRIK-key-ith), 5 mi. west of Porthmadog, the remains of **Criccieth Castle** stand on a windy hilltop tucked into Tremadog Bay. Conquered and held by many, it has been attacked by more, and its walls still bear the scars of Owain Glyndwr's attempt to scorch this symbol of English hegemony. Little remains, but the site itself is breathtaking enough to merit exploration. (☎522 227. Open daily June-Sept. 10am-6pm; Oct. and Apr.-May 10am-5pm. £3, concessions £2.40. Nov.-Mar. M-Th free, unstaffed, and always open; use side gate. Nov.-Mar. F-Su regular entrance fees apply.)

B&Bs (£18-25) are scattered on **Marine Terrace** and **Marine Crescent,** by the beach near the castle. At **Dan-Y-Castell ❷,** 4 Marine Crescent, guests are treated to spacious rooms with ocean views. (☎522 375. Singles £19. Cash only.) Spar **market,** 62 High St., in the center of town, stocks basic food items. (☎522 410. Open daily 7am-10pm.) Tiny, popular **Poachers Restaurant ❷,** 66 High St., is just a few doors down. The three-course meal (£11) is a gastronome's delight. (☎522 512. Open M-Sa from 6pm, Su noon-2pm and from 6pm. Reserve ahead. MC/V.) Located just opposite their namesake on 29 Castle St., the **Castell Tea Rooms ❶** occupy a building that has been used as a bakery for over a hundred years. Current baker and proprietor John still bakes a solid array of cakes, pies, and pastries (from £1.10) and serves basic lunch items. (☎523 528. Open daily 11am-5pm. Cash only.) Though **Cadwalader's ❶** ice cream store has expanded across the Ll̂yn, its world-famous vanilla is still light and oh-so-creamy. (Open M-F 11am-8pm, Sa-Su 11am-9pm. Cash only.) The beer garden of **Bryn Hir Arms ❶,** 24 High St., is the ideal setting for a relaxed pint, and the downstairs "Bistro Bach" serves upscale pub food for downscale prices. (☎522 493. Open daily noon-11pm. Food served noon-9pm. AmEx/MC/V.)

Trains arrive from Pwllheli and Machynlleth via Porthmadog. From the station, turn right on High St. for the town center. Arriva **bus** #3 comes from Porthmadog and Pwllheli (15min.; M-Sa 2 per hr., Su 6 per day). The closest **TIC** is in Porthmadog (p. 511), but most services are right in town. HSBC **bank** is at 51 High St. (Open M-F 9:15-11:30am). The only public **Internet access** on the peninsula is at Roots Bookshop, 46 High St. (☎523 564; 5p per min., open M-Sa 10am-5pm). The **post office** is around the corner from the station. (Open M-Tu and Th-F 9am-5:30pm, W and Sa 9am-12:30pm.) **Post Code:** LL52 OBU.

🔆 DAYTRIP FROM CRICCIETH

LLANYSTUMDWY. Just 1½ mi. north of Criccieth, tiny Llanystumdwy (HLAN-ih-stim-doo-ee) was the boyhood home of **David Lloyd George,** British Prime Minister from 1916 to 1922, and the town lovingly ballyhoos its native son at every turn. The **Lloyd George Museum** has become a village centerpiece. It chronicles Lloyd George's life and displays numerous relics from his career, among them his working copy of the Treaty of Versailles and the pen he used to sign it. Exit the museum, turn right, and follow the path behind it to **Highgate,** George's boyhood home, humble but well-restored. The cobbler's **workshop** next door features a mannequin fashioned after George's uncle, who tells long-winded family anecdotes on audiotape. A jaunt through the museum carpark and across the street leads to George's solemn **gravesite,** a monolith behind a wrought-iron gate overlooking the gurgling brook in which young George played. *(Arriva bus #3 stops twice per hr. 20min. from Pwllheli, 15min. from Porthmadog, 4min. from Criccieth. ☎ 01766 522 071. Open July-Sept. daily 10:30am-5pm; Apr.-June M-F 10:30am-5pm; Oct. M-F 11am-4pm. Last admission 1hr. before close. £3, concessions £2, families £7.).*

PWLLHELI   ☎ 01758

The Cambrian Coaster rail line terminates at Pwllheli (poohl-HEL-ly), 8 mi. west of Criccieth, but there are many buses to aid transportation from this convenient hub. While antique shops and touristy stores dominate the main stretches, farther afield are two **beaches**—Abererch Beach, with windsurfers and a shallow grade that attracts families, and less known South Beach.

Bank Place Guest House ❷, 29 High St., is convenient, well-priced, and all rooms have TVs. (☎ 612 103. £18 per person. Cash only.) Area **camping** is good; try **Hendre ❶,** 1½ mi. down the road to Nefyn at Efailnewydd. (☎ 613 416. Open Mar.-Oct. From £10 per tent. Laundry and showers. Cash only.) Get local pastries (like Welsh cakes and *bara brith*) and produce at the open-air **market** in front of the bus station (open W 9am-5pm). The Spar **supermarket** is on Y Maes Sq. (☎ 612 993; open daily 8am-10pm). **Jane's Sandwich Bar ❶,** 55 High St. specializes in provencettes, from £1.60-2. (☎ 614 464. Open M-Sa 7am-2:30pm, Su 8am-2pm. Cash only.) **Taro Deg ❷,** 17 Lon Dywod, across from the train station, offers sandwiches, soups, and quiche in a venue with sleek minimalist design. (☎ 701 271. Open M-Sa 9:30am-4:30pm. MC/V.)

The **train** station is in Station Sq. The **bus** station is farther down Ffordd-y-Cob. Call **999 Taxi** at ☎ 740 999. The **Tourist Information Centre,** Station Sq., books B&Bs for a £2 charge plus a 10% deposit. (☎ 613 000. Open Apr.-Oct. daily 9am-5pm; Nov.-Mar. M-W and F-Sa 10:30am-4:30pm.) Other services include: HSBC **bank,** 48 High St. (☎ 632 700; open M-F 9am-4:30pm); **police** (☎ 701 177) on Ala Rd.; free **Internet access** at the library, in Neuadd Dwyfor (the Town Hall, Stryd Penlan; ☎ 612 089; open M 2-7pm; Tu, Th, Sa 10am-1pm; W and F 10am-1pm and 2-7pm); and the **post office,** New St., inside a general store (☎ 612 658; open M-F 9am-5:30pm, Sa 9am-12:30pm). **Post Code:** LL53 5HL.

ABERDARON AND TRE'R CEIRI   ☎ 01758

Once the next-to-last stop on the holy Ynys Enlli (Bardsey Island) pilgrimage, the tiny village of Aberdaron sits on the tip of Llŷn Peninsula. In a quiet inlet bounded by steep green hills, Aberdaron has managed to retain some of the small-town serenity that other Llŷn towns have lost. Right next to the ocean, the **Church of Saint Hywyn** has held fast against the tides and winds since medieval times. The 20th century has witnessed the construction of a sturdy seawall and the arrival of celebrity vicar **R.S. Thomas** (the other Welsh poet named Thomas) whose experiences working with this rural congregation feature prominently in his works. (Open daily in summer 10am-5pm; Aug. 10am-6pm; in winter 10am-4pm. Free.) **St. Mary's Well,** 1½ mi. west of town, is located surprisingly close to the ocean, and lore has it that its water stays fresh even when flooded by high tide. Follow road signs from Aberdaron 2 mi. to **Porthor,** where footfall causes the "whistling sands" to live up to their name. Long a religious site—its first monastery was allegedly built in the 6th century—the "Island of Twenty Thousand Saints" was once so holy that three pilgrimages there equaled one to Rome. Because so many holy men made the pilgrimage late in life, the "twenty thousand" in its name allegedly refers to the number of pilgrims buried there. Visitors can admire the ruins of the old abbey and observe hundreds of migratory birds. (☎760 667. Trust open daily Easter to Sept. 1-5pm. Ferries 15-20min., allowing 3½hr. visits; frequency depends on weather and demand. £20, children £10. Longer stays in the island's croglofts and Victorians are available.) A **National Trust information point** occupies the Coast Guard hut overlooking Bardsey at the Uwchmynydd headland.

Tre'r Ceiri (trair-KAY-ree; "Town of the Giants"), on the peninsula's north shore, is Britain's oldest fortress, dating back 4000 years. Take the Pwllheli-Caernarfon bus #12 to Llanaelhaearn (15min.; M-Sa every hr., Su 4 per day), go uphill to the B4417, turn left, then look for the footpath signposted 1 mi. southwest of town. At the path's upper reaches, keep to the stony track, a direct uphill route (elevation 1600 ft.). The well-preserved remains of 150 circular stone huts are clustered within a defensive wall, which, however strong, fails to protect against the weather; dress warmly.

Follow the sign pointing toward Whistling Sand, or simply head up the hill behind the bus stop to the lovely **Bryn Mor ❷,** where elegant rooms have sea views and TVs. (☎760 344. £23. Cash only.) A small Spar provides **groceries.** (☎760 234. Open Apr.-Sept. M-Sa 8am-9pm, Su 8:30am-9pm; Oct.-Mar. until 5:30pm.) Food has been served since 1300 in the small building now occupied by **Y Gegin Fawr ❶** ("The Big Kitchen") cafe. Enjoy a "Pilgrim's Lunch" (£5) on the creekside patio or in the pleasant tea room. (☎760 359. Open daily July-Aug. 10am-6pm; Easter to June and Sept.-Oct. 10am-5:30pm. Cash only.) **Bus** #17 runs from Pwllheli (40min., M-Sa 9 per day); #17B follows a more scenic, coastal route and takes 5min. longer (2 per day). The **Bardsey Island Trust Booking Office,** in the center of the village, provides information on boats to Bardsey Island. The **post office** is inside the Spar market. (Open M-Tu and Th-F 9am-12:30pm and 1:30-5:30pm, W and Sa 9am-noon.) **Post Code:** LL53 8BE.

SCOTLAND

Half the size of England but with only a tenth the population, Scotland possesses open spaces and wild natural splendor its southern neighbor cannot rival. The craggy Highlands, beaches of the west coast, and mists of the Hebrides are awe-inspiring, and the farmland to the south and tiny fishing villages in the east convey a more subtle beauty. The Scots revel in a distinct and diverse culture, from the fevered nightlife of Glasgow to the festival atmosphere in Edinburgh and the isolated communities of the Orkney and Shetland Islands. The Scots defended their independence for hundreds of years before reluctantly joining with England to create Great Britain in 1707; they regained a separate parliament in 1999. The mock kilts and bagpipes of the big cities can grow tiresome. Rather, travel afar to discover a B&B owner speaking Gaelic to her grandchildren, a crofter cutting peat, or a fisherman setting out in his skiff at dawn.

TRANSPORTATION

GETTING THERE

Reaching Scotland from outside Britain is often easiest and cheapest through London, where the **Scottish Tourist Board,** 19 Cockspur St., SW1 Y5BL (☎08452 255 121; www.visitscotland.com), has brochures and reserves train, bus, and plane tickets.

BY PLANE. The cheapest fares between England and Scotland are available from no-frills airlines. **easyJet** (☎08706 000 000; www.easyjet.com) flies to Edinburgh from London Luton, Stansted, and Gatwick and to Glasgow from Luton or Stansted. The fares are web-only; book far in advance and fly for as little as £10. **Ryanair** (☎08712 460 000; www.ryanair.com) flies to Edinburgh and to Glasgow Prestwick (1hr. from the city) from Dublin and London for close to nothing. **EUjet** (☎08704 141 414; www.eujet.com) flies to Glasgow and Edinburgh from Kent. **British Airways** (☎08457 733 377; www.ba.com) sells round-trip tickets between England and Scotland from £80. **British Midland** (☎08706 070 555; www.flybmi.com) offers Saver fares from London to Glasgow (from £78 round-trip). With all airlines, book as far in advance as possible for the best fares.

BY TRAIN AND BUS. From London, **GNER** runs **trains** (☎08457 225 333; www.gner.co.uk) to Edinburgh and Glasgow, which take 4½-6hr. Fares vary depending on how far in advance you buy (£27-£100). A pricier option is the **Caledonian Sleeper,** run by **First Scotrail** (☎08457 550 033; www.firstgroup.com/scotrail), which leaves London Euston near midnight and gets to Edinburgh at 7am (reclining chair £60; cabin £95-£125). Although the **bus** from London can take anywhere from 8 to 12 hours, it may be significantly cheaper than rail travel. **National Express** (☎08705 808 080; www.nationalexpress.com) connects England and Scotland via Glasgow and Edinburgh.

GETTING AROUND

BY TRAIN AND BUS. In the Lowlands (south of Stirling and north of the Borders), trains and buses run many routes frequently. In the Highlands, Scotrail and GNER **trains** snake slowly on a few routes. Many stations are unstaffed—buy tickets on board. **Buses** tend to be the best way to travel. They're usually more frequent and far-reaching than trains and are always cheaper. **Scottish Citylink** (☎08705 505 050; www.citylink.co.uk) runs most intercity routes; **Traveline Scotland** has the best information on all routes and services (☎08706 082 608; www.travelinescotland.com). Bus service is infrequent in the northwest Highlands and grinds to a halt on Sundays almost everywhere. **Postbuses** (Royal Mail customer service ☎08457 740 740) are a unique British phenomenon. Red mail vans pick up passengers and mail once or twice a day in the most remote parts of the country, charging 40p–£4 (and often nothing). They're a reliable way to get around the Highlands.

The **Freedom of Scotland Travelpass** allows unlimited train travel and transportation on most **Caledonian MacBrayne** ("CalMac") ferries, with discounts on some other ferry lines. Purchase the pass *before* traveling to Britain at any BritRail distributor (see **By Train,** p. 30).

BY BUS TOUR. A thriving industry of tour companies is eager to whisk travelers into the Highlands. ◪ **HAGGiS** (☎01315 579 393; www.haggisadventures.com) and **MacBackpackers** (☎01315 589 900; www.macbackpackers.com) cater to the young and adventurous, with a number of tours departing from Edinburgh. Both run hop-on, hop-off excursions that let you travel Scotland at your own pace (usually within three months). HAGGiS is geared toward set tours with specific itineraries, run by witty and super-knowledgeable local guides; the company guarantees accommodation at a few favorite stopping points. MacBackpackers guarantees accommodation at any of the social **Scotland's Top Hostels** in Edinburgh, Fort William, Skye, Oban, and Inverness. (See **Bus Tours,** p. 32.) **Celtic Connection** (☎01312 253 330; www.thecelticconnection.co.uk) covers Scotland in a variety of 5- to 12-day tours, with one-way, round-trip, and hop-on, hop-off options.

BY CAR. Driving affords travelers access to Scotland's remote corners without the fear of being stranded by complicated bus services. As in the rest of Britain, driving in Scotland is on the left, seatbelts are required at all times, the minimum age to drive with a foreign license is 17, and the legal minimum age to rent is 21. In rural areas, roads are often **single-track;** vehicles share one lane and may have to slow to a crawl to negotiate oncoming traffic. Often one car must pull into a **passing place** (shoulder turn-off) to enable another to pass or overtake. Many rural roads are also traversed by **livestock.** Cute, sure, but drivers should take caution.

BY BICYCLE. Scotland's biking terrain is scenic and challenging. You can usually rent bikes even in very small towns and transport them by ferry for little or no charge. Fife and regions south of Edinburgh and Glasgow offer gentle country lanes. Orkney, Shetland, and the Western Isles are negotiable by bicycle, though bicyclists should be aware of strong winds and wet roads. In the Highlands, touring is more difficult. Most major roads have only one lane, and locals drive at high speeds. Transporting a bike by public transportation in the Highlands can be difficult. Many trains can carry only four or fewer bikes; reservations are essential.

BY THUMB. Hitchers report that drivers tend to be most receptive (and often downright friendly) in the least-traveled areas. Far to the northwest and in the Western Isles, the Sabbath is strictly observed, making it difficult or impossible to get a ride on Sundays. *Let's Go* does not recommend hitchhiking.

BY FOOT. Two long-distance footpaths, established under the Countryside Act of 1967, traverse Scotland. The **West Highland Way** begins just north of Glasgow in Milngavie and snakes 95 mi. north along Loch Lomond, through Glen Coe to Fort William and Ben Nevis. The **Southern Upland Way** runs 212 mi. from Portpatrick on the southwest coast to Cockburnspath on the east coast, passing through Galloway Forest Park and the Borders. Most Tourist Information Centres (TICs) distribute simple maps of the Ways and a list of accommodations along the routes. For infor-

Scotland

N

0   20 miles
0   20 kilometers

NORTH ATLANTIC
OCEAN

Shetland Islands

Unst

Fetlar

Yell

Mainland

Scalloway

Lerwick

TO SHETLANDS

Orkney Islands

Westray

Sanday

Eday

Rousay

Stronsay

Shapinsay

Stromness

Kirkwall

Hoy

Burwick

North
Sea

Cape
Wrath

Scrabster

Durness

Tongue

John
O'Groats

Thurso

Wick

Ben Hope
(3041 ft.)

Ben Loyal
(2507 ft.)

Helmsdale

OUTER HEBRIDES

Eddrachillis
Bay

Ben Kilbreck
(3153 ft.)

Stornoway

Lochinver

Lewis

Achiltibuie

Ullapool

HIGHLANDS

Tarbert

Gairloch

Achnasheen

Moray Firth

Elgin

Harris

Leverburgh

Berneray

Torridon

Forres

North
Uist

Uig

Applecross

Inverness

GRAMPIAN

Spey River

Lochmaddy

Skye

Portree

Cannich

Drumnadrochit

Don River

Benbecula

Plockton

Broadford

Kyle of Lochalsh

**Loch
Ness**

CAIRNGORM
NATIONAL PARK

Aberdeen

South
Uist

Kyleakin

Aviemore

Dee River

Lochboisdale

Armadale

Caledonian Canal

CAIRNGORM MTS.

Tomintoul

Stonehaven

Barra

Canna

Rum

Mallaig

Fort
William

Braemar

GRAMPIAN MTS.

Castlebay

Muck

Eigg

**Ben
Nevis**
(4406 ft.)

TAYSIDE

Montrose

INNER HEBRIDES

Coll

Kilchoan

Glencoe

Aberfeldy

Pitlochry

Tiree

Tobermory

**Loch
Etive**

Killin

**Loch
Tay**

Dunkeld

Treshnish
Islands

Staffa

Mull

Craignure

Crianlarich

Ben More
(3852 ft.)

Loch Tay R.

Birnam

Dundee

Iona

Oban

Inveraray

**Ben
Lomond**
(3196 ft.)

LOCH LOMOND
AND THE TROSSACHS
NATIONAL PARK

Perth

FIFE

St. Andrews

Colonsay

Jura

**Loch
Lomond**

**THE
TROSSACHS**

Falkland

Crail

Anstruther

Port
Askaig

Argyll

Dunoon

Balloch

CENTRAL

Stirling

Kirkcaldy

Elie

Firth of Forth

Islay

Tarbert

Rothesay

Berwick-
upon-
Tweed

Port Charlotte

Bowmore

Lochranza

Ardrossan

LOTHIAN

Edinburgh

Port Ellen

Lamlash

Prestwick

Glasgow

Galashiels

Melrose

Tweed R.

Kintyre

Brodick

Arran

AYRSHIRE

Culter Fell
(2454 ft.)

Peebles

Selkirk

Kelso

Campbeltown

Firth of Clyde

Ayr

Nith River

Broad Law
(2756 ft.)

Jedburgh

BORDERS

CHEVIOT HILLS

ENGLAND

**DUMFRIES AND
GALLOWAY**

Galloway
Forest
Park

Dumfries

Glencaple

Hadrian's Wall

Hexham

Cairnryan

Castle
Douglas

Carlisle

Stranraer

Portpatrick

Kirkcudbright

**NORTHERN
IRELAND**

Larne

Luce
Bay

Wigtown
Bay

Whithorn

Solway
Firth

Penrith

TO BELFAST

Mull of Galloway

Keswick

The Minch

Firth of Lorne

North
Sea

S C O T L A N D

mation on these paths, write or call the **Scottish Tourist Board,** 23 Ravelston Terr., Edinburgh EH4 3EU (☎ 0845 2255 121; www.visitscotland.com) or visit www.walk-scotland.com. Detailed guidebooks are available at most bookstores.

Mountain ranges, like the Cuillins, the Torridons, the Cairngorms, Glen Nevis, and Glen Coe, have hostels that are bases for hillwalking or biking. Walk along mainland Britain's highest **cliffs** at Cape Wrath or ramble across the eerie **moors** of the Outer Hebrides. One of the most attractive aspects of hiking in Scotland is that you can often pick your own route. The wilds do pose certain dangers: stone markers can be unreliable and expanses of open heather can be disorienting. Heavy mists are always a possibility, and blizzards occur even in July; never go up into the mountains without proper equipment (see **Wilderness Safety,** p. 46). Many trails (even those in national parks) cross privately owned land. Be respectful and ask permission from the landowner. Leave a copy of your route and timetable at a hostel or rescue station, and if you're out between mid-August and mid-October, be sure to ask about areas in which deer hunters might be at work. For information on walking and mountaineering in Scotland, consult Poucher's *The Scottish Peaks* (£13), the Scottish Mountaineering Club's *The Munros* (£18), or the introductory Tourist Board booklet, *Walk Scotland.*

LIFE AND TIMES

HISTORY

EARLY TIMES. Little is known of the early inhabitants of Scotland, except that they managed to repel Roman incursions into their land and inspired **Emperor Hadrian** to shield Roman England behind an immense 73 mi. long wall (p. 429). Later invaders were more successful, however, and by AD 600 four groups inhabited the Scottish mainland. The **Picts,** the original inhabitants, are the most mysterious—only references in Latin histories and a collection of carved stones betray their existence. The Celtic **Scots** arrived from Ireland in the 4th century, bringing with them the Gaelic language and Christian religion, and the Germanic **Angles** and **Saxons** invaded Scotland from northern England in the 6th century. In AD 843, the Scots decisively defeated the Picts and formed the beginnings of a consolidated kingdom. United by the threat of encroaching **Vikings,** various groups gathered under the first king of all Scotland, **Duncan** (later killed by a certain Macbeth in 1040), and the House of Canmore ("big-headed," after Duncan's son Malcolm and his gargantuan cranium) reigned over Scotland for 200 years. In the early 12th century, Scotland grew prodigiously under the popular and pious King **David I** (1124-53), who built castles, abbeys, and cathedrals all over the Lowlands. Subsequent Scottish monarchs found their independence threatened by the increasingly powerful nation to the south. During the 13th century, Scottish kings struggled to contend with civil revolts and Scandinavian attacks; the nation held a tenuous peace punctuated by occasional fighting.

WARRING WITH ENGLAND. In 1286 King **Alexander III** died without an heir, and the resulting contest over the Scottish crown fueled the territorial ambitions of **Edward I** of England. Edward promptly seized most of Scotland and commenced a long history of English oppression, his not-so-gentle governing hand earning him the nickname the "Hammer of the Scots." The **Wars of Independence** bred heroic figures like William Wallace (yes, the *Braveheart* guy), but it was the cunning **Robert the Bruce** who emerged as Scotland's leader after a spate of assassinations. Against all odds, Robert led the Scots to victory over Edward II's forces at **Bannockburn** (p. 588) in 1314 and won Scotland its independence. In the next centuries the Scottish kings frequently capitalized on an **"Auld Alliance"** with France to stave off the English.

The reigns of **James IV** (1488-1513) and **James V** (1513-42) witnessed the arrival of both the **Renaissance** and the **Reformation** (p. 65). Following the death of James V, the infant **Mary, Queen of Scots** (1542-67), ascended to the throne and was promptly sent to France, where she later married the future François II. Lacking a strong ruler during Mary's absence, Scotland was vulnerable to the revolts of the Reformation, as a Protestantism piloted by iconoclastic preacher **John Knox** spread through the social strata. In 1560 the monarchy finally capitulated, and the **Scottish Parliament** denied the Pope's authority in Scotland and established the Presbyterian Church as Scotland's new official church.

In 1561, after the death of her husband, staunchly Catholic Mary returned to Scotland. Unpopular amongst Scottish nobles and Protestants, Mary's rule fanned the flames of discontent, and civil war resulted in her forced abdication and imprisonment in 1567. She escaped her Scottish captors only to find another set of shackles across the border, where her cousin Elizabeth I ruled. As Mary languished in an English prison, her son **James VI** was crowned king of Scotland. Nine years later, with Catholic Spain a rising threat, Queen Elizabeth made a tentative alliance with the nominally Protestant James (which didn't stop her from executing his mother in 1587).

UNION WITH ENGLAND. When Elizabeth died without an heir in 1603, James VI was crowned **James I**, uniting both countries under a single monarch. James ruled from London, and his half-hearted attempts to reconcile the Scots to British rule were tartly resisted. Scottish Presbyterians supported Parliamentary forces against James's successor **Charles I** during the **English Civil Wars** (p. 65). But when the Parliamentarians executed Charles, the Scots shifted alliances and declared the deceased king's son to be King Charles II. **Oliver Cromwell** quickly defeated Charles II, but in a conciliatory gesture gave Scotland representation in the English Parliament. The Protestant victory of William of Orange over James II in the **Glorious Revolution** (p. 65) convinced Scotland's Presbyterian leaders that its interests were safer with the Anglicans than with longtime Catholic ally France. (That, and the fact that many Scots were impoverished and famine-stricken after defending their independence for four centuries.) The Scottish Parliament was subsumed by England in the 1707 **Act of Union.**

THE JACOBITE REBELLION. Scottish supporters of James II (called **Jacobites**) never accepted the Union, and after a series of unsuccessful uprisings they launched the **"Forty-Five"**—the 1745 rebellion that snared the imaginations of Scots and Romantics everywhere. James's grandson Charles (or **Bonnie Prince Charlie**) landed in Scotland, where he succeeded in mustering unseasoned troops from various Scottish clans. He rallied the troops in **Glenfinnan** (p. 628) and marched to Edinburgh, where he kept court and prepared a rebellion. Desertions on the march to London and the uncertainty of help from France prompted a retreat to Scotland. Despite the materialization of modest French support and Jacobite victories at Stirling and Falkirk in 1746, the rebellion once again collapsed. Although Charles eventually escaped back to France, his Highland army fell heroically on the battlefield of **Culloden** (p. 621). The English subsequently enacted a new round of oppressive measures: they forbade the wearing of hereditary **tartans** and the playing of **bagpipes,** discouraged the speaking of **Gaelic,** and forcibly eradicated much of traditional Scottish culture. Sir Walter Scott's novel *Waverley*, written 60 years after the Forty-Five, expresses the next generation's nostalgia for a lost way of life.

ENLIGHTENMENT AND THE CLEARANCES. Despite Jacobite agitation and reactionary English counter-measures, the 18th century proved to be one of the most prosperous in Scotland's history. As agriculture, industry, and trading boomed, a vibrant intellectual environment and close links to Continental **Enlightenment** thought produced such luminaries as **Adam Smith, David Hume,** and **Thomas Carlyle.**

Although political reforms did much to improve social conditions in the 19th century, economic problems proved disastrous. The Highlands in particular were affected by a rapidly growing population combined with limited arable land, archaic farming methods, and the demands of rapacious landlords. The resulting poverty led to mass **emigration,** mostly to North America, and the infamous **Highland Clearances.** Between 1810 and 1820, the Sutherland Clearances, undertaken by the Marquis of Stafford, forcibly relocated thousands of poor farmers from their lands to smaller landholdings called **crofts** to make way for expanded sheep ranching. Resistance to the relocations was met with violence—homes were burned and countless people killed. Other clearances occurred throughout the Highlands, in some cases evicting entire villages, whereupon the inhabitants were not just displaced within Scotland but were packed into boats and shipped overseas. The **Industrial Revolution** led to growth in Glasgow and the rest of southern Scotland and increasingly poor living conditions for new industrial laborers.

THE 20TH CENTURY. Scotland, like the rest of Britain, lost countless young men in the Great War and suffered the ensuing economic downturn. In the 1930s the **Depression** hit Scotland as hard, if not harder, than the rest of the world. The **Home Rule** (or **Devolution**) movement, begun in 1886 and put on hold during WWI, continued the push for a separate parliament in Edinburgh, and the **Scottish National Party (SNP)** was founded in 1934 on the strength of nationalist sentiments. Four young tartan-blooded agitators broke into Westminster Abbey on Christmas of 1950 and liberated the **Stone of Scone** (or "Stone of Destiny"; see sidebar), which previously had been removed from Scotland by Edward I. Home Rulers neither managed to score a real victory on the floor of Parliament during the years following WWII nor dissolved as a movement. The discovery of North Sea oil gave Scotland an economic boost and incited a new breed of nationalism embodied by the SNP's 1974 political slogan, "It's Scotland's Oil!" Polls in the 70s indicated as much as three-quarters of Scotland's population favored devolution, but the crucial **1979 referendum** failed to win the required proportion of the electorate.

After the World Wars, Labour governments nurtured Scotland's **industrial boom,** nationalizing many industries. **Thatcherism,** however, removed many of the public-funding props sustaining industries in the north of Britain, and Scotland's work-force was reduced by 20%. The country faced economic downturn similar to, if not more intense than, that of the industrial meccas of Northern England.

SCOTLAND TODAY

Stands Scotland where it did?
—William Shakespeare, *Macbeth*

CURRENT POLITICS. September 1997 brought a victory for the proponents of home rule; Scottish voters supported **devolution** by an overwhelming three-to-one margin, and the first elections for the new **Scottish Parliament** occurred in 1999, leaving a Labour-Liberal Democrat coalition in power and the SNP in the position of primary opposition. Although Scotland has a new Parliament house at **Holyrood,** Edinburgh (p. 537), it still has seats in the United Kingdom's House of Commons. The precise nature of Scotland's relationship with England remains disputed. On the one hand, even the mention of "Bannockburn" still stirs nationalist feeling among Scots, and the last party supporting union with England has been scourged from the Scottish Parliament. On the other, there are many Scottish politicians more closely tied to London than to their own constituents.

SCOTLAND AT CENTURY'S TURN. Out of the post-industrial ruins, Glasgow began a cultural revitalization in the late 80s that continues today. **Edinburgh,** long a cultural magnet, has recently seen its 55-year-old **International Festival** (and attendant events like **The Fringe** that have come to dominate the festival on their own; p. 525) make headlines around the world—today, over 15% of the revelers come from overseas. Edinburgh's festival energies peak during August but fuel the economy year round, generating millions of pounds in revenue and thousands of jobs.

Cultural tourism draws droves of heritage-seekers and Celtic devotees to the country each summer. Though the industrial trades still comprise Scotland's largest workforce, tourism employs more people than any other field in holiday spots like the Highlands and islands. Still others have turned to new technologies as economic alternatives. On July 5, 1996, Dolly the sheep was born in the labs of the Roslin Institute, conceived by Dr. Ian Wilmut. Scotland also has a stake in microtechnologies, producing a large portion of all the superconductors in the UK and earning central Scotland the nickname "Silicon Glen."

CULTURE AND CUSTOMS

The cold, drizzly skies of Scotland loom over some of the warmest people on earth. The Scottish reputation for openness and good nature is well-founded. Reserve and etiquette are somewhat less important here than in London's urban sprawl; life is generally slower and less frenetic outside—and even within—the densely populated belt running between Glasgow and Edinburgh. But all this is no reason to forget your manners. As in the few other unharried corners of the world, **hospitality** and **conversation** are highly valued; most Scots will welcome you with geniality and pride (unless you call them English). In certain areas of the Highlands,

IN-RECENT NEWS

PARLIAMENT WOES

Visitors to the palace of Holyroodhouse in Edinburgh may notice a rather bizarre-looking modern building across the street. This edifice has already been a symbol, in its short history, of both Scotland's bright future and its deepest misgivings.

With a giant chunk of prime real estate, a team of international architects, and a huge budget, the Scottish Parliament building was to be an exuberant celebration of Scotland's new degree of independence. Then came delays, mishaps, unforeseen costs, and other issues. The just-finished building was three years behind schedule and almost £400 million over budget. Construction problems were at times flat-out embarrassing. In one famous incident, workers received the glass for the building's windows only to find that the plates were too big. Parliament, desperate to avoid further delays and expenditures, ordered that the windows be installed anyway. Architects complained that the building's quality was compromised by a "dash to finish" attitude. A panel has already been established to investigate what went wrong.

In a summer 2005 television series, *Demolition,* the Parliament building was voted one of the 12 ugliest in Britain. The public seems to have no patience for the panel; several petitions have recommended bulldozing the expensive eyesore.

nationalism runs deep and strong; using the (technically) correct "British" will win you no friends. **Religion** and **football**, and the religion of football, are topics best left untouched if you're not prepared to defend yourself—verbally and otherwise. Even the sweetest little old lady can turn out to be a hot-blooded football fanatic.

A WORD ABOUT KILTS. The kilt is not a purely romanticized, Hollywoodized concept, though it's unlikely you'll see very many during your travels. Criminalized as Highland garb after the Jacobite rebellion, kilts were revived during the mid-19th-century collective nostalgia for Highland culture. **Tartan** plaids originally denoted the geographic base of the weaver. Today, few Scots still wear their family tartan, though many do own one for use at formal gatherings (and often sporting events).

KILT IT UP. You don't have to be Scottish to wear a kilt. Hiring a kilt costs upwards of £25, or £30 for the whole nine yards, including kilt, **hose** (socks), **flashes** for the hose (worn facing outwards), **Ghillie Brogues** (shoes), **sgian dubh** (ceremonial dagger, usually false, that goes tucked into the right sock with only the handle showing), **Bonnie Prince Charlie jacket** (a tuxedo-like top), **waistcoat** (vest), and the important **sporran**, worn across the front and serving as your only pocket (besides just looking sexy). What goes under is up to you.

LANGUAGE

The early Picts left no record of their language, a **Celtic** language related to Welsh and used until the 7th century. Settlers in southern Scotland transported their native tongues—Gaelic from Ireland, Norse from Scandinavia, and an early form of English (Inglis) brought by the Angles from northern England. By the 11th century, **Scottish Gaelic** (pronounced GAL-ick; Irish Gaelic is GAYL-ick), had subsumed other dialects and become the official language of Scottish law. As the political power of southern Scotland increased, Gaelic speakers migrated to the Highlands and islands. Inglis, a dialect of English now called **Scots,** became the language of the Lowlands and, eventually, of the monarchy.

While a number of post-1700 Scottish literati, most notably Robert Burns and the contemporary poet Hugh MacDiarmid, have composed in Scots, union with Britain and the political and cultural power of England led to the rise of the English language in Scotland. Today, **standard English** is spoken throughout Scotland, but with a strong Scots influence. In the Highlands, for example, "ch" becomes a soft "h," as in the German "ch" sound. Modern Scottish Gaelic, a linguistic cousin of modern Irish, is spoken by approximately 60,000 people in Scotland today, particularly in the western islands. Recent attempts to revive Gaelic have led to its introduction in the classroom and even on street signs in the Hebrides, assuring that some form of the language will continue to exist in Scotland for years to come. (For a **glossary** of Scottish Gaelic and Scots words and phrases, see the Appendix.)

THE ARTS

LITERATURE. In a nation where stories have long been recounted by fireside, **oral literature** is as much a part of literary tradition as novels. Unfortunately, most medieval Scottish manuscripts have been lost—not surprising, as raids on monastic centers of learning were fierce and frequent—effectively erasing pre-

14th-century records. **John Barbour** is the best-known writer in Early Scots. His *The Bruce* (c. 1375) preceded Chaucer and favorably chronicled the life of Robert I in an attempt to strengthen national unity. **William Dunbar** (1460-1521) composed in Middle Scots and his work is considered representative of Scots poetry.

In 1760, **James Macpherson** published the works of **"Ossian,"** supposedly an ancient Scottish bard to rival Homer; Macpherson was widely discredited when he refused to produce the manuscripts that he claimed to be translating. **James Boswell** (1740-95), the biographer of Samuel Johnson (p. 73), composed Scots verse as well as voluminous journals detailing his travels with the good Doctor. "Scotland's National Bard," **Robert Burns** (1759-96), ignored pressure from the south urging him to write in English, instead composing in his native Scots. New Year's Eve revelers owe their anthem to him, though most mouth "Auld Lang Syne" (Old Long Time) without a clue what it means. **Sir Walter Scott** (1771-1832) was among the first Scottish authors to achieve international accolades for his work. The chivalric *Ivanhoe* is one of the best-known, if sappiest, novels of all time. Scott was also quite nostalgic, and his historic novels (such as *Waverley*) may have single-handedly sparked the 19th-century revival of Highlands culture. **Robert Louis Stevenson** (1850-94) is most famous for his tales of high adventure, including *Treasure Island* and *Kidnapped*, which still fuel children's imaginations. His *Strange Case of Dr. Jekyll and Mr. Hyde* is nominally set in London, but any Scot would recognize Edinburgh's streets. Another of Edinburgh's authorial sons is **Sir Arthur Conan Doyle** (1859-1930), whose *Sherlock Holmes* series is beloved by mystery fans the world over.

Scotland's literary present is as vibrant as its past. A series of 20th-century poets—most notably **Hugh MacDiarmid** and **Edwin Morgan**—have returned to the language of Burns, fueling a renaissance of Scottish Gaelic, particularly the Lowlands ("Lallands") dialect. **Neil Gunn** (1891-1973) wrote short stories and novels about Highland history and culture. More recent novelists include **Alasdair Gray, Tom Leonard, Janice Galloway,** and **James Kelman,** who won 1995's Booker Prize for his controversial, sharp-edged novel *How Late It Was, How Late*. **Irvine Welsh's** *Trainspotting*, the 1993 novel about Edinburgh heroin addicts that was adapted into a 1996 film, has been simultaneously condemned as immoral and hailed as the chronicle of a new generation.

ART. Scotland has produced fewer visual artists than it has writers and musicians, but the extraordinary galleries and museums of Glasgow and Edinburgh display a rich, if circumscribed, aesthetic history. Eighteenth and 19th-century portraitists like **Allan Ramsay** and **Sir Henry Raeburn,** and genre painter **David Wilkie** are recognized figures in the world of art. As a celebrated participant in both the Arts and Crafts movement (p. 75) and the Art Nouveau scene, Glaswegian artist and architect **Charles Rennie Mackintosh** (1868-1928) considerably boosted Scotland's artistic prestige with his elegant designs.

MUSIC. The Gaelic music of western Scotland has its roots in the traditional music of Irish settlers. As in Ireland, **ceilidhs** (KAY-lees)—spirited gatherings of music and dance—bring jigs, reels, and Gaelic songs to halls and pubs. Evidence suggests the *clarsach*, a Celtic harp, was the primary medium for musical expression until the 16th century, when the Highlander's **bagpipes** (one of the oldest instruments in the world) and the violin introduced new creative possibilities. **Ballads**—dramatic narrative songs often performed unaccompanied—form a central point in Scottish musical heritage. The strong folk tradition is

HAGGIS AND TATTIES AND NEEPS, OH MY!

Scotland's regional cuisine usually comes beer-battered and deep-fried. But the country does offer delicacies beyond fish and chips. Here is a culinary translation of a traditional and coronary-inducing Scottish meal.

Haggis: Perhaps the best-known Scottish dish, haggis consists of minced and boiled offal (organ meats), which is encased in stomach lining and shaped into sausage. Don't be fooled by the locals who tell you it's made from a three legged bird, and don't believe weak-kneed foreigners who tell you it's disgusting.

Neeps: They're technically rutabagas, although the nickname comes from the word turnip. Neeps are delicious stir-fried, mashed, baked, or deep-fried, especially accompanying haggis.

Tatties: Yet another name for the humble potato. Chips are served with fish. Tatties, more like steak fries, go well with heartier fare.

Irn-Bru: Wash down your Scottish dinner with this peculiar caffeinated orange soda. It takes a little like liquid bubblegum and is often mixed with liquor.

Cranachan: For dessert, try this semi-sweet fruit parfait, made with raspberries, honey, whipped cream, oatmeal, and (unsurprisingly) whisky.

evident in the Scottish contribution to popular music, including native Scots **The Proclaimers,** folk-rockers **Belle and Sebastian,** and Britpop entries **Texas** and **Travis.** Glasgow alone has been a thriving exporter of musical talent since the 80s, generating bands like **Simple Minds** and **Tears for Fears.** Today, Glaswegians are most proud of their stylish rock gods **Franz Ferdinand.**

FOOD AND DRINK

The frequenter of B&Bs will encounter a glorious **Scottish breakfast,** consisting of beans, fried eggs, potato cakes, fried tomato, and a rasher of bacon. In general, Scottish cuisine greatly resembles English food. Although delicious, buttery **shortbread** will please everyone, only adventurous travelers are likely to sample more traditional dishes, which include **Scotch eggs** (boiled eggs wrapped in sausage, breaded, and fried) and the (in)famous **haggis,** made from a sheep's stomach (see sidebar). Those courageous enough to try it will be rewarded with a zesty, if mushy, delicacy. The truly bravehearted will seek out Scotland's least known specialty, the **fried Mars bar.** While the fad may be over, many chip shops will still make you a crispy, gooey treat.

If the food is not for you, Scotland's **whisky** (spelled without the "e") is certainly more welcoming. Scotch whisky is either "single malt" (from a single distillery), or "blended" (a mixture of several different brands). The malts are excellent and distinctive, with flavors and strengths varied enough to accommodate novices and lifelong devotees alike. Raise a glass yourself at the **distilleries** in Pitlochry (p. 583), the Speyside area (p. 615), or on the Isles of Islay and Jura (p. 595). Due to heavy taxes on alcohol sold in Britain, scotch may be cheaper at home or from duty-free stores than it is in Scotland. The Scots do know how to party: they have the highest alcohol consumption rate in Britain, and, no surprise, are more generous in their licensing laws than in England and Wales—drinks are served later and pubs are open longer (often until midnight or later).

SPORTING AND MERRYMAKING

The Scottish are as passionate about **football** as their English neighbors are, and the intensity of devotion in Glasgow in particular rivals any English fervor. Scottish **rugby** takes a close second to football, with three professional teams drawing crowds in the thousands. **Golf,** the "tyrannising game" that continues to dominate St. Andrews (p. 572), was first invented in 15th-century Scotland.

The over 400 golf courses in Scotland testify to the persistent influence of this sport. Traditional Scottish or **Highland games** originated from competitions under English military oppression, when participants could use only common objects such as hammers, rounded stones, and tree trunks. Although **"tossing the caber"** may look easy, it actually requires a good deal of talent and practice to chuck an 18 ft., 150 lb. pine trunk. Weekend clan gatherings, bagpipe competitions, and Highland games occur frequently in Scotland, especially in summer; check for events at TICs and in local newspapers. In addition, the Scottish Tourist Board publishes the annual *Scotland Events*, which details happenings across Scotland.

Each year a slew of festivals celebrate Scotland's distinctive history and culture. June and July's **Common Ridings** in the Borders (p. 545) and the raucous **Up-Helly-Aa'** in Shetland on the last Tuesday in January (p. 665) are among the best known. Scotland is also famous for its New Year's Eve celebration, known as **Hogmanay.** The party goes on all over the country, taking over the streets in Edinburgh and Glasgow (check www.hogmanay.net for events and locations). Above all events towers the **Edinburgh International Festival** (Aug. 14-Sept. 4 in 2005; ☎0131 473 2000; www.eif.co.uk), one of the largest in the world. The concentration of musical and theatrical events in the space of three weeks is dizzying; Edinburgh's cafes and shops stay open all hours and pipers roam the streets. Be sure to catch the **Fringe Festival** (Aug. 7-29 in 2005; ☎0131 226 0000; www.edfringe.com), the much less costly sibling of the International Festival. There are literally hundreds of performances every day, including drama, comedy acts, jazz, and a bit of the bizarre. Travelers planning to travel to Scotland in August should plan well ahead and be sure to swing by Edinburgh.

SOUTHERN SCOTLAND

Southern Scotland offers a rich past and a promising present. In the Borders region, castles and ruined abbeys commemorate Scotland's struggles with England. East of the tranquil Isle of Arran, nearly 80% of Scots cluster in the metropolitan areas of Edinburgh and Glasgow. A fountainhead of the Enlightenment and Scotland's capital, Edinburgh is a singularly beautiful city and draws enormous crowds each summer during its festivals. Glasgow hosts formidable art collections and a kinetic, student-fed nightlife.

HIGHLIGHTS OF SOUTHERN SCOTLAND

CATCH a play or 19 at world's biggest arts festival—the simultaneous Edinburgh International and Fringe—held every August (p. 544).

PONDER the past at the four Border Abbeys, a ring of medieval ruins with a bloody past, set today amidst quiet villages and hills (p. 549).

SURVEY magnificent architecture, free museums, hundreds of pubs, and Britain's highest concentration of Indian restaurants in Glasgow (p. 561).

EDINBURGH ☎0131

A city of elegant stone, Edinburgh (ED-in-bur-ra; pop. 500,000) is set on an ancient volcano amid rolling hills. Since King David I granted it burgh (town) status in 1130, Edinburgh has been a site of political and cultural significance. Here the medieval Stuarts created a center for the arts and the seeds of the Scottish Reformation and Enlightenment were sown. Infused with cosmopolitan verve, today's city endures as a cultural beacon, its medieval spires rising above streets lined with rollicking pubs. In August, Edinburgh becomes an arts mecca, drawing talent and crowds from around the globe to its festivals.

✈ INTERCITY TRANSPORTATION

Edinburgh lies 45 mi. east of Glasgow and 405 mi. northwest of London on Scotland's east coast, on the southern bank of the Firth of Forth.

Flights: Edinburgh International Airport (☎333 1000), 7 mi. west of the city. Lothian **Airlink** (☎555 6363) shuttles between the airport and Waverley Bridge (25min.; every 10-15min., every hr. after midnight; £3, children £2). An **Airsaver** ticket buys a trip on Airlink and 1 day unlimited travel on Lothian buses (£4.20, children £2.50).

Trains: Waverley Station, in the center of town, lies between Princes St., Market St., and Waverley Bridge. Luggage storage £5 per item per day. Free bike storage beside Platform 1. Ticket office open M-Sa 4:45am-12:30am, Su 7am-12:30am. Trains (☎08457 484 950) from: **Aberdeen** (2½hr.; M-Sa every hr., Su 8 per day; £31.60); **Glasgow** (1hr., 4 per hr., £7.80-8.60); **Inverness** (3½hr., every 2hr., £31.60); **London King's Cross** (4¾hr., every hr., £82.70-88.50); **Oban** via Glasgow (4½hr., 3 per day, £25.50); **Stirling** (50min., 2 per hr., £5.30); **Thurso** and **Wick** (7½hr., M-Sa 1 per day, £40.20).

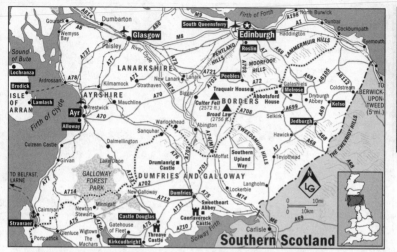

Southern Scotland

Buses: The modern **Edinburgh Bus Station** is on the eastern side of St. Andrew Sq. Open daily 6am-midnight. Ticket office open daily 8am-8pm. **National Express** (☎08705 808 080) from **London** (10hr., 4 per day, £28.50). **Scottish Citylink** (☎08705 505 050) from: **Aberdeen** (4hr., every hr., £15); **Glasgow** (1hr.; M-Sa 3 per hr., Su 2 per hr.; £3.80); **Inverness** (4½hr., 8-10 per day, £14.70). A bus-ferry route via Stranraer goes to **Belfast** (2 per day, £20) and **Dublin** (1 per day, £28).

▣ LOCAL TRANSPORTATION

Public Transportation: Though your feet will usually suffice (and are often faster) within the city center, Edinburgh has a comprehensive bus system. **Lothian** (☎555 6363; www.lothianbuses.co.uk) buses provide most services. Exact change required (40p-£1). Buy a 1-day **Daysaver** ticket (£2.30, children £2) from any driver or in the **Lothian Travelshops** on Waverley Bridge (☎475 4615), Hanover St. (☎475 0650), and Shandwick Pl. (☎475 0675). Open M-Sa 8:30am-6pm, Su 9:30am-5pm. **Night buses** cover selected routes after midnight (£2). **First Edinburgh** (☎0870 872 7271) also operates buses locally. **Traveline** (☎0800 232 323) has information on local public transport.

Taxis: Taxi stands are located at all stations and on almost every corner on Princes St. **City Cabs** (☎228 1211); **Central Radio Taxis** (☎229 2468); **Central Taxis Edinburgh** (☎229 2468; www.taxis-edinburgh.co.uk).

Car Rental: The TIC has a list of rental agencies, from £25 per day. **Thrifty,** 42 Haymarket Terr. (☎337 1319); **Avis,** 100 Dalry Rd. (☎337 6363).

Bike Rental: Biketrax, 11 Lochrin Pl. (☎228 6633; www.biketrax.co.uk). Mountain bikes £12 half-day, £16 full. Open M-Sa 9:30am-5:30pm, Su noon-5pm. **Edinburgh Cycle Hire,** 29 Blackfriars St. (☎556 5560, or 07796 886 899), off High St. Organizes cycle tours. Mountain bikes £10-15 per day, £50-70 per week. Open daily 10am-6pm.

▦ ORIENTATION

Edinburgh is a glorious city for walking. **Princes Street** is the main thoroughfare in **New Town,** the northern section of the city. From New Town you can view the impressive stone facade of the towering **Old Town,** the southern half of the city. The

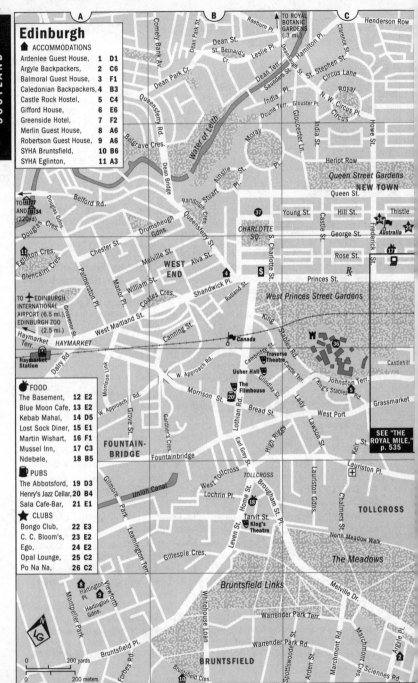

SOUTHERN SCOTLAND

Edinburgh

🏠 **ACCOMMODATIONS**

Ardenlee Guest House,	**1 D1**
Argyle Backpackers,	**2 C6**
Balmoral Guest House,	**3 F1**
Caledonian Backpackers,	**4 B3**
Castle Rock Hostel,	**5 C4**
Gifford House,	**6 E6**
Greenside Hotel,	**7 F2**
Merlin Guest House,	**8 A6**
Robertson Guest House,	**9 A6**
SYHA Bruntsfield,	**10 B6**
SYHA Eglinton,	**11 A3**

🍴 **FOOD**

The Basement,	**12 E2**
Blue Moon Cafe,	**13 E2**
Kebab Mahal,	**14 D5**
Lost Sock Diner,	**15 E1**
Martin Wishart,	**16 F1**
Mussel Inn,	**17 C3**
Ndebele,	**18 B5**

🍺 **PUBS**

The Abbotsford,	**19 D3**
Henry's Jazz Cellar,	**20 B4**
Sala Cafe-Bar,	**21 E1**

⭐ **CLUBS**

Bongo Club,	**22 E3**
C. C. Bloom's,	**23 E2**
Ego,	**24 E2**
Opal Lounge,	**25 C2**
Po Na Na,	**26 C2**

SEE "THE ROYAL MILE," p. 535

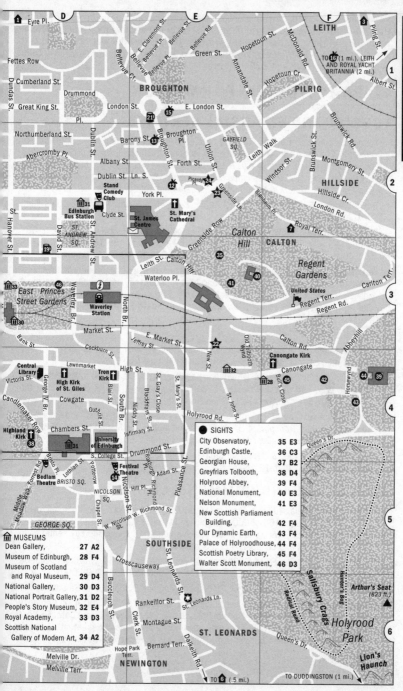

SIGHTS

Sight	Ref
City Observatory,	35 E3
Edinburgh Castle,	36 C3
Georgian House,	37 B2
Greyfriars Tolbooth,	38 D4
Holyrood Abbey,	39 F4
National Monument,	40 E3
Nelson Monument,	41 E3
New Scottish Parliament Building,	42 F4
Our Dynamic Earth,	43 F4
Palace of Holyroodhouse,	44 F4
Scottish Poetry Library,	45 F4
Walter Scott Monument,	46 D3

MUSEUMS

Dean Gallery,	27 A2
Museum of Edinburgh,	28 F4
Museum of Scotland and Royal Museum,	29 D4
National Gallery,	30 D3
National Portrait Gallery,	31 D2
People's Story Museum,	32 E4
Royal Academy,	33 D3
Scottish National Gallery of Modern Art,	34 A2

Royal Mile (Castle Hill, Lawnmarket, High St., and Canongate) is the major road in the Old Town and connects Edinburgh Castle in the west to the Palace of Holyroodhouse in the east. **North Bridge, Waverley Bridge,** and **The Mound** connect Old and New Town, with Waverly Station between the two. Two miles northeast, **Leith** is the city's seaport on the Firth of Forth.

▨ PRACTICAL INFORMATION

TOURIST AND FINANCIAL SERVICES

Tourist Information Centre: Waverley Market, 3 Princes St. (☎473 3800), north of Waverley Station. Slick, helpful, and often mobbed, the mothership of all Scottish TIC's books rooms for a £3 charge plus a 10% deposit; sells bus, museum, tour, and theater tickets; and has excellent free maps and pamphlets. Bureau de change. Open Oct.-Apr. 9am-6pm; Nov.-Mar. M-W 9am-5pm, Th-Sa 9am-6pm, Su 10am-5pm.

Budget Travel: STA Travel, 27 Forrest Rd. (☎226 7747). Open M-W and F 10am-6pm, Th 10am-7pm, Sa 10am-5pm.

Financial Services: Banks are everywhere. **Thomas Cook,** 52 Hanover St. (☎226 5500). Open M-Sa 9am-5:30pm. **American Express,** 69 George St. (☎718 2505, or 08706 001 600). Open M-Tu and Th-F 9am-5:30pm, W 9:30am-5:30pm, Sa 9am-7pm.

Work Opportunities: In summer hordes of young travelers are employed by festival organizers to help manage offices, set up, and help with publicity. In addition, employment agencies are always seeking temporary workers. **Temp Agency** (☎478 5151); **Wesser and Partner** (☎01438 356 222, www.wesser.co.uk); **Kelly Services** (☎220 2626).

LOCAL SERVICES

Camping Supplies: Outdoor Edinburgh, Princes Mall, Waverly Bridge (☎558 7777). All the essentials, but no rentals. Open M-Sa 9am-7pm, Su 11am-6pm.

GLBT Services: Pick up the *Gay Information* pamphlet at the TIC, or drop by the **Edinburgh Lesbian, Gay, and Bisexual Centre,** 58a-60 Broughton St. (☎478 7069), inside the Sala Cafe-Bar. See also **Gay and Lesbian Nightlife,** p. 543.

Disabled Services: The TIC has info on access to restaurants and sights, and stocks *The Access Guide* and *Transport in Edinburgh.* **Shopmobility,** The Mound (☎225 9559), by the National Gallery, lends motorized wheelchairs for free. Open Tu-Sa 10am-3:45pm.

Public Showers: In the "Superloo" at the train station. Shower, toilet, and towel £3. Toilet 20p. Open daily 4am-12:45am.

EMERGENCY AND COMMUNICATIONS

Police: Headquarters at Fettes Ave. (☎311 3901; www.lbp.police.uk). Other stations at 14 St. Leonard's St. (☎662 5000); Torphichen Pl. (☎229 2323); 188 High St. (☎226 6966). Blue **police information boxes** are scattered throughout the city center, with tourist information and an emergency assistance button.

Hospitals: Royal Infirmary of Edinburgh, 41 Lauriston Pl. (☎536 1000, emergencies 536 6000). **Royal Hospital for Sick Children,** 9 Sciennes Rd. (☎200 2000).

Pharmacy: 101-103 Princes St. (☎225 8331). Open M-F 8:30am-6pm, Sa 9am-6pm.

Internet Access: Free Internet access at the **Central Library** (☎242 8000), on George IV Bridge. Open M-Th 10am-8pm, F 10am-5pm, Sa 9am-1pm. **easyInternet Cafe,** 58 Rose St. (☎220 3577), inside Cafe Nero, has hundreds of terminals and great rates. £1 per 30min. Open M-Sa 7am-10pm, Su 9am-10pm. **Bytes & Slices Internet Lounge,** Waverley Sq., on the steps leading from Princes St. to Waverley Station. Slightly higher prices but more advanced technology, like DVD burners and scanner. Also serves food. £1 per 15min., £2.50 per hour. Open M-F 8am-9:30pm, Sa-Su 10am-8pm.

Post Office: (☎556 9546), in the St. James Centre beside the Bus Station. Bureau de Change. M-Sa 9am-5:30pm. Branch at 46 St. Mary's St. (☎556 6351) Open M-Tu and Th-F 9am-12:30pm and 1:30-5:30pm, Sa 9am-noon. **Post Code:** EH1 3SR.

ACCOMMODATIONS

Hostels and **hotels** are the only city-center options, while **B&Bs** and **guest houses** begin on the edges. It's a good idea to book ahead in summer, and essential to be well ahead of the game during festival time (late July to early September) and New Year's. Many locals let their apartments; the TIC's booking service works magic.

HOSTELS AND CAMPING

This backpacker's paradise offers a bevy of convenient hostels, many of them smack-dab in the middle of town, ranging from the small and cozy to the huge and party-oriented. Expect cliques of long-term residents. Several also offer more expensive private rooms with varying amenities.

▧ **High St. Hostel,** 8 Blackfriars St. (☎557 3984). Good facilities, party atmosphere, and a Royal Mile location. Friendly staff leads a daily tour. 4- to 16- bed rooms, co-ed available. Part of the Scotland's Top Hostels chain (www.scotlands-top-hostels.com), which hosts MacBackpackers tours. 18+. Continental breakfast £1.90. Internet access and laundry. Dorms £12.50. Ask about working for a free night's stay. AmEx/MC/V. ❶

▧ **Castle Rock Hostel,** 15 Johnston Terr. (☎225 9666). Just steps from the castle, this friendly hostel has regal views and a top-notch cinema room. Nightly movies. 220 beds in 8- to 16-bed dorms. Continental breakfast £1.90. No lockable dorms. Laundry. Internet access 80p per 30min. Dorms £12.50, £14 during festival. AmEx/MC/V. ❶

Brodies Backpackers 2, 93 High St. (☎556 2223; www.brodieshostels.co.uk). This Royal Mile hostel is a sweet deal, with a luxurious common room, kitchen, clean showers and heavenly beds. Family rooms available. 4- to 10-bed all-female and co-ed dorms. Valuables lockers available. Free Internet access. Dorms £11-16, £17.50 during festival; doubles £34-45; quads from £55. MC/V. ❷

Brodies Backpackers 1, 12 High St. (☎556 6770; www.brodieshostels.co.uk). Party environment at this small Royal Mile hostel. 50 beds in large, dorm-style rooms (3 co-ed, 1 all-female) with rustic wooden bunks, stone walls, and tartan spreads. No lockable dorms; valuables lockers available. Laundry and free Internet access. 24hr. key card access. Dorms £10.90-13.90. MC/V. ❶

Edinburgh Backpackers, 65 Cockburn (CO-burn) St. (☎220 1717; www.hoppo.com). Friendly and energetic, with common areas, pool table, ping-pong, and TV. 15% discount at the downstairs cafe. 96 beds in 8- to 16-bed co-ed dorms. Lockable dorms; valuables lockers available. Laundry and Internet access. Reception 24hr. Check-out 10am. Dorms £13-15.50, £18 during festival; private rooms £44.50-72. MC/V. ❷

Argyle Backpackers, 14 Argyle Pl. (☎667 9991). Take bus #41 from The Mound to Melville Dr. 2 renovated townhouses with a backyard and cafe. An alternative to louder city hostels; private rooms, many with TV. 60 beds in 3- to 8-bed dorms. Lockable dorms. Internet access £1.50 per hr. Dorms £12-15; doubles £34-40. AmEx/MC/V. ❶

Royal Mile Backpackers, 105 High St. (☎557 6120; www.scotlands-top-hostels.com). A small hostel with community feel, largely due to the many long-term residents. Guests can use amenities at nearby High St. Hostel. 38 beds in 8-bed dorms. Continental breakfast £1.90. No lockable dorms. Dorms £12.50. AmEx/MC/V. ❶

St. Christopher's Inn, 9-13 Market St. (☎226 1446; www.st-christophers.co.uk), across from Waverley Station. A clean and friendly outpost of a chain. Good security. Wheelchair accessible. No kitchen. Lockable dorms; lockers, £2-3 padlocks available. Laundry and Internet access. Dorms £15-18; doubles £42-46. MC/V. ❶

City Centre Tourist Hostel, 5 W. Register St. (☎556 8070; www.scotland-hostels.com), shares an entrance with Princes St. East Backpackers but completely separate. Small, comfortable New Town hostel close to Waverley Station. Very clean with a relaxed atmosphere. 40 beds in 4- to 10-bed dorms. No lockable dorms; no lockers. Reception 24hr. Dorms £10-18. Cash only. ❷

Caledonian Backpackers, 3 Queensferry St. (☎476 7224; www.caledonianbackpackers.com), at the west end of Princes St. This large, recently renovated hostel has spacious dorms and a backpackers' bar that stays open late with live music F-Sa and Tu open mic. 284 beds. 2 kitchens. Lockable dorms; lockers. Laundry and Internet access. Dorms £11-18, from £14 during festival; private rooms from £36. MC/V. ❷

SYHA Hostels (www.syha.org.uk). Not always fun, but always clean, safe, and well-run.

Eglinton, 18 Eglinton Cres. (☎227 1120). An impressive Victorian house near Haymarket Station in the west of the city. 150 beds in 2- to 10-bed dorms. Self-catering kitchen. Continental breakfast £2.80, full English breakfast £3.95, dinner £5.95. Lockable dorms and lockers. Laundry and internet access. Check-out 10am. Dorms £11.75-18, under 18 £10.50-14. MC/V. ❷

Bruntsfield, 7 Bruntsfield Cres. (☎447 2994). Take bus #11, 15-17, or 23. Standard hostel overlooking a park, still relatively close to the city center. Kitchen. Sony PlayStation £1. Bag breakfast £1.30. Laundry and Internet access. Dorms £12.50-20, under 18 £11-20. MC/V. ❷

International and Central. Apart from the two permanent hostels, the SYHA turns two University of Edinburgh dorms into hostels during July and August. **International,** Kincard's Ct., Guthrie St. (☎0871 330 8519) and **Central,** Robertson's Close, Cowgate (☎0871 330 8517). Offer plain but spacious single rooms, self-catering kitchens on each floor, laundry facilities, Internet access, and in-room phones. Dorms £20-22. MC/V. ❷

Camping: Edinburgh Caravan Club Site, Marine Dr. (☎312 6874), by the Forth. Take bus #8A from North Bridge. Electricity, showers, hot water, laundry, and shop. £4-5 per person, £3 per pitch. Cash only. ❶

HOTELS

Most of the independent city center hotels have stratospheric prices. At the affordable end are budget **chain hotels**—lacking in character, but comfortable.

Grassmarket Hotel, 94 Grassmarket (☎0870 990 6400), formerly Premier Lodge, offers tiny rooms at a reasonable rate in the heart of Old Town. Singles £30. MC/V. ❸

Greenside Hotel, 9 Royal Terr. (☎557 0022), is a refurbished Georgian building with views of the Firth from its top floors. Singles £25-65; doubles £45-90. AmEx/MC/V. ❸

B&BS AND GUEST HOUSES

B&Bs cluster in three well-stocked colonies, all of which you can walk to or reach by bus from the city center. Try Gilmore Pl., Viewforth Terr., or Huntington Gardens in the **Bruntsfield** district, south from the west end of Princes St. (bus #11, 16, or 17 west/southbound); Dalkeith Rd. and Minto St. in **Newington,** south from the east end of Princes St. (bus #7, 31, or 37, among others); or **Pilrig,** northeast from the east end of Princes St. (bus #11 east/northbound).

⊠ Ardenlee Guest House, 9 Eyre Pl. (☎556 2838). Bus #23 or 27 from Hanover St. northbound to the corner of Dundas St. and Eyre Pl. Near the Royal Botanic Gardens, this friendly guest house has big, comfy rooms. £30-45 per person. MC/V. ❸

Merlin Guest House, 14 Hartington Pl. (☎229 3864), just over 1 mi. southwest of the Royal Mile. Bus #10 or 27 from Princes St. Comfortable, well-priced rooms. £17-22.50 per person; student discounts in winter. Cash only. ❷

Gifford House, 103 Dalkeith Rd. (☎667 4688), under 2 mi. from the city center. Bus #33 from Princes St. Enormous rooms and good views of Arthur's Seat. Singles £27-55; doubles £55-95; family rooms £80-140. MC/V. ❸

Robertson Guest House, 5 Hartington Gardens (☎229 2652; www.robertson-guesthouse.com). Bus #10 or 27 from Princes St. Quiet and welcoming, with a nice garden patio. £30-35 per person, £40-50 during festival. MC/V. ❸

Balmoral Guest House, 32 Pilrig St. (☎554 1857; www.balmoralguesthouse.co.uk). Bus #11 from Princes St. Wrap yourself in the warm welcome at this well-furnished guest house. Singles £30-40; doubles £50-70. MC/V. ❸

◨ FOOD

Edinburgh features a wide range of cuisines and restaurants. If it's traditional fare you're after, the capital won't disappoint, with everything from pub haggis to creative "modern Scottish" at the city's top restaurants. For food on the cheap, many **pubs** offer student and hosteler discounts in the early evening, while fast-food joints are scattered across New Town. Takeaway shops on **South Clerk Street, Leith Street,** and **Lothian Road** have well-priced Chinese and Indian fare. For **groceries,** try **Sainsbury's,** 9-10 St. Andrew Sq. (☎225 8400. Open M-Sa 7am-10pm, Su 10am-8pm.)

OLD TOWN

▧ **The City Cafe,** 19 Blair St. (☎220 0125), right off the Royal Mile behind the Tron Kirk. This Edinburgh institution is popular with the young and tightly-clad; a cafe by day and a flashy pre-club spot by night. Try the herb chicken and avocado melt (£6). Incredible milkshakes. Happy hour daily 5-8pm. Open daily 11am-1am (3am during festival). Food served until 11pm. MC/V. ❶

▧ **The Elephant House,** 21 George IV Bridge (☎220 5355). Here Harry Potter and Hogwarts were born on hastily scribbled napkins. A perfect place to chill, chat, or read a newspaper. Exotic teas and coffees, the best shortbread in the universe, and filling fare for less than £5. Great views of the castle. Live music Th 8pm. Happy hour daily 8-9pm. Open daily 8am-11pm. MC/V. ❶

Kebab Mahal, 7 Nicolson Sq. (☎667 5214). This unglamorous, student-filled hole-in-the-wall will stuff you with authentic Indian tandoori for under £5. Worth the wait, but takeaway is available. Open Su-Th noon-midnight, F-Sa noon-2am. AmEx/MC/V. ❶

The Last Drop, 74-78 Grassmarket (☎225 4851). Tourist-friendly pub by the old gallows—hence the name. "Haggis, tatties, and neeps" for carnivores or herbivores (£5). Student and hosteler discounts until 7pm. Open daily 10am-2am. AmEx/MC/V. ❶

NEW TOWN

The Basement, 10a-12a Broughton St. (☎557 0097; www.thebasement.org.uk). The menu changes daily, with plenty of vegetarian options. Draws a lively mix of locals to its candlelit cavern for Mexican Sa-Su and Thai W nights. Entrees £6-9.50. Reservations recommended. Food served daily noon-10:30pm; drinks until 1am. AmEx/MC/V. ❷

Jekyll and Hyde, 112 Hanover St. (☎235 2022 www.eeriepubco.com). This themed establishment offers "food to die for" (entrees £4.75-7.95) and "throat warmers." Open daily 11am-1am, until 3am during festival. Food served daily 11am-9pm. MC/V. ❷

Lost Sock Diner, 11 E. London St. (☎557 6097). Order a delicious dinner (£4-8) while waiting for your clothes to dry. Open M 9am-4pm, Tu-Th 9am-10pm, F-Sa 10am-11pm, Su 11am-5pm. Cash only. ❷

Mussel Inn, 61-65 Rose St. (☎225 5979; www.mussel-inn.com). Muscle your way in for superior local shellfish. Entrees under £10. Open M-Th noon-3pm and 6pm-10pm, F-Sa noon-10pm, Su 12:30-10pm. MC/V. ❷

Hadrian's Brasserie, 2 North Bridge (☎557 5000). Despite its suave decor and location in the swanky Balmoral Hotel, Hadrian's classic British dishes are reasonably priced. All-day 3-course menu £11. Dinner £14. Open M-Sa 7-10:30am, noon-2:30pm, 6:30-10:30pm; Su 7:30-11am, 12:30-3pm, 6:30-10:30pm. AmEx/MC/V. ❸

ELSEWHERE

🏠 **Ndebele,** 57 Home St., Tolcross (☎221 1141; www.ndebele.co.uk), ¾ mi. south from the west end of Princes St. Serves generous portions. Try an ostrich and mango chutney sandwich (£3.80, £2.60 takeaway) or a piece of chocolate chili cheesecake (£2). South African food and handicrafts in the basement. Open daily 10am-10pm. MC/V. ❶

Restaurant Martin Wishart, 54 The Shore, Leith (☎553 3557; www.martin-wishart.co.uk), near the Royal Yacht Britannia. An exquisite and imaginative showcase of French cooking. Open Tu-F noon-2pm and 7-9:30pm, Sa 7-9:30pm. AmEx/MC/V. ❺

⬅ SIGHTS

TOURS

While a great array of tour companies in Edinburgh tout themselves as "the original" or "the scariest," the most worthwhile of the bunch is 🏠**McEwan's Edinburgh Literary Pub Tour.** Led by professional actors, this 2hr., alcohol-friendly crash course in Scottish literature meets outside the Beehive Inn on Grassmarket. (☎226 6665; www.scot-lit-tour-co.uk. Daily May-Sept. 7:30pm; Mar-Apr. and Oct. Th-Su 7:30pm; Nov.-Feb. F 7:30pm. £8, concessions £6. £1 discount for online booking.) The **City of the Dead Tour,** 40 Candlemaker Row, and its promised one-on-one encounter with the MacKenzie Poltergeist is the most popular. (☎225 9044; www.blackhard.uk.com. Daily Easter to Halloween 8:30, 9:15, 10pm; Halloween to Easter 7:30 and 8:30pm. £7, concessions £5, children £4.) **Mercat Tours,** leaving from Mercat Cross, enter Edinburgh's spooky underground vaults, although they rely upon long-winded ghost stories rather than real frights. (☎557 6464; www.mercattours.com. £3-7.50, families £16-19.)

Edinburgh is best explored by foot, but should you begin to tire, several similar hop-on, hop-off open-top bus tours stop at the major sights, beginning at Waverley Bridge. **City Sightseeing Edinburgh** (www.edinburghtour.com) buses run most frequently (£8, concessions £6.50, children £2.50, families £19.50); others include the **Majestic Tour** to New Haven and the Royal Yacht Britannia (£8.50, concessions £7.50, children £2.50, families £19.50), **MacTours** (www.edinburghtours.com), and the **Britannia Tour,** which runs to Leith. (General tour bus information ☎220 0770.)

THE OLD TOWN AND THE ROYAL MILE

Edinburgh's medieval center, the **Royal Mile,** runs through **Old Town** and by many fascinating sights. Once lined with narrow shopfronts and slums, this famous strip is now a playground, buzzing with bars and attractions. Cheesy souvenir stores overcrowd more interesting shops, but treasures can still be found. Try the outstanding 🏠**Royal Mile Whiskies,** 379 High St. Offering a staggering selection

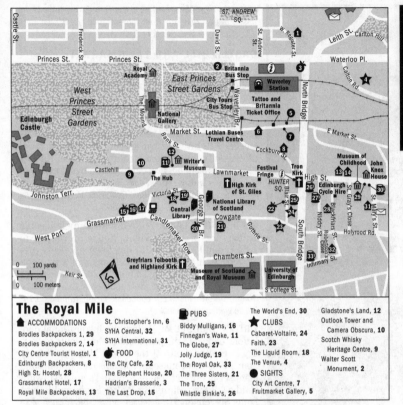

The Royal Mile

ACCOMMODATIONS

Brodies Backpackers 1, **29**
Brodies Backpackers 2, **14**
City Centre Tourist Hostel, **1**
Edinburgh Backpackers, **8**
High St. Hostel, **28**
Grassmarket Hotel, **17**
Royal Mile Backpackers, **13**

St. Christopher's Inn, **6**
SYHA Central, **32**
SYHA International, **31**

FOOD

The City Cafe, **22**
The Elephant House, **20**
Hadrian's Brasserie, **3**
The Last Drop, **15**

PUBS

Biddy Mulligans, **16**
Finnegan's Wake, **11**
The Globe, **27**
Jolly Judge, **19**
The Royal Oak, **33**
The Three Sisters, **21**
The Tron, **25**
Whistle Binkie's, **26**

The World's End, **30**

CLUBS

Cabaret-Voltaire, **24**
Faith, **23**
The Liquid Room, **18**
The Venue, **4**

SIGHTS

City Art Centre, **7**
Fruitmarket Gallery, **5**

The World's End, **30**
Gladstone's Land, **12**
Outlook Tower and
  Camera Obscura, **10**
Scotch Whisky
  Heritage Centre, **9**
Walter Scott
  Monument, **2**

of whiskies and ales, the knowledgeable staff will help even the most novice drinkers find something to suit them. (☎ 225 3383; www.royalmilewhiskies.com. 18+. Open M-Sa 10am-6pm, Su 12:30-6pm; open until 8pm during festival.)

■**EDINBURGH CASTLE.** Perched atop an extinct volcano, Edinburgh Castle dominates the city skyline. Its oldest surviving building is tiny, 12th-century **St. Margaret's Chapel,** built by King David I in memory of his mother. The castle compound developed over the course of centuries; the most recent additions date to the 1920s. The central **Palace,** begun in the 1430s, was home to Stewart Kings and Queens and contains the room where Mary, Queen of Scots, gave birth to the eventual King James VI. It also houses the **Scottish Crown Jewels,** which are older than those in London. The storied (though visually unspectac-ular) Stone of Scone, more commonly known as the **Stone of Destiny** (p. 536) is also on permanent display. Other sections of the sprawling compound, like the Scottish National War Memorial, the National War Museum of Scotland, and the 15th-century monster cannon Mons Meg, definitely merit a visit, despite the uphill climb (or bus ride). The **One O'Clock Gun** fires Monday to Saturday. *(Looming over the city center. ☎ 225 9846. Open daily Apr.-Oct. 9:30am-6pm; Nov.-Mar. 9:30am-5pm.*

LOCAL LEGEND

STONE OF DESTINY

Traveling from the Holy Land to Egypt, Sicily, and Spain before arriving in Ireland in 700 BC, the Stone of Scone (sometimes called "The Stone of Destiny") covered a lot of ground before it began its more recent commute between England and Scotland. The stone gained prominence by its association with the corona-ion of Scottish kings, but its recent shuttling between the two countries has created a contem-porary folklore almost as legend-ary as the origins of the stone.

On Christmas Day, 1950, Scottish patriot Ian Hamilton hid in Westminster Abbey, where the stone had resided since 1296. He intended to steal the 440 lb. (31 stone) stone and return it to Scotland, but he was detected before the heist was completed. Hamilton (later a prominent Scot-ish MP) convinced the watch-man that he had been locked in accidentally.

That same night, Hamilton and accomplices pulled the stone from its stand, breaking it into two pieces in the process. The stone was sent to a Glasgow workyard for repairs; while in Scotland, it was displayed at the altar in Arbroath Abbey before returning to Westminster. But according to some, the stone never made it back. Glasgow councilor Bertie Gray later revealed that the stone was copied and a fake returned. The real deal is now on display at Edinburgh Castle, where it stays under heavy guard.

Last admission 45min. before close. Free guided tours of the castle depart regularly from the entrance. £9.80, children £3.50, under 5 free. Excellent audio guide £3.)

CASTLE HILL AND LAWNMARKET

CASTLE HILL. The Scotch Whisky Experience at the **Scotch Whisky Heritage Centre,** provides a Disney-style 50min. tour through the "history and mystery" of Scotland's most famous export. *(354 Castle Hill. ☎ 220 0441. Open daily 9:45am-5:30pm; reduced winter hours. Tours every 15min. £8.50, concessions £6.40, children £4.50, families £20.)* Across the street, the **Outlook Tower** affords city views from a rooftop terrace. Its 150-year-old **camera obscura** captures a moving image of the streets below. *(Open daily July-Aug. 9:30am-7:30pm; Apr.-June and Sept.-Oct. 9:30am-6pm; Nov.-Mar. 10am-5pm. £6, concessions £4.70, children £3.80.)*

GLADSTONE'S LAND. Staffed with knowledgeable guides, the oldest surviving house on the Royal Mile (completed in 1620) has been carefully pre-served, with hand-painted ceilings and a fine col-lection of 17th-century Dutch art. *(477b Lawnmarket. ☎ 226 5856. Open Apr.-Oct. daily 10am-5pm. Last admission 30min. before close. £5, concessions £4, families £14. Braille guidebook available.)*

WRITER'S MUSEUM. Follow the inspirational quo-tations etched in the pavement to this tribute to liter-ary personae, just off the Royal Mile down Lady Stair's Close. The museum contains memorabilia and manuscripts from three of Scotland's greatest word-smiths—Robert Burns, Sir Walter Scott, and Robert Louis Stevenson. *(Lawnmarket. ☎ 529 4901. Open M-Sa 10am-5pm; during Festival also Su 2-5pm. Free.)*

PRINCES STREET GARDENS. Located directly in the city center and affording fantastic views of Old Town and the castle, this lush park is on the site of now-drained Nor' Loch, where Edinburghers used to drown accused witches. The Loch has been replaced with an impeccably manicured lawn, stone fountains, winding avenues lined with benches, and enough shady trees to provide shelter from the Scottish "sun." On a fine summer day all of Edinburgh eats lunch here.

HIGH STREET

⊠HIGH KIRK OF ST. GILES. The kirk is Scotland's principal church, sometimes known as **St. Giles Cathedral.** From its pulpit, protestant reformer John Knox delivered the sermons that drove the Catholic Mary, Queen of Scots, into exile. Spectac-ular stained-glass windows illuminate the structure, whose crown spire is one of Edinburgh's hallmarks. The 20th-century **Thistle Chapel** honors the Most Ancient and Most Noble Order of the Thistle, Scotland's prestigious chivalric order. St. Giles is flanked on the east by the stone **Mercat Cross,** marking the site of the medieval market (hence, "mercat") and on the west by the **Heart of Midlothian,** inlaid in the pavement. According to city legend, spitting on the Heart protects you from being hanged in the square. (Watch out for tour groups.) The cathedral hosts free organ and choral concerts throughout the year. *(Where Lawnmarket becomes High St. ☎225 4363. Open Easter to mid-Sept. M-F 9am-7pm, Sa 9am-5pm, Su 1-5pm; mid-Sept. to Easter M-Sa 9am-5pm, Su 1-5pm. Suggested donation £1.)*

TRON KIRK. A block downhill from St. Giles rises the high-steepled Tron Kirk—built to deal with the overflow of 16th-century religious zealots from St. Giles. Today, it houses the **Old Town Information Centre,** inside the kirk beside an open archaeological dig, and is the focus of Edinburgh's Hogmanay celebrations. *(Open daily Apr.-Oct. 10am-5:30pm; Nov.-Mar. noon-5pm; extended hours during Festival. Free.)*

CANONGATE

Canongate, the steep hill that constitutes the last segment of the Royal Mile, was once a separate burgh and part of an Augustinian abbey. Here, the Royal Mile's furious tourism and, not coincidentally, much of its appeal, begins to dwindle.

CANONGATE KIRK. Royals used to worship in this 17th-century chapel when in residence. Adam Smith, founder of modern economics, lies in the slope to the left of the entrance. Down the hill from his grave, find the famous joint effort of three literary Roberts: Robert Louis Stevenson commemorated a monument erected here by Robert Burns in memory of Robert Fergusson. Great acoustics for festival concerts. *(Open Apr. to mid-Sept. M-F 9am-7pm, Sa 9am-5pm, Su 1-5pm; mid-Sept. to Mar. M-Sa 9am-5pm, Su 1-5pm. Free.)*

SCOTTISH POETRY LIBRARY. A relaxing refuge from the main tourist drag in an award-winning piece of expansive modern architecture, the library treasures a fine collection of Scottish and international poetry. *(5 Crichton's Close. ☎557 2876; www.spl.org.uk. Open M-F 11am-6pm, Sa 1-5pm. Free.)*

HOLYROOD

PALACE OF HOLYROODHOUSE. This Stewart palace at the base of the Royal Mile remains Queen Elizabeth II's official Scottish residence. As a result, only parts of the ornate interior are open to the public, though these still merit a visit. Once home to Mary, Queen of Scots, whose bedchamber is on display, the palace is every bit a royal residence. Dozens of portraits inside the **Great Gallery** confirm its proud history. On the palace grounds lie the ruins of **Holyrood Abbey,** built by King David I in 1128 and ransacked during the Reformation. Only a single doorway remains from the original construction; most of the ruins date from the 13th century. Located in a recently renovated 17th-century schoolhouse near the palace entrance is the **Queen's Gallery,** which displays exhibits from the royal art collection. *(At the bottom of the Royal Mile. ☎556 5100. Open Apr.-Oct. daily 9:30am-6pm; Nov.-Mar. M-Sa 9:30am-4:30pm. Last admission 45min. before close. No admission while royals are in residence (often June-July). Palace £8, concessions £6.50, children £4, families £20. Queen's Gallery £5/4/3/13. Joint £11/9/5.50/27.50. Audio guide free.)*

HOLYROOD SCOTTISH PARLIAMENT BUILDING. After years of controversy and massive budget overruns, the new Scottish Parliament Building is functional and open to visitors. Built from steel, oak, and stone, the building is an attempt to recenter cosmopolitan craziness on the natural. Famed architect Enric Miralles designed a building influenced by the surrounding landscapes, the flower paintings

LOCAL LEGEND

GREYFRIARS BOBBY

Undoubtedly the most famous resident of the Greyfriars Tolbooth and Highland Kirk's ancient cemetery is a certain John Gray. The night after Gray's burial in 1858, his scruffy Skye terrier, Bobby, lay down on his master's grave. The next night Bobby returned and again held vigil, as he would every night for the next 14 years. As word spread of this extraordinary display of canine loyalty, the legend of Greyfriars Bobby became permanent part of Edinburgh lore.

After living to the age of 16, Greyfriars Bobby finally passed away, having spent all but two of his years guarding the tombstone. To honor his loyalty, the city erected a statue of the dog and buried him near his beloved master in the very same kirk.

Over the years this sweet story has found its way into numerous books and even a Disney film. The statue, which sits at the intersection of George IV Bridge and Candlemaker Row, is the most photographed statue in Scotland. Still, there are those who have their doubts about this touching saga. Some claim that the grave that Bobby so admirably watched over belonged in fact to another John Gray and not his master. Others claim that the dog's real affection was for a nearby bakery. Such spoilsports have been unsuccessful in tarnishing the legend, however, which is still alive and well.

of Charles Rennie MacKintosh, and upturned boats on the seashore. (☎ 348 5200; www.scottish.parliament.uk. Open Apr.-Oct. M and F 10am-6pm, Tu-Th 9am-7pm, Sa-Su 10am-4pm; Nov.-Mar. M, F, Sa-Su 10am-4pm, Tu-Th 9am-7pm. Hours may vary; call ahead. Guided tours on non-business days £3.50, concessions £1.75, children under 6 free. Free tickets to the parliamentary sessions; book in advance.)

HOLYROOD PARK. A true city oasis, Holyrood Park is replete with hills, moorland, and lochs. At 823 ft., 🖾**Arthur's Seat,** the park's highest point, affords stunning views of the city and Highlands. Considered a holy place by the Picts, Arthur's Seat is probably derived from "Ard-na-Saigheid," Gaelic for "the height of the flight of arrows." Traces of forts and Bronze Age terraces dot the surrounding hillside. From the Palace of Holyroodhouse, the walk to the summit takes about 45min. **Queen's Drive** circles the park and intersects with Holyrood Rd. by the palace.

ELSEWHERE IN THE OLD TOWN

GREYFRIARS TOLBOOTH AND HIGHLAND KIRK.
Off George IV Bridge, the 17th-century kirk rests in a churchyard that, while lovely, is estimated to contain 250,000 bodies and has long been considered haunted. A few centuries ago, the infamous bodysnatchers Burke and Hare dug up corpses here before resorting to murder in order to keep the Edinburgh Medical School's anatomy laboratories wellsupplied. A more endearing claim to fame is the loyal pooch Greyfriars Bobby, whose much-photographed statue sits at the southwestern corner of George IV Bridge in front of the kirkyard's gates. (Beyond the gates, atop Candlemakers Row. ☎ 225 1900. English services daily 11am, Gaelic services Su 12:30pm. Open for touring Apr.-Oct. M-F 10:30am-4:30pm, Sa 10:30am-2:30pm; Nov.-Mar. Th 1:30-3:30pm. Free.)

NATIONAL LIBRARY OF SCOTLAND. The library rotates exhibitions from its vast archives, which include a Gutenberg Bible, the last letter of Mary, Queen of Scots, and the only surviving original copy of The Wallace, a wildly popular epic poem that inspired a certain wildly popular movie. (George IV Bridge. ☎ 226 4531. Open M-F 9:30am-8:30pm, Sa 9:30am-1pm, Su 2-5pm; during Festival until 8:30pm. Free.)

THE NEW TOWN

Edinburgh's New Town is a masterpiece of Georgian design. James Craig, a 23-year-old architect, won the city-planning contest in 1767, and his rectangular grid of three parallel streets (**Queen, George,** and **Princes**) linking two large squares (**Charlotte** and **St. Andrew**) reflects the Scottish Enlightenment belief in order. Queen St. and Princes St., the outer streets, were built up on only one side to allow views of the Firth of Forth and the Old Town. Princes St., Edinburgh's main shopping drag, is also home to the venerable **Jenner's**, the Harrods of Scotland. (☎225 2442. Open M-Sa 9am-6pm, Su 11am-5pm. AmEx/MC/V.)

⬛WALTER SCOTT MONUMENT. Statues of Sir Walter and his dog preside inside the spire of this Gothic "steeple without a church." Climb 287 winding steps past the carved figures of 64 of Scott's most famous characters to reach the top. An eagle's-eye view of Princes St., the castle, and the surrounding city awaits. *(Princes St. between The Mound and Waverley Bridge. ☎529 4098. Open Apr.-Sept. M-Sa 9am-6pm, Su 10am-6pm; Oct.-Mar. M-Sa 9am-3pm, Su 10am-3pm. £2.50.)*

GEORGIAN HOUSE. Guides staff each room of this elegantly restored home, which provides a fair picture of how Edinburgh's elite lived 200 years ago, during the reign of George III. *(7 Charlotte Sq. ☎226 3318. Open daily Apr.-Oct. 10am-5pm; Mar. and Nov. 11am-3pm. Last admission 30min. before close. £5, concessions £4. Subtitled video and braille guidebook available.)*

CALTON HILL. This somewhat neglected hill at the eastern end of New Town provides a fine view of the city and the Firth of Forth. Climb 143 steps inside the castellated **Nelson Monument,** built in 1807 in memory of the great admiral and the Battle of Trafalgar. *(☎556 2716. Open Apr.-Sept. M 1-6pm, Tu-Sa 10am-6pm; Oct.-Mar. M-Sa 10am-3pm. £2.50.)* The hilltop grounds are also home to the old **City Observatory** (1818) and the **National Monument** (1822), affectionately known as "Edinburgh's Disgrace." The structure, an ersatz Parthenon designed to commemorate those killed in the Napoleonic Wars, was scrapped when civic coffers ran dry after a mere 12 columns were erected. For all its faults, it does give the town an ancient-looking "ruin"; watch the sun rise between its columns from Waverley Bridge in the spring.

BEYOND THE CITY CENTER

LEITH AND THE BRITANNIA. Two miles northeast of city center, the neighborhood of **Leith** has undergone a dramatic revival, its abandoned warehouses replaced (or at least supplemented) by upmarket flats, restaurants, and bars. The **⬛Royal Yacht Britannia,** used by the royal family from 1953 to 1997 (when the government decided it was too expensive and decommissioned it), sailed around the world on state visits and royal holidays. Visitors can follow a free audio tour of the entire flagship, which remains exactly as it was when decommissioned. Highlights include the officers' mess, the royal apartments, and the gleaming engine room. *(Entrance on the Ocean Terminal's 3rd fl. Take bus #22 from Princes St. or #35 from the Royal Mile to Ocean Terminal, £1. ☎555 5566; www.royalyachtbritannia.co.uk. Open daily Mar.-Oct. 9:30am-4pm; Nov.-Feb. 10am-4:30pm. £8.50, concessions £4.50.)*

DEAN VILLAGE. In the **Water of Leith Valley,** northwest of the city, Dean Village was once a busy milling community. Many of the mills remain—some now trendy apartments. The graceful sandstone **Dean Bridge,** a great feat of engineering when it opened in 1832, flies high above the river. A visit to this area might be combined with the **Scottish National Gallery of Modern Art** and **Dean Gallery** (p. 540), both 10min. west of Dean Village along the scenic **Water of Leith Walkway.** *(Walk north on Queensferry St. from the west end of Princes St. Buses #41 and 42 depart from The Mound.)*

CRAIGMILLAR CASTLE. This finely preserved 15th-century castle stands 3½ mi. southeast of central Edinburgh. Mary, Queen of Scots, fled here after the murder of her secretary at Holyroodhouse. While she was here, plans emerged for the murder of her second husband, Lord Darnley. *(Take bus #2, 14 or 32 from Princes St. to* *the corner of Old Dalkeith Rd. and Craigmillar Castle Rd., then walk 10min. up the castle road. ☎661 4445. Open Apr.-Sept. daily 9:30am-6pm; Oct.-Mar. M-W and Sa 9:30am-4:30pm, Th 9:30am-1pm, Su 2pm-4:30pm. £3, seniors £2.25, children £1.20.)*

EDINBURGH ZOO. At long last, your search for the world's largest penguin pool has come to an end. You'll find it along with exhibits featuring some 1000 other animals, 2½ mi. west of the city center. *(Take bus #12, 26, or 31 westbound from Princes St. ☎334 9171; www.edinburghzoo.co.uk. Open daily Apr.-Sept. 9am-6pm; Oct. and Mar. 9am-5pm; Nov.-Feb. 9am-4:30pm. £9, children and seniors £6.)*

ROYAL BOTANIC GARDENS. Edinburgh's herbaceous oasis has plants from around the world. Guided tours wander across the lush grounds and greenhouses crammed with orchids, tree ferns, and towering palms. *(Inverleith Row. Take bus #23 or 27 from Hanover St. ☎552 7171. Open daily Apr.-Sept. 10am-7pm; Mar. and Oct. 10am-6pm; Nov.-Feb. 10am-4pm. Free. Glasshouses £3.50, concessions £3, children £1, families £8.)*

🏛 MUSEUMS AND GALLERIES

NATIONAL GALLERIES OF SCOTLAND

Edinburgh's four major galleries form an elite group, all connected by a free shuttle that runs every 45min. (☎624 6200; www.nationalgalleries.org. All open daily 10am-5pm; during festival 10am-6pm, Th until 7pm. All free.)

🖼 NATIONAL GALLERY OF SCOTLAND. Housed in a grand 19th-century building designed by William Playfair, this compact gallery has a superb collection of works by Renaissance, Romantic, and Impressionist masters, including Raphael, Titian, Gauguin, Degas, and Monet. Don't miss the octagonal room, which displays Poussin's entire *Seven Sacraments*. The basement houses a selection of Scottish art. *(On The Mound between the halves of the Princes St. Gardens.)* The **Royal Academy** hosts exhibits from the National Gallery while also running a high-profile show of its own each summer. *(At the corner of The Mound and Princes St.)*

SCOTTISH NATIONAL PORTRAIT GALLERY. Set in an august red brick building, the gallery displays the faces of the famous men and women who have shaped Scotland's history. Military, political and intellectual figures are all represented, including the definitive portraits of wordsmith Robert Louis Stevenson, renegade Bonnie Prince Charlie, and royal troublemaker Mary, Queen of Scots. The gallery also hosts excellent visiting exhibitions. *(1 Queen St., north of St. Andrew Sq.)*

SCOTTISH NATIONAL GALLERY OF MODERN ART. In the west end of town, this permanent collection includes works by Braque, Matisse, and Picasso. The newly completed landscaping in front of the museum, a bizarre spiral of grass set into a pond, represents the concepts of chaos theory with dirt and greenery. *(75 Belford Rd. Take the free shuttle, bus #13 from George St., or walk along the Water of Leith Walkway.)*

DEAN GALLERY. Part of the Gallery of Modern Art, the newest addition to the National Galleries is dedicated to Surrealist and Dadaist art. The gallery owes much of its fine collection to the landmark sculptor Eduardo Paolozzi, whose towering, three-story statue, *Vulcan*, stands at the main entrance. *(73 Belford Rd., across from the Gallery of Modern Art. Special exhibits £3.50.)*

OTHER MUSEUMS AND GALLERIES

MUSEUM OF SCOTLAND AND ROYAL MUSEUM. The superbly designed **🖼 Museum of Scotland** traces the whole of Scottish history through an impressive collection of treasured objects and decorative art. Highlights include the working

Corliss Steam Engine and the Maiden, Edinburgh's pre-French Revolution guillotine, used on High St. around 1565. The rooftop terrace provides a 360° view of the city. Gallery tours and audio guides in various languages are free. Less modern and more motley (though still fascinating), the **Royal Museum** has exhibits on natural history, European art, and ancient Egypt, to name a few. The **Millennium Clock,** a towering and ghoulish display of mechanized figures that represent the darker periods in the last millennium of human history, chimes every hour. *(Chambers St. Museum of Scotland* ☎ *247 4422. Royal Museum 247 4219. Both open M and W-Sa 10am-5pm, Tu 10am-8pm, Su noon-5pm. Free.)*

OUR DYNAMIC EARTH. This glitzy, high-tech lesson in geology is part amusement park, part science experiment; it appeals mainly to young children. Look for the white tent-like structure next to Holyroodhouse. *(Holyrood Rd.* ☎ *550 7800. Open daily July-Aug. 10am-6pm; Apr.-June and Sept.-Oct. 10am-5pm; Nov.-Mar. W-Su 10am-5pm. Last entry 1hr. before closing. £9, concessions £6.50, children £5.45, families £24.50.)*

OTHER MUSEUMS. The **Museum of Childhood** displays an array of antique and contemporary childhood toys, from nineteenth-century dollhouses to 1990s teletubbies. *(42 High St.* ☎ *529 4142. Open M-Sa 10am-5pm; during festival also Su noon-5pm. Free.)* The picturesque **John Knox House,** 43 High St., offers an engaging look at former inhabitants John Knox, protestant reformer, and James Mosman, Catholic loyalist. *(*☎ *556 9579. Open July-Aug. M-Sa 10am-4:30pm, Su noon-5pm; Sept.-June M-Sa 10am-4:30pm. £3, concessions £2, children £1.)* **Canongate Tolbooth** (c. 1591), with a beautiful clock face projecting over the Royal Mile, once served as a prison and gallows for "elite" criminals. Now it houses the **People's Story Museum** an eye-opening look at the ordinary people of Edinburgh. *(163 Canongate.* ☎ *529 4057. Open M-Sa 10am-5pm; during festival also Su 10am-5pm. Free.)* Across the street in 16th-century Huntly House, the **Museum of Edinburgh** charts the city's advance from prehistory to the present, with a hodgepodge of artifacts such as the original 1638 National Covenant. *(142 Canongate.* ☎ *529 4143. Open M-Sa 10am-5pm; during festival also Su 2-5pm. Free.)*

SMALLER ART GALLERIES. The **City Art Centre** houses the city's collection of modern Scottish work and hosts international exhibitions. *(2 Market St.* ☎ *529 3993. Open M-Sa 10am-5pm, Su noon-5pm. Free.)* Across the street, the **Fruitmarket Gallery,** 45 Market St., shows contemporary Scottish and world art. *(*☎ *225 2383; www.fruitmarket.co.uk. Open M-Sa 11am-6pm, Su noon-5pm. Free.)*

◪ NIGHTLIFE

PUBS

Pubs on the **Royal Mile** tend to attract a mixed crowd of old and young, tourists and locals. Students and backpackers gather in force each night in the Old Town. Casual pub-goers groove to live music on **Grassmarket, Candlemaker Row,** and **Victoria Street.** The New Town also has its share of worthy watering-holes, some historical, and most strung along **Rose Street,** parallel to Princes St. Gay-friendly **Broughton Street** is increasingly popular for nightlife, though its pubs are more trendy than traditional. Wherever you are, you'll usually hear last call sometime between 11pm and 1am, or 3am during the Festival.

▨ **The Tron,** 9 Hunter Sq. (☎ 226 0931), behind the Tron Kirk. Wildly popular. Downstairs is a mix of alcoves and pool tables. Frequent live music. Students and hostelers get £1 drinks on W nights, burgers and a pint all the time for £4.50. Open M-Sa noon-1am, Su 12:30pm-1am; during Festival 8:30am-3am. Food served noon-9pm.

The Globe, 13 Niddry St. (☎557 4670). This hole-in-the-wall is recommended up and down the Royal Mile. International sports, DJs, quiz nights, and karaoke. Open M-F 4pm-1am, Sa noon-1am, Su 12:30pm-1am; during Festival until 3am.

The Three Sisters, 139 Cowgate (☎622 6801). Loads of space for dancing, drinking, and lounging. Attracts a young crowd to its 3 bars (Irish, Gothic, and American). Beer garden and barbecue see close to 1000 people pass through on Sa nights. Open daily 9am-1am. Food served M-F 9am-9pm, Sa-Su 9am-8pm.

Finnegan's Wake, 9b Victoria St. (☎226 3816). Drink the Irish way with several stouts on tap, road signs from Cork, and live music every night, starting at 10pm. During the summer, broadcasts Gaelic football and hurling on a big screen. Open daily 1pm-1am.

The Abbotsford, 3 Rose St. (☎225 5276). One of the most authentic of the Rose St. pubs. Built in 1902, this family-run bar and restaurant retains the era's elegant ambience with an ornate wooden bar. Open daily 11am-11pm. Above-average grub served noon-2:30pm and 5:30-10pm.

Jolly Judge, 7 James Ct. (☎226 2669). Hidden just off the Royal Mile, with a cozy atmosphere. 17th-century painted ceiling. M quiz night, Th live music, both 9pm. Open M and Th-Sa noon-midnight, Tu-W noon-11pm, Su 12:30-11pm. Food served noon-2pm.

Biddy Mulligans, 94-96 Grassmarket (☎220 1246). Kick things off early at this Irish-themed pub, which serves big breakfasts. M open mic; Th-F and Su live music; Sa DJ. Open daily 9am-1am. Food served until 9pm.

The World's End, 2-8 High St. (☎556 3628), at the corner of St. Mary's St. and the Royal Mile. The bar stands at the site of a gate in the 16th-century city wall, hence the name. Traditional and frequented by locals. Open M-F 11am-1am, Sa-Su 10am-1am. Food served until 9pm.

CLUBS

Edinburgh may be best known for its pubs, but the club scene is none too shabby. It is, however, in constant flux, with venues continuously closing down and reopening under new management—you're best off consulting *The List* (£2.20), a comprehensive guide to events, available from any local newsagent. Clubs cluster around the city's historically disreputable **Cowgate,** just downhill from and parallel to the Royal Mile, and most close at 3am (5am during the Festival). Smart street-wear is necessary for clubbing everywhere in Edinburgh.

▨ **Cabaret-Voltaire,** 36-38 Blair St. (☎220 6176). With a wide range of live music, dance, and art, this innovative club knows how to throw a party. A great, smaller spot with a friendly crowd. Some gigs at 7pm during festival. Cover up to £15.

Bongo Club, 14 New St. (☎558 7604), off Canongate. Particularly noted for its hip-hop and the long-running and immensely popular Messenger (reggae, every other Sa) and Headspin (funk and dance, one Sa per month) nights. Cover up to £20.

The Venue, 17-23 Calton Rd. (☎557 3073). It's big. 3 dance floors run the whole musical gamut. Hosts live gigs; call ahead. Cover usually £5-6, but ranges up to £20.

Faith, 207 Cowgate (☎225 9764). Located inside an old church, this purple-hued club specializes in R&B. Very popular Su Chocolate. Cover up to £6.

Po Na Na, 43b Frederick St. (☎226 2224), beneath Cafe Rouge. Go down the steps to a yellow cartoon image of a man in a fez. Moroccan-themed, with parachute ceilings, red velvet couches, and an eclectic blend of R&B, hip hop, disco, and funk. Cover £2.50-6, free before 11pm on Th.

Opal Lounge, 51a George St. (☎226 2275). A great New Town spot that attracts a mixed crowd of smartly dressed backpackers, locals, and students. DJs spin all day as the restaurant lounge morphs into a club around 9pm. Fantastic drinks. Cover £3-5.

GAY AND LESBIAN NIGHTLIFE

The Broughton St. area of the New Town (better known as the Broughton Triangle) is the center of Edinburgh's gay community.

C.C. Bloom's, 23-24 Greenside Pl. (☎556 9331), on Leith St. A gay club with no cover and a new DJ each night. F has a drag DJ.

Blue Moon Cafe, 36 Broughton St. (☎557 0911), at the corner of Barony St. A popular place with great food (served 10am-4pm).

Sala Cafe-Bar, 60 Broughton St. (☎478 7069). Formerly known as the Nexus. A relaxed atmosphere with regular live music and an eclectic menu. Tapas from £2.20. Open Tu-Su 10am-11pm.

Ego, 14 Picardy Pl. (☎478 7434). Not strictly a gay club, but hosts several gay nights, including **Vibe** (every Tu) and **Blaze** (3 F per month). Cover £2-10.

🎵 ENTERTAINMENT

For all the latest listings, check out *The List* (£2.20), available at newsstands.

THEATER AND FILM

Festival Theatre, 13-29 Nicholson St. (☎529 6000; www.eft.co.uk). Stages predominantly ballet and opera, turning entirely to the Festival in August. Box office open M-Sa 10am-6pm and before curtain. Tickets £5-55.

King's Theatre, 2 Leven St. (☎529 6000; www.eft.co.uk). Promotes serious and comedic performances, musicals, opera, and pantomime. Box offices open 1hr. before show and between matinee and evening performances; tickets also available through the Festival Theatre.

Royal Lyceum Theatre, 30 Grindlay St. (☎248 4848; www.lyceum.org.uk). The finest in Scottish, English, and international theater. Box office open M-Sa 10am-6pm; on performance nights until 8pm. Tickets £8-20, students half-price.

Traverse Theatre, 10 Cambridge St. (☎228 1404; www.traverse.co.uk). A real launching pad, this theater performs almost exclusively new drama with lots of local Scottish work. Box office open daily 10am-6pm. Tickets £5, concessions £3.50.

Bedlam Theatre, 11b Bristo Pl. (☎225 9873). A university theater presenting excellent student productions, ranging from comedy and drama to F night improv, all in a converted church. A Fringe Festival hotspot. Box office open M-Sa 10am-6pm. Tickets £4-5.

The Stand Comedy Club, 5 York Pl. (☎558 7272; www.thestand.co.uk). Acts every night and all day Su. Special 17-shows-per-day program for the Fringe Festival. Tickets £1-10.

The Filmhouse, 88 Lothian Rd. (☎228 2688). European and arthouse films, though quality Hollywood fare appears as well. Tickets £3.50-5.50. For mainstream cinema, try **Odeon,** 7 Clerk St. (☎667 0971), or **UGC Fountainpark,** Dundee St., Fountainbridge (bus #1, 28, 34, 35; ☎0870 902 0417).

LIVE MUSIC

Thanks to an abundance of university students who never let books get in the way of a good night out, Edinburgh's live music scene is vibrant and diverse. Excellent impromptu and professional folk sessions take place at pubs (p. 541), and many university houses sponsor live shows—look for flyers near Bristol Sq. *The List* (£2.20) has comprehensive listings. **Ripping Records,** 91 South Bridge (☎226 7010), sells tickets to rock, reggae, and pop performances.

Henry's Jazz Cellar, 8a Morrison St. (☎538 7385; www.henrysjazz.co.uk), downstairs off Lothian Rd, hosts both local and international jazz musicians in a laid-back atmosphere. Cover £5. Open daily 8pm-3am.

The Liquid Room, 9c Victoria St. (☎ 225 2528; www.liquidroom.com), in **The Venue** (p. 542) hosts rock and progressive shows. Open daily until 3am.

Whistle Binkie's, 4-6 South Bridge (☎ 557 5114), is a subterranean pub with two live music shows every night, always open to new bands. Open daily until 3am.

The Royal Oak, 1 Infirmary St. (☎ 557 2976), hosts live traditional and folk music in an intimate setting. Open M-F 10am-2am, Sa 11am-2am, Su 12:30pm-2am. Live music from 7pm. Tickets £3.

▦ FESTIVALS

Edinburgh has special events year-round, but the real show is in August. Prices rise, pubs and restaurants stay open later than late (some simply don't close), and street performers have the run of the place. What's commonly referred to as "the Festival" actually encompasses a number of independently organized events. For more information and links to all the separate festivals, check out www.edinburghfestivals.co.uk.

▩ **EDINBURGH INTERNATIONAL FESTIVAL.** Begun in 1947, the **Edinburgh International Festival** attracts the top performers from around the globe, mainly in classical music, ballet, opera, and drama. The most popular single event is the festival's grand finale: a spectacular **Fireworks Concert** with pyrotechnics choreographed to orchestral music. Most tickets go on sale in early April, and a full program is published by then. The biggest events sell out well in advance, but all hope is not lost; at least 50 tickets for major events are held and sold on the day of the performance at the venue; queue early. Throughout the festival, visitors can buy tickets at **The Hub** or at the door 1hr. prior to showtime. Selected shows are half-price on the day of performance. (*Aug. 13-Sept. 2, 2006. Bookings can be made by post, phone, web, or in person at The Hub, Edinburgh's Festival Centre, Castlehill, Edinburgh EH1 2NE. ☎ 473 2000 or 473 2001; www.eif.co.uk. Open M-Sa from early Apr.; daily from late July. Tickets £7-58, students and children half-price; £5 tickets held at the door for sale 1hr. before curtain.*)

▩ **EDINBURGH FESTIVAL FRINGE.** Longer and more informal than the International Festival, the Fringe is the world's biggest arts festival, showcasing everything from Shakespeare to coconut-juggling dwarves. It began in 1947, when eight theater companies arrived to Edinburgh uninvited and had to book "fringe" venues to perform. Today, the Fringe draws more visitors to Edinburgh than any other event or sight. Anyone who can afford the small registration fee can perform; this orgy of eccentricity attracts a multitude of good and not-so-good acts and guarantees a wild month. (*Aug. 6-28, 2006. ☎ 226 0000; www.edfringe.com. Tickets available online, by phone, in person, or by post at The Fringe Office, 180 High St., Edinburgh EH1 1QS. Open M-F 10am-5pm; during festival daily 10am-9pm. Tickets up to £25.*)

HOGMANAY. The party doesn't stop despite the long, dark winter. Hogmanay is Edinburgh's traditional New Year's Eve festival, a serious street party with a week of associated events. Hogmanay has deep pagan roots and is observed all over Scotland—it celebrates the turn of the calendar and the return of the sun. It also celebrates the consumption of copious amounts of alcohol. Check out The Old Town Information Centre in Tron Kirk or www.edinburghshogmanay.org. The Hub (see above) also provides ticket information.

OTHER SUMMER FESTIVALS. The following festivities are just a few of the events that take place during the five-week period surrounding the Festival in August. **Military Tattoo** is a magnificent spectacle of military bands, bagpipes, and drums performed before the gates of the castle. (*Aug. 4-26, 2005. Tattoo Ticket Sale*

Office, 33-34 Market St., Edinburgh EH1 1QB. ☎225 1188; www.edintattoo.co.uk. Book well in advance. Tickets £9-31.) One highlight of the **Jazz and Blues Festival** is the free **Jazz on a Summer's Day** in Ross Theatre. *(www.jazzmusic.co.uk. July 28-Aug. 6, 2006. Program available in June; bookings by phone, web, or at The Hub. Tickets £5-27.50.)* Charlotte Sq. Gardens hosts the **International Book Festival,** Europe's largest book celebration, in early and mid-August. *(Scottish Book Centre, 137 Dundee St. ☎228 5444; www.edbookfest.co.uk. Program available mid-June. Tickets £3-9; some free events.)* The **International Film Festival** occurs during the 2nd and 3rd weeks of August. *(Film Festival, The Filmhouse, 88 Lothian Rd. ☎229 2550; www.edfilmfest.org.uk. Box office sells tickets from late July.)*

▶ DAYTRIPS FROM EDINBURGH

SOUTH QUEENSFERRY. Eight miles west of Edinburgh and easily accessed by the #43 bus, the town of South Queensferry lies at the narrowest part of the Firth of Forth, where two bridges—the **Forth Road Bridge** and the splendid **Forth Rail Bridge**— cross the waterway. In the town center, on High St., the **Queensferry Museum** catalogues the history of the bridges and the town. *(☎331 5545. Open M and Th-Sa 10am-1pm and 2:15-5pm, Su noon-5pm. Free.)* From Hawes Pier, under Forth Rail Bridge, the **Maid of the Forth** ferries to Inchcolm Island, site of the well-preserved 12th-century **Inchcolm Abbey.** *(Ferry ☎331 5000; www.maidoftheforth.co.uk. Runs daily mid-July to early Sept.; Apr.-June and Oct. Sa-Su. Round-trip ticket includes admission. £13, concessions £11, children £4.50.)* Two miles west of South Queensferry stands **Hopetoun House.** Begun around 1700 and designed by Sir William Bruce (also responsible for Holyroodhouse), it offers lovely views of the Forth. *(☎331 2451; www.hopetounhouse.com. Open daily Apr.-Sept. 10am-5:30pm. Last admission 4:30pm. £7, concessions £6, children £4. No public transport runs to Hopetoun; take a taxi from South Queensferry.)*

ROSLIN. The exotic stone carvings of ◪**Rosslyn Chapel,** in the village of Roslin, 7 mi. south of Edinburgh, raised eyebrows in 15th-century Scotland. Filled with occult symbols, the chapel is one of the many British sites claiming to harbor the Holy Grail. Its mention in Dan Brown's *The Da Vinci Code* brought thousands of recreational Grail-hunters to view its intricately carved walls. Outside the chapel, footpaths lead to the ruined Roslin Castle in Roslin Glen. *(From Edinburgh, take bus #15A from St. Andrew Sq. (40min.) ☎0131 440 2159; www.rosslynchapel.org.uk. Chapel open M-Sa 9:30am-6pm, Su noon-4:45pm. £6, concessions £5, children free.)*

THE BORDERS

From the arrival of the Roman legions in the second century to the failure of the Jacobite Rebellions in the 18th, the Borders were caught in a violent tug-of-war between Scotland and England. Present-day Borderers, however, suffer no crisis of identity: grooms wear tartan kilts at their weddings and the blue and white cross of St. Andrew reigns over the Union Jack. Evidence of past strife lingers in the fortified houses dotting the landscape and the spectacular abbey ruins at Dryburgh, Jedburgh, Kelso, and Melrose. These grim reminders of warfare contrast with the gentle countryside, which inspired the poetry of Sir Walter Scott.

▣ TRANSPORTATION

There are no trains in the Borders, but **buses** are frequent. The main travel hub of the Borders is tiny Galashiels, or "Gala." (Bus station open M-F 9am-12:30pm and 1:30-5pm. Luggage storage 50p.) First (☎01896 752 237) is the largest operator. Ask at TICs for the *Central Borders Travel Guide*, which contains all of the area's bus schedules. Traveline (☎08706 082 608) also has schedules. Bus #23 runs from Berwick to Kelso (1hr.; M-F 5 per day, Sa 6 per day, Su 3 per day). Bus #60 (M-F 10 per day, Sa-Su 6 per day) goes from Berwick to Galashiels (1¾hr.) via Melrose (1½hr.). The following routes depart from Edinburgh: #62 (every hr.) to Peebles (1hr.), Galashiels (1¾hr.), Melrose (2¼hr.) and Kelso (2¾hr.); #29 to Jedburgh (2hr.; M-F 5 per day, Sa-Su 3 per day); #30 to Kelso (2hr.; M-Sa 9 per day, Su 3 per day). First #131 (1 per day) and National Express #383 (1 per day) head from Edinburgh to Newcastle via Galashiels, Melrose, and Jedburgh. Limited-stop bus #95/X95 (8 per day) travels from Edinburgh to Carlisle (3½hr.) via Galashiels (1¼hr.). #68/71 travels from Galashiels to Jedburgh (1½hr.) via Melrose (15min.).

█ ACCOMMODATIONS

TICs can help you find a bed, usually for a 10% deposit. For advance bookings call Scottish Borders Customer Service Centre (☎08706 080 404). The following **SYHA hostels** in the Borders are strategically dispersed—a fourth is in **Melrose** (p. 547). All have a 10:30am-5pm lockout and are only open from April to September.

Broadmeadows (☎08700 041 107), 5 mi. west of Selkirk off the A708 and 1¼ mi. south of the Southern Upland Way. The first SYHA hostel (opened 1931), close to the Tweedsmuir Hills. 26 beds. Dorms £10.75-14, under 18 £8.25-11. Cash only. ●

Coldingham Sands (☎08700 041 111), a 20min. walk from Coldingham at St. Abbs Head, 5min. from the ocean. 40 beds. Dorms £11-13.50, under 18 £5-10. MC/V. ●

Kirk Yetholm (☎08700 041 132), at the junction of the B6352 and B6401, near Kelso. Bus #81 runs from Kelso (20 min.; M-Sa 7 per day, Su 3 per day). The end of the Pennine Way. 20 beds. Dorms £10.50-13, under 18 £8.25-10. Cash only. ●

█ █ HIKING AND OUTDOORS

Hikers of all levels enjoy the Borders; take a late afternoon stroll in the hills or wander the wilds. The valley of the **River Tweed** offers many beautiful stretches for a day's trek. At the river's source in the west, the **Tweedsmuirs** provide difficult terrain. In the north, the **Moorfoots** and **Lammermuir** hills are well-suited to the country rambler. In addition, two long-distance paths cross the Borders. Marked by a thistle in a hexagon symbol, the **Southern Upland Way** winds through the region for 82 mi., passing near Galashiels and Melrose on its route to the sea. **Saint Cuthbert's Way** runs 62 mi. from Melrose to Holy Island on the English coast and is marked by a simple cross. The Borders are extensively covered by Ordnance Survey Landranger (#72-75, 79, 80; £6.50) and Explorer (#330, 331, 336-340, 346; £7.50) maps, which are a necessity. Upon arriving in the Borders, grab a copy of the superb *Walking the Scottish Borders* (free) at any TIC, which details 30 day-long walks in the area. *Short Walks on the Eastern Section of the Upland Way* (£2.50), available at TICs, is also helpful. The Borders also caters to on- and off-trail **bikers.** A number of well-maintained and well-marked trails cross the region, including the **Tweed Cycleway,** a 90 mi. route that hugs the Tweed River from Biggar to Berwick, and the **Four Abbeys Cycle Route,** which connects the abbeys at Melrose, Dryburgh, Jedburgh, and Kelso. The 250 mi. **Borderloop** offers more strenuous trails. *Cycling in the Scottish Borders* (free at TICs) outlines these routes and 20 shorter trails, lists local cycle shops, and dispenses good advice. The *Scottish Borders* series also offers guides to golfing and fishing.

MELROSE   ☎01896

The loveliest of the region's towns, Melrose draws visitors for its abbey. The town is within convenient reach of Dryburgh Abbey and Abbotsford, Sir Walter Scott's country home. A stop on the **Four Abbeys Cycle Route,** Melrose is also the start of **Saint Cuthbert's Way** and lies near both the **Southern Upland Way** and **Tweed Cycleway,** making it the best base camp for outdoor activities in the Borders. The fascinating ▨**Melrose Abbey** dates to the 12th century, though it was later remade in an ornate Gothic style after a particularly harsh pillaging by the English. Search the grounds for the tombstone marking Robert the Bruce's embalmed heart. The abbey has famed gargoyles, including a bagpipe-playing pig and a winged cow. The **Abbey Museum** displays objects unearthed from the abbey grounds and regional Roman forts. It also details Sir Walter Scott's life, death, and poetic dishonesty. (☎822 562. Open Apr.-Sept. daily 9:30am-6:30pm; Oct.-Mar. M-Sa 9:30am-4:30pm, Su 2-4:30pm. £4, seniors £3, children £1.60. Last admission 30min. before close.) Come, see, and briskly conquer the one-room **Trimontium Exhibition,** in Market Sq., a quirky jumble of a museum packed to the gills. (☎822 651. Open daily Mar.-Oct. 10:30am-4:30pm. £1.50, concessions £1, families £4.) The Roman fort featured in the museum spanned the three volcanic summits of the **Eildon Hills,** which tower above the town (guided walks to the fort leave from the museum Tu, Th 1:30pm). Legend has it that King Arthur and his knights lie asleep in a cavern beneath the hills. (That is, if they're not in Wales, Glastonbury, or any of the other places making similar claims.) The bare peaks afford fabulous views of the town. The relatively easy **Eildon Hills Walk** (4 mi.) leaves right from the abbey.

With a convenient location close to the town center and abbey ruins, the ▨**SYHA Melrose ❶,** off High Rd., resembles a stately manor more than a backpackers' abode and has an excellent kitchen. Some rooms even have views of the Abbey, which is lit at night and makes a haunting spectacle as it looms behind the trees. (☎822 521. From Market Pl., follow the footpath between Anderson fishmonger and the Ship Inn. Bear right going through the parking lot. Laundry £4. Internet access £1 per 20min. Reception 7am-11pm. Curfew 11:30pm. Dorms £11.50-13.75, under 18 £5-10.25. MC/V.) **Braidwood B&B ❸,** Buccleuch St., strikes a good balance between cost and comfort. (☎822 488. No smoking. Singles £30; doubles £50-55. Cash only.) Camp at the **Gibson Park Caravan Club Park ❶,** off High St., which provides clean facilities in a central location. (☎822 969. Open June-Sept. £4.80. MC/V.) Walter's, Market Sq., sells **groceries** (open M-Sa 7am-10pm, Su 8am-10pm).

Buses to Melrose stop in Market Sq. Active Sports, Annay Rd., beside the River Tweed, **rents bikes** and leads river trips. (☎822 452. Take the road going out of town past the Abbey and bear left at the fork, heading toward the footbridge over the river. Bikes £15 per day. 24hr. rental. Open daily 9am-9pm.) The **Tourist Information Centre** is across from the abbey on, appropriately, Abbey St. (☎08706 080 404. Open July-Aug. M-Sa 9:30am-5:30pm, Su 10am-2pm; June and Sept. M-Sa 9:30am-5pm, Su 10am-2pm; Apr.-May M-Sa 10am-5pm, Su 10am-2pm; Oct. M-Sa 10am-4pm, Su 10am-1pm; Nov.-Mar. M-Sa 10am-2pm.) Get free **Internet access** at the Melrose Library, Market Sq. (☎823 052. Open M and W 10am-1pm and 2:30-5pm, F 2:30-5pm and 5:30-7pm.). The **post office** is on Buccleuch St. (☎822 040. Open M-F 9am-1pm and 2-5:30pm, Sa 9am-noon.) **Post Code:** TD6 9LE.

▶ DAYTRIPS FROM MELROSE

▨**DRYBURGH ABBEY.** The grounds of Dryburgh Abbey host extensive ruins and the grave of Sir Walter Scott. The serenity that permeates the crumbling ruins makes it worth the effort to get there. Its views of the Tweed Valley are among the best around. Built in 1150, the abbey was inhabited by Premonstratensian monks for nearly two centuries. When Edward II began removing his English troops from Scotland in 1322, the abbey's monks prematurely rang their bells in celebration. Angry soldiers retraced their steps and set the abbey aflame. If driving, head for Scott's View, north of Dryburgh on the B635. *(From Melrose take bus #67 or 68 (10min., frequent) to St. Boswell's, turn left from the bus station, then follow St. Cuthbert's Way along the River Tweed, eventually crossing a metal footbridge to reach the abbey (30min.). The Four Abbeys Cycle Route also connects Melrose and Dryburgh. ☎01835 822 381. Open Apr.-Sept. daily 9:30am-6:30pm; Oct.-Mar. M-Sa 9:30am-4:30pm, Su 2-4:30pm. Last admission 30min. before close. £3.30, concessions £2.50, children £1.30.)*

ABBOTSFORD. Sir Walter Scott wrote most of his Waverley novels in this mock-Gothic estate 2 mi. west of Melrose and died here in 1832. It's easy to picture the writer toiling away in the dark interior. The house holds 9000 rare books, a collection of weapons, Rob Roy's gun, a lock of Bonnie Prince Charlie's hair, and a piece of the gown worn by Mary, Queen of Scots, at her execution. The gardens extend toward the river, and a few peacocks wander about. *(Frequent buses between Galashiels and Melrose stop nearby. Ask the driver to let you off at the first Tweedbank stop, walk back to the roundabout, and follow the sign to the house, which is ¼ mi. down B6360. ☎752 043; www.scottsabbotsford.co.uk. Open June-Sept. daily 9:30am-5pm; Mar.-May and Oct. M-Sa 9:30am-5pm, Su 2-5pm. £4.75, children £2.40.)*

THIRLESTANE CASTLE. The ancient seat of the Duke of Lauderdale, Thirlestane Castle stands 10 mi. north of Melrose on the A68, near Lauder. The defensive walls in the panelled room and library are 13 ft. thick. The beautiful restoration can't remedy the castle's bloody history—jealous nobles hanged a host of King James III's supporters here in 1482. *(From Melrose or Galashiels, take bus #61 toward Lauder and ask to be let off at the castle. ☎01578 722 430; www.thirlestanecastle.co.uk. Open May-Oct. M-F, Su 10:30am-5pm; last admission 4:15pm. £5.50, families £15. Grounds only £2.)*

PEEBLES
☎01721

Eighteen miles west of Galashiels, Peebles lies along the River Tweed. The **Tweed Cycleway** and numerous other trails pass through town. One excellent short walk departs from the Kingsmeadow car park and sets off for a 5 mi. circular route down and back along the River Tweed. Perched majestically above a bend in the river, ▨**Neidpath Castle** is about 20min. into the walk. The 11 ft. thick walls were breached only once in their long history. Today visitors can explore its many preserved levels, admiring the view from the top. Inside, batiks depict the life of Mary, Queen of Scots. (☎720 333. Open May-Sept. W-Sa 10:30am-5pm, Su 12:30-5pm. £3, concessions £2.50, children £1.) The free **Tweeddale Museum and Gallery,** in the Chambers Institute on High St., houses rotating exhibits and copies of Greek friezes. (☎724 820. Open Apr.-Oct. M-F 10am-noon and 2-5pm, Sa 10am-1pm and 2-4pm; Nov.-Mar. M-F 10am-noon and 2-5pm.)

Try the inviting **Rowanbrae ❸,** 103 Northgate (☎721 630; singles £25; doubles from £38; no smoking; cash only), or **Viewfield ❸,** 1 Rosetta Rd., in a room above the wonderful garden. (☎721 232. Singles from £22; doubles from £40. Cash only.) Campers will find comfort at the **Rosetta Caravan Park ❶,** Rosetta Rd., 10min. from town. (☎720 770. Open Apr.-Oct. £6 per person, children 50p. Cash only.) Grab your **groceries** at Somerfield, Edinburgh Rd. (☎724 518. Open M-Sa 8:30am-8pm, Su 9am-6pm.) The **Sunflower Restaurant ❸,** 4 Bridgegate, prepares modern Mediterranean cuisine in a classy setting (entrees £12-14), including a daily vegetarian option. (☎722 420; www.thesunflower.net. Open M-W and Su 10-11:30am, noon-3pm; Th-Sa 10-11:30am, noon-3pm, and 6-9pm. MC/V.)

The **Tourist Information Centre,** 23 High St., books rooms for a £3 charge and a 10% deposit. (☎08706 080 404. Open July-Aug. M-Sa 9am-6pm; Su 10am-4pm; June and Sept. M-Sa 9am-5:30pm, Su 10am-4pm; Apr.-May M-Sa 9am-5pm, Su 11am-4pm; Oct. M-Sa 9:30am-5pm, Su 11am-4pm; Nov.-Dec. M-Sa 9:15am-5pm, Su 11am-3pm; Jan.-Mar. M-Sa 9:30am-4pm.) Other services include: **banks** along High St.; **bike rental** at Border Bikesport, 3 High St. (☎723 423; www.thebicycleworks.co.uk; £12 per half-day, £16 per day; open daily 10am-6pm); free **Internet access** at the library, High St. (www.scotborders.gov.uk/libraries; open M, W, F 9:30am-5pm, Tu and Th 9:30am-7pm, Sa 9am-12:30pm); and the **post office,** 14 Eastgate (☎720 119; open M-F 9am-5:30pm, Sa 9am-12:30pm). **Post Code:** EH45 8AA.

▶ DAYTRIP FROM PEEBLES

TRAQUAIR HOUSE. 12th-century ▧**Traquair House** (trar-KWEER), the oldest inhabited house in Scotland, stands 6 mi. east of Peebles and about 1 mi. south of the A72. The interior offers a maze of low-ceilinged rooms, creaky wood floors, and narrow spiral staircases. Present resident Catherine Stuart brews what may be Scotland's finest ale in the 200-year-old brewery and holds tastings on Fridays in summer, when more visitors than usual find themselves entangled in the hedge maze. *(From Peebles, take bus #62 toward Galashiels to Innerleithen, and walk 1½ mi. There is also a scenic back road running 7 mi. from Peebles to the house; biking is a good option. For a taxi, call Alba Taxis ☎01896 831 333. Traquair House ☎01896 830 323; www.traquair.co.uk. Open daily June-Aug. 10:30am-5:30pm; Apr.-May and Sept.-Oct. noon-5:30pm. £5.80, concessions £5.35, children £3.25, family £16.80.)*

JEDBURGH   ☎01835

In Jedburgh (known to locals as "Jethart"), 13 mi. south of Melrose, King David I founded ▧**Jedburgh Abbey.** While pillaging English were successful in sacking the abbey on repeated occasions, much of the magnificent 12th-century structure endures. To appreciate its original grandeur, climb the narrow spiral staircase at the end of the nave. (☎863 925. Open Apr.-Sept. daily 9:30am-6:30pm; Oct.-Mar. M-Sa 9:30am-4:30pm, Su 2-4:30pm. Last admission 30min. before close. £4, concessions £3, children £1.60.) For the best free view of the abbey, try Abbey Close St., off Castlegate. The **Mary Queen of Scots House,** down Smiths Wynd on Queen St., stands as a rare example of a 16th-century fortified house. (☎863 331. Open Mar.-Nov. M-Sa 10am-4:30pm, Su 11am-4:30pm. £3, concessions £2, children free.) The 19th-century **Jedburgh Castle Jail and Museum** looms atop a hill on Castlegate on the site of the original Jethart Castle, which was destroyed in 1409. (☎864 750. Open Mar.-Oct. M-Sa 10am-4:30pm, Su 1-4pm. Last admission 30min. before close. £2, concessions £1.50, children free.) Walkers may enjoy the circular route leaving from the TIC, which temporarily follows **Dere Street,** an old Roman road, before tracing Jed Water back to town (roughly 5 mi.). Cyclists can join the **Four Abbeys Cycle Route** in town or pedal out to the **Borderloop.**

B&Bs are scattered throughout town. Family-friendly **Meadhon House ❸,** 48 Castlegate, has a secluded garden right in town. (☎862 504; www.meadhon.com. Singles £32; doubles £45. No smoking. Cash only.) **Craigowen Guest House,** 30 High St., is a cheaper town-center option. (☎862 604. £20 per person. Cash only.) Fun-loving campers can head to **Jedwater Caravan Park ❶,** 4 mi. south of the town center off the A68; watch for signs. (☎869 595; www.jedwater.co.uk. Showers, laundry, fishing, and trampolines. Open Mar.-Oct. 2-person site, including car, £9. Cash only.)

For **groceries,** visit the Co-op Superstore, at the corner of Jeweller's Wynd and High St. (☎862 944. Open M-Sa 8am-10pm, Su 9am-6pm.) At **Simply Scottish ❷,** 6-8 High St., well-prepared specials go for £7-10, and a fine 3-course dinner is a steal at £12. (☎864 696. Open M-Sa 10am-9pm, Su 11am-9pm.)

Buses stop on Canongate, near the abbey and next to the **Tourist Information Centre.** The TIC sells National Express tickets, books rooms for a 10% deposit, and has a commissionless bureau de change. (☎08706 080 404. Open July-Aug. M-Sa 9am-7pm, Su 10am-6pm; June and Sept. M-Sa 9am-6pm, Su 10am-5pm; Oct. M-Sa 9:15am-5pm, Su 10am-5pm; Nov.-Mar. M-Sa 9:15am-4:45pm.) Other services include: **bike rental** at The Rush, 39 High St. (☎869 643; open M-F 10am-6pm, Sa 9am-5pm; £12 per day, £10 per half-day); free **Internet access** at the library, Castlegate (open M-Tu, Th-F 9:30-11:30am); and the **post office,** 37 High St. (☎862 268; open M-F 9am-5:30pm, Sa 9am-12:30pm). **Post Code:** TD8 6DG.

KELSO   ☎01573

The peaceful market town of Kelso sits at the meeting of the Tweed and Teviot Rivers, near the English border. One mile from the town center along the Tweed, the Duke and Duchess of Roxburgh reside in the palatial **Floors Castle.** The largest inhabited castle in Scotland, Floors has vast riverside grounds, stately rooms, and a window for each day of the year. No, really. James II met his noble end while inspecting a cannon in the yard. (☎223 333. Open Apr.-Oct. daily 10am-4:30pm. £6, concessions £5, children £3.25. Grounds only £3.) Sadly, very little remains of **Kelso Abbey,** near Market Sq., another victim of English invasion. (Open Apr.-Sept. M-Sa 9:30am-6pm, Su 2-6pm; Oct.-Mar. M-Sa 9:30am-4pm, Su 2-4pm. Free.) **Mellerstain House,** one of Scotland's finest Georgian homes, is 6 mi. northwest of Kelso on the A6089. Begun in 1725 by William Adam and completed by his son Robert, the house is noted for its exquisite plaster ceilings and art collection. Take bus #689 (10min.; M-F every hr., Su 8 per day; round-trip £1.20) toward Gordon and ask the driver to drop you near the house. (☎410 225; www.mellerstain.com. Open May-Sept. M, W-F, Su 11:30am-5pm. House and gardens £5.50, children free. Grounds only £3.) Those interested in a long walk should try the 13 mi. section of the **Borders Abbeys Way,** running alongside the River Teviot, that joins Kelso to Jedburgh. Cyclists can join the **Four Abbeys Cycle Route** and the **Borderloop** in Kelso.

The **SYHA Kirk Yetholm ❶** (p. 546) is 6 mi. southeast of Kelso. The footpath up the hill from Croft Rd. reaches **Mrs. Ferguson ❸,** 11 King's Croft, which offers basic lodgings for a good price. (☎225 480. Singles £25; doubles £44. Cash only.) Closer to town, the relatively large **Bellevue Guest House ❹,** Bowmont St., makes a comfortable touring base. (☎224 588. Singles £35; doubles £58. MC/V.) Restock at Somerfield **grocery,** Roxburgh St. (☎225 641. Open M-Sa 8am-8pm, Su 9am-6pm.) At **Oscar's ❷,** 35-37 Horsemarket, lively music and an early evening menu (entrees £10; until 7pm) make for the best deal in town. (Open daily 5-10pm.)

The **bus** stops on Bridges St., near Market Sq., and on Bowmont St. The **Tourist Information Centre,** Market Sq., books rooms for a 10% deposit. (☎08706 080 404. Open July-Aug. M-Sa 9:30am-5pm, Su 10am-2pm; Apr.-June and Sept.-Oct. M-Sa 10am-5pm, Su 10am-2pm; Nov.-Mar. M-Sa 10am-4pm.) Get free **Internet access** at the library, Bowmont St. (Open M and F 10am-1pm and 2-5pm; Tu and Th 10am-1pm, 2-5pm and 5:30-7pm; W 10am-1pm; Sa 9:30am-12:30pm.) The **post office** is at 13 Woodmarket. (☎224 795. Open M-F 9am-5:30pm, Sa 9am-12:30pm.) **Post Code:** TD5 7AT.

DUMFRIES AND GALLOWAY

Though Dumfries and Galloway see less of the tourism that the north and south of Scotland enjoy, this southwest corner of Scotland does possess fine castles and abbeys, stately gardens, and local heroes like Robert the Bruce and Robert Burns. Wise visitors head for the country, where high mountains, dense forest, and 200 mi. of coastline supply rugged and rewarding scenery.

▐ TRANSPORTATION

Trains serve Dumfries and Stranraer. Though **buses** reach other towns, service is infrequent. Call Traveline (☎0870 608 2608) for schedule information. A **Day Discoverer Ticket**, available on buses, allows unlimited travel in Dumfries and Galloway, and on Stagecoach buses in Cumbria (£5, children £2, family £10).

▐ ACCOMMODATIONS

Each town has its own clutch of B&Bs and hotels. Two of the region's three **SYHA hostels** are probably of most interest to walkers; only Minnigaff is easily reached by public transport.

> **Kendoon** (☎08700 041 130), 20 mi. from Threave Castle. Near Loch Doon and the Southern Upland Way. Open Apr.-Sept. Dorms £10.50-13, under 18 £8.25-10. Cash only. ❶

> **Minnigaff** (☎01671 402 211), in Minnigaff village, across the bridge, ½ mi. from Newton Stewart. Accessible by bus from Dumfries, Stranraer, and Kirkcudbright. Popular with hikers and anglers. 36 beds. Open Apr.-Sept. Dorms £10, under 18 £8. MC/V. ❶

> **Wanlockhead** (☎01659 58581). In Scotland's highest village, on the Southern Upland Way. 28 beds. Open Apr.-Sept. Dorms £10.75, under 18 £8.25-9.50. Cash only. ❶

▓ ▐ HIKING AND OUTDOORS

The best of Dumfries and Galloway lies outdoors, and with some 1300 mi. of marked trails there is something for everyone. **Merrick** (2765 ft.) in the **Galloway Hills** and **White Coomb** (2696 ft.) in the **Moffat Hills** will provide a challenge for seasoned hikers, along with the region's main draw—the **Southern Upland Way.** Beginning in Portpatrick on the coast of the Irish Sea and snaking 212 mi. clear across Scotland, this long-distance route cuts through Dumfries and Galloway, passing near to each of the region's three SYHA hostels. The official *Southern Upland Way* guide (£16) breaks the route into 15 manageable sections and includes a complete Ordnance Survey map (1:50,000) of its course. In the west, the **Galloway Forest Park** is Britain's largest at over 300 sq. mi., though its excellent walking, cycling, and horseback riding trails can be difficult to reach without a car. The park has three ranger-manned visitor centers: **Clatteringshaws** (☎01644 420 285), 6 mi. west of New Galloway; **Glen Trool** (☎01671 402 420), 12 mi. north of Newton Stewart; and **Kirroughtree** (☎01671 402 165), 3 mi. east of Newton Stewart. (All are open daily Apr.-Sept. 10:30am-5pm; Oct. 10:30am-4:30pm.) The free *Walks In and Around* guides detail day outings and afternoon walks. Along the coasts and inland, Dumfries and Galloway are popular with serious birdwatchers, particularly around the **Mull of Galloway;** its sea cliffs are home to thousands of marine birds. **Cyclists** will find *Cycling in Dumfries and Galloway* (free at TICs) useful. The #7 and 74 **National Cycle Routes** cross Dumfries and Galloway. Among local routes, the **KM Cycle Trail** runs from Drumlanrig down to Dumfries. The Forest Enterprise puts out a number of leaflets describing on- and off-trail routes in Galloway and other area forests.

DUMFRIES
☎ **01387**

Dumfries (DUM-freez, pop. 37,000) boasts little but the tales of two Roberts. In 1306, Robert the Bruce proclaimed himself King of Scotland in Dumfries after stabbing Red Comyn at Greyfriars. Beloved scribbler Robert Burns made Dumfries his home from 1791 until his death in 1796, and the town has devoted many (many) a site to him. Its central location make this otherwise dull city a travel hub.

◗◢ TRANSPORTATION AND PRACTICAL INFORMATION. The **train station** is on Station Rd. (☎ 255 115. Open M-Sa 6:35am-7:30pm, Su 10:30am-7:55pm.) Trains (☎ 08457 484 950) come from: Carlisle (40min., every hr., £3.50); Glasgow Central (1¾hr.; M-Sa 8 per day, Su 2 per day; £10); London Euston (change in Carlisle; 5¼hr., 10 per day, £70); Stranraer via Ayr (3hr., 3 per day, £20.60). **Buses** arrive and depart along Whitesands and #974 runs from Glasgow (2hr.; M-Sa 3 per day, Su 2 per day; £6.40). Bus #100 travels from Edinburgh (2¾hr.; M-Sa 3 per day, Su 2 per day; £6.40) via Penicuik (2¼hr.), while #500/X75 connects Dumfries to Carlisle (1hr., 2 per day, £2.40) and Stranraer (2¼hr., 8 per day, £5).

The **Tourist Information Centre,** 64 Whitesands Rd., books rooms for a £3 charge plus a 10% deposit and sells National Express tickets. (☎ 253 862. Open Easter to June M-Sa 9:30am-5pm, bank holiday Su noon-4:30pm; July-Aug. M-Sa 9am-6pm, Su 11am-4:30pm; Sept. M-Sa 9am-5:30pm, Su 11am-4:30pm; Oct. M-Sa 9:30am-5pm, Su 11am-4pm, Nov. M-Sa 9am-5pm; Dec. to Easter M-F 9:30am-5pm, Sa 9:30am-4pm.) Other services include: **banks** along High St.; free **Internet access** at Ewart Library, Catherine St. (☎ 253 820; open M-W and F 9:15am-7:30pm, Th and Sa 9:15am-5pm); **bike rental** at the Nithsdale Cycle Centre, 46 Brooms Rd. (☎ 254 870; £8 per day, 3 days £20; open M-Sa 10am-5pm); and the **post office,** 7 Great King St., with a bureau de change (☎ 256 690; open M 8:45am-5:30pm, Tu-F 9am-5:30, Sa 9am-12:30pm). **Post Code:** DG1 1AA.

◗◖ ACCOMMODATIONS AND FOOD. If your plans call for a night's layover in town, welcoming **Torbay Lodge ❸,** 31 Lover's Walk, is just steps from the train station. (☎ 253 922; www.torbaylodge.co.uk. From £25 per person. MC/V.) Less expensive abodes lie along **Lockerbie Road,** north of the city across the tracks. Close to the Whitesands bus stop, **The Haven ❷,** 1 Kenmore Terr., is a riverfront home that was once the home of actor John Laurie, a great fan of Burns. (☎ 251 281. Singles £25-30; doubles £40-50. MC/V.) Find **groceries** at Somerfield, Leafield Rd. (Open M-Sa 8am-8pm, Su 9am-6pm.) Plenty of cheap eateries line **High Street** and **Whitesands.** Be like Burns and stop for a pint at **The Globe Inn,** 56 High St., one of the poet's favorite haunts. (☎ 252 335; www.globeinndumfries.co.uk. Open M-W 10am-11pm, Th-Sa 10am-midnight, Su noon-midnight. Food served M-Th and Su 10-11:30am and noon-3pm; F-Sa 10-11:30am, noon-3pm, and 7-9pm.)

◖ SIGHTS. The sights in Dumfries cater to extreme Robert Burns fans. Pick up a free copy of *Dumfries: A Burns Trail* in the TIC for an easy-to-follow walking Burns tour. Across the river, the **Robert Burns Centre,** Mill Rd., contains Burns memorabilia, including a cast of his skull; next door is a theater that shows an audio-visual presentation on Burns' life. (☎ 264 808. Open Apr.-Sept. M-Sa 10am-

8pm, Su 2-5pm; Oct.-Mar. Tu-Sa 10am-1pm and 2-5pm. Free.) At the **Burns Mauso-leum** in St. Michael's Kirkyard, a marble Burns leans on a plow and gazes at the attractive muse hovering overhead. Burnsmania reaches messianic proportions at the wee **Burns House,** where memorabilia on display includes a tiny box made with wood from the bed the poet died in. (☎255 297. Open Apr.-Sept. M-Sa 10am-5pm, Su 2-5pm; Oct.-Mar. Tu-Sa 10am-1pm and 2-5pm. Free.) The top floor of the **Dumfries Museum,** Rotchell Rd., has Britain's oldest camera obscura. (☎253 374; www.dumgal.gov.uk. Open Apr.-Sept. M-Sa 10am-5pm, Su 2-5pm; Oct.-Mar. Tu-Sa 10am-1pm and 2-5pm. Museum free. Camera obscura £1.80, concessions 90p.)

◪ DAYTRIPS FROM DUMFRIES

▥ **CAERLAVEROCK CASTLE.** Eight miles southeast of Dumfries, on the B725 just beyond Glencaple, moated and triangular Caerlaverock Castle (car-LAV-rick) is one of Scotland's finest medieval ruins. Though no one is sure whether this strategic marvel was built for Scottish defense or English offense, it was seized by England's Edward I in 1300 and passed around like a hot kipper thereafter. Beyond the castle is a path that runs down to the shore of the Solway Firth (10min.). The mountains of the Lake District rise up in the distance beyond the firth, which at low tide is nothing but sand for 20 mi. *(Stagecoach Western Bus #371 runs to the castle from the Loreburn Shopping Centre, off Irish St. in Dumfries (20min.; M-Sa 12 per day, Su 2 per day; round-trip £3). ☎770 244. Open daily Apr.-Sept. 9:30am-6:30pm; Oct.-Mar. 9:30am-4:30pm. £4, concessions £3, children £1.60.)*

SWEETHEART ABBEY. This abbey, 8 mi. south of Dumfries along the A710, was founded in the late 13th century by Lady Devorguilla Balliol in memory of her husband, John. She was later buried here with John's embalmed heart clutched to her breast. Now an impressively well-preserved ruin, the high arches and central spire of the abbey stand in a rather grisly testament to their love. *(Take MacEwan's bus #372 to New Abbey from Dumfries (15 min.; M-Sa 12 per day, Su 5 per day; round-trip £2.40). ☎350 397. Open Apr.-Sept. daily 9:30am-6:30pm; Oct.-Mar. M-W and Sa 9:30am-4:30pm, Th 9:30am-12:30pm, Su 2-4:30pm. £2, concessions £1.50, children 80p.)*

RUTHWELL CHURCH. Nine miles southeast of Dumfries, the church contains the magnificent 7th-century **Ruthwell Cross,** whose worn stone bears dense Celtic carvings of vine, scrolls, and beasts. The Anglo-Saxon poem (and Scotland's oldest surviving fragment of written English) "The Dream of the Rood" crowds its margins. *(Take Stagecoach bus #79 to Annan via Clarencefield (30min.; M-Sa every hr., Su every 2hr.; round-trip £4) and get off at Ruthwell. Free.)*

DRUMLANRIG CASTLE. 18 mi. north of Dumfries off the A76, Drumlanrig Castle is the home of the Duke of Buccleuch. Surrounded by formal gardens and a large country park, the castle's noted art collection includes works by Rembrandt and Da Vinci. Take a time out in the classy cafe, or browse the many shops and galleries in the converted stableyard. *(From Dumfries, Stagecoach Western bus #246 (45min., Su 2 per day, £2.50) stops 1½ mi. away. ☎01848 331 555; www.buccleuch.com. Castle open by guided tour May-Aug. M-Sa 11am-4pm, Su noon-4pm. Grounds open Easter to Sept. 11am-5pm. £7, concessions £5, children £3; grounds only £3, children £2.)*

CASTLE DOUGLAS ☎01556

Between Dumfries and Kirkcudbright, Castle Douglas resembles most other towns in Scotland's southwest. One mile west, however, the 60-acre **Threave Garden** deserves a visit, with native and exotic blooms pruned by students of the nearby School of Gardening. Buses #501 and 502 (10min., 1 per hr.) between Kirkcudbright and Castle Douglas pass the garden turnoff; ask the driver to stop, then walk 15min. (☎502 575. Garden open daily 9:30am-sunset. Walled garden and greenhouses open daily 9:30am-5pm. £6, concessions £5.) The **Threave Estate Walk** (2½-7½ mi.) meanders pleasantly through the countryside. Leaving from the garden car park, it leads hikers to a number of good bird-watching spots as well as the scenic ruins of 14th-century ▩**Threave Castle.** A stronghold of the Earls of Douglas and built by Archibald the Grim, this massive tower-castle sits in a commanding position on an island in the River Dee. The Kirkcudbright bus can drop you off at the roundabout on the A75; from there follow the signs for 1½ mi. along a one-lane road and then a marked footpath. Once at the river, ring the ship's bell and a boatman will appear to ferry you across to the castle. (Open daily Apr.-Sept. 9:30am-6:30pm; last boat 6pm. £3, concessions £2.25, children £1.20.)

The ensuite rooms at the **Crown Hotel ❸,** 25 King Street, provide rest (☎502 031; www.thecrownhotel.co.uk. Across from the TIC and the bus station. Singles £35; doubles £66. Cash only.) For **groceries,** the Co-op Superstore is on Cotton St. (Open M-Sa 8am-10pm, Su 9am-6pm.) A number of small cafes line **King Street.** **MacEwan's** buses #501 and 502 zip from **Dumfries** to **Kirkcudbright** via Castle Douglas (40min. from Dumfries, 20min. from Kirkcudbright; 2 per hr.; £3.50). For local lodgings, ask the staff at the **Tourist Information Centre.** (☎502 611. Open July-Aug. M-Sa 9:30am-6pm, Su 10am-4pm; Apr.-June M-Sa 10am-5pm, Su 11am-4pm; Sept. M-Sa 10am-4pm, Su 11am-4pm; Oct. M-Sa 10am-4pm.)

KIRKCUDBRIGHT ☎01557

Situated at the mouth of the River Dee, Kirkcudbright (ker-COO-bree) is a quiet town with rows of colorful Georgian homes and sights that have nothing to do with Robert Burns. In the 1890s, the town attracted a group of artists known as the Glasgow Boys, and Kirkcudbright still fancies itself an artists' colony.

▣❼ TRANSPORTATION AND PRACTICAL INFORMATION. Buses #501 and 502 travel from Dumfries via Castle Douglas (every hr.), and bus #431 comes from Gatehouse of Fleet (20 min.; M-Sa 12 per day, Su 6 per day). The **Tourist Information Centre,** Harbour Sq., books rooms for a £3 charge. (☎330 494. Open July-Aug. M-Sa 9:30am-6pm, Su 10am-5pm; Sept.-Nov. M-Sa 10am-5pm, Su 11am-4pm; Feb.-June M-Sa 10am-5pm, Su 11am-4pm.) Other services include: Shirley's **launderette,** 20 St. Cuthbert St. (☎332 047; laundry £5; open M-F 9am-4pm, Sa 9am-1pm); free **Internet access** at the Library, High St. (☎331 240; open M 2-7pm, Tu and F 10am-7:30pm, W noon-7:30pm, Th and Sa 10am-5pm); and the **post office,** 5 St. Cuthbert's Pl. (☎330 578; open M-F 9am-5:30pm, Sa 9am-12:30pm). **Post Code:** DG6 4DH.

▐▣ ACCOMMODATIONS AND FOOD. If you plan on spending the night, **Parkview ❷,** 22 Millburn St., is a good choice. (☎330 056. Singles £19; doubles £38. No smoking. Cash only.) The Georgian townhouse **Number 3 B&B ❸,** 3 High St., is in a perfect location and comes with luxurious amenities. (☎330 881; www.number3-bandb.co.uk. Singles £40; doubles £60. MC/V.) Get **groceries** at Somerfield, 52 St. Cuthbert St., at Millburn St. (☎330 516; www.somerfield.co.uk. Open M-Sa 8:30am-6pm, Su 10am-5pm.) The **Royal Hotel ❷,** St. Cuthbert St., has spacious seating and regular carveries. (☎331 213. Open daily 10am-9pm. Food served 8-9am, noon-2pm, 6-9pm.)

◪ SIGHTS. The **Tollbooth Art Centre,** High St., has displayed work of resident artisans since 1890. (☎331 556. Open May-June and Sept. M-Sa 11am-5pm, Su 2-5pm; July-Aug. M-Sa 10am-5pm, Su 2-5pm; Oct. M-Sa 11am-4pm, Su 2-5pm; Nov.-Dec. M-Sa 11am-4pm. Free.) **MacLellan's Castle,** a 16th-century tower house, dominates the town on Castle St. Sneak into the "Laird's Lug," a secret chamber behind a fireplace from which the lord could eavesdrop on conversations in the Great Hall. (☎331 856. Open Apr.-Sept. daily 9:30am-1pm and 2-6:30pm. £2.25, concessions £1.90, children £1.) One fine walk in the area departs from the TIC and runs along the coastal headland to Torrs Point (8½ mi. round-trip). **Broughton House and Garden**, 12 High St., displays the artwork (mostly carefree girls cavorting amid wildflowers) of E.A. Hornel. The backyard contains manicured lawns, lily ponds, sundials, and a greenhouse. (☎330 437. Garden open Feb.-Apr. daily 11am-4pm. House and garden open Good Friday to June and Sept.-Oct. daily noon-5pm; July-Aug. daily 10am-5pm. £8, concessions £5, families £20.)

STRANRAER ☎01776

On the westernmost peninsula of Dumfries and Galloway, Stranraer (stran-RAHR) provides ferry access to Northern Ireland—and that's about it. Locals have a unique accent, and as most early residents came from Ireland, they are often referred to as the Galloway Irish. Four miles east of Stranraer on the A75, the **Castle Kennedy Gardens** includes lovely landscaping between a pair of lochs. Tree-lined walks offer great picnic spots. Buses (#430, 416, and 500) from Stranraer pass the castles; ask the driver to let you off and walk about a mile from the main road. (☎702 024. Open Apr.-Oct. daily 10am-5pm. £4, concessions £3, children £1. Guidebooks £2.) In town, see the **Castle of St. John**, George St., a 1510 edifice that affords good views. (☎705 088. Open Apr.-Sept. M-Sa 10am-1pm and 2-5pm. Free.)

Friendly **Jan Da Mar Guest House ❷**, 1 Ivy Pl., on London Rd., is just up from the ferry pier. (☎706 194. www.jandamar.co.uk. Singles £20-25; doubles £40-50. Cash only.) The **Harbour Guest House ❸**, 11 Market St., near the west pier, provides spacious rooms that look out over the water. (☎704 626. No smoking. Singles £25-30; doubles £50-60. MC/V.) A Tesco **grocery** is on Charlotte St., near the ferry terminal. (Open M-Sa 7am-8pm, Su 10am-6pm.)

The **train station**, by the ferry pier, is open daily 9:30am-3pm and 4-6:30pm. **Trains** (☎08457 484 950) arrive from Ayr (1¼hr.; M-Sa 7 per day, Su 3 per day; £10) and Glasgow (2½hr.; M-Sa 4-7 per day, Su 3 per day; £16.20). Scottish Citylink (☎08705 505 050) **buses** arrive in town at Port Rodie from: Ayr (#923; 1½hr., 2 per day, £4.50); Dumfries (#500/X75; 2hr.; M-Sa 10 per day, Su 3 per day; £4.50); Glasgow (#923, 2½hr., 2 per day, £8.50). National Express (☎08705 808 080) runs from: Carlisle (2½hr., £15); London (10hr., 1 per day, £33); Manchester (6hr., 2 per day, £27). **Ferries** travel from Northern Ireland across the North Channel. Stena Line (☎08705 707 070) sails from Belfast (1¾hr.-3¼hr.; 5-7 per day; £14-24, concessions £10-19, children £7-12). Five miles up the coast at Cairnyan, P&O Ferries (☎08702 424 777) arrive from Larne (1-1¾hr., 5-8 per day, £18-25). Sea passage is sometimes discounted with a rail ticket.

The **Tourist Information Centre**, 28 Harbour St., books rooms for a £3 charge and a 10% deposit. (☎702 595. Open Jan.-Mar. M-Sa 10am-4:30pm; Apr. to June M-Sa 10am-4:30pm; July-Aug. M-Sa 9:30am-5pm, Su 11am-3pm; Sept. M-Sa 10am-4:30pm; Oct. to Easter M-Sa 10am-4pm.) Other services include: **banks,** throughout the town; free **Internet access** at the Stranraer Library, 2-10 N. Strand St. (☎707 400; open M-F 9:15am-7:30pm, Sa 9:15am-1pm and 2-5pm); **bike rental** at the George Hotel, 49 George St. (☎702 487; £10 per day; open daily 9am-5pm); and the **post office**, in the Tesco on Charlotte St. (☎702 587; open M-F 7am-6pm, Sa 7am-5pm). **Post Code:** DG9 7EF.

WESTERN GALLOWAY

The two peninsulas of Western Galloway extend from Stranraer and are fringed with cliffs, beaches, and great views. The tricky public transport affords some worthwhile stops, such as the beautiful and windswept coast around **Sandhead,** south of Stranraer. Take **bus** #407 (20min., M-Sa 10 per day, Su 3 per day). The **Galloway Forest Park** features 300 sq. mi. of hikeable peaks surrounding Glen Trool (northeast of Stranraer). At the **Mull of Galloway,** the southernmost point in Scotland, a lighthouse and thousands of sea birds teeter atop sheer cliffs. Live video cameras in the visitor center allow for non-disruptive observation. On a clear day Northern Ireland and the Isle of Man are visible. **Portpatrick,** 8 mi. southwest of Stranraer, is a low-key seaside town, its rocky coastline fronted by comely pastel buildings. The coast-to-coast **Southern Upland Way** (p. 545) begins here, and there's also a coastal path leading back to Stranraer. Another path runs along the cliffs south of town to the ruins of **Dunskey Castle,** an empty shell perched high above the pounding surf. From the castle, a thin hint of a path leads down to a small cove, where a smuggler's cave can be reached at low tide.

Braefield Guest House ❸, Braefield Rd., has spacious rooms with steps leading down to the harbor. (☎ 810 255; www.portpatrick-braefield.co.uk. No smoking. Singles £23-25. MC/V.) **Buses** #358, 367, and 411 serve Portpatrick from Stranraer (25min., M-Sa 16 per day, Su 3 per day). The **post office** is just up the street. (☎810 212. Open M-Tu, Th-F 9am-1:15pm and 2:15-5:30pm, W 9am-1pm, Sa 9am-12:30pm.) **Post code:** DG9 8GU.

AYRSHIRE

AYR   ☎01292

A pleasant seaside town, Ayr (as in fresh sea AIR; pop. 50,000) is little more than a base for exploring the surrounding area. Locally, most tourists set their sights on Robert Burns's birthplace at Alloway, 3 mi. to the south, though Ayr is also home to Scotland's top horse racetrack, which hosts the **Scottish Grand National** in April and the **Ayr Gold Cup** in September. (☎264 179. Call for race dates. Tickets £10-25.) Perhaps the best way to see the coastal islands of the Firth of Clyde is to take a cruise on the **Waverly,** the world's only remaining ocean paddle steamer. Departing from the south side of Ayr's harbor during July and August, the steamer tours many of the nearby islands, including the Isle of Arran. (☎0845 130 4647; www.waverlyexcursions.co.uk. Cruises July-Aug. M-W. Full-day tour £25.)

Among the many **B&Bs** clustered near the beach, the **Tramore Guesthouse ❷,** 17 Eglinton Terr., has Moroccan decor a pebble's toss from the sand. (☎266 019. Singles £25; doubles £42. Cash only.) **Craggallan Guest House ❹,** 8 Queens Terr., has a pool table and access to the Ayrshire golf courses. (☎264 998; www.craggallan.com. Breakfast included. Singles from £35; doubles or twins from £56; triples £60-65. AmEx/MC/V.) Diagonally across from the train station on Castlehill Rd., Morrison's **supermarket** has everything you need. (☎283 906. Open M-W 8:30am-8pm, Th-F 8:30am-9pm, Sa 8am-8pm, Su 9am-5pm.) Probably your best bet for a meal out, **Fouters Bistro ❸,** 2a Academy St., off Sandgate, serves up a mix of Scottish and French cuisine in its subterranean digs. (☎261 391; www.fouters.co.uk. Entrees £9-15. Open Tu-Th noon-2pm and 6-9pm, F-Sa noon-2pm and 6-9:30pm.)

Ayr's **train station** is a 10min. walk from the center of town at the crossroads of Station Rd., Holmston Rd., and Castle Hill Rd. (Open M-Sa 5:30am-11:10pm, Su 8:30am-11:10pm.) Trains (☎08457 484 950) run from Dumfries (2 per day, £10.20); Glasgow (1hr., 2 per hr., £5.30); and Stranraer (1½hr.; M-Sa 7 per day, Su 3 per day; £10). The **bus station,** in the town center on Fullerton St. off Sandgate, has **luggage storage** for £1. (Open M-F 8:30am-5pm, Sa 9am-1pm.) It receives Stagecoach Western (☎613 500) buses from Glasgow (1¾hr., every 30min., £3.15) and Stranraer (1¼hr., 2 per day, £5.70). The **Tourist Information Centre** is at 22 Sandgate. (☎290 300. Open June daily 9am-5pm; July-Aug. M-Sa 9am-6pm, Su 10am-5pm; Sept. M-Sa

9am-5pm, Su 11am-4pm; Oct.-May M-Sa 9am-5pm. Other services include: **banks** on High St.; free **Internet access** at the Carnegie Library, 12 Main St. (☎286 385; open M-F 10am-7:30pm, Sa 10am-5pm); **bike rental** at AMG Cycles, 55 Dalblair Rd. (☎287 580; £12.50 per day, £35 per week; open M-Sa 9:15am-5:15pm, Su noon-4pm); and the **post office**, 65 Sandgate, with a bureau de change (☎0845 601 122; open M-Sa 9am-5:30pm). **Post Code:** KA7 1AA.

▧ DAYTRIPS FROM AYR

▧ CULZEAN CASTLE AND COUNTRY PARK

From Ayr take bus #60 (30min., 2 per hr.) to the Culzean stop. The castle is signposted about 1 mi. from the main road. ☎01655 844 400; www.culzeancastle.net. Castle open daily Apr.-Oct. 10:30am-5pm; last admission 4pm. Park open year-round 9:30am-sunset. Free tours daily July-Aug. 11am and 3:30pm. £10, concessions £7.50, families £24. Park only £6/4.50/15.

Twelve miles south of Ayr along the A719, Culzean (cul-LANE) Castle perches imposingly on a coastal cliff. According to legend, one of the cliff's caves shelters the Phantom Piper, who plays to his lost flock when the moon is full. Much of the castle was designed by renowned architect Robert Adam. The people of Scotland gave the building's top floor to Dwight Eisenhower for use during his lifetime— with a presidential budget you can rent his digs for the night. (☎01655 884 455. £375; other castle accommodations from £160. MC/V.) Popular during the summer, the castle is surrounded by a 560-acre country park that includes one of the nation's finest walled gardens, an enclosed deer park, and miles of wooded walkways. At the entrance to the castle and country park, close to the bus stop, the **Glenside Culzean Caravan and Camping Park ❶** provides a great place to pitch your tent, with fresh sea air and views of the Isle of Arran. (☎01655 760 627. Showers and laundry. No calls after 8pm. Open mid-Mar. to Oct. Car and tent £3.05-4.55 for members of Camping and Caravanning Club; nonmembers £4.20-5.85. MC/V.)

ALLOWAY

From Ayr, take bus #57 M-Sa or #60 Su (10min., every hr.).

Three miles south of Ayr, the village of Alloway seems to exist solely to ensure that the memory of Robert Burns never dies. Here the **Burns National Heritage Park** encompasses a number of attractions devoted to the bard, included under a single admission charge. (☎443 700; www.burnsheritagepark.com. Open daily Apr.-Oct. 9:30am-5:30pm; Nov.-Mar. 10am-5pm. £5, concessions £3, children £2.50, families £12.) Burns was born under the thatched roof of **Burns Cottage and Museum,** which has succeeded in preserving the era's barnyard smell. (☎01292 441 215. On the main road.) The **Tam o' Shanter Experience,** Murdochs Lone, presents a lyrical multimedia reading. (☎01292 443 700.) A short walk from the Experience will bring you to the bridge **Brig o' Doon,** the setting of the climax in Burns's "Tam o' Shanter" poem. Also nearby are the **Burns Monument and Gardens** and the ruined **Kirk Alloway,** where, according to Burns, the devil played the bagpipes.

ISLE OF ARRAN   ☎01770

The glorious Isle of Arran (AH-ren; pop. 4750) justifiably bills itself as "Scotland in Miniature." Gentle lowland hills, majestic highland peaks, peaceful meadows, and dense forests crowd into an island less than 20 mi. long. Every year thousands of walkers visit the isle's beautiful and varied terrain. Although the tourist population swells in the summer months, you will still find plenty of room to ramble on your own. The crags of Goatfell and the Caisteal range dominate the northern skyline. Near the western coast, prehistoric stone circles rise incongruously out of boggy grass. Linked by a reliable transportation network, the eastern coastline winds south from Brodick Castle past Holy Island into meadows and white beaches.

▐ TRANSPORTATION

To reach Arran, take a **train** (☎ 08457 484 950) to Ardrossan from Glasgow Central (1hr., 4-5 per day, £4.50), or **bus** #585 from Ayr (1hr.; M-Sa 2 per hr., Su 6 per day; £2.75). From Ardrossan, the CalMac **ferry** (☎ 302 166) makes the crossing to Brodick on Arran in sync with the train schedule (1hr.; M-Sa 5-6 per day, Su 4 per day; £4.80, bikes £1). There's also a summer ferry service to Lochranza on Arran from Claonaig on the Kintyre Peninsula (30min.; mid-Apr. to mid-Oct. 8-9 per day; £4.35, bikes £1). The *Area Transport Guide*, distributed free at the TIC and on the ferry, contains transport information and all bus schedules for the island. Stagecoach Western (☎ 302 000; office at Brodick pier) operates a comprehensive **local bus** service; a connection to and from every part of the island meets each Adrossan-Brodick ferry. Additional services are run by the Royal Mail **postbus** (☎ 302 507). Available on board, the Rural Rover Ticket grants a full day of bus travel (£4, children £2). From April to October, Stagecoach offers half- and full-day **island tours** departing from Brodick pier (full-day £7.50, half-day £5).

✦ ▐ ORIENTATION AND PRACTICAL INFORMATION

The A841 completes a 56 mi. circuit around the Isle of Arran. Ferries from Ardrossan arrive at **Brodick**, on the eastern shore; those from Claonaig arrive at **Lochranza**, in the north. In the southeast of the isle are **Lamlash**, the largest settlement, and the small village of **Whiting Bay. Blackwaterfoot** is the largest town on the sparsely populated western shore. Home to a virgin wilderness of green hills, deep valleys, and pine forests, the interior of the island is practically uninhabited. Brodick has the widest range of tourist services. Arran's only **Tourist Information Centre** is across from the ferry pier in Brodick. It books B&Bs for a 10% deposit plus a £3 charge. (☎ 303 774. Open June-Sept. M-Sa 9am-7:30pm, Su 10am-5pm; Oct.-May M-Sa 9am-5pm.) From April to September, a tourist information desk on the Ardrossan-Brodick ferry answers questions and can book rooms for you by calling the mainland TIC (May-June M-Sa 8:20am-4:10pm; July-Aug. M-F 8:20am-4:10pm). The island's **police** station (☎ 302 574) is located on Shore Rd. in Lamlash.

▐ ▐ HIKING AND OUTDOORS

Despite Arran's proximity to Glasgow, swaths of wilderness in the north and southwest remain untouched. Ordnance Survey Landranger #69 (£6) and Explorer #361 (£13) maps cover the island in extraordinary detail. Among the available literature, the Forestry Commission produces the small and popular *A Guide to the Forest Walks of The Isle of Arran* (£1) and the more comprehensive *Walking on The Isle of Arran* (£11). Highlights include the signposted path up popular **⚑Goatfell,** Arran's highest peak (2866 ft.). Beginning on the road between Brodick and Brodick Castle, this hike passes forest, heather, and mountain streams before the final rocky ascent into the clouds (7 mi. round-trip). The route takes 4-5hr. and only becomes challenging in the last 300 ft. The view (on a clear day, all the way to Ireland) from the cold and windy peak is worth the last scramble. The walk up **Glen Rosa** offers some great mountain scenery without the mountain climb. The terrain remains mostly flat as it follows the glen into the heart of Arran's peaks. From Brodick, head about a mile north, take the left turn onto "The String" road towards Blackwaterfoot, then take the first right. Another fine walk is the 8 mi. **Cock of Arran** route, which departs from Lochranza and circles the northern tip of

To Do:
Buy Let's Go Europe
Buy Eurail Pass
Check euro conversion rate
Ask about Roman hostels
Visit letsgo.com

Photo credits, clockwise from top left: Jeremy Todd, Samuel Perwin, Kristin Lee, Yaa Bruce, Nick Elprin, Dham Choi

LETSGO.COM
Here today, wherever you're headed tomorrow.

Whether you're planning your next adventure or are already far afield, LETSGO.COM will help you satisfy your wanderlust. Peruse our feature articles and destination write-ups as you select the spots you're off to next. Consult fellow travelers on our discussion and photo forums or search for anecdotal advice in our researchers' blogs. From embassy locations to passport laws, we keep track of all the facts, so discover what you need to know, book that high-season hostel bed, and hit the road. *READY. SET. LETSGO.COM.*

the island, passing the ruins of **Lochranza Castle** and running along miles of beach, along which basking sharks are common. Well-marked shorter walks depart from Whiting Bay and north of Blackwaterfoot.

Biking on the hilly island is a rewarding challenge; pedaling all or part of the 56 mi. circuit ringing the island affords splendid views, and traffic is light in most stretches, except at the height of summer. Adrenaline junkies will want to try the 11 mi. off-road route between Lamlash and Kilmory, which winds through hills and woods. Located about 300 yd. from Brodick pier along Shore Rd., the expedition leaders at Arran Adventure tackle everything from rock climbing to gorge walking and also offer mountain **bike rental**. (☎302 244; www.arranadventure.com. Bikes £15 per day, £45 per week. Open Apr.-Sept. daily 9am-7:30pm.) For bike rental elsewhere on Arran, try Blackwaterfoot Garage, in Blackwaterfoot. (☎860 277. £8 per day, £20 per week. Open M-F and Su 8:30am-5:30pm, Sa 9am-5pm.)

 Deer-hunting season on Arran runs from August to February (peak August to September), when hunting parties trek through estates in the northern part of the island. To avoid unfortunate run-ins with hunter or hunted, call Hillphones (☎01770 302 363) for a list of a estates to avoid each day.

BRODICK ☎01770

Not quite picture-perfect, Brodick sits on a bay against a backdrop of rugged mountains. North of town, **Brodick Castle** overlooks the harbor. Built on the site of an old Viking fort, the castle resembles a Victorian manor and contains a collection of paintings and deer hunting trophies. Giant rhododendrons bloom in the jungle-like garden. If you can't manage a visit, look on the back of a Scottish £20 note. (☎302 202. Castle open Easter to Sept. daily 11am-4:30pm; Oct. daily 11am-3:30pm; Nov.-Dec. F-Su 11am-4pm. Garden open daily 9:30am-sunset. Castle and gardens £10, concessions £7, family £25. Gardens only £5/4/14.) All northbound buses from Brodick stop at the castle; Stagecoach also operates a vintage coach service. (Easter to Sept. 7-9 per day; round-trip £2, children £1.)

As the nexus of island transportation, Brodick is a fine place to spend the night. Try the spacious, seafront **Glenflorol Guest House ❷**, Shore Rd. (☎302 707. Singles £20; doubles £40. Cash only.) Upscale and closer to the ferry is **Dunvegan House ❸**, Shore Rd. (☎302 811; www.dunveganhouse.co.uk. No smoking. Dinner £18. No singles. £33 per person. Cash only.) Another option is sandstone **Carrick Lodge ❸**, a converted manse 5min. uphill left from the ferry pier. (☎302 550. £28 per person. MC/V.) **Glen Rosa Farm ❶**, just over 2 mi. north of Brodick pier, provides basic camping facilities and a lush valley in which to spend the night. (☎302 380. Toilets and cold water. £3.50 per person. Cash only.) The Co-op sells **groceries** across from the ferry. (☎302 515. Open M-Sa 8am-10pm, Su 9am-7pm.) A number of bars and inexpensive restaurants line Shore Rd. Travel by car or bus to **Creelers ❹**, north of town along the A841, a highly regarded seafood restaurant with fresh fish served in simple styles. (☎302 810. Lunch £7.50-9.50. 3-course dinner £25. Open Mar.-Oct. Tu-Sa 12:30-2:30pm and 6-9:30pm, Su 1-3pm and 6-9:30pm; call ahead during winter. MC/V.)

Brodick is spread out along **Shore Road,** just north of the ferry pier; take a right with your back to the water. Services include: the only **banks** and **ATMs** on the island, along Shore Rd.; a **launderette** at Collins' Good Food Shop, Auchrannie Rd., just over the bridge as you head north of town (☎302 427; wash £3.05, dry 35p per 5min.; open M-Tu and Th-Sa 9am-5pm, W 9am-1pm); free **Internet access** at the Arran Library, Shore Rd. (open Tu 10am-5pm, Th and F 10am-7:30pm, Sa 10am-1pm); and the **post office**, set back from Shore Rd. on Mayish Rd. (☎302 245; open June-Sept. M-F 9am-5:30pm, Sa 9am-12:45pm; Oct.-May M-F 9am-1pm, 2-5pm). **Post Code:** KA27 8AA.

WHITING BAY AND LAMLASH

Lamlash, the largest town on Arran, is a popular sailing center. **Holy Island** rises dramatically from the water, dominating the Lamlash horizon. Presently owned and inhabited by a group of Tibetan Buddhist monks, the island has an exotic feel to it, with shrines, painted rocks, and Buddhist mottoes sharing the stark hills with herds of wild ponies. The island also provides a number of walking paths including one up **Mulloch Mor** (1030 ft.), the highest point on the island, with splendid views of Arran's mountains and the bright blue sea below. A regular **ferry** (☎ 600 349) departs Lamlash for Holy Island (15min., May-Sept. 8 per day, round-trip £9), though special arrangements must be made in winter. Farther south, **Whiting Bay** is a sleepy seaside village stretched along the A841. From a trailhead toward the southern end of town, two relatively easy walks lead to the **Glenashdale Falls** (1 mi.) and the megalithic stone structures at **Giant's Graves.**

In Lamlash a Co-op sells **groceries** along the A841 (open M-Sa 8am-10pm, Su 10am-6pm). Just past where the A841 veers from the coast toward Brodick, the **Shore B&B ❸,** Shore Rd., has Scandinavian-style lodgings with fantastic views of Holy Island. (☎ 600 764. No singles. Doubles £60. MC/V.) The **Craig Ard B&B ❸,** Shore Rd., offers one ensuite double. (☎ 700 378. £48. Cash only.) Several hotels serve food; **◪The Coffee Pot ❶,** toward the southern end of town on the coastal road, is a picturesque spot for afternoon tea (£1-2) or a bowl of scrumptious homemade soup. (☎ 700 382. Open daily 10am-5pm. Food served until 4pm. Cash only.)

LOCHRANZA

Northern Arran is a spectacular land of rich green hillsides, bare peaks, and rocky coast. Idyllic **Lochranza,** 14 mi. from Brodick at the island's northern tip, shelters the remains of a 13th-century **castle.** (Always open. Free.) The whisky produced in the **Isle of Arran Distillery,** on the road to Brodick, is less peaty than other malts and thus more palatable to the uninitiated. (☎ 830 264. Open mid-Mar. to Oct. daily 10am-6pm. Tours start at 30min. past the hour, 10:30am-4:30pm, and include a wee dram. £3.50, concessions £2.50, under 12 free.) One mile down the coast, the fishing village of **Catacol Bay** harbors the **Twelve Apostles,** a dozen connected white houses that differ only in the shapes of their windows. A number of the northern peaks, including **Caisteal Abhail** (2817 ft.), are within a day's walk.

Though lacking in services and less accessible by bus than its southern neighbors, Lochranza's simple beauty is worth the added effort. Toward the southern end on the main road to Brodick, the **SYHA Lochranza ❶** has 64 beds and two friendly and helpful managers. (☎ 08700 041 140. Laundry and Internet access. Curfew 11:30pm. Lights out 11:45pm. Open Mar.-Oct. Dorms £12, under 18 £9.50. MC/V.) In the former town church across from the castle, the **Castlekirk B&B ❸** has high, arched ceilings, a lounge with stained-glass windows, and a peaceful ambience. (☎ 830 202; www.castlekirkarran.co.uk. No smoking. £20-22.50 per person. Cash only.) Campers can pitch at the **Lochranza Golf Course Caravan and Camping Site ❶** and buy very basic groceries and necessities at the shop. (☎ 830 273. Toilets, showers, and laundry. Open Apr.-Oct. £3.70 per person, £2.60 per tent. Cash only.) The restaurant at the **Isle of Arran Distillery ❷** features a daily menu of local Arran produce that ranges from a traditional cullen skink (£7) to sirloin steak flavored with Arran Malt. (Open daily mid-Mar. to Oct. noon-5pm; June-Sept. noon-6:30pm. MC/V.) In the evening, the **Lochranza Hotel ❷,** just along from the ferry pier, serves more typical pub grub. (☎ 830 223. Open daily 11am-9pm. Cash only.) For a cheap, ready-to-go alternative, stop by **The Sandwich Station ❶,** located across from the pier and to the right. Call in advance for picnic lunches. (☎ 07766 627583. Open daily 8am-6pm. Cash only.) Lochranza has **no banks or ATMs. Post Code:** KA27 8HJ.

WESTERN ARRAN

The western shore of Arran harbors a handful of tiny settlements separated by miles of coastline. The **Machrie Moor Stone Circle,** a mysterious Bronze-Age arrangement of standing stones and boulders, lies at the end of an easy 3 mi. walk. Follow the farm path 1 mi. south of Machrie village along the A841. Another mile south, the trail leading to the **King's Cave** (3 mi.) begins from a Forestry Commission carpark. Passing along coastal cliffs, the walk terminates at the caves where Robert the Bruce allegedly hid before returning to the mainland to claim the throne. From here it is another 2½ mi. south to **Blackwaterfoot,** where you can reconnect with island transportation and find a few places to eat and sleep.

GLASGOW   ☎ 0141

Glasgow (pop. 610,000) is a hip and unpretentious city. Its grand Victorian architecture, known as the Glasgow Style and spearheaded by luminary Charles Rennie MacKintosh, still characterizes the city center. But cranes littering the river Clyde and the blackened stones of Glasgow Cathedral recall the city's sooty past as the world's leading shipbuilder and steel producer. Now the daring curves of the multi-million pound Science Centre glint along the river, drawing crowds to Scotland's only IMAX theater. The renowned Glasgow School of Art and the city's world-class art museums, galleries, and collections give Glasgow a thriving pulse. With the largest student population in Scotland, Glasgow has no shortage of pubs and clubs to keep revelers entertained well into the wee hours of the morning.

✈ INTERCITY TRANSPORTATION

Glasgow lies on the River Clyde, 40 mi. west of Edinburgh. The M8 motorway links the two cities. Glasgow is the northern end of the M74, which connects with England.

Flights: Glasgow is served by 2 international airports.

Glasgow International Airport (GLA), (☎08700 400 008; www.baa.co.uk/glasgow), 10 mi. west in Abbotsinch. Scotland's major airport, served by KLM, British Airways, and others. Scottish Citylink bus #905 runs to the airport from Buchanan Station (25min.; every 10min. 6am-6pm, every 15-30min. 6pm-midnight; £3.30).

Prestwick International Airport (PIK), (☎08712 230 700; www.gpia.co.uk), southwest of the city center. Ryanair flies to England and other countries in Europe. Trains from Central Station leave every hr. M-Sa 6am-11pm, Sun 8am–11pm (30min.; £5.20, £2.60 with Ryanair flight printout). Express bus #X99 runs every hr. from the terminal building to Buchanan St. (50min., £3.40).

Trains: Bus #88 (50p) connects Glasgow's 2 main stations, but it's only a 5-10min. walk. Book in advance online (www.nationalrail.co.uk) for discounts.

Central Station, Gordon St. U: St. Enoch. Toilets 20p; shower with soap and towel £2. Open daily 5:30am-midnight. Ticket office open M-Sa 6am-9:30pm, Su 7:10am-11pm. Trains from: **Ardrossan** (1hr., 10-12 per day, £4.80); **Carlisle** (1½hr., every hr., £27); **Dumfries** (1¾hr.; M-Sa 7 per day, Su 2 per day; £10.30); **London King's Cross** (6hr., every hr., £90.60); **Manchester** (4hr., every hr., £40); **Stranraer Harbor** (2½hr.; M-Sa 8 per day, Su 3 per day; £16.30).

Queen Street Station, George Sq. U: Buchanan St. Serves trains from the north and east. Toilets 20p. Lockers £3-5 per day. Open M-Sa 5am-11:15pm, Su 7am-11pm. Travel center open M-Sa 6:15am-9:45pm, Su 7am-10pm. Trains (☎0845 748 4950) from: **Aberdeen** (2½hr.; M-Sa every hr., Su 7 per day; £34); **Edinburgh** (50min., 4 per hr., £8.20); **Fort William** (3¾hr., 2-4 per day, £19.50); **Inverness** (3¼hr.; M-Sa 7 per day, Su 4 per day; £34).

Buses: Buchanan Station, Killermont St. (☎331 3708, M-Sa 9am-5pm), 2 blocks north of Queen St. Station. National Express and Scottish Citylink buses. Toilets 20p. Luggage storage £3-5. Ticket office open M-Su 7am-9:30pm. Lockers open daily 6:30am-10:30pm. Scottish Citylink (☎08705 505 050) from: **Aberdeen** (4hr., every hr., £17);

Edinburgh (70min., every 20min., £4); **Perth** (1½hr., every hr., £7); **Inverness** (3½-4½hr., every hr., £17); **Oban** (3hr., 5 per day, £13.10). National Express (☎08705 808 080) arrives from **London** (8½hr., 3 per day, £30).

✱ ORIENTATION

George Square is the center of town; the stations and TIC are within a few blocks' radius. Sections of **Sauchiehall Street** (Sackie-HALL), **Argyle Street,** and **Buchanan Street** are lined with stores and open only to pedestrians, forming bustling outdoor shopping districts. **Charing Cross,** where Bath St. crosses the M8, can be used as a locator. The vibrant **West End** revolves around **Byres Road** and **Glasgow University,** 1 mi. northwest of George Sq. The city extends south of the **River Clyde** toward Pollok Country Park and the Science Centre.

⊟ LOCAL TRANSPORTATION

Travel Center: Strathclyde Passenger Transport Authority, St. Enoch's Sq. (☎0870 608 2608), 2 blocks from Central Station. U: St. Enoch. Immensely useful advice, passes, and Underground maps. Open M-Th 8:30am-4:45pm, F 8:30am-4pm. **STA Travel,** 122 George St. (☎552 6505). Student and budget travel arrangements. Open M-Th 9:30am-5:30pm, F-Sa 10:30am-5:30pm.

Public Transportation: Glasgow's transportation system includes suburban rail, private local bus services, and the circular **Underground (U)** subway line, a.k.a. the "Clockwork Orange." U trains run every 4-8min. M-Sa 6:30am-11pm, Su 11am-5:30pm. £1, children 50p. **Underground Journey** and **Season Tickets** are a good deal; bring a photo ID to the office at St. Enoch station. 10 trips £8, children £4; 20 trips £13/7; 7 days £8/4.50; 28 days £26/13. The **Discovery Ticket** (£1.70) for 1 day of unlimited travel is valid on the Underground after 9:30am M-Sa and all day Su. A **Roundabout Ticket** covers 1 day of unlimited Underground and train travel; valid after 9am M-F and all day Sa-Su (£4.50, children £2.25). Inquire about other discounts for families and travel using multiple modes of transport. The **Traveline** service (☎08706 082 608; www.traveline.org.uk) helps travelers coordinate bus, train, and ferry trips in Scotland.

Taxis: Airport Taxi Services (☎848 4900, airport free phone 4900) provides 24hr. service from Glasgow International Airport. Wheelchair-accessible services available. **Glasgow Taxis LTD** (☎429 7070). 1-3hr. tours available.

Bike Rental: With narrow streets that can unpredictably change direction and buses, taxis, and cars everywhere, biking in Glasgow can be a challenge. For the adventurous, however, **West End Cycles,** 16 Chancellor St. (☎357 1344) rents bikes for £15 per day. £100 or ID deposit.

⊉ PRACTICAL INFORMATION

Tourist Information Centre (TIC): 11 George Sq. (☎204 4400; www.seeglasgow.com), off George Sq. south of Queen St. Station, northeast of Central Station. U: Buchanan St. Books accommodations for £3 and 10% deposit, sells CalMac ferry tickets, and arranges car rentals. Also contains a travel bookshop, a Western Union, and a **bureau de change.** Pick up the free *Essential Guide to Glasgow* and *Where to Stay.* Open July-Aug. M-Sa 9am-8pm, Su 10am-6pm; Sept.-June M-Sa 9am-7pm, Su 10am-6pm.

Tours: City Sightseeing (☎204 0444; www.scotguide.com) bus tours allow unlimited hop-on, hop-off access. Look for the bus stop signs or get on in George Sq. £8.50, concessions £6.50. **Walkabout Tours** provides day-long audio tours (£5; English only) available at the TIC. Through **Glasgow City Walk** (☎946 4542), members of the Scottish Tour Guides Association will provide groups with excellent tours and copious historical information (£40 per group).

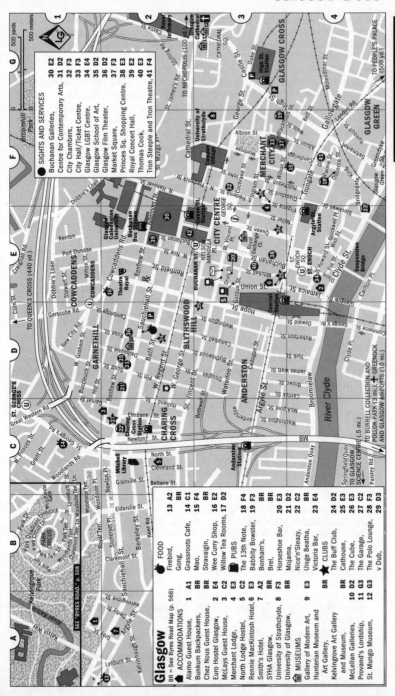

SOUTHERN
SCOTLAND

Glasgow

BR = See Byres Road Map (p. 568)

◆ ACCOMMODATIONS

Alamo Guest House,	1 A1
Bunkum Backpackers,	BR
Chez Nous Guest House,	BR
Euro Hostel Glasgow,	2 E4
McLays Guest House,	3 C2
Merchant Lodge,	4 E3
North Lodge Hostel,	5 C2
Rennie MacKintosh Hotel,	6 E3
Smith's Hotel,	7 A2
SYHA Glasgow,	8 F3
University of Strathclyde,	8 F3
University of Glasgow,	BR

🏛 MUSEUMS

Gallery of Modern Art,	9 E3
Hunterian Museum and	
Art Gallery,	BR
Kelvingrove Art Gallery	
and Museum,	BR
McLellan Galleries,	10 D2
Provand's Lordship,	11 G3
St. Mungo Museum,	12 G3

♦ FOOD

Firebird,	13 A2
Gong,	BR
Grassroots Cafe,	14 C1
Mao,	15 E3
Stravaigin,	BR
Wee Curry Shop,	16 E2
Willow Tea Rooms,	17 D2

🍺 PUBS

The 13th Note,	18 F4
Babbity Bowster,	19 F3
Bonham's,	20 E3
Brel,	BR
Horseshoe Bar,	21 D2
Mojama,	22 C2
Nice'n'Sleazy,	BR
Uisge Beatha,	23 E4
Victoria Bar,	BR

★ CLUBS

The Buff Club,	24 D2
Cathouse,	25 E3
The Cube,	26 E3
The Garage,	27 C2
The Polo Lounge,	28 F3
v Dub,	29 D3

● SIGHTS AND SERVICES

Buchanan Galleries,	30 E2
Centre for Contemporary Arts,	31 D2
City Chambers,	32 F3
City Hall/Ticket Centre,	33 F3
Glasgow LGBT Centre,	34 E4
Glasgow School of Art,	35 D2
Glasgow Film Theater,	36 D2
Market Square,	37 F3
Princes Sq. Shopping Centre,	38 E3
Royal Concert Hall,	39 E2
Thomas Cook,	40 E3
Tron Steeple and Tron Theatre,	41 F4

Financial Services: Banks are plentiful; **ATMs** are on every corner. **Thomas Cook,** 15-17 Gordon St. (☎201 7200), just beyond Central Station. Open M-Sa 8:30am-5:30pm, Su 10am-4pm. **American Express,** 115 Hope St. (☎0870 600 1060). Open M-Tu and Th-F 8:30am-5:30pm, W 9:30am-5:30pm, Sa 9am-noon.

Work Opportunities: Tourists descend upon Glasgow during the summer. If you are fluent in 2 or more European languages, you can apply to Glasgow's TIC for a seasonal position. Work in Scotland can also be found by visiting www.s1jobs.com.

GLBT Services: Glasgow LGBT Centre, 11 Dixon St. (☎221 7203; www.glgbt.org.uk). The first center of its kind in Scotland, with support groups, get-togethers, and information on gay and lesbian clubs, bars, and activities. Open daily 11am-midnight.

Launderette: Bank Street Laundry, 39-41 Bank St. (☎339 8953). U: Kelvin Bridge. Wash £2, dry 20p per 5min. Open M-F 9am-7:30pm, Sa-Su 9am-5pm.

Police: 173 Pitt St. (☎532 2000).

Hospital: Glasgow Royal Infirmary, 84-106 Castle St. (☎211 4000).

Pharmacy: Boots, 200 Sauchiehall St. (☎332 1925). Open M-W and F-Sa 8am-6pm, Th 8am-7pm, Su 11am-5pm.

Internet Access: Mitchell Library, North St. Free. Open M-Th 9am-8pm, F-Sa 9am-5pm. **Hub,** 8 Renfield St. (☎222 2227). £1.80 per hr.; £3.50 for a day pass or wireless connection. Open M-Th 7:30am-10pm, F-Sa 7:30am-9pm, Su 10am-9pm. **easyInternet Cafe,** 57-61 St. Vincent St. (☎222 2365), adjoining Caffe Nero. £1 per 30min. Open daily 7am-10:45pm.

Post Office: 47 St. Vincent St. (☎08457 223 344). Open M-F 8:30am-5:45pm, Sa 9am-5:30pm. Branches at Hope St. and Bothwell St. **Post Code:** G2 5QX.

◪ ACCOMMODATIONS

Glasgow has hostels, B&Bs, and hotels to suit any budget. Places fill up in the summer, so book well ahead. Those on a tight budget need not worry; hostels run only £10-14 per night. Most of Glasgow's B&Bs are scattered on either side of **Argyle Street** in the university area or east of the Necropolis near **Westercraigs Road.** The universities offer summer housing, but it fills quickly; book ahead.

HOSTELS

▨ **SYHA Glasgow,** 7-8 Park Terr. (☎332 3004). U: St. George's Cross. Take bus #44 from Central Station, ask for the 1st stop on Woodlands Rd., and follow the signs to the heart of the West End. Once the residence of a nobleman, later an upscale hotel, now the best hostel in town. All rooms (4-8 beds) ensuite. TV and game rooms, bike shed, and kitchen. Coin laundry. Internet access (£1 per 20min.). Dorms June-Sept. £14, under 18 £12; Oct.-May prices vary by month, starting at £12. MC/V. ❶

▨ **North Lodge Hostel,** 163 North St. (☎221 3852). Take the rail from Queen St. to Charing Cross. Next to Mitchell Library. The friendliest hostel in town, with a communal, jovial atmosphere; banter with the owner and the other guests. Pleasant space, with a living room and kitchen. Light breakfast included. No lockers. Internet and laundry free. Dorms £10. MC/V. ❶

Euro Hostel Glasgow (☎222 2828; www.euro-hostels.co.uk), at the corner of Clyde St. and Jamaica St., opposite Central Station. U: St. Enoch. Glasgow's largest hostel is comfortable, clean, quiet, and convenient to the city center. A gray, 8-story behemoth overlooking the Clyde. Cozy Osmosis bar, 2 lounges, and a small kitchen. Breakfast included. Laundry £2. Internet access £1 per 15min. Dorms £14-19. MC/V. ❷

Bunkum Backpackers, 26 Hillhead St. (☎581 4481; www.bunkumglasgow.co.uk), just up the hill from Glasgow University and the West End. U: Hillhead. Behind the tarnished facade, find spacious, colorful rooms, a kitchen, and a quiet location. Lockers £10 deposit. Laundry £2.50. Free parking, but call ahead to reserve. Dorms £12. MC/V. ❷

UNIVERSITY DORMS

University of Strathclyde, Office of Sales and Marketing, 50 Richmond St. (☎553 4148; www.rescat.strath.ac.uk). Rooms and B&B available in summer. Shared apartments and furnished rooms, with 1 kitchen per floor, laundry, and towels. Book well in advance. Open mid-June to mid-Sept. Singles £21.50, with breakfast £26.50-32.50. MC/V. ❸

University of Glasgow, 73 Great George St. (☎330 4116, bookings 08000 272 030; www.cvso.co.uk). Off Hillhead St. Summer housing at several dorms. Office open daily 9am-5pm. For those on a budget, **Cairncross House,** 20 Kelvinhaugh Pl. has self-catering rooms off Argyle St., near Kelvingrove Park. Tea, coffee, soap, towels, and linens provided. Singles from £15.10; doubles from £26.80. MC/V. ❷

B&BS

McLays Guest House, 268 Renfrew St. (☎332 4796; www.mclays.com). With 3 dining rooms, satellite TV, and phones in each of the 62 rooms, this posh B&B looks and feels like a hotel. Singles from £24, ensuite £32; doubles £40/48. MC/V. ❸

Merchant Lodge, 52 Virginia St. (☎552 2424; www.the-merchant-lodge.sagenet.co.uk). Quiet, upscale lodgings right next to stores and entertainment venues in the city center. Originally a tobacco store built in the 1800s; still boasts the original stone spiral staircase. All rooms ensuite. Big breakfast included. Singles £40; doubles £62; triples £80; quads £90. AmEx/MC/V. ❹

Alamo Guest House, 46 Gray St. (☎339 2395; www.alamoguesthouse.com). Posh Victorian house with family atmosphere, complete with housecat overlooking Kelvingrove Park. On a quiet street with access to the West End and Sauchiehall St. Pets welcome. Singles from £26; doubles £56. MC/V. ❸

Chez Nous Guest House, 33 Hillhead St. (☎334 2977; www.cheznousguesthouse.co.uk), just north of Glasgow University, across the street from Bunkum Backpackers. U: Hillhead. Lovely, comfortable nook with easy access to the West End. Attractive rooms are small but well-kept, and often booked through the summer; call well in advance. Free parking. Singles from £30, ensuite £45; doubles £50. MC/V. ❸

HOTELS

Smith's Hotel, 963 Sauchiehall St. (☎339 7674; www.smiths-hotel.com), 1 block east of Kelvingrove Park in the West End. This large, homey hotel is between the West End and the city center and provides welcome respite from the hubbub. Book in advance for long-term budget rooms. Singles £21-36; doubles £38-52; triples £69. MC/V. ❸

Rennie Mackintosh Hotel, 59 Union St. (☎221 0050; www.renniemac.com). Inspired, not built, by the famous architect. A standard but central hotel, inexpensive given its location. Ask for a Mackintosh-style room. Breakfast included. Singles £30-35; doubles £45-50. Discounts for students and long stays. AmEx/MC/V. ❹

⬛ FOOD

Glasgow is called the curry capital of Britain, and for good reason. The area bordered by **Otago Street** in the west, **St. George's Road** in the east, and along **Great Western Road, Woodlands Road,** and **Eldon Street** brims with kebab and curry joints. Currently, Italian and Asian eateries are all the rage—try one of the many pasta, pizza, sushi, or hot pot cafes. A number of hole-in-the-wall restaurants with excellent food at low prices. **Byres Road** and **Ashton Lane,** a tiny cobblestone alley parallel to Byres Rd., thrive with cheap, trendy cafes and bistros. Bakeries along **High Street** below the cathedral serve scones for as little as 20p.

▨ **Willow Tea Rooms,** 217 Sauchiehall St. (☎332 0521; www.willowtearooms.co.uk), upstairs from Henderson Jewellers. U: Buchanan St. Branch at 97 Buchanan St. A Glasgow landmark, this cozy upstairs room has beautiful MacKintosh revival design. Sample any of the more than 20 teas (£1.80 per pot) or indulge in a 3-course high tea (£9.50). Open M-Sa 9am-4:30pm, Su 11am-4:15pm. MC/V. ❷

▨ **Grassroots Cafe,** 97 St. George's Rd. (☎333 0534). U: St. George's Cross. Bold colors, excellent creative organic dishes, and an open kitchen make this the hottest vegetarian restaurant in town. Try the "kaboodles" (fritters; £4.15). A mecca for Glasgow veggie culture, with Green Party offices upstairs. Open daily 10am-10pm. AmEx/MC/V. ❷

Firebird, 1321 Argyle St. (☎334 0594). U: Kelvinhall. With imaginative and outstanding nosh, including glazed duck and quince salad (£8.50) and specialty pizzas (£12.50). Hip interior, perfectly realized down to the faux fireplace. DJs F-Sa nights. Open M-Th 11:30am-midnight, F-Sa 10:30-1am, Su 12:30pm-midnight. MC/V. ❸

Gong, Vinicombe St., off Byres Rd. (☎576 1700). U: Hillhead. One of Glasgow's most creative spots; the room resembles a futuristic art installation or bamboo forest. For the best deals, go for the set menu (£10 for 2 courses, £12.50 for 3; M-Th and Su all day, F-Sa 5-7pm) or the Supper Club deal (dishes £3.75; F-Sa 10:30pm-2am). Open M-Th and Su 5-9:30pm, F-Sa 5pm-2am. AmEx/MC/V. ❸

Wee Curry Shop, 7 Buccleuch St., off Sauchiehall St. (☎353 0777). U: Cowcaddens. Branch at 23 Ashton Ln. (☎357 5280). U: Hillhead. From famous Glasgow restauranteurs. The best bang for your buck in a town full of *pakora* and *puri*. Book a table in advance. 2-course lunch £4.75; entrees £5.50-7. Open M-Sa noon-2:30pm and 5:30-10:30pm. Buccleuch St.: cash only. Ashton Ln.: MC/V. ❶

Mao, 84 Brunswick St. (☎564 5161; www.cafemao.com). U: St. Enoch. With Andy Warhol-esque portraits of Mao in the window, this Asian-fusion restaurant provides tempura of lemon sole (£11) and other tasty dishes. Open daily noon-11pm. AmEx/MC/V. ❷

Stravaigin, 28 Gibson St. (☎334 2665; www.stravaigin.com). U: Kelvinbridge. The mantra "think globally, eat locally" inspires the dishes of fresh seafood, game, and produce. Exotic spices and a menu that changes daily (entrees £14-26). With a second, less-pricey location, **Stravaigin 2,** 8 Ruthaven Ln., off Byres Rd. (☎334 7165; U: Hillhead). Both open Tu-Th and Su 5-11pm, F-Sa noon-2:30pm and 5-11pm. AmEx/MC/V. ❹

◉ SIGHTS

A city dotted by free museums, with festivals and splendid period architecture, Glasgow is a paradise for budget sightseers. Many of the best sights are part of the **Glasgow Museums** network, whose free collections are scattered across the city. *The List* ($2.40), available from newsagents, is an essential guide that reviews current exhibitions and lists galleries, music, and nightlife.

THE CITY CENTER

▨ **GLASGOW CATHEDRAL AND NECROPOLIS.** The imposing Glasgow Cathedral is a spectacular example of 13th-century Gothic architecture. A front lawn littered with horizontal gravestones and the tomb of St. Mungo in the lower half of the Cathedral complete the spooky atmosphere. (*Castle St.* ☎552 6891. *Open Apr.-Sept. M-Sa 9:30am-6pm, Su 1-5pm; Oct.-Mar. until 4pm. Excellent personal tours of the Cathedral are free. Organ recitals and concerts held July-Aug. Tu at 7:30pm. Recitals and concerts free-£7.*) At the chilling, tiered hilltop **Necropolis,** tombstones, statues, and obelisks lie aslant and broken on the ground. A 50 ft. statue of reformer John Knox looms atop the hill. (*Behind the cathedral over the Bridge of Sighs. Be careful after dark. Open 24hr. Free.*)

GEORGE SQUARE. This grand, red-paved landmark has always been the physical, cultural, commercial, and historical center of Glasgow. Named for George III, the square's 80 ft. central column instead features a statue of Sir Walter Scott; the author wears his plaid, as always, over the wrong shoulder. The **City Chambers**, on the east side of George Sq., house an elaborate Italian Renaissance interior; crouch down with the other sightseers to capture a picture of a design reminiscent of the work of MC Escher. *(☎287 4017. Free 1hr. tours M-F 10:30am and 2:30pm.)* The eclectic **Gallery of Modern Art (GoMA)**, Queens St., south of George Sq., occupies a classical-style building that was once the Royal Exchange. *(☎229 1996. Open M-W and Sa 10am-5pm, Th 10am-8pm, F and Su 11am-5pm. Free.)*

ST. MUNGO MUSEUM OF RELIGIOUS LIFE AND ART. The museum surveys religions from Islam to Yoruba. Its prized possessions are Dalí's *Christ of St. John's Cross*, a bronze sculpture of Shiva Nataraja, and Britain's first Japanese Zen garden. *(2 Castle St. ☎553 2557. Open M-Th and Sa 10am-5pm, F and Su 11am-5pm. Free.)*

CENTRE FOR CONTEMPORARY ARTS (CCA). Three free galleries, a theater, artists' residences, a cafe, and a cinema comprise this avant-garde mecca, which houses the prestigious Beck's Futures prize every June and July. *(350 Sauchiehall St. ☎352 4900; www.cca-glasgow.com. Open Tu-W 9am-11pm, Th 9am-midnight, F-Sa 9-1am. Free galleries. Performances begin at 8pm. Films £8, concessions £2.50.)*

OTHER CENTRAL SIGHTS. Built in 1471, **Provand's Lordship** is the oldest house in Glasgow, and has the squeaky wooden floors to prove it. A collection of antique furniture attempts to transform its musty rooms into a recreation of medieval life, while Gregorian chants reverberate through the halls. *(3-7 Castle St. ☎552 8819. Open M-Th and Sa 10am-5pm, F and Su 11am-5pm. Free.)* In their enthusiasm for the Industrial Revolution, Glaswegians destroyed most of the city's medieval architecture, only to recreate it later in the **People's Palace** on Glasgow Green. *(☎271 2951. Open M-Th and Sa 10am-5pm, F and Su 11am-5pm. Free.)*

THE WEST END

KELVINGROVE PARK, MUSEUM, AND ART GALLERY. Along the River Kelvin, **Kelvingrove Park** is a genteel, wooded expanse, studded with statues and fountains. By day, it is lovely and peaceful, but be cautious at night. Rumored to have been built back to front (the true entrance faces the park, not the street), the spires of the **Kelvingrove Art Gallery and Museum** rise from the park's southwest corner. The museum is closed for renovations until summer 2006. In the meantime, the collection, including works by Rembrandt and van Gogh, is on display at the **McLellan Galleries** in the city center. *(270 Sauchiehall St.; look for the big purple awning. ☎565 4137. McLellan Galleries open M-Th and Sa 10am-5pm, F and Su 11am-5pm. Free.)*

UNIVERSITY OF GLASGOW. The central spire of the neo-Gothic university towers over University Ave. The best views of the university buildings are from Kelvingrove Park or up the 228 steps of the spire. Pick up *Welcome to the University of Glasgow*, free at the TIC, or stop by the **Visitor Centre** for a free map and self-guided tour. *(☎330 5511. U: Hillhead. Open M-Sa 9:30am-5pm. Free tours and tower access F 2pm.)* The oldest museum in Scotland, the **Hunterian Museum**, houses the university's Blackstone chair, in which all students had to sit for oral examinations while timed by an hourglass suspended overhead. Other attractions include a coin collection, Japanese Samurai armor, and £1 million turned into pulp. *(☎330 4221. Open M-Sa 9:30am-5pm. Free.)* Across University St. on Hillhead St., the ▧**Hunterian Art Gallery** displays 19th-century Scottish art, the world's largest Whistler collection, and a variety of Rembrandts, Pissarros, and

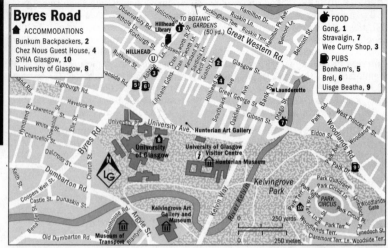

Byres Road

🏠 ACCOMMODATIONS
Bunkum Backpackers, **2**
Chez Nous Guest House, **4**
SYHA Glasgow, **10**
University of Glasgow, **8**

🍴 FOOD
Gong, **1**
Stravaigin, **7**
Wee Curry Shop, **3**

🍺 PUBS
Bonham's, **5**
Brel, **6**
Uisge Beatha, **9**

Rodins. Next door are the reconstructed rooms of the **MacKintosh House**. (☎330 5434. *Open M-Sa 9:30am-5pm; closed during exam period. Gallery free. House £2.50, students free; free after 2pm on W.*)

BOTANIC GARDENS. Colorful gardens stretch along the River Kelvin at the northern end of Byres Rd. Look for the wall of carnivorous plants as well as the Scottish national collection of tree ferns, orchids, and begonias in the **Main Range** hothouse and wander around the herb, rose, and uncommon vegetable gardens outside. A wrought-iron greenhouse, **Kibble Palace** has an elegant fish pond surrounded by Neoclassical statues, but will be closed until late 2006 for a makeover. (*730 Great Western Rd. and Byres Rd.* ☎334 2422. *U: Hillhead. Gardens open daily 7:30am to sunset. Kibble Palace and Main Range open daily Apr. to early Oct. 10am-4:45pm; late Oct. to Mar. 10am-4:15pm. Tours available by reservation. Free.*)

SOUTH OF THE CLYDE

🖼 POLLOK COUNTRY PARK AND BURRELL COLLECTION. The **Pollok Country Park** is an expanse of forest paths and colorful flora 3 mi. south of Glasgow. The famous **Burrell Collection** was once the private stash of ship magnate William Burrell, reflecting his diverse tastes: paintings by Cezánne and Degas, European tapestries, Persian textiles, and fine china. (☎287 2550. *Open M-Th and Sa 10am-5pm, F and Su 11am-5pm. Tours daily 11am, 2pm. Free.*) Also in the park is the less spectacular **Pollok House**, a Victorian mansion with a small collection of paintings, most notably pieces by El Greco, Goya, and William Blake. (*Take bus #45, 47, 48, or 57 from Jamaica St. (15min., £1.20).* ☎616 6410. *Open daily 10am-5pm. £5, students £3.75; Nov.-Mar. free.*)

GLASGOW SCIENCE CENTRE. The UK's only titanium-clad exterior gives the center the unmistakable appearance of a giant space-armadillo. The three buildings require three tickets; the first houses Scotland's only **IMAX theater**. (*Open daily 10am-6pm. £5.50, concessions £4.50.*) The second contains hundreds of interactive exhibits. (*Open Tu-Su 10am-5pm. £6.50/4.50.*) The 417 ft. **Glasgow Tower** is the only building in the world that rotates 360°. Built as an airfoil to move with the wind, Scotland's tallest freestanding structure tells the city's story and offers amazing views. (*Open M-Th and Su noon-6pm, F-Sa noon-8pm. £5.50/4.50.*) The entire complex cost $75 million—one-tenth the cost of London's Millennium Dome but 10 times more successful. (*50 Pacific Quay. U: Cessnock, accessible by Bells Bridge.* ☎420 5010; *www.gsc.org.uk.*)

◗ SHOPPING

You'll pass kilted mannequins and Charles Rennie MacKintosh jewelry for blocks on end as you make your way up **Sauchiehall Street** and down **Buchanan Street.** The two streets form a pedestrian-only zone and provide excellent shopping. Shops stay open late on Thursdays, but close early on the weekends. The three main indoor shopping centres are **Princes Square,** 48 Buchanan St., a high-end shopping mall; **St. Enoch Centre,** 55 St. Enoch Sq.; and the **Buchanan Galleries** at the end of Buchanan St. The (ugly) latter two opened to protests in 1999, but became hugely popular among capitalists and tourists.

◤ NIGHTLIFE

Glaswegians have a reputation for partying hard; three universities and the highest student-to-resident ratio in Britain guarantee a kinetic after-hours vibe. *The List* (£2.40), available from newsagents, has detailed nightlife and entertainment listings, while *The Gig* (free at newsstands) highlights the live music scene.

PUBS

You'll never find yourself far from a frothy pint in this city. Students at the prestigious University of Edinburgh love intellectual debate, and many have identified this crawl as the real avenue to enlightenment. The infamous **Byres Road** slithers past the university, beginning at Tennant's Bar and proceeding toward the River Clyde. Watch for happy hours, but pace yourself for the midnight closing time.

▧ **Uisge Beatha,** 232 Woodlands Rd. (☎564 1596). U: Kelvinbridge. "Uisge Beatha" (ISH-ker VAH) is Gaelic for "water of life" (whisky), and this pub has over 100 malts (from £2.35). Live Scottish music Su after 6pm, Irish tunes Th after 8pm. Happy hour daily 4-7pm. Open M-Sa noon-midnight, Su 12:30pm-midnight. Food served M-Th noon-3pm.

▧ **Mojama,** 426 Sauchiehall St. (☎332 4760). Charing Cross rail. Bright fuchsia walls, chandeliers, and a multitude of slatted mirrors make this bar the one of the trendiest hangouts in Glasgow, not surprising considering its location right down the hill from the Glasgow School of Art. Cheap, decent food; £3 for 1 dish, £5 for 2. Stick with the basics—full breakfasts or burgers. M night DJ competition. Open daily noon-midnight.

Bonham's, 192 Byres Rd. (☎357 3424). U: Hillhead. Relax on the extended leather couch and enjoy some of the best bar food in Glasgow in this cross between a hip student hangout and an old-fashioned hotel. Enjoy bangers and mash (£7) or a variety of sandwiches (£4-5) as you overlook Byres Rd. Open daily 11am-11pm.

The 13th Note, 50-60 King St. (☎553 1638; www.13thnote.net). U: St. Enoch. A reasonably priced all-organic, all-vegetarian menu (veggie haggis £5.40) and excellent local music. Also good for a pint. The large room is peppered with fliers and student art exhibitions, and gets smoky late. Open daily noon-midnight. Food served noon-10pm.

Babbity Bowster, 16-18 Blackfriars St. (☎552 5055). U: Queen St. An authentic Glaswegian experience: few kilts and little Gaelic music, but many drinks and conversations about the footie. Tasty grub offers good value and the small patio on a quiet street makes for a pleasant afternoon. Open M-Sa 10am-midnight, Su 11am-midnight.

Nice'n'Sleazy, 421 Sauchiehall St. (☎333 0900). Charing Cross rail. Sleazy's, as the die-hard alt music crowdsters call it, features up-and-coming local bands in its cavernous underground belly nearly every night. More nice than sleazy, this colorful hotbed of funk and punk captures the Glasgow music scene. Open daily 11:30am-11:45pm.

Brel, Ashton Ln. (☎342 4966; www.brelbarrestaurant.com). U: Hillhead. In summer, people spill out onto the cobblestones of tiny Ashton St. Stocks all manner of Belgian brews, including an odd, delicious collection of fruit (black currant, raspberry, banana, and cherry) beers. Open daily 10am-midnight.

SOUTHERN SCOTLAND

Victoria Bar, 157-159 Bridgegate (☎552 6040). U: St. Enoch. A fine assortment of beer and whisky, guitars strumming in the corner, and a mellow crowd of locals make this a cozy spot to wind down. Open M-Sa 11am-midnight, Su 12:30pm-midnight.

Horseshoe Bar, 17-21 Drury St. (☎229 5711), in an alley off Renfield St. Near Buchanan St. This Victorian pub has etched mirrors and a famed wooden bar. 3-course lunch (£3.20; M-Sa noon-2:30pm) and dinner (£2.60; M-Sa 3-7:30pm) served upstairs. Karaoke M-Sa 8pm, Su 5pm. Open M-Sa 11am-midnight, Su 12:30pm-midnight.

CLUBS

The Buff Club, 142 Bath Ln., behind Bath St. (☎248 1777). *The* after-hours club in Glasgow. Hard to find, but packed, with a disco ball and booths surrounding a dance floor. Dance until dawn to indie and funky house music. Cover M-Th and Su £3, F-Sa £6. Open M-Th and Su 11pm-3am, F-Sa 10:30pm-3am.

v Dub, 165 Hope St. (☎248 2004). Tunisian design, hidden alcoves, and thumping world beats create an other-worldly feel in this hip after-hours club. Cover £2-8. Drink specials (as low as £1) make v Dub a deal. Open daily 10pm-3am.

The Polo Lounge, 84 Wilson St. (☎553 1221; www.pololounge.co.uk). This labyrinthine club has Glasgow's biggest gay scene. Dance on the dance stairs or boogie back to the 80s in the Trophy Room. Chill out with a martini in the adjoining cocktail bar, Moda, 62 Virginia St. (same contact information). Both open M-Th 5pm-1am, F-Sa 5pm-3am.

The Cube, 34 Queen St. (☎226 8990). Home to some of the longest queues in Glasgow. Ultra-cool, with padded leather walls and heavily misted dance floor. Arrive early or know someone important. W R&B. Cover £8, Th students £6. Open daily 11pm-3am.

The Garage, 490 Sauchiehall St. (☎332 1120). Look for the yellow truck hanging over the door. One of Glasgow's biggest clubs, with flashing neon signs and several dance floors. Music can be cheesy, but upstairs **Attic** plays indie with an occasional DJ. Cover £2-6; frequent student discounts. Open M-F and Su 11pm-3am, Sa 10:30pm-3am.

Cathouse, 15 Union St. (☎248 6606; www.glasgowcathouse.co.uk). Grunge, goth, and indie please a younger crowd in this 3-floor club. Under-18 rockers can headbang downstairs in the Voodoo Room. Cover £2-5, students £1-3. Open Th-Su 11pm-3am.

🎵 🎆 ENTERTAINMENT AND FESTIVALS

The city's dynamic student population ensures countless film, food, and music events from October to April. **Ticket Centre,** City Hall, Candleriggs, has information on plays, films, and concerts taking place at Glasgow's dozen-odd theaters. (☎287 5511. Open M-Sa 9:30am-9pm.) Theaters include the **Theatre Royal,** Hope St. (☎332 9000) and the **Tron Theatre,** 63 Trongate (☎552 4267). The **Cottier Theatre,** 935 Hyndland St. (☎357 3868), hosts a variety of musical and theatrical events, from avant-garde to opera. The **Royal Concert Hall,** Sauchiehall St., is a frequent venue for the Royal Scottish National Orchestra. (☎353 8000. Box office open M-Sa 10am-6pm.) The **Glasgow Film Theatre,** 12 Rose St., screens both mainstream and sleeper hits. (☎332 8128. Box office open M-Sa noon-9pm, Su 30min. before first film. £5, concessions £4; matinees £4.50/3.50.)

Summer brings tourists and festivals. During the **West End Festival** (www.westendfestival.co.uk) in June, the city comes alive with longer bar hours and guest musicians. **Glasgow International Jazz Festival** (☎552 3552; www.jazzfest.co.uk), in late June, draws international jazz greats. **Bard in the Botanics** (Shakespeare in the Park) takes place in the West End Botanic Gardens during June and July. Take advantage of the fine dining during 🍴**Gourmet Glasgow,** when for two weeks in July over 50 restaurants and bars offer fixed-price meals and free tastings. Pick up *Gourmet Glasgow,* free at the TIC, or visit www.gourmetglasgow.com. On the second Saturday of August, over 100 bagpipe bands compete on the Glasgow Green for the **World Pipe Championships** (☎221 5414).

Red Sox versus Yankees, eat your heart out. England versus Argentina? Think again. Rocky Balboa versus Apollo Creed? Get real. When it comes to sporting rivalries, the 111-year-old contest between the Glasgow Rangers and Glasgow Celtic football clubs puts all other contenders to shame, both for the magnificence of its matchups on the pitch, and for the ferocity of the antagonism it engenders.

On the field of play, the "Auld Firm" rivalry (so named because of the aged status of the clubs involved) has been sublime, with home-grown footballing legends like Jim Baxter and Ally McCoist leading Rangers to Scottish soccer's most ever titles, and top-flight internationals like Sweden's Henrik Larsson carrying Celtic to its current championship form. Since 1891 one of the two clubs has won 86 of 105 possible premier-league titles, their seesawing periods of supremacy infusing nearly every head-to-head match with a sense of urgency rarely witnessed at such a high level of play. 2002 saw the two sides pitted against one another in both of Scotland's Cup competitions, the frenzied excitement of which was surely enough to inspire even the most apathetic of onlookers.

Indeed, off the pitch too, the passion that Auld Firm aficionados expend on the rivalry can scarcely be equaled. A study of any given Rangers-Celtic showdown yields ample proof of their exuberance: the briefest of glances bleacherwards meets with the spectacle of a stadium bedecked in swaths of Rangers blue and Celtic green, and the stands are rocked by songs and chants which repeatedly reverberate from one supporters' section to the other. Oddities also abound, not the least of which is the bewildering sight—unimaginable elsewhere in this normally nationalistic country, but commonplace on the grounds of Celtic Park and Ibrox—of dyed-in-the-wool Scotsmen waving Irish and even *English* flags, in keeping with club ties to Catholic (Celtic) and Protestant (Rangers) movements at home and in Northern Ireland.

Most of the time the rival revels are meant in a spirit of merriment. At times, however, the good fun can turn bad, even ugly. The dark side of the Auld Firm's association with sectarian strife in Ulster is driven home when, nearly every time the sides do battle on the pitch, Unionist Rangers fans and rival Nationalist Celtic supporters shed each other's blood on the streets of Belfast. A similar style of hooliganism afflicts Scotland itself, where "No Football Colours" signs adorning the doors of Glaswegian pubs don't always succeed in preventing clashes between confrontational fans. And not even an ongoing ban on the sale of alcohol at matches has managed to forestall such appalling exchanges as occurred in March 2002, when Rangers fans directed racist pantomimes at Celtic's French defender Dianbobo Balde, or in September 2001, when a Celtic fan affronted Rangers American midfielder Claudio Reyna by simulating an airplane impacting a building. Perhaps this Mr. Hyde-like side of an otherwise glorious rivalry has contributed to Scottish football's recent money-motivated threat to oust the Auld Firm from its ranks. But whether Rangers and Celtic will surrender a greater share of their revenue for the right to remain in Scotland, or whether they will choose instead to compete in the more lucrative (and more challenging) English leagues, one thing is certain: wherever the clubs choose to vest their future interests, their fortunes will be followed by throngs of fans whose devotion ensures that their rivalry will remain a conspicuous aspect of Scottish culture.

Brian Algra, a former researcher for Let's Go: California, *is currently pursuing a doctoral degree in English Literature at the University of Edinburgh.*

CENTRAL SCOTLAND

Less lofty than the Highlands to the north and more subdued than the cities to the south, central Scotland has draws all its own. The eastern shoulder, curving from Fife to the Highland Boundary Fault along the North Sea, is peppered with centuries-old communities and historical treasures. To the west, the landscape flattens from snow-covered mountains into the plains of the Central Lowlands. Castles of all shapes and sizes testify to the region's strategic importance. The remote Inner Hebrides, separated by mountains and a strip of sea, have an enchanting beauty.

HIGHLIGHTS OF CENTRAL SCOTLAND

ADMIRE the 5½ ft. sword of William Wallace and one of Britain's grandest castles in the historic royal seat of Scotland, Stirling (p. 586).

SING about the bonnie, bonnie banks of Loch Lomond before exploring the Trossachs, in Scotland's first national park (p. 588).

ISLE HOP between the pastel, palm-treed Tobermory (p. 600) and the stunning, cave-pitted Isle of Staffa (p. 602).

ST. ANDREWS ☎ 01334

Would you like to see a city given over,
Soul and body to a tyrannising game?
If you would, there's little need to be a rover,
For St. Andrews is the abject city's name.
—Robert F. Murray

The "tyrannising game" of golf overruns the small city of St. Andrews. Driving through the surrounding Fife countryside, with its softly rolling hills and seemingly endless grass, it is not hard to imagine that this landscape provided the inspiration for the first golf courses. But St. Andrews has other attraction: for the last millennium, what was once Scotland's largest cathedral, now an extensive ruin on the coast, has attracted pilgrims from across Europe. Today, golfers, students, beach bums, and history buffs converge on its medieval streets. The town is worth spending the night, especially during term-time; thanks no doubt to Scotland's oldest university, tiny St. Andrews has the highest concentration of pubs in the UK.

▐ TRANSPORTATION

Drivers can take the A917, or Fife Coastal Tourist Route, from Edinburgh. All **trains** (☎ 08457 484 950) stop 5 mi. away in Leuchars (LU-cars). Most trains to Leuchars travel from Perth (1hr., every hr., £8.10), a transfer point for trains from Aberdeen, Edinburgh, Inverness, and London. From Leuchars, buses #94 and 96 run to St. Andrews (5 per hr. 6am-10:30pm, £1.85). The **bus station** is on City Rd. (☎ 474 238). Scottish Citylink (☎ 01383 621 249) **bus** X60 comes from Edinburgh

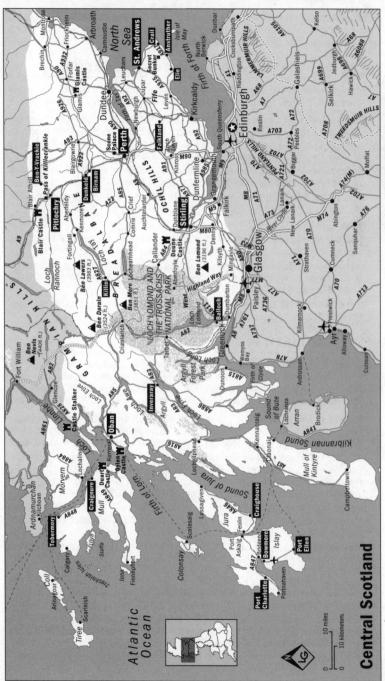

Central Scotland

(2hr., M-Sa 1-2 per hr., £6.50); the X24 comes from Glasgow (2½hr., M-Sa every hr., £6.50). Buses in Fife run reduced service in the evenings and on Sundays; schedules change often. Call Traveline (☎08706 082 608) for info.

✦ 🛈 ORIENTATION AND PRACTICAL INFORMATION

The three main streets—**North Street, Market Street,** and **South Street**—run nearly parallel to each other, terminating by the cathedral at the town's east end.

Tourist Information Centre: 70 Market St. (☎472 021). Ask for the free *St. Andrews Town Map and Guide.* Books accommodations for £3 plus a 10% deposit. Bureau de change. Open Apr.-June M-Sa 9:30am-5:30pm, Su 11am-4pm; July-Sept. M-Sa 9:30am-7pm, Su 9:30am-5pm; Oct.-Mar. M-Sa 9:30am-5pm.

Financial Services: Royal Bank of Scotland, 113-115 South St. (☎472 181). Bureau de change. Open M-Tu and Th-F 9:15am-4:45pm, W 10am-4:45pm.

Launderette: 14b Woodburn Terr. (☎475 150), outside of town. £5 per load. Open M-Sa 9am-7pm, Su 9am-5pm. Last wash 1½hr. before close.

Police: 100 North St. (☎418 700).

Hospital: St. Andrews Memorial, Abbey Walk (☎472 327), southeast of town. 24hr. medical attention also available at the **Health Centre,** Pipeland Rd. (☎476 840).

Internet Access: St. Andrews Library, Church Sq. (☎412 685). Free. Open M and F-Su 9:30am-5pm, Tu and Th 9:30am-7pm. Also **Costa Coffee,** 83 Market St. £1 per 20min. Open M-Sa 8am-6pm, Su 10am-5:30pm.

Post Office: 127 South St. (☎08457 223 344). Bureau de change. Open M-F 9am-5:30pm, Sa 9am-12:30pm. **Post Code:** KY16 9UL.

▚ ACCOMMODATIONS

St. Andrews is a plausible daytrip from Edinburgh, an ideal base for visiting the Fife Seaside, and a headquarters for golf enthusiasts. The town has only one year-round hostel, but is packed with delightful B&Bs (£18-29); over 20 line **Murray Park** and **Murray Place** alone. Prices are often lower in term time, from October to May.

☒ **St. Andrews Tourist Hostel,** St. Mary's Pl. (☎479 911), tucked above the Grill House restaurant. From bus station, turn right on City Rd., then left on St. Mary's Pl. Colorfully painted, sparkling clean, and spacious. In the center of town. Dorms £16. MC/V. ❷

SYHA St. Andrews, Buchanan Gardens (☎476 726), in the David Russell Apartments. From City Rd., turn right onto Argyle St., continue on Hepburn Gardens, and take the right fork at Buchanan Gardens. The city's newest hostel, in university housing. Hotel-style rooms. Open mid-July to Sept. Singles £25; doubles £38. MC/V. ❸

Brownlees, 7 Murray Pl. (☎473 868; www.brownlees.co.uk). Feel like your own clan lord—each room has its own tartan (and TV). Singles £26-33; doubles from £50. Cash only. ❸

Cameron House, 11 Murray Park (☎472 306). Chat with the owner about golf in this traditionally furnished and very friendly family-run B&B. Singles £25-30. MC/V. ❸

◖ FOOD

Although St. Andrews is famed for its pubs, you'll virtually trip over all the bakeries this small city supports. With classier restaurants to handle the tourists and takeaways open late, you won't go hungry. The Tesco **supermarket** is at 130 Market St. (☎413 600. Open M-Sa 7:30am-midnight, Su 10am-10pm.)

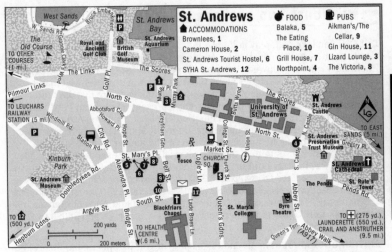

St. Andrews

FOOD

PUBS

▲ ACCOMMODATIONS
Brownlees, 1
Cameron House, 2
St. Andrews Tourist Hostel, 6
SYHA St. Andrews, 12

Balaka, 5
The Eating
Place, 10
Grill House, 7
Northpoint, 4

Aikman's/The
Cellar, 9
Gin House, 11
Lizard Lounge, 3
The Victoria, 8

CENTRAL SCOTLAND

Balaka, 3 Alexandra Pl. (☎ 474 825). Celebrities and royalty, including the King of Malaysia, make pilgrimages to this den of gastronomical wonders. Best Indian food in the UK? *Let's Go* doesn't doubt it. Fantastic chicken tikka masala (£10.85). Open M-Th noon-3pm and 5pm-1am, F-Sa noon-1am, Su 5pm-1am. AmEx/MC/V. ❸

Northpoint, 24 North St. (☎ 473 997). Serves up a great lunch. A hip, bustling crowd, local artwork lining the walls, and superb griddle melt sandwiches; try the baked brie, cranberry chutney, and caramelized onion (£4.75). MC/V. ❷

Grill House Restaurant, St. Mary's Pl. (☎ 470 500), between Alexandra Pl. and Bell St. Conveniently situated downstairs from the hostel. Continental fare. Order a la carte or take advantage of the 2-course prix-fixe (£11). AmEx/MC/V. ❸

The Eating Place, 177-179 South St. (☎ 475 671). Scottish pancakes (under £5)—smaller and less sweet than your average flapjack—served all day in this diner. Open M 9:30am-5pm, Tu-Sa 9:30am-9:30pm, Su 11:30am-5pm. MC/V. ❷

PUBS

After a long day of golf, it's the 19th hole that's most important, and St. Andrews has plenty to choose from. Get a lesson in whisky while you stamp your feet to live Scottish music at **Aikman's/The Cellar,** 32 Bell St. The spot is fun and vivacious; old golfers unwind to the beat upstairs while young rugby players sample the weekly rotating ales downstairs. (☎ 477 425; www.cellar-bar.co.uk. Aikman's open M-W and Su 10am-midnight, Th-Sa 10am-1am. Cellar open M-W and Su 6pm-midnight, Th-Sa 6pm-1am. The trendy **Gin House,** 116 South St. (next to the Blackfriars ruin) serves up posh martinis in a club with comfy leather couches and a huge flat-screen TV. (☎ 473 473; www.gin-house.co.uk. Open M-W and Su 10am-midnight, Th-Sa 10am-1am.) **The Victoria,** 1 St. Mary's Pl., offers deep leather chairs, live music, and many drink specials. (☎ 476 964. Open M-W and Su 10am-midnight, Th-Sa 10am-1am.) The **Lizard Lounge,** 127 North St., in the basement of the Inn at North St., is a cozy affair, with eclectic design and live bands most nights. (☎ 473 387. Open M-W 11am-midnight, Th-Sa 11am-1am, Su noon-midnight.)

CENTRAL SCOTLAND

👁 🏔 SIGHTS AND OUTDOOR ACTIVITIES

GOLF. If you love golf, play golf, or think that you might ever want to play golf, this is your town. The game was such a popular pastime in St. Andrews that Scotland's rulers outlawed the sport three times. At the northwest edge of town, the **Old Course** stretches along the **West Sands,** a beach as well-manicured as the greens. Mary, Queen of Scots, supposedly played here just days after her husband was murdered. Nonmembers must present a handicap certificate or letter of introduction from a golf club. Book at least a year or two in advance, enter your name into a near-impossible lottery by 2pm the day before you hope to play, or get in line before dawn by the caddie master's hut as a single. Tee times are easier to obtain at the less-revered but still excellent **New, Jubilee, Eden,** and **Strathtyrum** courses. The budget option is the nine-hole **Balgove Course.** (☎466 666. Old Course Apr.-Oct. £80-115 per round; Nov.-Mar. £56. New, Jubilee, Eden, and Strathtyrum courses £16-55 per round. Balgove course £10 per round. Club rental £20-30 per day.) The newest and priciest of the Royal and Ancient courses, the **Kingsbarns Golf Links,** is farther east along the coast. (☎460 860; www.kingsbarns.com. £125 per round.)

BRITISH GOLF MUSEUM. An endless display of golf paraphernalia, this collection includes examples of the earliest spoons (clubs) and feathers (balls). Enthusiasts will find the exhibits fascinating; others, less so. (Bruce Embankment. ☎460 046. Open mid-Mar. to Oct. M-Sa 9:30am-5:30pm, Su 10am-5pm; Nov. to mid-Mar. daily 10am-4pm. £5, concessions £4.)

ST. ANDREWS CATHEDRAL. The haunting, romantic ruin of what used to be Scotland's largest building is still the heart and soul of St. Andrews, especially since its stones make up most of the facades along South St. The square **St. Rule's Tower** still stands above the site where the Greek monk St. Rule buried the relics of St. Andrew, patron saint of Scotland. Climb the tower for a spectacular view of the town, sea, and countryside. The St. Andrews Cathedral Museum houses ancient Pictish carvings and modern tombs. (☎472 563. Open daily Apr.-Sept. 9:30am-5:45pm; Oct.-Mar. 9:30am-3:45pm. Cathedral free. Museum and tower £4. Joint ticket with the castle £5.)

ST. ANDREWS CASTLE. The castle features siege tunnels (not for the claustrophobic) and bottle-shaped dungeons (not for anyone). The walls were designed to keep out religious heretics, who nevertheless stormed the castle in 1546. For stellar views, descend the path south of the castle fence, where seagulls make their nests in the crags. (On the water at the end of North Castle St. ☎477 196. Open daily Apr.-Sept. 9:30am-6:30pm; Oct.-Mar. 9:30am-4:30pm. £4. Joint ticket with cathedral museum £5.)

UNIVERSITY OF ST. ANDREWS. Founded in 1410, Scotland's oldest university maintains a well-heeled student body (including recent alumnus Prince William) and a strong liberal arts program. Meander into placid quads through the parking entrances on North St., including **St. Mary's,** where a thorn tree planted in 1563 by Mary, Queen of Scots, still grows. The **official tour** grants access to the building interiors. (Between North St. and The Scores. Buy tickets from the Admissions Reception, Butts Wynd, beside St. Salvator's Chapel Tower on North St. ☎462 245. 1hr. tours mid-June to Aug. M-F 11am and 2:30pm. £4, concessions £3, under 6 free, families £10.)

OTHER SIGHTS AND ACTIVITIES. The **St. Andrews Museum** insists there are religions practiced off the fairways and that golf is but "a small dot" in the town's history. (Kinburn Park, down Doubledykes Rd. ☎412 690. Open daily Apr.-Sept. 10am-5pm; Oct.-Mar. 10:30am-4:30pm. Free.) An olde chemist's shoppe and painful-looking den-

tistry tools are among artifacts in the tiny **St. Andrews Preservation Trust Museum.**
(North St. ☎477 629. Open daily June-Sept. 2-5pm. Donations welcome.) The **St. Andrews
Aquarium** houses a legion of eels, rays, and orphaned seals. *(The Scores. ☎474 786.
Open daily 10am-6pm. Seal feeding 11:30am and 3pm. £6, concessions £5, children £4.)*
From Shakespeare to off-Broadway hits, **Byre Theatre** puts on plays year-round.
(Abbey St. ☎475 000; www.byretheatre.com. Tickets £5-14. Student discounts available.) And
for beach-goers, the immaculate **West** and **East Sands** on either side of town are
perfect for a stroll, but perhaps not a dip; it is the North Sea, after all. *(Free.)*

⚡ DAYTRIP FROM ST. ANDREWS: FIFE SEASIDE

"A fringe of gold on a beggar's mantle" is how James II of Scotland described these
burghs, built among the sheltered bays and farmland of the Kingdom of Fife. The
tidy gardens and gabled roofs of the fishing villages in the East Neuk (East Corner) stretch from Edinburgh to St. Andrews. Throughout most of the Middle Ages,
the Earls of Fife ranked highest among Scottish nobility and the Archbishop of St.
Andrews made his home here. Today, Fife maintains a peaceful coastal character.
In summer, golfers cram onto the nearly 50 coastal courses. Smaller villages may
be seen as daytrips from Edinburgh or St. Andrews; the meandering coastal road
A917 **(Fife Coastal Tourist Route)** links villages. Non-drivers need not worry: buses
cruise by frequently. **Fife Coastal Walk** runs along the shore and allows for walking,
hiking, and biking within and between towns.

CRAIL. The oldest of Fife's villages, Crail developed around a 12th-century castle and presents a maze of cobblestone streets and moss-covered stone cottages
above a craggy outcropping and sleepy harbor. Crail's **Tourist Information Centre,**
62-64 Marketgate, adjoins a small local history museum. (☎01333 450 869. Open
Apr.-Sept. M-Sa 10am-1pm and 2-5pm, Su 2-5pm.) Guided walks leave the
museum (1½-hr. tours July-Aug. Su 2:30pm; £2, children £1). Visit **Crail Pottery,**
75 Nethergate, for ceramics handmade by a family of master potters, displayed
in their 17th-century cottage. (☎01333 451 212. Open M-F 9am-5pm, Sa-Su
10am-5pm.) In the last week of July, the **Crail Festival** brings concerts, parades,
and craft shows.

ANSTRUTHER. The largest of the seaside towns, Anstruther lies 5 mi. west of
Crail on the A917 and 9 mi. southeast of St. Andrews on the B9131. The **Scottish
Fisheries Museum,** Shore St., relates the history of the fishing, trade, and smuggling that brought Fife to prominence. (☎01333 310 628. Open Apr.-Oct. M-Sa
10am-5:30pm, Su 11am-5pm; Nov.-Mar. M-Sa 10am-4:30pm, Su noon-4:30pm.
Last admission 45min. before close. £4.50, concessions £3.50.) Six miles off the
coast, the stunning mile-long **Isle of May Nature Reserve** is home to a large population of puffins, kittiwakes, razorbills, guillemots, shags, seals, and if you're
lucky, dolphins and whales. Inland from the towering cliffs stand the ruins of
Scotland's first lighthouse and the haunted 12th-century **St. Adrian's Chapel,**
named after a monk murdered on the lonely island by the Danes in AD 875.
From June to August, weather and tides permitting, the *May Princess* sails
from Anstruther to the Isle. (☎01333 310 103. 5hr. round-trip, including time
ashore. May-Sept. £15, concessions £13, children £7.) Call ahead for times, or
check with Anstruther's **Tourist Information Centre,** beside the museum. (☎01333
311 073. Apr.-Nov. M-Sa 10am-5pm, Su 11am-4pm.) On the way back from the
bay and lighthouse, the **Anstruther Fish Bar and Restaurant ❶,** 44-46 Shore St., has
divine fish and chips (£6.30, takeaway £4.10), renowned throughout Fife.
(☎01333 310 518. Open daily 11:30am-10pm. MC/V.)

(NOT SO) SECRET BUNKER. In the 1950s, the British government built a subterranean shelter halfway between Anstruther and St. Andrews (off the A917) to house British leaders in the case of nuclear war. Over 20,000 sq. ft. of cheesy displays, strategy rooms, sensory equipment, and weapons-launching systems lie 100 ft. below an unassuming Scottish farmhouse. Locals claimed knowledge of the bunker long before the "secret" broke in 1993. Take bus #61 Anstruther-St. Andrews, ask to get off near the Bunker, walk 1 mi. east on B940, then follow a winding road for half a mile. (☎01333 310 301. Open daily Apr.-Oct. 10am-5pm. ₤7.50, concessions ₤6.) Free Internet access in underground computer room.

ELIE. Don't let the retirement golfing developments along A917 deter you from discovering the sweeping sandy bay of Elie (EEL-y), 5 mi. west of Anstruther. Legend has it that the fishermen of Elie (then the 11th-century burgh of Earlsferry) helped Macduff, Earl of Fife, escape from Macbeth by ferrying him across the Firth to Dunbar. Elie is an ideal spot for watersports and walks along the accessible beaches. The town boasts an ancient granary on its rebuilt 15th-century pier. The picturesque **Ruby Bay,** named for the garnets occasionally found on its red-tinted sands, is an ideal swimming spot for any soul hardy enough to brave the chilly waters. It is worth the short walk to the 18th-century **Lady's Tower,** where Lady Janet Anstruther built an odd stone changing room on the cliffs and sent a bell-ringing servant to warn villagers to keep away when she was swimming, lest some commoner see her in her scanties. **Elie Watersports,** down Stenton Row, on The Toft, gives instruction on watersports. (☎01333 330 962; www.eliewatersports.com. Bikes ₤7 per half-day, ₤10 per day, ₤35 per week; wetsuits ₤10 per day; windsurfers, canoes, dinghies, and paddleboats ₤8-14 per hr.; lessons ₤14-25 per hr.; water ski pull ₤18 per hr.) South Street is home to the oldest houses in Elie, including the **Castle** (from the 16th century). While on The Toft, check out the **Ship Inn ❷**, a charming bar with rustic outdoor seating just feet from the sea. Watch cricket being played on the beach or enjoy delicious barbecues in the beer garden. (☎01333 330 246. Entrees ₤7-10. Open M-Th 11am-midnight, F-Sa 11am-1am, Su 12:30pm-midnight. Garden open Apr.-Aug. Su 12:30-3pm. Food served M-Sa noon-2:30pm, Su 12:30-3pm. MC/V.) If St. Andrews (p. 572) is all booked up, golf at **Elie Sports Club** (☎01333 330 955; from ₤7 per round).

FALKLAND. The Renaissance **Palace** dominates the gorgeous Royal Burgh of Falkland, at the base of the Lomond Hills. James IV built the palace in the early 1500s to replace the original fortified castle built by the Macduffs (of Shakespeare's *Macbeth*). James' granddaughter, Mary, Queen of Scots, enjoyed more peaceful days riding, hawking, and hunting on the grounds and in the beautifully maintained **Falkland Gardens.** While admiring the old castle ruins and rose hedges behind the palace, peek into the unceremonious stone **Royal Tennis Court,** built in 1539; a club still plays Royal Tennis (versus lawn tennis) here. (☎01337 857 397. Open Mar.-Oct. M-Sa 10am-6pm, Su 1-5:30pm. Last admission 1hr. before close. ₤10, concessions ₤7, families ₤25.) Though the castle is best seen as a daytrip, Falkland's **Burgh Lodge Hostel ❶**, 1 Back Wynd, is a great deal. (☎01337 857 710; www.burghlodge.co.uk. Dorms ₤12; doubles ₤24. MC/V.) Across the street is the **Hayloft Tearoom ❶**, where freshly baked scones and pastries are all around ₤1. (☎01337 857 590. Open daily 10:30am-5:30pm. Cash only.) To reach Falkland by car, follow the M90, A92, or A912 from the south or the A91 or A912 from the north and west. Public transportation is trickier: take Stagecoach Fife buses #36 or 66 from Glenrothes (20min., 2-4 per day) or #36 from Perth (1hr., every hr.).

PERTH
☎ 01738

Scotland's capital until 1452, today Perth is a town buzzing with cosmopolitan shops and restaurants. Busy year-round, Perth lives up to its self-promoting (if modest) titles, the "perfect centre" and the "fair city," with several beautiful walks in its Kinnoull Hill Wood and convenient access to nearby historical sites. Travelers on the go may not stay more than an afternoon, but the city makes a nice stop.

▐ TRANSPORTATION. The **train station** is on Leonard St. (Open M-Sa 6:45am-8:45pm, Su 8:15am-8:25pm.) **Trains** (☎08457 484 950) from: Aberdeen (1½hr., every hr., £23.50); Edinburgh (1hr., 7 per day, £10.70); Glasgow (1hr., every hr., £10.70); Inverness (2½hr., 7 per day, £15.50). The **bus station** is a block away on Leonard St. Ticket office open M-F 7:45am-5pm, Sa 8am-4:30pm. Scottish Citylink (☎08705 505 050) **buses** arrive from: Aberdeen (2hr., 8 per day, £13.60); Dundee (35min., every hr., £4.20); Edinburgh (1½hr., every hr., £6.60); Glasgow (1½hr., 2 per hr., £6.80); Inverness (2½hr., every hr., £10.80); Pitlochry (40min., every hr., £6). For more information, call Traveline. (☎08706 082 608. Open M-Su 8am-8pm.)

▌ PRACTICAL INFORMATION. The **Tourist Information Centre,** Lower City Mills, books local rooms for £3 plus a 10% deposit. From either station, turn right on Leonard St., bear right to South Methven St., and take a left on Old High St. (☎450 600; www.perthshire.co.uk. Open Apr.-June and Sept.-Oct. M-Sa 9am-5pm, Su 11am-4pm; July-Aug. M-Sa 9am-6:30pm, Su 10am-5pm; Nov.-Mar. M-F 9am-5pm, Sa 9:30am-4:30pm.) City Sightseeing runs **bus tours** in summer, making transport to far-off attractions like Scone Palace and Kinnoull Hill easy. Buy tickets at the TIC or on the bus at the Mill St. stop. (☎629 339. Tours June-Aug. M-Sa every hr. £6.50, seniors and students £4, children £2.) Other services include: numerous **banks;** Fair City **launderette,** 44 N. Methven St. (☎631 653; wash £3, dry £1.60 per 30min.; open M-F 9am-6pm, Sa 9am-5pm); **police,** Barrack St. (☎621 141); **Perth Royal Infirmary,** Taymount Terr. (☎623 311); Superdrug **pharmacy,** 100 High St. (☎639 746; open M-Sa 8:30am-5:30pm, Su 1:30-4:30pm); **Internet access** at Gig@Bytes, 5 St. Paul's Sq. (☎451 580; £1.50 per 15min.; open M-Sa 10am-6:30pm) and free at the library, York Pl. (☎444 949; open M, W, F 9:30am-5pm, Tu and Th 9:30am-8pm, Sa 9:30am-4pm); and the **post office,** 109 South St., with a bureau de change (☎624 413; open M and W-Sa 9am-5:30pm, Tu 9:30am-5:30pm). **Post Code:** PH2 8AF.

▐▐ ACCOMMODATIONS AND FOOD. The last hostel in Perth shut its doors several years ago. Try one of the numerous B&Bs on **Glasgow Road,** a 10min. walk from the city center, and on **Pitcullen Crescent,** across the river. **Darroch Guest House ❸,** 9 Pitcullen Crescent, has friendly owners and airy rooms. (☎636 893. Singles £20-25. MC/V.) Just up the road, **Pitcullen Guest House ❸,** 17 Pitcullen Crescent, provides similar, more-modern accommodation and a quiet garden. (☎626 506. Singles £23-35. MC/V.) Those on a budget can **camp** at **Scone Camping and Caravanning ❶,** 4 mi. from the city center, next to the racetrack. Head to Scone Palace and then follow signs for the racetrack or take bus #58 to Old Scone. The site has great facilities, including laundry and ping-pong, and quiet areas to pitch, away from the caravans. (☎552 323. Tents £3.80-5.40. MC/V.)

An enormous Morrison's **supermarket** is located on Caledonian Rd. (☎442 422. Open M-W 8:30am-8pm, Th-F 8:30am-9pm, Sa 8am-8pm, Su 9am-8pm.) Restaurants crowd the city's main streets but finding something affordable can be tricky. **Scaramouche ❶,** 103 South St., is packed and homey, and serves cheap, ample portions. Stay into the evening for drinks and dancing. (☎637 479. Open M-Th 11am-11pm, F 11am-11:45pm, Sa 11am-12:30am, Su 12:30-11pm. Food served noon-8pm. MC/V.) **Redrooms ❸,** 185 High St., attached to the Perth Theatre, has an elegant, arty vibe that befits its theater crowd clientele. Try the excellent breakfasts (black pudding and mushroom omelette £3.75) and the modern Scottish cuisine. (☎472 707. Entrees £7-13. Open M-Sa 10am-9:30pm, Su noon-9:30pm. MC/V.) Grab a hot panini and two salads for £3-6 at **Cafe Canto ❶**, 64 George St., by the Perth Museum. (☎451 938. Open M-W and Su 8:30am-5:30pm, Th-Sa 8:30am-8pm. MC/V.)

🄖 🅐 **SIGHTS AND OUTDOOR ACTIVITIES.** In 1559, John Knox delivered a fiery sermon from the pulpit of **St. John's Kirk,** on St. John's Pl., sparking the Scottish Reformation. (☎638 482. Open for Su services 9:30, 11am. Knock daily 10am-4pm; the pastors will open the church if they're there.) The **Perth Museum and Art Gallery,** at the intersection of Tay St. and Perth Bridge, chronicles city life and hosts exhibits by local artists. Visitors are invited to try the medieval toilet seat. (☎632 488. Open M-Sa 10am-5pm. Free.) The **Fergusson Gallery,** in the Old Perth Water Works, at the corner of Marshall Pl. and Tay St., is small and focused, with displays of the glamorous work of local artist J.D. Fergusson. (☎441 944. Open M-Sa 10am-5pm. Free.) The **Perth Theatre,** 185 High St., hosts shows and concerts year-round. (☎621 031. Box office open M 10am-5pm, Tu-Sa 10am-7pm.) The 16th-century home of the Earls of Kinnoull, **Balhousie Castle,** off Hay St., north of the city, now functions as a regimental headquarters and houses the **Black Watch Regimental Museum.** It includes weapons, medals, the back-door key to Spandau prison in Berlin, and an occasional real member of the Watch. (☎01313 108 530. Open May-Sept. M-Sa 10am-4:30pm; Oct.-Apr. M-Sa 10am-3:30pm. Free.)

A 20min. walk across the **Perth Bridge** leads to **Kinnoull Hill Woodland Park** and its four nature walks, all of which finish at a magnificent summit with gorgeous vistas. Beginners can try the **Tower Walk,** while experienced hikers might choose the **Nature Walk,** which winds through the thick of the forest. Across the **Queen's Bridge,** near the Fergusson Gallery, the 1 mi. **Perth Sculpture Trail** begins in the Rodney Gardens and surveys 24 pieces of modern art along the river. **Bell's Cherrybank Gardens** provides another pleasant place to stroll amid 900 types of heather. Take bus #7 from South St. (every 20min.) or walk 20min. uphill along Glasgow Rd. (☎472 800. Hours change seasonally; call ahead. Open Mar.-Oct. M-Sa 10am-5pm, Su noon-5pm; Nov.-Dec. M-Sa 10am-4pm, Su noon-4pm; Jan.-Feb. Th-Sa 10am-4pm, Su noon-4pm. £3.75, concessions £3.40, children £2.50.)

▣ DAYTRIPS FROM PERTH

▨SCONE PALACE. Scone (SKOON), 3 mi. northeast of Perth on the A93, is a regional jewel. With an impressive collection of china, portraits, ivories, and furniture, as well as the Earl of Mansfield's spectacular orchids, Scone is a fine example of a 19th-century aristocrat's house. Find the unique holographic portrait of Queen Elizabeth II amid the descriptions of the nation's rulers. Macbeth, Robert the Bruce, and Charles II were crowned on the humble **Stone of Scone.** A horticulturist's utopia awaits in the endless grounds patrolled by showy peacocks and hedged by purple rhododendrons. Try the fun, if not challenging, **Murray Star Maze.** *(Directly off the A94. Take bus #58 from South St. (every hr.) and tell the driver where you're going, or hop on a bus tour from the TIC.* ☎01738 552 300; www.scone-palace.co.uk. *Open daily Apr.-Oct. 9:30am-5pm. £7, concessions £6, under 16 £4. Grounds only £3.50/3/2.20.)*

GLAMIS CASTLE. Macbeth's purported home, Glamis (GLAMZ) is the dynastic home of the Earls of Strathmore and was the childhood playground of the Queen Mum. The castle and its dozen handsome turrets lie 35 mi. northeast of Perth on the A94. Royal-watchers will find a treasure trove of stories and artifacts highlighted in a free tour (every 45min. in summer). The original interiors, collections of armor, paintings, and furniture are significant, but the trek to the castle is inconvenient without a car. *(Take Scottish Citylink from Perth to Dundee, then catch Strathtay bus #22 or 22A to Glamis (35min., 5 per day). Call Traveline (☎08706 082 608) for updated information. Castle ☎01307 840 393. Open Mar.-Oct. 10am-6pm; Nov.-Feb. call for hours. Last tour 4:30pm. £7, concessions £5.70, children £3.80. Grounds only £3.50/2.50/2.50.)*

DUNKELD AND BIRNAM   ☎01350

Huddled amid the forested hills of Perthshire's "Big Tree Country" on either side of the River Tay, the medieval towns of Dunkeld (dun-KELD) and Birnam (separated by a short bridge) have deep historical roots. The towns inspired figures such as Wolf of Badenoch, who burnt Elgin and Forres in retribution for his papal excommunication, and the children's author Beatrix Potter, creator of Peter Rabbit. The area has long welcomed day walkers and ruin-spotters, and local artists energetically contribute to a thriving culture of traditional Scottish folk music.

⚏ TRANSPORTATION. The unstaffed **train station** in Birnam is on the Edinburgh-Inverness line. **Trains** (☎08457 484 950) run from: Edinburgh (2hr., 7 per day, £10.70); Glasgow (1½hr., 7 per day, £10.70); Inverness (1½hr., 8 per day, £18); Perth (15min., 7 per day, £5.10). Scottish Citylink **buses** (☎08705 505 050) stop at the Birnam House Hotel from: Edinburgh (1½hr., 3 per day, £9.30); Glasgow (2hr., 3 per day, £9.30); Inverness (2½hr., 3 per day, £11); Perth (20min., 3 per day, £5); Pitlochry (20min., 3 per day, £4.70). Grab the essential *Highland Perthshire and Stanley Area Local Public Transportation Guide* (free) from any TIC or call Traveline (☎08706 082 608).

⚏ PRACTICAL INFORMATION. Nearly all public transport arrives in Birnam (a popular Victorian vacation spot) but most tourist amenities are in more historic Dunkeld. The Dunkeld **Tourist Information Centre,** by the fountain in the town center, 1½ mi. from the train station, books beds for £3 plus a 10% deposit. (☎727 688. Open Apr.-June and Sept. M-Sa 9:30am-5pm, Su 11am-4pm; July-Aug. 9:30am-6:30pm, Su 10am-5pm; Nov.-Mar. M and Th-Sa 9:30am-4:30pm, Su 10am-4pm.) Other services include: **Bank** of Scotland, High St. (☎727 759; open M-F 9am-12:30pm and 1:30-5pm); Davidson's Chemists **pharmacy,** 1 Bridge St. (open M-F 9am-1pm and 2-5:30pm, Sa 9am-1pm and 2-5pm); **Internet access** at the Birnam Institute, Station Rd., Birnam (☎727 674; £1 per hr.; open daily 10am-4pm) and free at the Birnam Library next door (☎727 674; open M 6am-8pm, W 2-4 and 6-8pm, F-Sa 10am-noon); the **post office,** Bridge St. (☎727 257; open M-W and F 9am-1pm and 2-5:30pm, Th 9am-1pm, Sa 9am-12:30pm). **Post Code:** PH8 0AH.

⚏⚏ ACCOMMODATIONS AND FOOD. The town hostel owners throw a mean *ceidleh,* but quiet B&Bs are easy to find throughout the two towns—the TIC has a handy list outside its office. The **Wester Caputh Hostel ❷** has a gorgeous countryside location, a garden with roses and raspberries, and fantastic Highland hospitality. The hostel has nightly *ceidlehs,* or open jams (join in!). From Dunkeld, head east on the A984, turn right after the church in Caputh and right on the next block; the hostel is in the second group of buildings. (☎01738 710 449. Dorms £12. Bikes £6-10 per day. Cash only.) The happening **Taybank Hotel ❸,** once owned by legendary folk musician Dougie Maclean of "Caledonia" fame, is by the Dunkeld Bridge and offers stylishly rustic rooms. (☎727 340; www.taybank.com. Singles from £22.50; doubles from £45. MC/V.) **Campers** should head for the **Inver Mill Caravan Park ❶,** on the riverside, across from Dunkeld and to the north. (☎727 477. Open Apr.-Oct. £9-11 for 2 people; £1 each additional person. Cash only.)

The Co-op **supermarket,** 15 Bridge St., is in Dunkeld. (☎727 321. Open M-Sa 8am-10pm, Su 9am-6pm.) Don't miss out on a "session" (a wee dram of something local and a song) at the **Taybank Hotel pub ❶,** where they serve "stovies" (potatoes mashed with meat or veggies; £4.35) and host casual gatherings of musicians. Spare instruments hang on the walls. (☎727 340. Open M-Th 11am-11pm, F-Sa 11am-11:45pm, Su noon-11pm. MC/V.) For lunch, head to the **Palmerston's Coffee House & Bistro ❶**, 20 Atholl St., for freshly prepared contemporary Scottish cuisine, like a baguette with venison and salad (£4.25). The eclectic menu changes daily. (☎727 231. Open M-Sa 10am-5pm, Su 11am-5pm. Cash only.)

◧⋔ SIGHTS AND OUTDOORS. Carefully maintained 18th-century houses line the way to the towns' main attraction, █**Dunkeld Cathedral,** High St., just steps from the TIC. A peaceful spot on the grand banks of the River Tay, the grassy nave is a picture-perfect ruin. The nefarious Wolf of Badenoch rests inside the cathedral. (Open Apr.-Sept. M-Sa 9:30am-6:30pm, Su 2-6:30pm; Oct.-Mar. M-Sa 9:30am-4pm, Su 2-4pm. Free.) Beatrix Potter spent most of her childhood holidays in Birnam and drew on her experiences for *The Tale of Peter Rabbit.* The **Beatrix Potter Garden** at the **Birnam Institute,** Station Rd., celebrates her work. (☎727 674; www.birnaminstitute.com. Open daily 10am-4pm. Free.)

The TIC's *Dunkeld & Birnam Walks* (50p) provides maps of area rambles. Paths lead north from Birnam to the great **Birnam Oak,** the sole remnant of the Birnam Wood in *Macbeth.* The roaring waterfalls of the █**Hermitage** tumble 1½ mi. away in a gorge in the middle of the ancient forest. A well-marked 1 mi. path passes through designated photo-ops. The **Birnam Hill Walk** ascends 1000 ft. but rewards dedicated climbers with vast views. Birdwatchers will enjoy the **Loch of the Lowes,** a wildlife reserve east of Dunkeld and just south of the A923 (20min. on a path from the TIC). Since 1969, the Loch has served as a summer home for ospreys who fly all the way from Gambia. (☎727 337; www.swt.org.uk. Open daily mid-July to mid-Aug. 10am-6pm; Apr. to mid-July and mid-Aug. to Oct. 10am-5pm.) To **fish,** obtain a license (£3-5) from **Kettles,** 15 Atholl St. (☎727 556. Open M-Sa 9am-5pm, Su 11am-5pm.) Trout season lasts from mid-March to mid-October.

▶ DAYTRIP FROM DUNKELD AND BIRNAM

THE CATERAN TRAIL. Highland Perthshire, northeast of Dunkeld and Birnam, is home to the spectacular Cateran Trail, a 64 mi. hike past the cairns and ruins lining a loop between the Bridge of Cally, Alyth, Blairgowrie, and the Spittal of Glenshee. The route approximates the "Cateran Brands" trail of medieval cattle rustlers and is well-marked, though visitors are strongly encouraged to equip themselves with Ordnance Explorer Maps #381 and 387 before setting off (available at TICs; £7). Five of the six trails are for beginners, and each ends in a town with several B&Bs. *(For more information visit www.pkct.org/caterantrail or call the Blairgowie Tourist Information Centre ☎01250 872 960. The Cateran Trail Company (☎0800 277 200) can arrange accommodations and will cart your pack from £150.)*

KILLIN AND LOCH TAY ☎01567

Southwest of Pitlochry sits beautiful Loch Tay, a remote respite from the touristy surrounding areas. The Loch is bookended by the towns of Aberfeldy in the north and Killin in the south, with the A87 winding from end to end. Killin, with its accommodations and hostel, is a better base for exploring the lake.

▣ TRANSPORTATION. One **postbus** per day circles Loch Tay, passing through Killin and Aberfeldy (#213; 3hr.). Other postbuses travel from Crianlarich (#973; 45min., 1 per day) and Tyndrum (#97; 45min., 1 per day). Pick up a copy of *Highland Perthshire & Stanley Area Buses* from the Aberfeldy TIC.

⁊ PRACTICAL INFORMATION. The **Tourist Information Centre,** by the Falls of Douchart on Main St., offers information on St. Fillan, the local McGregor clan, and countless walks. (☎820 254. Open daily June-Sept. 10am-6pm; Oct. and Mar.-May 10am-5pm.) Aberfeldy also has a TIC. (☎01887 820 276. Open July-Aug. M-Sa 9:30am-6:30pm, Su 10am-4pm; Sept.-June M-Sa 10am-4pm.) Other services in Killin include: a **Bank** of Scotland (☎01877 302 000; open M-F 10am-12:30pm and 1:30-4pm); Grant's **launderette** (☎820 235; wash £2, dry 20p per 15min.; open M-Sa 9am-10pm, Su 11am-10pm); **police** on Main St. (☎820 222); **Internet access** at the Killin **Library,** Main St. (☎820 571; 30min. free, then £1 per hr.; open M 10am-1pm and 2-5pm, Tu and F 10am-1pm and 3-7pm, W 2-5pm); and the **post office** (open M-Tu and Th-F 8:30am-5pm, W 8:30am-2pm, Sa 8:30am-1pm). **Post Code:** FK21 8UH.

⌐◻ ACCOMMODATIONS AND FOOD. The **SHYA hostel ❶,** 1 mi. from town on the A827, is in a Victorian townhouse and is a well-located base camp for ramblers. (☎820 546. Open Mar.-Oct. F-Sa. Dorms £11-12.50, under 18 £5-9.75. MC/V.) Pick up **groceries** at the Co-op, Main St. (☎820 255. Open M-Sa 8am-10pm, Su 8am-8pm.) Grab home-cooked food from the **Coach House ❷,** Locay Rd., just down the A827 from the SYHA hostel. With live music, pool, tasty dishes (£6-8), and a bar dog, this pub provides an authentic Highland experience. If you're running low on cash, or imbibe too much, you can camp on the lawn opposite for £5. (☎820 349. Open M-Th and Su 8:30am-midnight, F-Sa 8:30am-1am. MC/V.) Enjoy a full farmhouse breakfast (£6) or an elegant dinner of traditional Scottish food (entrees £7-9) at the cozy **Shutters Restaurant ❸,** Main St. (☎820 314. Open daily 10am-8pm. MC/V.)

◙⧉ SIGHTS AND ENTERTAINMENT. At the two-room **Breadalbane Folklore Centre,** you can learn about kelpies, urisks, and faeries. (Main St. Open June-Sept. 10am-6pm; Oct. and Mar.-May 10am-5pm. £2.50, concessions £1.65.) A free 2hr. hike starts from behind the schoolyard on Main St. and leads to a sheep's-eye view of the loch. Encircling Loch Tay on the A87 and A827 by foot, in a car, or on local postbuses makes an excellent daytrip. Heading north on the western shore of the lake, a spectacular single track road takes you off the A827 for a scenic route up the side of mighty **Ben Lawers** to its **Visitor Centre.** (☎820 397. Open daily Easter to Sept. 10:30am-5pm. £1, concessions 60p.) Beware the flocks of sheep that call the mountain home. Continue along the narrow but well-paved road for unparalleled views of the mountains. The tiny village of **Fortingall,** on the northern end of Loch Tay, is home to a 5000-year-old yew tree, the oldest living organism in Europe and the supposed birthplace of Pontius Pilate. **Dewar's World of Whisky,** half a mile north of Aberfeldy on the A827, has an interactive audio-guided whisky exhibit, recreated blender's lab, and a guided tour through the Aberfeldy Distillery. (☎01887 822 010. Open Apr.-Oct. M-Sa 10am-6pm, Su noon-4pm; Nov.-Mar. M-Sa 10am-4pm. £5, concessions £3.50.) About 5 mi. past Aberfeldy on the southern shore (A827) resides the **Crannog Centre,** a replica of an ancient Celtic loch dwelling. Visitors can listen to the history of Scottish crannogs, walk inside one, and try to use the prehistoric tools. (☎01887 830 583; www.crannog.co.uk. 1hr. tour. Open mid-Mar. to Oct. daily 10am-5:30pm; Nov. W 10am-4pm. £4.75, concessions £4.)

PITLOCHRY ☎01796

The small Victorian town of Pitlochry, the "gateway to the Highlands," sits where lush lowlands give way to rugged, barren mountains. Pitlochry's beautiful setting has attracted tourists from around the world, transforming the town into a tidy strip of shops selling tacky knick-knacks, wool sweaters, and plush Nessies. With two distilleries, numerous accommodations, and access to walking and hiking routes, the town makes for a good stopover on a journey to or from the Highlands.

TRANSPORTATION. Trains (☎08457 484 950) stop near the town center from: Edinburgh (2hr., 7 per day, £20.80); Glasgow (1¾hr., 7 per day, £21.70); Inverness (1¾hr., 9 per day, £12.50); Perth (30min., 9 per day, £5.40). Scottish Citylink **buses** (☎08705 505 050) stop outside the Fishers Hotel on Atholl Rd. from: Edinburgh (2hr., 10 per day, £9.40); Glasgow (2½hr., 8 per day, £9.40); Inverness (2hr., every hr., £ 9.60); Perth (40min., every hr., £6). From Perth, Pitlochry is accessible by various local buses; call Traveline (☎08706 082 608) for information. Call ahead to **rent bikes** at Escape Route, 3 Atholl Rd. (☎473 859. £10 per half-day, £18 per day. Open M-Sa 9am-5:30pm, Su 10am-5pm.) Pitlochry Backpackers (listed below) also rents bikes.

PRACTICAL INFORMATION. The **Tourist Information Centre,** 22 Atholl Rd., stocks *Pitlochry Walks* (50p), an essential map for hikers, and has a bureau de change. (☎472 751. Open July-Aug. M-Sa 9am-7pm, Su 9:30am-6pm; Sept.-May M-Sa 9am-6pm, Su 9:30am-4pm.) Other services include: the Royal **Bank** of Scotland, 84 Atholl Rd. (☎472 771; open M-Tu and Th-F 9:15am-12:30pm and 1:30-4:45pm, W 10am-12:30pm and 1:30-4:45pm); a **launderette,** 3 West Moulin Rd. (☎474 044; wash £3, dry £2; open M-W and F 8:30am-5pm, Th and Sa 9am-5pm); Lloyds **pharmacy,** 122-124 Atholl Rd. (☎472 414; open M-F 9am-5:30pm, Sa 9am-5pm); **Internet access** at the Computer Services Centre, 67 Atholl Rd. (☎473 711; £2.90 per hr.; open M-F 9am-5:30pm, Sa 9am-12:30pm); and a **post office,** 92 Atholl Rd. (open M-F 9am-12:30pm and 1-5:30pm, Sa 9am-12:30pm). **Post Code:** PH16 5BL.

ACCOMMODATIONS AND FOOD. Pitlochry Backpackers ❷, 134 Atholl Rd., in the center of town, has dorms, twins, and doubles (some ensuite), plus a friendly staff, cheap bike rentals (£6 per half-day), and a pool table. (☎470 044. Curfew 2am. Open Apr.-Oct. Dorms £12. AmEx/MC/V.) Across from the TIC, **Atholl Villa ❸,** 29 Atholl Rd., provides comfortable ensuite rooms, parking, award-winning gardens, and spacious family areas. (☎473 820. Singles from £26; doubles from £45. Cash only.) The **SYHA Pitlochry ❶,** at Knockard and Well Brae Rd., has spacious rooms and a dining room with a fantastic view of the town. From the train and bus stations, turn right on Atholl Rd. and go uphill onto Bonnethill Rd., from which the hostel is signposted. (☎472 308. Laundry £2. Internet access £1 per 20min. Reception 7-11am and 5-11:45pm. Curfew 11:45pm. Dorms £11.50-13.50, under 18 £5-10.75. MC/V.) Two miles past town on Atholl Rd., camp in comfort at **Faskally Caravan Park ❶.** (☎472 007; www.faskally.co.uk. Open mid-Mar. to Oct. £6.80-7.50 per person. Surcharge for electricity, sauna, pool, and jacuzzi. MC/V.)

On West Moulin Rd., the Pitlochry Co-op provides **groceries.** (☎474 088. Open daily 8am-10pm.) The 300-year-old **Moulin Inn ❷,** Moulin Sq., in the wee village of Moulin, just north of Pitlochry, brews its own "Braveheart Ale" and serves standard pub food, including veggie options. (☎472 196. Entrees £6-12. Open M-Th and Su noon-11pm, F-Sa noon-11:45pm. Food served until 9:30pm. Free brewery tours M-F noon-3pm.) For Mediterranean food, head to the cute and upscale **Fern Cottage Restaurant and Tea House ❷,** Ferry Rd., just off Atholl Rd. The mousaka (£9.50) and whole stuffed vegetables (£9-13) are especially tasty. (☎473 840. Open daily 10:30am-9pm. MC/V.) End the night at **McKays,** 138 Atholl Rd., across the street from Pitlochry Backpackers. (☎473 888. Open M 9am-11pm, Tu-W 9am-12:30am, Th 9am-1am, F- Sa 9am-1:30am, Su 9am-midnight.)

SIGHTS AND OUTDOORS. Hikers should arm themselves with *Pitlochry Walks* (50p), available at the TIC. For a quick jaunt, take the path over the suspension footbridge or the road down behind the train station to the **Pitlochry Dam and Salmon Ladder.** From the observation chamber, watch the fish struggle ceaselessly against the current as an electronic fish counter keeps tally. (☎473 152. Open Apr.-

June and Sept.-Oct. M-F 10am-5:30pm; July-Aug. daily 10am-5:30pm. Observation chamber and dam free; Visitor Centre £3, concessions £2.) **Fishing permits** (£3-5 per day; £15 for salmon fishing) are available at the TIC.

If **whisky** is the water of life, Pitlochry just might live forever. At the **Blair Athol Distillery,** half a mile from the TIC down the main road, kilted guides take you from mashing malt to sampling the wares. (☎482 003. Open Easter to May M-Sa 9:30am-5pm; June-Sept. M-Sa 9:30am-5pm and Su noon-5pm; Oct. to Easter M-F 10am-4pm. Tours 11am, 1, 3pm. £4.) Nearby **Edradour,** Scotland's smallest distillery, produces only 40 bottles a day. Enjoy the folksy video and tour, also with kilted tourguides, and a handmade sample. Edradour is a 2½ mi. walk from Pitlochry, past Moulin along the A924. (☎472 095; www.edradour.co.uk. Open Apr.-Oct. M-Sa 9:30am-6pm, Su noon-5pm; Nov.-Dec. M-Sa 9:30am-5pm, Su noon-5pm; Jan.-Mar. M-Sa 10am-4pm, Su noon-4pm. Distilling ends at 3pm. Free.)

📓 **ENTERTAINMENT.** The **Pitlochry Festival Theatre,** over the Aldour Bridge, features an array of splendid performances throughout the year. (☎484 626. Tickets £15.50-21.50, students £7.75-10.75.) In the recreation fields southwest of town, near Tummel Crescent, **Highland Nights** features local pipe bands and traditional folk dancing. (May-Sept. M 8pm. Tickets available at the gate. £5, concessions £3.50, children £1.) Pick up the free *What's On in Perthshire* at the TIC for other entertainment ideas.

🏁 DAYTRIPS FROM PITLOCHRY

■**BLAIR CASTLE.** Seven miles north of Pitlochry on the A9, a mile-long row of spectacular elm trees leads up to the gleaming white turrets and tall windows which belie the castle's name: it's certainly more palace than castle, with 30 rooms filled with paintings, weaponry, and luxurious furniture. The grand entrance room is one of the most impressive armories in Scotland, and the great hall is likewise filled with relics of a bellicose past. The castle grounds, frequented by pedestrians and equestrians alike, are used to train the Duke of Atholl's army, the only private army in Britain. Though they prepared to fight in both the American Revolution and WWI, the farthest the Atholl troops have ever gone is Ireland. *(Take the train to Blair Atholl and walk 10min., or hop on bus #87 from the West End Car Park in Pitlochry. ☎481 207; www.blair-castle.co.uk. Open daily Apr.-Oct. 9:30am-4:30pm. £7. Grounds only £2.20.)*

BEN-Y-VRACKIE. The 2757 ft. **Ben-y-Vrackie** provides stellar views of Edinburgh on a clear day. Turn left onto the road directly behind the Moulin Inn in Moulin and follow the curve until you reach a fork. At the fork, the Dane's Stone, a solitary standing stone, will be in the field right in front of you. Take the right-hand road to Ben-y-Vrackie. The left-hand road leads **Craigower Hill** for a western view from Loch Tommel and Loch Rannoch to the Glencoe Mountains. From Pitlochry, a 5 mi. walk from the dam leads to the Pass of Killiecrankie (signposted, and included in *Pitlochry Walks*).

PASS OF KILLIECRANKIE. A few miles north of Pitlochry, right off the A9, the valley of the River Garry narrows into a stunning gorge. In 1689, a Jacobite army slaughtered William III's troops here in an attempt to reinstall James VII of Scotland to the English throne. One soldier, Donald MacBean, preferring to risk the steep fall than to surrender, vaulted 18 ft. across **Soldier's Leap.** The area is home to an intriguing array of wildlife, from the buzzard to the great tit. For information or a guided walk, stop at the **National Trust Visitors Centre,** down the path from the pass. *(Elizabeth Yule bus #87 runs from the West End Car Park to the pass in summer. ☎473 233. Open daily Apr.-Oct. 10am-5:30pm.)*

STIRLING ☎ 01786

Located at the narrowest point of the Firth of Forth and between Edinburgh and Glasgow, Stirling historically controlled the flow of goods into and out of much of Scotland. As a result of this economic power, it has been the locus of various political struggles. At the 1297 Battle of Stirling Bridge, William Wallace outwitted and overpowered the English army; Robert the Bruce led Scotland to independence 17 years later. Despite recent development, this former royal capital certainly hasn't forgotten its heroes; Stirling now swarms with *Braveheart* fans set on recapturing the Scotland of old.

⌐ TRANSPORTATION

The **train station** is in the town center on Goosecroft Rd. (☎ 08457 484 950. Travel Centre open M-F 6am-9pm, Sa 6am-8pm, Su 8:50am-10pm.) **Trains** arrive from: Aberdeen (2hr.; M-Sa every hr., Su 6 per day; £30.90); Edinburgh (50min., 2 per hr., £5.30); Glasgow (40min.; M-Sa 2-3 per hr., Su every hr.; £5.40); Inverness (3hr.; M-Sa 4 per day, Su 3 per day; £30.50); London King's Cross (5½hr., every hr., £44-84). The **bus station** is also on Goosecroft Rd. (☎ 446 474. Luggage storage £1. Ticket office open M-Sa 9am-5pm. Station open M-Sa 6:45am-10pm, Su 10:15am-5:45pm.) Scottish Citylink (☎ 0870 505 050) **buses** run from: Fort William (2¾hr., 1 per day, £14.20); Glasgow (40min., 2-3 per hr., £4); Inverness (3¾hr., every hr., £13). First (☎ 01324 613 777) bus M9 runs express to Edinburgh (1¼hr., every hr., £4).

⚡ PRACTICAL INFORMATION

The **Tourist Information Centre** is at 41 Dumbarton Rd. (☎ 200 620. Open Apr. to early June M-Sa 9am-5pm; June and early Sept. M-Sa 9am-6pm; July-Aug. M-Sa 9am-7pm, Su 9:30-6pm; mid-Sept. to mid-Oct. M-Sa 9:30am-5pm; mid-Oct. to Mar. M-F 10am-5pm, Sa 10am-4pm.) Next to the castle, the **Stirling Visitor Centre** is high-altitude and high-tech, with books, maps, and a 12min. movie on the city's history. They'll exchange your currency for a £3 commission and book you a room for £3 plus a 10% deposit. For £4.95 you can look up the history of your family name. (☎ 462 517. Open Apr.-Oct. 9:30am-6pm; Nov.-Mar. 9:30am-5pm.) City Sightseeing Stirling runs a hop-on, hop-off **tour** that departs frequently from the train station, traveling to Bannockburn, Stirling Castle, the Wallace Monument and Stirling University. (☎ 08707 200 620. £7, concessions £5, children £3.) Other services include: free **Internet access** at the library, Corn Exchange (☎ 432 107; open M, W, F 9:30am-5:30pm; Tu and Th 9:30am-7pm; Sa 9:30am-5pm); **police**, Randolphfield (☎ 456 000); the **hospital** (434 000); and the **post office**, 84-86 Murray Pl. (☎ 465 392; open M-F 9am-5:30pm, Sa 9am-12:30pm), with a bureau de change. **Post Code:** FK8 2BP.

🏠🍴 ACCOMMODATIONS AND FOOD

The excellent **SYHA Stirling ❷**, St. John St., halfway up the hill to the castle, occupies the front wall of the first Separatist Church in Stirling. (☎ 473 442. 126 beds in 2- to 5-bed dorms. Self-catering kitchen, laundry, and Internet access. Curfew 2am. Dorms £12-14, under 18 £9-13.50. MC/V.) At the bright and colorful **Willy Wallace Hostel ❶**, 77 Murray Pl., the warm staff fosters a fun atmosphere. (☎ 446 773. 54 beds. 1 all-female dorm. No lockable dorms; no lockers. Self-catering kitchen, laundry, and Internet access. Dorms £10-12. MC/V.) Near the train station, **Forth Guest House ❸**, 23 Forth Pl., is a comfortable Georgian house with ensuite rooms. (☎ 471 020. Singles £25-40; doubles from £40. MC/V.) Tucked into an alley, The Greengrocer **market**, 81 Port St., has fresh fruits and

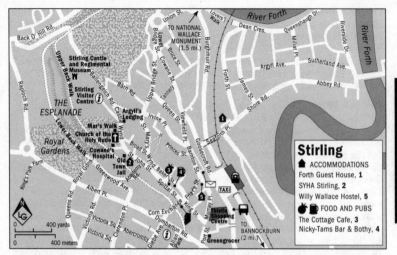

Stirling

▲ ACCOMMODATIONS
Forth Guest House, 1
SYHA Stirling, 2
Willy Wallace Hostel, 5

🍴 FOOD AND PUBS
The Cottage Cafe, 3
Nicky-Tams Bar & Bothy, 4

veggies. (☎479 159. Open M-Sa 9am-5:30pm.) Get **groceries** at Iceland, 5 Pitt Terr. (☎464 300. Open M-F 8:30am-8pm, Sa 8:30am-6pm, Su 10am-5pm.) Find hearty French fare (toasties £3) at **The Cottage Cafe ❸**, 52 Spittal St. (☎446 124. Open M-Tu and Th-Su 11am-3pm, Th-Sa also 5:30-9pm. Cash only.) **Nicky-Tams Bar & Bothy,** 29 Baker St., is a favorite nighttime hangout. (☎472 194; www.nicky-tams.co.uk. W live music, Th DJs, and Su quiz night, all at 9pm. Open M-Th and Su 11am-midnight, F-Sa 11am-1am. MC/V.)

👁 SIGHTS

■**STIRLING CASTLE.** Situated on a defunct volcano and surrounded on all sides by the scenic Ochil Hills, Stirling Castle has superb views of the Forth Valley and prim gardens that belie its turbulent history. The castle's regal gargoyles presided over the 14th-century Wars of Independence, a 15th-century royal murder, and the 16th-century coronation of Mary, Queen of Scots. The last military action at the site occurred in 1746, when Bonnie Prince Charlie besieged it while retreating from England. Beneath the cannons pointed at Stirling Bridge lie the 16th-century **great kitchens;** visitors can walk among the recreated chaos of cooks preparing all manner of game for a royal banquet. Near the kitchens, the sloping **North Gate,** built in 1381, is the oldest part of the sprawling complex. Beyond the central courtyard, make your way into **Douglas Garden,** named for the Earl of Douglas, who was murdered in 1452 by James II and whose body was dumped here. Free 30min. **guided tours** leave twice per hour from inside the castle gates. (☎450 000. Open daily Apr.-Oct. 9:30am-6pm; Nov.-Mar. 9:30am-5pm; last admission 45min. before close. £8, concessions £4, children £3. Audio tours £3, concessions £1.50, children £1.) The castle also contains the **Regimental Museum of the Argyll and Sutherland Highlanders,** a fascinating assemblage of a proud military tradition. (Open daily Easter to Sept. 9:30am-5pm; Oct. to Easter 10am-4:15pm. Last admission 15min. before close. Free.) **Argyll's Lodging,** a 17th-century Earl's mansion below the castle, has been impressively restored, with the original staircases and fireplaces intact. (Open daily Apr.-Sept. 9:30am-6pm; Oct.-Mar. 9:30am-5pm. £3.30, concessions £2.50, children £1.30. Free with castle admission.)

THE NATIONAL WALLACE MONUMENT. This 19th-century tower offers incredible views to those determined enough to climb its 246-step, wind-whipped spiral staircase. Halfway up you can catch your breath to admire William Wallace's actual 5½ ft. sword. *(Hillfoots Rd. ☎472 140; www.nationalwallacemonument.com. 1½ mi. from Stirling proper. Sightseeing Stirling runs here, as do local buses #62 and 63 from Murray Pl. Open daily July-Aug. 9:30am-6pm; June 10am-6pm; Sept. 9:30am-5pm; Mar.-May and Oct. 10am-5pm; Nov.-Feb. 10:30am-4pm. £5, concessions £3.75, children £3.25, families £13.25.)*

THE OLD TOWN. On Mar's Walk, **Castle Wynd,** an elaborate Renaissance facade, is all that was completed of a 16th-century townhouse before its wealthy patron died. Next door stands the **Church of the Holy Rude,** which witnessed the coronation of James VI and shook under the fire and brimstone of John Knox (p. 519). Check out the stained-glass windows and the organ, each considered among the finest in the country. *(Open May-Sept. daily 11am-4pm; Su service July-Dec. 10am, Jan.-June 11:30am. Organ recitals May-Sept. W 1pm. Donations appreciated.)* Down the church driveway lies 17th-century **Cowane's Hospital,** built as an almshouse for poor members of the merchant guild. *(Open M-Sa 9am-5pm, Su 1-5pm. Free.)* The **Old Town Jail,** St. John St., features enthusiastic reenactments of 19th-century prison life. Ascend to the roof for an exhibit on prisons today and views of the Forth Valley. *(☎450 050. Open daily Apr.-Sept. 9:30am-6pm; Oct. and Mar. 9:30am-5pm; Nov.-Feb. 9:30am-4pm. £5.75, students £4.30, other concessions £3.80, families £15.)* Stirling's old **town walls** are some of the best-preserved in Scotland; follow them along the circular **Back Walk.**

BANNOCKBURN. Two miles south of Stirling at **Bannockburn,** a statue of a battle-ready Robert the Bruce overlooks the field where his men decisively defeated the English in 1314, initiating 393 years of Scottish independence. Come in mid-September for a reenactment of this famous battle. *(☎812 664 for details.)*

⚡ DAYTRIP FROM STIRLING

DOUNE CASTLE. Perched above a peaceful bend in the river Teith, Doune Castle is an impressively well-preserved 14th-century fortress. Many of the castle's original rooms are entirely intact, most notably the towering great hall and the kitchen, with a fireplace large enough to roast a cow. Today, scholars of medieval architecture share the castle with those well-versed in Monty Python; many scenes from *Monty Python and the Holy Grail* were filmed here. The ticket desk kindly provides coconut shells for eager re-enactors. *(From Stirling, First bus #59 stops in Doune on its way to Callander (25min., hourly). The castle is a 5min. walk from town; ask the bus driver for directions. ☎01786 841 742. Open Apr.-Sept. daily 9:30am-6:30pm; Oct.-Mar. M-W and Sa-Su 9:30am-4:30pm. £3, concessions £2.30, children £1.)*

THE TROSSACHS ☎01877

The most accessible tract of Scotland's wilderness, the mountains and misty lochs of the Trossachs (from the Gaelic for "bristly country") are very popular for their moderate hikes and unbeatable beauty. Today, the Trossachs and Loch Lomond form Scotland's first national park, justifiably billed as the "Highlands in miniature." Here you will find long cycle routes winding through dense forest, peaceful loch-side walks, and some of Scotland's more manageable peaks.

📁 **TRANSPORTATION.** By public transport, access to the Trossachs is easiest from **Stirling.** First (☎01324 613 777) **bus** connects the region's main towns, running bus #59 from Stirling to Callander (45min., 12 per day, £3) and bus #11 to

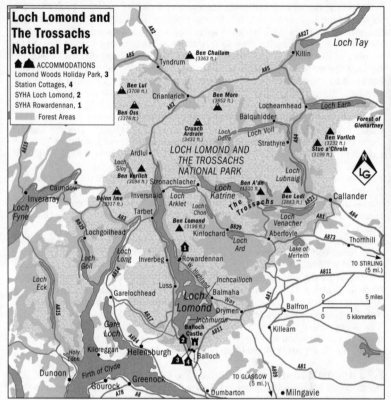

Loch Lomond and The Trossachs National Park

▲▲ ACCOMMODATIONS
Lomond Woods Holiday Park, **3**
Station Cottages, **4**
SYHA Loch Lomond, **2**
SYHA Rowardennan, **1**
Forest Areas

Aberfoyle (45min., 4 per day, £2.50). Scottish Citylink runs a bus from Edinburgh to Callander via Stirling (1¾hr., 1 per day, £8). From Glasgow, reach Aberfoyle by changing buses at Balfron. During the summer, the useful Trossachs Trundler (☎01786 442 707) travels between Callander, Aberfoyle, and the Trossachs Pier at Loch Katrine; one daily trip begins and ends in Stirling (June-Sept. M-Th 4 per day; Day Rover £5, concessions £4, children £1.75; including travel from Stirling £7.50/6/2.50). **Postbuses** reach some more remote areas of the region; find timetables at TICs or call the **Stirling Council Public Transport Helpline** (☎01786 442 707).

🏃 **OUTDOORS ACTIVITIES.** The A821 winds through the heart of the Trossachs between Aberfoyle and Callander. Named the **Trossachs Trail,** this scenic drive passes near majestic Loch Katrine, the Trossachs' original lure and the setting of Sir Walter Scott's *The Lady of the Lake*. The popular **Steamship Sir Walter Scott** cruises from Trossachs Pier and tours the loch, stopping at Stronachlachar on the northwest bank. (☎376 316. Apr.-Oct. M-Tu and Th-Su 11am, 1:45pm, 3:15pm; W no 11am sailing. £6-7, concessions £4.40-5.) At the pier, **rent bikes** from Katrinewheelz (☎376 284; £14 per day, £10 per half-day). For a good daytrip, take the ferry to Stronachlachar and then walk or ride back along the 14 mi. wooded shore road to the pier. Above the loch hulks **Ben A'an** (1512 ft.), a reasonable 2 mi. ascent that begins from a car park a mile along the A821.

Set beside the quiet River Teith, the town of **Callander** makes a good base for exploring the Trossachs and lies close to many outdoor attractions. Dominating the horizon, **Ben Ledi** (2883 ft.) provides a strenuous though not overly challenging trek. A six mile trail up the mountain begins just north of town along the A84. A number of fine walks depart from Callander itself: **The Crags** (6½ mi.) heads up through the woods to the ridge above town, while the popular walk to **Bracklinn Falls** (5 mi.) wanders along a picturesque glen. In Callander, cyclists can join **The Lowland Highland Trail,** a lovely stretch of which runs north to Strathyre along an old railway line. Passing through forest and beside Loch Lubnaig, a side-track from the route runs to **Balquhidder,** where **Rob Roy,** Scotland's legendary patriot, and his family find peace at last under a stone which reads, "MacGregor Despite Them." Callander's **Rob Roy and Trossachs Visitor Centre,** Main St., is a combined TIC and exhibit on the 17th-century local hero. Pick up Ordnance Survey maps, Explorer #378 (£7.50) or Landranger #57 (£6.50). Walkers will find the *Callander Walks & Fort Trails* pamphlet (£2) useful, and cyclists can consult *Rides around The Trossachs.* (☎330 342. Open daily Mar.-May and Oct. daily 10am-5pm; June-Sept. 10am-6pm; Nov.-Feb. 11am-4pm. Exhibit £3.60, concessions and children £2.40, families £9.60.) Rent bikes at **Cycle Hire Callander,** Ancaster Sq., beside the TIC. (☎331 052. £10 per day, £7 per half-day. Open daily 9am-6pm. MC/V.)

Aberfoyle is another springboard into the surrounding wilderness. The **Queen Elizabeth Forest Park,** established in 1953 to celebrate her coronation, covers a vast territory from the shore of Loch Lomond to the slopes of the Strathyre Mountains, with Aberfoyle right at its heart. For more information on trails, visit the **Trossachs Discovery Centre,** a TIC right in town. (☎382 352. Open July-Aug. daily 9:30am-6pm; Apr.-June and Sept.-Oct. daily 10am-5pm; Nov.-Mar. Sa-Su 10am-5pm.) A walk from town leads to the top of **Doon Hill** (2 mi.), where the ghost of Reverend Robert Kirk is supposedly trapped in an ancient pine. After publishing *The Commonwealth* in 1693, which exposed the world of elves and pixies, the good reverend was spirited away and replaced by a changeling who assumed his human form.

■❖ ACCOMMODATIONS AND FOOD. For lodgings, the star of the region lies 1½ mi. south of Callander Center at ◪**Trossachs Backpackers ❷,** Invertrossachs Rd. This hostel's location in a forest clearing makes it an ideal walking and cycling base. The hostel features a cable-TV lounge, barbecues, kitchen, and cycle hire. (Hostel ☎331 200, bike hire 331 100. 32 beds in 2- to 8-bed rooms. Breakfast included. Laundry and Internet access. Bikes £12.50 per day, £7.50 half-day. Dorms £13.50-18.50. MC/V.) In Callander Center, **Norwood B&B ❷,** 12 S. Church St., is well-kept. (☎330 665. Doubles £19-22. Cash only.) The **Abbotsford Lodge ❸,** Stirling Rd., is a cottage with hotel-style facilities. (☎330 066. £21.50-27 per person. MC/V.) In Aberfoyle, the owners welcome visitors to **Crannaig House ❸,** Trossachs Rd., with large, spacious rooms. (☎382 276. Wheelchair accessible. Singles from £30; doubles £50-60. MC/V.) **Camping** is available at the well-equipped **Trossachs Holiday Park ❶,** 2 mi. south of Aberfoyle on the A81. (☎382 614. Toilets, showers, laundry, and bike rental. Open Mar-Oct. £10-18. AmEx/MC/V.) Co-op **grocery** stores and **banks,** as well as a number of eateries, are found in both Callander and Aberfoyle. **Munchy's Restaurant,** Main St., Callander, has wholesome, home-cooked vittles (☎331 090; open in summer M and W-Sa 10:30am-7pm, Su noon-7pm).

LOCH LOMOND AND BALLOCH ☎01389

Immortalized by the famous ballad, the wilderness surrounding Loch Lomond continues to awe visitors. Britain's largest lake is dotted by 38 islands, whose proximity to Glasgow makes them the perfect destination for a day trip. As a result, these bonnie banks can get crowded, especially during summer, when daytrippers pour into Balloch, the area's largest town. A short walk from the southern tip of the lake, the town sits astride the River Leven and is a convenient transportation hub.

◨◪ TRANSPORTATION AND PRACTICAL INFORMATION. The Balloch **train station** is on Balloch Rd., across the street from the TIC. **Trains** (☎08457 484 950) arrive from Glasgow Queen St. Monday through Saturday, and from Glasgow Central on Sundays (45min., 2 per hr., £3.40). Scottish Citylink (☎08705 505 050) runs frequent **buses** from Glasgow (45min., 7 per day, £3.60) that drop off about 1 mi. from the town center, north of the Balloch roundabout. These buses then continue along the loch's western shore to Luss and Tarbet. First runs #12, 13, 313 from Stirling via Balfron (1½hr., M-Sa 4 per day, £3.80). To reach the eastern side of the loch, take bus #309 from Balloch to Balmaha (25min., 7 per day, £1.80). Bus #305 heads for Luss (15min., 9 per day, £1.50). Balloch's **Tourist Information Centre,** Balloch Rd., is in the Old Station Building, across the street from the end of the platform. Bureau de change, with a £3 surcharge. (☎200 607. Open daily July-Aug. 9:30am-6pm; May 10am-5pm; June 9:30am-5:30pm; Sept. 10am-5:30pm.) The **National Park Gateway Centre** sits 1 mi. away along a dirt and gravel road at the Loch Lomond Shores complex, a mobbed shopping mall set right on the lake. (☎722 199. Open daily Apr.-Sept. 9:30am-6:30pm; Oct.-Mar. 10am-5pm.)

▛ ACCOMMODATIONS. Two miles north of Balloch, the ▨**SYHA Loch Lomond ❷** is one of Scotland's largest hostels, with 153 beds in a stunning 19th-century castle-like structure. The grandeur of this palatial mansion makes it well worth the effort to get here. From the train station, turn left and follow the main road ¾ mi. to the second roundabout. Turn right, continue 1½ mi., and turn left at the sign for the hostel; it's a short walk up the hill. Bus #305 runs from Balloch to the foot of the hill—just be sure to tell the driver where to let you off. (☎0870 004 1136. Self-catering and far from a grocer; be sure to bring food with you. Laundry and Internet access. Book in advance. Open Mar.-Oct. Dorms £13-14.50, under 18 £5-12.25. MC/V.) On Loch Lomond's eastern shore, the **SYHA Rowardennan ❶,** the first hostel along the West Highland Way, overlooks the lake and makes a great base for exploring this more remote region. From Balloch take the bus to Balmaha, and walk 7 mi. along the well-marked way. (☎0870 004 1148. 75 beds. Laundry and basic groceries. Curfew 11:30pm. Open Apr.-Oct. Dorms £11-12.50, under 18 £5-9.25.) **B&Bs** congregate on Balloch Rd., close to the train station and TIC. Across from the train station, **Station Cottages ❸,** Balloch Rd., provides a peaceful and fairly luxurious environment. (☎750 759. Singles £25-40; doubles £35-60. MC/V.) The **Lomond Woods Holiday Park ❶,** Old Luss Rd., up Balloch Rd. from the TIC, is a convenient place to park your caravan. (☎755 000. Laundry, pool table, and table tennis all available. No young groups. Jul.-Aug. £20-22; Sept.-Jun. £15-17. MC/V.)

▛▟ HIKING AND OUTDOORS. Stock up on supplies and information at the TIC or Gateway Centre. Ordnance Survey Explorer maps #347 and 364 (£7) chart the south and north of the loch, respectively, while Landranger map #56 (£6) gives a broader view of the entire region. The **West Highland Way** runs 95 mi. from Milngavie to Fort William and skirts Loch Lomond's eastern shore, allowing for long walks. *The West Highland Way* official guide (£15) includes maps for each section of the route. Experienced hikers can try the 7½ mi. portion that runs from Rowardennan to Inversaid, passing through dense oak forests on Lomond's eastern shore. Rising above all, **Ben Lomond** (3195 ft.), is the southernmost of Scotland's 284 Munros (peaks over 3000 ft.). A popular walk departs from the 19th-century **Balloch Castle and Country Park,** across the River Leven from the train station, where you will find both a visitors center and park ranger station. (Castle

☎722 230. Open Apr.-Oct.). Outside of **Balmaha,** the strenuous 5 mi. hike up **Conic Hill** rewards hikers with magnificent views of the loch. Visitors can arrange a short boat ride (☎01360 870 214) from Balmaha to the island of **Inchcailloch,** where a 1½ mi. walk circumnavigates a nature preserve. The **Glasgow-Loch Lomond Cycleway** runs 20 mi. from city to lake along mostly traffic-free paths. At Balloch, where the route terminates, **National Cycle Route #7** heads east to the Trossachs while the smaller **West Loch Lomond Cycle Path** wraps around the lake to the west.

At **Loch Lomond Shores,** the region's lakeside visitor complex and shopping mall, the National Park Gateway Centre was designed as a "modern-day castle." Its centerpiece, **Drumkinnon Tower,** runs two short films; one explores Loch Lomond's namesake ballad, the other, suited to children, explores the underwater life of the lake. (☎722 406. Open daily June-Sept. 10am-6pm; Oct.-May 10am-5pm. ₤5, concessions ₤3.70.) Across from Drumkinnon Tower, rent bikes or canoes from **Can You Experience,** which also offers guided paddling and cycling tours. (☎602 576; www.canyouexperience.com. Bikes ₤15 per day, ₤10 for 4hr. Canoes ₤15 per hr. Guided tours Th and Su, ₤18-43. MC/V.) Departing from Loch Lomond Shores and the Balloch TIC on the River Leven, 1hr. **Sweeney's Cruises** provide one of the best introductions to the area. (☎752 376; www.sweeney.uk.com. Every hr. 10:30am-5:30pm. ₤9, children ₤4.50.) A daily 2½hr. cruise sails around the loch (2:30pm, ₤8.50/5.20). Avert your eyes (or don't) from the nudist colony on one of the islands.

INVERARAY   ☎01499

A pretty town with a splendid lochside setting, Inveraray was completely torn down and rebuilt in the 18th century to make room for the Duke of Argyll's castle. The resulting village retains a regal air, though Loch Fyne is the main attraction. Currently home to the Duke and Duchess of Argyll, palatial **Inveraray Castle** is the traditional seat of Clan Campbell. The 3rd Duke of Argyll built the castle to replace an earlier building as a sign of a more peaceful era in Scottish history, although it still bristles with an impressive array of weapons. (☎302 203. Open Apr.-May and Oct. M-Th and Sa 10am-1pm and 2-5:45pm, Su 1-5:45pm; June-Sept. M-Sa 10am-5:45pm, Su 1-5:45pm; last admission 5pm. ₤6, concessions ₤5, children ₤4, families ₤16. Guidebook ₤3.50. Grounds free.) A number of walks (1-2½ mi.) tour the forest and the top of **Dun na Cuaiche,** which provides a beautiful view. The **Inveraray Jail** welcomes with a "Torture, Death, and Damnation" exhibit. Guests are invited to try the Whipping Table and sit in on a 17th-century court scene. (☎302 381. Open daily Apr.-Oct. 9:30am-5pm; Nov.-Mar. 10am-5pm. Last admission 1hr. before close. ₤6, concessions ₤4, children ₤3, families ₤16.40. Guidebook available for ₤2.)

The small, basic **SYHA Inveraray ❶** is just north of town on Dalmally Rd. Take a left through the arch next to the Inveraray Woollen Mill onto Oban Rd. (☎08700 041 125. 26 beds in 2- to 4-bed rooms. Self-catering kitchen. Lockout 11am-5pm. Curfew 11:30pm. Open Apr.-Sept. Dorms ₤11.50, under 18 ₤8.75. MC/V.) For a B&B, the loch-side **Creag Dhubh ❸,** a 7 min. walk from town, south along Newton Rd., has unbeatable views of the loch and a luxurious lounge. (☎302 430. ₤24-28 per person. Cash only.) Cafes and **grocery** stores line Main St.

Scottish Citylink **buses** (☎08705 505 050) connect Inveraray with Glasgow (1¾hr., 6 per day, ₤6.90) and Oban (1hr., 3 per day, ₤6.40). The small **Tourist Information Centre,** Front St., books accommodations for a ₤3 charge plus a 10% deposit. (☎302 063. Open July-Aug. daily 9am-6pm; early to mid-Apr. M-Sa 9am-5pm; late April to June M-Sa 9am-5pm, Su 11am-5pm; Sept.-Oct. daily 9am-5pm; Nov.-Mar. daily 10am-3pm.) The **post office** is on Arkland St. (☎302 062. Open M-Tu and Th-F 9am-1pm and 2-5:30pm, Sa 9am-12:30pm.) **Post Code:** PA32 8UD.

OBAN
☎ 01631

The busiest ferry port on Scotland's west coast, Oban (OH-ben; pop. 8500) welcomes thousands of visitors bound for the Inner Hebrides every summer. Though the town lacks notable attractions, it makes a fine base for exploring the islands and Argyll countryside. As the sun sets on the hills, the streets of Oban fill with folks strolling along the harbor, chatting with neighbors, or heading to the pub.

TRANSPORTATION. The **train station** is on Railway Pier. (☎ 08457 484 950. Ticket office open M-Sa 7:15am-6pm, Su 10:45am-6pm.) **Trains** run to Oban from Glasgow Queen St. (3hr., 3 per day, £15). Scottish Citylink **buses** (☎ 08705 505 050) arrive at the bus stop in front of the train station from: Fort William (1½hr., M-Sa 4 per day, £7.60); Glasgow (3hr.; M-Sa 6 per day, Su 3 per day; £12.30); and Inverness via Fort William (3½hr., M-Sa 3 per day, £12.70). Caledonian MacBrayne **ferries** sail from Railway Pier to the Inner Hebrides and the southern Outer Hebrides. Pick up a timetable at the ferry terminal or TIC. Ferries go to: Craignure, Mull (45min.; M-Sa 6 per day, Su 5 per day; extra sailings July-Aug.; £3.85); Lismore (50min., M-Sa 2-4 per day, £2.65); Colonsay (2½hr., 1 per day, £10.90); Tiree (3¾hr., every day, £12.30) via Coll (2¾hr.); South Uist (7hr., M and Th-Su every day, £20.20) via Barra (5hr.). Call for times; those with a car should book ahead. Ferry services are reduced in winter. (☎ 566 688, reservations 08705 650 000. Terminal open M 6am-6pm, T and Th 6:45am-6pm, W 4:45am-8pm, F 4:45am-10:30pm, Sa 5:45am-8pm, Su 7:45am-6pm.) From Oban, several operators offer **day tours** to the isles of Mull, Iona, and Staffa. From April to October, Bowman's Tours, across from Railway Pier, runs daily to Mull and Iona and adds Staffa for a bit more. (☎ 812 313. Mull and Iona £30, children £15; including Staffa £40/20.) On Railway Pier, Turus Mara operates a day tour that includes Iona, Staffa, and the Treshnish Isles. (☎ 0800 0858 786. Iona and Staffa £30. Including Treshnish Isles £30-35.)

ORIENTATION AND PRACTICAL INFORMATION. **Corran Esplanade** runs along the coast north of town, **Gallanach Road** along the coast to the south. Fronting the harbor, **George Street** is the heart of Oban; a block inland, **Argyll Square** is actually a roundabout. The **Tourist Information Centre**, Argyll Sq., inhabits the vaulted interior of an old church and books beds for a £3 charge plus a 10% deposit. (☎ 563 122. Open late June to Aug. M-Sa 9am-8pm, Su 9am-7pm; late Apr. to mid-June M-Sa 9am-5:30pm, Su 10am-5pm; mid- to late June and early to mid-Sept. M-Sa 9am-6:30pm, Su 10am-5pm; mid-Sept. to Oct. M-Sa 9am-5:30pm, Su 10am-4pm; Nov.-Mar. M-F 9:30am-5pm, Sa 10am-5pm, Su noon-5pm.) Free **Internet access** is available at Corran Halls in the Oban Library, Corran Esplanade (check with reception first; open M, W, and F 10am-1pm and 2-7pm; Th 10am-1pm and 2-6pm; Sa 10am-1pm), and at the TIC (£1 per 12min.). Boots **pharmacy**, 34-38 George St., is on the harbor on the north side of town (open M-Sa 8:45am-5:30pm). **Rent bikes** at Oban Cycles, 29 Lochside St., off Argyll Sq., across from the Tesco. (☎ 566 996; www.obancycles.com. £15 per day, £10 per half-day, £55 per week. Open M-F 9am-5:30pm, Sa 9am-5pm.) There are **post offices** in the nearby Tesco, Lochside St. (☎ 510 450; open M-Sa 8am-6pm, Su 10am-1pm) and on Corran Esplanade across town (open M-F 9am-5:30pm, Sa 9am-1pm). **Post Code:** PA34 4HP.

⌂ ACCOMMODATIONS. The waterfront **SYHA Oban ❶**, Corran Esplanade, lies ¾ mi. north of the train station, just past St. Columba's Cathedral. Enjoy spacious dorms and a self-catering kitchen. (☎ 562 025. 128 beds in 6- to 10-bed dorms plus 42 beds in 4-bed ensuite rooms. Laundry and Internet access. Reception until 11:30pm. Curfew 2am. Wheelchair accessible. Dorms £10.50-13.50, under 18 £8.50-11.75; private rooms £12.50-15.50/10.50-13.75. MC/V.) To reach the lively **Oban Backpackers** ❷, 21 Breadalbane St., take George St. away from Railway Pier and bear right at the first fork; the hostel will appear on your right. (☎ 562 107. 48 beds in 6- to 12-bed single-sex dorms. Self-catering kitchen. Breakfast £1.90. No lockable dorms; no lockers. Laundry £2.50. Internet access 80p per 30min. Lockout 10am-5pm. Curfew 2:30am. Bicycle rental £12 per day, £6 per half-day. Open Apr.-Oct. Dorms £12-13. AmEx/MC/V.) Almost entirely comprised of nooks and crannies, Victorian **Corran House** ❷, 1-2 Victoria Crescent, sits near the water ½ mi. north of the train station. (☎ 566 040. 36 beds in 2- to 6-bed dorms and 11 private rooms with TV. Self-catering kitchen. Guests expected to make donation for breakfast. No lockable dorms; no lockers. Laundry £5. Dorms £12-14; private rooms £20-30 per person. MC/V.) Seven rooms, all with bath and TV, comprise the bright blue **Maridon House** ❷, Dunuaran Rd., where guests dine on a full Scottish breakfast. From Argyll Sq., walk to the end of Albany St. and look up. (☎ 562 670. £22-27 per person. MC/V.)

🎛🖥 FOOD AND PUBS. Tesco, Lochside St., covers **grocery** needs. (Open M-Sa 8am-10pm, Su 9am-6pm.) Seafood shops cluster around the ferry terminal on Railway Pier. In the summer, **McTavish's Kitchens** ❶, 34 George St., puts on a nightly show of traditional Scottish song and dance in its restaurant (Cover £4.50, £2.50 if dining; shows 8 and 10pm). A ground-floor self-serve cafeteria offers cheap food throughout the day. (☎ 563 064; www.mctavishs.com. Restaurant open daily noon-2pm and 6-10pm. Cafeteria open daily in summer 9am-10pm; in winter 9am-6pm. MC/V.) **O'Donnell's Irish Pub**, Breadalbane St., across the street from Oban Backpackers, draws a young crowd to its underground digs with live music, karaoke, and quiz nights. (☎ 566 159. Open Su-W 2pm-1am, Th-Sa 2pm-2am; reduced off-season hours.) Competing for local drinkers and cheery hostelers, **Markie Dan's**, Victoria Crescent, off Corran Esplanade under Corran House, has live music, drink specials, and a friendly bar staff. (☎ 564 448. Open daily 11am-1am.)

◙ SIGHTS. The town's only real tourist draw is the small but renowned **Oban Distillery**, which offers 1hr. tours ending with free samples of the local malt. (☎ 572 004. Open July-Sept. M-F 9:30am-7:30pm, Sa 9:30am-5pm, Su noon-5pm; Apr.-June and Oct. M-Sa 9:30am-5pm; Mar. and Nov. M-F 10am-5pm; Dec.-Feb. M-F 12:30-4pm. Tours every 15min. in summer, less frequent in off-season; call ahead for reservations. £4.) The hilltop Colosseum-esque structure dominating the skyline is **McCaig's Tower**. Commissioned at the end of the 19th century by John Stuart McCaig, it was intended as an art gallery, but construction was abandoned when McCaig died. Take the steep stairway at the end of Argyll St., then turn left along Ardconnel Rd. and right up Laurel St. (Open 24hr. Free.) North of town, the ivy-eaten ruins of 7th-century **Dunollie Castle**, Oban's oldest building, sit atop a cliff. From town, walk 20min. north along the water until you've curved around the castle, then take the overgrown path up the hill. (Open 24hr. Free.)

🔰 DAYTRIPS FROM OBAN

KERRERA. Across the bay from Oban is the beautiful and nearly deserted isle of Kerrera (CARE-er-uh), where a no-car policy guarantees a peaceful habitat for seals and sea eagles. Ringed by a network of gravel roads, Kerrera makes for great walking and mountain biking. From the ferry landing, turn left and follow the road for 2½ mi. to the southern tip of Kerrera, where tiny ▓Gylen Castle stands atop the cliffs in an isolated spot overlooking lush scenery and the sea. Enjoy a hearty soup and sandwich (£3) or spend the night in the cozy **Kerrera Bunkhouse and Tea Garden** ❶, 2 mi. from the pier near the castle. (☎ 570 223. Tea Garden open Apr.-Sept. W-Su 10:30am-4:30pm. 10 beds. Self-catering kitchen. Laundry £3. Dorms £10. Cash only.) A **ferry** crosses to Kerrera from a pier 2 mi. south of Oban along Gallanach Rd. Turn the board to the black side to signal the ferryman that you wish to cross. The ferryman also dispenses helpful maps of the island. (☎563 665. In summer daily 2 per hr. 10:30am-12:30pm and 2-6pm, also M-Sa 8:45am; in winter 6 per day, but call ahead. Maps 50p. Round-trip £3.50; bikes 50p.)

LOCH ETIVE. Twelve miles northeast of Oban lies Loch Etive. This body of water spans nearly 20 miles, from the **Falls of Lora** (more like rapids), which change direction with the shifting of the tides, to the mountains of Glen Coe. North of Taynuilt, the family-run **Loch Etive Cruises** sends tours into otherwise inaccessible countryside. Bring a pair of binoculars to scan for seals, otters, red deer, and golden eagles. (☎01866 822 430. Easter to Oct. Su-F noon and 2pm; Sa charters only; call in advance. 1½hr. tour £6, children £4, families £16; 3hr. tour £11/6/28.) Both **trains** and Scottish Citylink **buses** traveling from Oban to Glasgow stop in Taynuilt, and you can call the night before you arrive to arrange a free shuttle from the town to the pier. Monty Python fans can glimpse Castle Aaargh (actually **Castle Stalker**) on Loch Linnhe; cross Connel Bridge at the mouth of Loch Etive and take the A828 10min. from Appin. Scottish Citylink bus #918 from Oban to Appin passes by; ask the driver. (☎01631 730 234; www.castlestalker.com. Call 1-2 days in advance; visits by appointment only.)

ISLE OF ISLAY   ☎01496

Though known to many as "Whisky Island," the Isle of Islay (EYE-luh) has much more to offer than the famed "liquid sunshine." This barely inhabited outpost is a walker's paradise. Islay's real beauty lies in the patches of preserved nature, vaguely scented by the intoxicating fumes of newly-cut peat and some of the world's finest single malts from the island's distilleries.

▐ TRANSPORTATION

CalMac **ferries** (☎302 209) leave from **Kennacraig Ferry Terminal,** 7 mi. south of Tarbert on the Kintyre Peninsula, sailing either to Port Askaig or to Port Ellen (Port Ellen Terminal 2¼hr.; M-Tu and Th-Sa 3-4 per day, W 2 per day, Su 1-4 per day; £8). To reach Kennacraig, take the Scottish Citylink **bus** (☎08705 505 050) that runs between Glasgow and Campbeltown (Glasgow to Kennacraig 3½hr.; M-Sa 4 per day, Su 1-2 per day). Travelers from Arran can catch bus #448 to Kennacraig at the Claonaig ferry landing (☎01880 730 253; 20min., M-Sa 3 per day, £2.45) or call a taxi (☎01880 820 220). Wednesday in summer, a ferry leaves Oban, stops on Colonsay, and continues to Port Askaig (4hr., £10.85). The comprehensive *Islay and Jura Area Transport Guide* at TICs has more on these services as well as island bus timetables. Most bus schedules follow ferry times quite closely, but call ahead or risk being stranded. Islay Coaches (☎840 273) operates a few daily buses between Islay towns. Bus #451 connects Port Ellen and Port Askaig via Bowmore (M-Sa about 4 per day, Su 1 per day); #450 runs from Port Ellen to Port Charlotte via Bowmore (M-Sa 3 per day). **Postbuses** (☎01246 546 329) cross the island a few times a day. Many bus times apply to one day only, so read schedules carefully. Purchase single tickets; roundtrip tickets aren't cheaper, and aren't valid on different bus services. British Airways Express **planes** (☎08705 444 000) fly from Glasgow Airport to the Islay Airport, located between Port Ellen and Bowmore (2 per day, 40min., £75). For **taxis,** contact Carol's Cabs (☎302 155, mobile 0777 578 2155; www.carols-cabs.co.uk), which provides 24hr. service and **island tours.**

PORT ELLEN

Port Ellen serves as an immediate signal to those arriving by ferry that life on Islay is different from that on the mainland. To the west, the windswept **Mull of Oa** (OH-uh) drops dramatically into the sea. A 1½ mi. walk along the Mull of Oa road leads to the solar-powered **Carraig Fhada lighthouse,** which is one of the few square lighthouses in Scotland. Beyond the lighthouse lies crescent-shaped **Traigh Bhan,** a favorite beach of

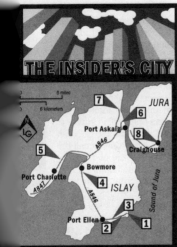

THE INSIDER'S CITY

JURA

7

6

Port Askaig ● 8

A846

5

Craighouse

Bowmore ●

Port Charlotte ●

A847

4 ISLAY

A846

3

Port Ellen ● 2

1

Sound of Jura

THE WHISKY TRAIL

Islay is renowned for its malt whiskys and boasts seven distilleries; Jura adds one more. The malts are known for their peaty flavor—not surprising; half of Islay is peat bog. The island's clean environment and fresh water supply are ideal for a flourishing whisky trail. What gives each malt its distinctive flavor? A plethora of determinants: water supply, air quality, temperature, the barley—even the shape of the pot-still (large kettle-like distilling structure). Pick up *The Islay and Jura Whisky Trail*, free at TICs, or use our guide:

1 Ardberg: (☎302 244), on the southeast coast, 4 mi. from Port Ellen. The peatiest of the island's malts. Ardberg is rapidly emerging as one of Islay's best malts. Tours M-Sa 10:30am and 2:30pm. £2.

2 Lagavulin: (☎302 400), 3 mi. from Port Ellen. Check out the massive washbacks that overflow with foam during the fermenting process. Tours M-F 10, 11:15am, and 2:30pm. £4.

many locals who frequent its "singing sands" in the summer heat. A longer trek (about 6 mi.) will bring you to the end of the peninsula and a massive **American Monument**, built to commemorate two ships that were sunk off this point in 1918, drowning hundreds. Heading east along the A846, you will pass three of Islay's finest distilleries, ▣**Laphroaig** (2 mi.), **Lagavulin** (3 mi.), and **Ardbeg** (4 mi.). They're relatively easy to get to, especially with a bike; it's the getting back that may pose a problem. Bus #451 runs from Port Ellen to Laphroaig, Lagavulin, and finally Ardbeg (M-Sa 2-3 per day, more on school days). Behind Lagavulin, the grass-covered rubble of 16th-century **Dunyveg Castle** looms beside the sea. Just past Ardbeg you will come across the **Loch an t-Sailein**, known as "Seal Bay" for its breeding colonies. Another 3 mi. east along the A846 from Ardbeg, 12th-century **Kildalton Chapel** holds the miraculously preserved **Kildalton High Cross**, a Celtic carved blue stone thought to date from the mid-9th century. This journey is best made by bicycle (see below).

If you choose to stay in town, Mr. and Mrs. Hedley's **Trout Fly Guest House ❸**, 8 Charlotte St., has decent rooms close to the ferry. (☎302 204. No smoking. Singles £21.50; doubles £45. Cash only.) Another good option is the simple but comfortable **Mingulay Guest House ❷**, 5 Charlotte St., just past the Trout Fly (☎302 085. From £18 per person. Cash only). On the Eastern coast, the **Kintra Farmhouse B&B ❷** stands in solitary coastal splendor on a working farm. (☎302 051. From £18 per person. Cash only.) Kintra also welcomes ▣**camping ❶** in the dunes at the southern end of the Big Strand (p. 597), where you can enjoy beach fires. (Toilet and showers. Open Apr.-Sept. £5 for 1 person, £8 for 2 people, including tent.) To reach Kintra from Port Ellen, take the Mull of Oa road 1 mi., then follow the right fork for 2¼ mi. In Port Ellen, Frederick Crescent rings the harbor and holds a Co-op for **groceries**. (☎302 446. Open M-Sa 8am-8pm, Su 12:30-7pm.) The **Mactaggart Community Cyber Cafe ❶**, 30 Mansfield Pl., offers diner-style meals (cheeseburger and fries £3.20), satellite TV, and a pool table. (☎302 693. Internet access £1 per 30min. Pool 30p per 30min. Open Tu-Su noon-10pm. Food served until 6:30pm.) **Bike rental** is available from Port Ellen Playing Fields, on the edge of town, on B846 toward Bowmore. (☎302 349 or 07831 246 911. £7 per day, £5 per half-day. Open May-Sept. daily noon-4pm and 6-9pm.) There is a **bank** in town, but no ATM. Port Ellen's tiny **Kildalton and Oa Information Point**, Frederick Crescent, opposite the **police**, is not an official TIC but stocks bus schedules and leaflets. (☎302 434. Open Mar.-Oct. M-Sa 9:30am-noon; Nov.-Mar. M-Sa 11am-noon.)

BOWMORE

Located 10 mi. from both Port Ellen and Port Askaig, Bowmore is Islay's largest town, though it is still in keeping with the island's charm. Arranged in a grid, the town is centered on **Main Street,** with the 18th-century **Bowmore Round Church** at the top, built perfectly circular to keep Satan from hiding in the corners. (Open daily 9am-6pm. Free.) Diagonally across from the TIC, the **Bowmore Distillery,** School St., is the island's oldest. (☎810 671. Tours M-F 10, 11am, 2, 3pm, Sa 10am. ₤2, under 18 free.) The **Big Strand,** 7 mi. of white-sand beach with waves perfect for **bodysurfing,** lines the coast between Bowmore and Port Ellen.

Among a flock of similarly priced Bowmore B&Bs, the friendly proprietors of the **Lambeth Guest House ❸**, Jamieson St., offer homey lodgings and good conversation. They also serve a great dinner (₤7.50 for 2-course meal)—ask in advance. (☎810 597. No singles. ₤22 per person. AmEx/MC/V.) The waterfront **Harbour Inn ❹**, The Square, offers luxurious (and more expensive) lodging. (☎810 330; www.harbour-inn.com. Singles ₤65; doubles ₤95. No smoking. MC/V.) There is a Co-op **market** on Main St. (☎810 201. Open M-Sa 8am-8pm, Su 12:30-7pm.) The Harbour Inn (p. 597) also runs a **restaurant ❺** with a small bar that serves all varieties of Islay single malt whisky. (3 courses ₤25. Food served daily noon-2pm and 6-9pm; bar open 11am-1am, Su noon-1am. MC/V.)

Islay's **Tourist Information Centre,** Main St., books accommodations for a ₤3 charge plus a 10% deposit. Ordnance Survey Explorer #352 and #353 (₤7.50) and Landranger #60 (₤6.50) maps cover Islay. Pick up *The Isles of Islay, Jura & Colonsay Walks* (₤2), which details hikes. (☎810 254. Open Apr. M-Sa 10am-5pm; May-June M-Sa 9:30am-5pm, Su 2-5pm; July-Aug. M-Sa 9:30am-5:30pm, Su 2-5pm; Oct. M-Sa 10am-5pm; Nov.-Mar. M-F 10am-4pm.) Other services include: two **banks** with ATMs; a **launderette** in the Mactaggart Leisure Centre, School St., where you swim while your clothes take a spin (☎810 767; wash ₤3.50, dry ₤1.60; swimming ₤2.50, children ₤1.50; open Tu 12:30-9:30pm, W 11am-9:30pm, Th-F 12:30-9pm, Sa 10:30am-6pm, Su 10:30am-5:30pm); **Internet access** at the office of Ileach newspaper, Main St. (☎810 355; ₤1.50 per 30min.; open M-F 10am-12:30pm and 1-4pm) or free Internet at the island's Servicepoint, on Jamieson St. (☎301 301; open M-Th 9am-4pm, F 9am-3pm; call in advance for an appointment); and the **post office,** Main St. (☎810 366; open M-W, F 9am-5:30pm, Th 9am-1pm, Sa 9am-12:30pm), which also **rents bikes** (₤10 per day, ₤8 per day for 1-4 days). Post Code: PA43 7JH.

PORT CHARLOTTE

On the western arm of Islay, across Loch Indaal from Bowmore, Port Charlotte is a quiet village set on a peaceful stretch of the coast. The **Museum of Islay Life,** Main St., exhibits a vast collection of artifacts, with displays on illicit whisky production and the evolution of the radio. (☎850 358. Open July-Aug. M-Sa 10am-

3 **Laphroaig** (la-FROYG): (☎302 418), 2 mi. from Port Ellen. Its name in Gaelic means "beautiful hollow by the broad bay." Considered by many to be Islay's finest malt.

4 **Bowmore:** (☎810 441), in town. The oldest (est. 1779) of Islay's distilleries in full operation and one of the last to malt its own barley. Tours M-F 10:30, 11:30am 10, 11am, 2 and 3pm, Sa 10:30am. ₤2.

5 **Bruichladdich** (brook-LADdee): (☎850 221), 2 mi. from Port Charlotte. A smoother malt, produced with 19th-century equipment. The only one on the island that bottles its own product. Tours M-F 10:30, 11:30am, and 2:30pm; Sa 10:30am and 2:30pm. ₤3.

6 **Caol Ila** (cool-EE-la): (☎840 207), 1 mi. from Port Askaig. Fine views across the sound and a complimentary swig. Tours by appointment. ₤4.

7 **Bunnahabhainn** (bun-na-HAVen): (☎840 646). Home to the "Black Bottle," containing all seven of Islay's malts. Tours M-Th 10:30am, 1, and 3pm; F 10:30am. Free.

8 **Jura:** (☎820 240). In Craighouse. Check out the warehouses where the "angels' share" evaporates out of the casks, producing a divine aroma. Produces a vintage label aged at least 36 years. Tours daily 10, 11am, and 2:30pm.

5pm, Su 2-5pm; Apr.-Oct. M-Sa 10am-5pm; Nov.-Mar. call in advance. £2.50, concessions £1.50, children £1.) Two miles along the A847 toward Bowmore, the ▓**Bruichladdich Distillery** uses only its original, antiquated equipment. It's the only distillery on Islay that ages and bottles its whisky on-site. (☎850 190; www.bruichladdich. Tours Easter to Oct. M-F 10:30, 11:30am, 2:30pm; Sa 10:30am, 2:30pm; Oct. to Easter M-F 11:30am, 2:30pm; Sa 10:30am.) The basic **SYHA Islay ❶**, above the Wildlife Information Centre, was once a distillery. (☎0870 004 1128. 30 beds. Laundry and kitchen. Reception closed 10:30am-5pm. Curfew 11:30pm. Open Apr.-Sept. Dorms £11-12.50, under 18 £5-8.75. MC/V.) There are a couple of **B&Bs** near Port Charlotte, including the luxurious **Port Charlotte Hotel ❹**, Main St. (☎850 360. Singles £60; doubles £105. MC/V.) **The Croft Kitchen ❸**, Main St., across from the Museum of Islay Life, uses only local produce. Outside tables make it ideal for a lunchtime picnic. (☎850 230. Lunch £5-10. Dinner £10-15. Open mid-Mar. to early Jan. daily 10am-8:30pm. MC/V.) The tiny Spar, Main St., has basic **groceries** and a **post office.** (☎850 232. Open Easter to Sept. M-Sa 9am-12:30pm and 1:30-5pm, Su 11am-1pm; Oct. to Easter M-Sa 9am-12:30pm and 1:30-5pm, Su 3:30-5:30pm.)

ISLE OF JURA   ☎01496

Separated from Islay by a narrow strait, the Isle of Jura ("Deer Island") has grown more wild and isolated during the past century. A census in 1841 showed that 2299 people lived there; today, only 170 call the island home. Living in scattered houses along a single-track road on the eastern shore, these hardy souls are outnumbered by deer nearly forty to one. Jura was remote enough to satisfy novelist George Orwell, who penned *1984* here in a cottage free from watchful eyes. The entire western coast and center of the island is uninhabited, offering the adventurous true wilderness. Its great **hiking** country includes a series of tough ascents up the three **Paps of Jura** (all over 2400 ft.), scaled by runners in the annual Jura Fells Race in May. The land surrounding **Loch Tarbet** is pristine and harsh. At the island's northern tip, the **Corryvreckan Whirlpool**—the third largest in the world—churns violently and can be heard from over a mile away. Ordnance Survey Explorer #353 (£7.50) and Landranger #361 #61 (£6.50) maps cover the island while *Jura: A Guide for Walkers* (£2) details various hikes. Jura also caters to the more conservative walker with the captivating **Jura House Walled Garden,** a paradise of rare plant species both native and Australian. Though the distance between Islay and Jura is short, do not attempt the swim; tidal currents are powerful. The Jura **Ferry** (☎840 681) ferries cars and passengers across the Sound of Islay from Port Askaig to Feolin (5min.; in summer M-Sa 13-16 per day, Su 6 per day; in winter M-Sa 12 per day, Su 2 per day; £1.40). During the summer and on weekdays during the school year, the Jura **Bus Service** (☎820 314 or 820 221) connects Feolin with Craighouse and other island points (6-8 per day).

Jura's only village is a tiny, one-road settlement 10 mi. north of the ferry landing. At the center of Craighouse, the **Isle of Jura Distillery** employs 20% of the island's working population. Nearby, a small, unstaffed **information center** has walking and wildlife guides. More detailed information and free **Internet access** can be found a 5min. walk down the street from the distillery, headed away from the ferry, at the **Jura Service Point,** which provides the community with its Internet, faxing, and photocopying needs. Craighouse is home to one hotel and a couple of B&Bs. The only restaurant in Craighouse is in the **Jura Hotel ❷**, where bar lunches (noon-2pm) and evening meals (7-9pm) average £5-8. The hotel also offers **camping ❶** on its front lawn, beside the harbor. (☎820 243; www.jurahotel.co.uk. Laundry £3. From £35 per person. Camping free. Showers and toilets £1. AmEx/MC/V.) Jura has **no banks,** but the hotel will give cash back on purchases. A van run by the Royal Bank of Scotland that functions as a **bank on wheels** and rolls into town for about an hour on Wednesdays at 1:30pm. Down the road and across from the distillery, Jura Stores sells **groceries** and houses a **post office.** (☎820 230. Store open M-Th 9am-1pm and 2-5pm, F-Sa 9am-1pm and 2-4:30pm. Post office open M-Tu and Th-F 9am-12:30pm, W 9-9:30am, Sa 9am-1pm and 2-4:30pm.) **Post Code:** PA60 7XS.

ISLE OF MULL

As the most accessible of the Inner Hebrides, Mull is also the most popular. With towering mountains, remote glens, and miles of untouched coastline, Mull rewards explorers who venture beyond the well-trodden routes. The tiny isles scattered to the east are attractions themselves (p. 601). Much of Mull's Gaelic heritage has given way to the pressure of English settlers and to the annual tourist herd, but life-long locals keep tradition alive.

■ TRANSPORTATION

CalMac (Craignure Office ☎01680 812 343) runs a **ferry** from Oban to Craignure (45min.; M-Sa 6 per day, Su 5 per day; extra sailings July-Aug.; £3.85). Smaller car and passenger ferries run from Lochaline on the Morvern Peninsula, north of Mull, to Fishnish, on the east coast 6 mi. northwest of Craignure (15min.; M-Sa 13-14 per day, Su 9 per day; £2.40), and from Kilchoan on the Ardnamurchan peninsula to Tobermory (35min.; M-Sa 7 per day; June-Aug. also Su 5 per day; £3.70). Winter schedules are reduced. **Day tours** run to Mull from Oban (p. 593).

Check the sometimes erratic **bus** times to avoid stranding yourself. Bowman Coaches (☎01680 812 313) operates the main bus routes. Bus #496 meets the Oban ferry at Craignure and goes to Fionnphort (1¼hr.; M-F 5 per day, Sa 4 per day, Su 2 per day; round-trip £6). #495 runs between Craignure and Tobermory via Fishnish (50min.; M-F 6 per day, Sa 5 per day, Su 3-4 per day; round-trip £6). R.N. Carmichael (☎01688 302 220) #494 links Tobermory and Calgary (45min.; M-F 4 per day, Sa 2 per day; round-trip £3.60). **Postbus** (☎01680 300 321) #187 runs from Salen, which lies between Fishnish and Tobermory, to Ulva Ferry and Burg on the west coast (1hr., M-Sa 2 per day, round-trip £6.50). TICs stock copies of the comprehensive *Mull and Iona Area Transport Guide*.

■ ORIENTATION

Mull's settlements cling to the sunnier shoreline. Its three main hubs, **Tobermory** (northwest tip), **Craignure** (east tip), and **Fionnphort** (FINN-a-furt; southwest tip), form a triangle bounded on two sides by the A849 and A848. A left turn off the **Craignure Pier** leads 35 mi. along the southern arm of the island to Fionnphort. There, the ferry leaves for **Iona,** a tiny island to the southwest.

■ HIKING AND OUTDOORS

The Isle of Mull features a range of terrain for walkers, from headland treks and sea-to-summit ascents to gentle forest strolls. While the coastline has some of the most scenic paths, inland you can hike among mountains and deep glens. Ordnance Survey Landranger maps #47-49 (£6) cover Mull, while *Walking in North Mull* and *Walking in South Mull* (£4 each) highlight individual trails. From Tobermory, a 2 mi. walk departs from the Royal Lifeboat Station at the end of Main St. and follows the shore to a **lighthouse.** Outside of Craignure, the **Dun da Ghaoithe Ridge** walk begins past the entrance to Torosay Castle on the A849. This 11 mi. route ascends 2513 ft., follows a ridge with fabulous views over the Sound of Mull, and finishes on the A848 near a bus stop. Popular climbs up **Ben**

More (3169 ft.) and **Ben Buie** (2352 ft.) start from the sea. You can also take the bus to **Calgary Bay,** where stretches of beautiful white-sand beach and rocky headland border the bright blue water. The single-lane main street from Craignure to Tobermury makes for a smooth and scenic bike route. In Tobermory, **Tackle and Books,** 10 Main St., runs 3hr. **fishing trips** that can be suited to experienced anglers or first-timers. (☎302 336. Trips Apr.-Oct. 2-5pm. Call in advance to arrange a sailing. ₤16, children ₤12. Store open M-Sa 9am-5:30pm, Su 11am-4pm.) Tobermory is also home base for whale-watching tours. On Main St. by the bus stop, **Sea Life Surveys** boasts a 96% whale sighting rate and a basking shark watch. (☎01688 302 916; www.sealifesurveys.com. 3-5 trips per day. ₤6-55, children ₤4-35.)

CRAIGNURE ☎01680

Craignure, Mull's main ferry port, is a tiny town with one main street. From the pier, turn left and take the first left again to reach **Mull Rail,** a vintage narrow-gauge toy of a train that will make you feel like a giant. (☎812 494; www.mullrail.co.uk. Runs mid-Mar. to mid-Oct. 4-11 per day. Round-trip ₤4, children ₤3, families ₤10.75. MC/V.) The train rolls 1 mi. south to the still-inhabited **Torosay Castle,** a Victorian mansion, where visitors are urged to sit on the chairs and explore the gardens. A 1 mi. walk leads from Craignure to the house; take the footpath that veers off the main road past the police station. (☎812 421. Open Apr.-Oct. daily 10:30am-5pm. Gardens open Apr.-Oct. daily 9am-7pm. ₤5.50, concessions ₤5, children ₤2.25, families ₤14. Gardens only ₤4.50/3.50/2/11.) Farther along the coast, spectacular ▨**Duart Castle,** a 700-year-old stronghold 4 mi. from Craignure, remains the seat of the MacLean clan chief. The bus runs to the end of Duart Rd., 1½ mi. from the castle. (☎812 309; www.duartcastle.com. Open May-Oct. daily 10:30am-5:30pm; Apr. Su-Th 11am-4pm. ₤4.50, concessions ₤4, children ₤2.25, families ₤11.25.) The Duart Castle Coach (4 per day, leaving the pier M-F and Su 10:15am, 12:30, 2:30, 4:30pm; Sa 9:45am, noon, 2, 4:30pm) runs from the pier to the castle.

To reach **Shieling Holidays Campsite ❶** from the ferry terminal, turn left onto the main road, and then take the next left. Super-clean toilet and shower facilities, a TV lounge, and a variety of permanent tents with gas cookers provide hostel-like accommodation. (☎812 496; www.shielingholidays.co.uk. Open late Mar. to Sept. Tent sites from ₤12, with car from ₤14; beds in permanent tent ₤10 per person. Bedding ₤2. AmEx/MC/V.) **Aon a'Dha ❷,** 1-2 Kirk Terr., ½ mi. left from the ferry, has friendly, family-run accommodations at bargain prices. (☎812 318. Breakfast ₤3. ₤15 per person. Cash only.) Just past the Spar, **MacGregor's Roadhouse ❷** serves up hearty burgers for ₤6-8 and excellent pizzas for ₤7-11. (☎812 471. Internet access ₤1 per 15min. Open Su-F 10am-10pm, Sa 9am-10pm. Food served until 9pm. MC/V.)

Across from the ferry, the **Tourist Information Centre** books rooms for a ₤3 charge plus a 10% deposit. (☎812 377. Open July-Aug. M-F 8:30am-7pm, Sa-Su 10am-6:30pm; Apr.-June and Sept.-Oct. M-F 8:30am-5:15pm, Sa-Su 10:30am-5:30pm; Nov.-Mar. M-Sa 9am-5pm, Su 10:30am-noon and 3:30-5pm.) The adjoining CalMac **ferry** office is Mull's largest. (☎08705 650 000. Open from 1hr. prior to the first ferry until the last ferry leaves.) **Rent bikes** at Kells Gallery and Craft Shop, near the TIC. (☎812 580. ₤12 per day, ₤6 per half day. Open daily 9am-7pm.) The **post office** is in the Spar on the main street. (☎812 301. Store open M 7:15am-7:15pm, Tu-Sa 8am-7:30pm, Su 10am-7:30pm. Post office open M-W and F 9am-1pm and 2-5pm, Th and Sa 9am-1pm.) **Post Code:** PA65 6AY.

TOBERMORY ☎01688

Colorful cafes and pastel houses characterize the Mediterranean-style harbor village of Tobermory (pop. 1000). Nestled at the foot of steep slopes, Mull's largest town is centered along **Main Street,** which hugs the harbor. Just across from the bus stop is the **Tobermory Distillery,** on the opposite side of the harbor from the TIC, which conducts 30min. tours and offers generous samples of the final product. (☎302 645. Open M-F 10am-5pm. Tours every hr. 11am-4pm. ₤2.50, seniors ₤1, children free.) The tiny **Mull Museum,** Main St., chronicles the island's history with local artifacts and folklore. (Open Easter to Oct. M-F 10am-4pm, Sa 10am-1pm. £1, children 20p.) During the last weekend of April, Tobermory hosts the **Mull Music Festival.** June's **Mendelssohn Festival** celebrates the composer's work, much of which was inspired by the Hebridean Isles. Concerts are held in churches and castles. The **Mull Highland Games** feature caber-tossing, hammer-throwing, bagpipes, and *ceilidhs* (folk music jams) on the third Thursday of July.

The waterfront **SYHA Tobermory ❶**, on the far end of Main St. from the bus stop, is painted pink and has a kitchen, lounge, and backyard terrace. (☎302 481. 39 beds. Internet available. Lockout 10:30am-5pm. Open Mar.-Oct. Dorms £10.50-11.50, under 18 £8-8.50. MC/V.) **B&Bs** line the bay, including **Failte Guest House ❸**, 27 Main St., which spoils visitors with comfortable ensuite rooms and great breakfasts. (☎302 495. Singles £25-35; doubles £48-70. MC/V.) The Co-op **supermarket,** Main St., sits opposite Fisherman's Pier. (☎302 004. Open M-Sa 8am-8pm, Su 12:30-7pm.) Grab fish and chips (£3.50) from the stall on **Fisherman's Pier ❶**. (Open in summer M-Sa 12:30-9pm.) The **Island Bakery and Delicatessen ❶**, 26 Main St., offers sandwiches, pizzas, and an impressive array of local cheeses. (☎302 225. Open Apr.-Oct. M-Sa 9am-7:30pm, Su 12:30-4pm; Nov.-Mar. M-Sa 9am-5:30pm. Cash only.)

Tobermory's **Tourist Information Centre,** on the ferry pier across the harbor from the bus stop, sells boat tickets and books rooms for a £3 charge plus a 10% deposit. (☎302 182. Open Apr. M-F 9am-5pm, Sa-Su noon-5pm; late Apr.-June M-F 9am-5pm, Sa-Su 11am-5pm; July-Aug. M-Sa 9am-6pm, Su 10am-5pm; Sept.-Oct. M-Sa 9am-5pm, Su noon-5pm.) Other services include: a CalMac office next to the TIC (☎302 517; open M-F 9am-5:30pm, Sa 9am-1pm and 2-4pm); **bike rental** at Archibald Brown & Son, 21 Main St. (☎302 020; £10 per half-day, £15 per day; open M-Sa 8:45am-1pm and 2:15-5:30pm); Clydesdale **bank,** Main St., the only bank and ATM on the island (open M-Tu and Th-F 9:15am-4:45pm, W 9:45am-4:45pm); **Internet access** with printer- and webcam-equipped computers at Posh Nosh Cafe/Restaurant, on Main St. next to the Co-op (☎302 499. £1.50 for 30 min., 75p for each subsequent 15 min.; open daily 10am-10pm); and the **post office,** 36 Main St. (open M-Tu and Th-F 9am-1pm and 2-5:30pm, Sa 9am-1pm). **Post Code:** PA75 6NT.

IONA, STAFFA, AND TRESHNISH ISLES

The isolation and rugged beauty offered by these tiny islands off Mull's west coast make them worth the effort to see. Serene **Iona,** birthplace of Christianity in Scotland, is the largest and most accessible. **Staffa,** one of the world's geological marvels, rises from the sea 8 mi. north of Iona, its towering basalt columns a natural masterpiece. Wildly remote, the **Treshnish Isles** teem with wildlife.CalMac **ferries** (Fionnphort office ☎01681 700 559) sail to Iona from Fionnphort (5min., frequent, round-trip £2.55). There are no other direct ferries between the islands; it's easiest to see them by **tour.** During the summer, Gordon Grant Tours (☎01681 700 338; www.staffatours.com) send boats from Fionnphort to Staffa (2½hr., £14) and the Treshnish Isles (5½hr., £27). The Kirkpatricks (☎01681 700 358) offer daily cruises to Staffa from Fionnphort and Iona (3hr.; from Iona 9:45am, 1:45pm; from Fionnphort 10am, 2pm; £17.50, children £7.50). Turus Mara operates tours leaving from the town of Ulva Ferry on Mull. (☎08000 858 786. Staffa and Iona £27.50, children £14. Staffa and Treshnish Isles £35/17.) Day tours also operate from Oban (p. 593).

IONA   ☎01681

The isle of Iona (pop. 150) beckons travelers with white-sand beaches, brilliant blue waters, and rugged hills. For nearly two centuries after Ireland's St. Columba landed on this island in AD 563, Iona was one of Europe's cradles of Christianity. The centerpiece of the island's offerings, **Iona Abbey,** is a 13th-century Benedictine structure on the site of St. Columba's original monastery. Follow signs from the pier to reach the abbey. (☎700 512. Open daily Apr.-Sept. 9:30am-6:30pm; Oct.-Mar.

9:30am-4:30pm. Services daily 9am, 2, 9pm; Su 10:30am, 9pm. £3.30, concessions £2.50, children £1.30.) Adjacent to the abbey, intimate **St. Columba's Shrine** contained relics of St. Columba until they were brought back to Ireland in the 10th century for protection from Viking raids. At the **Columba Centre** in Fionnphort, an exhibition charts the saint's story. (☎700 660. Open Easter to Sept. daily 10:30am-1pm, 2-5pm. Free.) Tiny 12th-century **St. Oran's Chapel** is the oldest ecclesiastical building on the isle. The surrounding burial ground supposedly contains a number of kings, including the pious Macbeth. At the start of the road to the abbey lie the ruins of a 13th-century **nunnery,** one of the better-preserved medieval convents in Britain. Signs lead from the nunnery to the **Iona Heritage Centre,** which traces the history of the island, from St. Columba through WWII. (☎700 576. Open Easter to Oct. M-Sa 10:30am-4:30pm. £2, concessions £1.50.)

On the isle's north end, isolated **Iona Hostel ❷**, about 1½ mi. from the pier, seeks to reunite its guests with nature with no TV, radio, or Internet, but postcard-perfect beaches nearby. (☎700 781; www.ionahostel.co.uk. 21 beds in 2- to 6-bed dorms. Dorms £15, children £10.50. Cash only.) The island has scattered **B&Bs** by the pier. Get your **groceries** at the Spar, uphill from the ferry. (☎700 321. Open Apr.-Oct. M-Sa 9am-5:30pm, Su noon-5pm; Nov.-Mar. 10am-1pm and 2-4pm.) The **Argyll Hotel ❸** serves fine cuisine, offering a range of home-grown organic produce. (☎703 334; www.argyllhoteliona.co.uk. Dinner entrees £8.50-£12.50. Food served 12:30-2pm, 3-5pm, 7-8:30pm. MC/V.) For slightly cheaper local seafood try the waterfront **Martyr's Bay Bar and Restaurant ❸**, immediately to the left of the pier. (☎700 382. Open daily 10am-11pm. Food served until 9pm. MC/V.) Left of the pier, Finlay, Ross, Ltd. **rents bikes** and runs the island's only **launderette.** (☎700 357. Bikes £4.50 per half-day, £8 per day. £10 deposit. Laundry £5. Open M-Sa 10am-5:15pm, Su 11am-4:30pm.) The **post office** is near the ferry pier. (☎700 515. Open M-Tu and Th-F 9am-1pm and 2-5pm, Sa 9am-12:30pm.) **Post Code:** PA76 6SJ.

STAFFA

Sixty million years ago, lava cooled by the sea formed the hexagonal basalt columns that have made Staffa famous. Ringed by treacherous cliffs, the 80 acres of soil that blanket this stone miracle were inhabited by a handful of hardy souls as recently as the late 18th century. All that remains today are the remnants of a building erected in 1820 and a colony of puffins. At low tide, you can enter **Fingal's Cave** and marvel at its natural basalt cathedral. When rough seas roar into the cavern, the noise reverberates; the pounding of wave against rock so inspired the great composer Felix Mendelssohn that he recreated its sound with surging strings in his *Hebrides Overture.*

TRESHNISH ISLES

The Treshnish Isles are a paradise for all kinds of wildlife, especially birds. Unthreatened by humans, the animals tolerate up-close examination on these isolated islands. Along the cliffs of Lunga, birds perch on one of the only remnants of human habitation, a 13th-century **chapel.** Legend holds that monks from Iona buried their library on one of the Treshnish Isles to save it from pillage during the Reformation. Many have tried digging, as yet without luck. Staffa **tours** visit the Treshnish Isles. (☎700 338; www.staffatours.com. Apr.-July M-F and Su, departing Fionnphort 12:10pm, Iona noon, returning 5pm. Adults £32, children £16.)

HIGHLANDS AND ISLANDS

Misty and remote, the Scottish Highlands have long been the stuff of fantasy and romance. These sheep-dotted moors, sliced by the narrow lochs of the Great Glen and framed by towering granite mountain ranges, maintain a miraculous isolation and genuine wilderness. But the Highlands haven't always been so unpopulated. Three centuries ago, almost a third of all Scots lived north of the Great Glen as members of clan-based societies; the cruel 19th-century Clearances (p. 520) emptied the landscape.

HIGHLIGHTS OF THE HIGHLANDS AND ISLANDS

CLIMB Ben Nevis, the highest mountain in the Britain, whose 4406 ft. peak hides behind a layer of clouds. On a clear day, you can see all the way to Ireland (p. 626).

DISCOVER an unparalleled wealth of ancient ruins set amid sheep, sky, and ocean in the Orkney and Shetland Islands (p. 653).

TREK the mighty Cuillin Mountains and misty waters of the Isle of Skye (p. 629).

◧ TRANSPORTATION IN THE HIGHLANDS AND ISLANDS

Traveling in the Highlands requires a great deal of planning. Transport services are, as a rule, drastically reduced on Sundays and during the winter, and making more than one or two connections per day on any form of transportation is difficult. A county's *Public Transport Travel Guide* (£1), available from TICs, is essential. **Trains** (☎08457 484 950), while offering the best views, will only get you so far, and Scottish Citylink **buses** (☎08705 505 050) do not travel far beyond the main rail routes. Citylink offers an **Explorer Pass** (3 consecutive days £39, 5 days in 10 £62, 8 days in 16 £85), which includes a 50% discount on CalMac ferry passages. **Driving** in the Highlands is more convenient but potentially treacherous (see **By Car,** p. 33). Watch out for livestock. No, seriously. Most **ferries** are operated by Caledonian MacBrayne (CalMac; ☎08705 650 000; www.calmac.co.uk). Peruse the website for the combination ticket that best suits your trip.

NORTHEAST SCOTLAND

ABERDEEN
☎01224

Whoever dubbed Aberdeen (pop. 210,000) the "Granite City" wasn't off the mark: most days, the city's buildings—by law a uniform gray—blend in with the sky. Though city planners have added parks and beach promenades, Aberdeen is still dominated by the 19th-century style of a handful of architects. This melancholy mecca of the North Sea oil industry nevertheless shelters many students and an array of pubs, clubs, and museums.

⌐ TRANSPORTATION

Flights: Aberdeen Airport (☎722 331). Stagecoach Bluebird #10 runs to the airport from the bus station (every hr. until 8:40pm, £1.25) and First Aberdeen (☎650 065) #27 runs from Guild St. (every hr. until 5:20pm, £1.45). British Airways (☎08457 733 377) flies from **London Heathrow** and **Gatwick** (11 per day, £30-£105).

Trains: Station on Guild St. Ticket office open M-F 6:30am-7:30pm, Sa 7am-7pm, Su 8:45am-7:30pm. Trains (☎08457 484 950) from: **Edinburgh** (2½hr., every hr., £33.90); **Glasgow** (2½hr., every hr., £33.90); **Inverness** (2¼hr., every 1½hr., £22.70); **London King's Cross** (7½hr.; 3 per day, 1 sleeper per day; £102.80).

Buses: Station on Guild St. (☎212 266). Ticket office open M-F 8:30am-6pm, Sa 8:30am-5pm. National Express (☎08705 808 080) from **London** (2 per day, £39). Megabus (☎09001 600 900) from **London** (2 per day, £18). Scottish Citylink (☎08705 505 050) from **Edinburgh** and **Glasgow** (both 4hr., every hr., £17.20). Stagecoach Bluebird (☎212 266) from **Inverness** (4hr., every hr., £8.10).

Ferries: Aberdeen Ferry Terminal, Jamieson's Quay (☎08456 000 449). Turn left at the traffic light off Market St. onto Commercial Quay and follow the road until it dead-ends. Open Tu, Th, Sa-Su 7am-5pm; M, W, F 7am-7pm. Northlink Ferries run to **Kirkwall, Orkney** (6hr.; Tu, Th, Sa-Su 5pm; roundtrip £30.90-46.20) and **Lerwick, Shetland** (12-14hr.; M, W, F, Su 7pm; Tu, Th, Sa 5pm; round-trip £39.60-60.60).

Local Transportation: First Aberdeen, 47 Union St. (☎650 065), runs public **buses.** Office open M-Sa 8:45am-5:30pm. Unlimited day travel £2.70.

Car Rental: Major car rental companies have offices at the airport and in town. **Arnold Clark Car Hire** (☎249 159) is one of the cheapest. 23+. Open M-F 8am-8pm, Sa 8am-5pm, Su 9am-5pm. From £19 per day, £99 per week.

Taxis: Com Cabs (☎353 535).

⁊ PRACTICAL INFORMATION

Tourist Information Centre: 23 Union St. (☎288 828; www.agtb.org), in the center of the city. From the bus station, turn right and head east on Guild St., then left on Market St.; take the second right on Union St. Books rooms for a £3 charge plus a 10% deposit. Open June-Aug. M-Sa 9am-7pm, Su 10am-4pm; Sept.-May M-Sa 9am-7pm.

Tours: Grampian Coaches (☎650 024) runs various day tours to nearby castles, Royal Deeside, the Whisky Trail, and beyond. June-Sept. £9-24, concessions £8-16.

Financial Services: Banks are ubiquitous. **Thomas Cook,** 335-337 Union St. (☎807 000). Open M-W and F-Sa 9am-5:30pm, Th 10am-5:30pm.

Launderette: A1, 555 George St. (☎621 211). Full service £9.50. Open daily 8am-6pm.

Police: Queen St. (☎08456 005 700).

Hospital: Aberdeen Royal Infirmary, on Foresterhill Rd. (☎681 818).

Pharmacy: Boots, Bon Accord Shopping Centre (☎626 080). Open M-W and F-Sa 8:30-6pm, Th 8:30am-8pm, Su 10:30am-5:30pm.

Internet Access: Free in the Media Centre of the **Aberdeen Central Library,** on Rosemount Viaduct. (☎652 532.) Open M-Th 9am-7pm, F-Sa 9am-5pm. The city is littered with cafes offering Internet access, including **The Hub,** 22 John St. (☎658 844). £1.50 per 30min. Open M-F 8am-5pm, Sa-Su 11am-5pm. **Books and Beans,** 22 Belmont St. (☎646 438). £3 per hr. Open M-Sa 10am-5pm, Su 11am-4pm.

Post Office: 489 Union St. Bureau de change. Open M-F 9am-5:30pm, Sa 9am-12:30pm. **Post Code:** AB11 6AZ.

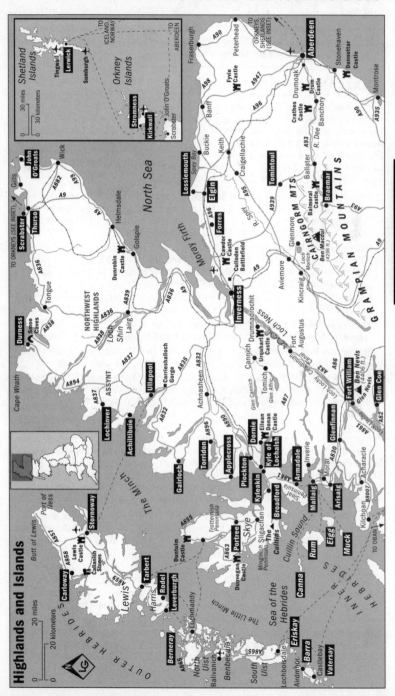

Highlands and Islands

TIP The weekend is the best time for a quick stopover in Aberdeen. During the week, oil rig workers fill up hotel and B&B rooms, driving up prices. When the workers leave the city, rates are slashed up to fifty percent.

ACCOMMODATIONS

For the budget traveler, Aberdeen has few options. Be sure to book a hostel bed or dorm room in advance. If you do get stuck, **B&Bs** are the next best option, lining the streets near the train station between **Crown Street, Springbank Terrace,** and **Bon Accord Street.** From the bus and train stations, turn south from Guild St. on College St., then west on Wellington Pl., which melds into Springbank Terr. Generally, the farther away from Union St., the cheaper the accommodation; be prepared, however, to spend £10-20 more than you would for a hostel.

SYHA Aberdeen, 8 Queen's Rd. (☎646 988). A long walk on Union St. and Albyn Pl. or a short ride on bus #14, 15, or 27. A handsome old house with high-ceilinged rooms and free parking. Breakfast £2.40. Laundry. Internet access £1 per 20min. Reception 7am-11pm. Curfew 2am. Dorms £11.50-13.75, under 18 £7.50-13.75. MC/V. ❶

University of Aberdeen, Crombie Johnston Hall (☎273 301). Take bus #1, 2, 5, or 15 from the city center or walk down King St. Turn left on University Rd., right on High St., and go through the fairy-tale turrets. Breakfast included. Open June to mid-Sept.; call ahead. Singles £20.50, ensuite £26. MC/V. ❸

Roselea Hotel, 12 Springbank Terr. (☎583 060). Walk up the rose-lined path to this warm, welcoming B&B. Singles from £26; doubles from £37. Cash only. ❸

Roselodge Guest House, 3 Springbank Terr. (☎586 794). Comfortable quarters in a converted home with standard rooms. Singles from £25; doubles £40. Cash only. ❸

Springbank Bed & Breakfast, 6 Springbank Terr. (☎592 048). Tidy, quiet, ensuite rooms, run by a hospitable couple. Singles £28; doubles £40. Cash only. ❸

Highland Hotel, 91-95 Crown St. (☎583 685; www.highlandhotel.net). Decked out in Scottish design, this hotel offers a more upscale experience with reasonable rates. Breakfast included. Singles from £37.50; doubles from £50. AmEx/MC/V. ❸

FOOD

Budget travelers will appreciate the centrally located Somerfield **supermarket,** 204 Union St. (☎645 583. Open M-W and Sa 8am-8pm, Th-F 8am-9pm, Su 10am-7pm.) The streets are lined with takeaways and restaurants offering early meal deals. A number of venues do triple duty as restaurants, pubs, and clubs; see **Soul,** the **Monkey House,** and the **Illicit Still,** listed under Nightlife.

▨ **The Ashvale,** 42-48 Great Western Rd. (☎596 981). An Aberdeen institution and 3-time winner of Scotland's "Fish and Chip Shop of the Year" award. The fish and chips (£6.65) can't be beat. Open daily 11:45am-1am. Cash only. ❷

La Lombarda, 2-8 King St. (☎640 916), by the TIC. An extensive menu of pasta, pizza, and risotto (£8-9) and pleasant outdoor seating in ancient Castle Sq. Open M-Th and Su 10am-2pm and 5-9:30pm, F-Sa 10am-2pm and 5-10pm. AmEx/MC/V. ❷

Black Olive Brasserie, 32 Queens Rd. (☎208 877). Simple modern Italian cuisine served in an elegant glass-enclosed brasserie. Inventive, moderately priced fare. Entrees £6-12. Open M-Sa 10am-10pm. AmEx/MC/V. ❷

Gourmet Kama, 20 Bridge St. (☎575 754). This authentic Indian restaurant serves up hearty, spicy dishes in a traditional setting. Entrees £7-10. Takeaway available. Open daily noon-midnight. MC/V. ❷

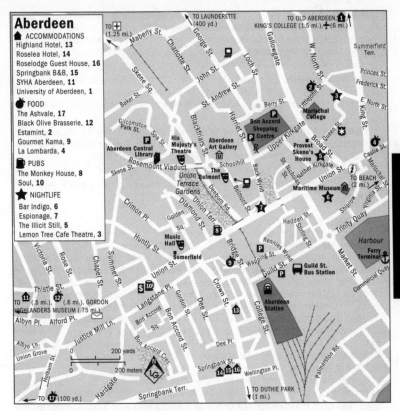

Aberdeen

ACCOMMODATIONS
Highland Hotel, 13
Roselea Hotel, 14
Roselodge Guest House, 16
Springbank B&B, 15
SYHA Aberdeen, 11
University of Aberdeen, 1

FOOD
The Ashvale, 17
Black Olive Brasserie, 12
Estamint, 2
Gourmet Kama, 9
La Lombarda, 4

PUBS
The Monkey House, 8
Soul, 10

NIGHTLIFE
Bar Indigo, 6
Espionage, 7
The Illicit Still, 5
Lemon Tree Cafe Theatre, 3

HIGHLANDS AND ISLANDS

Estamint, 7 Littlejohn (☎ 622 657). Serves up spicy tapas (£3-4) and tasty entrees (£6-8). University trendy, with leather couches and foosball table. Popular bar after 10pm. Open M-Th and Su noon-2am, F-Sa noon-3am. Food served noon-10pm. MC/V. ②

🎵📷 ENTERTAINMENT AND NIGHTLIFE

Seagulls aren't the only things to listen to in Aberdeen; the city comes alive at night with music from opera to trip-hop. Obtain tickets and information from the **Aberdeen Box Office,** next to the Music Hall. (☎ 641 122. Open M-Sa 9:30am-6pm.) The **Music Hall,** on Union St., features pop bands, musicals, and orchestra recitals (☎ 632 080; www.musichallaberdeen.com). **His Majesty's Theatre,** Rosemount Viaduct, hosts dance, opera, ballet, and theater (☎ 641 122; www.hmtheatre.com). The **Aberdeen Arts Centre,** 33 King St., stages avant-garde and traditional plays year-round. (☎ 641 122; www.aberdeenartscentre.org.uk. Tickets £7.50-9, concessions £5-7.) Catch the latest independent flick at **The Belmont Picture House,** 49 Belmont St. (☎ 343 536; tickets £3.70-6.10). **Estamint,** listed under Food (above), turns into a nightspot.

Lemon Tree Cafe Theatre, 5 West-North St. (☎ 642 230; www.lemontree.org), near Queen St. Serves food and drink in front of its mainstage. Tickets £9-12, concessions £6-8. Hours vary depending on show or event; check website or call ahead. Box office open M 11am-6pm, Tu-Sa 10am-6pm, Su noon-4pm.

Soul, 333 Union St. (☎211 150). A posh club with distinctive dishes—splurge on the fondant with Irn Bru sorbet (£4). In a converted church with stained glass windows and pulpit turned into a DJ area. Free wireless Internet access. Turns into club at 10pm; wear your best or be disappointed at the door. Entrees £5-8. Open M-Th and Su 10am-midnight, F-Sa 10am-1am. Food served noon-9:30pm. MC/V.

The Monkey House, 1 University Terr. (☎251 120). Pub-fare restaurant and upscale club. Lofty ceilings and prices (entrees £8-13), but packed and friendly. Open M-Th and Su noon-midnight, F-Sa noon-1am. Food served M-F noon-8:30pm, Sa-Su noon-9:30pm. MC/V.

Espionage, 120 Union St. (☎561 006; www.espionage007.co.uk). Enjoy a martini (shaken, not stirred; £5), at this popular themed club. 3 floors resembling different Bond film scenes. Open M-Th and Su 007pm-2am, F-Sa 007pm-3am.

Bar Indigo, 20 Adelphi Ln. (☎586 949), off Union St. by the TIC. Popular gay venue, with an intense, smoky dance floor and great harbor view. F-Sa cover £3. Open M-Th 5pm-2am, F-Sa 5pm-3am, Su 8pm-2am.

◉ SIGHTS

The **Aberdeen Art Gallery,** on Schoolhill, houses rotating exhibits of striking 20th-century art and older British works. (☎523 681. Open M-Sa 10am-5pm, Su 2-5pm. Free.) The **Maritime Museum,** on Shiprow, provides a comprehensive history of Aberdeen's long affair with the sea, from whaling to drilling for oil. (☎337 700. Open M-Sa 10am-5pm, Su noon-3pm. Free.) Just up Broad St., **Provost Skene's House,** 45 Guestrow, is one of the few 17th-century Aberdonian mansions that has escaped demolition. Its rare and mysterious **Painted Gallery** boasts grand, if undistinguished, depictions of the life of Christ. (☎641 086. Open M-Sa 10am-5pm, Su 1-4pm. Free.) Across the street, inside the deceptively slender Gothic facade of **Marischal College,** the **Marischal Museum** chronicles northeast Scotland's history. (☎274 301. Open M-F 10am-5pm, Su 2-5pm. Free.)

Aberdeen's architecture, though uniform to the untrained eye, ranges in age from the very old to the even older. **Old Aberdeen** and **King's College,** a short bus ride (#1, 2, 5, or 15) from the city center or a long walk along King St., have beautiful gothic buildings. Stop at the **Chapel** to see the 16th-century "misery seats"; students were forced to sit on the un-orthopedic chairs for hours. (☎272 137. Open daily 9am-4:30pm. Tours July-Aug. Su 2-5pm. Free.) Stroll around the 11-acre **Cruikshank Botanic Gardens,** St. Machar Dr. (☎493 288. Open May-Sept. M-F 9am-4:30pm, Sa-Su 2-5pm; Oct.-Apr. M-F 9am-4:30pm. Free.) Continue up High St. as it turns into Chanonry to find the 14th-century **St. Machar's Cathedral,** with its stained glass and coffins. (☎485 988; www.stmachar.com. Open daily 9am-5pm. Services Su 11am and 6pm.) After visiting, take a walk through **Seaton Park,** where the **Brig O' Balgownie**—a gift from Robert the Bruce—spans the River Don.

At the other end of town lies **Duthie Park** (DA-thee), by the River Dee at Polmuir Rd. and Riverside Dr. and accessible by bus #16 and 17. The expanse sports an extensive rose garden and the **Winter Gardens Hothouse,** home to enormous bougainvillea, hibiscus, and thistle. (☎585 310. Hothouse open daily May-Aug. 9:30am-7:30pm; Apr. and Sept.-Oct. 9:30am-5:30pm; Nov.-Mar. 9:30am-4:30pm. Free.) The **Gordon Highlanders Museum,** Viewfield Rd., displays the pomp, circumstance, and heroism of the kilted fighting regiment in a 15min. film and exhibit. (Walk down Queens Rd. or take bus #14 or 15 from Union St. ☎311 200; www.gordonhighlanders.com. Open Apr.-Oct. Tu-Sa 10:30am-4:30pm, Su 1:30-4:30pm. £2.50.) Aberdeen's long, sandy **beach** stretches 2 mi. north from city's edge and has an amusement park in the north, a promenade in the center, and golf at the end.

▣ DAYTRIPS FROM ABERDEEN: THE GRAMPIAN COAST

Make your way north or south from Aberdeen to encounter two of Scotland's spectacular castles—one in glorious cliffside ruin, the other intact, nestled inland, and straight out of a fairy tale. The rugged cliffs and picturesque hillocks of the Grampian coast afford many spots perfect for picnicking by the tempestuous surf.

▩ **DUNNOTTAR CASTLE.** The breathtaking, extensive ruins of Dunnottar Castle (dun-AHT-ur) stand at the edge of a cliff. Built in the 14th century, this mighty fortress has experienced infamous cruelty, intrigue, and war. Here Presbyterians were imprisoned in the Reformation, the crown jewels of Scotland were stolen during Cromwell's reign, and **William Wallace** burned an English garrison. *(Trains (20min., 1-2 per hr.) and Bluebird Northern buses #107 and 117 (1hr., 2 per hr.) connect Aberdeen to Stonehaven. 30min. walk south from town; follow signs. ☎01569 762 173. Open Easter to Oct. M-Sa 9am-6pm, Su 2-5pm; Nov. to Easter M-F 9am-dusk. £4, children £1.)*

▩ **FYVIE CASTLE.** Northwest on the A947, 25 mi. from Aberdeen, the 13th-century Fyvie remains intact despite its cursed status. A ghost called the "Green Lady" (who appears in about 10 other Scottish castles) likes to tap visitors on the shoulder. The lived-in interior contains a collection of tapestries and paintings, including a spectacular set of Raeburns and Gainsboroughs, while the striking exterior is adorned with five turrets—one added by each family that has owned the castle since the 14th century. *(Stagecoach Bluebird (☎01224 212 266) #305 runs from Aberdeen (1hr., every hr.). ☎01651 891 266. Open July-Aug. daily 11am-5pm; Easter to June M-W and Sa-Su noon-5pm. Last admission 4:15pm. Grounds open daily 9:30am-dusk. £8, concessions £5, families £20.)*

BRAEMAR ☎01339

Situated on the River Dee, 60 mi. west of Aberdeen, Braemar is the southern gateway to the Cairngorms and an excellent base for seeing the Royal Deeside.

▣ **TRANSPORTATION.** The only way into and out of Braemar by public transportation is the Stagecoach (☎08706 082 608) **bus** from Aberdeen (#201; 2¼hr.; 6-7 per day; £11), which stops at Crathie for Balmoral 15min. away. Drivers can reach Braemar en route from Perth or Aberdeen on the A93.

▣ **PRACTICAL INFORMATION. Rent bikes** from the Mountain Sports Shop, Invercauld Rd., at the town's eastern edge. (☎741 242. Bikes £15 per day, skis £16. Open daily 9am-6pm.) The **Tourist Information Centre,** on Mar Rd., at the Mews, efficiently finds you places to sleep, shows you where to hike, and can change your currency. (☎741 600. Open daily July-Aug. 9am-6:30pm; Mar.-June and Sept. M-Sa 10am-5pm, Su noon-5pm; Nov.-Feb. M-Sa 10:30am-4:30pm, Su noon-4:30pm.) The **post office** can be found in the Alldays Co-op, across from the TIC (☎741 201; open M-W and F 9am-noon and 1-5:30pm, Th 9am-1pm). **Post Code:** AB35 5YL.

▣▣ **ACCOMMODATIONS AND FOOD.** The **Rucksacks Bunkhouse ❶,** 15 Mar Rd., behind the TIC, is a warm, friendly hostel with a great kitchen. (☎741 517. Laundry £2. Internet access £1 per hr. Dorms £10; bunks £7. Cash only.) The forest-surrounded, 64-bed **SYHA Braemar ❷,** 21 Glenshee Rd., occupies a stone house 5min. south of town. Relax in the house and fear not the 11:30pm curfew—most of Braemar is closed by then. (☎741 659. Reception 7-10:30am and 5-11pm. Dorms £10.50-12.50, under 18 £8-8.75. MC/V.) Smell the pine in the all-wood, shotgun-style **Braemar Lodge Bunkhouse ❶,** 6 Glenshee Rd., behind the hotel of the same name.

The Bunkhouse has comfortable, traditional mountain lodging for 12, with home-cooked breakfasts (£6.50) and a self-catering kitchen. (☎741 627. Dorms £11. Cash only.) The **SYHA Inverey ❶**, Linn of Dee Rd., 4 mi. from Braemar, is a good place to spend the night if hiking Ben Macdui. The daily postbus stops at the hostel before swinging by the Linn. (☎01339 741 969. No showers. Open May to Oct. Dorms £11.75, under 18 £8. MC/V.) The elegant **Callater Lodge ❸**, 9 Glenshee Rd., has leather couches and fine china that almost seem out of place in rugged Braemar. (☎741 275. £28-30 per person. MC/V.) Stock up at the Alldays Co-op **supermarket.** (☎41 201. Open M-Sa 7:30am-9pm, Su 8:30am-7pm. Cash only.)

◨ ◪ SIGHTS AND HIKING. On the first Saturday in September, the town hosts the ◪**Braemar Gathering,** part of the Highland Games. In this 900-year-old tradition, athletes compete in events like caber-tossing, pipers entertain, and Her Majesty's military forces take part in an inter-services tug of war. (☎755 377; www.braemar-gathering.org. Seats £13-15; field admission £7. Book seating in advance.) Make sure to stop at the 17th-century Braemar Castle even if you decide to skip the tour of its "treasures," including a 19th-century fire escape (read: rope and pulley) and several taxidermied animals. (☎741 219. Open Easter to June and Sept.-Nov. M-Th and Su 10am-5:30pm; July-Aug. daily 10am-5:30pm. £4.)

The area around Braemar has hikes for all skill levels, centering around the frothy **Linn of Dee.** Along the river, the leisurely 2hr. round-trip **Derry Lodge Walk** promises sightings of red deer, red squirrels, and grouse. The more challenging **Lairig Ghru Trail** also starts at the Linn but stretches 20 mi. north to Aviemore. The name means "gloomy pass," which is accurate—the desolate path winds between steep mountainsides and past snow-covered **Ben Macdui.** It's also difficult, so don't overestimate your ability or underestimate your need for a map (Ordnance Survey #43; £6.50; ask for other applicable maps at the TIC). To get to the Linn, drive 20min. west of Braemar on the Linn of Dee Rd. or catch the daily **postbus** from the Braemar post office between 1:30 and 2:30pm (no round-trip); check at the TIC. Otherwise, walk or bike the scenic 7 mi. alongside the Linn of Dee Rd. Hikers should start early to finish the Lairig Ghru in one day.

▣ DAYTRIPS FROM BRAEMAR: ROYAL DEESIDE

The River Dee winds from Aberdeen to Braemar through a castle-studded valley of lofty pines and lush glens. The Cairngorms lie to the east and the hills of the Highlands to the north and south. Queen Victoria made this her Scottish retreat, and tourists have followed suit. These sights can be accessed on the A93 or by Stagecoach (☎08706 082 608) bus #201.

BALMORAL CASTLE AND ESTATE. An hour along the A93 from Braemar, Balmoral Castle and Estate rests on the southern side of the River Dee. The Queen's holiday palace, Balmoral was a gift to Queen Victoria from Prince Albert. The traversable landscape is fittingly majestic and worth a stroll, but, as a royal residence, only the ballroom and its exhibits are open to the public. (☎01339 742 534; www.balmoralcastle.com. Open daily Apr.-July 10am-5pm. Audio tour £6, under 16 £1, seniors £5. 2hr. pony treks 9:30am and 1:30pm. 12+. £30.)

DRUM CASTLE. The modest and pleasantly under-touristed Drum Castle sits two hours down the A93 from Braemar. Drum looks, feels, and actually is ancient, inhabited continuously from 1323 to 1975. A long driveway leads to the magnificent edifice and its **Garden of Historic Roses,** a collection of flowers that has been cultivated for over 400 years. (☎01330 811 204. Open daily June-Aug. 10am-5:30pm; Apr.-May and Sept. 12:30-5:30pm. Grounds open daily 9:30am-dusk. £8, concessions £5, families £20. Grounds and garden only £2.50/1.80/5.)

CRATHES CASTLE. Crathes Castle is a fine example of a 16th-century manor, with overhanging turrets and round towers. Grand but not extravagant, with brilliant painted ceilings, the castle contains curiosities like the Horn of Leys, a 1323 gift from Robert the Bruce, and a "trip step" designed to bungle burglars. Another "Green Lady" allegedly haunts this castle (p. 609), perhaps contributing to the superlative **gardens,** whose blooms deck alcoves and hedge-lined passages. (☎01330 844 525. Castle open daily Apr.-Sept. 10am-5:30pm; Oct. 10am-4:30pm. Last admission 45min. before close. Garden open daily 9am-sunset. Castle £8, concessions £5. Castle and garden £10, concessions £7, families £25.)

CAIRNGORM MOUNTAINS   ☎01479

At the center of the greater Grampian Mountain range, in Britain's largest national park, stand the awesome Cairngorms. Misty, mighty, and arctic even in summer, these rugged peaks provide both hard-core "Munro Bagger" expeditions and accessible short day excursions. The peaks are bare, covered only with heather, reindeer, and snow for much of the year. In addition to winter sports, the Cairngorms offer stellar hiking, climbing, biking, and horseback riding.

⌐ TRANSPORTATION

The largest town in the Cairngorms, **Aviemore** is located on the main Inverness-Edinburgh rail and bus lines. The **train station** is on Grampian Rd., just south of the TIC. (☎08457 484 950. Open M-F 7:30am-9:25pm, Sa 7:35am-2:40pm, Su 9:55am-5:35pm.) **Trains** arrive from Edinburgh and Glasgow (both 2hr., 3-5 per day, £33.20) and Inverness (45min., 5-7 per day, £8). Southbound **buses** stop at the shopping center north of the train station, northbound buses at the Cairngorm Hotel. Scottish Citylink (☎08705 505 050) runs every hour from Edinburgh (3hr., £14.80), Glasgow (3½hr., £14.80), and Inverness (40min., £5.50). **Kincraig,** 6 mi. south of Aviemore on the A9, is accessible by Scottish Citylink #957 from Perth (2 per day). For updates and detailed information, call Traveline (☎08706 082 608).

The principal path into Glenmore Forest Park, the Ski Road, begins south of Aviemore (on B970) and jogs eastward. The road passes the sandy beaches of **Loch Morlich** before carrying on to **Glenmore** and ending at the base of mighty **Cairn Gorm.** From Aviemore's train station, Highland Country #31 travels the same route (every hr.). The Cairngorm Service Station, on Aviemore's Main St., **rents cars.** (☎810 596. £36-42 per day, £190-210 per week. Open M-F 8:30am-5pm.) For **bike rental,** head to Bothy Bikes, Grampian Rd. (☎810 111. £10 per half-day, £15 per day. Open daily 9am-5pm. MC/V.) Ellis Brigham, two doors down from the TIC on Grampian Rd., **rents skis** during the winter and climbing equipment during the summer. (☎810 175. Open daily 9am-6pm.) The Glenmore Shop and Cafe, opposite the SYHA Cairngorm in Glenmore, rents bikes, skis, snowboards, and mountainboards. (☎861 253. Bikes £9 per half-day, £15 per day. Open daily 9am-5pm.)

⚑ ⚐ ORIENTATION AND PRACTICAL INFORMATION

Britain's busiest ski village in the winter, **Aviemore** remains invaluable to tourists in the summer, offering accommodations, amenities, and a prime location from which to explore the surrounding region. **Glenmore** offers an up-close view of the range, and **Kincraig,** though farther away, sustains visitors with a welcome breath of non-touristed air on the tranquil shores of **Loch Insh.** Smaller towns like **Boat-of-Garten** also offer places to stay, often at lower rates, and are worth a look.

THE HIDDEN DEAL

RUDOLPH, THE SCOT, AND OTHER ANIMALS

Britain's only reindeer herd was established in 1952 by a Swedish reindeer herder, who thought the arctic conditions of the Cairngorm mountains would be ideal for the gentle lichen-eating grazers. The ·Cairngorm Reindeer Centre offers visitors the opportunity to hike up to the free-range herd and interact. Visitors can hand-feed grain to the cheeky, awkward-looking yearlings and Christmas-card-ready bulls. There is also a petting paddock behind the center. *(Glenmore, 6 mi. from Aviemore, by the funicular.* ☎ *01479 861 228. Open daily 10am-5pm. Visits to the herd daily May-Sept. 11am and 2:30pm; Oct.-Apr. 11am. Free-range herd £8, children £4. Paddock £2/£1. Hiking boots recommended.)*

Neil Ross of Leault Farm directs a flock of 16 dogs around an unruly flock of sheep with just one whistle. Neil won the 1995 National Brace Championships, among other herding accolades—to watch him work his dogs is inspiring. After herding, visitors can help shear a sheep the old-fashioned way, bottle-feed orphaned lambs, and watch Neil hone his pups' herding instincts. *(Leault Farm, Kincraig, 10min. south of Aviemore on the B9152.* ☎ *01540 651 310. Demonstrations May-June and Sept.-Oct. M-F, Su noon, 4pm; July-Aug. M-F, Su noon, 2, 4pm; Nov.-Apr. call ahead. £4.)*

The **Aviemore and Spey Valley Tourist Information Centre,** on Grampian Rd.,books B&Bs for a £3 charge plus a 10% deposit, sells bus tickets, and exchanges currency. (☎ 810 363. Open July to mid-Sept. M-Sa 9am-6pm, Su 9:30am-4pm; mid-Sept. to June M-F 9am-5pm, Sa 10am-4pm.) The **Rothiemurchus Estate Visitors Centre** near Inverdruie, 1 mi. east on the Ski Rd. from Aviemore, sells a wide range of Highland gifts and provides information on tours and activities in the area. (☎ 812 345. Open daily 9:30am-5:30pm.) **Glenmore Forest Park Visitors Centre,** at the end of the Ski Rd. in Glenmore, offers maps and advice on walks west of the mountains. Travelers planning longer walks should stop there. (☎ 861 220. Open daily 9am-5pm.) Other services in Aviemore include: a **Bank** of Scotland, on Grampian Rd., across from Tesco (☎ 887 000; open M-Tu and Th-F 9am-5pm, W 9:30am-5pm); **police,** Grampian Rd. (☎ 810 222); free **Internet access** at Aviemore **Library,** Grampian Rd., behind the bank (☎ 811 113; open Tu 2-5 and 6-8pm; W 10am-12:30pm, 2-5, and 6-8pm; F 10am-12:30pm and 2-5pm); and the **post office,** Grampian Rd. (☎ 811 056; open M-F 9am-5:30pm, Sa 9am-12:30pm). **Post Code:** PH22 1RH.

ACCOMMODATIONS

■ **Lazy Duck Hostel** (☎ 821 642; www.lazyduck.co.uk), on Nethy Bridge. Catch Highland Country bus #34 or 15 from Aviemore (20min., 6-9 per day). The cottage sleeps 6-8, and between the loft, garden, and wood burning stove, this little escape is pure Highland comfort. Call ahead. Dorms £9.50. Credit cards online only. ●

Glen Feshie Hostel (☎ 01540 651 323), 11 mi. south of Aviemore, 5 mi. from Kincraig. Call ahead for a lift from the station; otherwise it's a 9 mi. walk along Loch-an-Eilein. Homey atmosphere with loft dorms and a den-like common room close to numerous hikes. Breakfast and lunch £4, dinner £7-12. Porridge free. Dorms £10. Cash only. ●

Fraoch Lodge (☎ 831 331), on Deshar Rd. in Boat of Garten, 6 mi. northeast of Aviemore on the A95. Free pickup from Aviemore. Also home to a mountaineering outfit (www.scotmountain.co.uk) that's busiest in winter; you're apt to find pleasant privacy in summer. Dorms £10; doubles £28. Cash only. ●

SYHA Aviemore, 25 Grampian Rd. (☎ 810 345), south of the TIC. The usual SYHA amenities. 106 beds, 4-8 per room. Curfew 2am. Dorms £12-13, under 18 £5-13. MC/V. ❷

Insh Hall Lodge (☎01540 651 272), 1 mi. downhill from Kincraig on Loch Insh; take Highland Country bus #35 or 38 from Aviemore (15 min., 3 per weekday). A B&B, but think traditional mountain lodge with breakfast. Beautiful location right on the water. Use of watersports equipment is free with 2-night stay. Singles from £20.50. MC/V. ❷

SYHA Cairngorm Lodge (☎0870 004 1137), Glenmore. Catch Highland Country Bus #31 from the Cairngorm Hotel opposite the rail station and ask to be dropped off. Newly refurbished with Loch Morlich beach across the road. 7 mi. from Aviemore, 2 mi. from Cairn Gorm ski area. Family, double, and dorm rooms available in a secluded, timeless 2-story lodge. £11.50-13 per person, under 18 £5-13. MC/V. ❶

Camping:

Glenmore Forest Camping and Caravan Park (☎861 271), opposite the SYHA Cairngorm Lodge. Ample space and good facilities, with a beautiful mountain view. Crowded in summer. Open Dec.-Oct. £6-7.30 per person. MC/V. ❶

Rothiemurchus Camp and Caravan Park (☎812 800), 1½ mi. south of Aviemore on Ski Rd. Lacks Glenmore's view, but is closer to town. £5 per person. Cash only. ❶

▐ FOOD

Standard pubs and restaurants line **Grampian Road.** For **groceries,** the local Tesco is north of the train station. (☎08456 779 017. Open M-Sa 8am-10pm, Su 9am-6pm.) **Cafe Mambo ❷,** 12-13 Grampian Rd., has burgers (£7-8.50) and soothing hot chocolate (£1.60). If you've had one too many "fetish" cocktail pitchers (£12), stay to dance it off. (☎811 670. M-Sa noon-1am, Su 12:30pm-1am. Food served M-Th and Su until 8:30pm, F-Sa until 7:30pm. MC/V.) **Royal Tandoori ❶,** 43 Grampian Rd. offers a 10% discount on takeaway. Plus, the Bangladeshi joint stays open late by Aviemore standards. (☎811 199. Open daily noon-2pm and 5-11:30pm. MC/V.)

▲ ▓ HIKING AND SKIING

The Cairngorms have Scotland's highest concentration of ski resorts. Outdoors enthusiasts and snowbunnies converge at **CairnGorm Mountain** (on the mountain **Cairn Gorm**) for skiing. On the **funicular railway,** sit facing down the mountain for great views on the ride up to **Ptarmigan Centre,** Britain's highest train station (3600 ft.). Catch the peak of **Ben Nevis** to the west from the observation deck. Due to conservation concerns, railway-riders may not set foot outside the center. The only way to wander about the peak is to do it the old-fashioned way: by hiking from the bottom. Although a relatively short hike for such a splendid view (3hr. round-trip), certain trails up Cairn Gorm are steep and rocky. (Highland County Bus #31 from Aviemore. ☎861 261; www.cairngormmountain.com. Trains every 15-30min. Ticket office opens 9:30am. Trains 10am-4:30pm. **Funicular** £8.50.)

 SAFETY PRECAUTIONS. Although the Cairngorms rise only 4000 ft., the region can have the weather patterns of the **Arctic tundra.** Explorers may be at the mercy of bitter winds and unpredictable mists any day of the year. Many trails are not posted and trekkers must rely on a map, compass, good navigational skills, and basic common sense. Make sure to use an **Ordnance Survey map** (Landranger #35 and 36), available at the TIC. Explain your route to the staff to find out exactly which maps apply. Be prepared for **sub-freezing temperatures.** Leave a description of your intended route with the police or at the mountain station, and learn the locations of the shelters (known as bothies) along your trail. For more information see **Wilderness Safety,** p. 52.

To reach the peak of **Ben Macdui**, Britain's second highest at 4296 ft., take the **Northern Corries Path** from the carpark to its terminus, and navigate the unmarked route. Beware, this 7hr. undertaking is suggested only for experienced hikers. Be prepared for all weather, at any time of year, and bring a stock of food. The strenuous but shorter **Windy Ridge Trail** reaches the top of Cairn Gorm (3-4hr. round-trip). Before setting out, consult the helpful **Cairngorm Rangers** about trail and weather conditions and fill out a route plan sheet. (Office next to CairnGorm Mountain carpark. ☎ 861 703. Open daily 9am-5pm, weather permitting.)

The Cairngorm Rangers also host free **guided hikes.** For forest walks, **Glenmore Visitors Centre** has several trails; the most popular is the easy-going 3hr. **Ryovan Trek** through the woods and along **Green Lochen.** Closer to Aviemore, the daunting but renowned **Lairig Ghru** trail (p. 631) heads south through 20 mi. of lush valley to Braemar. This one's only for the bravest of souls, so make sure you have your Ordnance Survey Landranger map (#36; £7) and a full day's supply of stamina.

For **skiers,** a day ticket with a railpass at Cairngorm costs £26 (concessions £20). Several companies run ski schools and rent equipment; pick up a copy of *Ski Scotland* at the Aviemore TIC for details. Three miles west of the furnicular, the interactive **Cairngorm Reindeer Centre** is home to dozens of the majestic creatures. Visit them in the pen attached to the center, or take the trek to the hillside to hand-feed the free-rangers. The guides know all the reindeer by name and rotate the ones in the pen every few weeks. (☎ 861 228. Open daily 10am-5pm. Paddock viewing £2, concessions £1; trek to the herd £8, concessions £4, families £20.) The 269 acres of **Highland Wildlife Park** in Kincraig are dedicated to preserving native beasties. (☎ 01540 651 270; www.kincraig.com/wildlife. Open daily June-Aug. 10am-7pm; Apr.-May and Sept.-Oct. 10am-6pm; Nov.-Mar. 10am-4pm. Last admission 2hr. before close. £8.50, seniors £7.50, concessions £6, families £29.) The **Carr Bridge Pony Trekking Centre,** off Station Road in Carrbridge, offers a wonderful way to see the area on horseback, with 2hr. treks at 10am and 2pm (£25), a 1hr. trek at 4:30pm (£15). (☎ 01479 841 602. Call ahead for reservations and seasonal prices.)

ELGIN
☎ 01343

Elgin (whose "g" is pronounced as in Guinness, not gin; pop. 20,000) is a small town halfway between Aberdeen and Inverness. The ruins of **Elgin Cathedral,** nicknamed the "Lantern of the North," warrant a stopover. Once the largest of Scottish churches, the cathedral was looted and burned by the Wolf of Badenoch in the late 14th century, then further tormented by fire, Edward III, the Reformation, Cromwell, and the townspeople who carted off its stones. Half a millennium of neglect has reduced the 200 ft. towers to 90 ft., but they still allow a breathtaking view. (☎ 547 171. Open Apr.-Sept. daily 9:30am-6:30pm; Oct.-Mar. M-W and Sa-Su 9:30am-4pm. £3.30, seniors £2.50.) Next door, all 104 plants mentioned in the Good Book thrive in the **Biblical Garden.** (Open daily May-Sept. 10am-7:30pm. Free.) The **Elgin Museum,** 1 High St., in the city center, traces the history of the Moray area. (☎ 543 675. Open Apr.-Oct. M-F 10am-5pm, Sa 11am-4pm. £2, concessions £1.)

Unless you're prepared to camp, Elgin has few options for the budget traveler. The town is full of **B&Bs,** especially on the two blocks north of the train station. The splendid **Richmond Bed & Breakfast ❸,** 48 Moss St., has ensuite rooms, plush beds, soft linens, and a garden ideal for enjoying the northern summer. (☎ 542 561. Singles £30; doubles £48. Cash only.) Situated next to the Elgin Bowling Club, the Victorian **Auchmillan Guest House ❸,** 12 Reidhaven St., has a large selection of rooms furnished in a contemporary style. Guests can use the bowling lanes for a bargain £1. (☎ 549 077. Singles £30; doubles £45. MC/V.) If you have a tent, head to **Riverside Caravan Park ❶,** West Rd. (☎ 542 813. Open Apr.-Oct. £5 per person. Cash only.) For **groceries,** try Tesco, 99 Batchen St. (☎ 08456 779 792; open M-F 7:30am-

8pm, Sa 7:30am-6pm, Su 10am-5pm). Two-course lunches are only £3.50 at the **Thunderton House Pub ❶**, Thunderton Pl. (Off High St. ☎554 921. Open M-Th and Su noon-11pm, F-Sa noon-12:30am. MC/V.) **Scribbles ❶**, 154 High St., is a coffee house, ice cream parlor, and a pizza joint. The fancy pizzas (Peking duck £6.85) and waffle ice-cream cones (£1.20) are delicious. (☎542 835. Open M-Sa 9am-10pm, Su noon-10pm. MC/V.) **Quismat ❷**, 202-204 High St., has a voluminous menu of delectable Indian cuisine, from the common tikka to *sharabi*, which is made with Scotch. (☎541 461. Entrees £7.50-9. Open M-Sa noon-2pm and 5-11:30pm, Su 5-11:30pm. AmEx/MC/V.)

The **train station** is 5min. south of the city center, at the end of South Guildry St. (Ticket office open M-Sa 6:15am-9:30pm, Su 10:30am-5:30pm.) Trains (☎08457 484 950) hail from Aberdeen (1½hr., 10 per day, £12.40) and Inverness (45min., 11 per day, £8.20). **Buses** stop behind High St. and the St. Giles Centre. Stagecoach Bluebird (☎01343 544 222) buses #10 and 305 arrive at the **bus station,** on Alexandra Rd., across from the Town Hall, from Aberdeen (2¼hr., every hr., £8.10) and Inverness (1¼hr., 2 per hr., £8.10). Call Traveline (☎08706 082 208) for complete schedules and information. The **Tourist Information Centre,** 17 High St., books accommodations for a £3 charge plus a 10% deposit. (☎542 666. Open July-Sept. M-Sa 9am-6pm, Su 11am-4pm; Mar. and May-June M-Sa 10am-5pm, Su 11am-3pm; Apr. and Oct. M-Sa 10am-5pm; Nov.-Feb. M-Sa 10am-4pm.) Other services include: free **Internet access** at Elgin **Library** in Cooper Park (☎562 600; open M-F 10am-8pm, Sa 10am-4pm); the **post office,** 99 Batchen St., in the large Tesco (☎546 466; open M-F 8:15am-6pm, Sa 8:15am-4pm). **Post Code:** IV30 1BH.

🔖 DAYTRIPS FROM ELGIN

FORRES. A perennial winner of the cutthroat "Britain in Bloom" competition, the small town of Forres boasts the magnificent **Sueno's Stone,** a richly carved Pictish cross-slab viewable day and night in a locked glass case. *(Stagecoach Bluebird #10 and 305 make the 30min. trip to Forres, halfway between Elgin and Inverness. 2 per hr., £2.40.)*

LOSSIEMOUTH. Secluded Lossiemouth has two sandy, windswept beaches: **East Beach,** connected to the mainland by a footbridge, and **West Beach.** The hardy can body-surf the medium-sized waves; the sensible can picnic. Bus #328 connects "Lossie" to Elgin (20min., 2-3 per hr., £2). Halfway to Lossie, climb the ruins of **Spynie Palace** for a sweeping view of the countryside. Once the digs of the Bishop of Moray, the palace is the largest surviving tower house in Scotland. *(6 mi. north of Elgin on the A941. ☎01343 546 358. Open daily Apr.-Sept. 9:30am-6:30pm; Oct.-Mar. Sa-Su 9:30am-4:30pm. £2.50, seniors £1.90.)* Campers pitch tents under the watchful lighthouse at **Silver Sands Leisure Park ❶.** *(☎813 262; www.silver-sands.co.uk. Open Mar.-Oct. £6-15 per tent. MC/V.)*

THE MALT WHISKY TRAIL. The world-famous Speyside area has 57 working distilleries. The 62 mi. trail staggers past seven of them, all of which dispense free booze. *(Stagecoach Bluebird bus #10 covers Keith, Elgin, and Forres. Always tell the driver where you want to go. Day Rover ticket £11.)* The whisky trail starts at **Strathisla Distillery,** established in 1786 as the "home and heart" of Chivas Regal, and the Highlands' oldest working distillery. *(Just outside of Keith on the A95. ☎01542 783 044; www.chivas.com. Open mid-Mar. to Nov. M-Sa 10am-4pm, Su 12:30-4pm. £4.50. No charge—and no drinking—for those under 18.)* Bus #336 to Glenfiddich (glen-FID-ick) will stop on request at the **Speyside Cooperage,** where visitors can watch casks being handmade. *(¼ mi. south of Craigellachie on the A941. ☎01340 871 108; www.speysidecooperage.co.uk. Open M-F 9:30am-4:30pm. Last admission 4pm. £3.10, concessions £2.50.)* The world's most popular whisky is bottled at the **Glenfiddich Distillery** in Dufftown. The free, slick tour begins with the requisite cheesy video, but the guides and dram more than compensate. *(17 mi. south of Elgin. Take Bluebird bus #336 from Elgin (40min., every hr.) to the distillery. ☎01340 820 373; www.glenfiddich.com. Open Jan. to mid-Dec. M-F 9:30am-4:30pm; Easter to mid-Oct. M-Sa 9:30am-4:30pm, Su noon-4:30pm. Free.)*

TOMINTOUL AND THE SPEYSIDE WAY. The **Speyside Way,** an 84 mi. trail along the river from Buckie at Spey Bay to Aviemore in the Cairngorms, isn't for the weak. The trail branches off to the Highlands' highest village, **Tomintoul,** which is surrounded by the rolling hills of the **Glenlivet Estate.** *(Speyside Way Ranger Service, ☎01340 881 266. Consult the free and indispensable* Speyside Way Long Distance Route *pamphlet and* Land Ordnance *maps (£7-8) at the Tomintoul or Elgin TIC.)* The famous **Glenlivet Distillery,** Ballindalloch, is worth the 7 mi. hike from Tomintoul. Where its competitors' tours are professional and efficient, Glenlivet's is folksy and rambling. One's preference, like for the whisky itself, is a matter of personal taste. You can sample the malted barley, and, for £1, whisky-flavored ice cream. *(☎01542 783 220; www.theglenlivet.com. Open Apr.-Oct. M-Sa 10am-4pm, Su 12:30-4pm. £3, under 18 free.)* Restless backpackers can enjoy relative comfort at **SYHA Tomintoul ❶,** Main St., in a converted schoolhouse. *(☎08700 041 152. Open Mar.-Oct. £11.50, under 18 £8.25. MC/V.)* The resilient can **camp** on the Glenlivet Estate, half a mile from the TIC, where Main St. ends. *(Glenlivet Estate Ranger Service ☎01807 580 283. Free. Toilets available.)* If you're not driving, biking, or long-distance hiking, Tomintoul is difficult to reach. Roberts *(☎544 222)* **buses** run from Keith and Dufftown *(#362; Tu and Sa 1 per day)* and Elgin *(#363; Th 1 per day, £4).* The **Tourist Information Centre,** in The Square, dispenses information on trails and books rooms. *(☎01807 580 285. Open July-Aug. M-Sa 9:30am-6pm, Su 1-6pm; Apr.-June and Sept.-Oct. 9:30am-1pm and 2-5pm.)*

THE GREAT GLEN

INVERNESS ☎01463

Inverness is rightly termed the "hub of the Highlands." It's a departure point for those headed to Scotland's remote islands and wilderness and a great base for exploring nearby castles, hills, and Loch Ness. Split by the River Ness, the city is a fascinating mixture of old and new. A turn-of-the-century-style market and the many kilt shops stand alongside elegant, contemporary restaurants, a modern mall, and pubs and nightclubs packed with partying youth.

▣ TRANSPORTATION

Flights: Inverness Airport (☎01667 464 000; www.hial.co.uk), 9 mi. east of the city and accessible by bus (M-Sa every hr.). **British Airways** (☎08457 733 377; www.britishairways.com) flies from **Dublin, Edinburgh, Glasgow, London, Orkney,** and **Shetland.** EasyJet (☎08706 000 000; www.easyjet.co.uk) flies from London and Dublin.

Trains: Station on Academy St., in Station Sq. Travel center open M-Sa 6:30am-8:30pm, Su 9:15am-8:30pm. Luggage storage £3. Trains (☎08457 484 950) to: **Aberdeen** (2½hr., 10 per day, £20.70); **Edinburgh** (3½hr., 8 per day, £33.90); **Glasgow** (3½hr., 8 per day, £33.90); **Kyle of Lochalsh** (2½hr., 4 per day, £15.20); **London** (8-11hr., 1 per day, £103.50); **Thurso** (3½hr., 3 per day, £13.50).

Buses: Farraline Park Bus Station (☎233 371), off Academy St. Scottish Omnibuses sells tickets for most companies. Office open M-Sa 8:30am-5:30pm, Su 9am-5:30pm.

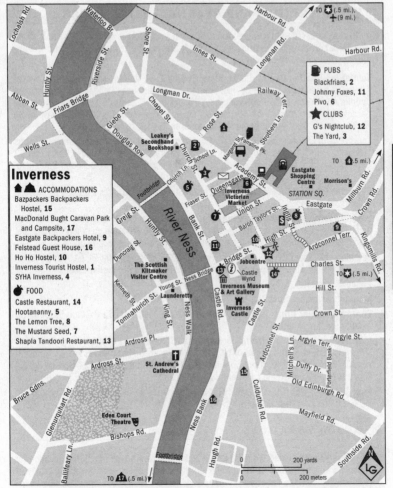

Inverness

▲■ ACCOMMODATIONS
Bazpackers Backpackers
  Hostel, 15
MacDonald Bught Caravan Park
  and Campsite, 17
Eastgate Backpackers Hotel, 9
Felstead Guest House, 16
Ho Ho Hostel, 10
Inverness Tourist Hostel, 1
SYHA Inverness, 4

🍴 FOOD
Castle Restaurant, 14
Hootananny, 5
The Lemon Tree, 8
The Mustard Seed, 7
Shapla Tandoori Restaurant, 13

📖 PUBS
Blackfriars, 2
Johnny Foxes, 11
Pivo, 6

★ CLUBS
G's Nightclub, 12
The Yard, 3

National Express (☎08705 808 080) to **London** (13hr., 1 per day, £39). Scottish Citylink (☎08705 505 050) to: **Edinburgh** (4½hr., every hr., £16.70); **Glasgow** (4hr., every hr., £16.70); **Kyle of Lochalsh** (2hr., 2 per day, £12); **Perth** (3hr., every hr., £12.20); **Thurso** (3½hr., 4-5 per day, £12.30). Both Citylink and Rapsons Coaches (☎01463 222 244) to **Ullapool** (1½hr., M-Sa 2 per day, £6.90-7.70).

Taxis: Inverness Taxis (☎222 900). Taxis queue by the Eastgate Shopping Center.

Car Rental: Budget (☎713 333; www.albacarhire.com) is on Railway Terr., behind the station. **Europcar** (☎235 525; www.northernvehiclehire.co.uk) has a Telfer St. office, though rates may be slightly higher. **Thrifty,** 33 Harbour Rd. (☎224 466; www.thrifty.co.uk) has delivery service to airport and a fleet of automatic vehicles.

Bike Rental: Barney's, 35 Castle St. (☎232 249). £7.50-8 per half-day, £11-12 per day. Open M-Sa 7:30am-10:30pm, Su 8am-10:30pm. Return bikes before dark.

HIGHLANDS AND ISLANDS

▄ 🔋 ORIENTATION AND PRACTICAL INFORMATION

The **River Ness** divides Inverness; most of what you need is on the east bank along **Bridge Street** and the pedestrian area of **High Street.** The train and bus stations are to the north on **Academy Street.**

Tourist Information Centre: Castle Wynd (☎234 353), up the steps toward the castle. The staff helps track Nessie by bus, boat, or brochure; books CalMac ferry tickets; and books non-hostel beds for £3 plus a 10% deposit. Bureau de change and Internet access (£1 per 20min., £2.50 per hr.). Open mid-June to Aug. M-Sa 9am-6pm, Su 9:30am-4pm; Sept. to mid-June M-Sa 9am-5pm, Su 10am-4pm.

Tours: Puffin Express (☎717 181; www.puffinexpress.co.uk) runs daily summer minibus tours to John O'Groats and several Scottish isles (£25-60). **Inverness Taxis** (☎222 900) leave from the TIC and give tours to nearby sights, including Culloden Battlefield. Numerous tours hit **Loch Ness** (p. 621).

Financial Services: Thomas Cook, 9-13 Inglis St. (☎882 200), has a bureau de change. Open M-W and F-Sa 9am-5:30pm, Th 10am-5:30pm.

Work Opportunities: Inverness JobCentre, 31-33 High St. (☎888 200 or 888 100) places temporary workers. Inverness revolves around tourism—in summer, the best bet for jobs is to go knocking on hostel, restaurant, and tourist attraction doors.

Launderette: New City, 17 Young St. (☎242 507). Wash £3, dry £1 per 15min. Open M-F 8am-8pm, Sa 8am-6pm, Su 10am-4pm. Last wash 1½hr. before close.

Police: Burnett Rd. (☎715 555).

Hospital: Raigmore Hospital, Old Perth Rd. (☎704 000).

Pharmacy: Super Drug, 12-22 High St. (☎232 587). Open M-Sa 8:30am-5:30pm, Su noon-4pm.

Internet Access: Library, Farraline Park (☎236 463), north of the bus station. Free. Photo ID required. Call ahead or be prepared to wait. Open M and F 9am-7:30pm, Tu and Th 9am-6:30pm, W 10am-5pm, Sa 9am-5pm. **Mailboxes, Etc.,** 24 Station Rd. £2 per 15min., £3 per 30min., £5 per hr. (☎234 700.)

Post Office: 14-16 Queensgate (☎243 574). Open M and W-Sa 9am-5:30pm, Tu 9:30am-5:30pm. **Post Code:** IV1 1AA.

🏠 ACCOMMODATIONS

▨ **Inverness Tourist Hostel,** 34 Rose St. (☎241 962). New hostel in an ideal location for travelers arriving by bus or train. Relax on the leather couches and watch a movie or football game on the flat-screen TV. May-Aug. dorms £11-14; Oct.-Apr. £10. MC/V. ❷

▨ **Bazpackers Backpackers Hotel,** 4 Culduthel Rd. (☎717 663). Home-like atmosphere and great views of the city from the barbecue area. Kitchen, fireplace, co-ed rooms, and clean bathrooms. No smoking. Reception 7:30am-midnight. Check-out 10:30am. Mid-June to Sept. dorms £12; doubles £28. Oct. to mid-June £10/24. MC/V. ❷

Eastgate Backpackers Hostel, 38 Eastgate (☎718 756; www.eastgatebackpackers.com), in the pedestrian Eastgate Precinct. 38 beds. Relaxed vibe in a fun hostel resembling an urban apartment. Dorms £9-11; twins £26-30. MC/V. ❷

Ho Ho Hostel, 23 High St. (☎221 225; www.hohohostel.force9.com), right in the middle of town. Simple lodging in a beautiful old building. Dorms £10-12. MC/V. ❷

Felstead Guest House, 18 Ness Bank (☎231 634; www.jafsoft.com/felstead/felstead.html). A great location along the eastern bank of the Ness River; 1min. south of the city center. Built by a lucky gambler, this 4-star B&B antes up spacious rooms, tartan rugs, and comfortable beds. £28-42 per person. MC/V. ❸

SYHA Inverness, Victoria Dr. (☎231 771). From the station, turn left on Academy St., go up Millburn Rd., and turn right on Victoria Dr. With card-swipe access, this high-tech hostel has an Orwellian feel. Lockers and kitchen. Laundry wash £2, dry 20p per 15min. Internet access £1 per 20min. Curfew 2am. Dorms £14, under 18 £12. MC/V. ❶

Camping: MacDonald Bught Caravan Park and Campsite, Bught Ln. (☎236 920). By the River Ness; easy to access from the A82. This manicured campsite has a host of amenities. Laundry wash £3, dry £3. Internet £1 per 30min. Open Apr.-Sept. £6 per 1- or 2-person tent, £3 per additional person. MC/V. ❶

 FOOD

Inverness is loaded with new restaurants and old pubs. Buy **groceries** from the colossal Morrison's, 15 Millburn Rd. (Follow Academy St. east and then north. ☎250 260. Open M and Sa 8:30am-8pm, Tu-W 8:30am-9pm, Th-F 8:30am-10pm, Su 9am-7pm.) Many of Inverness's pubs and bars have excellent food and many restaurants have good nightlife; see **Nightlife and Pubs** below for additional options.

🥘 **Hootananny,** 67 Church St. (☎233 651; www.hootananny.com). The place to be, whether you aim to drink whisky and stamp your feet to lively ceilidh bands or groove upstairs. Mouth-watering Thai food served downstairs (entrees £5-6). Upstairs Mad Hatter Club cover Sa £3. Downstairs open M-Th and Su noon-midnight, F noon-1am, Sa noon-12:30am. Mad Hatter Club open W-Th 8pm-1am, F-Sa 8pm-3am. MC/V. ❶

The Lemon Tree, 18 Inglis St. (☎241 114), north of High St. Cozy upstairs nook featuring sweet homemade goods and all-day breakfast (£3.25). Try the sweet orange lemonade (£1) or one of the fabulous soups (£2). Open M-Sa 8:30am-5:45pm. ❶

The Mustard Seed, 16 Fraser St. (☎220 220; www.themustardseedrestaurant.co.uk). With a wonderful view of the River Ness and poetry from Kipling enlarged on the wall, a perfect place to ruminate and enjoy a creative meal. Early dinner 5:30-7pm £12. Open noon-3pm and 6-10pm. MC/V. ❸

Castle Restaurant, 41 Castle St. (☎230 925). An American-style diner with red leather booths and waitresses in checkered maroon outfits. Enjoy a milkshake, cheeseburger, crinkly fries, and apple pie. Entrees £4-6. Open M-Sa 9am-8:15pm. Cash only. ❷

Shapla Tandoori Restaurant, 2 Castle Rd. (☎241 919). Enormous, sizzling Balti dishes (£7-9) and river views make this dining experience a sensual pleasure. Open daily noon-11:30pm. ❷

> **TIP** In Inverness, beware of an odd law that might give you an unexpected curfew. Although clubs and pubs often stay open until 2 or 3am, Highland Council law dictates that all patrons must be inside any liquor-selling establishment before midnight. Head out early, or be left out in the cold.

NIGHTLIFE AND PUBS

The pub/bar/cafe/club trend pervades Inverness; see Hootananny (**Food**) to start your night. The city's pubs pull an excellent pint, and visitors should try a whisky at one of the classic bars before testing the clubbing waters.

Blackfriars, 93-95 Academy St. (☎233 881). Purists will take heart: Scottish beer, Scottish whisky, and Scottish folk music. Open W-Th 11am-midnight, F 11am-1am, Sa 11am-12:30am, Su 12:30pm-midnight. Food served noon-9pm.

The Yard, 28 Church St. (☎713 005). Dance the night away to top 40 and early 90s hits with this young crowd. Open M-F 10am-1am, Sa 10am-12:30am, Su noon-midnight.

G's Nightclub, 21 Castle St. (☎ 233 322). Has great live music, but arrive early to avoid a long wait in the cold. Cover Th-Sa £3-6. Open W-Th 9:30pm-2am, F-Su 9:30pm-3am.

Pivo, 38-40 Academy St. (☎ 713 307). An addition to the Inverness international-themed pub and restaurant scene. Pivo's steely, trendy design and vodka drinks recall Eastern Europe. Entrees £6-7. Open M-Th 11am-midnight, F-Sa 11am-12:30am, Su 12:30pm-midnight.

Johnny Foxes, 26 Bank St. (☎ 236 577). An Irish bar near the main bridge. Draws a backpacker crowd. Entrees £6-8. M-Sa live music. Su karaoke. Open M-Th 11am-1am, W-Sa 11am-2am, Su 12:30pm-2am. Food served noon-3pm. MC/V.

◉ SIGHTS

The original wood **Inverness Castle** was built in the 12th century, captured by a vindictive Mary, Queen of Scots, and rebuilt in stone in 1726, only to be blown up by the Jacobites. The present castle was built in 1836; the 40min. **Castle Garrison Encounter** tries to fill the void by recreating life in 1745, complete with a swearing army sergeant. (☎ 243 363. Open Easter to Nov. M-Sa 10:30am-5pm. £5, concessions £4, families £14.) Down the hill, the **Inverness Museum and Art Gallery,** in Castle Wynd, has an enormous collection of Highland photographs, archaeological artifacts, and contemporary art exhibits. (☎ 237 114. Open M-Sa 9am-5pm. Free.) Browse the large collection of books and antique prints in **Leakey's Secondhand Bookshop,** at the northern end of Church St. in Greyfriars Hall. Enjoy a cup of tea with your new old read at the upstairs cafe. (☎ 239 947. Open M-Sa 10am-5:30pm. MC/V.) Across the river at Bridge St., the **Scottish Kiltmaker Visitor Centre,** 4-9 Huntly St., demonstrates plaid production and answers such burning questions as "how many pleats make it hang properly?" (At least 4. ☎ 222 781. Open mid-May to Sept. M-Sa 9am-9pm, Su 10am-5pm; Oct. to mid-May M-Sa 9am-5pm. £2, concessions £1.)

♫ ※ ENTERTAINMENT AND FESTIVALS

Dolphins are sometimes spotted on **Inverness Dolphin Cruises,** especially 3hr. before high tide (tidal information available at TIC). Boats leave from the Shore St. quay, downstream from the city center. (☎ 717 900. 1½hr. Mar.-Oct. 6 per day. £12.50.) In late July, strongmen hurl cabers (logs) during the **Inverness Highland Games** (☎ 724 262; www.invernesshighlandgames.com; tickets £5), while fife-and-drum bands dominate the **Inverness Tattoo Festival.** (☎ 242 915. £5-7.) In August, the **Marymas Fair** recreates 19th-century life with craft stalls and proletarian strife (☎ 715 760).

▶ DAYTRIPS FROM INVERNESS

Travelers may wish to invest in a Highland Country **Tourist Trail Day Rover** ticket, which allows one day of unlimited bus travel between Inverness, Culloden Battlefield, Cawdor Castle, and other sights. Buses leave from the Inverness bus station or Queensgate. (☎ 222 244. £6.) Car rental is a pricier option (p. 617).

▨**DUNROBIN CASTLE.** The largest house in the Highlands, Dunrobin offers an extravagant interior, elaborate grounds, and a spectacular perch above the sea. Though sections of the mansion date to the 14th century, most of the architecture is Victorian. Many of the castle's finest rooms are on display, and the grounds, modeled after Versailles, are dramatically situated. The castle still belongs to the Sutherlands, once the largest landowners in Europe. Its **museum** has a large collection of animal heads and other collectibles. Outdoors, the **Falconry Display** allows visitors the opportunity to have birds of prey fly overhead; a lucky few even get to handle the birds. *(300 yd. north of Dunrobin station, 1½ mi. north of Golspie. Train from Inv-*

erness 2hr., 2 per day, day return £13.90. Castle ☎01408 633 177; www.highlandescape.com. Open Apr.-June and Sept. to mid-Oct. M-Sa 10:30am-4:30pm, Su noon-4:30pm; July-Aug. M-Sa 10:30am-5:30pm, Su noon-5:30pm. Last admission 30min. before close. £6.60, students £6.) Dunrobin is a bit of a long haul from Inverness, and an all-but-impossible daytrip for those without cars. You can, however, bunk for the night at the simple **SYHA Helmsdale ❶**, in Helmsdale, right off the A9, 12 mi. from the castle and accessible by train and bus from both Dunrobin and Inverness. *(☎01431 821 577. Open Easter to Sept. Dorms £9.50, under 18 £8.)*

CULLODEN BATTLEFIELD. This field sits east of Inverness on the B9006. Wander around the heath where Bonnie Prince Charlie, charismatic but no genius in battle, lost 1200 men in 40min. A pretty 1½ mi. south, a grove hides the stone circles of the Bronze-Age **Cairns of Clava.** *(Highland Country bus #7 15min., every hr., round-trip £2.40. Visitor center ☎790 607. Open daily Apr.-May and Sept.-Oct. 9:30am-5pm; June-Aug. 9am-6pm; Feb.-Mar. and Nov.-Dec. 10am-4pm. Fields free. Centre £5. Guided tour £5.)*

CAWDOR CASTLE. The fairy-tale-like castle, complete with a drawbridge and garden maze, has been the residence of the Thane of Cawdor's descendants since the 15th century (long after Machabees, the best-known Thane) and is still inhabited for much of the year. The late Lord Cawdor IV detailed its priceless items in a series of witty signs. The gorgeous 1-5 mi. hikes through the forest behind the gardens are an added bonus. *(Between Inverness and Nairn on the B9090, off the A96. Highland Country bus #7 30min., every hr., round-trip £5; departs from the post office at Queensgate. ☎01667 404 401; www.cawdorcastle.com. Open daily May-Oct. 10am-5pm. Last admission 5pm. £6.80, concessions £5.80. Golf £8 per round.)*

MONIACK WINERIES. A 20min. tour explains everything you'd ever want to know about country wine and jam production. The tour culminates in an unlimited tasting of wines made from local flora, including elderflower and silver birch. *(7 mi. west of Inverness on the A862. ☎831 283. Open Apr.-Dec. M-Sa 10am-5pm; Jan.-Mar. 11am-4pm. £2.)*

LOCH NESS   ☎01456

The expansive loch and its famous resident draw thousands of tourists each year. In AD 565, St. Columba repelled a savage sea monster as it attacked a monk; whether a prehistoric leftover, giant sea snake, or product of an overactive saintly imagination, the **Loch Ness monster** has captivated the world ever since. The loch is 700 ft. deep just 70 ft. from its edge; no one has definitively determined how vast it really is, or what life exists at its bottom. The easiest way to see the loch is with one of the dime-a-dozen tour groups. **Jacobite Cruises,** Tomnahurich Bridge, Glenurquhart Rd., whisk you around any number of ways, on coach and boat trips. (☎01463 233 999. $8-20, includes castle admission.) Multiple **boat cruises** leave Drumnadrochit and tour Loch Ness for $8-20, including **Castle Cruises Loch Ness** (the Art Gallery; ☎450 695) and **Loch Ness Cruises** (Original Loch Ness Visitor Centre; ☎450 395), whose boats are equipped with underwater cameras.

In tiny **Drumnadrochit,** 13 mi. south of Inverness on the northwest shore of the loch, two visitors centers expound upon the Nessie legend. The **Original Loch Ness Visitors Centre** is steeped in Scottish lore. (☎450 342. Open daily 9am-9pm. $5, students $4.25.) The **Official Loch Ness Exhibition Centre,** with its 40min. visual display (available in 17 languages) gives the more thorough scientific version, explaining all the hoaxes; both have monstrous gift shops. (☎450 573; www.loch-ness-scotland.com. Open daily July-Aug. 9am-8pm; June and Sept. 9am-6pm; Oct. 9:30am-5:30pm; Nov. to Easter 10am-3:30pm. £6.) Three miles south on the A82 sits 🄰**Urquhart Castle** (URK-hart). One of the largest castles in Scotland before it was blown up in 1692 to prevent Jacobite occupation, the ruins now overlook the water of Loch Ness. Tours from Inverness stop at the ruins and multiple Nessie photos have been fabricated there. (☎450 551. Open June-Aug. daily 9:30am-6:30pm; Apr.-May and Sept. 9:30am-5:45pm; Oct.-Mar. M-Sa 9:30am-3:45pm. £6.) The **Great Glen Cycle Route** careens past the loch on its way to Fort William. The River Foyers empties into the loch in a series of waterfalls 18 mi. down.

Within walking distance of Loch Ness, the homey **Loch Ness Backpackers Lodge ❶**, Coiltie Farm House, East Lewiston, features cozy, cabin-like rooms, a TV room, friendly staff, and a warm fireplace. Continue along the A82 from Drumnadrochit just south to Lewiston, turn left at the sign beyond the gas station, and look for the white building with a gigantic Nessie mural. The lodge provides an entire wall of maps to get you to pubs and vistas, including to the 100 ft. **Divach Falls**, a lovely 1hr. walk from the hostel. (☎450 807. Continental breakfast £2. Internet access £1 per 20min. Dorms £11.50; doubles £28.) The more remote **SYHA Loch Ness ❶** stands alone on the loch's western shore, 7½ mi. south of the castle. (☎01320 351 274. Laundry £2. Internet access £1 per 20min. Reserve in advance July-Aug. Open mid-Mar. to Oct. Dorms £13, under 18 £10.75.) Both hostels lie on the Scottish Citylink bus routes between Inverness and Fort William (#919 and 917; every 2hr., £4.90 from Inverness). **Fiddler's ❷**, the Village Green, opposite the TIC, has pleasant patio seating, a huge selection of whisky (£3-6), and entrees (£7-15) one step above the usual pub fare. (☎450 678. Open daily 8am-9pm. MC/V.)

Scottish Citylink **buses** from Inverness to the Isle of Skye (#917; 3-5hr., 3 per day) stop at Drumnadrochit, Urquhart Castle, and Fort William (#919; 2hr., 6 per day). The Drumnadrochit **Tourist Information Centre**, located on the main road through the village, has all the information you need about tours, transportation, and lodging. (☎459 050. Open June-Sept. M-Sa 9am-6pm, Su 10am-4pm; Oct.-Apr. M-Sa 10am-1:30pm.)

GLEN AFFRIC AND GLEN CANNICH ☎01456

Full of hiking trails through dense pine forest, this remote area has been spared the throngs of tourists attracted by Nessie's tall tales. Various walks into Glen Cannich depart from behind the Glen Affric Hotel, beside the Cannich bus stop. A 4 mi. walk or bike west on the forest road out of Cannich leads to the trailhead for the popular **Dog Falls Walk** on the eastern edge of the **Glen Affric Caledonian Forest Reserve**. Passing by the waterfall, you'll get a good look at the heart of the 400-year-old pine forest, home to red deer, fox, adders, and otters. **Tomich** offers easier access to the more spectacular Glen Affric, including the breathtaking **Plodda Falls Walk**. Walk or bike 6 mi. east on the forest road out of Tomich to reach the trailhead. Your efforts won't go unrewarded—from a restored bridge spanning the gorge or from a viewing platform above the falls, watch the narrow cascades of Plodda Falls crash 100 ft. down into the gorge below. Ordnance Survey Map Landranger #25 will help you navigate successfully.

The antiquated **Glen Affric Backpackers Hostel ❶**, in Cannich, sleeps 70 in double rooms. The easygoing wardens are knowledgeable about the area. (☎415 263. Doubles £10. Cash only.) To ease into the wilderness or back to civilization, stay at the birthplace of the Golden Retriever, **The Kennels ❸**, 1 mi. west of Tomich on the road to Plodda Falls. The hotel has only one spacious room. (☎415 400. Dorms £22.50 per person. Book far in advance. Cash only.) Three miles farther west sits the basic but utterly charming **Cougie Lodge ❶**. Situated in a valley, and surrounded by ponies (available for treks) this small lodge is perfect for those looking to escape the tourist hordes. (☎415 459. Open Apr.-Sept. Singles £10. Cash only.) Farther in the same direction, the remote but popular **SYHA Glen Affric ❶**, Alltbeithe, is little more than a cabin, located where the trails to Tomich, Ratagan, and Clunie cross, roughly a 5 mi. hike from end of a dirt road. (SYHA central reservations ☎08701 553 255. No phone, showers, or garbage bin. Bring a sleeping bag. Open Apr.-Oct. Dorms £10.50, under 18 £8.50. Cash only.) The **Cannich Caravan and Camping Park ❶** rents **caravans** (from £165 per week) and **bikes.** (☎415 364; www.highlandcamping.co.uk. Bikes £10 per day. Open Apr.-Oct. £4, cars £1.) **Slater's Arms ❷**, on the northern end of Cannich, just down the road to Glen Affric, serves hearty meals, including Hungarian goulash (£8), to hillwalkers. (☎415 215. Open daily 9am-11pm. Cash only.)

The main access points for the glens are the villages of **Cannich**, at a turn in the A831, and **Tomich**, farther on; the towns don't offer much more than a point of entry. In summer, Rapson's (☎01463 222 244) **buses** run from Inverness to Cannich (#17; 1hr., M-Sa 2 per day), some extending to Tomich (M-Sa 2 per day). Purchase **groceries** at the Spar in Cannich, which contains the **post office.** (☎415 201. Spar open Apr.-Oct. M-Sa 9am-7pm, Su 10am-6pm; Nov.-Mar. M-Sa 9am-6pm, Su 11am-2pm. Post office open M-Sa 9am-noon.) **Post Code:** IV4 7LN.

FORT WILLIAM AND BEN NEVIS   ☎01397

In 1654, General Monck founded the town of Fort William among Britain's highest peaks to keep out "savage clans and roving barbarians." But the town's lofty location on the banks of Loch Linnhe caused his plan to backfire; today thousands of Highlands-bound hikers regularly invade Fort William. Despite the tourists, the town makes an excellent base for exploring some of Scotland's most impressive wilderness, including Ben Nevis.

▐ TRANSPORTATION

The **train station** is just beyond the north end of High St. **Trains** (☎08457 484 950) come from Glasgow Queen St. (3¾hr.; M-Sa 3 per day, Su 2 per day; £19.50) and Mallaig (1½hr.; M-Sa 4 per day, Su 1-3 per day; £8.10). The magnificent ▉West Coast Railways (☎01463 239 026; www.westcoastrailway.co.uk) Jacobite Steam train, currently billed as the "Harry Potter train" for its prominent role in the films, provides a spectacular alternate mode of transport to Mallaig. The rail line is a triumph of Victorian engineering, skirting some of Scotland's best rugged scenery. (Runs June-Oct. M-F; July-Aug. M-F and Su. Departs Fort William at 10:20am and Mallaig at 2:10pm. £19.50, round-trip £26.) The Caledonian sleeper train runs to London Euston (12hr., 1 per day, £ 99). **Buses** arrive next to the Morrison's by the train station. Scottish Citylink (☎08705 505 050) travels from: Edinburgh (4hr., 3 per day, £20.90); Glasgow (3hr., 4 per day, £14); Inverness (2hr., 7-8 per day, £8.80); Kyle of Lochalsh (2hr., 3 per day, £13.30); Oban (1½hr., M-Sa 2-4 per day, £8.40). Scottish Citylink/Shiel sends a bus from Mallaig (1½hr., M-F 1 per day, £4.25).

Locally, Highland Country Buses (☎702 373) travel around Fort William and the surrounding area. From June to September, #42 departs from the bus station and heads to the SYHA Glen Nevis and the Ben Nevis trailhead (10min.; M-Sa 7 per day, Su 4 per day; £1.30). Bus #45 runs to Corpach from the carpark behind the post office (15min.; M-Sa 3 per hr., Su every hr.; £1). **Taxis** queue outside the Tesco on High St.; try Al's Tours & Taxi (☎700 700). **Rent bicycles** at Offbeat Bikes, 117 High St. (☎704 008. £10 per half-day, £15 per day. Open daily 9am-5:30pm.)

⊞ ▐ ORIENTATION AND PRACTICAL INFORMATION

From the bus and train stations, an underpass leads to **High Street,** Fort William's main pedestrian avenue. The bustling **Tourist Information Centre,** Cameron Sq., books accommodations for a £3 charge plus a 10% deposit. (☎703 781. Open July-Aug. M-Sa 9am-6pm, Su 10am-4pm; Sept.-Oct. and Apr.-June M-Sa 9am-5pm, Su 10am-4pm; Nov.-Mar. M-Sa 9am-5pm.) Fort William keeps its droves of hikers well-outfitted with numerous **outdoors shops;** try Nevisport, Airds Crossing, at the north end of High St. (☎704 921. Hiking boots £3.50 per day plus deposit. Ski, boot, and pole rental £15-25 per day. Open daily 9am-5:30 pm.) Other services include: **banks** on High St.; **police** and the Lochaber Mountain Rescue Post, High St. (☎702 361); Belford **hospital,** Belford Rd. (☎702 481); Boots **pharmacy,** High St. (☎01463 715 555; open M-F 8:45am-6pm, Sa 8:45am-5:30pm); **Internet access** at One World, 123 High St. (☎702 673; £3 per hr.; open daily 10am-9pm) and the Fort William **library,** High St., across from Nevisport (open M and Th 10am-8pm, Tu and F 10am-6pm, W and Sa 10am-1pm); and the **post office,** 5 High St., with a bureau de change (☎702 827; open M-F 9am-5:30pm, Sa 9am-12:30pm). **Post Code: PH33 6AR.**

▟ ACCOMMODATIONS

Fort William's accommodations fill up quickly in summer. In town, hostels and **B&Bs** abound, with many streets consisting of nothing but the latter; try **Belford Road** or **Achintore Road.** For a more wooded setting, try just a mile or two outside of Fort William proper along the road through **Glen Nevis.** From the train station, turn left onto Belford Rd. away from the town center and follow the right fork at the roundabout to Glen Nevis.

▨ **Farr Cottage Lodge** (☎772 315), on the A830 in Corpach. Take Highland Country bus #45 from Fort William. One town over, this modern backpackers' lodge has a friendly, communal vibe. The perfect place to plan an outdoor adventure. Delicious full or continental breakfast (£2.50-5). Dorms £11-13; singles from £17. Discounts for longer stays. MC/V. ❷

Fort William Backpackers, 6 Alma Rd. (☎700 711; www.scotlands-top-hostels.com). From the train station, turn left on Belford Rd., right on Alma Rd., and bear left at the split. A fun and welcoming atmosphere. Watch the sun setting over Loch Linnhe from the back deck. 38 beds in 6- to 8-bed co-ed dorms; single-sex arrangements available. Self-catering kitchen. Breakfast £1.90. Laundry £2.50. Internet access 80p per hr. Curfew 2am. Dorms £11-14. AmEx/MC/V. ❶

Calluna, Connochie Rd. (☎700 451; www.fortwilliamholiday.co.uk), past the West End Roundabout; call for a lift. A self-catering, and spacious lodge with a modern wooden design. Stay longer in one of the two apartments or book a kayak or mountain trek with the owner, a local guide. 22 beds in 2- to 4-bed rooms. Dorms £10.50-12. MC/V. ❶

Achintee Farm B&B and Hostel, Achintee Farm (☎702 240; www.achinteefarm.com), across the river from the Glen Nevis Visitor Centre, 2 mi. from town on the Glen Nevis Rd. Walk or call for a lift. Ideal for exploring Glen Nevis, with large, comfortable rooms and a self-catering kitchen. 14 beds in 2- to 5-bed dorms. Lockable dorms; no lockers. Laundry available. Dorms £11-13; doubles £60. MC/V. ❶

SYHA Glen Nevis (☎702 336), 3 mi. from town on the Glen Nevis Rd. Walk or take Highland Country Bus #42. Backpackers' hub with ideal location—the front door opens up to the trail to Ben Nevis. 88 beds in 6- to 8-bed single-sex dorms. Self-catering kitchen. Laundry available. Internet access £1 per 20min. Lockout 9:30am-12:30pm. Curfew 2am. Dorms £11.50-13.50, under 18 £9-11.50. MC/V. ❶

Distillery House, North Rd. (☎700 103). From the train station, turn left on Belford Rd. and continue to the roundabout; the stately white house lies immediately beside the left fork. Enjoy breakfast and a dram of whisky while relaxing in a posh room. The fully equipped cottages are ideal for a longer stay. No smoking. Singles £38-45; doubles £76-90; self-catering cottages £70-95. AmEx/MC/V. ❸

Bank Street Lodge, Bank St. (☎ 700 070; www.bankstreetlodge.co.uk), just off High St. opposite the post office, above the Stables Restaurant. No-frills dorm accommodations with kitchen and TV lounge. 43 beds in 4- to 8-bed dorms. Lockable dorms; valuables locker. Laundry available. Dorms £12.50; singles from £15. AmEx/MC/V. ❷

Camping: Glen Nevis Caravan & Camping Park (☎ 702 191), 2½ mi. from town on the Glen Nevis Rd. Camp amidst the awe-inspiring Nevis Range in this 30-acre park with an informative staff. Toilets, showers, electricity, and laundry. Reservations July-Aug. Open mid-Mar. to Oct. £5.70-9 per tent plus £1.60-2.50 per person. MC/V. ❶

🌼🍖 FOOD AND PUBS

Grab **groceries** at Tesco, at the north end of High St. (Open M-Sa 8am-9pm, Su 9:30am-6pm.) Before heading to the hills, pick up a packed lunch (£3) and provisions from the Nevis Bakery, 49 High St. (☎ 704 101).

McTavish's Kitchen, 100 High St. (☎ 702 406). The Scottish equivalent of a luau in Honolulu: seriously touristy, but fun if you're in the mood. There's no missing the bagpipe show during dinner—even if you skip it, the sound reverberates down High St. Self-service entrees £4.50-7.50; dinner £10-16. Scottish show daily 8pm. Open in summer daily 9am-10pm; in winter 9am-6pm. MC/V. ❶

Crannog Seafood Restaurant (☎ 705 589), on the pier. Enjoy top-notch seafood. The dining room resembles the deck of a ship, right down to the star-like ceiling lights. Entrees £10-17. Open daily noon-2:30pm and 6pm until late. MC/V. ❸

Everest Indian Restaurant, 141b High St. (☎ 700 919). Escape the crowds down a small alley at this hole-in-the-wall restaurant overlooking the loch. With light, buttery *naan*, tasty vegetarian options, and friendly servers. Entrees £5.50-9. Open daily noon-2pm and 5:30-11pm. MC/V. ❷

Grog & Gruel, 66 High St. (☎ 705 078). The lively and always packed Grog has good Cajun and Tex-Mex cuisine and an excellent selection of beer. Entrees £6-10. Food served at bar noon-9pm, in restaurant 5-9:30pm. Open daily noon-10pm. MC/V. ❷

👁 SIGHTS

The breathtaking natural environment is Fort William's main attraction. For the shopaholic, High St. is Scottish souvenir heaven, abounding with Nessie dolls and modern kilts. Departing from Fort William's train station, ▧**The Jacobite,** a.k.a. the Harry Potter train, is a vintage steam-powered locomotive that travels 42 mi. to Mallaig as part of the fantastic **West Highland Railway.** (☎ 01463 239 026. Runs June and Sept.-Oct. M-F; July-Aug. M-F and Su. Departs Fort William at 10:20am. £19.50, return £26.) Two miles outside of town, on the A82 to Inverness, the **Ben Nevis Distillery** leads tours that conclude with a dram. (☎ 700 200. Open July to Aug. M-F 9am-5pm, Sa 10am-4pm, Su noon-4pm; Easter to June and Sept. M-F 9am-5pm, Sa 10am-4pm; Oct. to Easter M-F 9am-5pm. £4.) Hop aboard **Crannog Cruises** to scope out a local seal colony. Boat trips along Loch Linnhe leave from the town pier. (☎ 700 714; www.crannog.net. 1½hr. cruises depart Mar. to mid-May 11am, 2pm; mid-May to mid-Sept. 10am, noon, 2, 4pm. £7.50.) In nearby Corpach, **Treasures of the Earth** has an unexpectedly large collection of gemstones on display, even though your eye may be drawn to the hanging pterodactyl and mural of a T-Rex. (☎ 772 283. Open daily July-Sept. 9:30am-7pm; Feb.-June 10am-5pm. £3.50.)

⚡🏔 HIKING AND OUTDOORS

GLEN NEVIS. Just outside of Fort William, beautiful Glen Nevis runs southeast into the heart of the mountains. By far the biggest draw to the region and Britain's tallest mountain, **Ben Nevis** (4406 ft.) proves a challenging but manageable hike. The 10 mi. ascent is difficult more for its length than its terrain. Weather conditions can and do prove deadly to the unprepared. Pick up safety information from the visitor center, and be sure to inform someone of your route. The trailside waterfalls and views are breathtaking even in poor conditions. Expect to spend between 6 and 8 hours round-trip. The record, set in 1984 during the annual **Ben Nevis Race** (www.bennevisrace.com), is an incomprehensible 85 min. up and back. For those not planning on tackling Ben Nevis, venturing into the glen will provide spectacular views of mountains, gorges, rivers, and waterfalls. The drive up the glacial valley will bring you to some fine day hikes. At the end of Glen Nevis Rd., a popular 3 mi. walk heads to **Nevis Gorge** and **Steall Falls.** Follow a rugged path along a steep rocky gorge to a plain and you'll get a look at the breathtaking falls, even if you decide not to play Indiana Jones and pull yourself across the rope bridge at the three-quarter mark. Head to the **Glen Nevis Visitor Centre** to stock up on information and to get the latest area weather information. (☎ 705 922. Open daily Apr.-Sept. 9am-5pm.) Walkers will find the Pathfinder Guide #7 (£11) useful. Ordnance Survey Explorer #392 (£7) and Landranger #41 (£7) maps cover the entire area with a focus on Ben Nevis.

AONACH MOR AND THE NEVIS RANGE SKI AREA. Seven miles northeast of Fort William, along the A82 and on the slopes of Aonach Mor (4006 ft.), the Nevis Range is Scotland's highest ski area. Journey beyond the clouds, up 2150 ft., on the resort's gondola. (☎ 705 825. Open July-Aug. M-W and F-Su 9:30am-6pm, Th 9:30am-8pm; Sept. to mid-Nov. and mid-Dec. to June daily 9am-4pm. Weather permitting. Round-trip £8.) Highland Country buses #41 and 42 travel to Aonach Mor from Fort William's bus station (15min.; M-Sa 7 per day, Su 4 per day).

OTHER ACTIVITIES. The **West Highland Way** completes its 95 mi. track in Fort William. Hikers or cyclists hungry for more can venture another 60 odd miles along the **Great Glen Way,** which runs north to Inverness Castle. The 75p *Cycling in the Forest—The Great Glen* pamphlet breaks the route into 11 manageable sections and includes maps. Numerous adventure sports are offered around Fort William, from canyoning, abseiling (rapelling), and kayaking around the unreal **Inchree Falls** to river rafting and hang gliding in the Glen; check out ⚡**Vertical Descents** (☎ 01855 821 593; www.verticaldescents.com) to plan and outfit your adventure.

GLEN COE ☎ 01855

Surrounded by craggy mountains, the truly breathtaking enclosed valley of Glen Coe seems to glow a lush green. In 1692, the Clan MacDonald welcomed a company of Campbell soldiers, henchmen of William III, into their chieftan's home. The soldiers proceeded to murder their hosts, betraying the sacred trust of Highland hospitality. Every February 13, members of the Clan MacDonald gather as lone bagpipers play throughout the valley in commemoration of the massacre.

◧☷ TRANSPORTATION AND PRACTICAL INFORMATION. The valley is comprised of the villages of Glencoe and Ballachulish, which rest near the edge of Loch Leven, at the mouth of the River Coe. The A82 runs the length of the valley. Food and accommodations lie on a parallel road that winds from Ballachulish

through Glencoe. Scottish Citylink (☎08705 505 050) **buses** travel from Fort William to Glasgow (4 per day) and provide direct access to the valley. Highland Country bus #44 serves Glencoe village from Fort William (35min.; M-Sa 9 per day). Buses for Glen Coe stop at Glencoe village and down from the gas station.

South of Fort William, you'll find the **Tourist Information Centre** (☎811 866; open daily Apr.-Sept. 9am-6pm; Oct.-Mar. M-Sa 9am-5pm, Su 10am-5pm) just off the A82 in Ballachulish. Situated next to a former slate quarry, the center provides transportation information and good home-cooked fare in the adjoining cafe. Just off A82, 1 mi. southeast of Glencoe village, ◪**Glen Coe Visitor Centre** provides succinct, detailed information on a dozen mountain trails. To walk from the village to the center and avoid the highway, take the Woodland Trail, a short hike that passes by the ruins of one of the massacre homesteads. The center also features extensive displays on the history and topography of the area. (☎811 307. Open Apr.-Aug. daily 9:30am-5:30pm; Sept.-Oct. daily 10am-5pm; Nov.-Feb. M and F-Su 10am-4pm; Mar. daily 10am-4pm. Exhibit £5, concessions £4.) The Mace **market** (☎811 367; open in summer daily 9am-9pm; reduced winter hours) and the **post office** can both be found along the parallel road, just beyond the TIC. **Post Code:** PH49 4HS.

⌂⌃ ACCOMMODATIONS AND FOOD. Many of Glen Coe's accommodations are situated along or just off the minor road that runs 4 mi. up the valley to Glencoe village, roughly parallel to the A82. The **SYHA Glencoe ❶** rests 1½ mi. southeast of Glencoe village on this minor road. (☎811 219. 60 beds in 6- to 8-bed dorms. Self-catering kitchen, laundry, and Internet. Book in advance. Curfew 11:45pm. Dorms £11-13, under 18 £8.50. MC/V.) With a front lawn at the base of a mountain, the family-run **Clachaig Inn ❹** provides comfortable B&B lodging with spectacular views of nearby summits. Walk about 3 mi. along the minor road from the village or trace the A82 until the highway and river converge. (☎811 252. £38-42 per person. MC/V.) The **Glen Coe Caravan and Camping Site ❶**, next to the visitor center, is well-maintained, has a wide range of facilities, and is a good hiking base. (☎811 397. Toilets, showers, laundry, and cooking shelters. Open Apr.-Oct. £4.20-6.40 per person. Cash only.) Beside the River Coe, the **Red Squirrel Campsite ❶**, 1¾ mi. along the minor road from the village, just beyond SYHA hostel, is fine for those accustomed to roughing it. (☎811 256. £5.50 per person. Showers 50p. Cash only.) The Clachaig Inn is the place to go for food and entertainment. The restaurant is romantically lit; the lively **public bar ❷**, a traditional trail's-end pub, serves Scottish fare such as steak pie and venison burgers (£6-10). The Inn will also provide packed lunches (from £4.45) for hikers. (☎811 252. Open M-Th and Su 11am-11pm, F 11am-midnight, Sa 11am-11:30pm. Food served noon-9pm. Cash only.)

⛰⛏ HIKING AND OUTDOORS. Glen Coe offers excellent outdoor activities. Walkers stroll the floor of the valley; climbers head for the cliffs; in winter, skiers race down the slopes and ice-climbers ascend frozen waterfalls. Many of the trailheads lie several miles beyond Glencoe. With the right timing, you can use the Scottish Citylink **buses** that travel up the A82. For a small fee, most area hostels will shuttle hikers to the trailheads. Always bring a map; Landranger #41 (£7), Pathfinder Guide #7 (£11), and Short Walks #30 (£6) detail the area. Short but challenging daytrips abound. A 1 mi. trail leads to the base of the wooded and boulder-strewn **Lost Valley,** a hidden bowl where Clan MacDonald used to keep stolen cattle. In the upper valley, the **Two Passes** route (9 mi.) climbs some 2100 ft., passing through two U-shaped glacial scars. For serious climbing and hiking, ask rangers about route and safety specifics for ascending the **Three Sisters,** Glen Coe's signature triumvirate of peaks along the **Aonach Eagach Ridge.** Over the Pass of Glen Coe just off the A82, find ski fields and the **Glen Coe Ski Centre Chairlift.** During the winter, daily lift passes (£20-25) are available. (☎851 226. Open June-Aug. 9:30am-4pm, weather permitting. £5.) When the weather behaves, **Glencoe Cruises & Fishing Trips** (☎811 658) scud across Loch Leven, leaving from the pier in **Ballachulish.**

ROAD TO THE ISLES

The A830 travels from Fort William to Mallaig, following the historic Road to the Isles route (Rathad Iarainn nan Eilean). The drive to the coast captures the many landscapes of Scotland—rocky mountains, shady forests, and shallow lochs. Still single-lane in parts, the road often requires as much attention as the scenery. The ▨**West Highland Railway** (originating in Glasgow; p. 623) runs alongside the road, providing sublime views at a fast clip (3-4 per day, £8.10). In summer, **"The Jacobite"** steam train (p. 623) runs from Fort William to Mallaig (via Glenfinnan and the famous 21-arched viaduct) in the morning and back in the afternoon, stopping at towns along the way. (June and Sept.-Oct. M-F; July-Aug. M-F and Su. Departs Fort William at 10:20am and Mallaig at 2:10pm. £19.50, return £26). Buses make the same trip (1½hr.; July-Sept. M-Sa 1 per day, Oct.-June M-F 1 per day; £4.25.)

GLENFINNAN. The road runs westward from Fort William along Loch Eil, arriving after 12 mi. at Glenfinnan, on **Loch Shiel.** Trains often stop on trestle-bridged **Glenfinnan Viaduct.** A towering monument recalls Bonnie Prince Charlie's row up Loch Shiel to rally the clans around the **Stewart Standard** (see **The Jacobite Rebellion,** p. 519). For a panoramic view of the loch and the viaduct, visitors can climb a spiral staircase and stand atop the monument next to the statue of the Young Pretender. Look for gliding golden eagles as you drift on 2hr. **Loch Shiel Cruises** as far as **Acharacle,** at the loch's far shore. Trips depart from the Glenfinnan House Hotel. (☎01687 470 322; www.highlandcruises.co.uk. £12-18. MC/V.)
▨**Glenfinnan Sleeping Car ❶,** a railway-car-turned-hostel at the train station, provides unique lodgings. (☎01397 722 295. Food served from 8:30am. Linen £2. Dorms £10. Cash only.) For a twilight loch view, opt for pub grub at the **Glenfinnan House Hotel ❷.** (☎01397 722 235. Open M-Sa 11am-midnight, Su noon-midnight. Food served noon-9pm. MC/V.) The **Visitor Centre** provides pamphlets on local history, which you can read with a prawn sandwich (£3) in the **cafe ❸.** (☎01397 722 250. Open daily Apr.-June and Sept.-Oct. 10am-5pm; July-Aug. 9:30am-5:30pm. £3.) By **train,** Glenfinnan is 30min. from Fort William (£4.20) and 50min. from Mallaig (£5.30); by Scottish Citylink **bus,** the trips are both 30min. (£3).

ARISAIG AND LOCH MORAR. The road meets the west coast at the sprawling settlement of Arisaig. A popular spot for caravans and camping, Arisaig has patches of rocky beach with views of the outer islands. Stop at the volunteer-run **Land, Sea and Island Centre,** 7 New Buildings, for tide tables and other outdoor information. (☎01687 450 263. Open M-Sa 10am-3pm, Su noon-4pm.) Compact white beaches with hidden coves are 3 mi. south of town on the A830; from the Camusdarach campsite (below), follow the signposted path. A winding 5½ mi. walk west of the town center follows the banks of **Loch Morar,** Britain's deepest freshwater loch (1017 ft.), home to Morag, Nessie's cousin. Three miles south on the A830 from Arisaig, the placid **Camusdarach campsite ❶,** as well-groomed as the golf course around the corner, overlooks the beach. (☎01687 450 221. £8 per tent. Laundry £1. Showers free with £5 key deposit. Cash only.) The Spar on Main St. is the only **supermarket** between Fort William and Mallaig; inside is an **ATM.** (Open M-Sa 8:30am-6pm, Su 9:30am-5pm.) Dine on haggis (£2.40) as you surf the Internet at the **Rhu Cafe ❶** in Arisaig. (☎01687 450 707. Internet £1 per hr. Open M-Sa 9am-8pm, Su 10am-8pm.) MV Shearwater (☎01687 450 224) operates regular **ferries** and **day cruises** from Arisaig to Rum, Eigg, and Muck.

MALLAIG
☎ 01687

At the end of the road sits the port town of Mallaig (MAL-egg), where the railway terminates and ferries depart for the Inner Hebrides. Mallaig has few attractions of its own, but is a key transport hub to the Isles. Mallaig offers access to Inverie—the only mainland village disconnected from all roads—on the wild **Knoydart Peninsula**. From Mallaig, travel by boat.

Sheena's Backpackers Lodge ❶ fills its 12 beds quickly after early train and ferry arrivals. Turn right from the station; the bright, airy hostel is past the bank, above the Tea Garden. (☎ 462 764. Dorms £13. Cash only.) The **Moorings Guest House ❸**, East Bay offers harbor views. (☎ 462 225. £20-25 per person. Cash only.) Just up the street, the **Marine Hotel ❸**, Station Rd., provides a restful place for ferry stopovers. (☎ 462 217. Singles £35; doubles £60. MC/V.) The **Tea Garden ❸** at Moorings Guest House has a jungle of flowering plants and fresh fish (entrees £9-15; cash only). The **Fisherman's Mission ❶** is a muted cafeteria with tasty, inexpensive food. Get a full breakfast (£4.50) before you leave to avoid the ferry grub. (☎ 462 086. Open M-F 8:30am-10pm, Sa 8:30am-noon. Food served M-F 8:30am-1:45pm and 5:30-10pm, Sa 8:30am-noon. Cash only.) For delicious seafood, head to the **Fishmarket Restaurant ❷**, in front of the pier. (☎ 462 299. Open daily noon-9:30pm. MC/V.)

CalMac **ferries** (☎ 08705 650 000; www.calmac.co.uk) sail from Mallaig to Armadale, Skye (May-Sept. daily 8 per day; Oct.-Apr. M-Sa 8 per day. £3.25, 5-day round-trip £5.55; car £17.65/30.50) and to the Small Isles. Bruce Watt (☎ 462 320) runs ferries and **day cruises** from Mallaig along Loch Nevis to Tarbert and Inverie (June to mid-Sept. M-F; mid-Sept. to May M, W, F; £8-15). Just north of the pier, the Water's Edge **Tourist Information Centre** handles all tourist inquiries and has a free telephone for booking accommodations. (☎ 07876 518 042; www.thewatersedgetic.co.uk. Open M-F 10am-4pm, Sa 10:15am-3:45pm, Su 1:45-3:45pm.) Other services include: a **Bank** of Scotland by the train station (☎ 462 265; open M-Tu and Th-F 9:15am-1pm and 2-4:45pm, W 9:30am-1pm and 2-4:45pm); **Internet access** at the TIC (£2.50 per hr.) and in the Mallaig **Library** in the Mallaig Community Centre, at the top of the pier (☎ 460 097; open M 1-5pm, Tu 10:30am-2pm, W 9:30am-1:30pm, Th 5-8pm, Sa 10am-noon; free); and the **post office**, located in the Spar (☎ 462 419; post office open M-F 9am-5pm, Sa 9am-12:30pm; Spar open M-Sa 8am-10pm, Su 9:30am-9pm). **Post Code:** PH41 4PU.

THE INNER HEBRIDES

ISLE OF SKYE

From the serrated peaks of the Cuillin Hills to the commanding cliffs of the Trotternish Peninsula, the Isle of Skye possesses unparalleled natural beauty. Most visitors keep to the main roads and vast swaths of terrain remain empty. The islanders preserve the small towns by banning chain restaurants, stores, and shopping malls. Despite the summer throngs, travelers to Skye encounter a lively celebration of Scottish heritage in music, games, and storytelling. The isle's strong Scottish Gaelic (see Appendix, p. 705) influence is apparent in the prevalence of genealogy centers and the use of bilingual signs.

◩ GETTING THERE

The tradition of ferries that carried passengers "over the sea to Skye" ended with the construction of the Skye Bridge, which links the island to the mainland's Kyle of Lochalsh. **Pedestrians** can take either the bridge's 1½ mi. footpath or the **shuttle bus** (every hr., 70p). **Trains** (☎ 08457 484 950) reach Kyle from Inverness (2½hr.; M-

Sa 4 per day, Su 2 per day; £15.20). Scottish Citylink **buses** arrive daily from: Fort William (2hr., 3 per day, £13.30); Glasgow (6hr., 3 per day, £22); Inverness (2hr., 2 per day, £12). From the Outer Hebrides, CalMac **ferries** (☎08705 650 000) sail to Uig from Tarbert, Harris, and Lochmaddy, North Uist (1½hr.; M-Sa 1-2 per day; £9.40, 5-day round-trip £16.05; cars £45/77). Ferries also run to Armadale in southwest Skye from Mallaig on the mainland (30min.; June-Aug. daily 8-9 per day, Sept.-May M-Sa 8-9 per day; £3.25, 5-day round-trip £5.55; cars £17.65/30.50).

▐ LOCAL TRANSPORTATION

To avoid headaches, pick up the handy *Public Transport Guide to Skye and the Western Isles* at any TIC. On Sundays, buses run only to meet the Rassay and Armadale ferries (June-Aug.).

Buses: Highland Country buses traverse Skye. They are not necessarily timed to coordinate travel with other means of transport, or even other buses. The most reliable service is Scottish Citylink; bus #913 travels from **Kyleakin** to **Broadford** to **Portree** on the A87. The **Skye Rover** ticket offers unlimited travel on buses on Skye and can be purchased on any local bus (1-day £6, 3-day £15).

Bike rental: Cycling is possible and potentially enjoyable, but be prepared for steep hills, nonexistent shoulders, and rain. Most buses will not carry bikes. To rent bikes in Kyleakin, try the **Dun Caan Hostel** (☎01599 534 087; £10 per day); in Broadford, **Fairwinds Cycle Hire** (☎01471 822 270; £8 per day, £10 deposit for overnight rental); in Portree, **Island Cycles** (☎01478 613 121; £14 per day, discounts for longer rentals). Reserve ahead, especially in summer.

Car Rental: Kyle Taxi Company (☎01599 534 323) has a low delivery fee. 23+. £35-42 per day.

Tours: The **National Trust of Scotland** (☎01599 511 231) has 3hr. guided walks (£5) through the countryside and longer trips to the Three Sisters and the Falls of Glomach. Advance booking is required. For the eager and intrepid, the stellar ▨ **MacBackpackers Skye Trekker Tour** (☎01599 534 510), which departs from the hostel in Kyleakin, offers a 1-day tour emphasizing the mystical-historical side of the island (£18) or a 2-day, eco-conscious hike in the Cuillin Hills (£30). Weekly departure Sa 7:30am. For personalized treks, call **A1** (☎01478 611 112) in Portree. £25 per hr.

♫ ▨ ENTERTAINMENT AND FESTIVALS

Skye's cultural life is vibrant, with weekend festivals in summer. Snag a copy of the monthly *The Visitor* newspaper for a list of special events, or consult the TIC. Traditional music is abundant, especially in pubs. Dances to folk and rock music take place frequently in village halls. In mid-July, **Feis an Eilein** (☎01471 844 207), on the Sleat Peninsula, is a 10-day celebration of Gaelic culture, featuring concerts, *ceilidhs*, workshops, and films. Additional revelry can be found at the **Highland Games** (☎01478 612 540), a day of bagpipes and boozing in Portree on the first Wednesday of August, and **Highland Ceilidh**, with *ceilidhs* (p. 523) in Portree, Broadford, and Dunvegan. (☎01470 542 228. June M and W; July-Aug. M-W.)

KYLE AND KYLEAKIN ☎01599

Kyle of Lochalsh ("Kyle" for short) and Kyleakin (Ky-LAACK-in) bookend the Skye Bridge. Kyle, on the mainland, wishes travelers would dally—its slogan is "Kyle: Stay a While"—but the town is most often used en route to Skye. Though Kyleakin, across the bridge, is short on conveniences, it operates three hostels and countless tours, making it a backpacker's hub with a boisterous atmosphere.

⚡ TRANSPORTATION AND PRACTICAL INFORMATION. The Kyle **train station** is near the pier; the **bus stop** is just to the west. Highland Country buses meet incoming trains and head for Kyleakin (every 30min., 15p). The Kyle **Tourist Information Centre,** by the pier, has a free phone for accommodations booking. (Open May-Oct. M-F 9am-5pm, Sa-Su 10am-4pm.) Other services include a **Bank** of Scotland, Main St. (☎534 220; open M-Tu and Th-F 9am-5pm, W 9:30am-5pm) and a **post office** (☎534 246; open M-F 9am-5:30pm, Sa 9am-12:30pm). **Post Code:** IV40 8AA.

ⅱ ACCOMMODATIONS. In Kyle of Lochalsh, **Cu'chulainn's Backpackers Hostel ❶,** Station Rd., behind a popular pub of the same name, is a good stopping point for weary travelers with its especially cozy beds. (☎534 492. Laundry £2.50. Internet £2 per hr. Key deposit £5. Dorms £9-12.50. MC/V.) The comfortable **Kyle Hotel ❹,** Main St., provides traditional Scottish breakfasts. (☎534 204; www.kyle-hotel.co.uk. Singles £40-52; doubles £80-120. MC/V.)

In Kyleakin, hostels huddle near the pier. The friendly owners of ✉**Dun-Caan Hostel ❶** have renovated a 200-year-old cottage; enjoy a movie in the lounge or concoct a meal spiced with herbs from the garden. (☎534 087; www.skyerover.co.uk. Bike rental £10 per day. Dorms £11-12. MC/V.) The easygoing warden of the **SYHA Kyleakin ❷,** in the large white building on the village green, is a great source for outdoors information. (☎534 585. Laundry £3. Internet access £1 per 20min. Dorms £10.50-13, under 18 £5-13. MC/V.) Hang out in the comfy lounge at social **Skye Backpackers ❷** next door, a good base for trekkers. (☎534 510; www.scotlands-top-hostels.com. Laundry £2.50. Internet access 80p per 30min. Curfew 2am. Dorms £11-13. AmEx/MC/V.)

◧▨ FOOD AND PUBS. In Kyle, grab **groceries** at the Co-op, up the hill to the west of the Kyle bus station. (☎530 190. Open M-Sa 8am-10pm, Su 10am-6pm.) For a taste of local fish, hop off the train at Kyle and into the **Seafood Restaurant ❸,** in the railway building next to the bay. (☎534 813. Entrees £11-16. Open M-Sa 6:30-9pm. Cash only.) Play pool or foosball at the packed **Saucy Mary's,** next door to the SYHA hostel. (Open M-Th 5pm-midnight, F 5pm-1am, Sa 5-11:30pm, Su 5-11pm.)

The amiable staff of **Harry's ❶,** on the pier in Kyleakin, serves steaming pots of tea (£1), tasty sandwiches, and hot dishes (£4-7) to backpackers and seafarers. (☎534 641. Open M-Tu and Th-Sa 9am-5:30pm, Su 10am-3pm. Cash only.) **Cu'chulainn's ❶** offers pub fare in its beer garden. (☎534 492. Open M-Sa 11am-12:45 am. Food served 11am-8pm. MC/V.) Though it has few restaurants, Kyleakin's nightlife is enlivened by a steady stream of backpackers and tourists. The hopping **King Haakon Bar ❶,** at the east end of the village green, has a gorgeous view of the lighthouse and live music on weekend nights. (☎534 061. Open M-Th and Sa noon-12:30am, F noon-1am, Su 12:30pm-midnight. Food served 12:30-8:30pm. MC/V.)

◧ SIGHTS. The **Bright Water Visitor Centre,** on the pier in Kyleakin, offers a child-oriented look at local history. (☎530 040. Open Apr.-Oct. M-F 10am-4pm. Free.) The center runs 1½hr. walking tours to **Eilean Ban,** the island under the Skye Bridge. Departure times vary and are limited, so call ahead. (M-F 1 trip per day; £6.) Quiet **Kyleakin Harbor** lights up in oranges and purples during clear sunsets—for the best views, climb up to the memorial on the hill behind the Dun-Caan Hostel. A slippery scramble to the west takes you to the small ruins of **Castle Maol.** Cross the bridge behind the hostel, turn left, follow the road, and then the path. Look for tiles that mark the way and the forboding "Beware the Tides" stone. Heed its warning, for the ruins are accessible only when the tide is out. According to legend, Norwegian princess "Saucy Mary" built the original castle and stretched a chain across the water, charging a toll to ships. She supposedly flashed those who paid the toll—hence her spicy moniker. (Always open. Free.)

BROADFORD ☎ 01471

Situated on a rocky bay 8 mi. west of Kyleakin, Broadford is more road-strip than town, with most amenities and attractions lining the A87. The **SYHA Broadford** ❶ is the only hostel in the area and has views of the harbor through a lush garden. Head east on the first road north of the bridge and walk for a ½ mi. (☎ 822 442. Laundry £2. Reception 7-10am and 5-11pm. Curfew midnight. Open Mar.-Oct. Dorms £11.25-12.50, under 18 £5-9.75. MC/V.) More elaborate accommodation (and dramatic views) can be found at the **Dunnollie Hotel** ❹, on the main strip just south of the Co-op. (☎ 822 253. Singles from £40; doubles from £80. MC/V.) Stock up on **groceries** at the Co-op, next to Skye Surprises. (☎ 822 203. Open M-Sa 9am-6pm, Su 10am-6pm.) **Fig Tree Restaurant and Tea Room** ❷, near the post office, has a serene setting and serves entrees and cafe fare. (☎ 822 616. Open M-Sa 10am-6pm. MC/V.)

The **Tourist Information Centre** sits in the carpark along the bay south of the bus stop. (☎ 822 713. Open Apr.-Oct. M-Sa 9:30am-5pm, Su 10am-4pm.) Five minutes north on the road is a **Bank** of Scotland. (☎ 822 216. Open M-Tu and Th-F 9am-12:30pm and 1:30-5pm, W 9:30am-12:30pm and 1:30-5pm.) Skye Surprises, by the TIC, combines a convenience store, petrol station, bureau de change, **launderette,** and **Internet** cafe; look for the hairy Highland cow model out front. (☎ 822 225. Laundry £3. Internet access £1 per 30min. Always open.) Broadford also has a **post office** (☎ 822 201; open M-F 9am-5:30pm, Sa 9am-12:30pm). **Post Code:** IV49 9AB.

SLEAT PENINSULA AND ARMADALE ☎ 01471

Two miles south of Broadford, the single-lane A851 veers southwest through the foliage of the Sleat Peninsula, dubbed the "Garden of Skye." In town, the **Armadale Castle Gardens** and **Museum of the Isles** boast a disintegrating MacDonald castle, expansive gardens, and an excellent (if biased) exhibit on the Isles' clans. Its study center is one of the best places in Scotland for **genealogical research.** (☎ 844 305; www.clandonald.com. Open daily Apr.-Oct. 9:30am-5:30pm. Last admission 5pm. Research from £5 per half-day; first 15min. free. Gardens and museum £4.80, concessions £3.50, families £14.) The **Sleat Peninsula** has some of Skye's most verdant terrain, including the **Kinloch Forest** on the Broadford-Armadale bus route. From the Forestry Commission carpark, a footpath traces a circular route past the deserted settlement **Letir Fura,** from which **Loch na Dal** is visible (2½hr. round-trip). A longer hike (3-3½hr. round-trip) reaches Skye's southernmost tip, the **Point of Sleat,** with its lighthouse and views of the Cuillins to the north. The trailhead begins at the end of the A851, south of **Ardvasar** at the **Aird of Sleat.** An hour's walk rewards with awesome views of western island **Rum** from the watery inlet of **Acairseid an Rubha.** Consult the Broadford TIC (p. 632) for the correct Ordnance Survey maps and advice before heading out. The owner of **Flora MacDonald Hostel** ❶ will pick you up at the Armadale ferry and proudly show you rare Eriskay ponies. (☎ 844 272. Kitchen and TV. Dorms £11. Cash only.) The **SYHA Armadale** ❶ has a convenient location overlooking the water. (☎ 844 260. Lockout 10:30am-5pm. Curfew 11:30pm. Open Apr.-Sept. Dorms £11.25, under 18 £8.25. MC/V.) North of Armadale at Ostaig, the famous Gaelic college **Sabhal Mor Ostaig** ❸ teaches the Gaelic language, promotes Gaelic music, throws Gaelic dances, and hosts Gaelic festivals. They also offer summer courses in—you guessed it—all things Gaelic. (☎ 844 373; answered in Gaelic. Courses £120-200. Singles £25; twins £40. MC/V.) Armadale, 17 hilly miles to the south, sends **ferries** to Mallaig. Highland Country **buses** run between Armadale and Broadford (4-6 per day, £3).

CENTRAL SKYE   01478

Visible from nearly every part of Skye, the Cuillin Hills (COO-leen)—the highest peaks in the Hebrides—dominate central Skye and beckon walkers and climbers. Legend says the warrior Cúchulainn loved the Amazon ruler of Skye, who named the hills for him when he returned to Ireland. The Kyleakin-Portree road wends its way through the Red Cuillins, which present a foreboding face to the aspiring hillwalker. At the junction of the A863 to Portree and the A850 to Dunvegan, the village of Sligachan (SLIG-a-chan) is little more than bunkhouse, hotel, pub, and campsite in a jaw-dropping setting. The famous trail through Glen Sligachan (p. 633) begins in Sligachan.

⬛⬛ ACCOMMODATIONS AND FOOD. The **Sligachan Bunkhouse ❶**, a bungalow with new facilities, is hidden behind a copse of trees. (☎650 204. Linen £2. Dorms £10. MC/V.) The **Sligachan Hotel ❹**, a classic hillwalker's and climber's haunt, has more private accommodations. (☎650 204. Singles £40-50; doubles £60-80. MC/V.) The **Sligachan Campsite ❶** is across the road. (Open May-Sept. £4. Cash only.) Expert mountaineers give tips at the **SYHA Glenbrittle ❶**, near the southwest coast. Down a single-lane track lined with evergreens, the town of Glenbrittle can be reached by Highland Country bus #53 from Portree, which runs twice per day. (☎640 278. Open Apr.-Sept. Dorms £11-11.50, under 18 £8.75-9.75 MC/V.) The **Glenbrittle Campsite ❶** is at the foot of the Black Cuillins and has a breathtaking view of the loch. (☎640 404. Open Apr.-Oct. Reception 8am-7pm. £4.50. MC/V.) The Sligachan Hotel's **Seumas' Bar ❷** offers a broad selection of beers (try their own ale, Slig 80 Shilling), the usual selection of pub grub (£4-8), and nearly every malt in existence. (Live music F-Sa. Open daily 8am-11:30pm. MC/V.)

⬛⬛ HIKING AND OUTDOORS. The Cuillin Hills are great for experienced hikers but risky for beginners. TICs, campsites, and hostels are well-stocked with maps and books for walks throughout the region (see **Wilderness Safety,** p. 46). The pitted peat is always drenched, so expect sopping wet feet. ⬛**MacBackpackers Skye Trekker Tour** (p. 630) hikes the gorgeous coastal path from Elgol, camping overnight at Camasunary and moving north through Glen Sligachan the next day. The tour includes transport to and from trailheads. A short but scenic path follows the stream from Sligachan to the head of **Loch Sligachan.** After crossing the old bridge, fork right off the main path, and walk upstream along the right-hand bank. The narrow, boggy path leads past pools and waterfalls, in some places tracing the top of a small cliff (3 mi. round-trip). In 1899, a fit (and barefoot!) Gurkha soldier ascended and descended the 2537 ft. **Glamaig** in just 55min. Set aside your ambition, and start the 3½hr. hike only if you feel at ease on steep slopes. A smaller trail branches off the main trail after 1 mi. and leads up the ridge.

Experienced climbers can try to climb **Sgurr nan Gillean,** to the southwest of Glamaig, towering 3167 ft. above a tiny lake. For more level terrain, take the 8 mi. walk down **Glen Sligachan** through the heart of the Cuillins to the beach of **Camasunary,** with views of the isles of Rum and Muck. From Camasunary, you can hike 5 mi. along the coast to **Elgol.** From there, a sailing trip to **Loch Coruisk** with **Bella Jane Boat Trips** reveals extraordinary views. (☎01471 866 244. Runs Apr.-Oct. M-Sa; for reservations call from 7:30-10am. Round-trip £20-30.) Harder to reach is the gleaming **Spar Cave,** near **Glasnakille,** with the glistening "Frozen Waterfall." It is accessible only during low tide, and there are no facilities, so only seasoned cave explorers should attempt it. Bring a flashlight. From Camasunary beach, you can also hike to the loch along a coastal trail that encounters steep rocks at the intimidating "Bad Step" (1½hr.). Elgol is 14 mi. southwest of Broadford on the B8083; **postbus** #50B rumbles in from Broadford (M-F 2 per day, Sa 1 per day).

THE MINGINISH PENINSULA ☎01478

Few make the journey 10 mi. west of the Cuillins to the quiet Minginish Peninsula, despite its two hostels and plenty of B&Bs. The **Talisker Distillery** sits on serene Loch Harport. The 45min. distillery tour is bland, but the whisky isn't: Skye's only malt packs a fiery finish. (☎614 300. Open Apr.-Oct. M-Sa 9:30am-4:30pm; Nov.-Mar. M-F 2-5pm. £5.) The **Skyewalker Independent Hostel ❶**, Fiskavaig Rd., Portnalong, runs the best (and only) **cafe ❶** on the peninsula. (☎640 250. Dorms £8.50-9. Tents £2.50. MC/V.) The spacious **Croft Bunkhouse ❶** has dorms, private rooms, bothies (traditional sleeping shelves), wooden wigwams, and lawn space for camping. The bunkhouse has kitchen and bath facilities. (☎640 254. Dorms and bothies £8. Cash only.) Up the road, the inviting and stylish B&B **Taigh Ailean ❸** accommodates weary and hungry travelers with comfy bedrooms and an attached restaurant and bar. (☎640 271. £25-30 per person. MC/V.) Highland Country **buses** #53 and 54 arrive from Portree and Sligachan (M-F 4 per day, Sa 1-2 per day), stopping at Carbost and the Talisker Distillery, and continuing to Portnalong. The **post office** is in the hostel (open M and W-Th 9-11am). **Post Code:** IV47 8SL.

PORTREE ☎01478

Named *Port na Righ* (the King's Port) after James V visited in 1540, Portree is Skye's flourishing center of Gaelic music, arts, and crafts and the island's hub of public transportation. With pastel buildings and bright flags crisscrossing the streets, Portree is reminiscent of a tropical island village.

You can't miss the brightly painted **Portree Independent Hostel ❶**, The Green, which has a prime location, spacious kitchen, and enthusiastic staff. (☎613 737. Dorms £12-13. MC/V.) Head to the self-catering **Harbor Lodge ❸**, by the pier, for ocean views. (☎613 332. £22 per person. Cash only.) Right as you enter Portree, the **Easdale B&B ❸**, Bridge Rd., is hidden up a stone pathway and behind an impressive garden, but its distant nature ends there—the genial proprietor will make you feel at home. (☎613 244. £20-25 per person. Cash only.) For higher-end lodgings, the **Portree Hotel ❹**, Somerled Sq., has occupied its corner of the square since 1865. (☎612 511. £35-55 per person. MC/V.) The Somerfield **supermarket** is on Bank St. (☎612 855. Open M-Sa 8:30am-8pm, Su 10am-5pm.) ■**Cafe Arriba ❷**, Quay Brae, has an imaginative menu of toasties and falafels. Vegetarian options abound. (☎611 830. Entrees £4-10. Open daily 7am-10pm. MC/V.) With sweet smells wafting down the street, the **Granary ❶**, Somerled Sq., lures lucky travelers into its den with donuts, filled rolls, and warm bread. (☎612 873. Open July-Aug. M-Sa 9am-5pm, Su 10am-4pm; Sept.-June M-Sa 9am-5pm. MC/V.) Enjoy fresh local seafood in the elegant **Bosville Hotel ❷**, Bank St. (☎612 856. Entrees £8-16. 2 courses £28, 3 courses £37. Open daily 11am-10pm. MC/V.) For a quiet pint, try upstairs at the **Caledonian Hotel pub** on Wentworth St. (☎612 641. Live music F-Su. Open M-F 2pm-1am, Sa 12:30pm-12:30am, Su 12:30-11:30pm.) The **Isles Inn,** Somerled Sq., has Scotland's answer to the tiki bar: the recreated croft. (☎612 129. Open M-Sa 11am-midnight, Su 12:30-11:30pm.)

Scottish Citylink and Highland Country **buses** stop at Somerled Sq. from Kyle and Kyleakin (M-Sa 8-10 per day, Su 5 per day). To reach the **Tourist Information Centre,** Bayfield Rd., from the square, face the Bank of Scotland, turn left down the lane, and left again onto Bridge Rd. The welcoming staff explains bus schedules and books lodgings for a £3 charge plus a 10% deposit. (☎612 137. Open July-Aug. M-Sa 9am-6pm, Su 10am-4pm; Sept.-Oct. and Apr.-June M-F 9am-5pm, Su 10am-

4pm; Nov.-Mar. M-Sa 9am-4pm.) Other services include: a Royal **Bank** of Scotland, Bank St. (☎612 822; open M-Tu and Th-F 9:15am-4:45pm, W 10am-4:45pm); a **launderette,** underneath the Independent Hostel (☎613 737; open M-Sa 9am-9pm); **Internet access** at the TIC (£2.50 per hr.) or up the street at the library (☎612 697; free; open M and W 1-8pm, Th-F 10am-5pm, Sa 10am-1pm); and the **post office,** on Wentworth St. (☎612 533; open M-Sa 9am-4pm). **Post Code:** IV51 9DB.

▶ DAYTRIPS FROM PORTREE AND NORTHERN SKYE

From Portree, Highland Country **buses** run to the various sights (M-Sa 3-8 per day).

▧TROTTERNISH PENINSULA. The east side of Trotternish is a geological masterpiece with thundering waterfalls, while the west side has a softer landscape of rolling hills. A steep hike (1hr. round-trip) leads to the black stone monolith that is the **Old Man of Storr;** begin from the nearby carpark to attempt this ascent. North of Staffin, a footpath to the unique **Quirang** rock pinnacles ascends to the **Prison,** loops upward to the **Needle,** and arrives at the **Table,** a flat, grassy promontory where locals once played shinty, an extreme form of field hockey (3hr. round-trip). Nearby **Staffin Bay** abounds with fossils. **Kilt Rock** has lava columns that appear pleated above a rocky base crumbling into the sea. Strong, well-shod walkers can try the challenging but magnificent 12 mi. hike along the **Trotternish Ridge,** which runs the length of the peninsula from the Old Man of Storr to Staffin.

DUNVEGAN CASTLE. Majestic Dunvegan holds the title of longest-inhabited Scottish castle, occupied since the 13th century. As the ancient (and current) seat of clan MacLeod—one of the few strongholds still owned by a clan chief—it delivers a thorough dose of clan history. The current chief, John MacLeod of MacLeod, narrates the informative video, owns a restaurant and a wool shop, and appears throughout Skye on many a glossy poster. Get lost amid the sculpted gardens surrounding the castle. Highland Country bus #56 (M-Sa 3 per day) runs from Portree to the castle. (☎521 206; www.dunvegancastle.com. Open daily mid-Mar. to Oct. 10am-5:30pm; Nov. to mid-Mar. 11am-4pm. £6.80, concessions £5.80. Gardens only £4.50.)

DUNTULM CASTLE. Perched at the tip of the peninsula, Duntulm Castle was once the stronghold of the MacDonald clan. According to legend, the house was cursed when a nurse dropped the chief's child from a window. (Always open, but be careful of the edge. Free.) Near Duntulm at Kilmuir, the **Skye Museum of Island Life** has preserved a crofter village of 18th-century stone and thatch blackhouses. (☎552 206. Open Easter to Oct. M-Sa 9:30am-5:30pm. £2.) Along the same road, **Flora MacDonald's Monument** pays tribute to the Scottish folk hero who sheltered Bonnie Prince Charlie. On a bluff 5 mi. north of **Staffin,** the excellent **Dun Flodigarry Hostel ❶** has bright rooms, a commanding view of the cliffs, and is the starting point for many hikes. Take the Staffin bus from Portree and ask to be let off. (☎552 212. Internet access £1 per 15min. Dorms £11-12.50, with discounts for longer stays. Cash only.)

UIG ☎01470

Flanking a windswept bay on the peninsula's west coast, Uig (OO-ig) is little more than a ferry terminal and parking lot for hardy travelers headed to the Hebrides. While waiting for a ferry, stop by the **Isle of Skye Brewery,** next to the pier. When not busy brewing, employees will give you a brief tour. (☎542 477. Open M-F 10am-6pm. £2. Advance booking requested.) The **SYHA Uig ❶** has a fantastic ocean view and is a 30min. walk from the pier. The hostel is 2 mi. up the main road from the pier, past the tower. (☎542 211. Reception closed 10am-5pm. Curfew midnight. Open Apr.-Oct. Dorms £11-11.50, under 18 £8.75. MC/V.) Convenient for ferry connections, **Orasay B&B ❷** is by the pier; all rooms are ensuite, and **bike rental** is available. (☎542 316. £20-25 per person. MC/V.) The **Pub at the Pier ❷** serves standard grub (entrees £7-10) with sides of scenery and an occasional garnish of live music. (☎542 212. Open M-W 11am-11pm, Th-F 11am-1am, Sa 11am-12:30am, Su 12:30pm-11pm. Food served 11:30am-3pm and 5-9pm. MC/V.) CalMac runs a **ferry** connecting Uig to Tarbert, Lewis and to Lochmaddy, North Uist (1½hr.; M-Sa 1-2 per day; £9.40, 5-day round-trip £16.40; with car £45/77). Highland Country **buses** #57A and 57D and Scottish Citylink buses also run from Portree (M-Sa, every hr., £3).

THE SMALL ISLES   ☎01687

Virtually untouched by tourists, Rum, Eigg, Muck, and Canna are four remote jewels. From the national nature reserve of Rum to the privately owned Eigg, each island has its own distinct landscape and community. Although the journey no longer requires governmental permission or a jump from a small dinghy, careful planning and plenty of hiking is necessary to fully experience these four isles.

◣ GETTING THERE

CalMac **ferries** (☎462 403) sail from Mallaig to Rum (£8, 5-day round-trip £14), Eigg (£5.40/9.45), Muck (£8.20/14.50), and Canna (£10.15/17.60); call for schedules. Ferries do not allow cars, but are timed to connect with trains from Glasgow and Fort William and charge £2 per bicycle. Susan Grant (☎450 224) sails at 11am from Arisaig (p. 628) to: Rum (June-Aug. Tu, Th, Sa-Su; Easter to June and Sept. Tu, Th; round-trip £20, under 16 £10, under 12 £7); Eigg (daily except Th; £15, under 16 £10, under 12 £7); Muck (M, W, F; £11).

RUM. The largest and most striking of the Small Isles, diamond-shaped Rum is managed by Scottish Natural Heritage (SNH). Highland cattle, feral goats, golden eagles, Rum ponies, and migrating Manx shearwater birds are the main inhabitants. The island's 30 residents, all SNH employees, restore and preserve the island's natural woodlands. The friendly locals gladly give newcomers an introduction to the island's wildlife, geography, and trails, which are marked by beaters (large shovel-like instruments). Walk along the jagged coastline on the **Loch Scresort Trail** (2hr. round-trip) or head out on a day-long excursion to the Harris mausoleum. Don night-vision goggles as you trek to see the nesting Manx—one of several free guided walks. The opulent ◪**Kinloch Castle,** built in 1901, is a sight to see. Dashing playboy George Bullough squandered his family's fortune on imported stone and soil for his extravagant summer house and gardens. In summer, take one of the excellent daily tours to view the mint-condition rooms and antiques. (☎462 037. Tours M, W 1:15pm; Tu, Th, Sa 2pm; F 2:30pm. £5.) Ferry daytrips leave very little time; stay overnight. Sleep in the castle's former servants' quarters, now **Kinloch Castle Hostel ❷.** (☎462 037. Kitchen. Breakfast £3, packed lunch £5, 3-course dinner £12. Advance booking required. £13 per person; B&B £30 per person. MC/V.) For information on camping on Rum contact the Chief Warden, Scottish Natural Heritage, Isle of Rum, PH43 4RR (☎462 026; tent £1.50; cash only).

EIGG. The silhouette of Eigg (pop. 78) is easily recognized by the curious **Sgurr of Eigg** (1290 ft.), a massive lava cliff that juts up from the center of the island. Eigg sports vertical cliffs, sandy beaches, green hills, and palm trees; the sheltering rock wall of the Sgurr creates a sub-tropical micro-climate. According to local legend, St. Donnan and 52 companions were martyred by the warrior women of the pagan Queen of Moidart at **Kildonnan** in AD 617. Almost a thousand years later, the island's entire population (395 MacDonalds) were slaughtered by rival MacLeods in **Massacre Cave.** Today, however, life is much more genial—in 1997 the islanders raised £1.5 million to buy Eigg. With governmental oversight, this small community now runs the island. Ranger John Chester offers guided historical and wildlife walks. (☎482 477. £3. Call in advance to schedule a tour.) A minibus meets each ferry for a trip to the **Singing Sands** (round-trip £4). For **bicycles**, look for the shed just north of the grocery store. (☎482 432. £4 per half-day, £9 per day.) **Glebe Barn** ❶ is a hostel with pristine modern comforts, a wood-burning stove, and superb views. (☎482 417. Dorms £9-12. Book ahead. Cash only.) For B&Bs, the best value is **Laig Farm Guest House** ❸, nestled in a private valley with a nearby beach. (The hostel is 1 mi. from the pier, and the guest house 3 mi. farther. ☎482 412. £35 per person. Cash only.) For a **taxi**, call ☎482 494.

MUCK. The tiny (2 mi. by 1 mi.) southernmost isle, Muck is an experiment in communal living. The entire island is a single farm owned by the MacEwen family, which handles farming, transport (hop aboard the tractor-pulled trailer for a guided tour, £1), and shopping on the mainland. If you intend to stay on the island bring food. Stay at **Port Mor Guest House** ❹. (☎462 365. Full board £36. Cash only.) Next door is the cozy **Isle of Muck Bunkhouse** ❶. (☎462 042. £10.50. Linens £1. Cash only.) A tearoom/craftshop/information center is just up the hill from the pier.

CANNA. On Wednesdays and Saturdays, the CalMac **ferry** gives travelers time to spend a few hours on the isle of Canna (Gaelic for "porpoise"), which has just 14 residents. Walk the harbor road to find two one-room chapels and the **Harbor View Tearoom** ❶, which has scrumptious pastries. When the tide is out, ambitious powerwalkers can access the ruins of St. Columba's Chapel, a 7th-century nunnery. For those staying longer, the SNH runs **Kate's Cottage** ❷, a simple converted cottage with views of Rum and the Cuillins. (☎462 466. Singles £20. Cash only.)

THE OUTER HEBRIDES

With cairns, standing stones, and the remnants of generations against a landscape of exposed rock, the ancient past comes to life in the Outer Hebrides. The islands live in on tradition; you're more likely to get an earful of Gaelic here than anywhere else in Scotland. On the Calvinist islands of Lewis, Harris, and North Uist, most establishments close and public transportation ceases on Sundays (though one or two places may assist lost souls with a pint), while to the south, on Benbecula, South Uist, and Barra, tight-shuttered Sabbatarianism gives way to pictures of the Pope. The extreme seclusion, quiet, and isolation of the islands make the Western Isles one of Scotland's most undisturbed and unforgettable realms.

▧ TRANSPORTATION

CalMac (☎08705 650 000) has a near-monopoly on passenger and car **ferries** along major routes. It runs from Ullapool to Stornoway, Lewis (2¾hr.; M-Sa 2 per day; £14.40, 5-day round-trip £24.65; car £70/120); from Uig, Skye to Lochmaddy, North Uist (1¾hr.; 1-2 per day; £9.40, 5-day round-trip £16.05, car £45/77); and to Tarbert, Harris (1½hr.; 1-2 per day; £9.40, 5-day round-trip £16.05, car £45/77) and from Oban to Castlebay, Barra and Lochboisdale, South Uist (6½hr.; 1 per day; £20.70, 5-day round-trip £35.50, car £76/129). Call ahead if you wish to take a car.

In the archipelago, ferries brave rough sounds and infrequent buses cross causeways connecting the islands. Find the invaluable, free *Discover Scotland's Islands with Caledonian MacBrayne, Lewis and Harris Bus Timetables*, and *Uist and Barra Bus Timetables* at TICs. **Cycling** is popular, though windy hills and sudden rains often wipe out novice riders. Traffic is light, but **hitchhikers** report frequent lifts on all the islands. Let's Go does not recommend hitchhiking. Inexpensive **car rental** (from £25 per day) is available. Except in bilingual Stornoway and Benbecula, road signs are in Gaelic only. Although many names are similar in English, TICs often carry translation keys, and Let's Go lists Gaelic equivalents after English place names where appropriate.

▌ ACCOMMODATIONS

Mobility on the islands is limited by infrequent ferries and inconsistent ferry schedules. If you plan to stay overnight near a ferry terminal, try to book a bed ahead. Area TICs book **B&Bs** for a £3 charge plus a 10% deposit. **Camping** is allowed on public land in the Hebrides, but freezing winds and sodden ground often make it a miserable experience. Lewis's remote **SYHA Kershader ❶**, Ravenspoint, Kershader, South Lochs, is a standard small hostel, with a shop next door in the community center. (☎01851 880 236. Laundry £2. Dorms £9, under 18 £8. MC/V.)

The Outer Hebrides are home to the unique ◪**Gatliff Hebridean Trust Hostels ❶** (www.gatliff.org.uk), four 19th-century thatched croft houses turned into simple year-round hostels. The hostels accept no advance bookings but very seldom turn travelers away. Aside from basic facilities, all provide cooking equipment, range tops, cutlery, crockery, and hot water. Blankets and pillows are provided, but the hostels only have coal fires; you'll want a good sleeping bag. Hostels cost £8 per person (under 18 £5.50) and **camping** is £4.50. (Cash only.)

Berneray (Bhearnaraigh): Off North Uist. Frequent buses W19 and W17 shuttle between the hostel, the Otternish pier (where ferries arrive from Harris), the Lochmaddy pier on North Uist, and the Sollas Co-op food store (30min., M-Sa 6-9 per day, £1). A beautifully thatched and whitewashed building overlooking a picture-perfect beach.

Garenin (Na Gearranan): Lewis, 1½ mi. north of Carloway. Buses on the W2 "West Side Circular" route from Stornoway (M-Sa 10-11 per day) go to Carloway, if not Garenin village itself. Free taxi service meets some buses at Carloway. Unsurpassed surroundings.

Howmore (Tobha Mòr): South Uist, about 1hr. north of Lochboisdale by foot. W17 buses from Lochboisdale to Lochmaddy stop at the Howmore Garage (M-Sa 5-8 per day, £1); from there, follow the sign 1 mi. west from the A865. Overlooks a ruined chapel; near the rubble that was once Ormiclate Castle.

Rhenigidale (Reinigeadal): North Harris. Take the free minibus from the carpark next to the Tarbert TIC (☎01859 502 221; M-Sa 2 per day; call ahead). The bus will take your pack if you want to attempt the tough 6 mi. hike along the eastern coast. From Tarbert, take the road toward Kyles Scalpay for 2 mi. and follow the signposted path left to Rhenigidale. The path ascends 850 ft. before zig-zagging down steeply (3hr. total). By car, follow the turn-off to Maaruig (Maraig) from the A859, 13 mi. north of Tarbert.

LEWIS (LEODHAS)

With 20,000 inhabitants, Lewis is the most populous of the Outer Hebridean Islands. More than 8000 people live in Stornoway, the capital; most other islanders live in crofting settlements. The gentle slopes of moor make Lewis a good place for biking and hiking. The Callanish Stones predate the pyramids; archaeologists flock to the site. The isle is also a surfing mecca, with impressive swells attracting board-riders from around the world.

STORNOWAY (STEORNOBHAIGH)   ☎01851

Stornoway is a splash of urban life in the otherwise rural Outer Hebrides. But the city, with its castle and museums, maintains a rough-hewn Highland charm.

TRANSPORTATION AND PRACTICAL INFORMATION. The only things running on Sundays are planes and churchgoers late for service. CalMac **ferries** sail from Ullapool (2¾hr.; M-Sa 2 per day; £14.40, 5-day round-trip £24.65; car £70/120). **Buses** operated by Western Isles depart from the Beach St. station; pick up a free *Lewis and Harris Bus Timetable.* (☎704 327. Luggage storage 20p-£1. Station open M-Sa 8am-6pm.) Destinations include Callanish (Calanais; 1hr., M-Sa 4-6 per day); Port of Ness (Nis; 1hr., M-Sa 6-8 per day); Tarbert (An Tairbeart; M-Sa 3-7 per day, £4.15). **Car rental** is cheaper here than on the mainland. Try Lewis Car Rentals, 52 Bayhead St. (☎703 760; £25-45 per day; 21+; open M-Sa 9am-6pm), or Lochs Motors, across from the bus station (☎705 857; £21-25 per day; 21+; open M-Sa 9am-6pm). **Rent bikes** at Alex Dan's Cycle Centre, 67 Kenneth St. (☎704 025. £10 per day, £30 per week. Open M-Sa 9am-6pm.)

The **Tourist Information Centre** is on 26 Cromwell St. From the ferry terminal, turn left onto South Beach and right on Cromwell St. (☎703 088. Open Apr.-Oct. M-F 9am-6pm and 8-9pm; Nov.-Mar. M-F 9am-5pm.) From April to October, **Stornoway Trust** (☎702 002) organizes free **walks** through the town and countryside. Other services include: a **Bank** of Scotland, across from the TIC (☎705 252; open M-Tu and Th-F 9am-5pm, W 9:30am-5pm); a **pharmacy**, 29-31 Cromwell St. (☎703 131; M-Tu and Th-Sa 9am-6pm, W 9am-5pm); free **Internet access** at the Stornoway Library (☎708 631; open M-W and Sa 10am-5pm, Th-F 10am-6pm); and the **post office,** 16 Francis St. (open M-F 9am-5:30pm, Sa 9am-12:30pm). **Post Code:** HS1 2AA.

ACCOMMODATIONS AND FOOD. Fairhaven Hostel ❶, at the intersection of Francis St. and Keith St., is a second home for wayward kahunas; go here for the inside scoop on Lewis's best waves. The hostel is lively, airy, and basic. From the bus station, walk north on Kenneth St. and turn right onto Francis St. (☎705 862. Dorms £10. Cash only.) **Mr. and Mrs. Hill ❸,** Church St., has friendly service in a cozy space, removed from the hustle and bustle of the main square. From the town center, take Matheson Rd. north, turn left onto Robertson Rd. and right onto Church St. (☎706 553. £25 per person. Cash only.) The **Stornoway Backpackers Hostel ❶,** 47 Keith St., down the road from Fairhaven Hostel, is similarly basic; rooms are spacious but spartan. (☎703 628; www.stornoway-hostel.co.uk. Dorms from £10. Cash only.) The **Laxdale Bunkhouse ❶** sleeps 16 in four modern rooms on the Laxdale Holiday Park campgrounds. (1½ mi. from town center. ☎706 966; www.laxdaleholidaypark.com. Bunks £10-11. Cash only.)

Cheap chow is plentiful in takeaway-heavy Stornoway. Stock up on **groceries** at the Co-op on Cromwell St. (☎702 703. Open M-Sa 8am-8pm.) **Thai Cafe ❷,** 27 Church St., serves inexpensive, mouthwatering entrees (£4-6) by candlelight. (☎701 811. Open M-Sa noon-2:30pm and 5-11pm. Cash only.) The old-fashioned **Stag Bakery Tea Room ❶,** 3 Cromwell St., offers delicious pastries, wraps, and sandwiches in the heart of downtown (☎706 300; open M-Sa 9am-5pm).

SIGHTS. The **An Lanntair Arts Centre,** on Kenneth St., has a year-round program of visual and performing arts, a cafe, a restaurant, and an evening film series. (☎703 307. Open M-Sa 10am-11pm. Free.) The **Museum nan Eilean,** Francis St., has fascinating exhibits on 9000 years of Hebridean history, including a display on the Lewis Chessmen. (☎709 266; www.cne-siar.gov.uk. Open Apr.-Sept. M-Sa 10am-5:30pm; Oct.-Mar. Tu-F 10am-5pm, Sa 10am-1pm. Free.) Meander the shaded grounds of majestic **Lewis Castle,** northwest of town. Built in the 19th century by an opium smuggler, the castle now shelters a college. The entrance is on Cromwell St., but you can admire it from across the water at the end of N. Beach St.; turn left after the footbridge from New St.

NIGHTLIFE AND FESTIVALS. Don't miss out on Stornoway's vibrant nightlife. **Pubs** and **clubs** crowd the area between Point St., Castle St., and the two waterfronts. There's no better place to watch a big-time sporting event than on the screen at the **Crown Inn,** N. Beach St. (☎703 181. Open M-W 11am-11pm, Th-F

11am-1am, Sa 11am-11:30pm.) **The Heb,** Point St., is a hip club-bar-cafe like nothing you'd ever expect in the Outer Hebrides. (F-Sa disco 10pm. Cover £2. Open July-Aug. M-W 11am-11pm, Th-Sa 11am-1am; Aug.-June F-Sa 11am-1am.) The **Hebridean Celtic Festival** (☎621 234) in mid-July draws top musical talent from Scotland and all over the world; the main acts often sell out far in advance.

▶ DAYTRIPS FROM LEWIS

Lewis's rich history is visible along the island's **west coast,** with the Callanish Stones, Carloway Broch, reconstructed crofters' houses, and several archaeological sites situated along the A858. They can be reached via the W2 bus, which operates on a circuit beginning at the Stornoway bus station (M-Sa 4-6 per day). **Galson Motors** (☎840 269) offers a day pass on this route (£6), or a round-trip ticket to see one, two, or three of the sights from May to October (£4-5). Alternatively, travel with **Out and About Tours** (☎612 288; half-day £67, full day £102). **Albannach Guided Tours** offers personalized tours (☎830 433; from £10 per hour per person).

▨CALLANISH STONES (CALANAIS). The Callanish Stones, 14 mi. west of Stornoway on the A858, are second only to Stonehenge in grandeur and are considerably less overrun with tourists. The speckled stones, hewn from three-billion-year-old Lewisian gneiss, form a pattern resembling a cross. Archaeologists believe that prehistoric peoples used Callanish and two nearby circles to track the movements of the heavens. *(Always open. Free.)* The **Visitor Centre** has a comprehensive exhibit and a short video. *(☎621 422. Open Apr.-Sept. M-Sa 10am-6pm; Oct.-Mar. W-Sa 10am-4pm. Exhibit and film £1.85, concessions £1.35.)* Nibble scones at the **Callanish Tea House ❶** in the only privately owned blackhouse on the island. *(Open M-Sa 9am-6pm. Cash only.)* A mile south of Callanish, the W3 bus makes its way across the bridge to the island of **Great Bernera** (Bearnaraigh), where the **Bostadh Iron Age House** is being excavated from beneath the sands. *(Open June-Aug. M-F noon-4pm. £2, concessions £1.)* Perhaps more spectacular are the island's idyllic **white beaches.**

CARLOWAY BROCH (DÙN CHARLABHAIGH). Five miles north of Callanish along the A858 lies the crofting settlement (a "town" only by local standards) of **Carloway** (Carlabhaigh), dominated by the Iron-Age **Carloway Broch.** Dating from the first century BC, this double-walled stone tower is hailed as the most impressive broch in the Western Isles—it once protected farmers and their cattle from Vikings. The **Gearrannan Blackhouse Village** is a well-restored traditional croft house. *(Carloway Broch ☎643 338. Visitor Centre open Apr.-Oct. M-Sa 10am-5pm. Broch always open. Free. Blackhouse Village ☎643 416. Open M-Sa 9:30am-5:30pm. £2.20.)*

ARNOL BLACKHOUSE. Farther north on the A858, beyond **Shawbost,** lies a restored crofter's cottage known as the Arnol Blackhouse. The roof has no chimney in order to conserve heat from the peat fire. Inhale a hearty lungful inside the cottage, which was a working home until 1960. *(☎710 395. Open Apr.-Sept. M-Sa 9:30am-6:30pm; Oct.-Mar. M-Sa 9:30am-4:30pm. Last admission 30min. before close. £4.)*

BUTT OF LEWIS. Besides being the butt of terrible puns, the Butt of Lewis stands where the Atlantic crashes into the cliffs with deafening ferocity. On your way north you'll pass the village of Galson and the **Galson Farm Guesthouse and Bunkhouse ❶,** which sleeps a comfortable eight and has excellent vegetarian options for dinner. Be sure to call ahead. *(Butt of Lewis always open. Free. Galston Farm ☎850 492; www.galsonfarm.freeserve.co.uk. Bunks £10. MC/V.)*

DALMORE BEACH AND SURF SPOTS. White sandy beaches, clean water, 15 ft. tides, warm currents, and long daylight hours lure surfers to Lewis and Harris. In Lewis, the most popular spot is **Dalmore Beach,** near the town of Dalbeg. Competitions take place at the beaches of **Valtos** and **Europie,** where amateur archaeologists and shellhunters search for Neolithic artifacts and the pink shells fabled to be mermaid fingernails. With its rips and currents, the **Port of Ness** is a dangerous place to surf; only the experienced should head there. The best swells migrate according to wind and tidal cycles; check forecasts at the local surf shops. **Hebridean Surf Holidays** (☎ 705 862), on the corner of Keith St. and Francis St. in Stornoway, offers all-inclusive surfing lessons (from £35 per day), rents equipment, and shuttles surfers to the beach (board and ride to beach from £20). The W2 **bus** route (M-Sa 6-10 per day) runs past Dalbeg and Dalmor beach, while W4 buses (M-Sa 2-4 per day) from Stornoway pass other spectacular surf spots further down the coast. The W1 bus (M-F 8-9 per day, Sa 6 per day) travels along the northwest coast to the Butt and the Port of Ness.

HARRIS (NA HEARADH)

Harris shares an island with Lewis, but they're different worlds; when the ruling MacLeod clan split, so did the isle. The deserted flatlands of Lewis in the north yield to the rugged peaks of Harris. Tufts of grass dispersed between slabs of rock give the landscape an eerie, moon-like appearance. Toward the west coast, the Forest of Harris (in fact a treeless, heather-splotched mountain range) descends onto brilliant crescents of yellow sand bordered by indigo waters and machair (sea meadows). The A859, or "Golden Road" (named for the king's ransom spent blasting it from the rock), winds to Harris's southern tip; it's a trip for seasoned cyclists or bus travelers ready for a bumpy ride. Roads branch from Tarbert to the small fishing community Scalpay (Scalpaigh), connected to Harris by a causeway.

TARBERT (AN TAIRBEART)   ☎ 01859

Tarbert is the main town in Harris, straddling the narrow isthmus that divides the island into North and South. The lengthy rocky stretches and heathered slopes of Harris's hills provide some of the best **hiking** in the Hebs. The tallest peaks lie in the **Forest of Harris,** whose main entrances are off the B887 to Huishinish Point, at Glen Meavaig, and farther west at 19th-century **Amhuinnsuidhe Castle,** 15 mi. from Tarbert. The infrequent summertime W12 bus from Tarbert serves these points (3 per day). If you don't have a lot of time, use one of the unmarked eastern trails to hike up **Gillaval** (1554 ft.; at least 1hr.) or take a coastal stroll from Taobh Tuath to Horgabost. For the most comprehensive walk, try the **Harris Walkway,** a long but light ramble from Clisham in the south to

HARRIS (WORLDWIDE) TWEED

Harris tweed, a fine woven wool, once brought the small, windswept island of Harris fame and fortune. But during the 20th century, few young persons learned the craft and the industry declined. Unexpectedly, international giant Nike resuscitated the industry, granting a contract to local weaver Donald John MacKay.

On the industry: "In the 50s, 60s, and 70s, every 2nd house had a loom. Today there are two dozen people, tops, who continue to weave on Harris."

On the quality: "The material has to be hand-woven. That's what makes it unique. The day that changes is the day Harris tweed goes out the door."

On the Nike order: "They wanted 44,000 meters of material. Fifty old boys in the Hebrides were kept busy with that order. My wife worked the hardest, taking phone calls from the company in the small hours of the morning."

On the future: "The Nike order isn't the end. I'm confident when the work is there, more youngsters will take up weaving."

On his current work: "At any time, I'm probably four or five months behind. Right now, I'm doing an order of gents' jackets for a company in Japan."

With a glint in his eye, he adds, "But I'm not complaining."

Scaladal in the north, via Tarbert. Ordnance Survey maps for these remote areas are available in the TIC. Tarbert itself has few attractions. **Rent bicycles** from Paula Williams. (☎520 319. £10-12 per day.)

Less than a 5min. walk from the pier on Main St. is the basic **Rockview Bunkhouse ❶**. It's run by two postal clerks; you can check in at the post office. (☎502 211. Dorms £10. MC/V.) The stately **Harris Hotel ❹** has amenities aplenty and boasts J.M. Barrie's graffiti on its dining room window. (☎502 154. £40-60 per person, with dinner £61.50-81.50. MC/V.) A.D. Munro **market,** Main St., serves Tarbert as grocer, butcher, and baker. (☎502 016. Open M-Sa 7:30am-6pm.) Nestled behind fragrant flowering bushes, the **Firstfruits Tearoom ❶,** across from the TIC, pours hot drinks in a homey setting. (☎502 439. Open Apr.-Sept. 10:30am-4:30pm. Cash only.) The **Harris Hotel Restaurant and Bar ❷** serves food (entrees £14-18) in the main hotel building. (☎502 154. Bar open M-Sa 11am-11pm, Su 7-8:45pm. MC/V.)

Ferries serve Tarbert from Uig, Skye. (W and F 1 per day; M-Tu, Th, Sa 2 per day. £9.40, 5-day round-trip £16.05.) Check with CalMac (☎502 444), at the pier in Tarbert, for timetables. Hebridean Transport runs **buses** (☎01851 705 050) from Leverburgh and Stornoway (1hr., M-Sa 3-7 per day, £4.15). The **Tourist Information Centre** is on Pier Rd. and proudly boasts Tarbert's only **ATM.** (☎502 011. Open Apr. to mid-Oct. M-Sa 9am-5pm, Tu, Th, Sa 7:30-8:30pm; mid-Oct. to Mar. for ferry arrivals.) A **Bank** of Scotland is uphill from the pier. (☎502 453. Open M-Tu and Th-F 10am-12:30pm and 1:30-4pm, W 11:15am-12:30pm and 1:30-4pm.) **Internet access** is available in the public library in Sir E. Scott School, a cream-colored building 10min. along the A859 to Stornoway. (☎502 926. Open M 9:30am-6pm; Tu-Th and F 9:30am-4:20pm; W 9:30am-4:20pm and 6-7:45pm; Sa 10am-12:30pm. Free.) The **post office** is on Main St. (☎502 211. Open M-Tu and Th-F 9am-1pm and 2-5:30pm, W 11:15am-12:30pm.) **Post Code:** HS3 3DB.

RODEL AND LEVERBURGH   ☎01859

Rodel (Roghadal), at Harris's southern tip, is the site of **St. Clement's Church,** which houses three MacLeod tombs. Gaze at the 500-year-old images of knights etched into the black gneiss rock. Up the road is **Leverburgh,** a small port. The funky ■ **Am Bothan Bunkhouse ❷** has spacious rooms and a nautical-themed common area. It's located ¼ mi. from the Leverburgh pier. (☎520 251; www.ambothan.com. Dorms £14. MC/V.) The **Anchorage Restaurant ❷** serves good seafood on Leverburgh's pier. Enjoy a casual dinner (entrees £7-12) or a full breakfast (£4.50) in the morning. (☎520 225. Open M-Sa 7:30am-8pm. MC/V.) CalMac (☎01876 500 337) **ferries** sail to Leverburgh from Ardmaree, Berneray (M-Sa 3-4 per day; £5.30, 5-day round-trip £9.05). **Buses** W10 and W13 run from Tarbert (1hr., M-Sa 3-7 per day, £4.15).

THE UISTS (UIBHIST)

In contrast with the peak-strewn Highlands, the flatness of the Uists (YOO-ists) is a shock. Save for a thin strip of land along the east coast, the islands are almost completely level and are pocked with so many lochs that it's difficult to discern where land ends and water begins. In the summer, the Uists are a vision in yellow, blanketed with wildflowers. Bursts of sunlight reveal narrow beaches, crumbling blackhouses, ancient cairns, and streams filled with salmon. The islands' tiny population is scattered across small crofts, and the main villages of Lochmaddy (Loch nam Madadh) on North Uist (Uibhist a Tuath) and Lochboisdale (Loch Baghasdail) on South Uist (Uibhist a Deas) are pleasant communities. The small island of Benbecula (Beinn na Faoghla), which possesses the Uists' sole airport, is the stepping stone between the two larger isles.

▐ TRANSPORTATION

CalMac **ferries** travel to Lochmaddy from Uig, Skye (1¾hr.; 1-2 per day; £9.40, 5-day round-trip £16.05; car £45/77). Ferries travel to Ardmaree, Berneray from Leverburgh, Harris (1¼hr.; M-Sa 3-4 per day; £5.30, 5-day round-trip £9.05; with car £24.30/41.50) and to Lochboisdale from Oban (7hr.; Tu, Th, Sa-Su 1 per day; £20.70, 5-day round-trip £35.50; car £76/129). The island council also runs the tiny Sound of Barra Ferry (☎08151 701 702) to Eriskay from Airdmhor and Barra (1hr.; 4-5 per day; £5.80, 5-day round-trip £9.85; car £17.10/29.50). **Airplanes** operated by British Airways (☎08457 799 977) travel from Barra to Benbecula (1 per day, £30).

Pick up the latest bus schedule from the TIC. **Bus** W17 runs along the main road from Lochmaddy to the airport in Balivanich and Lochboisdale (M-Sa 5-6 per day, £3.20). Buses W17 and W19 meet at least one ferry per day in Ardmaree for departures to Harris; W17 and W29 go to Eriskay in the south for connections to Barra (5-9 per day). If you arrive on a late ferry, there may not be a bus until the next day. Call ahead to book a B&B or prepare to camp. Get the *Uist and Barra Bus Timetables* in the Lochmaddy or Lochboisdale TIC and plan ahead. For **car rental,** call MacLennan's Self Drive Hire, Balivanich, Benbecula. (☎01870 602 191. From £25 per day. 21+. Open M-F 9am-5:30pm, Sa 9am-noon.) **Bicycles** can be rented or repaired at Rothan Cycles, in Howmore, on the road to the Gatliff Trust hostel. (☎01870 620 283; www.rothan.com. £8 for the first day, £6 thereafter. Call ahead.)

▟ ▐ ORIENTATION AND PRACTICAL INFORMATION

The Uists, part of the Outer Hebrides and Western Isles, are 125 windswept, hilly miles from north to south. The Uists lie south of the Isle of Lewis, separated from the Isle of Skye and the Scottish mainland by the Sea of the Hebrides. A smaller island, Benbecula, separates North Uist and South Uist. There are only two cities to speak of: Lochmaddy on North Uist and Lochboisdale on South Uist.

There are **Tourist Information Centres** on the piers at Lochmaddy (☎01876 500 321; open Apr.-Oct. M-F 9am-5pm, 9:30am-5:30pm) and Lochboisdale (☎01878 700 286; open Apr.-Oct. M-Sa 9am-1pm and 2-5pm), which book accommodations and stay open late for ferry arrivals. **Banks** are scarce: Lochboisdale has a Royal Bank of Scotland (☎01878 700 399; open M-Tu and Th-F 9:15am-4:45pm, W 10am-4:45pm), Lochmaddy a Bank of Scotland (☎01876 500 323; open M-Tu and Th-F 9:30am-4:30pm), and Benbecula a Bank of Scotland (☎01870 602 044; open M-Tu and Th-F 9am-5pm, W 9:30am-5pm). Benbecula has the Uists' sole **launderette,** Uist Laundry, by Balivanich Airport. (☎01870 602 876. Wash £3.50, dry £2, kilts £8. Open M-F 8:30am-4:30pm, Sa 9am-1pm.) **Internet access** is available at Cafe Taigh Chearsabhagh, Lochmaddy (50p donation).

▐ ACCOMMODATIONS

The only **hostel** near Lochmaddy is the **Uist Outdoor Centre ❶,** which offers overnight expeditions and courses in rock climbing, canoeing, and water sports from £25 per half-day. Follow signposts west from the pier for 1 mi. (☎01876 500 480. Bring a sleeping bag and book ahead. Linen £2. Dorms £10. Cash only.) The other hostels are far from town and require clever navigation if you don't have a car. To reach the excellent **Taigh Mo Sheanair ❶** ("My Grandfather's House"), in an original croft house near Clachan, take bus W17 or W18 (20min., 12 per day) from Lochmaddy. The driver can let you off at the Clachan shop on Balishare Rd.; the house is a signposted 1 mi. walk west. (☎01876 580 246. Linen £2. Laundry £3. Internet access £1 per hr. Dorms £12. Camping £5. Cash only.) Easier to reach but without the creature comforts is the **Gatliff Hebridean Trust Hostel** on **Berneray** (p. 638). Another basic Gatliff Trust Hostel is on South Uist at **Howmore** (p. 638). **B&Bs** are scattered throughout the island; the TICs can help find vacancies. In Lochboisdale, **Mrs. MacLellan's ❷**, Bay View, is just up the street from the ferry terminal. (☎01878 700 329. From £18 per person. Cash only.) In Lochmaddy, **Mrs. Johnson ❸** greets guests in the Old Courthouse. (☎01876 500 358. £20 per person, with breakfast £25. Cash only.) You can camp almost anywhere, but ask the crofters first.

🔦🍴 FOOD AND PUBS

The cheapest **groceries** on the islands are the Co-ops in Sollas (Solas) on North Uist (☎01876 560 210; open M-W and Sa 8:30am-6pm, Th-F 8:30am-7pm), Creagorry at the bottom of Benbecula (☎01870 602 231; open M-Sa 8am-8pm, Su 12:30pm-6pm), and Daliburgh (Dalabrog) on South Uist (☎01878 700 326; open M-Sa 8am-8pm, Su 12:30-6pm). Groceries are also available at MacLennan's in Balivanich, Benbecula (open M-W 9am-6pm, Th-F 9am-8pm, Sa 9am-7pm, Su noon-3pm). Across the street from the Lochmaddy Hotel, the **Cafe Taigh Chearsabhagh ❶** sells baked goods and sandwiches for £1.50-4. (☎01876 500 293. Open M-Sa 10am-5pm. Cash only.) For a sit-down supper in either ferry hub, the only option is pub grub (£6-12) at the **Lochmaddy Hotel ❷** (☎01876 500 331; M-Sa noon-9pm; MC/V) or the **Lochboisdale Hotel ❷** (☎01878 700 332; food served noon-2pm and 5:30-9pm; MC/V). An upscale restaurant in Benbecula, **Stepping Stone ❸**, provides delicious local cuisine, like venison and scallops. (☎01870 603 377. Entrees £10-16. Open M 11am-6pm, Tu-Sa 11am-9pm, Su noon-9pm. Dinner served Tu-Su 6-8:45pm. MC/V.) Further down the B892 toward Lochboisdale, the **Dark Island Hotel Restaurant ❸** has an extensive menu, including pizza, sandwiches, omelets, Indian cuisine, and local fare. (☎01870 603 030. Sandwiches £4. Entrees £10-20. Bar open daily noon-9pm. Dinner served 6:30-8:30pm. Reservations recommended. MC/V.) If you're going out to Bharpa Langass, follow the signs to **Langass Lodge ❹** for a post-cairn pint. Halfway between Lochmaddy and Clachan, this hunting lodge serves superb seafood. (☎01876 580 285. 2 courses £22, 3 courses £27. Open daily noon-9pm. MC/V.) Down at the bottom of the island chain on the isle of Eriskay (p. 645), the **Am Politician,** fondly referred to by locals as the "Polly," serves grub, tea, and lots of whisky. (☎01878 720 246. Open M-Sa 11am-midnight, Su 12:30pm-1am.)

👁 SIGHTS

The vibrant 🎨**Taigh Chearsabhagh** (tie KEAR-sa-vah) **Museum and Arts Centre** in Lochmaddy is home to exhibits of contemporary Scottish artwork and an extensive photo exhibit on life in the Uists. The cafe (see above) has good eats and the only Internet access in North Uist. (☎01876 500 293. Open daily 10am-5pm. Free.) The path behind the museum leads to displays of public art, like a mackerel mosaic. Just up the road is the **Hut of the Shadow,** a camera obscura set in a cairn-like structure. The image of the bay is reflected onto the wall of the faux-primitive hut. Cairns, war memorials, old croft houses, and other historic sites stand proud across the flat expanse of land. Easiest to spot from the road are the 3000-year-old chambered cairn **Barpa Langass,** 2 mi. past Locheport Rd. on the A867, and stone circle **Pobull Fhinn,** down a short path from Langass Lodge. On North Uist's southern tip at **Carinish,** 13th-century **Trinity Temple** is now no more than a pile of rubble. Bus W17 from Lochmaddy swings near Langass and Carinish. Birdwatchers get frustrated by the elusive corncrake at the **RSPB Balranald Reserve** on western North Uist, north of Bayhead, signposted from the A867. But the warden offers guided walks to see local animals. (☎01876 560 287. M-Sa 3-4 per day. Walks £3-4.) There are pleasant walks around the Uists; hike along the sweeping beaches with crystal-blue water at **Sollas** to the **Scolpaig Tower.** The Victorian building is surrounded by water and a sea of grass. Several other walks and sights are described in detail by pamphlets available at the TIC (50p-£2). On Benbecula, the **North Uist Riding School** provides lessons and rides on the beach. (☎ 077 8681 7577. £20.)

SMALLER ISLANDS

BERNERAY (BEÀRNARAIGH). Connected to North Uist's north coast by a causeway, the tiny island of Berneray is a gem. The island features a gorgeous coast of white sand, machair (MA-hur, or sea meadow), a thriving seal population, standing stones, and a friendly human population of 140 that first saw electricity in 1969. The island is home to the ▨**Gatliff Trust Hostel ❶,** which is on the coast on the far side of Bays Loch. No reservations; simply show up and ask to stay for the night. (www.gatliff.org.uk. Dorms £8. Cash only.) Trails to the beach leave from the road behind the welcoming **Burnside Croft ❸.** (☎ 01876 540 235; www.burnsidecroft.fsnet.co.uk. Open Feb.-Nov. Singles from £27. Cash only.) Berneray is the **ferryport** for Harris arrivals; frequent **buses** W17 and W19 run from Lochmaddy (30min., M-Sa 6-9 per day, £1).

ERISKAY (EIRIOSGAIGH). Home to rare feral ponies and sandy beaches, Eriskay has a quirky history. On February 4, 1941, with wartime alcohol rationing in effect, the S.S. *Politician*, carrying 207,000 cases of whisky to America, foundered. Concerned islanders mounted a salvage operation; the local pub displays some of the bottles. Bonnie Prince Charlie first set foot on Scottish soil at **Prince Charles's Bay.** The unique pink flower that grows on the island is said to have been brought by seeds stuck to the Prince's shoe. Eriskay is connected to South Uist by a causeway; **buses** W17 and W29 run from Lochboisdale (45min., 10 per day).

BARRA (BARRAIGH)   ☎ 01871

The southern outpost of the Western Isles, Barra is the Hebrides in a nutshell. A breathtaking blend of moor, machair, and beach, the island is home to over 1000 species of wild plants. On sunny days, the island's colors are unforgettable: yellow and pink wildflowers crown golden sand dunes. Barra is also home to a small number of Gaelic-speaking Scots. The best times to visit are May and early June, when the primroses bloom, or in July during the Feis Festival, a two-week-long celebration of music and craftsmanship.

▌ **TRANSPORTATION.** CalMac **ferries** (☎ 01878 700 288) sail to Castlebay (Bagh A Chaisteil) from: Oban (5hr.; 1 per day; £20.70, 5-day round-trip £35.50; car £76/129), Lochboisdale (1¾hr.; M-W, F-Sa 1 per day; £5.90, 5-day round-trip £10; car £34/58), and Eriskay (1hr.; M-Sa 4-5 per day; £5.80, 5-day round-trip £9.85; car £17.10/29.50). Times change frequently; call the TIC or CalMac for help. Hebridean Coaches (☎ 01870 620 345) runs **buses** W17 and W29 to Eriskay from Benbecula and Lochboisdale (M-Sa 5-9 per day). An **airplane** operated by British Airways (☎ 08457 799 977) lands on the beach from Benbecula (1 per day, £30).

See all of Barra in a day by **bicycle.** To rent from Cycle Hire, drop by the long wooden shed on the main road. (☎ 810 438. From £10 per day. Discounts for longer rentals. Open daily 10am-5pm.) You can also hop on and off **bus** W32 as it zooms around the circular island road (☎ 810 262, 90min. circuit, M-Sa 1-2 per hr.). **Car rental** is available from Peter Brown (☎ 810 243; 25+, from £30 per day). If you tire of dry land, try a guided **sea-kayaking tour** with Chris Denehy. (☎ 810 443. £10 per evening, £15 per half-day, £25 per day.)

🔋🔧 ORIENTATION AND PRACTICAL INFORMATION. Castlebay is Barra's only town. The A888 rings the island, passing through Barra; the airport sits opposite Barra on the A888. A helpful **Tourist Information Centre** is around the bend to the east of the pier. They'll find you a B&B for a £3 charge plus a 10% deposit, but book ahead—a wedding, festival, or positive weather forecast can fill every bed on the island. (☎810 336; www.isleofbarra.com. Open Easter to Oct. M-Sa 9am-5pm, Su noon-4pm. Remains open for late ferries.) Barra has one **ATM**, at the Royal **Bank** of Scotland across from the TIC. (☎810 281. Open M-F 9:15am-12:30pm and 1:30-4:45pm.) **Internet access** is available at the Castlebay School Library, 10min. west of the Castlebay Hotel. (☎810 471. Book ahead. Open M and W 9am-1pm and 2-4:30pm; Tu and Th 9am-1pm, 2-4:30pm, and 6-8pm; F 9am-1pm and 2-3:30pm; Sa 10am-12:30pm.) The **post office** is next to the bank. (☎810 312. Open M-W and F 9am-1pm and 2-5:30pm, Th 9am-1pm, Sa 9am-12:30pm.) **Post Code:** HS9 5XD.

🔲🔳 ACCOMMODATIONS AND FOOD. Barra is home to the excellent 🔳**Dunard Hostel ❶**, up the hill from the pier. This colorful hostel has a knowledgeable staff; inquire about weekend events, island walks, adventure treks, and upcoming festivals. (☎810 443. Dorms £11. Cash only.) The **Isle of Barra Hotel ❹**, at Tangasdale Beach, overlooks the Atlantic at a picturesque spot; its restaurant has fresh meals and a good wine list. (☎810 383. Singles £48; doubles £84. MC/V.) The neighboring **Craigard Hotel ❸** has typical hotel accommodations, a gorgeous view of the ocean, a restaurant, and a pub. (☎810 200. Singles £55; doubles £80. MC/V.) The **restaurant ❷** overlooks the ocean and serves nightly specials of half a dozen types of local fish. (Open M-Sa noon-9pm, Su noon-8pm. MC/V.) Just below the Craigard Hotel is the Co-op **grocery** store. (☎810 308. Open M-W and Sa 8:30am-6pm, Th-F 8:30am-7pm, Su 12:30-6pm.) The cheerful 🔳**Cafe Kisimul ❶**, Main St., across from where the boat departs from the pier for the castle, has creative Indian food and the usual cafe fare. (☎810 645. Open M-Sa 10am-5pm. Cash only.) Feast on local salmon or lamb shank (£9) at the **Castlebay Hotel Restaurant ❸**, or sip a drink while listening to live music at its pub. (Uphill from the harbor. ☎810 223; www.castlebay-hotel.co.uk. Bar open 11am-midnight. Food served 5:30-8:30pm. MC/V.)

🔲 SIGHTS. Kisimul Castle, medieval bastion of the Clan MacNeil, rests in solitude in the middle of Castle Bay. It was recently leased to Historic Scotland for 1000 years, for £1 and one bottle of Talisker whisky per year. Take a motorboat from the pier in front of the TIC to the castle gate. (☎810 313. Open Apr.-Oct. M-Sa 9:30am-6:30pm. £3.30, concessions £2.50.) A sampling of island life and Gaelic culture is found at the rotating exhibits of the **"Dualchas" Barra Heritage and Cultural Centre,** near the school. (☎810 413. Open Apr.-Sept. M-Sa 11am-4pm. £2, concessions £1.50.) The road west from Castlebay passes the brooding, cloud-topped mass of **Ben Tangasdale** before arcing north to an amazing stretch of beach at **Halaman Bay.** From there, the road extends northward past turquoise waters and more white sand. Opposite Allasdale to the north, **Seal Bay** makes a great picnic spot. A map of Barra can guide you to numerous **standing stones** and **cairns** dotting the hills in the middle of the island. Farther north is **Eoligarry** is **Cille Bharra Cemetery**, containing "crusader" headstones thought to have served as ballast in a clan warship. Inside the neighboring **St. Barr's Church,** weave through candlelit shrines and Celtic crosses. To see the whole island, follow the one-lane A888, which makes a 14 mi. circle around the 1260 ft. slopes of **Ben Heavel,** Barra's highest peak.

🔁 DAYTRIP FROM BARRA: VATERSAY AND MINGULAY. A short causeway connects Barra to **Vatersay** (Bhatarsaigh; pop. 70), the southernmost inhabited isle in the Outer Hebrides. The island is home to two shell-sand beaches on the narrow isthmus connecting Barra and Vatersay. A monument commemorates the *Annie Jane*, which sank off Vatersay in 1853. **Camping** is available at a site next to the public hall; contact the **TIC** in Castlebay for more information (£4, toilet facilities). **Bus** W33 runs to Vatersay from the Castlebay post office by the pier (M-Sa 4-5 per day). Bird-watchers should visit the deserted island of **Mingulay,** to the south. Call Donald MacLeod at Barra Fishing Charters to inquire about **boat trips** from Castlebay in summer. (☎ 890 384. 2 per week, weather permitting. From £30 per day.)

NORTHWEST HIGHLANDS

Striking in its isolation and marked by a variety of natural landscapes—from gentle, sloping hills to diving cliffs to rocky mountains—northwest Scotland begs to be explored. Travelers will marvel up-close at seals, dolphins, and seabirds, climb the peaks of Torridon's mountains, and bathe by Britain's highest waterfalls at Eas-coul-Aulin, near Kylesku. The region is easiest to tour on foot or by car. Although possible to navigate, the public transportation system is limited.

▐ TRANSPORTATION

Without a car, traversing the northwest coast is tricky in summer and nearly impossible in winter. Inverness is the area's main transport hub. Scotrail (☎ 08457 484 950) runs **trains** from Inverness to Kyle of Lochalsh (2½hr., 4 per day, £15.20) and Thurso (4hr., 3 per day, £13.50). Scottish Citylink (☎ 08705 505 050) and Rapson **buses** travel from Inverness to: Kyle (2½ hr., 6 per day, £12); Thurso (3½hr., 5 per day, £12.20); Ullapool (1½hr., M-Sa 2-4 per day, £7.70). From April to October, the **Northern Explorer Ticket,** available at bus stations, provides unlimited travel between Inverness and Thurso (3 consecutive days £39; 5 of 10 £62; 8 of 16 £85). **Postbuses** are another option; consult the public transport guide. The few locals drive like hell-bats on narrow, winding roads, but pick up any hikers they don't run over. Let's Go does not recommend hitchhiking.

DORNIE   ☎ 01599

Though the tourist mobs rush to Skye, the **Eilean Donan Castle** (EL-len DOE-nin), near the village of Dornie, is a must-see. The restored 13th-century seat of the MacKenzie family and the setting for the films *Highlander* and *The World is Not Enough,* the castle juts out over three converging lochs. Tours provide in-depth explanations of the castle's secrets and treasures, including a dungeon next to the castle's kitchen, where prisoners were forced to smell sumptuous meals as they starved to death. (☎ 555 202. Open daily Apr.-Oct. 10am-5:30pm; Mar. and Nov. 10am-3:30pm. £4.75, concessions £3.75, families £9.75.) The trek to the 370 ft. **Falls of Glomach** is an amazing but tough 1½hr. from Glen Elchig. Farther east, the 3505 ft. **Five Sisters of Kintail** tower above the A87, and, on the other side of the highway, the spectacular **Mam Ratagan Pass** leads to secluded Glenelg.

Easily reachable by car, but a long trek on foot, the ▓**Tigh Iseaball Bunkhouse ①** can be found 7 mi. north of Dornie on the A87. The self-catering croft cottage has a lovely, remote setting at the base of a mountain. (☎ 588 205; www.holidaysinhighlands.com. Dorms from £7.50. Cash only.) The **Silver Fir Bunkhouse ②** sleeps a cozy four. Ask if you can use the herbs in the organic garden. (From Dornie, 10min. east along the loch, 200 yards past the chapel. ☎ 555 264. Linen £1. Dorms £12. Cash only.) Scottish Citylink and Highland Country **bus** #60 links Dornie to Inverness and Kyle (2 per day, £4.80).

PLOCKTON ☎01599

You may encounter your first Highland traffic jam in Plockton, as cattle and sheep roam freely and find the warm pavement perfect for napping. The idyllic harbor village, 6 mi. north of Kyle of Lochalsh, has hand-swept streets, a row of painted houses, and a grove of palm trees. The **Leisure Marine Office,** on the waterfront rents canoes, rowboats, and paddleboats (£5-15 per hr.). Keep your eyes peeled for seals, otters, and porpoises in the cove. **Calum's Seal Trips,** at the Main Pier or the pontoon next to the carpark, are free if no seals show. (☎544 306. 1hr. tours daily Apr.-Oct. at 10am, noon, 2, 4pm. £6. MC/V.) Just outside of Plockton is the **Craig Highland Farm,** where you can feed rare breeds of livestock. (☎544 205. £1.50, children £1. Open daily 10am to dusk.) Opposite the train station, the **Station Bunkhouse ❶,** offers a comfortable hostel. (☎544 235. Dorms £10. Cash only.) The owners also run a B&B, **Nessun Dorma ❷,** next door to the bunkhouse. (Singles from £20.) Scotrail runs **trains** from Inverness and Kyle (5 per day, £1.70). Plockton is also served by the Kyle-Plockton-Ardnarff **postbus** (#119; 1-3 per day).

APPLECROSS ☎01520

The tiny, serene village of Applecross is a well-hidden gem. The drive across the harrowing **Bealach na Ba ("Cattle") Pass** is an adventure for the iron-hearted only. At 2054 ft., the steep, single-track pass is Britain's highest road, punctuated by hairpin turns and livestock with little regard for their own lives and even less for yours. On a clear day, drivers are rewarded with expansive views of Skye and the Small Isles; with rain, it's a white-knuckle affair with a near-invisible cliff drop 5 ft. away; with snow, the road is impassible. The circuitous **coastal route** is a less death-defying option, offering views of the rocky seashore. A 9500-year-old dwelling in **Sand** and a **Viking lime kiln** in Keppoch, along with other pre-historic and natural wonders, are described in the free *Applecross Scenic Walks.* **Mountain & Sea Guides** offers kayaking and trekking trips. (☎744 394; www.applecross.uk.com. 2hr. session £15, half-day £25; discounts for longer excursions.)

After successfully navigating Bealach na Ba Pass, take the left-hand road at the junction and turn right at the red barn to discover the **Applecross Flower Tunnel Cafe ❶,** a breezy conservatory festooned with flowers and offering jazzy tunes, lattes, and mouthwatering carrot cake. (☎744 268. Open daily 9am-9pm. MC/V.) **Camping** is available in the grassy field next to the cafe (£6 per person, children free. MC/V). The elegant ⊠**Applecross Inn ❷,** down the hill on the waterfront, offers heartwarming Scottish hospitality and award-winning local seafood and game. The delightful upstairs **B&B ❸** has sunny rooms with ocean views. (☎744 262. Bar-restaurant open 10am-midnight. Singles £30-35, doubles £60-70. MC/V.) Applecross is served by **postbus** #92 from Torridon and Shieldaig (1 per day, departs Torridon at 10:45am). The nearest train station is 17 mi. away in Strathcarron.

TORRIDON ☎01445

The teensy village of Torridon (pop. 230) lies between **Loch Torridon** and the Torridon Hills. Although the town itself doesn't have much to offer, the surrounding peaks draw adventurous hikers; the highest and closest is the challenging **Liathach** (3456 ft.). The staff at the **Torridon Countryside Centre,** at the crossroads in Torridon, 100 yards east of the hostel, possesses an encyclopedic knowledge of the region and sells guides to area walks. (☎791 221. Open daily Easter to Sept. 10am-6pm.)

At the base of the daunting Liathach, the **SYHA Torridon ❷** is a large ranch-style lodge with a friendly staff and rowdy hillwalkers trumpeting their latest exploits. (☎791 284. Open Mar.-Oct. Dorms £11-12, under 18 £9.75. MC/V.) The rangers allow **camping** between their office and the SYHA. The small general store 300 yards west along the road is your lone bet for **groceries.** (☎791 400. Open M-Sa

9:30am-5:30pm, Su 9:30-11:30am and 3-5:30pm.) From Inverness, **trains** (☎08457 484 950) run to Achnasheen (1¼hr.; M-Sa 4 per day, Su 2 per day; £9.70); there, **postbus** #91 (12:10pm) connects to Torridon. Buses do not meet every train; Duncan Maclennan (☎01520 755 239) shuttle **buses** connect with the Inverness train at Strathcarron (1hr.; June-Sept. M-Sa 12:30pm, Oct.-May M, W, F only; £3).

GAIRLOCH   ☎01445

With a road that travels along miles of beautiful coastline culminating in the Rua Reidh lighthouse, Gairloch is a perfect seaside village. Just outside the mountains, Gairloch often escapes the rain and fog that clings to the surrounding region. Its pleasant coastal spread has made it a popular resort town; book ahead if coming in summer. The **Gairloch Heritage Museum** houses a giant lighthouse bulb. (☎712 287. Open Mar-Sept. M-Sa 10am-5pm; Oct. 10am-1pm; in winter call ahead. £3.) Horseback riders can ride at the **Gairloch Trekking Centre,** just south of the pier. (☎712 652. £6.75 per 30min.; lessons available.) Six miles north along the coastal road, the **Inverewe Gardens** grow flowers in a tropical microclimate heated by the passing jetstream. Free guided walks are available from mid-April to mid-September. Westerbus runs from Gairloch to the gardens at least twice per day during the week (£1); check the timetable at the TIC first. (☎781 200. Garden open daily mid-Mar. to Oct. 9:30am-9pm; Nov. to mid-Mar. 9:30am-4pm. £8.)

The 12 mi. drive out to the ⬛**Rua Reidh Lighthouse ❶** will reward you with hot showers, delicious food, and incredible views. From Gairloch, take the road signposted to Melvaig. (☎771 263; www.ruareidh.co.uk. Dorms £9.50; private rooms £28-38. MC/V.) Find a quiet, lochside bed at the **SYHA Carn Dearg ❶,** 2 mi. northwest of town on the B8021. Get off the Gairloch bus at the village of **Strath** and walk toward the sea from there. (☎712 219. Reception 7-10:30am and 5-11:30pm. Curfew 11pm. Open mid-May to Sept. Dorms £11, under 18 £8.75. MC/V.) Just half a mile west of the hostel, campers can pitch at the beachside **Sands Holiday Centre ❶** (☎712 152; www.sandsholidaycentre.co.uk. £8-11 per tent.) The **Old Inn ❹,** at the south end of town, meets the needs of diverse travelers in an elegant atmosphere. You'll find fresh local ingredients, an experienced chef, and live music. (☎712 006. Food served noon-9:30pm. Singles £32-45; doubles £45-89. MC/V.) In Strath village on B8021, head to the pleasantly cluttered **Mountain Coffee Company ❶** for a latte and scone (☎712 316; open daily 9:30am-5:45pm; MC/V). Dine on pasta and local seafood in the stylishly sparse **Cafe Blueprint ❷,** right across the street (☎712 397; entrees £6-9; open daily 10am-4:30pm and 6:30-9pm; MC/V).

For a £3 charge plus a 10% deposit, the **Tourist Information Centre** books B&Bs in Gairloch and Dundonnell, just east of the Ardessie Gorge. (☎712 130. Open June-Aug. M-F 9:30am-5:30pm, Sa 10am-6pm, Su 11am-3pm; Sept.-Oct. and Easter to June M-Sa 10am-5pm; Nov. to Easter M-Sa 10am-4pm.) Buy **groceries** at Somerfield, on the A832 just south of its intersection with the B8021. (☎712 242. Open M-F 7:30am-9pm, Sa 8am-9pm.) There is **Internet access** (£1 per 30min.) upstairs at **Strath Stores** on the B8021 in Strath's village center (☎712 499; open M-Sa 8am-6pm) and at **Wordworks,** above the Harbour Centre on Pier Rd. (☎712 712; £1 per 30min.). The **post office** is in Strath's center. (☎08457 223 344. Open M-W and F 9am-1pm and 2-5:30pm.) **Post Code:** IV21 2BZ.

ULLAPOOL   ☎01854

Compared to its neighbors, buzzing Ullapool feels downright cosmopolitan. With plenty of pubs, tea rooms, and gift shops, this lively port town will keep shoppers busy and travelers entertained. The area also abounds with **hikes,** including an excellent ramble through the shaded woodlands of **Ullapool Hill.** Its summit offers impressive views of Glenn Achall (2hr. round-trip). Footpaths are marked with yellow signs and begin 200 yd. northwest of the school on North Rd. and behind the Royal Hotel on Shore St. The SYHA hostel (p. 650) provides free leaflets detailing longer walks that traverse **Scots Pine** and the **Inverpolly Nature Reserve.** Wardens can also suggest how to **cycle** to nearby hostels in **Carbisdale** and **Achiniver.** The **Ullapool Museum,** W. Argyle St., uses audiovisual displays to recount local history. (☎612 987. Open Apr.-Oct. M-Sa 10am-5pm; Nov.-Mar. by arrangement. £3, concessions £2, children 50p.) Explore the **Summer Isles** (p. 650) with an adventurous powerboat expedition with **Seascape Expeditions** (☎633 708; £23) or a more leisurely float aboard the **Summer Queen** (☎612 472).

 ⧉Scotpackers West House ❶, W. Argyle St., has towering bunks, easy chairs, a computer room, and a lounge. (☎613 126; www.scotpackers-hostels.co.uk. Internet access £1 per hr. Dorms £13-14. AmEx/MC/V.) The affiliated **Crofton House ❸** has doubles, but phone the hostel first (£30 per person, AmEx/MC/V.) Sleep overlooking the harbor at the bright, well-situated **SYHA Ullapool ❶,** Shore St., 200yd. east of the pier. The friendly staff can give you lots of information on walks around Ullapool. (☎612 254. Laundry £2. Bike rental £6-12 per day. Curfew M-F and Su midnight; Sa 12:30am. Dorms £11-12, under 18 £8.75-9.25. MC/V.) Somerfield, Seaforth Rd., supplies **groceries** (☎01854 613 291; open M-Sa 8am-8pm, Su 9am-6pm). Costcutter, across from the post office, has a smaller selection. (☎612 261. Open M-Sa, Su 8am-8pm.) At **⧉The Seaforth ❷,** try a half-pint of winkles (£2) or the award-winning fish and chips. (☎612 122; www.theseaforth.com. Entrees £5-13. Open M-F 9am-12:45am, Sa 9am-11:45pm, Su noon-11:45pm. MC/V.) **The Ceilidh Place ❸,** 14 W. Argyle St. (☎612 103), is a hotel, cafe, bar, bookstore, and gallery enclosed by honeysuckle and roses. In summer, lively Celtic music is performed. (Entrees £13-18. Open daily 8:30am-9pm. AmEx/MC/V.) **Jasmine Tandoori ❶,** West Ln., serves excellent Indian food, offering a 3 course lunch for £7. (☎613 331. Entrees £7-9. Open daily noon-2pm and 5-11pm.)

 Except for the 1am arrivals, **ferries** from Stornoway, Lewis (M-F 2-3 per day; £14.40, 5-day round-trip £24.65; with car £70/120) are met by Scottish Citylink and Rapsons Coaches **buses** (☎01463 222 244). Buses run from Inverness (1½hr., 2 per day, £7.50), including a Tim Dearman (☎01349 883 585) bus with an attachment for bicycles (1¾hr., 1 per day, £8.50). The **Tourist Information Centre** is on Argyle St. (☎612 486. Open July-Aug. M-Sa 9am-6pm, Su 10am-5pm; Apr.-June and Sept.-Oct. M-Sa 9:30am-5pm, Su 10am-4pm.) An **ATM** can be found at the **Bank of Scotland** on W. Argyle St. (08457 801 801, Open M-T, Th-F 9am-12:30pm, 1:30pm-5pm; W 9:30am-12:30pm, 1:30pm-5pm.) The **post office** is on W. Argyle St. (☎612 228. Open M-Tu and Th-F 9am-1pm and 2-5:30pm.) **Post Code:** IV26 2TY.

🏊 DAYTRIPS FROM ULLAPOOL

⧉CORRIESHALLOCH GORGE. Twelve miles south of Ullapool on the A835, the River Broom cascades 150 ft. down the **Falls of Measach** into a menacing gorge. Corrieshalloch slices through the earth like a deep scar. Turn right on the footpath across from the bus stop; 40 yards northwest on the path, a short fenced plank thrusts over the gorge and serves as a **viewpoint** for the falls upstream to the southeast. Follow the footpath 100 yd. to the **suspension bridge** (built 1867) that balances over the falls. Though it sways unsettlingly with every step, six normal-sized hikers can safely traverse the (oft-inspected) relic. The gorge has been intermittently closed for repairs to the bridge; check at a TIC. The gorge is easily accessible by any Ullapool-Inverness **bus;** double-check that a return exists before you set out.

ACHILTIBUIE. (Ah-KILL-ta-boo-ee) Northwest of Ullapool, caught between coastal waters and towering rocks, Achiltibuie is a sleepy village where visitors can climb the hills or stroll a trio of sandy beaches. Off the coast, local crofters graze their sheep on the lovely **Summer Isles,** also home to rock formations and a seal colony. The **Hydroponicum** grows rows of strawberries, a choice selection of salad greens, and the only native Highland banana, all without soil. (☎ 622 202. Tours every hr. Open daily mid-Apr. to Sept. 10am-6pm. £5, concessions £4.) At the **Achiltibuie Smokehouse,** 4 mi. northwest in Altandhu, customers can watch as fish are slit, sliced, and smoked. (☎ 622 353. Open M-Sa 9:30am-5pm. Free.)

Hike down a short, ferned path and cross the bridge over a gushing stream to the idyllic **SYHA Achininver ❶,** ¼ mi. from a sandy beach and 3 mi. from Achiltibuie. (☎ 613 701. Open mid-May to Sept. Dorms £10.75, under 18 £8.25. MC/V.) The **Culross Vegetarian B&B ❸** has creative cuisine and decor, as well as local art in the gallery next door. (☎ 622 426. Singles £20-25; doubles £36-40. Gallery open M-F 10am-5pm, Sa-Su 10am-1pm. MC/V.) The ingredients at the **Lily Pond Cafe ❷** are straight from the Hydroponicum's garden. (Open daily mid-Apr. to Sept. 10am-6pm. MC/V.)

Tour Achiltibuie from Ullapool (p. 649) or on the passenger vessel M.V. *Hectoria* from **Badentarbet Pier,** at the western end of Achiltibuie. (☎ 01854 622 200. 3½hr. tours Apr.-Oct. M-Sa 10:30am and 2:15pm. £15. 7hr. tours Apr.-Oct. M-Sa 10:30am; £20.) Spa Coaches runs **buses** from Ullapool (M-F 2 per day, Sa 1 per day; £4). If driving, take the A835 north 10 mi. from Ullapool, then go west along the signposted single-track road, following it 15 mi. to the coast. On the main road in town, Achiltibuie Store sells **groceries.** (Open M-Sa 9am-5:30pm.) Fifty yards down the road, the **post office** offers info about the village. (☎ 622 200. Open M-W and F 9am-noon and 1-5:30pm, Th 9am-1pm, Sa 9am-12:30pm.) **Post Code:** IV26 2YG.

LOCHINVER AND ASSYNT   ☎ 01571

Thirty miles up the northwest coast, the unremarkable town of Lochinver is a food-and-petrol outpost for the wild region of Assynt, a breathtaking region nearly impossible to penetrate without a car. Treks (8-10hr.) go up the imposing mountains of **Suilven** and **Canisp;** though lengthy, these trails are accessible to walkers of all levels. Going south from the Visitor Centre, the second left leads to **Glencanisp Lodge,** where a footpath famed for wildlife sightings skirts the River Inver (2hr. round-trip). The shorter **Culag Wood Walk** (1hr. round-trip) starts west of the field near the pier. From the SYHA hostel (see below), a **nature trail** crosses the town of **Alt-na-Bradhan** before reaching the striking rock formation at **Clachtoll** (2-3hr. round-trip). For longer expeditions, buy a map—Ordnance Survey Landranger #15 is available at the TIC (£6.50). The Ranger Service (☎ 844 654) offers free **guided walks** in summer. Assynt Angling Group (☎ 844 076) or Assynt Crofters' Trust (☎ 855 298) can recommend **fishing** holes and the TIC can get permits (£5 per day).

There are a number of decent B&Bs in town; the **Ardglas Guest House ❷,** across the stone bridge, is one of Lochinver's cheapest, with fine views and spacious rooms. (☎ 844 257. Singles from £20.) **Hostels** are far away but compensate with dramatic views and access to hiking and cycling trails. The bare-bones **SYHA Achmelvich ❶,** Recharn, is 3 mi. west on a stunning footpath, or 20min. by the 11:15am postbus. (☎ 844 480. Reception 7-10:30am and 5-11pm. Open Apr.-Sept. Dorms £8.75, under 18 £7.50. MC/V.) The nearby **Achmelvich campsite ❶** sits along a beach with icy water. (☎ 844 393. Tent £7.) Another 13 mi. inland, the ruins of **Ardvreck Castle** on Loch Assynt sit 1 mi. from the social **Inchnadamph Lodge ❶,** Assynt Field Centre, which has endless amenities. Local deer lurk nearby, waiting for table scraps. Ullapool-Lochinver buses stop upon request. (☎ 822 218. Breakfast included. Laundry £1.50. Dorms £12.50; doubles £37. MC/V.)

The only public transport that enters this forbidding country is the KSM Motors **bus,** which runs once or twice per day from Ullapool (£3.50). Check with the TIC for times. **Postbus** #123 trundles in from the Lairg train station (M-Sa 12:45pm). The **Assynt Visitor Centre,** on the waterfront in Lochinver, serves as a TIC. (☎ 844 330.

Open Easter to Oct. M-Sa 10am-5pm, Su 10am-4pm.) A Royal **Bank** of Scotland is at the west end of town, just before the pier. (☎844 215. Open M-Tu and Th-F 9:15am-12:30pm and 1:30-4:45pm, W 10:30am-12:30pm and 1:20-4:45pm.) The Spar **supermarket** is on the far end of the same street. (☎844 207. Open M-Sa 8am-6:30pm.) The **post office** is next door to the Spar. (☎844 201. Open M, W, F 8:30am-1pm and 2-5pm, Tu 8:30am-1pm, Sa 8:30am-12:30pm.) **Post Code:** IV27 4JY.

DURNESS   ☎01971

A quiet village on Scotland's north coast, Durness is a popular stop on tours of the region, and for good reason. One mile from the town center lie the ◪**Smoo Caves**— deep holes in the limestone that take their name from *smuga*, Old Norse for "hiding place." Legend claims that the bastard son of a McKay chieftain hid the bodies of 18 murdered men here. Take a tour and float via rubber dinghy past the interior waterfall. (☎511 704; ask for Colin. 20min. tours depart from cave entrance daily Apr.-Sept. 10am-5pm. £3.) **Smoo Cave Tours** runs wildlife boat tours, taking in Faraid Head, the Cliffs of Moine Schist, and glimpses of gray seals, dolphins, and minke whales. (☎511 704. Easter to Oct. 11am-4pm. £4.) Cliffs soar at **Cape Wrath,** 12 mi. west of Durness. From the Cape Wrath Hotel (1½ mi. west of the town center), a ferry crosses to Kyle of Durness (☎511 376; 3-4 per day; round-trip £4.30), where it's met by a minibus that completes the trip to Cape Wrath (☎511 287; round-trip £7). Ferries and buses operate on demand May-Sept. from 9:30am. The Cape may be closed for Royal Air Force training; call the TIC to check.

The best budget lodgings are provided by the amiable ◪**Lazycrofter Bunkhouse ❶,** whose dull exterior does little justice to its luxurious bunks. (☎511 202; www.durnesshostel.com. Dorms £11.) Right next to Smoo, the **SYHA Durness ❶,** 1 mi. north of town along the A838, sports a bland exterior that hides eclectic design, a friendly staff, and a peat-burning stove. (☎511 244. Reception 7-10:30am and 5-11pm. Open Apr.-Sept. Dorms £10.50, under 18 £8. MC/V.) More private respite awaits at **Smoo Falls B&B ❸,** across from the Smoo Caves. (☎511 228. £23-30 per person. Cash only.) **Sango Sands Camping Site ❶** overlooks the sea next to the visitor center. To the south find a beach, to the north, the campground's pub. (☎511 726. Reception 9-9:30am and 6-6:30pm. Tent £4.50. Cash only.)

To reach Durness, hop **postbus** #104 from the Lairg train station or #105 from the post office (☎01463 256 228; M-Sa 2 per day). Postbus # 136 (1 per day) goes from Thurso to Tongue; buses will shuttle you from Tongue to Durness, but schedules change, so call ahead. Tim Dearman buses also pull in from Inverness (5hr., 1 per day, £14) and Ullapool (3hr., 1 per day, £8). The **Tourist Information Centre** books B&Bs for a £3 charge plus a 10% deposit. (☎511 368. Open daily Apr.-Oct. 10am-5pm; Nov.-Mar. 10am-1:30pm.) The **post office** is up the road in the Mace store. (☎511 209. Store open M-F 8am-5:30pm, Sa 9am-5:30pm. Post office open M-Tu and Th-F 9am-5:30pm, W and Sa 9am-12:30pm.) **Post Code:** IV27 4QF.

THURSO AND SCRABSTER   ☎01847

A big fish in a very small pond, Thurso (pop. 9000) is considered a veritable Tokyo by the crofters and fishermen of Scotland's desolate north coast. The city has no museums and doesn't seem to care. But Thurso sports **castle ruins** just east of town and one of Europe's best **surfing beaches** near the castle. Rent wetsuits (£10 per day) and surfboards (£10 per day) from Tempest Surf, Thurso Harbor, at the end of the waterfront road. (☎892 500. Open daily 10am-6pm. MC/V.) Scrabster, 2½ mi. east, is no more than a ferry port for Orkney (p. 653); spend the night in Thurso.

Infectiously friendly ◪**Sandra's Backpackers Hostel ❶,** 26 Princes St., features a kitchenette and ensuite dorms with TVs. The owners provide lifts to Scrabster for noon ferry connections. (☎894 575; www.sandras-backpackers.ukf.net. Continental breakfast included. Facilities for the disabled available. Bike rental and Internet access free. Dorms £10; private rooms £30. Cash only.) The countryside **Thurso Youth Club Hostel ❶** is in the echoing halls of a converted mill. From the train station, walk east down Lover's Ln., turn north on Janet St., cross the river, and follow the park path to the right. (☎892 964. Continental breakfast included. Open July-Aug. Dorms £9. Cash only.) **Sandra's Snack Bar and Takeaway ❶,** beneath the hostel, is a happening backpacker hangout with rock-bottom prices. (☎894 575. Open M-F 10am-11pm, Sa 10am-midnight, Su 12:30-10:30pm. 10% discount for hostelers. Cash only.) A more sophisticated menu of crepes, fish, fajitas, and steak awaits at **Le Bistro ❷,** 2 Traill St., Thurso, with comfy window seats for people-watchers. (☎893 737. Entrees £8-14. Open M-F 10am-9pm, Sa 9:30am-3:45pm and 5:15pm-9pm.) On Wednesday nights, young and old come together at the **Commercial ("Comm") Bar,** 1 Princes St., for live local music. (☎893 366. Open M-Th 11am-midnight, F-Sa 11am-1am, Su noon-11pm.) The **Central Pub,** Traill St., attracts a young, lively crowd in the late afternoons. (☎893 129. Open M-Th and Su 11am-11:45pm, F-Sa 11am-12:45am.)

Highland Country **bus** #77 travels to Thurso between Wick train station and John O'Groats. (1hr.; M-F 9 per day, Sa 3 per day). A **Tourist Information Centre,** Riverside Rd., treats Thurso's sights with casual indifference but its visitors with warmth. (☎892 371. Open June-Aug. M-Sa 10am-5pm and Su 10am-4pm; Apr.-May and Sept.-Oct. M-Sa 10am-5pm.)

JOHN O'GROATS ☎01955

Named for the first man to arrange ferries to the islands (Jan. de Groot, a Dutchman), John O'Groats is known for its position as mainland Britain's northernmost town. The surrounding islands are the real destination. **Wildlife Cruises,** run by John O'Groats Ferries, leave the docks daily at 2:30pm in July and August to cruise the waters of Pentland Firth, home to kittiwakes, great black backs, and other obscure animals. (☎611 353. 1½hr. tours £14.) **Dunnet Head,** halfway from John O'Groats to Thurso, is the northernmost point on the Isle, but **Duncansby Head,** 2 mi. east of town, has a better view overlooking the Pentland Firth toward Orkney. If stuck on the mainland, make your way 2½ mi. west to Canisbay and the quaint **SYHA John O'Groats ❶.** (☎08700 041 129. Reception 7-10am and 5-11:30pm. Curfew 11:30pm. Open Easter to Sept. Dorms £11, under 18 £8.25. MC/V.) To reach town from the **Wick train station,** take Highland Country **bus** #77 (40min., 4-5 per day), which also runs to Thurso (1hr.; M-F 9 per day, Sa 3 per day) and passes the hostel. From May to August, John O'Groats Ferries's Orkney Bus runs from Inverness (daily 2:20pm, June-Aug. also 7:30am; £14). The **Tourist Information Centre,** County Rd., by the pier, helps plan escapes to surrounding areas and can arrange accommodations if you miss a ferry. (☎611 373. Open daily June-Aug. 9am-6pm; Apr.-May and Sept.-Oct. 10am-5pm.)

ORKNEY ISLANDS

The magnificent Orkneys are a world in and of themselves. The islands sport fertile farmland, archaeological sites, a reef of scuttled German WWII warships, and vertigo-inducing cliffs. The residents, mostly farmers and fishers, of the 70-island archipelago have a unique ancestry; Orcadians, part Scottish, part Viking, part Pictish, have lived on the islands for millennia. And with 337 species of birds, the feathered outnumber the flightless 100 to 1. On Mainland (the largest island, sometimes called Pomona), the capital city of Kirkwall has a stunning 12th-century

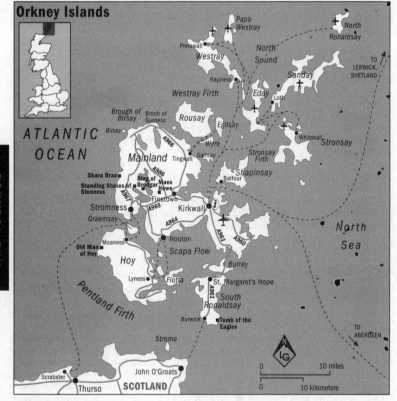

Orkney Islands

cathedral and bustling, shop-lined streets. The quieter city of Stromness offers an arts center and Orkney museum. The most interesting sights lie in the sparsely populated northern islands and rocky southern islands.

▐ GETTING THERE

Ferries are the main mode of transport between the Orkneys and mainland Scotland. The affordable Pentland Ferry (☎01856 831 226) runs from Gills Bay, west of John O'Groats on the A836 (1hr.; 2-4 per day; £11, children £5.50, cars £27; cash only). Ferries land at St. Margaret's Hope on Orkney. Orkney Coaches runs a bus service between there and Kirkwall (M-Sa 4 per day). John O'Groats Ferries (☎01955 611 353; www.jogferry.co.uk) travel from John O'Groats to Burwick, Orkney, where a free bus takes passengers to Kirkwall (ferry 40min., bus 35min.; June-July 4 per day; May 2 per day; Sept. 2 per day; round-trip £24-28). John O'Groats Ferries also offers several **ferry-tour packages.** Their Maxi Day Tour makes stops at major sights and includes a 2hr. break in Kirkwall (9am-7:45pm, last boarding 8:50am; £36; book ahead). The Highlights Day Tour hits the same sights but only stops in Kirkwall for 20min. (10:30am-6pm; £33). Northlink Ferries (☎08456 000 449) offers trips from Scrabster to Stromness on the posh *Hamnavoe*

(1½hr.; M-F 3 per day, Sa-Su 2 per day; round-trip £24.60-29). A bus departs from the Thurso rail station for Scrabster before each crossing. Northlink also sails from Aberdeen to Kirkwall (6-8hr., round-trip £30.40-46.20).

LOCAL TRANSPORTATION

Orkney Coaches (☎ 01856 870 555; www.rapsons.co.uk) runs **buses** between Kirkwall bus station and Stromness Pier Head (30min., M-Sa every hr., £2.20). The friendly staff of Orkney **Ferries** (☎ 01856 872 044), based on Shore St. at the Kirkwall harbor, can help travelers island-hop. Some ferries are foot-passengers only (no vehicles), all ferries offer student discounts, and schedules are likely to change; call ahead. Ferries (£3-6, concessions £1.50-3, cars £9-13.50) depart from Kirkwall to: Shapinsay (25 min.), Westray & Papa Westray (1½hr.), Stronsay (1½hr.), Eday (1¼hr.), and Sanday (1½hr.). Ferries also depart Tingwall to Rousay, Egilsay, and Wyre (30-60min.). Ferries leave Houton (20min. west of Kirkwall on the A964) to Lyness in the south of Hoy (20-45min.), and Flotta (45min.). A passenger-only ferry runs from Stromness to Moaness in the north of Hoy (15min.).

Car rental is by far the most convenient way of getting around Orkney; try W.R. Tullock, Castle St., Kirkwall Airport. (☎ 876 262. 21+. From £32 per day.) Orkney Car Hire, Junction Rd., Kirkwall (☎ 872 866; www.orkneycarhire.co.uk; 21+; from £28 per day) and Stromness Car Hire, John St., Kirkwall (☎ 850 973; 21+; from £28 per day, £159 per week) also rent cars. **Biking** is an alternative, though the rain and wind can be problematic. You can rent wheels in Kirkwall from Cycle Orkney, Tankerness Ln., off Broad St. (☎ 875 777; www.bobbyscycles.co.uk; £8 per day; open M-Sa 9am-5:30pm) or in Stromness at Orkney Cycle Hire, 54 Dundas St. (☎ 850 255. Helmet and map included. £6 per day. Open daily 8:30am-9pm.)

THE ORKNEY MAINLAND

KIRKWALL   ☎ 01856

The bustling center of Orkney becomes a full-fledged tempest during the day, as cars fight their way down the pedestrian-packed Albert St. and Broad St., before quieting when the shops close and daytrippers depart. Kirkwall is at its best (and most expensive) during the **St. Magnus Festival** (St. Magnus Festival Office, 60 Victoria St.; ☎ 871 445; www.stmagnusfestival.com), which takes place during the third week of June. Musicians, from folk singers to the BBC Philharmonic, migrate north for the festival and entertain around the clock in the almost 24hr. daylight.

🔢 **PRACTICAL INFORMATION.** The Kirkwall **Tourist Information Centre**, 6 Broad St., books B&Bs for a £3 charge plus a 10% deposit and distributes transport info. (☎ 872 856. Open May M-F 9am-5pm, Sa 10am-4pm, Su 10am-4pm; June-Sept. daily 8:30am-8pm; Oct.-Apr. M-F 9am-5pm, Sa 10am-4pm.) Guidebooks are also available at The **Orcadian Bookshop** on Albert St. (☎ 878 888). Inter-island ferry information and bookings are best obtained at Orkney Ferries, Shore St. (☎ 872 044; www.orkneyferries.co.uk.) Other services include: **Bank** of Scotland, 56 Albert St. (☎ 682 000; open M-Tu and Th-F 9am-5pm, W 9:30am-5pm); Kelvinator **launderette**, 47 Albert St. (☎ 872 982; open M-F 8:30am-5:30pm, Sa 9am-5pm); **police**, Watergate (☎ 872 241); Boots **pharmacy**, 49-51 Albert St. (☎ 872 097; open M-Sa 9am-5:30pm); **Internet access** at Support Training Limited, 2 W Tankerness Ln., one block west of Broad St. (☎ 873 582; £1 per 10min., £5 per hr.; open M-F 8:30am-7pm, Sa 10am-

5pm) or free next door at the **public library** (☎873 166; M-Th 9am-8pm, F 9am-6pm, Sa 9am-5pm); and the **post office,** 15 Junction Rd. (☎874 249; open M-Tu and Th-F 9am-5pm, W 9am-4pm, Sa 9:30am-12:30pm). **Post Code:** KW15 1AA.

⌐ ACCOMMODATIONS. A number of hostels, B&Bs, and crofthouses can be found by consulting the Orkney Tourist Board's annual publication, available around town and at the TIC. Keep in mind that sometimes the best accommodations are in the most remote areas. Kirkwall's simple **SYHA hostel ❶** is on Old Skapa Rd. Follow the main pedestrian road south from the TIC for 1 mi. as it evolves from Broad St. into Victoria St. Cross Union St., heading southwest to Main St., and turn on Wellington St. (☎872 243. Reception 7:30-10:30am and 5-11:30pm. Lockout 10:30am-5pm. Curfew midnight. Open Apr.-Oct. Dorms £11.50, under 18 £9.25.) It's an easy walk to the cozy **Peedie Hostel ❶**, 1 Ayre Rd., across from the pier, with televisions and a harbor view. (☎875 477. Dorms £10.) At **Mr. and Mrs. Flett's B&B ❷**, Cromwell Rd., climb a ship's staircase to cozy rooms with views of the harbor and sea. (☎873 160. £18-20 per person.) For a more upscale environment, head to the peaceful **West End Hotel ❹**, Main St., just outside the main drag. (☎872 368. Breakfast included. Singles £43; doubles £59.) Right near the Scrabster ferry is the elegant **Kirkwall Hotel ❹**, Harbour St. (☎872 232. Singles £20-48; double £40-82.) **Camp** at **Pickaquoy Centre Caravan & Camping Site ❶**, on Pickaquoy Rd. just south of the A965. (☎879 900. £7.50 per caravan, £4-7.20 per tent.) You can pitch a tent almost anywhere on the islands, but always ask the landowner first.

◖ FOOD. Stock up on **groceries** before a trip to the islands at Somerfield, on the corner of Broad St. and Great Western Rd. (☎228 876; open M-W and Sa 8am-8pm, Th and F 8am-9pm, Su 9am-6pm) or at the Co-op next door (☎873 056; open M-F 9am-5pm, Sa 9am-7:30pm, Su 9am-6pm). **Buster's Diner ❶**, 1 Mounthoolie Pl., is draped in tacky Americana and cooks up pizza and burgers for less than £5—all under the front end of a Ford Mustang. (☎876 717. Open May-Sept. M-F noon-2pm and 4:30-9:30pm, Sa noon-11pm, Su 4:30pm-9pm. Cash only.) **Trenabies Cafe ❶**, 16 Albert St., has delicious sandwiches (£4-5), cappuccino, and pastries. (☎874 336. Open M-Tu 8am-6pm, W-Th 8am-7pm, F 8am-9pm, Sa 9am-5pm, Su noon-6pm. MC/V.) For a rollicking time with a mixed crowd of young and old, locals and travelers, head to **The Bothy Bar ❶**. (☎876 000. Live folk music Su night. Open M-W 11am-midnight, Th-Sa 11am-1am, Su noon-midnight. Food served 5-9:30pm.)

◙ SIGHTS. Next to the TIC on Broad St., **St. Magnus Cathedral,** begun in 1137 and constructed from beautiful bands of red and yellow sandstone, is the town's central landmark. (Open Apr.-Sept. M-Sa 9am-6pm, Su 1-6pm; Oct.-Mar. M-Sa 9am-1pm and 2-5pm. Free.) Across Palace Rd. from the cathedral, the **Bishop's and Earl's Palaces** once housed the Bishop of Orkney and his enemy, the wicked Earl Patrick Stewart. The houses were joined when the earl was executed for treason. (☎871 918. Both open daily Apr.-Sept. 9:30am-6:30pm. £2.50. Ticket for both palaces, Skara Brae, Maes Howe, and the Broch of Gurness £13, concessions £10, children £5.) For a thorough history of the islands, check out the **Orkney Museum,** Broad St., in the center of town across from the chapel. (☎873 191. Open Apr.-Sept. M-Sa 10:30am-5pm, Su 2-5pm; Oct.-Mar. M-Sa 10:30am-12:30pm and 1:30-5pm. Free.) The 200-year-old **Highland Park Distillery,** 20min. south of town on Holm Rd., is the world's northernmost whisky distillery and purveyor of acclaimed single malts. The distillery has a tour, a sampling, and an informative (if goofy) video. Walk to the southern end of Broad St., turn west on Clay Loan, then south on Bignold Park Rd. and take the right fork on Holm Rd. (☎874 619; www.highlandpark.co.uk. Open Apr. and Oct. M-F 10am-5pm; May-Sept. M-F 10am-5pm, Sa-Su noon-5pm; Nov.-Mar. M-F 1-5pm. Tours 2pm. £5, concessions £4.)

STROMNESS ☎ 01856

Originally named "Hamnavoe" by the Vikings and once a thriving fishing and whaling port, the town of Stromness is rich in maritime history. With narrow cobblestone streets and historic buildings, Stromness has a distinct Old-World charm and a beautiful view of the bay. The **Pier Arts Centre,** Victoria St., which is closed until summer 2006, displays the work of contemporary Scottish artists and a brilliant collection of 20th-century British artists, including Hepworth and Wallis. (☎850 209. Open Tu-Sa 10:30am-12:30pm and 1:30-5pm. Free.) The **Stromness Museum,** 52 Alfred St., tackles the history of local boating and boasts a collection of stuffed Orkney birds. (☎850 025. Open Apr.-Sept. daily 10am-5pm; Oct.-Mar. M-Sa 11am-3:30pm. £2.50, concessions £2.)

The small and simple **Brown's Hostel ❶,** 45-47 Victoria St., has 14 beds and is centrally located on Stromness's main street. (☎850 661. Dorms £11. Cash only.) **Orca's Hotel ❸,** 76 Victoria St., offers friendly B&B-style service in the middle of town and keeps a stellar, unpretentious restaurant, ▓**Bistro 76 ❸,** below. Enjoy the fresh catch of the day amid romantic nautical decor. (Hotel ☎850 447; www.orcahotel.com. £20-25 per person, MC/V. Restaurant ☎851 308. Entrees £8-13. Open M-Sa 5:30-9:30pm. Cash only.) Pricier accommodations are available at the recently refurbished 100-year-old **Stromness Hotel ❹,** at the Pier Head on Victoria St., which has two bars and a restaurant. (☎850 298; www.stromnesshotel.com. May-Sept. £48 per person; Apr. £41; Oct.-Mar. £29. MC/V.) One mile south of town on Victoria St., the **Point of Ness Caravan and Camping Site ❶** has a beautiful view. (☎851 235. Open May to mid-Sept. £7.50 per caravan, £4-7.20 per tent. Showers 20p. Laundry wash £1, dry 40p. Cash only.) Across from the pier, **Julia's Cafe & Bistro ❶,** 20 Ferry Rd., has baked goods, vegetarian options, and sandwiches (£3-6). Sunlight pours in through the bay windows. (☎850 904. Open Easter to Sept. M-Th 9am-5pm, F-Sa 9am-8:30pm, Su 10am-8:30pm; Oct. to Easter M-Th 9am-5pm, F-Sa 9am-8:30pm. Cash only.)

The **Northlink Ferry** runs the *Hamnavoe* from Scrabster to Stromness (p. 654); almost everything you'll need (and almost everything in town) is on **Victoria Street,** which parallels the harbor. The **Tourist Information Centre,** in an 18th-century warehouse on the pier, provides free maps. (☎850 716. Open May-Sept. daily 9am-5pm; Oct.-Apr. M-Sa 9:30am-3:30pm.) The **Bank** of Scotland, 99 Victoria St., has an ATM (☎682 000. Open M-Tu and F 9:45am-12:30pm and 1:30-4:45pm, W 10:45am-12:30pm and 1:30-4:45pm.) The **library,** 2 Hellihole Rd., offers free **Internet access.** (☎850 907. Open M-Th 2-5pm and 6-8pm, F 2-6pm, Sa 10am-1pm and 2-5pm.) The **post office** is at 37 Victoria St. (☎850 225. Open M-F 9am-1pm and 2-5:15pm, Sa 9am-12:30pm.) **Post Code:** KY16 3BS.

▶ DAYTRIPS ON THE ORKNEY MAINLAND

A journey across the verdant mainland is a journey through 5000 years of Orkney history. The Stone-Age, Bronze-Age, and Viking-era sites around the island are the finest examples of their kind in the world. Although public transportation can be scant, tour buses service the four main archaeological sites between Kirkwall and Stromness: **Maes Howe Tomb,** the **Standing Stones of Stenness,** the **Ring of Brodgar,** and **Skara Brae.** Reaching these sites by **bicycle** is also an option, but beware the harsh winds and unpredictable weather. Ranger-naturalist Michael Hartley of **Wildabout Tours** squires visitors around Mainland and Hoy in his minibus on half- and full-day tours. (☎851 011; www.wildabout-orkney.co.uk. Tours daily Mar.-Oct. From £18; student and hosteler discounts.) Orkney native John Grieve leads **Discover Orkney Tours,** which tailors trips to individual visitors' interests (☎872 865; from £30 per person per day). Both guides leave from the TICs in Kirkwall and

Stromness; if you arrange ahead, they will also pick you up from your ferry, plane, or accommodation. Alternatively, take one of the packaged ferry-and-tour trips (p. 654). The **Orkney Explorer Pass,** for sale at all Historic Scotland sites on Orkney, saves you several pounds on admission to popular attractions (£13).

⬛ SKARA BRAE. Five thousand years ago, Skara Brae was a bustling Stone-Age village; eventually, ocean waves destroyed the houses and forced the inhabitants away. Sand preserved the village until 1850, when a storm revealed the remnants of nine houses, a workshop, and covered town roads. You can make your way via a beach path to the site until closing. (19 mi. northwest of Kirkwall on the B9056; take the A965 from Kirkwall to Stromness and turn right at the sign after Maes Howe. Continue along the road until the signs for Skara Brae. ☎ 841 815. Open Apr.-Sept. daily 9:30am-6:30pm; Oct.-Mar. M-Sa 9am-4:30pm. Last admission 45min. before close. £6.)

RING OF BRODGAR. Six miles east of Skara Brae and 5 mi. northeast of Stromness on the B9055 stands a great circle of standing slabs of sandstone. The Ring of Brodgar may once have witnessed gatherings of local chieftains or burial ceremonies; no two archaeologists agree. The 60 stones (only 27 of which still stand) have stayed true to their heritage as a venue for unusual assemblies—a motley crew congregates annually for the summer solstice. (Always open. Free.)

STANDING STONES OF STENNESS. One mile east of the Ring on the B9055, the berm-enclosed Standing Stones of Stenness have been reduced over time to a humble few, but they are still impressive. A solitary stone between the two monuments implies that Stenness and Brogdar were once part of the same ceremonial process. By 1760 only four of the original 12 stones remained—locals angered by the monument's pagan origins likely knocked down the others. (Always open. Free.)

MAES HOWE TOMB. Between Kirkwall and Stromness on the A965, this tomb may have held the bones of the area's earliest settlers (from 2700 BC). Vikings arrived in the mid-12th century and plundered the settlement's treasures; their carvings constitute the largest collection of runic inscriptions in the world. This site enabled linguists to crack the runic alphabet and translate the profound statements: "This was carved by the greatest rune carver" and "Ingigerth is the most exquisite of women." (☎ 761 606; www.maeshowe.co.uk. Open Apr.-Sept. daily 9:30am-6pm; Oct.-Mar. M-Sa 9:30am-4pm, Su 2-4pm. £4. Call ahead.)

BROCH OF GURNESS. Off the A966, on the north coast of the Evie section of Mainland, this broch is the site of a preserved Iron-Age village, fortuitously unearthed by the ultimate Orcadian Renaissance man, Robert Rendall, in 1929. The reconstructed Pictish and Viking settlements are worth a stop on the way between towns. (☎ 751 414. Open Apr.-Sept. daily 9:30-12:30pm and 1:30-6pm. £3.30.)

BROUGH OF BIRSAY. At the northwest tip of the mainland, this brough is an island at high-tide; in low tide, a man-made path atop the wet, rocky ground makes it accessible by foot. Check the tidal charts at the TIC or Skara Brae before making the journey. The island's kirkyard holds a Pictish stone engraving of a crowned royal figure, suggesting that Orcadian kings once ruled from here. Bird-watching is absorbing, but linger too long and the puffins may become your bedfellows. (Open mid-June to Sept.; only accessible during low tide. Free.)

CHURCHILL BARRIERS AND SCAPA FLOW. At the end of WWII, the German High Seas Fleet sunk at **Scapa Flow,** the bay south of Houton on Mainland; the German Admiral von Reuter ordered all 74 of his ships to be scuttled rather than remain in British hands. To the delight of scuba divers from around the world, seven of the wrecks remain. **Scapa Scuba,** in the Lifeboat House on Dundas St., Stromness, offers non-certified "try-a-dive" lessons, equipment, and a dive to the wrecks. They also offer more involved tours for experienced divers. (☎851 218. £60 per half-day.) If you don't want to get wet, **Roving Eye Enterprises** does the marine work for you via a roaming underwater camera; the boat leaves from Houton Pier and stops on Hoy. (☎811 360; www.orknet.co.uk/rov. Tours daily 12:30pm. £25, children £12.50.) In 1939, German U-boats re-entered the straits leading to the Scapa Flow naval anchorage during an exceptionally high tide, sinking a warship, killing 800 seamen, and escaping unscathed. The next year, Prime Minister Churchill erected massive barriers to seal the seas from attack. The POWs who built the barriers exhausted over a quarter-million tons of rock, and the barrier's **causeways** now provide access from Mainland to the smaller southeast islands.

ORKNEY CRAFT TRAIL AND ARTISTS STUDIO TRAIL. Founded in the 1990s, the Orkney Craft Industry Association, a group of local artists, weavers, jewelers, woodworkers, and other artisans designed a route connecting their workshops (usually also their homes). The stops include shops with varying prices and styles, from **Hoxa Tapestry Gallery** in St. Margaret's Hope (☎831 395) to **Orkney Stained Glass,** on Shapinsay (☎771 276). Brown signs (sometimes faded to orange) direct drivers to hidden hamlets of tradition and creativity. Pick up the *Craft Trail* brochure in the TIC or visit www.orkneydesignercrafts.com.

SMALLER ISLANDS ☎01856

The smaller islands, most accessible by car or ferry from Kirkwall or Stromness, have fascinating sights—Iron- and Bronze-Age monuments, wildlife, and gorgeous scenery. Take particular care when traveling here; with erratic ferry schedules dependant upon tides, you could end up sleeping with the seals and birds. Make sure to tell someone where you're going and to bring warm clothing with you.

HOY. Hoy, the second-largest of the Orkney Islands (57 sq. mi.), gets its name from the Norse word "Haey," meaning "high island." Hoy is spectacularly hilly in the north and west (more "Highland" in character), while the south and east are lower and more fertile, like the rest of Orkney. Its most famous landmark, the ▧**Old Man of Hoy,** is a 450 ft. sea stack of sandstone off the west coast of the island. Hikers can take the steep, well-worn footpath from the partially abandoned crofting village of Rackwick, 2 mi. away (3hr. round-trip). The North Hoy Bird Reserve offers respite for guillemots and a host of other species. Puffins roost during breeding season, from late June to early July. The **SYHA Hoy ❶,** near the pier, and the eight beds of the simple **SYHA Rackwick ❶,** at the start of the path toward the Old Man, offer accommodations and share a telephone number. Visitors must bring a sleeping bag. (☎873 535. Hoy open May to mid-Sept. Rackwick open mid-Mar. to mid-Sept. Dorms £7.70-10.60, under 18 £7.70-8.25.) If you plan to stay overnight on Hoy, make sure to bring adequate provisions. The tiny isle of Flotta, off Hoy's coast, was home to "that irascible and belligerent Jacobite" James Stewart, who murdered Captain James Moodie on Kirkwall's Broad St. A strategic military base in both World Wars, Flotta is now a quiet, flat isle with gorgeous 360-degree views.

SHAPINSAY. Only 45min. from Kirkwall, with frequent ferry services, Shapinsay is the most accessible of the outer isles. Shapinsay's relatively flat landscape is interrupted by **Ward Hill,** the island's highest point at 210 ft. From its peak on a (rare) clear day you can see almost all the islands. An excellent example of the Victorian Baronial style, 19th-century **Balfour Castle** was once home to the influential lairds of Balfour and is now a posh guest house. Romantics can rent the castle and its chapel for weddings. Guided tours of the castle depart from Kirkwall pier and include the ferry ride and tea. For those without the curiosity or cash to see inside, the castle is perfectly visible from the ferry. (☎711 282, tours 872 856. Tours May-Sept. Su 2:15pm. £18.) **Burroughston Broch,** an Iron-Age shelter, lies 5 mi. north of the ferry pier. Archaeology buffs will be thrilled by the crumbling round home, which was excavated in the 1860s. There are no hostels on Shapinsay, but the award-winning **Girnigoe B&B ❹,** near the beach, has two rooms in a converted farmhouse. (☎711 256; www.girnigoe.net. Twins or doubles £40-50. Cash only.)

ROUSAY. Many argue that Orkney's finest archaeological sights lie not on Mainland, but on Rousay. The **Midhowe Broch** and **Cairn** has Stone-, Bronze-, and Iron-Age remnants. The **Knowe of Yarso Cairn** stands on a cliff overlooking Eynhallow Sound, and the **Westness Walk** winds past sites from the Neolithic, Pictish, Viking, medieval, and crofting eras. Just above the ferry terminal, a visitor center displays an exhibition on the points of interest in Rousay and nearby Egilsay and Wyre. Stay at the **Rousay Hostel ❶** on Trumland Farm near the pier; turn left from the ferry port and walk 5min. down the main road. (☎01856 821 252. Linen £2. Dorms £8. Cash only.)

STRONSAY. Seven miles long, this island is a collection of bays and beaches. Along the east coast, between Lamb Ness and Odiness, is the stunning Vat of Kirbister, an opening ("gloup") spanned by a dramatic natural stone arch. There are Pictish settlements and an Iron-Age fort on the southeastern bay. Stay at **Stronsay Fishmart ❶,** in Whitehall Village, which also has a cafe. (☎616 385. £10, with bedding and towel £13. Cash only.)

EDAY. The peat-covered hills of Eday hide Stone-Age field walls, chambered tombs like the **Vinquoy** and **Huntersquoy Cairns,** the towering **Stone of Setter,** and, on the Calf of Eday, the remnants of an Iron-Age roundhouse. The island also provides the standard, desolate Orkney landscape. The **SYHA Eday ❶,** London Bay, is on the main north-south road, 4 mi. from the pier. (☎01857 622 206. Laundry £2. Open Mar.-Oct. Dorms £8, under 18 £7. Camping £2. Cash only.)

SANDAY. As its name suggests, Sanday's greatest feature is its sweeping white sand beaches. Seal pups can be seen swimming at Otterswick in June, and grey seals are born on the beaches in November. Elusive otters are hard to spy, but their tell-tale tracks (five-toed prints and a trailing line) speckle the sands. Head out at low tide along Cata Sand Bay for a spectacular barefoot walk across the white sands to the sea. The unexpected **Orkney Angora Craft Shop,** in Upper Breckan, is home to enormous white fluffy Angora rabbits, who are sheared like sheep every few months. The hair is hand-spun, dyed, and knitted in the shop. (☎600 421; www.orkneyangora.co.uk. Open daily 1:30-5:30pm or by arrangement.) Diane runs ◪**Ayre's Rock Hostel and Campsite 1,** a meticulously kept bunkhouse with two double rooms, a family room, a kitchen, towels as big and fluffy as Angora rabbits, and sunsets over the ocean. (☎600 410. Internet access 50p per hr. £10. Cash only.)

WESTRAY. Just west of Papa Westray, (mama) Westray features ruined **Noltland Castle,** the **Knowe O'Burristae Broch,** ancient rubble, and magnificent cliffs. Legend holds that the windowless castle, marked by over 60 gun holes, is linked underground to the **Gentlemen's Cave,** which hid supporters of Bonnie Prince Charlie. The castle's first owner, Gilbert Balfour, was implicated in two royal assassination plots, the second of which got him executed. Bird-watchers rejoice on **Noup Head Reserve,** while budget travelers welcome two top-notch hostels. You'll feel like one of the family at ◪**The Barn ❶,** Chalmersquoy, at the southern end of Pierowall village, in a wonderfully converted stone barn. (☎01857 677 214. £11.75, children £8.80.)

Cash only.) ◼Bis Geos Hostel ❶, 2 mi. west of Pierowall, on the edge of the world, is a fabulous croft ruin-turned-hostel, complete with Internet access (£1 per 30min.), heated flagstone floors, and a gorgeous sunroom overlooking the cliffs. If you're lucky, you might dine on crabs and lobsters just pulled from the ocean cliffs. (☎01857 677 420; www.bisgeos.co.uk. Open Apr.-Oct. Dorms £11. Cash only.)

PAPA WESTRAY. "Papay" is home to a mere 60 or so Orcadians. This northern "isle of the priests" once supported an early Christian Pictish settlement. The island lies where the Atlantic Ocean and the North Sea meet; at the right tidal moments, fearsome waves break both above and below the water's surface. Fly from Kirkwall (LoganAir ☎872 494; M-F 3 per day, Sa 2 per day, Su 1 per day; £15); if the plane stops at Westray, you get a certificate for world's shortest commercial flight. On the west coast, the **Knap of Howar** marks the location of the oldest standing house in northern Europe (c. 3500 BC), built centuries before the pyramids of Egypt. The **Bird Sanctuary** at North Hill has Europe's largest colony of Arctic terns. Two miles north of the pier, **Beltane House ❶** is open year-round; hostelers enjoy ensuite dorms, while B&B guests get a sitting room. All have access to the only liquor-licensed place on the island—a closet full of booze. (☎644 267. Dorms £12, children £8; B&B £25 per person. Cash only.) Bring enough food for at least a day.

NORTH RONALDSAY. Due to the warm Gulf Stream, this northernmost Orkney is an average of 10°F warmer than its latitudinal neighbors. North Ronaldsay offers archaeological wonders, like the **Broch of Burrian,** an unusual standing stone with a hole through it, and two weathered lighthouses. The lighthouse keeper gives excellent tours (☎07703 112 224; £4, children £2). The island's famous ◼seaweed-eating sheep graze on the beaches, producing coveted wool. Viciously protective nesting birds are all over—take a cue from them and stay at the solar- and wind- powered **North Ronaldsay Bird Observatory Hostel ❶.** (☎01857 633 200. Internet access free. Call ahead for a lift from the airport. Dorms £10-11, full board £23.50. Cash only.)

SOUTHEAST ISLANDS. Accessible by road from Mainland, this string of islands, including Lamb Holm, Burray, and South Ronaldsay, is quiet and full of wonderful craft shops and an organic farm hostel. On Lamb Holm, the **Italian Chapel** is all that remains of Camp 60, a prison that held hundreds of Italian POWs in WWII. When not at work on the Churchill Barriers, the Italians transformed their bare cement hut into a beautiful house of worship that is still in use today. (Open daily Apr.-Sept. 9am-10pm; Oct.-Mar. 9am-4:30pm. Occasionally closed F afternoons, the traditional time for Orkney weddings. Services 1st Su of the month. Free.) During the summer, **buses** chug over the Churchill Barriers from Kirkwall to the pier at St. Margaret's Hope (3-4 per day), on the larger isle of South Ronaldsay.

A fantastic 8-bed hostel and organic farm, **Wheems Bothy ❶,** stands on the blustery promontory of South Ronaldsay. The proprietors run a treasure of a silkscreen and feltmaking studio. Fresh eggs and produce available. Call ahead for pickup. (☎831 537. Open Apr.-Oct. Dorms £6.50; camping £2-3 per person.) The greatest treasure to be found on South Ronaldsay, however, is the family-run ◼Tomb of the Eagles. Farther south, outside of St. Margaret's Hope in Isbister, lies the farm of the Simison family. They own and operate a fantastic visitor's center, where you can handle 5000-year-old artifacts, including marvelously intact human skulls and eagle talons. A quarter of a mile from the visitor's center is a Bronze-Age burnt mound, a stone dwelling with a plumbing system, the dramatic sea cliffs, and the spectacular Stone-Age tomb after which the property is named. (☎831 339; www.tomboftheeagles.co.uk. Open daily Apr.-Oct. 9:30am-6pm; Nov.-Mar. 10am-noon or by appointment. £5, concessions £4.25, children £2-3.)

HIGHLANDS AND ISLANDS

SHETLAND ISLANDS   ☎ 01595

Prosperous from the discovery of oil in the 1970s, the Shetlands and Orkneys became part of Scotland in the 15th century, when King Christian I of Denmark and Norway mortgaged them to pay his daughter's dowry. Closer to Norway than to Great Britain, the Shetlands seem a country unto themselves; their Viking heritage is apparent in the architecture and in festivals like the longship-burning Up Helly Aa Festival (p. 665).

✈ GETTING THERE

Air travel is the fastest and most expensive way to the Shetlands. Flights are usually cheaper if you stay over a Saturday night. British Airways (☎08457 733 377) flies from: Kirkwall, Orkney (35min., 1 per day, round-trip £80-170); Inverness (1½hr., 1 per day, round-trip £124-294); Aberdeen (1hr.; M-F 3 per day, Sa-Su 2 per day; £80-110); Edinburgh (1½hr., 1 per day, £181-250); Glasgow (2½hr.; M-F 2 per day, Sa-Su 1 per day; £96-200). **Travel agents** Shetland Travelscope (☎696 644) and John Leask & Son (☎693 162; www.leaskstravel.co.uk) purchase tickets and organize trips. All flights land at **Sumburgh Airport,** on the southern tip of Shetland's Mainland, which also has a visitor's center with a knowledgeable staff and Internet access (£1 per 20min.). The airport is 25 mi. (and a hefty £30-35 taxi ride) from Lerwick, the islands' capital and largest town. John Leask & Son buses make the journey to Lerwick (1hr.; M-Sa 5 per day, Su 3 per day; £2.20). Buses arrive at the **Viking Bus Station** (☎694 100), 5min. from the city center on Commercial Rd.

Ferries are the other means of travel to the Shetlands. Though cheaper, they take far longer than flights. Most ferries arrive at **Holmsgarth Terminal,** a 20min. walk northwest of Lerwick's town center, or the smaller **Victoria Pier,** across from the TIC. Northlink Ferries (☎08456 000 449; www.northlinkferries.co.uk) arrive from Aberdeen (12-14hr.; M, W, F 7pm; Tu, Th, Sa-Su 5pm; £19.80-30.30) and Kirkwall, Orkney (7¾hr.; Tu, Th, Sa-Su 11:45pm; £12.90-18.20). Arrive 30min. in advance. P&O Smyril Line (☎690 845; www.smyril-line.com) runs in summer from Lerwick to Bergen, Norway (12hr., M 11:30pm, £77.50) and to Iceland (30hr.; W 2am; £149.50, with car from £184) via the Faroe Islands (13hr., £77.50). Call ahead for prices and times from mid-September to April.

▄ LOCAL TRANSPORTATION

Infrequent public transport makes getting around Shetland difficult without a car. **Car rental** companies include John Leask & Son (☎693 162; £31-42 per day), the more extensive Bolts Car Hire, 26 North Rd. (☎693 636, airport branch 01950 460 777; www.boltscarhire.co.uk; 21+; £35-49 per day), and Grantfield Garage, 44 North Rd. (☎692 709; www.grantfieldgarage.co.uk. 23+. £24-30 per day.)

Travel between the islands is heavily subsidized; **ferries** sail to the larger islands nearly every hour, to the smaller islands at least once a day, and no trip costs more than £5. All ferries except those to Fair Isle transport bikes for free. Shetland's main **bus** provider is John Leask & Son (☎693 162). Whites Coaches (☎809 443) handles the North Mainland services. The TIC stocks the vital *Shetland Transport Timetable* (£1) with bus, ferry, and plane schedules. Eric Brown's Cycle Hire, on the second floor of Grantfield Garage, offers **bike rental.** (☎692 709. £7.50 per day, £45 per week. Helmets £1. Open M-W 8am-9pm, Th-Sa 8am-10pm, Su 11am-9pm.) Winds and hills can make biking difficult.

Tour companies offer convenient ways of seeing Shetland. Dr. Jonathan Wills runs ▓**Seabirds-and-Seals,** a 3hr. tour which includes cliffs, caves, and wildlife. Tea and coffee are served on deck. Trips depart from Victoria Pier, Lerwick. (☎693 434; www.seabirds-and-seals.com. £30. Daily May-Aug. 9:30am, 2pm.) A 2hr. cruise

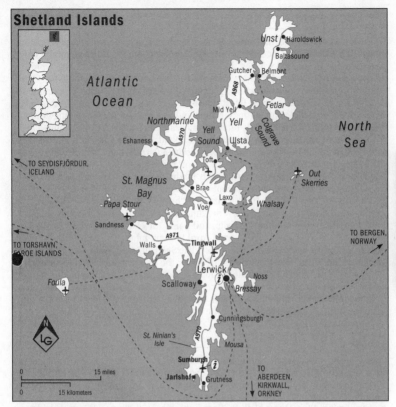

Shetland Islands

Atlantic Ocean

Unst Haroldswick
Baltasound
Gutcher Belmont
A968
Fetlar
Mid Yell
Northmarine *Yell* *Yell* Colgrave Sound
A970 Sound
Eshaness Ulsta
North Sea

Toft

TO SEYDISFJÖRDUR, ICELAND

St. Magnus Bay
Brae
Papa Stour Laxo Out Skerries
Voe *Whalsay*
Sandness

A971
TO TORSHAVN, FAROE ISLANDS
Walls **Tingwall**

TO BERGEN, NORWAY

Foula **Lerwick**
Scalloway Noss
Bressay

Cunningsburgh

St. Ninian's Isle
A970 *Mousa*
Sumburgh
Jarlshof Grutness
TO ABERDEEN, KIRKWALL, ORKNEY

0   15 miles
0   15 kilometers

through Bressay Sound allows travelers to view the kelp forest below with a live feed from a mini-sub (daily 6pm, £25). Most affordable are the **Leasks Coach Tours,** on the Esplanade in Lerwick. (☎693 162. Mainland tours Tu and Su £12, Yell and Unst W £30, Northmavine Th £18.) Walking tours include the **Shetland Ranger Service's** guided treks across the islands, which are great for bird-watching (☎01957 711 528 or 0195 694 688; May-Aug. £2.50), **Geo Tours'** day-long geology and land-scape-themed expeditions (☎859 218), and the folklore-oriented **Island Trails** with local Elma Johnson. (☎01950 422 408. May-Sept. 2hr., £10-12, children £4.)

ORIENTATION AND PRACTICAL INFORMATION

On the eastern coast of Mainland, Lerwick sits on the island's central artery, the A970. The **Tourist Information Centre,** Market Cross, books beds for £3 plus a 10% deposit. (☎693 434; www.visitshetland.com. Open Apr.-Oct. M-F 8am-6pm, Sa-Su 8am-4pm; Nov.-Mar. M-F 9am-5pm.) Other services include: the Royal **Bank** of Scotland, 81 Commercial St. (☎694 520; open M-Tu and Th-F 9:15am-4:45pm, W 10am-4:45pm); free **Internet access** in the Learning Centre adjacent to the Shetland **Library,** on Lower Hillhead (☎693 868; open M and W-Th 10am-7pm, Tu and F-Sa 10am-5pm); and the **post office,** 46-50 Commercial St. (☎08457 223 344; open M-F 9am-5pm, Sa 9am-12:30pm). **Post Code:** ZE1 0EH.

HIGHLANDS AND ISLANDS

ACCOMMODATIONS

The community-run **SYHA Lerwick** ❷, at King Harald and Union St., is perhaps the finest SYHA hostel you'll come across, with has excellent facilities, a popular cafe, and gardens. Bruce, the warden, knows everything Shetland. (☎692 114. Laundry £2. Reception 9-9:30am, 4-4:30pm, and 9:45-10:15pm; at other times, go to the Community Centre next door. Curfew 11:45pm. Open Apr.-Sept. Dorms £15, under 18 £12.50. MC/V.) The **Glen Orchy Guest House** ❹, 20 Knab Rd., is a comfortable B&B overlooking Breiwick Bay, with 24 rooms and many amenities, including complimentary fresh fruit. (☎692 031. Internet access free. Singles £42.50; doubles £69. MC/V.) There are three **campgrounds** on Mainland, but you can pitch almost anywhere with the landowner's permission. **Clickimin Caravan and Camp Site** ❶ is closest to the Lerwick ferry terminal; turn left on Holmsgarth Rd. (A970), go through the roundabout, and merge onto North Lochside; it's on the right. (☎741 000. Showers, pool, bar, and cafe. Reception 8:30am-10pm. Open May-Sept. Pitches £6.70-9.40. MC/V.) **Böds** ❶ (Old Norse for "barns"; www.camping-bods.co.uk), are converted fishing cottages now serving as "camping barns." Bring a sleeping bag, camping stove, cooking utensils, and coins for electricity (when available). Mainland's six böds are available from April to September. Try **Betty Mouat's,** near the airport (with hot water and showers); The **Sail Loft,** next to the pier in Voe; the **Voe House,** in Waas; **Skeld,** southeast of Waas; the newly refurbished **Nesbister,** in Whiteness; and **Johnnie Notions,** at Hamnavoe, Eshaness, in the extreme northeast. **Grieve's House** is on tiny Whalsay, near Lerwick by bus; the **Windhouse Lodge** is on Yell; and **Aithbank** is on Fetlar. All böds cost £6-8 per night and must be booked in advance through the Lerwick TIC or the Shetland Amenity Trust (☎694 688).

FOOD AND PUBS

Stock up on **groceries** at Somerfield, South Rd., or at the Co-op, Holmsgarth Rd., one block from the ferry station. (Somerfield ☎692 426. Co-op ☎693 419. Both open M-W and Sa 8am-8pm, Th-F 8am-9pm, Su 9am-6pm.) Jivin' **Osla's Cafe** ❶, 88 Commercial St., specializes in pancakes (£3.50-4.50). They're worth a stop. (☎696 005. Open M-W 9:30am-7pm, Th-Sa 9:30am-8:30pm, Su 11am-5pm.) On the Esplanade, the **Peerie Shop Cafe** ❶ serves sandwiches, baked goods, organic cider, and a sinful special hot chocolate (£1.65, with rum £2.75). The shop next door sells funky woollens and crafts. (☎692 817. Open M-Sa 9am-6pm.) **Raba** ❸, 26 Commercial St., offers traditional Indian cuisine and atmosphere. (☎695 554. All-you-can-eat Su buffet £8.50. Open M-Sa noon-2pm and 5pm-midnight, Su noon-midnight.) For Lerwick's hostelers, the city's most convenient food awaits at the **Isleburgh Community Centre Cafe** ❶, on the first floor of the hostel, and the **Blue Rock Cafe** ❶, next door at the Community Centre. Both are happening backpacker hangouts. (Both ☎692 114. Isleburgh Community Centre Cafe open M-Sa 8am-2:30pm, Su 8-11am. Blue Rock Cafe open M-Sa 9:45am-11pm, Su noon-4pm and 8:30-11pm.)

The Lounge, 4 Mounthooly St., is the busiest pub; the downstairs is the main hangout and the upstairs is thick with smoke and lively Shetland fiddling. Jam sessions happen on Wednesday nights and some Saturday afternoons. (☎692 231. Open M-Sa 11am-1am.) Lively **Market Cross** has a great harbor view. (☎692 249. Happy hour F 5-7pm. Open M-Sa 8am-1am, Su 12:30pm-1am. Food served M-Sa noon-2:15pm, Su 12:30-2:15pm.) Young crowds put pool tables to good use at **Thule Bar,** near the ferry docks. (☎692 508. Open M-Sa 11am-1am, Su 12:30pm-1am.)

SHOPPING

Logically enough, Shetland is one of the best places in the world to buy ▓Shetland wool. Several shops in the center of Lerwick are chock full of hand-knit sweaters (£42-120). **Anderson & Co.**, 60-62 Commercial St., has a good selection within its larger clothing store. (☎693 714. Open M-Sa 9am-5pm.) The **Spider's Web**, 41 Commercial St., showcases various local artisans' high-quality knitwork. (☎695 246. Open M-Sa 9am-5pm.) On northerly Unst, you can shop for knits and enjoy apple pie at **NorNova Knitwear** in Muness. (☎01957 755 373. Open M-F 10am-4pm.)

MAINLAND SIGHTS

LERWICK. Shetland's capital began as a small fishing town in the 17th century. Weather permitting, you can cruise around the bay on the ▓**Dim Riv**, a full-scale replica of a Viking longship. (☎07970 864 189. Open June-Aug.; call ahead for times. Book in advance. £5) The **Isleburgh Exhibition,** in the Isleburgh Community Centre, features traditional music, dance, crafts, artwork, and film. (☎692 114. Open M and W 7-9:30pm. £5, children £3.) Not much of a sight in itself, the giant pentagonal **Fort Charlotte,** just off Commercial St. at the north end of town, offers the best views of Lerwick and its harbor. (Open daily 9am-10pm. Free.) The **Knab**, a small but impressive promontory at the end of Knab Rd., is a short coastal walk from **Clickimin Broch,** 1 mi. west of the city center. The broch, a stronghold from 400 BC, stands in the middle of a loch. Climb to the grassy top for a great view. (Always open. Free.) Shetland's Norse heritage is on display in longship form at the **Up-Helly-Aa' Exhibition** in the **Galley Shed,** Saint Sunniva St., Lerwick. (Open mid-May to mid-Sept. Tu 2-4pm and 7-9pm, F 7-9pm, Sa 2-4pm. £3, concessions £1.)

SCALLOWAY. Though Scalloway was Shetland's capital in the 17th century and is still a busy fishing port, 7 mi. west of Lerwick, there's not much to see. Crumbling **Scalloway Castle** was once home to villainous Earl Patrick Stewart and later become the sheriff's headquarters. Get the key from the Scalloway Hotel. (☎880 444. Castle open daily 9am-5pm. Free.) Popular ▓**Da Haaf Restaurant ❶**, North Atlantic Fisheries College, in the harbor, has the best fish and chips on the island. Call to reserve a table. (☎880 747. Open M-F 12:30-2pm and 5-8pm.) John Leask & Son sends **buses** from Lerwick (☎693 162; M-Sa 10 per day, round-trip £1.20).

UP HELLY AA

It has been nearly a millennium since the Vikings set sail in their sleek longships to conquer the Shetland Isles, but the wild Norsemen of Lerwick still party like, well, like Vikings. In the endless darkness of the last Tuesday of January, a thousand or so revelers bearing shields and torches bedeck themselves in the sartorial splendor of their Nordic ancestors—animal skins, armor, and horned helmets. The *guizers,* or revelers, elect a Shetlander to be the presiding Guizer Jarl (Earl), who organizes the event. On the morning of Up Helly Aa, a proclamation known as the "Bill," which contains the year's best gossip and local humor, is nailed to the Market Cross in the center of Lerwick. That night the guizers march through the streets bearing a meticulously reconstructed 30 ft. Viking longship (galley), which they eventually attack with burning torches to welcome the springtime daylight, singing the traditional song "The Norseman's Home."

The blazing pyre signals just the beginning of the festivities, and the procession then dashes off to the first of a dozen halls where the guizer squads perform with song and dance until dawn. The next day is a public holiday in Lerwick, and the streets are deserted while the town recovers from the previous night's merriment. *(Visitors welcome; call the Lerwick TIC ☎01595 693 434; www.shetland-tourism.co.uk.)*

JARLSHOF AND SOUTH MAINLAND. At the southern tip of Mainland, southwest of Sumburgh Airport, **Jarlshof** is one of Europe's most remarkable archaeological sites. In 1896 a storm uncovered stone walls and artifacts, some over 4000 years old. (☎01950 460 112. Open daily Apr.-Sept. 9:30am-6:30pm. Last admission 6pm. £3.30.) A mile up the road, the **Old Scatness Broch** is the site of ongoing excavation. Remains were discovered in 1975 during airport construction; since then an entire Iron-Age village and over 20,000 artifacts have surfaced. Guided tours provide helpful re-enactments. (☎694 688. Open July to mid-Aug. M-Th 10am-5pm, Sa-Su 10:30am-5:30pm. £2.) On nearby **Sumburgh Head,** gulls, guillemots, and puffins rear their young on steep cliff walls. All South Mainland sights can be reached by the Leask **bus** that runs to Sumburgh Airport from Lerwick (☎693 162; 5 per day). Four miles north of the airport at Voe, the ◙**Croft House Museum,** signposted off of A970, is a restored working croft house, barn, mill, and byre from the 19th century. (☎01950 460 557. Open daily May-Sept. 10am-1pm and 2-5pm. Free.)

NORTHMAVINE. Across Mavis Grind, a 100-yard-wide isthmus, lies the wild and remote northern part of the Mainland known as Northmavine. Continue northwest to the imposing volcanic seacliffs on ◙**Eshaness.** The wide-standing arch of **Dore Holm** sits offshore. ◙**Da Bod Cafe ❷**, on the waterfront in Hillswick, serves outstanding vegetarian food. The cafe donates proceeds to the seal and otter sanctuary. (☎01806 503 348. Open May Sa-Su 11am to late; June-Sept. Tu-Su 11am to late.) On Thursdays, John Leask & Son runs **tours** of Northmavine. (☎693 162. £18.)

◙ SMALLER ISLANDS

BRESSAY AND NOSS. Hike to the summit of the conical **Ward of Bressay,** locally called "Da Wart" (742 ft.), for a sweeping view of the sea. From Bressay's east coast, 3 mi. past the Lerwick ferry port (follow the "To Noss" signs), dinghies go to the tiny isle of **Noss;** stand at the "Wait Here" sign and wave to flag one down. Great skuas and arctic terns dive-bomb visitors at the **bird sanctuary;** wave a hat or stick over your head to ward them off. **Ferries** (☎980 317; 7min.; every hr.; £3, cars £7) sail from Lerwick to Bressay. (National Nature Reserve ☎693 345. Open June-Sept. Tu-W and F-Su 10am-5pm. Round-trip £3, concessions £1.50. Noss open Tu-W and F-Su 10am-5pm. Overnight stays forbidden.)

MOUSA. The tiny, uninhabited island of Mousa, just off the east coast of Mainland, is famous for its 6000 pairs of the miniscule nocturnal Storm Petrels. It also holds the world's best preserved Iron-Age **broch,** a 50 ft. drystone fortress that has endured 1000 years of Arctic storms. Catch a Sumburgh-bound Leask bus in Lerwick and ask the driver to let you off at the Setter Junction for Sandsayre (round-trip £5); it's a 15min. walk from there to the ferry. (☎01950 431 367. Ferry departs Apr.-May and Sept. M-Th and Sa 2pm, F and Su 12:30 and 2pm; June-Aug. M, W-F, Su 12:30 and 2pm, Tu and Sa 2pm. £9.)

ST. NINIAN'S ISLE. Off the southwest coast of Mainland, an unusual **tombolo**—a beach surrounded on both sides by the sea—links St. Ninian's Isle to Mainland, just outside of **Bigton.** Inhabited from the Iron Age to the 18th century and the site of an early monastery, the isle is now home to a ruined church, rabbits, and sheep. It achieved brief fame in 1958 when a hoard of silver was discovered. In order to visit St. Ninian's in a day—necessary, since there are no accommodations—take the noon Sumburgh-bound bus from Lerwick to Bigton, and the 1:50pm bus from Bigton to Lerwick, allowing 1¼hr. to explore the island.

YELL. The long, uninhabited coast of Yell is home to otters and seals and is free of humans. If you tire of wildlife-watching, head for the north end of the main road at **Gloup;** a 3 mi. hike from here takes you to the desolate eastern coast. The remains of an **Iron-Age fort** sit on the Burgi Geos promontory; jagged outcroppings face the sea and a 3 ft. ridge leads between cliffs to Mainland. Killer whales are occasionally spotted in **Bluemull Sound** between Yell and Unst. **Ferries** run from Toft on Mainland to Ulsta on Yell (20min.; 1-2 per hr.; £3, cars £7).

UNST. Unst, the northernmost inhabited region in Britain, has stupendous cliffs and jagged sea stacks. Get the key and a torch from Mrs. Peterson to explore roofless **Muness Castle,** built in the late 16th century and often raided by pirates. (Open all year. Free.) At **Haroldswick Beach,** gannets dive into the ocean near crumbling, abandoned air-raid shelters. A pair of black-browed albatrosses and countless puffins grace the celebrated **bird reserve** at Hermaness. The Leask bus stops along the way at **Gardiesfauld Hostel ❶,** in Uyeasound in the south of Unst, where you'll find a gorgeous coastal view. (☎01957 755 279. No smoking, no pets, and no alcohol. Open Apr.-Sept. Dorms £10, under 16 £8, tents £6. Cash only.) Only one bus per day runs by the hostel; it's easy to get stranded. Those without private means of transport should consider riding the bus to Unst's main town, Baltasound, which has a few **B&Bs.** Ferries from Belmont (Unst) and Gutcher (northern Yell) divert routinely to Oddsta on the island of Fetlar, where birdwatchers catch sight of the crimson-tailed finch. To get to Unst, take a **ferry** from Gutcher to Belmont (10min.; 1-2 per hr.; £3 per person, £7 per car). A daily Leask **bus** leaves Lerwick at 7:50am, 2:30pm (M-F), and 3:45pm (Th-F) and connects with ferries to Haroldswick on Unst (2¼hr., £4.80). The Baltasound **post office** (open M-Tu and F 9am-1pm and 2-5:30pm, W 9am-1pm and 2-4:30pm, Th and Sa 9am-1pm) features Britain's northernmost **Post Code:** ZE2 9DP.

OTHER ISLANDS. Shetland's outer islands are perfect for the traveler looking to leave civilization and head out into wild, remote natural landscapes. Advance planning is necessary as getting there can be a challenge. **Planes** depart for the islands from Tingwall on Mainland, but **ferries** are cheaper. Rooms and transport are hard to find; book several weeks ahead. Bring supplies to last at least a week, as ferries often do not operate in inclement weather. Many ferries run from Walls, Vidlin, and Laxo on Mainland, which can be reached by bus from Lerwick (generally under 1hr.; consult the *Shetland Transport Timetable*).

Whalsay ("whale island" in Norse; pop. 1000) is the center of Shetland's fishing industry. The prosperous isle is accessible by bus and ferry from Lerwick and home to coastal walks and Stone-Age relics. **Symbister House,** an impressive example of Georgian architecture, bankrupted its owners. Ferries depart Laxo every hour (30min.; £3 per person, £7 per car). The **Out Skerries** settlement supports 80 hardy fishermen. Planes (☎840 246; M and W-Th 1-2 per day, £20) arrive from Tingwall, while ferries come from Lerwick and Vidlin (1½hr. from Vidlin, 2½hr. from Lerwick; both 12 per week; £2.60 per person, £3.50 per car).

Papa Stour's (pop. 24) frothy coastline features sea-flooded cliff arches, and used to house a colony of "lepers" on the southwest side of the isle. As it turns out, the poor folk simply suffered from terrible malnutrition and vitamin deficiencies. Backpackers can camp or head to **Hurdiback ❶.** (☎873 229. May-Sept. £10, under 16 £8.50. Cash only.) To get to Papa Stour, fly (Tu only, £17.50) or sail (☎810 460; 8 per week; £2.60, cars £3.50; book ahead) from Tingwall.

Far to the west, rugged **Foula** is home to 35 humans, 2000 sheep, and the highest sheer cliff in Britain (1220 ft.). Barely Scottish, the inhabitants of Foula had their own monarch until the late 17th century, spoke the now-extinct Nordic language of Norn until 1926, and still celebrate Christmas and Easter according to the now-defunct Julian calendar. From May to September, ferries (☎ 753 254) travel from Walls (Tu, Th, Sa; £2.60, cars £12.40) and Scalloway (every other Th; £2.60, cars £12.40), while planes (☎ 840 246) fly from Tingwall (1¼hr., 5-6 per week, £25).

Fair Isle, midway between Shetland and Orkney, is home to the Fair Isle knitting patterns and 70 self-sufficient souls. Unusual but ideal accommodation for bird-watchers is available at the **Bird Observatory Lodge ❸.** (☎ 760 258; www.fairislebirdobs.co.uk. Open Apr.-Oct. Full board £30-42. Free guided walks.) In summer, a ferry (☎ 760 222) braves the North Sea from Lerwick or Grutness (Apr.-Sept. Tu, Sa, and every other Th; £2.60, cars £12.40). Planes (☎ 840 246) depart from Tingwall (25min.; mid-Feb. to mid-Oct. M, W, F 2 per day; May to mid-Oct. M, W, F 2 per day, Sa 1 per day; £28) and Sumburgh (May-Oct. Sa 1 per day, £28).

❊ FESTIVALS

Shetland's remoteness, endless daylight in the summer, and endless darkness in the winter make for long summer festivals and fiery winter ones. The TIC is an excellent source for info. The **Shetland Folk Festival** (☎ 741 000; www.sffs.shetland.co.uk), at the end of April, lures fiddlers from around the world, while the **Shetland Fiddle and Accordion Festival** takes place in Lerwick in mid-October. Enjoy live music and a lamb burger at the **Flavour of Shetland** on Victoria Pier in mid-July. The wild annual **Up Helly Aa Festival** (www.uphellyaa.com) is held in Lerwick the last Tuesday in January (see p. 665).

HIGHLANDS AND ISLANDS

NORTHERN IRELAND

The calm tenor of everyday life in Northern Ireland has long been over-shadowed by media headlines about riots and bombs. While the violence has subdued and the Irish Republican Army (IRA) has agreed to total disarmament, the observable divisions in civil society continue. Protestants and Catholics usually live in separate neighborhoods, attend separate schools, patronize different stores and pubs, and even play different sports. The 1998 Good Friday Agreement, designed by leaders of Northern Ireland, Great Britain, and the Republic of Ireland to lead Northern Ireland out of the Troubles, began a slow march to peace. All sides have renewed their efforts to make their country as peaceful as it is beautiful.

NORTHERN IRELAND HIGHLIGHTS

BEHOLD ballet at Belfast's historical Grand Opera House (p. 679).

EXPLORE the geological wonder of the Giant's Causeway in Co. Antrim (p. 684).

GET TIPSY at the Bushmills Distillery, the oldest licensed whiskey producer in the world (p. 685).

MONEY. Legal tender in Northern Ireland is the British pound. Northern Ireland has its own bank notes, which are identical in value to English and Scottish notes. These notes are not accepted outside of Northern Ireland; English and Scottish notes, however, are accepted in the North. Euro are generally not accepted in the North, with the exception of some border towns.

SAFETY AND SECURITY. Although sectarian violence is much less common than in the height of the Troubles, some neighborhoods and towns still experience unrest during sensitive political times. It's best to remain alert and cautious while traveling in Northern Ireland, especially during **Marching Season,** which reaches its peak July 4-12. August 12th, when the **Apprentice Boys** march in Derry/Londonderry, is also a testy period. Despite these concerns, Northern Ireland has one of the lowest tourist-related crime rates in the world. Unattended luggage is always considered suspicious and is often confiscated. It is generally unsafe to hitch in Northern Ireland. *Let's Go* never recommends hitchhiking.

 The **phone code** for every town in the North is **028.**

HISTORY AND POLITICS

Since the partition of 1920, the people of Northern Ireland have retained their individual cultural and political identities, even at the cost of lasting peace. Many continue to defend the lines that define their differences, whether ideological divisions across the chambers of Parliament or actual streets marking the end of one culture and the beginning of the next. Generally speaking, the 950,000 Protestants are **Unionists,** who want the six counties of Northern Ireland to remain in the UK; the 650,000 Catholics tend to identify with the Republic of Ireland, not Britain, and many are **Nationalists,** who wish the six counties to be part of the Republic. The more extreme (generally working-class) members of either side are known respectively as **Loyalists** and **Republicans.** These groups have historically defended their turf with rocks and gas bombs.

A DIVIDED ISLAND: IT STARTS. In the 13th century, the English took control of Ireland, and King Henry VIII declared himself King of Ireland in 1542. Irish uprisings encouraged King James I to begin a series of plantations in six of the nine counties of **Ulster** (a British name for Northern Ireland) in the 17th century. Two of the main events currently commemorated by Protestants in Northern Ireland took place during this early period: in 1688 the gates of Derry were shut against the troops of the Catholic James II (commemorated each August by the **Apprentice Boys of Derry**) and in 1690 William III defeated James II at the **Battle of the Boyne** (commemorated in July by the **Orange Order**). The **Orange Order** (named after the uniforms of Protestant William III's army) formed in County Armagh in 1795 and provided explosive opposition to the first **Home Rule Bill** in 1886. After the **Easter Rising** in the Republic in 1916, the 1920 **Government of Ireland Act** split Ireland into two self-governing units: 28 counties in the south and six counties in northeast Ireland, soon to be Northern Ireland. In 1949 the Republic was officially established and the **Ireland Act** recognized Northern Ireland's right to autonomy; violence (barring the occasional border skirmish) diminished. Between 1956 and 1962, the IRA launched attacks on the border, but this ended for lack of support in 1962.

THE TROUBLES. In 1966, Protestant Unionists founded the **Ulster Volunteer Force (UVF),** which was declared illegal. The UVF and the IRA actively bombed each other (and civilians) throughout 1966. In response, the religiously mixed **Northern Ireland Civil Rights Association (NICRA)** sponsored a march in Derry/Londonderry in 1968. The march became a bloody mess, eventually broken up by the **Royal Ulster Constabulary (RUC)** and several water cannons. Rioting during parades became so common and violent that police stopped entering parts of some cities, particularly Derry/Londonderry, where the slogan **"Free Derry"** became famous. The IRA later split in two; the more violent and extreme faction, the **Provisional IRA** or **Provos,** took over with less ideology and more guns.

On January 30, 1972, British troops fired into a peaceful crowd of protesters in Derry/Londonderry. **Bloody Sunday,** and the ensuing reluctance of the British government to investigate, increased Catholic outrage. In 1978, Nationalist prisoners in the **Maze Prison** began a campaign for political prisoner status, going on a **hunger strike** in 1981. Republican leader **Bobby Sands** was elected to Parliament while imprisoned and leading the strike. He died at age 26 after 66 days of fasting; he remains one of the conflict's most powerful symbols. Bombings and factioning continued on both sides throughout the 80s and 90s. The IRA attained an estimated 30 tons of arms, used in Northern Ireland and England. In 1991, the **Brooke Initiative** led to the first multiparty talks in Northern Ireland in over a decade.

1994 CEASEFIRE. On August 31, 1994, the IRA announced a "complete cessation of military activities." The **Combined Loyalist Military Command,** speaking on behalf of all Loyalist paramilitary organizations, offered "to the loved ones of all innocent victims...abject and true remorse" as they announced their ceasefire. The peace held for over a year. The ceasefire ended in 1996, when the IRA bombed an office building in London's Docklands. The stalled peace talks, chaired by US Senator **George Mitchell,** were planned but fell apart when a blast

Northern Ireland

in a Manchester shopping district injured more than 200 people. In May 1997, the Labour party swept British elections; **Tony Blair** became Prime Minister, and the government ended its ban on talks with **Sinn Féin** (the political wing of the IRA). Hopes for a renewed ceasefire were dashed when the car of a prominent Republican was bombed. In retaliation, the IRA shot two members of the RUC.

GOOD FRIDAY AGREEMENT. After long negotiations between politicians and paramilitaries from Northern Ireland, the Republic, and Britain, during which Blair physically blocked a door to prevent participants from walking out, the delegates approved a draft of the 1998 Northern Ireland Peace Agreement—better known as the **Good Friday Agreement.** The pact emphasized that change in Northern Ireland could come about only with majority will and the recognition of "birthright," allowing citizens of Northern Ireland to adopt British, Irish, or dual citizenship.

On May 22, 1998, in the first island-wide vote since 1918, residents of Northern Ireland and the Republic voted the agreement into law; 71% of Northern Ireland and 94% of the Republic voted to reform Northern Ireland's government. As per the agreement, the main body, a 108-member **Northern Ireland Assembly,** assigns committee posts and chairs proportionately to the parties' representation and is headed by a First Minister. The second strand of the new government, a **North-South Ministerial Council,** serves as a cross-border authority across the isles. The final strand, the **British-Irish Council,** controls governance across the isles.

But shortly after these leaps forward, Marching Season began. The July 4 **Drumcree parade** was forbidden from marching down war-torn Garvaghy Road, spurring a stand-off between Republican and Loyalist paramilitaries. On the night of July 11, three young boys died in the firebombing of a Catholic home. The attack was condemned universally and the **Drumcree Standoff** lost support. On August 15, a bombing in **Omagh,** intended to undermine the Good Friday Agreement, left 29 dead and 382 injured; a splinter group called the **Real IRA** claimed responsibility. The cycle of attacks, counter-attacks, splintering, appeasement, peace talks, disarmament, and rearmament seemed to continue in perpetuity.

CURRENT EVENTS. At midnight on May 29, 2000, Britain restored a power-sharing Northern Irish government (as outlined in the Good Friday Agreement) after the IRA promised to begin disarming. On July 28, 2005, the IRA ordered a formal paramilitary disarmament, announcing that it would pursue its political ends only through peaceful means. All sides now are making efforts to reconcile the past. The **Bloody Sunday Inquiry** records testimonies from British military and IRA figures. In 2001, the RUC became **Police Service of Northern Ireland.** Sinn Féin has a plurality (as voted in November, 2003), but the Assembly remains suspended.

BELFAST (BÉAL FEIRSTE)

The second-largest city on the island, Belfast (pop. 330,000) is the focus of Northern Ireland's cultural, commercial, and political activity. Queen's University testifies to the city's rich academic history—luminaries such as Nobel Laureate Seamus Heaney and Lord Kelvin (of chemistry fame) once roamed the halls of Queen's, and Samuel Beckett taught the young men of Campbell College. The Belfast pub scene ranks among the best in the world, combining the historical appeal of old-fashioned watering holes with more modern bars and clubs. While Belfast has suffered from the stigma of its violent past, it has rebuilt and now surprises most visitors with its neighborly, urbane feel.

✈ INTERCITY TRANSPORTATION

Flights: Belfast is served by two airports.

Belfast International Airport (☎9442 2448; www.belfastairport.com) in Aldergrove. **Aer Lingus** (☎08450 844 444; www.aerlingus.com), **British Airways** (☎08458 509 850; www.ba.com), **easyJet** (☎08706 000 000; www.easyjet.com) and many other airlines arrive from London and other European cities. **Airbus** (☎9066 6630) runs to the Laganside and Europa bus stations in the city center (40min.; M-Sa every 30min. 5:45am-10:30pm, Su every hr. 6:15am-9:30pm; £6). **Taxis** (☎9448 4353) do the same for £22.

Belfast City Airport (☎9093 9093; www.belfastcityairport.com), at the harbor, has arrivals from regional carriers. Trains run to **Central Station** (M-Sa frequent, Su 12 per day; £1).

Trains: For info on trains and buses, contact **Translink** (☎9066 6630; www.translink.co.uk. Inquiries daily 7am-8pm). Trains arrive at Belfast's **Central Station,** E. Bridge St. from **Derry/Londonderry** (2hr.; M-Sa 9-10 per day, Su 4 per day; £8.20) and **Dublin** (2hr.; M-Sa 8-9 per day, Su 5 per day; £20). The **Metro** buses are free with rail tickets.

Buses: Europa Bus Terminal (☎9066 6630), off Great Victoria St. Ticket office open M-Sa 7:30am-6:30pm, Su 12:30-5:30pm. Buses from: **Derry/Londonderry** (1¾hr.; M-Sa 19 per day, Su 7 per day; £7.50) and **Dublin** (3hr.; M-Sa 7 per day, Su 6 per day; £12). The Centrelink bus connects the station with the city center.

Ferries: To reach the city center from **Belfast SeaCat Terminal** (☎08705 523 523; www.seacat.co.uk), off Donegall Quay, late at night or early in the morning, a **taxi** is the best bet. SeaCat arrives from: **Isle of Man** (2¾hr.; Apr.-Nov. M, W, F 1 per day; £10-30) and **Troon, Scotland** (2½hr., 2-3 per day, £10-30). Norse Merchant Ferries (☎08706

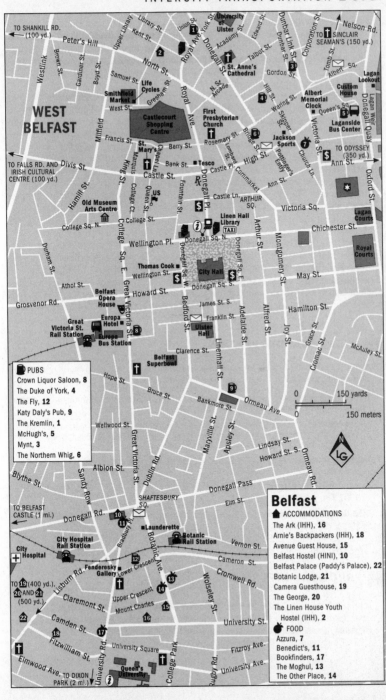

NORTHERN IRELAND

Belfast

🛏 ACCOMMODATIONS

The Ark (IHH), **16**
Arnie's Backpackers (IHH), **18**
Avenue Guest House, **15**
Belfast Hostel (HINI), **10**
Belfast Palace (Paddy's Palace), **22**
Botanic Lodge, **21**
Camera Guesthouse, **19**
The George, **20**
The Linen House Youth
Hostel (IHH), **2**

🍴 FOOD

Azzura, **7**
Benedict's, **11**
Bookfinders, **17**
The Moghul, **13**
The Other Place, **14**

🍺 PUBS

Crown Liquor Saloon, **8**
The Duke of York, **4**
The Fly, **12**
Katy Daly's Pub, **9**
The Kremlin, **1**
McHugh's, **5**
Mynt, **3**
The Northern Whig, **6**

004 321; www.norsemerchant.com) run from **Liverpool, England** (8hr., from £59). P&O Irish Ferries (☎08702 424 777) run from **Cairnryan, Scotland** and other locations in Ireland, England, and France. Stena Line (☎08705 707 070; www.stenaline.com) has service to **Stranraer, Scotland** (1¾hr., £18).

✳ ORIENTATION

Buses arrive at the Europa Bus Station on **Great Victoria Street.** To the northeast is **City Hall** in **Donegall Square.** Donegall Pl. turns into **Royal Avenue** and runs from Donegall Sq. through the shopping area. To the east, in **Cornmarket,** pubs in narrow **entries** (small alleyways) offer an escape. The stretch of Great Victoria St. between the bus station and Shaftesbury Sq. is known as the **Golden Mile,** for its highbrow establishments and Victorian architecture. **Botanic Avenue** and **Bradbury Place** (which becomes **University Road**) extend south from Shaftesbury Sq. into **Queen's University's** turf. The city center, Golden Mile, and the university are relatively safe. Though locals advise caution in the east and west, central Belfast is safer for tourists than most European cities.

Westlink Motorway divides working-class **West Belfast,** historically more politically volatile than the city center, from the rest of Belfast. The Protestant district stretches along Shankill Road, just north of the Catholic neighborhood, centered around Falls Road. **River Lagan** splits industrial **East Belfast** from Belfast proper. The shipyards and docks extend north on both sides of the river as it grows into **Belfast Lough.** During the week, the area north of City Hall is essentially deserted after 6pm. Though muggings are infrequent in Belfast, it's wise to use taxis after dark, particularly near clubs and pubs in the northeast.

▐ LOCAL TRANSPORTATION

Transport cards and tickets are available at the kiosks in Donegall Sq. W. (open M-F 8am-6pm, Sa 8:30am-5:30pm) and around the city.

Buses: Belfast has two bus services. Many local bus routes connect through Laganside Bus Station, Queen's Sq.

Metro buses (☎9066 6630; www.translink.co.uk) center at Donegall Sq. 12 routes cover Belfast. Ulsterbus "blue buses" cover the suburbs. Travel within the city center £1, under 16 50p; 10-journey passes £9-13/5.25-7.25; day passes £3. Concessions available.

Nightlink Buses shuttle the tipsy from Donegall Sq. W. to various towns outside of Belfast. Sa 1 and 2am. £3.50

Taxis: 24hr. metered cabs abound. **Value Cabs** (☎9080 9080); **City Cab** (☎9024 2000); **Fon a Cab** (☎9033 3333).

Bike Rental: McConvey Cycles, 183 Ormeau Rd. (☎9033 0322; www.mcconvey.com). £10 per day, £40 per week, M and F-Su £20. Locks supplied. Deposit £50. Open M-W and F-Sa 9am-6pm, Th 9am-8pm. **Life Cycles,** 36-37 Smithfield Market (☎9043 9959; www.lifecycles.co.uk). £9 per day. Also offers **bicycle city tours** (see **Tours,** p. 674).

❷ PRACTICAL INFORMATION

Tourist Information Centre: Belfast Welcome Centre, 47 Donegall Pl. (☎9024 6609; www.gotobelfast.com). Has a comprehensive free booklet on Belfast and info on surrounding areas. Books reservations in Northern Ireland (£2 charge) and the Republic (£3). Open June-Sept. M-Sa 9am-7pm, Su noon-5pm; Oct.-May M-Sa 9am-5pm.

Financial Services: Find 24hr. ATMs at **Bank of Ireland,** 54 Donegall Pl. (☎9023 4334) and **First Trust,** 92 Ann St. (☎9032 5599). Most banks open M-F 9am-4:30pm. **Thomas Cook,** 10 Donegall Sq. W. (☎9088 3800). Open M-W and Sa 8am-7pm, Th 8am-9pm, F 8am-8pm, Su 1-5pm.

Launderette: Globe, 37-39 Botanic Ave. (☎9024 3956). £4.65. Open M-F 8am-9pm, Sa 8am-6pm, Su noon-6pm. Last wash 70min. before close.

Police: 6-18 Donegall Pass or 65 Knock Rd. (both ☎9065 0222).

Hospital: Belfast City Hospital, 91 Lisburn Rd. (☎9032 9241). From Shaftesbury Sq. follow Bradbury Pl. and take a right at the fork.

Internet Access: Belfast Central Library, 122 Royal Ave. (☎9050 9150). £1.50 per 30min. for non-members. Wheelchair accessible. Open M and Th 9am-8pm, Tu-W and F 9am-5:30pm, Sa 9am-1pm. **Belfast Welcome Centre,** 47 Donegall Pl. £1.25 per 15min., students £1. Open M-Sa 9:30am-7pm, Su noon-5pm.

Post Office: Central Post Office, 25 Castle Pl. (☎08457 223 344). Open M-Sa 9am-5:30pm. **Post Code:** BT1 1BB.

ACCOMMODATIONS

Nearly all budget accommodations are near Queen's University. If hindered by baggage, catch **Citybus** #69, 70, 71, 83, 84, or 86 from Donegall Sq. to areas in the south. Reservations are necessary in summer. Most accommodations accept cash only, unless otherwise noted; call ahead.

HOSTELS

Arnie's Backpackers (IHH), 63 Fitzwilliam St. (☎9024 2867). From Europa Bus Station, take a right on Great Victoria St. and go through Shaftsbury Sq. to Bradbury Pl., which becomes University Rd.; then take a right on Fitzwilliam, across from Queen's University. Relaxed, friendly, and comfortable. Kitchen. 8-bed dorms £7; 4-bed dorms £9.50. ❶

Belfast Palace (Paddy's Palace), 68 Lisburn Rd. (☎9033 3367; www.paddyspalace.com), at the corner of Fitzwilliam St. This sociable new hostel offers satellite TV and a kitchen. Breakfast included. Laundry available. Internet access free. Reception M-Th and Su 8am-8pm, F-Sa 8am-10pm. Book ahead in summer. Dorms from £8.50. ❶

The Ark (IHH), 18 University St. (☎9032 9626). A 10min. walk from Europa bus station. Offers clean and spacious dorms and a kitchen with free tea and coffee. Books tours of Belfast (£8) and Giant's Causeway (£16). Laundry £5. Internet £1 per 20min. Curfew 2am. Coed 4- to 6-bed dorms £11; doubles £36. ❶

Belfast Hostel (HINI), 22 Donegall Rd. (☎9031 5435; www.hini.org.uk), off Shaftesbury Sq. A clean, inviting interior with a cafe and modern rooms. Cafe open daily 7:30-11am. Full breakfast £4. Wheelchair accessible. Laundry £3. Internet £1 per 20min. Reception 24hr. 4- to 6-bed dorms M-Th and Su £7.50-9.50, F-Sa £10.50-12; singles £18; doubles £26-28; triples £33-36. MC/V. ❶

The Linen House Youth Hostel (IHH), 18-20 Kent St. (☎9058 6444; www.belfasthostel.com), bordering West Belfast. Converted 19th-century linen factory now packs 130 bunks into bare rooms. Downtown location is a mixed blessing: the area empties out at night. Bike and luggage storage 50p. Towels 50p. Laundry £4. Internet £1 per 30min. 18- to 20-bed dorms £7; 6- to 10-bed dorms £9; singles £15-20; doubles £24-30. Discounted long term stays available. ❶

BED AND BREAKFASTS

B&Bs cluster south of Queen's University between **Malone** and **Lisburn Roads.**

Camera Guesthouse, 44 Wellington Park (☎9066 0026). This pristine Victorian house offers organic breakfasts. Singles £35, ensuite £45; doubles £54/60. AmEx/MC/V with 3% surcharge. ❸

Avenue Guest House, 23 Eglantine Ave. (☎9066 5904; www.avenueguesthouse.com). Four airy rooms equipped with TV, phone, and wireless internet. £25 per person. ❸

Botanic Lodge, 87 Botanic Ave. (☎9032 7682), the corner of Mt. Charles Ave. In the heart of the Queen's University area. All rooms with sinks and TV. Singles £25, ensuite £35; doubles £35/40. MC/V with 5% surcharge. ❸

The George, 9 Eglantine Ave. (☎9068 3212). Stylish furniture. Fresh fruit at breakfast. All rooms ensuite. Singles £25; doubles £45. ❸

▐ FOOD

Dublin Rd., Botanic Ave., and the Golden Mile, around **Shaftsbury Sq.,** have the highest concentration of restaurants. The huge Tesco **supermarket,** 2 Royal Ave., has better prices than the city's convenience stores. (☎9032 3270. Open M-W and Sa 8am-7pm, Th 8am-9pm, F 8am-8pm, Su 1-5pm.)

▨**Azzura,** 8 Church Ln. (☎9024 2444). Tiny cafe with excellent meat and vegetarian dishes. Gourmet pizzas, pastas, soups, and sandwiches arrive warm from the oven for under £5. Peppers grown fresh by the owners. Open M-Sa 9am-5pm. ❷

The Other Place, 79 Botanic Ave. (☎9020 7200). This bustling eatery dishes out decadent fried breakfasts (from £3, until 5pm). Open M-Su 8am-10pm. ❷

Bookfinders, 47 University Rd. (☎9032 8269). Check the walls for occasional poetry readings and local artwork. Soup and bread £2.50. Open M-Sa 10am-5:30pm. ❶

The Moghul, 62a Botanic Ave. (☎9032 6677). Sit overlooking the street from 2nd fl. corner windows. Outstanding Indian Thali lunch M-Th £3. Lunch buffet F £5. Takeaway available. Open M-Th and Su noon-2pm and 5-11pm, F-Sa noon-2pm. ❷

Benedict's, 7-21 Bradbury Pl. (☎9059 1999; www.benedictshotel.co.uk), near Queen's University. "Beat the Clock" meal deal—5:30-7:30pm the time you order is the price of your meal. Curried chicken, seafood, and veggie options. Open M-Sa noon-2:30pm and 5:30-10:30pm, Su noon-3:30pm and 5:30-9pm. ❸

▐▨ NIGHTLIFE AND PUBS

The city center becomes deserted late at night. Many begin a night out downtown, move to Cornmarket's historic entries, and then party late near the university. For extra suggestions, check *The List*, available at the tourist office and hostels.

▨**The Duke of York,** 7-11 Commercial Court. (☎9024 1062). From City Hall, go up Donegall Pl., take a right on Castle Pl., a left on Waring, and a quick left on Donegall St. The pub is through a small entry marked "Duke of York." Old boxing venue turned Communist printing press, rebuilt after being bombed by IRA in the 60s; now home to the city's largest selection of Irish whiskeys. Th trad 10pm. Sa disco £5. Open M-W 11:30am-11pm, Th-F 11:30am-1am, Sa 11:30am-2am.

▨**Katy Daly's Pub,** 17 Ormeau Ave. (☎9032 5942), behind City Hall. This high-ceilinged, wood-paneled pub is a true stalwart of the Belfast music scene. Local bands W; singer/songwriters Th-Sa. Su night Club "No Dancing"—figure out what to do over a quiet drink.

The Northern Whig, 2 Bridge St. (☎9050 9888). Occupying the building of its demised namesakes' press, the Whig boasts a full list of cocktails (£3.75). DJ Th-Sa. 21+. Open M-Tu 10am-11pm, W-Sa 10am-1am, Su 1-11pm.

McHugh's, 29-31 Queen's Sq. (☎9050 9999; www.mchughsbar.com), across from the Custom House, sells native Belfast ale. Sleek wrought-iron banisters, a colorful collection of contemporary art, and a chess set featuring caricatures of political figures add to the allure of this historic pub, open since 1711. Trad sessions in basement W 9-11pm. Live music F-Sa £3. Open M-Tu and Su noon-midnight, W-Sa noon-1am.

Crown Liquor Saloon, 46 Great Victoria St. (☎9027 9901; www.crownbar.com). The only pub owned by the National Trust in Belfast. The Crown's windows were blown in by a bomb attack, but pubbers would never know it: the stained glass and Victorian snugs have been restored. Open M-F 11:30am-midnight, Su 11:30am-11pm.

The Fly, 5-6 Lower Crescent (☎9050 9750). 1st floor bar for pints, 2nd for dancing, 3rd for the test-tube-shot bar with 40 flavors of vodka—from cinnamon to Starburst. Promotions, theme nights, and 5-9pm happy hour most nights. Free tapas M for "game-show" participants. Open M-W 7pm-1am, Th-Sa 5pm-1:15am.

Mynt, 2-16 Dunbar St. (☎9023 4520; www.myntbelfast.com). A bastion of the Belfast gay scene. The casual cafe-bar in front leads into two floors of clubbing. F separate gay and lesbian parties £5. Sa karaoke downstairs and DJ upstairs. Cover £6-9. Open M and Su 11:30am-1am, F-Sa 11:30am-3am.

The Kremlin, 96 Donegall St. (☎9031 6061; www.kremlin-belfast.com). Look for the statue of Lenin. Beautiful, gelled boys and girls sip and flirt in this gay bar until they spill onto the dance floor around 10:30pm. Tight security. F theme night. Cover varies, but free Su. Bar open Tu-Th 4pm-3am, F-Su 1pm-3am. Doors close 1am.

◥ TOURS

Black Taxi Tours: These tours, a cottage industry of well-informed cabbies, are often the best way to see the sights; the tours give balanced commentary on the murals and cover both sides of the Peace Line.

Original Belfast Black Taxi Tours (☎08000 322 003; www.tobbtt.com). One of five Protestant or five Catholic drivers will answer any question. 1½hr. £8 per person.

Black Taxi Tours (☎08000 523 914; www.belfasttours.com). Michael Johnson has made a name for himself with his witty, objective presentations. £8 per person for groups of 3 or more.

Backpackers Black Taxi Tours (☎07721 067 752). Walter, in his 11th year as a tour guide, covers all bases with insight and wry humor. Around £10 per person.

Pub Tours: Several companies offer guided pub crawls; for other options, ask at the TIC. **Bailey's Historical Pub Tours** (☎9268 3665; www.belfastpubtours.com). Offers a primer in Pint Studies. Guides visitors through 7+ of Belfast's oldest and best pubs with a little sightseeing and history. One tumbler of Bailey's Irish Cream included. 2hr. tours depart from above the Crown Liquor Saloon. May-Oct. Th 7pm, Sa 4pm. £6, £5 per person for groups of 10 or more.

Bike Tours: Life Cycles (see **Bike Rental,** p. 674). **Irish Cycle Tours,** 27 Belvoir View Pk. (☎667 128 733; www.irishcycletours.com). £15 per day.

Bus Tours: Mini-Coach (☎9031 5333). Tours depart from the Belfast International Youth Hostel. Tickets available at the TIC. 1hr. tours of Belfast M-F noon; £8, children £4. 4hr. tours of the Giant's Causeway M-Sa 9:40am-7pm, Su 9am-5:45pm; £15/10.

THE INSIDER'S CITY

THE CATHOLIC MURALS

The murals of West Belfast are a powerful testament to the volatile past and fierce loyalties of the divided neighborhoods. Many of the most famous Catholic murals are on Falls Rd., an area that saw some of the worst of the Troubles.

1 Mural illustrating protestors during the **Hunger Strikes of 1981,** in which they fasted for the right to be considered political prisoners.

2 Portrayal of **Bobby Sands,** the first hunger-striker to die, is located on the side of the Sinn Féin Office, Sevastopol St. Sands was elected as a member of the British Parliament under a "political prisoner" ticket during this time and is remembered as the North's most famous martyr.

3 Formerly operating as Northern Ireland's National RUC Headquarters, the most bombed of any police station in England, the Republic, or the North. Its fortified, barbwire facade is on Springfield St.

👁 SIGHTS

BELFAST CITY HALL. The most dramatic and impressive piece of architecture in Belfast is also its administrative and geographic center. Dominating the grassy square that serves as the locus of downtown Belfast, its green copper dome is visible from nearly any point in the city. Inside, a grand staircase ascends to the second fl., where portraits of the city's Lord Mayors line the halls. The City Council's oak-paneled chambers, used only once a month, are deceptively austere, considering the Council's reputation for rowdy meetings (fists have been known to fly). The interior of City Hall is accessible only by guided tour. (☎9027 0456. 1hr. tours June-Sept. M-F 11am, 2, and 3pm, Sa 2:30pm; Oct.-May M-F 11am and 2:30pm, Sa 2:30pm. Tour times prone to change. Free.)

ST. ANNE'S CATHEDRAL. Belfast's newspapers set up shop around St. Anne's, the **Belfast Cathedral.** This Church of Ireland cathedral was begun in 1899, but to keep from disturbing regular worship, it was built around a smaller church already on the site; upon completion of the new exterior, builders extracted the earlier church brick by brick. (Donegall St., a few blocks from the city center. Open M-Sa 10am-4pm, Su before and after services at 10, 11am, and 3:30pm.)

ODYSSEY. The posterchild of Belfast's riverfront revival, this complex packs attractions into one entertainment center. The **Odyssey Arena,** with 10,000 seats, is the largest indoor arena in Ireland. When the Belfast Giants ice hockey team isn't on the ice, big name performers such as Destiny's Child heat up the stage. The **W5 Discovery Centrem** (short for "whowhatwherewhywhen?") is a playground for curious minds and hyperactive schoolchildren. (2 Queen's Quay. ☎9045 1055; www.theodyssey.co.uk. Box office ☎9073 9074; www.odysseyarena.com. Hockey ☎9059 1111; www.belfastgiants.com. W5 ☎9046 7700; www.w5online.co.uk. Wheelchair accessible. Open M-Th 10am-5pm, F-Sa 10am-6pm, Su noon-6pm. Last admission 1hr. before close. W5 £6, students and seniors £4.50, children £4, families £17.)

LAGAN LOOKOUT AND LAGAN WEIR. The refurbished lookout has a near 360° view, a room of displays on the history of Belfast and the purpose of the weir, and a short video highlighting the city's major sights. (Donegall Quay, across from the Laganside bus station. ☎9031 5444. Lookout open Apr.-Sept. M-F 11am-

5pm, Sa noon-5pm, Su 2-5pm; Oct.-Mar. Tu-F 11am-3:30pm, Sa 1-4:30pm, Su 2-4:30pm. £1.50, students and seniors £1, children 75p, families £4.)

SINCLAIR SEAMEN'S CHURCH. Designed to accommodate the hordes of sinning sailors landing in Belfast port, this quirky church does things its own way—the minister delivers his sermons from a pulpit carved in the shape of a ship's prow, collections are taken in miniature lifeboats, and an organ from a Guinness barge—with port and starboard lights—carries the tune. *(Corporation St. ☎ 9071 5997. Su service at 11:30am and 7pm. Also open W 2-5pm.)*

ALBERT MEMORIAL CLOCK. Belfast has its own leaning tower of Pisa and Big Ben, in one towering timepiece: the **Albert Memorial Clock Tower,** which keeps watch over Queen's Sq. Named for Victoria's prince consort and designed in 1865 by W. J. Barre, the tower slouches precariously at the entrance to the docks. The story goes that it gained its tilt from the young ladies leaning on one side of the clock while awaiting their special sailors.

GRAND OPERA HOUSE. The city's pride and joy, the opera house was cyclically bombed by the IRA, restored to its original splendor at enormous cost, and then bombed again. Visitors today enjoy the calm in high fashion, while tours on Saturday offer a look behind the ornate facade. *(☎ 9024 1919; www.goh.co.uk. Office open M-F 8:30am-9pm. Tours Sa 11am. Times vary, so call ahead. £3, concessions £2.)*

QUEEN'S UNIVERSITY BELFAST. Charles Lanyon modeled the beautiful Tudor and Gothic brick campus after Magdalen College, Oxford. The **visitors centre,** in the Lanyon Room to the left of the main entrance, offers Queen's-related exhibits, merchandise, and a free pamphlet detailing a walking tour of the grounds. A gallery upstairs displays rotating exhibits of contemporary art. *(University Rd. Visitors Centre ☎ 9033 5252; www.qub.ac.uk/vcentre. Wheelchair accessible. Open May-Sept. M-F 10am-4pm, Sa 10am-4pm; Oct.-Apr. M-F 10am-4pm. Gallery open M-F noon-4pm and Sa 10am-4pm.)* Join birds, bees, and Belfast's student population in the peaceful botanic gardens behind the university. The rare spurt of sunshine brings people to the park in droves. Inside the gardens lie two 19th-century greenhouses, the humid **Tropical Ravine,** and the more temperate Lanyon-designed **Palm House,** which shelters an impressive array of flowers. *(☎ 9032 4902. Open daily 8am-dusk. Tropical House and Palm House open Apr.-Sept. M-F 10am-noon and 1-5pm, Sa-Su 1-5pm; Oct.-Mar. M-F 10am-noon and 1-4pm, Sa-Su 1-4pm. Free.)*

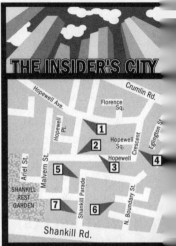

THE INSIDER'S CITY

THE PROTESTANT MURALS

The Protestant murals, in the Shankill area of West Belfast, tend to be overtly militant. Most are found near Hopewell St. and Hopewell Cr., to the north of Shankill Rd., or down Shankill Parade, and are accessed by traveling south from Crumlin Rd.

1 Mural commemorating the **Red Hand Commando,** a militant Loyalist group.

2 Painting of a **Loyalist martyr,** killed in prison in 1997.

3 Depiction of the **Grim Reaper,** with gun and British flag.

4 A collage of Loyalist militant groups including the **UVF, UDU,** and **UDA.**

5 Mural of the **Battle of the Boyne,** commemorating William of Orange's 1690 victory over James II.

6 The **Marksman's** gun seems to follow you as you pass by.

7 Portrait of the infamous **Top Gun,** a man responsible for the deaths of many high-ranking Republicans.

SIR THOMAS AND LADY DIXON PARK. The most stunning of the parks sits pretty on Upper Malone Rd. 20,000 rose bushes of every variety imaginable bloom here each year. The gardens were founded in 1836 and include stud China roses, imported between 1792 and 1824. *(Open M-Sa 7:30am-dusk, Su 9am-dusk.)*

BELFAST ZOO. Set in the hills alongside Cave Hill Forest Park, the zoo's best attribute is its natural setting—catching sight of a lumbering elephant against the backdrop of Belfast Lough can be a surreal experience. *(4 mi. north of the city on Antrim Rd. Take Metro bus #1. ☎ 9077 6277. Open daily Apr.-Sept. 10am-6pm; Oct.-Mar. 10am-2:30pm. Last admission 1hr. before close. Apr.-Sept. £7, children £3.60, families £19.50; Oct.-Mar. £5.70/2.80/15.30.)*

BELFAST CASTLE. Constructed in 1870 by the Third Marquis of Donegall, the castle sits atop **Cave Hill,** long the seat of Ulster rulers. It offers the best panoramas of the Belfast port—on a clear day views extend as far as the Isle of Man. The ancient King Matudan had his McArt's Fort here, where the United Irishmen plotted rebellion in 1795, though these days it sees more weddings than skirmishes. *(☎ 9077 6925; www.belfastcastle.co.uk. Open M-Sa 9am-10:30pm, Su 9am-6pm. Free.)*

WEST BELFAST AND THE MURALS

The neighborhoods of West Belfast have been at the heart of political tensions in the North; there were 1000 bomb explosions and over 400 murders in 1972 alone. The **peace line,** a wall, separates the Catholic and Protestant neighborhoods, centered on **Falls Road** and the **Shankill** respectively. The grim, gray peace line's gates close at nightfall. West Belfast is not a tourist site in the traditional sense, though the walls and houses along the area's streets display political **murals,** the city's most striking and popular attraction. Those traveling to these sectarian neighborhoods often take **black taxis** (see p. 677). *Let's Go* offers two **neighborhood maps** (see **Catholic and Protestant murals,** p. 678) of the Protestant and Catholic murals, allowing individuals to explore the murals for themselves.

Visitors should avoid the area during Marching Season, around July 12; the parades can inflame sectarian violence. Visitors are advised not to wander across the peace line. Rather, travelers should return to the city center between visits to Shankill and the Falls to prevent misunderstandings.

THE FALLS. This Catholic and Republican neighborhood, west of the city center along Castle St., is larger than Shankill. When Castle St. crosses the A12/Westlink, it becomes **Divis Street.** A high-rise apartment building marks **Divis Tower,** an ill-fated housing development built by optimistic social planners in the 1960s. The project soon became an IRA stronghold and saw some of the worst of Belfast's Troubles in 1970s. The British Army still occupies the top floors.

Continuing west, Divis St. turns into **Falls Road.** The **Sinn Féin** office is easily spotted: one side of it is covered with an enormous portrait of Bobby Sands and an advertisement for the Sinn Féin newspaper, *An Phoblacht.* A number of murals line the side streets off of Falls Rd. In the past, the Falls and the Shankill were home to paramilitaries; the murals reflected the tense times with depictions of the violent struggle. Today, both communities have focused on historical and cultural representations, even replacing older murals. The newest Falls murals recall the ancient Celtic heritage of myths and legends and events like the Great Hunger.

The Falls Rd. soon splits into **Andersontown Road** and **Glen Road,** urban areas with a predominately Irish-speaking population. On the left are the Celtic crosses of **Milltown Cemetery,** the resting place of many Republican dead. Inside the entrance to the right, find a memorial to Republican casualties and Bobby Sands's grave. Nearby **Bombay Street** was the first street firebombed during the Troubles. Another mile along Andersontown Rd. lies Andersontown, a housing project that was once a wealthy Catholic enclave. On Springfield Rd., the **Police Service of Northern Ireland** (once the RUC station) was the most-attacked police station in the British Isles. It was recently demolished, but the Police Service's **Andersonstown Barracks,** at the corner of Glen and Andersonstown Rd. are still heavily fortified and in use.

SHANKILL. The Shankill Rd. (always with an article) begins at the Westlink and turns into Woodvale Rd. as it crosses Cambrai St. Woodvale Rd. intersects Crumlin Rd. at the Ardoyne roundabout, and can be taken back into city center. The Shankill Memorial Garden honors 10 people who died in a bomb attack on Fizzel's Fish Shop in October 1993; the garden is on the Shankill Rd. facing Berlin St. On the Shankill Rd., farther toward the city center, is a mural of James Buchanan, the 15th President of the United States (1857-1861), who was of Ulster Scots (Scots-Irish) descent. Other cultural murals depict the 50th Jubilee of the coronation of Queen Elizabeth in 1952 and the death of the Queen Mother in 2002. These are at the beginning of the Shankill on the road near the Rex bar. Historical murals include a memorial to the UVF who fought at the Battle of the Somme in 1916 during WWI, also near the Rex Bar. In the Shankill Estate, streets off to the left of the road, some murals represent Cromwell putting down the 1741 Rebellion against the Protestant plantation owners. The densely decorated Orange Hall sits on the left at Brookmount St. McClean's Wallpaper, on the right, was formerly Fizzel's Fish Shop. Through the estate, Crumlin Rd. heads back to the city center, passing an army base, the courthouse, and the jail.

SANDY ROW AND NEWTOWNARDS ROAD. This area's Protestant population is growing steadily, partly due to the redevelopment of the Sandy Row area, and also because many working-class residents are leaving the Shankill. Nearby murals show the Red Hand of Ulster, a bulldog, and William crossing the Boyne. Use caution when traveling in this area around Marching Season. A number of murals line Newtownards Rd. One mural depicts the economic importance of the shipyard and the industrial history. On the Ballymacart road, which runs parallel to Newtownards Rd., is a mural of local son C.S. Lewis's *The Lion, the Witch, and the Wardrobe.* One likens the UVF to the ancient hero Cú Chulainn, Ulster's defender.

🎵 ARTS AND ENTERTAINMENT

Belfast's many cultural events and performances are covered in the monthly *Arts Council Artslink,* free at the tourist office, while the bi-monthly *Arts Listings* covers arts and entertainment throughout Northern Ireland. **Fenderesky Gallery,** 2 University Rd., inside the Crescent Arts building, hosts contemporary shows and sells the work of local artists. (☎9023 5245. Open Tu-Sa 11:30am-5pm.) The **Old Museum Arts Centre,** 7 College Sq. N., is Belfast's largest venue for contemporary artwork. (☎9023 5053; www.oldmuseumartscentre.org. Open M-Sa 9:30am-5:30pm.) The **Grand Opera House,** 4 Great Victoria St., shows a mix of opera, ballet, musicals, and drama. Tickets for most shows can be purchased either by phone until 9pm or in person at the box office. (☎9024 0411, 24hr. info line 9024 1919; www.goh.co.uk. Tickets from £12.50. Open M-F 8:30am-9pm.) The **Lyric Theatre,** 55 Ridgeway St., presents a mix of classical and contemporary plays with an emphasis on Irish productions. (☎9038 1081; www.lyrictheatre.co.uk. Box office open M-Sa 10am-7pm. Tickets M-W £13.50, concessions £10; Th-Sa £16.50.) **Waterfront Hall,** 2 Lanyon Pl., is one of Belfast's newest concert centers, hosting a varied series of performances. (☎9033 4400. Tickets £10-35, student discounts usually available.)

◪ **DAYTRIP FROM BELFAST: MOUNT STEWART**

To reach Mount Stewart from Belfast, take the Portaferry bus from Laganside Station. 1hr.; M-F 16 per day, Sa 14 per day, Su 4 per day; £2.40. From Newtownards take the Portaferry Rd. (C4). ☎ 4278 8387. House open May-June M and W-F 1-6pm, Sa-Su noon-6pm; July-Aug. daily noon-6pm; Sept. M and W-Su noon-6pm; Oct. Sa-Su noon-6pm; Mar.-Apr. Sa-Su and bank holidays noon-6pm. Garden open May-Sept. daily 10am-8pm; Mar. Sa-Su 10-4pm; Apr. and Oct. daily 10am-6pm. Temple open Apr.-Oct. Su and bank holidays 2-5pm. House tours every 30min. noon-5pm. House and garden £5.45, children £2.70, families £13.60. Garden only £4.40/2.30/11.10.

Fifteen miles southeast of Belfast sits ◪**Mount Stewart House and Gardens.** Held by many a Marquess of Londonderry, the Mount Stewart House was brought to its current splendor as an upper-crust Shangri-La in the 1920s by Lady Edith, First Viscount of Chaplin. Both house and garden are now National Trust property. The stately 18th-century Mount Stewart House is packed with eccentricities, and its halls have been graced by visitors such as Winston Churchill, George Bernard Shaw, and European royalty. Among the treasures are George Stubbs's life-sized painting of the Stewart family horse and race champion, Hambletonian.

Mount Stewart's **gardens,** covering 80 acres, are more of an attraction than the house itself; they are currently nominated as a UNESCO World Heritage Site. Lady Edith took advantage of Ireland's temperate climate to create a landscape of flowers, shrubs, and trees from as far as Africa and Australia. Her **Dodo Terrace** contains a menagerie of animal statues representing the members of her upper-crust circle of friends dubbed "the Ark Club." Each member adopted an animalian alter-ego, with Lady Edith, the group's matriarch, named "Circe the Sorcerer" after the character in the *Odyssey.* Other elite critters include Winston "the Warlock" Churchill and Nelson "the Devil" Chamberlain. The **Shamrock Garden,** whose name belies its shape, contains a Red Hand of Ulster made of begonias, and a topiary Irish Harp planted, appropriately enough, over a cluster of the Emerald Isle's shamrocks. The Lake Walk leads to **Tír Nan Óg** ("the land of the ever young"), the beautiful family burial ground above the lake. The gardens also host the popular **Summer Garden Jazz Series** on the last Sunday of each month from April through September, as well as murder mystery evenings and car and railway engine shows. Based on the Tor of the Winds in Athens, the **Temple of the Winds,** used by Mount Stewartians for "frivolity and jollity," sits atop a hill with a superb view of Strangford Lough.

ANTRIM AND DERRY

The A2 coastal road connects the attractions of Counties Antrim and Derry to Belfast, providing a fantastic and easily accessible journey for visitors. The scenery of the nine Glens of Antrim sweeps visitors north toward the Giant's Causeway, which spills its geological honeycomb into the ocean off the northern coast.

PORTRUSH (PORT RUIS)

Portrush's name should be taken literally: when the universities reopen in fall, students flood the city; in July, when their summer holidays begin, they give way to an even more vicious influx of tourists on their way to the Giant's Causeway.

◪▨ **TRANSPORTATION AND PRACTICAL INFORMATION. Trains** run to Eglinton St. in the center of town from Belfast (2hr.; M-Sa 10 per day, Su 4 per day; £7.60, children £3.80). Most **buses** stop at Dunluce Ave. #252, the "Antrim

Coaster," traveled between Portrush and Belfast, stopping at sights along the Antrim coast (M-Sa 3 per day, Su 2 per day). For **taxis,** try Radio Taxis (☎0800 032 339 or 7035 5055) or Cromore Cabs (☎7083 4550).

The **Tourist Information Centre,** Sandhill Dr., in the Dunluce Centre, is south of the town center. (☎7082 3333. Open mid-June to Aug. daily 9am-7pm; Apr. to mid-June and Sept. M-F 9am-5pm, Sa-Su noon-5pm; Mar. and Oct. M-F 9am-5pm, Sa-Su noon-5pm.) For **banks,** try First Trust, 25 Eglinton St. (☎7082 2726. Open M-Tu and Th-F 9:30am-4:30pm, W 10am-4:30pm.) Find **Internet access** at the public **library** across from MacCool's on Causeway St. (☎7082 3752. £1.50 per 30min. Open M and Th-F 10am-1pm and 2-5:30pm, Tu 10am-1pm and 2-8pm, Sa 10am-1pm and 2-5pm.) The **post office** is on Eglinton St. (☎7082 3700. Open M-Tu and Th-F 9am-12:30pm and 1:30-5:30pm, Sa 9am-12:30pm.) **Post Code:** BT56.

⌐⌐ ACCOMMODATIONS AND FOOD. Although it takes its name from a giant, **Portrush Hostel (MacCool's) ❶,** 35 Causeway St., is a smallish hostel. However, the clean rooms ensure a comfortable stay. (☎7082 4845; www.portrush-hostel.com. Breakfast included. Internet available. Laundry wash £2, dry £3. Dorms £10; doubles £24; triples £28.) Or stay at the more luxurious **Clarmont Guest House ❸,** 10 Landsdowne Crescent, with jacuzzi baths. (☎7082 2397; www.clarmont.com. Singles from £30. MC/V.) Family-run **Ashlea House ❷,** 52 Mark St., has eight comfortable rooms. (☎7082 3094. Wheelchair accessible. Singles from £16.)

Greasy chippers and pricey eateries dominate Portrush's culinary offerings. **Groceries** are available at Costcutter, 106 Lower Main St. (☎7082 5447. Open daily 7am-10pm.) At **▨D'Arcy's ❹,** Main St., adventurous options, like ostrich steak (£13.25), add a touch of flair to the menu. (☎7082 2063. Entrees £9-14. Open M-Th and Su noon-9:30pm, F-Sa noon-10pm. MC/V.) Find solace in the fishy arms of **Spinnaker ❸,** 25 Main St., where the spoils of the sea are broiled, grilled, sauteed, and smothered in butter. (☎7082 2348. Entrees £6-10.) Late at night, try the Chinese food at **Lucky House ❷,** 53 Eglinton St. (☎7082 3855. Entrees £4.30-5.80. Open Tu-Th and Su 5pm-midnight, F 5pm-2am, Sa 5pm-2:30am.) **Coast ❷,** North Pier, serves up stone-baked pizzas (from £4.25) in a sleek interior. (☎7082 3311. Open W-Th 5-10pm, F-Sa 4-10:30pm, Su 3-9:30pm.)

▨▨ PUBS AND CLUBS. Portrush plays host to the premiere club scene in the North. Weekend partiers come from as far as Belfast and Derry/Londonderry to black out at the town's multi-venue nightlife complexes. **Springhill Bar,** Causeway St., features the best trad on Thursday nights and live bands on Fridays and Saturdays. The upstairs lounge has pool and darts and hosts a 60s-80s themed disco Friday and Saturday nights. (☎7082 3361. Open M-Sa 11am-1am, Su noon-midnight.) The laidback **Harbour Bar,** 5 Harbour Rd., tries its best to remain a sailor pub with bands rocking on weekends. (☎7082 2430. Open M-Sa noon-10pm, Su noon-9pm.) **Ramore Wine Bar,** sitting pretty atop North Pier off Harbour Rd., boasts three restaurants, a pub, a wine bar, and a lounge. (☎7082 4313. Open M-Sa 12:15-2:15pm and 5-10pm, Su 12:30-3pm and 5-9pm.) **Kelly's,** outside of town on Bushmills, is the North's top clubbing venue, regularly drawing big-name DJs. The wonderland of club kitsch features 10 themed bars and three clubs. (☎7082 2027. Cover £5-10. Open W and Sa 9pm-2am.)

▨▨ SIGHTS AND OUTDOOR ACTIVITIES. Sandy **East Strand Beach** stretches 1½ mi. from town toward the **Giant's Causeway** (see p. 684). The best **surfing** on the North Antrim coast is at **Portballintree Beach,** where the waves soar almost as high as the nearby castle. Outfit a surfing excursion at **Trogg's,** 88 Main St. (☎7082 5476. Boards £10. Wet suits £5. Open daily July-Aug. 10am-9pm; Sept.-June 10am-6pm.) Martin Kelly gives **surf lessons,** teaching the timid to hang ten

THE LOCAL STORY

GIANT GEOLOGY

Just over 60 million years ago, after the last dinosaurs had died, the supercontinent Laurasia began to split up. The movement of the earth's plates caused zones of weakness in crustal rock. The lava that erupted through fissures in the weakened northern Irish coastline eventually pooled into a lake 90m deep, and cracks in the cooling lava formed the 40,000 basalt coulmns of the Giant's Causeway. Many are hexagonal, but others have seven or eight sides.

Some deposits of fresh lava were broken down by the Irish wind and rain, forming the mineral-rich red soil that still delights farmers many millions of years later. Others stood up to the elements as well as the Causeway steps did, creating formations like the Giant's Harp (a hardened lava waterfall) and the Giant's Eye (the cross-section of a column that weathered in many colorful, concentric rings).

At the end of the second Ice Age, about 15,000 years ago, glaciers carved out Ireland's dramatic coastline. Eventually the ice melted and sea levels rose around the Causeway columns and the surrounding cliffs.

Though the Causeway Coast is the only place in Ireland with such dramatic geology, similar volcanic structures can also be found in Scotland, Israel, Thailand, and New Zealand. Those countries just don't have giants to blame for them.

like a pro. (☎7082 5476 or 07748 257 717. From £25 per hr.) Before hitting the amazing Antrim waves, make sure to check the **surf report** (☎09061 337 770). Portrush's **Summer Theatre**, St. Patrick's Hall, Causeway St., is a venue for several Northern Irish theater companies. (☎7082 2500; www.audf.org.uk/portrush.html. Box office open W-Sa 11am-noon and 6-8pm. Shows W-Sa 8pm. Tickets £4-6.)

▓ DAYTRIPS FROM PORTRUSH

▓ THE GIANT'S CAUSEWAY

Ulsterbuses #172, 252 (the Antrim Coaster), the Causeway Rambler, and the Bushmills Bus drop visitors at Giant's Causeway Visitors Centre. The Causeway Coaster minibus runs to the columns; 2min., every 15min., £1.20. On the Giant's Causeway and Bushmills's Railway. ☎2073 2594; www.giantscausewayrailway.org. Runs Mar.-Sept. daily 11:15am-4:30pm; Dec.-Feb. call ahead. 2 per hr. £3.50, children £2. Centre info ☎2073 1855; www.northantrim.com. Centre open May daily 10am-5:30pm; June daily 10am-6pm; July-Aug. daily 10am-7pm; Sept.-Oct. M-F 10am-5pm, Sa-Su 10am-5:30pm. Movie every 15min. 10am-5pm. £1, children 50p. The Causeway is free and always open.

The Giant's Causeway is a profoundly awesome sight to behold. Comprising over 40,000 perfectly symmetrical, hexagonal basalt columns, it resembles a large descending staircase leading from the cliffs to the ocean's floor. Geologists believe the unique rock formations were created some 60 million years ago by ancient lava outpourings that left curiously shaped cracks in their wake. Several other formations stand within the Great Causeway: the **Giant's Organ**, the **Wishing Chair**, the **Granny**, the **Camel**, and the **Giant's Boot**. Advertised as the eighth natural wonder of the world, the Giant's Causeway is Northern Ireland's most famous sight, so don't be surprised if 2000 other travelers pick the same exact day to visit. Visit early in the morning or after the center closes to avoid crowds.

The informative Giant's Causeway Visitors Centre is inland from the Causeway. From the visitors center there are two routes to the coast. The low road is a well-signposted 20min. walk. But do take the high road, which rambles 4½ mi. up a sea cliff to the romantic Iron-Age ruins of **Dunseverick Castle.** Buses #172 and 252 (the Antrim Coaster) also stop in front of the castle. A free map of the area is available at the visitors center. The visitors center also offers a 12min. film about the legend of Finn MacCool and geological explanation for the formations.

OTHER SIGHTS

DUNLUCE CASTLE. This 16th-century castle is built so close to a cliff's edge that the kitchen fell into the sea during a grand banquet, resulting in the arrest of the host and the relocation of the lady of the house to an inland residence. Beneath the castle, a covert **sea cave** offers a quick escape route to Rathlin Island or Scotland. The most spectacular views of the cliffs above the Atlantic are afforded by stopping along the A2 on the way to the castle. *(The castle is along the A2 between Bushmills and Portrush. The Causeway Rambler bus travels from Portrush. ☎ 7032 5400 or 9066 6630; www.translink.co.uk. Runs daily 10:15am-5pm. Castle open Oct.-Mar. daily 10am-4:30pm; Apr.-Sept. 10am-5:30pm. £2, concessions £1.)*

BUSHMILLS DISTILLERY. Ardently Protestant Bushmills has been home to the Old Bushmills Distillery since 1608, when a nod from King James I established it as the oldest licensed whiskey producer in the world. Travelers have stopped here since ancient days, when the whiskey's strength was determined by gunpowder's ability to ignite when doused with the fiery liquid. When the plant is operating, the tour shows the various stages involved in the production of Irish whiskey, distilled three times rather than the paltry two for Scotch "whisky." During the three weeks in July when production halts for maintenance, the far-less-interesting experience is redeemed only by the free sample. Serious whiskey fans should shoulder their way to the front as the tour winds down to get a chance at eight different whiskeys by volunteering when the guide makes his cryptic request for "help." *(At the intersection of the A2 and B17, 3 mi. east of Portrush and 2 mi. west of the Causeway. On the Causeway Rambler bus route. ☎ 7032 5400 or 9066 6630; www.translink.co.uk. Runs daily 10:15am-5pm. Also on the Giant's Causeway and Bushmills's Railway. ☎ 2073 2594; www.giantscausewayrailway.org. Runs Mar.-Sept. daily 11:15am-4:30pm; Dec.-Feb. call ahead. 2 per hr. £5, children £3.50. Distillery ☎ 2073 1521; www.whiskeytours.ie. Open M-Sa 9:30am-5:30pm. Tours Apr.-Oct. frequently; Nov.-Mar. M-F at 10:30, 11:30am, 1:30, 2:30, 3:30pm; Sa-Su at 1:30, 2:30, 3:30pm. £5, concessions £4.)*

NORTHERN IRELAND

DUBLIN (BAILE ÁTHA CLIATH)

Not as cosmopolitan or as large, but just as eclectic as New York or London, Dublin cultivates a culture so magnetic that weekending suburbanites and international hipsters come body-slamming into its hotel mattresses. The capital on the rise supports innovative theatrical and musical enclaves but never forgets its artists of the past—nearly every street boasts a literary landmark, a statue, a birthplace, or a favorite pub. Watering holes remain centers of neighborhood communities. Gangs of tourists have danced their way into Temple Bar, but the nightlife hub remains as lively as ever. New late-night hotspots glimmer farther south along Great Georges St., while the area around Grafton St. continues to flourish under an oligarchy of designer fashion. Despite murmurs that the capital has contracted the growl of big-city crime and poverty, its cultural and pub-happy attractions retain the Irish charm. At the same time, Dublin exudes an air of urban sophistication, making it an exhilarating and deservedly popular destination.

IRELAND	❶	❷	❸	❹	❺
ACCOMMODATIONS	under €17	€17-26	€27-41	€42-56	€57 and up
FOOD	under €6	€6-10	€11-15	€16-20	€21 and up

PHONE CODES	Country code: 353. Dublin City Code: 01. From outside Ireland, dial int'l prefix + 353 + city code (drop the first zero; Dublin's code would be 1 + local number. If calling within Dublin, dial 01 + local number.

◰ TRANSPORTATION

Airport: Dublin Airport (☎814 1111; www.aer-rianta.ie). **Dublin buses** #41, 41B, and 41C run directly to Eden Quay in the city center (40-45min., every 20min., €1.75). **Airlink shuttle** (☎703 3092) runs directly to **Busáras Central Bus Station** and O'Connell St. (20-25min., every 10-20min. 5:45am-11:30pm; €5), and to **Heuston Station** (50min., €5). **Taxis** to the city center cost €20-25.

Trains: Tickets are sold at Dublin's three major stations or at the **Irish Rail Travel Centre (Iarnród Éireann),** 35 Lower Abbey St. Open M-F 9am-5pm, Sa 9am-1pm. ☎836 6222; www.irishrail.ie. Call center open M-Sa 9am-6pm, Su 10am-6pm.

Connolly Station, Amiens St. (☎703 2358). Ticket office open daily 7am-11pm. Bus #20B heads south of the river and #130 goes to the city center.

Heuston Station (☎703 3299), south of Victoria Quay and west of the city center. Ticket office open daily 6:30am-10:30pm. Buses #26, 78, and 79 run from Heuston to the city center.

Pearse Station (☎888 0226), east of Trinity College at the intersection of Pearse St. and Westland Row. Ticket office open daily 7:45am-11pm. Receives southbound trains from Connolly Station.

Buses: Buses arrive at **Busáras Central Bus Station,** Store St. (☎836 6111), behind the Customs House and next to Connolly Station. The **Bus Éireann** (www.buseireann.ie) window is open M-F 10am-5pm and Sa 10:30am-2pm. **Dublin Bus,** 59 O'Connell St. (☎873 4222; www.dublinbus.ie) runs local bus service. Office open M-F 9am-5:30pm.

Taxis: Blue Cabs (☎802 2222), **ABC** (☎285 5444), **City Metro Cabs** (☎872 7272). €3.25 plus €0.15 every sixth of a kilometer (tenth of a mile); €1.50 call-in charge.

Hitchhiking: Hitchhiking in Dublin and its vicinity is extremely unsafe, especially for women.

⚜ ORIENTATION

The **River Liffey** forms a natural boundary between Dublin's North and South Sides. Most of the notable sights, shops, and restaurants are on the **South Side.** The rival **North Side** claims most of the hostels, Busáras, Connolly Station, and a whole lot of heart. The core of Dublin is ringed by **North** and **South Circular Roads,** each with its own creative assortment of name changes. Most of the city's major sights are located within this area; the walk from one end to the other should take about 1hr. **O'Connell Street,** three blocks west of Busáras, is the primary link between north and south Dublin. The streets running alongside the Liffey are called **quays** (KEEZ); the name of the quay changes with every block. Dubliners are more likely to direct by quays than by street name or address. If a street is split into "Upper" and "Lower" (which occurs on both sides of the river) the "Lower" is the section closer to the Liffey. The North Side has the reputation of being a rougher area, especially after dark. Tourists should avoid walking in unfamiliar areas on either side of the Liffey at night, especially when alone. Solo travelers should stay on well-lit streets and should **avoid Phoenix Park after dark.**

ⓘ PRACTICAL INFORMATION

TOURIST AND FINANCIAL SERVICES

Tourist Information: Main Office, Suffolk St. (☎669 792 083; www.visitdublin.com). From Connolly Station, walk left down Amiens St., take a right on Lower Abbey St., pass Busáras, and continue until O'Connell St. Turn left, cross the bridge, and walk past Trinity College; the office is on the right, down Suffolk St., in a converted church.

Banks: Bank of Ireland, AIB, and **TSB** branches with bureaux de change and 24hr. ATMs cluster on Lower O'Connell St., Grafton St., and near Suffolk and Dame St. On F evenings, long lines form outside the ATMs, which aren't replenished over the weekends. Most banks open M-W and F 10am-4pm, Th 10am-5pm.

GLBT Travelers: Gay Community News (GCN), Unit 2 Scarlet Row, W. Essex St. (☎671 9076; www.gcn.ie), a gay-life monthly. **Gay Switchboard Dublin** sponsors a hotline (☎872 1055; M-F and Su 8-10pm, Sa 3:30-6pm). **OUThouse,** 105 Capel St. (☎873 4932), is a queer community resource center. Open for drop-in M-F noon-6pm.

EMERGENCY AND COMMUNICATIONS

Emergency: ☎999 or 112; no coins required.

Police (Garda): Dublin Metro Headquarters, Harcourt Terr. (☎666 9500); Store St. Station (☎666 8000); Fitzgibbon St. Station (☎666 8400); Pearse St. Station (☎666 9000). **Police Confidential Report Line:** ☎800 666 111.

Pharmacy: O'Connell's, 56 Lower O'Connell St. (☎873 0427). Convenient to city bus routes. Open M-F 7:30am-10pm, Sa 8am-10pm, Su 10am-10pm. **Dowling's,** 6 Baggot St. (☎678 5612), near the Shelbourne Hotel and St. Stephen's Green. Open M-W and F 8am-7pm, Th 8am-8pm, Sa 9am-7pm.

Hospital: St. James's Hospital, James St. (☎410 3000). Bus #123. **Mater Misericordiae Hospital,** Eccles St. (☎803 2000), off Lower Dorset St. Buses #3, 10, 11, 16, 22, and 121. **Beaumont Hospital,** Beaumont Rd. (☎809 3000). Buses #27B, 51A, 101, 103, and 300.

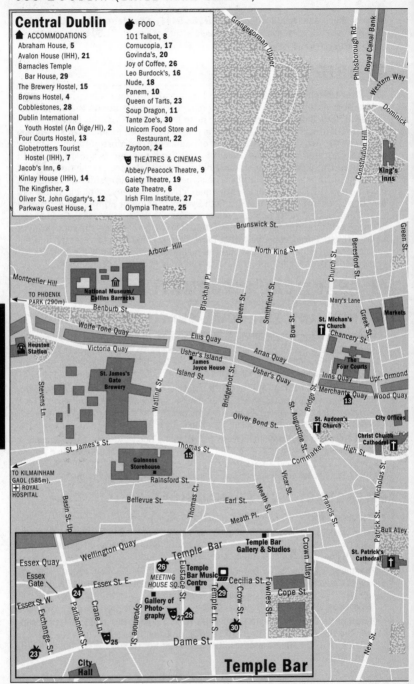

Central Dublin

⌂ ACCOMMODATIONS
Abraham House, **5**
Avalon House (IHH), **21**
Barnacles Temple
  Bar House, **29**
The Brewery Hostel, **15**
Browns Hostel, **4**
Cobblestones, **28**
Dublin International
  Youth Hostel (An Óige/HI), **2**
Four Courts Hostel, **13**
Globetrotters Tourist
  Hostel (IHH), **7**
Jacob's Inn, **6**
Kinlay House (IHH), **14**
The Kingfisher, **3**
Oliver St. John Gogarty's, **12**
Parkway Guest House, **1**

♣ FOOD
101 Talbot, **8**
Cornucopia, **17**
Govinda's, **20**
Joy of Coffee, **26**
Leo Burdock's, **16**
Nude, **18**
Panem, **10**
Queen of Tarts, **23**
Soup Dragon, **11**
Tante Zoe's, **30**
Unicorn Food Store and
  Restaurant, **22**
Zaytoon, **24**

♥ THEATRES & CINEMAS
Abbey/Peacock Theatre, **9**
Gaiety Theatre, **19**
Gate Theatre, **6**
Irish Film Institute, **27**
Olympia Theatre, **25**

DUBLIN

Grangegorman Upper
Philsborough Rd.
Royal Canal Bank
Western Way
Dominick
Constitution Hill
King's Inns
Green St.
Brunswick St.
Arbour Hill
North King St.
Church St.
Beresford St.
Montpelier Hill
National Museum/
Collins Barracks
Benburb St.
Mary's Lane
Markets
Greek St.
St. Michan's Church
Chancery St.
TO PHOENIX PARK (290m)
Wolfe Tone Quay
Blackhall Pl.
Queen St.
Smithfield St.
Bow St.
Victoria Quay
Ellis Quay
Arran Quay
Heuston Station
Usher's Island
James Joyce House
Island St.
Bridgefoot St.
Usher's Quay
The Four Courts
Inns Quay
Merchants Quay
Upr. Ormond
Wood Quay
St. James's Gate Brewery
Watling St.
Stevens Ln.
St. Augustine St.
Bridge St.
City Offices
Oliver Bond St.
St. Audoen's Church
Christ Church Cathedral
St. James's St.
Thomas St.
High St.
Cornmarket
Nicholas St.
Guinness Storehouse
Rainsford St.
TO KILMAINHAM GAOL (585m),
ROYAL HOSPITAL
Bellevue St.
Thomas Ct.
Earl St.
Meath St.
Vicar St.
Francis St.
Patrick St.
Bull Alley
Meath Pl.
Basin St. Up.
St. Patrick's Cathedral
Crown Alley

Temple Bar
Essex Quay
Wellington Quay
Temple Bar
Temple Bar Gallery & Studios
Essex Gate
Essex St. E.
Eustace St.
Temple Bar Music Centre
Cecilia St.
Essex St. W.
MEETING HOUSE SQ.
Temple Ln. S.
Crow St.
Fownes St.
Cope St.
Exchange St.
Crane Ln.
Sycamore St.
Gallery of Photography
New St.
Dame St.
Parliament St.
City Hall

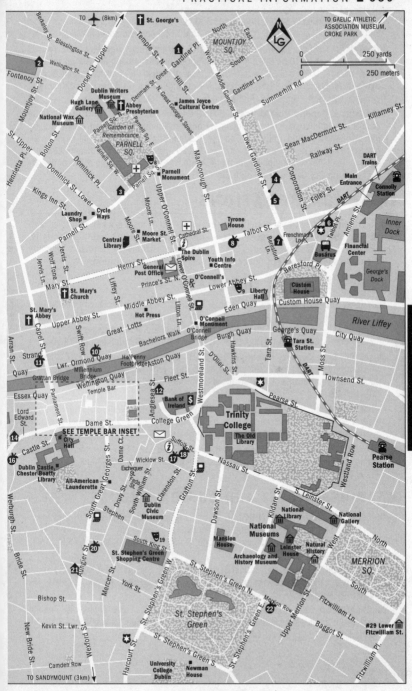

TO ✈ (8km)

⛪ St. George's

TO GAELIC ATHLETIC
ASSOCIATION MUSEUM,
CROKE PARK

MOUNTJOY
SQ.

1

0   250 yards

0   250 meters

Dublin Writers
Museum

Hugh Lane
Gallery

2

James Joyce
Cultural Centre

Abbey
Presbyterian

National Wax
Museum

Garden of
Remembrance

PARNELL
SQ.

Summerhill Rd.

Sean MacDermott St.

Railway St.

DART
Trains

Main
Entrance

Connolly
Station

Parnell
Monument

6

4

5

Laundry
Shop

Cycle
Ways

Moore St.
Market

Central
Library

3

Tyrone
House

8

Talbot St.

7

6

Frenchman's
Ln.

Inner
Dock

Financial
Center

St. Mary's
Church

The Dublin
Spire

General
Post Office

Youth Info
Centre

O'Connell's

Busáras

George's
Dock

St. Mary's
Abbey

Hot Press

9

Liberty
Hall

Custom
House

Custom House Quay

River Liffey

O'Connell
Monument

O'Connell
Bridge

Ha'Penny
Footbridge

10

Millennium
Bridge

11

Temple Bar

12

George's Quay

Tara St.
Station

City Quay

Bank of
Ireland

Trinity
College

The Old
Library

Pearse
Station

SEE TEMPLE BAR INSET!

City
Hall

14

College Green

Lord
Edward
St.

16

Dublin Castle
Chester Beatty
Library

All-American
Launderette

17 18

Dublin Civic
Museum

Wicklow St.

National
Museums

National
Library

National
Gallery

Mansion
House

Leinster
House

Natural
History

MERRION
SQ.

St. Stephen's Green
Shopping Centre

19

20

Archaeology and
History Museum

21

22

St. Stephen's
Green

#29 Lower
Fitzwilliam St.

University
College
Dublin

Newman
House

TO SANDYMOUNT (3km)

DUBLIN

Directory Inquiries: ☎11811 (free) or 11850 (€0.65 1st min., €0.10 each additional min.); international ☎11866 (€1.20 1st min., €0.60 each additional min.).

Internet: Free access available at the **Central Library,** Henry and Moore St. (☎873 4333). Open M-Th 10am-8pm, F-Sa 10am-5pm. The best chains are **Global Internet Cafe,** 8 Lower O'Connell St. (☎878 0295; www.globalcafe.ie) and its partner **Central Cyber Cafe,** 6 Grafton St. (☎677 8298; www.centralcafe.ie). €6 per hr., students €5. Wireless €2 per hr. Open M-F 8am-10pm, Sa-Su 10am-9pm.

Post Office: General Post Office (GPO), O'Connell St. (☎705 7000). Open M-Sa 8am-8pm. Smaller post offices, including one on Suffolk St. across from the tourist office, open M-Tu and Th-F 9am-6pm, W 9:30am-6pm. **Post Code:** The city is organized into regions numbered 1-18, 20, 22, and 24; even-numbered codes are for areas south of the Liffey, odd numbers are for the north. The numbers radiate out from the city center: North City Centre is 1, South City Centre is 2.

⌂ ACCOMMODATIONS

It is necessary to reserve accommodations in Dublin at least a week in advance. If the accommodations below are full, consult Dublin Tourism's annually updated *Dublin Accommodation Guide* (€3.50) or ask hostel staff for referrals. Virtually all of Dublin's hostels accept only cash; hotels usually accept credit.

TEMPLE BAR AND THE QUAYS

Barnacles Temple Bar House, 19 Temple Ln. (☎671 6277). Patrons can nearly jump into bed from Temple Bar pubs. Sky lit lounge with open fire and TV, and a colorfully tiled and well-kept kitchen. Continental breakfast included. Free luggage storage. 10- to 12-bed dorms €14-18.50; 6-bed €20-24; 4-bed €24-26.50; doubles €65-78. ❶

Oliver St. John Gogarty's Temple Bar B&B, 18-21 Anglesea St. (☎671 1822; www.gogartys.ie). Bright, clean dorms in an old, well-maintained building above a pub of the same name. Elevator access. Dorms €18-33; doubles €60-90; triples €93-114. ❷

Litton Lane Hostel, 2-4 Litton Ln. (☎872 8389), off Bachelor's Walk. Bold furniture and Warhol-esque silk screens keep things hip. Dorms €19-21; doubles €90; 1-bedroom apartments (sleep up to 4) €120. ❷

Cobblestones, 29 Eustace St. (☎677 8154 or 677 5422). Fantastic location. Snug rooms with large windows and a patio roof. Continental breakfast included. Dorms €16-21; doubles €50-55. ❷

GARDINER STREET AND CUSTOMS HOUSE

▨ **Globetrotters Tourist Hostel (IHH),** 46-47 Lower Gardiner St. (☎878 8808; www.town-houseofdublin.com). Trendy pop art, tropical fish, and a lush courtyard. Irish breakfast included. Free Internet and luggage storage. Dorms €21.50-23; singles €66; triples €114; quads €127. ❷

Browns Hostel, 89-90 Lower Gardiner St. (☎855 0034). Closets and A/C in every room, TVs in most. Large single-sex baths in the basement. Breakfast included. 12-bed dorms €11-18; 8-bed €17.50-20; 4- to 6-bed €20-25. ❶

Abraham House, 82-83 Lower Gardiner St. (☎855 0600). Large dorms with ensuite baths. Light breakfast included. Free luggage storage. 16- and 10-bed dorms €10-20; 8- and 6-bed €18-25; 4-bed €23-32; private rooms €76-90. ❷

Jacob's Inn, 21-28 Talbot Pl. (☎855 5660; www.isaacs.ie). 2 blocks north of the Custom House. Ensuite rooms are spacious and clean. Light breakfast included. Luggage storage. Lockers €1.50 per night. Towels €2. Lockout 11am-3pm. Dorms €18-20; doubles €66; triples €87. ●

WEST OF TEMPLE BAR

▨ **Four Courts Hostel,** 15-17 Merchants Quay (☎672 5862), on the south bank. The #748 bus from the airport stops next door. A quiet lounge and a game room provide plenty of space to wind down. Continental breakfast included. 4- to 16-bed dorms €16.50-27; singles €45-50; doubles €60-66; triples €87. ●

Kinlay House (IHH), 2-12 Lord Edward St. (☎679 6644). Great location a few blocks from Temple Bar, across from Christ Church Cathedral. Continental breakfast included. Free luggage storage. 16- to 24-bed dorms €17-20; 4- to 6-bed €24-29; singles €44-56; doubles €29-33; triples €27-33. ●

Avalon House (IHH), 55 Aungier St. (☎475 0001; www.avalon-house.ie). A few blocks from Grafton St., Avalon revs with the energy of transcontinental travelers. Kitchen and pool. Light breakfast included. Large dorms €13-20; 6-bed €23-30; 4-bed €20-30; singles €30-37; doubles €60-70. ●

The Brewery Hostel, 22-23 Thomas St. (☎453 8600). Bus #123. 15-20min. walk from Temple Bar. Picnic area with grill for cookouts. Continental breakfast included. Free luggage storage. 8- and 10-bed dorms €16; doubles €70. ●

NORTH OF O'CONNELL STREET

Abbey Court Hostel, 29 Bachelor's Walk (☎878 0700; www.abbey-court.com). Clean, narrow rooms overlook the Liffey. Continental breakfast included. Free luggage storage. 12-bed dorms €18-21; 6-bed €23-26; 4-bed €26-29; doubles €76-88. ●

Parkway Guest House, 5 Gardiner Pl. (☎874 0469; www.parkway-guesthouse.com). Run by a cheery hurling veteran who offers advice on restaurants and pubs. Irish breakfast included. Singles €35; doubles €55-65, ensuite €65-80. ●

Dublin International Youth Hostel (An Óige/HI), 61 Mountjoy St. (☎830 4555; www.irelandyha.org). A huge, rambling hostel housed in a converted convent. Complimentary breakfast served in the former chapel. Free shuttle to Temple Bar. €2 discount for HI members. Dorms €20-21; doubles €52; triples €75; quads €92-100. ●

The Kingfisher, 166 Parnell St. (☎872 8732; www.kingfisherdublin.com). Bathrooms clean enough to sleep in, but the rooms are more comfortable. Singles from €35. ●

◘ FOOD

TEMPLE BAR

▨ **Queen of Tarts,** Dame St. (☎670 7499), across from City Hall. Addictive pastries and light meals. Scones, flaky and baked to perfection, €3. Breakfast €3-8. Open M-F 7:30am-6pm, Sa 9am-6pm, Su 9:30am-6pm. ●

Tante Zoe's, 1 Crow St. (☎679 4407). Mellow instrumental music may whisper "elevator," but the Cajun-Creole food shouts "delicious." Su live jazz 1-4pm. Entrees €14-22, lunch €5-12. Open daily noon-4pm and 5:30pm-midnight. ●

Joy of Coffee, 25 Essex St. (☎679 3393). Large tables encourage conversation mergers over lunch or coffee. Wide selection of coffee drinks €2-3.50. Panini and salads €6-7. Open M-Th 9am-10:30pm, F-Sa 9am-12:30pm, Su 10am-10pm. ●

Zaytoon, 14-15 Parliament St. (☎677 3595). Top-grade Persian food is a healthy way to satisfy the raging post-pub munchies. Döner plate €9. Open daily noon-4am. ❷

GRAFTON AND SOUTH GREAT GEORGES STREETS

🖾 **Unicorn Food Store and Café,** Merrion Row (☎678 8588), offers Italian food from the famed Unicorn Café and Restaurant kitchen at a fraction of the price. Pastas €5-7. Open daily 8am-7pm. ❷

🖾 **Leo Burdock's,** 2 Werburgh St. (☎454 0306), behind the Lord Edward pub across from Christ Church Cathedral. Lip-smacking fish and chips served the real way, in brown paper. Takeaway only. Fish €3.50-6; chips €2.20. Open daily noon-midnight. ❶

Cornucopia, 19 Wicklow St. (☎677 7583). Popular spot for a delicious and filling meal (€9.50-10.50) or a cheaper but equally tasty salad (€3-8 for choice of 2 to 6 salads). Open M-W and F-Sa 8:30am-8pm, Th 8:30am-9pm, Su noon-7pm. ❷

Nude, 21 Suffolk St. (☎677 4804). Imperialists may feel slightly out of place at this free-range, free-trade restaurant. Smoothies (€2-4), salads (€4), and wraps (€5). Branch on Grafton St. above BT2. Open M-Sa 7:30am-10pm, Su 10am-8pm. ❶

Govinda's, 4 Aungier St. (☎475 0309). Vegetarian Indian food in a colorful oasis with a karma-conscious menu. Dinner special €9. Open M-W and Su noon-9pm. ❷

NORTH OF THE LIFFEY

🖾 **101 Talbot,** 101 Talbot St. (☎874 5011), between Marlborough and Gardiner St., one flight up through the red doors. Italian-Mediterranean menu changes frequently but always has vegetarian specialties. Entrees €14-20. Open Tu-Sa 5-11pm. ❹

Panem, 21 Lower Ormond Quay (☎872 8510). Cheap and delicious. Crafts some of the best sandwiches (€4) in the city in its little storefront overlooking the Liffey. ❶

Soup Dragon, 168 Capel St. (☎872 3277). Choose from a dozen homemade soups (€4-11.50). Open M-F 8am-5:30pm, Sa 11am-5:30pm. ❷

🎦 PUBLIN

Note that a growing number of bars are blurring the distinction between pub and club by hosting live music and staying open late into the night on weekdays; pay attention and hit two birds with one pint.

GRAFTON STREET AND TRINITY COLLEGE AREA

McDaid's, 3 Harry St. (☎679 4395), off Grafton St. across from Anne St. The center of the Irish literary scene in the 50s. Today the gregarious crowd spills out onto the street. Open M-W 10:30am-11:30pm, Th-Sa 10:30am-12:30am, Su 12:30-11pm.

The International Bar, 23 Wicklow St. (☎677 9250), on the corner of South William St. A great place to meet kindred wandering spirits. Downstairs lounge hosts excellent improv comedy M; stand-up W-Sa; jazz Tu; house Su. W-F cover €10, students €8. Open M-W 10:30am-11:30pm, Th-Sa 10:30am-12:30am, Su 12:30-11pm.

Café en Seine, 40 Dawson St. (☎677 4567; www.capitalbars.com). The 3-story atrium belongs in an Egyptian palace but is resigned to this yuppie bar. Live jazz M 10pm-midnight, Su 3-5pm. DJ F-Sa. Open M-W 11am-1:30am, Th-Sa 11am-2:30am, Su 11am-1:30am. Food served daily noon-3pm and 4-10pm.

Bruxelles, Harry St. (☎677 5362), across from McDaid's. Glass chandeliers hang above a constant crowd of young trendsetters. Blues and soul music M-Tu and Su. Open M-W 10:30am-1:30am, Th-Sa 10:30am-2:30am, Su 10:30am-1am.

Dublin Pub Crawl

4 Dame Lane, **15**
The Bleeding Horse, **23**
The Brazen Head, **1**
Brogan's Bar, **12**
Bruxelles, **18**
Café en Seine, **20**
The Celt, **6**
Davy Byrne's, **17**
The Globe, **13**
The International Bar, **16**
The Long Stone, **8**

McDaid's, **19**
Messrs. Maguire, **4**
Mulligan's, **7**
The Odeon, **24**
Oliver St. John Gogarty, **9**
The Porter House, **11**
Pravda, **3**
Solas, **21**
The Stag's Head, **14**
Temple Bar Pub, **10**
Whelan's, **22**
Zanzibar, **2**

DUBLIN

Davy Byrne's, 21 Duke St. (☎677 5217; www.davybyrnespub.com), off Grafton St. The pub where Joyce set *Ulysses*'s Cyclops chapter; come on Bloomsday for a taste of Joycean Dublin. Open M-W 9am-11:30pm, Th-Sa 9am-12:30am, Su 12:30-11pm.

HARCOURT, CAMDEN, AND WEXFORD STREETS

▨ **Whelan's,** 25 Wexford St. (☎478 0766). Live traditional music and rock every night starting at 8:30pm. DJs spin the popular "Fear and Loathing" night Th. Cover €7-15. Open late daily, M-W until 2am and Th-Sa until 3am.

The Bleeding Horse, 24 Upper Camden St. (☎475 2705). A labyrinth of cozy nooks for private affairs surround a sprawling central bar. Late bar with DJ F-Sa. Open M-Th and Su until midnight, F-Sa until 2am.

The Odeon, Old Harcourt Train Station (☎478 2088). The longest bar in Ireland (nearly 100 ft.). Young, well-heeled clientele come to be seen. DJ Th-Sa; other nights lounge and dance. Cover €10. Open M-W until 11pm, Th 12:30am, F-Sa 2:30am.

Solas, 31 Wexford St. (☎478 0583). Popular with students. DJ spins urban and soul nightly at 9pm. Open M-W noon-11:30pm, Th-Sa noon-12:30am, Su 4-11pm.

AROUND SOUTH GREAT GEORGES STREET

▨ **The Stag's Head,** 1 Dame Ct. (☎679 3701). The student crowd dons everything from t-shirts to tuxes and spills into the alleys (especially now that they can't smoke indoors). Excellent pub grub. Entrees €7.50-11. Open M-Th 10:30am-11:30pm, F-Sa 10:30am-12:30am. Food served M-F noon-3:30pm and 5-7pm, Sa noon-2:30pm.

The Globe, 11 S. Great Georges St. (☎671 1220). Frequented by a laid-back crowd imbibing Guinness or frothy cappuccino. Open M-Sa noon-3am, Su 4pm-1am.

4 Dame Lane, 4 Dame Ln. (☎679 2901). Look for the 2 flaming torches. 2 DJs on 2 floors play mostly house in this votive-lit space. 23+. Open daily 5pm-3am.

TEMPLE BAR

▨ **The Porter House,** 16-18 Parliament St. (☎671 5715). Way, way more than 99 bottles of beer on the wall, including 10 self-brewed porters, stouts, and ales. 3 spacious floors fill nightly for trad, blues, and rock. Open M-W 11:30am-11:30pm, Th 11:30am-2am, F-Sa 11:30am-2:30am, Su 11:30am-1:30am.

Temple Bar Pub, Temple Ln. S. (☎672 5286). Sprawling pub with outdoor beer garden. Tourists rule, but locals still come. 2hr. trad sessions M-Th 4:30pm and 8:30pm, F-Sa 4:30pm. Open M-Th 11am-12:30am, F-Sa 11am-1:30am, Su noon-12:30am.

Brogan's Bar, 75 Dame St. (☎671 1844). Unassuming spot ignored by tourists despite its location. Somewhat fatherly crowd. Open M-W 4-11:30pm, Th 4pm-12:30am, F-Sa 1pm-12:30am, Su 1-11:30pm.

Messrs. Maguire, Burgh Quay (☎670 5777). Explore this classy watering hole under the spell of homemade brews. Trad M 9:30-11:30pm, ballads Su 9-11pm. Late bar W-Sa, with DJ. No cover. Open M-Tu 10:30am-12:30am, W 11am-1:30am, Th 10:30am-2am, F-Sa 11am-2:30am, Su noon-12:30am. Food served all day.

THE BEST OF THE REST

▨ **Zanzibar** (☎878 7212), at the Ha'penny Bridge. Dances between club and pub, and the result is explosive. Unique private rooms on the balcony are free to reserve. M-Th and Su €5 mixed drinks before midnight. Live DJ Tu-Su. Cover after 11pm F €5, Sa €7. Open M-Th 5pm-2:30am, F 4pm-2:30am, Sa 2pm-2:30am, Su 2pm-1:30am.

■ **The Long Stone,** 10-11 Townsend St. (☎671 8102). The strains of the live bands (W and Sa 8-10pm) reach everywhere in this multi-level maze of comfortable booths. Open M-Th noon-11:30pm, F-Sa noon-12:30am, Su 4-12:30am.

Pravda, 35 Lower Liffey St. (☎874 0090), on the north side of the Ha'penny Bridge. Trendy, gay-friendly, and crowded. DJ W-Sa. Late bar Th-Sa until 2:30am.

The Celt, 81-82 Talbot St. (☎878 8665). Filled with locals of all ages who stay for the nightly trad sessions. Some of the cheapest pints in the city center (€3.80). Open M-Th 10:30am-11:30pm, F-Sa 10:30am-12:30am, Su 12:30-11pm.

Mulligan's, 8 Poolbeg St. (☎677 5582), behind Burgh Quay, off Tara St. Upholds its reputation as one of the best pint-pourers in Dublin. Strictly drinks, with no touristy trad to be found. Open M-Th 10:30am-11:30pm, F-Sa 10:30am-12:30am, Su noon-11pm.

The Brazen Head, 20 North Bridge St. (☎679 5186), off Merchant's Quay. Dublin's oldest pub was once where the United Irishmen met to plan their attacks on the British. The cobbled courtyard doesn't waste any time getting lively on summer nights. Nightly trad. Open M-W 10:30am-11:30pm, Th-Sa 10:30am-12:30am, Su 12:30pm-midnight.

Life, Lower Abbey St. (☎878 1032). The young, the beautiful, and the hangers-on trickle in after work, so the pink-tinted skylights don't heat up until late in this live music venue. Lunch €8-12. DJ F-Sa. Late bar F-Sa until 2:30am.

▌ CLUBLIN

Clubbing is an expensive end to the evening, since covers run €5-20 and pints can surpass €5. To save some money, find a club with an expensive cover but cheap drink prices and stay all night.

■ **The PoD,** 35 Harcourt St. (☎478 0225), corner of Hatch St. A club that's serious about its music. Upstairs is the **Red Box** (☎478 0225), with music that crushes brains and a crowd so deep it seems designed to winnow out the weak. The more mellow train-station-turned-bar **Crawdaddy** hosts musical gigs, including some world stars. Cover €10-20, Th students €5. Open until 3am on weekends.

■ **Spirit,** 57 Mid. Abbey St. (☎877 9999). Huge club with a daunting queue on weekends. "Soul," the blindingly colorful main bar, plays R&B. "Body," first floor, has a giant egg-shaped fortress for the DJs to hatch pounding house music. The top floor, "Virtue," may be the coolest of all, but it's only for VIPs and clubbers with invisibility cloaks. Su gay night. Cover €10-20, Th students €5. Open Th-Su 10:30pm-3:30am.

Spy, Powerscourt House, South William St. (☎677 0014). **Wax** is a thumping dance club in the basement. The mellow lounge rooms on the first floor go unnamed. Th gay night. No cover. Open F-Su until 2:30am.

The Village, 26 Wexford St. (☎475 8555). Bands play Th-Sa from 7-10:30pm (tickets around €20), then DJs come in for chill-out, jungle, and house downstairs. Club cover F €7, Sa €9. Bar open until 1:30am; club open Th-Sa until 3am.

Gaiety, S. King St. (☎679 5622; www.gaietytheatre.com), off Grafton St. Elegant theater shows its late-night wild side every F-Sa. Salsa, jazz, swing, latin, and soul. Cover around €10. Open F-Sa 11:45pm-4am.

Traffic, 54 Middle Abbey St. (☎873 4038; www.traffic54.net). Nightly DJ spins hip-hop or techno from his throne at the end of the long bar. Cover Th €6, F-Sa €8-10; free before 11pm. Open M-W 3-11:30pm, Th-Sa 3pm-2:30am, Su 3pm-midnight.

Club M, Blooms Hotel (☎671 5622), on Cope St. in Temple Bar. One of Dublin's largest clubs. Younger crowd; conversation closer to gym class than career moves. Cover M-Th €5, F-Sa €12-15. Open M-Th 11pm-2:30am, F-Sa 10pm-2:30am.

The Mezz, 21-25 Eustace St. (☎670 7655). A quiet pub by day, The Mezz turns into a cauldron of loud live-music at night. No cover.

GAY AND LESBIAN NIGHTLIFE

Gay and lesbian nightlife centers around several options mentioned below; also keep a lookout for clubs like **Spy** (see above), which have running gay nights.

■ **The Dragon,** S. Great Georges St. (☎478 1590), a few doors down from The George. Dublin's newest gay club, although everyone is welcome. It's packed to its trendy rafters on weekend nights. Open M-W 5-11:30pm, Th-Sa 5pm-2:30am, Su 5pm-1am.

The Front Lounge, Parliament St. (☎670 4112). The red velvet seats of this more subdued gay bar are filled nightly by a young crowd. Open M and W noon-11:30pm, Tu noon-12:30am, Th noon-1:30am, F-Sa noon-2am, Su 4-11:30pm.

The George, 89 S. Great Georges St. (☎478 2983; www.capitalbars.com). Dublin's oldest and most prominent gay bar seems to draw a decidedly older male crowd. The attached nightclub opens W-Su until 2am. Cover €8-10 after 10pm. Open M-Tu 12:30-11:30pm, W-Su 12:30pm-2:30am.

◙ TOURS

SELF-GUIDED WALKING TOURS

The first three walking tours listed below are mapped out in the *Dublin Walkabout City Map and Guide.* Trail pamphlets can be purchased for the Ulysses Trail. All guides are available at the tourist office (€1-4).

The Cultural Experience. Visit the shopping mecca of Henry St., the Custom House, the Municipal Gallery, and the Dublin Writers Museum.

The Heritage Experience. Begin on College Green and weave your way past theaters, churches, and markets to end at Grafton St.

The Georgian Experience. Stroll past Dublin's best-preserved Georgian streets and public buildings, including Merrion Square and Newman House.

Ulysses Map of Dublin. Chart Poldy's haunts and retrace his heroic actions, beginning with kidneys for breakfast. The walk takes 18hr. (including drinking), but it's faster than reading *Ulysses.* Walking while reading is not recommended.

GUIDED WALKING TOURS

Historical Walking Tour (☎878 0227). Trinity College history graduates seamlessly transition from one era to another and from one street to the next, protecting their listeners from ignorance and maniacal drivers. Meet at Trinity's front gate. May-Sept. daily 11am and 3pm, Apr.-Oct. daily 11am; Nov.-Mar. F-Su 11am. €10, students €8.

Trinity College Walking Tour. Moderately irreverent and sufficiently stuck-up, this student-led tour concentrates on university lore. All that pretentiousness does serve some good: their guests skip to the front of the line at the *Book of Kells* exhibit. Tours depart from the info booth inside the front gate. 30min. tours every 40min. May-Oct. daily 10:15am-3:40pm; Oct.-Jan. Sa-Su 10:15am-3:40pm. €4, with admission to the Old Library and the Book of Kells €10.

1916 Rebellion Walking Tour (☎086 858 3847). See the scars the 1916 Rebellion left and the state it created. Meet inside the International Bar, 23 Wicklow St. 2hr. tour Mar.-Oct. Tu-Th 11:30am, F-Sa 11:30am and 2:30pm, Su 1pm. €10.

👁 🏛 SIGHTS AND MUSEUMS

SOUTH OF THE LIFFEY

TRINITY COLLEGE AND NEARBY

To get to Trinity from North of the Liffey, follow O'Connell St. across the river and bear right onto Westmoreland St.

TRINITY COLLEGE. Bullet holes from the 1916 Rebellion still mar the stone entrance to Trinity, built by the British as a seminary in 1592. The college later became a stop on the life-track of Anglo-Irish elite and has educated Jonathan Swift, Oscar Wilde, and Samuel Beckett. Until the 1960s, the Catholic Church deemed it a cardinal sin to attend Trinity; when the Church lifted the ban, the size of the student body tripled. (*Between Westmoreland and Grafton St., in South Dublin. Main entrance fronts the College Green.* ☎ *608 1724; www.tcd.ie. Grounds always open. Free.*)

THE OLD LIBRARY. On display is the famous **Book of Kells,** a four-volume edition of the Gospels beautifully illustrated by Irish monks in AD 800 with ink made from bugs and plants. Upstairs, the library's **Long Room** contains Ireland's oldest harp and one of the original copies of the **1916 proclamation** of the Republic of Ireland. (*From the main gate, the library is to the right, on the south side of Library Sq.* ☎ *608 2320; www.tcd.ie/Library. Open June-Sept. M-Sa 9:30am-5pm, Su 9:30-4:30pm; Oct.-May M-Sa 9:30am-5pm, Su noon-4:30pm.* €*8, students and seniors* €*7.*)

GRAFTON STREET. The few blocks south of College Green are off-limits to cars. The area's nucleus, Grafton St., meanders southward and connects with St. Stephen's Green. Its shops showcase everything from fast-food to haute couture and its wide variety of **street performers** keeps the crowds entertained.

KILDARE STREET

The block bordered by Kildare St., Nassau St., Upper Merrion St., and Merrion Row is loaded with impressive buildings and many of the city's major museums.

▒THE NATURAL HISTORY MUSEUM. This museum showcases Victorian taxidermy at its strangest and best. Three giant Irish deer skeletons stare out from old Victorian cabinets, the dodo skeleton fights Irish parasitic worms for prime facetime, and mysterious red tarps, when lifted, reveal the complex world of preserved insects. (*Upper Merrion St.* ☎ *677 7444. Open Tu-Sa 10am-5pm and Su 2-5pm. Free.*)

THE NATIONAL GALLERY. Paintings by Brueghel, Goya, Caravaggio, Vermeer, and Rembrandt fill the European sections, while a major part of the collection is dedicated to the Irish tradition. The works of **Jack Yeats,** brother of poet W.B., are of particular interest. (*Merrion Sq. W.* ☎ *661 5133. Open M-W and F-Sa 9:30am-5:30pm, Th 9:30am-8:30pm, Su noon-5:30pm. Free guided tours July M-Sa 3pm, Su 2, 3, 4pm; Aug.-June Sa 3pm, Su 2, 3, 4pm. Admission free. Temporary exhibits* €*10, students and seniors* €*6.*)

THE NATIONAL MUSEUM OF ARCHAEOLOGY AND HISTORY. One room gleams with the **Tara Brooch,** the **Ardagh Hoard,** and other Celtic goldwork. Another section flaunts the bloody vest of nationalist hero **James Connolly.** (*Kildare St., next to Leinster House.* ☎ *677 7444; www.museum.ie. Open Tu-Sa 10am-5pm and Su 2-5pm. Admission free. Guided tours* €*2; call for times.*)

THE NATIONAL LIBRARY. The library chronicles Irish history and exhibits literary treasures in its entry hall. A genealogical center helps visitors trace even the thinnest twiglets of their Irish family trees. Don't miss the reading room and its

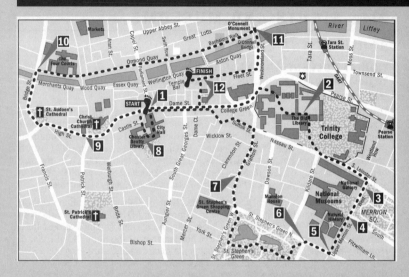

1 QUEEN OF TARTS CAFE. Begin the day with a delicious scone (p. 691).

2 TRINITY COLLEGE The Old Library, one of the many stately edifices of Dublin's most famous university, holds the **Book of Kells** (p. 697).

3 NATIONAL GALLERY This gallery has a major collection of international works, from paintings by Picasso and Goya to a wing dedicated to the Yeats family (p. 697).

START: Queen of Tarts Cafe, Dame St.

FINISH: Temple Bar Pub, Temple Bar; Brogan's Bar, Dame St.

DISTANCE: 3.5km

DURATION: 8hr.

WHEN TO GO: Begin the tour at 8am

4 NATURAL HISTORY MUSEUM A marvel of taxidermy and preservation; everything from beetles to bears are jam-packed into three floors of flora and fauna (p. 697).

5 UNICORN FOOD STORE This Italian bistro is a great place to grab some lunch. Bring some pasta or a sandwich with you to St. Stephen's Green (p. 692).

6 ST. STEPHEN'S GREEN Linger over a picnic and enjoy the streams, trees, and flowers in Dublin's answer to Central Park (p. 699.).

7 GRAFTON STREET Try to catch some of the street performers or window-shop on Dublin's trendiest shopping avenue (p. 697).

8 CHESTER BEATTY LIBRARY Walk through the grounds of Dublin Castle to reach this library of treasures, and gawk over the ancient illuminated texts (p. 699).

9 CHRIST CHURCH CATHEDRAL Dublin's oldest structure is also, supposedly, the burial place of Strongbow (p. 699).

10 RIVER WALK Pass St. Audeon's Church, turn right and cross the river, then follow the quays past The Four Courts toward the city center (p. 701).

11 O'CONNELL STREET Stop to admire the O'Connell Monument (p. 700).

12 PUB STOP Because no day in Dublin is complete without a pub experience, seek out Temple Bar Pub's daily trad session at 4:50pm (p. 694). Alternatively, drink with the locals at Brogan's Bar, Dame St. (p. 694).

soaring domed ceiling. *(Kildare St., adjacent to Leinster House. ☎ 603 0200. Open M-W 10am-9pm, Th-F 10am-5pm, Sa 10am-1pm. Free. Academic reason required to obtain a library card and entrance to the reading room; being a student is usually enough.)*

ST. STEPHEN'S GREEN AND MERRION SQUARE

Home to Ireland's trendiest shops and priciest homes, Merrion Sq. draws shoppers and gawkers, while the grass of Dublin's finest park is cause to relax nearby.

ST. STEPHEN'S GREEN. St. Stephen's was a private estate until the Guinness clan bequeathed it to the city. Today, the 9 hectares of artificial lakes and hills are a welcome return to the elements. *(Kildare, Dawson, and Grafton St. lead to the park. ☎ 475 7826. Open M-Sa 8am-dusk, Su 10am-dusk.)*

MERRION SQUARE. After leaving 18 Fitzwilliam St., **W.B. Yeats** took up residence at 82 Merrion Sq. Farther south on Harcourt St., **George Bernard Shaw** and *Dracula*'s creator, **Bram Stoker**, were neighbors at numbers 61 and 16, respectively. **#29 Lower Fitzwilliam St.,** a townhouse-turned-museum, demonstrates the lifestyle of the 18th-century Anglo-Irish elite. *(☎ 702 6165; www.esb.ie/numbertwentynine. Open Tu-Sa 10am-5pm, Su 1-5pm. €4.50, students €2.)* The Georgians continue up Dawson St. to the Mansion House, where the Irish state declared its independence in 1919.

TEMPLE BAR

The government has spent €40 million to build a flock of arts-related tourist attractions in Temple Bar. Even so, weekend nights tend to be wild, with stag and hen (bachelor and bachelorette) parties pub-hopping with the throngs of tourists.

▧**THE IRISH FILM INSTITUTE.** Two theaters screen new releases, focusing on independent and foreign cinema, and also hold festivals and special retrospectives. The inner sanctum, the **Irish Film Archive,** is dedicated to Irish film. *(6 Eustace St. ☎ 679 5744, box office 679 3477; www.irishfilm.ie. Open M-F 10am-6pm.)*

TEMPLE BAR MUSIC CENTRE. The center holds terrific musical events virtually every night of the week and has its own pub and cafe. *(Curved St. ☎ 670 9202; www.tbmc.ie. Music nightly 7:30pm, club 11pm. Cover varies according to act; call ahead.)*

TEMPLE BAR GALLERY AND STUDIOS. One of Europe's largest studio complexes, the gallery draws artists from all over Ireland. Though the studio has several dozen live-in artists, the gallery is free and open to the public. *(5-9 Temple Bar. ☎ 671 0073; www.templebargallery.com. Open Tu-W and F-Sa 11am-6pm, Th 11am-7pm.)*

DAME STREET AND THE CATHEDRALS

The Dame Street area hosts some of Dublin's oldest religious and state buildings.

▧**CHESTER BEATTY LIBRARY.** Everything from Chinese snuff bottles to some of the earliest fragments of the Gospels are arranged by world region. The serene rooftop garden hovers above the urban landscape. *(Behind Dublin Castle. ☎ 407 0750; www.cbl.ie. 45min. tours W 1pm, Su 3 and 4pm. Open May-Sept. M-F 10am-5pm, Sa 11am-5pm, Su 1-5pm; Oct.-Apr. Tu-F 10am-5pm, Sa 11am-5pm, Su 1-5pm. Free.)*

DUBLINIA. This interactive exhibition ushers visitors through Dublin's medieval history. One room recreates a 13th-century fair, where you can don period clothes and get a taste for the archaic world of medieval medicine. *(Across from Christ Church Cathedral. ☎ 679 4611; www.dublinia.ie. Open Apr.-Sept. daily 10am-5pm; Oct.-Mar. M-F 11am-4pm, Sa-Su 10am-4pm. Last admission 45min. before close. €6, students and seniors €5. Combined admission with Christ Church Cathedral €9.50.)*

CHRIST CHURCH CATHEDRAL. The King of the Dublin Norsemen built a wooden church on this site around 1038, and Strongbow rebuilt it in stone in 1169. Stained glass sparkles above the raised crypts, one of which supposedly belongs to Strongbow. *(At the end of Dame St., uphill and across from the Castle. Bus #50 from Eden Quay or 78A from Aston Quay. ☎ 677 8099. Open daily 9:45am-5pm. €5, students and seniors €2.50.)*

ST. PATRICK'S CATHEDRAL. Jonathan Swift spent his last years as Dean of St. Patrick's; his grave is in the south nave. *(Patrick St. ☎ 475 4817; www.stpatrickscathedral.ie. Open Mar.-Oct. daily 9am-6pm; Nov.-Feb. Sa 9am-5pm, Su 10am-3pm. Church closed to touring Su during services. €4.50, students and seniors €3.50.)*

GUINNESS BREWERY AND KILMAINHAM GAOL

If you're within walking distance of central Dublin, it's best to take a bus west along the quays or to hop on a train to nearby Heuston Station.

GUINNESS STOREHOUSE. Seven floors of glass and metal catwalks coax you through the production of Ireland's most famous brew. *(St. James's Gate. Bus #51B or 78A from Aston Quay, or #123 from O'Connell St. ☎ 408 4800; www.guinness-storehouse.com. Open daily July-Aug. 9:30am-8pm, Sept.-June 9am-5pm. €14, students and seniors €9.50.)*

KILMAINHAM GAOL. Many Irish rebels spent time here, including the jail's last occupant, **Éamon de Valera,** the former leader of Éire. The 1hr. tour of the dank chambers ends in the wasteland of an execution yard. *(Inchicore Rd. Bus #51b, 51c, 78a, or 79 from Aston Quay. ☎ 453 5984. Open Apr.-Sept. daily 9:30am-5pm, Oct.-Mar. M-F 9:30am-4pm and Su 10am-5pm. Tours every 30min. €5, students €2, seniors €3.50.)*

NORTH OF THE LIFFEY

O'CONNELL STREET AND PARNELL SQUARE

The elusive real Dublin lies just a dart off onto one of the many side streets, where fresh fruit and fish markets abound.

■**ST. MICHAN'S CHURCH.** The church's creepy limestone vaults may have inspired Bram Stoker's *Dracula*. Touch the hand of the Cavalier, the oldest mummy on display, and be blessed with good luck. *(Church St. ☎ 872 4154. Open mid-Mar. to Oct. M-F 10am-12:45pm and 2-4:30pm, Sa 10am-12:45pm; Nov. to mid-Mar. M-F 12:30-3:30pm, Sa 10am-12:45pm. Crypt tours €3.50, students €3.*

O'CONNELL STREET. Facing the Liffey and O'Connell Bridge is **O'Connell's statue;** the winged women aren't angels but Winged Victories, and one has a bullet hole from 1916 in a rather inglorious place. At the other end of the street, **Parnell's statue** points toward nearby Parnell Mooney's pub. In front of the General Post Office stands the 300 ft. **Dublin Spire,** which commemorated the new millennium three years too late.

THE GENERAL POST OFFICE. Today, it may just be the place to send a postcard, but in 1916 the GPO was the eye of the 1916 Easter Rising. Padraig Pearse read the Proclamation of Irish Independence from its steps. In the main hall, paintings recount the struggle for independence. *(O'Connell St. ☎ 705 7000. Open M-Sa 8am-8pm.)*

THE DUBLIN WRITERS MUSEUM. The upstairs Gallery of Writers harbors one of the most personal items of the collection: James Joyce's piano. *(18 Parnell Sq. N. ☎ 872 2077. Open June-Aug. M-F 10am-6pm, Sa 10am-5pm, Su 11am-5pm; Sept.-May M-Sa 10am-5pm, Su 11am-5pm. €6.50, students and seniors €5.50.)*

ALONG THE QUAYS

On a (rare) sunny day, a walk along the river can be pleasant, especially if broken up by visits to the following sights, listed from east to west.

THE CUSTOM HOUSE. The Custom House was designed in the 1780s by London-born **James Gandon.** The Roman and Venetian columns and domes give a hint of what the city's 18th-century Anglo-Irish brahmins wanted Dublin to become. *(East of O'Connell St. at Custom House Quay, where Gardiner St. meets the river. ☎ 888 2538.)*

FOUR COURTS. This Gandon masterpiece now houses the Supreme Court and the High Court. *(Inn's Quay, several quays west of O'Connell Bridge. ☎888 6000. Open M-F 9am-4:30pm. No scheduled tours. Free.)*

ARTS AND ENTERTAINMENT

MUSIC

Hot Press (€2) has up-to-date music listings, particularly for rock. The intimate ▓Whelan's, 25 Wexford St., hosts international acts (see p. 694). Big-deal bands frequent the **Baggot Inn**, 143 Baggot St. (☎676 1430) and **Olympia Theatre**, 72 Dame St. (☎677 7744). Tickets for major shows are available through **Ticketmaster** venues (www.ticketmaster.ie). Many pubs in the city center hold nightly trad (traditional music) sessions (see **Publin**, p. 692).

THEATER

Check the *Event Guide*, available in restaurants and hostels throughout the city, and look for flyers for shows in any given week.

▓ **Abbey Theatre,** 26 Lower Abbey St. (☎878 7222; www.abbeytheatre.ie). Founded by W.B. Yeats and Lady Gregory in 1904 to promote the Irish cultural revival and modernist theater. Today, the Abbey serves as Ireland's National Theatre. Tickets €15-30; Sa 2:30pm matinee €15, students €9.50. Box office open M-Sa 10:30am-7pm.

Peacock Theatre, 26 Lower Abbey St. (☎878 7222). The Abbey's experimental downstairs studio theater. Tickets €10-17; Sa 2:45pm matinees €12.50; available at Abbey box office. Doors open M-Sa at 7:30pm.

Gate Theatre, 1 Cavendish Row (☎874 4045, www.gate-theatre.ie). Contemporary Irish and classic international dramas. Tickets €16-27; M-Th student ticket at curtain €10 with ID, subject to availability. Box office open M-Sa 10am-7:30pm.

SPORTS

Gaelic football and **hurling** runs from mid-February to November. Games are played on **Phibsborough Road** and in **Croke Park.** Contact the Gaelic Athletic Association for details. (Clonliffe Rd., 15min. from Connolly station. Buses #3, 11, 11A, 16, 16A, 51A, 123. ☎836 3222; www.gaa.ie. Tickets €20-60.)

FESTIVALS

BLOOMSDAY. James Joyce's Dublin comes to life on June 16, the date of protagonist Leopold Bloom's 18hr. journey in *Ulysses*. Festivities are held the week leading up to the big day and culminate on the 16th with a slate of events, including reenactments, concerts, and guided tours. *(Contact the James Joyce Cultural Centre. 35 N. Great Georges St. ☎878 8547; www.jamesjoyce.ie. Center open Sept.-June M-Sa 9:30am-5pm, Su 12:30-5pm; July-Aug. M-Sa 9:30am-5pm, Su 11am-5pm.)*

ST. PATRICK'S DAY. The week of March 17 occasions a city-wide carnival of concerts, fireworks, street theater, and intoxicated madness. *(☎676 3205; also contact the tourist center for more information.)*

THE DUBLIN THEATRE FESTIVAL. This premier cultural event is held from late September to early October at major theaters across the city. Tickets may be purchased year-round at participating theaters or at the Festival Booking Office. *(44 E Essex St. ☎677 8439, box office 677 8899; www.dublintheatrefestival.com. Tickets €13-20, student discounts vary by venue.)*

APPENDIX

CLIMATE

Avg Temp (lo/hi), Precipitation	January			April			July			October		
	°C	°F	mm	°C	°F	mm	°C	°F	mm	°C	°F	mm
London	2/6	36/43	54	6/13	43/55	37	14/22	57/72	57	8/14	46/57	57
Cardiff	2/7	36/45	108	5/13	41/55	65	12/20	54/68	89	8/14	46/57	109
Edinburgh	1/6	34/43	57	4/11	39/52	39	11/18	52/64	83	7/12	45/54	65

2006 BANK HOLIDAYS

Government agencies, post offices, and banks are closed on the following days (hence the term "Bank Holiday"). Businesses, if not closed, may have shorter hours. Transportation in rural areas grinds to a halt, while congestion in urban areas can reach ridiculous levels. Holiday destinations are usually open.

DATE	HOLIDAY	AREAS
Jan. 2	New Year's Day	UK
Jan. 2-3	New Year's Day and 2nd January	Scotland
Mar. 17	St. Patrick's Day	Northern Ireland
Apr. 14	Good Friday	UK
Apr. 17	Easter Monday	UK except Scotland
May 1	May Day Bank Holiday	UK
May 29	Spring Bank Holiday	UK
July 12	Battle of the Boyne (Orange Day)	Northern Ireland
Aug. 7	Summer Bank Holiday	Scotland
Aug. 28	Summer Bank Holiday	UK except Scotland
Dec. 25	Christmas Day	UK
Dec. 26	Boxing Day/St. Stephen's Day	UK

MEASUREMENTS

Britain uses the metric system, though its conversion is still in progress; road signs indicate distances in miles. Gallons in the US and those across the Atlantic are not identical: one US gallon equals 0.83 Imperial gallons. Pub aficionados will note that an Imperial pint (20 oz.) is larger than its US counterpart (16 oz.). Below is a list of Imperial units and their metric equivalents.

MEASUREMENT CONVERSIONS	MEASUREMENT CONVERSIONS
1 inch (in.) = 25.4mm	1 millimeter (mm) = 0.039 in.
1 foot (ft.) = 0.30m	1 meter (m) = 3.28 ft.
1 yard (yd.) = 0.914m	1 meter (m) = 1.09 yd.
1 mile (mi.) = 1.61km	1 kilometer (km) = 0.62 mi.
1 ounce (oz.) = 28.35g	1 gram (g) = 0.035 oz.

MEASUREMENT CONVERSIONS	MEASUREMENT CONVERSIONS
1 pound (lb.) = 0.454kg	1 kilogram (kg) = 2.20 lb.
1 fluid ounce (fl. oz.) = 29.57ml	1 milliliter (ml) = 0.034 fl. oz.
1 UK gallon (gal.) = 4.546L	1 liter (L) = 0.264 gal.
1 square mile (sq. mi.) = 2.59km²	1 square kilometer (km²) = 0.386 sq. mi.

LANGUAGE

The worldwide use of a single language has given rise to countless variations. Below is a list of British words that travelers are most likely to encounter.

BRITISH ENGLISH	AMERICAN ENGLISH	BRITISH ENGLISH	AMERICAN ENGLISH
aubergine	eggplant	give a bollocking to	shout at
bap	a soft bun	high street	main street
barmy	insane, erratic	hire	rental, to rent
bed-sit, or bed sitter	studio apartment	holiday	vacation
beer mat	coaster	hoover	vacuum cleaner
biro	ballpoint pen	ice-lolly	popsicle
biscuit	a cookie or cracker	interval	intermission
bobby	police officer	"in" a street	"on" a street
bonnet	car hood	jam	jelly
boot	car trunk	jelly	Jell-O
braces	suspenders	jumper	sweater
brilliant	awesome, cool	kip	sleep
caravan	trailer, mobile home	kit	sports team uniform
car park	parking lot	knackered	tired, worn out
cheeky	mischievous	lavatory, "lav"	restroom
cheers, cheerio	thank you, goodbye	lay-by	roadside turnout
chemist/chemist's	pharmacist/pharmacy	legless	intoxicated
chips	french fries	lemonade	lemon soda
chuffed	pleased	let	to rent
coach	intercity bus	lift	elevator
concession	discount on admission	loo	restroom
courgette	zucchini	lorry	truck
crisps	potato chips	mate	pal
dear	expensive	motorway	highway
dicey, dodgy	sketchy	naff	cheap, in poor taste
the dog's bollocks	the best	pants	underwear
dual carriageway	divided highway	petrol	gasoline
dustbin	trash can	pissed	drunk
ensuite	with attached bathroom	plaster	Band-Aid
fag	cigarette	prat	stupid person
fanny	vagina	pudding	dessert
first floor	second floor	pull	to seduce
fortnight	two weeks	public school	private school
full stop	period (punctuation)	punter	average person
geezer	adult male	queue up, queue	to line up
grotty	grungy	quid	pound (in money)

APPENDIX

BRITISH ENGLISH	AMERICAN ENGLISH	BRITISH ENGLISH	AMERICAN ENGLISH
roundabout	rotary road intersection	toilet	restroom
rubber	eraser	torch	flashlight
self-catering	with kitchen facilities	tosser	term of abuse; see prat
self-drive	car rental	trainers	sneakers
serviette	napkin	trousers	pants
a shag, to shag	sex, to have sex	trunk call	long-distance call
single carriageway	non-divided highway	vest	undershirt
sod it	forget it	waistcoat (weskit)	men's vest
snogging	making out	wanker	masturbator; see prat
sweet(s)	candy	way out	exit
swish	swanky	W.C. (water closet)	toilet, restroom
take the piss	to make fun of	"zed"	the letter Z

BRITISH PRONUNCIATION

Berkeley	BARK-lee	Magdalen	MAUD-lin
Berkshire	BARK-sher	Norwich	NOR-ich
Birmingham	BIRM-ing-um	Salisbury	SAULS-bree
Derby	DAR-bee	Shrewsbury	SHROWS-bree
Dulwich	DULL-idge	Southwark	SUTH-uk
Edinburgh	ED-in-bur-ra	Thames	TEMS
Gloucester	GLOS-ter	Woolwich	WOOL-ich
Greenwich	GREN-ich	Worcester	WOO-ster
Hertfordshire	HART-ford-sher	gaol	JAIL
Grosvenor	GROV-nor	quay	KEY
Leicester	LES-ter	scones	SKONS

WELSH WORDS AND PHRASES

Consult **Language**, p. 438, for the basic rules of Welsh pronunciation. Listed below are a number of words and phrases you may encounter on the road.

WORD/PHRASE	PRONUNCIATION	MEANING
allan	ahl-LAN	exit
ar agor	ahr AG-or	open
ar gau	ahr GUY	closed
bore da	boh-RA DAH	good morning, hello
croeso	CROY-so	welcome
diolch	dee-OLCH	thank you
dydd da	DEETH dah	good day
dynion	dihnion	men
Ga i peint o cwrw?	gah-EE "pint" oh coo-roo?	Can I have a pint of beer?
hwyl	huh-will	cheers
ia	eeah	yes
iawn	eeown	well, fine
llwybr cyhoeddus	hlooee-BIR cuh-HOY-this	public footpath
merched	mehrch-ED	women
na, nage	nah, nahgah	no
nos da	nos dah	good night
noswaith dda	nos-WAYTHE tha	good evening

WORD/PHRASE	PRONUNCIATION	MEANING
os gwelwch yn dda	ohs gwell–OOCH uhn tha	please
perygl	pehr-UHGL	danger
preifat	"private"	private
safle'r bws	savlehr boos	bus stop
stryd Fawr	strihd vahor	high street
dwn i ddim	dun ee thim	I don't know

IRISH WORDS AND PHRASES

You may come across the following words and phrases in your travels in Northern Ireland. Spelling conventions almost never match English pronunciations: "mh" sounds like "v," and "dh" sounds like a soft "g."

WORD/PHRASE	PRONUNCIATION	MEANING
an Lár	on lahr	city center
Conas tá tú?	CUNN-us thaw too?	How are you?
Dia dhuit	JEE-a dich	Good day, hello
dia's Muire dhuit	JEE-as MWUR-a dich	reply to "good day"
Éire	AIR-uh	Ireland; official name of the Republic of Ireland
fáilte	FAWLT-cha	welcome
go raibh maith agat	guh roh moh UG-ut	thank you
ní hea	nee hah	no (lit. "it is not")
oíche mhaith dhuit	EE-ha woh ditch	good night
Oifig an Phoist	UFF-ig un fwisht	Post Office
sea	shah	yes (sort of–it's tricky)
sláinte	SLAWN-che	cheers, to your health
slán agat	slawn UG-ut	goodbye
sraid	shrawd	street

SCOTTISH GAELIC WORDS AND PHRASES

Consult **Language,** p. 522, for information on Scottish Gaelic. Listed below are a number of words and phrases you may encounter on the road.

WORD/PHRASE	PRONUNCIATION	MEANING
allt	ALT	stream
baile	BAL-eh	town
beinn	BEN	mountain
Ciamar a tha sibh?	KI-mer a HA shiv?	How are you?
De an t-ainm a th'oirbh?	JAY an TEN-im a HO-riv?	What's your name?
Failte gu...	FAL-chuh goo	Welcome to...
gleann	GLAY-ahn	valley
Gle mhath	GLAY va	very well
Gabh mo leisgeul	GAV mo LESH-kul	excuse me
Is mise...	ISH MISH-uh	My name is...
Latha ma	LA-huh MA	good day
ionad	EE-nud	place, visitor center
Madainn mhath	MA-ting VA	good morning
Oidhche mhath	a-HOY-chuh VA	good night
rathad	RAH-hud	road
Slainte mhath	SLAN-che VA	cheers, good health
sraid	SRAHJ	street

WORD/PHRASE	PRONUNCIATION	MEANING
Tapadh leibh	TA-pa LEEV	Thank you
Tha gu math	HA gu MA	I'm fine

SCOTS WORDS AND PHRASES

Consult **Language,** p. 522, for more info on Scots, a distinct dialect of English. Listed below are a few of the many Scots words and phrases used in standard Scottish English and their pronunciation, if applicable:

WORD/PHRASE	MEANING	WORD/PHRASE	MEANING
aye	yes	eejit	idiot
ben	mountain	nae	no (NAY)
blether, or guid blether	talk idly, chat (good BLA-ther)	sassenach	Lowlander (SAS-uh-nach)
bonnie	beautiful	strath	broad valley
brae	hill near water (BRAY)	tatty	potato
braw	bright, strong, great	thane	minor noble
burn	stream	tipple	a drink
cannae	cannot (CAN-eye)	weegie	Glaswegian (WEE-gee)

INDEX

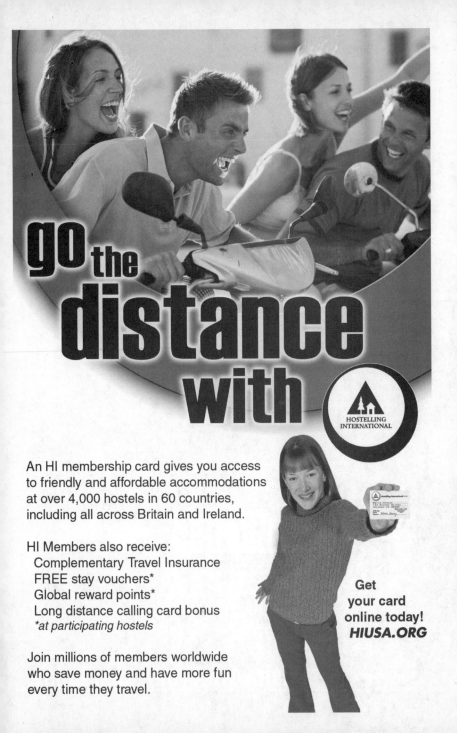

MAP INDEX

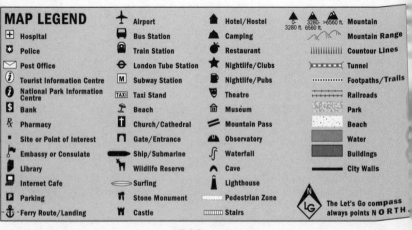

MAP LEGEND

✚ Hospital	✈ Airport
✇ Police	🚌 Bus Station
✉ Post Office	🚆 Train Station
ⓘ Tourist Information Centre	⊖ London Tube Station
ⓘ National Park Information Centre	Ⓜ Subway Station
$ Bank	TAXI Taxi Stand
℞ Pharmacy	⚓ Beach
▪ Site or Point of Interest	�🂠 Church/Cathedral
⚑ Embassy or Consulate	⊓ Gate/Entrance
📕 Library	Ship/Submarine
🖥 Internet Cafe	Wildlife Reserve
P Parking	Surfing
⚓ Ferry Route/Landing	⚑ Stone Monument
	Castle

♠ Hotel/Hostel	
▲ Camping	
🍎 Restaurant	
★ Nightlife/Clubs	
Nightlife/Pubs	
Theatre	
🏛 Museum	
Mountain Pass	
Observatory	
Waterfall	
Cave	
Lighthouse	
Pedestrian Zone	
Stairs	

0-3280 ft. 3280-6560 ft. >6560 ft. Mountain	
Mountain Range	
‖‖‖‖‖ Countour Lines	
Tunnel	
Footpaths/Trails	
Railroads	
Park	
Beach	
Water	
Buildings	
City Walls	

The Let's Go compass
always points NORTH